RELIGIOUS FREEDOM

HISTORY, CASES, AND OTHER MATERIALS ON THE INTERACTION OF RELIGION AND GOVERNMENT

by

JOHN T. NOONAN, JR.
Circuit Judge, United States Court of Appeals for the Ninth Circuit
Robbins Professor of Law Emeritus
University of California at Berkeley

EDWARD McGLYNN GAFFNEY, JR.
Professor of Law
Valparaiso University School of Law

NEW YORK, NEW YORK
FOUNDATION PRESS
2001

COPYRIGHT © 2001 By FOUNDATION PRESS

        395 Hudson Street
        New York, NY 10014
        Phone Toll Free 1–877–888–1330
        Fax (212) 367–6799
        fdpress.com

ISBN 1–56662–962–4

 TEXT IS PRINTED ON 10% POST CONSUMER RECYCLED PAPER

In Memory of David Daube (1909-1999)

*Student of secular and religious law,
master of both Testaments,
bridger of continents and worlds.*

Foundation Press Library of Constitutional Law
Related Student Textbooks to Assist
in the Study of Law

The First Amendment, ISBN 1-56662-611-0 (1998) by Dan Farber at the University of Minnesota

American Constitutional Law, Second Edition, ISBN 0–88277–601–0 (1988) by Laurence H. Tribe, Harvard University

American Constitutional Law, Third Edition–Volume One, ISBN 1–56662–714–1 (2000) by Laurence H. Tribe, Harvard University.

Please visit your local bookstore for these student friendly texts or go to fdpress.com to place your order.

ACKNOWLEDGMENTS
TO FIRST EDITION

I am grateful to the Oxford University Press, the University of Chicago Press, the University Press of Virginia, the Princeton University Press, Herald Press, and the *American Journal of Comparative Law* for permission to use excerpts from works to which they hold the copyright.

I am greatly indebted to Julie Oseid and Christine Huang for checking citations and authorities, to my daughter Becky for general editorial assistance, and to Pat Boyd for her typing of the manuscript.

JOHN T. NOONAN, JR.

*

ACKNOWLEDGMENTS
TO SECOND EDITION

We are grateful to the National Council of Churches of Christ in the United States of America, the University of Chicago Press, the University Press of Virginia, the Princeton University Press, Herald Press, and the *American Journal of Comparative Law* for permission to use excerpts from works to which they hold the copyright.

Professor Gaffney is grateful to Terry Bloede, Karen Koelemeyer, and Nancy Young for valuable secretarial assistance, and to Professor Mary Persyn, Director of the Law Library, Valparaiso University School of Law, and her able staff, for assistance with library research.

He is deeply grateful to Professor Joseph Blenkinsopp, University of Notre Dame, Professor Frederick Niedner, Valparaiso University, and Professor Felix Just, Loyola Marymount University, for their comments on a draft of the materials in Chapter One; to Professor Robert Wilken, University of Virginia, for his comments on a draft of the materials in Chapter Two; to Bishop Thomas J. Curry for his comments on a draft of the materials in Chapter Six; and to Professor Sarah Baringer Gordon, Pennsylvania University, for her comments on a draft of the materials in Chapter Nine.

He is also grateful to Valparaiso University for a sabbatical year in which to complete the research on the second edition, to the Rockefeller Foundation for a fellowship at the Foundation's Study Center in Bellagio, Italy, where he completed the writing of this edition, and to his wife, Aine O'Healy, for nearly two decades of patient understanding and support.

JOHN T. NOONAN, JR.
EDWARD MCGLYNN GAFFNEY, JR.

*

PREFATORY NOTE
TO FIRST EDITION

John T. Noonan, Jr.'s book is one of several publications commissioned by a project on church and state funded by the Lilly Endowment through Princeton University and intended both to interest scholars and students in the churchstate issue in American culture and to enlarge general appreciation of this neglected topic. In addition to this casebook, the project has commissioned two volumes of bibliographical essays and listings, nine monographic studies, and a summary volume that will review the issue from the colonial period to the present day. Of the monographic studies, four will analyze important developments in churchstate relations in various periods of United States history and five will address the topic in societies whose experience contrasts sharply with that of the United States, including Western Christendom, modern Europe, India, modern Japan, and contemporary Latin America. We are grateful to Judge Noonan for his work.

JOHN F. WILSON
Project Director
STANLEY N. KATZ
ALBERT J. RABOTEAU
ROBERT T. HANDY

*

INTRODUCTION TO FIRST EDITION

Prior to 1940 the Supreme Court of the United States had never upheld a claim of free exercise of religion, had never found any governmental practice to be an establishment of religion, and had never applied the religion clauses of the First Amendment to the states. The religion clauses were part of the American vision; they were not at work in the judicial process. They were alive in the sense that the ideals they embodied were regularly, if vaguely and inconsistently, acknowledged. Their force and power were yet to be realized.

Beginning in 1940 the Court changed all that. It applied the religion clauses to the states. It vindicated a claim of free exercise of religion. In due time it found an unconstitutional establishment of religion. With the sonorous simplicity of John Marshall laying out the foundations, the Court set out basic principles in the new area of law it was creating. The course of development for the next two generations, from 1940 to 1986, has been vigorous. No area of modern law, it may be boldly asserted, has been so marked by sectarian struggle, so strained by fundamental fissures, so reflective of deep American doubts and aspirations.

Cases have been chosen for inclusion here because they are controlling precedents—for example, the great trio of the early 1940s, *Cantwell, Barnette, and Ballard*—because they, as it were, continue the conversation, refining, elaborating, and qualifying—for example, the 1985 cases of *Aguilar, Ball,* and *Jaffree*—or because they are representative of a pattern—for example, the decisions of the Supreme Judicial Court of Massachusetts in the first part of the nineteenth century. Being concrete, the cases exemplify principles, challenge principles, qualify principles, generate principles. Issuing from conflict, they reveal the losing as well as the winning arguments. Being brought by litigants, they reflect the play of persons in the process.

"A page of history is worth a volume of logic." "The life of the law has not been logic but experience." These two axioms of Holmes—always given lip service by law schools but rarely taken seriously in academic milieus where the arts of logic flourish—are here, if anywhere, the keys of understanding. It is not only a matter of grasping the intentions of the Founding Fathers (a necessity if our national notion of a written Constitution as bedrock is to have validity). It is also a matter of empathetically appropriating the experience that undergirds the constitutional principles of free exercise and no establishment. The experience that made the law is capturable only through history. To know the price other systems have exacted, to know the prize we have, we must immerse ourselves in history.

In law school everything gets classified. Religion becomes a category, and categories are easy to manipulate. A sense of the hard, living reality of religion for believers—the sense that they believe that they are responding to a living transcendent intelligent Being—is easy to lose. One function of history is to put its student in the perspective of those for whom the overriding reality was that God was making demands of them. Without that awareness of a power higher than the physical power of the state there would have been nothing to keep separate from the state; the law would have been the measure of obligation. Judaism, followed by Christianity, brought an obligation to obey God and established criteria for conscience that surpassed the law. Society was split by this spiritual requirement. In theory at any rate, conscience was made supreme because of each person's higher allegiance. From this higher sphere, too, came the paradigms of justice and mercy and constancy that provided guidance as the law was formed. To sense the reality of religion for the believers is to glimpse how the law was modeled.

Interacting, religion and law have affected each other. The history of that interaction is Jewish, Catholic, Protestant. It is scriptural, patristic, scholastic, Reformation, Enlightenment. It is Near Eastern, Roman, European, North American. It consists in theology, philosophy, political science, jurisprudence. It is exemplified in the earliest great treatise on the common law, *The Law and Customs of England*. It is illustrated by the assassination of Thomas Becket at Canterbury, the burning of Joan of Arc at Rouen, the martyrdom of Thomas More at Tyburn and of Hugh Latimer at Oxford. It is contained in the writings of the great Welsh defender of religious freedom, Roger Williams, and the writings and acts of the American fathers of religious freedom, Thomas Jefferson and James Madison. It involves the active persecution in America in the eighteenth century of the Baptists, in the nineteenth century of the Mormons, and in the twentieth century of the Jehovah's Witnesses and the strain throughout American history of hostility to the Catholics. It involves the crusades conducted under religious auspices for the abolition of slavery, the end of polygamy, the prohibition of alcohol, the vindication of civil rights, and the elimination of abortion. The history consists in specific speeches, memorable declarations, public and private letters, concrete deeds. It carries the most precious values and most terrible memories of our culture.

Religious liberty exists more fully today in America than in 1770 when Baptists were flogged in Virginia, or in 1790 when Catholics could not hold office in Massachusetts, or in 1870 when neither a Catholic nor a Jew could be a governor or legislator in New Hampshire, or in 1890 when the Church of LatterDay Saints of Jesus Christ was dissolved by act of Congress, or in 1930 when conscientious pacifists could not become citizens. Absolute religious liberty never existed and still does not exist. It has been approached asymptotically.

To often the votaries of religion forget the evil that has been done in God's name. Too often the critics of religion forget that the cultural concepts on which they depend are owed to religion. Impartial history—impartial at least in so far as "the lot of humanity allows"—presents the bad and the good that religion has bestowed on our civilization. The religious impulse, like the sexual, is powerful, not easily trammeled and not easily eliminated from any phase of life. A history of mankind might be written in terms of the foolishness and wickedness that sexual desire or religious aspiration has caused. But it would be incomparably foolish to think humankind could get along without either impulse.

No believer in God need deny that religion has often been the excuse for cruelty and wickedness. In Scripture itself the hypocrites who cry "Lord, Lord" are assured of their condemnation, and our religious traditions from Isaiah onward have rung with denunciations of the folly and the lethargy and the corruption of official leaders of God's flock. No enemy of the exploitation of human beings by religion should deny that the very terms he invokes in judgment—justice and truth and judgment itself—come from religious roots.

Religion is the realm of the spirit. But the good and the bad effected by religion have very often been achieved through the impact of religion on the organs of government. Recurrent problems are these:

1. *Limits.* What is the limit to the logic that the truth is to be brought to everyone? What is the limit to the logic that everyone is entitled to the full free exercise of religion? The first question was once the problem of believers. Underlying the question is the assumption that you have to doubt either your power or your premises if you do not use force in support of the truth. The second question is the more modern problem. The question is faced not only by those who are skeptical about religious truth and by those pragmatically committed to tolerance to secure peace but also by those who from their view of religion or the requirements of human dignity are constrained not to coerce conscience. The problem is most severe when recognition for the rights of conscience endangers the ability of the nation to defend itself by arms. Dependence on nuclear arms has made the dilemma acute.

Separation of sex and state is a popular idea today—to get the government out of the bedroom is axiomatic. It is urged that if we can accept religious pluralism, we can live with a variety of sexual styles, none specially favored or disfavored by the government. The approach converges with religious pluralism as it is seen that the foundation of the laws on sexual conduct is religious. If we proclaim liberty of choice as to the foundations, why not as to the derivative propositions? This extension of religious freedom has yet to be fully tested. The present compromise, not wholly stable, sees marriage as a secular enterprise that can survive separated from religion. The problem of limits recurs.

2. *Neutrality.* Is it possible for a government to govern without taking positions affecting religion? For example, every government must tax. The tax will fall on religious bodies or it will not; there is no third option. Are there neutral rules of law to decide intrachurch disputes and are the neutral state agencies to adjudicate between believers and nonbelievers? Are the judges marvelously above doctrinal prejudice so that they among all Ameri-

cans are truly neutral or are they selfdeluded in their claim to be enforcing impartial principle?

3. *The Definition and Special Place of Religion.* Is religion one of many expressions of the human mind so that it is best understood and treated legally as a subdivision of speech? What religion does not largely consist in the communication of words? Can religion be defined to differentiate it from nonreligious verbal systems? Is religion indeed susceptible of a single definition? Religion was once defined in terms of duty to God. In a society where Buddhism is commonly viewed as a religion this definition no longer works. Is secular humanism, as the Supreme Court has suggested, a religion? Is Marxist communism a religion by metaphor or in reality?

Because of the magnitude of its claims or the intensity of the devotion it inspires, are believers in religion (a) to be peculiarly favored by the law in relation to fraud, medical malpractice, and the use of hallucinogens? (b) to be specially helped or handicapped in relation to the education of their children? (c) to be permitted to participate in the political system only if their ideas meet with the approval of the elite or only if they do not win too often or too much?

This book sets out documents by which these recurrent questions may be explored. But why speak of such abstractions as "religion" and "government?" The existent realities are persons—persons who are religious or not religious, who wield power or do not, but who invariably and necessarily incorporate in their own beings a mixture of beliefs and functions that can be separated only at the level of abstraction. Very few Justices of the United States Supreme Court, for example, have been irreligious men. Justice Holmes is the best known counterinstance, and he had little impact on the law in this area. The Justices who have shaped the law here have been predominantly Christian, mostly Protestant, sometimes the descendants of Protestant ministers—for example, Stephen J. Field, Charles Evans Hughes, and William O. Douglas. The strength of their religious commitment has varied, but no one could fairly charge them with antireligious opinions. They have embodied the state in its most concentrated form — judicial power. They have embodied Christian faith in ways well within the bounds of accepted Christian belief.

Litigants have been identified and lawyers named in many of the cases here collected. The identification of names functions as a reminder that "the law" set out in cases does not fall from heaven and would not be set out at all unless litigants sued and lawyers had experience, skill, persistence. Where would modern case law in this area be without Hayden Covington, Leo Pfeffer, and William Ball? Legal development has been affected by their beliefs.

"Church and State"—the title under which the subject of this book is conventionally classified—is a profoundly misleading rubric. The title triply misleads. It suggests that there is a single church. But in America there are myriad ways in which religious belief is organized. It suggests that there is a single state. But in America there is the federal government, fifty state governments, myriad municipalities, and a division of power among executive, legislative, administrative, and judicial entities, each of whom embodies state power. Worst of all, "Church and State" suggests that there are two distinct bodies set apart from each other in contrast if not in conflict. But everywhere neither churches nor states exist except as they are incorporated in actual individuals. These individuals are believers and unbelievers, citizens and officials. In one aspect of their activities, if they are religious, they usually form churches. In another aspect they form governments. Religious and governmental bodies not only coexist but overlap. The same persons, much of the time, are both believers and wielders of power.

"The power"—often translated as "the powers that be"—is St. Paul's phrase for the force that resides in governments. It is stunningly impersonal. French employs a similar expression, *le pouvoir,* to designate the locus of authority. "The power" conveys the reality, that the force at the state's disposition is greater than that of any individual. The phrase also misleads if it dehumanizes this force so that one forgets that it is human beings who embody it.

Those human beings wielding power are linked by law, and it is the linkages of law as affected by and affecting religious belief that are the subject of this book. American law, dominated by case law climaxing in decisions of the Supreme Court, is a complex and comprehensive process. By "law" I mean constitutional provisions, statutes, and judicial decisions, but I also include a variety of other phenomena that are part of the legal process —legislative debates, presidential proclamations and addresses, the commentary of legal scholars, and the arguments of lawyers. Too truncated a vision of American law is conveyed if these other lawmaking, lawasserting activities are not noticed.

To capture the legal process relating to religion in time, to push back to the experience at its roots and carry it forward to the present, is the purpose of this book as it sets out salient moments in the articulation of the relationship between religious beliefs and legal power. The presentation is generally chronological (how else is history to be understood?). But there is a large exception. When one goes from Part I, "Roots," and Part II, "The American Experience," to Part III, "Current Controversies," one enters an area where decisions of the Supreme Court shape the problematic. If one is not to be completely a captive of the Court's categories, there is need to create one's own. I contend that the six divisions proposed here—Sacred Duties; Belief and Its Organization; Double Effect; Education; Political Participation; and Sexual Morals—produce more intelligibility than does a tracking of the Court's analysis.

John T. Noonan, Jr.

Berkeley
August 15, 1986

*

INTRODUCTION TO SECOND EDITION

This casebook is a reworking of Judge Noonan's collection of materials published by Macmillan in 1987 under the title, *The Believer and the Powers That Are: Cases, History and Other Data Bearing on the Relation of Religion and Government*. That edition has not been available for classroom use for a period of over ten years. The frequent requests of teachers for these materials has led to this updated version. I have the responsibility for the changes that were made to Judge Noonan's materials, which I describe below.

One of the greatest strengths of Judge Noonan's materials is that they illustrate the powerful interaction between law and religion over many centuries. Part III describes various approaches to religious freedom that have emerged in contemporary controversies since 1940, when the Supreme Court first applied the Religion Clause of the First Amendment to the states. One might be tempted to leap over the historical materials in Parts I and II, but that would be short-sighted. In our view, one cannot understand, let alone intelligently criticize, the approaches of the courts and the political branches to religious freedom in the recent past, without a deep appreciation of the roots of these controversies in the ancient and medieval world (Part I) and in the American experience (Part II).

For this reason I have not altered the historical materials in Parts I and II significantly. Occasionally I have added a few new texts and bibliographical citations. For example, I added materials to Chapter One illustrating that many of our legal principles (e.g., privileges and immunities, due process of law, and equal protection of the laws) find their roots in the Hebrew Bible and in the New Testament, and that the problem of exemption of religious adherents from generally applicable laws is an ancient one, involving Jews and well as Christians.

Important differences between Jews and Christians are lost when reference is too easily made to "Judeo-Christian values," a term avoided in this book. I have added materials in the first two chapters that expressly describe the Jewish experience. Symbols have meaning too, so this edition adopts the convention of reckoning time under the increasingly common designations "BCE" (before the common era) and "CE" (common era) rather than under the more familiar designation of time referring to Jesus, "BC" (before Christ) and "AD" (anno Domini, in the year of the Lord).

I acknowledge with candor and sadness that religion has too often been used to deny freedom and even to eliminate lives. The deepest tragedy of the past century—the Holocaust—stems in part from the Christian teaching (a heresy in my view) of contempt for Jews. The Holocaust was an atrocity committed by a pagan secular regime that had contempt for Christianity, but many Christians were bystanders at a time of crisis because they and their ancestors had been taught both by church leaders such as Ambrose, John Chrysostom, Aquinas and Luther and by the law itself to think of Jews as second-class citizens at best. Established religion begets denial of free exercise.

I added notes that address these concerns for two reasons. First, the relation between religion and government has not always been smooth or error-free, and religion has sometimes been the sinner. I illustrate this with a note on the troubled period in European history from the Peace of Augsburg to the Thirty Years' War and the Peace of Westphalia [Chapter Five, section 1]. Second, sins against religious freedom have also been committed by those who do not believe in sin. The greatest outrages in the century just past were committed not by religious communities but by secular totalitarian regimes of the Left and Right. From the Turkish genocide against the Armenians to the Nazi genocide against the Jews, gays, and gypsies; from Stalin's elimination of millions of his adversaries to the killing fields of Cambodia; and from the tribal slaughter in Rwanda to the ethnic cleansing in the former Yugoslavia, the recurrent mega-problem of the past century has been that lawless authority could acknowledge no power greater than itself, no transcendent point of reference to call it to judgment.

I also address the issue of violence as a religious problem. This edition retains the section containing the modern cases on conscientious objection to military service [Chapter Eleven, § 4]. I added a note in Chapter Two on "Christians and Military Service in the Early Church: From Pacifism to the Augustinian Tradition on Justifiable War." This note is meant to explain the development of thinking within early Christianity on the deeply problematic character of the relationship between a believer and a governmental authority that commands a believer to kill.

I also added a note in Chapter Two about the critical transition in the fourth century, in which Christianity first became tolerated by Roman law under Emperor Constantine and then became the official established religion of the empire under Emperor Theodosius.

The principal additions to Judge Noonan's materials are edited versions of intervening decisions of the Supreme Court in Part III. I have tried to be generous with the text of decisions to enable students to see how divided the Court is on these matters and to challenge the whole enterprise of its jurisprudence, including evanescent standards for safeguarding free exercise of religion, as well as contrived tests for evaluating when there is a violation of the nonestablishment principle. Not being able to define hard core pornography didn't keep Justice Stewart from knowing it when he saw it. But familiarity with the historical materials in Parts I and II should equip students to recognize an establishment of religion more readily than can the memorization of judicial tests (from stream-lined "endorsement" or "coercion" tests, to the aptly styled *Lemon* test with its famous three parts, or to a recent proposal for an eleven-part "test" that promises more criteria to come!).

In Chapter Eleven, I added materials from the sacred scriptures of Jews, Christians and Muslims to enable readers to understand the source of a sacred duty that conflicts with the law. And I report several instances in which the political branches have been more vigilant in safeguarding our first liberty than the Court has deemed necessary. I also report the struggle between the Court and Congress over what is "necessary and proper" in these matters. The text just cited—a phrase from Article I of the Constitution echoed in section 5 of the Fourteenth Amendment—refers to congressional power, not to judicial interpretation. In Chapter Fourteen, I report the latest efforts of the Court to eliminate some of the confusion that has come from its decisions on the funding of education in religious schools.

Judge Noonan and I express our gratitude to colleagues who were willing to use the preliminary draft of this second edition, and favor us with comments that were useful in the process of revision. We are especially grateful to the late William Bentley Ball, who used these materials in a course on this subject that he taught regularly at Widener University School of Law. Ball was a champion of religious liberty identified in this book as a frequent litigator in the Supreme Court, notably in *Wisconsin v. Yoder* (1972) [Chapter Eleven, section 7]. Even when the Court was to announce a sea-change in free exercise standards in *Employment Division v. Smith* (1990) [Chapter Eleven, section 10], it did not abandon *Yoder*, which still stands as a valid precedent requiring States and local public school boards to accommodate the religious concerns of parents. Richard John Neuhaus, a distinguished commentator on religion in public life, wrote of Ball: "From the Supreme Court to school board hearings in humble villages, the voice of Bill Ball has championed the cause of `little people' who have dared to question the authority of their supposed betters. His advocacy joins fortitude to compassion, learning to eloquence, and earnestness to humor." Ball died in January of 1999, and will be sorely missed among those litigate in this field.

I also wish to honor the memory of another giant in our religious community, John Courtney Murray, S.J. (1904-1967). Like Madison, Fr. Murray knew the difference between toleration and free exercise. He once said that intolerance is a terrible vice, but that toleration is not much of a virtue.

He battled mightily against racial injustice in our country because it was a denial of the self-evident truth that all are created equal. Like David Daube, to whom this book is dedicated, Murray fostered civil dialogue between Christians and Jews, between believers and unbelievers. Tocqueville and Murray were Catholics who—over a century apart from one another—offered the world precious reflections on the American experience. Unlike Tocqueville, Murray lived under a cloud of suspicion in his church because of his writings on religious freedom. But he lived to see his thinking affirmed at the highest teaching level of his church in a declaration of an ecumenical council. Vatican II taught: "The right to religious freedom has its foundation" neither in the church nor in the state, but "in the very dignity of the human person." On the day the Council approved the final draft of the Decree on Religious Freedom, I asked Fr. Murray to autograph his book, *We Hold These Truths: Reflections on the American Experience*. He inscribed it: "Now we must hold these truths more than ever." It is a great honor for me to repeat those words to the readers of this book many years after Murray's death, when religious freedom has become so vulnerable to governmental trivialization and even to judicial assault.

In 1998 the University of California Press published Judge Noonan's book, *The Lustre of Our Country: The American Experience of Religious Freedom*. A paper edition appeared in 1999, making it an affordable companion to this volume. With Judge Noonan's permission I offer here ten commandments on religious freedom in America. They formed the final chapter in *The Lustre of Our Country*, summarizing succinctly the major themes of that volume. I repeat them here because I view them as a disclosure of where we are coming from and as a guide to where you may be willing to go. Perhaps these commandments may seem obscure at first. The structure and content of this book should clarify what these commandments mean as you read on. You might profit by coming back to these commandments at the end of your study of these materials.

First. You shall conclude that the genealogy, the domestic environment, the educational exposure, the intellectual adventures, the friendships, and the professional life of anyone treating this topic influence the treatment; and you shall suspect that the spiritual life of the writer is relevant as well; and you shall know that no person, man or woman, historian or law professor or constitutional commentator or judge, is neutral in this matter.

Second. You shall acknowledge that the foundation of freedom in religion is the concept of the individual conscience; and you shall not worship an empty idol attributing to "the Enlightenment" an insight of deeper and more ancient root.

Third. You shall respect the content and the context of the fifteen words creating religious freedom in the Constitution, and you shall not artfully divide the words from one another, nor omit any of them, nor impose two meanings on a single word.

Fourth. You shall read Tocqueville for his celebration of the holy union of freedom and religion, discount his excesses and omissions as an advocate, and meditate on his conviction that religion is the foremost of our political institutions.

Fifth. You shall observe that the free exercise of religion generated the moral energy and the bitter passions that produced the Civil War and led to the liberation of the millions held in bondage.

Sixth. You shall mark that government when it seeks to adjudicate the truth of a religion falls afoul of the First Amendment and when it attempts to adjudicate the sincerity of a believer enters an enterprise beset by hazards.

Seventh. You shall realize that the words safeguarding religious freedom in the Constitution must be applied in order to achieve that end; that their application invites interpretation; that interpretation breeds disputes; that disputes result in distinctions; and that only over time do the dominant distinctions become palpable, only then does a development of doctrine occur.

Eighth. You shall substitute neither State nor society for God nor suppose that religion may be analytically reduced to the self-worship of society.

Ninth. You shall recognize that the free exercise of religion can be divisive and dangerous to established institutions and customary ways as well as beneficent for believers and empowering for the forgotten, and that the price of our constitutional liberty is acceptance of this precarious condition.

Tenth. You shall acknowledge that religion itself requires religious freedom. Heart speaks to heart, spirit answers Spirit, freely.

I certainly count myself within the scope of Judge Noonan's commandments, especially the first, which requires that I acknowledge that I am not neutral in the matters discussed below. I state my own views candidly, but I also try to also report some of the important discussion occurring among scholars of differing perspectives. My hope is to be able to foster serious conversation between students and professors about issues that are not only—in the language of First Amendment discourse—of "public concern," but also—in the famous phrase of the theologian Paul Tillich—of "ultimate concern." Finally, I would be grateful if you would call my attention to any errors you might detect, or to any pedagogical concerns you might have either as teachers or as students.

Edward McGlynn Gaffney, Jr.

Valparaiso
Shevuot-Pentecost (The Giving of the Law) 2000

*

SUMMARY OF CONTENTS

TABLE OF CONTENTS

TABLE OF CASES

Principal cases are in bold type. Non-principal cases are in roman type. References are to Pages.

*

RELIGIOUS FREEDOM

HISTORY, CASES, AND OTHER MATERIALS ON THE INTERACTION OF RELIGION AND GOVERNMENT

*

PART ONE

ROOTS

CHAPTER ONE

"YOU SHALL HAVE NO OTHER GOD TO SET AGAINST ME": BIBLICAL RELIGION AND LAW IN THE ANCIENT WORLD

1. THE COVENANT WITH NOAH: UNIVERSAL PROHIBITION OF MURDER

From the ancient world to the present, stories of catastrophic floods contain several common elements: inundated land, drowned multitudes, survivors in a boat. The legend of a hero who survives a flood to repopulate the earth is found in many cultures in the ancient Near East. The most famous of these pre-biblical flood narratives is a Babylonian tale called the Gilgamesh Epic. The epic narrates the story of a "pious hero warned by his god to build a great ship and to load it with his family and selected animals in order to escape the coming deluge. Once all others have perished, the ship grounds on a mountain in Armenia, a sacrifice pleases the god, and a divine oath follows never to send another flood." Alan Millard, "The Flood" in Bruce M. Metzger and Michael D. Coogan, eds., *The Oxford Companion to the Bible* 231 (1993); *see also* Cyrus H. Gordon, "Gilgamesh Epic," *id.* at 254; and Maureen Gallery Kovacs, trans., *The Epic of Gilgamesh* (1989).

In the biblical imagination of the universe, a vast reservoir of "waters above" was kept in place by the sky, called a "firmament" or superdome (*see* Gen. 1:6). All that was necessary for these "waters above" to cover the earth below was for God to open gates in the dome-like firmament of heaven. The opening of these floodgates is represented in the biblical account as a response to a situation where "the wickedness of humankind was great in the earth, and every inclination of the thoughts of their hearts was evil" (Gen. 6:5). Although the flood is intended to punish pervasive rebellion against God's will, God identifies Noah as a second Adam (or man) to whom would again be given the divine command to "be fruitful, and multiply, and fill the earth" (Gen. 9:1; *see* Gen. 1:22, 28). Noah and his family and representatives of many animals ride out the flood and emerge as the progenitors of post-diluvial life. God promises never to destroy the earth again with floodwaters, placing the rainbow in the sky as a perpetual reminder of this promise. The text forges a crucial connection between law and religion. God enters into a covenant—a legal term for a solemn treaty or agreement—not with Israel, but with the entire human family; and he announces basic commands—prohibition of consumption of meat with the blood of the animal, and murder—that bind all.

Genesis 9: 1–7, 14–17

God blessed Noah and his sons, and said to them, "Be fruitful and multiply, and fill the earth. The fear and dread of you shall rest on every animal of the earth, and on every bird of the air, on everything that creeps on the ground, and on all the fish of the sea; into your hand they are delivered. Every moving thing that lives shall be food for you; and just as I gave you the green plants, I give you everything. Only, you shall not eat flesh with its life, that is, its blood. For your own lifeblood I will surely require a reckoning: from every animal I will require it and from human beings, each one for the blood of another, I will require a reckoning for human life. Whoever sheds the blood of a human, by a human shall that person's blood be shed; for in his own image God made humankind. And you, be fruitful and multiply, abound on the earth and multiply in it.... I have set my bow in the clouds, and it shall be a sign of the covenant between me and the earth. When I bring clouds over the earth and the bow is seen in the clouds, I will remember my covenant that is between me and you and every living creature of all flesh; and the waters shall never again become a flood to destroy all flesh. When the bow is in the clouds, I will see it and remember the everlasting covenant between God and every living creature of all flesh that is on the earth." God said to Noah, "This is the sign of the covenant that I have established between me and all flesh that is on the earth."

2.   THE TEN COMMANDMENTS: STIPULATIONS OF COVENANTAL LIFE

The first five books of the Bible, known as the Pentateuch or Torah, contain three principal collections of legal materials: (1) the book of the covenant (Ex 20:23–24:19), (2) the Deuteronomic law (Dt. 12–28), and (3) the holiness code (Lev. 17–26) and priestly law (Ex. 25–31; 35–40; Num. 1–10). *See* Dale Patrick, *Old Testament Law* 63–188 (1985). The best known of all the legal materials in the Bible are the ten commandments, a succinct statement of the human ethical obligations toward God and neighbor. Anthony Phillips, *Ancient Israel's Criminal Law: A New Approach to the Decalogue* (1970). There are two versions of the commandments. The first occurs in Exodus 20:1–17, immediately after the narrative of the covenant between God and Israel at Mount Sinai (Ex. 19) three months after the Israelites had come out of Egypt (ca. 1300 BCE, or before the common era). God promises Israel that it will be God's "very own" if it obeys His will and holds fast to His covenant (Ex. 19:1–18). The ten commandments follow, spoken by God (Ex. 20:1–17) and then inscribed by God or Moses on two stone tablets (Ex. 34:28). Biblically presented, the law is not from the beginning or set in a timeless past. Instead, the law has a date, a place where it was issued, and a direct sanction: God's favor. From biblical times to the seventeenth century most Jews and Christians read the Bible to state that in these concrete historical circumstances God gave the commandments to Moses. Many Jews and Christians still read the ten commandments in this way.

The text that follows is the second version of the commandments, found in Deuteronomy. This book is structured in the form of a treaty or covenant: (1) preamble naming the lawgiver (Dt. 1:1); (2) list of historical kindnesses of the great king to the covenanting people (Dt. 1:2–4:40); (3) stipulations of the covenant (Dt. 4:44–26:19); (4) provision for annual reading of the treaty (Dt. 27:8); and (5) curses for breaking the stipulations of the covenant and blessings for keeping them (Dt.27–28). Gerhard von Rad, *Deuteronomy* (1966) 21–23; *see also* von Rad, *The Problem of the Hexateuch and Other Essays* (1966) 26–33.

As the Note below indicates, there is a great variety of views on the dating, numbering, and exact meaning of the ten commandments. Whatever may be said about the original context within which these commandments emerged in the ancient world, little doubt exists that they have been the most influential law code in history. *See* Walter Harrelson, *The Ten Commandments and Human Rights* (1980). Among the religious traditions that were most influential in early America, the commandments recognized a Lawgiver above the nation, law based on God's will, and a sanction that depended on obedience to Him. Life, property, truth, marriage, and worship of God were given special status by the ten commandments. These basic moral prescriptions are described by the Bible itself as "ten words" (Dt. 4:13). This designation links the image of God as lawgiver with the image of God as creator using words to bring forth order from the "formless void" of the universe (Gen. 1:3,6,9,11,14,20,24). With these "ten words," permanent criteria for judging human enterprises, including governments, came into written existence.

Deuteronomy 5:1–22

Moses convened all Israel, and said to them:

Hear, O Israel, the statutes and ordinances that I am addressing to you today; you shall learn them and observe them diligently. The Lord our God made a covenant with us at Horeb. Not with our ancestors did the Lord make this covenant, but with us, who are all of us here alive today. The Lord spoke with you face to face at the mountain, out of the fire. (At that time I was standing between the Lord and you to declare to you the words of the Lord; for you were afraid because of the fire and did not go up the mountain.) And he said:

I am the Lord your God, who brought you out of the land of Egypt, out of the house of slavery; you shall have no other gods before me.

You shall not make for yourself an idol, whether in the form of anything that is in heaven above, or that is on the earth beneath, or that is in the water under the earth. You shall not bow down to them or worship them; for I the Lord your God am a jealous God, punishing children for the iniquity of parents, to the third and fourth generation of those who reject me, but showing steadfast love to the thousandth generation of those who love me and keep my commandments.

You shall not make wrongful use of the name of the Lord your God, for the Lord will not acquit anyone who misuses his name.

Observe the sabbath day and keep it holy, as the LORD your God commanded you. Six days you shall labor and do all your work. But the seventh day is a sabbath to the LORD your God; you shall not do any work—you, or your son or your daughter, or your male or female slave, or your ox or your donkey, or any of your livestock, or the resident alien in your towns, so that your male and female slave may rest as well as you. Remember that you were a slave in the land of Egypt, and the LORD your God brought you out from there with a mighty hand and an outstretched arm; therefore the LORD your God commanded you to keep the sabbath day.

Honor your father and your mother, as the LORD your God commanded you, so that your days may be long and that it may go well with you in the land that the LORD your God is giving you.

You shall not murder.

Neither shall you commit adultery.

Neither shall you steal.

Neither shall you bear false witness against your neighbor.

Neither shall you covet your neighbor's wife.

Neither shall you desire your neighbor's house, or field, or male or female slave, or ox, or donkey, or anything that belongs to your neighbor.

These words the LORD spoke with a loud voice to your whole assembly at the mountain, out of the fire, the cloud, and the thick darkness, and he added no more. He wrote them on two stone tablets, and gave them to me.

NOTES AND QUESTIONS

Should the Ten Commandments be posted in public buildings, such as schools or courts? *See Stone v. Graham* [Chapter 14, Section 2]. All of the commandments? Which ones? Why some and not others?

One of the striking features of Deuteronomy is its homiletic style, that of a preacher exhorting a liturgical assembly. It is cast as a day long sermon of Moses on the day before he dies in the wilderness. Although ascribed to Moses, this collection of sermons is directed to a people living long after the events of the Exodus. This community is urged to recall and observe the teaching of the great prophet, Moses. Many of the legal ideas of Deuteronomy, such as de novo appeal of difficult cases to the central sanctuary in Jerusalem (Dt. 17:8–13), presuppose the developed governmental form established under Kings David and Solomon (ca. 1000–930 BCE). There are important parallels between central themes in Deuteronomy—such as social justice and national identity—and the preaching of prophets such as Micah, who had a direct effect on the reform activity of King Hezekiah (716–687 BCE) described in 2 Kings 23. The centrality of these concerns in Deuteronomy (on the abolition of the worship of other or foreign deities, *see* Dt. 7:15; 12:1–32; 16:1–8; 17:3; 18:11; 23:18) led Wilhelm de Wette in the early nineteenth century to identify the core legal element of Deuteronomy (5–26) with the discovery in Jerusalem of a "book of the law" during the reign of King Josiah around 622 BCE. There is a strong consensus among biblical scholars that Deuteronomy reached its present form as a result of a long process of formation that may have included the Josianic reign, but that may also have preceded that period. *See* Joseph Blenkinsopp, "Deuteronomy," in Raymond E. Brown, Joseph A. Fitzmyer, and Roland E. Murphy eds., *New Jerome Biblical Commentary*, 95 (1990); Norbert Lohfink, "Deuteronomy," 5 *Interpreter's Dictionary of the Bible* 229–32 (1976). Eventually Deuteronomy was conjoined with the other four books of the Torah (Genesis, Exodus, Leviticus, and Numbers) some time after 538 BCE, when Cyrus the Persian issued an edict permitting the Jews to return to Jerusalem from their exile in Babylon. The Babylonian captivity began with the first deportation of Jews from Jerusalem in 587 BCE. The early Persian period (538–440 BCE), also known as the period of Ezra and Nehemiah, was a time of great renewal focused on the legal traditions of Israel and on worship in the Second Temple in Jerusalem. Blenkinsopp, *Ezra-Nehemiah* (1988).

Although the order of the ten commandments became standard by the time of Deuteronomy, several versions of Israel's moral catechism may have circulated before this time. For example, the prophet Hosea notes: "There is swearing, lying, killing, stealing, and committing adultery; they break all bounds, and murder follows murder" (Hos. 4:2). And the prophet Jeremiah asks of major sins in a different order: "Will you steal, murder, commit adultery, burn incense to Baal, and go after gods that you have not known, and then come to stand before me in this house?" (Jer. 7:9–10). The canonical list of commands is preserved in a slightly different order in the New Testament (Mt. 19:18–19; Rom. 13:9).

Different numbering systems are used to reach the number ten. Jews begin with Dt. 5:6 ("I brought you out of slavery"). Greek Orthodox and most Protestants treat Dt. 5:7 (no other gods) as the first and Dt. 5:8–10 (no images) as the second, and then agree with Jews in treating Dt. 5:11 (no misuse of name) as the third, Dt. 5:12 (the Sabbath) as the fourth, Dt. 5:16 (honor parents) as the fifth, and so on. Catholics and Lutherans, following St. Augustine, treat Dt. 5:7–10 (no other gods, no images) as the first, Dt. 5:11 (no misuse of name) as the second, Dt. 5:12 (the Sabbath) as the third, Dt. 5:16 (parents) as the fourth, Dt. 5:17 (murder) as the fifth, and so forth, then separating into the ninth and tenth commandments the prescriptions against coveting a neighbor's wife and a neighbor's goods, Dt. 5: 21.

Opinion also divides as to the meaning of particular commands. For example, the sixth commandment could mean "You shall not kill" under any circumstances. The more likely meaning of the original text is a narrower prohibition of intentional homicide: "You shall not murder." *See* John Howard Yoder, "Exodus 20:13-'Thou Shalt Not Kill,' " 34 *Interpretation* 394–99 (1980); Patrick, *Old Testament Law* 53–54. Whatever its original meaning, this text and other passages in the Bible about the sacred value of life have important consequences for later understandings of pacifism [Chapter Two, section 1; Chapter Eleven, section 4] and other moral questions related to killing.

Note. *Covenants and the Process of Formation of Biblical Law.* In all the law codes of the ancient Near East that have been discovered since the last century, the king was the lawgiver. The most complete and undoubtedly the most famous of these legal collections is the Code of Hammurabi, king of Babylon (1792–1750 BCE), with which there are parallels in the case laws in Exodus 21–23. *See* G.R. Driver and J. C. Miles, eds. *The Babylonian Laws* (2 vols. 1952–55), and James Pritchard, ed., *Ancient Near Eastern Texts Relating to the Old Testament* (1969). In Israel, however, the function of lawgiver is attributed not to a king, but to Moses, a prophet (Dt. 18:15) who speaks for God to the community. Thus God himself is ultimately the lawgiver in the first books of the Bible. *See* E.W. Nicholson, "The Decalogue as the Direct Address of God," 27 *Vetus Testamentum* 422–33 (1977).

Although all of the legal materials from Exodus to Deuteronomy are presented in the Bible as belonging to the Mosaic age, they refer to institutions that were in place only after the entry of people of Israel into the land of Canaan. There are, moreover, significant differences between the laws in these collections. For example, the law in Ex. 23:10–11 demands that farmers leave the land unplanted every seventh year, so that the poor can find food to survive. The parallel law in Dt. 15:1–11 adds elaborate regulations for forgiving debt owed by the poor every seven years; the regulations even extend to foreign borrowing and lending. Deuteronomy thus addresses an urban culture and economy, in a situation found not at the time of Moses, but centuries later. According to Exodus (19:1), the place where the covenant was formed is called Sinai; in Deuteronomy (1:2; 5:1) it is called Horeb. Textual differences such as these raise problems for those who would insist that all of the legal materials were literally written down in the Mosaic period.

Other readings are also possible. One reading concentrates on the form of the ten commandments. The collections of ancient Near Eastern law referred to above typically take the form of case histories, with a statement of facts (if X) followed by their legal consequences (then Y). The ten commandments do not follow this form. Instead, they are cast as "broad moral imperatives and prohibitions universally binding as a direct expression of the divine will." Joseph Blenkinsopp, *The Pentateuch: An Introduction to the First Five Books of the Bible* (1992) 205. Some scholars, notably Sigmund Mowinckel and Albrecht Alt, have argued that such commands addressed directly by God to the people must have originated in the setting of a worshipping community. Mowinckel, *Le Décalogue* (1927); Alt, "The Origins of Israelite Law," *Essays on Old Testament History and Religion* (1966) 79–132. Other scholars, notably Erhard Gerstenberger and Joseph Blenkinsopp, rejected this hypothesis, noting that the collections of legal materials in the Bible, including the ten commandments, appear to have earlier roots in Egyptian and Mesopotamian instructions on prudent behavior or in the collective wisdom transmitted by tribal elders. Gerstenberger, *Wesen und Herkunft des Apodiktischen Rechts* (1965); Blenkinsopp, *The Pentateuch*, 205; and *see* Blenkinsopp, *Wisdom and Law in the Old Testament* (2d ed. 1995).

Another reading situates the commandments in the political context of international suzerainty treaties between great kings and vassal city-states in the ancient Near East. In the first stage of the scholarship on this theme, emphasis was laid upon the antiquity of the covenant formulary in the Bible on the ground that the biblical texts closely resembled Hittite treaties from the fourteenth and thirteenth century BCE. Victor Korosec noted that these treaties included the following elements: (1) a *preamble* identifying the name and title of the overlord, (2) an *historical prologue* reciting the deeds performed on behalf of the client state that form the basis for the duty of the vassal to obey, (3) *stipulations* that the covenanted community must observe, (4) *deposit of the treaty in a sacred place*, with provision for public reading of the treaty at regular intervals, (5) invocation of *divine witnesses*, and (6) *blessings* on those who observe the stipulations and *curses* on those who do not. Korosec, *Hethi-*

tische Staatsverträge (1931). George Mendenhall applied Korosec's work to the biblical text. He noted that the ten commandments are preceded in Ex. 20:2 with a *preamble* ("I am the Lord, your God") and a brief *historical prologue* ("who brought you out of the land of Egypt, out of the land of slavery"). Then follow the ten commandments, which Mendenhall characterized as *stipulations* that the members of the covenanted community must observe to remain in the alliance spelled out in the treaty (Ex. 20:3–17). As with Near Eastern treaties, the stone tablets of the law were *deposited in a sacred place*, the ark of the covenant, which resided in the central sanctuary of the community (Ex. 25:10–22). Joshua 24:1–28 records a covenant renewal ceremony after the entrance of the tribes into Canaan. According to Dt. 24:10–11, Israel was enjoined to observe a ritual covenant renewal every seven years. *See* Sigmund Mowinkel, *The Psalms in Israel's Worship* (1962); Blenkinsopp, *The Pentateuch* 208. The monotheistic character of the Sinai covenant precludes any other deities as *witnesses*, but *blessings* for observance of the covenant and *curses* for disobedience of the covenant laws are found in Dt. 28:1–46. *See* Mendenhall, *Law and Covenant in the Ancient Near East* (1955); Mendenhall, "Covenant," in 1 *Interpreter's Dictionary of the Bible* 714–723 (1962); Delbert Hillers, *Covenant: The History of a Biblical Idea* (1969); Klaus Baltzer, *The Covenant Formulary* (1971); Edward McGlynn Gaffney, "Of Covenants Ancient and New: The Influence of Secular Law on Biblical Religion," 2 *J. Law & Relig.* 117 (1984).

Subsequent scholarship on ancient Near Eastern treaties cast doubt on an early dating of the covenant formulary. On the one hand, a closer inspection of the Hittite treaties yielded less clarity about the typical form of these treaties, which vary significantly in the content of the historical prologue and which frequently omit the provision for deposit and public reading. On the other hand, attention to Assyrian treaties dating from the eighth century BCE disclosed closer parallels with the biblical text. *See* Dennis McCarthy, *Covenant and Treaty* (1963); McCarthy, *Old Testament Covenant: A Survey of Current Opinions* (1972); Patrick, *Old Testament Law* 223–48; R. Frankena, "The Vassal–Treaties of Esarhaddon and the Dating of Deuteronomy," 14 *Old Testament Studies* 122–54 (1965); P.A. Reiman, "Covenant, Mosaic," 5 *Interpreter's Dictionary of the Bible* 192–99 (1976).

Despite different answers to questions of authorship and dating of the biblical laws, there is strong consensus that all of the law codes found in the Bible are cast within the framework of a covenant that forms and reforms a people gathered together in that covenant. One commentator notes the significance of this way of thinking about law for our generation. "Laws about crime, property, torts, family relations, judicial procedure, as well as laws about sacred days, priests and religious rituals, are all located within the structure of the covenant. Thus the meaning of the laws derives from the covenant. They are interpreted in light of the covenant. Their violation is understood as a betrayal of the covenant. They are changed and amended as the covenanted people discern the shifting needs of changing times. What remains constant as the overarching reality and demand is the covenant itself and its qualities and obligations. Curiously, a covenant is honored even in its breach, for a broken covenant is just that.... A rift in a relationship does not totally destroy the relationship, otherwise it could not be rendered as a rift. Under the conditions of a broken covenant, a people stands in contradiction to itself. Its identity is a judgment against its existence. The myth of the covenant is not merely a story about times past.... It is a communication about the real world, the world of human existence. It is a statement of ontological and anthropological significance. The claim of a myth is that it divulges important truths about our own reality, truths that we should understand if we would be indeed realistic. The myth of the covenant is cast in narrative form. It has the appearance of historical description. But it is more than historical description of a unique set of events that occurred in past times. It is, in addition, a paradigmatic statement. The narrative should be comprehended as a presentation about the structure and dynamics, the meaning and import of the world. It is a world view. What is the alleged truth symbolized in and conveyed through the myth of the covenant? Negatively, it is a rejection of both individualism and corporativism as understandings of human association. That is, according to the myth of the covenant, we are not and cannot adequately understand ourselves as essentially isolated individuals who may make and break social relations at will. Rather we are and should understand ourselves as responsible participants in a whole host of relationships—natural, social, political, economic. On the one hand, these relationships constitute the given context of our individuality. On the other hand, these relationships bear the imprint of our personal creativity. Life is a constant give and take. We receive and we give. How we receive and how we give make all the difference in the world. Some ways of receiving and giving enhance life. Other ways of receiving and giving degrade, delimit, and destroy. That is the narrative of human life. That is the narrative of a covenantal way of looking at and living in the world. If in our receiving and in our giving we are constituted by the qualities of liberation, faithfulness, justice, and peace, then life is enhanced. If, on the contrary, in our receiving and in our giving we are constituted by the qualities of oppression, disloyalty, injustice and alienation, the result is destructiveness and degradation of life." Douglas Sturm, "American Legal Realism and the Covenantal Myth: World Views in the Practice of Law," 31 *Mercer L. Rev.* 487, 502–3 (1980).

3. ANOTHER DECALOGUE: BIBLICAL FOUNDATIONS FOR DUE PROCESS OF LAW AND EQUAL PROTECTION OF THE LAWS

The phrase "due process of law" traces its pedigree in English legal history to article 39 of the Magna Carta of 1215 [Chapter Three, section 2]. In the Great Charter the crown pledged that "No freeman shall be taken or imprisoned or disseised or exiled or in any way destroyed ... except by the legal judgment of his peers and *by the law of the land*." The Latin text for the last phrase reads: "*per legem terrae*." In a fourteenth century statute, 28 Edward III, chapter 3, this phrase was rendered in Norman French as "*par due process de ley*." Sir Edward Coke (1552–1634), the British jurist and politician whose defense of the supremacy of the common law against Stuart claims of the royal prerogative had a profound influence on the development of the English common law and constitution, emphasized the protection afforded to persons by this provision in Magna Carta. In Coke's *Second Institute*, published in 1642, he cited the fourteenth century restatement, translated into English as "*without due process of law*," the expression that occurs in the Fifth and Fourteenth Amendments to the United States Constitution.

The twin concepts of procedural fairness and equality of all persons before the law actually have a more ancient, biblical pedigree. For example, the laws in Exodus (20:22–23:19) and in Deuteronomy (16:18–20; 17:8–13) describe duties attaching to civil and criminal procedure in ancient Israel. *See* Roland deVaux, *Ancient Israel: Its Life and Institutions* 143–63 (1961).

One scholar suggested that the following text contains another decalogue that might have served as an inaugural oath for judges in ancient Israel. J.W. McKay, "Exodus XXIII 1–3, 6–8: A Decalogue for the Administration of Justice in the City Gate," 21 *Vetus Testamentum* 311–25 (1971). Blenkinsopp notes that this decalogue reflects usage in a Hebrew court of law, but doubts that it was for "the exclusive use of judges, who, among other things, did not serve as witnesses. It seems more likely that it would have served to guide the entire community in the vital task of preserving the judicial process from subversion and corruption." Blenkinsopp, *The Pentateuch*, 200. The translation of these ten commandments is that of McKay, *id.*

Exodus 23:1–3,6–8

You shall not utter a false report.

You shall not conspire with the one in the wrong by being a malicious witness.

You shall not follow the majority in evildoing.

When testifying, you shall not follow the majority in perverting justice.

You shall not be partial to a person of standing in his suit.

You shall not pervert the justice due to the poor person in his suit.

Be far removed from a false charge.

Do not slay the innocent or the one in the right.

Do not give judgment in favor of the one in the wrong.

Do not accept a bribe, for a bribe blinds clear-sighted men and is the ruin of the just man's cause.

---

4. LAW AND PROPHETIC RELIGION: THE DEMANDS OF SOCIAL JUSTICE AND OF INTERIORITY (THE CIRCUMCISED HEART)

In the excerpt that follows, three things are especially notable. First the bold use of symbolic language—"circumcise your heart"—which cannot be meant or understood in any literal way; by act and example this text points from letter to spirit. Second, God is imaged as an impartial judge who "does not lift up faces and does not take offerings." "To lift up faces" is related to an Akkadian expression meaning "to stand surety," a legal action accomplished by extending one's hand to the other's face in token of identification. God, this text teaches, will not identify in this way with those He judges; He will not be partial. Noonan, *Bribes* 16 (1984). Similarly He will not as Judge receive offerings *(shohadh),* the usual placatory tribute brought a superior by an inferior. *id.* 25. The model of God as non-*shohadh*-taking judge breaks the regular pattern of reciprocity with a powerful, potentially hostile stranger. *id.* 3–4. God as impartial Judge becomes the paradigm for judges in Israel (Dt.

16:18–20). Third, God commands the Israelites to remember the powerless—"the orphan and the widow," traditional figures of the poor since at least 2000 BCE, and the alien. Implicit in the command is that God is the owner of the land. Israel's ownership is not so absolute that the alien can be treated as a thing or as a nothing. To revere the poor is to give God the respect or "fear" he is due. It is to give him true worship, not shallow piety. The connection between law and prophetic religion may be seen in a parallel text from an eighth century prophet who wrote: "What does the LORD require of you but to do justice, to love kindness, and to walk humbly with your God?" (Micah 6:8).

Deuteronomy 10:12–20

So now, O Israel, what does the LORD your God require of you? Only to fear the LORD your God, to walk in all his ways, to love him, to serve the LORD your God with all your heart and with all your soul, and to keep the commandments of the LORD your God and his decrees that I am commanding you today, for your well-being. Although heaven and the heaven of heavens belong to the LORD your God, the earth with all that is in it, yet the LORD set his heart in love on your ancestors alone and chose you, their descendants after them, out of all the peoples, as it is today. Circumcise, then, the foreskin of your heart, and be not stubborn any longer. For the LORD your God is God of gods and Lord of lords, mighty and awesome, who is not partial and takes no bribe, who executes justice for the orphan and the widow, and who loves the strangers, providing them food and clothing. You shall also love the stranger, for you were strangers in the land of Egypt. You shall fear the Lord your God; him alone shall you worship; to him you shall hold fast, and by his name shall you swear.

An older contemporary of Micah, Isaiah received a call to be a prophet (Is. 6:1) at the end of the reign of King Uzziah of Jerusalem (ca. 783–742 BCE). Isaiah is a critic of existing religious practices in Israel and by the same token a critic of those in power. The existence of a Ruler above the rulers, of Law above current conventions are the predicates of his preaching. The dualism of governmental power and a Higher Power is at the foundation of his fierce message. "Whatever is right" is not a norm Isaiah can accept. His attack on a religion based on shallow external sacrifices to God appears to be absolute. It is paralleled by his attack on *shohadh* offered to human judges (Is. 1:23). Note again that the full measure of a right relationship with God (called "righteousness") is not ritual worship, but moral conduct—justice, especially toward the oppressed, the orphan and the widow.

Isaiah 1:10–17,23

Hear the word of the LORD,
    you rulers of Sodom!
Listen to the teaching of our God,
    you people of Gomorrah!

What to me is the multitude of your sacrifices?
   says the LORD;
I have had enough of burnt offerings of rams
   and the fat of fed beasts;
I do not delight in the blood of bulls,
   or of lambs, or of goats.
When you come to appear before me,
   who asked this from your hand?
   Trample my courts no more;
bringing offerings is futile;
   incense is an abomination to me.
New moon and sabbath and calling of convocation—
   I cannot endure solemn assemblies with iniquity.
Your new moons and your appointed festivals
   my soul hates;
they have become a burden to me,
   I am weary of bearing them.
When you stretch out your hands,
   I will hide my eyes from you;
even though you make many prayers,
   I will not listen;
   your hands are full of blood.
Wash yourselves; make yourselves clean;
   remove the evil of your doings
   from before my eyes;
cease to do evil,
learn to do good;
seek justice,
   rescue the oppressed,
defend the orphan,
   plead for the widow ...
Your princes are rebels
   and companions of thieves.
Everyone loves a bribe
   and runs after gifts.
They do not defend the orphan,
   and the widow's cause does not come before them.

———

Amos was not a professional prophet employed at the court, but a simple farm worker who was suddenly called to tell the truth to power. His message exemplifies classically that biblical prophecy is concerned not about prediction of future events, but about calling people to live faithfully and honestly here and now. It is not foretelling, but telling forth. This passage repeats the concern of Isaiah for justice, especially for the poor and the needy, dispossessed by those with wealth and power. The term "in the gate" refers to the place where legal disputes were resolved in the ancient world, the great plaza near the city gate. It is there, the prophet insists, that justice must be established.

Amos 5: 10–15

They hate the one who reproves in the gate, and they abhor the one who speaks the truth. Therefore because you trample on the poor and take from them levies of grain, you have built houses of hewn stone, but you shall not live in them; you have planted pleasant vineyards, but you shall not drink their wine. For I know how many are your transgressions, and how great are your sins—you who afflict the righteous, who take a bribe, and push aside the needy in the gate. Therefore the prudent will keep silent in such a time; for it is an evil time. Seek good and not evil, that you may live; and so the LORD, the God of hosts, will be with you, just as you have said. Hate evil and love good, and establish justice in the gate.

————

The biblical narrative of the original covenant with Israel describes how Moses destroyed the original two tablets of the law because of Israel's idolatry at Sinai–Horeb, worshipping a metal calf (Ex. 32; Dt. 9:15–21). This act signifies the rupture of the covenant. The narrative, however, does not end there, but emphasizes that God graciously gave Israel a new covenant, inscribing the Ten Words on two new tablets (Ex. 34:1–9; Dt. 10:1–11). The remaking of a covenant functions as a spiritual conviction about the passage from sin and guilt to acceptance and forgiveness. After the extinction of two kingdoms—Israel in the eighth century at the hands of the Assyrians and Judah in the sixth century at the hands of the Babylonians—the theme of covenant renewal was also politically charged with the hope of restoration of nationhood. Blenkinsopp, *The Pentateuch* 184. In the promise of a new covenant Torah and prophets concur. In an oracle written after the destruction of Jerusalem by the Babylonians in 587 BCE, the prophet Jeremiah employs the covenant formulary to promise not only a new political reality, but also a renewed people who will observe the law written not on stone tablets, as at Sinai–Horeb, but deep within their hearts (*see* Jer. 32:36–41; Ezek. 11:19; Hos. 2:20).

Jeremiah 31:31–34

The days are surely coming, says the LORD, when I will make a new covenant with the house of Israel and the house of Judah. It will not be like the covenant that I made with their ancestors when I took them by the hand to bring them out of the land of Egypt—a covenant that they broke, though I was their husband, says the LORD. But this is the covenant that I will make with the house of Israel after those days, says the LORD: I will put my law within them, and I will write it on their hearts; and I will be their God, and they shall be my people. No longer shall they teach one another, or say to each other, "Know the LORD," for they shall all know me, from the least of them to the greatest, says the LORD; for I will forgive their iniquity, and remember their sin no more.

————

Any attempt to regulate human behavior by law, whether ancient or modern, can degenerate into formalism and legalism, but the possibility of deep

interior commitment by a community to a covenanted way of life explains why
the law was celebrated in Israel as a source of wisdom, enlightenment, and joy.
Psalm 119 is the longest psalm in the Bible. To assist in its memorization it is
an acrostic, each stanza of eight verses beginning with the same letter in
Hebrew until all the letters of the alphabet are included. The psalm exalts in
the Torah, with all its ordinances and precepts, commandments, and statutes.
Those taunting the psalmist could be the external foes who destroyed Israel in
the eighth and sixth centuries. In a later period it could be a fellow Jew who
has become assimilated to Greek or Roman legal culture, [sections 5 and 6
below].

Psalm 119:33–48

Teach me, O Lord, the way of your statutes;
   and I will keep it to the end.
Give me understanding, that I may keep your law,
   and observe it with my whole heart.
Lead me in the path of your commandments,
   for I delight in it.
Incline my heart to your testimonies,
   and not to gain!
Turn my eyes from looking at vanities;
   and give me life in your ways.
Confirm to your servant your promise,
   which is for those who fear you.
Turn away the reproach which I dread,
   for your ordinances are good.
Let your steadfast love come to me, O Lord,
   your salvation according to your promise.
Then shall I have an answer for those who taunt me,
   for I trust in your word.
And take not the word of truth utterly out of my mouth,
   for my hope is in your ordinances.
I will keep your law continually,
   for ever and ever.
And I shall walk at liberty,
   for I have sought your precepts.
I will also speak of your testimonies before kings,
   and shall not be put to shame.
For I find delight in your commandments,
   which I love.
I revere your commandments, which I love,
   and I will meditate on your statutes.

5. THE PRIMACY OF GOD'S LAW AND THE DUTY OF DISOBEDIENCE OF HUMAN LAW

Israel came under the foreign domination of successive empires that waxed
and waned in the ancient Near East: the Egyptians, the Assyrians, the

Babylonians, the Persians, the Greeks, and the Romans. Each of these experiences tested Israel's fidelity to the central law of its covenanting God: "You shall have no other God to set against me" (Dt. 5:7) [section 1]. The Hebrew Bible clarified the duty of disobeying conflicting human law not only through law codes, but also through narratives illustrating the primacy of God's law. One of the earliest stories of a dramatic conflict between an imperial edict and God's law is located in the period of Israel's sojourn in Egypt. The Pharaoh has issued a decree that all male babies of the Hebrews are to be executed as soon as they are born. The midwives who disobeyed this decree set in motion the saving events of the exodus, for the great liberator and lawgiver Moses was rescued from destruction. Their disobedience sets an example for all successive generations reading the Torah. This narrative and others like it form a sort of biblical "supremacy clause."

Exodus 1:15–21

The king of Egypt said to the Hebrew midwives, one of whom was named Shiphrah and the other Puah, "when you act as midwives to the Hebrew women, and them on the birthstool, if it is a boy, kill him; but if it is a girl, she shall live." But the midwives feared God; they did not do as the king of Egypt commanded them, but they let the boys live. So the king of Egypt summoned the midwives and said to them, "Why have you done this, and allowed the boys to live?" The midwives said to Pharaoh, "Because the Hebrew women are not like the Egyptian women; for they are vigorous and give birth before the midwife comes to them." So God dealt well with the midwives; and the people multiplied and became very strong. And because the midwives feared God, he gave them families.

The Hellenistic period began with the stunning military victories of Alexander the Great (356–323 BCE), first over Greece and Asia Minor, then over Darius III at Issus in 333 BCE, and finally at Gaugamela in modern Iraq in 331 BCE. Alexander planned a universal empire dominated by Greek culture; at its zenith it included Egypt, Mesopotamia, and Persia. Before his death in 323 BCE Alexander divided up his empire among his generals, who quarreled over the control of the empire for over three decades (319–287 BCE). Throughout most of the third century the Ptolemies granted local autonomy to the provinces they administered. Seleucus I Nicator prevailed in Syria and Babylonia, establishing the Seleucid dynasty. Judea fell subject to the Seleucids for a period of about fifty years (197–142 BCE). At the outset of Seleucid rule, the charter of Antiochus III the Great sanctioned the theocratic status of the Jewish nation (2 Mac. 4:11). His son, Antiochus IV Epiphanes (176–163 BCE), a strong devotee of Greek culture, came to power after getting rid of several rival claimants. Committed to a systematic program of Hellenization, this Antiochus presented the gravest threat to the religious freedom of the Jews by encouraging and then demanding conformity to pagan practices (1 Mac. 1:10–15). An assimilated Jew named Joshua first abandoned his Jewish heritage by taking a Greek name, Jason. He then offered Antiochus a bribe to obtain the office of High Priest (2 Mac. 4: 7–8), and he promised to collaborate in the Hellenization program that compromised the identity of the covenanted people on critical points of the Law. "There was such an extreme of Hellenization and increase in the adoption of foreign ways because of the surpassing wickedness of Jason, who was ungodly and no high priest, that the priests were no longer intent upon their services at the altar. Despising the sanctuary and neglecting the sacrifices, they hastened to take part in the wrestling arena after the call to the discus, disdaining the honors prized by their fathers and putting the highest value upon Greek forms of prestige" (2 Mac. 4:13–15). The Greek customs referred to included a gymnasium in which young athletes would compete with one another naked in mini-Olympic games. Assimilated Jews "disguised their circumcision, and abandoned the holy covenant, submitting to the heathen rule as willing slaves of impiety" (1 Mac. 1:15).

The program of "voluntary" Hellenization (2 Mac. 4:9–17) swiftly led to the brutal coercion of a decree aimed at obliterating Judaism (2 Mac. 6:1). "A man could neither keep the sabbath, nor observe the feasts of his fathers, nor so much as confess himself to be a Jew" (2 Mac. 6:6). Antiochus desecrated and pillaged the Jerusalem Temple (1 Mac. 1:19–24; 2 Mac. 5:15–16), where he erected the "abomination of desolation" (Dan. 11:31), a statue of the Olympian deity Zeus, within its sacred precincts (1 Mac. 1:54). His imperial law created an unavoidable conflict with the central prohibitions of idol worship contained in the first three commandments of the covenant: "You shall have no other god to set against me. You shall not make a carved image for yourself nor the likeness of anything in the heavens above, or on the earth below, or in the waters under the earth. You shall not bow down to them or worship them" (Dt. 5: 7–9). These outrages prompted further resistance by observant Jews, which led in turn to a full-scale program of massacre of Jews remaining faithful to the Torah (2 Mac. 5:11–26). This brutal persecution lasted from 167 to 164 BCE. *See* Menahem Stern, "The Decrees Against the Jewish Religion and the Establishment of the Hasmonean State," in Haim Hillel Ben–Sasson, ed., *A History of the Jewish People* 201–16 (1976).

Nearly fifty years after these events, the Second Book of Maccabees, a Greek composition addressed to the Jews of Alexandria and found in the Apocrypha, was the occasion for celebrating obedience to God unto death. Chapters 6–7 of this book contain the earliest martyrologies. Designed to encourage fidelity to the covenant in time of suffering, this literary form later became popular among Christians during their persecution by the Romans [Chapter Two, section 1] or, in the sixteenth century, by the royal authority in England [Chapter Four, section 4]. The text describes how Eleazar, a leading teacher of the law, refused the ruler's order to eat pork and so was flogged to death (2 Mac. 6:18–30). Seven brothers were then tortured to turn them into porkeaters. After six have died, the story continues:

2 Maccabees 7:20–31

The mother was especially admirable and worthy of honorable memory. Although she saw her seven sons perish within a single day, she bore it with good courage because of her hope in the Lord. She encouraged each of them in the language of their ancestors. Filled with a noble spirit, she reinforced her woman's reasoning with a man's courage, and said to them, "I do not know how you came into being in my womb. It was not I who gave you life and breath, nor I who set in order the elements within each of you. Therefore the Creator of the world, who shaped the beginning of humankind and devised the origin of all things, will in his mercy give life and breath back to you again, since you now forget yourselves for the sake of his laws.''

Antiochus felt that he was being treated with contempt, and he was suspicious of her reproachful tone. The youngest brother being still alive, Antiochus not only appealed to him in words, but promised with oaths that he would make him rich and enviable if he would turn from the ways of his ancestors, and that he would take him for his Friend and entrust him with public affairs. Since the young man would not listen to him at all, the king called the mother to him and urged her to advise the youth to save himself. After much urging on his part, she undertook to persuade her son. But, leaning close to him, she spoke in their native language as follows, deriding the cruel tyrant: "My son, have pity on me. I carried you nine months in my womb, and nursed you for three years, and have reared you and brought you up to this point in your life, and have taken care of you. I beg you, my child, to look at the heaven and the earth and see everything that is in them, and recognize that God did not make them out of things that existed. And in the same way the human race came into being. Do not fear this butcher, but prove worthy of your brothers. Accept death, so that in God's mercy I may get you back again along with your brothers."

While she was still speaking, the young man said, "What are you waiting for? I will not obey the king's command, but I obey the command of the law that was given to our ancestors through Moses."

In 167 BCE Mattathias led an open rebellion against Greek rule in Judea. When Mattathias died a year later, his son, Judas Maccabeus, led the guerrilla resistance movement (2 Mac. 8–9). Antiochus ordered his regent Lysias to depopulate the whole of Judea, enslave its population, and lay it waste. Judas defeated a vastly superior Syrian army under the Greek general Gorgias at Emmaus in 166 BCE. In the following year Judas defeated a still larger army under Lysias at Beth-zur, and restored Judea and its capital Jerusalem to Jewish rule. At one level this revolt was a courageous peasant rebellion against the might of the Hellenistic empire. Its success against formidable odds meant the end of an early attempt to impose a "final solution" to the "Jewish question" either by genocidal destruction of observant Jews or by destroying Jewish identity through enforced assimilation. The recapture and rededication of the sacred precincts of the Jerusalem Temple (1 Mac. 4:36–61; 2 Mac. 10) gave rise to the Festival of Lights or the Feast of Chanukah, which celebrates a major victory for religious freedom in the ancient world. The Maccabean movement, however, was also intended as a purging of the Jewish community, or as a civil war in which observant Jews struggled against Jewish assimilators personified by Jason, the pseudo high priest.

Both points have poignant counterparts in this century. From the Nazi laws discriminating against Jews as early as 1933, Lucy Dawidowicz, *The War Against the Jews*, 1933–1945 63–92 (1975), to the death camps that claimed six million Jews, *id.* 173–200, the Third Reich represented the most intense effort in the long history of anti-Jewish hatred to impose a "final solution." In modern America, by contrast, many contemporary Jewish leaders think that Jews now face the other peril of the Maccabean period, that of gradual but steady erosion of their unique character as a religious people. *See* Jonathan D. Sarna, "Christian America or Secular America?: The Church–State Dilemma of American Jews," in Richard John Neuhaus, ed., *Jews in Unsecular America* (1987) 8–19; David Novak, "American Jews and America: The Mission of Israel Revisited," *id.* 41–60; Alan M. Dershowitz, *The Vanishing American Jew* (1997).

One form of this difficulty was reflected in the demand by the dominant Protestant Christian communities that Jews assimilate to their beliefs or be denied public benefits available only to those willing to swear to a Protestant oath [Chapter Six, section 2]. A more pervasive form of the difficulty presents itself as a demand for radical secularization of the culture, neutering all religious faith by relegating religion exclusively to the private sphere. These views are contentious, but they insinuate themselves into many of the controversies in the modern period of constitutional litigation, including the cases on keeping holy the sabbath [Chapter Seven, section 4; Chapter Eleven, section 5; and Chapter Thirteen, section 2], on wearing religious garb [Chapter Eleven, section 8], on religious displays sponsored by the government [Chapter Thirteen, section 6], on public aid to education in religious schools [Chapter Fourteen, section 1], and on religion in the curriculum of public schools [Chapter Fourteen, section 2].

6.   Jews, Christians, and the Roman Empire

"Rome is the only example in history of a single city-state growing to a world empire." Seán Freyne, *The World of the New Testament* 49 (1989). Neither the city of Rome nor its empire was "built in a day." Unlike the brief military campaign of Alexander the Great, the expansion of Roman rule or *imperium* throughout the Mediterranean world took centuries to achieve. By the same token the Roman empire endured for centuries longer than its Hellenistic antecedents. The Jewish attitude toward Rome varied considerably over the centuries. The next excerpt hails the eastward expansion of Roman rule in second century BCE. Shortly after the persecution of the Jews under Antiochus Epiphanes, Rome appeared as a friend with whom a strategic alliance should be forged.

————

1 Maccabees 8:1–4,17–29

Now Judas heard of the fame of the Romans, that they were very strong and were well-disposed toward all who made an alliance with them, that they pledged friendship to those who came to them, and that they were very strong. He had been told of their wars and of the brave deeds that they were doing among the Gauls, how they had defeated them and forced them to pay tribute, and what they had done in the land of Spain to get control of the silver and gold mines there, and how they had gained control of the whole region by their planning and patience, even though the place was far distant from them. They also subdued the kings who came against them from the ends of the earth, until they crushed them and inflicted great disaster upon them; the rest paid them tribute every year. . . . So Judas sent [emissaries] to Rome to establish friendship and alliance, and to free themselves from the yoke; for they saw that the kingdom of the Greeks was completely enslaving Israel. They went to Rome, a very long journey; and they entered the senate chamber and spoke as follows: "Judas, who is also called Maccabeus, and his brothers and the people of the Jews have sent us to establish alliance and peace with you, that we may be enrolled as your allies and friends." The proposal pleased them, and this is a copy of the letter which they wrote in reply, on bronze tablets, and sent to Jerusalem, to remain with them there as a memorial of peace and alliance: "May all go well with the Romans and with the nation of the Jews at sea and on land for ever, and may sword and enemy be far from them. If war comes first to Rome or to any of their allies in all their dominion, the nation of the Jews shall act as their allies wholeheartedly, as the occasion may indicate to them. To the enemy who makes war they shall not give or supply grain, arms, money, or ships, just as Rome has decided; and they shall keep these obligations and do so without deceit. In the same way, if war comes first to the nation of the Jews, the Romans shall willingly act as their allies, as the occasion may indicate to them. And to their enemies there shall not be given grain, arms, money, or ships, just as Rome has decided; and they shall keep these obligations and do so without deceit." Thus on these terms the Romans make a treaty with the Jewish people.

––––––––

    The Romans granted to the Jews special "privileges and immunities"—a phrase that was to make its way into the United States Constitution, Art. IV, § 1, and Amend. XIV, § 1. This policy of special consideration for the Jews in Roman law began with the approach by Judas after the attempted annihilation of the Jews by Antiochus Epiphanes. "The Romans were interested in embarrassing and weakening Syria, and agreed to a declaration of friendship. In the following century, the Jews lent valuable military assistance first to [Julius] Caesar and then to Octavian in the civil wars, moved by outrage at Pompey's capture of Jerusalem and violation of the Holy of Holies, and by the diplomatic necessity of rallying to the victor of Actium. The outcome was a series of official edicts and letters to Greek cities in the East instructing them to permit resident Jews to observe their traditional religion." Peter Garnsey & Richard Saller, *The Roman Empire: Economy, Society and Culture* 169–70 (1987). Rome thus provided the powerful social matrix within which Judaism and Christianity were shaped in the critical first centuries of the common era. Roman law explicitly protected the freedom of Jews to form religious associations throughout the empire. This enabled Jews to travel throughout the Mediterranean without abandoning their religious practices. The establishment of synagogues in virtually every province of the empire proved critical for the survival of Judaism in the diaspora communities outside of Judea. Most critically, Roman law provided exemptions for Jews "from many external acts of the Roman cult [and] from all secular activities on the Sabbath, [holding] them only to prayers for the emperor. Before the Christian era began, Judaism was recognized as the only *religio licita* in the empire save the imperial cult itself." Edward H. Flannery, *The Anguish of the Jews* 16 (1965).

The Apostle Paul used the synagogues as his first point of entry into the communities he visited in the journeys described in Acts of the Apostles (9:20, Damascus; 13:5, Salamis; 13:14, Antioch of Pisidia; 14:1, Iconium; 17:1, Thessalonica; 17:10, Beroea; 17:17, Athens; 18:4, Corinth; 18:19, Ephesus). Thus Roman law helped both Jews and Christians to expand in a relatively peaceful, stable environment throughout the Mediterranean world.

The associational freedom of Jews is clarified in a letter to the citizens of Alexandria in 41 CE [common era] from the emperor Claudius (41–54 CE). Claudius wrote that the Jews of Alexandria—longtime citizens of that city— should enjoy religious freedom "to observe the rites in the worship of their god," but that they should not "agitate for more privileges than they formerly possessed." C.K. Barrett, ed., *New Testament Background: Selected Documents* 47–50 (1987). Seutonius (*Claudius*, 25:4) reports that eight years later, when a disturbance arose in the city of Rome—presumably between orthodox Jews and Christians over the messianic character of Jesus—the same emperor did not distinguish between Jews and Christians, expelling both from the city; this story is mentioned in Acts 18:2.

Like the Greeks, the Romans thought of law as an aspect of a pervasive culture, which included obligations of religious worship as a demonstration of civic loyalty or patriotism. There was a substantial overlap between Greek and Roman religion. The Olympian deities were given Roman names (e.g., Zeus Pater became Jupiter), and the Romans tried to accommodate diverse religious practices among their conquered subjects. The centrality of the Jewish commitment to monotheism and the repudiation of any graven image led to recurrent difficulties with the principal Roman innovation in civil religion exported from the East, emperor worship, instituted under caesar Augustus (22 BCE–14 CE). *See* D.S. Potter, "Persecution in the Early Church," in David Noel Freedman, ed., 5 *Anchor Bible Dictionary*, 231–35 (1992).

Flavius Josephus had been a military leader in Galilee during the First Jewish War against Roman rule (66–73 CE), but went over to the other side in the middle of the war and for that reason was viewed by many Jews with the suspicion, if not repugnance, reserved for traitors. Around 93 CE he wrote *The Antiquities of the Jews*. In part *The Antiquities* served as an important chronicle of historical events seen from a Jewish perspective. "The Jews were a sizeable minority group within the Roman Empire, numbering from four to six million people out of a population of approximately sixty million." Robert L. Wilken, *The Christians as the Romans Saw Them* 113 (1984). Hence Josephus wrote *The Antiquities* in part to allay any fear that the Roman authorities might have that this large group might constitute a serious threat to the empire. One of the arguments used to assuage the Romans was that sensible accommodation of Jewish religion had been an effective policy in the past. For example, Josephus recounts that more than 6,000 Pharisees refused to take an oath to caesar Augustus on the occasion of a census, perhaps that referred to in Lk. 2:1, without any serious breakdown in imperial rule. Josephus, *The Antiquities of the Jews* 17:2, in *The Works of Flavius Josephus* 453 (William Whiston trans., 1987). Oaths to the *genius* of the emperor were commonly required throughout the empire, and the breaking of such an oath was an act of *lege-majesté* regarded as high treason. Hence the willingness of Rome to exempt Jews on this matter was a significant accommodation of their religious beliefs.

Josephus also reports that around the year 26 CE a delegation of Jews appeared in Caesarea, the capital of the Roman province of Judea, before Pontius Pilate, the Roman procurator, to protest Pilate's posting of images of the emperor as divine within the sacred precincts of the Jerusalem Temple. When Pilate replied that anyone who would refuse to worship these divine images should be executed, all of the delegates immediately offered their bared necks to the Roman sword, saying "they would take their deaths willingly, rather than the wisdom of their laws should be transgressed." Moved by this courageous display of devotion to the commandment prohibiting the making of images [section 1 above], Pilate ordered the standards removed from the Temple and brought to Caesarea. Josephus, *Antiquities* 18:3, *id.* 479–80; *see also* Josephus, *The Jewish Wars* 2:9, *id.* 608–9 (reflecting that the sit-in lasted five days and nights). *See* Carl Kraeling, "The Episode of the Roman Standards at Jerusalem," *Harv. Theological Rev.* 35 (1942) 263. The courage of these Jewish leaders in confronting Pilate is underscored by the propensity of the procurator for brutality. For example, he crushed the movement of a Samaritan prophet who was about to lead a crowd to Mt. Gerizim to recover the sacred vessels thought to be hidden there by Moses. Josephus was well aware of the staggering loss of life in this episode. Josephus, *Antiquities* 18:4, *id.* 482.

Conflicts between the Jews and the Romans over the Jerusalem Temple did not end with Pilate. The emperor Caligula (37–41 CE) ordered his governor in Syria to have his statue erected in the Temple, by force if necessary. Josephus, *Antiquities*, 18:8, *id.* 494–97; Tacitus, *Histories*, 5.9. Once again, Jews were prepared to die in defiance of a law that required them to violate the commandment against worshiping any other god. Caligula's effort at exporting emperor worship to Jerusalem failed in part because of an agricultural strike by Jewish peasants, who refused to plant their crops in protest of the imperial insensitivity to Jewish law. A full-blown crisis was averted by the emperor's death in 41 CE.

Although collective nonviolence had proven successful twice within a short period, some Jews began to plot a full-blown military confrontation with the Roman authorities. The Galilean countryside was the base of a resistance movement that was to erupt into open war with the Romans in 66 CE. The leaders of this movement were the Zealots; their name in Latin, *sicarii*, "is probably derived from their tactic of using the small Roman *sica* or dagger disguised under their cloaks, as they engaged in what can be described as urban guerilla warfare." Freyne 66. Like the Maccabees before them, the Zealots were determined not only to overthrow their foreign overlords for religious reasons, "but they also directed their ire against the wealthy Jewish aristocracy who were seen as collaborationists with Rome." *Id.*; *see also* 118–22. Like Antiochus Epiphanes, the procurator Florus (64–66 CE) confiscated the Temple treasury. This provided the lighting of the tinder box that sparked the outburst of First Jewish War (66–73 CE). The Zealots then occupied the Temple and prohibited any further sacrifice on behalf of the Emperor. "This was tantamount to an open declaration of war since the daily sacrifice to their god was the Jewish equivalent to worship of the Emperor, which was expected of every loyal inhabitant of the empire as an act of civic duty.... [A]fter four years of bloodshed and siege the Jerusalem Temple was burned to the ground by storming Roman troops, and a chapter of Jewish history that had begun with the rebuilding of the Temple by the Babylonian exiles in 515 BCE—the second temple period, as Jewish historians call it—had come to an end" in 70 CE. *Id.* 67. The resistance fighters who survived the destruction of Jerusalem fled to the mountain fortress of Masada, where—after a bitter siege lasting three years—they committed mass suicide rather than surrender to the Romans. *See* Menahem Stern, "The Great Revolt," in Ben–Sasson, ed., *A History of the Jewish People,* 296–303.

The probable date of the letter that follows is 57–58 CE; the place of composition, Corinth; the author certainly the man who called himself Paul, converted about twenty years earlier from Judaism to being a follower of Jesus Christ. *See* Joseph A. Fitzmyer, "The Letter to the Romans," and "Paul," *New Jerome Biblical Commentary* 830, 1336 (1990). The ruling caesar was Nero (54–68 CE). The famous fire in the Circus Maximus, which he blamed on the Christians [section 8 below], did not occur until 64 CE. Paul confidently took an "appeal to Caesar" (Acts 25:11) as late as 60 CE. His advice on the proper attitude to the authorities immediately follows exhortations not to be conformed to this world, to bless one's persecutors, to forgo vengeance, and to live in peace (Rom. 12:14–21). Paul refers to the government as the *"exousiai" or* "the powers," not as "the state." He personifies the powers as God's agent but does not cease to think of it as an "it" rather than as individual men. No criteria of this agency of the divine are suggested, but one probably would be mistaken to read these lines as contrary to the long prophetic tradition of criticizing "the powers." A similar attitude of respect for imperial authority is reflected in 1 Peter 2:13–17. *See* John Howard Yoder, *The Politics of Jesus* 193–214 (1972); Oscar Cullmann, "Paul and the State," in *The State in the New Testament* 50–70 (1956).

Romans 13:1–8

Let every soul be subject to the higher powers, for there is no power except by God, and those that are have been ordained by God. Hence he who resists the power has opposed the ordinance of God. Those who oppose will receive judgment for themselves. Rulers are not a terror for good work but for evil. Do you want not to fear the power? Do good, and you will have praise from it. It is God's minister to you for the good. But if you do evil, fear. It does not carry the sword in vain. God's minister, it is an avenger for wrath to the one practicing evil. Therefore it is necessary to be subject, not only because of wrath but also because of conscience. So pay taxes. For they are servants of God who attend to this very thing. Pay each what you owe him—the tax to whom you owe the tax, the tribute to whom you owe the tribute, fear to whom you owe fear, honor to whom you owe honor. Owe nothing to anyone except to love one another, for he who loves the other has fulfilled the law.

———

Paul founded the Christian community at Corinth during one of his missionary journeys, lived there for a number of years, and had on-going contact with this community. As a devout Pharisee, he was familiar with the teaching that the Torah is summed up in the two commands of love of God (Dt.

6:5) and love of neighbor (Lev. 19:18). For example, immediately after the previous excerpt he provides a summary of the commandments culminating in the thought, "Love is therefore the fullness of the law" (Rom. 13:10). He may have been familiar with the teaching of Jesus to the same effect (Mt. 19:34–40). Paul expressly teaches that bearing one another's burdens fulfills the "Torah of the Messiah" (Gal. 6:1), and he holds that the greatest of all the gifts that God can bestow is patient, generous, self-giving love of others (1 Cor. 12:31–13:13). To preserve the unity of the church then under the stress of factions, Paul teaches that Christians—who will soon judge this fleeting world—should not have recourse to the pagan courts of the Roman empire, but should settle their differences with one another in the spirit of familial love. This teaching is also relevant to the resolution of intrachurch disputes [Chapter Eight, Section 5, and Chapter Twelve, Section 3].

1 Corinthians 6:1–8

When any of you has a grievance against another, do you dare to take it to court before the unrighteous, instead of taking it before the saints? Do you not know that the saints will judge the world? And if the world is to be judged by you, are you incompetent to try trivial cases? Do you not know that we are to judge angels—to say nothing of ordinary matters? If you have ordinary cases, then, do you appoint as judges those who have no standing in the church? I say this to your shame. Can it be that there is no one among you wise enough to decide between one believer and another, but a believer goes to court against a believer—and before unbelievers at that? In fact, to have lawsuits at all with one another is already a defeat for you. Why not rather be wronged? Why not rather be defrauded? But you yourselves wrong and defraud—and believers at that.

NOTES AND QUESTIONS

At the time the above passage was written, Christians were a tiny minority within a large pagan environment. Both the author of the text, Paul, and the people to whom he was writing, expected the imminent return of Jesus to pronounce final judgment on the world. Would a shift in either of these predicates—the growth of Christianity to a point of significant influence on legal culture, or the postponement of the expectation of the return of Jesus—alter the binding effect of this text? Is the text as urgent if Christians began to doubt that they were living in the last days of a world that they would judge, but accepted that they would need to rely on institutions of government for such mundane, this-worldly matters as the peaceful resolution of "trivial cases" and "ordinary matters"? There is evidence that in the early third century at least some Christians believed themselves bound by this passage. In chapter 11 of his treatise on military service, *De corona militum*, Tertullian, Bishop of Carthage, asked: "Shall the son of peace take part in battle when it does not become him even to sue at law?" [Chapter Two, Note 2]. Beginning in the fourth century CE, under the emperor Constantine [Chapter Two, Note 1] the civil courts of the empire were staffed not by "unrighteous ... unbelievers," but by fellow Christians. Does this fact change the moral relevance of the text? Numerous Christians still read this text as binding them to attempt to reconcile differences with fellow Christians rather than resort to litigation against one another. Whatever your answer to these questions, this text—in harmony with the teaching of Jesus on the imperative of reconciliation with one's "brother," whom Christians are to befriend on the way to court (Mt. 5:21–26)—forms the basis for many Christians who attempt conciliation before resorting to litigation in the civil courts. *See* Ken Sande, *The Peacemaker: A Biblical Guide to Resolving Personal Conflict* (1991). For different reasons than those articulated by Paul in the text above, Jews have maintained an elaborate system of alternative dispute resolution for members of their own community. "Jewish law is the oldest applied legal system in the world, spanning more than three thousand years." Aaron M. Schreiber, *Jewish Law and Decision–Making: A Study Through Time* 3 (1979); *see also* Elliot N. Dorff and Arthur Rosett. *A Living Tree: The Roots and Growth of Jewish Law* (1988).

7.   Jesus and The Tribute Coin: "Render to Caesar Only What Is Due to Caesar"

Like many other teachings of Paul, the teaching about rulers in Romans 13 stated in Greek abstractions ideas that can be found in, or in harmony with, the sayings of Jesus. *See* Harald Riesenfeld, *The Gospel Traditions* (1970). That more concrete teaching, as preserved in the Gospel of Mark, commonly dated as written between 65 and 70 CE, occurs in a dialogue set by Mark in Jerusalem not long before Jesus' death. The "they" referred to are "the chief priests and scribes and elders."

Mark 12:13–17

Then they sent to him some Pharisees and some Herodians to trap him in what he said. And they came and said to him, "Teacher, we know that you are sincere, and show deference to no one; for you do not regard people with partiality, but teach the way of God in accordance with truth. Is it lawful to pay taxes to the emperor, or not? Should we pay them, or should we not?" But knowing their hypocrisy, he said to them, "Why are you putting me to the test? Bring me a denarius and let me see it." And they brought one. Then he said to them, "Whose head is this, and whose title?" They answered, "The emperor's." Jesus said to them, "Give to the emperor the things that are the emperor's, and to God the things that are God's." And they were utterly amazed at him.

———

The question of financial tribute by believers to the state (the exact reverse of the American question of financial support by the state for believers) is crucial. Jesus' answer is on the surface neutral, but structured so that the emphasis is on giving what is God's to God. J. Duncan M. Derrett, *Law in the New Testament* 313–38 (1970); and "Luke's Perspective on Tribute to Caesar," in Richard Cassidy and Philip Scharper, eds., *Political Issues in Luke–Acts* 33–48 (1983). According to Lk. 23:2, his enemies twist his teaching into a flat command not to "pay taxes to Caesar" and make this a principal charge against him before Pilate. Reminiscence of this incident colors Paul's teaching to the Romans where the injunction to pay taxes is clearer than in Jesus' saying and where the duty to pay taxes is the final and climactic obligation. David Daube draws attention to the analogous treatment by Jesus of the obligation to pay a tax to the Temple in Jerusalem (Mt. 17:24–27). Daube, "Responsibilities of Master and Disciples in the Gospels," 19 *New Testament Studies* 13 (1972); Derrett, *Law in the New Testament* 247–65. Both sayings about the tribute coin—rendering to caesar and to God—are examples of another teaching of Jesus: "Be wise as serpents and harmless as doves" (Mt. 10:16), a verse with perennial attraction to believers pressed by duties imposed by the ruling authorities and conflicting duties to God.

8. Luke-Acts and the Christian Challenge to the Roman Empire

One of the purposes of the third Gospel and the Acts of the Apostles, written in the 80s CE, was to convince the Roman powers that the Christians did not pose any threat of violent insurrection. It is significant that this Gospel is addressed to "Theophilus," an unnamed distinguished official of the Roman empire. The author intends Paul's defense before the Roman procurator, below, to refer to Christians generally: they have "committed no offense whatever either against Jewish law, or the Temple, or Caesar" (Acts 25:8). Yet Luke's gospel narrative portrays a Jesus who acts in ways that contradict core values underlying the stable hierarchical order of the empire. According to Luke, women play a very significant role in the mission and teaching of Jesus (Lk. 4:38–39; 7:11–17, 36–50; 8:1–3, 43–48; 10:38–42; 13:10–13; 18:1–8; 21:1–4); and Jesus associates with the poor, the sick and infirm (Lk. 7:21–23; 14:7–24), all of whom were outcasts in the empire; *see* Richard Cassidy, *Jesus, Politics and Society: A Study of Luke's Gospel* (1978) 20–24. Relief of poverty and hunger (Lk. 6:20–21) could be seen as an implicit "critique of the Roman tax system, which was placing an intolerable burden, at least in Judea, on an already overstrained peasant economy." Loveday C.A. Alexander, "Rome, Early Christian Attitudes to," in David Noel Freedman, ed., 5 *The Anchor Bible Dictionary* 836 (1992).

Luke's companion work, Acts of the Apostles, is also addressed to "Theophilus." In this document Luke discusses a central concern of the early Christian community about legal matters: the extent to which they must obey the Mosaic law and the leadership of the Jewish community in Jerusalem. Although far from being the laws of a pagan emperor, the Torah was felt as a constraint by the new Gentile Christians. For Paul the law is holy but "now we are rid of the law" (Rom. 7:6). The author of Luke–Acts, sharing Paul's perspective and writing about 80 CE, shows Peter and the apostles in confrontation with the council of Jewish authorities in Jerusalem. Peter gives a reason for his defiance, which was to afford an analogy applicable to later conflicts between caesar and Christians. According to an ancient tradition preserved in a second century document, Peter was executed by crucifixion. Acts of Peter, 30–41, in William Schneemelher, ed., *New Testament Apocrypha* (1992). The death of Peter occurred during the reign of the caesar Nero, who instigated a persecution of Christians in the city of Rome in 64 CE. *See* Potter, "Persecution in the Early Church," and Karl Baus, *From the Apostolic Community to Constantine* 111–18 (1965). Nero blamed the Christians for a fire in the Circus Maximus, but the Roman historian Tacitus gives an account of this persecution that suggests that Christianity was viewed as suspect for darker reasons: "Nero ... inflicted most extreme punishments on those, hateful by reasons of their abominations, who were commonly called Christians. Christus, the originator of that name, had been executed by the procurator Pontius Pilate. The pernicious superstition, checked for the moment, was bursting out again not only throughout Judea, the birthplace of the plague, but also throughout the city [Rome] into which all that is horrible and shameful streams from every quarter and is constantly practiced. Therefore first those who confessed were arrested, then on information a huge throng was convicted not so much on a charge of arson as because of their hatred of the human race." Tacitus, *Annals* 15.44.2–8. *See also* Wilken 48–50.

One of the purposes for the writing of Luke–Acts was to serve as an apologia or defense of Christianity against charges such as those leveled against it by Tacitus. Luke strove to explain to the Romans that the new movement that admitted Gentiles was grounded in the ancient religion of Israel, and was thus not a "pernicious superstition," but a venerable religion worthy of the same exemptions from Roman law as those enjoyed by the Jews. Luke also had to explain how Christianity had become distinct from Judaism, as the following story illustrates. The concluding line of the story explains why Christians, like the midwives in the Exodus story [section 5 above], resisted laws that are not in harmony with the dictates of conscience.

Acts of the Apostles 5:27–29

When they had brought them, they had them stand before the council. The high priest questioned them, saying, "We gave you strict orders not to teach in this name, yet here you have filled Jerusalem with your teaching and you are determined to bring this man's blood on us." But Peter and the apostles answered, "We must obey God rather than any human authority."

————

Luke also set out to explain to the Romans how Christianity moved beyond Judea, described by Tacitus as "the birthplace of the plague," and came to the capital of the Empire. He achieved this goal through a long journey narrative centered around the mission of the Apostle Paul. A Pharisee who followed the strict observance of the Torah (Acts 22:3), Paul became a convert to "the way" of Christianity (Acts 9:1–22; 22:4–16; 26:9–18). He sought thereafter to bring the good news or gospel about Jesus first to his fellow Jews (Acts 14:1; 16:13; 17:1; 18:4; 19:8; 28:23). But when many of the Jews rejected Paul's message, he turned to the Gentiles (Acts 13:46–47; 18:6), travelling throughout the empire on a mission that is "not a replacement of Israel but its legitimate continuation." Luke Johnson, *The Acts of the Apostles* 9 (1992). Many Jewish Christians, such as Peter and Paul, continued to worship faithfully in the Jerusalem Temple (Acts 3:1; 5:12) or in synagogues throughout the empire (Acts 13:14; 14:1). As the divergent rabbinical schools of Hillel and Gamaliel illustrate, Judaism in the first century of the common era could readily accommodate diverse interpretations of Torah. But Christian faith in the messianic and divine character of Jesus strained Jewish pluralism to the breaking point. In the year 90 CE a group of rabbis in Jamnia made a decision about the Jewish liturgy that quickly led to the exclusion of Christians from synagogues and to separation of the communities in most parts of the Empire.

Another critical legal issue for early Christians was the extent to which they were protected by exemptions, privileges and immunities under Roman law. Luke addresses this issue in a story that also illustrates the mounting tension between Jews and Jewish Christians. On one of his missionary journeys, Paul took up a collection for the poor of Jerusalem (Romans 15:25; 2 Cor. 8–9). When he returned to Jerusalem around 58 CE with this alms, he went to the Temple to join in the worship at the time of the feast of Weeks (Pentecost). Jews from Asia Minor recognized Paul in the Temple and identified him as one "who preaches to everyone everywhere against our people, against the Law, and against this place [the Temple]" (Acts 21:28). When a riot broke out in the Temple, the Roman authorities arrested Paul. A Roman citizen by virtue of his birth in the city of Tarsus (Acts 16:37–38; 21:39; 22:25–27), Paul invoked the privilege of trial before punishment (Acts 22:24–29). At a hearing before the Sanhedrin, Paul provoked a divisive dispute between the two principal parties in the Sanhedrin, the Pharisees and the Sadducees, by insisting that the reason why he was on trial was his belief as a Pharisee in the resurrection of the dead (Acts 23:6–9). He was then transferred to the provincial capital, Caesarea, to face charges before the Roman procurator, Felix, who kept Paul imprisoned without bringing his case to trial for two years in the hope of receiving a bribe (Acts 24:26), and who left Paul's fate to his successor, Festus. When Festus intimated that he would decline to exercise Roman jurisdiction and remand the prisoner back to the Sanhedrin, Paul exercised another right of Roman citizens by transferring jurisdiction over his case from the provincial tribunal in Caesarea to the central imperial tribunal in Rome (*see* Pliny the Younger, *Letters* 10:96). "Paul knows his legal rights, and makes use of them." Johnson, 423 *The Acts of the Apostles*; *see* also Richard Cassidy, *Society and Politics in the Acts of the Apostles* (1987); H.J. Cadbury, "Roman Law and the Trial of Paul," 5 *The Beginnings of Christianity* 312–19 (1933); and A.N. Sherwin–White, *Roman Society and Roman Law in the New Testament* 57–70 (1973). According to an ancient Roman tradition preserved in an early second century letter, 1 Clement 5:7, and a mid-to late-second century document known as the "Acts of Paul," Paul was held under house arrest in Rome, was released and was later beheaded by the Romans, perhaps during the persecution under Nero. William Schneemelher, ed., *New Testament Apocrypha* (1992).

Acts of the Apostles 25:1–12

Three days after Festus had arrived in the province, he went up from Caesarea to Jerusalem where the chief priests and the leaders of the Jews gave him a report against Paul. They appealed to him and requested, as a favor to them against Paul, to have him transferred to Jerusalem. They were, in fact, planning an ambush to kill him along the way. Festus replied that Paul was being kept at Caesarea, and that he himself intended to go there shortly. "So," he said, "let those of you who have the authority come down with me, and if there is anything wrong about the man, let them accuse him."

After he had stayed among them not more than eight or ten days, he went down to Caesarea; the next day he took his seat on the tribunal and ordered Paul to be brought. When he arrived, the Jews who had gone down from Jerusalem surrounded him, bringing many serious charges against him, which they could not prove. Paul said in his defense, "I have in no way committed an offense against the laws of the Jews, or against the temple, or against the emperor." But Festus, wishing to do the Jews a favor, asked Paul, "Do you wish to go up to Jerusalem and be tried there before me on these charges?" Paul said, "I am appealing to the emperor's tribunal; this is where I should be tried. I have done no wrong to the Jews, as you very well know. Now if I am in the wrong and have committed something for which I deserve to die, I am not trying to escape death; but if there is nothing to their charges against me, no one can turn me over to them. I appeal to the emperor." Then Festus, after he had conferred with his council, replied, "You have appealed to the emperor; to the emperor you will go."

9. ROMAN RESPONSIBILITY FOR THE DEATH OF JESUS

According to all four of the Gospels Jesus had confrontations with the religious authorities in Jerusalem. These confrontations came to a head in the trial scenes in the Passion narratives of the Gospels. Although these texts are not verbatim transcripts of an historical trial, they do preserve the historical memory that some of the Jewish religious authorities in Jerusalem rejected the claim of Jesus to teach with divine authority (Mt. 27:1–2,20; Mk. 15:1–11; Lk. 23:1–5,13–25; and Jn. 18:38–40; 19:12–16). From the first century to the present, that fact has tragically undergirded deep misunderstanding between Jews and Christians. In some passages in the New Testament Christians appear to blame Jews for the death of Jesus. But the starkest confrontation of Jesus with "the powers that are" was with the Roman procurator of Judea, Pontius Pilate. Chronologically this confrontation preceded Paul's letter to the Romans, [Section 6 above]. The Gospel of John was probably composed after the expulsion of Christians from the synagogue in 90 CE. *See* Pheme Perkins, "The Gospel According to John," *New Jerome Biblical Commentary* 946 (1960).

The contrast between Jesus' kingdom and the Roman empire is sharper in the fourth Gospel than in any exchange related in the Synoptic Gospels. The relation of religious truth to civil power is suggested with Pilate's secular skepticism noted to his discredit. Readers of John know that earlier Jesus had identified himself as "the way, the truth, and the life" (John 14:6).

Roman law made efforts to accommodate regional differences in legal culture, especially in the remote provinces. In Judea the Romans allowed the Jewish religious authority tightly circumscribed rights to impose the death penalty when the Temple was expressly under attack, "and different Roman procurators may have exercised varying degrees of vigilance over the way in which this right was exercised." Freyne, *The World of the New Testament* 65. But the manner of the execution of Jesus—crucifixion–points to Roman responsibility for imposing the death penalty on Jesus. *See* Cullmann, "Jesus' Condemnation by the Roman State," in *The State in the New Testament* 24–49 (1956). A later articulation of the Christian faith known as the *Apostles' Creed* underlines this by stating that Jesus "was crucified under Pontius Pilate, suffered, died and was buried."

Unlike Paul, Jesus was not a Roman citizen and could not transfer his case to Rome. The provincial procurator's decision was final and unreviewable. In the following excerpt from the Gospel according to John Pilate is about to order this punishment for Jesus. Jesus' acceptance of the penalty that "this world" imposes upon him is the fulfilment of a mission higher than any duty performed by a secular functionary of the empire. A stark dualism is set out between "this world" and the world over which Jesus exercises his royal rule.

John 18:33–38

Then Pilate entered the headquarters again, summoned Jesus, and asked him, "Are you the King of the Jews?" Jesus answered, "Do you ask this on your own, or did others tell you about me?" Pilate replied, "I am not a Jew, am I? Your own nation and the chief priests have handed you over to me. What have you done?"

———

NOTE. *The Cross as a "Stumbling Block" for Jews*. From the perspective of Christian faith the execution of Jesus under Pontius Pilate on a Roman cross is the central event of saving grace (e.g., 1 Cor. 1:23,30). From the Jewish perspective, the cross signified a brutal and ignominious form of Roman torture. Under Jewish law (Deut. 21:23; Josh. 8:29; 10:26–27; 2 Sam. 4:12) hanging a criminal on a tree after execution was regarded as the greatest disgrace. Only criminals regarded as accursed were subjected to this ignominy. Paul is aware of this tradition, and turns it into a theological argument that Jesus redeemed the world by rescuing us from that curse (Gal. 3:13). For the vast majority of Jews, the very fact that Jesus had died in this accursed manner meant that they could not believe that Jesus was the awaited Messiah in the royal line of David.

Jews suffered death by asphyxiation on Roman crosses by the thousands. During the First Jewish War (66–73 CE) the revolt against Rome was crushed with severity. According to Josephus, *War* 2:14.9, in 66 CE the Roman governor of Judea, Gessius Florus, executed—either by sword or by crucifixion—3,600 Jews for taking part in the resistance. The Temple in Jerusalem was destroyed under Titus in 70 CE. When the caesar Hadrian (117–138) banned circumcision and other basic observances of Jewish law, a Second Jewish War (132–135) broke out against Roman rule. Led by Simon Bar Kokhba, the Jewish resistance inflicted severe losses on the Romans, who retaliated with overwhelming force, killing more than 580,000 Jews. Shortly after the war, the prefect Varus (139–169), crucified 2,000 Jews within view of the holy city of Jerusalem. Flannery, *The Anguish of the Jews* 17. Hence it is small wonder that Jews over the centuries have regarded this instrument of Roman torture as a "stumbling block" (1 Cor. 1:23). It would be a marvel, indeed, if Jews could even honor the death of Jesus as the loss of one of the thousands of Jews executed in this denigrating, accursed manner of execution under the Roman eagle.

10. Christian and Jewish Martyrdom and the Apocalyptic View of the Roman Empire

By the end of the first century, Christians had ample experience of being tested in their faith. Their convictions about the messianic and divine character of the identity and mission of Jesus led to their expulsion from the Jewish synagogues around 90 CE. Their faith in Jesus as Lord led them into conflict with Roman law as well. Unlike the Jews, Christians had no special exemption from the generally applicable duty under Roman law to worship the full pantheon of Roman deities (Jupiter, Juno, Eros, Diana, Hera, Apollo, and Saturn). Roman religion, moreover, was not a private affair. It involved public festivities known as *dies feriae* in which all were expected to participate. One such holiday worshipped Saturn, the Roman god of agriculture. "It was a week-long celebration terminating on December 25. There was much partying, gift giving, and conviviality; all business was put aside; and slaves were released temporarily from their work. The debauchery that occurred during the Saturnalia did not sit well with the Christians. In retaliation for lack of participation, they were charged with constituting a felonious covert society that drank blood and ate human flesh [a reference to the Christian celebration of the Eucharist] as a part of their religious rituals." Yaseen, 68. In addition to the official celebration of the Roman deities, Roman religion also included acknowledging the quasi-divine status of the caesar. For example, Romans were expected to add a pinch of incense before the images of the caesar at the public baths. If insisted upon, as they were in periods of persecution, such practices were utterly inconsistent with the Christian view of Jesus as Lord (Rom. 1:4; 1 Cor. 12:3). Thus, like the Jews at the time of the persecution under Antiochus Epiphanes [section 5 above] and the 6,000 Pharisees who refused to take the oath to caesar Augustus at the beginning of the first century of the common era [section 6 above], early Christians were forced to contemplate professions of political loyalty to the empire and its deities that implicated them in apostasy, or abandonment of their faith in the great commandment: "You shall have no other god to set against me" (Dt. 5:7) [section 1 above].

Witnessing (in Greek, "*marturia*") to the faith that Jesus, not caesar, is Lord literally became a life or death decision. Under these circumstances the Christian community began to rethink its relationship to the caesar. The last book of the New Testament, the Book of Revelation, was circulating sometime during the last decade of the first century, shortly after the church in Asia Minor suffered sporadic local persecution during the time of the caesar Domitian (81–96 CE), who ordered strict observance of emperor worship in the provinces. *See* Adela Yarbro Collins, "The Apocalypse (Revelation)," *New Jerome Biblical Commentary* 999 (1990). The title of the book literally means "unveiling" or "disclosure," but the strange literary form in which it is cast, known as "apocalyptic," in fact obscures its message to those, such as Roman officials, who were unfamiliar with the devices of this form. For the biblical prophets revelation occurred by "hearing" a word of the Lord, which they communicated orally in the style of a preacher. The authors of apocalyptic literature, by contrast, were given revelation through visions, which they passed on in written form charged with rich symbolism that was never meant to be taken literally.

Apocalyptic flourished as a literary form for about three centuries from the second century BCE to the end of the first century CE. This literary form is basic to much of the New Testament thought, which expects a sudden cataclysm and end to the world (*see, e.g.*, Mark 13). But only two whole books of this sort are found in the biblical canon: the Book of Daniel (written during the persecution of the Jews under Antiochus Epiphanes) and the Book of Revelation (written during the persecution of the Christians under the caesar Domitian). Apocalyptic presents two urgent messages to the persecuted faithful, constancy and consolation. The faithful should stand firm in the faith during time of suffering, and they should take hope in the divine promise that although the powers seem to be destroying the faith, God will ultimately vindicate his people in a stunning reversal of human history that will dethrone the powers and establish His reign forever. In the central vision of the Book of Daniel, four great empires of the ancient world—Babylon, the Medes, Persia, and Greece—represented by four beasts, fall subject to the rule of God, who promises to destroy both the persecutor and his persecution shortly (Dan. 7). Similarly, the great "throne vision" (Rev. 4) discloses that the real emperor of the universe is not the caesar Domitian, but the God of the Christians enthroned in heaven. In the concluding vision (Rev. 21–22), the saints reign forever, and they worship before the throne of God and of his Lamb, an unmistakable reference to Jesus, the wounded yet victorious servant of God. Between these visions the Roman empire is identified variously as the Beast, the great enemy of Christ and his people, and the fallen decadent city Babylon (Rev. 17:1–18:24), which is ultimately to be annihilated before the final judgment.

As a rallying cry to persecuted Christians, the Book of Revelation has served over the centuries as an epic of hope. For example, this book is the source of many of the arias and choruses of George Friedrich Handel's famous oratorio, "The Messiah." At the end of the first century, however, the document functioned both as an unmistakable condemnation of imperial Rome and as an urgent call to Christians to persevere in their faith even at the enormous cost of their lives. Some of these visions may have been written as early as the reign of Nero [sections 6 & 8 above]. The Book of Revelation was finished and began circulating among Christian communities in Asia Minor toward the close of the first century, when the early church was suffering persecution during the reign of the emperor Domitian. It employs symbolic language that would have been obscure to Roman imperial officials, but unmistakable for readers familiar with Jewish apocalyptic literature. "Two Jewish apocalypses written at about the same time as the Book of Revelation, 4 Ezra and 2 Baruch, speak of the suffering and disorientation felt by some Jews after the Romans had destroyed Jerusalem in A.D. 70. Like Revelation, they are concerned with the question why God does not send the messianic age soon and destroy the forces of evil, especially the Roman empire. . . . They both reassure the faithful that the end of the evil age is coming and that faithfulness to God will not be lost or forgotten." Pheme Perkins, *Reading the New Testament* 319–20 (1988). Cullmann, "The State in the Johannine Apocalypse," in *The State in the New Testament* 71–86 (1956).

As with the vision in Daniel 7, the text below is replete with animal symbols referring to the Roman empire under which the church was now suffering persecution. The second beast in the vision is a servant of the first beast. Like Antiochus Epiphanes, he erected an idol and commanded the faithful to worship before it on pain of death. "Apocalypses written at the same time as Revelation [4 Ezra & 2 Baruch] use the code name 'Babylon' for the Roman empire. No first century semitic reader would have any difficulty figuring that the number of the beast is the spelling of 'Nero Caesar' in a semitic alphabet." Perkins, 321. Not only does Jewish apocalyptic refer to Rome as Babylon; so does the New Testament (1 Pet. 5:13). Thus the faithful of Asia Minor could be warned against the danger of associating with emperor worship, while the device of gematria (using numbers to signify letters) would obscure its meaning for Roman officials into whose hands the Book of Revelation might fall. Josephine Massyngberde Ford, *Revelation* 227 (1975). Hebrew and Greek are alphanumeric languages; thus aleph in Hebrew and alpha in Greek corresponds to the number 1, beth and beta to the number 2, and so on. In this numbering system 666 represents the total of the numbers indicated by the following Hebrew letters: **q**oph [=100], **s**amech [=60], **r**esh [=200]; **n**un [=50], **r**esh [=200], **w**aw [=6], **n**un [=50]. These letters spell out two words: "kaisar Neron," or "caesar Nero." Ford 226; *see also* William Barclay, "Revelation 13, Great Themes of the New Testament," 70 *Expository Times* 260–64, 292–96(1958/59); Delbert Hillers, "Revelation 13:18 and the Scroll from Murabba'at," 170 *Bulletin of the American Schools of Oriental Research* 65 (1963). Even with some other interpretation of the name of the beast, the passage marks a clear contrast with the passage in the letter to the Romans cited above [section 6]. Note the description of the divine titles given to Roman emperors as "blasphemous."

Revelation 13:1–18

And I saw a beast rising out of the sea, having ten horns and seven heads; and on its horns were ten diadems, and on its heads were blasphemous names. And the beast that I saw was like a leopard, its feet were like a bear's, and its mouth was like a lion's mouth. And the dragon gave it his power and his throne and great authority. One of its heads seemed to have received a death-blow, but its mortal wound had been healed. In amazement the whole earth followed the beast. They worshiped the dragon, for head had given his authority to the beast, and they worshiped the beast, saying, "Who is like the beast, and who can fight against it?"

The beast was given a mouth uttering haughty and blasphemous words, and it was allowed to exercise authority for forty-two months. It opened its mouth to utter blasphemies against God, blaspheming his name and his dwelling, that is, those who dwell in heaven. Also it was allowed to make war on the saints and to conquer them. It was given authority over every tribe and people and language and nation, and all the inhabitants of the earth will worship it, everyone whose name has not been written from the foundation of the world in the book of life of the Lamb that was slaughtered.

> Let anyone who has an ear listen:
> If you are to be taken captive,
> into captivity you go;
> if you kill with the sword,
> with the sword you must be killed.

Here is a call for the endurance and faith of the saints.

Then I saw another beast that rose out of the earth; it had two horns like a lamb and it spoke like a dragon. It exercises all the authority of the first beast on its behalf, and it makes the earth and its inhabitants worship the first beast, whose mortal wound had been healed. It performs great signs, even making fire come down from heaven to earth in the sight of all; and by the signs that it is allowed to perform on behalf of the beast, it deceives the inhabitants of earth, telling them to make an image for the beast that had been wounded by the sword and yet lived; and it was allowed to give breath to the image of the beast so that the image of the beast could even speak and cause those who would not worship the image of the beast to be killed. Also it causes all, both small and great, both rich and poor, both free and slave, to be marked on the right hand or the forehead, so that no one can buy or sell who does not have the mark, that is, the name of the beast or the number of its name. This calls for wisdom: let anyone with understanding calculate the number of the beast, for it is the number of a person. Its number is six hundred sixty-six.

NOTES

The Ambivalence of Judaism toward Roman Rule and the Urgency of the Reign of God in Jewish Apocalyptic. Just as the Christian attitude of respect for the empire reflected in Romans 13 [section 6 above] yielded to a different perspective toward the empire during a period of intense persecution, Jewish attitudes toward Roman rule were similarly ambivalent. As long as Roman law enabled Jews to follow the Torah, Rome could be thought of benevolently. As was noted above [section 6 above], Julius Caesar and Octavian bestowed "privileges and immunities" on the Jews in gratitude for their support in the civil wars. But Roman rule was not always benign to Jews. For example, Avilus Aulus Flaccus, the Roman prefect of Egypt (32–38 CE) was particularly insensitive to the Jews in Alexandria. In 37 CE, with the accession of caesar Caligula, he ordered pagan idols to be erected within the Jewish synagogues, and issued an edict declaring Jews to be "aliens," though they had a venerable history of Alexandrian citizenship for centuries. Lea Roth, "Flaccus, Avilus Aulus," 6 *Encyclopaedia Judaica* 1333 (1971). The Jewish philosopher Philo records that Flaccus subjected Jews to the cruelest form of torture and mutilation before their execution. Philo, *In Flaccum* IX.62–72, X.73–77 (trans. C.D. Yonge 1993) 730–31. Flaccus was recalled to Rome and was put on trial for his atrocities, and was banished to Andros and later executed. Nearly a century before this Flaccus, the famous Roman orator, Cicero, delivered a powerful defense of another Flaccus, praising him for opposing the "barbarous superstition" of the Jews. Cicero's *Pro Flacco* stands at the head of classical anti-Semitism. Flannery, *The Anguish of the Jews* 19.

The banishment and exile of 4,000 Jews under caesar Tiberius (14–37 CE) and later under caesar Claudius [section 5] also served as an effective means of confiscating their property. The exemption for Jews came under greater pressure during the reigns of Nero (54–68 CE), Vespasian (69–79 CE) and Titus (79–81 CE). Nero dispatched Vespasian to Judaea to deal with the Jewish rebellion. Shortly after Nero died in 68, Vespasian became the new caesar and left his son Titus to finish the job of crushing the rebellion. The Roman legion under Titus destroyed the city of Jerusalem, including the Second Temple, in 70 CE. Under the standard practice of the day, Titus seized many of the survivors as prisoners of war and took them to Rome, where they were sold as slaves and forced into public works projects such as the construction of the Colloseum, much as their ancestors had done in Egypt (Ex. 1:11–14). The arch constructed in honor of Titus in the Roman Forum depicts Jewish slaves in his triumphal procession. The half-shekel temple tax that Jews used to send to

Jerusalem to support the Temple [section 7 above] was now to be sent to Rome as a *fiscus judaicus* or Jewish tax to finance the temple of Jupiter Capitoline. Jews, however, retained the exemption from emperor worship under Vespatian and Titus. The succeeding caesar, Domitian, began to call this tradition into question, opening the prospect that Jews would be obliged to engage in emperor worship.

When a government does not protect personal liberty and private property, it often has scant regard for human life. As was noted above [section 9 above], the Romans subjected to crucifixion large numbers of Jewish rebels. Under these circumstances Jews no longer prayed: "May all go well with the Romans . . . at sea and on land for ever, and may sword and enemy be far from them." 1 Mac. 8: 23 [section 6 above]. Instead they recognized that it was now the Romans, not the Greeks, who were "completely enslaving Israel." 1 Mac 8:18. Thus they began to refer to Rome under the code word, "Edom," one of the ancient enemies of Judah repeatedly denounced by the prophets (Amos 1:6,9,11;2:1; Is. 11:14;34:5–17; Jer. 49:7–22; Ezek. 35; Obadiah; Mal. 1:2–4; Ps. 137:7). *See, e.g.,* 4 Ezra 6:9; Michael A. Knibb, *The First and Second Book of Esdras* 147 (1979). Moshe David Herr argues that the identification of Edom with Rome appeared for the first time in the revolt of Bar Kokhba in 132–135 CE: "The intense hatred of Rome after the cruel crushing of the revolt of the Diaspora in the time of Trajan [98–117 CE] and still more after the harsh suppression of the Bar Kokhba revolt and the decrees of persecution in Hadrian's days; the fact that Rome, like Edom, had destroyed the Temple; the similarity of Edom, compared to a pig, with Rome, for whom the pig . . . was an important symbol; the allusions to Edom dwelling on high like an eagle and that fact that the eagle, too, was an important Roman symbol; and perhaps finally even the similarity to the name Rome and Romans in several verses that speak of Edom . . . —all these apparently combined to cause the application to Rome of the biblical references to Edom, the eternal enemy of Israel." Herr, "Edom," 6 *Encyclopaedia Judaica* 379 (1971). Rabbinical commentaries also allude to Rome as Edom; *see* Jacob Levy, 1 *Wörterbuch über die Talmudim und Midraschim: Neuhebräische und chaldaisches Wörterbuch* 29 (1963). For example, a midrash on Psalm 68:30 ("Out of Thy Temple at Jerusalem, whither kings shall bring presents unto Thee") notes that this will happen when the kingdom of Edom [Rome] is destroyed." Commenting on Ps. 68:31 ("Rebuke the wild beast of the reed"), the same text identifies the wild beast with Edom [Rome], whose decrees, all done with an undeviating reed, impose only persecution upon the children of Israel and command them to worship idols." Commenting on Ps. 97:1 ("The Lord rules; let the earth rejoice"), the midrash states that "as long as the kingdom of Edom [Rome] abides, there will be no rejoicing in the earth." William G. Braude, trans., *The Midrash on Psalms* I:548, II:141 (1959). *See also* Judah Goldin, *The Song at the Sea* 102 (1971) (a commentary on the late fourth century midrash on Exodus, *Mekhilta of Rabbi Ishmael*).

Whatever the precise dating of the Jewish designation of Rome as "Edom," it is similar to the Christian reference to Rome as the "Babylon the great, mother of harlots and of the earth's abominations, . . . the woman drunk with the blood of the saints and the blood of the martyrs of Jesus." (Rev. 17:5–6). Lest anyone miss the reference to Rome, the city of seven hills, the author of Revelation expressly states that the seven-headed monster can be identified "by a mind with wisdom: the seven heads are the seven hills on which the woman is seated" (Rev. 17:9). The message announced by a revealing angel is: "Fallen, fallen is Babylon the great!" (Rev. 18:2,10,21).

In this situation Jews begged God for an end to Roman rule and for the imminent dawning of God's rule or kingdom. Christians prayed, "Thy Kingdom come" with eschatological urgency. Raymond E. Brown, "The Pater Noster as an Eschatological Prayer," 22 *Theological Studies* 175–208 (1961). Similarly, Jews prayed in the spirit of the *Kaddish*: "May He establish His kingdom in your lifetime and during your days ... speedily and soon." Joseph Heinemann, "The Background of Jesus' Prayer in the Jewish Liturgical Tradition," in Jakob J. Petruchowski and Michael Briocke, eds., *The Lord's Prayer and Jewish Liturgy* 81–89 (1978).

Jewish expectation of the end-time during the first century of the common era is complex. For example, the members of the community at Khirbet Qumran—the proximity of which to the Dead Sea led to the designation of their writings as the "Dead Sea Scrolls"—expected the coming not only of the traditional royal messiah known as the Messiah of David, but also that of a priestly leader known as the Messiah of Aaron, and of a third figure known as the Prophet, who would fulfill the promise of the return of Moses (Dt. 18:15). This view is reflected in two places in the Dead Sea Scrolls, *Community Rule* IX and *Damascus Rule* B II. Although Jews did not believe that Jesus was the Messiah, they expected that the Messiah (or Messiahs) would come swiftly to establish God's rule, not Roman rule. *See* John Collins, *The Apocalyptic Imagination: An Introduction to the Jewish Matrix of Christianity* (1984), and Norman Cohn, *Cosmos, Chaos, and the World to Come: The Ancient Roots of Apocalyptic Faith* (1993).

CHAPTER TWO

THE ESTABLISHED CHURCH: CHRISTIAN BISHOP AND IMPERIAL OFFICIAL, 413–417 CE

NOTES

1. *From Persecution of Christianity to Toleration under Constantine, and from Toleration to Official Establishment of Christianity under Theodosius.* Four letters below from a Christian bishop to a Roman official illustrate the interaction between church and empire in the fifth century of the common era [CE]. For this correspondence to have occurred, a major shift had to precede it. This NOTE traces the path from the first century, in which the empire was closely identified with pagan religion, to the fourth century, in which the empire first allowed Christianity to exist as one of the "licit religions" of the empire and then came to replace paganism with Christianity as the official religion of the empire.

With the establishment of Christianity in the fourth century CE came a remarkable expansion of imperial power over religious matters. Before exploring this development in detail below, a word of general explanation may be helpful at the outset. It is easy to understand that the church would be interested in doctrinal unity among in its own members. This result flows from the imperatives of deeper clarity of understanding of the faith and of stronger charity among the disciples of Jesus. The Fourth Gospel reports Jesus as praying that his followers would "abide in [his] love" (John 14:7) and "that they may all be one. As you, Father, are in me and I am in you, may they also be in us, so that the world may believe that you have sent me" (John 17:21). But a biblical basis for Christian unity does not necessarily mean that this goal should be part of the government's agenda. Why would the empire care about such matters of faith? The short answer is that by the fourth century the imperial task was conceived to include the building of a Christian society. *See* Oliver O'Donovan, *The Desire of Nations: Rediscovering the Roots of Political Theology* (1996). In that effort unity of faith came to have a political dimension as well as a religious one. From the imperial perspective the divisive squabbling among Christians inhibited the power of Rome to control its subjects. There is no doubt that the fourth century entailed a paradigm shift in the understanding of "the things that belong to Caesar" from the time Jesus used a Roman coin to foil his adversaries in the first century of the common era.

In that first century the small Christian community–numbering perhaps 50,000 throughout the empire–seemed to the Romans similar enough to the Jews with respect to the fundamental issue of the First Commandment–"have no other god to set against me" [Chapter One, section 1]—as not to require fine distinctions between these communities. Christians and Jews were lumped

36

together as monotheists. The church had a strong presence in the very capital of the empire. St. Paul wrote a letter to the Christians in Rome that contains his most important theological themes [Chapter One, section 6]. St. Peter, given a leadership role among the Apostles (Mt. 16:16), also went to Rome.

There were imperial outbursts against the Christians, but they were sporadic rather than systematic. For example, the emperor Claudius expelled both Christians and Jews from Rome in 41 CE (Acts 18:2), apparently because of conflict between them over the identity of Jesus as the Messiah and Lord [Chapter One, section 6]. Christians soon returned to Rome, for in 64 CE the emperor Nero subjected the church to persecution in the city [Chapter One, section 6]. Under emperor Domitian (81–96 CE) persecution of Christians spread to the Roman provinces, where imperial officials were enjoined to enforce the observance of emperor worship [Chapter One, section 10]. *See* R.L.P. Milburn, "The Persecution of Domitian," 139 *Church Q. Rev.* 154–64 (1945).

In the early second century CE the Roman empire began to examine more closely the question whether Christians should enjoy a "privilege and immunity"–the Roman term for exemption–from the generally applicable laws about emperor worship. There was no specific Roman law targeting Christians in a particular way. Neither was Roman law specific about what to do in proceedings against Christians. The lack of procedural clarity about such cases triggered correspondence written around 111 CE between Pliny the Younger, governor of the province of Bithynia (in modern Turkey), and the emperor Trajan (98–117 CE). Pliny sought guidance from the emperor about how to proceed with cases involving those who were accused as Christians. He indicated that imperial officials were aware of Christian beliefs from descriptions provided to them by apostates. In passing, Pliny noted that the Christians "before dawn on a stated day sang alternately a hymn to Christ as to a god." For an early example of such a hymn, *see* Phil. 2:5–11 ("at the name of Jesus every knee should bow and every tongue should proclaim Jesus Christ as Lord, to the glory of God the Father"); R.P. Martin, *Carmen Christi: Philippians ii.5–11 in Recent Interpretation and in the Setting of Early Christian Worship* (1967). Pliny then described his customary procedure for handling these cases. "I asked them whether they were Christians, and I asked them a second and third time with threats of punishment. If they kept to it, I ordered them taken off for execution, for I had no doubt that whatever it was they admitted, in any case they deserve to be punished for obstinacy and unbending pertinacity.... As for those who said they neither were nor ever had been Christians, I thought it right to let them go, when they recited a prayer to the gods at my direction, and made supplication with incense and wine to your statue, which I had ordered to be brought into court for this purpose, and moreover, cursed Christ—things which (so it is said) those who are really Christians cannot be made to do." Pliny the Younger, *Ep.* 10.96. Trajan replied immediately, approving of Pliny's actions: "You have adopted the proper course, my dear Pliny, in your examination of the cases of those who were accused before you as Christians, for it impossible to lay down a general rule to a fixed formula. They are not to be hunted out; but if they are brought before you and the charge is proved, they must be punished—but in the case of anyone who denies that he is a Christian, and makes that fact plain by his action, that is, by offering prayers to our gods, he is to be pardoned as a result of his repentance, however suspicious his past conduct may be. But the pamphlets circulated anonymously must play no part in any accusation. They create the worst sort of precedent and are quite out of keeping with the spirit of our age." Pliny, *Ep.* 10.97. See Karl Baus, *From the Apostolic Community to Constantine* 132–135 (1984), and Robert L. Wilken, *The Christians as the Romans Saw Them* 1–30 (1984).

There is no evidence of systematic persecution of the church by the Romans, but the profession of the Christian faith did entail significant risk. A leading church historian describes the situation as follows: "We are not certain that any of the persecutions of the first two centuries was Empire-wide. Presumably Christians were always in danger, for their legal status was at best precarious, a local or provincial official might at almost any time proceed against them, and some action of an Emperor might stiffen the backbone of otherwise lenient authorities. They were chronically regarded with suspicion by large elements in the populace and among the respectable citizens. Their peril was further accentuated by a procedure which gave their possessions to those who brought a successful accusation against them. Confiscation of goods, imprisonment, and torture might overtake them at any time, followed by hard labour in the mines or execution." Kenneth Scott Latourette, *A History of Christianity* 86 (1953).

By the mid-third century, a loosely defined policy of general toleration yielded to a more aggressive campaign against all Christians. The emperor Decius (249–251 CE) regarded Christians as enemies of the empire on the view that their "atheism," or refusal to worship the traditional Roman deities, was responsible for many of the troubles in the empire. In 249 CE Decius issued an edict requiring all persons throughout the Empire—with the single exception of Jews—to offer sacrifice to the gods, including emperor worship. Those who performed these ritual acts of worship were given *libelli*, or certificates of compliance. Refusal to conform to imperial religion carried severe penalties, including confiscation of property and capital punishment. From the Roman perspective the edict may have seemed simply to be a facially neutral, generally applicable law, *see Employment Division v. Smith* [Chapter Eleven, section 11]. On this view Decius did not single Christians out for unique treatment or intentionally target Christians for discriminatory treatment, *see Church of the Lukumi Babulu Aye v. City of Hialeah* [Chapter Eleven, section 12]. For Christians, however, the edict presented a Hobson's choice, *see Sherbert v. Verner* [Chapter Eleven, section 5]. They could survive only by surrendering their consciences either by sacrificing at a pagan altar and thereby committing the unpardonable sin of apostasy, or by purchasing *libelli* from venal officials without actually performing the sacrifice. *See* Cyprian, *The Lapsed*, (Maurice Bevenot, trans., 1971), vol. 3; Jacques Paul Migne, Ed., 4 *Patrologia Latina* [hereafter PL] cols. 486–487; Baus 222–26; F.L. Cross and E.A. Livingstone, eds., *Oxford Dictionary of the Christian Church* 441 (3d ed. 1997). The Decian persecution strengthened the Christian movement in two ways: non-Christians began to be appalled at the brutality of official violence against the Christians, and non-Christians began to admire the passive resistance of the Christians who showed that their faith was worth dying for. The Decian persecution ended in 251 CE

From 251 to 257 CE Christians experienced a brief respite from official hostility, followed by a fresh wave of persecution under emperor Valerian (253–260 CE) with redoubled fury. "The bishops, as heads of the Church, were singled out and were commanded to do homage to the old gods under pain of exile. Christians were threatened with the death penalty if they so much as went to any of the meetings or services of the Church or even visited a Christian cemetery.... In the year 258 a new and more drastic edict ... ordered death for bishops, priests, and deacons; first confiscation of property and then, if this were not enough to induce apostasy, death for Christians of high rank in the state, confiscation of goods for Christian matrons, and slavery for Christian members of the imperial household. By hitting at the persons of prominence in the Church the latter would be deprived of its leadership." Latourette 88–89; and *see* Baus 226–28, and W.H.C. Frend, *Martyrdom and Persecution in the Early Church* (1965). For example, Cyprian was executed under the Valerian in 258 CE, becoming the first bishop-martyr of Africa. This persecution came to an abrupt end with the death of Valerian in 260. It was followed by a period of toleration for Christians, first officially proclaimed by Valerian's son, emperor Gallienus (260–268 CE); *see* Eusebius, *Ecclesiastical History* 7.13.1. By now, Christians were present in the civil service, the army, and the imperial household. This period of toleration lasted for nearly four decades.

Toward the end of the third century emperor Diocletian (284–305 CE) launched another general persecution of the church. He attempted in 295 CE to purge the army of Christians, and in 303 CE he ordered the destruction of all Christian churches and books; in 304 CE he prescribed death for Christians refusing to offer pagan sacrifice. Baus 396–404.

In 311 CE Diocletian's successor, Galerius, issued an Edict of Toleration for Christians, Eusebius, *Ecc. Hist.*, 8.16.9. On October 28, 312, Constantine won supreme power in the West by his victory at the Milvian bridge on the Tiber. He was convinced that his victory was due to divine inspiration and achieved under the sign of the cross of Christ; *see* Eusebius, *The Life of Constantine* 1, 27–32. In February of 313 CE Constantine met in Milan with his co-emperor in the East, Licinius; both agreed to a document known as the "Edict of Milan," which Licinius promulgated in the East in June of that year. The Edict of Milan was not technically an imperial edict, but it had broad impact, instructing provincial officials throughout the empire that Christians within their jurisdiction were to be tolerated as practicing a *religio licita* and that the churches should receive back property that had been confiscated. The Edict of Milan made sense politically as Christians became more numerous, but Lactantius, a third century Latin writer, saw a deeper meaning in this document. Since, he noted, toleration is rooted in religious choice as a distinctively human activity, coercion about matters of the heart makes no sense. Lactantius, *The Deaths of the Persecutors*, 44; PL 7, 261. There is an important difference between toleration and establishment of Christianity. As one historian notes, "The policy of Constantine was one of toleration. He did not make Christianity the sole religion of the state. That was to follow under later Emperors. He continued to support both paganism and Christianity.... To the end of his days he bore the title of *pontifex maximus* as chief priest of the pagan state cult. The subservient Roman Senate followed the long-established custom and classed him among the gods. He did not persecute the old [pagan] faiths." Latourette 92. On the other hand, Constantine almost at once used his office to promote the end of the Donatist schism in Africa; Eusebius, *Ecclesiastical History* 10.5.11–20. He used bishops such as Eusebius as counselors of state. In 318 he gave legal force to the bishops' decisions in civil cases; *Theodosian Code* 1.27.1. (Clyde Pharr, trans., 1952). He recognized full liberty of leaving legacies to the church; *id.* 16.2.4. And he declared Sunday a holiday in the courts; *id.* 2.8.1, creating a preference for Christian worship later reflected in the law codes of colonial America [Chapter Seven, section 4], and a free exercise problem for sabbatarians in the twentieth century [Chapter Eleven, section 5].

As Constantine moved in the direction of supporting Christianity, his rival in the East, Licinius, moved in an opposite direction. Within a decade of the Edict of Milan Licinius revived old antagonisms against the Christians in his half of the empire, locking up or razing churches, imprisoning bishops, and banning episcopal synods. In 323 CE Constantine moved eastward with his army to clear the lower Danube of invading Goths. Licinius viewed this act as a violation of his territorial jurisdiction, and formally declared war on Constantine. The civil war that broke out a year later "engaged armies bigger than any seen since the second century, and not to be seen again for a thousand years." Ramsey Macmullen, *Constantine* 134 (1987). Rather than rely on a claim of legitimacy as the senior Augustus, or on his military skill in defending the empire where Licinius had proved inept, Constantine emphasized that his cause was just since his fellow Christians needed to be rescued from the oppression of a tyrant. Macmullen 135. Though outnumbered in each engagement with Licinius, Constantine's army prevailed in 324 CE at Hadrianople, Byzantium (soon to be renamed Constantinople), and finally at Chrysopolis, "with decisive slaughter." Macmullen 138. With the defeat and later the execution of Licinius, "Constantine might now freely multiply his titles, as 'Constantine Maximus Augustus, Conqueror,' 'Victor Everywhere,' 'Triumpher over All Peoples,' and, at long last, 'Ruler of the Entire Globe.' The empire stood united." *Id.*

The political unification of the empire impelled Constantine to seek the doctrinal unity of Christians as a means of cementing political unity. In the year that Constantine became the sole emperor of East and West, he convened the first ecumenical or general council of the Church, the Council of Nicaea, and even presided in person over the council when it assembled in 325 CE. Under Constantine Christians confronted a new phenomenon: an empire whose head was actively pro-Christian. Baus writes: "It must have been a temptation for many bishops especially in the East, after being oppressed for so long, to sun themselves in the imperial favour and so lose their freedom. More dangerous was the tendency, deriving from the emperor's view, not to consider the Church as a partner *sui generis*, but to make her serviceable to the interests of the State and so to stifle her independence and necessary freedom in the realm of internal Church affairs." Baus 432.

Although the short rule of emperor Julian (361–363 CE) interrupted imperial support for the Catholic church, the fourth century as a whole saw the Christians move from a persecuted minority first to a position of toleration as a *religio licita,* and then to a position of official preference or establishment, at least within the ruling class. In 380 CE a decree of emperors Valentinian, Theodosius, and Arcadius announced the emperors' will that all the people they ruled should "practice that religion which the divine Apostle Peter transmitted to the Romans. . . . We command that those persons who follow this rule shall embrace the name of Catholic Christians. The rest, however, whom We adjudge demented and insane, shall sustain the infamy of heretical dogmas, their meeting places shall not receive the name of churches, and they shall be smitten first by divine vengeance and secondly by the retribution of Our own initiative, which we shall assume in accordance with the divine judgment."

Theodosian Code, 16.1.2. Bishops and other clerics were granted exemption from public service, *id.* 16.2.1–3, and a variety of tax exemptions, *id.* 16.2.8, 10 and 36. As of 355, it was provided that a bishop could be sued only before a bishop, *id.* 16.2.12; and as of 412, any cleric could be accused only before a bishop, *id.* 16.2.41. Illegal entry into a Catholic church was to be capitally punished, *id.* 16.2.31.

The establishment of Christianity as the official religion of the empire marks an important turn in which the doctrinal unity of Christians was transformed from a religious concern into a political one. The government purported to have authority to resolve doctrinal disputes by decrees favoring those who confessed that the Father, Son, and Holy Spirit are "of the same glory," *id.* 16.1.3. And the government actively intervened in the internal discipline of the church, prohibiting priests to have unrelated women in their homes, *id.* 16.2.44. All privileges were denied "heretics and schismatics," *id.* 16.5.1. Indeed, imperial law forbade "all heresies," *id.* 16.5.5. Extensive legislation was enacted against the Manichees, depriving them of the right to bequeath or to inherit, *id.* 16.5.7. Apollinarians, Arians, Donatists, Eunomians, Macedonians, Montanists, Phrygians, and Priscillianists were all subjected to penalties as heretics, *id.* 16.5.12, 25, 34, and 38–39.

Under Constantine and other Christian emperors in the first half of the fourth century CE, pagans continued to hold high office. By the mid-century the tide had begun to turn against pagans. An edict under the emperors Constantius and Constans sought to "eradicate completely all superstitions," but allowed pagan temples outside of Rome to remain untouched so that plays, circus performances, contests, and other "long established amusements" could continue to be performed, *id.* 16.10.3. In 356 Constantius ordered that any persons proven to devote their attention to pagan "sacrifices or to worship images" would be subject to capital punishment, *id.* 16.10.6. By 392 CE the emperor Theodosius prohibited not only public worship through pagan sacrifices "to senseless images in any place at all or in any city," but also forbade the observance of ancient pagan religion in the home, including burning lights or placing incense before statutes of the deities or suspending wreaths for them, *id.* 16.10.12. Three years later the emperors Arcadius and Honorius directed the provincial governors to enforce the decrees prohibiting access to any pagan shrine or temple throughout the empire, *id.* 16.10.13. They revoked the privileges of the "civil priests" or ministers of the ancient pagan religion, *id.* 16.10.14. And finally in 399 CE they ordered pagan temples "in the country districts" to be torn down so that "the material basis for all superstition [would] be destroyed." *Id.* 16.10.16.

By the dawn of the fifth century CE, after decades of preferential treatment of Christians, no one could doubt that Christians played the major part in governing the empire. "God does not reject the powerful, because He is powerful," Jerome mistranslated Job 36:5. The mistranslation was significant. As part of the Latin Vulgate, it was to assure Christian officeholders, and reflect their belief, that God was with them in the exercise of governmental power.

2. *Christians and Military Service in the Early Church: From Pacifism to the Augustinian Tradition on Justifiable War.*

The question of military service in the Roman army did not become a significant problem in the biblical period studied in Chapter One. According to a distinguished church historian, "Till about 175 A.D. there were, as far as we can tell, no Christian soldiers, and therefore, no actual question about military service arose." Hans von Campenhausen, "Christians and Military Service in the Early Church," in *Tradition and Life in the Church: Essays and Lectures on Church History* 162 (1968). Campenhausen goes further, suggesting that when the problem did arise in the late second century, attempts to adduce answers to this problem from the New Testament were fruitless. *Id.*

Although it is generally a sound principle of interpretation that a text does not provide an answer for a question that was not asked when the text was written, Campenhausen understates the possibility that the New Testament had clear ethical implications for the followers of Jesus with respect to violence. Differences in interpretation of the prohibition against killing in the Ten Commandments [Chapter One, section 2] affect the question of military service, which at least implicitly entails a willingness to kill. Differences in interpretations of the teaching of the New Testament on the use of force likewise affect this theme. Attempts by Christians to come to terms with the biblical teaching on nonviolence have in fact led at least some Christians to refuse to follow a command of the state to kill [Chapter Five, section 1].

The church in the post-biblical period tried to live with fidelity to the apostolic witness to Jesus reflected in the books of the New Testament. Hence a brief overview of some of the New Testament texts relevant to the issue of military service is essential to an understanding of the problematic from the second century onwards. One text reporting the preaching of John the Baptist admonishes soldiers to abstain from violent theft and false accusation (Luke 3:14). The text is not very flattering about the behavior of the occupying imperial forces, but it at least implies that a hearer of the Gospel might be a soldier; see also Luke 7:1–10 (healing of slave of Roman centurion). Even if a Christian might be a soldier, that does not resolve the question whether a Christian soldier could take another's life and remain faithful to the teachings of Jesus. For example, in the Sermon on the Mount Jesus is portrayed as a new Moses offering instruction on nonviolence. The law of the talion ("an eye for an eye, a tooth for a tooth," Ex. 21:23–24; Lev. 24:19–20; Dt. 19:21) had not been taken literally in biblical law, but functioned as a principle of equivalency of monetary compensation for tort claims. *See, e.g.*, Dale Patrick, *Old Testament Law* 76–77 (1985). Jesus taught more than the law of the talion: "Do not resist one who is evil. But if any one strikes you on the right cheek, turn to him the other also" (Mt. 5:39). Jesus acknowledged the ethic of love of one's neighbor in the Hebrew Bible (Lev. 19:2,18; Prov. 25:21–22), but taught his disciples: "Love your enemies and pray for those who persecute you" (Mt. 5:44). In the famous parable of the Good Samaritan (Luke 10:25–37), Jesus expanded the duty of care considerably by enlarging the definition of a neighbor as any human person in need of help. And in the passion narratives, he told his disciples to put away their swords on the ground that "those who live by the sword die by the sword" (Matthew 26:52).

Although Jesus had at least one disciple in his company who is identified as a Zealot (Lk. 6:15; Acts 1:13), this fact cannot be stretched into a proof that Jesus was a military revolutionary. Oscar Cullmann, "Jesus and the Resistance Movement of the Zealots," in *The State in the New Testament* 8–23 (1956) ("Jesus' attitude is to be sought beyond any uncritical absolutising of the Roman State, and at the same time beyond any thoroughgoing political resistance to it"); *see also* Cullmann, *Jesus and the Revolutionaries* (1970). On the contrary, the principal theological understanding of the mission and purpose of Jesus was that he was not an earthly, political messiah who came to overthrow the Romans, but was the servant of Israel who suffered and died under the yoke of Roman power [Chapter One, section 9]; *see*, e.g., Mt. 12:18–21 (citing servant song in Is. 42:1–4); Mt. 26:63–64 (repudiating title of Messiah); and *see* Cullmann, *New Testament Christology* 111–36 (1959); Ferdinand Hahn, *The Titles of Jesus in Christology* 136–223 (1969); Reginald H. Fuller, *The Foundations of New Testament Christology* 23–31, 63–64, 109–11, 158–62, 191–92, 230 (1965).

At least some Christians, notably those from the perspective of the "radical," Mennonite tradition of the Reformation [Chapter Five, section 1], have found these and similar teachings of Jesus on nonviolence to be a binding norm in their lives. These Christians include leaders of the civil rights movement in recent American history. *See*, *e.g.*, Martin Luther King, Jr., *Letter from Birmingham Jail* (1963) [Chapter Fifteen, section 3]. In this perspective, to be a disciple or follower of Jesus means not only to attend carefully to his teaching about nonviolence, but also to live as he did—nonviolently—and to follow the path he walked, the way of the cross. *See*, *e.g.*, G.H.C. MacGregor, *The New Testament Basis of Pacifism* (1953); John Howard Yoder, *Nevertheless: The Varieties of Religious Pacifism* (1971); Yoder, *The Politics of Jesus* 115–134 (1972); and Jean–Michel Hornus, *It is Not Lawful for Me to Fight* (1980).

One of the earliest voices in the Christian community raised against military service is that of Tertullian (160–230 CE), Bishop of Carthage. Acknowledging that some Christians have begun to serve in the Roman army by the end of the second century, Tertullian objects to such service on the ground that it is inconsistent with the non-violent character of the Christian community. *Apologeticum* 37.3. "How will [a Christian] wage war," asks Tertullian, "nay, how will he even in peace do military service without the sword, which the Lord has taken away.... [E]very soldier of later times was ungirded by the Lord, when he disarmed Peter." J.H. Waszink and J.C.M. Van Winden, *Tertullianus. De idololatria* 63 (1987). The "disarming" of Peter referred to in this passage is found in the Gospel according to John, 18:10–11; cf. Mt. 26:51–52.

Campenhausen explains the ambivalent view of the early church on military service as follows. "If [Christians] comply with and accept some factor in the outside world, that does not mean that they approve it; it is simply that they cannot change the world and make it the Church. At the same time, if definite obligations are imposed on Christians by the Church ... , that does not mean that they are intended as principles to which all law must conform; it is simply that they cannot commit themselves wholly to the law of this world. This explains the seemingly inconsistent ways in which the ancient Church judged war and military service. Not a single one of the Fathers doubted that, in the world as it is, war is inevitable, and consequently, they saw no reason to condemn the military profession in particular.... It is only by force that external peace is preserved, for which Christians also are grateful. They themselves, however, would not have anything to do with war service. The world may need its Caesars, but no emperor can be a Christian nor a Christian ever be an emperor [citing Tertullian]. The Church knows no war [citing Clement of Alexandria]. Christians are peacemakers and adhere to the commandments in the Sermon on the Mount. They are ready to suffer and die in testimony to their truth; but they do not kill [citing Justin, Irenaeus, Tertullian, and Minucius Felix]." Campenhausen 160–61. He notes that since "there was practically no conscription" at the time, "it was easy to avoid anything to do with the army." *Id.* 161.

Recent scholarship has shed light on the many ways in which military service entailed not only an ethical problem for the followers of Jesus, but also a profound religious conflict. Service in the Roman army was by no means secular. On the contrary, the pagan religion of Rome pervaded the military, with its sacred oath of fealty to the emperor, its cult of the standards, and its elaborate calendar of liturgical festivals and sacrifices timed to coincide with similar pagan rituals in Rome. A Roman soldier could not help confronting an all-pervasive religious dimension to service in the imperial army. *See, e.g.,* John Helgeland, Robert Daly, and J. Patout Burns, *Christians and the Military: The Early Experience* (1985) 51–54; and Helgeland, "Christians and the Roman Army: A.D. 173–337," 43 *Church History* 149–63 (1974). For example, soldiers were required to swear an oath of obedience to the caesar as lord. *Id.* 48. The oath was known as the "*sacramentum fidei,*" embodying two terms that had rich theological resonance for Christians. For pagan Romans the term "*sacramentum*" meant a solemn oath or promise; for Christians the term also signified a ritual encounter with Christ. For pagan Romans the term "*fides*" referred to fealty, loyalty, or obedience; for Christians the term comprehended two deeply connected religious concepts, fidelity and belief [Chapter Four, section 1]. Christians would later use the term "sacrament of faith" to refer to the Eucharist. In this context, then, the Roman loyalty oath presented a direct conflict with the central command of Deuteronomy 5:7 "You shall have no other god to set against me" [Chapter One, section 1], and with the fundamental Christian belief that "Jesus is Lord" (Rom. 1:4; 1 Cor. 12:3). Thus Tertullian could write: "The oath of allegiance to God and that to man, the standard of God and the standard of the devil, the camp of light and the camp of darkness are incompatible.... All uniforms are prohibited to us, since they are signs of a forbidden calling." *De Cor.* 11. Campenhausen notes: "What Tertullian feared was the denial of Christ and the taint of pagan worship, which seemed inevitable in view of the strictness of military discipline and the role played by pagan religion in the whole ceremonial and life of the army." *Id.* 163. As long as military service was connected at least implicitly with emperor worship, it presented a religious problem of idolatry and apostasy. For a succinct and balanced discussion of the treatment of military service in early Christianity, *see* David Hunter, "A Decade of Research on Early Christians and Military Service," 18 *Religious Studies Rev.* 87–94 (1991); *see* also Geoffrey Nuttall, *Christian Pacifism in History* 1–14 (1958); Stephen Gero, "*Miles Gloriosus*: The Christian and Military Service according to Tertullian," 39 *Church History* 285–298 (1970); and Louis J. Swift, *The Early Fathers on War and Military Service* (1983).

As noted above, the reign of Constantine produced a important turn in Christian attitudes about the imperial army. "When the supreme commander had himself become a Christian [on his deathbed in 337], the 'idealistic approach' was seen to be obviously untenable. It was no longer possible to shift the responsibility for wars to the heathen population exclusively. Christians had themselves to become members of the army—no longer just in isolated cases and by way of concession, but in general and on principle. The Church did not reach this decision easily. Indeed, the atrocities committed in the preceding persecutions and civil wars powerfully reinforced the general horror of war on the part of civilians, as well as the Church's own impressions of the sordid character of the military profession." Campenhausen, 167. A canon or church law issued at a synod at Hippo in northern Africa held: "Persons who have authority to put to death [judges] and soldiers must, under no circumstances, kill, even when they are commanded to." Canon 13f, Synod of Hippo. *Id.* 168. By the year 416 CE, an edict of the Emperor Theodosius II decreed that only Christians could enter the army.

Campenhausen concludes: "Notwithstanding the basic assertion that certain duties, political and military, are incumbent on all citizens, including Christians, war service is not held simply as an absolute law. There are possible exceptions, and from the Christian standpoint, necessary ones. Monks, clerics, and 'spiritual persons' of all kinds are not obliged to fight, but may always restrict themselves to sacrifice and suffering . Perseverance and stability in these callings are a sign and a constant reminder of the possibility of exemption as a live issue [Chapter Eleven, section 4]. For, in fact, the main thing is the freedom of such 'exceptions,' which persist in full view of the world. The Christian readiness to share in all the burdens and responsibilities of civic life is not thereby revoked. It subsists unimpaired, and holds good even when—as in the case when war has become inevitable—it is clearly a matter of the *consequence* of human sin. . . . On the other hand, the impression should never be given that sin is itself a power to which Christians must submit, instead of fighting; and so their compliance with the political and military authorities never means that they take war to be an ultimate truth and a reality of life that suffers no impairment. The real and always valid truth is, rather, the truth of the peace given to the world, and this truth be witnessed to at all times. The forces of enmity must be breached by those of the spirit, and this must be done repeatedly. . . . In this way, both war service and the renunciation of war on the part of Christians belong, in a sense, together. In this case, the 'exception,' rightly understood, is the necessary explanation and ratification of the 'rule' rightly understood." *Id.* 169–70. *See also* Adolph Harnack, *The Mission and Expansion of Christianity in the First Three Centuries* (1962); Harnack, *Militia Christi: The Christian Religion and the Military in the First Three Centuries* (1981); C. John Cadoux, *The Early Christian Attitude to War* (1982; orig. ed. 1919); and Roland H. Bainton, *Christian Attitudes toward War and Peace: A Historical Survey and Critical Re-evaluation* 66–84 (1960). For an assessment of the impact of the Constantinian shift on the teaching of Christianity on violence, see John Howard Yoder, "The Constantinian Sources of Western Social Ethics," in *The Priestly Kingdom* 135–47 (1984); and Stanley Hauerwas, *The Peaceable Kingdom* (1983).

With the major shift in the fourth century from persecution of Christianity to the status of a tolerated religion and then to official establishment, the ethical questions about war posed new dimensions. Now Christians had to ponder not whether it was ever permissible to serve in an imperial army replete with pagan religion, but whether the State could ever wage war (*jus ad bellum*), and if so, whether the Christian religion placed any limits on the conduct of warfare (*jus in bello*). The leading Christian theologian to address these questions systematically was Augustine (354–430 CE), who wrote about these realities after almost a century of open Christian influence at the center of power. He was born in Tagaste, Numidia. "An African," as his enemies taunted him, he was familiar with the imperial court but was basically a man from the provinces. He had been a pagan, then a Manichee; he became a Catholic in 387. He was elected bishop of Hippo in northern Africa in 395. The preeminence of his theological insights and rhetorical skills, his energetic delight in argument and mental combat, his encyclopedic range, his personality, his personal experience, and his willingness to speak personally made him the most influential writer on morals for the Christian West. Starting with his own experience of human weakness articulated powerfully in his autobiographical *Confessions* (ca. 397 CE), and elaborating his theological anthropology more systematically in *The City of God* (413–426 CE), Augustine held a view of the human condition that was deeply pessimistic. The Augustinian doctrine of original sin meant that all persons are selfish and prone to sin; without redeeming grace we are full of depravity. This perspective influenced Augustine's views both as the founder of the justifiable war tradition and as the great political theorist whose writings were to dominate the medieval period. Robert A. Markus, *Saeculum: History and Society in the Theology of St. Augustine* (2d ed. 1989)

Although Augustine viewed the pacifism of earlier Christian writers cited above as too great a concession to evil and injustice, "Augustine was no militarist; there is no glorification of war in *The City of God*." George Weigel, *Tranquilitas Ordinis: The Present Failure and Future Promise of American Catholic Thought on War and Peace* 29 (1987). On the contrary, he expressly condemned wars of military conquest such as the destruction of Rome by Alaric, leader of the Goths, in 410 CE. Bainton 93–95. For Augustine, the fallenness of the world does not make war necessary, let alone desirable, but simply inevitable. Once Augustine posited the inevitability of war, his moral question was how to set limits upon it. *See* Louis J. Swift, "Augustine on War and Killing: Another View," 66 *Harv. Theol. Rev.* 369–83 (1973); Robert A. Markus, "St. Augustine's Views of the 'Just War,' " in W.J. Shiels, ed., *The Church and War* (1983) 1–14; and David A. Lenihan, "The Just War Theory in the Work of St. Augustine," 19 *Augustininan Studies* 19 37–70 (1988).

"In Augustine's theory, three kinds of war were morally defensible: a defensive war against aggression, a war to gain just reparations for a previous wrong, and a war to recover stolen property. But historical circumstances alone did not create the conditions for a 'just' war. A properly constituted authority must decide that the resort to war is necessary. Once that decision has been made, it is the soldier's duty to obey. Further, war must be waged with a 'right intention': not for revenge, or lust for glory and spoils, but with a sober commitment to conduct the war as an instrument of punishment necessary to protect the innocent and to prevent malefactors from doing worse. Right intentions would be expressed, not only in the decision to go to war, but also in the just conduct of a war. Here, 'the rules were taken from classical antiquity. Faith must be kept with the enemy. There should be no wanton violence, profanation of temples, looting, massacre, or conflagration. Vengeance, atrocities, and reprisals were excluded, though ambush was allowed.' Thus, Augustine, who counseled against self-defense in the case of individual threat, outlined the skeleton of a just-war theory rooted in a moral passion for peace as the tranquility of order." Weigel 29. (citations omitted); *see* Bainton 89–100; John Langan, "The Elements of St. Augustine's Just War Theory," 12 *J. of Religious Ethics* 19–38 (1984); John Howard Yoder, *When War is Unjust: Being Honest in Just–War Thinking* 8–18 (1996). Paul Ramsay noted that Augustine did not justify Christian participation in war on grounds of self-defense, but on grounds of defense of the innocent, a defense that required the State to use no more force than is necessary to prevent the attacker from destroying the innocent. Ramsay, *War and the Christian Conscience* (1961); *see also* Stanley Hauerwas, *Against the Nations: War and Survival in a Liberal Society* 138 (1985).

Augustine's seminal work on a theory to limit warfare has been refined over time by scholars such as Thomas Aquinas (1225—1274), *see Summa Theologiae*, II–II, q. 40, art.1, and discussion in Weigel 33–38, Francisco Suárez (1548–1617), *see* John Eppstein, *The Catholic Tradition of the Law of the Nations* 97–123 (1935), and Hugo Grotius (1583–1645), *see* Wolfgang Friedman, "Hugo Grotius," in 3 *Encyclopedia of Philosophy* 393–95 (1967).

The result of centuries of reflection on the justification of war is that there is now fairly strong consensus in international law that war may be justified only if: (1) declared and waged by legitimate authority, (2) resorted to after all efforts to resolve the conflict peacefully have failed, (3) waged for a just cause (e.g., restoration of peace and justice) and with reasonable hope of success, (4) waged within the principle of proportionality, according to which the good sought to be achieved must outweigh the evil inherent in all war, and (5) waged within the limits of the law of war, providing, for example, immunity for noncombatants. Eppstein 92–93; Weigel 41. Although these principles derive from the thinking of Augustine, they are no longer bound up with the belief that there is a God who discloses himself to human persons through some form of revelation. The contemporary consensus on the just war tradition rests not only on religious insight, but also on secular norms that are empirically grounded and accessible to human reason. *See, e.g.*, James Turner Johnson, *Ideology, Reason and the Limitation of War: Secular and Religious Concepts, 1200–1740* (1975), and Johnson, *The Quest for Peace: Three Moral Traditions in Western Cultural History* (1987); Richard A. Falk, *Law, Morality, and War in the Contemporary World* (1963); Richard A. Falk, *Legal Order in a Violent World* (1968); Richard A. Falk & Saul H. Mendlovitz, eds. *The Strategy of World Order* (4 vols. 1966); Richard A. Falk & Samuel S. Kim, *The War System: An Interdisciplinary Approach* eds. (1980).

Augustine also turned his attention to the problems of government at a higher level of abstraction. The givens of the situation when he wrote were these. The government was deeply involved with religion. Christians were deeply involved with the government. Christian rulers listened to but did not always follow Catholic bishops. The recent disasters of the empire (for example, the capture and sacking of Rome by the king of the Goths, Aleric, in 410 CE) made pagans wonder whether Christianity was at the root of the empire's problems. Augustine's lengthy reply to this charge is set forth in the first ten "books" or major units of his magisterial work, *The City of God*, written in 413 CE. *See* Hans von Campenhausen, "Augustine and the Fall of Rome," in *Tradition and Life in the Church*, 201–16. In the remaining fifteen books of *The City of God*, Augustine differentiated between the earthly city and the heavenly city. This distinction is not the same as the distinction between church and state, both of which are part of the earthly city. The dualism Augustine proposes is not spatial, between two contemporaneous entities, but temporal, between the world as we know it and the world of God's eternal peace that this world can only glimpse. *See* Peter Dennis Bathory, *Political Theory as Public Confession: The Social and Political Thought of St. Augustine of Hippo* (1981); Markus, *Saeculum;* Herbert Deane, *The Political and Social*

Ideas of St. Augustine (1963); and John Neville Figgis, *The Political Aspects of S. Augustine's City of God* (1921).

The letters that follow were addressed by Augustine to three Roman rulers in Africa. Marcellinus, imperial state secretary and tribune, had been picked by the imperial administrators as a Catholic official with an interest in theology and was sent to represent the emperor at Carthage in 411 in a conference between Catholic and Donatist bishops planned by the government to abolish "the pestilence" of Donatism (*Theodosian Code* 16.5.44).

Marcellinus had presided and then gone on to judge the cases of certain Donatist extremists, the Circumcellions, who were charged with actual violence. The first letter to him here was written after these trials; the second addresses the kind of problem a conscientious Christian using power had to face at every moment.

Marcellinus was himself the victim of imperial power. In 413 he was executed on nonreligious grounds as a rebel, but he entered the Roman Martyrology as a saint. Augustine thought enough of him to address *The City of God* to him (Book 1, Chapter 1). He did not remove his name after his disgrace and execution.

1.   THE DUTY OF MERCY

Augustine to Marcellinus (Letter 133)

To the Excellent and Deservedly Distinguished Lord, his Very Dear Son, Marcellinus, health in the Lord from Augustine.

Several of the Circumcellions and clerics of the Donatist party whom care of public discipline had removed from Hippo for trial of their actions have, I learn from Your Nobility, confessed what they committed against the Catholic priest, Restitutus, and that as to the mutilation of another Catholic priest, Innocent, they dug out an eye and cut off a finger. I have been filled with the greatest worry that Your Highness judge that they be struck with such severity of law that they suffer the kind of things that they have done. By this letter I beg the faith which you have in Christ that, through the mercy of Christ the Lord, you do not do this nor permit it to be done under any circumstances.

We can distance ourselves from their death when they are seen to be presented for trial, not at our accusation, but at that of those to whom vigilance belongs for the safeguarding of public peace. Nonetheless we do not want the sufferings of the servants of God to be vindicated with equal punishments as if by the law of the talion. Not that we forbid taking from wicked men license to do crimes, but we want this to suffice, so that alive and mutilated in no part of their bodies they may be directed from their mad restlessness to healthful rest by the coercion of the law or assigned from their evil works to some useful work. This is also called condemnation, but who does not understand that it should be called a benefit rather than a punishment where neither bold savagery is given rein nor the medicine of penance is withheld?

Christian judge, fulfill the office of a father. Be angry at wickedness in such a way that you take care to remember humanity. Do not let yourself exercise the lust of revenge against the atrocities of sinners. Apply your will to care for the sinners' wounds. Do not lose that fatherly diligence which you kept in your investigation when you extracted the confession of such great crimes, not by stretching on the rack, not by tearing on hooks, not by burning in fire, but by the blows of rods. This form of coercion is used by teachers of the liberal arts, by parents themselves, and often by bishops in public trials.

Do not, then, punish severely what you found out gently. There is a greater need to investigate than to punish. For this reason even the mildest men diligently and pressingly investigate a hidden crime to find those they then spare. It is generally necessary that an investigation be carried out sharply, so that, when the crime is clear, mildness may appear. All good things assuredly love to be set in the light, not on account of human glory, but, as the Lord says, that "they may see your good works and glorify your Father who art in heaven." And so it is not enough for the Apostle to advise us to be mild but to make it known to all. "Let your mildness," he says, "be known to all"; and elsewhere "showing mildness to all men." Hence that most celebrated clemency of Saint David when he mercifully spared the enemy delivered into his hands would not have shone unless his power had equally appeared. Do not, then, let your power of punishment make you harsh, when the necessity of inquiry did not shake your spirit of mildness. You have found out the crime, do not seek the executioner when you refused to use the torturer in discovering it.

Finally, you have been sent for the welfare of the Church. This, I contend, is expedient for the Catholic Church or—that I may not appear to surpass the limit of my concern—this benefits the Church belonging to the diocese of Royal Hippo. If you do not hear a friend asking, hear a bishop advising. Since I speak to a Christian, especially on such a matter, I shall say without arrogance: it is appropriate for you to hear a bishop commanding, Excellent and Deservedly Distinguished Lord and Very Dear Son.

I know the ecclesiastical cases have been mostly referred to Your Excellency, but because I believe responsibility for them belongs to that very illustrious and distinguished man, the proconsul, I have also sent a letter for him. I ask you not to mind giving it to him yourself and if necessary citing it to him. I beg you both not to judge inopportune our intercession or suggestion or solicitude, and not to cheapen, by reciprocal punishments of the enemies by whom they suffered, the sufferings of the Catholic servants of God which ought to be useful for the spiritual building up of the weak. Rather, break judicial severity. You are sons of the Church. Do not fail to commend your faith and the mildness of your Mother.

May almighty God increase all good things for Your Nobility, Excellent and Deservedly Distinguished Lord and Very Dear Son.

2. CHRISTIAN AS RULER

Augustine to Marcellinus (Letter 138)

Now let us see what follows in your letter. You added that they say that "Christ's preaching and teaching are in no part fit for the morals of the commonwealth: it is clear that his commandment is that we must return evil for evil to no one, and that to him who strikes us we must offer the other cheek and give our coat to him who takes our shirt and walk twice as far with him who makes us go." All these they assert to be contrary to the morals of the commonwealth. "Who," they say, "would suffer something to be taken from him by the enemy? Who would not wish by the law of war to return evil to the ravagers of a Roman province?"

Words of this kind from objectors or from those who are not objecting but inquiring, I could perhaps only refute with labor, but these discussions are held with men who have been liberally educated. What need then for me to work longer and not ask them how they who made the commonwealth large and rich when it was small and poor could have governed and enlarged it when "they preferred to pardon rather than pursue the injuries they received?" How could Cicero, extolling the morals of Caesar the ruler of the commonwealth, say, "He was accustomed to forget nothing, except injuries." He said this either as a great admirer or as a great flatterer. If he spoke as an admirer, he had known such a Caesar. If he spoke as a flatterer, he showed that the prince of the city ought to be as he inaccurately proclaimed him to be.

But what is it not to return evil for evil except to abhor the lust of revenge? What is it to prefer to pardon rather than pursue injuries received except to forget them? When they read these things in their authors, they exclaim over them and applaud them. Morals appear to be described and proclaimed by which a city which would rule over so many people was worthy to rise, because "they preferred to pardon rather than pursue injuries received." But when they read that divine authority commands that evil is not to be returned for evil and when this healthy advice sounds from a higher place to congregations of the people, in public schools for both sexes and for every age and rank, religion is accused as if it were the enemy of the commonwealth....

How many great commandments of harmony, not worked out by human arguments but written by divine authority, are read in the churches of Christ! Who so foreign to that religion or so deaf that he does not know? To this belong these things which pertain to action more than learning. "Offer your other cheek to the one striking you. Give your shirt to one wanting to take your coat. Walk twice the way with one forcing you to go." Assuredly these things are done to overcome evil with good or rather that, in the evil man, the evil be conquered by the good and the man be freed not from an exterior and alien evil but from his own interior evil by which he is more seriously and ruinously wasted than by the inhumanity of any exterior enemy.

Therefore he who overcomes evil by good patiently loses temporal advantages in order to teach how for the sake of faith and justice those things are to be despised by which the other loving them too much became evil. So the wrongdoer learns from him to whom he did the injury what sort of things they are on account of which he did the injury; and repentant, he is won to harmony, than which nothing is more useful to the city—conquered not by the strength of savagery but by the benevolence of patience. This is rightly done when it appears that it will benefit him for whose sake it is done, working amendment and harmony in him. It is certainly to be done with this intention, even if another result follows and he refuses to be corrected or pacified. This medicine must be applied for the sake of the one to be corrected and pacified as if he were to be cured and healed.

Otherwise if we attend to the words and think they are to be kept literally, the right cheek is not to be offered if the left is struck; for He says, "If anyone strikes you on the right cheek, offer him the left." But the left is struck more often because the blow is easier for the right hand of the striker. But it is usually understood as if it said, "If anyone pursues your better goods, offer him your worse; lest being zealous for vengeance rather than patience, you despise eternal things for temporal, when temporal are to be despised for eternal as the left is for the right."

This intention has always been that of the holy martyrs: they justly demand an ultimate judgment when no place of amendment longer remains—the final and supreme Judgment. Now we must beware that out of desire for vengeance we lose (to say nothing more) patience itself which is to be held above all that an enemy can take from us against our will.

Another Gospel-writer of the same opinion made no mention of the right cheek but named only "one cheek" and "the other" and that "the other" may be somewhat more understood he simply commands the same patience. Therefore a just and devout man ought to bear patiently the malice of those whom he seeks to become good; so that the number of the good will increase rather than that he add himself by equal malice to the number of the evil.

Finally, these commandments relate more to the preparation of the heart, which is within, than to the deed which is done openly. Patience with benevolence is to be held in the secret place of the spirit and to be made manifest when it appears it will benefit those to whom we ought to wish well. This is clearly shown because the Lord Jesus himself, a singular example of patience, replied when He was struck on the face: "If I have spoken wrongly, prove the wrong; if well, why strike me"? He did not—if we look at the words—fulfill his own commandment; for He did not offer the other side to the one striking him but instead prohibited the one who did the injury from increasing it. But He came prepared not only to be struck on the face but even to be killed, crucified, for the sake of those by whom He suffered these things. For them He said as He hung on the cross: "Father, pardon them because they know not what they do."

The Apostle Paul did not seem to have fulfilled the commandment of his Lord and Teacher. When he himself was struck on the face, he said to the chief priest: "God shall strike you, whitewashed wall. You sit judging me according to the law and you order me to be struck contrary to the law." And when the bystanders said, "You do injury to the chief priest," he wanted to warn them by his mockery so that those who were wise would understand that now at the coming of Christ the whitewashed wall was to be destroyed—that is, the hypocrisy of the priesthood of the Jews. Indeed he said: "I did not know, brother, that he is the chief, for it is written, 'You shall not curse the chief of your people.' " Beyond doubt he had grown up in this people and had there learned the law and could not not know that this man was the chief priest nor could he in any way have deceived those to whom he was known into believing that he did not know.

These commandments of patience are therefore always to be kept in the heart, and benevolence is to be fulfilled in the will, so that evil is not returned for evil. But many things must be done with those who are unwilling, beating them with a certain kindly severity and taking into account not their will but what is useful for them. Their literature had lavishly praised such acts at the start of the commonwealth. In correcting a son, however severely, paternal love is surely never lost. Yet what he who is to be cured by pain against his will does not want and is pained by, happens.

In the same way if this earthly commonwealth keeps the Christian commandments, wars themselves will be waged not without benevolence so that thought is more readily taken for the conquered in a fellowship pacified in piety and justice. He whose license to do iniquity is snatched away is beneficially conquered, for nothing is less happy than the happiness of sinners. Impunity from punishment nourishes this happiness while an evil will like an internal enemy is strengthened. Depraved and distorted mortal hearts think human affairs are happy when they notice the splendor of the coverings and do not notice the fall of the souls; when a mass of theaters are thrown up while the foundations of the virtues are dug away; when there is a glorious madness of expenditure while the works of mercy are laughed at; when actors luxuriate in the midst of riches, while the poor scarcely have necessities; when God, who cries out against this public evil with the public voice of his teaching, is blasphemed by impious peoples; and such gods are sought in whose honor these theatrical decorations of bodies and souls are celebrated.

If God permits these things to go on, He is the more gravely angered. If He lets them go unpunished, He punishes more terribly. But when He overturns what supports vices, and turns rich lusts into poverty, He opposes them mercifully. Mercifully, if it can be done, let even wars be waged by the good so that those dominated by licentious desires will lose these vices which ought to be extirpated or suppressed by just rule.

If Christian discipline faulted all wars, when the soldiers in the Gospel asked for advice as to salvation it should have been said: "Throw away your arms. Separate yourself entirely from the soldiery." But what was said to them was: "Shake down no one. Blackmail no one. Let your wages suffice for you." He who commands that their own wages should suffice surely does not forbid them to fight. Hence, let those who say that the teaching of Christ is against the commonwealth grant the kind of army with such soldiers as the teaching of Christ orders that these should be; let them grant such provincial administrators, such husbands, such spouses, such parents, such sons, such masters, such slaves, such kings, such judges, even such tax collectors and agents for debts due the Treasury as Christian teaching commands, and let them dare to say that it is against the commonwealth. Let them not hesitate to acknowledge that, if it is observed, it is the great salvation of the commonwealth.

3. THE DUTY TO INTERCEDE

In 414, the year after Marcellinus' death, Augustine wrote to Macedonius, governor of Africa. Roman law recognized the right of a Catholic bishop to intervene where a judge's "negligence or favoritism" threatened the safety of a defendant, *Theodosian Code* 9.40.16. Augustine apparently understood this concession broadly, and Macedonius had challenged his practice. The letter that follows not only defended the bishop's right to plead for mercy but, in a later passage not quoted here, referred to the obligation of a judge not to take money for his judgment. Delicately and by allusion only, Augustine indicated that a bribed judge was under obligation like other criminals to make restitution. He does not say that Macedonius is in this posture but in this letter so eloquently stressing the need for mercy, Augustine discreetly reminds Macedonius that he may need it too.

Augustine to Macedonius (Letter 153)

Augustine, bishop, the servant of Christ and his household, to his beloved son, Macedonius, greetings in the Lord.

A man so very busy as you are in human affairs with matters of state and so very attentive not to his own interest but others'—as to which I congratulate you—I ought not to deprive of conversation or detain with a preamble. Receive then what you either wanted to know through me or to find out if I knew. If you judged the matter trivial or excessive, you would have thought that among so many and great necessary cares there was no need to take care for it.

You ask me why I say that it belongs to the office of the priesthood to intervene for the guilty and why I am offended if I fail, as if I had not been discharging what was my duty. You say that you seriously doubt whether this arises from religion. Then you add why are you so aroused. You say, "If sins are so prohibited by the Lord that indeed no opportunity of repenting is granted after the first sin, how can I argue from religion that whatever the crime was, it is to be forgiven"? More passionately, you further urge, "What I want to be unpunished, I approve. If it is clear that he who approves an act, no less than its author, is bound in any matter of sin, it is certain that I am bound in fellowship of fault as often as I want a guilty man to be unpunished."

Whom would you not frighten by these words if one did not know your kindness and humanity? I who know you do not doubt that you wrote these things in order to inquire and not to give a decision. I answer the more quickly with other words of yours. As though you did not want me to delay with this question or foresaw what I would say or advised me what I should say, you said: "Besides, here is what is more serious. All sins seem forgivable when the guilty promise amendment."

Therefore, before I discuss that more serious point which follows in your letter, I shall take what you have given and use it to remove that barrier by which our intercessions seem repressible. Assuredly we intercede for all sins as much as opportunity is granted, because "all sins seem forgivable when the guilty promise amendment." This is your judgment; and it is mine.

In no way, then, do I approve the fault which I want corrected; nor what is done wrongly do I want to be unpunished because it pleases me. But I pity the man and I detest his crime or outrage. The more his vice displeases me, the less I want the vicious man to die without being corrected. Common and easy it is to hate evil men because they are evil. Rare and dutiful it is to love the same men because they are men, so that in one man you simultaneously disapprove his fault and approve his nature and more justly hate the fault because it befouls the nature you love. He who is the foe of crime in order to be the liberator of the man is, therefore, not bound in a partnership of iniquity but in that of humanity.

Moreover, there is no other place to correct morals except in this life. After it, one will have whatever he found pleasure in. Therefore, I am compelled by charity for humankind to intercede for the guilty, so that they do not so finish this life by punishment that when it is finished they cannot finish the punishment.

Do not doubt that this my duty arises from religion. God "with whom there is no iniquity," whose power is supreme, who sees not only how each one is but also how each one will be, who alone cannot slip in judging because He cannot be deceived in judging, nevertheless as the Gospel says, "makes his sun rise upon the good and the bad, and rains upon the just and the unjust." Of His wonderful goodness I am an imitator, the Lord Christ exhorting, "Love your enemies. Do good to those who hate you and pray for those who persecute you so that you may be sons of your Father who is in heaven, who makes his sun rise upon the good and the bad, and rains upon the just and unjust." That many abuse this divine pardon and mildness to their own destruction, who does not know? Rebuking such and seriously reproving them, the Apostle says, "But do you think, man, you who judge those who do such things, and do them yourself, that you will escape the judgment of God? Do you despise the riches of his kindness and patience and long-suffering? Are you unaware that the kindness of God leads you to penitence? But according to your hardness and impertinent heart, you heap up wrath for yourself on the day of wrath and of the just revelations of the judgment of God, who returns to each one according to his work." These persevere in their weakness: should God therefore not persevere in his patience, punishing by means of a few things in this world lest divine providence not be believed to be, and keeping many things for the final examination, so that his future judgment will be justified?

That heavenly Teacher does not, I think, command us to love iniquity when He commands us to love our enemies, to do good to those who hate us, to pray for those who persecute us, although beyond doubt if we devoutly worship God we cannot have any enemies or any aroused against us with bitter hatreds and persecutors except the godless. Are the godless therefore to be loved? Are we to do good to the godless? Are the godless even to be prayed for? Assuredly, yes. For He who commands this is God. Yet He does not by this compact add us to the fellowship of the godless, just as by sparing them and granting them life and safety He does not become their fellow. His intention, so far as it is given a devout man to know it, is what the Apostle sets out, saying, "Are you unaware that the patience of God leads you to penitence?" To this I want to add that the sins of those for whom I intervene I do not spare or favor.

Certain men whose crimes are evident, when they have been freed by your severity, I still keep from the fellowship of the altar, so that by doing penance and punishing themselves they can please Him whom by sinning they despised. For he who truly repents does nothing less than this: the evil he did he does not permit to be unpunished. God—whose high and just judgment so despises evil—spares him who in this way does not spare himself. He spares the unjust and the wicked and grants them life and safety, even the many whom He knows will not do penance, and shows his patience. How much more should I be merciful to those who promise amendment when I am uncertain whether they will do what they promise, so that I bend your rigor by interceding for them. For them I pray to the Lord from whom nothing about their future morals is hidden; and I do so without rashness, because He himself commands this.

Iniquity sometimes so makes progress among men that even after they have done penance, even after they have been reconciled to the altar, they commit similar or more serious things. Yet God makes his sun also rise on such; nor less than before does He bestow on them the very ample gifts of life and health. Although in the Church the humble place of penance is not granted them, still God does not forget his patience upon them. Suppose one of this number were to say, "Either give me again the place of doing penance or allow me in despair to do whatever shall please so far as I can with my own resources and am not prohibited by human laws, in fornication and every lust condemned by God but praiseworthy among most men; or if you call me back from this wickedness, say whether it benefits me at all for my future life if in this life I despise the enticements of the most seductive pleasure, if I resist the enticements of lust, if I withdraw my body even from many lawful and conceded things in order to chastise it, if I punish myself by doing penance more fiercely than before, if I groan more miserably, weep more fully, live better, support the poor more generously, burn more ardently with the charity that covers a multitude of sins"— which of us would be so mad as to say to this man, "None of these things will help you later. Go, at least savor the sweetness of this life." God avert such monstrous sacrilegious madness! Cautiously and salubriously it is provided that place for most humble penance is granted only once in the Church, lest, for the sick, cheap medicine be less useful which is the more salubrious the less it is held in contempt. Nonetheless who would dare to say to God, "Why do you again spare this man who has bound himself in the toils of iniquity after his first repentance?" Who would dare to say that what the Apostle says, "Are you unaware that the patience of God leads you to repentance?" does not work as to them; or that these are excepted from the saying, "Blessed are all who trust in Him," or that "Act manfully and let your heart be comforted, all you who hope in the Lord'' does not apply to them.

Upon sinners, so great is the patience, so great is the mercy of God that those who amend their souls in this temporal life are not condemned in eternity. He looks to no one to furnish Him mercy for no one is more blessed than He, no one more powerful, no one more just. Is it necessary therefore for men to be like this toward men? Whatever praise we pile up in this life, we say it is not without sin—if we said otherwise, as it is written, ''We deceive ourselves and the truth is not in us.''

One role is the accuser's; another the defender's; another the intercessor's; another the judge's (it would be too long and it is unnecessary in this speech to discourse upon the duties proper to each). But the avengers of crimes—in this office moved not by their own anger but ministers of the laws and vindicators not of their own injuries but of those done to others, and so necessarily like judges—are themselves terrified by the divine judgment, so that they think God's mercy is needed on account of their own sins. They do not think it a fault in their duty if they act mercifully toward those over whose life or death they have lawful power.

4. THE DUTY TO COERCE

Three years later Augustine addressed another governor of Africa, Boniface, sending him a small treatise, *The Correction of the Donatists,* setting out the difference between the heretical Arians and the Donatists who are described as ''rebels against the unity of Christ,'' and going on to describe the imperial laws intended to increase peace and unity. The letter reflects a distinct evolution in Augustine's thought. The Donatists are to be driven into the Church by force. He still retains the notion of mild force expressed in the letter of 412 to Marcellinus. He still harbors the view, also expressed to Marcellinus, that the infliction of moderate punishment can be paternal and medicinal. Scourging is not execution. By embracing in principle the use of coercion against schismatics and heretics, however, he laid a general foundation for religious persecution. True, the death penalty would run counter to his rationale as well as to his repeated pleas for mercy; but it was to prove impossible to draw his nice line between the severe and lenient infliction of pain. From one perspective Augustine merely rationalized a century of religious persecution by Christian emperors and sets limits. From another perspective he provided the charter of the Inquisition by his use of two words from the parable of the great supper (Lk. 14:15–24), *coge intrare* (''*compel* people *to come in*, that my house may be filled''), to authorize the use of official force against heretics in northern Africa. See Markus, ''*Coge intrare*: the Church and Political Power,'' in *Saeculum* 133–53; Peter Brown, ''Religious Coercion in the later Roman Empire: The Case of North Africa,'' 48 *History* 283–305 (1963); and Brown, ''Saint Augustine's Attitude to Religious Coercion,'' 54 *J. of Roman Studies* 107–16 (9164).

Augustine, *The Correction of the Donatists* (Letter 185)

Those who refuse to have just laws enacted against their own impieties say that the Apostles did not seek such from the kings of the earth. They do not consider that the time then was something else and that all things are done at their own times. Then there was no emperor who had believed in Christ, no emperor who would serve Him by passing laws in favor of religion and against impiety ... not yet was the time as to which the psalm says, "And now, kings, understand: learn you who judge the earth, serve the Lord in fear and rejoice in Him with fear." In what way, then, do kings serve the Lord in fear except by prohibiting and punishing with religious severity those things that are done against the commandments of the Lord? For he serves in one way because he is a man and in another way because he is king. Because he is man he serves by living faithfully; but because he is also king he serves by prescribing just laws and prohibiting the contrary, providing sanction with due vigor, just as Ezechias served by destroying the groves and temples of idols in those high places which had been set up against the commandments of God.

Why since free will has been divinely given to man, are adulteries punished by the laws and sacrileges permitted? Is it a lighter matter for a soul not to keep faith in God than for a woman not to keep it with her husband?

Or if these things which are committed not in contempt but in ignorance of religion are to be punished more mildly, are they therefore to be neglected?

Will anyone doubt that it is better for men to be led by teaching, rather than forced by fear of punishment or suffering, to worship God? But that one way is better is not reason that the other should be neglected. It has benefited many, as we have proved by experience and do prove, that they first be compelled by fear of suffering so that afterward they can be taught or carry out in act what they have learned in words. Many as it were bad slaves and in a way wicked runaways are called back to the Lord by the lash of temporal scourges.

Who can love us more than Christ who laid down his life for his Church? Yet while He had called Peter and the other Apostles by word alone, He not only compelled Paul (formerly Saul, afterward a great builder of His Church but first a ferocious destroyer) by word but He also prostrated him with power, and in order to lead him from the savagery of his dark unbeliefs to the desire of the light of the heart, he first struck him with bodily blindness.... They are accustomed to cry, "To believe or not believe is free. On whom would Christ use force? Whom would He compel?" Look, they have the Apostle Paul. Let them recognize in him that Christ first compelled and then taught, first struck and then compelled. It is wonderful how he who, compelled by bodily pain, entered into the gospel, labored more in the gospel than all those who were called by word alone and that in him whom greater fear drove to charity, "perfect charity drove out fear."

Why, then, should the Church not compel her lost sons to return if the lost sons have compelled others to be lost? ...

Hence the Lord Himself first commands the guests to be brought to his great wedding feast but afterward has them compelled; for when the slaves cried, "Lord it is done as you command," he said, "Go out into the highways and hedges and whomever you find compel them to enter." In those, therefore, who were first brought in gently obedience was fulfilled, but in those who were compelled disobedience was coerced.... Therefore if the power which the Church has received by divine gift through religion and faith in the time of kings is exercised as it should be, those who are found in the highways and hedges—that is, in heresies and schisms—are compelled to come in. Let them not blame her because they are compelled but let them pay attention when they are compelled.

But before those laws by which they are compelled to enter the sacred banquet were sent to Africa, it seemed to some of our brothers, and to me as well, that although the madness of the Donatists raged everywhere, we should not ask the emperors to have a punishment set against this heresy....

But the greater mercy of God, who knew the terror of these laws and a certain medicinal harassment to be necessary for the wicked and cold minds of many and for the hardness which could not be changed by words but could by some degree of severity of discipline, then so acted that our representatives could not obtain what they sought. Very heavy complaints of some bishops from other districts came ahead of us—bishops who had suffered many evil things and had been thrown out of their sees, especially the horrible and unbelievable maltreatment of Maximian, Catholic Bishop of Bagai. The result was that our mission had nothing to do, for a law had already been promulgated that the heresy of the Donatists was of such monstrousness that it seemed crueler to spare it.

NOTES AND QUESTIONS

Augustine's interpretation of the compulsion used on Paul would have justified the use of force to make Jews and pagans convert. Neither he nor the Church nor the empire went so far. The thrust of Augustine's exegesis was restrained by the practice of the empire until the accession of Theodosius II (408–450 CE) as Emperor of the East. As the following note suggests, the tide was turning against the Jews both in Christian teaching and in Roman law. And the day would come when Christian princes throughout Europe would require Jews to convert to Christianity or to forfeit their homes, their property, and even their lives.

Christians and Jews From Roman Law to the Holocaust ant Its Aftermath

The period between the early fourth century and the early fifth century was a decisive epoch for Christians and Jews for several reasons. First, this was a period in which Christian preaching about Jews took a sharply negative rhetorical turn. Second, Roman law gradually turned in favor of Christians, and eventually against Jews in significant ways during this period. Third, the momentous political changes of the fourth century shaped the religious discourse of Judaism in a profound way. This was the period in which the Jewish sages moved past the stage of "Judaism without Christianity" reflected in the Mishnah, to an elaborate response to Christianity preserved in the first iteration of the Talmud. This NOTE explores all three of these inter-related themes.

The first issue is the way in which Christian leaders contributed a discourse of hatred relating to the "Jewish question." The term "Judenfrage" or "Jewish question" is a twentieth century invention. This "question" is not one that Jews ask. Jews do not wonder whether they should exist or have equal dignity with others. Gentiles do. More specifically, only people who are hostile to Jews ask about the "Jewish question." One of the terrors of the Third Reich is that hundreds of lawyers and judges took part in a massive conspiracy to implement the so-called "final solution" to the "question," implementing a plan to exterminate all Jews in Europe. Ingo Muller, *Hitler's Justice: The Courts of the Third Reich* (1991). The Nazis created the bureaucracy to implement the plan with a ruthless technology of death. But they did not invent antisemitism. That core of Nazi doctrine–to which the Nazis added a theory of racial purity and a theory of absolute governmental power with no transcendental referent point to challenge its abuses–is imbedded in Christian preaching and teaching centuries before the Third Reich.

The shift in Christian rhetoric about the Jews that occurred in this period has had terrible consequences for the relationship between Jews and Christians for many centuries since then. The first NOTE in this chapter discussed the revolution in the political status of Christianity that occurred in the fourth century. It must now be added that Christian preaching about Jews in this period produced a discourse that lies at the root of the antisemitism that stained the Christian centuries. Most scholars acknowledge that this discourse has roots in passages in the Christian scriptures of the first century. There is an intensive debate about whether or not the New Testament as a whole can properly be described as antisemitic. For opposing views on this, *see, e.g.,* Rosemary Radford Reuther, *Faith and Fratricide: The Theological Roots of Anti–Semitism* (1979) and Gregory Baum, *Is the New Testament Anti–Semitic? A Re-examination of the New Testament* (1965). Whatever one concludes about that issue, nothing in the Christian literature of the first century matches the severity and excesses of the anti-Jewish preaching of the fourth century. *See also* Edward H. Flannery, *The Anguish of the Jews: Twenty-three Centuries of Anti–Semitism* (2d ed. 1985), and Jules Isaac, *The Teaching of Contempt: Christian Roots of Anti–Semitism* (1964).

In a series of eight sermons preached at Antioch in 387 CE, John Chrysostom (349–407 CE), charged that Jews "sacrificed their own sons and daughters to devils." Although—in observance of the prohibition against images in the second commandment [Chapter One, section 2]—Jews had no religious art in their synagogues, Chrysostom refers to synagogues as "homes of idolatry and devils," and as "worse than heathen circuses." Wilken argues that the pastoral reason for the sermons was the clarification of the boundary between Judaism and Christianity for people who were straddling the fence by observing both Jewish and Christian practices. Robert L. Wilken, *John Chrysostom and the Jews: Rhetoric and Reality in the Late Fourth Century* (1983). Noting that at the time Christianity was no longer in danger from the Roman empire, Parkes describes the sermons, known collectively as *Adversus Judaeos* ("Against the Jews"), as containing a "bitterness and lack of restraint unusual even in that place and century." James Parkes, *Conflict of the Church and the Synagogue* 163 (1961). Chrysostom—his Greek nickname means "golden tongued"—

served as the Christian Patriarch of Constantinople from 398 to 407, the period immediately preceding a series of disastrous turns in Roman law for the Jews.

A year after Chrysostom's sermons anti-Jewish words were matched by violent deeds. In 388 the bishop of Callinicum, a small town on the Euphrates, incited a Christian mob to burn down a synagogue. The provincial governor punished the hateful arsonists and required the bishop to rebuild the synagogue. Emperor Theodosius I (379–395 CE) confirmed this decision. Upon hearing of the imperial disposition of the case, Saint Ambrose, bishop of Milan—who had previously served as a provincial governor himself—sent the emperor a long letter denouncing the emperor for condemning the destruction of the synagogue. Ambrose referred to the synagogue as a "miserable hovel, ... a place of unbelief, a home of insanity, which God himself has condemned." Ambrose urged that it was monstrous that Jews who despise Roman law should look to it for support. Letter XL and XLI, PL 16:1101 ff. The following Sunday, in the presence of the emperor, Ambrose preached a sermon on the church and the synagogue; he then refused to continue the service until the emperor agreed to reverse his decision in the case. Parkes 166–168. The emperor repealed the order, but in 393 CE he issued a new edict clarifying that Judaism was a *religio licita* and directing the supreme military command in the East to protect synagogues from destruction. *Theodosian Code,* 16.8.9; Amnon Linder, *The Jews in Roman Imperial Legislation* 189–191 (9187) (containing texts of imperial decrees, edicts, and rescripts, with contextual commentary). The fact that there were at least ten imperial interventions against damaging synagogues in the period from 393 to 426 indicates both the growing hostility of Christians against Jews and the importance of the Roman law in protecting the Jewish minority. Alfredo Mordechai Rabello, "Theodosius I," 15 *Encyclopaedia Judaica* 1101 (1971); Linder 73–74.

The most startling development in this period was the transformation of the teaching of the New Testament on the responsibility of the Romans for the death of Jesus [Chapter One, section nine] into the most serious charge against Jews. In this view, Jews in the first century, not Romans, were responsible for the death of Jesus; worse yet, their descendants were a "deicide race." This unjust charge remained a powerful subtext, and at times an overt central theme in church-state relations for centuries.

One of the most egregious instances of Christian violence against Jews occurred in the First Crusade (1096–1099), a war called by Pope Urban II (1088–1099) to liberate Palestine from Muslim control. Emperor Henry IV forbade his soldiers to attack Jews on the way to Palestine. Another Christian prince, the Duke of Lorraine, raised money for his army by promising to kill Jews to avenge the death of Jesus. An estimated 10,000 Jews were killed in France and Lorraine by undisciplined soldiers marked with the sign of the Cross–and for that reasons known as "Crusaders," The massacres continued in the Rhine Valley, where another 12,000 Jews were slaughtered in 1096. A contemporary witness of the killings in the Rhineland, Albert of Aix, wrote: "I know not whether by a judgment of the Lord, or by some error of mind;, they rose in a spirit of cruelty against the Jewish people scattered throughout these cities and slaughtered them without mercy, especially in the Kingdom of Lorraine, asserting it to be the beginning of their expedition and their duty against the enemies of the Christian faith. This slaughter of Jews was done first by citizens of Cologne. These suddenly fell upon a small band of Jews and severely wounded and killed many; they destroyed the houses and synagogues of the Jews and divided among themselves a very large amount of money. When the Jews saw this cruelty, about two hundred in the silence of the night began flight by boat to Neuss. The pilgrims and crusaders discovered them, and after taking away all their possessions, inflicted on them similar slaughter, leaving not even one alive." August C. Krey, ed., *The First Crusade: The Accounts of Eyewitnesses and Participants* 54 (1921).

The Bishop of Mainz offered sanctuary in the great hall of his residence to the Jews of his city. The Crusaders breached the city walls and one Emico discovered the episcopal hiding place. Albert of Aix also chronicled the next slaughter: "Emico and the rest of his band held a council and, after sunrise, attacked the Jews in the hall with arrows and lances. Breaking the bolts and doors, they killed the Jews, about seven hundred in number, who in vain resisted the force and attack of so many thousands. They killed the women, also, and with their swords pierced tender children of whatever age and sex. The Jews, seeing that their Christian enemies were attacking them and their children, and that they were sparing no age, likewise fell upon one another, brother, children, wives, and sisters, and thus they perished at each other's hands. Horrible to say, mothers cut the throats of nursing children with knives and stabbed others, preferring them to perish thus by their own hands rather than to be killed by the weapons of the uncircumcised." Krey 56. Some Jewish writers to refer to these events as the "first holocaust."

The atrocity continued when the Crusaders reached Jerusalem and broke through the walls of the city of peace. The soldiers engaged in wholesale, indiscriminate slaughter of all the inhabitants that they could find (men, women, children, and infants). When the soldiers discovered the Jewish community in the synagogue, they set the building on fire and burned alive thousands of the Jews of "royal David's city." The Crusaders also slaughtered tens of thousands of Muslims who had fled to the al-Aqsa Mosque. The sign of the Cross–once a symbol of nonviolent love–had become a symbol of violent hatred for the other two people of the book, Jews and Muslims. The misconduct is impossible to reconcile either with Christian pacifism or with the Augustinian tradition on justifiable war. [See NOTE above on *Christians and Military Service in the Early Church*].

Canon law–the law governing the church–also became a vehicle for antisemitism. In 1215 CE the Roman Catholic Bishops of the Fourth Lateran Council issued decrees on the Jews that directed Christian princes to supervise the lending practices of Jews lest they exact exorbitant interest on Christian debtors. Baptized Jews were forbidden to observe Jewish customs. Jews were prohibited from appearing in public during Easter week. Jews were required to contribute to the church a tithe on their houses and other property and to pay a yearly tax at Easter. Christian princes were prohibited under pain of excommunication from giving an office to a Jew. And Jews were required to wear a distinctive badge from their twelfth year to distinguish them from Christians. *See* Edward A. Synan, *The Popes and the Jews in the Middle Ages* (1965).

In the sixteenth century the principal leader of the Protestant Reformation in Germany, Martin Luther spoke at first with great admiration and respect for Jews, whose command of their scriptures was a marvel for the monk who wished to reform the church by returning to its biblical roots. Later in his career, after it had become apparent that Jews had no greater desire to convert to his "purified" version of Christianity than to Catholicism, Luther spoke against Jews with as much vehemence as the bishop of Callinicum had done in urging a mob of Christians to burn a synagogue in 388. For example, Luther wrote that Jews should be deprived of "all their cash and jewels and silver and gold" and "that their synagogues or schools be set on fire, that their houses be broken up and destroyed ... and they be put under a roof or stable, like the gypsies ... in misery and captivity as they incessantly lament and complain to God about us."

For the full text of Luther's infamous recommendations, *see* Franklin Sherman, ed. 47 *Luther's Works*, ("The Christian in Society," IV), 268–274 (1971). Two distinguished Reformation scholars have explored the teaching of Luther on the Jews; *see* Heiko A. Oberman, *The Roots of Anti–Semitism in the Age of Renaissance and Reformation* (1984), and Mark U. Edwards, Jr., *Luther's Last Battles: Politics and Polemics, 1531–46* (1983).

A popular historian of the Holocaust noted that Nazi propagandists in the twentieth century cited Luther in support of their atrocities, and suggested that Hitler, Goering and Himmler "literally followed [Luther's advice] four centuries later." William L. Shirer, *The Rise and Fall of the Third Reich: A History of Nazi Germany* (1960) 236; *see also* Lucy S. Dawidowicz, *The War Against the Jews: 1933–1945* (1986) 23. Throughout the Christian centuries no leader—neither Chrysostom nor Luther, neither Pope nor Emperor—had ever urged the full horror of the genocidal attack on Jews effected by the Nazis, but there was enough hatred being taught by Christians against Jews that Nazi propagandists could easily distort prior statements for their own ends. *See also* John G. Gager, *The Origins of Anti–Semitism* (1985). As this NOTE indicates below, Christian communities after the Holocaust have repudiated the tragic teaching of contempt for Jews that marked too much of the Christian past. But repentance for misdeeds can only proceed from clarity about their evil.

The second issue is the way in which Roman law challenged or confirmed the hostility of Christians toward Jews. It is not correct, as some maintain, that as soon as the Roman empire allowed Christianity to thrive, it abandoned its role as an enforcer of public values when it came to the protection of Jews. It is fair to say, however, that once Roman law established Christianity as the official religion of the empire, the legislators reexamined the privileged position that Judaism had held under Roman law for several centuries.

From the time of the Maccabees Jews sought a special arrangement with Rome that would enable them to live within the protection of Roman rule while remaining faithful to their religious beliefs and practices [Chapter One, section 6]. Under Julius Caesar and Caesar Augustus the granting of "privileges and immunities" to the Jews enabled a compromise of this sort. Even the curbing of the Jewish rebellions in the first and second centuries by the Roman legion did not lead to wholesale revocation of the privileges and immunities of Jews under Roman law. Neither did the Constantinian shift toward Christianity or the Theodosian establishment of Christianity entail so drastic a consequence for Jews. For example, in 321 CE Constantine issued a general law requiring the nomination of Jews to serve in regional curias, while preserving a "perpetual privilege" exempting "two or three [Jews] in every curia." Linder, *The Jews in Roman Imperial Legislation* 120–124 (1987). It is possible to interpret this law as an abrogation of an "ancient privilege" exempting Jews from this service, but it is more plausible to read it as imperial protection of the place of Jews in public life. In 330 CE Constantine clarified that those exempted from curial service under the earlier law are those whom the autonomous Jewish leader known as the Palestinian patriarch designated as essential for service within his administration. Linder, 132–38. This law amounted to imperial recognition of the Patriarch and the Sanhedrin [Jewish court] as the supreme authority over the diaspora Jews. Linder 133. Many acts of legislation in this period confirm that Rome extended to the Jewish leadership what we now call the "autonomy" of religious organizations in deciding internal religious matters [Chapter Eight, section 5; Chapter Twelve, section 3]. For example, Theodosius "prohibited the provincial governors from all interference in questions of excommunication and release from excommunication among the Jews, leaving the entire matter in the hands of the Jewish authorities." Linder 70, see 186–189. The patriarch's court could hear all cases pertaining to religion, but was proscribed from adjudicating civil disputes unless the parties agreed to the jurisdiction of the Jewish court. Linder 71.

Difficulties mounted for Jews in the fifth century. Theodosius II was the emperor of the East (408–450) who collected the imperial statutes from the time of Constantine to the year 438. His reign marked a "serious deterioration in the position of the Jews." Rabello, "Theodosius II," 15 *Encyclopaedia Judaica* 1101. His first law, in May of 408, prohibited Jews from mocking Christian rituals in the feast of Purim, in which Jews celebrate the story of their deliverance—recounted in the Book of Esther—from the destruction intended against them by Haman. The legislator threatened that future instances of mocking of Christianity may result in a loss of the Jews' traditional privileges. *Theodosian Code,* 16.8.18; Linder 236–38. In 415 Theodosius demoted Gamaliel, a Jewish patriarch who had become an honorary praetorian prefect. The prefect was expressly stripped of power to hear disputes between a Christian and a Jew; and Jews were to be subjected to "the severity of the laws" if they attempted "to pollute a Christian ... with the Jewish stigma [circumcision]." More ominously, the emperor forbade the construction of new synagogues, and even ordered the destruction of existing ones "in desert places," if this could be accomplished "without sedition" or a Jewish uprising; *Theodosian Code,* 16.8.22; Linder 267–72. In 417 the emperor issued an edict forbidding Jews, described as adherents of a "nefarious superstition," from purchasing or being given a slave of the "true [Christian] religion"; if a Jew violated this edict, he suffered the loss of the slave and was subject to the death penalty. *Theodosian Code,* 16.9.4; see 16.9.5 (stating in 423 that the emperor finds it "abominable that very religious [Christian] slaves should be defiled by the ownership of very impious [Jewish] purchasers."); Linder 277–80. In 418 Theodosius issued an edict barring Jews from public office in the imperial service. *Theodosian Code,* 16.8.24, Linder 280–83. In 423 the emperor repeated the ban on construction of new synagogues, but clarified that Jews were entitled to compensation for the loss of synagogues seized by Christians under the previous decree. *Theodosian Code,* 16.8.26; Linder 287–89. In the same year Theodosius issued an edict describing previous decrees as having "suppressed the spirit and audacity of the abominable pagans, of the Jews also, and of the heretics," but he ordered that Christians should "refrain from injuring and persecuting [the Jews], and that ... no person shall seize or burn their synagogues." *Theodosian Code,* 16.8.26 & 27; Linder 289–95. In 429 the emperor ended imperial recognition of Jewish government of the Land of Israel and took advantage of abolition of the Jewish patriarchate to impose a new tax to be paid to the imperial treasury by the entire Jewish community. *Theodosian Code,* 16.8.29; Linder 320–23. In 438, the year of the compilation of the Theodosian Code, a statute described Jews not only as "monstrous heretics," but also as "enemies of the Supreme Majesty and of the Roman laws." Theodosius II, *Novella,* 3; Linder 323–37. Theodosius wrote in this law: "we perceive the search for the true religion as the Imperial Majesty's foremost care." Jews may no longer exercise public office lest they "have the power to judge and pronounce sentence against Christians, very often even against priests of the sacred religion, to the insult of our faith." By the mid-fifth century the establishment of Christianity as the official religion of the empire amounted to treatment of Jews as civilly inferior to Christians under Roman law. Establishment of Christianity had come to mean official discrimination against Jews, because "our faith" required it.

The third issue is the development of a different mode of discourse within Judaism that defined itself more intentionally in relationship to Christianity. In the first century Christianity emerged as a distinct community within Judaism. Even when the separation became complete, the common ground these groups occupied was more important–at least to the Romans—than the things that marked Jews and Christians as different. When Christianity became the official religion of the empire, the differences loomed much larger. Was Jesus the Messiah, the anointed of Israel? Was he the Savior of the world who had imposed so radical change in history that time was now to be reckoned from the date of his birth? In the Mishnah–the defining documents of Judaism formed from the second to the end of the third century–the Jewish sages had been indifferent to such questions. They invented a "Judaism without Christianity." Jacob Neusner, *Judaism and Christianity in the Age of Constantine* 4–7 (1987).

According to Neusner, the work of the fourth century sages who produced the Palestinian Talmud was forged in response to the political triumph of Christianity. "When the Roman Empire and Israelite nation had to assess the meaning of epochal change, when each had to reconsider the teleology [end, goal, purpose] of society and system as the identity of the Messiah defined that teleology, when each had to reconsider the appropriate metaphor for the political unit, namely, people, nation, extended family, only then did chronic disagreement become acute difference. It was the progressive but remarkable change in the character of the Roman government–at the beginning of the century pagan and hostile to Christianity, at the end of the century Christian and hostile to paganism—that was decisive. In the age of Constantine the terms of the fifteen-hundred-year confrontation between Judaism and Christianity reached conclusive formulation." *Id.* 3. See also Neusner, *Judaism in the Matrix of Christianity* (1986), and *The Death and Birth of Judaism* (1987). Reuther agrees: "The classical form of both Judaism and Christianity was shaped by sages and theologians whose systems of thought found their fullest ripening in the fourth century after Christ." Rosemary Radford Reuther, "Judaism and Christianity: Two Fourth–Century Religions," 2 *Studies in Religion* 1–10 (1972); *see also* Jaroslav Pelikan, *The Emergence of the Catholic Tradition (100–600)* (1971).

After the enormity of the Holocaust, Christians began a process of rebuilding a better relationship with Jews. The most vicious and tenacious justification offered for hatred of Jews was the charge of deicide—the killing of God—leveled against Jews throughout the Christian centuries because of the involvement of some of the Jewish authorities in Jerusalem at the time of Jesus in seeking his execution under Roman law [Chapter One, section 9]. In the late twentieth century the highest authorities within Christian communities have formally repudiated this charge and have clearly condemned antisemitism. For example, the World Council of Churches of Christ–the largest ecumenical body of Christian churches in the world—met in New Delhi in 1961. Its General Assembly issued a statement acknowledging the involvement of a common guilt for anti-Semitism and a common responsibility for making "such amends as are possible." World Council of Churches, *The New Delhi Report* (1962).

In 1965 the Roman Catholic Bishops of the Second Vatican Council issued a "Decree on the Relationship of the Church to Non–Christian Religions," ¶ 4 of which states: "The Church repudiates all persecutions against any man. Moreover, mindful of her common patrimony with the Jews, and motivated by the gospel's spiritual love and by no political considerations, she deplores the hatred, persecutions, and displays of anti-Semitism directed against the Jews at any time and from any source." Walter Abbott, ed., *The Documents of Vatican II* 666–67 (1966). A commentary on this text mentions the decrees of the Fourth Lateran Council cited above as explicit examples of anti-Semitism imbedded in the law and "here repudiated by the Second Vatican Council ('at any time and from any source')." *Id.* 667. During the debate on this document the German Bishops stated: "We German bishops welcome the Council Decree on the Jews.... We are convinced that this Council Declaration provides an opportunity for renewed contact and a better relationship between the Church and the Jewish people. We German bishops welcome the Decree especially because we are conscious of the grave injustice done to the Jews in the name of our own people." As cited in John M. Oesterreicher, "Declaration on the Relationship of the Church to Non–Christian Religions," in Herbert Vorgrimler, ed., 3 *Commentary on the Documents of Vatican II* 68 (1969). The Archbishop of St. Louis, Cardinal Joseph Ritter, stated more bluntly: "With all my heart I gladly make this Declaration my own. Quite clearly, it meets a need of our time. I speak of a need, not of some political or national pressure to be evaded or appeased, nor of some human approval to be sought for, but quite simply of a centuries-old injustice that cries aloud for reparation. For many centuries we Christians have been guilty of error and injustice towards the Jews. In many ways we have assumed that God ... had abandoned this people. Christians, and even ecclesiastical documents, have charged the Jewish people with the suffering and death of Christ. In prayers they were called the 'perfidious', the 'deicidal' people, who 'once called down upon themselves the blood of the Saviour'. We who are gathered here in this Ecumenical Council have today been given an opportunity to root out such errors and injustices and to make reparation (for the injuries these have caused)." *Id.*

On April 18, 1994, the Evangelical Lutheran Church in America issued a "Declaration to the Jewish Community," stating that "in the long history of Christianity there exists no more tragic development than the treatment accorded the Jewish people on the part of Christian believers" and acknowledging the "special burden" felt by Lutherans "because of certain elements in the legacy of the reformer Martin Luther and the catastrophes, including the Holocaust of the twentieth century, suffered by Jews in places where the Lutheran churches were strongly represented." The document continued: "In the spirit of ... truth-telling, we who bear [the] name and heritage [of Luther] must with pain acknowledge also Luther's anti-Judaic diatribes and violent recommendations of his later writings against the Jews. As did many of Luther's own companions in the sixteenth century, we reject this violent invective, and yet more do we express our deep and abiding sorrow over its tragic effects on subsequent generations. In concert with the Lutheran World Federation, we particularly deplore the appropriation of Luther's words by modern anti-Semites for the teaching of hatred toward Judaism or toward the Jewish people in our day.... We recognize in anti-Semitism a contradiction and an affront to the Gospel, a violation of our hope and calling, and we pledge this church to oppose the deadly working of such bigotry, both within our own circles and in the society around us."

In a speech to a symposium on the roots of anti-Judaism, Pope John Paul II acknowledged on October 31, 1997 that in the Christian world "erroneous and unjust interpretations of the New Testament regarding the Jewish people and their alleged culpability have circulated for too long, engendering feelings of hostility towards this people." In 1998 the Vatican's Commission for Religious Relations with the Jews issued a document entitled "We Remember: A Reflection on the *Shoah*." The document affirmed a duty of Christians to remember the events of the Holocaust. More specifically, it stated: "While bearing their unique witness to the Holy One of Israel and to the *Torah,* the Jewish people have suffered much at different times and in many places. But the *Shoah* was certainly the worst suffering of all. The inhumanity with which the Jews were persecuted and massacred during this century is beyond the capacity of words to convey. All this was done to them for the sole reason that they were Jews.... In the lands where the Nazis undertook mass deportations, the brutality which surrounded these forced movements of helpless people should have led to suspect the worst. Did Christians give every possible assistance to those being persecuted, and in particular to the persecuted Jews? Many did, but others did not. Those who did help to save Jewish lives as much as was in their power, even to the point of placing their own lives in danger, must not be forgotten.... [A]longside such courageous men and women, the spiritual resistance and concrete action of other Christians was not that which might have been expected from Christ's followers. We cannot know how many Christians in countries occupied or ruled by the Nazi powers or their allies were horrified at the disappearance of their Jewish neighbors and yet were not strong enough to raise their voices in protest. For Christians, this heavy burden of conscience of their brothers and sisters during the Second World War must be a call to penitence."

On March 12, 2000, Pope John Paul II led Roman Catholics in a Day of Pardon. He prayed: "God our Father, merciful and compassionate, slow to anger, great in love and fidelity, accept the repentance of his people who humbly confess their sins." Among the sins acknowledged by the spiritual leader of Catholics were the following: that "men of the Church, in the name of faith and morals, have sometimes used methods not in keeping with the Gospel," and that many Christians over the centuries had committed "sins against the people of the Covenant and the blessings" that inflicted "sufferings endured by the people of Israel throughout history." "Deeply saddened by the behavior of those who in the course of history have caused these children of yours to suffer," the Pope specifically asked for forgiveness for sins against the Jews and pledged to commit the Catholic community to "genuine brotherhood with the people of the Covenant."

Are these developments within Roman Catholicism and Protestant Christianity in the late twentieth century too little too late? Although making amends for atrocity cannot undo the past, can it keep atrocity from recurring in the name of religion?

CHAPTER THREE

THE FREEDOM OF THE CHURCH: THE ENGLISH EXPERIENCE, 1160–1260

In England, only seven centuries after Augustine, secular princes were as selectively attentive to bishops as Roman governors had been. But bishops now enjoyed such secular possessions and popular influence that princes paid great attention to their selection and often arranged that their own candidate be chosen. Apart from local bishops, the pope himself was an international figure with whom princes had to reckon. Beginning in the eleventh century, reformers of the Church had placed their hopes on a strong papacy. A monk with the nickname of Hildebrand ("bright flame") fulfilled this hope when he was elected pope in the late eleventh century. Building on the ideals of his predecessor Gregory I (590–604), whose name he chose, Gregory VII (1073–1085) challenged the empire in the name of reform. A distinguished legal historian regards the reforms in canon law undertaken by Hildebrand as the spark of a revolution in legal thinking and method that produced the system of Western jurisprudence. Harold J. Berman, *Law and Revolution: The Formation of the Western Legal Tradition* 199–224 (1983). By the mid-twelfth century the organization the reformers had desired was in place. The pope had his own bureaucracy, the Curia, and he sat as the acknowledged head of related judicial and administrative systems whose reach extended to every corner of Europe from Ireland in the West to Hungary in the East.

A new kind of law book was in circulation in the courts of the Church—*Gratian's Concordia discordantium canonum (Harmony of the Unharmonious Canons)*. The *Harmony* (also known as the *Decretum*) had been put together in the 1130s and 1140s at the center of European legal studies, Bologna. It was a law professor's case book; a resolution of conflicting texts; and a giant compendium of canons (excerpts from Scripture and the Fathers, especially Augustine; decrees of church councils; case decisions and legislation by popes). The book exhibited the complex and developed legal system the Church now possessed to decide such questions as when a marriage existed and when an heir was legitimate; who had title to a see or a parish or a tithe; what heresy was and how it was to be adjudicated. Its completion also assured more complexity and development. Its existence was a challenge to a more embryonic legal system such as England's.

Nearly everyone in England was in name a Christian. A small Jewish population was sporadically persecuted both for religious and economic reasons until 1290, when 16,000 Jews were expelled by Edward I. *See* Robin R. Mundill, *England's Jewish Solution: Experiment and Expulsion, 1262–1290* (1998). Jews were not permitted to return to England until the interregnum or Commonwealth period under Oliver Cromwell. Heresy was rare and unorganized. No one disputed that the pope was the head of the Church, although sometimes there were two popes claiming election, between whom a choice had to be made. The real problems lay in the interaction of the overlapping legal systems of pope and prince, problems mostly handled ad hoc by mutual accommodation. "Interpenetration" is the term used by a great historian to describe the relationship, and he finds it "thoroughgoing." David Knowles, *Becket* 59 (1970). The prince did not think it alien to his duties to be involved with both the personnel and the property of the Church. The Church could not be uninvolved with issues that affected public policy and public peace. The murder of Thomas Becket dramatized the difficulties when accommodation failed.

1.   THE BECKET CONTROVERSY

Thomas Becket was born about 1118 in London, the son of Norman gentry. He studied the liberal arts in Paris from 1136 to 1138, served as private secretary to a baron, and at age twenty-five set out on an ecclesiastical career as a member of the staff of Theobald, archbishop of Canterbury. A decade later, Theobald recommended him to Henry II as his chancellor; the easy movement of clerical personnel into royal service was normal. Knowles 6–9, 27.

Henry was twenty-one, fifteen years Thomas's junior, and just beginning his reign. Thomas became his "heart and wisdom, without whose will nothing happened." *Foliot to Thomas,* 1166, Rolls Series 67, 522. Jean Anouilh's play, *Becket: Or the Honor of God* (1960), portrays Thomas as the king's lustful boon companion. This portrayal is inaccurate, Knowles 41, but Thomas was devoted to Henry's political interests, for example, plotting the conquest of Ireland, an excursion for which the pope's blessing was thought desirable and was secured. John of Salisbury, *Metalogion* 4,4. As John's letter to Bartholomew of June 1166, indicates, he also encroached on the Church's domain to get revenue for the crown. In those days, Thomas was "a great gamesman." *John of Salisbury to Bartholomew of Exeter* (Letter 187), in John of Salisbury, *Letters* 2:244.

In 1162, at the king's urging, the monks of Christ Church, Canterbury, chose Thomas to succeed Theobald as archbishop. Thomas not only accepted but—to the king's chagrin—resigned as chancellor. He was now his own master and the steward, as he saw it, of Christ. Within the year he was at odds with Henry over whether clerics could be punished by the royal courts after conviction of a crime and punishment by a church court. Beyond any political disagreement, Henry felt the bitterness of a patron who sees his protégé thwart his will.

In 1164 Thomas and the other bishops swore to observe the Constitutions of Clarendon, which let the Church try clerics, the royal judges punish them, and in other ways limited the immunity and freedom of action of the bishops. Berman 255–69. Thomas almost instantly repented his surrender, suspended himself from saying mass for forty days, and wrote the pope asking to be absolved from his oath to the king. Knowles 92–93. Henry retaliated by summoning Thomas to answer a charge against him by one of his tenants. When Thomas failed to appear, he was fined all his movable goods for contempt, and the king went on to have his barons try Thomas for not accounting for all the funds he had received as chancellor. In October 1164 he was found guilty. Knowles 94, 98. By these maneuvers within his own legal system, the king, as he thought, challenged Thomas on turf where the king set the rules. But in Thomas's view the king was violating the ancient tradition of a bishop's immunity from civil suit. Thomas appealed to the pope, Alexander III, to quash the verdicts. The other bishops of England—some of them hostile to Thomas, some of them pressured by the king—filed a separate appeal with the pope. The bishops eventually asked the pope to condemn the archbishop or at least let the case be tried by a papal legate in England. Knowles 97–98, 104.

For the next six years the only litigation that went on was in the canonical system with the pope as Supreme Judge acting in person or by legates. Thomas issued excommunications against various bishops, clerics, and royal officials. As John's letter to Bartholomew, July 1166, indicates, Thomas was hesitant to anathematize Henry in person, but a canon adopted in 1139 excommunicated a person who laid violent hands on a Cleric; the king appeared to fall within this class. Gratian 17.4.29.

Thomas was a Marcellinus teaching by example more than by word [Chapter Two, sections 1 & 2]. The intellectual through whose eyes the controversy is captured was John of Salisbury, the greatest literary genius of the twelfth century. John was also the author of the *Policraticus (The Ruler of the City)*, a treatise on government enriched by classical allusions and many concrete examples, a work on politics unequaled in Western Europe up to the sixteenth century. In the course of it John advanced the doctrine that the sword of the king is given by the Church, so that "the prince is a certain kind of deputy of the priesthood." C.I. Webb, ed., *Policraticus* 4.3 (1909).

Thomas inherited John from Theobald's staff, and John stayed with him in exile, returned with him to England, and was present when he was killed. His letters from exile, which follow, describe how Thomas's party scorned the bishops on the king's side, doubted the pope's constancy, and saw the fight as one for the freedom of the Church against evil incarnate. The translation is based on the Latin text of W. J. Millor and C.N.L. Brooke, *The Letters of John of Salisbury* (1979), vol. 2, Letters 168 and 174.

John of Salisbury to Bartholomew, Bishop of Exeter, June 1166

All things are said to be full of snares so that it is not safe for good men to have oral or written commerce with each other. I know not what game wickedness is plotting against innocence. The prick of conscience stings and burns continually, so that all men and all things are felt suspect. . . .

Someone will say that this imposition of tax and the harassment of the churches is to be wholly turned back on his [the king's] chancellor [Thomas] who now rules as archbishop, as I believe (or, as his rivals lie, *claims* to rule as archbishop)—at that time the king was directed by him as he chose in everything, and he [Thomas] led him to this as he did to many other evils. I know this to be false, since I know that at that time he [Thomas] did not obey the authority of lust but the dictate of necessity. Nonetheless, I do not doubt that he [Thomas] was the servant of wickedness, and so I judge him punishable by the highest law. . . .

Recently, he [the king] gathered in conference at Chinon his nobles and staff, who are known to have energy and practice in evil pursuits and to be wise in suggesting and doing evil. He zealously inquired, using promises, threats, and much protestation, what plan he should use against the Church. Most bitterly he complained about the Archbishop of Canterbury.... He wept and said this Canterbury would take away both his body and his soul. Finally he said they were all traitors who refused to apply work and care to save him from the trouble of one man.

[Meanwhile Archbishop Thomas excommunicated various clerics and royal officials and summoned the king to give satisfaction.] Now the archbishop has made the summons public and has invited him [the king] to the fruit of penance. He has threatened shortly to pass a judgment of anathema against him unless he has a good flavor and makes satisfaction for his audacities against the Church. But yet he will not do that willingly, nor do I know any of his household who is inclined to this judgment.

That document [the Constitutions of Clarendon] which contains the wickedness of the malignant against the Church (which they call grandfatherly customs) he [Thomas] publicly condemned, binding with the chain of the anathema all who rely on its authority. With the advice of the Roman Church he especially condemned these chapters by name:

That it is not lawful for a bishop to excommunicate a tenant of the king without the king's permission.

That it is not lawful for a bishop to try any members of his diocese for perjury or breach of faith.

That clerics may be brought to secular courts.

That the king or other laymen may try cases concerning churches and tithes.

That except after seeking the pardon of the king and his officials, no case may be appealed to the Apostolic See.

That it is not lawful for an archbishop or bishop or any other person to respond to the summons of the Lord Pope apart from the king's permission.

Also other things in this fashion which are found contrary to divine laws and the constitutions of the Holy Fathers.

But he [Thomas] has absolved all the bishops from the promise they made of observing this document contrary to ecclesiastical rule. He also proclaimed this by letter to the archbishops and bishops, just as he had been advised by the Roman Church.

John of Salisbury to Bartholomew, Bishop of Exeter, July 1166

Whatever the bishops wrote in haste in their appeal, whatever they proclaimed of his [the king's] piety and kindness, justice and lovability and respect for the priesthood, the French and the Latins would more readily believe anything about him that was impious toward God and inhuman toward humans. Hence all who hear greatly wonder and are amazed at the conscience, the impudence, the chutzpah with which you bishops dared to assert, commit to writing and confirm with evidences of episcopal authority the innocence of a man whose injustices are a legend to all, whose deceits and acts of violence the whole world has known. In what fashion did a venerable body composed of so many and so great Fathers give false testimony in subversion of justice and for the benefit of malice? For these are the words of your document on behalf of the king, whose cause your notary is trying to justify: "The king promises all justice and is ready to do it with deeds. He thinks it a sweet service to be warned to correct any offense he has committed against God. He is not only ready to make satisfaction in general but to make satisfaction in this matter if the law demands it."

People say, "How sound, how saintly is the preaching of the bishops of England! How sincere and uncorrupted is their witness for the liberty of the Church! How true is the declaration of the priests! They proclaim what a jester or actor would not speak without suffering shame".…

The bishops say (perhaps more truly the bishop) that it is peace. But all cry out that it is not peace but bitterness most bitter. But if indeed he [the king] demands only due customs, as your Demosthenes asserts, he surely ought to be content with those that are not the enemies of divine laws, that are not against good morals, that do not dishonor the priesthood, that do not offer danger to souls, that do not subvert the liberty of Mother Church, from whose hand he received the sword to guard her and beat off her wrongs. But in his desire, all things are contrary just as that writing of his condemned by the authority of the Holy Fathers and by the mouth of the Supreme Pontiff bears witness, as do the daily complaints of the clergy and the people. I fear that the bishops themselves will be compelled to act against their own document and to unpreach what they preach and to justify the cause they now condemn and to condemn the cause they justify.

The signed attestation is indeed drafted in the name of all of them, but it is confirmed only by the seals of three bishops, to wit, the chief of the London synagogue my lord and friend, the bishop of Winchester, whom I now spare; and Hereford, indeed an old scholastic but a novice bishop, equally powerful in learning and in eloquence. Their authority would be high if their good reputation was not prejudiced by their consent to wickedness and attestation of manifest falsehood; of this both the letter and attachment of their seal convicts them.

But I hear that all [of the bishops] have given authority to the document. If they saw it first, it was most impious to offer witness to such wickedness. If they did not see it, it was most stupid to give authority to another's wickedness by placing on it their characters.…

Since God disposed otherwise, your scribe [Gilbert] could not be what he ambitioned to be, archbishop of Canterbury. Hence with the consent, counsel, and authority of those in the English Church who persecute Christ, he became chief of the synagogue. Recently the king wrote him by his archdeacon Ralph de Diceto that he commits to his judgment as to that of a father and most faithful friend his whole kingdom and the case which is between him and the Church.…

Christ, I issue a summons for you. I call you to judgment, you who are unfailing truth. On the Last Day of Judgment, I shall, if reason allows, prove your lie, unless each one is judged by the judgment by which he has judged and receives reciprocal measure for measure.…

[The archbishop] does not believe the appeal which the bishops have made against him to be of any moment. But for those who do think it to have some force, such as the king, the bishops, and the nobles, making the prudence of the flesh their aim, it was necessary to allow everything belonging to the archbishop to stay in the same state, because nothing should be changed while an appeal is pending. But later, by the king's command, the Chaplain William and other clerics were taken prisoner (I say nothing of the laymen); the property of the Church was removed; and they were abominably treated. Therefore the archbishop has reported to the Lord Pope that the king himself has fallen under the canon and by his own deed is excommunicate, unless perhaps the Apostolic See believes ecclesiastical laws are to be compared to those civil laws which, as Anacharsis the Scythian said, are like spiders' webs catching flies but letting larger flying things through....

Know this for certain that unless the king surrenders William the Chaplain, his head shall carry the judgment of anathema, and he will not now be spared in anything if he dares to try such things.

Appeals from Thomas's excommunications were lodged with the pope, who sometimes but not always restrained the archbishop. At no point were the issues treated from only a legal viewpoint. Alexander III was seriously threatened by a rival pope, who had the backing of the German emperor; Alexander was not anxious to make a permanent enemy of Henry. Realistically he was also aware of how hard it would be to make Henry act against his will within his kingdom. Yet he did not desire to desert Thomas or the legal principles Thomas was defending. For Alexander the obvious solution was compromise, not a clearcut judicial verdict.

Thomas, an exile in France, thought Henry was untrustworthy and knew him to be cruel; he had exiled all of Thomas's relations including "babes in the cradle and those still clinging to the breasts of their mothers" and told them to go to Thomas as the one responsible. Knowles 109. Thomas found the pope's diplomacy disheartening, and he became convinced the king's money played a corrupt part in producing policy shifts at the Curia. Under the principle of restitution set out by Augustine to Macedonius and now established in the canon law, Gratian C.14, q.6, c.1, the king should have restored the profits he illegally derived from the estates of Canterbury; instead Thomas thought he was using the profits to pay off certain cardinals. Noonan, *Bribes* 165–169. Disgusted and worn down, Thomas went through a pro forma reconciliation with Henry, with all the real problems left to be worked out later.

The following, Letter 303, was written after Thomas had gone through the formal reconciliation with Henry. The last sentence of the second paragraph can be read as unconscious prophecy.

John of Salisbury to William Brito, subprior; to Robert, the sacristan; and to the magistrates of the Canterbury Church, Mid–October 1170

Your prayers and the desires of the faithful, the merciful and mercy-hearted Lord has heard to, his own honor as many and sure signs show. He restores peace to the English Church and recalls your father from exile. Would that your ears had been near the mouth of the Lord King when at the conference of the kings recently held between Blois and Amboise [Fréteval] he sent away the archbishop to receive permission swiftly from the French, to whom he was bound, and to return with all speed to him, then to cross over to England.

Therefore, as it has been arranged, God willing, he will depart here on the feast of All Saints and will purposely and by agreement return to his own. As quickly as he can, he will make the city of the saints shine by his return to Canterbury.

You, then, as you wish there to be provision in the future for the honor and welfare of your church, run to meet your father. Do not delay to send across the sea something of faith, of friendship, of devotion or counsel by which he can lessen his burden and be perpetually bound harmlessly to you. Now redeem your delay . . . .

———

Thomas returned to England, renewed an excommunication of three disobedient bishops, and in so doing roused again the wrath of Henry. On the afternoon of December 29, 1170, four knights of Henry's entourage burst into his cathedral. John had once advised Thomas to stand on principle at the risk of martyrdom but when the armed knights were on the premises he told Thomas that he was not anxious for death. He accompanied Thomas into the cathedral but dove into a recess before the assault began. Knowles 114, 144, 147. In Letter 305 he writes not necessarily as an eyewitness, but as one who was very close to the scene, which he survived to become, six years later, bishop of Chartres.

John of Salisbury to John, Bishop of Poitiers, Early 1171

But he was ready to suffer, as I said, in the church before the altar of Christ—a martyr before he was struck .. When he heard that he was asked for—when the knights who had come for this shouted out in the crowd of clerics and monks, "Where is the archbishop?"—he met them on the steps which he had mostly climbed. With an intrepid countenance he said, "Here I am. What do you want?" One of the deadly knights, in a spirit of fury, flung at him, "That now you die. For it is impossible that you live longer." But the archbishop replied with as much steadiness of speech as of spirit (in my opinion, with respect to all the martyrs, I confidently say that none of them was steadier in his passion): "And I for my God am ready to die, and for the declaration of justice and the liberty of the Church. But if you seek my head, I forbid on the part of Almighty God and under anathema that you harm any other, whether monk or cleric or layman, of high or low degree. They are immune from punishment as they have stood apart from the case. Not to them but to me is it to be imputed if any of them undertook the cause of the Church in her labor. I embrace death freely, as long as the Church obtains peace and liberty in the shedding of my blood."

Who has seemed more fervent in love? He was offering himself to his persecutors for the law of God. He took care only that his neighbors be harmed in nothing. Did not his words seem to express Christ who in his passion said, "If you seek me, let these go" [John 18:8].

After he said these things, he saw that the butchers had drawn their swords, He lowered his head in the fashion of one who prays and uttered these last words, "To God and Blessed Mary and to the holy patrons of this Church and to Blessed Denis I commend myself and the Church's cause."

Who will tell what followed without sighs, sorrow, tears? Piety does not permit one to relate each individual thing which the most cruel butchers did. They held the fear of God in contempt. They were forgetful of faith and of all humanity.

It was not enough for them to profane the church and stain a most sacred day with the blood of a priest and his killing. The crown of his head which the anointing of the sacred chrism had dedicated to God they—it is terrible even to say it—cut off and with their deadly swords drew out the brain of the dead man and most cruelly scattered it over the pavement with his blood and bones. More inhuman were they than those who crucified Christ who judged that his legs should not be broken as had been the legs of those who were alive, when they saw that he had died.

In all these tortures the martyr, with unconquered spirit and wonderful steadiness, spoke not a word nor let out a cry nor emitted a groan. He opposed neither his arm nor a garment to the one striking him, but he held his bowed head immobile, which he had exposed to the swords with wonderful virtue until it was consummated, and at length falling on the ground he did not move foot or hand, and his body lay straight.

———

To see this controversy as Church versus State is an anachronism. The Church was divided; the king was not a modern bureaucracy ideologically hostile to the Church's claims. Henry was at least in part responding to what he saw as pride and disloyalty and was acting with personal meanness to reach Thomas in his relatives. That the bishops were divided was important to him not only politically but personally. In good conscience he could say that he was not attacking the Church when learned churchmen were on his side. The pattern is familiar. But from the viewpoint of the universal Church, Thomas died for his defense of its claims. Two years and two months after his death, he was proclaimed a saint, canonized by Alexander III himself. His cult was celebrated from a mosaic in his honor in the Norman cathedral in Monreale, Sicily, to stories about his integrity told in the schools of Paris. Noonan, *Bribes* 176. During the next 600 years the Church was often to be in conflict with Christian monarchs who had their own ideas as to how to limit the jurisdiction of the Church. For popes or bishops involved in any of these encounters Thomas was an exemplar of adherence to principle and resistance to royal pretensions. By his life and by his death he had an impact on European views of the relation of bishop to prince.

2.   THE GREAT CHARTER: "THE ENGLISH CHURCH SHALL BE FREE, AND SHALL HAVE HER RIGHTS ENTIRE"

A favorite stumper in English history classes is: Who signed Magna Carta? The answer is: No one, the document was agreed to but not signed by King John. A comparable conundrum is: How long was Magna Carta the law of England? The answer is: About two months. The grant was then formally invalidated by John's legal overlord. Only Magna Carta as reissued by Henry III had the long life into the mid-nineteenth century that is popularly credited to the famous document. This history, and the origins of Magna Carta, both arise from the interaction of the Church with the English crown.

The see of Canterbury became vacant in 1205. The monks of Christ Church, the normal electors were challenged by the suffragan bishops as to who would choose the new archbishop. King John, the talented Henry II's untalented youngest son, backed the bishops. The monks appealed to Pope Innocent III (1198–1216) the most energetic of all the medieval popes.

As a student at Paris, Innocent had made a pilgrimage to the shrine of St. Thomas. From his perspective, St. Thomas had "laid down his life for the Church's liberty" and yet "his blood" had borne no fruit. The English king continued to dominate the Church. The pope now saw his opportunity. The king's agents intimated that they were ready to pay over 11,000 silver marks for the right result, but Innocent detested such bribes and stayed on "the royal road" of impartiality. *Gesta Innocentii III*, c. 131, Migne, *PL*, vol. 214. He quashed the election that had already been held and called the electors of Christ Church to Rome. Voting in his presence, they chose his candidate, Cardinal Stephen Langton. *Gesta,* c. 131.

Langton was an admirable choice—an honest, highly intelligent Englishman who had made a great reputation as a scholar in Paris and had been called to Rome from Paris by Innocent, who may already have had him in mind as the ideal man for Canterbury. It was, however, intolerable to the king that a man so unknown to him should hold the premier see of his realm. He asked the pope to reconsider and put papal relatives on his payroll to influence the reconsideration. Noonan, *Bribes* 195. "Strong and steady," as he saw himself, Innocent consecrated Langton with his own hands. *Gesta,* c. 131.

John reacted as his father would have reacted. He expelled from their monastery the monks whose representatives had elected Langton. He put Langton's own father to flight in fear of his life and confiscated his estate. He announced that the new archbishop could not land in England. Innocent replied with the threat of a general interdict of England. After months of fruitless negotiations, the interdict took effect in March 1208. While it lasted, the only sacraments that could lawfully be administered in the country were those to the dying. To restrain their ruler the English as a whole were subjected to sacramental starvation. Christopher R. Cheney, *Pope Innocent III and England* 298–302 (1976).

Protracted conflict between pope and prince went on for five years. John confiscated clerical properties of various kinds. Innocent insisted on the interdict. In 1213 John faced invasion by France. Unrest among his own subjects and the desire for papal support impelled him to abject surrender. On May 13, 1213, he submitted to the papal legates and offered to make restitution for the damages the Church had suffered. On May 15, 1213, he made restitution by a remarkable gesture—the conveyance of England and Ireland to the pope and his successors in office. "We have offended God and Our Mother Holy Church in many things," he declared. "We will to humble ourselves" (John to All Christ's Faithful, May 15, 1213, *PL* vol. 216, 878–880). After conveyance, the pope gave the countries back to John as fiefs. John became the vassal of the pope. He continued to hold the kingdoms in consideration of doing homage as a liegeman to his overlord, the pope, vowing henceforth to defend "the Patrimony of Blessed Peter and in particular the kingdom of England and the kingdom of Ireland," and agreeing to pay an annual cash tribute—700 silver marks for England, 300 for Ireland, the whole 1,000 to be paid in two semiannual installments. *Id.*.

Cardinal Stephen Langton then set off for England and within a year had drafted reforms which the king must carry out. Among them was the proposition, "King John grants that he will not take men without judgment nor accept anything for doing justice, nor perform injustice" W.L. Warren, *King John* 215–47 (1978). Clause 40 of Magna Carta existed in embryo.

In early 1215 mutinous barons were in revolt against the king. The pope was now on John's side. As overlord, it was his duty to protect his vassal. Moreover, the pope was planning a crusade, the king had taken the crusader's cross, and the barons could not be allowed to disrupt the crusade. Langton was rebuked for stirring up the barons. Cheney 368–79.

On June 15, 1215, the bishops of England led by Langton, a party of barons, and the papal legate Pandulph secured John's consent at Runnymede to the document that was to be celebrated as "The Great Charter." A remarkably heterogeneous set of reforms was outlined within its limits, from provisions on the dowry of widows to provisions pledging the king not to sell justice and to respect the freedom of the Church. A month later John duplicitously appealed to Rome to annul his agreement.

The case was put to Innocent, not in terms of the substantive provisions of the document but in terms of how it had been secured. A familiar legal doctrine was that a promise was voidable if the promisor had been subjected to the kind of fear that would cow "a steady man." John, Innocent held, had been subjected to fear that would have cowed "the steadiest man." In a decretal letter issued on August 24, 1215, not long after Magna Carta had reached Rome, Innocent annulled it. Innocent and John both died in 1216. Only after their deaths was Magna Carta reissued without challenge in the reign of Henry III (1216–1272). There follows a portion of Magna Carta, based on the Latin text in James C. Holt, *Magna Carta* (1965); and Innocent III's annulment of it, the letter *Etsi Karissimus*, is based on the Latin text in Christopher R. Cheney and W.H. Semple, eds., *Selected Letters of Pope Innocent III concerning England, 1198–1216* (1953).

Magna Carta, June 15, 1215

The Preamble

John, by the grace of God King of England, Lord of Ireland, Duke of Normandy and Aquitaine and Count of Anjou, to his archbishops, bishops, abbots, earls, barons, justices, foresters, sheriffs, stewards, servants, and to all his officials and loyal subjects, Greetings.

Know that before God, for the health of our soul and the souls of our ancestors and heirs, to the honour of God, the exaltation of the holy Church, and amendments of our kingdom by the advice of our reverend Fathers, Stephen, Archbishop of Canterbury, Primate of all England, and Cardinal of the holy Roman Church; Henry, Archbishop of Dublin; William of London, Peter of Winchester, Jocelin of Bath and Glastonbury, Hugh of Lincoln, Walter of Worcester, William of Coventry, Benedict of Rochester [the seven bishops of England], Master Pandulf subdeacon and member of the Pope's household, Aymeric, Master of the Knights Templar in England; William Marshal, Earl of Pembroke; William, Earl of Salisbury; William, Earl of Warren; William, Earl of Arundel; Alan de Galloway, Constable of Scotland, Warin Fitz Gerald, Hubert de Burgh, Seneschal of Poitou, Peter Fitz Herbert, Hugh de Neville, Matthew Fitz Herbert, Thomas Basset, Alan Basset, Philip Daubeny, Robert de Roppeley, John Marshal, John Fitz Hugh, and other our loyal subjects:

Clause 1: In the first place we have granted to God, and by this present charter have confirmed for us and our heirs in perpetuity, that the English Church shall be free, and shall have her rights entire, and her liberties inviolate. That we wish this to be observed is evident that of our own free will, before the outbreak of the disputes before us and our barons, we granted and confirmed by charter the freedom of the elections, which is considered to be of the greatest necessity and importance to the English Church. . . .

Preamble to Clauses 2–63: To all free men of our kingdom, we have also granted, for us and for our heirs for ever, all the underwritten liberties, to be had and held by them and their heirs ... forever. . . .

Clause 62: All the ill will, hatreds, and bitterness, that have arisen between us and our subjects, clergy and laity, from the date of the quarrel, we have completely remitted and pardoned to every one. . . . We have caused letters patent to be made to the barons, as a testimony to this security and to the concessions set out above, over the seals of the lord Stephen, Archbishop of Canterbury, of the lord Henry, Archbishop of Dublin, the other bishops named above and Master Pandulf.

Clause 63: Wherefore it is our will and command that the English church shall be free, and that men in our kingdom shall have and keep all these liberties, rights and concessions, freely and quietly, fully and wholly, for themselves and their heirs, of us and our heirs, for ever.

Given under our hand in the meadow that is called Runnymede, between Windsor and Staines, on the fifteenth day of June, in the seventeenth year of our reign.

Innocent III to all Christ's Faithful, *Etsi Karissimus,* August 24, 1215

Innocent, bishop, servant of the servants of God, to all the faithful of Christ who will see this document, health and apostolic blessing.

Although our most well-beloved son in Christ, John, illustrious king of the English, violently offended God and the Church, in consequence of which we bound him with the knot of excommunication and subjected his kingdom to ecclesiastical interdict, nonetheless he himself, by the merciful inspiration of Him who does not will the death of the sinner but that he be converted and live, at length returned to his heart. Humbly he made satisfaction to God and the Church so that he not only gave recompense for losses and restitution of what had been taken but also granted plenary liberty to the English Church. Further when we lifted both our sentences, he granted his own kingdom of England and of Ireland to Blessed Peter and the Roman Church, receiving it from us as a fief under an annual return of 1,000 marks after he had sworn an oath of fidelity to us, as appears in his privilege furnished with a gold seal. Desiring to please Almighty God still further, he reverently put on the sign of the life-giving cross, intending to go to the relief of the Holy Land and splendidly prepared to go.

But the enemy of the human race, who is always accustomed to envy good deeds, by his cunning arts stirred up against him the barons of England, so that those who helped him when he was offending the Church, now when he had converted and made satisfaction to the Church, perversely rose against him.

Matters of dispute had arisen between them, and several days had been fixed to treat of peace between them. Meanwhile, formal envoys had been sent to us. With them we had careful conversation and after full deliberation we wrote by them to the English archbishop and bishops, charging and commanding them to apply diligent zeal and effective effort to reformation, so that there would be true and full harmony between them. By apostolic authority they were to declare void all leagues and agreements which perchance had been formed from the time discord arose between the kingdom and the priesthood. By sentence of excommunication they were to forbid anyone to form such things in the future. They were prudently to warn and effectively to enjoin the magnates and nobles of England to strive to please the king himself by manifest proofs of devotion and humility; and then if they did decide to ask anything of him to implore him not arrogantly but humbly, maintaining the royal honor and rendering the customary services which they and their predecessors gave to him and his predecessors; for the king should not be despoiled of these without judgment. In this way they could more easily obtain what they sought. We by our letters asked the king, and warned him for the remission of his sins to treat the aforesaid magnates and nobles benignly and to attend mercifully to their just petitions, so that they, rejoicing with us, might recognize how he was changed to a better state by divine grace, and so that by this they and their heirs might serve him more readily and more loyally. We also asked him to grant them full security in coming, staying, and returning, so that if perchance they could not come to harmony, the dispute might be decided by their peers in his court according to the laws and customs of the kingdom.

But, before the envoys had returned with this provident and just command, the barons treated their oath of fidelity with utter contempt. If the king had unjustly injured them, they nonetheless should not have acted against him as if in their own case they were the judges and executors of judgment. Vassals, they publicly conspired against their lord; and knights, they conspired against the king. They not only presumed to make war against him; they joined with his most open enemies; and they occupied and devastated his lands and even invaded the city of London, which is the seat of the kingdom and was treacherously surrendered to them.

Meanwhile, the aforesaid envoys returned to England, and the king offered them the fullness of justice according to the form of our mandate. The barons spurned this completely and began to stretch out their hands to worse things. Hence the king himself appealed to our tribunal and offered to show them justice before us, to whom judgment of this case belonged by reason of our lordship. This they wholly rejected. Then he offered that four prudent men chosen by him and by them should, together with us, end the dispute which had arisen with them. He promised that before anything else he would repeal all abuses whatever which had been introduced into England in his time. But they did not deign to accept this. Finally, the king declared to them that since the lordship of the kingdom belonged to the Roman Church, he himself could not and ought not to change anything affecting it to our prejudice without our special mandate. Hence he again appealed to our tribunal and put himself and his kingdom with all his honor and right under Apostolic protection. When he made no progress in this way, he demanded that the archbishop and bishops execute our mandate, defend the rights of the Roman Church, and safeguard him according to the form of the privilege conceded to those signed with the cross. When they wished to do nothing of the sort, he saw himself almost bereft of all advice and aid, and he did not dare deny what they dared to ask. Hence, compelled by the force and fear which could fall on even the steadiest man, he accepted a settlement with them which is not only vile and shameful but also illegal and unjust in undue diminution and derogation of both his right and his honor.

But the Lord has spoken to us in the Prophet: "I have set you over peoples and kingdoms to root out and to destroy, to build and to plant"; and by another Prophet: "Loose the bonds of wickedness, undo the oppressive bundles." Therefore we refuse to ignore audacity of such great malignity in contempt of the Apostolic See, to the loss of royal rights, the shame of the English people, and the serious endangering of the whole enterprise of the Crucified, which would surely be imminent unless we by our authority entirely revoked things extorted in this way from such a just prince, signed with the cross, even if he wanted to observe them. On behalf of Almighty God, Father and Son and Holy Spirit, and by the authority also of the blessed Apostles Peter and Paul, and by our own authority, with the common advice of our brethren, we utterly reject and condemn this sort of settlement. Under threat of anathema we forbid that the aforesaid king dare to observe it and that the barons with their accomplices ask him to observe it. We completely annul and hold void both the Charter and the obligations and guarantees made on its account or flowing from it, so that never shall they have any force.

Let it be lawful for no man to infringe this document of annulment and prohibition or temerariously dare to oppose it. If anyone should presume to attempt this, let him know he will incur the wrath of Almighty God and His Blessed Apostles Peter and Paul.

Given at Anagni, August 24, in the eighteenth year of our pontificate.

3.   THE LAWS AND CUSTOMS OF ENGLAND

In the same generation in which Magna Carta was reissued, work was begun on what was to be for the next 500 years the most remarkable treatise on English law—*De legibus et consuetudinibus Angliae (The Laws and Customs of England)*. Its "prime mover" was William de Ralegh. Samuel E. Thorne, Introduction, 3 *The Laws and Customs of England* xxxvi (1968). Ralegh in the 1220s was the law clerk of the royal judge Martin de Pateshull, and in 1229 he became a royal judge himself. In 1234 Henry III made him Chief Justice. At this time he possessed "the talent of friendship with the king." Robert Grosseteste to William de Ralegh, 1236, Rolls Series 25, 94. He represented the king in a request to magnates of the realm for a contribution of property. He was not afraid in 1234 to hold null an outlawry passed by the king. *Bracton's Notebook,* ed. F. W. Maitland, Case 857.

Ralegh's career changed dramatically in 1239 when he was elected bishop of Norwich and left judicial office. In 1240 the monks of Winchester chose him as bishop of Winchester. Henry had his own candidate for the see, and there ensued a battle between king and former counselor which, while it never reached the depths of Henry II's quarrel with Becket, showed that Henry III could be rough. In the end Ralegh was vindicated by litigation before the pope and took possession of his see in 1244; the king let himself be reconciled.

The treatise that Ralegh presumably began as a law clerk and continued as a judge (the great bulk of the cases are from the 1220s and 1230s) passed into the hands of Ralegh's protégé, Henri de Bratton, who became a royal judge in 1245. Bratton added to the manuscript, revised it a little, and left it unpublished on his death in 1268. Nine years later his heirs circulated copies, and it began its career as a legal authority attributed to Bratton. In 1569 the first printed edition erroneously fixed the spelling of the author's name as Bracton.

The treatise for our purposes is of great interest in its bland fusion of canon law, Roman law, cases, and customs as together constituting the common law of England. "Interpenetration" was still going on. The authors did not care what the sources of the rules were if they believed the rules were current in England. In this way, for example, the canon law on cooperation in homicide— set out by decretal letters of Alexander III to cover the accomplices in Thomas Becket's death—became here the common law of England.

Divine sanctions, as will be seen below, are used as the chief deterrent to bribery. Their description in Book I is taken bodily from a popular tract written by Innocent III as a young cardinal, *The Misery of the Human Condition*, Book III, chapter 20. For Ralegh–Bratton the terrors of the Last Judgment are as integral to the English legal system as a writ for appointing justices. The heavenly sanction is the only effective insurer of the integrity of the judge. God's punishments are also a chief, though not the only, sanction against a lawless king.

Faith in a future accounting to the Lord and papal case law were no strangers to Ralegh and Bratton, both clerics, both holding ecclesiastical appointments that gave them independent incomes. They incorporated their beliefs into English law as easily as the king used them to provide royal justice. But there were also tensions of which they were acutely aware. They made express acknowledgment of the two different jurisdictions of the crown and the priesthood. They tacitly ignored areas where canon law clashed with English custom.

Three examples will suffice:

1. Canon law provided an elaborate system for determining the existence of a marriage, of which the Church was taken to be the only judge. Ralegh–Bratton, in some cases involving the existence of marriage, cut off all appeal to the pope. *Laws and Customs*, 3:372–73; 4:302–5.

2. Canon law expressly held that if a child was born from intercourse outside of marriage to parents otherwise free to marry, their subsequent marriage legitimated the child. Alexander III to Bartholomew, bishop of Exeter, *Decretals of Gregory IX*, 4.17. 6, *Tanta est vis matrimonii*. English law expressly held such a child to be a bastard, incapable of inheriting as a lawful heir. *Laws and Customs* 4:294. Robert Grosseteste, the outspoken bishop of Lincoln, wrote Ralegh reminding him of his duty to follow canon law on this point. Grosseteste thought the divine law also acknowledged the child's legitimacy. He threatened Ralegh with damnation at the Last Judgment if he did not conform. Grosseteste to Ralegh, 1236, Rolls Series 25, 94. But Ralegh stuck to the hard laws and customs of his country.

3. Canon law forbade a cleric to participate in any way in a judgment of blood. Innocent III's Fourth Lateran Council in 1215 had legislated this prohibition for the universal church. J. Alberigo, Ed. *Conciliorum oecumenicorum decreta*, (1973) c. 18. Ralegh, like many other bishops, enacted the prohibition in legislation for his own diocese of Norwich. F.W. Powicke and Christopher R. Cheney, eds., 1 *Councils and Synods with Other Documents Relating to the English Church* 348 (1964). Nonetheless, when *Laws and Customs*, 2:340, treated of the death penalty, nothing was said as to the disqualification of clerics to pronounce it. Both Ralegh and Bratton as royal judges must have had to pronounce it many times. James B. Given, *Society and Homicide in Thirteenth–Century England* 101 (1977). Their obligation to the crown was silently permitted to override their obligation to the Church.

No ideological formula, no neat allotment of the roles of the prince and the pope, no clear logic govern the way Ralegh–Bratton handle the two spheres of the secular and the spiritual. They did not use Magna Carta, fresh and comprehensive though it was, to determine what was "the liberty of the Church." Their one true guide was experience, largely their own experience which had been molded by custom. The spiritual and secular interpenetrated. Experienced ecclesiastics who were also royal judges were able to decide what the relation should be.

Ralegh-Bratton, *The Laws and Customs of England*, Introduction, 1277

The purpose of this undertaking is that quarrels may be quieted and vices repressed and peace and justice kept in the kingdom. But it must be set under ethics as if it were moral science, because it treats of morals....

Let no fool or ignoramus presume to ascend the judgment seat which is as if the throne of God, lest for light be put darkness and for darkness light, and in the manner of a madman with ignorant hand he strike the innocent with the sword and free the injurious; lest he fall from on high as from the throne of God—he who began to fly before he had wings. And if one should judge and be made a judge, let him take care for himself lest by judging perversely and against the laws for prayer or price, for the stipend of a small temporal gain, he presume to purchase for himself the sorrow of eternal lamentation.

What the Punishment Is for Him Who Judges Evilly

And let him not on the day of the Lord's wrath feel Him avenging, Him who said, "Vengeance is mine, and I shall reciprocate"—on that day when the kings and princes of the earth shall weep and moan when they see the Son of Man because of terror of his tortures where gold and silver will not free them. Who may not fear that trial in which the Lord will be accuser, advocate, and judge? From his judgment there cannot be appeal, because the Father has given all judgment to the Son. He closes and no one opens. He opens and no one closes. Strict judgment! There men shall render account not only as to deeds but even of every idle word they have spoken.

Who therefore will be able to flee the anger that is to come? For the Son of Man shall send his angels who will gather from the kingdom of God all scandals and those who do wickedness and make of them bundles to be burnt. They shall send them into the furnace of fire. There, there will be weeping and gnashing of teeth, groans and moans, outcries, lamentations and agonies, shrieking and screeching, fear and trembling, suffering and travail, fire and stink, darkness and dread, bitterness and boisterousness, calamity and craving, distress and dejection, oblivion and orderlessness, torturings and tearings, torments and terrors, hunger and thirst, frigidity and heat, brimstone and fire burning forever and ever.

Let each one beware of that judgment where the Judge is frighteningly strict, unbearably severe, immeasurably offended, violently angered; His judgment not commutable; the prison inescapable; the tortures without end, without intermission; the torturers, who never tire and never pity, horrible. Fear unsettles; conscience condemns; thoughts reproach; it is not permitted to flee. Hence Blessed Augustine, "My great sins are too many! When anyone has God as just Judge and his own conscience as the witness, he need fear nothing except his own case...."

Persons

The king in his kingdom has no peer because otherwise he would lose command; for a peer has no power over a peer. Much less ought he to have a superior or one more powerful than he, because then he would be inferior to those subject to him, and inferiors cannot be peers with superiors. But the king himself ought to be under no man but under God and under the law; for the law makes the king.

Let the king therefore render to the law what the law renders to him, to wit, domination and power. For there is no king where will and not law dominates. And because he ought to be under the law since he is the vicar of God, he is clearly close to the likeness of Jesus Christ, whose vice-regent he is on earth. The true mercifulness of God chose this most powerful way to destroy the work of the devil, although for the ineffable recovery of the human race many ways were open to Him; and so He used not the power of force but the reason of justice. And so He willed to be under the law that He might buy back those who were under the law. He did not will to use strength but judgment. So also the Blessed Procreator of God, the Virgin Mary, Mother of the Lord, who by a singular privilege was above the law, nonetheless in order to give an example of humility did not refuse to be subjected to established laws. So then the king—lest his power stay unbridled.

Therefore there ought not to be anyone in his kingdom greater in attention to the law. But he ought to be the last or as if the last in receiving judgment if he seeks it. If it is sought from him, although a writ does not run against him, there will be place for a petition to correct and amend his act. If he will not do it, it is sufficient penalty for him that he wait for God the Avenger....

Actions
What Judgment Is, and In What the Duty of a Judge
Consists, Namely Three Things

We must see, therefore, what a judgment is. And it must be known that in any action whatsoever a judgment is the act of three persons—the judge, the plaintiff, and the defendant. Persons of this sort are to be understood broadly, to wit, that there be at least two persons between whom the dispute lies and at least a third who judges.

It is said: "Look at what you do, for you do not exercise the judgment of man but of God, and that which you judge shall redound upon you. Let the fear of the Lord be with you and do everything with care. For with our Lord God there is no wickedness nor taking up of persons nor desire for offerings which blind the eyes of the wise and twist the words of the just," as is read in Ecclesiasticus, Chapter 20: "Courtesy-presents and gifts blind the eyes of judges."

He who said gifts or offerings meant every kind of offering: (1) an offering from the hand—that sort of thing is something corporeal that is offered; (2) an offering from the tongue, which is a flattering and fawning petition, a public proclamation of praise, a symphony celebrating vain glory; (3) an offering from obedience, which is service bestowed and received in return for which the straightness of judgment is twisted. Nor does an offering from blood kinship merit being called anything less when for the blood line the line of straight judgment is made crooked; for, in this, blood responds to blood. Offerings of these kinds are assuredly described by the name of "defilements," and human law inflicts a serious punishment on the judge corrupted by defilements, that is, by dirty offerings: if a judge or justice contracts with a litigant for a certain part of the lawsuit, the *Codex* at the Julian law, *Repetundae,* says, "Let all triers of cases and judges keep their hands from money, and let them not think another's lawsuit to be booty for them. The final judge in even private litigation who is the same as a merchant shall be compelled to undergo the loss established by law." The loss or penalty shall be that he shall restore what he receives fourfold, as the *Codex* says at the very end of the same law; for there they are bound to repay the fourfold whether they received something during their administration or afterward, whatever the title or veil when they pretend that a title of gift or sale has intervened. In truth, he is defiled whom the truth of judgment does not adorn. Where favoritism or hatred, fear, envy or reward induce its contrary, the truth of judgment falls into the courtyard. As to this it can be said, "Woe to that defiled man through whom truth became defiled in the swamps of the courtyards." He shall not be numbered among the blessed of whom it is said, "Blessed is he who shakes his hands free from every offering."

Nonetheless, one must not abstain from every offering. It is most avaricious and most vile to receive from everyone and everywhere. But to receive from no one will be inhuman. A friend may receive from a friend at the sole prompting of friendship and love.

The Power of the Judge

It is necessary that he who judges have jurisdiction, ordinary or delegated, if his judgments are to be valid. And it does not suffice that he have jurisdiction unless he have the power of coercion. If he could not require execution of his judgments, they would be illusory. An ordinary judge does not have jurisdiction and execution in every case, for laws are separate and limited.

The Division of the Jurisdictions of the Priesthood and the Kingdom

There are spiritual cases in which a secular judge has neither power to try them nor (since he lacks power of coercion) execution. In these cases the judgment belongs to the ecclesiastical judges who rule and defend the priesthood.

There are also secular cases whose judgment belongs to the kings and princes who defend the kingdom. Ecclesiastical judges must not meddle with them, for their laws or jurisdictions are limited and separate, except when sword ought to help sword. For there is a great difference between the priesthood and the kingdom.

The Regulation of the Jurisdictions of the Kingdom ...
(Nothing for the Present as to the Priest)

Since nothing as to the regulation of the priesthood belongs to this treatise, we must see about those things that belong to the kingdom. Who, primarily and powerfully, can and ought to judge? And it must be known that it is the king himself, and no other, if he alone is sufficient. To this he is bound by power of an oath, for at his coronation he must in an oath offered in the name of Jesus Christ promise the people subject to him these three things:

The Oath Which the King must Make at his Coronation

First, that he will command, and as his strength allows work, that for the Church of God and for the whole Christian people true peace be observed in all his time. Second, that he will prevent rapacity and all wickedness to men of every degree. Third, that in all judgments he will command equity and mercy, so that a clement and merciful God may grant him His mercy and by his justice all may enjoy a firm peace.

CHAPTER FOUR

"Bound That I Should Not Obey My Prince": The Contested Supremacy of Conscience, 1250–1560

1. Thomas Aquinas on Force and Faith

Fides—faith—is the central value Thomas is defending in the texts below. Modern translators translate *fides* in a feudal relation as "fealty." They translate *fides* in marriage as "fidelity." They translate *fides* in religion as "belief." They lose the triple tie that binds the analogues of the concept together. Thomas is for keeping faith to an overlord, faith to a spouse, faith in God. The same principle that justifies the Church in making the married or members of a religious order keep their vows justifies making those who have accepted the faith keep it. The *infidelis*—the infidel, the unfaithful—is to be forced back into the fold.

Thomas Aquinas has the title "the Angelic Doctor," and he writes like an angel—that is, with a clarity, sobriety, and dispassionateness that suggest a being outside this world. Nonetheless, what he has to teach on religion and governmental power is far from angelic, and it is possible to see in his position the convergence of various earthly currents. First, he came from a family of seven children, of whom he was the youngest boy; he always felt secure, he never felt persecuted. Second, he came from a family of feudal lords who ruled Roccasecca under the emperor; fealty was a high value. Third, he had spent years in the neighborhood of the papal court and was the friend of Pope Clement IV and Pope Urban IV: he had a strong regard for the papal government and the canon law. Fourth, intellectually speaking most important, he had become an admirer of Aristotle and at the very time that he was writing the Second Part of the *Summa Theologiae (S.T.)* quoted below, he was also commenting on Aristotle's *Nicomachean Ethics*.

From Aristotle came Thomas's language of whole and part. Human beings are parts, the community is a whole. The parts are, naturally, subordinated to the whole. The parts can be sacrificed to the whole. With this vocabulary, Thomas defends the death penalty in general, arguing that the community has the right to lop off a putrid member; *S.T.*, 2–2, 64, 4. The Christian view that human destiny transcends the state is somehow lost from his account.

Aristotle helps to explain his intellectual stance, but Aristotle had nothing to say on heresy. Important here was what was accepted by other authorities he acknowledged: Aristotle above all, and the canon law found in Gratian and Gregory IX's *Decretals*. Authority as such was not, however, decisive. As will be seen in the argument below, there were venerable teachers—the Gospel itself, never a small authority—that pointed to more merciful and more magnanimous conclusions. Practice was decisive. In the world Thomas knew, heretics were sent to the flames. The most chilling statement, perhaps, in what follows—startling in a religion built on the imitation of God—is that where forgiveness of heretics is concerned, the Church "cannot imitate God."

Another reflection of the accepted environment is the statement that "the Jews are the slaves of the Church," made as part of a legal justification for the canon that directs the gratuitous manumission of a slave who becomes a Christian, whose owners are Jewish. The Church, Thomas argues, can dispose of Jewish property this way because the Jews themselves are her slaves. The argument is legal, but Thomas provides no legal citations, and no canon embodied this precise teaching. Nonetheless, the statement reflected a common belief of medieval Christendom and can be found in decretal letters of such thirteenth-century popes as Innocent III and Gregory IX; *see* Edward A. Synan, *The Popes and the Jews in the Middle Ages* 108, 226 (1965); for the two relevant decretals of Innocent III, translated by Synan, 221–229, *see* Innocent III, *Epistolae, PL* 215, 501, and 1291. The idea was never taken to its logical legal conclusion with Christians or ecclesiastics feeling free to sell Jews as chattels, but it undoubtedly contributed to the oppressive social conditions in which Jews were often subjected to extortion and pillage [see Chapter Two, Note, *Christians and Jews from Roman Law to the Holocaust and its Aftermath*].

Thomas, aged about forty-five, and a master of the University of Paris, wrote what follows at Paris between 1270 and 1272. What he had to say on any topic proved to be extraordinarily influential. Canonized in 1323, he was named a Doctor of the Church in 1567. Pope Clement VIII declared that "no error is to be found in his works." As recently as the *Code of Canon Law* (1917), canon 1366.2 prescribed that all priests were to be educated "according to the method, doctrine and principles of the Angelic Doctor." The following text is a translation of the Latin of the Leonine edition of the *Summa Theologiae*. For further reading in English, the Blackfriars translation of the 1970s is recommended.

Aquinas, *Summa Theologiae*
2–2 Question 10 Infidelity in General

Article 8. Are infidels to be forced to the Faith?

1.   It appears that infidels are in no way to be forced to the faith. For it is said in Matthew [13:28] that the slaves asked the householder in whose field the tares were sown, "Shall we go and gather them?" and he replied, "No, lest in gathering up the tares, you eradicate the wheat with them." On this Chrysostom says [*PG* 58:477]: "The Lord says these things to forbid killings. For it is necessary not to kill the heretics, because if you kill them you must kill many of the saints at the same time." Therefore it seems by a parallel reason that other infidels are not to be forced to the faith.

2.   Moreover, the *Decretum* [Gratian, 45, 5] reads as follows: "The holy synod commands as to the Jews that force is henceforth not to be

inflicted on any of them to make them believe." Therefore by parallel reason other infidels are not to be compelled to the faith.

3. Further, Augustine says [*On John*, Tract 26, c.2, *PL* 35, 1607]: A man can do other things unwillingly, but "he cannot believe except willingly." But the will cannot be forced. Therefore it appears that infidels are not to be forced to the faith.

4. Further, Ezekiel in the person of God says [18:23]: "I do not will the death of sinners." But we ought to conform our will to the divine will, as said above. Therefore we too should not will that infidels be killed.

But to the contrary is what is said in Luke [14:23]: "Go out into the highways and hedges and force them to enter that my house may be filled." But men enter by faith into the house of God, that is, into Holy Church. Therefore, some are to be forced to the faith.

Reply: It must be said that some infidels have not received the faith, such as the gentiles and the Jews; and such are in no way to be forced to the faith so that they believe, because to believe depends on the will. They are nonetheless to be forced by the faithful, if they can, not to impede the faith by blasphemies or evil persuasions or open persecutions. And on this account the faithful of Christ frequently wage war against infidels, not to force them to believe (because even if they conquered them and held them captive they should leave them in their liberty as to whether they wish to believe), but on this account, to force them not to impede the faith of Christ.

But there are other infidels who once received the faith and professed it, such as heretics and every apostate; and such are to be forced even physically to fulfill what they promised and to hold to what they once received.

1. To the first objection, it must be said that by that text some have understood that not the excommunication but the killing of heretics is forbidden, as is clear from the cited text of Chrysostom. And so Augustine to Vincentius says in regard to himself [*PL* 33, 330]: "This was my first opinion, that no one should be forced to the unity of Christ, but we should act by words and fight by argument.... But my opinion was overcome not by the words of those contradicting it but by the example of facts...." [For terror of the law was so advantageous that many say], "Thank the Lord, who has broken our chains." Therefore when the Lord says, "Let them both grow until the harvest," how it is to be understood appears from what follows: "lest perchance in gathering up the tares you eradicate the wheat with them." This sufficiently shows, Augustine says, "when that danger is not present—that is, when the crime of anyone is known to everyone and appears hateful so that he has no defenders or none such by whom a schism could occur, let severe discipline not sleep."

2. To the second objection, it must be said that Jews, if in no way they accept the faith, are in no way to be forced to the faith. But if they have received the faith, they must by necessity be forced to retain the faith, as is said in the same chapter.

3.   To the third objection, it must be said that to vow depends on the will, to fulfill the vow is a matter of necessity. In this way to accept the faith depends on the will, but to keep it, once accepted, is a matter of necessity. And therefore heretics are to be forced to keep the faith. For Augustine says to Count Boniface [*The Correction of the Donatists, supra,* I]: "What is that these men are accustomed to cry, 'to believe or not, to believe is free? On whom does Christ inflict force?' Let them recognize in Paul Christ first forcing and then teaching. . . ."

4.   To the fourth objection, it must be said as Augustine says in the same epistle [PL 33:807]: "None of us wants any heretic to perish. . . . But the house of David did not deserve to have peace until Absalom, David's son, was extinguished in the war he waged against his father. . . ." Thus too the Catholic Church, if by the loss of some she gathers up others, cures the sorrow of her motherly heart by the liberation of many peoples. . . .

Article 10. Can infidels have authority or dominion over the faithful?

[Thomas holds that if the faithful are not subject to infidels, the Church will not permit them to become subject to them. But if the infidels already possess such authority, it continues unless the Church determines to the contrary.]

But this the Church sometimes does and sometimes does not. As to those infidels who are subjected in temporal subjection to the Church and her members, the Church has decreed this law, that a slave of Jews, when he becomes a Christian, shall be at once liberated from slavery without any price being paid, if he had been a slave from birth. But if he were purchased for commerce, then within three months he should be offered for sale [Gregory IX, *Decretals* 5, 6, 1]. Nor does the Church do any injury by this law, for the Jews themselves are the slaves of the Church, so she can dispose of their property, just as secular princes issue many laws about their subjects in favor of liberty. But as to infidels who are temporally not subject to the Church or her members, the Church has not decreed the said law, although legally she could establish it; and she acts in this way to avoid scandal, just as the Lord showed He could excuse himself from the tax because the sons are free, but yet He ordered the tax to be paid to avoid scandal. . . .

Article 11. Are the rites of infidels to be tolerated?

3.   Further, the sin of infidelity is the gravest, as was said above. But other sins such as adultery, theft, and things of this sort are not tolerated but punished by law. Therefore the rites of infidels should not be tolerated.

But to the contrary is what Gregory says in the *Decretum* concerning the Jews [of Naples] [Gratian, D. 45,3]: "Let them have free permission to observe and celebrate all their festivals, just as they themselves till now and their forefathers for ages past have held them."

Reply: It must be said that human rule is derived from divine rule and ought to imitate it. But although God is almighty and supremely good, yet He permits some evils to happen in the universe which He could forbid, because if they were removed greater goods would be taken away or even worse evils would follow. Therefore those who preside in human government in the same way rightly tolerate some evils lest some goods be taken away or even some worse things be incurred. [Thomas goes on to argue that Jewish ceremonies are related to Christian ones as a kind of foreshadowing and so should be tolerated. He continues:]

But the rites of other infidels, which bear nothing true or useful, are not to be tolerated in the same way except perhaps to avoid some evil, to wit, scandal or a division that could arise from this or an obstacle to the salvation of those who would gradually be converted to the faith if they were tolerated. On this account the Church has sometimes tolerated the rites of even heretics and pagans when there was a great multitude of infidels.

Question 11 Heresy

Article 3. Should Heretics Be Tolerated?

1. It seems that heretics should be tolerated. For the Apostle says [2 Tim 2:24]: "The servant of God must be mild, correcting with modesty those who resist the truth so that God may grant them repentance and they will know the truth and escape from the snares of the devil." But if heretics are not tolerated but handed over to death, the opportunity of repenting will be taken from them. Therefore this seems to be contrary to the commandment of the Apostle.

2. Moreover, what is necessary to the Church is to be tolerated. But heresies are necessary in the Church. For the Apostle says [1 Cor. 11:19]: "It is necessary that there be heresies in order that those who are approved may be manifest among you." Therefore it seems that heretics should be tolerated.

3. Further, the Lord commanded his servants to let the tares grow until the harvest [Matt 13:30], that is, until the end of the world, as it is explained there. But by tares are meant heretics, according to the exposition of the saints. These heretics are to be tolerated.

But to the contrary is what the Apostle says: "After the first and second correction, avoid the heretical man. You know that one of this sort is perverted [Titus 3:10]."

Reply: It must be said that two things about heretics are to be considered: one on their part, the other on the part of the Church. On their part there is sin for which they deserve not only to be separated by excommunication from the Church but even by death to be excluded from the world. For it is much more serious to corrupt the faith through which the soul lives than to counterfeit money through which temporal life is supported. Hence, if counterfeiters of money or other malefactors are justly handed over at once to death by secular princes, so much more heretics, once they are convicted by heresy, cannot only be excommunicated but justly killed.

But on the part of the Church there is mercy for the conversion of the errant. And therefore she does not condemn at once but "after the first and second correction," as the Apostle says. Then, if he is still found pertinacious, the Church, no longer hoping for his conversion, provides for the welfare of others, separating him from the Church by sentence of excommunication; and she further leaves him to secular judgment to be eliminated from the world by death. For Jerome says, and the *Decretum* has it [Gratian, C. 24, 3, 16]: "Putrid flesh is to be cut off, and the scabby sheep is to be driven off from the fold, lest the whole house, mass, body, and flock burn, become corrupt, putrify, and die. Arius was one spark in Alexandria, but when he was not at once crushed, his flame devastated the whole world."

1. To the first objection, it must therefore be said that it is modesty to correct the first and second times. But if he refuses to return, he is then held as one perverted, as is clear in the text of the Apostle that was cited.

2. To the second objection, it must be said that the usefulness arising from heresy happens beyond the heretics' intention, that is, the steadiness of the faithful is proved, as the Apostle says, and we shake off sluggishness, more attentively searching the divine Scriptures, as Augustine says [*About Genesis, Against the Manichees, PL* 34, 173]. But their intention is to corrupt the faith, and this is the maximum harm. And therefore we must look at that which is per se from their intention, so that they are excluded; rather than at that which is beyond their intention, that they may be borne with.

3. To the third objection, it must be said as it is put in the *Decretum* [Gratian, C. 24, 3, 37]: "Excommunication is one thing, eradication is another." For someone is excommunicated for this purpose, as the Apostle says, that his spirit may become saved on the day of the Lord. If nonetheless heretics are totally eradicated by death, it is not contrary to the commandment of the Lord, which is to be understood of that case where the tares cannot be extirpated without extirpation of the wheat, as was said above about unbelievers in general.

Article 4. Shall those returning from heresy be received by the Church?

... 2. Further, the Lord commands Peter to forgive his sinning brother not only seven times but up to seventy times seven [Matt. 18:22]....

But to the contrary, the decretal *Ad Abolendam, Heretics,* c. 9, [Gregory IX, *Decretals* 5, 7, 9]: If any, after abjuring error, shall be found to have relapsed into the heresy they have abjured, they shall be left to secular judgment.

Reply:.... If returning heretics were always received so as to be preserved in their lives and other temporal goods, this could be to the prejudice of the salvation of others: both because if they relapsed again they would infect others, and because if they escaped without punishment, others would more securely lapse again into heresy....

1. To the first objection, it must therefore be said that in the judgment of God those who return are always received: for God is the searcher of hearts and He knows who are truly returning. But the Church cannot imitate this. She presumes that they did not truly return who after

they had been received again relapsed. Therefore she does not deny them a way of salvation but she does not safeguard them from the peril of death.

2. To the second objection, it must be said that the Lord is speaking to Peter about forgiving a sin committed against oneself, which must always be forgiven so that the returning brother is spared. But it is not to be understood as to a sin against a neighbor or against God, which, as Jerome says [*Glossa ordinaria* on Matthew 18:15], "is not in our discretion to forgive." In this matter a measure is set by law according to what fits the honor of God and the advantage of our neighbors.

3. To the third objection, it must be said that other infidels who have never received the faith, when they are converted to the faith, have not yet shown any sign of unsteadiness about the faith as do relapsed heretics. And so there is no similarity in the character of the two cases.

Question 12 Apostasy

Article 1. Does apostasy belong to infidelity?

[Among kinds of infidelity, Thomas distinguished between heresy, a sin committed by those "professing the faith of Christ" (q. 11, art. 1) and "apostasy," a sin committed by one "withdrawing from the faith" (q. 12, art. 1). As to the latter he concluded that in an absolute sense, apostasy is a species of infidelity; it is called "the apostasy of treachery."]

Article 2. Because of apostasy, does a prince lose rule over his subjects so that they are not bound to obey him?

1. It appears that on account of apostasy a prince does not lose rule over his subjects so that they are not bound to obey him, for Ambrose says, and the *Decretum* has it [Gratian, C. 11, q. 3, c. 94]: "The Emperor Julian, although he was an apostate, still had under him Christian soldiers, who, when he told them, 'Fight for the defense of the commonwealth,' obeyed him." Therefore, on account of the apostasy of a prince, subjects are not absolved from his rule. . . .

But to the contrary is what Gregory VII says [Gratian, C. 11, q. 6, c. 41: "We, holding to the statutes of our holy predecessors, by Apostolic authority absolve from their oath those who are bound by fidelity or oath to the excommunicated, and we forbid them in every way to observe fidelity until the latter make satisfaction." But as a decretal says, apostates such as heretics are excommunicated. Therefore, princes apostasizing from the faith are not to be obeyed.

Reply: . . . But it does not belong to the Church to punish infidelity in those who have never received the faith, according to the Apostle's dictum, "What is it to me to judge those who are outside?" [I Cor. 5:12]. But she can punish by a sentence the infidelity of those who have received the faith. And they are conveniently punished by providing that they cannot rule over believing subjects, for this could tend to great corruption of the faith: as has been said [Prov. 6:14], "An apostate man plots evil with his heart and sows discord," intending to separate men from the faith. And so as soon as anyone is declared by a sentence to be excommunicate on account

of apostasy from the faith, his subjects are *ipso facto* absolved from his rule
and the oath of fidelity by which they were bound to him....

3.　To the third objection, it must be said that apostasy from the faith
totally separates a man from God, as has been said; which does not happen
in any other sin.

———

Thomas scarcely emerges as a liberal, but on one important point his
commitment to reason and the primacy of reason in moral conduct leads to
what was liberal in comparison to the dominant opinion of the day. Alexander
of Hales—a teacher at Paris who might justly be regarded as the first English
jurisprudent—taught that an erring conscience did not oblige. An erring
conscience was contrary to the law of God; it could not be right to follow it.
Alexander, *"De conscientia,"* in Odon Lottin, *Psychologie et morale aux XIIe et
XIIIe siecles* (1948) 2:356–57. Thomas, as will be seen, teaches to the contrary
that a man must follow his conscience.

Taken seriously this doctrine carried the seed of religious liberty. Thomas
took away nearly all that he had established by arguing in the next article,
below, that an erring conscience, although it must be followed, did not always
excuse from sin: the error could be voluntary or negligent and therefore sinful.
He nonetheless left open the possibility that the error, whatever it was, could
be without fault. His illustrations suggest that he thinks a mistake of fact will
excuse, a mistake of law will not.

But nothing in his analysis confines an excusable mistake to a mistake of
fact. A mistake of law, even a mistake of faith, would seem in some cases to be
as involuntary as the hypothetical case he supposes of a man mistaking another
woman for his wife. If mistake can be involuntary, and if error is excusable, and
if a man must follow his conscience, however mistaken, with what justice can
he be punished if he is conscientiously a heretic or apostate?

Thomas did not engage in that kind of reasoning. But contemporaries saw
where his thought led. The Franciscan Matthaeus of Aquasparta objected that
if Thomas were right, "the heretics would act correctly in doing what they
think they ought to do." Joseph Lecler, *Toleration and the Reformation* 1,99–
100 English trans. (1960). Lecler, a historian of the idea of tolerance, concludes
that Thomas's position was of real importance for the future. Id. 1, 99.

Aquinas, *Summa Theologiae* 1–2
Question 19 The Goodness and the Malice of the
Interior Act of the Will

Article 5. Whether Erring Reason is Binding

1.　It appears that will differing from erring reason is not bad. For, as
has been said, reason is the rule of the human will inasmuch as reason is
derived from the eternal law. But erring reason is not derived from the
eternal law. Therefore, erring reason is not the rule of a human will;
therefore, the will is not bad if it differs from erring reason.

2.　Further, according to Augustine [Sermon 62, c. 8, *PL* 38, 421] the
commandment of an inferior power does not bind if it is contrary to the

commandment of a superior power, as if the proconsul ordered something which the emperor prohibits. But erring reason sometimes proposes something that is against the commandment of a superior, namely God, Whose power is supreme. Therefore, the dictate of erring reason does not bind; therefore, the will is not bad if it differs from erring reason.

3. Further, every bad will is reduced to some species of malice. But the will differing from erring reason cannot be reduced to some species of malice—for example, if erring reason errs in this, that it dictates that one is to commit fornication, the will of him who did not will to fornicate could not be reduced to any malice. Therefore, will differing from erring reason is not bad.

But, to the contrary, as was said in the First Part, conscience is nothing else but the application of knowledge to some action. But knowledge is in the reason. Therefore, will differing from erring reason is against conscience. But also the will is bad; for it is said by the Apostle in Romans [14:3], "All which is not from faith is sin," that is, all that is against conscience. Therefore, will differing from erring reason is bad.

Reply: It must be said that since conscience is in a certain way the dictate of reason—for, as has been said, it is a certain application of knowledge to action—it is the same thing to ask, "Whether will differing from erring reason is bad" as to ask, "Whether erring conscience binds."

About this some [*e.g.*, Alexander of Hales] have distinguished three kinds of acts—some are generically good, some are indifferent, some are generically bad. They say, therefore, that if reason or conscience dictates something to be done that is generically good, there is no error there; similarly, if it dictates something not to be done that is generically bad, by the same reason the good is commanded and the bad prohibited. But if reason or conscience dictates to someone that he is bound to do from command those things that are in themselves bad, or that those things that are in themselves good are prohibited, it will be an erring reason or conscience. Similarly, if reason or conscience dictates to someone that what is in itself indifferent (for instance, to pick up a stalk from the earth) is prohibited or commanded, it will be an erring reason or conscience. They say, therefore, that reason or conscience erring about indifferent things, whether commanding or prohibiting, is binding, so that will differing from such erring reason will be bad and a sin. But erring reason or conscience commanding those things that are not themselves bad or prohibiting those that are not themselves good and necessary to salvation does not bind; hence, in such matters the will differing from erring reason or conscience is not bad.

But this is said irrationally, for in indifferent things the will differing from erring reason or conscience is bad in some way because of the object on which the goodness or badness of the will depends—not because of the object according to its own nature but according to what by accident is apprehended by the reason as good to be done or bad to be avoided. And because the object of the will is that which is proposed by the reason, as has been said, in that something is proposed by the reason as bad, the will, as long as it is borne toward that, takes on the character of the bad.

This happens not only in indifferent things but even in those good or bad in themselves. For not only that which is indifferent can accidentally take on the character of good or bad, but that which is good can take on the character of bad, or that which is bad can take on the character of good because of the apprehension of the reason.

For example, to abstain from fornication is a certain good, yet the will is not borne to this good except as it is proposed by reason. If, therefore, it is proposed as bad by erring reason the will is borne toward this under the character of bad. Hence, the will will be bad because it wills the bad, not indeed what is bad in itself, but what is accidentally bad because of the apprehension of the reason.

Similarly, to believe in Christ is good in itself and necessary for salvation, but the will is not borne toward this except according to what is proposed by reason. Hence, if it is proposed by reason as bad, the will will be borne to this as bad, not because it is bad in itself, but because it is accidentally bad from the apprehension of reason. That is why the Philosopher [Aristotle] says in the *Ethics* [7, 1 and 2] that strictly speaking one is lacking in self-control who does not follow right reason, but accidentally he is lacking in self-control who does not follow false reason.

Hence it must be said absolutely that every will differing from reason, whether right or erring, is always bad.

1. To the first objection, it must be said that the judgment of erring reason, although it is not derived from God, yet is proposed by erring reason as true. Consequently it is derived from God, from Whom is every truth.

2. To the second objection, it must be said that the statement of Augustine has place when it is recognized that an inferior power is commanding something against the commandment of a superior power. But if someone should believe that the commandment of the proconsul was the commandment of the emperor, he would flout the commandment of the emperor in flouting the commandment of the proconsul. Similarly, if any man should recognize that human reason is dictating something against the commandment of God, he would not be obliged to follow reason; but then reason would not be totally erring. But when erring reason proposes something as the commandment of God, then it is the same thing to flout the dictate of reason and the commandment of God.

To the third objection it must be said that when reason apprehends something as bad it always apprehends it under some character of badness, for example, because it is contrary to a divine commandment or because it is a scandal or something of this kind; and then such bad will is reduced to such a species of malice.

Article 6. Is Will Agreeing with Erring Reason Good?

1. It seems that will agreeing with erring reason is good. For, just as will disagreeing with reason tends toward that which the reason judges bad, so will agreeing with reason tends toward that which reason judges

good. But will disagreeing with even an erring reason is bad. Therefore the will agreeing with even an erring reason is good.

2.   Further, will agreeing with a commandment of God and the eternal law is always good. But the eternal law and the commandment of God is proposed to us by the apprehension of even an erring reason. Therefore the will agreeing with even erring reason is good.

3.   Further, the will disagreeing with erring reason is bad. If, therefore, will agreeing with erring reason is also bad, it seems that every will of one who has an erring reason is bad, and so such a man will be entangled and will sin from necessity—which is awkward. Therefore the will agreeing with erring reason is good.

But, to the contrary, the will of the killers of the apostles was bad, but yet it agreed with their erring reason, according to John [16:7]: "The hour comes when everyone who kills you will think he is offering service to God." Therefore the will agreeing with erring reason can be bad.

Reply: It must be said that just as the previous question was the same as the question. "Whether an erroneous conscience obliges," so this question is the same as "Whether an erroneous conscience excuses."

But this question depends on what was said above [q. 6, Art. 81] about ignorance. It was said above that ignorance sometimes causes something involuntary but sometimes does not. And because moral good and evil consist in an act insofar as it is voluntary, as is evident from what has gone before, it is clear that that ignorance which causes something involuntary takes away the character of moral good and evil, but not that ignorance which does not cause something involuntary. I speak of ignorance directly willed as that on which the act of the will bears, and indirectly, when because of negligence someone does not wish to know what he is bound to know, as said above.

If, therefore, reason or conscience errs by an error that is voluntary either directly or indirectly because of negligence, because it is in error about that which one is bound to know, then such an error of reason or conscience does not excuse the will agreeing with the reason of conscience erring in such a way. But if the error which causes the involuntary comes from ignorance of some circumstance apart from any negligence, then such error of reason or conscience excuses so that the will agreeing with the erring reason is not bad—for example, if the erring reason dictates that a man is bound to approach another's wife, the will agreeing with this reason is bad in that this error arises from ignorance of the law of God, which he is bound to know; but if reason errs in this, that one believes some woman is his wife and when she seeks the marital debt he wishes to know her, his will is excused so that it was not bad because this error arises from ignorance of a circumstance that excuses and causes the involuntary.

1.   To the first objection, it must be said therefore as Dionysius says [PG 3, 729], "Good is caused from the wholeness but evil from any particular defect," and, therefore, that to which the will is borne should be called bad, it suffices either that it be in its nature bad or that it be

apprehended as bad; but that to be good it is required that it be good in both ways.

2. To the second objection, it must be said that the eternal law cannot err, but human reason can err; and therefore will agreeing with human reason is not always right and is not always agreeing with the eternal law.

3. To the third objection, it must be said that just as in logic when one thing is inappropriately given, others necessarily follow, so in morals when one inappropriate thing is posited, others necessarily follow. Suppose that someone seeks empty glory, whether he does what he is bound to do because of the empty glory or fails to do it, he will always sin. Yet he is not entangled because he can always set aside his bad intention. Similarly, supposing there is an error of reason or conscience which proceeds from a nonexcusable ignorance, it is necessary that evil always follow in the will. Yet the man is not entangled because he can withdraw from his error since his ignorance is conquerable and voluntary.

2. Joan of Arc at the Stake

The system for punishing heretics, enacted into canon law and endorsed by Thomas Aquinas and the rest of the theologians, assumed and assured maximum cooperation between the ecclesiastical courts, which tried the suspected heretic, and the secular authorities, which put him or her to death if he or she were found to have relapsed. Such cooperation was a thin legal fiction protecting the position taken at the Fourth Lateran Council that clerics were forbidden to participate in blood judgments [Chapter Three, section 3]. Sometimes, as in the case of Joan of Arc, the fiction was so thin when the death penalty was imposed by the prince that it was abandoned altogether; the only judgment was the Church's. But even where the form was maintained, ecclesiastics permitted themselves to take this Pilate-like posture at the cost of enabling the secular authorities to manipulate the canonical system to produce verdicts desired by the secular power. The trial of Joan of Arc is a spectacular example of such manipulation.

Joan was born in Domrémy, Lorraine, in 1412. At the age of thirteen she heard voices telling her it was her mission to save France. At seventeen, a peasant girl, she acted on her voices, left home and presented herself at the French court. King Charles VII, harried by the English who claimed a large part of his domain, agreed to see her, had her examined by theologians, and was convinced enough to give her a try. Four months after leaving home Joan was put at the head of a French army and sent to relieve besieged Orléans. She raised the siege, then led the troops to a second spectacular victory that opened the way to Reims and Charles's coronation. The following year, 1430, Joan was taken prisoner by the Burgundians, who for a price delivered her to their English allies.

The English could scarcely have been expected to believe that it was God's will that they be driven from France and that Joan was His agent. In all good faith, they thought she must be aided by diabolical powers. They were certain that an ecclesiastical court would penetrate her sophistries and uncover her true character. They were aware that not only she but her patron Charles VII would be disgraced by a trial in which she was shown not to be a true Christian.

Henry VI of England directed Pierre Cauchon, bishop of Beauvais, the diocese where Joan had been taken captive, to proceed against her as a heretic. Such royal directives to begin an inquisitional process were standard procedure in both England and France; *see* P. Doncoeur and Y. Lanhers, *La Réhabilitation de Jeanne La Pucelle. L'enquête ordonnée par Charles VII* 9 (1956).

The trial began on February 21, 1431. At a decisive moment in the process, on May 19, 1434, a group of consultants to the court from the faculty of theology of the University of Paris subscribed to the statement that they found her "a liar, inspired by the devil, erring in the Faith, a sorcerer, an idolator, a blasphemer of God and the saints, a schismatic, a heretic, and an apostate"; *id.* 15. On May 24 she was found guilty of heresy. She abjured all her errors and, as was common where the heretic's sin was great, was not released but committed to prison. Five days later she was found to have relapsed, for the reason that appears in the testimony below. She was burned the next day.

Moving with unaccountable sluggishness, Charles VII ordered a royal inquiry eighteen years later into the validity of the trial of the girl to whom he owed his crown. The close relation of the secular powers with the Church is again excellently illustrated by this procedure, which had no warrant in canon law. The king's extralegal investigations, whose results were communicated to the pope, resulted in a papal commission being set up by Calixtus III. After further inquiries, this commission in 1456 quashed the original verdict. In May 1920, in the aftermath of the French victory in World War I, Joan was canonized.

The record of the royal inquiry gives a remarkable picture of the collaboration of churchmen with their rulers and a picture of the kind of persons whose cooperation was needed to produce the conviction. Cauchon, the presiding bishop, was not quite sixty, an accomplished diplomat, whose patron in promotion to office had been the duke of Burgundy and whose services had been used before by Henry VI of England; C. Laplatte, "Cauchon," *Dictionnaire d'histoire et de géographie ecclésiastiques* (1953) 12:4–6. He was a political bishop, who knew who his masters were. Defenders still assert that he was no worse than others of his time *id*. The defense is an indictment of the institutional arrangements that put such men in the dress of pastors. It is hard to read the testimony that follows without applauding Paul Claudel's pun on his name in the script for Poulenc's oratorio where "Cochon, Cochon, Cochon" mocks the murderous judge. It is certainly "Peter Pig" who plays a game of Gotcha with Joan and on the flimsiest of pretexts finds that she has relapsed. The legal fiction the bishop so cynically exploits is brushed aside by Joan who exclaims, "It is by you I die." Peter Pig advises her at this moment to be patient.

Cauchon himself had once been the rector of the University of Paris, and the theology faculty of the University was "the soul of the trial"; *id.* 6. Beaupère is an example. The willingness of such learned men to put their skills at the service of the prosecution is an instance of that misplaced *machismo* all too frequently found in academics dabbling in practical affairs. In Beaupère's case it is accompanied by a decided whiff of misogyny; and no one can doubt that the fact that Joan was an extraordinary woman was a goad to some of those who condemned her.

Two members of religious orders, Ladvenu and Ysambart, recall in their testimony the kindnesses they did for Joan and celebrate her heroism. They are having it both ways. They signed the declaration that she was a lying, devil-inspired heretic. Ysambart was one of those who found she had relapsed. Doncoeur and Lanhers 15.

Lohier, the distinguished canon lawyer whose behavior is described by Manchon, is another type. He pointed out all that was illegal about the trial with a fine eye for procedural irregularities. He then left town. He did not want to die. Few do. Manchon himself is the most interesting witness of all—Mr. Average Man, the honest notary, who tries to keep the record he makes free from error, who genuinely regrets Joan's death, but whose willingness to work at the trial makes it possible for the trial to go on. "If I don't do it then someone else will," he surely thought. The gesture he makes at the end, using some of his fee to buy a missal to pray for Joan, reflects a wonderful mixture of piety and guilt.

Peter Pigs, chauvinists, lawyers who went somewhere else like Lohier, pious priests whom fear could bend, honest men like Manchon—these were the kind of men that made the system work by which governmental force was used to maintain religion and, as had been long before predicted, ended by killing saints.

Inquiry Before a Royal Commission, March 4 and 5, 1450

1. Brother Ysambart de la Pierre of the Augustinians of the convent of Rouen, a priest, being sworn and examined the fifth day of March, A.D. 1449, declares:

Once, in my presence and that of may others, Joan, exhorted and solicited to submit to the Church, replied that she willingly would submit to the Roman Pontiff and asked that she be taken to him, but that in no way would she submit to those present who were conducting her trial, be-cause—as she often said—they were her enemies. I counseled her to submit to the Council of Basel then in session. She asked what a General Council was. I replied that it was a universal assembly of the whole Church and of Christianity itself, and that in this Council there were many men on her side as well as on the side of the English. When she heard that, she declared, "Oh, are there people there on our side?" I said, "Yes." She at once replied that she indeed wanted to submit to that Council. But the Bishop of Beauvais, full of fury and contempt, shouted at me, "In the devil's name, shut up!" And he immediately ordered the notary not to record the submission which she had made to the General Council. Because of this and many other things, I suffered grave threats from the English and their officials that unless I was silent in the future, I would be tied and tossed in the Seine. . . .

I went in person to Monseigneur the bishop of Avranches, a very old and wise man, who like others had been requested to give his opinion on this case. He asked me what Saint Thomas taught as to the submission that ought to be made to the Church. I gave him in writing my view, to wit, that in matters of doubt bearing on the faith, recourse is always to be had to the Supreme Pontiff or a General Council. And the good bishop was of the same opinion. And the other bishop appeared to be unhappy with this reply. This opinion was not transcribed in the record, which seems to have been composed maliciously.

After her confession and partaking of the Eucharist, the judgment against her was promulgated, and she was declared a heretic and excommunicate. I saw well and perceived very clearly—because I was always near her during the whole business and at her end—that she was in no way condemned by the secular judge to death or to burning, even though the secular judge was present and seated on the platform or scaffolding where she was preached to and finally abandoned to secular judgment. But without sentence or judgment she was delivered to the executioner and to burning. They said to the executioner without further sentence, "Do your duty...."

The executioner came to me and my associate, Brother Martin Ladvenu, immediately after the burning, impelled by a wonderful and terrible penitence. It was as if he despaired of receiving pardon from God after what he had done to her, who, as he said, was such a holy woman. He also affirmed that although he had several times put the wood and coals upon her entrails and heart, he could in no way consume her heart or reduce it to cinders; and at this he was amazed, as if it were an evident miracle.

2. The venerable and religious man, Brother Jean Toutmouille of the Order of Preachers, distinguished professor of sacred theology, of the convent of St. Jacques of Rouen belonging to the said order, aged forty-two or thereabouts, having been sworn and examined on the fifth day of March, declares:

On that day on which Joan was abandoned to secular judgment and delivered to the fire, I was in the morning in the jail with Brother Martin Ladvenu, who was sent to her by the bishop of Beauvais to announce her approaching death to her, to lead her to true patience, and to hear her confession. All these things Martin very carefully and charitably did. And he told Joan that it was necessary because of her relapse that she die that day by fire and burning and so her judges had ordained. When she heard the terrible death that awaited her, she began to cry out very sorrowfully, loudly, and tearfully, with every gesture of intense pain, "Alas, how cruelly they treat me. My body, which is whole and uncorrupted, will be burned by fire. I would choose rather, if it could be done, to have my head cut off seven times than be burnt by fire."

She wept and said, "If I had been in the custody of the Church, to whom I had submitted, and been guarded by men of the Church and not by armed men and enemies, it would never have happened to me. And as to this as from so many injuries I appeal to God the Supreme Judge." She then complained in a remarkable way about the harassment and violence which had been offered her or attempted against her by her guards and others brought into her from the time of her abjuration.

Afterwards the bishop of Beauvais, the judge, arrived and she at once said to him, "Bishop, I die by you." He replied, "Joan, you will not have patience. You are in this case because you did not keep what you promised and you relapsed." She replied, "Alas, if you had put me in your jail with fit church guards, this would not have happened to me. That is why I appeal from you to God."

3. The religious and respectable man, Brother Martin Ladvenu of the Order of Preachers and of the said convent of St. Jacques in Rouen, the special confessor and director of Joan at the end of her life, was questioned on the same day, on certain points as above, and declares:

Joan revealed to me that in that prison, after her abjuration, she was very violently attacked with violence and seduction by a certain English lord; and she said publicly that this was the reason why she was moved to resume male dress. Hence near the end of her life Joan said to the bishop, "Look, by you I am dying. If you had put me in Church jails and I had been kept by men of the Church and not by my English enemies, it would not have happened to me this way."

4. A venerable and discreet man, Monsieur Guillaume Manchon, a priest fifty years old or thereabouts, canon of the collegial church of Notre Dame d'Andeley, curé of the parish church St. Nicholas of Rouen, notary of the archiepiscopal court of Rouen, sworn and examined March 4, 1449, deposes:

I was a notary at the trial of Joan from the beginning to the end, and with me was Monsieur Guillaume Colles, called Boscguillaume.

In my opinion, on the part of those who had charge of conducting and managing the trial—to wit, Monseigneur of Beauvais and the masters sent from Paris to investigate the cases, and the English too, at whose instigation the trial was had—the proceeding was rather with hatred and contempt for the cause of the king of France than for anything she had done. My reasons follow.

First, one Nicolas Loyseleur, who was of the household of Monseigneur of Beauvais and was totally on the side of the English (for, another time, when the king was before Chartres, he went to get the king of England to raise the siege) pretended that he was from the land of the Maid and by this means found a way of having access, speech and familiarity with her, telling her news of the land that pleased her; and he asked to be her confessor; and what she told him in secret he found a way of getting to the ears of the notaries. Indeed at the beginning of the trial I and Boscguillaume, with witnesses, were secretly placed in an adjoining room where there was a hole through which we listened, so that we could report what she said or confessed to Loyseleur. And it seems to me that what the Maid said or related familiarly to Loyseleur, he reported to the notaries, and from these things a memorandum was made up for interrogatories at the trial, so a way could be found of catching her.

Again, after the trial had begun, Master Jean Lohier, a grave Norman cleric, came to the city of Rouen, and it was communicated to him what the bishop of Beauvais had written hereon and Lohier asked a delay of two or three days to look at it. To this it was replied that he give his opinion at the next session, and he was forced to do so. And Master Jean Lohier, having looked at the trial, said that it was worth nothing, for several reasons. First, it did not have the form of an ordinary trial. Then, it was being carried on in an enclosed and shut-up place where those in attendance did not have plain and pure freedom to speak their pure and plain will. Then, it treated in this way the honor of the king of France, on whose side she was, without calling him or anyone who was on that side. Then, an indictment had not been framed, nor any charges, and so this woman, who was a simple girl, did not have any guide to reply to these numerous masters and doctors on the great matters, especially those which, as she said, touched upon revelations. For these reasons it seemed to him that the trial was worthless.

At this Monseigneur of Beauvais was indignant at Lohier, and although Monseigneur of Beauvais told him that he might remain to see the trial, Lohier replied that he would not stay longer. And Monseigneur of Beauvais, who was staying at the house where Master Jean Bidault now lives near St. Nicholas the Painter, left at once and went to the masters—to wit, Master Jean Beaupère, Jacques de Touraine, Nicolas Midi, Pierre Morice, Thomas de Courcelles, and Loyseleur—and said to them, "Look at Lohier who wants us to frame beautiful interrogatories for our trial. He discredits everything and says it's worth nothing. To believe him we would have to begin everything again, and all we have done would be worth nothing." After reciting the reasons why Lohier wanted to discredit it, Monseigneur of Beauvais exclaimed, "I see on what foot he limps. By Saint John we will do nothing about it. We will continue our trial as we have begun."

And this was a Saturday afternoon in Lent; and the next morning I spoke to Lohier at Notre Dame and asked him what he thought of the trial and of Joan. He answered me, "You see how they are proceeding. They will catch her in words, if they can—as in assertions where she says, 'I know for certain as regards the apparitions.' If she said, 'It seems to me' instead of 'I am certain,' it is my opinion that no one could condemn her. They seem to me to proceed more out of hatred than otherwise. And for that reason I'll no longer stay here. I do not want to be in it." And indeed the rest of his days he stayed in Rome, where he died the dean of the Rota.

At the beginning of the trial, for five or six days I put in writing the answers and excuses of the Maid; and sometimes the judges, speaking in Latin, wanted to force me to change the sense of her words and to say what I had not heard. By command of Monseigneur of Beauvais, two men sat in a window near the judges with a curtain drawn so that they could not be seen. These men wrote and reported what there was in the charges against Joan, leaving out her excuses. And I think they were Loyseleur and the cleric Beaupère, who were not notaries. After the session was over, in the afternoon, when I compared what had been written, these two had reported differently and had not put in any excuses; at which Monseigneur of Beauvais got very angry at me. And in those parts of the record where "Note" is written, there was a controversy, and new interrogations had to be made about it; and it was found that what I had written was true.

In writing the record I was asked several times by Monseigneur of Beauvais and these masters to write what they imagined and contrary to the sense of the Maid. And several times where there were things that did not please them they would say, "Don't write it down. It doesn't serve the trial." Nonetheless I never wrote anything except according to my understanding and conscience.

I saw Joan led to the scaffold. There were 700 or 800 soldiers around her carrying swords; and there was no man so bold to speak to her to advise her, except Brother Martin Ladvenu and Monsieur Jean Massieu. Patiently she heard the sermon straight through. Afterwards she made thanksgiving and prayed and lamented most notably and devoutly, so that the judge-prelates and everyone else in attendance, hearing it, were moved to great weeping. And I never wept so much for anything that happened to me. And one month later I could not put myself at peace, and with part of the money I had from the trial I bought a small missal which I still have so that I could pray for her. As for her final penitence, I never saw greater signs of a Christian.

5. Monsieur Jean Massieu, priest, *curé* of one of the sections of the parish church of St. Candre of Rouen, formerly dean of the clergy of Rouen, fifty years old or thereabouts, sworn and examined the fifth day of March, declares:

I was present at the trial of Joan every time she was present before judges and clerics; and because of my office I was appointed clerk to Monsieur Jean Benedicite, the Promoter in the case, to cite Joan and all the others who were summoned in this case. And it seems to me from what I saw that the proceedings were taken out of hatred and with favoritism, in order to disparage the honor of the king of France whom she served, and for vengeance, in order to make her die; and not according to reason and the honor of God and the Catholic faith. . . .

I mean also by this that when I was leading her back to prison from being before the judges on the fourth or fifth day, a priest named Monsieur Eustace Turquetil asked me, "What do you think of her answers? Will she burn? What will happen?" To which I replied, "Up to now I have only seen goodness and honor in her, but as to the end I don't know what it will be, God knows!" The priest reported my reply to the king's people and it was said that I was not friendly to the king. And on this occasion I was sent for in the afternoon by Monseigneur of Beauvais, the judge, and he spoke to me of these things and told me to take care not to be misunderstood or they would make me drink one more time than I should. And I think that if it had not been for Notary Manchon, who excused me, I would never have escaped. . . .

That day, after dinner, in the presence of the counselors of the Church, she took off her men's clothes and put on women's dress as she had been directed. That was Thursday or Friday after Pentecost; and the men's clothes were put in a bag in the same room where she was held prisoner. She stayed guarded there by five Englishmen, three of whom stayed during the night in the room and two outside, at the door of the room. I know for certain that at night she slept chained by the legs with two pairs of iron chains and tightly tied by a chain crossing the feet of her bed, held to a great piece of wood, five or six feet long, that locked with a key. And when Sunday morning came, the day of the Trinity, and she had to rise, as she reported and said to me, she asked her English guards, "Unchain me so I may get up." Then one of the Englishmen took away from her the women's garments she had on her, and they emptied the bag that held the men's clothes; and they threw the clothes at her saying, "Get up." And they threw the women's garments in the bag. At this, she reported, they told her to dress in the men's clothes which they had given her, and she replied, "Sirs, you know it is forbidden me. Without fail I will not take it again." And still they refused to give her the other, so the contention lasted until noon. And finally, out of bodily necessity, she was forced to go outside and to wear the men's clothes. When she returned, they refused to give her the other, whatever prayer or request she made.

This she told me the following Tuesday after dinner. On this day the Promoter had taken me with him to the prison. And the Promoter left to go with Monseigneur of Warwick; and I stayed with her. Immediately I asked her why she had resumed the men's clothing; and she declared what I just said....

When she was released by the Church, I was still with her; and with great devotion she asked to have a cross. Hearing this, one of the English who was there made a little one of wood with the ends of a stick, which he gave her; and devoutly she received it and kissed it, making piteous lamentations and acknowledgements to God our Redeemer who had suffered on the cross for our redemption, of which cross she had the sign and image. And she put the cross in her breast, between her flesh and her clothes. And besides, she humbly asked me to have the cross brought from the church so that she could constantly see it up to death. And I had the cleric from the parish of St. Sauveur bring it. When it was brought, she embraced it very lightly for a long time, and she held it until she was tied to the stake.

While she was making these devotions and piteous lamentations, I was much hurried by Englishmen, even by some of their leaders, to leave her in their hands, so they could make her die sooner. They said to me who as best I could was comforting her on the scaffold, "What, priest, will you make us dine here?" And immediately, without any form or indication of judgment, they sent her to the fire, saying to the master of the business, "Do your duty." And so she was led out and tied; and she continued her praises and devout lamentations toward God and his saints. With her last words, as she passed, she loudly cried, "Jesus."

6. The venerable and careful man, Master Jean Beaupère, master of theology, canon of Rouen, seventy years old or thereabouts, declares:

With regard to the apparitions mentioned in the trial of Joan, I was and still am very much of the opinion that the apparitions were rather from natural causes and human invention than from a supernatural cause; but I always refer to the trial.

Before she was taken to St. Ouen to be preached to in the morning, I by myself with permission entered into Joan's prison and warned Joan that she would soon be led to the scaffold to be preached to; and I said to her that if she was a good Christian, she would say on the scaffold that she put all her deeds and sayings in the ordering of our Holy Mother Church and especially of the ecclesiastical judges. She answered that she would do so.

And so she did on the scaffold, on being asked by Master Nicholas Midi. This being observed and considered this time, she was sent back after her abjuration, although some of the Englishmen accused the Bishop of Beauvais and the men from Paris of favoring Joan's errors.

After this abjuration and after she had put on her women's dress which she had received in the prison, it was reported to the judges the next Friday or Saturday that Joan had repented of having put aside men's clothing and had taken up women's clothing. For that reason, Monseigneur of Beauvais, the judge, sent me and Master Nicholas Midi to the castle in the hope of speaking to Joan and inducing and admonishing her to persevere and take care not to relapse. But we could not find the one who had the key of the prison; and while we were waiting for the prison guard, several Englishmen in the courtyard of the castle spoke threatening words, as Midi told me—to wit, any one who would throw us both in the river would be well employed. Because of these words we returned; and on the castle bridge, Midi, as he told me, heard similar words, or something like them, pronounced by other Englishmen; at which we were frightened and came away without speaking to Joan.

In my opinion, if Joan had had wise and frank directors, she would have spoken many words useful for her justification and not spoken several which made for her condemnation.

As to Joan's innocence, she was very subtle, with the subtlety that belongs to a woman, as it seems to me. And I did not know from any words of hers that she had been corrupted in her body.

In regard to her final penitence, I do not know what to say, for the Monday after the abjuration I left Rouen to go to Basle on behalf of the University of Paris, and she was condemned the following Tuesday, and I had no news of her condemnation until I heard it spoken of at Lisle in Flanders.

3.   THE FOUR THOMASES: WOLSEY, CROMWELL, CRANMER AND MORE

Thomas More might have written this. The four, whose baptismal name testifies to the continued popularity in England of the martyred defender of the freedom of the Church, were the four principal actors as constitutional change occurred in the position of the Church in England. Their master was the king himself, Henry VIII, a figure with a will, an ego, and a theological temper of his own; *see* J.J. Scarisbrick, *Henry VIII* (1968); but without the four Thomases the scenario of change would not have been the same.

Thomas Wolsey (1475–1530) was "the great cardinal," who in person unified ecclesiastical interests and the power of the state, enjoying the special privileges of a papal legate as well as the almost unlimited confidence of young Henry VIII, and ruling as chief minister from 1515 until his abrupt fall in October 1529. Wolsey's pursuit of personal profit, his failure to reform recognized abuses in the Church, his cynical and unrealistic attempt to have Henry's marriage to Catherine of Aragon annulled set the stage on which the constitutional change occurred.

When Wolsey was removed from office for his failure to get the annulment, he was at once indicted for having violated the Statute of Praemunire, a fourteenth-century enactment making it a "contempt," with unspecified but awful penalties, to take "out of the realm" a case that should have been tried in the king's court or suing "in any other court, to defeat or impeach the judgments given in the King's Court"; 27 Edw. III, Stat. 1, c.1 [2 Pickering Stat. 72] (1353). The statute was a typical medieval check on papal claims and had been successfully enforced against papal appointees to benefices contested by Englishmen; Robert E. Rodes, Jr., *Lay Authority and Reformation in the English Church* 28, 47, 63 (1982). Its application to Wolsey was another matter. He had exercised his legatine powers with the enthusiastic support of the king; the first hearings of the great annulment case had been before him as co-legate. Nonetheless he pleaded guilty and forfeited all his property; G.R. Elton, *Reform and Reformation* 112 (1977). His case is instructive: the king already had in medieval legislation a supple tool for controlling his clergy's relations with Rome.

The recognized jurisdiction of the clergy was very wide. Marriages and their annulment; wills and their probate; tithes, ecclesiastical dues (e.g., fees for presiding at funerals, known as "mortuaries"), and their collection; and a variety of moral offenses—sexual misbehavior, breach of any promise, usury, defamation—all fell within the jurisdiction of ecclesiastical courts; Rodes 12–21. Clerical immunity and sanctuary had provided oases of mercy and a constant irritant to anyone seriously interested in law enforcement; *id.*, 29–33, 70–71. The Parliament that met in 1529 was to be "the Reformation Parliament" and was to stay in session until 1536. Its concerns were not merely anticlerical. For example, it enacted a statute making a homosexual act punishable by death, the Buggery Act, 25 Hen. VIII, c. 6 [4 Pick. Stat. 267] (1533). But in this first session it showed its sensitivity to old grievances about the clergy. It limited benefices and made it a crime to seek a dispensation to hold several, 21 Hen. VIII, c. 3 [4 Pick. Stat. 180] (1529). It limited what could be charged for probate (c. 5). It limited what could be charged as mortuaries (c. 6). These laws trenched on the spiritual jurisdiction and arguably invaded it. They would not have been enacted if reform had not been in the air, but they were not radical. When Henry VIII encouraged such legislation, he was already in the anticlerical camp. Scarisbrick 245.

Thomas More (1477–1535) succeeded Wolsey as chancellor, the first layman ever to hold the office. Ironically, as it was to seem, the very appointment of a layman was a signal by Henry VIII of the king's new turn of mind. More was fifty-two, a London lawyer's son, who had gone from a successful legal practice to service as a royal counselor in 1518. In his *Utopia*, published before he held high office, he had imagined a Nowhere where no one was molested for his religious opinion, although disbelievers in God or a future life were barred from office. In the 1520s he had become a polemicist against the new heretics, and as chancellor he encouraged enforcement of the statute against heresy. The king knew from the start that More did not believe in his case for an annulment and for a time tolerated his noncooperation here while other agents continued to press in Rome.

The matter of the marriage, an accident on which so much was to turn, was constitutionally within the jurisdiction of the Church; and at the apex of that jurisdiction was the Pope, who had awarded Henry for his anti-Lutheran writing the title of "Defender of the Faith." Exasperated by delay, seeing clearly that whatever the legal merits of his case (they were little) the pope would never decide in his favor because the pope was politically under the thumb of the Emperor Charles, Henry soured on his propapal attitude and listened to the counsels of those who proposed a new and daring course. The chief counselors were Thomas Cromwell (1485–1540) and Thomas Cranmer (1489–1556).

Cromwell, who had gained his administrative experience serving Wolsey, was a layman who turned out to believe in such reforms as the Bible in English. He had convictions, energy, organizing ability, and legal skill. By 1530 he was a member of the royal Council; Elton 137, 168–133. Thomas Cranmer was an academic and cleric from Cambridge who in the same year was enlisted to win academic support for Henry's annulment. As yet there was no break with Rome. But early in 1531 fresh charges of praemunire were brought against selected English bishops for having recognized Wolsey as legate. Yielding to this legal blackmail, the Convocation of southern bishops voted 100,000 pounds to the king. In the same year, the payment of an annual tribute known as annates to the pope was in effect suspended; the pope was put on notice not only of the king's displeasure but of the king's ability to hurt him; 23 Hen. VIII c. 20 (1531).

In May 1532, the Convocation asked the king to protect the liberties of the Church: Magna Carta was invoked. Henry, steeled by his more radical counselors, replied by demanding subservience, and the cowed clerics surrendered, the Convocation passing a declaration entitled "The Submission of the Clergy," granting the king power to approve or disapprove their canons; Elton 154–155. This concession can be interpreted as small, as Rodes 84–85, does, an acknowledgement that canons could not be the law of the land without the royal assent; or major, as Elton does, an abandonment of the pope as legislator for the Church. Thomas More resigned the day after it was passed; it may reasonably be inferred that he read the concession as fatal and foresaw the course the king would now follow. Parliament passed a statute whose preamble referred to England as an empire "governed by one supreme head and king," beneath whom there was a "spirituality [sic] and temporalty [sic]"; 24 Hen. VIII c. 12 [4 Pick. Stat. 257] (1532). The germ of revolution was planted.

In August 1532 the old archbishop of Canterbury died and Henry seized the opportunity to ask the pope that Cranmer, a mere archdeacon, succeed him. Cranmer had secretly gone through a marriage ceremony with the niece of a leading Lutheran in Germany; Scarisbrick 401. According to the law of the Church and of England, he was living with a concubine. He had to choose between keeping this woman in sin and abandoning Rome. Pope Clement VII, although warned that there was something unsuitable about Cranmer, was eager to oblige Henry and sent the bull of nomination; *id.* 310. In March 1533 Cranmer was consecrated, taking the usual oath of obedience to the pope; Elton 175. In the same month Parliament enacted The Submission of the Clergy and Restraint of Appeals Act, confirming the clergy's subordination to the crown as to legislation; 25 Hen. VIII c. 19 (1533). The act also made a broad expansion of praemunire, cutting off appeals to Rome in cases such as annulment suits where appeals traditionally had been taken.

In late May Cranmer annulled Henry's marriage to Catherine on the ground of affinity, her previous marriage to his brother Arthur, allegedly consummated and invalidly dispensed; *see* Henry Ansgar Kelly, *The Matrimonial Trials of Henry VIII* 210 (1976). Anne Boleyn was crowned queen on June 1, 1533. In July the pope excommunicated Henry.

Parliament then passed the Act of Succession declaring Henry and Catherine's marriage void and Henry and Anne's marriage "perfect," and requiring from every adult male an oath of allegiance to Anne and her issue; to refuse was to be guilty of "misprision of high treason," 25 Hen. VIII c. 22 [4 Pick. Stat. 305] (1533). Commissioners to enact the oath were appointed, and on April 17, 1534, Thomas More, two years in retirement, was summoned to take the oath. The remarkable letter that follows was written soon afterward, addressed to Margaret, his oldest daughter, aged 29. It is, of course, not an unqualified defense of the supremacy of conscience; but it is a defense of even a doubtful conscience against coercion by the secular power.

More's silence sealed his fate. In November 1534, under Cromwell's management, a special bill of attainder was passed condemning him to death for his failure; Elton 188. In the same session two general laws were passed—the Act of Supremacy, declaring the king to be "the only supreme head in earth of the church of England," without any qualifying reference to the law of Christ; 26 Hen. VIII c. 1 [4 Pick. 312] (1534); and the Treason Act, making it treason maliciously to say in writing or by mouth that the king was a schismatic or heretic or to deny him any of his titles; 26 Hen. VIII c. 13 [4 Pick. 337] (1534).

Elton describes what happened as a "revolution"; Elton 196. Rodes, on the other hand, stresses the continuity with the medieval church and, a Catholic, emphasizes the reformers' view that what they were achieving was only an "updating," Rodes 93. Was it revolution or only *aggiornamento*?

There was a great deal of continuity. Ecclesiastical jurisdiction of marriages and wills, for example, was not touched. No new regime, however revolutionary, writes on a *tabula rasa*. But destruction of the monasteries and dissolution of the religious orders liquidated two main institutions of the old church with revolutionary thoroughness. The coercive means used were not extraconstitutional but their purpose was: to compel consent to a religious proposition whose truth depended upon a statute. Even more significant from the perspective of this book, the elimination of papal government of the Church tilted the balance in favor of greater governmental control of the Church. "The freedom of the Church," as proclaimed in Magna Carta, [Chapter Three, section 2], was a formula weighted toward the preeminence of the Church. The king as "supreme head" was a formula weighted toward preeminence of the state. Paradoxically, in the long run, the formula was to make for greater freedom of conscience for everyone. Secular governments did not have a jealous interest in doctrinal purity. But the argument here is not whether the results were good or ill, but whether constitutional revolution was effected.

More himself was not disposed of by the bill of attainder, but was proceeded against under the Treason Act. Convicted in June 1535 of denying the king's supremacy over the church, he was executed on July 6, 1535; he was canonized as a martyr in 1933. The following letter is from the *Correspondence of Thomas More*, edited by Elizabeth Frances Rogers (1947).

Thomas More to His Daughter Margaret
(Written from the Tower of London, about April 17, 1534)

When I was before the Lords at Lambeth, I was the first that was called in, although Master Doctor the Vicar of Croydon had come before me, and several others. After the cause of my being sent for was declared to me (whereof I somewhat marveled in my mind, considering that they sent for no more temporal men but me) I desired the sight of the oath, which they showed me under the great seal. Then I desired the sight of the Act of Succession, which was delivered to me in a printed roll. After which I read separately by myself and considered the oath with the act, and I showed them that my purpose was not to put any fault either on the act or any man that made it, upon the oath or any man that swore it, nor to condemn the conscience of any other man. But as for myself in good faith my conscience so moved me in the matter that though I would not refuse to swear to the succession, yet unto the oath that there was offered me I could not swear without the risking of my soul to perpetual damnation. And that if they doubted whether I would refuse the oath only for the grudge of my conscience, or for any other fantasy, I was ready therein to satisfy them by my oath. Which if they trusted not, what should they be the better to give me any oath? And if they trusted that I would therein swear true, then trusted I that of their goodness they would not move me to swear the oath that they offered me, perceiving that the swearing was against my conscience.

Unto this my Lord Chancellor said that they all were sorry to see me say this and see me thus refuse the oath. And they all said that on their faith I was the very first that ever refused it; which would cause the King's Highness to conceive great suspicion of me and great indignation toward me. And therewith they showed me the roll and let me see the names of the lords and the commons who had sworn and subscribed their names already. Which notwithstanding, when they saw that I refused to swear the same myself, not blaming any other man that had sworn, I was in conclusion commanded to go down into the garden and thereupon I tarried in the old burned chamber that looks into the garden and would not go down because of the heat. During that time I saw Master Doctor Latimer come into the garden, and there he walked with various other doctors and chaplains of my Lord of Canterbury, and very merry I saw him, for he laughed and took one or two about the neck so handsomely that if they had been women I would have believed that he had become wanton. After that came Master Doctor Wilson from the lords and was with two gentlemen brought past me and in a gentlemanly way sent straight to the Tower. What time my Lord of Rochester was called in before them, that I cannot tell. But at night I heard that he had been before them, but where he remained that night and so forth until he was sent hither, I never heard. I heard also that Master Vicar of Croydon and all the remnant of the priests of London that were sent for were sworn, and that they had such favor at the Council's hand that they were not made to linger nor to dance any long attendance to their travail and cost as suitors are sometimes wont to be, but were sped apace to their great comfort, so far forth that Master Vicar of Croydon, either for gladness or for dryness, or else that it might be seen (*quod ille notus erat pontifici*) went to my lords buttery bar and called for drinks, and drank (*valde familiariter*).

When they had played their pageant and were gone out of the place, then was I called in again. And then was it declared to me what a number had sworn, even since I went aside, and gladly without any sticking. Wherein I laid no blame on any man but for my own self answered as before. Now as well then as before, they somewhat laid into me for obstinacy that, whereas before since I refused to swear, I would not declare any special part of that oath that grudged my conscience and open the causes why. For thereunto I had said to them that I feared lest the King's Highness would, as they said, take displeasure enough toward me for the mere refusal of the oath. And that if I should open and disclose the causes why, I should therewith but further exasperate his Highness, which I would in no wise do, but rather would I abide all the danger and harm that might come towards me than to give his Highness any occasion for further displeasure more than the offering of the oath to me of pure necessity constrained me. However, when they various times imputed this to me as stubbornness and obstinacy, that I would neither swear the oath nor yet declare the causes why, I inclined thus far toward them, that, rather than be accounted obstinate, upon the King's gracious license, or rather his commandment—as might be my sufficient warrant—that my declaration should not offend his Highness nor put me in danger of any of his statutes, I would be content to declare the causes in writing and beyond that to give an oath at the beginning that if I might find those causes by any man answered in such a way as I might think my own conscience satisfied, I would after that with all my heart swear the principal oath too.

To this I was answered that although the King would give me license under his letters patent, yet it would not serve against the statute, to which I said that if I had them I would stand to the trust of his honor at my peril for the rest. But yet I thought that if I might not declare the causes without peril, then to leave them undeclared is no obstinacy.

My Lord of Canterbury taking hold upon that which I had said, that I condemned not the conscience of them that swore, said to me that it appeared well that I did not take it for a very sure and certain thing that I might not lawfully swear, but rather as a thing uncertain and doubtful. But then, said my Lord, you know for a certainty and a thing without doubt that you are bound to obey your sovereign lord, your King, and therefore you are bound to leave the doubt of your unsure conscience in refusing the oath and take the sure way in obeying your prince, and swear it. Now it was all so in my own mind I thought myself not defeated, yet this argument seemed suddenly so subtle and with such authority coming out from so noble a prelate's mouth that I could answer nothing thereto but only that I thought myself I might not well do so, because in my conscience this was one of the cases in which I was bound that I should not obey my prince, since whatever other folk thought in the matter (whose conscience and learning I would not condemn nor take upon myself to judge), yet in my conscience the truth seemed on the other side. Wherein I had not informed my conscience suddenly nor slightly but at long leisure and with diligent search in the matter. And of truth if that reason is conclusive, then have we a ready way to avoid all perplexities. For in whatsoever matters the doctors stand in great doubt the King's commandment given upon whatever side he chooses, resolves all the doubts.

Then said my Lord of Westminster to me that howsoever the matter seemed to my mind, I had cause to fear that my own mind was erroneous when I saw the Great Council of the Realm determine the contrary of my mind, and that, therefore, I ought to change my conscience. To that I answered that if there were no men but myself upon my side, and the whole Parliament upon the other, I would be sore afraid to lean to my own mind alone against so many. But on the other side, if it so be that in some things for which I refuse the oath, I have (as I think I have) upon my part as great a Council and a greater too, I am not then bound to change my conscience and would confirm it to the Council of one realm against the General Council of Christendom. Upon this, Master Secretary (as one that tenderly favors me) said and swore a great oath that he would rather that his only son (who is in truth a goodly young gentleman and shall I trust come to much worship) had lost his head than that I should thus have refused the oath. For surely the King's Highness would now conceive a great suspicion against me and think of the matter of the nun of Canterbury was all contrived by my drift. To which I said that the contrary was true and well known and whatsoever should mishap me, it lay not in my power to help it without peril of my soul. Then did my Lord Chancellor repeat before me my refusal to Mister Secretary, as to him that was going unto the King's Grace. And in the rehearsing, this Lordship repeated again that I denied not but was content to swear to the succession. Whereunto I said that as for that point I would be content so that I might see my oath in that point so framed in such a manner as might stand with my conscience.

Then said my Lord: "Mary! Master Secretary mark that too that he will not swear that either only in some certain manner." "Verily no, my Lord," quote I, "but that I will see it made in such wise first as I shall myself see that I shall neither be foresworn nor swear against my conscience." Surely as to swear to the succession I see no peril, but I thought and think it reason, that to my own oath I myself look well and be of counsel in the fashion, and never intend to swear for a piece and set my hand to the whole oath. How be it (as help me God) as touching the whole oath, I never withdrew any man from it nor never advised any to refuse it nor never put, nor will, any scruple in any man's head, but leave every man to his own conscience. And me thinks in good faith that so were it good reason that every man should leave me to mine.

4. A CANDLE NEVER EXTINGUISHED

Hugh Latimer (1492–1555) was "the most popular, as he was the most influential, preacher of the English Reformation." To his admirers, he was "the

Apostle to the English." Allan G. Chester, *Selected Sermons of Hugh Latimer* xiii (1968). That he died at the stake showed that Catholics had not yet learned anything from More's martyrdom.

Ordained a Catholic priest in 1515, a bachelor of divinity from Cambridge in 1524, Latimer at Cambridge came to reject scholasticism and to appeal to the Bible alone for his theology. By 1528 he was demanding that a Bible in English be authorized. By 1530 he was known at Cambridge as one working for a favorable opinion from the university on the invalidity of Henry's marriage to Catherine. A little later he was asked to preach before the king and given a royal preferment; *id*. xiii-xx.

Latimer then rose as Cranmer, his friend, rose. In 1534 he was made chaplain of the king. In the same year, in More's letter to Margaret, *supra*, we glimpse him in the garden with Cranmer as More watches critically. In the summer of 1535 he was chosen to open Convocation as it met to draw up articles of faith for the English Church; he rebuked the corruption in the Court of Arches and the inactivity of Convocation in the past; Latimer, "The Sermon Before Convocation," *id*. 15, 22.

In 1539, at Henry VIII's urging, Parliament passed "An Act Abolishing Diversity of Opinions," 31 Hen. VIII c. 14, making it a crime of heresy, punishable by death by burning, to write or "hold opinion" that after the consecration the bread and wine did not become "the natural body and blood of the Saviour Jesus Christ conceived of the Virgin Mary." This Article and five others, collectively called "the six whips," repudiated the Protestant wing of the Anglican Church. Latimer resigned his bishopric and was put under house arrest. Released in 1540, he was forbidden to preach and was banished from London. He spent six years in obscurity and was then imprisoned for doubting the statute's teaching on transubstantiation. He was related in 1547 under the new king, Edward VI, and in 1548 was invited to preach at Paul's Cross and before the king. He boldly denounced bribery in high places; Noonan, *Bribes* 313–315. When the Protector Somerset fell, he retired to Lincolnshire and kept on preaching.

In July 1533 Mary Tudor, a Catholic, became queen. Parliament enacted a statute declaring Henry and Catherine's marriage good, Cranmer's judgment on it corrupt, and Mary legitimate, 1 Mary c. 1, 6 Pick. Stat. 3. Two months later, Latimer and Cranmer were summoned before the Privy Council for examination. They were imprisoned in the Tower, then moved to Oxford and examined before thirty-three doctors of divinity and found to be heretical. Under Edward the statute on the burning of heretics had been repealed. Legality was observed, and nothing was done to the distinguished prisoners before the law was reenacted in December 1554, 1 Philip and Mary c. 6, 6 Pick. Stat. 32. Further delays put a final trial off until September 30, 1555.

John Foxe's work, commonly known as *The Book of Martyrs*, a martyrology culminating in an account of Protestants killed by those the author describes ad "the Persecutors of God's Truth, commonly called Papists." It has the perspective of a polemic by a Protestant who himself had lived through the Marian persecution; it was to count in English history "as much as Drake's drum." The work was first published in 1559 in Basel, four years after Latimer's death, under the title *Rerum in Ecclesia gestarum, quae postremis et periculosis his temporibus evenerunt*; it was published in English in 1563; D.M. Loades, *The Oxford Martyrs* 264–66 (1970). As the emphasis of the title on "these latter days" suggests, Foxe was a millenarian with an interest in the apocalyptic significance of the martyrdoms. Recent historical scholarship such as Loades's still relies on Foxe's account of Latimer's end. The following account is from Foxe's *Acts and Monuments of These Latter and Perilous Days* (1968 reprint of 1870 edition).

The Behavior of Dr. Ridley and Master Latimer, at the Time of Their Death, Which Was the 16th of October, 1555.

Upon the north-side of the town, in the ditch over against Balliol-college, the place of execution was appointed: and for fear of any tumult that might arise, to let the burning of them, the lord Williams was commanded, by the queen's letters, and the householders of the city, to be there assistant, sufficiently appointed. And when every thing was in a readiness, the prisoners were brought forth by the mayor and the bailiffs.

Master Ridley had a fair black gown furred, and faced with foins, such as he was wont to wear being bishop, and a tippet of velvet furred likewise about his neck, a velvet night-cap upon his head, and a corner cap upon the same, going in a pair of slippers to the stake, and going between the mayor and an alderman, etc.

After him came master Latimer in a poor Bristol frieze frock all worn, with his buttoned cap, and a kerchief on his head, all ready to the fire, a new long shroud hanging over his hose, down to the feet: which at the first sight stirred men's hearts to rue upon them, beholding on the one side, the honour they sometime had, and on the other, the calamity whereunto they were fallen.

Master doctor Ridley, as he passed toward Bocardo, looked up where master Cranmer did lie, hoping belike to have seen him at the glass-window, and to have spoken unto him. But then master Cranmer was busy with friar Soto and his fellows, disputing together, so that he could not see him, through that occasion. Then master Ridley, looking back, espied master Latimer coming after, unto whom he said, "Oh, be ye there?" "Yea," said master Latimer, "have after as fast as I can follow." So he, following a pretty way off, at length they came both to the stake, the one after the other, where first Dr. Ridley entering the place, marvellous earnestly holding up both his hands, looked towards heaven. Then shortly after espying master Latimer, with a wonderous cheerful look he ran to him, embraced, and kissed him; and, as they that stood near reported, comforted him, saying, "Be of good heart, brother, for God will either assuage the fury of the flame, or else strengthen us to abide it."

With that went he to the stake, kneeled down by it, kissed it, and most effectuously prayed, and behind him master Latimer kneeled, as earnestly calling upon God as he. After they arose, the one talked with the other a little while, till they which were appointed to see the execution, removed themselves out of the sun. What they said I can learn of no man.

Then Dr. Smith, of whose recantation in king Edward's time ye heard before, began his sermon to them upon this text of St. Paul, "If I yield my body to the fire to be burnt, and have not charity, I shall gain nothing thereby." Wherein he alleged that the goodness of the cause, and not the order of death, maketh the holiness of the person; which he confirmed by the examples of Judas, and of a woman in Oxford that of late hanged herself, for that they, and such like as he recited, might then be adjudged righteous, which desperately sundered their lives from their bodies, as he feared that those men that stood before him would do. But he cried still to the people to beware of them, for they were heretics, and died out of the church. And on the other side, he declared their diversity in opinions, as Lutherans, Ecolampadians, Zuinglians, of which sect they were, he said, and that was the worst: but the old church of Christ, and the catholic faith believed far otherwise. At which place they lifted up both their hands and eyes to heaven, as it were calling God to witness of the truth: the which countenance they made in many other places of his sermon, where as they thought he spake amiss. He ended with a very short exhortation to them to recant, and come home again to the church, and save their lives and souls, which else were condemned. His sermon was scant; in all, a quarter of an hour.

Dr. Ridley said to master Latimer, "Will you begin to answer the sermon, or shall I?" Master Latimer said, "Begin you first, I pray you." "I will," said master Ridley.

Then, the wicked sermon being ended, Dr. Ridley and master Latimer kneeled down upon their knees towards my lord Williams of Thame, the vice-chancellor of Oxford, and divers other commissioners appointed for that purpose, who sat upon a form thereby; unto whom master Ridley said, "I beseech you, my lord, even for Christ's sake, that I may speak but two or three words." And whilst my lord bent his head to the mayor and vice-chancellor, to know (as it appeared) whether he might give him leave to speak, the bailiffs and Dr. Marshall, vice-chancellor, ran hastily unto him, and with their hands stopped his mouth, and said, "Master Ridley, if you will revoke your erroneous opinions, and recant the same, you shall not only have liberty so to do, but also the benefit of a subject; that is, have your life." "Not otherwise?" said master Ridley. "No," quoth Dr. Marshal. "Therefore if you will not so do, then there is no remedy but you must suffer for your deserts." "Well," quoth master Ridley, "so long as the breath is in my body, I will never deny my Lord Christ, and his known truth: God's will be done in me!" And with that he rose up, and said with a loud voice, "Well then, I commit our cause to Almighty God, which shall indifferently judge all." To whose saying, master Latimer added his old posy, "Well! there is nothing hid but it shall be opened." And he said, he could answer Smith well enough, if he might be suffered.

Incontinently they were commanded to make them ready, which they with all meekness obeyed. Master Ridley took his gown and his tippet, and gave it to his brother-in-law master Shipside, who all his time of imprisonment, although he might not be suffered to come to him, lay there at his own charges to provide him necessaries, which from time to time he sent him by the serjeant that kept him. Some other of his apparel that was little worth, he gave away; other the bailiffs took.

He gave away besides, divers other small things to gentlemen standing by, and divers of them pitifully weeping, as to sir Henry Lea he gave a new groat; and to divers of my lord Williams's gentlemen some napkins, some nutmegs, and rases of ginger; his dial, and such other things as he had about him, to every one that stood next him. Some plucked the points off his hose. Happy was he that might get any rag of him.

Master Latimer gave nothing, but very quietly suffered his keeper to pull off his hose, and his other array, which to look unto was very simple: and being stripped into his shroud, he seemed as comely a person to them that were there present, as one should lightly see; and whereas in his clothes he appeared a withered and crooked silly old man, he now stood bolt upright, as comely a father as one might lightly behold.

Then master Ridley, standing as yet in his truss, said to his brother, "It were best for me to go in my truss still." "No," quoth his brother, "it will put you to more pain: and the truss will do a poor man good." Whereunto master Ridley said, "Be it, in the name of God;" and so unlaced himself. Then, being in his shirt, he stood upon the foresaid stone, and held up his hand and said, "O heavenly Father, I give unto thee most hearty thanks, for that thou hast called me to be a professor of thee, even unto death. I beseech thee, Lord God, take mercy upon this realm of England, and deliver the same from all her enemies."

Then the smith took a chain of iron, and brought the same about both Dr. Ridley's and master Latimer's middles: and, as he was knocking in a staple, Dr. Ridley took the chain in his hand, and shaked the same, for it did gird in his belly, and looking aside to the smith, said, "Good fellow, knock it in hard, for the flesh will have his course." Then his brother did bring him gunpowder in a bag, and would have tied the same about his neck. Master Ridley asked, what it was. His brother said, "Gunpowder." "Then," said he, "I take it to be sent of God: therefore I will receive it as sent of him. And have you any," said he, "for my brother;" meaning master Latimer. "Yea sir, that I have" quoth his brother. "Then give it unto him," said he, "betime; lest ye come too late." So his brother went, and carried of the same gunpowder unto master Latimer.

In the mean time Dr. Ridley spake unto my lord Williams, and said, "My lord, I must be a suitor unto your lordship in the behalf of divers poor men, and especially in the cause of my poor sister: I have made a supplication to the queen's majesty in their behalfs. I beseech your lordship for Christ's sake, to be a mean to her grace for them. My brother here hath the supplication, and will resort to your lordship to certify you hereof. There is nothing in all the world that troubleth my conscience, I praise God, this only excepted. Whilst I was in the see of London, divers poor men took leases of me, and agreed with me for the same. Now I hear say the bishop that now occupieth the same room, will not allow my grants unto them made, but, contrary unto all law and conscience, hath taken from them their livings, and will not suffer them to enjoy the same. I beseech you, my lord, be a mean for them: you shall do a good deed, and God will reward you."

Then they brought a faggot, kindled with fire, and laid the same down at Dr. Ridley's feet. To whom master Latimer spake in this manner: "Be of good comfort, master Ridley, and play the man. We shall this day light such a candle, by God's grace, in England, as I trust shall never be put out."

And so the fire being given unto them, when Dr. Ridley saw the fire flaming up towards him, he cried with a wonderful loud voice, "In manus tuas, Domine, commendo spiritum meum" ["Into your hands I commend my spirit, O Lord," the prayer of the dying Jesus, Luke 23:46, citing Ps 31:5]; "Domine, recipe spiritum meum" ["Lord, receive my spirit," the prayer of the dying martyr Stephen, Acts 7:59]. And after, repeated this latter part often in English, "Lord, Lord, receive my spirit;" master Latimer crying as vehemently on the other side, "O Father of heaven, receive my soul!" who received the flame as it were embracing of it. After that he had stroked his face with his hands, and as it were bathed them a little in the fire, he soon died (as it appeareth) with very little pain or none. And thus much concerning the end of this old and blessed servant of God, master Latimer, for whose laborious travails, fruitful life, and constant death, the whole realm hath cause to give great thanks to Almighty God.

CHAPTER FIVE

THE CRITICS OF PERSECUTION, 1554–1674

1. "IF THOSE IN GOVERNMENT TRULY KNEW CHRIST . . ."

The Reformation did not usher in a period of mutual respect among the divided Christian churches. On the contrary, it increased religious persecution. There were more heretics to be persecuted; moreover, the heretics themselves also persecuted for religion's sake. Martin Luther, Henry VIII, John Calvin, and Huldrych Zwingli all endorsed the principle that the secular sword should suppress Christian dissenters; all approved of actual persecutions. See Lecler, 1 *Toleration* 162 [Luther authorizes the death penalty for Anabaptists], 328 [Calvin agrees that Michael Servetus, a Unitarian, shall be burned], 200 [Zwingli persecutes the Anabaptists]. The Reformation, however, did smash the old system of Christendom sufficiently so that advocates of toleration appeared. In the first place it stimulated the spread of small sects that were doomed to be minorities and, if persecution was permissible, to be persecuted. Such splinter groups had far more practical incentive to embrace toleration as a principle than had the membership of a dominant church. In the second place, as Protestant churches spread, it became impracticable if not impossible to wipe out all the heretics. Stalemate was the practical situation. Acceptance of the stalemate began to look reasonable. In the third place, the Reformation freed some theological minds to think of the Christian Church as a wholly spiritual body or even a purely spiritual force, spurning worldly assistance. The Catholic Christian tradition was full of acknowledgements of the spiritual nature of the Church. Thomas Aquinas, for example, had defined the New Law as the life of the Spirit in the believer's heart; *Summa Theologiae* 1–2, q. 106, art. 1. But the close involvement of the pope and bishops with terrestrial goods and power had weighed down the spiritual. Now emphasis on the spiritual could predominate and with it a deliberate rejection of unspiritual means for the protection of the spiritual kingdom.

Erasmus (1466–1536) was a Catholic who in 1526 extended Thomas Aquinas's reason for tolerating pagans to the toleration of Lutherans in Germany; 1 Lecler, 119. His more general criticism of unnecessary dogma, his intellectual openness, and his love of peace also inclined him and those who followed him to toleration. The Erasmians encouraged the idea of religious reconciliation with Germany; *id.* 261. In line with Erasmian thought, Emperor Maximilian II in 1568 granted legal toleration to the Lutheran lords within his realm and practical toleration to other Lutherans; *id.* 268. In this *modus vivendi* the impossibility of the Catholic emperor ruling without good relations with his Lutheran subjects was acknowledged.

In 1573 at the Warsaw Confederation the nobles and gentry of Poland agreed to an even broader recognition of religious difference. "To preserve the

117

common peace between separated and differing people in faith and worship'' and "because in our commonwealth there is significant disagreement in the matter of the Christian religion.... we mutually pledge ... that those of us who disagree about religion shall keep peace among ourselves, refrain from bloodshed over differences of faith or changes of church, nor punish by imprisonment or confiscation...." The king was to swear to uphold this pact; A. Brückner, "The Polish Reformation in the Sixteenth Century," in M. Giergielwic, ed., *Polish Civilization* 81 (1979). This tolerance extended not only to Catholics, Lutherans, and Calvinists but also to groups denying the divinity of Christ such as the Socinians, Unitarians, and Antitrinitarians; (*id.* 83). For a period, Poland was the most tolerant Christian country in the world. The basis of tolerance was the pragmatic one of securing peace for the state.

Believers in a spiritual Church tended also to be minorities who experienced the pain of persecution. Sebastian Franck (1499–1542) was a minority of one. A Dominican priest who became a Lutheran, he ultimately took the position that "the spiritual, invisible Church" was to be ruled "without exterior means." For him a list of heretics of old became a list of martyrs; and the use of persecution became itself a mark of heresy. Marvelously, the tables were turned on the heresy-hunter, who by his very action proclaimed himself guilty of the sin he hunted. His brothers, Franck declared, were any who wished him well, "Papist, Zwinglian, Anabaptist, or even Turk ... even if he is a Jew or Samaritan I want to love him and do him as much good as in me lies." The great phrase from Deuteronomy on God as a judge was once more evoked: God is not an *acceptor personarum*, that is, God does not discriminate. Neither, then, should we. Lecler, 1: 166–75.

Other theologians denying that the material sword should be used to defend the spiritual church began to write, for example, Caspar Schwenckfeld (1489–1561), a layman from Silesia (Lecler, 1, 176–185; and Valentine Weigel (1537–1588), outwardly a Lutheran minister, in his heart a believer in a purely invisible Church that eschewed force; Lecler, 1: 186–88. A theologian who had greater impact than Franck or Weigel, because he gathered about him a community, was Menno Simons (1493–1559).

Menno Simons was the Catholic parish priest in his home parish of Witmarsum in Friesland when in 1534 he wrote his first book rebuking the Anabaptists who had resorted to force in ruling the town of Münster. In 1535 he announced that he was himself an Anabaptist, that is, one who believed in the necessity of "again baptizing" because infant baptism was ineffective, and a year later he became the leader of the scattered Anabaptist brethren in Holland. For the remainder of his life he labored as a bishop among the Anabaptists in Holland, Cologne, Holstein, and Baltic Germany. In 1542 the empire put a price of 100 guilders on his head and only sporadically was he safe from betrayal or capture, prosecution and death for heresy.

From the perspective of the empire the Mennonites were heretical on two counts. First, the rejection of infant baptism–on the view that baptism entails the willingness of adult Christians to accept Jesus as their sovereign Lord– meant that some members of the civil community—children—were not yet initiated into the Christian community. Second, their renunciation of all forms of violence–on the view that a follower of Jesus must be faithful to his teachings on nonviolence–meant that some members of the civil community– adult Christians–were prepared to disobey an order by the prince to take human life. Both the sacramental principle and the ethical conviction had the effect of challenging the unity of church and state and of requiring a rethinking of the relationship between church and state.

Menno is recognized not as the founder of the church that bears his name—the church had been founded in Zurich in 1525—but as its inspiring spirit when the faith was threatened by "dungeon, fire, and sword"; Harold S. Bender, "A Brief Biography of Menno Simons," in John Christian Wenger, ed., 1 *The Complete Writings of Menno Simons* 4–28 (1956). Appealing solely to Scripture, Menno developed a strong concept of the doctrine and moral conduct required of true believers. While the Church he had known as a young man had been tolerant of many sinners, he was clear that the ungodly should be excommunicated and shunned. The "obstinate schismatic ... and those who do not abide in the doctrine of Christ, who lead an offensive life, or greedy people who lead a soft and easy life at the expense of others shall not be allowed a place in the holy house" (Menno, *Instruction on Excommunication, 1 Works*, 968). Parents must shun excommunicated children; children, excommunicated parents; a spouse, an excommunicated spouse (*id.* 971). Strict spiritual discipline compensated for civil toleration.

Menno's main doctrinal work, *Fondamentboek*, was published in Dutch in 1539. (His followers were not called by his last name because that would have made them "Simonians," a term already established as a disparaging epithet for those who bought or sold the Spirit like Simon Magus.) Menno's reply to a Reformed minister in Emden, East Friesland, Gellius Faber, *Een klare beantwoordinge over eene schrift Gellii Fabri*, was composed in Northern Germany. The excerpt that follows is from the translation from the Dutch by Leonard Verduin, edited by John Christian Wenger, 1 *The Complete Writings of Menno Simons* 623.

Reply of Menno Simons to Gellius Faber (1554)

In the last place he writes of us, saying, "Experience has taught that their teachers and prophets are not such teachers and prophets of God. And that they are not the people of God, I have, perhaps, already proved too powerfully. From which, then, it is clear that our magistrates do right by not letting them proceed in their wicked course but obstructing them diligently. And we might, in pastoral and paternal faithfulness or solicitude for the church of Christ, lest the church be quite destroyed, speak and conclude a bit more sternly concerning them. But then we would be called persecutors and bloodhounds by them."

Reply. Jeremiah, Micah, Elijah, Christ Jesus, and Paul could not pass for the true prophets and servants of God with the perverse; neither can we. But the great Lord shall in due time make it manifest who are the faithful prophets and servants of God and who are hot.

Again, to this saying that we are not the people of God, we answer with holy Paul that it is a very small thing that we should be judged with the judgment of men, and especially by men who are so flatly opposed to the ordinance, will, and Word of God as may be seen in the case of Gellius from his writing. Yes, kind reader, if he and similar preachers acknowledged us to be the people of God, they would thereby acknowledge that they are not of that group, a thing which an ambitious carnal person who seeks reputation and fame never will do.

To his assertion that the magistracy does well in obstructing our course which he calls wicked, I reply, that the longer he writes, the more clumsy and offensive he becomes and the more he manifests his blindness. If he is a preacher called by the Spirit of God, then let him show a single letter in all the New Testament that Christ or the apostles have ever called on the magistrates to defend and protect the true church against the attack of the wicked, as, alas, he calls us. No, no, Christ Jesus and His powerful Word and the Holy Spirit are the protectors and defenders of the church, and not, eternally not, the emperor, king, or any worldly potentate! The kingdom of the Spirit must be protected and defended by the sword of the Spirit, and not by the sword of the world. This, in the light of the doctrine and example of Christ and His apostles, is too plain to be denied.

I would say further, if the magistracy rightly understood Christ and His kingdom, they would in my opinion rather choose death than to meddle with their worldly power and sword in spiritual matters which are reserved not to the judgment of man but to the judgment of the great and Almighty God alone. But they are taught by those who have the care of their souls that they may proscribe, imprison, torture, and slay those who are not obedient to their doctrine, as may, alas, be seen in many different cities and countries.

In short, kind reader, if the merciful Lord did not, in His great love, temper the hearts of sonic of the magistrates, but if they should proceed according to the partisan instigation and blood-preaching of the learned ones, no pious person could endure. But as it is, some are found who, notwithstanding the railing and writing of the learned ones, suffer and bear with the miserable, and for a time show them mercy, a thing for which we will forever give praise to God, the most High, and express our gratitude to such kind and fair governors.

But to his writing that in paternal and pastoral solicitude and faithfulness they might speak and decide a bit more sternly against us, I reply, if he had entered in at the right door of Christ, who is the Prince and Head of all true pastors, and if he had tasted in his heart the friendly and amiable Spirit, nature, and disposition of Christ, then he would not, by any means, think of such a resolution against the blood of others, much less write and mention it. This I know of a certainty, that the Spirit of Christ is not so inclined. Reader, observe, the reason that he does not write boldly that the magistracy may very well plunge its sword in us, is that he does not want to be called a bloodhound or persecutor; nevertheless he does make it plain that if they should do so, he would call it a praiseworthy thing. Whoever is not quite destitute of understanding, understands very well what his position is in the matter. Oh, doctrine of blood!

NOTES AND QUESTIONS

From the Peace of Augsburg to the Thirty Years' War and the Peace of Westphalia. Both Catholics and Lutherans frequently practiced their "doctrine of blood" by killing Mennonites as heretics. In the period immediately following the Reformation in Germany, Catholics and Lutherans killed one another as well. From each perspective, the other was a heretic worthy of death. A year after Menno's reply to Farber, Catholics and Lutherans put a halt to their mutual slaughter in a treaty called the Peace of Augsburg. The central principle of this arrangement was stated succinctly in Latin: "cuius regio, eius religio" (whose rule, his religion). Professor Laycock describes this principle as follows: "Each ruler in the empire would choose the religion of his realm; all his subjects would have to conform or emigrate.... This principle made the State supreme over fundamental religious choices, and to the extent it could be enforced, it required State suppression of minority faiths and made the population of each state religiously uniform...." As Laycock notes, the Peace of Augsburg led to "state supremacy over the established Church ... [in] England and some of the Lutheran states in Germany." Douglas Laycock, "Continuity and Change in the Threat To Religious Liberty: The Reformation Era and the Late Twentieth Century," 80 *Minn. L. Rev.* 1047, 1052–53 (1996). Which was worse, the warfare conducted by Christians against one another, or the coercive arrangements set up when the warfare was ended? Laycock suggests that the other major continental leader of the Reformation, John Calvin (1509–1564), avoided the extremes that the Reformation in Germany produced. "Calvin developed a theory of church and state as separate and independent entities with separate responsibilities, and no individual could hold both religious and political positions. But this was hardly separation of church and state: the State enforced religious uniformity, and when the Puritans developed their democratic version of this model, only members of the established Church could vote or hold political office." *Id.* 1053. Laycock does not mention that Calvin approved the death penalty in Geneva for the Unitarian Michael Servetus.

The Peace of Augsburg lasted from 1555 to 1618, collapsing with the Battle of Pilsen that took place on All Saints' Day, November 1, 1618. Tensions between Catholics and Protestants were mounting. When two emissaries of Ferdinand of Styria, hereditary ruler of the Hapsburg lands in central Europe and elected head of the Holy Roman Empire, were killed by Protestants in Prague, the emperor went on the attack. Ferdinand prevailed in subsequent conflicts for nearly a decade. Ferdinand met opposition both inside and outside the Empire. Germans resented paying taxes and making contributions to support his rapacious armies. The war spread in scope, intensity, and duration, eventually involving most of Europe. The slaughter was ferocious. Over 15% of the entire population of the contested areas of Europe were killed. The last battle of the war was fought at Lens on August 2, 1648. On October 24, 1648, one week short of thirty years, the war was ended by the Treaty of Westphalia. *See* Ronald G. Asch, *The Thirty Years War: The Holy Roman Empire and Europe, 1618–1648* (1997); and Geoffrey Parker, ed. *The Thirty Years War* (1997).

The war is frequently cited for conclusions that are larger than the facts of the war itself. For example, some secularists characterize the war as "religious," and conclude that the safest remedy for avoiding such conflict is to remove religion from politics. Two questions challenge this conclusion. First, was the Thirty Years' War simply a religious conflict? Laycock's account is ambivalent: "In general, subject to the conflicting political interests of each ruler, the war pitted Catholic states against Protestant states. But the decisive intervention came when Catholic France allied with Protestant Sweden against the Catholic Emperor, thereby fatally weakening France's traditional enemy Spain, and illustrating once again that the needs of the State were more important than the needs of the Church." Id. 1055. Second, can one verify the hypothesis that the political order will be safer if wholly secular, in the wake of the wars of mass destruction waged in the twentieth century by secular governments of the political Left, Right, and Center? For the view that religious discourse in American politics is noxious to Jews, see Suzanne Sherry, "Religion and the Public Square: Making Democracy Safe for Religious Minorities," 47 *DePaul L. Rev.* 499 (1998).

2.   THE CITY UPON A HILL; THE COVENANT; THE NEW ISRAEL AND THE SEPARATED GARDEN

In 1630 John Winthrop, leader of the Massachusetts Bay Colony, preached to his followers aboard the *Arabella* en route to the new land a sermon he called "Christian Charitee: Modell Hereof." Winthrop, 2 *Papers* 294–95.

John Winthrop, Sermon on Christian Charity, 1630

When God giues a speciall Commission he lookes to haue it stricktly obserued in every Article, when hee gaue Saule a Commission to destroy Amaleck hee indented with him vpon certaine Articles and because hee failed in one of the least, and that vpon a faire pretence, it lost him the kingdome, which should haue been his reward, if hee had obserued his Commission: Thus stands the cause betweene God and vs, wee are entered into Covenant with him for this worke, wee haue taken out a Commission, the Lord hath giuen vs leaue to drawe our owne Articles wee haue professed to enterprise these Accions vpon these and these ends, wee haue herevpon besought him of favour and blessing: Now if the Lord shall please to hear vs, and bring vs in peace to the place wee desire, then hath hee ratified this Covenant and sealed our Commission, [and] will expect a strickt performance of the Articles contained in it, but if wee shall neglect the observacion of these Articles which are the ends wee haue propounded, and dissembling with our God, shall fall to embrace this present world and prosecute our carnall intencions, seekeing great things for our selues and our posterity, the Lord will surely breake out in wrathe against vs be revenged of such a periured people and make vs knowe the price of the breache of such a Covenant.

Now the onely way to avoyde this shipwracke and to provide for our posterity is to followe the Counsell of Micah, to doe Justly, to loue mercy, to walke humbly with our God, for this end, wee must be knitt together in this worke as one man, wee must entertaine each other in brotherly Affeccion, wee must be willing to abridge our selues of our superfluities, for the supply of others necessities, wee must vphold a familiar Commerce together in all meekenes, gentlenes, patience and liberallity, wee must delight in eache other, make others Condicions our owne reioyce together, mourne together, labour, and suffer together, allwayes haueing before our eyes our Commission and Community in the worke, our Community as members of the same body, soe shall wee keepe the vnitie of the spirit in the bond of peace, the Lord will be our God and delight to dwell among vs, as his owne people and will commaund a blessing vpon vs in all our wayes, soe that wee shall see much more of his wisdome power goodnes and truthe then formerly wee haue been acquainted with, wee shall finde that the God of Israell is among vs, when tenn of vs shall be able to resist a thousand of our enemies, when hee shall make vs a prayse and glory, that men shall say of succeeding plantacions: the lord make it like that of New England: for wee must Consider that wee shall be as a Citty vpon a Hill [Mt.5.14] the eies of all people are vppon vs; soe that if wee shall deale falsely with our god in this worke wee haue undertaken and soe cause him to withdrawe his present help from vs, wee shall be made a story and a by-word through the world, wee shall open the mouthes of enemies to speake euill of the wayes of god and all professours for Gods sake; wee shall shame the faces of many of gods worthy seruants, and cause theire prayers to be turned into Cursses vpon vs till wee be consumed out of the good land whether wee are goeing: And to shutt vpp this discourse with that exhortacion of Moses that faithfull seruant of the Lord in his last farewell to Israell Deut. 30. Beloued there is now sett before vs life, and good, deathe and euill in that wee are Commaunded this day to loue the Lord our God, and to loue one another to walke in his wayes and to keepe his Commaundements and his Ordinance, and his lawes, and the Articles of our Covenant with him that wee may liue and be multiplyed, and that the Lord our God may blesse vs in the land whether wee goe to possesse it: But if our heartes shall turne away soe that wee will not obey, but shall be seduced and worshipp [Serue *cancelled*] other Gods our pleasures, and proffitts, and serue them; it is propounded vnto vs this day, wee shall surely perishe out of the good Land whether wee passe over this vast Sea to possesse it;

> Therefore lett vs choose life,
> that wee, and our Seede,
> may liue; by obeying his
> voyce, and cleaueing to him
> for hee is our life, and
> our prosperity.

———

Of this sermon a leading authority on contemporary America has written that "In relation to the principal theme of the American mind, the necessity laid upon it for decisions, Winthrop stands at the beginning of our consciousness," Perry Miller, *Nature's Nation* 6 (1967), and a contemporary sociologist sees the sermon as paradigmatic of the way biblical themes were adopted to define the enterprise of the settlers and their implications and obligations, Robert N. Bellah, *The Broken Covenant: American Civil Religion in Time of Trial* 13 (1967).

Imagery and sermon were biblical: the city on a hill from the Gospel, the covenant from Genesis, the whole metaphor from Exodus' story of Moses leading the people of Israel from Egypt to the promised land. Winthrop urged love, and he emphasized community. He did not stress liberty.The Puritan colony of New Haven, founded in the late 1630s, was even stricter than

Massachusetts, Thomas J. Curry, *The First Freedoms: Church and State in America to the Passage of the First Amendment* 3 (1986). The colony provided: "The laws of God as delivered to Moses ... shall be accounted of moral equity and generally binding on all offenders and be the rule of all courts," *id.* 224.

When in 1644 Roger Williams published his *Bloudy Tenent of Persecution*, he had had personal experience of what he wrote. Fourteen years earlier, aged about twenty-six, of Welsh antecedents, a graduate of Cambridge University, he had come to the year-old Massachusetts Bay Colony, had been invited to be minister of the church in Boston and had refused. The Puritan leaders of the colony, spiritual elect who had been born again—who were therefore "regenerate"—were dissatisfied with the Anglican Church that embraced the unregenerate, but they had refused to renounce her, "our dear Mother," Edmund S. Morgan, *The Puritan Dilemma* 52 (1958). Williams, a Separatist, not only renounced her but any church that held communion with her, *id.* 117. In the new colony, where each church was a congregation of the reborn—where no bishops existed to enforce uniformity of doctrine—William's view had a chance of being accepted by some congregation. In 1635 he was chosen by the church in Salem to be its minister.

The choice was a challenge to the colony. Williams was hailed before the General Court, the civil authority, and charged with teaching four doctrines: that the true owners of "our land," conferred by the king's charter, were the Indians; that one should not pray with the unregenerate or even accept an oath, an act of worship, from the unregenerate; that communion could not be had with the ministers of the Church of England; and that civil power could not be used to enforce religious opinions. Williams cheerfully acknowledged the truth of these charges, Williams, *Mr. Cottons Letter Lately Printed, Examined and Answered* (1644), 1 *The Complete Writings of Roger Williams* 325 (1963). As with Menno, rigidity of spiritual standard accompanied, or compensated for, latitude of civil freedom. On October 9, 1635, the Court ordered him to leave the colony.

Williams believed that the other churches of the colony had forfeited their purity by calling on the civil magistracy to act against him, so Salem should break with them. In the vernacular of modern politics, the General Court played hardball. It notified Salem that it would not have Marblehead Neck if it stayed with Williams. Many other considerations also tied Salem to the rest of the colony. Williams was deserted by the majority of his congregation. Acting on a suggestion by Governor Winthrop, he decided to start a new settlement to the south at Narragansett Bay, and, to avoid being deported to England, he departed abruptly in January 1636 for the southern wilderness.

As Williams saw it, he had voluntarily left "churches resolved to continue in those evils," but because the colony treated church and civil community as coterminous, he had been involuntarily banished from the civil state "in so sharp a time of New England's cold," *id.* He had not been put to death, he had been driven to extremities. Punished in part for his religious condemnation of religious persecution, he now conceived a passionate horror of such use of secular force.

Eight years after his exile from Massachusetts, Williams was in London to seek a charter for his new colony, Rhode Island. The English Civil War was in progress. Parliament was largely divided between Presbyterians, favoring control of local churches by a hierarchy of governing bodies, and Independents sympathetic to the Congregational model of New England. Neither side believed in religious tolerance. To the theologians of the independents, Williams addressed *Queries of Highest Consideration*, warning them against "spiritual rape" by using force to compel conscience, Perry Miller, *Roger Williams* 79, 83 (1953). Almost simultaneously he answered his chief critic from Massachusetts, John Cotton, "Teacher of the Church in Boston," attacking the unity of ecclesiastical and civil power that characterized the Bay Colony, *id.* 106–107.

The Christian church, Williams wrote, is "separate from the world." He continued: and when they opened a gap in the hedge or wall of separation between the garden of the church and the wilderness of the world, God hath ever broke down the wall itself, removed the candlestick, and made his garden a wilderness as at this day. Williams, *Mr. Cotton's Letter*, [1 *Writings*, 392].

The image of the garden was scriptural, beginning with the description of the Garden of Eden in Genesis. To describe the church as God's garden was commonplace, e.g., Thomas Aquinas, *In sententias Petri Lombardi*, Bk. 1, 140. The wilderness was also scriptural—Moses had led Israel in the wilderness, Christ had prayed in the wilderness, *cf.* George H. Williams, *Wilderness and Paradise in Christian Thought* (1962). What was different in Roger Williams was, first, his lively sense of what a physical wilderness was. It was "an howling wilderness, in frost and snow" that he reminded Cotton he had been forced to enter. Second, "the wall of separation" between garden and wilderness was an unusual metaphor. On the general use of the metaphor of law as wall or bulwark, *see also* Milner S. Ball, *Lying Down Together: Law, Metaphor and Theology* 23–27 (1985). The wall or hedge, which God himself would break down if a gap was allowed in it, was thought of as a structure protecting the holiness of the church, keeping it from contamination by the world. Third, as important as "wall"—probably more important to Williams—was "separation." Separateness for the holy was the great cause for which he had entered the wilderness. The "wall of separation" was a metaphor destined to have an extraordinary future in American political thought.

In March 1644 Parliament gave Rhode Island a charter. Williams's mission was accomplished. He stayed on to complete *The Bloudy Tenent, of Persecution, for cause of Conscience, discussed, in A Conference betweene Truth and Peace.* The preface addresses Parliament, dominated by Presbyterians, and then "every courteous reader." Saturated in Scripture, he pointedly appealed to the popularity of the English Bible in asking how England with the Bible was better than Spain without it, if the civil power was to determine doctrine. He equally appealed to experience—the experience of killing generated by religious disagreement. In the midst of war, Williams prophetically pointed the way to peace. But peace in his view was not achieved by sacrificing truth. His dialogists, Peace and Truth, are not adversaries.

For over 1300 years Christians had persecuted because they believed it was their duty to uphold the truth. No doubt in individual cases they had been cruel as well as intolerant. But always they had thought that because they were right in their doctrine, they were right in their persecution. Williams told them that they could not be right in doctrine if they believed that persecution was right. Like Sebastian Franck, he made persecution a sign of Christian heresy not faith. A persecuting Christian was a self-canceling phrase. On the foundation of the teaching of Jesus Christ, Williams proclaimed a gospel of liberty of religious belief.

**Roger Williams, The Blovdy Tenent, of PERSECUTION,
for Cause of CONSCIENCE, Discussed,
In *A* Conference *Betweene* Trvth And Peace. WHO,
in All Tender Affection, Present To The High Court Of PARLIAMENT,
(As The *Result* of Their *Discourse*) These,
(Amongst Other *Passages*) of *Highest Consideration* (1644)**

First, that the blood of so many hundred thousand souls of Protestants and Papists, spilt in the wars of present and former ages, for their respective consciences, is not required nor accepted by Jesus Christ the Prince of Peace.

Secondly, pregnant Scriptures and arguments are throughout the work proposed against the doctrine of persecution for the cause of conscience.

Thirdly, satisfactory answers are given to Scriptures, and objections produced by Mr. Calvin, Beza, Mr. Cotton, and the ministers of the New English Churches and others former and later, tending to prove the doctrine of persecution for cause of conscience.

Fourthly, the doctrine of persecution for cause of conscience is proved guilty of all the blood of the souls crying for vengeance under the altar.

Fifthly, all civil states with their officers of justice in their respective constitutions and administrations are proved essentially civil, and therefore not judges, governors, or defenders of the spiritual or Christian state and worship.

Sixthly, it is the will and command of God, that (since the coming of his son the Lord Jesus) a permission of the most paganish, Jewish, Turkish, or antichristian consciences and worships, be granted to all men in all nations and countries: and they are only to be fought against with that sword which is only (in soul matters) able to conquer, to wit, the sword of God's spirit, the word of God.

Seventhly, the state of the land of Israel, the kings and people thereof in peace and war, is proved figurative and ceremonial, and no pattern nor precedent for any kingdom or civil state in the world to follow.

Eighthly, God requireth not an uniformity of religion to be enacted and enforced in any civil state; which enforced uniformity (sooner or later) is the greatest occasion of civil war, ravishing of conscience, persecution of Christ Jesus in his servants, and of all hypocrisy and destruction of millions of souls.

Ninthly, in holding an enforced uniformity of religion in a civil state, we must necessarily disclaim our desires and hopes of the Jews' conversion to Christ.

Tenthly, an enforced uniformity of religion throughout a nation or civil state, confounds the civil and religious, denies the principles of Christianity and civility, and that Jesus Christ is come in the flesh.

Eleventhly, the permission of other consciences and worships than a state professeth, only can (according to God) procure a firm and lasting peace (good assurance being taken according to the wisdom of the civil state for uniformity of civil obedience from all sorts).

Twelfthly, lastly, true civility and Christianity may both flourish in a state or kingdom, not withstanding the permission of divers and contrary consciences, either of Jew or Gentile [Preface, 3 *Writings*, 3–4]. . . .

In vain have English Parliaments permitted English Bibles in the poorest English houses, and the simplest man or woman to search the Scriptures, if yet against their souls' persuasion from the Scripture, they should be forced (as if they lived in Spain or Rome itself without the sight of a Bible) to believe as the Church believes.

Fourthly, having tried, we must hold faith, I Thess. 5. upon the loss of a Crown, Revel. 3. We must not let go for all the flea-bitings of the present afflictions, etc. Having bought Truth dear, we must not sell it cheap, not the least grain of it for the whole World, no not for the saving of souls, though our own most precious; least of all the bitter sweetening of a little vanishing pleasure.

For a little puff of credit and reputation from the changeable breath of uncertain sons of men. For the broken bags of Riches on Eagles' wings: For a dream of these, any or all of these which on our death-bed vanish and leave tormenting stings behind them: Oh how much better is it from the love of Truth, from the love of the Father of lights, from whence it comes, from the love of the Son of God, who is the Way and the Truth, to say as he, John 18.37. For this end was I born, and for this end came I into the World that I might bear witness to the Truth ... [To Every Courteous Reader, *id*. 3:13].

Lastly, I ask, whether (as men deal with wolves) these wolves at Ephesus were intended by Paul to be killed, their brains dashed out with stones, staves, halberts, guns, etc. in the hands of the Elders of Ephesus, etc.?

Truth. Doubtless (comparing spiritual things with spiritual) all such mystical wolves must spiritually and mystically be slain. And the Witnesses of Truth, Revel. II. speak fire, and kill all that hurt them, by that fiery word of God, and that two edged sword in their hand, Psal. 149.

But oh what streams of blood of saints have been and must be shed (until the Lamb have obtained the victory, Rev. 17) by this unmerciful (and in the state of the New Testament, when the Church is spread all the world over) most bloody doctrine, viz. The wolves (heretics) are to be driven away, their brains knocked out and killed, the poor sheep to be preserved for whom Christ died, etc.

Is not this to take Christ Jesus, and make him a temporal king by force? John 6.15. Is not this to make his kingdom of this world, to set up a civil and temporal Israel? [ch. 43, *id*. 3:145]. . . . First, it will appear that in spiritual things they make the garden and the wilderness (as often I have intimated) I say the garden and the wilderness, the church and the world are all one: for thus,

If the powers of the world of civil state, are bound to propose external peace in all godliness for their end, and the end of the church be to preserve internal peace in all godliness, I demand if their end (godliness) be the same, is not their power and state the same also, unless they make the church subordinate to the commonwealth's end, or the commonweal subordinate to the church's end, which (being the governor and setter up of it, and so consequently the judge of it) it cannot be? [c. 86, *id.* 3:233].

PEACE. Yea but they say that "such laws as are conversant about religion, may still be accounted civil laws, as on the contrary an oath doth still remain religious, though conversant about civil matters."

TRUTH. Laws respecting religion are two-fold:

First, such as concern the acts of worship and the worship itself, the ministers of it, their fitness or unfitness, to be suppressed or established: and for such laws we find no footing in the New Testament of Jesus Christ.

Secondly, laws respecting religion may be such as merely concern the civil state, bodies and goods of such and such persons, processing these and these religions, viz. that such and such persons, notorious for mutinies, treasons, rebellions, massacres, be disarmed: again, that no persons Papists, Jews, Turks, or Indians be disturbed at their worship (a thing which the very Indians abhor to practice towards any.) Also that immunity and freedom from tax and toll may be granted unto the people of such or such a religion, as the magistrate pleaseth. Ezra 7.

These and such as are of this nature, concerning only the bodies and goods of such and such religious persons, I confess are merely civil [c. 92, *id.* 3, 252].

With less sin ten thousand fold may a natural father force his daughter, or the father of the commonweal force all the maidens in a country to the marriage beds of such and such men whom they cannot love, than the souls of these and other subjects to such worship or ministry, which is either a true or false bed ... [c. 94, *id.* 3:259].

PEACE. Their third reason is, it will dissolve the continuity of the state, especially theirs, where the walls are made of the stones of the churches.

TRUTH. I answer briefly to this bare affirmation thus, that the true church is a wall spiritual and mystical, Cant. 8.9.

Then consequently a false church or company is a false or pretended wall, and none of Christ's.

The civil state, power and government is a civil wall, etc. and

Lastly, the walls of earth or stone about a city are the natural or artificial wall or defense of it.

Now in consideration of these four walls I desire it may be proved from the Scriptures of truth, how the false spiritual wall or company of false worshipers suffered in a city can be able to destroy the true Christian wall or company of believers.

Again, how this false spiritual wall or false church permitted, can destroy the civil wall, the state and government of the city and citizens, any more than it can destroy the natural or artificial wall of earth or stone.

Spiritual may destroy spiritual, if a stronger and victorious, but spiritual cannot reach to artificial or civil.

Peace. Yea, but they fear the false spiritual wall may destroy their civil, because it is made of the stones of churches.

Truth. If this has reference to that practice amongst them, viz. that none but members of churches enjoy civil freedom amongst them (ordinarily) in imitation of that national church or state of the Jews, then I answer, they that follow Moses' church constitution (which the New English by such a practice implicitly do) must cease to pretend to the Lord Jesus Christ and his institutions.

Secondly, we shall find lawful civil states both before and since Christ Jesus, in which we find not any tidings of the true God or Christ.

Lastly, their civil New English state framed out of their churches may yet stand, subsist and flourish, although they did (as by the word of the Lord they ought) permit either Jews or Turks or antichristians to live amongst them subject unto their civil government [c. 102, *id.* 3:286].

In 1651 John Clark, the leader of the Baptists in Newport, Rhode island, and his colleague Obadiah Holmes, secretly visited a dying coreligionist in Lynn, Massachusetts. They were detected and tried; Clark was fined, Holmes was whipped. Williams addressed John Endecott, governor of Massachusetts, denouncing these punishments. He published the letter the following year in London where the English government, headed by Oliver Cromwell, was sure to take a hostile view of a colony that persecuted Protestants. To the extent that he could count on that reaction, Williams evened a score. But Cromwell's view of Catholics was less generous; Williams risked defending Catholics, too. An excerpt from the letter follows.

Roger Williams to John Endecott, August, 1651

Be pleased then (honored Sir) to remember that, that thing which we call Conscience is of such a nature, (especially in Englishmen) as once a Pope of Rome at the suffering of an Englishman in Rome, himself observed that although it be groundless, false, and deluded, yet it is not by any arguments or torments easily removed.

I speak not of the stream of the multitude of all nations, which have their ebbings and flowings in religion, (as the longest sword, and strongest arm of flesh carries it). But I speak of Conscience, a persuasion fixed in the mind and heart of a man, which enforceth him to judge (as Paul said of himself a persecutor) and to do so and so, with respect to God, His worship, & c.

This Conscience is found in all mankind, more or less, in Jews, Turks, Papists, Protestants, Pagans, & c. And to this purpose let me freely without offence remember you (as I did Mr. Clarke newly come up from his sufferings amongst you) I say, remember you of the same story I did him, 'twas that of William Hartley, in Queen Elizabeth her days, who receiving the sentence of hanging & c., drawing, spake confidently (as afterwards he suffered), what tell you me of hanging, & c. If I had ten thousand millions of lives, I would spend them all for the Faith of Rome, & c.

I confess, that for confidence no Romish Priest hath ever exceeded the martyrs or witnesses of Jesus: Witness (amongst so many) that holy English woman, who cried out, that if every hair of her head were a life or man, they should burn for the name of the Lord Jesus: But Sir, your principles and conscience bind you not to respect Romish or English, saints or sinners: William Hartley, and that Woman, with all their lives, you are bound by your Conscience to punish (and it may be) to hang or burn, if they transgress against your Conscience, and that because according to Mr. Cotton's monstrous distinction (as some of his chief brethren to my knowledge hath called it) not because they sin in matters of Conscience, (which he denies the magistrate to deal in) but because they sin against their Conscience [*Writings*, 6:219–221].

Roger Williams deplored in particular the "horrible *oppressions* and horrible *slaughters*" that the Jews had suffered from English kings and people and ventured the thought that to remove guilt and pacify God "a great and weighty Duty" lay upon the state to provide the Jews "some gracious *Expedients*." Roger Williams, "A *Testimony* to the 4th *Paper* presented by *Major* Butler to the Honorable *Committee* for propagating the *Gospel*," *Writings* 7:137.

Williams was not a champion of disestablishment or of pacifism. In the *Bloudy Tenet*, above, he had acknowledged that immunity from taxation could be granted by the civil magistrate on a religious basis. When in 1655 the town of Providence organized a militia, a number of Baptists objected, in the name of religious liberty, to bearing arms. As President of the Colony, Williams wrote as follows to the people of Providence. Williams, *Writings*, 6:278–279.

Roger Williams to the Town of Providence

Providence, January, 1654–5

That ever I should speak or write a tittle, that tends to such an infinite liberty of conscience, is a mistake, and which I have ever disclaimed and abhorred. To prevent such mistakes, I shall at present only propose this case: There goes many a ship to sea, with many hundred souls in one ship, whose weal and woe is common, and is a true picture of a commonwealth, or a human combination or society. It hath fallen out sometimes that both papists and protestants, Jews and Turks, may be embarked in one ship; upon which supposal I affirm, that all the liberty of conscience, that ever I pleaded for, turns upon these two hinges—that none of the papists, protestants, Jews, or Turks be forced to come to the ship's prayers or worship, nor compelled from their own particular prayers or worship, if they practice any. I further add, that I never denied that, notwithstanding this liberty, the commander of this ship ought to command the ship's course, yea, and also command that justice, peace, and sobriety, be kept and practiced, both among the seamen and all the passengers. If any of the seamen refuse to perform their services, or passengers to pay their freight; if any refuse to help, in person or purse, towards the common charges or defence; if any refuse to obey the common laws and orders of the ship, concerning their common peace or preservation; if any shall mutiny and rise up against their commanders and officers; if any should preach or write that there ought to be no commanders or officers, because all are equal in Christ, therefore no masters nor officers, no laws nor orders, nor corrections nor punishments;—I say, I never denied, but in such cases, whatever is pretended, the commander or commanders may judge, resist, compel and punish such transgressors, according to their deserts and merits. This, if seriously and honestly minded, may, if it so please the Father of lights, let in some light to such as willingly shut not their eyes.

I remain studious of your common peace and liberty.

Roger Williams

3. THE LIMITS OF POWER

Menno and Roger Williams were pastors and pioneers. Among the erudite of Europe only Erasmus had ever been a moderate champion of tolerance; even he had not stood for religious liberty. On the whole, intellectuals well into the seventeenth century stood with the old doctrine that some forms of religious dissent were literally intolerable. A new note is sounded in 1670 when a major philosopher used his pen to attack all, or nearly all, forms of civil intolerance. The writer is Baruch Spinoza, and his work *Tractatus theologico-politicus*.

The note is new in another way. It is sounded by one writing against the background of Jewish experience. In 1492–within a month of Columbus' first voyage of discovery—King Ferdinand and Queen Isabella required the Jews of Spain to convert to Christianity or be expelled from their mother land. The overwhelming majority chose exile from their beloved Sepharad (the Hebrew word for the Iberian peninsula), over apostasy to the faith of their ancestors. See Jane Gerber, *The Jews of Spain* (1992). After granting safe harbor to Spanish Jews, Portugal yielded to the demand of Ferdinand and Isabella, expelling its Jews in 1497. Spinoza's grandfather Abraham was one of the thousands of Sephardic Jews who fled from Portugal to the Netherlands, where Jews were granted asylum as refugees of conscience. Spinoza's father Michael was the head of the Jewish community in Amsterdam, and Baruch Spinoza himself was brought up on the Bible and the Talmud. But in 1656, at the age of twenty-four, he was excommunicated by the congregation of which he had been a member. He was thereafter a minority of one, religiously neither Jew nor Christian.

What Spinoza proceeded to do was to develop his own view of the world, retaining the vocabulary of earlier theology but redefining key terms such as "God" and pouring his own content into the redefinition. God, for example, is not for him an intelligent, omnipotent Lawmaker and Judge. In the *Tractatus*, Chapter 19, he specifically denies that God has given any laws. In the *Ethics* God is seen as an impersonal force. As Wolfson has expressed it, Spinoza's "work of rationalization" of religious dogma was to say in effect to the orthodox "I see no reason why I should not use your own formulae, but I must give them an interpretation of my own," Harry Wolfson, *The Philosophy of Spinoza* 1, 22 (1969). Spinoza examines religious toleration form the angle of a disbeliever in any religious creed.

Spinoza's friends had included Mennonites, and it is reasonable to see their benign influence in his interest in toleration. But while Menno had used Scripture to prove the rightness of toleration, Spinoza put his views forward in a book that was largely a critique of Scripture. Moreover, he had derived from Descartes a desire for demonstration in philosophy. He wanted to show not merely that religious freedom was desirable but that it was necessary.

The sequel showed how confined he was. The Synod of Delft, a body of the Reformed Church, condemned his book. The Supreme Powers, the States–General, condemned his book. It had been published anonymously—another caution—and he was not pursued in person. But his views were intolerable in tolerant Holland. Spinoza's reputation after his death was that of a dangerous atheist. Neither civil authorities nor Christian moralists were willing to be taught by him. The immediate impact of the *Tractatus* on the thought of Europe was therefore not tangible. The overwhelming fact of history is that a European philosopher for the first time treated liberty of though and speech as a major good.

The centerpiece of Spinoza's presentation is his treatment of *fides*, that marvelous Latin word meaning religious belief, marital fidelity, feudal fealty, commercial rectitude, and civic faithfulness. Shame on the translators of Spinoza who translate *fides* as "honesty"! Heresy in the Middle Ages had been suppressed in the name of faith. It was the breach of faith that was punished. Spinoza turns the tables. In the name of faith, heresy is *not* to be punished. Faithfulness is corrupted by persecution. As firmly as Franck or Williams, Spinoza inverts the old position and now, on philosophical grounds, makes persecution the enemy of *fides*.

A paradox: a champion of natural law, the Holy Spirit as law within the human heart and the strict limits of secular authority, such as Thomas Aquinas, is a defender of the suppression of heresy by force, an analyst who identifies power with right, like Spinoza, insists that opinion and its expression must be free. Perhaps the paradox proves no more than the inability of even very great philosophers to reason consistently, or no more than that in Thomas's case an institutional context dominated his conclusions, and he did not dwell on history. Spinoza's appeal is ultimately not to philosophical reasoning about power or to observations about irrepressible opinions, but to the history of religious strife. Experience spoke with an authority stronger than any syllogism.

Baruch Spinoza, *Theological-Political Treatise*, Chapter 20, 1670

If it were equally easy to command minds and tongues, everyone would reign in safety and no rule would be oppressive: for everyone would live according to the wish of the rulers and by their decree alone would judge what is true and false, good or bad, just or unjust. But this, as I have already noted at the start of Chapter 18, cannot be—that is, that a mind be absolutely under the right *[ius]* of another, because no one can transfer to another his own natural right or his faculty of reasoning freely, and judging about everything whatsoever; nor can he be compelled to do so. Hence it happens that that rule is regarded as oppressive which is over minds, and that supreme majesty appears to do injury to its subjects and usurp their right when it wants to prescribe to each one what is to be embraced as true and to be rejected as false and what opinions ought to move each mind with devotion to God. These things are the right of each one. No one, even if he wanted to, could yield them.

I grant that judgment can be prejudiced in many and almost incredible ways, so that although it be not directly under the rule of another, yet it so depends on the word of another that it could deservedly be said to be under his right. But whatever art can afford in this matter, it has never happened that human beings have not experienced that each one is full of his own meanings, and that there are as many differences between heads as between palates.

Moses, who not by deceit but by divine virtue had captivated the judgment of his people, was nevertheless not able to avoid their rumors and malignant misinterpretations. Much less any of the other monarchs. But if this could in any way be conceived of, it would be conceivable only in a monarchy, not at all in a democracy where all or a great part of the populace partake collegially in ruling. I think the reason for this is plain to everyone.

Although, then, the Supreme Powers are believed to have a right to everything as the interpreters of the law and of religion, they nevertheless can never achieve a condition where human beings do not judge about everything by their own judgment and are not affected by this or that affection. The Supreme Powers can indeed rightly hold as enemies all who do not absolutely agree with them in all things. But now I do not argue about what they can do with right but about what is useful.

I conceded that they can rightly rule most oppressively and send citizens to death for the most trivial reasons. But, because they cannot do such things without great risk to their rule as a whole, I can also deny that they have an absolute capability to do these and similar things, and I can consequently deny that they have an absolute right to do so. For, as I have shown, the rights of the Supreme Powers are determined by their capability.

If, therefore, no one can yield his freedom of judging and feeling what he wishes and if everyone by the greatest law of nature is master of his own thoughts, it follows that never in a commonwealth, except with unhappy results, can it be attempted to have human beings, who think diverse and contrary things, speak only what is prescribed for them by the Supreme Powers. Not even the most expert—I say nothing of the populace—know how to be silent. It is a common human vice to entrust one's plans, when one should be silent, to others.

Therefore, that rule will be most oppressive where each one is denied freedom to say and to teach what he thinks. On the contrary, that rule will be moderate where the same liberty is granted to each. But I also cannot deny that majesty can be injured by words as well as by deed; and so if it is impossible to take away this liberty from subjects entirely, it will be, on the other hand, most pernicious to concede it completely. Therefore I must here inquire how far this liberty can and should be granted, preserving the peace of the commonwealth and preserving the rights of the Supreme Powers. This ... is my particular object.

It follows most plainly from the foundations of the commonwealth set out above that its ultimate end is not to dominate or to hold human beings with fear and make them under another's right but on the contrary to free each one from fear to live as safely as possible—that is, to let each best keep his own natural right to exist and to work without loss to himself or to others. No, I say, the end of the commonwealth is not to make beasts or automatons out of rational human beings, but rather to let them enjoy their minds and bodies safely in their functions and to let them use reason freely and not to fight with hatred, anger, or deceit nor regard each other in an unjust spirit. The end of the commonwealth, therefore, is, in truth, liberty.

Further, to form a commonwealth we saw that this one thing was necessary: that all power to make decrees be in all, or some, or one; for the free judgment of human beings is so various, and everyone thinks he knows everything, that it cannot happen that all think the same things and speak with one mouth. They could not live peacefully unless each one gave up the right of acting only on the decree of his own mind. Therefore everyone has given up only the right of acting from his own decree, but not the right of reasoning and judging. Hence, preserving the right of the Supreme Powers, no one can act against their decree, but anyone can think and judge, and consequently also speak, against it, provided he merely speaks or teaches and defends what he says with reason, not with deceit, anger, hatred or intent of introducing something into the commonwealth on the authority of his own decree. For example, if anyone shows some statute to be repugnant to sound reason and judges that it should be repealed and submits his opinion to the Supreme Power (which alone can make or repeal statutes), and meanwhile does not act contrary to the statute, he deserves very well of the commonwealth as the best of citizens. But if he acts against the statute to accuse the magistrate of injustice and make him odious to the crowd or in a seditious way tries to abrogate a statute against the magistrate's will, he is simply an agitator and a rebel.

We see, then, how, preserving the rights and authority of the Supreme Powers (that is, preserving the peace of the commonwealth), each one can speak and teach the things he thinks—assuredly if he leaves to the Supreme Powers the decrees for doing everything and does nothing against their decree, even if he often judges it to be contrary to what he judges good and openly thinks ought to be done. He can do this preserving justice and religion; rather, he must do this if he wants to show himself as just and religious. For, as I have already shown, justice depends on the decree of the Supreme Powers. Hence no one can be just unless he lives according to their received decrees. Piety, as I have shown in the preceding chapters, is supreme when it is exercised by serving the peace and tranquility of the commonwealth, and these cannot be kept if each one lives according to his own decision. Hence it is impious to do something by one's own decision against a decree of the Supreme Power to whom one is subject, since if this was permitted to everyone, the ruin of their rule would necessarily follow. He cannot do anything against the decree and dictate of his own reason as long as he acts according to the decrees of the Supreme Power; for at the persuasion of his own reason he has decided to transfer his right of living according to his own judgment to the Supreme Power.

And I can confirm these things from practice. At meetings either of the Supreme Powers or lesser powers, anything is rarely done with the unanimous vote of all the members; yet everything is done by the common decree of all—that is, of those who voted against it as much as of those who voted for it. However, I return to my subject.

We have then seen that on the basis of the fundamentals of the commonwealth each one can use liberty of justice preserving the right of the Supreme Powers. It is not less determined by the fundamentals what opinions in the commonwealth are seditious. Assuredly they are those which as soon as they are proposed remove the compact by which everyone has yielded the right of acting by his own judgment. For example, if anyone thinks that the Supreme Power ought not to have its right, or that no one ought to keep his promises, or that it is necessary for everyone to live according to his own judgment, and other things of this sort directly repugnant to the compact, such a one is seditious—not so much indeed on account of his judgment and opinion as because of the action which such judgments involve, i.e., because by the very fact that he thinks such a thing he dissolves the faith he has tacitly or expressly pledged to the Supreme Power.

Hence other opinions which do not involve an act—that is, the breaking of the compact, vengeance, wrath, etc.—are not seditious; except perhaps in a commonwealth corrupted in some way, where the superstitious and the ambitious, who cannot stand liberal men, have gained such a reputation they have more authority with the populace than the Supreme Powers. I cannot deny that there are also opinions which, although they appear to concern only what is true or false, are proposed and circulated in an unjust spirit but I have already dealt with these ... in such a way that reason remained free. In short, if we attend to this, that the faith of anyone towards the commonwealth, as towards God, can only be known from his works, i.e., from charity towards his neighbor, we can never doubt that the best commonwealth concedes to each the same liberty of philosophizing as we have shown that faith concedes to each one. I admit that some inconveniences sometimes arise from such liberty, but what was ever so wisely established that no inconvenience could arise from it? He who wants to settle everything by laws will aggravate vices, not correct them. What cannot be prevented must necessarily be conceded, although loss often follows. How many evils arise from lust, envy, avarice, drunkenness and similar things? But these things are put up with because they cannot be prohibited by the command of laws, although in truth they are vices. So much the more should liberty of judgment be granted, which undoubtedly is a virtue and which cannot be suppressed. Add that no inconveniences arise from it which cannot be avoided (as I shall at once show) by the authority of the magistrates. I say nothing as to how this liberty is especially necessary to promote the arts and sciences, for these are cultivated with happy results by those who have free and unprejudiced judgment.

But suppose that this liberty can be suppressed and that human beings can be so restricted that they dare murmur nothing except what is prescribed by the Supreme Powers. It will never happen that they will think nothing except what the Supreme Powers want. Hence it will necessarily follow that human beings will think one thing and say another; and consequently, faith, which is especially necessary in a commonwealth, will be corrupted and an abominable flattery and faithlessness fostered, from which will come frauds and the corruption of every good act. But it is far from being possible that all should speak to order. On the contrary, the more care is taken to deprive human beings of liberty of speech, the more contumaciously they will resist—not indeed the avaricious, the flatterers and other powerless minds whose supreme salvation is to contemplate cash in a chest and to have their stomachs stretched, but those whom good education, integrity of morals, and virtue have made more free. Such human beings are generally so constituted that they bear nothing less patiently than having opinions which they believe to be true held to be criminal and to have held against them as wickedness what moves them to piety towards God and humans. On this account they detest such laws and think that whatever is attempted against the magistrate is not disgraceful but highly honest. For this reason they cause revolts and try every kind of crime.

Since, then, it is established that human nature can be so compared, it follows that laws about opinions do not affect the wicked but the good and are issued not to coerce the malignant but to harass the decent and cannot be defended without great danger to the government. Add that such laws are entirely useless, for those who believe that the opinions condemned by the laws are sound cannot obey the laws, while those who reject the opinions as false receive the laws by which they are condemned as privileges and so triumph in them that a magistrate could not, if he wished, repeal them. Then there are the matters we laid out in Chapter 18 from the history of the Hebrews. Finally, how many schisms have arisen in the Church because magistrates wanted to resolve controversies by laws? For if human beings were not bound by the hope of dragging the laws and the magistrates to their side, and triumphing over their adversaries with the applause of the crowd, and acquiring official honor, they would never fight in an unjust spirit in such a way, nor would such frenzy agitate their minds.

Not only reason but daily experience teaches these things. Laws by which it is commanded what each one should believe and by which it is forbidden to speak or write against this or that opinion are often established to gratify or, rather, to appease the anger of those who cannot stand free talent; such men by certain crooked authority can easily convert the devotion of a rebellious populace to madness and rouse it against whomever they want. How much better it would be to restrain the anger and frenzy of the crowd than to enact useless statutes that cannot be violated except by those who love the virtues and the arts and to reduce the commonwealth to such straits that it cannot support liberal men! . . .

If no servility but faithfulness be of value, and the Supreme Powers are to retain their rule in the best way and not be compelled to yield to the seditious, liberty of judgment must necessarily be granted and human beings must be ruled in such a way that although they openly think different and contrary things, yet they live in concord.

4. "THE TRUE BUSINESS OF RELIGION"

John Locke (1632–1704) is commonly thought of today as a philosopher or political theorist; but that is only because modern interests have been less theological than his. The author of *Infalliblis Interpres Scripturae Non Necessarius* ("An Infallible Interpreter of Scripture Not Necessary," a very early work), of *An Essay for Understanding St. Paul's Epistles by Consulting St. Paul Himself*, of *The Reasonableness of Christianity as Delivered in the Scriptures*, of *Vindication of the Reasonableness of Christianity*, and of *Second Vindication of the Reasonableness of Christianity*, Locke was not merely a religious man. He was a master theologian with his own view of revelation and its exposition, with his own very clear, very moderate, very persuasive vision of the essentials of Christianity free from the dogma and the controversies, the elaborations, and, as he thought, the quibbles that had marred that exposition up to his time. That he constantly appeals to reason and makes reasonableness his criterion should lead no one to suppose that he is a rationalist in the sense of a critic of Christianity superior to its influences. As Christopher Hill has pointed out, "reason" is a social construct, Hill, *Change and Continuity in Seventeenth Century England* 120 (1974). Locke's "reason" is that of a man brought up in the mild Anglicanism of mid-seventeenth-century Oxford, exposed to Latitudinarian influence, and thoroughly convinced that the moral teachings of Christ are binding norms. It is from the perspective of this theology—tolerant of much doctrinal squabbling, moralistic, firmly antipapal—that Locke wrote his famous *Letter on Toleration*.

Note in particular the opening sentence setting out "the chief characteristic mark of the true church." In the opening paragraphs he then quotes twice from the Gospel of Luke, and once each from Galatians, Romans, and Second Timothy. He proceeds to state what "the business of true religion is." He goes on to elucidate what is the purpose of a church. It is "the public worship of God and by means thereof acquisition of eternal life." A corollary for him is that a church has rules only relating to spiritual matters. As much as for Menno or Roger Williams, for Locke a church is conceived of as a purely spiritual society.

The *Letter* was written to another theologian, Philip van Limborch, professor of divinity at the Arminian or Remonstrant Church at Amsterdam. When the letter first appeared anonymously in Latin, it was plausibly attributed to Limborch himself or to another Arminian divine, Jean LeClerc, *see* Raymond Klibansky, Preface to John Locke, *Epistola de Tolerantia* (1968). The Arminians, who were strongly opposed to the dominant Dutch Calvinists, were already attached to the ideas Locke celebrated: that the essence of Christianity consisted in a few "fundamental articles" and that all who accepted them should treat their other institutional, ritual, and doctrinal differences as unimportant, Jean LeClerc quoted, *id.* xvii. Locke, as it were, restated for the Arminians their own convictions. They were precariously perched within the Calvinist commonwealth; Locke was an exile from an England ruled once more by a Catholic king.

Locke had one advantage over Spinoza: experience in political affairs. He had in fact been in the service of one of the most active politicians of the age, Anthony Ashley Cooper. Cooper—Lord Ashley when Locke joined his household in 1667—was on his way up. A Roundhead under Oliver Cromwell, he had made a smooth transition when General Monk brought King Charles II back. We see him in Samuel Pepys's *Diary*, ed. Robert Latham and William Matthews (1970), for May 20, 1666, and September 23, 1667, taking bribes for procurement contracts with imperturbable aplomb. By 1672 he was earl of Shaftesbury. Of him is told a famous story that when a lady asked his religion, he replied, "Wise men, madam, are of but one religion," and when she persisted with, "What is that?" he answered, "Wise men never tell," George Macaulay Trevelyan, *England under the Stuarts* 347 (1914). It is hard to read that answer except cynically. Shaftesbury's cynicism and his other vices are not to be attributed to his secretary; but it is clear that Shaftesbury thought of Locke as knowledgeable on religious matters. When Shaftesbury was Lord Chancellor in 1672 he made Locke his secretary for "ecclesiastical preferments"—that is, he put him in charge of patronage in the church, J. W. Gough, Introduction to Locke's *The Second Treatise of Government viii*. And on one religious issue on which Locke was his adviser, Shaftesbury was to stake his political career—the exclusion of Catholics from English political life.

In 1667 when Locke first joined Shaftesbury's staff, Locke wrote *An Essay on Toleration*, many of whose ideas are very similar to the *Letter* of 1686. In early drafts, the greatest difference was the view that if dissenters were organized as a distinct party so as to be "visibly" a danger to the state, the magistrate should suppress them, J. W. Gough, Introduction to Locke's *Epistola de Toleration* 18. This hostility was toned down in the final form of the essay; but Locke maintained a persistent intolerance toward "Papists." On the basis of Locke's reasoning, Shaftesbury presented a memorial to the king, urging toleration for all Protestants but not for Catholics, *id*. at 21.

In 1672, Shaftesbury pushed the enactment of the Tests Act, providing that all persons holding any civil or military office or receiving any pay or grant of the king should take an oath in court acknowledging the king's supremacy over the Church and a second oath denying that there is "any transubstantiation in the sacrament of the Lord's supper," and should obtain a certificate from the parish minister and churchwarden that they had received "the sacrament of the Lord's supper, according to the usage of the church of England." The statute was entitled "An act for preventing dangers which may happen from popish recusants" and provided that anyone obliged to take the oaths or sacrament who failed to do so would on indictment and conviction lose his office, become incapable of bringing a lawsuit or receiving a legacy, and be subject to a fine of 500 pounds, 25 Charles II, c. 2 (8 Pick. Stat. 389) (1672).

The Tests Act forced out of the Admiralty the king's brother James, a Catholic. In 1679 Shaftesbury, with Locke as one of his lieutenants (*see* Gough, *Introduction to Locke's Second Treatise* ix), began to push the Exclusion Bill that would eliminate James as a Catholic from succession to the throne. In 1681 the bill carried in the Commons. Shaftesbury meanwhile had attempted to have James indicted as a "popish recusant" in criminal violation of the Tests Act. The attempt failed, the king's party engineered a reaction, Shaftesbury himself was tried and acquitted, but in November 1682 he fled the kingdom. In July 1683 leaders of Monmouth's rebellion, for which Shaftesbury was blamed, were executed, Trevelyan 416–423. In September 1683, Locke judged it expedient to follow his master by leaving England for Holland, Gough, *Introduction to the Second Treatise* ix. It is with this deep experience of government, of political intrigue, of the role of religion in politics that Locke wrote the *Letter*.

Sharply different from Spinoza in belief, the religious minority and the exile saw with the same sharpness as Spinoza that religious toleration was a great good. But if toleration was good, was it a great one? As far as Locke's letter went in the late seventeenth century, it illustrates the limits of its central category. Toleration assumes a tolerator and a toleratee. The gist of Locke's objection to extending toleration to Catholics and Muslims is that they could not be trusted to be loyal subjects of the Crown. The tolerator imagines that all Catholics and Muslims "deliver themselves up to the protection and service of another prince," whether the Pope or the King of Spain, the Mufti of Constantinople or the Ottoman Emperor. Atheists could not be trusted either, though for a different reason: how could they be expected to tell the truth if they will not take an oath? The scope of toleration for Locke is for Anglicans and dissenting Protestants. Toleration, then, is not the same as "free exercise of religion," an American invention that would come a century later. [Chapter Six, section 1A].

When Locke wrote in Holland in the winter of 1685–1686, religious tolerance was much debated. It had been vigorously defended in 1682 by Pierre Bayle in an essay in French; Klibansky, x. In October 1685 Louis XIV had revoked the French charter of toleration, the Edict of Nantes, and the barbarous persecution of Protestants in France was causing suffering known to everyone. The intellectual and political currents of the day make Locke's topic vital and insured its immediate success. Three years after it was written in Latin—the language of the learned and of the Continent—it was translated into English. It is this translation, ascribed since 1765 to William Popple, that is used here; for it is the form in which Locke's ideas were disseminated to Englishmen.

Locke himself, apparently out of timidity, never acknowledged his authorship. He angrily rebuked Limborch in 1690 when Limborch was divulging it in Holland. Locke was apparently secure in England. A Protestant monarch held the throne. Locke held a royal appointment as commissioner of appeals. But he wrote Limborch, "You do not know what situation you have landed me in," *Locke to Limborch*, April 22, 1690, quoted in Klibansky, xxiii. What now seems so much to his credit did not seem wholly creditable then.

John Locke, *A Letter Concerning Toleration*, 1688

Honoured Sir,

Since you are pleased to inquire what are my thoughts about the mutual toleration of Christians in their different professions of religion, I must needs answer you freely that I esteem that toleration to be the chief characteristic mark of the true Church. For whatsoever some people boast of the antiquity of places and names, or of the pomp of their outward worship; others, of the reformation of their discipline; all, of the orthodoxy of their faith—for everyone is orthodox to himself—these things, and all others of this nature, are much rather marks of men striving for power and empire over one another than of the Church of Christ. Let anyone have never so true a claim to all these things, yet if he be destitute of charity, meekness, and good-will in general towards all mankind, even to those that are not Christians, he is certainly yet short of being a true Christian himself. "The kings of the Gentiles exercise lordship over them," said our Saviour to His disciples, "but ye shall not be so." The business of true religion is quite another thing. It is not instituted in order to the erecting of an external pomp, nor to the obtaining of ecclesiastical dominion, nor to the exercising of compulsive force, but to the regulating of men's lives, according to the rules of virtue and piety. Whosoever will list himself under the banner of Christ, must, in the first place and above all things, make war upon his own lusts and vices. It is in vain for any man to usurp the name of Christian, without holiness of life, purity of manners, benignity and meekness of spirit. "Let everyone that nameth the name of Christ, depart from iniquity." "Thou, when thou art converted, strengthen thy brethren," said our Lord to Peter. It would, indeed, be very hard for one that appears careless about his own salvation to persuade me that he were extremely concerned for mine. For it is impossible that those should sincerely and heartily apply themselves to make other people Christians, who have not really embraced the Christian religion in their own hearts. If the Gospel and the apostles may be credited, no man can be a Christian without charity and without that faith which works, not by force, but by love. Now, I appeal to the consciences of those that persecute, torment, destroy, and kill other men upon pretence of religion, whether they do it out of friendship and kindness towards them or no? And I shall then indeed, and not until then, believe they do so, when I shall see those fiery zealots correcting, in the same manner, their friends and familiar acquaintance for the manifest sins they commit against the precepts of the Gospel; when I shall see them persecute with fire and sword the members of their own communion that are tainted with enormous vices and without amendment are in danger of eternal perdition; and when I shall see them thus express their love and desire of the salvation of their souls by the infliction of torments and exercise of all manner of cruelties. For if it be out of a principle of charity, as they pretend, and love to men's souls that they deprive them of their estates, maim them with corporal punishments, starve and torment them in noisome prisons, and in the end even take away their lives—I say, if all this be done merely to make men Christians and procure their salvation, why then do they suffer whoredom, fraud, malice, and such-like enormities, which (according to the apostle) manifestly relish of heathenish corruption, to predominate so much and abound amongst their flocks and people? These, and such-like things, are certainly more contrary to the glory of God, to the purity of the Church, and to the salvation of souls, than any conscientious dissent from ecclesiastical decisions, or separation from public worship, whilst accompanied with innocence of life. Why, then, does this burning zeal for God, for the Church, and for the salvation of souls—burning I say, literally, with fire and faggot—pass by those moral vices and wickednesses, without any chastisement, which are acknowledged by all men to be diametrically opposite to the profession of Christianity, and bend all its nerves either to the introducing of ceremonies, or to the establishment of opinions, which for the most part are about nice and intricate matters, that exceed the capacity of ordinary understandings? Which of the parties contending about these things is in the right, which of them is guilty of schism or heresy, whether those that domineer or those that suffer, will then at last be manifest when the causes of their separation comes to be judged of. He, certainly, that follows Christ, embraces His doctrine, and bears His yoke, though he forsake both father and mother, separate from the public assemblies and ceremonies of his country, or whomsoever or whatsoever else he relinquishes, will not then be judged a heretic.

Now, though the divisions that are amongst sects should be allowed to be never so obstructive of the salvation of souls; yet, nevertheless, adultery, fornication, uncleanliness, lasciviousness, idolatry, and such-like things, cannot be denied to be works of the flesh, concerning which the apostle has expressly declared that "they who do them shall not inherit the kingdom of God." Whosoever, therefore, is sincerely solicitous about the kingdom of God and thinks it his duty to endeavour the enlargement of it amongst men, ought to apply himself with no less care and industry to the rooting out of these immoralities than to the extirpation of sects. But if anyone do otherwise, and whilst he is cruel and implacable towards those that differ from him in opinion, he be indulgent to such iniquities and immoralities as are unbecoming the name of a Christian, let such a one talk never so much of the Church, he plainly demonstrates by his actions that it is another kingdom he aims at and not the advancement of the kingdom of God.

That any man should think fit to cause another man—whose salvation he heartily desires—to expire in torments, and that even in an unconverted state, would, I confess, seem very strange to me, and I think, to any other also. But nobody, surely, will ever believe that such a carriage can proceed from charity, love, or goodwill. If anyone maintain that men ought to be compelled by fire and sword to profess certain doctrines, and conform to this or that exterior worship, without any regard had unto their morals; if anyone endeavour to convert those that are erroneous unto the faith, by forcing them to profess things that they do not believe and allowing them to practise things that the Gospel does not permit, it cannot be doubted indeed but such a one is desirous to have a numerous assembly joined in the same profession with himself, but that he principally intends by those means to compose a truly Christian Church is altogether incredible. It is not, therefore, to be wondered at if those who do not really contend for the advancement of the true religion, and of the Church of Christ, make use of arms that do not belong to the Christian warfare. If, like the Captain of our salvation, they sincerely desired the good of souls, they would tread in the steps and follow the perfect example of that Prince of Peace, who sent out His soldiers to the subduing of nations, and gathering them into His Church, not armed with the sword, or other instruments of force, but prepared with the Gospel of peace and with the exemplary holiness of their conversation. This was His method. Though if infidels were to be converted by force, if those that are either blind or obstinate were to be drawn off from their errors by armed soldiers, we know very well that it was much more easy for Him to do it with armies of heavenly legions than for any son of the Church, how potent soever, with all his dragoons.

The toleration of those that differ from others in matters of religion is so agreeable to the Gospel of Jesus Christ, and to the genuine reason of mankind, that it seems monstrous for men to be so blind as not to perceive the necessity and advantage of it in so clear a light. I will not here tax the pride and ambition of some, the passion and uncharitable zeal of others. These are faults from which human affairs can perhaps scarce ever be perfectly freed; but yet such as nobody will bear the plain imputation of, without covering them with some specious colour; and so pretend to commendation, whilst they are carried away by their own irregular passions. But, however, that some may not colour their spirit of persecution and unchristian cruelty with a pretence of care of the public weal and observation of the laws; and that others, under pretence of religion, may not seek impunity for their libertinism and licentiousness; in a word, that none may impose either upon himself or others, by the pretences of loyalty and obedience to the prince, or of tenderness and sincerity in the worship of God; I esteem it above all things necessary to distinguish exactly the business of civil government from that of religion and to settle the just bounds that lie between the one and the other. If this be not done, there can be no end put to the controversies that will be always arising between those that have, or at least pretend to have, on the one side, a concernment for the interest of men's souls, and, on the other side, a care of the commonwealth.

The commonwealth seems to me to be a society of men constituted only for the procuring, preserving, and advancing their own civil interests.

Civil interests I call life, liberty, health, and indolency of body; and the possession of outward things, such as money, lands, houses, furniture, and the like.

It is the duty of the civil magistrate, by the impartial execution of equal laws, to secure unto all the people in general and to every one of his subjects in particular the just possession of these things belonging to this life. If anyone presume to violate the laws of public justice and equity, established for the preservation of those things, his presumption is to be checked by the fear of punishment, consisting of the deprivation or diminution of those civil interests, or goods, which otherwise he might and ought to enjoy. But seeing no man does willingly suffer himself to be punished by the deprivation of any part of his goods, and much less of his liberty of life, therefore, is the magistrate armed with the force and strength of all his subjects, in order to the punishment of those that violate any other man's rights.

Now that the whole jurisdiction of the magistrate reaches only to these civil concernments, and that all civil power, right and dominion, is bounded and confined to the only care of promoting these things; and that it neither can nor ought in any manner to be extended to the salvation of souls, these following considerations seem unto me abundantly to demonstrate.

First, because the care of souls is not committed to the civil magistrate, any more than to other men. It is not committed unto him, I say, by God; because it appears not that God has ever given any such authority to one man over another as to compel anyone to his religion. Nor can any such power be vested in the magistrate by the consent of the people, because no man can so far abandon the care of his own salvation as blindly to leave to the choice of any other, whether prince or subject, to prescribe to him what faith or worship he shall embrace. For no man can, if he would, conform his faith to the dictates of another. All the life and power of true religion consist in the inward and full persuasion of the mind; and faith is not faith without believing. Whatever profession we make, to whatever outward worship we conform, if we are not fully satisfied in our own mind that the one is true and the other well pleasing unto God, such profession and such practice, far from being any furtherance, are indeed great obstacles to our salvation. For in this manner, instead of expiating other sins by the exercise of religion, I say, in offering thus unto God Almighty such a worship as we esteem to be displeasing unto Him, we add unto the number of our other sins those also of hypocrisy and contempt of His Divine Majesty.

In the second place, the care of souls cannot belong to the civil magistrate, because his power consists only in outward force; but true and saving religion consists in the inward persuasion of the mind, without which nothing can be acceptable to God. And such is the nature of the understanding, that it cannot be compelled to the belief of anything by outward force. Confiscation of estate, imprisonment, torments, nothing of that nature can have any such efficacy as to make men change the inward judgement that they have framed of things.

It may indeed be alleged that the magistrate may make use of arguments, and, thereby; draw the heterodox into the way of truth, and procure their salvation. I grant it; but this is common to him with other men. In teaching, instructing, and redressing the erroneous by reason, he may certainly do what becomes any good man to do. Magistracy does not oblige him to put off either humanity or Christianity; but it is one thing to persuade, another to command; one thing to press with arguments, another with penalties. This civil power alone has a right to do; to the other, goodwill is authority enough. Every man has commission to admonish, exhort, convince another of error, and, by reasoning, to draw him into truth; but to give laws, receive obedience, and compel with the sword, belongs to none but the magistrate. And, upon this ground, I affirm that the magistrate's power extends not to the establishing of any articles of faith, or forms of worship, by the force of his laws. For laws are of no force at all without penalties, and penalties in this case are absolutely impertinent, because they are not proper to convince the mind. Neither the profession of any articles of faith, nor the conformity to any outward form of worship (as has been already said), can be available to the salvation of souls, unless the truth of the one and the acceptableness of the other unto God be thoroughly believed by those that so profess and practise. But penalties are no way capable to produce such belief. It is only light and evidence that can work a change in men's opinions; which light can in no manner proceed from corporal sufferings, or any other outward penalties.

In the third place, the care of the salvation of men's souls cannot belong to the magistrate; because, though the rigour of laws and the force of penalties were capable to convince and change men's minds, yet would not that help at all to the salvation of their souls. For there being but one truth, one way to heaven, what hope is there that more men would be led into it if they had no rule but the religion of the court and were put under the necessity to quit the light of their own reason, and oppose the dictates of their own consciences, and blindly to resign themselves up to the will of their governors and to the religion which either ignorance, ambition, or superstition had chanced to establish in the countries where they were born? In the variety and contradiction of opinions in religion, wherein the princes of the world are as much divided as in their secular interests, the narrow way would be much straitened; one country alone would be in the right, and all the rest of the world put under an obligation of following their princes in the ways that lead to destruction; and that which heightens the absurdity, and very ill suits the notion of a Deity, men would owe their eternal happiness or misery to the places of their nativity.

These considerations, to omit many others that might have been urged to the same purpose, seem unto me sufficient to conclude that all the power of civil government relates only to men's civil interests, is confined to the care of the things of this world, and hath nothing to do with the world to come.

Let us now consider what a church is. A church, then, I take to be a voluntary society of men, joining themselves together of their own accord in order to the public worshipping of God in such manner as they judge acceptable to Him, and effectual to the salvation of their souls.

I say it is a free and voluntary society. Nobody is born a member of any church; otherwise the religion of parents would descend unto children by the same right of inheritance as their temporal estates, and everyone would hold his faith by the same tenure he does his lands, than which nothing can be imagined more absurd. Thus, therefore, that matter stands. No man by nature is bound unto any particular church or sect, but everyone joins himself voluntarily to that society in which he believes he has found that profession and worship which is truly acceptable to God. The hope of salvation, as it was the only cause of his entrance into that communion, so it can be the only reason of his stay there. For if afterwards he discover anything either erroneous in the doctrine or incongruous in the worship of that society to which he has joined himself, why should it not be as free for him to go out as it was to enter? No member of a religious society can be tied with any other bonds but what proceed from the certain expectation of eternal life. A church, then, is a society of members voluntarily uniting to that end.

It follows now that we consider what is the power of this church and unto what laws it is subject.

Forasmuch as no society, how free soever, or upon whatsoever slight occasion instituted, whether of philosophers for learning, or merchants for commerce, or of men of leisure for mutual conversation and discourse, no church or company, I say, can in the least subsist and hold together, but will presently dissolve and break in pieces, unless it be regulated by some laws, and the members all consent to observe some order. Place and time of meeting must be agreed on; rules for admitting and excluding members must be established; distinction of officers, and putting things into a regular course, and suchlike, cannot be omitted. But since the joining together of several members into this church-society, as has already been demonstrated, is absolutely free and spontaneous, it necessarily follows that the right of making its laws can belong to none but the society itself; or, at least (which is the same thing), to those whom the society by common consent has authorised thereunto.

Some, perhaps, may object that no such society can be said to be a true church unless it have in it a bishop or presbyter, with ruling authority derived from the very apostles, and continued down to the present times by an uninterrupted succession.

To these I answer: In the first place, let them show me the edict by which Christ has imposed that law upon His Church. And let not any man think me impertinent, if in a thing of this consequence I require that the terms of that edict be very express and positive; for the promise He has made us, that "wheresoever two or three are gathered together" in His name, He will be in the midst of them (Mt. 18:20), seems to imply the contrary. Whether such an assembly want anything necessary to a true church, pray do you consider. Certain I am that nothing can be there wanting unto the salvation of souls, which is sufficient to our purpose.

Next, pray observe how great have always been the divisions amongst even those who lay so much stress upon the Divine institution and continued succession of a certain order of rulers in the Church. Now, their very dissension unavoidably puts us upon a necessity of deliberating and, consequently, allows a liberty of choosing that which upon consideration we prefer.

And, in the last place, I consent that these men have a rule in their church, established by such a long series of succession as they judge necessary, provided I may have liberty at the same time to join myself to that society in which I am persuaded those things are to be found which are necessary to the salvation of my soul. In this manner ecclesiastical liberty will be preserved on all sides, and no man will have a legislator imposed upon him but whom himself has chosen.

But since men are so solicitous about the true church, I would only ask them here, by the way, if it be not more agreeable to the Church of Christ to make the conditions of her communion consist in such things, and such things only, as the Holy Spirit has in the Holy Scriptures declared, in express words, to be necessary to salvation; I ask, I say, whether this be not more agreeable to the Church of Christ than for men to impose their own inventions and interpretations upon others as if they were of Divine authority, and to establish by ecclesiastical laws, as absolutely necessary to the profession of Christianity, such things as the Holy Scriptures do either not mention, or at least not expressly command? Whosoever requires those things in order to ecclesiastical communion, which Christ does not require in order to life eternal, he may, perhaps, indeed constitute a society accommodated to his own opinion and his own advantage; but how that can be called the Church of Christ which is established upon laws that are not His, and which excludes such persons from its communion as He will one day receive into the Kingdom of Heaven, I understand not. But this being not a proper place to inquire into the marks of the true church, I will only mind those that contend so earnestly for the decrees of their own society, and that cry out continually, "The Church! the Church!" with as much noise, and perhaps upon the same principle, as the Ephesian silversmiths did for their Diana; this, I say, I desire to mind them of, that the Gospel frequently declares that the true disciples of Christ must suffer persecution; but that the Church of Christ should persecute others, and force others by fire and sword to embrace her faith and doctrine, I could never yet find in any of the books of the New Testament.

The end of a religious society (as has already been said) is the public worship of God and, by means thereof, the acquisition of eternal life. All discipline ought, therefore, to tend to that end, and all ecclesiastical laws to be thereunto confined. Nothing ought nor can be transacted in this society relating to the possession of civil and worldly goods. No force is here to be made use of upon any occasion whatsoever. For force belongs wholly to the civil magistrate, and the possession of all outward goods is subject to his jurisdiction.

But, it may be asked, by what means then shall ecclesiastical law be established, if they must be thus destitute of all compulsive power? I answer: They must be established by means suitable to the nature of such things, whereof the external profession and observation—if not proceeding from a thorough conviction and approbation of the mind—is altogether useless and unprofitable. The arms by which the members of this society are to be kept within their duty are exhortations, admonitions, and advices. If by these means the offenders will not be reclaimed, and the erroneous convinced, there remains nothing further to be done but that such stubborn and obstinate persons, who give no ground to hope for their reformation, should be cast out and separated from the society. This is the last and utmost force of ecclesiastical authority. No other punishment can thereby be inflicted than that, the relation ceasing between the body and the member which is cut off. The person so condemned ceases to be a part of that church.

These things being thus determined, let us inquire, in the next place: How far the duty of toleration extends, and what is required from everyone by it?

And, first, I hold that no church is bound, by the duty of toleration, to retain any such person in her bosom as, after admonition, continues obstinately to offend against the laws of the society. For, those being the condition of communion and the bond of the society, if the breach of them were permitted without any animadversion the society would immediately be thereby dissolved. But, nevertheless, in all such cases care is to be taken that the sentence of excommunication, and the execution thereof, carry with it no rough usage of word or action whereby the ejected person may any wise be damnified in body or estate. For all force (as has often been said) belongs only to the magistrate, nor ought any private persons at any time to use force, unless it be in self-defense against unjust violence. Excommunication neither does, nor can, deprive the excommunicated person of any of those civil goods that he formerly possessed. . . .

But, to speak the truth, we must acknowledge that the Church (if a convention of clergymen, making canons, must be called by that name) is for the most part more apt to be influenced by the Court than the Court by the Church. How the Church was under the vicissitude of orthodox and Arian emperors is very well known. Or if those things be too remote, our modern English history affords us fresh examples in the reigns of Henry VIII, Edward VI, Mary, and Elizabeth, how easily and smoothly the clergy changed their decrees, their articles of faith, their form of worship, everything according to the inclination of those kings and queens. Yet were those kings and queens of such different minds in point of religion, and enjoined thereupon such different things, that no man in his wits (I had almost said none but an atheist) will presume to say that any sincere and upright worshipper of God could, with a safe conscience, obey their several decrees. To conclude, it is the same thing whether a king that prescribes laws to another man's religion pretend to do it by his own judgement, or by the ecclesiastical authority and advice of others. The decisions of churchmen, whose differences and disputes are sufficiently known, cannot be any sounder or safer than his; nor can all their suffrages joined together add a new strength to the civil power. Though this also must be taken notice of— that princes seldom have any regard to the suffrages of ecclesiastics that are not favourers of their own faith and way of worship.

But, after all, the principal consideration, and which absolutely determines this controversy, is this: Although the magistrate's opinion in religion be sound, and the way that he appoints be truly Evangelical, yet, if I be not thoroughly persuaded thereof in my own mind, there will be no safety for me in following it. No way whatsoever that I shall walk in against the dictates of my conscience will ever bring me to the mansions of the blessed. I may grow rich by an art that I take not delight in; I may be cured of some disease by remedies that I have not faith in; but I cannot be saved by a religion that I distrust and by a worship that I abhor. It is in vain for an unbeliever to take up the outward show of another man's profession. Faith only and inward sincerity are the things that procure acceptance with God. The most likely and most approved remedy can have no effect upon the patient, if his stomach reject it as soon as taken; and you will in vain cram a medicine down a sick man's throat, which his particular constitution will be sure to turn into poison. In a word, whatsoever may be doubtful in religion, yet this at least is certain, that no religion which I believe not to be true can be either true or profitable unto me. In vain, therefore, do princes compel their subjects to come into their Church communion, under pretence of saving their souls. If they believe, they will come of their own accord, if they believe not, their coming will nothing avail them. How great soever, in fine, may be the pretence of good-will and charity, and concern for the salvation of men's souls, men cannot be forced to be saved whether they will or no. And therefore, when all is done, they must be left to their own consciences.

Having thus at length freed men from all dominion over one another in matters of religion, let us now consider what they are to do. All men know and acknowledge that God ought to be publicly worshipped; why otherwise do they compel one another unto the public assemblies? Men, therefore, constituted in this liberty are to enter into some religious society, that they meet together, not only for mutual edification, but to own to the world that they worship God and offer unto His Divine Majesty such service as they themselves are not ashamed of and such as they think not unworthy of Him, nor unacceptable to Him; and, finally, that by the purity of doctrine, holiness of life, and decent form of worship, they may draw others unto the love of the true religion, and perform such other things in religion as cannot be done by each private man apart.

These religious societies I call *Churches*; and these, I say, the magistrate ought to tolerate, for the business of these assemblies of the people is nothing but what is lawful for every man in particular to take care of—I mean the salvation of their souls; nor in this case is there any difference between the National Church and other separated congregations.

But as in every Church there are two things especially to be considered—the outward form and rites of worship, and the doctrines and articles of faith—these things must be handled each distinctly that so the whole matter of toleration may the more clearly be understood.

Concerning outward worship, I say, in the first place, that the magistrate has no power to enforce by law, either in his own Church, or much less in another, the use of any rites or ceremonies whatsoever in the worship of God. And this, not only because these Churches are free societies, but because whatsoever is practised in the worship of God is only so far justifiable as it is believed by those that practise it to be acceptable unto Him. Whatsoever is not done with that assurance of faith is neither well in itself, nor can it be acceptable to God. To impose such things, therefore, upon any people, contrary to their own judgment, is in effect to command them to offend God, which, considering that the end of all religion is to please Him, and that liberty is essentially necessary to that end, appears to be absurd beyond expression.

But perhaps it may be concluded from hence that I deny unto the magistrate all manner of power about indifferent things, which, if it be not granted, the whole subject matter of law-making is taken away. No, I readily grant that indifferent things, and perhaps none but such, are subjected to the legislative power. But it does not therefore follow that the magistrate may ordain whatsoever he pleases concerning anything that is indifferent. The public good is the rule and measure of all law-making. If a thing be not useful to the commonwealth, though it be never so indifferent, it may not presently be established by law.

And further, things never so indifferent in their own nature, when they are brought into the Church and worship of God, are removed out of the reach of the magistrate's jurisdiction, because in that use they have no connection at all with civil affairs. The only business of the Church is the salvation of souls, and it no way concerns the commonwealth, or any member of it, that this or the other ceremony be there made use of. Neither the use nor the omission of any ceremonies in those religious assemblies does either advantage or prejudice the life, liberty, or estate of any man. For example, let it be granted that the washing of an infant with water is in itself an indifferent thing, let it be granted also that the magistrate understand such washing to be profitable to the curing or preventing of any disease the children are subject unto, and esteem the matter weighty enough to be taken care of by a law. In that case he may order it to be done. But will any one therefore say that a magistrate has the same right to ordain by law that all children shall be baptised by priests in the sacred font in order to the purification of their souls? The extreme difference of these two cases is visible to every one at first sight. Or let us apply the last case to the child of a Jew, and the thing speaks itself. For what hinders but a Christian magistrate may have subjects that are Jews? Now, if we acknowledge that such an injury may not be done unto a Jew as to compel him, against his own opinion, to practise in his religion a thing that is in its nature indifferent, how can we maintain that anything of this kind may be done to a Christian?

Again, things in their own nature indifferent cannot, by any human authority, be made any part of the worship of God—for this very reason: because they are indifferent. For, since indifferent things are not capable, by any virtue of their own, to propitiate the Deity, no human power or authority can confer on them so much dignity and excellency as to enable them to do it. In the common affairs of life that use of indifferent things which God has not forbidden is free and lawful, and therefore in those things human authority has place. But it is not so in matters of religion. Things indifferent are not otherwise lawful in the worship of God than as they are instituted by God Himself and as He, by some positive command, has ordained them to be made a part of that worship which He will vouchsafe to accept at the hands of poor sinful men. Nor, when an incensed Deity shall ask us, "Who has required these, or such-like things at your hands?" will it be enough to answer Him that the magistrate commanded them. If civil jurisdiction extend thus far, what might not lawfully be introduced into religion? What hodgepodge of ceremonies, what superstitious inventions, built upon the magistrate's authority, might not (against conscience) be imposed upon the worshippers of God? For the greatest part of these ceremonies and superstitions consists in the religious use of such things as are in their own nature indifferent; nor are they sinful upon any other account than because God is not the author of them. The sprinkling of water and the use of bread and wine are both in their own nature and in the ordinary occasions of life altogether indifferent. Will any man, therefore, say that these things could have been introduced into religion and made a part of divine worship if not by divine institution? If any human authority or civil power could have done this, why might it not also enjoin the eating of fish and drinking of ale in the holy banquet as a part of divine worship? Why not the sprinkling of the blood of beasts in churches, and expiations by water or fire, and abundance more of this kind? But these things, how indifferent soever they be in common uses, when they come to be annexed unto divine worship, without divine authority, they are as abominable to God as the sacrifice of a dog. And why is a dog so abominable? What difference is there between a dog and a goat, in respect of the divine nature, equally and infinitely distant from all affinity with matter, unless it be that God required the use of one in His worship and not of the other? We see, therefore, that indifferent things, how much soever they be under the power of the civil magistrate, yet cannot, upon that pretence, be introduced into religion and imposed upon religious assemblies, because, in the worship of God, they wholly cease to be indifferent. He that worships God does it with design to please Him and procure His favour. But that cannot be done by him who, upon the command of another, offers unto God that which he knows will be displeasing to Him, because not commanded by Himself. This is not to please God, or appease his wrath, but willingly and knowingly to provoke Him by a manifest contempt, which is a thing absolutely repugnant to the nature and end of worship.

But it will be here asked: "If nothing belonging to divine worship be left to human discretion, how is it then that Churches themselves have the power of ordering anything about the time and place of worship and the like?" To this I answer that in religious worship we must distinguish between what is part of the worship itself and what is but a circumstance. That is a part of the worship which is believed to be appointed by God and to be well-pleasing to Him, and therefore that is necessary. Circumstances are such things which, though in general they cannot be separated from worship, yet the particular instances or modifications of them are not determined, and therefore they are indifferent. Of this sort are the time and place of worship, habit and posture of him that worships. These are circumstances, and perfectly indifferent, where God has not given any express command about them. For example: amongst the Jews the time and place of their worship and the habits of those that officiated in it were not mere circumstances, but a part of the worship itself, in which, if anything were defective, or different from the institution, they could not hope that it would be accepted by God. But these, to Christians under the liberty of the Gospel, are mere circumstances of worship, which the prudence of every Church may bring into such use as shall be judged most subservient to the end of order, decency, and edification. But, even under the Gospel, those who believe the first or the seventh day to be set apart by God, and consecrated still to His worship, to them that portion of time is not a simple circumstance, but a real part of Divine worship, which can neither be changed nor neglected.

In the next place: As the magistrate has no power to impose by his laws the use of any rites and ceremonies in any Church, so neither has he any power to forbid the use of such rites and ceremonies as are already received, approved, and practised by any Church; because, if he did so, he would destroy the Church itself: the end of whose institution is only to worship God with freedom after its own manner.

You will say, by this rule, if some congregations should have a mind to sacrifice infants, or (as the primitive Christians were falsely accused) lustfully pollute themselves in promiscuous uncleanness, or practise any other such heinous enormities, is the magistrate obliged to tolerate them, because they are committed in a religious assembly? I answer: No. These things are not lawful in the ordinary course of life, nor in any private house; and therefore neither are they so in the worship of God, or in any religious meeting. But, indeed, if any people congregated upon account of religion should be desirous to sacrifice a calf, I deny that that ought to be prohibited by a law. Meliboeus, whose calf it is, may lawfully kill his calf at home, and burn any part of it that he thinks fit. For no injury is thereby done to any one, no prejudice to another man's goods. And for the same reason he may kill his calf also in a religious meeting. Whether the doing so be well-pleasing to God or no, it is their part to consider that do it. The part of the magistrate is only to take care that the commonwealth receive no prejudice, and that there be no injury done to any man, either in life or estate. And thus what may be spent on a feast may be spent on a sacrifice. But if peradventure such were the state of things that the interest of the commonwealth required all slaughter of beasts should be forborne for some while, in order to the increasing of the stock of cattle that had been destroyed by some extraordinary murrain, who sees not that the magistrate, in such a case, may forbid all his subjects to kill any calves for any use whatsoever? Only it is to be observed that, in this case, the law is not made about a religious, but a political matter; nor is the sacrifice, but the slaughter of calves, thereby prohibited.

By this we see what difference there is between the Church and the Commonwealth. Whatsoever is lawful in the Commonwealth cannot be prohibited by the magistrate in the Church. Whatsoever is permitted unto any of his subjects for their ordinary use, neither can nor ought to be forbidden by him to any sect of people for their religious uses. If any man may lawfully take bread or wine, either sitting or kneeling in his own house, the law ought not to abridge him of the same liberty in his religious worship; though in the Church the use of bread and wine be very different and be there applied to the mysteries of faith and rites of Divine worship. But those things that are prejudicial to the commonweal of a people in their ordinary use and are, therefore, forbidden by laws, those things ought not to be permitted to Churches in their sacred rites. Only the magistrate ought always to be very careful that he do not misuse his authority to the oppression of any Church, under pretence of public good.

It may be said: "What if a Church be idolatrous, is that also to be tolerated by the magistrate?" I answer: What power can be given to the magistrate for the suppression of an idolatrous Church, which may not in time and place be made use of to the ruin of an orthodox one? For it must be remembered that the civil power is the same everywhere, and the religion of every prince is orthodox to himself. If, therefore, such a power be granted unto the civil magistrate in spirituals as that at Geneva, for example, he may extirpate, by violence and blood, the religion which is there reputed idolatrous, by the same rule another magistrate, in some neighbouring country, may oppress the reformed religion and, in India, the Christian. The civil power can either change everything in religion, according to the prince's pleasure, or it can change nothing. If it be once permitted to introduce anything into religion by the means of laws and penalties, there can be no bounds put to it; but it will in the same manner be lawful to alter everything, according to that rule of truth which the magistrate has framed unto himself. No man whatsoever ought, therefore, to be deprived of his terrestrial enjoyments upon account of his religion. Not even Americans, subjected unto a Christian prince, are to be punished either in body or goods for not embracing our faith and worship. If they are persuaded that they please God in observing the rites of their own country and that they shall obtain happiness by that means, they are to be left unto God and themselves. Let us trace this matter to the bottom. Thus it is: An inconsiderable and weak number of Christians, destitute of everything, arrive in a Pagan country; these foreigners beseech the inhabitants, by the bowels of humanity, that they would succour them with the necessaries of life; those necessaries are given them, habitations are granted, and they all join together, and grow up into one body of people. The Christian religion by this means takes root in that country and spreads itself, but does not suddenly grow the strongest. While things are in this condition peace, friendship, faith, and equal justice are preserved amongst them. At length the magistrate becomes a Christian, and by that means their party becomes the most powerful. Then immediately all compacts are to be broken, all civil rights to be violated, that idolatry may be extirpated and unless these innocent Pagans, strict observers of the rules of equity and the law of Nature and no ways offending against the laws of the society, I say, unless they, will forsake their ancient religion and embrace a new and strange one, they are to be turned out of the lands and possessions of their forefathers and perhaps deprived of life itself. Then, at last, it appears what zeal for the Church, joined with the desire of dominion, is capable to produce, and how easily the pretence of religion, and of the care of souls, serves for a cloak to covetousness, rapine, and ambition.

Now whosoever maintains that idolatry is to be rooted out of anyplace by laws, punishments, fire, and sword, may apply this story to himself. For the reason of the thing is equal, both in America and Europe. And neither Pagans there, nor any dissenting Christians here, can, with any right, be deprived of their worldly goods by the pre-dominating faction of a court-church; nor are any civil rights to be either changed or violated upon account of religion in one place more than another....

But some may ask: "What if the magistrate should enjoin anything by his authority that appears unlawful to the conscience of a private person?" I answer that, if government be faithfully administered and the counsels of the magistrates be indeed directed to the public good, this will seldom happen. But if, perhaps, it do so fall out, I say, that such a private person is to abstain from the action that he judges unlawful, and he is to undergo the punishment which it is not unlawful for him to bear. For the private judgement of any person concerning a law enacted in political matters, for the public good, does not take away the obligation of that law, nor deserve a dispensation. But if the law, indeed, be concerning things that lie not within the verge of the magistrate's authority (as, for example, that the people, or any party amongst them, should be compelled to embrace a strange religion, and join in the worship and ceremonies of another Church), men are not in these cases obliged by that law, against their consciences. For the political society is instituted for no other end, but only to secure every man's possession of the things of this life. The care of each man's soul and of the things of heaven, which neither does belong to the commonwealth nor can be subjected to it, is left entirely to every man's self. Thus the safeguard of men's lives and of the things that belong unto this life is the business of the commonwealth; and the preserving of those things unto their owners is the duty of the magistrate. And therefore the magistrate cannot take away these worldly things from this man or party and give them to that; nor change propriety amongst fellow subjects (no not even by a law), for a cause that has no relation to the end of civil government, I mean for their religion, which whether it be true or false does no prejudice to the worldly concerns of their fellow subjects, which are the things that only belong unto the care of the commonwealth.

But what if the magistrate believe such a law as this to be for the public good? I answer: As the private judgement of any particular person, if erroneous, does not exempt him from the obligation of law, so the private judgement (as I may call it) of the magistrate does not give him any new right of imposing laws upon his subjects, which neither was in the constitution of the government granted him, nor ever was in the power of the people to grant, much less if he make it his business to enrich and advance his followers and fellow-sectaries with the spoils of others. But what if the magistrate believe that he has a right to make such laws and that they are for the public good, and his subjects believe the contrary? Who shall be judge between them? I answer: God alone. For there is no judge upon earth between the supreme magistrate and the people. God, I say, is the only Judge in this case, who will retribute unto every one at the last day according to his deserts; that is, according to his sincerity and uprightness in endeavouring to promote piety, and the public weal, and peace of mankind. But what shall be done in the meanwhile? I answer: The principal and chief care of every one ought to be of his own soul first, and, in the next place, of the public peace; though yet there are very few will think it is peace there, where they see all laid waste.

There are two sorts of contests amongst men, the one managed by law, the other by force; and these are of that nature that where the one ends, the other always begins. But it is not my business to inquire into the power of the magistrate in the different constitutions of nations. I only know what usually happens where controversies arise without a judge to determine them. You will say, then, the magistrate being the stronger will have his will and carry his point. Without doubt; but the question is not here concerning the doubtlessness of the event, but the rule of right.

But to come to particulars. I say, first, no opinions contrary to human society, or to those moral rules which are necessary to the preservation of civil society, are to be tolerated by the magistrate. But of these, indeed, examples in any Church are rare. For no sect can easily arrive to such a degree of madness as that it should think fit to teach, for doctrines of religion, such things as manifestly undermine the foundations of society and are, therefore, condemned by the judgement of all mankind; because their own interest, peace, reputation can be no reason why they should not be tolerated, everything would be thereby endangered.

Another more secret evil, but more dangerous to the commonwealth, is when men arrogate to themselves, and to those of their own sect, some peculiar prerogative covered over with a specious show of deceitful words, but in effect opposite to the civil right of the community. For example: we cannot find any sect that teaches, expressly and openly, that men are not obliged to keep their promise; that princes may be dethroned by those that differ from them in religion; or that the dominion of all things belongs only to themselves. For these things, proposed thus nakedly and plainly, would soon draw on them the eye and hand of the magistrate and awaken all the care of the commonwealth to a watchfulness against the spreading of so dangerous an evil. But, nevertheless, we find those that say the same things in other words. What else do they mean who teach that faith is not to be kept with heretics? Their meaning, forsooth, is that the privilege of breaking faith belongs unto themselves; for they declare all that are not of their communion to be heretics, or at least may declare them so whensoever they think fit. What can be the meaning of their asserting that kings excommunicated forfeit their crowns and kingdoms? It is evident that they thereby arrogate unto themselves the power of deposing kings, because they challenge the power of excommunication, as the peculiar right of their hierarchy. That dominion is founded in grace is also an assertion by which those that maintain it do plainly lay claim to the possession of all things. For they are not so wanting to themselves as not to believe, or at least as not to profess themselves to be the truly pious and faithful. These, therefore, and the like, who attribute unto the faithful, religious, and orthodox, that is, in plain terms, unto themselves, any peculiar privilege or power above other mortals, in civil concernments; or who upon pretence of religion do challenge any manner of authority over such as are not associated with them in their ecclesiastical communion, I say these have no right to be tolerated by the magistrate; as neither those that will not own and teach the duty of tolerating all men in matters of mere religion. For what do all these and the like doctrines signify, but that they may and are ready upon any occasion to seize the Government and possess themselves of the estates and fortunes of their fellow subjects; and that they only ask leave to be tolerated by the magistrate so long until they find themselves strong enough to effect it?

Again: That Church can have no right to be tolerated by the magistrate which is constituted upon such a bottom that all those who enter into it do thereby *ipso facto* deliver themselves up to the protection and service of another prince. For by this means the magistrate would give way to the settling of a foreign jurisdiction in his own country and suffer his own people to be listed, as it were, for soldiers against his own Government. Nor does the frivolous and fallacious distinction between the Court and the

Church afford any remedy to this inconvenience; especially when both the one and the other are equally subject to the absolute authority of the same person, who has not only power to persuade the members of his Church to whatsoever he lists, either as purely religious, or in order thereunto, but can also enjoin it them on pain of eternal fire. It is ridiculous for any one to profess himself to be a Mahometan only in his religion, but in everything else a faithful subject to a Christian magistrate, whilst at the same time he acknowledges himself bound to yield blind obedience to the Mufti of Constantinople, who himself is entirely obedient to the Ottoman Emperor and frames the feigned oracles of that religion according to his pleasure. But this Mahometan living amongst Christians would yet more apparently renounce their government if he acknowledged the same person to be head of his Church who is the supreme magistrate in the state.

Lastly, those are not at all to be tolerated who deny the being of a God. Promises, covenants, and oaths, which are the bonds of human society, can have no hold upon an atheist. The taking away of God, though but even in thought, dissolves all; besides also, those that by their atheism undermine and destroy all religion, can have no pretence of religion whereupon to challenge the privilege of a toleration. As for other practical opinions, though not absolutely free from all error, if they do not tend to establish domination over others, or civil impunity to the Church in which they are taught, there.

*

PART TWO

THE AMERICAN EXPERIENCE

CHAPTER SIX

Freedom of Conscience and Religious Establishments in a Revolutionary Age

---

1. Virginia

Virginia was special—the most populous state in America, the home of a remarkable galaxy of political leaders, a community in which the claims of an established church and dissenters from it were in sharp conflict and had to be resolved.

A. "Quota of Imps": The Awakening of James Madison

Baptized as an infant in the Church of England, James Madison attended a Presbyterian institution, the College of New Jersey in Princeton, from 1769 to 1772. Back in Virginia, aged twenty-two, he wrote his fellow Princetonian William Bradford on Bradford's choice of a career. "Divinity" is the academic study of religion. Madison regarded theology as "the most sublime of all sciences."

Madison to William Bradford, September 25, 1773

You forbid any recommendation of Divinity by suggesting that you have insuperable objections therefore I can only condole with the Church on the loss of a fine Genius and persuasive Orator. I cannot however suppress thus much of my advice on that head that you would always keep the Ministry obliquely in View whatever your profession be. This will lead you to cultivate an acquaintance [sic] occasionally with the most sublime of all Sciences and will qualify you for a change of public character if you should hereafter desire it. I have sometimes thought there could not be a stronger testimony in favor of Religion or against temporal Enjoyments even the most rational and manly than for men who occupy the most honorable and gainful departments and are rising in reputation and wealth, publicly to declare their unsatisfatoriness [sic] by becoming fervent Advocates in the cause of Christ, & I wish you may give in your Evidence in this way. Such Instances have seldom occurred, therefore they would be more striking and would be instead of a "Cloud of Witnesses." William T. Hutchinson and William M.E.Rachal, eds., 1 *Papers of James Madison* [*Madison Papers*] 96 (1962).

"Cloud of Witnesses" was a reference to Hebrews 12:1–2: "With a cloud of witnesses to faith around us, we must throw off every encumbrance, every sin to which we cling, and run with resolution the race for which we are entered, our eyes fixed on Jesus...." The allusions chimed with Madison's interest in "Advocates for Christ" and the admonition (surely self-directed) to "keep the Ministry obliquely in view." *See* also William Lee Miller, *The First Liberty: Religion and the American Republic* 79–96 (1985).

Bradford replied on November 5, 1773. Madison had decided him for the law. He later became attorney general of the United States. Writing from Philadelphia, he added: "Yet in a place *where* deistical *sentiments* almost universally prevail I look upon it as absolutely *necessary* to be *able to defend as well as believe the Christian religion.*" 1 *Madison Papers* 98. Madison wrote back on December 1, 1773. His question marked his first interest in the great subject on which he was to leave his imprint: "Is an Ecclesiastical Establishment absolutely necessary to support civil society in a supream Government? & how far is it hurtful to a dependant State?" 1 *Madison Papers* 101. The next letter to Bradford linked religion with politics.

Madison to Bradford, January 24, 1774

However Political Contests are necessary sometimes as well as military to afford exercise and practise and to instruct in the Art of defending Liberty and property. I verily believe the frequent Assaults that have been made on America[,] Boston, especially, will in the end prove of real advantage. If the Church of England had been the established and general Religion in all the Northern Colonies as it has been among us here and uninterrupted tranquility had prevailed throughout the Continent, It is clear to me that slavery and Subjection might and would have been gradually insinuated among us. Union of Religious Sentiments begets a surprizing confidence and Ecclesiastical Establishments tend to great ignorance and Corruption all of which facilitate the Execution of mischievous Projects....

I have indeed as good an Atmosphere at home as the Climate will allow: but have nothing to brag of as to the State and Liberty of my Country. Poverty and Luxury prevail among all sort: Pride ignorance and Knavery among the Priesthood and Vice and Wickedness among the Laity. This is bad enough But It is not the worst I have to tell you. That diabolical Hell conceived principle of persecution rages among some and to their eternal Infamy the Clergy can furnish their Quota of Imps for such business. This vexes me the most of any thing whatever. There are at this [time] in the adjacent County not less than 5 or 6 well meaning men in close Gaol for publishing their religious Sentiments which in the main are very orthodox. I have neither patience to hear talk or think of any thing relative to this matter, for I have squabbled and scolded abused and ridiculed so long about it, to so little purpose that I am without common patience. So I [leave you] to pity me and pray for Liberty of Conscience [to revive among us]. 1 *Madison Papers* 105–106.

See John T. Noonan, Jr., "Quota of Imps," in Merrill Peterson and Robert Vaughan, eds., *The Virginia Statute for Religious Freedom: Its Evolution and Consequences in American History*, 171–199 (1988); and Noonan, *The Lustre of Our Country: The American Experience of Religious Freedom* 68 (1998). Madison was stirred to what his editors describe as this "unaccustomed fervor" by the imprisonment of a half-dozen Baptist preachers in Culpepper County, Virginia. Quakers, Presbyterians, and Regular Baptists existed in the colony, as did smaller groups of Lutherans, Dunkers, and Methodists. The English Act of Toleration of 1689 had been accepted by the colony, and those Protestant churches conforming to its terms, while not on a par with the Church of England, were not persecuted. H.J. Eckenrode, *Separation of Church and State in Virginia: A Study in the Development of the Revolution* 30–34 (1910). The tolerated churches applied for permits to preach and to build meeting houses. The Separate Baptists, present in force since the 1750s, did not. Their missionary methods were itinerant. They already had an independent attitude toward British law. Appealing with evangelical enthusiasm to the less affluent part of the white community, they were socially unsettling and, from 1770 on, were persecuted. *Id.* 36–37.

In 1771, for example, a Baptist preacher in Caroline County had been hauled off in the middle of his sermon and flogged by the sheriff. Baptists met at Blue Run church in Orange County (Madison's home) and protested this outrage; the crowd of 4,000 was the largest mass meeting ever assembled in Virginia to that date. *See* Rhys Isaac, " 'The Rage of Malice of the Old Serpent Devil': The Dissenters and the Making and Remaking of the Virginia Statute for Religious Freedom," in Peterson and Vaughan, eds., *The Virginia Statute for Religious Freedom* 139–69 (1988). Madison's indignation responded to feelings widespread in the community.

In the words of Isaac Backus, the New England Baptist leader: "In Virginia they [the Episcopalians] cruelly imprisoned Baptist ministers, only for preaching the gospel to perishing souls without license from their courts." Backus, 2 *A History of New England with Particular Reference to the Baptists* 197 (1871). Imps, in the eighteenth century, were a species of devil—in the words of Samuel Johnson's *Dictionary*, "subaltern devils" or "puny devils." Madison's characterization of the persecutors is theological. Madison's editors observe: "Apparently it was religious issues, more than tax and trade regulation disputes with England, which were rapidly luring JM away from his beloved studies." 1 *Madison Papers* 107.

Bradford replied on March 4, 1774, extolling the religious freedom of Pennsylvania, whose "inhabitants think, speak and act with a freedom unknown." 1 *Madison Papers* 109. Besides Roger Williams's pioneering views on tolerance in Rhode Island, three colonies had moved toward acceptance of all Christians. Cecil Lord Baron of Baltimore, proprietary ruler of Maryland, had on August 26, 1650, approved an act providing that no person "professing to believe in Jesus Christ" should henceforth be molested "for or in respect of his or her religion nor in the free exercise thereof," "An Act Concerning Religion," in William Hand Browne, ed., *Archives of Maryland: Proceedings and Acts of the General Assembly of Maryland, January 1637–September 1664* (1883) 244. New York in 1683 had provided that those professing "faith in God by Jesus Christ" should not be molested "for any difference in opinion or matter of religious concernment" if they did not "actually disturb the civill peace of the

Province." Hugh Hastings, 2 *Ecclesiastical Records of the State of New York* 864 (1901). William Penn had gone the furthest, providing in 1701 that no one acknowledging "One Almighty God, the Creator, Upholder, and Ruler of the World" should be molested because of his "conscientious Persuasion or Practice, nor be compelled to frequent or maintain any religious Worship, Place or Ministry." However, only those professing to "believe in Jesus Christ, the Saviour of the World" were eligible for public office, *Pennsylvania Charter of Privileges,* in Francis Thorpe, ed., 5 *The Federal and State Constitutions* 3077 (1909). For an in-depth study of the religious situation in eighteenth century America, *see* Thomas J. Curry, *The First Freedoms: Church and State in America to the Passage of the First Amendment* (1986). For a brief summary, *see* Forrest McDonald, *Novus Ordo Seclorum: The Intellectual Origins of the Constitution* 42–44 (1985).

Madison to Bradford, April 1, 1774

Our Assembly is to meet the first of May When It is expected something will be done in behalf of the Dissenters: Petitions I hear are already forming among the Persecuted Baptists and I fancy it is in the thoughts of the Presbyterians also to intercede for greater liberty in matters of Religion. For my part I can not help being very doubtful of their succeeding in the attempt. The Affair was on the Carpet during the last Session; but such incredible and extravagant stories were told in the House of the monstrous effects of the Enthusiasm prevalent among the Sectaries and so greedily swallowed by their Enemies that I believe they lost footing by it and the bad name they still have with those who pretend too much contempt to examine into their principles and Conduct and are too much devoted to the ecclesiastical establishment to hear of the Toleration of Dissentients, I am apprehensive, will be again made a pretext for rejecting their requests. The Sentiments of our people of Fortune & fashion on this subject are vastly different from what you have been used to. That liberal catholic and equitable way of thinking as to the rights of Conscience, which is one of the Characteristics of a free people and so strongly marks the People of your province, is but little known among the Zealous adherents to our Hierarchy. We have it is true some persons in the Legislature of generous Principles both in Religion & Politicks but number not merit you know is necessary to carry points there. Besides[,] the Clergy are a numerous and powerful body[,] have great influence at home by reason of their connection with & dependence on the Bishops and Crown and will naturally employ all their art & Interest to depress their rising Adversaries; for such they must consider dissenters who rob them of the good will of the people and may in time endanger their livings & security. You are happy in dwelling in a Land where those inestimable privileges are fully enjoyed and public has long felt the good effects of their religious as well as Civil Liberty. 1 *Madison Papers* 112.

On November 26, 1774, as the First Continental Congress met, Madison wrote Bradford: "I was told by a Quaker Gentleman from Phial that a complaint of being persecuted in New England was laid before the Congress by the People called Baptists. Did Truth or prejudice dictate to the Quaker in his report?" 1 *Madison Papers* 130. As in Virginia, the sufferers were Baptists [section 2 below]. Madison, now an active rebel, wrote Bradford about the day set by the Continental Congress as one of "public humiliation, fasting and prayer."

Madison to Bradford, July 28, 1775

A Scotch Parson in an adjoining County refused to observe the fast or preach on that day. When called on he pleaded Conscience, alledging that it was his duty to pay no regard to any such appointments made by unconstitutional authority. The Committee it seems have their Consciences too: they have ordered his Church doors to be shut and his salary to be stopped, and have sent to the convention for their advice. If the Convention should connive at their proceedings I question, should his insolence not abate if he does not get ducked in a coat of Tar & surplice of feathers and then he may go in his new Canonicals and act under the lawful Authority of Gen. Gage if he pleases. We have one of the same Kidney in the parish I live in. He was sometime ago published in the Gazette for his insolence and had liked to have met with sore treatment; but finding his protection to be not so much in the law as the favor of the people he is grown very supple & obsequious. 1 *Madison Papers* 161.

————

Madison's reaction on this occasion should be compared with his later view [Chapter Seven, section 1] on government-sponsored prayers. Madison was named on May 6, 1776, to a committee to prepare "a declaration of rights for revolutionary Virginia." George Mason, the senior member, a devout Anglican, proposed the following on religious freedom.

George Mason, Proposal on Religious Freedom, 1776

That as Religion, or the Duty which we owe to our divine and omnipotent Creator, and the Manner of discharging it, can be governed only by Reason and Conviction, not by Force or Violence; and therefore that all Men should enjoy the fullest Toleration in the Exercise of Religion, according to the Dictates of Conscience, unpunished and unrestrained by the Magistrate, unless, under Colour of Religion, any Man disturb the Peace, the Happiness, or Safety of Society, or of Individuals. And that is the mutual Duty of all, to practice Christian Forbearance, Love and Charity towards Each other. 1 *Madison Papers* 172–173.

————

Madison, the youngest member, was not only characterized by "extreme modesty" (Jefferson, *Autobiography, Writings* (1907) 1, 61) but was without legal training. Nonetheless, wanting to go beyond toleration, he proposed a crucial change. He eliminated the restriction about disturbing the peace, and he attacked state support of religion.

Madison's Revision of Mason's Proposal on Religious Freedom, 1776

That religion or the duty which we owe to our Creator, and the manner of discharging it, being under the direction of reason and conviction only, not of violence or compulsion; all men are equally entitled to the full and free exercise of it accordg to the dictates of Conscience; and therefore that no man or class of men ought, on account of religion to be invested with peculiar emoluments or privileges, nor subjected to any penalties or disabilities unless under & c. 1 *Madison Papers* 174.

———

Patrick Henry, in the past a defender of imprisoned Baptists, introduced the amendment to the Convention. But when asked if he intended to disestablish the Episcopal Church, he "disclaimed such an object." The amendment was doomed. 1 *Madison Papers* 171. Madison drafted a second proposal, which, slightly altered, was almost completely accepted.

Madison's Reply to Patrick Henry's Proposal on Religious Freedom, 1776

That religion, or the duty which we owe to our Creator, and the manner of discharging it, can be directed only by reason and conviction, not by force or violence; and therefore, all men are equally entitled to the free exercise of religion, according to the dictates of conscience; and that it is the mutual duty of all to practise Christian forbearance, love, and charity, towards each other. 1 *Madison Papers* 175.

———

The magic words "free exercise of religion"—so much stronger than "toleration"—were fixed in a public document of great importance. For a study of Madison's "original insight" on religious freedom, see Noonan, *The Lustre of Our Country* 61–91 (1998).

B. "COMFORTABLE LIBERTY": JEFFERSON ENTERS THE BATTLE

In Virginia, Madison was overshadowed by Thomas Jefferson. Jefferson, as a young lawyer, had made a short investigation into the question, "Whether Christianity is part of the common law?" His conclusion conveyed the anticlericalism—not anti-Christianity—that was to be characteristic of him.

Jefferson, "Whether Christianity is Part of the Common Law?"

In truth, the alliance between church and state in England, has ever made their judges accomplices in the frauds of the clergy; and even bolder than they are; for instead of being contented with the surreptitious introduction of these four chapters of Exodus, they have taken the whole leap, and declared at once that the whole Bible and Testament, in a lump, make a part of the common law of the land, the first judicial declaration of which was by this Sir Matthew Hale. And thus they have incorporate into the

English code, laws made for the Jews alone, and the precepts of the gospel, intended by their benevolent author as obligatory only in foro conscientiae; and they arm the whole with the coercions of municipal law. They do this, too, in a case where the question was, not at all, whether Christianity was a part of the law of England, but simply how far the ecclesiastical law was to be respected by the common law courts of England, in the special case of a right of presentment. Thus identifying Christianity with the ecclesiastical law of England. Appendix, *Jefferson's Report's in Virginia Reports Annotated* (1903).

NOTES

1. *The Position of Jews in Colonial America.* Jews were subjected to a variety of religious discriminations. In Maryland they were subject to the laws against blasphemy, in Virginia they could not employ Christian servants, and in eight states they had to pay taxes to support the established Christian church; Jacob Marcus, 1 *The Colonial American Jew, 1492–1776* 507–508 (1970). An insistence on Christian oaths made it impossible for Jews to be lawyers in most colonies and prevented them from being instructors in some schools and colleges; *id.* In all the colonies the Jews were ineligible for public office. *Id.* 511. In Connecticut, Delaware, Maryland, Pennsylvania, Rhode Island, South Carolina, and Virginia, they could not vote; *Id.* 510. Rhode Island was an especially ironic example. Roger Williams, its founder, had believed in religious freedom for all [Chapter Five, section 2]. There were traces of Jewish life in Newport in the seventeenth century, and by 1763 there was a synagogue and a Jewish community equal to about 1 percent of the population of this town of 6,000. *Id.* 319. But in Rhode Island, Jews were denied both office and the vote. They were not emancipated until the Rhode Island Constitution of 1842. *Id..*438. *See also* Morton Borden, *Jews, Turks, and Infidels* (1984).

2. *The Protestant Episcopal Church.* The legal status of the Church of England, whose legal head was the King of England, was peculiarly affected by the Revolution and the severing of all legalities with the old country. Central to the organization of the Church was the episcopate, but prior to the Revolution no bishops had existed in America. New England Congregationalists and the dissenters in England had worked on the English government to prevent the introduction of bishops in America, despite the strenuous efforts of the Reverend Samuel Johnson of Connecticut to create an American diocese. Nelson Rollin Burr, *The Story of the Diocese of Connecticut* 127–30 (1962). During the Revolution, on November 14, 1784, the Reverend Samuel Seabury, a native of Connecticut, was consecrated a bishop by three Scottish bishops who did not require him to swear allegiance to George III. *Id.* 138. A national convention, held in Philadelphia in September 1785, announced the formation of the Protestant Episcopal Church, distinct in its independent legal organization and to be ruled by elected bishops. *Id.* 148–149. Parliament enacted a statute permitting the bishops of England to consecrate without requiring the oath of allegiance to the crown, and in late 1786 two more Americans, Samuel Provoost and William White, sailed to England to be ordained as bishops. *Id.* 151. In October 1789 Seabury, White, and Provoost joined in consecrating Edward Bass of Newbury as a bishop. The episcopal line of succession was established. The church, no longer under the crown, now stood as an independent ecclesiastical

entity. *See also* Carl Bridenbaugh, *Mitre and Sceptre: Transatlantic Faiths, Ideas, Personalities, and Politics* (1962).

3. *Jeffersonian Arguments against Preferences for the Anglican Church in Virginia.* In October 1776 Jefferson, as a member of the Virginia House of Delegates, threw himself into what he described as "the severest contest in which I have ever been engaged," Albert E. Bergh, ed., *Autobiography, Writings of Thomas Jefferson* [*Writings of Jefferson*] 57 (1907). The papers of Jefferson contain several pages of shorthand notes, summarized below, that were written that fall in preparation for a speech in the House of Delegates. Julian P. Boyd, ed. *1 The Papers of Thomas Jefferson* [*Jefferson Papers*] (1950). Jefferson acknowledged that some civil rights may have to be surrendered when civil government is established, but even that should be as "lit[tle] as pos[si]ble." Religious rights, however, should not be surrendered to the civil government because the individual must answer on this matter to God, not the government. "God req[ui]res ev[er]y[one to] act ac[cor]d[in]g to Belief," and the evidence for belief is in some minds, but not others. A magistrate, wrote Jefferson, might restrain an overt act, but not an opinion or mere tendency [*see Reynolds v. United States*, Chapter Nine]. Jefferson contrasted religious freedom with governmental coercion [*see Lee v. Weisman*, Chapter Fourteen, section 2]. To the argument that "Religion will decline if not supported" by the government, Jefferson replied with a citation of the promise of Jesus that the "Gates of Hell shall not prevail" against his church [Gospel according to Matthew 16:18]. The purpose of a state religion, noted Jefferson, must be uniformity. But that is not a desirable goal because it would stifle free inquiry. Uniformity is the work of "Monk[i]sh impos[itio]ns, ignor[ance], darkness." Islam, he wrote, is supported by stifling free inquiry, while philosophy is reformed by free inquiry. Even if religious uniformity were theoretically desirable, experience has shown it to be unattainable except by means such as the Inquisition, torturing and burning heretics, or fining and imprisoning persons for their beliefs. Churches are strengthened when Presbyterians assign reasons to themselves for being Presbyterians or when Episcopalians decide why they are Episcopalians. Being on an equal footing is an advantage for religion. It obliges ministers to be industrious. Jefferson also argued from church history, noting that Christianity flourished for 300 years without establishment, and arguing that as soon as it was established it "declin[e]d from Purity" [see Chapter Two, NOTE, *From Persecution of Christianity to Toleration, and from Toleration to Official Establishment*]. Jefferson urged that it betrays a lack of confidence in the doctrines of the church to suspect that reason or intrinsic excellence is insufficient without a secular prop, again citing Mt. 16:18. Finally, Jefferson offered a practical political reason against the proposal to provide public support for the teaching of religion. Anglicans, who would be the primary beneficiaries of the proposal, are outnumbered by religious dissenters ("55,000 in all") such as the Free Baptists in Virginia. Jefferson's efforts to effect disestablishment had limited success, as he wrote later in Paris in his *Notes on Virginia*.

Jefferson, *Notes on Virginia*, 1784
Query XVII *The different religions received into that State?*

The first settlers in this country were emigrants from England, of the English church, just at a point of time when it was flushed with complete victory over the religious of all other persuasions. Possessed, as they became, of the powers of making, administering and executing the laws, they shewed equal intolerance in this country with their Presbyterian brethren, who had emigrated to the northern government. The poor Quakers were flying from persecution in England. They cast their eyes on these new countries as asylums of civil and religious freedom; but they found them free only for the reigning sect. Several acts of the Virginia assembly of 1659, 1662, and 1693, had made it penal in parents to refuse to have their children baptized; had prohibited the unlawful assembling of Quakers; had made it penal for any master of a vessel to bring a Quaker into the state; had ordered those already here, and such as should come thereafter, to be imprisoned till they should abjure the country; provided a milder punishment for their first and second return, but death for their third; had inhibited all persons from suffering their meetings in or near their houses, entertaining them individually, or disposing of books which supported their tenets. If no capital execution took place here, as did in New England, it was not owing to the moderation of the church, or spirit of the legislature, as may be inferred from the law itself, but to historical circumstances which have not been handed down to us. The Anglicans retained full possession of the country about a century. Other opinions began then to creep in, and the great care of the government to support their own church, having begotten an equal degree of indolence in its clergy, two thirds of the people had become dissenters at the commencement of the present revolution. The laws indeed were still oppressive on them, but the spirit of the one party had subsided into moderation, and of the other had risen to a degree of determination which commanded respect.

The present state of our laws on the subject of religion is this. The convention of May 1776, in their declaration of rights, declared it to be a truth, and a natural right: that the exercise of religion should be free; but when they proceeded to form on that declaration the ordinance of government, instead of taking up every principle declared in the bill of rights, and guarding it by legislative sanction, they passed over that which asserted our religious rights, leaving them as they found them. The same convention, however, when they met as a member of the general assembly in October 1776, repealed all acts of parliament which had rendered criminal the maintaining any opinions in matters of religion, the forbearing to repair to church, and the exercising any mode of worship; and suspended the laws giving salaries to the clergy, which suspension was made perpetual in October 1779. Statutory oppressions in religion being thus wiped away, we remain at present under those only imposed by the common law, or by our own acts of assembly. At the common law, heresy was a capital offence, punishable by burning. Its definition was left to the ecclesiastical judges, before whom the conviction was, till the statute of the 1 Eliz. I, c. 1 circumscribed it, by declaring that nothing should be deemed heresy but what had been so determined by authority of the canonical scriptures, or by one of the four first general councils, or by some other council having for the grounds of their declaration the express and plain words of the scriptures. Heresy, thus circumscribed, being an offence at the common law, our act of assembly of October 1777, c.17 gives cognizance of it to the general court, by declaring that the jurisdiction of that court shall be general in all matters at the common law. The execution is by the writ *De haeretico comburendo.* By our own act of assembly of 1705, c.30, if a person brought up in the christian religion denies the being of a God, or the trinity, or asserts there are more Gods than one, or denies the christian religion to be true, or the scriptures to be of divine authority, he is punishable on the first offence by incapacity to hold any office or employment ecclesiastical, civil, or military; on the second by disability to sue, to take any gift or legacy, to be guardian, executor or administrator, and by three years imprisonment, without bail. A father's right to the custody of his own children being founded in law on his right of guardianship, this being taken away, they may of course be severed from him and put, by the authority of a court, into more orthodox hands. This is a summary view of that religious slavery under which a people have been willing to remain who have lavished their lives and fortunes for the establishment of their civil freedom. The error seems not sufficiently eradicated, that the operations of the mind, as well as the acts of the body, are subject to the coercion of the laws. But our rulers can have authority over such natural rights, only as we have submitted to them. The rights of conscience we never submitted, we could not submit. We are answerable for them to our God. The legitimate powers of government extend to such acts only as are injurious to others. But it does me no injury for my neighbor to say there are twenty gods, or no god. It neither picks my pocket nor breaks my leg. If it be said his testimony in a court of justice cannot be relied on, reject it then, and be the stigma on him. Constraint may make him worse by making him a hypocrite, but it will never make him a truer man. It may fix him obstinately in his errors, but will not cure them. Reason and free inquiry are the only effectual agents against error. Give a loose to them, they will support the true religion by bringing every false one to their tribunal, to the test of their investigation. They are the natural enemies of error, and of error only. Had not the Roman government permitted free inquiry, christianity could never have been introduced [*see* Chapter One, section 6]. Had not free inquiry been indulged, at the era of the reformation, the corruptions of christianity could not have been purged away [*see* Chapter Five, section 1]. If it be restrained now, the present corruptions will be protected, and new ones encouraged. Was the government to prescribe to us our medicine and diet, our bodies would be in such keeping as our souls are now. Thus in France the emetic was once forbidden as a medicine, and the potatoe as an article of food. Government is just as infallible, too, when it fixes systems in physics. Galileo was sent to the inquisition for affirming that the earth was a sphere; the government had declared it to be as flat as a trencher, and Galileo was obliged to abjure his error. This error however at length prevailed, the earth became a globe, and Descartes declared it was whirled round its axis by a vortex. The government in which he lived was wise enough to see that this was no question of civil jurisdiction, or we should all have been involved by authority in vortices. In fact the vortices have been exploded, and the Newtonian principle of gravitation is now more firmly established, on the basis of reason, than it would be were the government to step in and to make it an article of necessary faith. Reason and experiment have been indulged, and error has fled before them. It is error alone which needs the support of government. Truth can stand by itself. Subject opinion to coercion: who will you make your inquisitors? Fallible men; men governed by bad passions, by private as well as public reasons. And why subject it to coercion? To produce uniformity. But is uniformity of opinion desirable? No more than of face and stature. Introduce the bed of Procrusses then, and as there is danger that the large men may beat the small, make us all of a size, by lopping the former and stretching the latter. Difference of opinion is advantageous in religion. The several sects perform the office of a Censor mourn over each other. Is uniformity attainable? Millions of innocent men, women and children, since the introduction of Christianity, have been burnt, tortured, fined, and imprisoned: yet we have not advanced one inch towards uniformity. What has been the effect of coercion? To make one half the world fools, and the other half hypocrites. To support roguery and error all over the earth. Let us reflect that it is inhabited by a thousand millions of people. That these profess probably a thousand different systems of religion. That ours is but one of that thousand. That if there be but one right, and ours that one, we should wish to see the 999 wandering sects gathered into the fold of truth. But against such a majority we cannot effect this by force. Reason and persuasion are the only practicable instruments. To make way for these, freer inquiry must be indulged; and how can we wish others to indulge it while we refuse it ourselves. But every state, says an inquisitor, has established some religion. "No two, say I, have established the same." Is this a proof of the infallibility of establishment? Our sister states of Pennsylvania and New York, however, have long subsisted without any establishment at all. The experiment was new and doubtful when they made it. It has answered beyond conception. They flourish infinitely. Religion is well supported; of various kinds indeed, but all good enough; all sufficient to preserve peace and order: or if a sect arises whose tenets would subvert morals, good sense has fair play, and reasons and laughs it out of doors, without suffering the state to be troubled with it. They do not hang more malefactors than we do. They are not more disturbed with religious dissentions. On the contrary, their harmony is unparalleled, and can be ascribed to nothing but their unbounded tolerance, because there is no other circumstances in which they differ from every nation on earth. They have made the happy discovery, that the way to silence religious disputes, is to take no notice of them. Let us too give this experiment fair play, and get rid, while we may, of those tyrannical laws. It is true we are as yet secured against them by the spirit of the times. I doubt whether the people of this country would suffer an execution for heresy, or a three years imprisonment for not comprehending the mysteries of the trinity. But is the spirit of the people an infallible, a permanent reliance? Is it government? Is this the kind of protection we receive in return for the rights we give up? Besides, the spirit of the times may alter, will alter. Our rulers will become corrupt, our people careless. A single zealot may commence persecutor, and better men be his victims. It can never be too often repeated, that the time for fixing every essential right on a legal basis is while our rulers are honest, and ourselves united. From the conclusion of this war we shall be going down hill. It will not then be necessary to resort every moment to the people for support. They will be forgotten therefore, and their rights disregarded. They will forget themselves, but in the sole faculty of making money, and will never think of uniting to effect a due respect for their rights. The shackles, therefore, which shall not be knocked off at the conclusion of this war, will remain on us long, will be made heavier and heavier, till our rights shall revive or expire in a convulsion. Merrill D. Peterson, ed., *Thomas Jefferson, Writings* 283–87 (1984).

————

If Jefferson's estimate of religious denominations in Virginia was correct, the Episcopalians were a minority. But "although the majority of our citizens were dissenters, as has been observed, a majority of the legislature were churchmen," *Autobiography,* Bergh, ed., 1 *Writings of Jefferson* 58. In 1779, Jefferson penned "A Bill for Establishing Religious Freedom"—"establishing" here being neatly turned to the advantage of liberty. The bill was introduced in the General Assembly in May 1779. Its author was certainly acceptable to many legislators; on June 1 the General Assembly, 67 to 61, elected Jefferson governor of the commonwealth. 2 *Jefferson Papers* 278. His bill read as follows.

Jefferson, A Bill for Establishing Religious Freedom, 1779

Well aware that the opinions and belief of men depend not on their own will, but follow involuntarily the evidence proposed to their minds; that Almighty God hath created the mind free, *and manifested his supreme will that free it shall remain by making it altogether insusceptible of restraint;* that all attempts to influence it by temporal punishments, or burthens, or by civil incapacitations, tend only to beget habits of hypocrisy and mean-ness, and are a departure from the plan of the holy author of our religion, who being lord both of body and mind, yet chose not to propagate it by coercions on either, as was in his Almighty power to do, *but to extend it by its influence on reason alone;* that the impious presumption of legislators and rulers, civil as well as ecclesiastical, who, being themselves but fallible and uninspired men, have assumed dominion over the faith of others, setting up their own opinions and modes of thinking as the only true and infallible, and as such endeavoring to impose them on others, hath estab-lished and maintained false religions over the greatest part of the world and through all time: That to compel a man to furnish contributions of money for the propagation of opinions which he disbelieves *and abhors,* is sinful and tyrannical; that even the forcing him to support this or that teacher of his own religious persuasion, is depriving him of the comfortable liberty of giving his contributions to the particular pastor whose morals he would make his pattern, and whose powers he feels most persuasive to righteousness; and is withdrawing from the ministry those temporary rewards, which proceeding from an approbation of their personal conduct, are an additional incitement to earnest and unremitting labours for the instruction of mankind; that our civil rights have no dependance on our religious opinions, any more than our opinions in physics or geometry; that therefore the proscribing any citizen as unworthy the public confidence by laying upon him an incapacity of being called to offices of trust and emolument, unless he profess or renounce this or that religious opinion, is depriving him injuriously of those privileges and advantages to which, in common with his fellow citizens, he has a natural right; that it tends also to corrupt the principles of that *very* religion it is meant to encourage, by bribing, with a monopoly of worldly honours and emoluments, those who will externally profess and conform to it; that though indeed these are criminal who do not withstand such temptation, yet neither are those innocent who lay the bait in their way; *that the opinions of men are not the object of civil government, nor under its jurisdiction,* that to suffer the civil magistrate to intrude his powers into the field of opinion and to restrain the profession or propagation of principles on supposition of their ill tendency is a dangerous fallacy, which at once destroys all religious liberty, because he being of course judge of that tendency will make his opinions the rule of judgment, and approve or condemn the sentiments of others only as they shall square with or differ from his own; that it is time enough for the rightful purposes of civil government for its officers to interfere when principles break out into overt acts against peace and good order; and finally, that truth is great and will prevail if left to herself, that she is the proper and sufficient antagonist to error, and has nothing to fear from the conflict unless by human interposition disarmed of her natural weapons, free argument and debate; errors ceasing to be dangerous when it is permitted freely to contradict them.

We the General Assembly of Virginia do enact that no man shall be compelled to frequent or support any religious worship, place, or ministry whatsoever, nor shall be enforced, restrained, molested, or burthened in his body or goods, nor shall otherwise suffer, on account of his religious opinions or belief; but that all men shall be free to profess, and by argument to maintain, their opinions in matters of religion, and that the same shall in no wise diminish, enlarge, or affect their civil capacities.

And though we well know that this Assembly, elected by the people for the ordinary purposes of legislation only, have no power to restrain the acts of succeeding Assemblies, constituted with powers equal to our own, and that therefore to declare this act irrevocable would be of no effect in law; yet we are free to declare, and do declare, that the rights hereby asserted are of the natural rights of mankind, and that if any act shall be hereafter passed to repeal the present or to narrow its operation, such act will be an infringement of natural right. Peterson, ed., *Jefferson, Writings* 346–348 (1984).

————

The bill was read twice, and was killed in August 1779, a death that reflected the political skill and strength of the establishment Jefferson had attempted to destroy. Jefferson lost the skirmish in 1779, but won the battle when his statute was enacted in 1786 [section 3 below]. Jefferson wrote his own epitaph. It does not mention that he served as Governor of Virginia, American Ambassador to France, Secretary of State, or President of the United States, but states simply: "Here was buried Thomas Jefferson Author of the Declaration of American Independence of the Statute of Virginia for religious freedom and Father of the University of Virginia."

C. "THE GREAT BARRIER WHICH DEFENDS THE RIGHTS OF THE PEOPLE"

On April 25, 1784, Madison reported to Jefferson, now the American minister in Paris, that Governor Patrick Henry, "the old fox," was friendly to a "general assessment" on behalf of the Christian religion. 8 *Madison Papers* 20. Petitions in favor of such a bill were introduced in the Virginia House of Delegates, but their supporters were nervous about the outcome and did not push for enactment. 8 *Madison Papers* 93. On November 11, 1784, the House, 47–32, called for a tax for "the support of the Christian religion," but no tax was actually passed, 8 *Madison Papers* 155. Jefferson on December 8, 1784, wrote from Paris: "I am glad the *Episcopalians* have again shown their teeth and fangs. The *dissenters* had almost forgotten them." 8 *Madison Papers* 178. Finally, on Christmas Eve 1784, Henry submitted his "modest tax" proposal before the House.

A Bill Establishing a Provision for Teachers of the Christian Religion, 1784

Whereas the general diffusion of Christian knowledge hath a natural tendency to correct the morals of men, restrain their vices, and preserve the peace of society; which cannot be effected without a competent provision for learned teachers, who may be thereby enabled to devote their time and attention to the duty of instructing such citizens, as from their circumstances and want of education, cannot otherwise attain such knowledge; and it is judged that such provision may be made by the Legislature, without counteracting the liberal principle heretofore adopted and intended to be preserved by abolishing all distinctions of preeminence amongst the different societies or communities of Christians;

Be it Hereford enacted by the General Assembly, That for the support of Christian teachers, ___ per centime on the amount, or ___ in the pound on the sum payable for tax on the property within this Commonwealth, is hereby assessed, and shall be paid by every person chargeable with the said tax at the time the same shall become due; and the Sheriffs of the several Counties shall have power to levy and collect the same in the same manner and under the like restrictions and limitations, as are or may be prescribed by the laws for raising the Revenues of this State.

And be it enacted, That for every sum so paid, the Sheriff or Collector shall give a receipt, expressing therein to what society of Christians the person from whom he may receive the same shall "direct the money to be paid," keeping a distinct account thereof in his books. The Sheriff of every County, shall, on or before the ___ day of ___ in every year, return to the Court, upon oath, two alphabetical lists of the payments to him made, distinguishing in columns opposite to the names of the persons who shall have paid the same, the society to which the money so paid was by them appropriated; and one column for the names where no appropriation shall be made. One of which lists, after being recorded in a book to be kept for that purpose, shall be filed by the Clerk in his office; the other shall by the Sheriff be fixed up in the Court-house, there to remain for the inspection of all concerned. And the Sheriff, after deducting five per centum for the collection, shall forthwith pay to such person or persons as shall be appointed to receive the same by the Vestry, Elders, or Directors, however denominated of each such society, the sum so stated to be due to that society; or in default thereof, upon the motion of such person or person to the next or any succeeding Court, execution shall be awarded for the same against the Sheriff and his security, his and their executors or administrators; provided that ten days previous notice be given of such motion. And upon every such execution, the Officer serving the same shall proceed to immediate sale of the estate taken, and shall not accept of security for payment at the end of three months, nor to have the goods forthcoming at the day of sale; for his better direction wherein, the Clerk shall endorse upon every such execution that no security of any kind shall be taken.

And be it further enacted, That the money to be raised by virtue of this Act, shall be by the Vestries, Elders, or Directors of each religious society, appropriated to a provision for a Minister or Teacher of the Gospel of their denomination, or the providing places of divine worship, and to none other use whatsoever; except in the denomination of Quakers and Menonists, who may receive what is collected from their members, and place it in their general fund, to be disposed of in a manner which they shall think best calculated to promote their particular mode of worship.

And be it enacted, That all sums which at the time of payment to the Sheriff or Collector may not be appropriated by the person paying the same, shall be accounted for with the Court in manner as by this Act is directed; and after deducting for his collection, the Sheriff shall pay the amount thereof (upon account certified by the Court to the Auditors of Public Accounts, and by them to the Treasurer) into the public Treasury, to be disposed of under the direction of the General Assembly, for the encouragement of seminaries of learning within the Counties whence such sums shall arise, and to no other use or purpose whatsoever.

THIS Act shall commence, and be in force, from and after the ___ day of ___ in the year ___.

————

NOTE. *Madison and Excessive Entanglement of Government with Religion.* Madison anticipated that Henry would eventually file his bill. Between December 12 and 24, 1784, Madison wrote shorthand notes, summarized below, of arguments against the proposal. 8 *Madison Papers* 197–199. One vice of Henry's proposal would be to give to courts the task of judging what Christianity is, and of entering into a host of theological questions, such as the edition of the Bible to be used (Hebrew, Septuagint translation into Greek, Vulgate translation into Latin), the list of the books in the biblical canon (noting differences between Catholics and Protestants on this point), the manner of interpretation (is Scripture "dictated" by inspiration in every letter, or in essential parts only, or only in general?), the sense in which a doctrine is true or "essential to Christianity," and the characterization of a belief as "Trinitarian or Arian." "What clue," asked Madison, "is to guide Judge thro' this labyrinth?" Inquiries of this sort, he noted, end up in questions such as "what is orthodoxy, what heresy?" See *United States v. Ballard* [Chapter Twelve, section 1]. By one vote the House voted to delay the bill, and then by a vote of 45–37, put off a third reading until the following November. 8 *Madison Papers* 200. Madison, writing Lafayette on March 20, 1785, rejoiced at the defeat of what he called "the Act for corrupting our Religious system." 8 *Madison Papers* 254.

In the spring, writing James Monroe on April 12, 1785, Madison analyzed the situation: "The Episcopal people are generally for it, tho' I think the zeal of some of them has cooled. The laity of the other sects are equally unanimous on the other side. So are all the Clergy except the Presbyterians...." 8 *Madison Papers* 261. George Nicholas urged Madison to organize petitions to show the true feeling of the "great majority," 8 *Madison Papers* 264, 328. Madison wrote Jefferson on April 27, 1785, that the bill had "produced some fermentation below the Mountains and a violent one beyond them," 8 *Madison Papers* 268. By the end of June 1785 Madison had prepared a petition for general use.

To the Honorable the General Assembly of the Commonwealth of Virginia A Memorial and Remonstrance, 1785

We the subscribers, citizens of the said Commonwealth, having taken into serious consideration, a Bill printed by order of the last Session of General Assembly, entitled "A Bill establishing a provision for Teachers of the Christian Religion," and conceiving that the same if finally armed with the sanctions of a law, will be a dangerous abuse of power, are bound as faithful members of a free State to remonstrate against it, and to declare the reasons by which we are determined. We remonstrate against the said Bill,

1. Because we hold it for a fundamental and undeniable truth, "that Religion or the duty which we owe to our Creator and the manner of discharging it, can be directed only by reason and conviction, not by force or violence." The Religion then of every man must be left to the conviction and conscience of every man; and it is the right of every man to exercise it as these may dictate. This right is in its nature an unalienable right. It is unalienable, because the opinions of men, depending only on the evidence contemplated by their own minds cannot follow the dictates of other men: It is unalienable also, because what is here a right towards men, is a duty towards the Creator. It is the duty of every man to render to the Creator such homage and such only as he believes to be acceptable to him. This duty is precedent, both in order of time and in degree of obligation, to the claims of Civil Society. Before any man can be considered as a member of Civil Society, he must be considered as a subject of the Governour of the Universe: And if a member of Civil Society, who enters into any subordinate Association, must always do it with a reservation of his duty to the General Authority; much more must every man who becomes a member of any particular Civil Society, do it with a saving of his allegiance to the Universal Sovereign. We maintain therefore that in matters of Religion, no mans right is abridged by the institution of Civil Society and that Religion is wholly exempt from its cognizance. True it is, that no other rule exists,

by which any question which may divide a Society, can be ultimately determined, but the will of the majority; but it is also true that the majority may trespass on the rights of the minority.

2.   Because if Religion be exempt from the authority of the Society at large, still less can it be subject to that of the Legislative Body. The latter are but the creatures and vicegerents of the former. Their jurisdiction is both derivative and limited: it is limited with regard to the coordinate departments, more necessarily is it limited with regard to the constituents. The preservation of a free Government requires not merely, that the metes and bounds which separate each department of power be invariably maintained; but more especially that neither of them be suffered to overleap the great Barrier which defends the rights of the people. The Rulers who are guilty of such an encroachment, exceed the commission from which they derive their authority, and are Tyrants. The People who submit to it are governed by laws made neither by themselves nor by an authority derived from them, and are slaves.

3.   Because it is proper to take alarm at the first experiment on our liberties. We hold this prudent jealousy to be the first duty of Citizens, and one of the noblest characteristics of the late Revolution. The free men of America did not wait till usurped power had strengthened itself by exercise, and entangled the question in precedents. They saw all the consequences in the principle, and they avoided the consequences by denying the principle. We revere this lesson too much soon to forget it. Who does not see that the same authority which can establish Christianity, in exclusion of all other Religions, may establish with the same ease any particular sect of Christians, in exclusion of all other Sects? that the same authority which can force a citizen to contribute three pence only of his property for the support of any one establishment, may force him to conform to any other establishment in all cases whatsoever?

4.   Because the Bill violates that equality which ought to be the basis of every law, and which is more indispensable, in proportion as the validity or expediency of any law is more liable to be impeached. If "all men are by nature equally free and independent," all men are to be considered as entering into Society on equal conditions; as relinquishing no more, and therefore retaining no less, one than another, of their natural rights. Above all are they to be considered as retaining an "*equal* title to the free exercise of Religion according to the dictates of Conscience." Whilst we assert for ourselves a freedom to embrace, to profess and to observe the Religion which we believe to be of divine origin, we cannot deny an equal freedom to those whose minds have not yet yielded to the evidence which has convinced us. If this freedom be abused, it is an offence against God, not against man: To God, therefore, not to man, must an account of it be rendered. As the Bill violates equality by subjecting some to peculiar burdens, so it violates the same principle, by granting to others peculiar exemptions. Are the Quakers and Menonists the only sects who think a compulsive support of their Religions unnecessary and unwarrantable? Can their piety alone be entrusted with the care of public worship? Ought their Religions to be endowed above all others with extraordinary privileges by

which proselytes may be enticed from all others? We think too favorably of the justice and good sense of these denominations to believe that they either covet pre-eminences over their fellow citizens or that they will be seduced by them from the common opposition to the measure.

5. Because the Bill implies either that the Civil Magistrate is a competent Judge of Religious Truth; or that he may employ Religion as an engine of Civil policy. The first is an arrogant pretension falsified by the contradictory opinions of Rulers in all ages, and throughout the world: the second an unhallowed perversion of the means of salvation.

6. Because the establishment proposed by the Bill is not requisite for the support of the Christian Religion. To say that it is, is a contradiction to the Christian Religion itself, for every page of it disavows a dependence on the powers of this world: it is a contradiction to fact; for it is known that this Religion both existed and flourished, not only without the support of human laws, but in spite of every opposition from them, and not only during the period of miraculous aid, but long after it had been left to its own evidence and the ordinary care of Providence. Nay, it is a contradiction in terms; for a Religion not invented by human policy, must have pre-existed and been supported, before it was established by human policy. It is moreover to weaken in those who profess this Religion a pious confidence in its innate excellence and the patronage of its Author; and to foster in those who still reject it, a suspicion that its friends are too conscious of its fallacies to trust it to its own merits.

7. Because experience witnesseth that ecclesiastical establishments, instead of maintaining the purity and efficacy of Religion, have had a contrary operation. During almost fifteen centuries has the legal establishment of Christianity been on trial. What have been its fruits? More or less in all places, pride and indolence in the Clergy, ignorance and servility in the laity, in both, superstition, bigotry and persecution. Enquire of the Teachers of Christianity for the ages in which it appeared in its greatest lustre; those of every sect, point to the ages prior to its incorporation with Civil policy. Propose a restoration of this primitive State in which its Teachers depended on the voluntary rewards of their flocks, many of them predict its downfall. On which Side ought their testimony to have greatest weight, when for or when against their interest?

8. Because the establishment in question is not necessary for the support of Civil Government. If it be urged as necessary for the support of Civil Government only as it is a means of supporting Religion, and it be not necessary for the latter purpose, it cannot be necessary for the former. If Religion be not within the cognizance of Civil Government how can its legal establishment be necessary to Civil Government? What influence in fact have ecclesiastical establishments had on Civil Society? In some instances they have been seen to erect a spiritual tyranny on the ruins of the Civil authority; in many instances they have been seen upholding the thrones of political tyranny: in no instance have they been seen the guardians of the liberties of the people. Rulers who wished to subvert the public liberty, may have found an established Clergy convenient auxiliaries. A just Government instituted to secure & perpetuate it needs them not. Such a Govern-

ment will be best supported by protecting every Citizen in the enjoyment of his Religion with the same equal hand which protects his person and his property; by neither invading the equal rights of any Sect, nor suffering any Sect to invade those of another.

9.   Because the proposed establishment is a departure from the generous policy, which, offering an Asylum to the persecuted and oppressed of every Nation and Religion, promised a lustre to our country, and an accession to the number of its citizens. What a melancholy mark is the Bill of sudden degeneracy? Instead of holding forth an Asylum to the persecuted, it is itself a signal of persecution. It degrades from the equal rank of Citizens all those whose opinions in Religion do not bend to those of the Legislative authority. Distant as it may be in its present form from the Inquisition, it differs from it only in degree. The one is the first step, the other the last in the career of intolerance. The magnanimous sufferer under this cruel scourge in foreign Regions, must view the Bill as a Beacon on our Coast, warning him to seek some other haven, where liberty and philanthrophy in their due extent, may offer a more certain repose from his Troubles.

10.   Because it will have a like tendency to banish our Citizens. The allurements presented by other situations are every day thinning their number. To superadd a fresh motive to emigration by revoking the liberty which they now enjoy, would be the same species of folly which has dishonoured and depopulated flourishing kingdoms.

11.   Because it will destroy that moderation and harmony which the forbearance of our laws to intermeddle with Religion has produced among its several sects. Torrents of blood have been spilt in the old world, by vain attempts of the secular arm, to extinguish Religious discord, by proscribing all difference in Religious opinion. Time has at length revealed the true remedy. Every relaxation of narrow and rigorous policy, wherever it has been tried, has been found to assuage the disease. The American Theatre has exhibited proofs that equal and compleat liberty, if it does not wholly eradicate it, sufficiently destroys its malignant influence on the health and prosperity of the State. If with the salutary effects of this system under our own eyes, we begin to contract the bounds of Religious freedom, we know no name that will too severely reproach our folly. At least let warning be taken at the first fruits of the threatened innovation. The very appearance of the Bill has transformed "that Christian forbearance, love and charity," which of late mutually prevailed, into animosities and jealousies, which may not soon be appeased. What mischiefs may not be dreaded, should this enemy to the public quiet be armed with the force of a law?

12.   Because the policy of the Bill is adverse to the diffusion of the light of Christianity. The first wish of those who enjoy this precious gift ought to be that it may be imparted to the whole race of mankind. Compare the number of those who have as yet received it with the number still remaining under the dominion of false Religions; and how small is the former! Does the policy of the Bill tend to lessen the disproportion? No; it at once discourages those who are strangers to the light of revelation from coming into the Region of it; and countenances by example the nations who

continue in darkness, in shutting out those who might convey it to them. Instead of Levelling as far as possible, every obstacle to the victorious progress of Truth, the Bill with an ignoble and unchristian timidity would circumscribe it with a wall of defence against the encroachments of error.

13. Because attempts to enforce by legal sanctions, acts obnoxious to so great a proportion of Citizens, tend to enervate the laws in general, and to slacken the bands of Society. If it be difficult to execute any law which is not generally deemed necessary or salutary, what must be the case, where it is deemed invalid and dangerous? And what may be the effect of so striking an example of impotency in the Government, on its general authority?

14. Because a measure of such singular magnitude and delicacy ought not to be imposed, without the clearest evidence that it is called for by a majority of citizens, and no satisfactory method is yet proposed by which the voice of the majority in this case may be determined, or its influence secured. "The people of the respective counties are indeed requested to signify their opinion respecting the adoption of the Bill to the next Session of Assembly." But the representation must be made equal, before the voice either of the Representatives or of the Counties will be that of the people. Our hope is that neither of the former will, after due consideration, espouse the dangerous principle of the Bill. Should the event disappoint us, it will still leave us in full confidence, that a fair appeal to the latter will reverse the sentence against our liberties.

15. Because finally, "the equal right of every citizen to the free exercise of his Religion according to the dictates of conscience" is held by the same tenure with all our other rights. If we recur to its origin, it is equally the gift of nature; if we weigh its importance, it cannot be less dear to us; if we consult the "Declaration of those rights which pertain to the good people of Virginia, as the basis and foundation of Government," it is enumerated with equal solemnity, or rather studied emphasis. Either then, we must say, that the Will of the Legislature is the only measure of their authority; and that in the plenitude of this authority, they may sweep away all our fundamental rights; or, that they are bound to leave this particular right untouched and sacred: Either we must say, that they may controul the freedom of the press, may abolish the Trial by Jury, may swallow up the Executive and Judiciary Powers of the State; nay that they may despoil us of our very right of suffrage, and erect themselves into an independent and hereditary Assembly or, we must say, that they have no authority to enact into law the Bill under consideration. We the Subscribers say, that the General Assembly of this Commonwealth have no such authority: And that no effort may be omitted on our part against so dangerous an usurpation, we oppose to it, this remonstrance; earnestly praying, as we are in duty bound, that the Supreme Lawgiver of the Universe, by illuminating those to whom it is addressed, may on the one hand, turn their Councils from every act which would affront his holy prerogative, or violate the trust committed to them: and on the other, guide them into every measure which may be worthy of his blessing, may redound to their own praise, and may

establish more firmly the liberties, the prosperity and the happiness of the Commonwealth.

———

Not anxious to alienate allies on other subjects who were in favor of Henry's bill, Madison had the petition circulated anonymously; it gained 1,552 signatures. Madison provided political leadership and rhetorical skill in the struggle, but he was by no means the only one to present a petition in opposition to the bill. The following petition, asserting the General Assessment to be against "the Spirit of the Gospel and the Bill of Rights," obtained 4,899 subscribers, over three times the number of those who signed Madison's petition.

Petition of the Inhabitants of Cumberland County, October 26, 1785

The petition of the Inhabitants of Cumberland County Humbly sheweth, that whereas it hath pleased your Honourable House to Publish a Bill Obliging the Inhabitants of this Common Wealth to pay the Teachers of the Christian Religion, and have requested their Opinion Concerning it Your Petitioners therefore do most earnestly declare Against it, Believing it to be Contrary to the Spirit of the Gospel and the Bill of rights.

Certain it is that the Blessed Author of the Christian Religion not only maintained and Supported his Gospel in the World for Several hundred Years Without the aid of Civil Power, but against all the Powers of the Earth, the Excellent Purity of its Precepts, and the unblamable behaviour of its Ministers, with the divine blessing made its way through all opposition,

Nor was it the better for the Church when Constantine the Great first Established Christianity by human Laws, true there was rest from Persecution but how soon was the Church overrun With error Superstition and Immorality how unlike Were Ministers now to what they were before both in Orthodoxy of Principle and Purity of Life,

But it is said religion is taking its flight and that deism with its baneful Influence is spreading itself over the State, if so it must be owing to the Laws, not the want of Religious Establishment, let Your Laws punish the Vices and Immoralities of the Times, and let there not be wanting Such men placed in Power and Authority, who by their Example shall recommend religion, and by their faithfulness, scurge the growing vices of the Times, Let Ministers Manifest to the World that they are inwardly Moved by the Holy ghost to take upon them that office, that they seek the Good of Mankind and not Worldly Interest, let their doctrine be Scriptural and their lives upright, Then shall religion (if Departed) Speedily return and Deism with it dreaded Consequences be removed,

But what Valuable Purpose would such Assessment answer, Would it introduce any More Useful and faithful men into the Ministry? Surely not, Those whom divine grace hath Called to that work, will esteem it their highest honour to do his Pleasure, on the Contrary it might call in Many Hirelings Whose chief Motive and design would be Temporal Interest,

That religious Establishment and Government is linked together, and that the latter cannot Exist without the former is Something new; Witness Pensylvania where no Such Establishment hath taken place, Their Government stands firm and which of the Neighbouring States has better Members of brighter Morals and more Upright Characters;

The [Virginia] bill of rights which Says that all men by nature are born equally free; so no person in this Commonwealth shall injoy Exclusive Privileges except for Services rendered the State, Shall not those then Who are not Professors of the Christian religion who were in this State at the Passing of this bill; and others who have been invited Since by the benefits it held out, When they shall be Obliged to Support the Christian Religion, think that such Obligation is a Departure from the True Spirit and meaning of it;

Finally if such Tax is against the Spirit of the Gospel if Christ for Several hundred Years not only without the aid of Civil Power but against all the powers of earth, Supported and defended it, if religious Establishment has never been a means of Prospering the Gospel, if no more faithful men would be Called by it into the Ministry, if it would not revive decayed Religion nor stop the Growth of Deism, nor serve the Purpose of Government and if against the bill of rights Your Petitioners trust that the Wisdom and uprightness of your Honourable House will leave them intirely free in Matters of religion and the Manner of Supporting its Teachers.

————

This petition and Madison's Memorial and Remonstrance were but two of several petitions relating to the special privileges of the Anglican Church in Virginia during the period from 1784 to 1802. For example, these petitions not only attacked the General Assessment, but also addressed the controversy over the incorporation of the Protestant Episcopal Church in Virginia. See, e.g., Petition of Anglican clergy, June 4, 1784, urging the repeal of "all those laws which direct Modes of faith and worship, and enjoin the observance of certain days" and allowing "an act of incorporation to regulate all the spiritual concerns of that Church, Alter its form of worship, and institute such Canons, bye laws, and rules for the government and good order thereof as are suited to their religious principles"; but see Petition of "united Clergy of the Presbyterian Church in Virginia," November 12, 1784, opposing the incorporation of "clergymen, independent of the religious communities to which they belong" because that would "form Clergymen into a distinct order in the community and especially where it would be possible for them to have the principal direction of a considerable public estate ... [it would have] a tendency to render them independent, at length of the churches whose Ministers they are". Other petitions attacked the system of setting aside public lands known as "glebes" for the support of the Anglican clergy; see Petition of "ministers and Lay representatives of the Presbyterian Church in Virginia," November 2, 1785, lamenting the "impolitic Partiality" of reserving lands "procured at the expense of the whole Community" for the use of only one religious community.

In all, 10,929 persons indicated opposition to Henry's bill, which died in the November 1785 session. 8 *Madison Papers* 295–298. The Evangelicals, especially the Baptists, provided the decisive numbers. Thomas E. Buckley, S.J., *Church and State in Revolutionary Virginia, 1776–1787* 175 (1977). The aftermath was glorious for Madison and Jefferson. Jefferson's bill, defeated in 1779, now passed. Madison wrote to Jefferson in Paris.

Madison to Jefferson, January 22, 1786

The steps taken throughout the Country to defeat the Genl. Assessment, had produced all the effect that could have been wished. The table was loaded with petitions & remonstrances from all parts against the interposition of the Legislature in matters of Religion. A General convention of the Presbyterian church prayed expressly that the bill in the Revisal might be passed into a law, as the best safeguard short of a constitutional one, for their religious rights. The bill was carried thro' the H of Delegates, without alteration. The Senate objected to the preamble, and sent down a proposed substitution of the 16th art: of the Declaration of Rights. The H. of D.disagreed. The Senate insisted and asked a Conference. Their objections were frivolous indeed. In order to remove them as they were understood by the Managers of the H. of D. the preamble was sent up again from the H. of D. with one or two verbal alterations. As an amendment to these the Senate sent down a few others; which as they did not affect the substance though they somewhat defaced the composition, it was thought better to agree to than to run further risks, especially as it was getting late in the Session and the House growing thin. The enacting clauses past without a single alteration, and I flatter myself have in this Country extinguished for ever the ambitious hope of making laws for the human mind. 8 *Madison Papers* 473–474.

———

The changes made by the legislature are indicated by italics in the copy of Jefferson's bill [section 2 above]. "Comfortable liberty" was established, even if Madison's estimation of the victory—the end of "making laws for the human mind"—was exaggerated. When Jefferson had attacked the belief that Christianity was part of the common law, he had found one ancient ecclesiastical phrase acceptable: *in foro conscientiae*, "in the forum of conscience" or internal tribunal where the old canonists said each one had to judge his own acts. Jefferson had abandoned external judgment of the morality of an act while retaining the sanction of conscience. That sanction, coupled with the idea of an avenging God, he invoked in his reflections on slavery in another portion of his Notes on Virginia.

Jefferson, *Notes on Virginia*, 1784
Query XVIII: *The particular customs and manners that may happen to be received in that State*

It is difficult to determine on the standard by which the manners of a nation may be tried, whether *catholic or particular*. It is more difficult for a native to bring to that standard the manners of his own nation, familiarized to him by habit. There must doubtless by an unhappy influence on the manners of our people produced by the existence of slavery among us. The whole commerce between master and slave is a perpetual exercise of the most boisterous passions, the most unremitting despotism on the one part, and degrading submissions on the other. Our children see this, and learn to imitate it; for man is an imitative animal. This quality is the germ of all education in him. From his cradle to his grave he is learning to do what he sees others do. If a parent could find no motive either in his philanthropy or his self-love, for restraining the intemperance of passion towards his slave, it should always be a sufficient one that his child is present. But generally it is not sufficient. The parent storms, the child looks on, catches the lineaments of wrath, puts on the same airs in the circle of smaller slaves, gives a loose to the worst of passions, and thus nursed, educated, and daily exercised in tyranny, cannot but be stamped by it with odious peculiarities. The man must be a prodigy who can retain his manners and morals undepraved by such circumstances. And with what execrations should the statesman be loaded, who permitting one half the citizens thus to trample on the rights of the other, transforms those into despots, and these into enemies, destroys the morals of the one part, and the amor patriae of the other. For if a slave can have a country in this world, it must be any other in preference to that in which he is born to live and labour for another: in which he must lock up the faculties of his nature, contribute as far as depends on his individual endeavours to the evanishment of the human race, or entail his own miserable condition on the endless generations proceeding from him. With the morals of the people, their industry also is destroyed. For in a warm climate, no man will labour for himself who can make another labour for him. This is so true, that of the proprietors of slaves a very small proportion indeed are ever seen to labour. And can the liberties of a nation be thought secure when we have removed their only firm basis, a conviction in the minds of the people that these liberties are of the gift of God? That they are not to be violated but with his wrath? Indeed I tremble for my country when I reflect that God is just: that his justice cannot sleep forever: that considering numbers, nature and natural means only, a revolution of the wheel of fortune, an exchange of situation, is among possible events: that it may become probable by supernatural interference! The Almighty has no attribute which can take side with us in such a contest—But it is impossible to be temperate and to pursue this subject through the various considerations of policy, of morals, of history natural and civil. We must be contented to hope they will force their way into every one's mind. I think a change already perceptible, since the origin of the present revolution. The spirit of the master is abating, that of the slave rising from the dust, his condition mollifying, the way I hope preparing, under the auspices of heaven, for a total emancipation, and that this is disposed, in the order of events, to be with the consent of the masters rather than by their extirpation. *Notes on Virginia* 266–267.

NOTE

The slaves were one large class of human beings whose minds were not permitted to be free. Slaves worshipped on the terms their masters and the commonwealth of Virginia allowed. Slaves learned what religious doctrine their masters thought suitable. Slaves supported the churches to which their masters contributed the income from their labor. Freeing the free population from external religious restraints, Madison and Jefferson did not acknowledge that they left at least half the population bound, religiously as well as physically. Was the price of religious liberty for one half of the population in Virginia in 1785 slavery for the other half? *See* Noonan, *Persons and Masks of the Law: Jefferson, Wythe, Cardozo, and Holmes as Makers of the Masks* (1976).

2.   MASSACHUSETTS

Meanwhile in Massachusetts, lawmaking had taken a different turn. The Baptists in Massachusetts had sent Isaac Backus to the Continental Congress in 1775 to complain of their being "obliged to support a ministry we cannot attend." Backus wrote as follows to the Massachusetts delegates.

Isaac Backus to Massachusetts Delegates to Continental Congress, 1775

In their plea, S. Adams tried to represent that regular Baptists were quite easy among us; and more than once insinuated that these complaints came from enthusiasts who made it a merit to suffer Persecution; and also that enemies had a hand therein. Paine said, there was nothing of conscience in the matter; it was only a contending about paying a little money; and also that we would not be neighborly and let them know who we were, which was all they wanted, and they would readily exempt us.

In answer, I told them they might call it enthusiasm or what they pleased; but I freely own, before all these gentlemen, that it is absolutely a point of conscience with me; for I cannot give in the certificates they require without implicitly acknowledging that power in man which I believe belongs only to God. This shocked them; and Cushing said: "*It quite altered the case*; for if it were a point of conscience, he had nothing to say to that." And the conference of about four hours continuance, closed with their promising to do what they could for our relief, though to deter us from thinking of their coming upon equal footing with us as to religion, John Adams at one time said, we might as well expect a change in the solar system, to expect they would give up their establishment. Isaac Backus, 2 *A History of New England with particular reference to the denomination of Christians called Baptists* 201–202 (1871; reprint ed. 1969).

————

A state constitution proposed in 1778 had been rejected partly because it lacked a declaration of rights. In 1780 a new Convention remedied this defect. The chief author of the constitution of 1780—a prototype of written American constitutions—was John Adams, who has described his part: "I was by the Convention put upon the Committee—by the Committee upon the Subcommittee—and by the Subcommittee appointed a Sub Committee—so that I had the honor to be principal Engineer," Adams to Edmund Jennings, June 7, 1800, quoted in L. H. Butterfield, Leonard C. Faber, Wendell D. Garrett, eds., 2 *Diary and Autobiography of John Adams* 401 (1961). The constitution of 1780 opened with a preamble that acknowledged "the goodness of the Great Legislature of the Universe" and prayed for his guidance. Part I proceeded as follows.

A Declaration of the Rights of the Inhabitants of the Commonwealth of Massachusetts, 1780

Art.I. All men are born free and equal, and have certain natural, essential, and unalienable rights; among which may be reckoned the right of enjoying and defending their lives and liberties; that of acquiring, possessing, and protecting property; in fine, that of seeking and obtaining their safety and happiness.

Art. II. It is the right as well as the duty of all men in society, publicly, and at stated seasons, to worship the SUPREME BEING, the great creator and preserver of the universe. And no subject shall be hurt, molested, or restrained, in his person, liberty, or estate, for worshipping GOD in the manner and season most agreeable to the dictates of his own conscience; or for his religious profession or sentiments; provided he doth not disturb the public peace, or obstruct others in their religious worship.

Art. III. As the happiness of a people, and the good order and preservation of civil government, essentially depend upon piety, religion and morality; and as these cannot be generally diffused through a community, but by the institution of the public worship of GOD, and of public instructions in piety, religion and morality: Therefore, to promote their happiness and to secure the good order and preservation of their government, the people of this Commonwealth have a right to invest their legislature with power to authorize and require, and the legislature shall, from time to time, authorize and require, the several towns, parishes, precincts, and other bodies-politic, or religious societies, to make suitable provision, at their own expense, for the institution of the public worship of GOD, and for the support and maintenance of public protestant teachers of piety, religion and morality, in all cases where such provision shall not be made voluntarily.

And the people of this Commonwealth have also a right to, and do, invest their legislature with authority to enjoin upon all the subjects an attendance upon the instructions of the public teachers aforesaid, at stated times and seasons, if there be any on whose instructions they can conscientiously and conveniently attend.

Provided notwithstanding, that the several towns, parishes, precincts, and other bodies-politic, or religious societies, shall, at all times, have the exclusive right of electing their public teachers, and of contracting with them for their support and maintenance.

And all monies paid by the subject to the support of public worship, and of the public teachers aforesaid, shall, if he require it, be uniformly applied to the support of the public teacher or teachers of his own religious sect or denomination, provided there be any on whose instructions he attends: otherwise it may be paid towards the support of the teacher or teachers of the parish or precinct in which the said monies are raised.

And every denomination of christians, demeaning themselves peaceably, and as good subjects of the Commonwealth, shall be equally under the protection of the law: And no subordination of any one sect or denomination to another shall ever be established by law.

NOTES

Ambiguities in the Meaning of "Establishment" The term "established church" comes not from an Act of Parliament, but from Canon 10, one of the religious rules for excommunicating Catholics and dissident Protestants from the Church of England. These canons were formulated and promulgated by the Archbishop of Canterbury, Richard Bancroft, in 1604. *See* J.V. Bullard, Ed., *Constitutions And Canons Ecclesiastical, 1604* (1934); and Robert E. Rodes, Jr., *Law and Modernization in the Church of England: Charles II to the Welfare State* 84 (1991). As used in that canon, the reference is clear. It meant the Church of England, which in Tudor and Stuart England had been given a special status and which was differentiated both from Recusant Catholics and Dissenting Protestants by a variety of burdens and penalties imposed upon non-members of the church. *See, e.g.,* Act against Jesuits and Seminary Priests, 27 Eliz. I c. 2 (1585); Act against Seditious Sectaries, 35 Eliz. I c 1 (1593); Act against Popish Recusants, 35 Eliz. I c. 2 (1593); Act concerning Jesuits and Seminary Priests, 1 & 2 James I c. 4 (1604); Act of Uniformity, 14 Chas. II c. 4 (1662); The Five Mile Act, 17 Chas. II c. 2 (1664); The Conventicle Act, 22 Chas. II c. 1 (1670); Test Act, 25 Chas. II c. 2 (1673); and The Second Test Act, 30 Chas. II c. 1 (1678).

The term "establishment" had greater clarity in England than in the American colonies. As one commentator notes, "In England 'establishment' clearly referred to the Anglican Church, officially approved and supported by the government, which excluded non-Anglicans, who probably constituted less than ten per cent of the population, from positions of power, privilege, and social influence. In America the constant need for more settlers made such exclusivity unachievable." Thomas J. Curry, *The First Freedoms* 105 (1986).

Further ambiguities about the meaning of the term "establishment" in the colonies "stemmed from such peculiarly American situations as that in New York, where the minority Anglicans claimed to be the establishment, or in New England, where Congregationalists—Dissenters within the Empire—in fact constituted the established church. Virginia, the Carolinas, Maryland, and Georgia established the Church of England and taxed all residents for its support, but none of those colonies confined officeholding to Anglicans. Though their inhabitants expressed considerable discontent with the established church, their dissatisfaction, at least until the eve of the American Revolution, centered on the operation of that church, not on the nature or principle of establishment itself." *Id.* 105. Curry notes, however, that throughout the eighteenth century ministers "consistently denounced throughout the colonies . . . any theoretical establishment that imposed a unity of belief on all subjects." *Id.* 98.

Massachusetts introduced yet another ambiguity. The Congregationalists maintained a set of relationships that clearly amounted to a form of establishment for themselves, but they differentiated their "good" establishment from the "evil" establishment in England "from which their ancestors had fled and that still oppressed their brethren in England." *Id.* 106. Meanwhile, back in England, "English Congregationalists, referred to as Dissenters since the reestablishment of the Church of England after the Restoration, were concerned lest their own pleas to a hostile English hierarchy be rendered ineffective by the intransigence of Massachusetts toward its own dissenters. New England ministers found this delicate situation somewhat trying and wished their English cohorts would cease reminding them of it." *Id.* 26.

Whatever an establishment meant in a particular colony, the very idea of an established religion came under intense fire as the colonies inched toward rebellion. Establishment–whether religious or political–was associated with the British Empire. The repudiation of the established order of British imperial rule entailed a repudiation of "the Church of England ... by law established." The demand for religious freedom sparked the call for revolution, and the revolution would not be complete without a thorough reexamination of the relationship between church and state in America. Two phrases intertwined in meaning were coined to express this commitment to freedom: nonestablishment of religion and free exercise of religion. These two terms—nonestablishment and free exercise—were virtually coterminous expressions of freedom.

Shortly after the Declaration of Independence, New York expressly repudiated its establishment of the Anglican church. The issue never arose in states like Delaware, New Jersey, Pennsylvania, and Rhode Island, which in the preRevolutionary period had "established no religion, provided public support for no ministers, and admitted all Protestants on an equal basis." *Id.* 106. But every state "altered the Church–State arrangements it had inherited from colonial times." *Id.* 134. Nonestablishment was accepted up and down the Atlantic seaboard.

After the Revolution, New England proceeded at a slower pace to dismantle the historical arrangements favoring the Congregationalists. To Baptists and Quakers in New England, these arrangements certainly seemed to amount to an establishment. See William G. McLoughlin, *New England Dissent: The Baptists and the Separation of Church and State, 1630–1833* (1971). But the political leaders of Massachusetts and Connecticut would never have conceded that they still had an officially established state religion in the same sense as was meant by the phrase the "Church of England ... by law established." Thus paragraph 5 of Article III above expressly commits the Commonwealth against establishing the "subordination of any one sect or denomination to another."

At the constitutional convention of 1780, Article III–a provision that John Adams accepted but did not draft—had been the most controversial. A distinguished American historian concluded that in effect this provision "virtually established Congregationalism as the state religion of Massachusetts." Samuel Eliot Morison, "The Struggle over the Adoption of the Constitution of Massachusetts, 1780" 50 Massachusetts Historical Society *Proceedings* 368 (1917). Morison's conclusion that Massachusetts had a de facto establishment is grounded on these facts. A "parish" was governed by the same male taxpayers who governed a town, and these taxpayers were Congregationalists. The "public teachers" who were to receive public support were Congregationalist ministers. *Id.* 370.

The dissenters wrung three concessions from the Congregationalists at the Convention. First, provision for church support could be "voluntary" (Article

III, Paragraph I, last clause). This provision acknowledged the system prevalent in Boston, where the churches supported themselves by pew rent, not public taxes. Baptists said they wanted no greater liberty. Morison 375. Second, the choice of the minister could be made by the town, parish, or *religious society* (Article III, Paragraph 3). The scope of this provision depended on what the term "religious society" included. Third, one's tax money went to one's own minister (Article III, Paragraph 4), but with two qualifications. One had to attend his services. Who counted as a minister or public teacher again depended on the definition of a "religious society," a matter that would trouble the courts of Massachusetts in the early nineteenth century [Chapter Seven, section 6].

The didactic part of Article III, explaining why the preservation of civil government was owed to the worship of God, gained the "full concurrence" of Isaac Backus. Backus, 2 *A History of New England* 228. Article III as a whole was still opposed by the Baptists. A petition offered the electorate three reasons to reject it.

Baptist Petition to Reject Article III of Massachusetts Constitution, 1780

First, because it asserts a right in the people to give away a power they never had themselves; for no man has a right to judge for others in religious matters; yet this article would give the majority of each town and parish the exclusive right of covenanting for the rest with religious teachers and so of excluding the minority from the liberty of choosing for themselves in that respect.

Second, Because this power is given entirely into the hands of men who vote only by virtue of money qualifications; without any regard to the Church of Christ.

Third, Because said article contradicts itself, for it promises *equal* protection of all sects, with an exemption from any subordination of one religious denomination to another; when it is impossible for the majority of any community to govern in any affair, unless the minority are in subordination to them in that affair. Morison 376.

The town meetings voted on the constitution. Twenty-nine towns objected that Article III interfered "in Matters that belong to Christ & Conscience." Morison 407 (citing Petition of Town of Granville). The popular vote was only 8,885 to 6,225 in favor of the Article. *Id.* 411. In terms of the total population of Massachusetts—about 378,000—a tiny fragment approved. 50 *Massachusetts Historical Society Proceedings* 55. The convention itself had specified that two-thirds of those voting must agree. *Journal of Convention of 1780* 169. By the convention's own criteria Article III had not been adopted. Nevertheless, the convention and everyone else proceeded to treat Article III as if it had been approved. The Declaration of Rights in Massachusetts thus entrenched the system that Adams had told Backus he might as well expect to change as the solar system. The constitution of 1780 had further provisions bearing on religion in Part II, "The Frame of Government." Two oaths were required.

Constitution of Massachusetts, 1780, Part II, Chapter VI

ART.I. Any person chosen Governor, Lieutenant–Governor, Counsellor, Senator, or Representative, and accepting the trust, shall, before he proceed to execute the duties of his place or office, make and subscribe the following declaration, viz—

I, AB do declare, that I believe the christian religion, and have a firm persuasion of its truth, . . .

And every person chosen to either of the places or offices aforesaid, as also any person appointed or commissioned to any judicial, executive, military, or other office under the government, shall, before he enters on the discharge of the business of his place or office, take and subscribe the following declaration, and oaths or affirmations, viz— . . .

And that I do renounce and adjure all allegiance, subjection and obedience to the King, Queen or Government of Great Britain, (as the case may be) and every other foreign power whatsoever: And that no foreign Prince, Person, Prelate, State or Potentate, hath, or ought to have, any jurisdiction, superiority, pre-eminence, authority, dispensing or other power, in any matter, civil, ecclesiastical or spiritual, within this Commonwealth; except the authority and power which is or may be vested by their Constituents in the Congress of the United States: And I do further testify and declare, that no man or body of men hath or can have any right to absolve or discharge me from the obligation of this oath, declaration or affirmation; and that I do make this acknowledgement, profession, testimony, declaration, denial, renunciation and abjuration, heartily and truly, according to the common meaning and acceptation of the foregoing words, without any equivocation, mental evasion, or secret reservation whatsoever. So help me GOD.

———

The convention did not acknowledge inconsistency between the first oath and the right of conscience recognized by Part I, Article II. However, the convention did express concern over the relation of the second oath to Article III's final clause about not subordinating one sect to another. Addressing the electorate, the convention declared:

Your Delegates did not conceive themselves to be vested with Power to set up one Denomination of Christians above another; Religion must at all Times be a matter between GOD and individuals: But we have nevertheless, found ourselves obliged by a Solemn Test, to provide for the exclusion of those from Offices who will not disclaim those Principles of Spiritual Jurisdiction which Roman Catholicks *in some Countries* have held, and which are subversive of a free Government established by the People. *Journal of Convention of 1780* 220–221.

———

That only some Catholics believed in the spiritual preeminence of the pope was a delusion the convention readily entertained to free itself from the implication of bigotry. Finally, the constitution made provision for the college that it acknowledged as valuable to both "Church and State."

Constitution of Massachusetts, 1780, Part II, Chapter V

The University at Cambridge, and Encouragement of Literature, etc.

Section I.   *The University*

Art.I. Whereas our wise and pious ancestors, so early as the year one thousand six hundred and thirty six, laid the foundation of Harvard–College, in which University many persons of great eminence have, by the blessing of GOD, been initiated in those arts and sciences, which qualified them for public employments, both in Church and State: And whereas the encouragement of Arts and Sciences, and all good literature, tends to the honor of GOD, the advantage of the christian religion, and the great benefit of this, and the other United States of America—It is declared, That the PRESIDENT AND FELLOWS OF HARVARD-COLLEGE, in their corporate capacity, and their successors in that capacity, their officers and servants, shall have, . . . all the powers, . . . which they now have, or are entitled to have, hold, use, exercise and enjoy . . . forever. . . .

And it being necessary, in this new Constitution of Government, to ascertain who shall be deemed successors to the said Governor, Deputy–Governor and Magistrates: IT IS DECLARED That the Governor, Lieutenant–Governor, Council and Senate of this Commonwealth, are, and shall be deemed, their successors; who, with the President of Harvard–College, for the time being, together with the ministers of the congregational churches in the towns of Cambridge, Watertown, Charlestown, Boston, Roxbury, and Dorchester, mentioned in the said act, shall be, and hereby are, vested with all the powers and authority belonging, or in any way appertaining to the Overseers of Harvard College. . . .

Divinity was part of the college curriculum. Congregationalist ministers were trained by instruction in the college courses. The constitution gave the legislature a basis for further encouraging, by the appropriation of tax money, this key institution of the de facto religious establishment.

3.   THE UNITED STATES OF AMERICA

The Massachusetts system was with minor variations the system of Connecticut and New Hampshire. South Carolina had its own distinctive form of privileges for the Episcopal church. None of these states accepted the anti-establishment views of Virginia. The makers of the new nation had to form it for constituents who came from both camps.

A.   THE DECLARATION OF INDEPENDENCE, 1776

Thomas Jefferson, the principal draftsman of the Declaration of Independence, referred to "the equal and independent station to which the laws of nature & of nature's god entitle [Americans]." He went on to say: "We hold these truths to be sacred & undeniable: that all Men are created equal and independent, that from that creation they derive rights inherent and inalienable," Jefferson's "original Rough draught," 1 *Jefferson Papers* 423. Equality was derived from creation; God was invoked as the author of nature's laws. After revisions by John Adams, Benjamin Franklin, Roger Sherman, and Robert R. Livingston, 1 *Jefferson Papers* 414, the draft read as follows.

When in the Course of human events, it becomes necessary for one people to dissolve the political bonds which have connected them with another, and to assume among the powers of the earth, the separate and equal station to which the Laws of Nature and of Nature's God entitle them, a decent respect to the opinions of mankind requires that they should declare the causes which impel them to the separation. We hold these truths to be self-evident, that all men are created equal, that they are endowed by their Creator with certain unalienable Rights, that among these are Life, Liberty and the pursuit of Happiness.

————

The theology embedded in this opening paragraph was acceptable to a wide spectrum of Christians and Deists. Congress added two ideas taken more specifically from Jewish and Christian theology.

We, therefore, the Representatives of the United States of America, in General Congress, Assembled, appealing to the Supreme Judge of the world for the rectitude of our intentions, do, in the Name, and by Authority of the good People of these Colonies, solemnly publish and declare, That these United Colonies are, and of Right ought to be Free and Independent States; that they are Absolved from all Allegiance to the British Crown, and that all political connection between them and the State of Great Britain, is and ought to be totally dissolved; and that as Free and Independent States, they have full Power to levy War, conclude Peace, contract Alliances, establish Commerce, and to do all other Acts and Things which Independent States may of right do. And for the support of this Declaration, with a firm reliance on the protection of divine Providence, we mutually pledge to each other our Lives, our Fortunes and our sacred Honor.

————

The Supreme Judge stepped out of Scripture. The belief in a superintending Providence was biblical. And, although the Declaration charged the king of England with many crimes, nothing was said about his fostering religious establishments or permitting the persecution of religious dissenters. The national consensus agreed on God, His bestowal of inalienable rights, His role as Judge, His help. Virginian ideas about religious freedom were postponed.

B. THE OATH OF OFFICE

Religion first reached the floor of the convention that made the Constitution of the United States on August 20, 1787, when Charles

Pinckney of South Carolina, aged twenty-four, put forward a proposal banning test oaths such as those that had excluded non-members of the Anglican church from serving in public office.

Proposal of Charles Pinckney, 1787

No religious test or qualification shall ever be annexed to any oath of office under the authority of the U.S. Max Farrand, ed., 2 *Records of the Federal Convention of 1787* [*Records of Convention*] 342 (1911).

———

On August 30, 1787, Pinckney saw his opportunity to move this language as an addition to the article on the oath of office to support the Constitution. A delegate from Maryland provided the fullest account of what happened next.

Luther Martin to Legislature of Maryland, August 30, 1787

The part of the system which provides, that *no religious test* shall ever be required as a qualification to any office or public trust under the United States, was adopted by a great majority of the convention, and without much debate; however, there were some members *so unfashionable* as to think, that a *belief of the existence of a Deity,* and of *a state of future rewards and punishments* would be some security for the good conduct of our rulers, and that, in a Christian country, it would be *at least decent* to hold out some distinction between the professors of Christianity and downright infidelity or paganism. Farrand, 3 *Records of Convention* 227, note 100.

———

According to Madison, Roger Sherman of Connecticut opposed the proposal as "unnecessary, the prevailing liberality being a sufficient security against such tests." Gouverneur Morris of Pennsylvania and Charles Cotesworth Pinckney supported young Pinckney. The provision was then adopted unanimously. Farrand, 2 *Records of Convention* 468.

United States Constitution, Article VI

The Senators and Representatives before mentioned, and the Members of the several State Legislatures, and all executive and judicial Officers, both of the United States and of the several States, shall be bound by Oath or Affirmation, to support this Constitution; but no religious Test shall ever be required as a Qualification to any Office or public Trust under the United States.

———

The oath as a special ritual required of officeholders rested on the assumption that an oath-taker believed in God and would out of respect, love, or fear not call on Him to witness his words unless he spoke the truth. Article VI employed this religious device.

An oath is a religious act. The phrase, "so help me God," was meant to invoke the presence of God to vouch for the truth of the statement made by the person taking the oath. Affirmation of the truth, an alternative to oath-taking, was originally an accommodation of the religious concerns of Quakers, who declined to take oaths because of the command in the sermon on the mount: "Let your word be 'Yes, Yes' or 'No, No'; anything more than this comes from the evil one." (Mt. 5:37). See Michael W. McConnell, "The Origins and Historical Understanding of Free Exercise of Religion," 103 *Harv.L.Rev.* 1409, 1428, 1467–68 (1990). The two words "or affirmation," were added to the Constitution without debate in the final days of the Constitutional Convention. These words are now thought to protect the right of agnostics and atheists to testify in court without committing themselves to the existence of God.

C. THE PROPOSED NATIONAL UNIVERSITY

On September 14, 1787, James Madison and Charles Pinckney moved to give Congress a power "to establish an University, in which no preferences or distinctions should be made on account of religion." Farrand, 2 *Records of Convention* 616. A national university had the potential of bringing the religious differences of the nation to the fore. The motion, however, was not opposed on that ground, but on the ground that the power was superfluous; Congress would be free to establish educational institutions in the federal district. The motion failed 4–6.

D. WRITTEN SECURITY: THE FIRST AMENDMENT

Thomas Jefferson was not in Philadelphia during the constitutional convention because he was serving as the American Ambassador to France. He wrote to James Madison from Paris.

Jefferson to Madison, December 20, 1787

I will now add what I do not like. First, the omission of a bill of rights providing clearly and without the aid of sophisms for freedom of religion, freedom of the press, protection against standing armies, restrictions against monopolies, the eternal and unremitting force of the habeas corpus laws, and trials by jury in all matters of fact triable by the laws of the land and not by the laws of Nations.... Let me add that a bill of rights is what the people are entitled to against every government on earth, general or particular, and what no just government should refuse or rest on inference. 10 *Madison Papers* 336–37.

————

A second letter from Jefferson on February 6, 1788, called the absence of a declaration of rights the Constitution's "principal defect," and he hoped that the first nine states would ratify and the last four refuse to ratify until the defect had been cured. 10 *Madison Papers* 474. Connecticut, Delaware, Georgia, Maryland, New Jersey, and Pennsylvania in fact asked for no amendments. Massachusetts asked for none relating to religion. South Carolina asked for a minor clarification of Article VI. Chester J. Antieau, Arthur T. Downey, and Edward C. Roberts, *Freedom from Federal Establishment* 112–113, 117 (1964).

The five other states made substantive proposals for amendments relating to religion. New Hampshire, on June 21, 1788, proposed a single sentence.

New Hampshire Proposal for a Religion Clause, 1788

Congress shall make no laws touching religion, or to infringe the rights of conscience. Jonathan Elliot, 1 *The Debates in the Several State Conventions on the Adoption of the Federal Constitution [Debates in State Conventions]* 326 (1836).

————

A provision in the New Hampshire Bill of Rights almost identical with Article III of the Massachusetts constitution extended to the Congregationalist churches a preference that amounted to a similar de facto establishment. Asking that Congress not "touch religion," New Hampshire wanted the hands of the national government off its arrangements with the Congregationalists. On June 27, 1788, Virginia submitted a very different proposal.

Virginia Proposal for a Religion Clause, 1788

That any person religiously scrupulous of bearing arms ought to be exempted, upon payment of an equivalent to employ another to bear arms in his stead.

That religion, or the duty which we owe to our Creator, and the manner of discharging it, can be directed only by reason and conviction, not by force or violence; and therefore all *men have an equal, natural, and unalienable right to the free* exercise of religion, according to the dictates of conscience; and *that no particular religious sect or society ought to be favored or established, by law, in preference to others*. Elliot, 3 *Debates in State Conventions* 659.

————

Italics indicate additions to the Virginia Declaration of Rights of 1776. That declaration's last clause as to the Christian duty of mutual charity was omitted. On August 1, 1788, North Carolina adopted the language of Virginia. Elliot, 4 *Debates in State Conventions* 244. So did Rhode Island on June 16, 1790. Elliot, 1 *Debates in State Conventions* 334–335. New York, on July 26, 1788, also used language almost identical with the last clause of Virginia's proposal. Elliot, 1 *Debates in State Conventions* 328. All of the proposals, including New Hampshire's, treated freedom of conscience as essential. The Virginia language forbade preference for one religion over another. James Madison, so active in securing religious liberty in Virginia, had shown much more interest in getting the Constitution adopted than amended by any bill of rights. In the Virginia convention on the Constitution, he answered Patrick Henry, an opponent of ratification, who had invoked Jefferson's known desire for a bill of rights.

Madison's Reply to Patrick Henry in the Virginia Ratifying Convention, June 12, 1788

The honorable member has introduced the subject of religion. Religion is not guarded—there is no bill of rights declaring that religion should be secure. Is a bill of rights a security for religion? Would the bill of rights in this state exempt the people from paying for the support of one particular sect, if such sect were exclusively established by law? If there were a majority of one sect, a bill of rights would be a poor protection for liberty. Happily for the states, they enjoy the utmost freedom of religion. This freedom arises from that multiplicity of sects, which pervades America, and which is the best and only security for religious liberty in any society. For where there is such a variety of sects, there cannot be a majority of any one sect to oppress and persecute the rest. Fortunately for this commonwealth, a majority of the people are decidedly against any exclusive establishment— I believe it to be so in the other states. There is not a shadow of right in the general government to intermeddle with religion. Its least interference with it would be a most flagrant usurpation. I can appeal to my uniform conduct on this subject, that I have warmly supported religious freedom. It is better that this security should be depended upon from the general legislature, than from one particular state. A particular state might concur in one religious project. But the United States abound in such a variety of sects, that it is a strong security against religious persecution, and is sufficient to authorise a conclusion, that no one sect will ever be able to out-number or depress the rest. Elliot, 3 *Debates in State Conventions* 330 (1836).

————

Madison's argument paralleled his argument in *The Federalist* No. 10, that the great security against oppression by a political factor was a multiplicity of interests contending with one other. *See* Edward McGlynn Gaffney, "Political Divisiveness Along Religious Lines: The Entanglement of the Court in Sloppy History and Bad Public Policy," 24 St. Louis Univ. L. J.205 (1980). When Virginia finally proposed several amendments, including the one on religion, Madison referred to them globally, saying that a number were "highly objectionable," Madison to George Washington, June 27, 1788. 11 *Madison Papers* 182. Madison wrote to Thomas Jefferson in Paris giving his views a little more explicitly.

Madison to Jefferson, October 17, 1788

One of the objections in New England was the Constitution by prohibiting religious tests opened a door for Jews Turks & infidels.3.because the limited powers of the federal Government and the jealousy of the subordinate Governments, afford a security which has not existed in the case of the State Governments, and exists in no other. 4.because experience proves the inefficacy of a bill of rights on those occasions when its controul is most needed. Repeated violations of these parchment barriers have been committed by overbearing majorities in every State. In Virginia I have seen the bill of rights violated in every instance where it has been opposed to a popular current. Notwithstanding the explicit provision contained in that instrument for the rights of Conscience it is well known that a religious establishment wd. have taken place in that State, if the legislative majority had found as they expected, a majority of the people in favor of the measure; and I am persuaded that if a majority of the people were now of one sect, the measure would still take place and on narrower ground than was then proposed, notwithstanding the additional obstacle which the law has since created. Wherever the real power in a Government lies, there is the danger of oppression.

Supposing a bill of rights to be proper the articles which ought to compose it, admit of much discussion. I am inclined to think that *absolute* restrictions in cases that are doubtful, or where emergencies may overrule them, ought to be avoided. The restrictions however strongly marked on paper will never be regarded when opposed to the decided sense of the public; and after repeated violations in extraordinary cases, they will lose even their ordinary efficacy. 11 *Madison Papers* 297–99, 14 *Jefferson Papers* 18–20.

————

Jefferson replied firmly on November 18, 1788: "As to the bill of rights however I still think it should be added," 11 *Madison Papers* 353. Madison's attitude changed when he ran for the House of Representatives in November 1788–February 1789. He wrote to George Eve, the Baptist pastor of Blue Run Church in Orange County, making a campaign promise to propose a Bill of Rights in the First Congress and to urge its prompt adoption.

Madison to George Eve, January 2, 1789

Sir, Being informed that reports prevail not only that I am opposed to any amendments whatever to the new federal Constitution; but that I have ceased to be a friend to the rights of Conscience; and inferring from a conversation with my brother William, that you are disposed to contradict such reports as far as your knowledge of my sentiments may justify, I am led to trouble you with this communication of them. As a private Citizen it could not be my wish that erroneous opinions should by entertained, with respect to either of those points, particularly, with respect to religious liberty. But having been induced to offer my services to this district as its representative in the federal Legislature, considerations of a public nature make it proper that, with respect to both, my principles and views should be rightly understood.

I freely own that I have never seen in the Constitution as it now stands those serious dangers which have alarmed many respectable Citizens. Accordingly whilst it remained unratified, and it was necessary to unite the States in some one plan, I opposed all previous alterations as calculated to throw the States into dangerous contentions, and to furnish the secret enemies of the Union with an opportunity of promoting its dissolution. Circumstances are now changed: The Constitution is established on the ratifications of eleven States and a very great majority of the people of America; and amendments, if pursued with a proper moderation and in a proper mode, will be not only safe, but may serve the double purpose of satisfying the minds of well meaning opponents, and of providing additional guards in favour of liberty. Under this change of circumstances, it is my sincere opinion that the Constitution ought to be revised, and that the first Congress meeting under it, ought to prepare and recommend to the States for ratification, the most satisfactory provisions for all essential rights, particularly the rights of Conscience in the fullest latitude, the freedom of the press, trials by jury, security against general warrants & c. 11 *Madison Papers* 403–4.

———

Madison's adviser, George Nicholas, urged him by letter on the same day to make further appeals to Reuben Ford, the Baptist minister at Goochland Church, and to get John Leland, the leader of the Virginia Baptists, to "exert himself." 11 *Madison Papers* 407–408. Leland had had his greatest success in converts that year—300 baptized—and was based in Orange, Madison's home county. 10 *Madison Papers* 516. The Reverend Eve responded by holding an election meeting at the Baptist church, taking "a very spirited and decided part" for Madison and recalling his "many important services" to the Baptists, Benjamin Johnson to Madison, January 19, 1789. 11 *Madison Papers* 423–424. Madison continued to campaign, announcing in the Fredericksburg, Virginia, *Herald* his view that the Constitution should have "specific provisions made on the subject of the Rights of Conscience." 11 *Madison Papers* 428. On February 2, 1789, Madison was elected to Congress. John Leland wrote him at once, congratulating him, reminding him that he had voted for him, and concluding: "One Thing I shall expect; that if religious Liberty is anywise threatened; that I shall receive the earliest Intelligence." 11 *Madison Papers* 442–443. On June 8, 1789, true to his campaign promises, Madison moved for amendments to the Constitution, including a Religion Clause.

Madison's First Proposal of a Religion Clause, June 8, 1789

That in article 1st, section 9, between clauses 3 and 4, be inserted these clauses, to wit: The civil rights of none shall be abridged on account of religious belief or worship, nor shall any national religion be established, nor shall the full and equal rights of conscience be in any manner, or on any pretext, infringed 1. *Annals of Congress* 451.

———

Fisher Ames, the most brilliant New Englander in the House, reacted to Madison's ideas.

Fisher Ames to George Richards Minot, July 23, 1789

We have had the amendments on the *tapis*, and referred them to a committee of one from a state. I hope much debate will be avoided by this mode, and that the amendments will be more rational, and less *ad populum*, than Madison's. It is necessary to conciliate, and I would have amendments. But they should not be trash, such would dishonor the Constitution, without pleasing its enemies. W.B.Allen, ed., 1 *Works of Fischer Ames* 694 (1983).

———

Quakers and Mennonites had been exempted from bearing arms by the revolutionary convention at Richmond in 1775; their exemption had been protested, R. K. MacMaster, S. L. Holste, and R. F. Ullie, *Conscience in Crisis: Mennonite and Other Peace Churches in America, 1739–1789* 273 (1979). The Schweckfelders and Amish were equally opposed to fighting. *Id.* 225. *See also* Peter Brock, *Pacifism in the United States, From the Colonial Era to the First World* (1968). A proposed amendment reflected these constituencies, chiefly in Pennsylvania and Virginia.

Debate in the House on the Bill of Rights, August 17, 1789

The House again resolved itself into a committee, Mr. BOUDINOT in the chair, on the proposed amendments to the constitution. The third clause of the fourth proposition in the report was taken into consideration, being as follows: "A well regulated militia, composed of the body of the people, being the best security of a free state, the right of the people to keep and bear arms shall not be infringed; but no person religiously scrupulous shall be compelled to bear arms."

Mr. GERRY.—This declaration of rights, I take it, is intended to secure the people against the mal-administration of the Government; if we could suppose that, in all cases, the rights of the people would be attended to, the occasion for guards of this kind would be removed. Now, I am apprehensive, sir, that this clause would give an opportunity to the people in power to destroy the constitution itself. They can declare who are those religiously scrupulous, and prevent them from bearing arms. . . .

Mr. JACKSON did not expect that all the people of the United States would turn Quakers or Moravians; consequently, one part would have to defend the other in case of invasion. Now this, in his opinion, was unjust, unless the constitution secured an equivalent: for this reason he moved to amend the clause, by inserting at the end of it, "upon paying an equivalent, to be established by law."

Mr. SMITH, of South Carolina, inquired what were the words used by the conventions respecting this amendment. If the gentleman would conform to what was proposed by Virginia and Carolina, he would second him. He thought they were to be excused provided they found a substitute.

Mr. JACKSON was willing to accommodate. He thought the expression was, "No one, religiously scrupulous of bearing arms, shall be compelled to render military service, in person, upon paying an equivalent."

Mr. SHERMAN conceived it difficult to modify the clause and make it better. It is well known that those who are religiously scrupulous of bearing arms, are equally scrupulous of getting substitutes or paying an equivalent. Many of them would rather die than do either one or the other; but he did not see an absolute necessity for a clause of this kind. We do not live under an arbitrary Government, said he, and the States, respectively, will have the government of the militia, unless when called into actual service; besides, it would not do to alter it so as to exclude the whole of any sect, because there are men amongst the Quakers who will turn out, notwithstanding the religious principles of the society, and defend the cause of their country. Certainly it will be improper to prevent the exercise of such favorable dispositions, at least whilst it is the practice of nations to determine their contests by the slaughter of their citizens and subjects.

Mr. VINING hoped the clause would be suffered to remain as it stood, because he saw no use in it if it was amended so as to compel a man to find a substitute, which, with respect to the Government, was the same as if the person himself turned out to fight.

Mr. STONE inquired what the words "religiously scrupulous" had reference to: was it of bearing arms? If it was, it ought so to be expressed.

Mr. BENSON moved to have the words "but no person religiously scrupulous shall be compelled to bear arms," struck out. He would always leave it to the benevolence of the Legislature, for, modify it as you please, it will be impossible to express it in such a manner as to clear it from ambiguity. No man can claim this indulgence of right. It may be a religious persuasion, but it is no natural right, and therefore ought to be left to the discretion of the Government. If this stands part of the constitution, it will be a question before the Judiciary on every regulation you make with respect to the organization of the militia, whether it comports with this declaration or not. It is extremely injudicious to intermix matters of doubt with fundamentals.

I have no reason to believe but the Legislature will always possess humanity enough to indulge this class of citizens in a matter they are so desirous of; but they ought to be left for their discretion.

The motion for striking out the whole clause being seconded, was put, and decided in the negative—22 members voting for it, and 24 against it. 1 *Annals of Cong.* 778–780.

————

Meanwhile another important amendment had also been adopted by the House.

Debate in the House on the Bill of Rights, August 15, 1789

The House again went into a Committee of the whole on the proposed amendments to the Constitution, Mr. BOUDINOT in the chair.

The fourth proposition being under consideration, as follows:

Article 1. Section 9. Between paragraphs two and three insert "no religion shall be established by law, nor shall the equal rights of conscience be infringed."

Mr. SYLVESTER had some doubts of the propriety of the mode of expression used in this paragraph. He apprehended that it was liable to a construction different from what had been made by the committee. He feared it might be thought to have a tendency to abolish religion altogether.

Mr. VINING suggested the propriety of transposing the two members of the sentence.

Mr. GERRY said it would read better if it was, that no religious doctrine shall be established by law.

Mr. SHERMAN thought the amendment altogether unnecessary, inasmuch as Congress had no authority whatever delegated to them by the constitution to make religious establishments; he would, therefore, move to have it struck out.

Mr. CARROLL As the rights of conscience are, in their nature, of peculiar delicacy, and will little bear the gentlest touch of governmental hand; and as many sects have concurred in opinion that they are not well secured under the present constitution, he said he was much in favor of adopting the words. He thought it would tend more towards conciliating the minds of the people to the Government than almost any other amendment he had heard proposed. He would not contend with gentlemen about the phraseology, his object was to secure the substance in such a manner as to satisfy the wishes of the honest part of the community.

Mr. MADISON said, he apprehended the meaning of the words to be, that Congress should not establish a religion, and enforce the legal observation of it by law, nor compel men to worship God in any manner contrary to their conscience. Whether the words are necessary or not, he did not mean to say, but they had been required by some of the State Conventions, who seemed to entertain an opinion that under the clause of the constitution, which gave power to Congress to make all laws necessary and proper to carry into execution the constitution, and the laws made under it, enabled them to make laws of such a nature as might infringe the rights of conscience, and establish a national religion; to prevent these effects he presumed the amendment was intended, and he thought it as well expressed as the nature of the language would admit.

Mr. HUNTINGTON said that he feared, with the gentleman first up on this subject, that the words might be taken in such latitude as to be extremely hurtful to the cause of religion. He understood the amendment to mean what had been expressed by the gentleman from Virginia; but others might find it convenient to put another construction upon it. The ministers of their congregations to the Eastward were maintained by the contributions of those who belonged to their society; the expense of building meetinghouses was contributed in the same manner. These things were regulated by by-laws. If an action was brought before a Federal Court on any of these cases, the person who had neglected to perform his engagements could not be compelled to do it; for a support of ministers, or building of places of worship might be construed into a religious establishment.

By the charter of Rhode Island, no religion could be established by law; he could give a history of the effects of such a regulation; indeed the people were now enjoying the blessed fruits of it. He hoped, therefore, the amendment would be made in such a way as to secure the rights of conscience, and a free exercise of the rights of religion, but not to patronize those who professed no religion at all.

Mr. MADISON thought, if the word national was inserted before religion, it would satisfy the minds of honorable gentlemen. He believed that the people feared one sect might obtain a pre-eminence, or two combine together, and establish a religion to which they would compel others to conform. He thought if the word national was introduced, it would point the amendment directly to the object it was intended to prevent.

Mr. LIVERMORE was not satisfied with that amendment; but he did not wish them to dwell long on the subject. He thought it would be better if it was altered, and made to read in this manner, that Congress shall make no laws touching religion, or infringing the rights of conscience.

Mr. GERRY did not like the term national, proposed by the gentleman from Virginia, and he hoped it would not be adopted by the House. It brought to his mind some observations that had taken place in the conventions at the time they were considering the present constitution. It had been insisted upon by those who were called antifederalists, that this form of Government consolidated the Union; the honorable gentleman's motion shows that he considers it in the same light. Those who were called antifederalists at that time complained that they had injustice done them by the title, because they were in favor of a Federal Government, and the others were in favor of a national one; the federalists were for ratifying the constitution as it stood, and the others not until amendments were made. Their names then ought not to have been distinguished by federalists and antifederalists, but rats and antirats.

Mr. MADISON withdrew his motion, but observed that the words "no national religion shall be established by law," did not imply that the Government was a national one; the question was then taken on Mr. Livermore's motion, and passed in the affirmative, thirty-one for, and twenty against it. 1 *Annals of Cong.* 757–759.

———

On August 17, the House proceeded to the fifth proposition.

Article I. section 10. between the first and second paragraph, insert, "no State shall infringe the equal rights of conscience, nor the freedom of speech or of the press, nor of the right of trial by jury in criminal cases."

Mr. TUCKER.—This is offered, I presume, as an amendment to the constitution of the United States, but it goes only to the alteration of the constitutions of particular States. It will be much better, I apprehend, to leave the State Governments to themselves, and not to interfere with them more than we already do; and that is thought by many to be rather too much. I therefore move, sir, to strike out these words.

Mr. MADISON conceived this to be the most valuable amendment in the whole list. If there was any reason to restrain the Government of the United States from infringing upon these essential rights, it was equally necessary that they should be secured against the State Governments. He thought that if they provided against the one, it was as necessary to provide against the other, and was satisfied that it would be equally grateful to the people.

Mr. LIVERMORE had no great objection to the sentiment, but he thought it not well expressed. He wished to make it an affirmative proposition; "the equal rights of conscience, the freedom of speech or of the press, and the right of trial by jury in criminal cases, shall not be infringed by any State." 1 *Annals of Cong.* 783–784.

———

The proposition ultimately adopted by the House on August 20, 1789, was formulated by Fisher Ames.

House Version of the Religion Clause, August 20, 1789

Congress shall make no law establishing religion, or to prevent the free exercise thereof, or to infringe the rights of conscience.

———

The Senate killed the provision on conscientious objection while keeping the right of the people to bear arms, *Journal of the First Session of the Senate*, September 4, 1789 (1820) 71. It also killed the article that Madison had thought "the most valuable," the resolution against interference with conscience by the States, *id*. 72. A revised form of the establishment and freedom proposal, advanced by Oliver Ellsworth of Connecticut, was adopted:

Senate Version of the Religion Clause, September 4, 1789

Congress shall make no law establishing *articles of faith or a mode of worship* or prohibiting the free exercise *of religion*. 1 *Annals of Cong.* 70. [Italics indicate changes from the House version.]

———

The House refused to concur and asked for a conference. The conferees were Senators Ellsworth, Charles Carroll of Maryland, William Paterson of New Jersey, and Representatives James Madison of Virginia, Roger Sherman of Connecticut, and John Vining of Delaware. From their deliberations emerged the First Amendment clause on religion.

The Religion Clause of the First Amendment

Congress shall make no law respecting an establishment of religion, nor prohibiting the free exercise thereof.

CHAPTER SEVEN

RELIGIOUS BELIEFS AND PRACTICES IN AMERICAN LAW, 1790–1840

A multitude of religious beliefs, presuppositions, and practices were incorporated into the laws of the United States and of the individual states. A number of them were so ingrained and generally accepted as to have been uncontroverted; others were the subject of doubt, debate, or denial.

1. PRAYER

In the House of Representatives, on September 24, 1789, the day on which the House concurred with the Senate in adopting the First Amendment, the following debate occurred:

Debate in First Congress on Day of Thanksgiving, September 24, 1789

Mr. BOUDINOT said, he could not think of letting the session pass over without offering an opportunity to all the citizens of the United States of joining, with one voice, in returning to Almighty God their sincere thanks for the many blessings he had poured down upon them. With this view, therefore, he would move the following resolution:

Resolved, That a joint committee of both Houses be directed to wait upon the President of the United States, to request that he would recommend to the people of the United States a day of public thanksgiving and prayer, to be observed by acknowledging, with grateful hearts, the many signal favors of Almighty God, especially by affording them an opportunity peaceably to establish a Constitution of government for their safety and happiness.

Mr. BURKE did not like this mimicking of European customs, where they made a mere mockery of thanksgivings. Two parties at war frequently sung *Te Deum* for the same event, though to one it was a victory, and to the other a defeat.

Mr. BOUDINOT was sorry to hear arguments drawn from the abuse of a good thing against the use of it. He hoped no gentleman would make a serious opposition to a measure both prudent and just.

Mr. TUCKER thought the House had no business to interfere in a matter which did not concern them. Why should the President direct the people to do what, perhaps, they have no mind to do? They may not be inclined to return thanks for a Constitution until they have experienced that it promotes their safety and happiness. We do not yet know but they may have reason to be dissatisfied with the effects it has already produced;

but whether this be so or not, it is a business with which Congress have nothing to do; it is a religious matter, and, as such, is proscribed to us. If a day of thanksgiving must take place, let it be done by the authority of the several States; they know best what reason their constituents have to be pleased with the establishment of this Constitution.

Mr. SHERMAN justified the practice of thanksgiving, on any signal event, not only as a laudable one in itself, but as warranted by a number of precedents in holy writ: for instance, the solemn thanksgivings and rejoicings which took place in the time of Solomon, after the building of the temple, was a case in point. This example, he thought, worthy of Christian imitation on the present occasion; and he would agree with the gentleman who moved the resolution.

Mr. BOUDINOT quoted further precedents from the practice of the late Congress; and hoped the motion would meet a ready acquiescence.

The question was now put on the resolution, and it was carried in the affirmative; and Messrs. BOUDINOT, SHERMAN, and SYLVESTER were appointed a committee on the part of the House. 1 *Annals of Cong.* 949–950.

———

George Washington issued the requested proclamation.

Washington's Proclamation of a National Day of Thanksgiving, October 3, 1789

Whereas it is the duty of all nations to acknowledge the providence of Almighty God, to obey His will, to be grateful for His benefits, and humbly to implore His protection and favor; and

Whereas both Houses of Congress have, by their joint committee, requested me "to recommend to the people of the United States a day of public thanksgiving and prayer, to be observed by acknowledging with grateful hearts the many and signal favors of Almighty God, especially by affording them an opportunity peaceably to establish a form of government for their safety and happiness:"

Now, therefore, I do recommend and assign Thursday, the 26th day of November next, to be devoted by the people of these States to the service of that great and glorious Being who is the beneficent author of all the good that was, that is, or that will be; that we may then all unite in rendering unto Him our sincere and humble thanks for His kind care and protection of the people of this country previous to their becoming a nation; for the signal and manifold mercies and the favorable interpositions of His providence in the course and conclusion of the late war; for the great degree of tranquillity, union, and plenty which we have since enjoyed; for the peaceable and rational manner in which we have been enabled to establish constitutions of government for our safety and happiness, and particularly the national one now lately instituted for the civil and religious liberty with which we are blessed, and the means we have of acquiring and diffusing useful knowledge; and, in general, for all the great and various favors which He has been pleased to confer upon us.

And also that we may then unite in most humbly offering our prayers and supplications to the great Lord and Ruler of Nations, and beseech Him to pardon our national and other trangressions; to enable us all, whether in public or private situations, to perform our several and relative duties properly and punctually; to render our National Government a blessing to all the people by constantly being a Government of wise, just, and constitutional laws, discreetly and faithfully executed and obeyed; to protect and guide all sovereigns and nations (especially such as have shown kindness to us), and to bless them with good governments, peace, and concord; to promote the knowledge and practice of true religion and virtue, and the increase of science among them and us; and, generally, to grant unto all mankind such a degree of temporal prosperity as He alone knows to be best.

Given under my hand, at the city of New York, the 3d day of October, A.D. 1789.

G. WASHINGTON. James D. Richardson, ed., 1 *Messages and Papers of the Presidents, 1789–1897* [*Papers of Presidents*] 64 (1896).

———

John Adams issued a similar proclamation, referring to the Holy Spirit and the Redeemer as well as the Father.

Adams's Proclamation of Day of Humiliation, Fasting, and Prayer, March 23, 1798

As the safety and prosperity of nations ultimately and essentially depend on the protection and the blessing of Almighty God, and the national acknowledgment of this truth is not only an indispensable duty which the people owe to Him, but a duty whose natural influence is favorable to the promotion of that morality and piety without which social happiness can not exist nor the blessings of a free government be enjoyed; and as this duty, at all times incumbent, is so especially in seasons of difficulty or of danger, when existing or threatening calamities, the just judgments of God against prevalent iniquity, are a loud call to repentance and reformation; and as the United States of America are at present placed in a hazardous and afflictive situation by the unfriendly disposition, conduct, and demands of a foreign power, evinced by repeated refusals to receive our messengers of reconciliation and peace, by depredations on our commerce, and the infliction of injuries on very many of our fellow-citizens while engaged in their lawful business on the seas—under these considerations it has appeared to me that the duty of imploring mercy and benediction of Heaven on our country demands at this time a special attention from its inhabitants.

I have therefore thought fit to recommend, and I do hereby recommend, that Wednesday, the 9th day of May next, be observed throughout the United States as a day of solemn humiliation, fasting, and prayer; that the citizens of these States, abstaining on that day from their customary worldly occupations, offer their devout addresses to the Father of Mercies agreeably to those forms or methods which they have severally adopted as the most suitable and becoming; that all religious congregations do, with the deepest humility, acknowledge before God the manifold sins and transgressions with which we are justly chargeable as individuals and as a nation, beseeching Him at the same time, of His infinite grace, through the Redeemer of the World, freely to remit all our offenses, and to incline us by His Holy Spirit to that sincere repentance and reformation which may afford us reason to hope for his inestimable favor and heavenly benediction; that it be made the subject of particular and earnest supplication that our country may be protected from all the dangers which threaten it; that our civil and religious privileges may be preserved inviolate and perpetuated to the latest generations; that our public councils and magistrates may be especially enlightened and directed at this critical period; that the American people may be united in those bonds of amity and mutual confidence and inspired with that vigor and fortitude by which they have in times past been so highly distinguished and by which they have obtained such invaluable advantages; that the health of the inhabitants of our land may be preserved, and their agriculture, commerce, fisheries, arts, and manufactures be blessed and prospered; that the principles of genuine piety and sound morality may influence the minds and govern the lives of every description of our citizens, and that the blessings of peace, freedom, and pure religion may be speedily extended to all the nations of the earth.

And finally, I recommend that on the said day the duties of humiliation and prayer be accompanied by fervent thanksgiving to the Bestower of Every Good Gift, not only for His having hitherto protected and preserved the people of these United States in the independent enjoyment of their religious and civil freedom, but also for having prospered them in a wonderful progress of population, and for conferring on them many and great favors conducive to the happiness and prosperity of a nation.

Given under my hand and the seal of the United States of America, at Philadelphia, [SEAL] this 23d day of March, A.D. 1798, and of the Independence of the said States the twenty-second. JOHN ADAMS. Richardson, 1 *Papers of Presidents* 268–270.

————

Thomas Jefferson made reference to the need for the nation to worship in his First Inaugural.

Jefferson's First Inaugural, March 4, 1801

Kindly separated by nature and a wide ocean from the exterminating havoc of one quarter of the globe; too high-minded to endure the degradations of the others; possessing a chosen country, with room enough for our descendants to the thousandth and thousandth generation; entertaining a due sense of our equal right to the use of our own faculties, to the acquisitions of our own industry, to honor and confidence from our fellow-citizens, resulting not from birth, but from our actions and their sense of them; enlightened by a benign religion, professed, indeed, and practiced in various forms, yet all of them inculcating honesty, truth, temperance, gratitude, and the love of man; acknowledging and adoring an overruling Providence, which by all its dispensations proves that it delights in the happiness of man here and his greater happiness hereafter—with all these blessings, what more is necessary to make us a happy and a prosperous people? Richardson, 1 *Papers of Presidents* 323.

————

Jefferson had occasion to reply to an address voted later in the year by the Danbury Baptist Association, twenty-six churches mostly in the Connecticut Valley. Yale, a more conservative institution than Harvard, was under the presidency of Timothy Dwight, a Congregationalist minister, known to the irreverent as "the Pope." At the start of the nineteenth century the Congregationalist dominance of Connecticut was a fundamental fact of political life, to the great discomfort of Baptist, Episcopalian, and Methodist minorities. "Connecticut," wrote an Episcopal priest, "is more completely under the administration of a Pope than Italy," Burr, *The Story of the Diocese of Connecticut* 163. By 1800 Connecticut was split between the ruling Congregationalist Federalist party and the Republican or Toleration Party favorable to the presidential aspirations of Thomas Jefferson. *Id*. Nehemiah Dodge, Ephraim Robbins, and Stephen S. Nelson, a committee of the Danbury Baptist Association, in the state of Connecticut, wrote Jefferson, "We have reason to believe that America's God has raised you up to fill the chair of state." William G. McLoughlin, 2 *New England Dissent: The Baptists and the Separation of Church and State, 1630–1833* 1004–1005 (1971). In a draft of a reply to this letter, Jefferson expressed the view that since Congress was inhibited by the Constitution from enacting legislation "respecting religion" [*sic*], and the executive was authorized only to execute their acts, he had refrained from prescribing "even occasional performances of devotion," such as the proclamations of thanksgiving or fasting by Presidents Washington and Adams [this section above]. Jefferson shared the draft with his chief political advisors on New England, his Postmaster General, Gideon Granger, and his Attorney General, Levy Lincoln. Granger urged Jefferson to send the letter as drafted. Lincoln cautioned against including the language about thanksgivings since this might give uneasiness "even to Republicans" in the eastern states, where they had long been accustomed to proclamations of thanksgiving by their governors. Jefferson accepted the advice of his Attorney General, deleting the reference to thanksgiving days. *See* Dumas Malone, *Jefferson the President: First Term, 1801–1805* 109 (1970). The letter used the metaphor of a "wall of separation between Church and State" for the first time in American literature, and ended with the president joining the Baptists in prayer to the Father and Creator.

Jefferson to the Danbury Baptist Association, January 1, 1802

Gentlemen,—The affectionate sentiments of esteem and approbation which you are so good as to express towards me, on behalf of the Danbury Baptist Association, give me the highest satisfaction. My duties dictate a faithful and zealous pursuit of the interests of my constituents, and in proportion as they are persuaded of my fidelity to those duties, the discharge of them becomes more and more pleasing.

Believing with you that religion is a matter which lies solely between man and his God, that he owes account to none other for his faith or his worship, that the legislative powers of government reach actions only, and not opinions, I contemplate with sovereign reverence that act of the whole American people which declared that their legislature should "make no law respecting an establishment of religion, or prohibiting the free exercise thereof," thus building a wall of separation between Church and State. Adhering to this expression of the supreme will of the nation in behalf of the rights of conscience, I shall see with sincere satisfaction the progress of those sentiments which tend to restore to man all his natural rights, convinced he has no natural right in opposition to his social duties.

I reciprocate your kind prayers for the protection and blessing of the common Father and Creator of man, and tender you for yourselves and your religious association, assurances of my high respect and esteem. Peterson, ed., *Jefferson: Writings* 510 (1984); Bergh, ed. *Jefferson Writings* 281–282.

————

Jefferson ended his Second Inaugural with a request for prayer as specific as Washington's Proclamation and with an explicit invocation of the Old Testament and God's deliverance of Israel after the Exodus.

Jefferson's Second Inaugural, March 4, 1805

I shall now enter on the duties to which my fellow-citizens have again called me, and shall proceed in the spirit of those principles which they have approved. I fear not that any motives of interest may lead me astray; I am sensible of no passion which could seduce me knowingly from the path of justice, but the weaknesses of human nature and the limits of my own understanding will produce errors of judgment sometimes injurious to your interests. I shall need, therefore, all the indulgence which I have heretofore experienced from my constituents; the want of it will certainly not lessen with increasing years. I shall need, too, the favor of that Being in whose hands we are, who led our fathers, as Israel of old, from their native land and planted them in a country flowing with all the necessaries and comforts of life; who has covered our infancy with His providence and our riper years with His wisdom and power, and to whose goodness I ask you to join in supplications with me that He will so enlighten the minds of your servants, guide their councils, and prosper their measures that whatsoever they do shall result in your good, and shall secure to you the peace, friendship, and approbation of all nations. Richardson, 1 *Papers of Presidents* 382.

————

· James Madison, as he revealed after he ceased to be president, believed that religious proclamations by the president were objectionable. Members of the government might speak "in their individual capacities as distinct from their official station," Madison, "Posthumously Published Essay," *Harper's*, March 1914. As president, however, he acted differently. The war with Great Britain was proceeding disastrously for the Americans. Congress asked the president to recommend a day of public humiliation and prayer, to be observed "with religious solemnity." Madison responded as follows.

Madison's Proclamation of Day of Humiliation and Prayer, July 23, 1813

I do, therefore, issue this my Proclamation, recommending to all, who shall be piously disposed to unite their hearts and voices in addressing, at one and the same time, their vows and adorations to the Great Parent and Sovereign of the Universe, that they assemble, on the second Thursday of September next, in their respective religious congregations, to render Him thanks for the many blessings He has bestowed on the people of the United States; that He has blessed them with a land capable of yielding all the necessaries and requisites of human life, with ample means for convenient exchanges with foreign countries; that He has blessed the labors employed in its cultivation and improvement; that He is now blessing the exertions to extend and establish the arts and manufactures, which will secure within ourselves supplies too important to remain dependent on the precarious policy, on the peaceable dispositions of other nations; and, particularly, that He has blessed the United States with a political Constitution, founded on the will and authority of the whole people, and guaranteeing to each individual the security, not only of his person and his property, but of those sacred rights of conscience, so essential to his present happiness, and so dear to his future hopes. 27 *Annals of Cong.* 2673–74.

———

President Madison issued other equally religious proclamations on July 9, 1812; July 23, 1813; November 16, 1814; and March 4, 1815. Richardson, 1 *Papers of Presidents* 513, 532, 558, 561. Subsequent presidents issued proclamations asking for public prayer without apparent hesitation.

In the second month of the first session of Congress, April 1789, the House and Senate set up committees to select chaplains, and in September 1789, as Congress adopted the First Amendment, a statute was enacted to pay the chaplains, 1 Stat. 70–71; *see Marsh v. Chambers* [Chapter Thirteen, section 4].

2. OATHS

George Washington's Farewell Address took up, among several subjects on which he offered counsel to his fellow citizens, the place of religion and specifically of oaths.

Washington's Farewell Address, September 17, 1796

Of all the dispositions and habits which lead to political prosperity, religion and morality are indispensable supports. In vain would that man claim the tribute of patriotism who should labor to subvert these great pillars of human happiness—these firmest props of the duties of men and citizens. The mere politician, equally with the pious man, ought to respect and to cherish them. A volume could not trace all their connections with private and public felicity. Let it simply be asked, Where is the security for property, for reputation, for life, if the sense of religious obligation *desert* the oaths which are the instruments of investigation in the courts of justice? And let us with caution indulge the supposition that morality can be maintained without religion. Whatever may be conceded to the influence of refined education on minds of peculiar structure, reason and experience both forbid us to expect that national morality can prevail in exclusion of religious principle.

It is substantially true that virtue or morality is a necessary spring of popular government. The rule indeed extends with more or less force to every species of free government. Who that is a sincere friend to it can look with indifference upon attempts to shake the foundation of the fabric? Promote, then, as an object of primary importance, institutions for the general diffusion of knowledge. In proportion as the structure of a government gives force to public opinion, it is essential that public opinion should be enlightened. . . .

Observe good faith and justice toward all nations. Cultivate peace and harmony with all. Religion and morality enjoin this conduct. And can it be that good policy does not equally enjoin it? It will be worthy of a free, enlightened, and at no distant period a great nation to give to mankind the magnanimous and too novel example of a people always guided by an exalted justice and benevolence. Who can doubt that in the course of time and things the fruits of such a plan would richly repay any temporary advantages which might be lost by a steady adherence to it? Can it be that Providence has not connected the permanent felicity of a nation with its virtue? The experiment, at least, is recommended by every sentiment which ennobles human nature. Alas! is it rendered impossible by its vices? Richardson, 1 *Papers of Presidents* 220–221.

————

In the most foundational case asserting the independence of the judiciary, Chief Justice John Marshall argued that the judicial oath to support the Constitution supports the central holding of the case, the Court's power and duty to pronounce on the constitutionality of federal law and to set aside statutes it finds unconstitutional.

Marbury v. Madison

5 U.S. (1 Cranch) 137, 179–180 (1803).

Why otherwise does it [the Constitution] direct the judges to take an oath to support it? This oath certainly applies in an especial manner, to their conduct in their official character. How immoral to impose it on them, if they were to be used as the instruments, and the knowing instruments, for violating what they swear to support!

The oath of office, too, imposed by the legislature, is completely demonstrative of the legislative opinion on this subject. It is in these words: "I do solemnly swear, that I will administer justice, without respect to persons, and do equal right to the poor and to the rich; and that I will faithfully and impartially discharge all the duties incumbent on me as—, according to the best of my abilities and understanding, agreeably to the constitution and laws of the United States." Why does a judge swear to discharge his duties agreeably to the constitution of the United States, if that constitution forms no rule for his government? if it is closed upon him, and cannot be inspected by him? If such be the real state of things, this is worse than solemn mockery. To prescribe, or to take this oath, becomes equally a crime.

————

Is Marshall's argument about the duty to support the Constitution well grounded in the text of the Constitution? The constitutional text he invoked–Article VI—also provides that legislators and members of the Executive must also take an oath to support the Constitution [Chapter Six, section 3B]. The judicial oath of office is unique to judges. It incorporated the ancient standard of Deuteronomy 16:19 "without respect to persons," an English translation of the Hebrew "without lifting faces." God, to whom the oath was sworn, was a Being believed to be living, intelligent, attentive to human actions, and punishing promise-breakers. Other governmentally prescribed oaths required not only belief in a caring God but doctrinal beliefs. Oaths of this kind—test oaths designed to exclude from public office those who could not take them—were outlawed by the federal Constitution [Chapter Six, section 3B] but the states did not understand this prohibition to apply to them. For example, the two test oaths required by the Massachusetts constitution of 1780 [Chapter Six, section 2] were retained for forty years. Under the anti-Catholic oath, no Catholic was "capable of holding any public office in this Commonwealth," Robert E. Lord, 1 *History of the Archdiocese of Boston* 776 (1945). Both oaths were finally abolished when the Massachusetts constitution was amended in 1820. *Journal of the Massachusetts Constitutional Convention of 1820* 284, 630–634 (1853).

————

3. SWEARING AND BLASPHEMY

Cursing and swearing, acts that are the mirror opposite of oath-taking, took significance from their use of God's name or invocation of His power. Even a state with as much religious freedom as Virginia treated cursing or swearing as an offense, albeit minor.

Virginia Prohibition of Swearing and Cursing, 1792

That if any person or persons shall profanely swear or curse, or shall be drunk ... [they] shall forfeit and pay the sum of eighty-three cents for every such offense. *Virginia Revised Laws*, c. 142 (*Statute* of 1792).

————

Other states had stiffer laws for what was classified as "blasphemy," that is, contemptuous public comments about God or matters held sacred by Christians. Without a statute, blasphemy was held to be a crime at common law and was so punished in New York in 1811. The opinion by Chief Judge James Kent, one of the most influential American authorities on the common law, became a classic.

The People Against Ruggles
8 Johns. 290 (N.Y. 1811).

The defendant was indicted at the General Sessions of the Peace, held at *Kingsbury,* in the county of *Washington,* in *December,* 1810, for that he did, on the 2d day of *September,* 1810, at *Salem, & c. wickedly, maliciously, and blasphemously,* utter, and with a loud voice publish, in the presence and hearing of divers good and christian people, & c. of and concerning the christian religion, and of and concerning JESUS CHRIST, the false, scandalous, malicious, wicked and blasphemous words following, to wit, *"Jesus Christ was a bastard, and his mother must be a whore,"* in contempt of the christian religion, and the laws of this state, to the evil and pernicious example of all others, & c. The indictment was removed into the Court of Oyer and Terminer and gaol delivery, held on the 11th *June,* 1811 in *Washington* county, before Mr. Justice *Spencer,* and the judges of the Common Pleas, when the defendant was tried and found guilty and was sentenced by the court to be imprisoned for three months, and to pay a fine of 500 dollars.

The record of the proceedings and conviction, & c. having been removed to this court,

Wendell, for the prisoner, now contended, that the offence charged in the indictment was not punishable by the law of this state, though, he admitted, it was punishable by the common law of *England,* where *christianity* makes part of the law of the land, on account of its connection with the established church. In *England,* apostacy, heresy, reviling the ordinances of the established church, and nonconformity, are made punishable by statute. But from the preamble, and the provisions of the constitution of this state, and the silence of the legislature, it was to be inferred that *christianity* did not make a part of the common law of this state. There are no statutes concerning religion, except those relative to the Sabbath, and to suppress immorality. The constitution allows a free toleration to all religions and all kinds of worship. The exception as to *licentiousness,* refers to conduct, not opinions. *Judaism and Mahometanism* may be preached here without any legal animadversion. For aught that appears, the prisoner may have been a *Jew,* a *Mahometan,* or a *Socinian*; and if so, he had a right by the constitution, to declare his opinions.

Kent, Ch. J., delivered the opinion of the Court. The offence charged is, that the defendant below did "wickedly, maliciously, and blasphemously utter, in the presence and hearing of divers good and christian people, these false, feigned, scandalous, malicious, wicked and blasphemous words, to wit," "Jesus Christ was a bastard, and his mother must be a whore;"

and the single question is, whether this be a public offence by the law of the land. After conviction, we must intend that these words were uttered in a wanton manner, and, as they evidently import, with a wicked and malicious disposition, and not in a serious discussion upon any controverted point in religion. The language was blasphemous not only in a popular, but in a legal sense; for blasphemy, according to the most precise definitions, consists in maliciously reviling God, or religion, and this was reviling christianity through its author [citing English authorities]. The jury have passed upon the intent or quo anima and if those words spoken, in any case, will amount to a misdemeanor, the indictment is good.

Such words, uttered with such a disposition, were an offence at common law. In *Taylor's* case [citation omitted] the defendant was convicted upon information of speaking similar words, and the court of [King's Bench] said, that christianity was parcel of the law, and to cast contumelious reproaches upon it, tended to weaken the foundation of moral obligation, and the efficacy of oaths. And in the case of *Rex v. Woolston* [citiation omitted] on a like conviction, the court said they would not suffer it to be debated whether defaming christianity in general was not an offence at common law, for that whatever strikes at the root of christianity, tends manifestly to the dissolution of civil government. But the court were careful to say, that they did not intend to include disputes between learned men upon particular controverted points. The same doctrine was laid down in the late case of *The King v. Williams*, for the publication of *Paine's* "Age of Reason," which was tried before Lord Kenyon in July, 1797. The authorities show that blasphemy against God, and contumelious reproaches and profane ridicule of Christ or the Holy Scriptures, (which are equally treated as blasphemy) are offences punishable at common law, whether uttered by words or writings [citations omitted]. The consequences may be less extensively pernicious in the one case than in the other, but in both instances, the reviling is still an offence, because it tends to corrupt the morals of the people, and to destroy good order. Such offences have always been considered independent of any religious establishment or the rights of the church. They are treated as affecting the essential interests of civil society.

And why should not the language contained in the indictment be still an offence with us? There is nothing in our manners or institutions which has prevented the application or the necessity of this part of the common law. We stand equally in need, now as formerly, of all that moral discipline, and of those principles of virtue, which help to bind society together. The people of this state, in common with the people of this country, profess the general doctrines of christianity, as the rule of their faith and practice; and to scandalize the author of these doctrines is not only, in a religious point of view, extremely impious, but, even in respect to the obligations due to society, is a gross violation of decency and good order. Nothing could be more offensive to the virtuous part of the community, or more injurious to the tender morals of the young, than to declare such profanity lawful. It would go to confound all distinction between things sacred and profane. . . . The [New York] act concerning oaths [citation omitted] recognises the common law mode of administering an oath, "by laying the hand on and kissing the gospels." Surely, then, we are bound to conclude, that wicked and malicious words, writings and actions which go to vilify those gospels, continue, as at common law, to be an offence against the public peace and safety. They are inconsistent with the reverence due to the administration of an oath, and among their other evil consequences, they tend to lessen, in the public mind, its religious sanction.

The court are accordingly of opinion that the judgment below must be affirmed.

NOTE. *Blasphemy in Massachusetts.* Massachusetts punished blasphemy under a statute enacted in 1782. According to Chief Justice Lemuel Shaw, the statue was "frequently enforced" for at least the next fifty years. There were "many prosecutions and convictions," *Commonwealth v. Kneeland*, 37 Mass. (20 Pick.) 206, 217 (1838). The statute reflected trinitarian theology—"reproaching Jesus Christ or the Holy Ghost" was as bad as "denying God"—but its constitutionality, when finally challenged in 1838, was upheld by Unitarians, *id.* at 220–221. Abner Kneeland, a newspaper editor, had jeered Jesus' Virgin Birth—how sensitive a subject this was *People v. Ruggles* had shown. Kneeland had also denied belief in the truth of the Gospels and the reality of the resurrection of the dead. His oral appeal to the Supreme Court of the Untied States was quickly denied by Chief Justice Shaw, and he spent sixty days in the Suffolk County Jail for his forceful assertions of skepticism about Christianity. Abner Kneeland, *A Review of the Trial, Conviction and Final Imprisonment in the Common Jail of the County of Suffolk, of Abner Kneeland, for the Alleged Crime of Blasphemy* (1938) reproduced in Leonard W. Levy, *Blasphemy in Massachusetts* (1973) 493–505. See also Levy, *Blasphemy: Verbal Offense Against The Sacred, From Moses To Salman Rushdie* (1993).

---

4.   THE LORD'S DAY

Observance of the Lord's Day—Sunday, the day associated with the Resurrection of Christ—was an early concern of the New York legislature, *see People v. Ruggles* [section 3 above]. Virginia, in the same 1792 statute that punished swearing, forbade laboring "on a sabbath day" under pain of paying $1.67 for the offense. Employing a slave was treated as sabbath-breaking too, *Virginia, Revised Laws* (1819) c. 141. The majority of Baptists in Virginia, as in Massachusetts, supported the measure, which imposed "the beliefs and values of the dominant Protestant churches upon the inhabitants of the state." Thomas P. Buckley, *Church and State in Revolutionary Virginia, 1776–1787* 181–82 (1977). The following sample of such sabbath laws was enacted October 22, 1782.

Massachusetts Sabbath Law, 1782

Whereas the observance of the Lord's Day is highly promotive of the welfare of a community, by affording necessary seasons for relaxation from labour and the cares of business; for moral reflections and conversation on the duties of life, and the frequent errors of human conduct; for publick and private worship of the Maker, Governour and Judge of the world, and for those acts of charity which support and adorn a Christian society: ... 1. Be it therefore enacted by the Senate and House of Representatives, in

General Court assembled, and by the authority of the same, That no person or persons whatsoever shall keep open his or their shop, ware-house or work-house, nor shall upon land or water do any manner of labour, business or work, nor be present at any concert of musick, dancing or any publick diversion, shew or entertainment, nor use any sport, game, play or recreation on the Lord's Day, or any part thereof (works of necessity and charity only excepted) upon penalty that every person so offending, shall forfeit and pay a sum not exceeding twenty shillings nor less than ten shillings. . . .

III. And be it further enacted, That no person shall recreate, disport or unnecessarily walk or loiter, or assemble themselves in the streets, lanes, wharves, highways, common fields, pastures or orchards of any town or place within this State, on the said day, or any part thereof, on penalty of the sum of five shillings. . . .

VII . . . And whereas the publick worship of Almighty God is esteemed by Christians an essential part of the due observance of the Lord's Day, and requires the greatest decency and reverence for a due performance of the same.

VIII. Be it therefore enacted, That each person being able of body, and not otherwise necessarily prevented, who shall for the space of one month together, absent him or herself from the publick worship of God on the Lord's Day, shall forfeit and pay the sum of ten shillings, provided there be any place of worship on which they can conscientiously and conveniently attend. Massachusetts, *Perpetual Laws* 198–199.

———

Compulsory church attendance was reduced to once every three months in 1792, Act of March 8, 1792, 2 *Massachusetts Laws* 538 (Nov. 1780 to Feb. 1807). The state constitutional convention of 1820 proposed taking away altogether the power to force attendance. *Journal of the Massachusetts Constitution Convention of 1820* 623 (1853). But the amendment was rejected when the people vetoed any tampering with Article III. *Id.* 634. Finally, in 1833, the Constitution was amended to abolish the legislature's power over the subject. Mass. Const. Amend. XI.

Observance of the Lord's Day continued to require the prohibition of secular work or play. Well after the Civil War the criminal law forbidding work on the Lord's Day was enforced by preventing persons injured by Sabbath-breaking from recovering compensation for their injuries. Timothy McGrath helped a mill owner fix his wheel pit on Sunday so that the mill could get started on Monday; injured, he was denied an action for negligence, because his "illegal act was inseparably connected with the cause of action and contributed to his injury," *McGrath v. Merwin*, 112 Mass. 467 (1873). For a thorough collection of materials on Sabbatarian legislation and litigation, *see* William Addison Blakely, ed. *American State Papers Bearing on Sunday Legislation* (1911, reprint: Da Capo, 1970).

5. MARRIAGE AND SEXUAL ACTIVITY

Without any special awareness that they were enacting Christian doctrine, all the states treated marriage as a privileged institution and punished various forms of sexual activity outside of monogamy. In Massachusetts only a justice of the peace for the county or the "stated and ordained Minister of the Gospel" of the town could perform a marriage. In 1784, for example, John Murray, the Universalist minister in Gloucester, was prosecuted for performing a marriage; in 1787, he was found liable under the statute to a fine of fifty pounds. John D. Cushing, "Notes of Disestablishment in Massachusetts, 1780–1833," 26 *William and Mary Quarterly* 169, 174 (1969).

Monogamy was protected by statutes making bigamy a crime punishable by public whipping, Act of February 17, 1785, Massachusetts, *Perpetual Laws* 203 (Oct. 1780 to May 1789), or by death, Virginia, *Acts in Force* ch. 104, 270, 274 (1814). Later legislation reduced the Virginia penalty to a penitentiary term, *Warner v. Commonwealth*, 4 Va. 95 (1817). Adultery was punishable in Massachusetts by the man or woman being put on the gallows "for the space of one hour" and "publickly whipped, not exceeding thirty-nine stripes," Act of February 17, 1785, Massachusetts, *Perpetual Laws* 203 (Oct. 1780 to May 1789). Whipping was also prescribed for "open gross lewdness and lascivious behaviour," *id.* at 204. Homosexual intercourse was punished by death, An Act against Sodomy, March 3, 1785, *id.* 182, a punishment reduced in 1804 to "not more than twenty years" in the state prison, Massachusetts, *Revised Statutes*, Ch. 130, Sect. 14, 741 (1835). The statute of 1785 took its inspiration from Leviticus; like it, it prescribed the death penalty for sex with an animal and the burning of the beast. Except for bigamy, sexual crimes were less severely treated in Virginia. Fornication by a free person there was a crime punishable by a fine; in 1845 the statute was interpreted to apply to a free person fornicating with a slave. *Commonwealth v. Jones*, 43 Va. 555 (1845).

6. FINANCIAL SUPPORT

A.   FEDERAL AID TO RELIGIOUS EDUCATION

Among the actions of Congress taken to further the religious education of Americans in general or the religious education provided by particular churches was "An ordinance for the Government of the Territory of the United States north-west of the river Ohio," a statute of the Continental Congress of 1787. The Northwest Ordinance's statement of purpose was to extend "the fundamental principles of civil and religious liberty" to the new federal domain.

Northwest Ordinance, 1 Stat. 50, 51–53 (1789)

Article I. No person, demeaning himself in a peaceable and orderly manner, shall ever be molested on account of his mode of worship or religious sentiments, in the said territory. . . .

Article III. Religion, morality, and knowledge, being necessary to good government and the happiness of mankind, schools and the means of education shall forever be encouraged.

On August 7, 1789, the same First Congress that a month later adopted the First Amendment took steps to adapt the Northwest Ordinance "to the present Constitution of the United States." No changes were made in the Ordinance's provision connecting schools and religion. Act of Aug. 7, 1789, ch. 8, 1 Stat. 50 (1789).

Grant to the Ohio Company. The Continental Congress gave the Ohio Company an enormous grant of land, specifying that a substantial acreage be reserved and used for the support of religion. Congress, during the presidency of Washington, confirmed this grant and reservation for religion on April 21, 1792, Act of Apr. 21, 1792, ch. 25, 1 Stat. 257 (1792). In 1833, during Jackson's presidency, Congress authorized the state of Ohio to sell the land appropriated "for the support of religion" and to use the proceeds "for ever" for "the support of religion." Act of Feb. 20, 1833, ch. 42, 4 Stat. 618 (1833).

Grant to Columbian College. In 1822 the Baptists founded a national university, Columbian College (later George Washington University), in the District of Columbia. McLoughlin 2 *New England Dissent* 1264. The Baptists were by now famous for their opposition to religious establishments. Ten years after its founding, during Jackson's presidency, Columbian College received a land grant from Congress. Act of July 14, 1832, ch. 248, 4 Stat. 603 (1832).

Grant to Georgetown College. Georgetown College, an institution for the education of Catholic boys, was owned and directed by the Society of Jesus; its president and directors were all Jesuits. In 1833 Congress granted Georgetown $25,000 worth of land in the District of Columbia for the establishment of such professorships as its president and directors should decide. Act of March 2, 1833, ch. 86, 6 Stat. 538 (1833).

Federal Missionaries. In 1819 Congress passed and President James Monroe signed an act appropriating $10,000 in order that the president might employ "capable persons of good moral character" to instruct the Indians. Act of March 3, 1819, ch. 85, 3 Stat. 516 (1819). But instruct them where? When gold is discovered in Georgia, pressure mounted to have the Cherokees expelled from their ancestral lands. The Cherokees challenged the constitutionality of the Removal Act, but the Court dismissed on the ground that that the Cherokee Nation was not a "sovereign state" within the meaning of the provision that confers jurisdiction on the Court to hear cases brought by such a party. *Cherokee Nation v. Georgia*, 30 U.S. 1 (1831). In the next phase of the litigation the Court could not turn the challenge aside on jurisdictional grounds. A Christian missionary, Samuel Worcester, was found guilty in a Georgia state court of residing in the Cherokee nation without a license from Georgia. He was sentenced to four years at hard labor in the penitentiary. Worcester pointed out that "he entered the aforesaid Cherokee nation, in the capacity of a duly authorized missionary of the American Board of Commissioners for Foreign Missions, under the authority of the President of the United States ... that he was, at the time of his arrest, engaged in preaching the

Gospel to the Cherokee Indians, and in translating the sacred Scriptures into their language." 31 U.S. 515, 529.

Worcester v. Georgia

31 U.S. (6 Pet.) 515 (1832).

■ CHIEF JUSTICE MARSHALL gave the opinion of the Court:

Will these powerful considerations avail the plaintiff in error? We think they will. He was seized, and forcibly carried away, while under guardianship of treaties guarantying the country in which he resided, and taking it under the protection of the United States. He was seized, while performing, under the sanction of the chief magistrate of the Union, those duties which the humane policy adopted by congress had recommended. He was apprehended, tried and condemned, under color of a law which has been shown to be repugnant to the constitution, laws and treaties of the United States. Had a judgment, liable to the same objections, been rendered for property, none would question the jurisdiction of this court. It cannot be less clear, when the judgment affects personal liberty, and inflicts disgraceful punishment—if punishment could disgrace, when inflicted on innocence. The plaintiff in error is not less interested in the operation of this unconstitutional law, than if it affected his property. He is not less entitled to the protection of the constitution, laws and treaties of his country. This point has been elaborately argued, and after deliberate consideration, decided, in the case of *Cohens v. Commonwealth of Virginia*, 6 Wheat. 264.

It is the opinion of this court, that the judgment of the superior court for the county of Gwinnett, in the state of Georgia, condemning Samuel A. Worcester to hard labor in the penitentiary of the state of Georgia, for four years, was pronounced by that court under color of a law which is void, as being repugnant to the constitution, treaties and laws of the United States, and ought, therefore, to be reversed and annulled.

The Court pronounced against the Removal Act, but a defiant President Jackson sent the army to expel the Cherokees from Georgia. In the winter of 1838–39, 14,000 Cherokees were forced to march 1,200 miles to Oklahoma through Tennessee, Kentucky, Illinois, Missouri, and Arkansas. Over 4,000 died on the "Trail of Tears" from hunger, exposure and disease.

B. STATE AID TO RELIGIOUS EDUCATION

At the state level, the key to the religious establishment in Massachusetts was Harvard College, first a Congregationalist, then a Unitarian institution for boys, from whom came the clergy of the establishment. The Massachusetts legislature in 1811, at the behest of the new Unitarian rulers of Harvard, altered the composition of the board of overseers. This alteration was debated in the Massachusetts Constitutional Convention of 1820. How, it was asked, could an institution that was "partly the property of the State" be put outside "the control of the State"? *Journal of the Massachusetts Constitutional Convention of 1820* 71 (1853).

Harvard, the recipient of many earlier bounties from the commonwealth, was at the time enjoying an annual grant of $10,000, voted for ten years in 1814. As Daniel Webster reported to the Convention, the sum loomed large in comparison with the college's own income of $17,000. *Journal of the Massachusetts Constitutional Convention of 1820* 527–531 (1853).

Debate on Subsidy to Harvard College, Massachusetts Constitutional Convention, January 4, 1821

Joseph Richardson of Hingham observed: This provision appears to me to place all the other denominations of christians in a degree of *subordination* to one, as if all others were disqualified for the high trust. What are the inferences naturally following such a provision? That this State from the first institution of this government and (as a province) long before, has with liberal munificence fostered Harvard University, for the encouragement of arts and sciences, and all good literature, (as expressed by the constitution) tending to the honor of God, the advantage of the christian religion, and the great benefit of this and the other United States—but entrusted, so far as depending on the care of the ministers of religion, to one denomination only. Does not the inference follow, from the exclusive words, or rather from the implied and actual exclusion, that ministers of other denominations are, in the view of the State, unworthy to be trusted with the care of an institution on which the "honor of God, and the advantage of christian religion depend?" It appears that all other denominations are taxed with large appropriations to support the character and dignity of an institution, which, as the constitution now stands, is a sort of holy of holies, which even the clergy of other denominations are not permitted to approach, only in subordination. Are there not respectable clergymen of other denominations in the several towns mentioned (admitting that the board of overseers must be limited to these towns) who might be safely permitted to share in the management of that University? In these several towns there are Episcopalians, Baptists, Methodists, Universalists, and perhaps other denominations, who have formed societies of high reputation, possessing great numbers and wealth, who have long contributed in the same proportion that others have done, to erect the numerous superb buildings, to endow liberally the many professorships, or at least to aid them, and in various ways to dignify this renowned institution. But these denominations are all excluded from the least participation in that department of trust assigned to the ministers of religion. If, sir, my views of this subject are erroneous, I hope to be convinced by fair arguments that they are so. But every feature of a free government that tends to cherish and perpetuate a spirit of intolerance among different denominations of christians, is inconsistent, in my view, with liberty, both civil and religious. I am constrained to view this policy of preference and exclusion as verging too much towards a national establishment of religion, and who has been conversant in history, and does not admit that religious establishments on narrow principles, maintained by civil power and authority, have not proved instruments of great calamity? Sir, I oppose the provision of the constitution on another ground. This partiality to Congregational tenets, in my view, is to render this denomination a spoiled child of the State.

The voters of Massachusetts, 20,123–8,020, rejected any change in Harvard's special place in the Constitution. *Id.* 633–34.

C. STATE SUBSIDY OF MINISTERS OF THE GOSPEL

No state did more to identify an official clergy and support it than Massachusetts. A generation after the adoption of the Constitution of 1780, litigation began to show the nature of the de facto religious establishment and to test its limits. Joseph Avery had been chosen minister in 1788 by a majority vote at "a legal town meeting" of Tyringham. The town meeting had agreed that if he would "settle with, and preach the gospel to said inhabitants, and instruct them in the principles and doctrines of the Christian religion," the town would provide him a parsonage and pay him 70 pounds annually in produce. In May 1803 a majority vote of a town meeting dissolved the contract. Avery sued for his salary.

Avery v. Inhabitants of Tyringham

3 Mass. 160 (1807).

■ PARSONS, C.J. In this cause, after a verdict for the plaintiff, the defendants move for a new trial, and also in arrest of judgment.

On the motion for a new trial, we are called upon to decide a question of the first importance to the good order and peace of society, and to the best interests of our fellow-citizens. The defendants' counsel insists that a Congregational minister of any parish, regularly called, ordained, and settled, according to the ancient usages of the country, and faithfully executing the duties of his office, according to his capacity, holds his office at the will of his parish, who may remove him at their pleasure. The plaintiff's counsel contend that he holds his office for life, determinable on sufficient cause exhibited and proved before a proper tribunal. If the office be holden at will, the evidence rejected ought to have been admitted, and the action must be sent to a new trial, otherwise the verdict must stand.

It is a general rule that an office is holden at the will of either party, unless a different tenure be expressed in the appointment, or is implied by the nature of the office, or results from ancient usage. A consideration of the nature and duties of the ministerial office is important in determining its tenure. It is the duty of a minister to adapt his religious and moral instructions to the various classes comprising his congregation. He ought, therefore, to have a knowledge of their situation, circumstances, habits, and characters, which is not to be obtained, but by a long and familiar acquaintance with them.

Vice is to be reproved by him in public and private; and the more prevalent and fashionable are any bad habits, the more necessary is it for the faithful minister to censure them, and to rebuke those who indulge them. But if it be a principle that his office and support depend on the will of his people, the natural tendency of such a principle, by operating on his fears, will be to restrain him from a full and plain discharge of his official duties. And it may be added, that the same principle, by diminishing his weight and influence, will render his exhortations and rebukes unavailing and ineffectual. And as it cannot be for the interest of the people to hold a power, probably dangerous, and certainly inconvenient to themselves, I cannot believe that a tenure at will, whence this power results, can accord with the nature and duties of the office. And it may be also observed, that if the tenure of his office be at will, a minister, after a life of exemplary diligence in the exercise of his official duties, may, when oppressed with the infirmities of age, be removed from office and be dismissed to poverty and neglect. A consequence of this power in a parish, will be the deterring of young men of information and genius, from entering into the clerical profession and devolving the public instruction in religion and morals, on incompetent persons, without talents, education, or any suitable qualifications. Thus an office, which, to be useful, ought to attract our respect and veneration, will be the subject of general contempt and disgrace. And an effect of this kind, surely every good citizen would wish the laws to prevent, so far as the laws may have power.

But considerations of irresistible weight result from the ancient usages established by our pious ancestors, and wisely continued to this day.

In the settlement of a minister, the parish invite some candidate to preach on probation, that they may have an opportunity to judge of his qualifications, and that he may have some knowledge of the state, temper, and principles of the people. If a settlement be agreed upon by both parties, it is the general practice of parishes, not having parsonages, to grant a sum of money, or other property, to the minister, exclusive of his annual salary, which is emphatically called his *settlement*. This name was derived from the uses to which it was intended the money should be applied by the minister. With it he usually purchased in his town some domicil, where he might have a permanent abode among his people, and be conveniently situated to attend to all the duties of his office.

But if the tenure of his office be at will, it is unquestionably at the will of either party. The minister, therefore, if the parish can remove him at their pleasure, may, at his own pleasure, immediately after he has availed himself of the grant, abandon his office, and carry away his settlement, to the great loss and damage of the parish. The usage of granting a settlement is satisfactory evidence that the tenure of his office is not at will, but that the ministerial relation must continue until it be dissolved for good cause.

As an encouragement to settle ministers in new towns where the property of the inhabitants is not large, the practice of granting permanent settlements had been long confirmed by grants from the former provincial legislature, and from the General Court of the commonwealth.

When new townships are sold, two rights are reserved by the government, one as a parsonage for the minister and his successors, and the other for the absolute use of the first settled minister and his heirs. Unwise indeed, and negligent, must have been the legislature, in making this charitable provision, if the first minister, soon after his settlement, might resign his office at his own will, and retain, for himself and his heirs, the fruits of the public beneficence.

[Chief Justice Parsons referred to "many cases" uniformly holding that "when no tenure was annexed to the office of a minister by the terms of settlement, he did not hold the office at will, but for life, determinable for some good and sufficient cause, or by the consent of both parties."]

The counsel for the defendants have contended that, admitting the contract of settlement before the revolution, was not at will, the constitution has altered the law; and that now the tenure of the minister must be at will. The part of the constitution relied on, is the provision in the *third* article of the declaration of rights, which secures to towns, & c., the exclusive right, *at all times*, of electing their public teachers, and of contracting with them for their support and maintenance. The argument is in this form; a town shall at all times elect its public teacher; but if, after one be elected, the town cannot remove him at pleasure, then there will be a time when the town cannot elect a public teacher, the office being full.

This argument certainly will prove much. If the town, in the election of a public teacher, contracts with him for a certain number of years, by this construction it must have a right to break its contract solemnly made. A conclusion so unreasonable and unjust, it is supposed, the counsel for the defendants are not willing to admit. The fair and natural construction of this provision is, that a town, & c, shall at all times, when it has no public teacher, have the exclusive right of election, but no right to violate its own contracts solemnly and deliberately made.

This article of the constitution has, without doubt, made some alteration in the ecclesiastical establishments of the state. Under the colonial laws, the church members in full communion had the exclusive right of electing and settling their minister, to whose support all the inhabitants of the town were obliged to contribute. And when the town neglected or refused suitably to maintain the minister, the county court was authorized to assess on the inhabitants a sum of money adequate to his support. Under the colony charter no man could be a freeman, unless he was a church member, until the year 1662; and a majority of the church constituted a majority of the legal voters of the town. After that time, inhabitants, not church members, if freeholders, and having certain other qualifications, might be admitted to the rights of freemen. In consequence of this alteration, a different method of settling a minister was adopted, under the provincial charter. The church made the election, and sent their proceedings to the town for their approbation. If the town approved the election, it also voted the salary and settlement. When the candidate accepted, he was solemnly introduced to the office by ordination, and became the settled minister, entitled to his salary and settlement under the votes of the town. If the town disapproved, and the church insisted on its election, it might call an ecclesiastical council; and if the council approved the election, the town was obliged to maintain the person chosen, as the settled minister of the town, by the interference of the Court of Sessions, if necessary; but if the council disapproved, the church must have proceeded to a new election.

By the constitution the rights of the town are enlarged, if it choose to exercise them, and those of the church impaired. If the church, when their election has been disapproved by the town, shall unwisely refuse to make a new election, or the town, for any cause, shall abandon the ancient usages of the country in settling a minister, it may, without or against the consent of the church, elect a public teacher, and contract to support him. And such teacher will have a legal right to the benefit of the contract, although he cannot be considered as the settled minister of the gospel, agreeably to the usages and practice of the Congregational churches in the state. An adherence to these usages so manifestly tends to the preservation of good order, peace, and harmony among the people, in the exercise of their religious privileges, it may be presumed that a departure from them will never be admitted by any town, but in cases of necessity.

It has been objected that a minister holds his office at his own will, because his town have no legal remedy, if he abandon his office, and therefore that he should also hold at the will of the town. The conclusion is certainly just, if the premises were correct. But a minister does not hold his office at his own will; and if he abandon it without cause, and without the consent of his town, the inhabitants may recover at law such damages as they have sustained by his injurious conduct. In *Cumberland,* before the revolution, Mr. *Wiswall,* a settled minister of the parish of *New Casco,* in the town of *Falmouth,* left his parish without its consent, and was ordained over the Episcopal church in that town. The parish brought an action against him to recover damages for his leaving his office. There was no objection made by the court, or the defendant's counsel, to the action, as not lying in such a case; but the cause went off from a variance between the declaration and the contract of settlement.

It is further objected that the minister ought to hold his office at the will of either party, because there is no jurisdiction competent to declare when the office is forfeited, or when the contract may be dissolved; and that the custom of applying to an ecclesiastical council may be rendered nugatory by either party refusing to concur in the appointment.

This objection deserves a particular consideration. It is the duty of a minister to teach by precept and example. If his example is vicious, he is worse than useless. Immoral conduct is then such misfeasance, as amounts to a forfeiture of his office. I do not mean to include mere infirmities incident to human nature, and to which an habitually good man is sometimes liable. Negligence also, or a willful and faulty neglect of public preaching, or of administering the ordinances, or of performing other usual parochial duties, is such a non-feasance, as will cause a forfeiture of the office. In either of these cases, or in both, the town may, at a legal meeting, declare the office forfeited, assigning in their votes the causes of the forfeiture, and of their dismission. If the minister do not resist, no further question will arise; if he still claim the office, and sue for his salary, the charges made by the town, as creating a forfeiture, are questions of fact properly to be submitted to the jury. If they find the allegations true, the minister will not be considered as holding his office after the vote of dismission. If the allegations are false, justice requires that he shall recover his salary. These allegations the jury are competent to inquire into, and on such inquiry ultimately to decide. And doubtless they would be as willing to relieve a town from the burden of supporting a vicious and unworthy minister, as they would to aid an exemplary and faithful one in recovering his stipulated salary.

There are also objections to a minister founded in questions of doctrine and discipline. A town may sometimes desire a dissolution of the ministerial contract, from its impoverishment, by a great part of its inhabitants annexing themselves to other denominations of Christians, or from other causes. A minister may also desire his dismission from various causes. In all these cases, therefore, and also on charges of immorality and neglect in the minister, the parties, if they cannot agree to dissolve the contract, may call to their assistance an ecclesiastical council mutually chosen; and their advice, technically called their result, is so far of the nature of an award made by the arbitrators, that either party conforming thereto will be justified. If, in a proper case for the meeting of an ecclesiastical council to be mutually chosen, either party should, unreasonably and without good cause, refuse their concurrence to a mutual choice, the aggrieved party may choose an impartial council, and will be justified in conforming to the result.

————

In 1810, the Supreme Judicial Court spoke in a case that had large implications for the nonestablished churches, *Barnes v. First Parish in Falmouth*. Thomas Barnes was the Universalist minister in Falmouth (now Portland, Maine, then part of Massachusetts). In 1807 he sued to recover from the town "the ministerial taxes" paid from 1798 to 1805 by two Universalists. Barnes claimed that under the Massachusetts constitution he was entitled to ministerial taxes paid by members of his denomination. The town had two defenses. First, the Universalists were not a separate denomination, for they agreed with the Congregationalists in discipline, though not in doctrine—the Universalists, unlike orthodox Congregationalists, believed in the certainty of the salvation of every human being. The second was that the Universalists of Falmouth were not an incorporated society and so their minister was ineligible for tax support. The case was argued twice before the Supreme Judicial Court and finally decided in May 1810.

Barnes v. First Parish in Falmouth

6 Mass. 401 (1810).

■ PARSONS, C.J. The plaintiff claims to be a public teacher of piety, religion, and morality, within the third article of the declaration of rights prefixed to the constitution of this commonwealth, but of a sect of Christians different from the inhabitants of the first parish in Falmouth, and publicly instructing several of the said inhabitants, who are of the same sect with himself, who usually attend on his preaching, and who have directed their taxes, paid for supporting public worship in the parish, to be paid over for his support; and he has instituted this suit to recover those taxes of the parish.

Not pretending to be the public teacher of any incorporated religious society obliged by law to maintain a public teacher, to maintain the issue on his part, he offered evidence, that in fact he was the teacher of a voluntary society of Universalists, who usually attended on his instruction. This evidence was rejected by the judge, on the ground that no person could maintain this action but a Protestant teacher of piety, religion, and morality, of some incorporated religious society; and to this rejection the plaintiff excepts.

The legal effect of evidence of this kind, in cases of this nature, has been often a subject of discussion; and among judges there have been different opinions. The subject certainly requires a diligent examination, exempt, as far as possible, from the influence of any prepossessions, or preconceived opinions. For this purpose, we shall consider the motives which induced this people to introduce into the constitution a religious establishment, the nature of the establishment introduced, and the rights and privileges it secured to the people, and to their teachers. If these points shall be clearly and justly explained, it will be easy to infer the principles by which the present action must be decided.

The object of a free civil government is the promotion and security of the happiness of the citizens. These effects cannot be produced, but by the knowledge and practice of our moral duties, which comprehend all the social and civil obligations of man to man, and of the citizen to the state. If the civil magistrate in any state could procure by his regulations a uniform practice of these duties, the government of that state would be perfect.

To obtain that perfection, it is not enough for the magistrate to define the rights of the several citizens, as they are related to life, liberty, property, and reputation, and to punish those by whom they may be invaded. Wise laws, made to this end, and faithfully executed, may leave the people strangers to many of the enjoyments of civil and social life, without which their happiness will be extremely imperfect. Human laws cannot oblige to the performance of the duties of imperfect obligation; as the duties of charity and hospitality, benevolence and good neighborhood; as the duties resulting from the relation of husband and wife, parent and child; of man to man, as children of a common parent; and of real patriotism, by influencing every citizen to love his country, and to obey all its laws. These are moral duties, flowing from the disposition of the heart, and not subject to the control of human legislation.

Neither can the laws prevent, by temporal punishment, secret offences, committed without witness, to gratify malice, revenge, or any other passion, by assailing the most important and most estimable rights of others. For human tribunals cannot proceed against any crimes, unless ascertained by evidence; and they are destitute of all power to prevent the commission of offences, unless by the feeble examples exhibited in the punishment of those who may be detected.

Civil government, therefore, availing itself only of its own powers, is extremely defective; and unless it could derive assistance from some superior power, whose laws extend to the temper and disposition of the human heart, and before whom no offence is secret, wretched indeed would be the state of man under a civil constitution of any form.

This most manifest truth has been felt by legislators in all ages; and as man is born, not only a social, but a religious being, so, in the pagan world, false and absurd systems of religion were adopted and patronized by the magistrate, to remedy the defects necessarily existing in a government merely civil.

On these principles, tested by the experience of mankind, and by the reflections of reason, the people of Massachusetts, in the frame of their government, adopted and patronized a religion, which, by its benign and energetic influences, might cooperate with human institutions, to promote and secure the happiness of the citizens, so far as might be consistent with the imperfections of man.

In selecting a religion, the people were not exposed to the hazard of choosing a false and defective religious system. Christianity had long been promulgated, its pretensions and excellences well known, and its divine authority admitted. This religion was found to rest on the basis of immortal truth; to contain a system of morals adopted to man, in all possible ranks and conditions, situations and circumstances, by conforming to which he would be meliorated and improved in all the relations of human life; and to furnish the most efficacious sanctions, by bringing to light a future state of retribution. And this religion, as understood by Protestants, tending, by its effects, to make every man submitting to its influence, a better husband, parent, child, neighbor, citizen, and magistrate, was by the people established as a fundamental and essential part of their constitution.

The manner in which this establishment was made, is liberal, and consistent with the rights of conscience on religious subjects. As religious opinions, and the time and manner of expressing the homage due to the Governor of the universe, are points depending on the sincerity and belief of each individual, and do not concern the public interest, care is taken, in the second article of the declaration of rights, to guard these points from the interference of the civil magistrate; and no man can be hurt, molested, or restrained, in his person, liberty, or estate, for worshipping God in the manner and season most agreeable to the dictates of his own conscience, or for his religious profession or sentiment, provided he does not disturb the public peace, or obstruct others in their religious worship in which case he is punished, not for his religious opinions or worships, but because he interrupts others in the enjoyment of the rights he claims for himself, or because he has broken the public peace.

Having secured liberty of conscience, on the subject of religious opinion and worship, for every man, whether Protestant or Catholic, Jew, Mahometan, or Pagan, the constitution then provides for the public teaching of the precepts and maxims of the religion, of Protestant Christians to all the people. And for this purpose it is made the right and the duty of all corporate religious societies, to elect and support a public Protestant teacher of piety, religion, and morality; and the election and support of the teacher depend exclusively on the will of a majority of each society incorporated for those purposes. As public instruction requires persons who may be taught, every citizen may be enjoined to attend on some one of these teachers, at times and seasons to be stated by law, if there be any on whose instructions he can conscientiously attend.

In the election and support of a teacher, every member of the corporation is bound by the will of the majority: but as the great object of this provision was to secure the election and support of public Protestant teachers by corporate societies, and as some members of any corporation might be of a sect or denomination of Protestant Christians different from the majority of the members, and might choose to unite with other Protestant Christians of their own sect or denomination, in maintaining a public teacher, who by law was entitled to support, and on whose instructions they usually attended, indulgence was granted, that persons thus situated might have the money they contributed to the support of public worship, and of the public teachers aforesaid, appropriated to the support of the teacher on whose instructions they should attend.

Several objections have at times been made to this establishment, which may be reduced to three: that when a man disapproves of any religion, or of any supported doctrines of any religion, to compel him by law to contribute money for public instruction in such religion or doctrine, is an infraction of his liberty of conscience; that to compel a man to pay for public religious instructions, on which he does not attend, and from which he can therefore derive no benefit, is unreasonable and intolerant; and that it is anti-christian for any state to avail itself of the precepts and maxims of Christianity, to support civil government, because the Founder of it has declared that his kingdom is not of this world.

These objections go to the authority of the people to make this constitution, which is not proper nor competent for us to bring into question. And although we are not able, and have no inclination, to assume the character of theologians, yet it may not be improper to make a few short observations, to defend our constitution from the charges of persecution, intolerance, and impiety.

When it is remembered that no man is compellable to attend on any religious instruction, which he conscientiously disapproves and that he is absolutely protected in the most perfect freedom of conscience in his religious opinions and worship, the first objection seems to mistake a man's conscience for his money and to deny the state a right of levying and of appropriating the money of the citizens, at the will of the legislature, in which they all are represented. But as every citizen derives the security of his property, and the fruits of his industry, from the power of the state, so, as the price of this protection, he is bound to contribute, in common with his fellow-citizen, for the public use, so much of his property, and for such public uses, as the state shall direct. And if any individual can lawfully withhold his contribution, because he dislikes the appropriation, the authority of the state to levy taxes would be annihilated; and without money it would soon cease to have any authority. But all money raised and appropriated for public uses, by any corporation, pursuant to powers derived from the state, are raised and appropriated substantially by the authority of the state. And the people, in their constitution, instead of devolving the support of public teachers on the corporations, by whom they should be elected, might have directed their support to be defrayed out of the public treasure to be reimbursed by the levying and collection of state taxes. And against this mode of support, the objection of an individual, disapproving of the object of the public taxes, would have the same weight it can have against the mode of public support through the medium of corporate taxation. In either case, it can have no weight to maintain a charge of persecution for conscience' sake. The great error lies in not distinguishing between liberty of conscience in religious opinions and worship, and the right of appropriating money by the state. The former is an unalienable right; the latter is surrendered to the state, as the price of protection.

The second objection is, that it is intolerant to compel a man to pay for religious instruction, from which, as he does not hear it, he can derive no benefit. This objection is founded wholly in mistake. The object of public religious instruction is to teach, and to enforce by suitable arguments, the practice of a system of correct morals among the people, and to form and cultivate reasonable and just habits and manners; by which every man's person and property are protected from outrage, and his personal and social enjoyments promoted and multiplied. From these effects every man derives the most important benefits; and whether he be, or be not, an auditor of any public teacher, he receives more solid and permanent advantages from this public instruction, than the administration of justice in courts of law can give him. The like objection may be made by any man to the support of public schools, if he have no family who attend; and any man, who has no lawsuit, may object to the support of judges and jurors on the same ground; when, if there were no courts of law, he would unfortunately find that causes for lawsuits would sufficiently abound.

The last objection is founded upon the supposed antichristian conduct of the state, in availing itself of the precepts and maxims of Christianity, for the purposes of a more excellent civil government. It is admitted that the Founder of this religion did not intend to erect a temporal dominion, agreeable to the prejudices of his countrymen; but to reign in the hearts of men, by subduing their irregular appetites and propensities, and by moulding their passions to the noblest purposes. And it is one great excellence of his religion, that, not pretending to worldly pomp and power, it is calculated and accommodated to meliorate the conduct and condition of man, under any form of civil government.

The objection goes further, and complains that Christianity is not left, for its promulgation and support, to the means designed by its Author, who requires not the assistance of man to effect his purposes and intentions. Our constitution certainly provides for the punishment of many breaches of the laws of Christianity, not for the purpose of propping up the Christian religion, but because those breaches are offences against the laws of the state; and it is a civil as well as a religious duty of the magistrate, not to bear the sword in vain. But there are many precepts of Christianity, of which the violation cannot be punished by human laws; and as obedience to them is beneficial to civil society, the state has wisely taken care that they should be taught, and also enforced by explaining their moral and religious sanctions, as they cannot be enforced by temporal punishments. And from the genius and temper of this religion, and from the benevolent character of its Author, we must conclude that it is his intention that man should be benefited by it in his civil and political relations, as well as in his individual capacity. And it remains for the objector to prove, that the patronage of Christianity by the civil magistrate, induced by the tendency of its precepts to form good citizens, is not one of the means by which the knowledge of its doctrines was intended to be disseminated and preserved among the human race.

The last branch of the objection rests on the very correct position that the faith and precepts of the Christian religion are so interwoven, that they must be taught together; whence it is inferred that the state, by enjoining instruction in its precepts, interferes with its doctrines, and assumes a power not intrusted to any human authority.

If the state claimed the absurd power of directing or controlling the faith of its citizens, there might be some ground for the objection. But no such power is claimed. The authority derived from the constitution extends no further than to submit to the understanding of the people the evidence of truths deemed of public utility, leaving the weight of the evidence, and the tendency of those truths, to the conscience of every man.

Indeed, this objection must come from a willing objector; for it extends, in its consequences, to prohibit the state from providing for public instruction in many branches of useful knowledge which naturally tend to defeat the arguments of infidelity, to illustrate the doctrines of the Christian religion, and to confirm the faith of its professors.

As Christianity has the promise not only of this, but of a future life, it cannot be denied that public instruction in piety, religion, and morality, by Protestant teachers, may have a beneficial effect beyond the present state of existence. And the people are to be applauded, as well for their benevolence as for their wisdom, that, in selecting a religion whose precepts and sanctions might supply the defects in civil government, necessarily limited in its power, and supported only by temporal penalties, they adopted a religion founded in truth; which in its tendency will protect our property here, and may secure to us an inheritance in another and a better country.

These objections to our constitution cannot be made by the plaintiff, who, having sought his remedy by an action at law, must support it as resting on our religious establishment, or his claim can have no legal foundation.

The last point for our consideration is, whether this establishment, according to the true intent and design of its provisions, will, or will not, enable the plaintiff to maintain his claim to the money he demands.

The objection against his claim is substantially this: that the constitution has not provided in any way for the legal support of any teacher of piety, religion, and morality, unless he be a public Protestant teacher of some incorporated religious society. It is admitted by the parties, that the plaintiff is a Protestant teacher of a voluntary society not incorporated, and which is under no legal obligation to elect or support a teacher; that he and his hearers are of a denomination of Christians different from that of the inhabitants of the first parish in Falmouth; and all other facts, necessary to support the action, may be presumed.

After a consideration of these facts, we are all of opinion that the constitution has not authorized any teacher to recover, by action at law, any money assessed pursuant to the third article of the declaration of rights, but a public Protestant teacher of some legally incorporated society; and that the objection must prevail. The societies, who may be enjoined to elect and support teachers of this description, are described as "towns, parishes, precincts, or other bodies politic, or religious societies," which last expression is merely explanatory of the words, "bodies politic," and confines them to bodies politic incorporated to act as religious societies. If we are to consider the words "religious societies" as descriptive of a class of societies not included in the words "bodies politic," the consequences would be, that all bodies politic, for whatever purposes incorporated, would be obliged to elect and maintain a teacher of religion—a consequence too absurd to be admitted. Indeed, the words "religious societies" must, from the nature of the duty imposed of them, necessarily mean societies having corporate powers; because, without those powers, the duty cannot be legally performed, a voluntary association having no legal authority to assess money on all the members, or to compel payment, or to elect a teacher by a vote of the greater part.

The plaintiff's claim is endeavored to be supported by the fourth paragraph of the third article, in which it is declared that "all moneys paid by the subject to the support of public worship, and of the public teachers aforesaid, shall, if he require it, be uniformly applied to the support of the teacher of his own religious denomination, on whose instruction he attends." And it is contended, that in this paragraph two descriptions of teachers are included—the first referring to the teachers of incorporated societies provided for in the first paragraph, and the latter embracing teachers of any voluntary society, who, in fact, have a teacher, although not obliged to elect and support one. We are, however, satisfied, that in every part of the third article, but one class of public teachers is contemplated, and which is particularly described in the first paragraph; and that, whenever teachers are mentioned, such teachers alone are intended, who by law are entitled to support. For, although the constitution contemplates different denominations of Protestant Christians, yet no religious societies are referred to, unless incorporated; and no teachers are mentioned as existing, who are not entitled to a maintenance.

If the construction which was contended for was right, then a Roman Catholic teacher might maintain an action similar to the plaintiffs. But in the case of *Matignon v. The Inhabitants of Newcastle*, in the county of Lincoln, decided some years since by this Court in Suffolk, it was determined, that the teacher mentioned in the latter part of the fourth paragraph so far referred to the first paragraph, as that he must be a Protestant teacher. And if a reference must be made to any part of the description, we know not why it must not be made to the whole of it, as the article has drawn no line of distinction.

In the latter part of this fourth paragraph, the teachers to whom the money may be applied, are described as public teachers. But a public teacher must be a teacher of some public, and not of any private religious society. And what society must be deemed a public society, is certainly a question of law, whether it be settled by a judge or by a jury. When, therefore, the facts, describing the nature or circumstances of any society, are established by evidence, from those facts the law must conclude whether the society be, in legal contemplation, public or private. Now, if the society be not incorporated, what rules are prescribed by law, by which its character may be defined? Does it depend on the number of the associates, or on the notoriety of the association? If on the former, what number is sufficient? If on the latter, what degree of notoriety is necessary?

On these points the law is silent. But there is a legal principle applicable to this subject, and which can at all times be applied with certainty. A public society is a society known in law, formed by the public authority of the state; and a private society is formed by the voluntary association of private persons, the powers of which are derived from the individual consent of each member.

To admit the plaintiff's construction, would render the first paragraph unreasonable and unjust. By that paragraph, a corporate religious society is obliged to support a public teacher; but by his construction, the means of support may be taken from it, without any fault on its own part. Any number of members, whether five or five hundred, (for a voluntary society may consist of any number, large or small,) may associate together, assume the denomination of Protestant Christians, and at their own pleasure withdraw their assistance from the corporation whose duty remains, by engaging a teacher upon any or no terms, and whom they are not obliged by law to maintain.

By this last paragraph, a reasonable indulgence is in particular cases granted. When there are teachers of two incorporated religious societies of different denominations, a member of one, who is of the sect and worships with the other, may direct his parish tax to be paid to the teacher on whose instructions he attends. This can be attended with little inconvenience, as both the teachers are entitled by law to a support, and the exchange of hearers may be mutual.

But to extend this indulgence to a teacher of an unincorporated society, who is entitled to no support, would be to grant him a remedy where he has no right, and to encourage disaffection and divisions in regular parishes, thereby also lessening or defeating the means they have of supporting a public teacher, to which they are obliged by this very article. . . .

———

To the further objection of Article III's caveat that "no subordination of one sect or denomination to another shall ever be established by law," Chief

Justice Parsons replied that this provision's "object was to prevent any hierarchy, or ecclesiastical jurisdiction of one sect of Christians over any other." But here "the only inferiority is founded on a social principle, essential to the existence of any society, the submission of the minority to the majority." The Baptists had made the same point when they made objection to the adoption of the constitution in 1780 [Chapter Six, section 2].

NOTE

Barnes, in the words of Governor Elbridge Gerry, "produced a great excitement," McLoughlin 2 *New England Dissent* 1098. Its author, Chief Justice Theophilus Parsons, was a leading Federalist, prominent in the Massachusetts constitutional convention of 1780 and active in assuring the ratification of the federal Constitution by Massachusetts. In the eyes of his admirers, he was "the great man of his time," Isaac Parker, "Address to the Grand Jury of Suffolk County, November 23, 1813," 10 Mass. 522. To his Jeffersonian enemies, he was "the Goliath of the Massachusetts Gentile–Army, a man as cunning as Lucifer and about half as good," Benjamin Waterhouse to Thomas Jefferson, March 20, 1813, printed in Samuel Eliot Morison, "The Great Rebellion in Harvard College, and the Resignation of President Kirkland," Colonial Society of America, 27 *Transactions* 59 (1920). He was also—as Chief Justice Parker later had inserted in the Massachusetts Reports—a convinced Christian believer in the Resurrection and a member of a Unitarian congregation, 10 Mass. 536. His enthusiastic exposition of how Massachusetts had "adopted a religion" showed how little the Federalists of the first generation thought that religious freedom and religious establishment were incompatible.

The practical effect of this decision was to require religious societies to incorporate if their members were not to be forced to support the established church of the town. Many Baptists and other dissenters had scruples about recognizing the legislature's power over their churches and accepting from the state a power to share in taxes. Less than half the Baptist societies were incorporated; even fewer of other dissenters' societies had applied for such legitimation by the state. McLoughlin 2 *New England Dissent* 1088. In the legislature, the dissenters presented a bill to override *Parsons*. John Leland (Madison's Baptist constituent now back in New England) declared that the Baptists did not want "the mischievous dagger" of civil power: governmental support of religion normally was "the first step in the case which leads in regular progression to inquisition." *Id.* 1097. The dissenters wanted only not to have to pay taxes to maintain a faith they did not believe in. Joseph W. Cannon, a Methodist from Nantucket, denounced the system outlined by Parsons as "an eternal disgrace to the state." *Id.* 1100. Religion became a political issue. A Federalist Unitarian judge had spoken in *Barnes*. A Republican, non-Unitarian legislature passed "An Act respecting Publick Worship and Religious Freedom," which put unincorporated religious societies on a par with incorporated ones, *Laws of Massachusetts from February 21, 1807 to December 14, 1816*, 227. The Baptists, despite their disclaimers, were given power to participate in tax revenues.

"Churches" were not mentioned in the Constitution of Massachusetts. The time came when it was necessary to define them legally. Jonathan Burr, the minister in Sandwich, had become more Calvinist than the parish. At a parish meeting, called by a warrant addressed to the town constable, Burr was dismissed by a vote of 83–80. Nine-tenths of "the church" supported Burr, and he sued for his salary, Jacob C. Meyer, *Church and State in Massachusetts from*

1740 to 1833: A Chapter in the History of the Development of Individual Freedom 168 (1930, reprint, 1968). Chief Justice Parsons held for the defendants. The case was appealed to the Supreme Judicial Court. Another Unitarian, Isaac Parker, wrote the opinion.

Burr v. The Inhabitants of the First Parish in Sandwich

9 Mass. 277 (1812).

■ JUSTICE PARKER delivered the opinion of the Court.

The last cause assigned by the plaintiff for his refusal, and the only cause stated by him to the committee, was, that his church would not concur with him in the choice of a mutual council; and it is in evidence that the church had refused their concurrence.

The sufficiency of this cause has had much attention, because the law on this point may have a general influence. And we have to decide upon the nature and powers of a Congregational church, as distinct from a parish. Formerly a question of this kind could not have arisen; because all the legal voters of any parish were members of the church. For no man was privileged to vote but a freeman; and for many years after the first settlement of the colony, church membership was an indispensable qualification of a freeman.

Now, a parish and church are bodies with different powers. A regularly-gathered Congregational church is composed of a number of persons, associated by a covenant or agreement of church fellowship, principally for the purpose of celebrating the rites of the supper and of baptism. They elect deacons: and the minister of the parish is also admitted a member. The deacons are made a corporation, to hold property for the use of the church, and they are accountable to the members. The members of a church are generally inhabitants of the parish: but this inhabitancy is not a necessary qualification for a church member. This body has no power to contract with or to settle a minister, that power residing wholly in the parish, of which the members of the church, who are inhabitants, are a part. The parish, when the ministerial office is vacant, from an ancient and respectable usage, wait until the church have made choice of a minister, and have requested the concurrence of the parish. If the parish do not concur, the election of the church is a nullity. If the parish concur, then a contract of settlement is made wholly between the parish and the minister, and is obligatory only on them. The proceedings of the church, so far as they relate to the settlement, are only a nomination of a minister to the parish, which may be concurred in or rejected. This view of the subject must be confined to parishes created by the general laws of the land, and not extended to parishes incorporated specially with different powers.

When, therefore, the parish should have a reasonable claim to a dissolution of their contract with the minister, on grounds proper to be inquired into by an ecclesiastical council, if the church, who have no pecuniary interest in this contract, could, by refusing their assent to the convening of a council, justify the minister in rejecting the offer of a mutual council, the parish would be without remedy. The parish could not legally dissolve the contract by their own vote, for a difference with their minister merely relating to points of doctrine, because a court of law has no means of deciding on those points. The minister refusing to join in calling a mutual council, the parish could not proceed to choose one *ex parte,* because the non-concurrence of the church would be sufficient cause of his refusal.

If, therefore, this cause of refusal, assigned by the plaintiff, were to be adjudged sufficient, the consequence would be, either the parish had no remedy, which would be unreasonable; or that they might dissolve the ministerial contract by their own vote, thus reducing the office of a minister to a mere tenure at will, which would be repugnant to the nature of the office, and the intent of the parties when the contract was made; or disputes in theology must come into courts of law for decision, when the law has not furnished the jury with weapons of polemic divinity. The conclusion is, therefore, necessary, that no interference of the church can justify the minister in refusing a mutual council; and this last cause assigned, resting on the non-concurrence of the church, cannot be admitted as sufficient.

This conclusion cannot be affected by an inference from a supposed peculiar relation between the plaintiff and his church. Although minister of his parish, it seems to have been supposed that he is emphatically the pastor of his church. This use of the terms may be adopted in common parlance, but we must look to the fact. A minister has no peculiar relation to his church, but as a member of it; and his right to administer the ordinances he claims from his ordination, which right may remain after his dismission from the church. The term pastor is correlative to flock, and is an expressive metaphor. Now, of whom is the flock composed? Of all whom it is the minister's duty to instruct and reprove. And these are the inhabitants of the parish; they compose the flock, of which the minister is the pastor.

We have the less regret in admitting this conclusion, because we are satisfied, from attending to the result of the very respectable council in this case, that the peace and happiness of both parties will be promoted by a separation; and we are satisfied, from all the facts which have been disclosed in this cause, that Mr. Burr's moral character remains fair and unimpeached. When he was settled, he and his people believed the same religious doctrines, which both parties then considered as essential. Mr. Burr has since, from honest conviction, as we trust, changed his opinion as to some of those doctrines; and, believing the doctrines which he has recently adopted to be essential, he has endeavored to support them in his public preaching, to the great pain and dissatisfaction of a majority of his parish, who for this cause have sought a separation.

Judgment is to be entered for the defendants on the verdict.

The parish appeared to rule the church. The Baptists of Bellingham drew the inference that when they became a majority in the town they owned the meeting house and the Congregationalists would have to go elsewhere. Their logic was unassailable, their sense of the allocation of power in the commonwealth deficient. A court ruled against their claim, Meyer, *Church and State in Massachusetts* 213. Only Unitarians had a chance of taking over the Congregationalist town establishment. But the Unitarian view of the relation of the church to the parish was scandalous to Trinitarian Congregationalists. Their basic theological position was expressed by Lyman Beecher (1775–1863), a graduate of Yale College, then, under Timothy Dwight, a Trinitarian stronghold. Beecher, ordained as a Presbyterian in 1799, had served as the minister in East Hampton, Long Island, and then in Litchfield, Connecticut. As the conflict between Trinitarians and Unitarians grew, it attracted his attention, and eventually in 1826 he was called as a minister by Trinitarians anxious to fortify their thinned ranks in Boston. Their approval was won by the views he set out in this excerpt from his *Autobiography*. Note the recurrence of the "wall" metaphor.

Lyman Beecher, *Autobiography* The Local Church.

The Unitarian controversy involved, in its progress, a discussion, not only of the principal doctrines of theology, but also of the principles of Congregational Church organization, which are but the outgrowth of that theology. According to the primitive Puritan faith, a local Church is not a voluntary association on purely human principles, but a divine family, a household of children spiritually born of God, heirs of God and joint heirs with Christ. "One is your Master, even Christ, and all ye are brethren," is the organic law of the local Church. God creates the Church by creating the spiritual children who are *ipso facto* its members. True sonship to God constitutes membership in the visible church, as really as natural birth in the natural family. All that the local Church can do, according to this view, is to recognize as members, on suitable evidence, those who are such by birth divine. All she can require of candidates she must require in the form of evidence of present spiritual sonship to God.

Now, in proportion as a system of theology is adopted which extenuates human guilt, explains away regeneration, and divests the Christian character of its distinctive supernatural peculiarity, in that proportion it tends to destroy that form of organization which avowedly depends on such peculiarity as its fundamental organic law.

This, however, was precisely what the system of Unitarianism did, and, as a natural consequence, the whole system of the local Church was shaken. By the inevitable operation of the laws of logical consistency, attempts were made to efface the distinction between the regenerate and the unregenerate, and enlarge the circle of Church fellowship to include the whole congregation. In progress of controversy, the endeavor was pushed in various ways, beyond the bounds of argument and moral influence, until the churches felt themselves invaded, robbed of their rights, and in peril of utter destruction.

It was the object of the sermon on "the Design, Rights, and Duties of Local Churches," given at Salem, Massachusetts in 1819, to meet the onset, and sound a note of defensive war so loud and clear that "all the churches of the land might feel the assault made upon their Christian liberty, and stand together upon the defensive."

Extracts from Sermon

"Wherever, therefore, a number of individuals, possessing the required qualifications, associate to maintain the ordinances of the Gospel, they become *a society incorporated by the God of heaven with specific chartered privileges.*

"The requisite qualifications for membership in a Church of Christ are *personal holiness in the sight of God, and a credible profession of holiness before me....* The commission given by our Savior to His apostles at His ascension directs them first to make disciples and then to baptize them, inculcating universal obedience. The qualifications for discipleship Jesus has before disclosed. They were love to Christ above father or mother; daily self-denial; real religion....

"A regularly ordained ministry, an orthodox creed, and devout forms of worship, can not constitute a Church of Christ without personal holiness in the members.... The attempt which is making to confound the scriptural distinction between the regenerate and the unregenerate blots out practically, as has been long done in theory, the doctrine of regeneration by the special influence of the Holy Ghost. To abolish the revealed terms of membership in the Church of God, and to form churches without reference to doctrinal opinion or experimental religion, and only by location within certain parish limits, and by certain civil qualifications, is the most pernicious infidelity that was ever broached. It breaks the spring of motion in the centre of God's system of good will to men and stops the work of salvation....

"That system of aggression which would break down the sacred inclosures about the Church, and throw the Church and the world together in one common field, and which, to accomplish its purpose, would bring into competition the rights of churches and of congregations, and, by designed invidious excitement, arouse and direct the stream of popular indignation against the Church, is a system of practical infidelity armed with the principles of the most efficient persecution.... All the churches of our Lord, and all ecclesiastical societies, and all men who wish well to the civil as promoted by the religious order of our fathers, have more cause to fear and to execrate such a system of aggression than all the infidel books that ever were printed....

"Local churches have the right to require a confession of faith and a satisfactory account of Christian experience as the condition of membership in their communion. A belief of the truth, attended by corresponding affection of heart, is a part of the evidence which is indispensable to constitute a profession of religion credible. If, then, churches have no right to interrogate a candidate for admission concerning the articles of his belief and the exercises of his heart, they are deprived of the only means of preserving the Church as a society of faithful men; for external actions, without any reference to belief or experience, do not furnish credible evidence of piety...." Notwithstanding the current of invective poured out against creeds, after the most deliberate attention to the subject I have not been able to perceive any rational ground of objection against them.... It is not the object of creeds to supplant the Bible, but to ascertain, for purposes of concentrated effort in the propagation of truth, how pastors and churches understand the Bible....

"If men attached invariably the same ideas to the language of the Bible, creeds would be superfluous, and the profession of a general belief in the Bible would suffice." But as men differ indefinitely as to the import of scripture language, a profession of a belief in the Bible, as a means of informing those who have a right to know in what particular sense the Bible is understood, has now become an intelligible profession of no one truth which it contains. And to profess that *Jesus is the Christ, the Son of God*—a phrase which in the apostolic age had known a definite meaning—does not now, when different circumstances exist and opposite meanings are attached to it, communicate any intelligible profession of our belief on that point; and all pretension of giving an account of our faith in that manner is an artifice for concealment unworthy of honest men, and an indignity offered to the understandings of those who desire to know in what manner we understand and doctrines of the Bible....

————

In 1820, the Massachusetts constitutional convention recognized that Article III was central to the legal controversy and proposed adopting the principle of the Republican legislation of 1811 as a kind of constitutional compromise. But country Trinitarians of one denomination or another combined to defeat the proposed amendment, Convention of 1820, *Journal* 613–614, 634. Article III of the constitution of 1780 continued in force. Meanwhile a new case decided by the Unitarian-dominated Supreme Judicial Court fueled the fire of controversy.

The minister in Dedham resigned in 1818. The *parish* chose Alvan Lamson, a Unitarian, to replace him. The *church*, 17 to 15, rejected Lamson. The *parish* called an ecclesiastical council dominated by such Unitarian luminaries as William Ellery Channing; Henry Ware, Hollis Professor of Divinity at Harvard; and John Thornton Kirkland, the president of Harvard. The council, unsurprisingly, approved Lamson. Meyer, *Church and State in Massachusetts* 174–175. In the person of Eiphalet Baker, represented by Daniel Webster, the *church* sued the deacons of the *parish* for possession of the money and documents that belonged to "the First Church in Dedham." Deacon Samuel Fales spent $3,000 of his own money to defend the parish's possession. *Id.* 177.

Chief Justice Parker traced the history of grants to the church in Dedham since the seventeenth century and held that the grants had created a trust, of which the church was the trustee, and that the beneficiary for whose benefit the trustee must act was the parish. The parish, he continued, was "the assembly of Christians in Dedham." This assembly he equated with the inhabitants of the town. Specifically, "as the particular trusts intended must have been the providing for the public worship of God in Dedham, the inhabitants at large of that town, as parishioners or members of the religious society'' were the proper beneficiaries of the trust.

Baker v. Fales

16 Mass. 488 (1820).

■ CHIEF JUSTICE PARKER delivered the Opinion of the Court.

If a church may subsist unconnected with any congregation or religious society, as has been urged in argument, it is certain that it has no legal qualities, and more especially that it cannot exercise any control over property which it may have held in trust for the society with which it had been formerly connected. That any number of the members of a church who disagree with their brethren, or with the minister, or with the parish, may withdraw from fellowship with them, and act as a church in a religious point of view, having the ordinances administered and other religious offices performed, it is not necessary to deny; indeed, this would be a question proper for an ecclesiastical council to settle, if any should dispute their claim. But as to all civil purposes, the secession of a whole church from the parish would be an extinction of the church; and it is competent to the members of the parish to institute a new church, or to engraft one upon the old stock if any of it should remain; and this new church would succeed to all the right of the old, in relation to the parish. . . .

It is said, in argument, that churches may subsist without connection with any parish or religious society; and the churches of Harvard College, Dartmouth College, and the Andover Institution, are cited as instances. We have before said that it was not intended to deny that there may be such churches in an ecclesiastical sense; but there is not appertaining to them, as churches, any civil rights or privileges, by virtue merely of their association as members of a church. These very churches may possibly be religious societies under the statute of 1811, called the religious freedom act, and may, as such, exercise power, *quasi* a body politic, to a certain extent; but this does not tend to show that a church, which had existed within a parish, and as such has had the custody and the disposition of property for parish purposes, can disunite itself from the parish, and retain, nevertheless, all the property, and dispose of it to other uses, or to similar uses, in another parish. If all the members of a church so situated should withdraw, leaving not even the deacons, or members enough to elect them, it might be necessary, perhaps, to apply to the legislature, in the absence of a court of chancery, to appoint some new trustee of the property, until a new church should be organized within the parish. But where members enough are left to execute the objects for which a church is gathered, choose deacons, & c., no legal change has taken place; the body remains, and the secession of a majority of the members would have no other effect than a temporary absence would have upon a meeting which had been regularly summoned.

That a church cannot subsist without some religious community to which it is attached, with the exceptions before stated, is not a new theory.

It has, we believe, been the understanding of the people of New England, from the foundation of the colonies. A few anomalous cases can have no bearing on the question. All the numerous laws, which were passed by the colonial and provincial legislature, in relation to churches, are predicated upon a supposed connection with some body politic; and, in the year 1800, a decisive expression of the public opinion was given in an act of the legislature, which provides for the public worship of God and for other purposes; for, by the first section of that statute, it is enacted, "That the respective churches, connected and associated in public worship with the several towns, parishes, precincts, districts, and other bodies politic, being religious societies, shall at all times have, use, exercise, and enjoy, all their accustomed privileges and liberties, respecting divine worship, church order and discipline, not repugnant to the constitution."

The consequences of the doctrine contended for by the defendant, will glaringly show the unsoundness of the principle upon which the argument is founded. The position is that, whenever property is given to a church, it has the sole control of it, and the members, for the time being, may remove to any other place, even without the commonwealth, and carry the property with them.

Now, property bestowed upon churches has always been given for some pious or benevolent purpose, and with a particular view to some associated body of Christians. The place in which the church is located, is generally had in view by the donor, either because he there had enjoyed the preaching of the gospel and the ordinances, or because it was the place where his ancestors or his family and friends had assembled together for religious purposes. These associations will be found to be the leading motive for the particular direction which his charity has received. If he gives to a church for the general purpose of promoting piety, or for the use of the poor of the church, he generally designates the body by the place where it is accustomed to worship. Thus, if a donation were made to the Old South church, Park-street church, Brattle-street church, or any other that might be thus designated by local qualities, it must be supposed that the donor had in view the society of Christians worshipping in those places; and as his donation is intended to be perpetual, that he had regard to the welfare of successive generations, who might become worshipping Christians and church members in the same place. If the whole society should find occasion to remove to some other place in the same town, the identity might be preserved, and the bounty enjoyed as he intended it. But if the church alone should withdraw, and unite itself to some other church, or to a new and different congregation, it would be defeating his intentions to carry the property with them, and distribute the proceeds in a community for the members of which he may have never entertained any particular feelings of kindness.

To divert the charity from the poor of the Old South church, to the poor of the church in Park-street, would be to violate the will and design of the donor, as effectually as to apply it to the support of the town's or state's poor. So, of property given for the support of public worship in any particular place.

It being, as we think, established that the members of the church, who withdrew from the parish, ceased to be the first church in Dedham, and that all the rights and duties of that body, relative to property intrusted to it, devolved upon those members who remained with and adhered to the parish; it remains to be considered whether the plaintiffs were duly chosen deacons of that church, and so became entitled to the possession of the property, as the trustees under the statute of 1754, as stated by the judge in his charge to the jury. And, as this was thought to depend upon the validity of the settlement and ordination of Mr. Lamson which took place in November, 1818, it has seemed to become necessary to look into the facts which led the judge to state to the jury, "that Mr. Lamson was legally ordained, as minister of said first parish, and that those members of the church who adhered to the parish and united with them on this occasion, must be considered as the church in said first parish in Dedham, and the successors of said ancient church, and that those members of the church who withdrew from the parish and refused to concur in the proceedings of the majority of the inhabitants of said parish in the ordination of Mr. Lamson, could not, in law, be considered as a church, so as to entitle them (through a majority) to hold, appropriate, or control, said ministerial or church fund or property."

The objection to the settlement of Mr. Lamson rests altogether upon the supposition that there could be no legal settlement and ordination, unless the church, as a distinct body from the parish or congregation, had assented to his call, and concurred in the proceedings preliminary to his settlement; and it is upon this ground, also, that the ordaining council are supposed to have had no authority in the matter, they being invited by the parish and a minority of the members of the church, but not by the church itself, to which body, it is alleged, belongs solely the right of convening a council upon such occasions.

That the proceedings of the parish and the council were not conformable to the general usage of the country, cannot be denied. But the parish alleged, in vindication of their departure from this usage, their constitutional right to elect and contract with their minister, exclusively of any concurrence or control of the church; and the necessity they were under to proceed as they did, because the church had refused to concur with them in the choice, and in the invitation to the ordaining council. That the parish have the constitutional right contended for, cannot be questioned by those who will pursue the clause of the third article of the Declaration of Rights, upon which this claim is asserted. It is there provided, "that the several towns, parishes, precincts, and other bodies politic or religious societies, shall at all times have the exclusive right of electing their public teachers, and of contracting with them, for their support and maintenance." This is too explicit to admit of cavilling or to require explanation, as every constitutional provision for the security of civil or religious liberty ought to be. All preexisting laws or usages must bow before this fundamental expression of the public will; and however convenient or useful it might be to continue the old form of electing or settling a minister, whenever a parish determines to assert its constitutional authority, there is no power in the state to oppose their claim.

It has been supposed by counsel in the argument, that there is a distinction between a public teacher, whose election is thus provided for in the Declaration of Rights, and a minister or pastor of a church, in the ecclesiastical or clerical sense of these terms; and that, although a civil contract may be made with the former, binding upon the parish, he is not vested with a religious character or office, so as to be entitled to the privileges of a minister of the gospel. But we see no ground for such distinction. A teacher of piety, religion and morality, is a minister of the gospel within the meaning of the Declaration of Rights; and it is a strange supposition, that the framers of the constitution, or the people, had respect, in this provision, to a class of men not known at the time the constitution was formed; to whom should belong only a part of the character, duties and privileges of ministers of the gospel. The term "teacher" was made use of as *nomen generalissimum*, to embrace the clerical head of every denomination of Christians in the state. It was well-known, that, in early times, certain titles used in the established church were offensive to our modest ancestors, as savoring of ecclesiastical distinction, and that the terms "teacher, teaching elder, teaching officer," & c., were commonly used, in lieu of other official designations known in the English church. By a colonial law of 1668, it is provided, that teaching officers of churches should be the ministers to all the inhabitants of the towns in which the churches over which they are placed shall be planted. If a teacher of piety, religion and morality, in the sense of the Declaration of Rights, does not mean ministers of the gospel, then the provision is senseless and nugatory; for there was not then, not is there now, any such officer known in the parishes or churches. It was supposed that this distinction was countenanced by the late Chief Justice Parsons, in the opinion delivered by him in the case of *Avery vs. The Inhabitants of Tyringham* [this section above]. His words are, "By the constitution, the rights of the town are enlarged, if it choose to exercise them, and those of the church impaired. If the church, when the election has been disapproved by the town, shall unwisely refuse to make a new election, or the town, for any cause, shall abandon the ancient usages of the country in settling a minister, it *may, without or against* the consent of the church, elect a public teacher, and contract to support him; and such a teacher will have a legal right to the benefit of the contract, although he cannot be considered a settled minister of the gospel, agreeably to the usages and practice of the Congregational churches in the state." He then goes on to recommend an adherence to those usages, and to deprecate a departure from them, except in cases of necessity.

We agree with him in estimating highly these ancient usages, protected as the people are by the constitutional provision, and in hoping they may be observed in future, as they have been in past times. But we cannot think, nor can it be inferred from his observations that he thought, that a teacher chosen by the parish, without the consent of the church, and publicly set apart by ordination over the parish, would not be a settled minister of the gospel; although he would not be so according to the usages and practice of the Congregational churches in the state. For the constitution supersedes those usages, where the parties do not choose to observe them; and to deny the character of ministers of the gospel to those who are chosen according to the constitution, would be to repeal the constitution and render it nugatory.

There is one religious society in the state at least [Brattle-street church, Boston], probably there are many, which, from its foundations, even before the adoption of the constitution, has departed from the general usage in the mode of settling their ministers. In this society there has been a long line of able, pious, learned ministers, teaching their flock for many generations, administering the holy ordinances of baptism and the Lord's supper, associating with the reverend clergy who may have been settled according to the common usage, and interchanging official duties with them. Will any one refuse to these teachers the character of ministers of the gospel, because they were not settled "according to the usages and practice of Congregational churches in the state?" We apprehend not. The practice in this society has been, immemorially, for the parish only to choose the minister, church members acting only as parishioners; and the church is requested, as a matter of courtesy, to invite the ordaining council. As in former times, particularly at the period of forming our constitution, many distinguished citizens belonged to this society, it is not improbable that the constitutional provision emanated from them, for it is exactly conformable to the practice of this society since its foundation. And, if uninterrupted harmony for near a century between church and society, and repeated unanimity in the choice of a minister, is any evidence of the merits of any system, there need be no apprehension of those disorders, which some have imagined will follow a general execution of the constitutional privilege. The distinction suggested is founded upon the hypothesis that the people, in establishing the provision in the third article, meant only to secure the right in towns, & c., to elect certain civil officers to be called teachers of piety, religion, and morality, like schoolmasters, who were not to be vested with a sacred or religious character or privileges; and that, in order to endow them with these, there must still be an appointment by the church, or some other body foreign to the town or parish. But this would have been going only half way in establishing the right of the people; for the most interesting, if not the principal, office of a minister is of a religious nature; such as administering the holy ordinances to those who should seek them; and of this benefit the people would be deprived at the will of the church, if such is to be the construction of the constitution. Indeed, if the church and congregation should concur in the choice of a minister, and other churches should, from disagreement with their creed, decline to advise to, and assist in the ordination; upon this close construction, the person chosen might be a teacher, but he could not be a minister of the gospel, because not settled according to the usages and practice of the Congregational churches; for those usages require a council, composed of the ministers and delegates of other churches, to give validity to an ordination.

What is the essential virtue and public benefit of an ordination? Surely, it is nothing but setting apart, installing or inaugurating, one who has been chosen to the office, and tendering to him the fellowship of the churches who assist in the ceremony. It will not now be contended, that any spiritual or temporal power is conferred by the imposition of hands. Ordination, according to the Platform, is nothing else but the solemn putting a man into his place and office in the church, whereunto he had a right before by election; being like the installation of a magistrate in the commonwealth. "Ordination is therefore not to go before, but to follow election." Again; "Ordination doth not constitute an office, nor give him the essentials of his office." *Cambridge Platform*, ch. ix. sec. 2. It is true, that the election here spoken of is an election by the church; but whenever, by change of law or usage, the right of election come to the congregation, the principles in regard to ordination are applicable. The people having the constitutional right to choose, they must have the right to have the minister of their choice set over them, or the former right would be in many important respects useless. If, then, the church would obstruct their wishes, by refusing to concur in calling a council, they have a right to invite one themselves; or if, upon prudential motives, or from adherence to old forms, they could find no ministers or churches to aid them, they would have the right, by some public solemn act, to carry into full effect their constitutional privilege, and thus to secure to their pastor all the privileges and immunities of a public teacher of piety, religion and morality, and of a minister of the gospel. This doctrine is as old as the history of the New England churches; for the first minister of Salem was set apart by the lay brethren, accident having prevented the clergy who were expected from attending; and though, after they arrived, they participated in the ceremony by giving the right hand of fellowship, this act was not an essential part of ordination. They seem not to have doubted the right of the people to give publicity to their choice; for although, after they formed themselves into a church state, they installed their ministers anew, it does not appear that any council was called in for this purpose. And the *Cambridge Platform* recognizes the principle; for in sec. 4, ch. 9, it is said, if the people may elect officers, which is the greater, and wherein the substance of the office doth consist, they may much more (need so requiring) impose hands in ordination, which is the less, and but the accomplishment of the other.

We consider, then, the non-concurrence of the church in the choice of the minister, and in the invitation to the ordaining council, as in no degree impairing the constitutional right of the parish. That council might have refused to proceed, but the parish could not by that have been deprived of their minister. It was right and proper, as they could not proceed according to ancient usage, because of the dissent of the church, to approach as near to it as possible by calling a respectable council, and having their sanction in the ordination. And it was certainly wise in that council, finding that the points of disagreement were such as would be likely to cause a permanent separation, to yield to the wishes of the parish, and give their sanction to proceedings which were justified by the constitution and laws of the land. They ordained him over the parish only; but, by virtue of that act, founded upon the choice of the people, he became not only the minister of the parish, but of the church still remaining there, notwithstanding the secession of a majority of the members. Mr. Lamson thus became the lawful minister of the first parish in Dedham, and of the church subsisting therein; and he had a right to call church meetings, and do all other acts pertaining to a settled and ordained minister of the gospel. The church had a right to choose deacons, finding that the former deacons had abdicated their office, and thus no legal objection is found to exist against their right to maintain this action....

Indeed, we apprehend those are mistaken, who imagine that the cause of religion would be served, public worship promoted, or instruction in piety, religion and morality more extensively encouraged, by restoring to the churches the power they once enjoyed, of electing the minister without concurrence of the people of the congregation, or by the aid of a council which they might select to sanction their choice. Nothing would tend more directly to break up the whole system of religious instruction; for the people never would consent to be taxed for the support of men in whose election they had no voice. It is an undoubted fact, that the male members of the churches form but a small part of the corporation which makes the contract, and is obliged to perform it; and it is not at all consistent with the spirit of the times, that the great majority should, in this particular, be subject to the minority. To arrogate such a power, would be to break up, in no distant period, every parish in the commonwealth.

The authority of the church should be of that invisible, but powerful nature, which results from superior gravity, piety, and devout example. It will then have its proper effect upon the congregation, who will cheerfully yield to the wishes of those who are best qualified to select the candidate. But as soon as it is challenged as a right, it will be lost. The condition of the members of a church is thought to be hard, where the minister elected by the parish is not approved by them. This can only be because they are a minority; and it is one part of the compensation paid for the many blessings resulting from a state of society. A difficulty of this nature surely would not be cured by returning to the old provincial system of letting the minority rule the majority; unless we suppose that the doctrines of a minister are of no consequence to any but church members. Besides, in the present state of our laws, and as they are likely to continue, there is no hardship, although there may be some inconvenience; for dissenting members of the church, the parish, may join any other church and society, or they may institute a new society; so as well as of that they are neither obliged to hear nor to pay a minister, in whose settlement they did not concur. It is true, if there are any parish funds, they will lose the benefit of them by removal; but an inconvenience of this sort will never be felt, when a case of conscience is in question.

Having established the points necessary to settle this cause, viz., that the property sued for belongs to the first church in Dedham, *sub modo;* that is, to be managed by its deacons under the superintendence of the church, for the general good of the inhabitants of the first parish, in the support of the public worship of God,—that the members of the church now associated and worshipping with the first parish, constitute the first church,—and that the plaintiffs are duly appointed deacons of that church; it follows that the verdict of the jury is right, and that judgment must be entered accordingly.

———

Mark DeWolfe Howe observed that the court avoided "abstruse problems of 'theology,' " and did its best "to make the litigants realize that the court was deciding nothing more than a controversy with respect to the control of property," Howe, *The Garden and the Wilderness: Religion and Government in American Constitutional History* 37, 40 (Chicago, 1965). But are not the nature of a church, its relations to a parish, and the status of a minister "abstruse questions of theology?" The Supreme Judicial Court could not help being embroiled in religious controversy when Massachusetts had adopted a religion.

Baker v. Fales was a blow to the Trinitarian Congregationalists. It was not made sweeter to them by the Chief Justice's unctuous words on their loss of the parish funds: "an inconvenience of this sort will never be felt, when a case of conscience is in question." Inconvenience of this sort, and feeling about it, were just what had led Deacon Eliphalet Baker to defend the suit and hire the great Daniel Webster as his lawyer. The Congregationalists did not feel better when, as the controversy continued in the political arena, Chief Justice Parker issued a long defense of his opinion in the *Christian Examiner*, an organ of the Unitarians. Meyer 206–206.

Between 1820 and 1834 nearly one hundred Congregationalist parishes fell under Unitarian control—over one-quarter of the Congregationalist parishes in the commonwealth. McLoughlin 2 *New England Dissent* 1175 n. 22, 1196. The Trinitarians estimated that the Unitarians took $608,000 worth of property. Meyer 177. The Trinitarians, as they watched the process, became champions of abolishing Article III. The entrenched Unitarians defended the establishment. "The government of this Commonwealth has uniformly distinguished itself by the spirit of religious freedom," declared their leader, William Ellery Channing, in the election sermon of 1830. "Intolerance, however rife abroad, has found no shelter in our halls of legislation." Meyer 217.

Reopening the issue of *Baker v. Fales,* the Trinitarian Congregationalists were again defeated in an opinion by the new Chief Justice, Lemuel Shaw, also a Unitarian, *Stebbins v. Jennings*, 27 Mass. (10 Pick.) 171 (1830). The Trinitarians now sounded the note that the Baptists had been sounding for generations: "To say that our religion cannot be supported without the aid of establishments and law is to disgrace it in the eyes of the world, and to cast reproach on its maker." *Spirit of the Pilgrims* 629–648 (1831) excerpted in Meyer 218.

Universalists, denouncing diehard Unitarians, took the lead in moving for constitutional reform. McLoughlin 2 *New England Dissent* 1245–1254. Trinitarian Congregationalists, Baptists, dissenters of every kind then voted for the eleventh amendment of the state constitution abolishing the right to tax for public worship. It was passed in 1833 by a vote of 32,324–3,273. *Id.* 1259.

The Eleventh Amendment left intact Article III's premise: The "public worship of GOD" promotes "the security of a republican government." It gave every religious society, incorporated or not, the right to elect "their pastors or religious teachers" and to raise money to support them. What it did not decide was who owned the property of the parishes. Legislation enacted in 1834 declared that all parishes continued to enjoy their existing rights. Massachusetts, *Revised Statutes*, 1835, c. 20, sec. 2. The churches, "connected and associated in public worship with such parishes," were to continue to "enjoy all their accustomed privileges." *Id*. sec. 3.

Under the principle established in *Baker v. Fales* it would have appeared that the voters of a parish could dispossess the churches and devote the church property to whatever Christian creed the majority of voters wanted. But the Trinitarian churches kept their church property and the Unitarians kept the property they had already won. On what basis? "That question has never been satisfactorily answered." Meyer 181. The result of the eleventh amendment and the 1834 legislation was to transfer a large amount of property, hitherto public, to the control of the two denominations. A kind of golden handshake was extended by the commonwealth to both the Trinitarian Congregationalist ministers and the Unitarian ministers no longer supported by public taxes. They took over as their own what had been trusts for "public worship." Disestablished in one sense, they were publicly endowed with the meeting-houses and parish funds of the towns of Massachusetts.

7.   "THE FOREMOST OF THE POLITICAL INSTITUTIONS"

In 1830 a Frenchman, Alexis de Tocqueville, aged twenty-five, began a nine-month tour of America. By training he was a lawyer, and he had had experience as a minor judge at Versailles. By temperament and intuition, he was a great observer, and he possessed, to the degree of genius, a Gallic capacity to generalize. His nine-month trip led in 1835 to the first volume of a masterpiece on the mores and government of the United States, *La Democratie en l'Amerique*, subsequently translated by Henry Reeve as *Democracy in America*. Religion and its relation to government were of great concern to Tocqueville.

Tocqueville to Eugene Stoffels, July 24, 1836

You seem to me to have well understood the general ideas on which my programme rests. What has most struck me about my country, more especially these last few years, is to see ranged on one side men who prize morality, religion, and order, and upon the other, those who love liberty and the equality of men before the law. This spectacle has struck me as the most extraordinary and the most deplorable ever offered to the eyes of a man; for all the things that we separate in this way, are, I am certain, united indissolubly in the eyes of God. They are *holy* things, if I may so express myself, because the greatness and the happiness of man in this world can result only from their simultaneous union. From this I believe to have perceived that one of the finest enterprises of our time would be to demonstrate that these things are not at all incompatible; that, on the contrary, they are bound together by a necessary tie, so that each of them is weakened in being separated from the others. Such is my general idea. Tocqueville, 1 *Oeuvres et correspondance inedites* (1861) 432 (emphasis in original).

Tocqueville's comments on religion in America are a mixture of observation, exhortations to his own countrymen, and prophecy of what was to come in America.

Tocqueville, *Democracy in America* (1835) Book I, Chapter XVII: Religion Considered as a Political Institution, Which Powerfully Contributes to the Maintenance of the Democratic Republic Amongst the Americans

North America peopled by men who professed a democratic and republican Christianity–Arrival of the Catholics—For what reason the Catholics form the most democratic and the most republican class at the present time.

Every religion is to be found in juxtaposition to a political opinion which is connected with it by affinity. If the human mind be left to follow its own bent, it will regulate the temporal and spiritual institutions of society upon one uniform principle; and man will endeavor, if I may use the expression, to harmonize the state in which he lives upon earth with the state which he believes to await him in heaven. The greatest part of British America was peopled by men who, after having shaken off the authority of the Pope, acknowledged no other religious supremacy; they brought with them into the New World a form of Christianity which I cannot better describe than by styling it a democratic and republican religion. This sect contributed powerfully to the establishment of a democracy and a republic, and from the earliest settlement of the emigrants politics and religion contracted an alliance which has never been dissolved.

About fifty years ago Ireland began to pour a Catholic population into the United States; on the other hand, the Catholics of America made proselytes, and at the present moment more than a million of Christians professing the truths of the Church of Rome are to be met with in the Union. The Catholics are faithful to the observances of their religion; they are fervent and zealous in the support and belief of their doctrines. Nevertheless they constitute the most republican and the most democratic class of citizens which exists in the United States; and although this fact may surprise the observer at first, the causes by which it is occasioned may easily be discovered upon reflection....

I happened to be staying in one of the largest towns in the Union, when I was invited to attend a public meeting which had been called for the purpose of assisting the Poles, and of sending them supplies of arms and money. I found two or three thousand persons collected in a vast hall which had been prepared to receive them. In a short time a priest in his ecclesiastical robes advanced to the front of the hustings: the spectators rose, and stood uncovered, whilst he spoke in the following terms: "Almighty God! the God of Armies! Thou who didst strengthen the hearts and guide the arms of our fathers when they were fighting for the sacred rights of national independence; Thou who didst make them triumph over a hateful oppression, and hast granted to our people the benefits of liberty and peace; Turn, O Lord, a favorable eye upon the other hemisphere; pitifully look down upon that heroic nation which is even now struggling as we did in the former time, and for the same rights which we defended with our blood. Thou, who didst create Man in the likeness of the same Image, let not tyranny mar Thy work, and establish inequality upon the earth. Almighty God! do Thou watch over the destiny of the Poles, and render them worthy to be free. May Thy wisdom direct their councils, and may Thy strength sustain their arms! Shed forth Thy terror over their enemies, scatter the powers which take counsel against them; and vouchsafe that the injustice which the world has witnessed for fifty years, be not consummated in our time. O Lord, who holdest alike the hearts of nations and of men in Thy powerful hand; raise up allies to the sacred cause of right; arouse the French nation from the apathy in which its rulers retain it, that it go forth again to fight for the liberties of the world.

"Lord, turn not Thou Thy face from us, and grant that we may always be the most religious as well as the freest people of the earth. Almighty God, hear our supplications this day. Save the Poles, we beseech Thee, in the name of Thy well-beloved Son, our Lord Jesus Christ, who died upon the cross for the salvation of men. Amen."

The whole meeting responded "Amen!" with devotion.

Indirect Influence of Religious Opinions Upon Political Society in the United States

Christian morality common to all sects—Influence of religion upon the manners of the Americans—Respect for the marriage tie—In what manner religion confines the imagination of the Americans within certain limits, and checks the passion of innovation—Opinion of the Americans on the political utility of religion—Their exertions to extend and secure its predominance.

I have just shown what the direct influence of religion upon politics is in the United States, but its indirect influence appears to me to be still more considerable, and it never instructs the Americans more fully in the art of being free than when it says nothing of freedom.

The sects which exist in the United States are innumerable. They all differ in respect to the worship which is due from man to his Creator, but they all agree in respect to the duties which are due from man to man. Each sect adores the Deity in its own peculiar manner, but all the sects preach the same moral law in the name of God. If it be of the highest importance to man, as an individual, that his religion should be true, the case of society is not the same. Society has no future life to hope for or to fear; and provided the citizens profess a religion, the peculiar tenets of that religion are of very little importance to its interests. Moreover, almost all the sects of the United States are comprised within the great unity of Christianity, and Christian morality is everywhere the same.

It may be believed without unfairness that a certain number of Americans pursue a peculiar form of worship, from habit more than from conviction. In the United States the sovereign authority is religious, and consequently hypocrisy must be common; but there is no country in the whole world in which the Christian religion retains a greater influence over the souls of men than in America; and there can be no greater proof of its utility, and of its conformity to human nature, than that its influence is most powerfully felt over the most "enlightened" and "free" nation of the earth.

I have remarked that the members of the American clergy in general, without even excepting those who do not admit religious liberty, are all in favor of civil freedom; but they do not support any particular political system. They keep aloof from parties and from public affairs. In the United States religion exercises but little influence upon the laws and upon the details of public opinion, but it directs the manners of the community, and by regulating domestic life it regulates the State.

I do not question that the great austerity of manners which is observable in the United States, arises, in the first instance, from religious faith. Religion is often unable to restrain man from the numberless temptations of fortune; nor can it check that passion for gain which every incident of his life contributes to arouse, but its influence over the mind of woman is supreme, and women are the protectors of morals. There is certainly no country in the world where the tie of marriage is so much respected as in America, or where conjugal happiness is more highly or worthily appreciated. In Europe almost all the disturbances of society arise from the irregularities of domestic life. To despise the natural bonds and legitimate pleasures of home, is to contract a taste for excesses, a restlessness of heart, and the evil of fluctuating desires. Agitated by the tumultuous passions which frequently disturb his dwelling, the European is galled by the obedience which the legislative powers of the State exact. But when the American retires from the turmoil of public life to the bosom of his family, he finds in it the image of order and of peace. There his pleasures are simple and natural, his joys are innocent and calm; and as he finds that an orderly life is the surest path to happiness, he accustoms himself without difficulty to moderate his opinions as well as his tastes. Whilst the European endeavors to forget his domestic troubles by agitating society, the American derives from his own home that love of order which he afterwards carries with him into public affairs.

In the United States the influence of religion is not confined to the manners, but it extends to the intelligence of the people. Amongst the Anglo–Americans, there are some who profess the doctrines of Christianity from a sincere belief in them, and others who do the same because they are afraid to be suspected of unbelief. Christianity, therefore, reigns without any obstacle, by universal consent; the consequence is, as I have before observed, that every principle of the moral world is fixed and determinate, although the political world is abandoned to the debates and the experiments of men. Thus the human mind is never left to wander across a boundless field; and, whatever may be its pretensions, it is checked from time to time by barriers which it cannot surmount. Before it can perpetrate innovation, certain primal and immutable principles are laid down, and the boldest conceptions of human device are subjected to certain forms which retard and stop their completion.

The imagination of the Americans, even in its greatest flights, is circumspect and undecided; its impulses are checked, and its works unfinished. These habits of restraint recur in political society, and are singularly favorable both to the tranquillity of the people and to the durability of the institutions it has established. Nature and circumstances concurred to make the inhabitants of the United States bold men, as is sufficiently attested by the enterprising spirit with which they seek for fortune. If the mind of the Americans were free from all trammels, they would very shortly become the most daring innovators and the most implacable disputants in the world. But the revolutionists of America are obliged to profess an ostensible respect for Christian morality and equity, which does not easily permit them to violate the laws that oppose their designs; nor would they find it easy to surmount the scruples of their partisans, even if they were able to get over their own. Hitherto no one in the United States has dared to advance the maxim, that everything is permissible with a view to the interests of society; an impious adage which seems to have been invented in an age of freedom to shelter all the tyrants of future ages. Thus whilst the law permits the Americans to do what they please, religion prevents them from conceiving, and forbids them to commit, what is rash or unjust.

Religion in America takes no direct part in the government of society, but it must nevertheless be regarded as the foremost of the political institutions of that country; for if it does not impart a taste for freedom, it facilitates the use of free institutions. Indeed, it is in this same point of view that the inhabitants of the United States themselves look upon religious belief. I do not know whether all the Americans have a sincere faith in their religion, for who can search the human heart? but I am certain that they hold it to be indispensable to the maintenance of republican institutions. This opinion is not peculiar to a class of citizens or to a party; but it belongs to the whole nation, and to every rank of society.

In the United States, if a political character attacks a sect, this may not prevent even the partisans of that very sect from supporting him; but if he attacks all the sects together, everyone abandons him, and he remains alone.

Whilst I was in America, a witness, who happened to be called at the assizes of the county of Chester (State of New York), declared that he did not believe in the existence of God, or in the immortality of the soul. The judge refused to admit his evidence, on the ground that the witness had destroyed beforehand all the confidence of the Court in what he was about to say. The newspapers related the fact without any further comment.

The Americans combine the notions of Christianity and of liberty so intimately in their minds, that it is impossible to make them conceive the one without the other; and with them this conviction does not spring from that barren traditionary faith which seems to vegetate in the soul rather than to live.

I have known of societies formed by the Americans to send out ministers of the Gospel into the new Western States to found schools and churches there, lest religion should be suffered to die away in those remote settlements, and the rising States be less fitted to enjoy free institutions than the people from which they emanated. I met with wealthy New Englanders who abandoned the country in which they were born in order to lay the foundations of Christianity and of freedom on the banks of the Missouri, or in the prairies of Illinois. Thus religious zeal is perpetually stimulated in the United States by the duties of patriotism. These men do not act from an exclusive consideration of the promises of a future life; eternity is only one motive of their devotion to the cause; and if you converse with these missionaries of Christian civilization, you will be surprised to find how much value they set upon the goods of this world, and that you meet with a politician where you expected to find a priest. They will tell you that "all the American republics are collectively involved with each other; if the republics of the West were to fall into anarchy, or to be mastered by a despot, the republican institutions which now flourish upon the shores of the Atlantic Ocean would be in great peril. It is, therefore, our interest that the new States should be religious, in order to maintain our liberties."

Such are the opinions of the Americans, and if any hold that the religious spirit which I admire is the very thing most amiss in America, and that the only element wanting to the freedom and happiness of the human race is to believe in some blind cosmogony, or to assert with Cabanis the secretion of thought by the brain, I can only reply that those who hold this language have never been in America, and that they have never seen a religious or a free nation. When they return from their expedition, we shall hear what they have to say.

There are persons in France who look upon republican institutions as a temporary means of power, of wealth, and distinction; men who are the *condottieri* of liberty, and who fight for their own advantage, whatever be the colors they wear: it is not to these that I address myself. But there are others who look forward to the republican form of government as a tranquil and lasting state, towards which modern society is daily impelled by the ideas and manners of the time, and who sincerely desire to prepare men to be free. When these men attack religious opinions, they obey the dictates of their passions to the prejudice of their interests. Despotism may govern without faith, but liberty cannot. Religion is much more necessary in the republic which they set forth in glowing colors than in the monarchy which they attack; and it is more needed in democratic republics than in any others. How is it possible that society should escape destruction if the moral tie be not strengthened in proportion as the political tie is relaxed? and what can be done with a people which is its own master, if it be not submissive to the Divinity?

Principal Causes Which Render Religion Powerful in America

Care taken by the Americans to separate the Church from the State— The laws, public opinion, and even the exertions of the clergy concur to promote this end—Influence of religion upon the mind in the United States attributable to this cause—Reason of this—What is the natural state of men with regard to religion at the present time—What are the peculiar and incidental causes which prevent men, in certain countries, from arriving at this state.

The philosophers of the eighteenth century explained the gradual decay of religious faith in a very simple manner. Religious zeal, said they, must necessarily fail, the more generally liberty is established and knowledge diffused. Unfortunately, facts are by no means in accordance with their theory. There are certain populations in Europe whose unbelief is only equalled by their ignorance and their debasement, whilst in America one of the freest and most enlightened nations in the world fulfils all the outward duties of religious fervor.

Upon my arrival in the United States, the religious aspect of the country was the first thing that struck my attention; and the longer I stayed there the more did I perceive the great political consequences resulting from this state of things, to which I was unaccustomed. In France I had almost always seen the spirit of religion and the spirit of freedom pursuing courses diametrically opposed to each other; but in America I found that they were intimately united, and that they reigned in common over the same country. My desire to discover the causes of this phenomenon increased from day to day. In order to satisfy it I questioned the members of all the different sects; and I more especially sought the society of the clergy, who are the depositaries of the different persuasions, and who are more especially interested in their duration. As a member of the Roman Catholic Church I was more particularly brought into contact with several of its priests, with whom I became intimately acquainted. To each of these men I expressed my astonishment and I explained my doubts; I found that they differed upon matters of detail alone; and that they mainly attributed the peaceful dominion of religion in their country to the separation of Church and State. I do not hesitate to affirm that during my stay in America I did not meet with a single individual, of the clergy or of the laity, who was not of the same opinion upon this point.

This led me to examine more attentively than I had hitherto done, the station which the American clergy occupy in political society. I learned with surprise that they filled no public appointments; not one of them is to be met with in the administration, and they are not even represented in the legislative assemblies. In several States the law excludes them from political life, public opinion in all. And when I came to inquire into the prevailing spirit of the clergy I found that most of its members seemed to retire of their own accord from the exercise of power, and that they made it the pride of their profession to abstain from politics.

I heard them inveigh against ambition and deceit, under whatever political opinions these vices might chance to lurk; but I learned from their discourses that men are not guilty in the eye of God for any opinions concerning political government which they may profess with sincerity, any more than they are for their mistakes in building a house or in driving a furrow. I perceived that these ministers of the gospel eschewed all parties with the anxiety attendant upon personal interest. These facts convinced me that what I had been told was true; and it then became my object to investigate their causes, and to inquire how it happened that the real authority of religion was increased by a state of things which diminished its apparent force: these causes did not long escape my researches.

The short space of threescore years can never content the imagination of man; nor can the imperfect joys of this world satisfy his heart. Man alone, of all created beings, displays a natural contempt of existence, and yet a boundless desire to exist; he scorns life, but he dreads annihilation. These different feelings incessantly urge his soul to the contemplation of a future state, and religion directs his musings thither. Religion, then, is simply another form of hope; and it is no less natural to the human heart than hope itself. Men cannot abandon their religious faith without a kind of aberration of intellect, and a sort of violent distortion of their true natures; but they are invincibly brought back to more pious sentiments; for unbelief is an accident, and faith is the only permanent state of mankind. If we only consider religious institutions in a purely human point of view, they may be said to derive an inexhaustible element of strength from man himself, since they belong to one of the constituent principles of human nature.

I am aware that at certain times religion may strengthen this influence, which originates in itself, by the artificial power of the laws, and by the support of those temporal institutions which direct society. Religions, intimately united to the governments of the earth, have been known to exercise a sovereign authority derived from the twofold source of terror and of faith; but when a religion contracts an alliance of this nature, I do not hesitate to affirm that it commits the same error as a man who should sacrifice his future to his present welfare; and in obtaining a power to which it has no claim, it risks that authority which is rightfully its own. When a religion founds its empire upon the desire of immortality which lives in every human heart, it may aspire to universal dominion; but when it connects itself with a government, it must necessarily adopt maxims which are only applicable to certain nations. Thus, in forming an alliance with a political power, religion augments its authority over a few, and forfeits the hope of reigning over all.

As long as a religion rests upon those sentiments which are the consolation of all affliction, it may attract the affections of mankind. But if it be mixed up with the bitter passions of the world, it may be constrained to defend allies whom its interests, and not the principle of love, have given to it; or to repel as antagonists men who are still attached to its own spirit, however opposed they may be to the powers to which it is allied. The Church cannot share the temporal power of the State without being the object of a portion of that animosity which the latter excites.

The political powers which seem to be most firmly established have frequently no better guarantee for their duration than the opinions of a generation, the interests of the time, or the life of an individual. A law may modify the social condition which seems to be most fixed and determinate; and with the social condition everything else must change. The powers of society are more or less fugitive, like the years which we spend upon the earth; they succeed each other with rapidity, like the fleeting cares of life; and no government has ever yet been founded upon an invariable disposition of the human heart, or upon an imperishable interest.

As long as a religion is sustained by those feelings, propensities, and passions which are found to occur under the same forms, at all the different periods of history, it may defy the efforts of time; or at least it can only be destroyed by another religion. But when religion clings to the interests of the world, it becomes almost as fragile a thing as the powers of earth. It is the only one of them all which can hope for immortality; but if it be connected with their ephemeral authority, it shares their fortunes, and may fall with those transient passions which supported them for a day. The alliance which religion contracts with political powers must needs be onerous to itself; since it does not require their assistance to live, and by giving them its assistance it may be exposed to decay.

The danger which I have just pointed out always exists, but it is not always equally visible. In some ages governments seem to be imperishable; in others, the existence of society appears to be more precarious than the life of man. Some constitutions plunge the citizens into a lethargic somnolence, and others rouse them to feverish excitement. When governments appear to be so strong, and laws so stable, men do not perceive the dangers which may accrue from a union of Church and State. When governments display so much weakness, and laws so much inconstancy, the danger is self-evident, but it is no longer possible to avoid it; to be effectual, measures must be taken to discover its approach.

In proportion as a nation assumes a democratic condition of society, and as communities display democratic propensities, it becomes more and more dangerous to connect religion with political institutions; for the time is coming when authority will be bandied from hand to hand, when political theories will succeed each other, and when men, laws, and constitutions will disappear, or be modified from day to day, and this, not for a season only, but unceasingly. Agitation and mutability are inherent in the nature of democratic republics, just as stagnation and inertness are the law of absolute monarchies.

If the Americans, who change the head of the Government once in four years, who elect new legislators every two years, and renew the provincial officers every twelvemonth; if the Americans, who have abandoned the political world to the attempts of innovators, had not placed religion beyond their reach, where could it abide in the ebb and flow of human opinions? where would that respect which belongs to it be paid, amidst the struggles of faction? and what would become of its immortality, in the midst of perpetual decay? The American clergy were the first to perceive this truth, and to act in conformity with it. They saw that they must renounce their religious influence, if they were to strive for political power; and they chose to give up the support of the State, rather than to share its vicissitudes.

In America, religion is perhaps less powerful than it has been at certain periods in the history of certain peoples; but its influence is more lasting. It restricts itself to its own resources, but of those none can deprive it: its circle is limited to certain principles, but those principles are entirely its own, and under its undisputed control.

NOTES AND QUESTIONS

Tocqueville's conclusion that "morality is everywhere the same" overlooked a profound debate on social ethics that was raging in America at the time of his visit, the debate over the abolition of slavery. As the materials in

Chapter Eight illustrate, this division resulted in violence in the civil order and in schism in mainline religious communities.

Do you agree with Tocqueville that "religion exercises but little influence upon the laws and upon the details of public opinion, but it directs the manners of the community, and by regulating domestic life it regulates the State"? When Tocqueville wrote in 1835, he contrasted the thorough secularism of his native France with the American attitude that "the spirit of religion and the spirit of freedom [are not] diametrically opposed to each other, but [are]... intimately united...." Is this view of American society still accurate? Tocqueville described the "influence of religious opinions upon political society" as "indirect"? Was the influence of religion on the abolitionist movement [Chapter Eight] and on the Civil Rights Movement [Chapter Fifteen] "little"? Was it "indirect"? For further analysis of Tocqueville on religion in America, see John T. Noonan, Jr., *The Lustre of Our Country: The American Experience of Religious Freedom* 95–115 (1998); and Joshua Mitchell, *The Fragility of Freedom: Tocqueville on Religion, Democracy, and the American Future* (1995).

CHAPTER EIGHT

EMANCIPATION, 1834–1870

At the very time that the churches of Massachusetts were being emancipated from tax support by the state, the energy of a nucleus of Christian laity and clergy was being turned to the emancipation of the slaves in the American South. The "abolitionist crusade"—an enterprise more religious in its origins and more single-minded in its object than the crusades to save the Holy Land—began in the administration of Andrew Jackson and reached its climax with the enactment of the Thirteenth Amendment in 1865. Christian motivation and fervor and biblical arguments and imagery created a massive religious intervention in American politics that could be read both to confirm Tocqueville's observations on the role of religion in America and to challenge his characterization of it as an indirect influence.

1. THE BIBLE AGAINST SLAVERY

In 1834, 124 ministers of the Gospel, predominantly from Massachusetts and predominantly Congregationalist, but with a sprinkling of names from other denominations and other northern states, issued an address to the public.

Declaration of Ministers of the Gospel on Slavery, 1834

We believe,

1. That Slavery in our land is a great and threatening evil.

2. That it is a great and crying national sin.

3. That every man whether he live at the North, South, East, or West, is personally responsible, and has personal duties to discharge in respect to it.

4. That every man, who adopts opinions or pursues practices, which adopted and pursued by all others, would go to perpetuate this sin, does thereby become personally guilty in respect to it.

5. We believe that slavery, like other sins, ought to be remedied as soon as the nature of the case admits; and further, that the nature of the case admits the *possibility* and therefore imposes the obligation of Immediate Emancipation. Amos A. Phelps, *Lectures on Slavery and Its Remedy* v-vi (1834; reprint, 1970).

In this manifesto, slavery is a religious, not a political issue; cooperation with the sin becomes sin, too; emancipation is not a far-off goal but a present duty. These themes were to be the themes of the abolitionist minority for the next thirty years. A minister, once converted to the cause, addressed other ministers "because this subject has been woefully and criminally overlooked and forgotten by ministers, who, of all other men, ought ever to be alive to it." *Id.* 13.

Ministers were already organizing for another great cause, "Temperance." Emancipation, like temperance, should be the work of all Christian denominations, "a common cause." *Id.* xi. Ministers were the key to public opinion. "Once get the public sentiment of the ministry right, and then inspire them with courage to speak that sentiment out, and you revolutionize the public sentiment of the community in a trice," *Id.* at 14–15. Some clergymen pleaded it was "a political subject" that they should not touch; as to which the pulpit should be silent. *Id.* 15. But like Jeremiah, the minister should not hesitate to pull down "the strong holds of Satan." Like Isaiah and Jesus Christ, he should "preach deliverance to the captives," *Id.* 16, 24.

The Christian attack on slavery was met with the Christian answer that slavery was sanctioned in the Old Testament, never criticized by Christ, and expressly approved by St. Paul. To these excuses, the answer was that servitude among the Jews was not like slavery in America, and that the entire spirit of the Bible condemned slavery. *Id.* 65–80. Slavery as practiced in America was clearly sinful because it denied God's moral government, reducing the slave from an intelligent, responsible human being to a chattel. William Goodell, "Slavery Tested by Its Own Code," 1 *Quarterly Anti–Slavery Magazine* 23–24 (1836). American slavery, moreover, denied the slave his religious rights by denying him literacy and with it the possibility of reading the Bible. *Id.* 25. American slave law also denied that slaves could marry. Doing so, "it blots out the seventh commandment" and "renders all this promiscuous concubinage inevitably certain!" *Id.* 26–27.

The ministers struck a vital spark, even though they were only a minority of the clergy, and the main church bodies—Methodist, Baptist, Presbyterian, Episcopalian, Roman Catholic—took no stand against the institution. The ministers alone would not have succeeded if their words had not influenced laymen who provided much of the leadership. Among the latter was Theodore Dwight Weld, the son of a Congregationalist minister in Utica, New York, and the descendant of a long line of New England ministers. Weld, like others in the antislavery cause, was first active as a temperance advocate. Under the influence of Charles Finney, a Presbyterian revivalist, Weld took the lead in bringing students to a new Presbyterian seminary, Lane, in Cincinnati, that became a center of abolitionist thought. He brought the gospel of emancipation to the Middle West, *Dictionary of American Biography* 19, 625. The title of his first book, *The Bible Against Slavery* (1837) shows the religious center of his zeal.

The most controversial of all the abolitionists, William Lloyd Garrison, had been crusading against intoxication and Sabbath-breaking before he was converted to the new cause by a Quaker, Benjamin Lundy. The first speech of his antislavery career was delivered on July 4, 1829, in the Park Street Church, Boston—the characteristic association of the celebration of American independence with religion and freedom for all human beings. Later, angry at the apathy of the mainline churches—"cages of unclean birds," as he described them—Garrison was less than orthodox but well within the doctrine of liberal Bostonian Christianity. For him as for the other leaders, the wicked wilderness of the world was a challenge to Christian reform. See Edward McGlynn Gaffney, Jr., "Politics without Brackets on Religious Convictions: Michael Perry and Bruce Ackerman on Neutrality," 64 Tulane L. Rev. 1143, 1158–1166 (1990) (discussing the role of religion in opposition to the law of slavery).

Christian belief also inspired the agents of abolitionism and provided a model for their martyrdom. In 1835 Amos Dresser, a student at Lane, brought abolitionist tracts into Nashville and was apprehended. At his trial he declared "slaveholding to be inconsistent with the Gospel, and a constant transgression of God's law." He was sentenced to a public whipping of twenty lashes. Dresser's narrative of what happened was much circulated in the North.

The Narrative of Amos Dresser, 1835

I knelt to receive the punishment which was inflicted by Mr. Braughton, the city officer, with a heavy cowskin. When the infliction ceased, an involuntary feeling of thanksgiving to God for the fortitude with which I had been enabled to endure it arose in my soul, to which I began aloud to give utterance. The death-like silence that prevailed for a moment was suddenly broken with loud exclamations, "G-d d-n him, stop his praying." "The Narrative of Amos Dresser," in John L. Thomas, ed., *Slavery Attacked: The Abolitionist Crusade* 43–44 (1965).

No reader familiar with stories of Christian endurance under Roman persecution could ignore the analogies.

The Christians for emancipation did not propose that force be used to effect it. Their program was to arouse ministers of the Gospel and stir the conscience of the community. Slaveholders, however, could not endure this kind of religious upbraiding; and they feared that the doctrines of the abolitionists would stir the slaves to armed rebellion. As early as 1835 President Andrew Jackson's postmaster general unofficially sought to close the United States mails in the South to abolitionist literature, see Thomas 41, 52. In 1836 the House of Representatives adopted "the gag rule" refusing to listen to or print petitions for the end of slavery in the District of Columbia.

The abolitionists' Christian critique had made the issue inflammatory. The dynamism of the situation was this: the more religious condemnation was heaped upon the institution, the more aggressive its beneficiaries became in asserting its rightness. They could not stand being put down as bad Christians and morally inferior beings. Their critics did not mind the effect of their words; they saw themselves as physicians provoking a crisis in an unhealthy body. The discomfort of the South would not alter their prescriptions. As Jefferson had done half a century ago, abolitionists appealed to the judgments of a "sin-avenging God," Phelps 150. They also appealed to the Last Judgment in chapter 25 of the Gospel according to Matthew, where Christ asks each what he has done for the needy. *See, e.g.*, Beriah Green, "Letter to a Minister of the Gospel," *I Quarterly Anti–Slavery Magazine* 340 (1836).

---

2.   NO COMPROMISE WITH SIN

The question of the annexation of Texas made slavery a major issue of national politics in the 1840s. Mexico had abolished slavery in Texas; but Texas wished to enter the Union as a slave state from which other slave states could be formed, giving the slave side preponderance in the United States Senate.

The center of opposition was New England where the "Conscience Whigs"–their name betraying their religious scruples—joined actual abolitionists in issuing *How to Settle the Texas Question* (1845) telling voters how to act and adding this direction: "To clergymen: You are entreated in the name of God and Christ to pray for the slave; and preach at least one sermon against the admission of Texas as a slave state, as soon as may be." Thomas *Slavery Attacked,* 105–106.

When the United States actually went to war with Mexico, the war was seen by the abolitionists and their allies–notably Abraham Lincoln and Henry David Thoreau—as a war to extend slavery. In Boston in 1846 it was denounced by the Reverend Theodore Parker, one of the purest products of the Unitarian culture of Harvard Divinity School and its Emersonian development. Too liberal for the established Unitarians, yet revering Jesus as "the highest known representative of God," Parker was the pastor of the Twenty–Eighth Congregationalist Society in Boston. He addressed a mass meeting at Faneuil Hall.

Theodore Parker on the Mexican–American War, 1846

Men and brothers, I call on you all to protest against this most infamous war, in the name of the States, in the name of the country, in the name of man—yes, in the name of God....

Leave not your memory infamous among the nations, because you feared men, feared the Government ... because you loved slavery, loved war, but loved not the eternal justice of all-judging God. Parker, "The Mexican War," in Parker, *The Slave Power* 31 (1969).

————

The Wilmot Proviso, banning slavery in land acquired from Mexico, failed of passage in Congress in 1847. After the war the terms on which California and New Mexico would become states had to be decided; by 1850 passions ran high over whether they should be slave or free. The sectional division was deep. Southern fire-eaters talked secession. General Winfield Scott, commander of the army, thought the country "on the eve of a terrible civil war." James Ford Rhodes, 1 *History of the United States* 131 (1910). In this crisis Henry Clay outlined a compromise embodied in a series of bills that preserved the Union for another decade. California was admitted as a free state. The question of slavery in New Mexico was left open. The Texas boundary was drawn not to include New Mexico. The slave trade in the District of Columbia was abolished. A new and harsher Fugitive Slave Act gave slaveholders more legal resources in the North in recapturing escaped slaves. Rhodes 182–183.

Slavery was now the single issue by which the religious abolitionists judged public men. A key speech in support of Clay's compromise was delivered on March 7, 1850, by Daniel Webster who, for three decades, had been a force in Massachusetts—a leader at the constitutional convention of 1820; a congressman from Boston in 1822; United States senator, 1828–1840; secretary of state, 1840–1843; senator again since 1846; a perennial prospect for the presidency. No past glory could outweigh the offense of his speech of March 7, 1850. On March 25, Parker again addressed a mass meeting in Faneuil Hall.

Theodore Parker on Mr. Webster's Speech, 1850

Four great men in the Senate of the United States have given us their decision; the four most eminent in the party politics of the nation—two great whigs, two great democrats. The Shibboleth of their party is forgotten by each; there is a strange unanimity in their decision. The Herod of free trade and the Pilate of protection are "made friends," when freedom is to be crucified. All four decide adverse to freedom; in favor of slavery; against the people. Their decisions are such as you might look for in the politicians of Austria and Russia. Many smaller ones have spoken on this side or on that. Last of all, but greatest, the most illustrious of the four, so far as great gifts of the understanding are concerned, a son of New England, long known, and often and deservedly honored, has given his decision. We waited long for his words; we held our peace in his silence; we listened for his counsel. Here it is; adverse to freedom beyond the fears of his friends, and the hopes even of his foes. He has done wrong things before, cowardly things more than once; but this, the wrongest and most cowardly of them all; we did not look for it. No great man in America has had his faults or his failings so leniently dealt with; private scandal we will not credit, public shame we have tried to excuse, or, if inexcusable, to forget. We have all of us been proud to go forward and honor his noble deeds, his noble efforts, even his noble words. I wish we could take a mantle big and black enough, and go backward and cover up the shame of the great man who has fallen in the midst of us, and hide him till his honor and his conscience shall return. But no, it cannot be; his deed is done in the face of the world, and nothing can hide it.

We have come together to-night in Faneuil Hall, to talk the matter over, in our New England way; to look each other in the face; to say a few words of warning, a few of counsel, perhaps something which may serve for guidance. We are not met here tonight to "calculate the value of the Union," but to calculate the worth of freedom and the rights of man; to calculate the value of the Wilmot Proviso. Let us be cool and careful, not violent, not rash; true and firm, not hasty or timid. . . .

Now, Mr. Foote of Mississippi—"Hangman Foote," as he has been called—understands the laws of the formation of the earth as well as the distinguished senator from Massachusetts. Why, the inhabitants of that part of the Northwest Territory, which now forms the States of Indiana and Illinois, repeatedly asked Congress to allow them to introduce slaves north of the Ohio; and but for the ordinance of '87, that territory would now be covered with the mildew of slavery!

But I have not yet adduced all the testimony of Mr. Foote. Last year, on the 23d of February, 1849, he declared: "No one acquainted with the vast mineral resources of California and New Mexico, and who is aware of the peculiar adaptedness of slave labor to the development of mineral treasures, can doubt for a moment, that were slaves introduced into California and New Mexico, being employed in the mining operations there in progress, their labor would result in the acquisition of pecuniary profits not heretofore realized by the most successful cotton or sugar planter of this country?" Does not Mr. Webster know this? Perhaps he did not hear

Mr. Foote's speech last year; perhaps he has a short memory, and has forgotten it. Then let us remind the nation of what its Senator forgets. Not know this—forget it? Who will credit such a statement? Mr. Webster is not an obscure clergyman, busy with far different things, but the foremost politician of the United States.

But why do I mention the speeches of Mr. Foote, a year ago? Here is something hardly dry from the printing-press. Here is an advertisement from the "Mississippian" of March 7th, 1850, the very day of that speech. The "Mississippian" is published at the city of Jackson, in Mississippi.

"CALIFORNIA,
THE SOUTHERN SLAVERY COLONY.

"Citizens of the slave States, desirous of emigrating to California with their slave property, are requested to send their names, number of slaves, and period of contemplated departure, to the address of 'SOUTHERN SLAVE COLONY,' Jackson, Miss....

"It is the desire of the friends of this enterprise to settle in the richest mining and agricultural portions of California, and to have the uninterrupted enjoyment of slave property. It is estimated that, by the first of May next, the members of this Slave Colony will amount to about five thousand, and the slaves to about ten thousand. The mode of effecting organization, & c., will be privately transmitted to actual members.

"Jackson (Miss), Feb. 24, 1850. dtf."

What does Mr. Webster say in view of all this? "If a proposition were now here for a government for New Mexico, and it was moved to insert a provision for the prohibition of slavery, I would not vote for it." Why not vote for it? There is a specious pretence, which is publicly proclaimed, but there is a real reason for it which is not mentioned!

In the face of all these facts, Mr. Webster says that these men would wish "to protect the everlasting snows of Canada from the pest of slavery by the same overspreading wing of an act of Congress." Exactly so. If we ever annex Labrador—if we "re-annex" Greenland, and Kamskatka, I would extend the Wilmot Proviso there, and exclude slavery forever and forever.

But Mr. Webster would not "reaffirm an ordinance of nature," nor "reenact the will of God." I would. I would reaffirm nothing else, enact nothing else. What is justice but the "ordinance of nature?" What is right but "the will of God?" When you make a law, "Thou shalt not kill," what do you but "reenact the will of God?" When you make laws for the security of the "unalienable rights" of man, and protect for every man the right to life, liberty, and the pursuit of happiness, are you not re-affirming an ordinance of nature? Not reenact the will of God? Why, I would enact nothing else. The will of God is a theological term; it means truth and justice, in common speech. What is the theological opposite to "The will of God?" It is "the will of the devil." One of the two you must enact—either the will of God, or of the devil. The two are the only theological categories for such matters. *Aut Deus aut Diabolus.* There is no other alternative, "Choose you which you will serve"....

It is a great question before us, concerning the existence of millions of men. To many men in politics, it is merely a question of party rivalry; a question of in and out, and nothing more. To many men in cities, it is a question of commerce, like the establishment of a bank, or the building of one railroad more or less. But to serious men, who love man and love their God, this is a question of morals, a question of religion, to be settled with no regard to party rivalry, none to fleeting interests of to-day, but to be settled under the awful eye of conscience, and by the just law of God.

Shall we shut up slavery or extend it? It is for us to answer. Will you deal with the question now, or leave it to your children, when the evil is ten times greater? In 1749, there was not a slave in Georgia; now, two hundred and eighty thousand. In 1750, in all the United States, but two hundred thousand; now, three millions. In 1950, let Mr. Webster's counsels be followed, there will be thirty millions. Thirty millions! Will it then be easier for your children to set limits to this crime against human nature, than now for you? Our fathers made a political, and a commercial, and a moral error—shall we repeat it? They did a wrong; shall we extend and multiply the wrong? Was it an error in our fathers; not barely a wrong—was it a sin? No, not in them; they knew it not. But what in them to establish was only an error, in us to extend or to foster is a sin!

Perpetuate Slavery, we cannot do it. Nothing will save it. It is girt about by a ring of fire which daily grows narrower, and sends terrible sparkles into the very centre of the shameful thing. "Joint resolutions" cannot save it; annexations cannot save it—not if we re-annex all the West Indies; delinquent representatives cannot save it; uninstructed senators, refusing instructions, cannot save it, no, not with all their logic, all their eloquence, which smites as an earthquake smites the sea. No, slavery cannot be saved; by no compromise, no non-intervention, no Mason's Bill in the Senate. It cannot be saved in this age of the world until you nullify every ordinance of nature, until you repeal the will of God, and dissolve the union He has made between righteousness and the welfare of a people. Then, when you displace God from the throne of the world, and instead of his eternal justice, reenact the will of the Devil, then you may keep Slavery; keep it forever, keep it in peace. Not till then.

The question is, not if slavery is to cease, and soon to cease, but shall it end as it ended in Massachusetts, in New Hampshire, in Pennsylvania, in New York; or shall it end as in St. Domingo? Follow the counsel of Mr. Webster—it will end in fire and blood. God forgive us for our cowardice, if we let it come to this, that three millions or thirty millions of degraded human beings, degraded by us, must wade through slaughter to their unalienable rights.

Mr. Webster has spoken noble words—at Plymouth, standing on the altar-stone of New England; at Bunker Hill, the spot so early reddened with the blood of our fathers. But at this hour, when we looked for great counsel, when we forgot the paltry things which he has often done, and said, "Now he will rouse his noble soul, and be the man his early speeches once bespoke," who dared to fear that Olympian head would bow so low, so deeply kiss the ground? Try it morally, try it intellectually, try it by the statesman's test, world-wide justice; nay, try it by the politician's basest test, the personal expediency of to-day—it is a speech "not fit to be made," and when made, not fit to be confirmed.

> "We see dimly in the distance what is small and what is great,
> Slow of faith how weak an arm may turn the iron helm of fate;
> But the soul is still oracular; amid the market's din,
> List the ominous stern whisper from the Delphic cave within—
> 'They enslave their children's children,
> who make compromise with sin.' "

3 *Works of Theodore Parker*, 37.

Parker's stark either/or alternative "Choose you which you will serve" was a citation of Joshua 24:15. The context of the biblical text in the ancient world was a covenant renewal ceremony; *see* Note. *Covenants and the Process of Formation of Biblical Law* [Chapter One, section 2]. According to Joshua, the successor of Moses, the crossing of the Jordan river into the land of promise was a moment for a critical decision. Would the people of Israel forsake the worship of Egyptian deities? Joshua made clear his own decision to accept the terms of the First Commandment: "I am the Lord your God, who brought you out of the land of Egypt, out of the house of slavery; you shall have no other gods before me." (Deut. 5:5). He called upon everyone at the ceremony to do likewise. So did Parker. The times demanded a stark alternative: "either God or the Devil." For a cento about Parker and a memorial service in his honor, see John T. Noonan, Jr., *The Lustre of Our Country* 117–37 (1998).

Note. *Chief Justice Shaw and the Compromise of 1850.* The Compromise of 1850—"compromise with sin" to its religious critics—settled nothing because more states applied for admission and the terms of their admission had to be settled. Moreover, the new Fugitive Slave Act of 1850 virtually assured that outrages to northern opinion would occur: persons would be carried off, under the authority of the law, from freedom to slavery. When Chief Justice Lemuel Shaw sustained the constitutionality of the act in 1851, he satisfied the mercantile class of Boston, anxious for concord with the South, but did nothing to reconcile religious antislavery feeling, *Sims' Case*, 61 Mass. (7 Cush.) 285 (1851). His son-in-law, Herman Melville, wrote *Billy Budd*, showing a scrupulously legalistic Captain Vere putting to death an innocent Billy Budd in defiance of a higher law. *See* Robert M. Cover, *Justice Accused: Antislavery and the Judicial Process* (1975).

By 1854 the issue of the terms on which Kansas and Nebraska would be admitted divided the country. The Missouri Compromise of 1820, long taken to be untouchable, prohibited slavery in the entire area. Stephen Douglas proposed the Kansas–Nebraska Act, letting Kansas determine by "popular sovereignty" whether it entered the Union as a free or a slave state. Northern moderates, who were not abolitionists but were against extension of slavery, took alarm. A petition against Douglas's bill was presented to the Senate by Hamilton Fish, senator from New York. The bishop of the Episcopal diocese of New York headed the signatories, and a majority of the clergymen of New York were reported to have signed it. The next day Edward Everett, senator from Massachusetts, presented a protest signed by 3,500 of the 3,800 clergymen in New England. Among them were not only names like Theodore Parker and

Lyman Beecher but also those of the clergymen presidents of Amherst, Brown, Williams, and Yale.

Statement of New England Clergy Against the Nebraska–Kansas Bill, 1854

The undersigned, clergymen of different religious denominations in New England, hereby, in the name of Almighty God, and in his presence, do solemnly protest against the passage of what is known as the Nebraska bill.... We protest against it as a great moral wrong, as a breach of faith eminently unjust to the moral principles of the community, and subversive of all confidence in national engagements; as a measure full of danger to the peace and even the existence of our beloved Union, and exposing us to the righteous judgments of the Almighty. Rhodes, *History of the United States* 478.

————

The intrusion of the clergy was strongly resented by Christians in favor of slavery, compromise, and peace. A third petition of 500 clergymen from Illinois and neighboring states was read aloud by Stephen Douglas, a sponsor of the bill. He added that he understood that in New England alone on one day between 1,500 and 2,000 sermons had been preached against the proposed legislation.

Stephen Douglas on the Nebraska–Kansas Bill, 1854

It is well known that there is an organization by which a copy of the New England protest has been sent to every preacher of every denomination, in all the free States of the Union, for his signature. Every minister has been appealed to, and yet they have been able to bring to their support but comparatively a small number. This shows that the great mass of the Christian ministers, the great mass of preachers of the Gospel, abhor this attempt to prostitute religion into the means of elevating men into power. The great mass are unwilling in the pulpit to utter a slander, and falsehood, and calumny against public men in a place where no answer can be made, and no vindication can be put forth. I submit, sir, whether it is fair as between man and man, whether it is honest, on the part of ministers of the Gospel towards their congregations, to pursue such a course. They take a partisan view of the subject in these sermons. They fix the character of each public man. They indorse this man; they condemn that. They indorse this political party; they excommunicate that. They give what pretends to be a true statement of the facts of the question; when that statement is derived from the address and speeches of the Abolition confederates, and contradicted by the records of the country, and these records are not allowed to be produced. If these statements are put forth upon the stump, we can refute them. If they should be put forth anywhere else than in the pulpit, or except upon the Sabbath day, we can disprove them. What would these gentlemen think of me if I were to violate the Holy Sabbath day by going into Chicago, and on that day making a stump speech in vindication of the Nebraska bill? If they have a right to discuss it on the

Sabbath day in opposition, may I not expose their slanders by vindicating the truth? Sir, this is an attempt to convert the Sabbath into the great day of the hustings, to make it a great day of electioneering, to get people out on the Sabbath for the purpose of hearing stump speeches; and in the most convenient of all modes, for if you wish to blacken the character of a man, you can do it then with security and with impunity, because no man can rise up and expose the slander, although a dozen living witnesses may be present and know it to be a slander.

I say, sir, that the purity of the Christian church, the purity of our holy religion, and the preservation of our free institutions, require that Church and State shall be separated; that the preacher on the Sabbath day shall find his text in the Bible; shall preach "Jesus Christ and him crucified," shall preach from the Holy Scriptures, and not attempt to control the political organizations and political parties of the day. 29 *Cong. Globe* 656 (1854).

————

The bill passed the House by three votes on May 22, 1854, and was signed by President Franklin Pierce on May 30. While the bill was awaiting the president's signature, Anthony Burns was arrested in Boston on May 24. Burns was a black Baptist preacher, who in February had escaped from his master in Richmond. The convergence of the application of the Fugitive Slave Act to Burns with passage of the Kansas–Nebraska Act excited the strongest emotions. At a meeting at Faneuil Hall on May 26, Parker advocated action, not mere words.

Theodore Parker on the Nebraska–Kansas Act of 1854

I have heard many hurrahs and cheers for liberty many times; I have not seen a great many *deeds* done for liberty. I ask you are we to have *deeds* as well as words? ... Gentlemen, there was a Boston once, and you and I had fathers—brave fathers; and mothers who stirred up fathers to manly deeds.... They did not obey the stamp act.... You know what they did with the *tea*. Rhodes, 502.

————

The crowd attempted to storm the court house; a marshal's aide was killed. Escorted by troops ready to fire without notice, Burns on May 31 was taken to a Treasury cutter and shipped back to Virginia. For details of the military preparations, see *Ela v. Smith*, 71 Mass. 121 (1855). Burns himself was subsequently purchased by Bostonians from a new owner, set free, and financed for study at Oberlin. He became a Baptist pastor in Indianapolis and later in Canada, 3 *Dictionary of American Biography* 308. The role of the authorities in Massachusetts became the subject of impassioned religious criticism at a mass meeting of 10,000 persons in Framingham on Independence Day, 1854.

"We have degenerated," William Lloyd Garrison told the meeting, "in our reverence for the higher law of God." In a scene modeled on the Old Testament, Garrison picked up a copy of the Fugitive Slave Act, set it on fire, and said, "And let the people say Amen." They did. He then set fire to a copy of the decision returning Burns and again asked the people to say amen. A third time he took up the Constitution itself. He described it as "the parent of all other atrocities," and citing the prophet Isaiah (Is. 28:18) called it "a covenant with death, an agreement with hell." He lit the paper and called out, "So perish all compromises with tyranny!" "And let the people say Amen." They did. Phillip S. Paludan, *A Covenant with Death: The Constitution, Law, and Equality* 2–3(1975). The scene was permeated by theology. The Constitution was seen as the reverse of Israel's life-giving covenant with God. The whole ritual was modeled on Deuteronomy 27 in which Moses tells the Levites to intone a curse "upon him who slights his father or his mother" and adds, "Let the people say Amen," and so on through several commandments of the Law. With the same solemnity Garrison cursed the Constitution.

3. THE GOSPEL TO KANSAS

In 1820, it will be recalled, Lyman Beecher had been a defender of the Congregational establishment. In 1826 he had been called to the new Hanover Street Church in Boston and conducted a powerful evangelical ministry there. In 1831 his zealous attacks on Catholicism were generally regarded as contributing to the state of mind in which a mob burned down a convent belonging to the Ursuline nuns in Charleston. Beecher then left Massachusetts to become the president of Lane in Cincinnati. So his career reflected the times. He was now an antislavery man. When the Kansas–Nebraska Act passed, he was among the leaders organizing an influx of antislavery men into Kansas, the prelude to a kind of civil war in the state. Beecher's appeal follows.

Lyman Beecher, Education, Temperance, Freedom, Religion in Kansas

Dear Sir: We are engaged in an effort to have all the "clergymen of New England," the life members of the New England Emigrant Aid Company.

By insuring thus their cooperation in the direction of this Company, and by engaging its funds at this period of its highest usefulness, we are satisfied that the Christians of New England will bring to bear a stronger influence in sustaining the principles of what was last year called the "Ministers' Memorial," than by any other means which Providence puts in their hands. We ask such cooperation as you can give us; supposing that you may have been one of those 3,050 ministers, who in the Senate of the United States were pronounced to know nothing of the facts, laws and votes involved in the Nebraska bill and to have "no time to understand them." We are certain that you belong to that body of Northern ministers who have been prohibited from entering northwestern Missouri Kansas, by those mobs of men who have attempted to take the law of that region in their own hands.

We beg your attention to the great work the New England Emigrant Aid Company has in hand. We ask your particular attention in the encouragement which divine providence has given to its efforts. We beg you to observe all the facts in the case, before you give way to the false and discouraging impressions, assiduously circulated before the pretended election in Kansas, of March 30, which was the work, simply, of an invading army. You may rely on the following statements of the work of the Emigrant Aid Company, since it was established:

1. *For Freedom*. It has assisted in establishing at commanding points the towns of Lawrence, Topeka, Osawatomie, Boston, Hampden, and Wabounse. In some of these towns it has mills—in most of them some investment of value to the settlers. These towns are all peopled by "Free-State men," whose whole influence goes to make Kansas free. There are other towns already started of similar character. The only "Slave-State" town of commanding influence in Kansas is Leavenworth, on the Missouri frontier, separated from the other settled parts of the Territory by Indian reservations. We may say, therefore, that all the most important centers of influence have been established or assisted by the Emigrant Aid Company, and that their influence tells for the cause of Freedom. This Company has, in fact, directly transported between two and three thousand emigrants to Kansas. Not one man of them is known to have ever given a "Slave-State" vote. More than ten thousand, from free States of the Northwest, have been led there by its indirect influence here. To prevent the return of this tide, and to provide those who go with the assistance which capital only can provide, this Company wishes to supply saw-mills at important points, and other conveniences. For such purposes will it use any enlargement of its funds. The emigration is still very large; and whenever this Company can establish a saw-mill, with other conveniences, a "Free-State" town can be gathered. From the best sources of information, from the officers of the Company, and well-informed persons in Kansas and Missouri, we are convinced, as the result of what has been done, that the great proportion of settlers now in Kansas wish it to become a free State. At the election held on the 22d ult., to fill vacancies in the Legislature, nine "Free-State" members were chosen, and only three "Slave-State" members—the last in Leavenworth, which is separated by a ferry only from Missouri.

2. *For Religion*. The officers of this Company have understood that, to make a free State, they needed, first of all, the Gospel. Every missionary sent there by different boards has received their active assistance. Divine service is regularly maintained in the towns where the company has influence, and, we believe, no where else. Every Sabbath school in the Territory has been formed with the assistance of the Company, or its officers. Every church organized has been organized with their cooperation.

3. For Education. Schools will be in operation at Lawrence, at Topeka, at Osawatomie and Hampden before the end of July. These, which are the only schools in the Territory of which we have any account, are due to the exertions of the New England Emigrant Aid Company and its officers.

4. *For Temperance*. The traffic in intoxicating liquors scarcely exists in any one of the towns founded with the Company's assistance, and any attempt to introduce it will be resisted by their citizens. This prohibition, intended in the first instance for the benefit of the towns, will approve

itself to you as the only hope for the Indians still remaining in that Territory.

Such has been the work of this Company in one year. To carry further such operations in these towns, and to plant more towns at once in Kansas, so as to secure its future destiny before next January, the Company needs $150,000. We think it highly desirable that that sum shall be furnished by those who will continue to the Company the Christian direction which has always guided it. We address this statement of facts, therefore, to every clergyman in New England, asking for it their careful attention. . . .

————————

In 1857 the Supreme Court decided the Dred Scott case, denying that a descendant of black slaves could ever be a citizen of the United States and denying the power of Congress to exclude slavery from the territories. *Dred Scott v. Sandford*, 60 U.S. (19 How.) 393. The dissenting opinion of Justice John McLean was read from the pulpit. George B. Cheever, author of *God Against Slavery* and pastor of the Church of the Puritans in New York City, declared that when sin and the devil usurped power, it was everyone's duty to disobey. *The Independent*, a Congregationalist weekly, edited by Henry Ward Beecher (Lyman's son) and other ministers, declared that the justices had "achieved only their own infamy." If the people obeyed, the paper said, "they disobey God." Don E. Fehrenbacher, *The Dred Scott Case: Its Significance in American Law and Politics* 422–423 (1978). Compromise with sin was once more denounced.

4.   "GOD IS MARCHING ON"

When the war came, religious support for the contestants was a major factor in morale on both sides. The identification of the war as God's battle was more intense in the North. Julia Ward Howe, a New Yorker married to a New Englander, made the Howes' Boston home, Green Peace, a center of Unitarian causes, editing from there the antislavery journal, *The Commonwealth*. Visiting Washington at the end of 1861, as the first year of war drew to a close, she wrote religious words to the tune of the popular song "John Brown's Body." Published in February 1862 in *The Atlantic Monthly*, her poem perfectly expressed the sense of religious mission that brought together God's judgment and Christ's redemptive sacrifice and perceived victory for the Union as both divine judgment and liberation.

Julia Ward Howe, Battle–Hymn of the Republic, 1861

Mine eyes have seen the glory of the coming of the Lord:
> He is trampling out the vintage where the grapes of wrath are stored;
> He hath loosed the fateful lightning of His terrible swift sword;
> His truth is marching on.

I have seen Him in the watch-fires of a hundred circling camps;
> They have builded Him an altar in the evening dews and damps;

I can read His righteous sentence by the dim and flaring lamps:
His day is marching on.

I have read a fiery gospel writ in burnished rows of steel:
"As ye deal with my contemners, so with you my grace shall deal;
Let the Hero, born of woman, crush the serpent with his heel,
Since God is marching on."

He has sounded forth the trumpet that shall never call retreat;
He is sifting out the hearts of men before His judgment-seat;
Oh, be swift, my soul, to answer Him! Be jubilant, my feet!
Our God is marching on.

In the beauty of the lilies Christ was born across the sea,
With a glory in his bosom that transfigures you and me:
As he died to make men holy, let us die to make men free,
While God is marching on.

The idea that God had a special interest in the cause was held in higher official quarters. Gideon Welles, secretary of the navy, described in his diary this meeting of Lincoln's cabinet, shortly after the quasi-victory of the Union at Antietam.

Gideon Welles, Diary, September 22, 1862

September 22. A special Cabinet-meeting. The subject was the Proclamation for emancipating the slaves after a certain date, in States that shall then be in rebellion. For several weeks the subject has been suspended, but the President says never lost sight of When it was submitted, and now in taking up the Proclamation, the President stated that the question was finally decided, the act and the consequences were his, but that he felt it due to us to make us acquainted with the fact and to invite criticism on the paper which he had prepared. There were, he had found, not unexpectedly, some differences in the Cabinet, but he had, after ascertaining in his own way the views of each and all, individually and collectively, formed his own conclusions and made his own decisions. In the course of the discussion on this paper, which was long, earnest, and, on the general principle involved, harmonious, he remarked that he had made a vow, a covenant, that if God gave us the victory in the approaching battle, he would consider it an indication of Divine will, and that it was his duty to move forward in the cause of emancipation. It might be thought strange, he said, that he had in this way submitted the disposal of matters when the way was not clear to his mind what he should do. God had decided this question in favor of the slaves. He was satisfied it was right, was confirmed and strengthened in his action by the vow and the results. His mind was fixed, his decision made, but he wished his paper announcing his course as correct in terms as it could be made without any change in his determination.

———

Victory at Gettysburg was announced by the president in terms that incorporated a portion of the Lord's Prayer.

Lincoln's Announcement of News from Gettysburg, July 4, 1863

The President announces to the country that news from the Army of the Potomac, up to 10 p.m. of the 3rd is such as to cover that Army with the highest honor, to promise a great success to the cause of the Union, and to claim the condolence of all for the many gallant fallen. And that for this, he especially desires that on this day, He whose will, not ours, should ever be done, be everywhere remembered and reverenced with profoundest gratitude. Roy P. Basler, ed., 6 *Collected Works of Abraham Lincoln* [*Works of Lincoln*] 314 (1953).

————

Eleven days later the president issued this proclamation.

Lincoln's Proclamation of Thanksgiving July 15, 1863

By the President of the United States of America, A Proclamation

It has pleased Almighty God to hearken to the supplications and prayers of an afflicted people, and to vouchsafe to the army and the navy of the United States victories on land and on the sea so signal and so effective as to furnish reasonable grounds for augmented confidence that the Union of these States will be maintained, their constitution preserved, and their peace and prosperity permanently restored. But these victories have been accorded not without sacrifices of life, limb, health and liberty incurred by brave, loyal and patriotic citizens. Domestic affliction in every part of the country follows in the train of these fearful bereavements. It is meet and right to recognize and confess the presence of the Almighty Father and the power of His Hand equally in these triumphs and in these sorrows:

Now, therefore, be it known that I do set apart Thursday the 6th. day of August next, to be observed as a day for National Thanksgiving, Praise and Prayer, and I invite the People of the United States to assemble on that occasion in their customary places of worship, and in the forms approved by their own consciences, render the homage due to the Divine Majesty, for the wonderful things he has done in the Nation's behalf, and invoke the influence of His Holy Spirit to subdue the anger, which has produced, and so long sustained a needless and cruel rebellion, to change the hearts of the insurgents, to guide the counsels of the Government with wisdom adequate to so great a national emergency, and to visit with tender care and consolation throughout the length and breadth of our land all those who, through the vicissitudes of marches, voyages, battles and sieges, have been brought to suffer in mind, body or estate, and finally to lead the whole nation, through the paths of repentance and submission to the Divine Will, back to the perfect enjoyment of Union and fraternal peace.

In witness whereof, I have hereunto set my hand and caused the seal of the United States to be affixed. Done at the city of Washington, this fifteenth day of July, in the year of our Lord one thousand eight hundred and sixty-three, and of the Independence of the United States of America the eighty-eighth.

By the President: ABRAHAM LINCOLN. 6 *Works of Lincoln* 332.

————

On November 19, 1863, the president gave the Gettysburg Address, classic in its compact statement of principle, and concluding "that we here highly resolve these dead shall not have died in vain—that this nation, under God, shall have a new birth of freedom—and that government of the people, by the people, for the people, shall not perish from the earth," 7 *Works of Lincoln* 23.

In March 1865, Lincoln delivered his Second Inaugural Address, a small summa of theology on the war, its divine cause, and the proper scriptural response to the war.

Lincoln's Second Inaugural Address, March 4, 1865

At this second appearing to take the oath of the presidential office, there is less occasion for an extended address than there was at the first. Then a statement, somewhat in detail, of a course to be pursued, seemed fitting and proper. Now, at the expiration of four years, during which public declarations have been constantly called forth on every point and phase of the great contest which still absorbs the attention, and engrosses the energies of the nation, little that is new could be presented. The progress of our arms, upon which all else chiefly depends, is as well known to the public as to myself; and it is, I trust, reasonably satisfactory and encouraging to all. With high hope for the future, no prediction in regard to it is ventured.

On the occasion corresponding to this four years ago, all thoughts were anxiously directed to an impending civil war. All dreaded it—all sought to avert it. While the inaugural address was being delivered from this place, devoted altogether to *saving* the Union without war, insurgent agents were in the city seeking to *destroy* it without war—seeking to dissolve the Union, and divide effects, by negotiation. Both parties deprecated war; but one of them would *make* war rather than let the nation survive; and the other would *accept* war rather than let it perish. And the war came.

One eighth of the whole population were colored slaves, not distributed generally over the Union, but localized in the Southern part of it. These slaves constituted a peculiar and powerful interest. All knew that this interest was, somehow, the cause of the war. To strengthen, perpetuate, and extend this interest was the object for which the insurgents would rend the Union, even by war; while the government claimed no right to do more than to restrict the territorial enlargement of it. Neither party expected for the war, the magnitude, or the duration, which it has already attained. Neither anticipated that the *cause* of the conflict might cease with, or even before, the conflict itself should cease. Each looked for an easier triumph, and a result less fundamental and astounding. Both read the same Bible, and pray to the same God; and each invokes His aid against the other. It may seem strange that any men should dare to ask a just God's assistance in wringing their bread from the sweat of other men's faces; but let us judge not that we be not judged. The prayers of both could not be answered; that of neither has been answered fully. The Almighty has His own purposes. "Woe unto the world because of offences! for it must needs be that offences come; but woe to that man by whom the offence cometh!" If we shall suppose that American Slavery is one of those offences which, in the providence of God, must needs come, but which, having continued through His appointed time, He now wills to remove, and that He gives to both North and South, this terrible war, as the woe due to those by whom the offence came, shall we discern therein any departure from those divine attributes which the believers in a Living God always ascribe to Him? Fondly do we hope—fervently do we pray—that this mighty scourge of war may speedily pass away. Yet, if God wills that it continue, until all the wealth piled by the bond-man's two hundred and fifty years of unrequited toil shall be sunk, and until every drop of blood drawn with the lash, shall be paid by another drawn with the sword, as was said three thousand years ago, so still it must be said "the judgments of the Lord, are true and righteous altogether."

With malice toward none; with charity for all; with firmness in the right, as God gives us to see the right, let us strive on to finish the work we are in; to bind up the nation's wounds; to care for him who shall have borne the battle, and for his widow, and his orphan—to do all which may achieve and cherish a just and lasting peace, among ourselves, and with all nations.

————

Presidential prayer; quotation of Psalm 19:9 (on the judgments of the Lord); invocation of duty to the widow and the orphan as in Deuteronomy 10:16–18; Jesus' words on not judging lest one be judged (Matt. 7:1–2); Jesus' words of woe to him by whom scandal comes (Matt. 18:7); finally an expression of charity reflecting the deepest of biblical doctrines—these were the themes of the president's formal message as the war neared its close. Less than six weeks later, on Good Friday, the president was assassinated. "Over and over again were the parallels drawn of Lincoln and Christ in blood of atonement dying for mankind," Carl Sandburg, 4 *Abraham Lincoln* 361 (1939). In the clerical-political interpretation of his death Lincoln legitimated the emancipation and confirmed the religious reading of its rightness.

5.   TWO MAINLINE CHURCHES AND THE WAR

The Methodist Church had an early history of antipathy to slavery. John Wesley had formed a "Society for the Suppression of the Slave Trade." John Newton, captain of a slave ship, and author of journals and letters that are the source of much of what is known about the eighteenth century slave trade, is more famous as the author of the hymn, "Amazing Grace." Once blind, he saw the light of the Gospel, accepted ordination as an Anglican priest, and renounced slavery. He aligned himself with Wesley's Evangelical revival, and as a pastor at St. Mary Woolchurch, in London, he influenced many, among them William Wilberforce, who would one day become a leader in the campaign for the abolition of slavery in England. In America several eighteenth-century

Methodist ministers in the South denounced slavery and freed their own slaves. The "Christmas Conference" of the American Methodist Church in 1784 forbade the purchase of slaves.

Most American Methodists lived in the slaveholding states, and many resisted the rule laid down without any religious sanctions being applied against them. By the time of the General Conference of 1808, the Methodists were willing to compromise and accept slaveholding. Charles Baumer Swaney, *Episcopal Methodism and Slavery* 1–19 (1926; reprint, 1962). When abolitionist sentiment mounted in New England, southern Methodists were advised to "shun abolition as you would the DEVIL." *Id.* 50. By 1839 the church had taken strong disciplinary steps to crush the abolitionists within it. *Id.* 100. Northern abolitionist ministers threatened secession, but in 1844 it was at the instance of Southerners that the General Conference divided the church. *Id.* at 143. The church's prosperous publishing house, the Book Concern, was not divided without litigation. In two circuit court cases, Supreme Court Justice Samuel Nelson, a New York proslavery Presbyterian, decided for the Southern Church; while Supreme Court Justice John McLean, the most prominent Methodist in the country and an antislavery man, decided for the Northern Church. Both justices urged compromise. When one case finally reached the Supreme Court itself, Justice Nelson wrote the opinion upholding the authority of the General Conference as "the sovereign power" in the church to divide it. *Smith v. Swormstedt*, 57 U.S. 288, 307 (1853). Justice McLean acquiesced but the disappointed side voiced its distrust of a court dominated by slaveholders. Swaney 184.

Northern Methodist journals such as *Zion's Herald* condemned the Compromise of 1850, denouncing politicians who were "pro-slavery men" or "dough-faces." The *Western Christian Advocate* summoned "the religious press" to condemn politicians favoring the Compromise. *Id.* 264–265. The *Dred Scott* decision was condemned by Northern Methodist conferences, the New Hampshire Conference stigmatizing it as contrary to "the Constitution, justice and religion." *Id.* 277. When the war came, the bishops of the church in the North vigorously supported the government against "this infernal rebellion, the most hellish since Satan seceded from the government of Heaven." *Id.* 300.

The Upper Iowa Conference of the Church in 1863 noted that there were 100,000 Methodists in the Union armies, and the General Conference of 1864 wrote Lincoln stating the Church's support for the Union cause. *Id.* 299.

Lincoln to the Upper Iowa Conference of the American Methodist Church, May 18, 1864

Gentlemen: In response to your address, allow me to attest the accuracy of its historical statements; indorse the sentiments it expresses; and thank you, in the nation's name, for the sure promise it gives.

I would utter nothing which might, in the least, appear invidious against any. Yet, without this, it may fairly be said that the Methodist Episcopal Church, not less devoted than the best, is by its greatest numbers, the most important of all. It is no fault in others that the Methodist Church sends more soldiers to the field, more nurses to the hospital, and more prayers to Heaven than any. God bless the Methodist

Church—less all the churches—and blessed be God, Who in this our great trial, giveth us the churches. Lincoln, 7 *Works of Lincoln* 350–51.

————

A historian of Methodism notes: "One of the most important addresses delivered in behalf of Lincoln during the campaign of 1864 was that of Bishop [Matthew] Simpson, November 3, 1864. Before an immense New York audience, he gave his great lecture on 'Our Country' which had created such an intense spirit of loyalty in many other cities. This speech was reported by the leading New York papers so that he spoke to the whole nation. It probably had a large part in completing the splendid victory obtained by the President in the November election." Swaney 306. At the direction of the secretary of war, Edward Stanton, Methodist churches in the South that did not have "loyal ministers" were turned over to bishops of the Northern Church. *Id.* 303–305.

General Assembly of the Presbyterian Church, Declaration on Slavery, 1818

We consider the voluntary enslaving of one part of the human race by another, as a gross violation of the most precious and sacred rights of human nature; as utterly inconsistent with the law of God, which requires us to love our neighbour as ourselves and as totally irreconcilable with the spirit and principles of the Gospel of Christ, which enjoin that, "all things whatsoever ye would that men should do to you, do ye even so to them." Slavery creates a paradox in the moral system—it exhibits rational, accountable, and immortal beings, in such circumstances as scarcely to leave them the power of moral action. It exhibits them as dependent on the will of others, whether they shall receive religious instruction; whether they shall know and worship the true God; whether they shall enjoy the ordinances of the Gospel; whether they shall perform the duties and cherish the endearments of husbands and wives, parents and children, neighbours and friends; whether they shall preserve their chastity and purity, or regard the dictates of justice and humanity. Robert Ellis Thompson, *A History of the Presbyterian Churches in the United States* 364 (1895).

By 1845 the General Assembly took a different view.

General Assembly of the Presbyterian Church, Declaration on Slavery, 1845

The Church of Christ is a spiritual body, whose jurisdiction extends only to the religious faith, and moral conduct of her members. She cannot legislate where Christ has not legislated, nor make terms of membership which he has not made. The question, therefore, which this Assembly is called upon to decide, is this: Do the Scriptures teach that the holding of slaves, without regard to circumstances, is a sin, the renunciation of which should be made a condition of membership in the church of Christ?

It is impossible to answer this question in the affirmative, without contradicting some of the plainest declarations of the word of God. *Id.* 369–370.

————

When the war came, however, the Assembly, over a strong minority protest, opted for the Union.

General Assembly of the Presbyterian Church, Declaration on Slavery, 1861

Resolved, 2. That this General Assembly, in the spirit of that Christian patriotism which the Scriptures enjoin, and which has always characterized this Church, do hereby acknowledge and declare our obligation to promote and perpetuate, so far as in us lies, the integrity of these United States, and to strengthen, uphold, and encourage the Federal Government in the exercise of all its functions under our noble Constitution; and to this Constitution, in all its provisions, requirements, and principles, we profess our unabated loyalty. *Id.* 380.

The Southern Presbyteries formed the Presbyterian Church in the Confederate States of America.

Declaration of the Presbyterian Church in the Confederate States of America, 1861

The first thing which roused our Presbyteries to look the question of separation seriously in the face, was the course of the Assembly in venturing to determine, as a Court of Jesus Christ, which it did by necessary implication, the true interpretation of the Constitution of the United States as to the kind of government it intended to form. A political theory was, to all intents and purposes, propounded, which made secession a crime, the seceding States rebellious, and the citizens who obeyed them traitors. We say nothing here as to the righteousness or unrighteousness of these decrees. What we maintain is, that, whether right or wrong, the Church had no right to make them—she transcended her sphere, and usurped the duties of the State. *Id.*

The services to the Confederate States of the moderator of this church were said to have been "worth more to the cause than a soldiery of ten thousand men." *Id.* 156.

After the war the 1866 Assembly of the northern Presbyteries declared secession a crime and made rejection of slavery as a divine institution a condition of membership in the Church. These resolutions deeply divided the Presbyteries in border states such as Missouri and Kentucky. Fifty-four ministers and 173 elders signed a "Declaration and Testimony" accusing the Assembly of acting on political questions. The Synods of Missouri and Kentucky supported this protest. The Assembly cut off these synods. The case of the Walnut Street Church in Louisville became a test as to which group should control the church property. *Id.* 167–69. The case reached the Supreme Court. The majority opinion was written by Samuel Miller, a Lincoln appointee and a Unitarian.

Watson v. Jones

80 U.S. (13 Wall.) 679 (1871).

This was a litigation which grew out of certain disturbances in what is known as the "Third or Walnut Street Presbyterian Church," of Louisville, Kentucky, and which resulted in a division of its members into two distinct bodies, each claiming the exclusive use of the property held and owned by that local church. The case was thus:

The Presbyterian Church in the United States is a voluntary religious organization, which has been in existence for more than three-quarters of a century. It has a written Confession of Faith, Form of Government, Book of Discipline, and Directory for Worship. The government of the church is exercised by and through an ascending series of "judicatories," known as Church Sessions, Presbyteries, Synods, and a General Assembly. . . .

The General Assembly, consisting of ministers and elders commissioned from each Presbytery under its care, is the highest judicatory of the Presbyterian Church, representing in one body all the particular churches of the denomination. Besides the power of receiving and issuing appeals and references from inferior judicatories, to review the records of Synods, and to give them advice and instruction in all cases submitted to them in conformity with the constitution of the church, it is declared that it "shall constitute the bond of union, peace, correspondence, and mutual confidence among all our churches." To the General Assembly also belongs the power of deciding in all controversies respecting doctrine and discipline; of reproving, warning, or hearing testimony against any error in doctrine or immorality in practice, in any Church, Presbytery, or Synod; . . . of superintending the concerns of the whole church; . . . of suppressing schismatical contentions and disputations; and, in general, of recommending and attempting reformation of manners, and the promotion of "charity, truth, and holiness through all the churches under their care." . . .

We have already adverted to the war of the insurrection, its action on the subject of slavery, and the feeling engendered by this action in the special congregation of the Walnut Street Church.

We now speak of the same subject of the war, of slavery, & c., in its more general relation with the judicatories above that local church, and of the way in which this local church was affected by and identified itself with the action of the more general church. From the beginning of the war to its close, the General Assembly of the Presbyterian Church at its annual meetings expressed in Declaratory Statements or Resolutions, its sense of the obligation of all good citizens to support the Federal government in that struggle; and when, by the proclamation of President Lincoln, emancipation of the slaves of the States in insurrection was announced, that body also expressed views favorable to emancipation, and adverse to the institution of slavery. At its meeting in Pittsburg in May, 1865, instructions were given to the Presbyteries, the Board of Missions, and to the Sessions of the churches, that when any person from the Southern States should make application for employment as missionary or for admission as members, or ministers of churches, inquiry should be made as to their sentiments in regard to loyalty to the government and on the subject of slavery; and if it was found that they had been guilty of voluntarily aiding the war of the rebellion, or held the doctrine announced by the large body of the churches in the insurrectionary States which had organized a new General Assembly, that "the system of negro slavery in the South is a divine institution, and that it is the peculiar mission of the Southern church to conserve that institution," they should be required to repent and forsake these sins before they could be received.

In the month of September thereafter the Presbytery of Louisville, under whose immediate jurisdiction was the Walnut Street Church, adopted and published in pamphlet form, what it called *"A Declaration and Testimony against the erroneous and heretical doctrines and practices which have obtained and been propagated in the Presbyterian Church of the United States during the last five years."* This Declaration denounced, in the severest terms, the action of the General Assembly in the matters we have just mentioned, declared an intention to refuse to be governed by that action, and invited the cooperation of all members of the Presbyterian Church who shared the sentiments of the Declaration, in a concerted resistance to what they called "the usurpation of authority" by the Assembly.

The General Assembly of 1866, denounced in turn the Declaration and Testimony and declared that every Presbytery which refused to obey its order should be *ipso facto* dissolved, and called to answer before the next General Assembly; giving the Louisville Presbytery an opportunity for repentance and conformity. The Louisville Presbytery divided, and the adherents of the Declaration and Testimony sought and obtained admission, in 1868, into "the Presbyterian Church of the Confederate States," a body which had several years previously withdrawn from the General Assembly of the United States and set up a new organization....

On the 1st of June, 1867, the Presbytery and Synod recognized by *Watson and his party,* were declared by the General Assembly to be "in no sense a true and lawful Synod and Presbytery in connection with and under the care and authority of the General Assembly of the Presbyterian Church in the United States of America;" and were permanently excluded from connection with or representation in the Assembly. By the same resolution the Synod and Presbytery adhered to by those whom *Watson and his party* opposed were declared to be the true and lawful Presbytery of Louisville and Synod of Kentucky.

■ JUSTICE MILLER now delivered the opinion of the court.

This case belongs to a class, happily rare in our courts, in which one of the parties to a controversy, essentially ecclesiastical, resorts to the judicial tribunals of the State for the maintenance of rights which the church has refused to acknowledge, or found itself unable to protect. Much as such dissensions among the members of a religious society should be regretted, a regret which is increased when passing from the control of the judicial and legislative bodies of the entire organization to which the society belongs, an appeal is made to the secular authority; the courts when so called on must perform their functions as in other cases.

Religious organizations come before us in the same attitude as other voluntary associations for benevolent or charitable purposes, and their rights of property, or of contract, are equally under the protection of the law, and the actions of their members subject to its restraints. Conscious as we may be of the excited feeling engendered by this controversy, and of the extent to which it has agitated the intelligent and pious body of Christians in whose bosom it originated, we enter upon its consideration with the satisfaction of knowing that the principles which we are to decide so much of it as is proper for our decision, are those applicable alike to all of its class, and that our duty is the simple one of applying those principles to the facts before us. . . .

[Justice Miller noted that among intrachurch controversies, properly disputes are "oftenest found in the courts," and "with reference to the number and difficulty of the questions involved," are in "every way the most important."]

It is the case of property acquired in any of the usual modes for the general use of a religious congregation which is itself part of a large and general organization of some religious denomination, with which it is more or less intimately connected by religious views and ecclesiastical government.

The case before us is one of this class, growing out of a schism which has divided the congregation and its officers, and the presbytery and synod, and which appeals to the courts to determine the right to the use of the property so acquired. Here is no case of property devoted forever by the instrument which conveyed it, or by any specific declaration of its owner, to the support of any special religious dogmas, or any peculiar form of worship, but of property purchased for the use of a religious congregation, and so long as any existing religious congregation can be ascertained to be that congregation, or its regular and legitimate successor, it is entitled to the use of the property. In the case of an independent congregation we have pointed out how this identity, or succession, is to be ascertained, but in cases of this character we are bound to look at the fact that the local congregation is itself but a member of a much larger and more important religious organization, and is under its government and control, and is bound by its orders and judgments. There are in the Presbyterian system of ecclesiastical government, in regular succession, the presbytery over the session or local church, the synod over the presbytery, and the General Assembly over all. These are called, in the language of the church organs, "judicatories," and they entertain appeals from the decisions of those below, and prescribe corrective measures in other cases.

In this class of cases we think the rule of action which should govern the civil courts, founded in a broad and sound view of the relations of church and state under our system of laws, and supported by a preponderating weight of judicial authority is, that, whenever the questions of discipline, or of faith, or ecclesiastical rule, custom, or law have been decided by the highest of these church judicatories to which the matter has been carried, the legal tribunals must accept such decisions as final, and as binding on them, in their application to the case before them. . . .

In this country the full and free right to entertain any religious belief, to practice any religious principle, and to teach any religious doctrine which does not violate the laws of morality and property, and which does not infringe personal rights, is conceded to all. The law knows no heresy, and is committed to the support of no dogma, the establishment of no sect. The right to organize voluntary religious associations to assist in the expression and dissemination of any religious doctrine, and to create tribunals for the decision of controverted questions of faith within the association, and for the ecclesiastical government of all the individual members, congregations, and officers within the general association, is unquestioned. All who unite themselves to such a body do so with an implied consent to this government, and are bound to submit to it. But it would be a vain consent and would lead to the total subversion of such religious bodies, if any one aggrieved by one of their decisions could appeal to the secular courts and have them reversed. It is of the essence of these religious unions, and of their right to establish tribunals for the decision of questions arising among themselves, that those decisions should be binding in all cases of ecclesiastical cognizance, subject only to such appeals as the organism itself provides for.

Nor do we see that justice would be likely to be promoted by submitting those decisions to review in the ordinary judicial tribunals. Each of these large and influential bodies (to mention no others, let reference be had to the Protestant Episcopal, the Methodist Episcopal, and the Presbyterian churches), has a body of constitutional and ecclesiastical law of its own, to be found in their written organic laws, their books of discipline, in their collections of precedents, in their usage and customs, which as to each constitute a system of ecclesiastical law and religious faith that tasks the ablest minds to become familiar with. It is not to be supposed that the judges of the civil courts can be as competent in the ecclesiastical law and religious faith of all these bodies as the ablest men in each are in reference to their own. It would therefore be an appeal from the more learned tribunal in the law which should decide the case, to one which is less so.

The Court of Appeals of Kentucky, in the case of *Watson v. Avery*, before referred to, while admitting the general principle here laid down, maintains that when a decision of an ecclesiastical tribunal is set up in the civil courts, it is always open to inquiry whether the tribunal acted within its jurisdiction, and if it did not, its decision could not be conclusive.

There is, perhaps, no word in legal terminology so frequently used as the word jurisdiction, so capable of use in a general and vague sense, and which is used so often by men learned in the law without a due regard to precision in its application. As regards its use in the matters we have been discussing it may very well be conceded that if the General Assembly of the Presbyterian Church should undertake to try one of its members for murder, and punish him with death or imprisonment, its sentence would be of no validity in a civil court or anywhere else. Or if it should at the instance of one of its members entertain jurisdiction as between him and another member as to their individual right to property, real or personal, the right in no sense depending on ecclesiastical questions, its decision would be utterly disregarded by any civil court where it might be set up. And it might be said in a certain general sense very justly, that it was because the General Assembly had no jurisdiction of the case. Illustrations of this character could by multiplied in which the proposition of the Kentucky court would be strictly applicable.

But it is a very different thing where a subject-matter of dispute, strictly and purely ecclesiastical in its character,—a matter over which the civil courts exercise no jurisdiction,—a matter which concerns theological controversy, church discipline, ecclesiastical government, or the conformity of the members of the church to the standard of morals required of them,—becomes the subject of its action. It may be said here, also, that no jurisdiction has been conferred on the tribunal to try the particular case before it, or that, in its judgment, it exceeds the powers conferred upon it, or that the laws of the church do not authorize the particular form of proceeding adopted; and, in a sense often used in the courts, all of those may be said to be questions of jurisdiction. But it is easy to see that if the civil courts are to inquire into all these matters, the whole subject of the doctrinal theology, the usages and customs, the written laws, and fundamental organization of every religious denomination may, and must, be examined into with minuteness and care, for they would become, in almost every case, the *criteria* by which the validity of the ecclesiastical decree would be determined in the civil court. . . .

The novelty of the questions presented to this court for the first time, their intrinsic importance and far-reaching influence, and the knowledge that the schism in which the case originated has divided the Presbyterian churches throughout Kentucky and Missouri, have seemed to us to justify the careful and laborious examination and discussion which we have made of the principles which should govern the case. For the same reasons we have held it under advisement for a year; not uninfluenced by the hope, that since the civil commotion, which evidently lay at the foundation of the trouble, has passed away, that charity, which is so large an element in the faith of both parties, and which, by one of the apostles of that religion, is said to be the greatest of all the Christian virtues, would have brought about a reconciliation. But we have been disappointed. It is not for us to determine or apportion the moral responsibility which attaches to the parties for this result. We can only pronounce the judgment of the law as applicable to the case presented to us, and that requires us to affirm the decree of the Circuit Court as it stands.

DECREE AFFIRMED.

■ THE CHIEF JUSTICE did not sit on the argument of this case, and took no part in its decision.

■ MR. JUSTICE CLIFFORD with whom concurred MR. JUSTICE DAVIS, dissented.

NOTE: *Bouldin v. Alexander*, 82 U.S. (15 Wall.) 131 (1872). Albert Bouldin, a black minister, founded the Third Colored Baptist Church in Washington, D.C. Some years later the congregation divided, each faction claiming to be the Third Colored Baptist Church. In June 1867 Bouldin and a minority of the congregation voted to "turn out" four of the seven trustees who had been elected in February 1867. The Bouldin group gained control of the building.

The Philadelphia Baptist Association, described in the statement of the case as "an ancient authoritative body of the Baptist Church," recognized the trustees aligned with the majority. In an action by these trustees to recover the money of the church from Bouldin, the Supreme Court held for the majority trustees. The trustees, the Court said, might be excommunicated but they could not be turned out as trustees "by a minority of the church society, or meeting, without warning, and acting without charges, without citation or trial, and in direction contravention of the church rules." The First Amendment was not mentioned in the opinion by Justice William Strong for a unanimous Court.

6.   THE CIVIL WAR AMENDMENTS

On January 31, 1865, months before the surrender of the Confederacy on April 9, the Thirty-ninth Congress proposed the amendment abolishing slavery. By December 6 of that year, twenty-seven of the thirty-six States had ratified the amendment. The adoption was not unanimous. It was rejected by New Jersey on Mar. 16, 1865 and subsequently ratified on Jan. 23, 1866. It was rejected by Delaware on Feb. 8, 1865 and subsequently ratified on Feb. 12, 1901. It was rejected by Kentucky on Feb. 24, 1865 and subsequently ratified on Mar. 18, 1976. It was rejected by Mississippi on Dec. 2, 1865 and subsequently ratified on Mar. 16, 1995.

United States Constitution, Amendment XIII

Section 1. Neither slavery nor involuntary servitude, except as a punishment for crime whereof the party shall have been duly convicted, shall exist within the United States, or any place subject to their jurisdiction.

Section 2. Congress shall have power to enforce this article by appropriate legislation.

NOTE. This amendment and each of the other civil war amendments expressly conferred upon Congress legislative authority to enforce the reshaping of the Constitution.

The second session of the same Congress adopted the Fourteenth Amendment on June 13, 1866. A little over two years later, the Secretary of State issued a proclamation declaring that the proposed amendment had been ratified by the legislatures of thirty of the thirty-six States. As with the Thirteenth Amendment, the Fourteenth Amendment was not adopted unanimously. It was rejected by Delaware, Georgia, Louisiana, North Carolina, South Carolina, Texas and Virginia. The State Legislatures of these States subsequently ratified the amendment. Three states—New Jersey, Ohio and Oregon—withdrew their consent to the ratification of this amendment in 1868. The State of New Jersey expressed support for this amendment on Nov. 12, 1980. Ohio and Oregon have yet to do so. As the Fourteenth Amendment was to become, much later, the chief vehicle for applying the First Amendment to the states, it is appropriate to note its terms and contemporaneous understanding of them.

United States Constitution, Amendment XIV

Section 1. All persons born or naturalized in the United States, and subject to the jurisdiction thereof, are citizens of the United States and of the State wherein they reside. No State shall make or enforce any law which shall abridge the privileges or immunities of citizens of the United States; nor shall any State deprive any person of life, liberty, or property, without due process of law; nor deny to any person within its jurisdiction the equal protection of the laws....

Section 5. The Congress shall have power to enforce, by appropriate legislation, the provisions of this article.

————

The amendment marked a sea change in the federal-state relationship. In 1789 Madison thought "the most valuable" amendment would be one prohibiting interference with conscience by the States, but his proposal was rejected. [Chapter Six, section 3 D]. Now the Constitution declared that no state could abridge the privileges and immunities of citizens, that no state could deprive any person of liberty, including religious liberty, without due process of law, and that Congress had authority to enforce these provisions "by appropriate legislation." The materials below illustrate that the privileges and immunities of citizens were meant by at least some of the framers to include religious freedom. The large open question would prove to be who decides when legislation is appropriate? In *City of Boerne v. Flores,* 521 U.S. 507 (1997) [Chapter Eleven, section 11] the Court took a restrictive view of the enforcement power of the Fourteenth Amendment, invalidating legislation aimed at protecting religious freedom more vigorously than the Court deemed necessary in *Employment Division v. Smith*, 494 U.S. 872 (1990) [Chapter Eleven, section 10].

NOTES

Cummings v. Missouri, 71 U.S. (4 Wall.) 277 (1866). While the Fourteenth Amendment was pending ratification, a case illustrated the existing narrow understanding of the protection accorded by the Constitution to the free exercise of religion. In 1865, Missouri by popular vote had amended its constitution and prescribed an oath to be taken by every officeholder, lawyer, teacher, and clergyman that declared that he had not "ever, by act or word, manifested his adherence to the cause of such enemies [the Confederate States] or his desire for their triumph over the arms of the United States or his sympathy with those engaged in exciting or carrying on rebellion against the United States," *Cummings v. Missouri*, 71 U.S. (4 Wall.) 277, 279–281 (1866). Father Cummings, a Catholic priest, was convicted of preaching without having taken the oath and fined $500; the Supreme Court of Missouri affirmed. On appeal to the Supreme Court of the United States, Cummings, represented by David Dudley Field, attacked the law as violating the Constitution of the United States, Article I, section 10, which provides "No State shall ... pass any Bill of Attainder, ex post facto Law or Law impairing the Obligation of Contracts." This provision had been applied by Chief Justice John Marshall in regard to contracts and described by him as "what may be deemed a bill of rights for the people of each state," *Fletcher v. Peck*, 10 U.S. (6 Cranch) 87, 137 (1810). Field made little of the statute's intrusion on religion except to say: "It would be strange, indeed, if a minister of the Gospel, whose sympathies are with all the children of men—the good and the sinful, the happy and the sorrowing—might not manifest such sympathy by an act of charity or a word of consolation." *Cummings*, 285.

Four pre-Civil War appointees voted against the statute. The swing vote was that of Stephen Field, whose brother David Dudley Field argued for Father Cummings. The Fields were sons of a country Congregationalist, a Massachusetts minister in Stockbridge. Stephen Field voted to uphold his brother's contention that Article I, section 10, had been violated. *Cummings*, 325, 327. Justice Field made no reference to religion as such having any special protection. The decision came down in the spring of 1867 and underscored the contemporary view that the Constitution did not extend the Bill of Rights to the states.

Four of five of Lincoln's appointees to the Court voted to uphold the statute. Their dissent was attached to *Ex parte Garland*, 71 U.S. (4 Wall.) 333 at 397 (1866). Samuel F. Miller, a Unitarian and religious liberal, wrote about religious rights.

Ex parte Garland, 71 U.S. (4 Wall.) 333 (1866)

In regard to the case of *Cummings v. The State of Missouri*, allusions have been made in the course of argument to the sanctity of the ministerial office, and to the inviolability of religious freedom in this country.

But no attempt has been made to show that the Constitution of the United States interposes any such protection between the State governments and their own citizens. Nor can anything of this kind be shown. The Federal Constitution contains but two provisions on this subject. One of these forbids Congress to make any law respecting the establishment of religion, or prohibiting the free exercise thereof. The other is, that no religious test shall ever be required as a qualification to any office or public trust under the United States.

No restraint is placed by that instrument on the action of the States; but on the contrary, in the language of Story, "the whole power over the subject of religion is left exclusively to the State governments, to be acted upon according to their own sense of justice and the State constitutions."

If there ever was a case calling upon this court to exercise all the power on this subject which properly belongs to it, it was the case of the Rev. B. Permoli.

An ordinance of the first municipality of the city of New Orleans imposed a penalty on any priest who should officiate at any funeral, in any other church than the obituary chapel. Mr. Permoli, a Catholic priest, performed the funeral services of his church over the body of one of his parishioners, inclosed in a coffin, in the Roman Catholic Church of St. Augustine. For this he was fined, and relying upon the vague idea advanced here, that the Federal Constitution protected him in the exercise of his holy functions, he brought the case to this court.

But hard as that case was, the court replied to him in the following language: "The Constitution (of the United States) makes no provision for protecting the citizens of the respective States in their religious liberties; this is left to the State constitutions and laws; nor is there any inhibition imposed by the Constitution of the United States in this respect on the States." Mr. Permoli's writ of error was, therefore, dismissed for want of jurisdiction.

In that case an ordinance of a mere local corporation forbids a priest, loyal to his government, from performing what he believed to be the necessary rites of his church over the body of his departed friend. This court said it could give him no relief.

In this case the constitution of the State of Missouri, the fundamental law of the people of that State, adopted by their popular vote, declares that no priest of any church shall exercise his ministerial functions, unless he will show, by his own oath, that he has borne a true allegiance to his government. This court now holds this constitutional provision void, on the ground that the Federal Constitution forbids it. I leave the two cases to speak for themselves.

———

That the Fourteenth Amendment was chiefly intended to protect the rights of the recently freed slaves is incontestable. The first sentence of section 1 denied the doctrine of *Dred Scott* that descendants of black slaves could never be citizens. The second sentence gave a constitutional basis for condemning laws discriminating against blacks. But did the amendment have implications for religious freedom and religious establishment?

Senate Debate on the Fourteenth Amendment, 1865

Senator Jacob M. Howard reported the amendment to the Senate from the Joint Committee on Reconstruction.

"Such is the character of the privileges and immunities spoken of in the second section of the fourth article of the Constitution. To these privileges and immunities, whatever they may be—for they are not and cannot be fully defined in their entire extent and precise nature—to these should be added the personal rights guaranteed and secured by the first eight amendments of the Constitution; such as the freedom of speech and of the press; the right of the people peaceably to assemble and petition the Government for a redress of grievances, a right appertaining to each and all the people; the right to keep and to bear arms; the right to be exempted from the quartering of soldiers in a house without the consent of the owner; the right to be exempt from unreasonable searches and seizures, and from any search or seizure except by virtue of a warrant issued upon a formal oath or affidavit; the right of an accused person to be informed of the nature of the accusation against him, and his right to be tried by an impartial jury of the vicinage; and also the right to be secure against excessive bail and against cruel and unusual punishments." *Cong. Globe,* 39th Cong., 1st Sess. 2765 (1865).

————

This statement does not mention freedom of religion, but purports to be illustrative, not comprehensive. As Professors Lash and Amar argue below, other legislators expressly mentioned religious freedom among the privileges and immunities secured under the new amendment.

Senator Luke Poland, former chief justice of Vermont, thought the privileges and immunities secured under the Fourteenth Amendment were coterminous with those secured in Article IV, section 2 of the original Constitution.

"The clause of the first proposed amendment, that 'no State shall make or enforce any law which shall abridge the privileges or immunities of citizens of the United States,' secures nothing beyond what was intended by the original provision in the Constitution, that 'the citizens of each State shall be entitled to all privileges and immunities of citizens in the several States'" *Id.* 296.

NOTES AND QUESTIONS

The nature of an amendment–even the first–is that it was not an "original provision in the Constitution." But is the focus on the founding generation misplaced? When the issue of the meaning of the religion clause after the Fourteenth Amendment, whose intent matters, the drafters of the First Amendment or of the Fourteenth? Professor Amar suggests that examining only the evidence of the late eighteenth century may be like looking for a set of lost keys at night time under a lamp post because that is where the light is. Akhil Reed Amar, *The Bill of Rights: Creation and Reconstruction* (1998). Precisely because of the passage of time after the founding period, attention must be paid to the intervening events that led up to the Civil War and the amendments adopted shortly after it.

Professor Lash has gathered evidence from the nineteenth century relevant to determining the meaning of the Fourteenth Amendment. Kurt T. Lash, "The Second Adoption of the Free Exercise Clause: Religious Exemptions under the Fourteenth Amendment," 88 *Northwestern L. Rev.* 1106, 1131–1137 (1994) (materials from abolitionist period). Contrary to the suggestion of Senator Poland, Lash argues skillfully that the framers of the Fourteenth Amendment intended the Privileges and Immunities of the newly emancipated slaves to include free exercise of religion, which had been violated by several states during the period of slavery. For example, Lash notes: "John Bingham, author of Section One of the Fourteenth Amendment, believed slavery violated basic principles of the Constitution, including the right 'to utter, according to conscience.' James Wilson, Chair of the House Judiciary Committee and sponsor of the Civil Rights Act of 1866, the provisions of which Section One was designed to embrace, noted slavery's 'incessant, unrelenting, aggressive warfare upon ... the purity of religion.' Lyman Trumbull, Wilson's cosponsor of the Civil Rights Act, reminded the Congress of the oppressive laws that existed under slavery, including provisions which prohibited blacks from 'exercising the function of a minister' and made it 'a highly penal offense for any person . . . to teach slaves.' Congressman James Ashley noted that 'slavery has silenced every free pulpit within its control.' According to Senator Henry Wilson, "religion, 'consisting in the performance of all known duties to God and our fellow men, never has been and never will be allowed free exercise in any community where slavery dwarfs the consciences of men.' " *Id.* at 1146 (notes omitted). Lash also argues that "the roots of the modern principle of nonestablishment are located in the contemporary understanding of personal freedom in the period just after the Civil War." Lash, "The Second Adoption of the Establishment Clause: The Rise of the Nonestablishment Principle," 27 *Ariz. St. L.J.* 1085 (1995).

The most explicit statement as to the meaning of section 1 was made by Representative John A. Bingham of Ohio, a member of the Joint Committee on Reconstruction and the actual draftsman of section 1. Charles Fairman, "Does the Fourteenth Amendment Incorporate the Bill of Rights?" 2 *Stan. L. Rev.* 5, 19, 21 (1949). On February 28, 1866, Bingham spoke on the floor of the House in "support of the proposed amendment to enforce the Bill of Rights." He asserted that the legislation he was reporting was "essential to the safety of all the people of every State" and repudiated the argument that the proposed amendment would "interfere with the reserved rights of the States." *Cong. Globe*, 39th Cong., 2d. Sess. ___ (1866). Running for reelection later that year, Bingham explained section 1 in a speech at Bowerstown, Ohio, on August 24.

"It is the spirit of Christianity embodied in your legislation. It is a simple, strong, plain declaration that equal laws and equal and exact justice shall hereafter be secured within every State of this Union by the combined power of all the people of every State. It takes from no State any right which hitherto pertained to the several States of the Union, but it imposes a limitation upon the States to correct their abuses of power, which hitherto did not exist within the letter of your Constitution, and which is essential to the nation's life. Look at that simple proposition. No State shall deny to any person, no matter whence he comes, or how poor, how weak, how simple—no matter how friendless—no State shall deny to any person within its jurisdiction the equal protection of the laws. If there be any man here who objects to a proposition as just as that, I would like him to rise in his place and let his neighbors look at him and see what manner of man he is. That proposition, I think, my fellow-citizens, needs no argument. No man can look his fellow-man in the face, surrounded by this clear light of heaven in which we live, and dare to utter the proposition that of right any State in the Union shall deny to any human being who behaves himself well the equal protection of the laws. Paralysis ought to strangle the utterance upon the tongue before a man should be guilty of the blasphemy of saying that he himself to the exclusion of his fellow man, should enjoy the protection of the laws. I hazard nothing, I think, in saying to the American people that the adoption of that amendment by the people, and its enforcement by the laws of the nation is, in the future, as essential to the safety and peace of this Republic, as is the air which surrounds us essential to the life of the people of the nation. Hereafter the American people can not have peace, if, as in the past, States are permitted to take away freedom of speech, and to condemn men, as felons, to the penitentiary for teaching their fellow men that there is a hereafter, and a reward for those who learn to do well." Fairman 76.

The reference to penalizing persons who teach "that there is a hereafter" probably is to slave-state laws against preaching to slaves. No reference is made to the establishment part of the First Amendment. Rather, Bingham endorses a kind of establishment: the embodiment in legislation of "the spirit of Christianity." Five years later Bingham returned to the scope of section 1 of the Fourteenth Amendment in a floor debate in the House of Representatives.

"Mr. Speaker, that the scope and meaning of the limitations imposed by the first section, fourteenth amendment of the Constitution may be more fully understood, permit me to say that the privileges and immunities of citizens of the United States, as contradistinguished from citizens of a State, are chiefly defined in the first eight amendments to the Constitution of the United States." *Cong. Globe,* 42nd Cong., 1st Sess. 151 (1871).

The statements of Howard and Bingham in 1866 are strong evidence that some sponsors of the Fourteenth Amendment intended to incorporate the Bill of Rights wholesale. Against this understanding, the amendment was ratified by states whose own constitutions were inconsistent with the Bill of Rights. Connecticut, the first to ratify, did not require indictment by grand jury as the Bill of Rights (Amendment VI) does. New Jersey did not require a jury trial in all civil suits as the Bill of Rights (Amendment VII) does. Most relevantly for our purposes, New Hampshire—the second state to ratify—had a Constitution modeled on that of Massachusetts of 1780, empowering the legislature to make provision through the towns for the support of "public Protestant teachers of piety, religion, and morality," and only Protestants were eligible to be governor or to sit in the legislature.

7. THE BLAINE AMENDMENT

On December 14, 1875, James G. Blaine, a leader of the Republican Party, introduced the following amendment to the Constitution.

House Version of Blaine Amendment, 1875

No State shall make any law respecting an establishment of religion or prohibiting the free exercise thereof; and no money raised by taxation in any State for the support of public schools, or derived from any public fund therefor, nor any public lands devoted thereto, shall ever be under the control of any religious sect, nor shall any money so raised or lands so devoted by divided between religious sects or denominations. 4 *Cong. Rec.* 205 (1875).

—————

The timing indicated that the Republicans saw the Blaine amendment as a campaign issue for 1876. It passed the House 116–5. *Id.* at 5192. The Senate Judiciary Committee made it much stronger.

Senate Version of Blaine Amendment, 1875

Sec. 1. No State shall make any law respecting an establishment of religion, or prohibiting the free exercise thereof; and no religious test shall ever be required as a qualification to any office or public trust under any State. No public property, and no public revenue of, nor any loan of credit by or under the authority of the United States, or any State, Territory, District, or municipal corporation, shall be appropriated to, or made or used for, the support of any school, educational or other institution, under the control of any religious or anti-religious sect, organization, or denomination, or wherein the particular creed or tenets of any religious or anti-religious sect, organization, or denomination shall be taught; and no such particular creed or tenets shall be read or taught in any school or institution supported in whole or in part by such revenue or loan of credit; and no such appropriation or loan of credit shall be made to any religious or anti-religious sect, organization, or denomination, or to promote its interests or tenets. This article shall not be construed to prohibit the reading of the Bible in any school or institution, and it shall not have the effect to impair rights of property already voted.

Sec. 2. Congress shall have power, by appropriate legislation, to provide for the prevention and punishment of violations of this article. *Id.* at 5580.

————

In debate, Senator George F. Edmunds read from the encyclical letter *Quanta cura* of Pius IX of December 8, 1864.

Senator Edmunds on the Blaine Amendment, 1867

Contrary to the teaching of the Holy Scriptures, of the Church, and of the holy fathers, these persons do not hesitate to assert that "the best condition of human society is that wherein no duty is recognized by the Government of correcting by enacted penalties the violators of the Catholic religion, except when the maintenance of the public peace requires it." From this totally false notion of social government they fear not to uphold that erroneous opinion most pernicious to the Catholic Church and to the salvation of souls which was called by our predecessor Gregory XVI ... "insanity" ... (*deliramentum*), namely, that "liberty of conscience and of worship is the right of every man; and that this right ought in every well governed state, to be proclaimed and asserted by law; and that the citizens possess the right of being unrestrained in the exercise of every kind of liberty, by any law, ecclesiastical or civil, so that they are authorized to publish and put forward openly all their ideas whatsoever, either by speaking, in print, or by any other method." But while these men make these rash assertions, they do not reflect or consider that they preach the liberty of perdition, (St. Augustine, Epistle 105, al. 106) and that, "if it is always free to human arguments to discuss men will never be wanting who will dare to resist the truth, and to rely upon the loquacity of human wisdom, when we know from the command of our Lord Jesus Christ how faith and Christian wisdom ought to avoid this most mischievous vanity" (St. Leo, Epistle 164, al. 133, section 2, Boll. edition).

————

Edmunds added a quotation from the *Syllabus of Errors*, a compendium of propositions also condemned by Pius IX:

45. The entire direction of public schools in which the youth of Christian states are educated, except (to a certain extent) in the case of episcopal seminaries, may and must appertain to the civil power, and belong to it so far that no other authority whatsoever shall be recognized as having any right to interfere in the discipline of the schools, the arrangement of the studies, the taking of degrees, or the choice and approval of the teachers.

———

In the light of this doctrine, Edmunds asked how the Democrats could oppose the amendment, *Congressional Record* 4: 5587–5588. The Democrats contended that the amendment would harm religious activities in all government hospitals, orphanages, prisons, and veterans' homes. *Id.* 5595. The amendment was rejected by the Senate. *Id.* 5595.

Both sides assumed and stated that without an amendment no federal constitutional provision controlled the states' support of religion. *See, e.g., id.* 5561 (Senator Freylinghuysen); 5589 (Senator Adlai Stevenson). Although the amendment was never adopted by the Congress, Senator Blaine wielded considerable influence in the Committee on Territories to ensure that some version of his proposed amendment was included in the state constitutions of Western territories seeking admission to the Union. For a clear contextual analysis of the bill, see Joseph P. Viteritti, "Choosing Equality: Religious Freedom and Educational Opportunity Under Constitutional Federalism," 15 *Yale L. & Policy Rev.* 113 (1996), and Stephen K. Green, "The Blaine Amendment Reconsidered," 36 *Am.J.Legal Hist.* 38, 54 (1992).

CHAPTER NINE

"THE CIVILIZATION WHICH CHRISTIANITY HAS PRODUCED": MARRIAGE, 1852–1890

NOTE. *The Latter-Day Saints.* On September 21, 1823, according to Mormon belief, the angel Moroni appeared to Joseph Smith telling him of the existence of a book of divine revelations, written by Moroni's father, Mormon. From this beginning came the organization, in 1830 in Fayette, New York, of the Church of Christ, later known as the Church of Jesus Christ of Latter–Day Saints. Jan Shipps, *Mormonism: The Story of a New Religious Tradition* (1987); Richard L. Bushman, *Joseph Smith and the Beginnings of Mormonism* 143 (1984); Leonard J. Arrington and Davis Bitton, *The Mormon Experience: A History of the Latter Day Saints* 8, 20–21 (1979). Tolerance, by now fairly general in the United States toward every variety of Protestant Christianity, was not extended to this new faith. It was hounded out of Missouri and Illinois. Joseph Smith was killed by a mob in 1844. Under Brigham Young, the Mormons emigrated West and founded a new "kingdom" of Deseret where, at first, religious services and civic meetings were generally combined. Arrington and Bitton 116, and Klaus J. Hansen, *Quest for Empire: The Political Kingdom of God and the Council of Fifty in Mormon History* (1970). In 1850, their community became a territory of the United States with Young as governor.

The novelty of a book added to Scripture, and the corporate enterprise of the Mormons and its substantial success, were irritants to their non-Mormon neighbors. But what led to the religious clash resulting in federal legislation challenging the church was more fundamental. In 1852 a general conference of the church announced that plural marriage was "justified" by the law of God for believing Saints. In fact polygamy was always less common than monogamy. But it was practiced by Mormon leaders, and exalted as the highest form of marriage. Richard S. Van Wagoner, *Mormon Polygamy, A History* (2d ed. 1989); B. Carmon Hardy, *Solemn Covenant: The Mormon Polygamous Passage* (1992). As late as 1880 the population of Utah consisted of 74,509 males and 69,454 females, a ratio suggesting how impractical widespread practice would have been. Polygamy, however, became the focal point of religious attention. It was opposed to the understanding of Scripture of virtually all other Christian denominations. Like slavery, the practice in the minds of its critics carried with it sinister suggestions of sexual licentiousness. Worse than slavery, it formally challenged the accepted sexual code of the rest of the country. Like the split on slavery, the division was deep; theological; past compromise. Either the Mormons were right about the relationship between the sexes or the challenged religious view was. The use of governmental power by those who believed in the traditional Christian sexual norms was seen as the way to meet the challenge. *See* Sarah Barringer Gordon, *The Mormon Question: Polygamy and Constitutional Conflict in Nineteenth–Century America* (2001).

Republican Party Platform, 1856

Resolved that the Constitution confers upon Congress sovereign power over the Territories of the United States for their government, and that in the exercise of this power it is both the right and the imperative duty of Congress to prohibit in the Territories those twin relics of barbarism, polygamy and slavery. George D. Ellis, ed., *Platforms of the Two Great Political Parties* [*Platforms*] 13 (1928).

————

The Democrats also saw political possibilities in the situation. Robert Taylor, a champion of southern rights, wrote President James Buchanan on April 27, 1857: "I believe that we can supersede the Negro–Mania with the almost universal excitements of an Anti–Mormon crusade," quoted in Norman F. Furniss, *The Mormon Conflict, 1850–1859* 74–75 (1960). When Buchanan later in 1857 ordered federal troops into the territory, it was seen by many as an effort to "root out polygamy as an affront to Christian morality." *Id.* 82. The "Mormon war" produced a truce of sorts, as the federal government asserted control over the territory, and Brigham Young and the Saints settled into a policy of resistance and agitation for statehood.

Not until the Civil War, however, did Congress actually legislate. It then passed "An Act to punish and prevent the Practice of Polygamy in the Territories of the United States." 12 *Stat.* 501–502 (1862). Bigamy was subjected to a $500 fine or five years' imprisonment. Acts of the territorial legislature incorporating the Church of Jesus Christ of the Latter-day Saints and countenancing polygamy were annulled, with the proviso that the act was to be "so limited and constructed" as not to affect existing property rights nor "the right 'to worship God according to the dictates of conscience.'" A further provision— "in the nature of a mortmain law," as Senator James Bayard told the Senate, *Cong. Globe*, 37th Cong. 2d Sess. 2506 (June 3, 1862)—limited future acquisitions by churches of real estate in any territory to $50,000. The measure had originated in the House, which had framed a bill as early as 1857. The sponsor in 1862 was Justin Morrill of Vermont; his measure passed the House without a record vote. *Cong. Globe*, 37th Cong. 2d Sess. 1847 (April 28, 1862). The most significant change made in the Senate was removal of a penalty for mere cohabitation without marriage. It was the formal institution of plural marriage to which Congress objected. *Cong. Globe*, 37th Cong. 2d Sess. 2506 (June 3, 1862). On July 2, 1862, Abraham Lincoln signed the bill into law. *Id.* 3082. The Morrill Act was not enforced during the Civil War. In the summer of 1865 Schuyler Colfax, Speaker of the House of Representatives, traveled to Salt Lake City to deliver a speech denouncing the "barbarism" of polygamy. Undertaking this journey before the completion of the transcontinental railroad was itself an indication of the seriousness of the polygamy issue for leaders in Washington. Dealing with polygamy so shortly after the end of the Civil War, when so much urgent business required the attention of the nation's leaders, was another sign that Congress was ready to focus on this issue with a greater level of intensity.

The completion of the Union Pacific in 1869 brought more non-Mormons— "Gentiles" to the Saints—into Utah. By 1869 there was also internal dissent. William Godbe was tried by the Church for heresy and was expelled, leading him to form the independent Church of Zion. Colfax, now vice-president of the

United States, seized upon this internal dissent as a reason to travel again to Salt Lake to urge the Mormons to give way on polygamy. Leonard J. Arrington, *Brigham Young: American Moses* 355, 361, 374–375 (1985). John Taylor, an apostle of the Church of Latter-day Saints, replied in the New York *Tribune*:

> Loyola did not invent and put into use the faggot, the flame, the sword, the thumbscrews, the rack and gibbet to persecute anybody; it was to purify the Church of heretics, as others would purify Utah. "Ours," says Mr. Colfax, "is a land of civil and religious liberty, and the faith of every man is a matter between himself and God alone," providing God don't shock our moral ideas by introducing something we don't believe in. If He does, let Him look out.

———

In 1870 the chaplain for the Senate, John P. Newman, a leading Methodist, traveled to Salt Lake City to debate Elder Orson Pratt, one of the "first ten" in Brigham Young's "first company" of pioneers to arrive in Utah in 1847. The debate took place in the Tabernacle, lasting three full days. The subject: "Does the Bible Sanction Polygamy?" Arrington and Bitton 178. Methodists and Presbyterians urged Congress to act. In 1874 Congress passed the proposal of Senator Luke Poland, another Vermonter, extending direct federal control over most legal cases in the territory. *Id.* 177.

In 1874 George Reynolds, secretary to Brigham Young, was indicted for bigamy. Married to Mary Ann Tuddenham, he had also married Amelia Jane Schofield. Reynolds was convicted and sentenced to two years at hard labor. He appealed to the Supreme Court of the United States. Chief Justice Morrison R. Waite delivered the opinion of the unanimous Court, treating Jefferson's political letter to the Danbury Baptists [Chapter Seven, section 1] as virtually on the same footing as the Annals of the First Congress. The Court adopted the "wall" metaphor for the first time.

Reynolds v. United States

98 U.S. 145 (1879).

As to the defence of religious belief or duty.

On the trial, the plaintiff in error, the accused, proved that at the time of his alleged second marriage he was, and for many years before had been, a member of the Church of Jesus Christ of Latter–Day Saints, commonly called the Mormon Church, and a believer in its doctrines; that it was an accepted doctrine of that church "that it was the duty of male members of said church, circumstances permitting, to practise polygamy; ... that this duty was enjoined by different books which the members of said church believed to be of divine origin, and among others the Holy Bible, and also that the members of the church believed that the practice of polygamy was directly enjoined upon the male members thereof by the Almighty God, in a revelation to Joseph Smith, the founder and prophet of said church; that the failing or refusing to practise polygamy by such male members of said church, when circumstances would admit, would be punished, and that the penalty for such failure and refusal would be damnation in the life to come." He also proved "that he had received permission from the recognized authorities in said church to enter into polygamous marriage; ... that Daniel H. Wells, one having authority in said church to perform the marriage ceremony, married the said defendant on or about the time the crime is alleged to have been committed, to some woman by the name of Schofield, and that such marriage ceremony was performed under and pursuant to the doctrines of said church."

Upon this proof he asked the court to instruct the jury that if they found from the evidence that he "was married as charged—if he was married—in pursuance of and in conformity with what he believed at the time to be a religious duty, that the verdict must be 'not guilty.'" This request was refused, and the court did charge "that there must have been a criminal intent, but that if the defendant, under the influence of a religious belief that it was right,—under an inspiration, if you please, that it was right,—deliberately married a second time, having a first wife living, the want of consciousness of evil intent—the want of understanding on his part that he was committing a crime—did not excuse him; but the law inexorably in such case implies the criminal intent."

Upon this charge and refusal to charge the question is raised, whether religious belief can be accepted as a justification of an overt act made criminal by the law of the land. The inquiry is not as to the power of Congress to prescribe criminal laws for the Territories, but as to the guilt of one who knowingly violates a law which has been properly enacted, if he entertains a religious belief that the law is wrong.

Congress cannot pass a law for the government of the Territories which shall prohibit the free exercise of religion. The first amendment to the Constitution expressly forbids such legislation. Religious freedom is guaranteed everywhere throughout the United States, so far as congressional interference is concerned. The question to be determined is, whether the law now under consideration comes within this prohibition.

The word "religion" is not defined in the Constitution. We must go elsewhere, therefore, to ascertain its meaning, and nowhere more appropriately, we think, than to the history of the times in the midst of which the provision was adopted. The precise point of the inquiry is, what is the religious freedom which has been guaranteed.

Before the adoption of the Constitution, attempts were made in some of the colonies and States to legislate not only in respect to the establishment of religion, but in respect to its doctrines and precepts as well. The people were taxed, against their will, for the support of religion, and sometimes for the support of particular sects to whose tenets they could not and did not subscribe. Punishments were prescribed for a failure to attend upon public worship, and sometimes for entertaining heretical opinions. The controversy upon this general subject was animated in many of the States, but seemed at last to culminate in Virginia. In 1784, the House of Delegates of that State having under consideration "a bill establishing provision for teachers of the Christian religion," postponed it until the next session, and directed that the bill should be published and distributed, and that the people be requested "to signify their opinion respecting the adoption of such a bill at the next session of assembly" [Chapter Six, section 1C].

This brought out a determined opposition. Amongst others, Mr. Madison prepared a "Memorial and Remonstrance," which was widely circulated and signed, and in which he demonstrated "that religion, or the duty we owe the Creator," was not within the cognizance of civil government [Chapter Six, section 1C]. At the next session the proposed bill was not only defeated, but another, "for establishing religious freedom," drafted by Mr. Jefferson, was passed. In the preamble of this act religious freedom is defined; and after a recital "that to suffer the civil magistrate to intrude his powers into the field of opinion, and to restrain the profession or propagation of principles on supposition of their ill tendency, is a dangerous fallacy which at once destroys all religious liberty," it is declared "that it is time enough for the rightful purposes of civil government for its officers to interfere when principles break out into overt acts against peace and good order" [Chapter Six, section 1B]. In these two sentences is found the true distinction between what properly belongs to the church and what to the State.

In a little more than a year after the passage of this statute the convention met which prepared the Constitution of the United States. Of this convention Mr. Jefferson was not a member, he being then absent as minister to France. As soon as he saw the draft of the Constitution proposed for adoption, he, in a letter to a friend, expressed his disappointment at the absence of an express declaration insuring the freedom of religion but was willing to accept it as it was, trusting that the good sense and honest intentions of the people would bring about the necessary alterations. Five of the States, while adopting the Constitution, proposed amendments. Three—New Hampshire, New York, and Virginia—included in one form or another a declaration of religious freedom in the changes they desired to have made, as did also North Carolina, where the convention at first declined to ratify the Constitution until the proposed amendments were acted upon. Accordingly, at the first session of the first Congress the amendment now under consideration was proposed with others by Mr. Madison. It met the views of the advocates of religious freedom, and was adopted. Mr. Jefferson afterwards, in reply to an address to him by a committee of the Danbury Baptist Association, took occasion to say: "Believing with you that religion is a matter which lies solely between man and his God; that he owes account to none other for his faith or his worship; that the legislative powers of the government reach actions only, and not opinions,—I contemplate with sovereign reverence that act of the whole American people which declared that their legislature should 'make no law respecting an establishment of religion or prohibiting the free exercise thereof' thus building a wall of separation between church and State. Adhering to this expression of the supreme will of the nation in behalf of the rights of conscience, I shall see with sincere satisfaction the progress of those sentiments which tend to restore man to all his natural rights, convinced he has no natural right in opposition to his social duties" [Chapter Seven, section 1]. Coming as this does from an acknowledged leader of the advocates of the measure, it may be accepted almost as an authoritative declaration of the scope and effect of the amendment thus secured. Congress was deprived of all legislative power over mere opinion, but was left free to reach actions which were in violation of social duties or subversive of good order.

Polygamy has always been odious among the northern and western nations of Europe, and, until the establishment of the Mormon Church, was almost exclusively a feature of the life of Asiatic and of African people. At common law, the second marriage was always void [citing Commentaries of Chancellor Kent], and from the earliest history of England polygamy has been treated as an offence against society. After the establishment of the ecclesiastical courts, and until the time of James I, it was punished through the instrumentality of those tribunals, not merely because ecclesiastical rights had been violated, but because upon the separation of the ecclesiastical courts from the civil the ecclesiastical were supposed to be the most appropriate for the trial of matrimonial causes and offences against the rights of marriage, just as they were for testamentary causes and the settlement of the estates of deceased persons.

By the statute of 1 James I, (c.11), the offence, if committed in England or Wales, was made punishable in the civil courts, and the penalty was death. As this statute was limited in its operation to England and Wales, it was at a very early period reenacted, generally with some modifications, in all the colonies. In connection with the case we are now considering, it is a significant fact that on the 8th of December, 1788, after the passage of the act establishing religious freedom, and after the convention of Virginia had recommended as an amendment to the Constitution of the United States the declaration in a bill of rights that "all men have an equal, natural, and unalienable right to the free exercise of religion, according to the dictates of conscience," the legislature of that State substantially enacted the statute of James I, death penalty included, because, as recited in the preamble, "it hath been doubted whether bigamy or polygamy be punishable by the laws of this Commonwealth" [citation omitted]. From that day to this we think it may safely be said there never has been a time in any State of the Union when polygamy has not been an offence against society, cognizable by the civil courts and punishable with more or less severity. In the face of all this evidence, it is impossible to believe that the constitutional guaranty of religious freedom was intended to prohibit legislation in respect to this most important feature of social life. Marriage, while from its very nature a sacred obligation, is nevertheless, in most civilized nations, a civil contract, and usually regulated by law. Upon it society may be said to be built, and out of its fruits spring social relations and social obligations and duties, with which government is necessarily required to deal. In fact, according as monogamous or polygamous marriages are allowed, do we find the principles on which the government of the people, to a greater or less extent, rests. Professor Lieber says, polygamy leads to the patriarchal principle, and which, when applied to large communities, fetters the people in stationary despotism, while that principle cannot long exist in connection with monogamy. Chancellor Kent observes that this remark is equally striking and profound [citation omitted]. An exceptional colony of polygamists under an exceptional leadership may sometimes exist for a time without appearing to disturb the social condition of the people who surround it; but there cannot be a doubt that, unless restricted by some form of constitution, it is within the legitimate scope of the power of every civil government to determine whether polygamy or monogamy shall be the law of social life under its dominion.

In our opinion, the statute immediately under consideration is within the legislative power of Congress. It is constitutional and valid as prescribing a rule of action for all those residing in the Territories, and in places over which the United States have exclusive control. This being so, the only question which remains, is, whether those who make polygamy a part of their religion are excepted from the operation of the statute. If they are, then those who do not make polygamy a part of their religious belief may be found guilty and punished, while those who do, must be acquitted and go free. This would be introducing a new element into criminal law. Laws are made for the government of actions, and while they cannot interfere with mere religious belief and opinions, they may with practices. Suppose one believed that human sacrifices were a necessary part of religious worship, would it be seriously contended that the civil government under which he lived could not interfere to prevent a sacrifice? Or if a wife religiously believed it was her duty to burn herself upon the funeral pile of her dead husband, would it be beyond the power of the civil government to prevent her carrying her belief into practice?

So here, as a law of the organization of society under the exclusive dominion of the United States, it is provided that plural marriages shall not be allowed. Can a man excuse his practices to the contrary because of his religious belief? To permit this would be to make the professed doctrines of religious belief superior to the law of the land, and in effect to permit every citizen to become a law unto himself. Government could exist only in name under such circumstances.

A criminal intent is generally an element of crime, but every man is presumed to intend the necessary and legitimate consequences of what he knowingly does. Here the accused knew he had been once married, and that his first wife was living. He also knew that his second marriage was forbidden by law. When, therefore, he married the second time, he is presumed to have intended to break the law. And the breaking of the law is the crime. Every act necessary to constitute the crime was knowingly done, and the crime was therefore knowingly committed. Ignorance of a fact may sometimes be taken as evidence of a want of criminal intent, but not ignorance of the law. The only defence of the accused in this case is his belief that the law ought not to have been enacted. It matters not that his belief was a part of his professed religion: it was still belief, and belief only.

In *Regina v. Wagstaff* [citation omitted], the parents of a sick child, who omitted to call in medical attendance because of their religious belief that what they did for its cure would be effective, were held not to be guilty of manslaughter, while it was said the contrary would have been the result if the child had actually been starved to death by the parents, under the notion that it was their religious duty to abstain from giving it food. But when the offence consists of a positive act which is knowingly done, it would be dangerous to hold that the offender might escape punishment because he religiously believed the law which he had broken ought never to have been made. No case, we believe, can be found that has gone so far.

As to that part of the charge which directed the attention of the jury to the consequences of polygamy.

The passage complained of is as follows: "I think it not improper, in the discharge of your duties in this case, that you should consider what are to be the consequences to the innocent victims of this delusion. As this contest goes on, they multiply, and there are pure-minded women and there are innocent children,—innocent in a sense even beyond the degree of the innocence of childhood itself. These are to be the sufferers; and as jurors fail to do their duty, and as these cases come up in the Territory of Utah, just so do these victims multiply and spread themselves over the land."

While every appeal by the court to the passions or the prejudices of a jury should be promptly rebuked, and while it is the imperative duty of a reviewing court to take care that wrong is not done in this way, we see no just cause for complaint in this case. Congress, in 1862 (12 Stat. 501), saw fit to make bigamy a crime in the Territories. This was done because of the evil consequences that were supposed to flow from plural marriages. All the court did was to call the attention of the jury to the peculiar character of the crime for which the accused was on trial, and to remind them of the duty they had to perform. There was no appeal to the passions, no instigation of prejudice. Upon the showing made by the accused himself, he was guilty of a violation of the law under which he had been indicted: and the effort of the court seems to have been not to withdraw the minds of the jury from the issue to be tried, but to bring them to it; not to make them partial, but to keep them impartial.

Upon a careful consideration of the whole case, we are satisfied that no error was committed by the court below. *Judgment affirmed.*

———

After a petition for rehearing, the judgment was remanded to enter the same verdict, except to the extent that it required imprisonment at hard labor.

NOTES AND QUESTIONS

Consider the function of the Court's citation to "Professor Lieber," a citation entirely derived from Chancellor James Kent's *Commentaries* (1844) 2:81, which stated that polygamy was prohibited because of "the precepts of Christianity and the laws of our social nature." Kent added, "Polygamy may be regarded as exclusively the feature of Asiatic manners, and of half civilized life, and to be incompatible with civilization, refinement and domestic felicity." In a footnote Kent referred to "Mr. Lieber," i.e., to the *Manual of Political Ethics* (1839) of Francis Lieber, a learned German immigrant who was professor of political science at South Carolina College.

Lieber and Kent both wrote before the Mormon experience of polygamy had been observed. By 1855, however, Lieber was asserting that polygamous Utah and its "theocracy" be denied statehood until the Church's power was broken. In 1865, now teaching at Columbia in New York, Lieber proposed a constitutional amendment outlawing polygamy. Lieber, "Contributions to Political Science," in 2 *Miscellaneous Writings* 173, 534 (1881). Lieber taught that the Mormons "deny the very first principles ... of our whole western civilization, as distinguished from oriental life." Lieber, *On Civil Liberty and Self-Government* 101 (1869). This unscientific assertion–which we would now brand as "pop sociology" was scarcely more than the hearty assertion of prejudice. It was supplemented by another guide, whom Waite did not acknowledge in the opinion: the historian George Bancroft, to whom he wrote on January 17, 1879: "As you gave me the information on which the judgment in the late polygamy case rests, I send you a copy of the opinion that you may see what use has been made of your facts." Bruce R. Trimble, *Chief Justice Waite* 244–245 (1938); see also C. Peter Magrath, "Chief Justice Waite and the 'Twin Relic': Reynolds v. United States," 18 *Vand. L. Rev.* 507, 531 (1965), and Carol Weisbrod & Pamela Sheingorn, "Reynolds v. United States: Nineteenth–Century Forms of Marriage and the Status of Women," 10 *Conn. L. Rev.* 828 (1978). It may reasonably be surmised that Waite owed to Bancroft the references to Jefferson's letter, now destined to be famous. Waite was an Episcopalian, regular and reverent in his practice. He described his opinion to a clergyman as "my sermon on the religion of polygamy." Trimble, 18, 244. Why did Waite invoke Jefferson's metaphor of the wall? Does that metaphor suggest at the very least that the government–in this case the judiciary–should not deliver such a "sermon on religion" in the official exercise of governmental power?

Note the reappearance of Locke's distinction between belief and acts. Most people would concede that the religious practices Waite mentions by way of analogy need to be restrained. Does he unfairly weight the argument by not noticing that the acts he mentions–human sacrifice and suicide—involve irremediable physical injury, while Mormons claimed that the act condemned by the statute was a consensual sexual relation?

Note, too the stark either/or alternative involved in Waite's position. For the criminal law to admit of exceptions based upon religious conscience would invite anarchy and would strip the government of all power. To excuse practices prohibited by the positive law on the basis of religious belief would be "to permit every citizen to become a law unto himself. Government could exist only in name under such circumstances."

The Republicans in 1880 again pressed on the nation the duty to "extirpate that relic of barbarism, polygamy." *Platforms* 46. Can a man excuse his practices to the contrary because of his religious belief? To permit this would be to make the professed doctrines of religious belief superior to the law of the land, and in effect to permit every citizen to become a law unto himself. Protestant criticism mounted. A new law was added in 1882, proposed by Senator George F. Edmunds, who like Morrill and Poland was a Vermonter. The 1862 act was amended. Persons practicing polygamy or believing it to be "right" were disqualified from sitting as jurors in polygamy cases. Practicing polygamists were disqualified from office and from voting. Cohabitation was made a misdemeanor, and persons cohabiting with more than one woman were disqualified like polygamists. A federal commission was created to supervise elections in Utah. Two provisions held out the carrot with the stick. The president was authorized to grant amnesty to polygamists. Their offspring born before January 1, 1883, were declared legitimate. Finally, careful provision was made that no one should be excluded from voting because of "any opinion" on polygamy, 22 Stat. 31–32. In 1884 the Republicans called for more action–including military action–to suppress polygamy and enforce the law against "the so-called Mormon Church."

Republican Party Platform, 1884

Resolved: That it is the duty of Congress to enact such laws as shall promptly and effectually suppress the system of polygamy within our Territories and divorce the political from the ecclesiastical power of the so-called Mormon Church; and that the laws so enacted shall be rigidly enforced by the civil authorities, if possible, and by the military if need be. *Platforms 65.*

―――――

Sections 5 of the Edmunds Act of 1882, 22 Stat. 30, provided "that in any prosecution for bigamy, polygamy, or unlawful cohabitation, under any statute of the United States, it shall be sufficient cause of challenge to any person drawn or summoned as a juryman ... that he believes it right for a man to have more than one living and undivorced wife at the same time." In 1884 Rudger Clawson was the first to be indicted under the new law. Fifteen of the prospective grand jurors were Mormons, all of whom were asked the following questions: "Do you believe in the doctrine and tenets of the Mormon church? Do you believe in the doctrine of plural marriage, as taught by the Mormon church? Do you believe it is right for a man to have more than one undivorced wife living at the same time?" Each prospective grand juror answering these questions in the affirmative was challenged for cause by the prosecuting attorney and was excluded from the grand jury. Composed exclusively of non-Mormons, the grand jury indicted Clawson on two counts, polygamy and cohabitation. The petit jury–from which all Mormons were likewise excluded–promptly convicted Clawson on both counts. On the first count–polygamy—the trial judge fined Clawson $500 and sentenced him to three and a half years in the Utah territorial penitentiary. On the second count–cohabitation–the judge fined Clawson an additional $350 and imposed a consecutive prison sentence of six months. Because of Clawson's defiance, the trial judge added that the defendant should be held in prison until the fines were paid. Clawson's appeal challenged the composition of the grand and petit juries. The Court, per Justice Samuel Blatchford, dismissed Clawson's challenge to the statute and sustained his conviction and penalties. *Clawson v. United States*, 114 U.S. 477 (1885). Clawson served four years for his crime, but is remembered among Mormons as a martyr. *See* Stan Larson, ed. *Prisoner for Polygamy: The Memoirs and Letters of Rudger Clawson at the Utah Territorial Penitentiary, 1884–87* (1994).

Emboldened by the *Clawson* case, the government announced that it would prosecute vigorously under the new statute. *See* Sarah Barringer Gordon, "The Erosion of Sympathy," chapter 5 in *The Mormon Question: Polygamy and Constitutional Conflict in Nineteenth–Century America* (2001) (95% of criminal prosecutions in the Utah territory were for polygamy and related offenses). As arrests and prosecutions increased, prominent churchmen in Utah went into hiding. This period of Mormon history is known as "the underground." Arrington and Bitton 181.

The Court made life a little easier for zealous prosecutors. Angus M. Cannon—a Mormon who lived with two women, Amanda and Clara, each of whom was known as "Mrs. Cannon" and each of whom alternated in sharing meals with him—was convicted in 1885. Angus Cannon claimed that there was no proof that he had actually "cohabited" with Amanda and Clara. The government had not established that he had actually had sexual intercourse with either Amanda or Clara. Reviewing the conviction immediately, the Supreme Court upheld the conviction, interpreting "cohabit" to mean "to live together as husband and wife." Proof of actual sexual intercourse was irrelevant. *Cannon v. United States*, 116 U.S. 55 (1885). Justices Miller and Field dissented.

Congress was now determined to push further. The Edmunds–Tucker Act, declared forfeit the property of the Church itself. John T. Caine, Utah's delegate to Congress, spoke warmly against the bill, emphasizing the honesty, prosperity, and patriotism of the Mormons and comparing their plight to persecuted English Puritans, Irish Catholics, and French Huguenots. 18 *Cong. Rec.* 585–586 (January 12, 1887). Congressmen supporting the bill did not disguise their target: the Church itself.

Rep. Ezra B. Taylor on the Edmunds–Tucker Act, January 12, 1887

That church governs all things with a steady and relentless hand; it disposes of liberty; it dictates laws and practices. . . . This people and this church defy the moral sense of the civilized world and are of necessity antagonistic to the principles and institution of the Republic. *Id.* 584.

Rep. Lucien Bonaparte Caswell on the Edmunds–Tucker Act, January 12, 1887

The bill strikes at the very root of the church. It absolutely repeals the charter which gave it existence. *Id.* 592.

———

John R. Tucker, closing on behalf of the House Committee on the Judiciary, focused on the Lockean distinction between belief and overt acts, but he cited the Gospel [Mark 10: 7–8] as the warrant for the "law of every state in Christendom."

Rep. John Tucker on the Edmunds–Tucker Act, January 12, 1887

I do not care what the Mormon believes. But he must not believe and act upon his belief if it violates the right of any other man or violates the power of the Government and its laws for the peace and good order of society. That is all. I do not object to his saying that he or some other man ought to have two wives or more; but I do not intend to let him or that other man have more than one. If you are not a polygamist in act I do not care what you believe; but I do care very much what you do. When religious belief breaks out into the overt act of polygamy it is time for the civil government to interfere to preserve the peace, purity, and good order of society.

Now, Mr. Speaker, that being the power of Congress, what is it the duty of Congress to do? What is polygamy? It is a crime by the law of every state in Christendom. Ever since Christ interpreted the Judaic law and gave it to us in His own express words it has been not only a sin against God, but has been made a crime by every Christian society. Mark His words:

"For this cause shall a man leave his father and mother, and cleave to his wife; and they twain—not a whole bundle of them, but they twain— shall be one flesh: so then they are no more twain, but one flesh."

Ever since Christ uttered that language all of the Japhetic race have adopted monogamy as the only foundation of a decent civilization. *Id.* 593.

————

On February 18, 1887, the Senate approved the conference report, which reconciled the House and Senate versions of the bill. The Edmunds–Tucker Act became law without the signature of President Grover Cleveland. The Idaho Territory went even further than Congress, using three devices with an old pedigree in ecclesiastical controversies: oaths, charges of conspiracy, and a ban on speech. Samuel D. Davis was prosecuted not for the prohibited conduct of polygamy, but for conspiracy to violate section 501 of the Revised Statutes of the Territory of Idaho, which barred from holding office or even from voting any "bigamist or polygamist, or [one] who teaches, advises, counsels, or encourages any person or persons to become bigamists or polygamists." Conspiracy was charged on the theory that Davis and other Mormons had agreed to take falsely the oath prescribed by the territorial statute.

Anti-Mormon Test Oath, Revised Statutes of the Territory of Idaho, Section 501

I am not a bigamist or polygamist. . . . I am not a member of any order, organization, or association . . . which practices bigamy or polygamy or plural or celestial marriage as a doctrinal rite of such organization. I do not and will not, publicly or privately, or in any manner whatever, teach, advise, counsel, or encourage any person to commit the crime of bigamy or polygamy. . . .

————

Like the anti-Catholic oath of the Massachusetts Constitution of 1780 [Chapter Six, section 2], this oath proscribed the objectionable belief, delicately avoiding mention of the Church whose beliefs were being condemned. Like that other oath, it anticipated evasion and tried to prevent it. Unlike that other oath, it even forbade advocacy. Davis was found guilty and sentenced to a $500 fine or 250 days in jail. He applied at once for habeas corpus. Counsel before the Supreme Court assailed the Idaho territorial statute on two grounds. It inhibited the free exercise of religion in violation of the First Amendment, and required an oath that violated Article VI of the Constitution. The author of the unanimous opinion of the Court was Justice Stephen J. Field. The Edmunds–Tucker Act contained one of the most invidious features of an established religion, imposing deprivation of civil liberties on non-members of the preferred group. The Court scarcely noticed the new issue the case raised. Unlike Waite, Field candidly acknowledged the relevance of Christianity.

Davis v. Beason

133 U.S. 333 (1890).

On this appeal our only inquiry is whether the District Court of the Territory had jurisdiction of the offence charged in the indictment of which the defendant was found guilty. If it had jurisdiction, we can go no farther. We cannot look into any alleged errors in its rulings on the trial of the defendant. The writ of *habeas corpus* cannot be turned into a writ of error to review the action of that court. Nor can we inquire whether the evidence established the fact alleged, that the defendant was a member of an order or organization known as the Mormon Church, called the Church of Jesus Christ of Latter–Day Saints, or the fact that the order or organization taught and counselled its members and devotees to commit the crimes of bigamy and polygamy as duties arising from membership therein. On this hearing we can only consider whether, these allegations being taken as true, an offence was committed of which the territorial court had jurisdiction to try the defendant. And on this point there can be no serious discussion or difference of opinion. Bigamy and polygamy are crimes by the laws of all civilized and Christian countries. They are crimes by the laws of the United States, and they are crimes by the laws of Idaho. They tend to destroy the purity of the marriage relation, to disturb the peace of families, to degrade woman and to debase man. Few crimes are more pernicious to the best interests of society and receive more general or more deserved punishment. To extend exemption from punishment for such crimes would be to shock the moral judgment of the community. To call their advocacy a tenet of religion is to offend the common sense of mankind. If they are crimes, then to teach, advise and counsel their practice is to aid in their commission, and such teaching and counselling are themselves criminal and proper subjects of punishment, as aiding and abetting crime are in all other cases.

The term "religion" has reference to one's views of his relations to his Creator, and to the obligations they impose of reverence for his being and character, and of obedience to his will. It is often confounded with the *cultus* or form of worship of a particular sect, but is distinguishable from the latter. The first amendment to the Constitution, in declaring that Congress shall make no law respecting the establishment of religion, or forbidding the free exercise thereof, was intended to allow every one under the jurisdiction of the United States to entertain such notions respecting his relations to his Maker and the duties they impose as may be approved by his judgment and conscience, and to exhibit his sentiments in such form of worship as he may think proper, not injurious to the equal rights of others, and to prohibit legislation for the support of any religious tenets, or the modes of worship of any sect. The oppressive measures adopted, and the cruelties and punishments inflicted by the governments of Europe for many ages, to compel parties to conform, in their religious beliefs and modes of worship, to the views of the most numerous sect, and the folly of attempting in that way to control the mental operations of persons, and enforce an outward conformity to a prescribed standard, led to the adoption of the amendment in question. It was never intended or supposed that the amendment could be invoked as a protection against legislation for the punishment of acts inimical to the peace, good order and morals of society. With man's relations to his Maker and the obligations he may think they impose, and the manner in which an expression shall be made by him of his belief on those subjects, no interference can be permitted, provided always the laws of society, designed to secure its peace and prosperity, and the morals of its people, are not interfered with. However free the exercise of religion may be, it must be subordinate to the criminal laws of the country, passed with reference to actions regarded by general consent as properly the subjects of punitive legislation. There have been sects which denied as part of their religious tenets that there should be any marriage tie, and advocated promiscuous intercourse of the sexes as prompted by the passions of its members. And history discloses the fact that the necessity of human sacrifices, on special occasions, has been a tenet of many sects. Should a sect of either of these kinds ever find its way into this country, swift punishment would follow the carrying into effect of its doctrines, and no heed would be given to the pretence that, as religious beliefs, their supporters could be protected in their exercise by the Constitution of the United States. Probably never before in the history of this country has it been seriously contended that the whole punitive power of the government for acts recognized by the general consent of the Christian world in modern times as proper matters for prohibitory legislation, must be suspended in order that the tenets of a religious sect encouraging crime may be carried out without hindrance....

It is assumed by counsel of the petitioner, that because no mode of worship can be established or religious tenets enforced in this country, therefore any form of worship may by followed and any tenets, however destructive of society, may be held and advocated, if asserted to be a part of the religious doctrines of those advocating and practising them. But nothing is further from the truth. Whilst legislation for the establishment of a religion is forbidden, and its free exercise permitted, it does not follow that everything which may be so called can be tolerated. Crime is not the less odious because sanctioned by what any particular sect may designate as religion....

NOTE. *Premature Rumors of the Death of a Church that Perseveres.* Shortly after *Davis* was decided, a case involving forfeiture of the property of the Church under the Edmunds–Tucker Act reached the Supreme Court. The statute itself exempted buildings used for worship from confiscation. The government valued the rest of the Church's property at $3,000,000. It seized both real property owned by the church and cash on hand, amounting to about $382,000. *See* Paul G. Kauper & Steven C. Ellis, "Religious Corporations and the Law," 71 *Michigan Law Review* 1499, 1517 (1973); Leonard J. Arrington, *Great Basin Kingdom: An Economic History of the Latter-day Saints, 1830–*

1900 (1960). After the argument in January 1889, the Supreme Court postponed decision, a suspended execution bringing pressure on the Church to prepare to conform. In May 1890, Justice Joseph Bradley wrote the majority opinion. Bradley had been brought up in the Dutch Reformed Church, but his religious opinions had evolved to the point where he believed that Christ "taught no dogmas but one—that God is our Father and that we are all brethren," Bradley, "Esoteric Thoughts on Religion and Religionism" (1876), in Charles Bradley, ed., *Miscellaneous Writings of Joseph Bradley* 431 (1902). As in other parts of the West, the government was the "grantor" of all or most of the Mormon-held land. In Bradley's legal reasoning, this meant that the land should revert to the government when it decided that a religious corporation should cease to exist. After all, as the Court would say a century later in the disposition of a free exercise claim by Native Americans, the government should be able to dispose of "its land" as "it sees fit." *Lyng v. Northwest Indian Cemetery Protective Association* [Chapter Eleven, section, 11]. The heart of Bradley's opinion, however, was his view of polygamy in relation to Christian civilization: it was "barbarous" and that ended the matter. In his eyes, the claim of the Mormons that their religious beliefs merited the "protection of the constitutional guaranty of religious freedom ... is altogether a sophistical plea." He echoed Chief Justice Waite's worry about human sacrifice in *Reynolds*. Plural marriage—consensual sex—was analogized to "the offering of human sacrifices by our own ancestors in Britain ... sanctioned by an equally conscientious impulse." Worse yet, Mormon polygamists were like the "Thugs of India imagin[ing] that their belief in the right of assassination was a religious belief." The assets of the church may be seized; no, they must be seized. The Saints think of themselves as privileged to have received a revelation from Jesus Christ in the "latter days." In the lethal styling of the case, however, their church was deemed "late," dead. The Mormons are now the fastest growing religious community in the world. It was the Court that dealt the death blow.

The Late Corporation of the Church of Jesus Christ of Latter–Day Saints v. United States, Romney v. United States

136 U.S. 1 (1890).

The next question is, whether Congress or the court had the power to cause the property of the said corporation to be seized and taken possession of, as was done in this case....

When a business corporation, instituted for the purposes of gain, or private interest, is dissolved, the modern doctrine is, that its property, after payment of its debts, equitably belongs to its stockholders. But this doctrine has never been extended to public or charitable corporations. As to these, the ancient and established rule prevails, namely: that when a corporation is dissolved, its personal property, like that of a man dying without heirs, ceases to be the subject of private ownership, and becomes subject to the disposal of the sovereign authority; whilst its real estate reverts or escheats to the grantor or donor, unless some other course of devolution has been directed by positive law, though still subject as we shall hereafter see to the charitable use. To this rule the corporation in question was undoubtedly subject. But the grantor of all, or the principal part, of the real estate of the Church of Jesus Christ of Latter–Day Saints was really the United States, from whom the property was derived by the church, or its trustees, through the operation of the town site act. Besides, as we have seen, the act of 1862 expressly declared that all real estate acquired or held by any of the corporations or associations therein mentioned, (of which the Church of Jesus Christ of Latter–Day Saints was one), contrary to the provisions of that act, should be forfeited and escheat to the United States, with a saving of existing vested rights. The act prohibited the acquiring or holding of real estate of greater value than $50,000 in a Territory, and no legal title had vested in any of the lands in Salt Lake City at that time, as the town site act was not passed until March 2, 1867. There can be no doubt, therefore, that the real estate of the corporation in question could not, on its dissolution, revert or pass to any other person or persons than the United States. . . .

It is distinctly stated in the pleadings and findings of fact, that the property of the said corporation was held for the purpose of religious and charitable uses. But it is also stated in the findings of fact, and is a matter of public notoriety, that the religious and charitable uses intended to be subserved and promoted are the inculcation and spread of the doctrines and usages of the Mormon Church, or Church of Latter–Day Saints, one of the distinguishing features of which is the practice of polygamy—a crime against the laws, and abhorrent to the sentiments and feelings of the civilized world. Notwithstanding the stringent laws which have been passed by Congress—notwithstanding all the efforts made to suppress this barbarous practice—the sect or community composing the Church of Jesus Christ of Latter–Day Saints perseveres, in defiance of law, in preaching, upholding, promoting and defending it. It is a matter of public notoriety that its emissaries are engaged in many countries in propagating this nefarious doctrine, and urging its converts to join the community in Utah. The existence of such a propaganda is a blot on our civilization. The organization of a community for the spread and practice of polygamy is, in a measure, a return to barbarism. It is contrary to the spirit of Christianity and of the civilization which Christianity has produced in the Western world. The question, therefore, is whether the promotion of such a nefarious system and practice, so repugnant to our laws and to the principles of our civilization, is to be allowed to continue by the sanction of the government itself; and whether the funds accumulated for that purpose shall be restored to the same unlawful uses as heretofore, to the detriment of the true interests of civil society.

It is unnecessary here to refer to the past history of the sect, to their defiance of the government authorities, to their attempt to establish an independent community, to their efforts to drive from the territory all who were not connected with them in communion and sympathy. The tale is one of patience on the part of the American government and people, and of contempt of authority and resistance to law on the part of the Mormons. Whatever persecutions they may have suffered in the early part of their history, in Missouri and Illinois, they have no excuse for their persistent defiance of law under the government of the United States.

One pretense for this obstinate course is, that their belief in the practice of polygamy, or in the right to indulge in it, is a religious belief, and, therefore, under the protection of the constitutional guaranty of religious freedom. This is altogether a sophistical plea. No doubt the Thugs of India imagined that their belief in the right of assassination was a religious belief, but their thinking so did not make it so. The practice of suttee by the Hindu widows may have sprung from a supposed religious conviction. The offering of human sacrifices by our own ancestors in Britain was no doubt sanctioned by an equally conscientious impulse. But no one, on that account, would hesitate to brand these practices, now, as crimes against society, and obnoxious to condemnation and punishment by the civil authority.

The State has a perfect right to prohibit polygamy, and all other open offenses against the enlightened sentiment of mankind, notwithstanding the pretense of religious conviction by which they may be advocated and practised. *Davis v. Beason* [above]. And since polygamy has been forbidden by the laws of the United States, under severe penalties, and since the Church of Jesus Christ of Latter–Day Saints has persistently used and claimed the right to use, and the unincorporated community still claims the same right to use the funds with which the late corporation was endowed for the purpose of promoting and propagating the unlawful practice as an integral part of their religious usages, the question arises, whether the government, finding these funds without legal ownership, has or has not, the right, through its courts, and in due course of administration, to cause them to be seized and devoted to objects of undoubted charity and useful-ness—such for example as the maintenance of schools—for the benefit of the community whose leaders are now misusing them in the unlawful manner above described; setting apart, however, for the exclusive posses-sion and use of the church, sufficient and suitable portions of the property for the purposes of public worship, parsonage buildings and burying grounds, as provided in the law....

As to the constitutional question, we see nothing in the act which, in our judgment, transcends the power of Congress over the subject. We have already considered the question of its power to repeal the charter of the corporation. It certainly also had power to direct proceedings to be institut-ed for the forfeiture and escheat of the real estate of the corporation; and, if a judgment should be rendered in favor of the government in these proceedings, the power to dispose of the proceeds of the lands thus forfeited and escheated, for the use and benefit of common schools in the Territory, is beyond dispute. It would probably have power to make such a disposition of the proceeds if the question were merely one of charitable uses, and not of forfeiture. Schools and education were regarded by the Congress of the Confederation as the most natural and obvious appliances for the pro-motion of religion and morality. In the ordinance of 1787, passed for the government of the Territory Northwest of the Ohio, it is declared, Art. 3, "Religion, morality and knowledge, being necessary to good government and the happiness of mankind, schools and the means of education shall forever be encouraged." Mr. Dane, who is reputed to have drafted the said ordinance, speaking of some of the statutory provisions of the English law regarding charities as inapplicable to America, says: "But in construing these laws, rules have been laid down, which are valuable in every State; as that the erection of schools and the relief of the poor are always right, and the law will deny the application of private property only as to uses the nation deems superstitious." 4 Dane's Abridg. 239.

The only remaining constitutional question arises upon that part of the 17th section of the act, under which the present proceedings were instituted. We do not well see how the constitutionality of this provision can be seriously disputed, if it be conceded or established that the corporation ceased to exist, and that its property thereupon ceased to have a lawful owner, and reverted to the care and protection of the government as *parens patriae*....

The application of Romney and others, representing the unincorporated members of the Church of Jesus Christ of Latter–Day Saints, is fully disposed of by the considerations already adduced. The principal question discussed has been, whether the property of the church was in such a condition as to authorize the government and the court to take possession of it and hold it until it shall be seen what final disposition of it should be made; and we think it was in such a condition, and that it is properly held in the custody of the receiver. The rights of the church members will necessarily be taken into consideration in the final disposition of the case. There is no ground for granting their present application. The property is in the custody of the law, awaiting the judgment of the court as to its final disposition in view of the illegal uses to which it is subject in the hands of the Church of Latter–Day Saints, whether incorporated or unincorporated. The conditions for claiming possession of it by the members of the sect or community under the act do not at present exist.

The attempt made, after the passage of the act on February 19, 1887, and whilst it was in the president's hands for his approval or rejection, to transfer the property from the trustee then holding it to other persons, and for the benefit of different associations, was so evidently intended as an evasion of the law, that the court below justly regarded it as void and without force or effect.

We have carefully examined the decree, and do not find anything in it that calls for a reversal. It may perhaps require modification in some matters of detail, and for that purpose only the case is reserved for further consideration.

Chief Justice Fuller, with whom concurred Justice Field and Justice Lamar, dissented as to the power of Congress to confiscate the property.

————

The Mormons had been confident that they were protected by the Constitution, which they believed to be divinely inspired. Joseph Smith in 1833 had received a revelation that God "established the constitution of this land, by the hands of wise men whom [He] raised up unto this very purpose." 98 *Book of Doctrine and Covenants, Reorganized Church of Jesus Christ of Latter–Day Saints* 10 (1970). When the Supreme Court permitted the Church's property to be confiscated, Mormons were confronted with circumstances that made polygamy the sure source of the church's obliteration. On September 25, 1890, Wilford Woodruff, the presiding officer of the Church, announced what became known as "the Manifesto."

Wilford Woodruff, The Mormon Manifesto, September 25, 1890

Inasmuch as laws have been enacted by Congress forbidding plural marriages, which laws have been pronounced constitutional by the court of last resort, I hereby declare my intention to submit to those laws, and to use any influence with the members of the Church over which I preside to have them do likewise. Arrington and Bitton 183; *see also* Thomas G. Alexander, *Things in Heaven and Earth: The Life and Times of Wilford Woodruff, A Mormon Prophet* (1994).

———

Without conceding a change in belief, President Woodruff acknowledged that circumstances no longer made the practice applicable. No matter how Woodruff was to explain the shift to the Saints, it is difficult to refrain from characterizing it as a change of belief that had come to pass because of federal law applied directly against a church. In 1893 the government returned personal property seized from the church. In 1896 Congress returned the church's real property confiscated under the statute. In the same year it admitted Utah as a state.

NOTE. *The Relevance of the Mormon Cases.* In *Reynolds* Chief Justice Waite suggested that to take the free exercise claim seriously would, in effect, invite anarchy. The Court moved beyond binary thinking of this sort when it required vigorous judicial protection of free exercise in cases such as *Sherbert v. Verner* [Chapter Eleven, section 5] and *Wisconsin v. Yoder* [Chapter Eleven, section 7]. These cases stood for the proposition that a statute burdening the free exercise of religion may stand only if the law in general, and the government's refusal to allow a religious exemption in particular, are justified by a compelling interest that cannot be served by less restrictive means. When the Court severely limited that approach in *Employment Division v. Smith* [Chapter Eleven, section 10], Justice Scalia invoked *Reynolds* for the view that anarchy–imagined to be the consequence of taking free exercise seriously–makes strict scrutiny of religious claims a "luxury" we cannot afford, and makes the repression of minority religions an "unavoidable consequence of democratic government." Concurring in *Smith*, Justice O'Connor wrote: "The compelling interest test reflects the First Amendment's mandate of preserving religious liberty to the fullest extent possible in a pluralistic society. For the Court to deem this command a 'luxury,' is to denigrate [t]he very purpose of a Bill of Rights." Before you turn to the study of these cases in Chapter Eleven, do you have an intuitive view about which approach seems more correct in light of your reflection on the Mormon cases?

In *Church of the Lukumi Babalu Aye, Inc. v. City of Hialeah* [Chapter Eleven, section 12], the Court ruled that a series of municipal ordinances expressly targeting the practices of an unpopular religious minority violated the free exercise principle. The Court reaffirmed *Employment Division v. Smith* in this decision. Again, without anticipating the details of these later cases, do they shed any light on the way that Congress targeted the practice of the Mormon church?

In *City of Boerne v. Flores* [Chapter Eleven, section 11], Justice Kennedy acknowledged that government "persecution" of a religion is impermissible. Whatever this comment on "persecution" might entail, it surely is not a very precise judicial standard for knowing when free exercise is inhibited. Even so, was this loose "standard" violated when 95% of the government's prosecutions in the Utah territory were for bigamy and related offenses, and were tried by juries from which all Mormons had been excluded? Justice Bradley alluded tentatively to the hostility directed at Mormons but denied its relevance to the case at hand. "Whatever persecutions they *may have suffered* in the early part of their history, in Missouri and Illinois, they have no excuse for their persistent defiance of law under the government of the United States." If the burning of a community's homes and buildings and the assassination of its leader do not suffice to establish a claim of persecution, what would it take to move a practice beyond the subjunctive: "whatever persecutions they *actually suffered*"? And if the test has no consequence on facts like these ("they have no excuse for their persistent defiance of laws"), of what ability is the persecution "test"?

Should the Mormon cases be reaffirmed today [Chapter Sixteen, section 1]? All of them? If not, which ones? Why?

Chapter Ten

"THE MASS OF ORGANIC UTTERANCES": GOVERNMENTAL BENEVOLENCE, 1890–1940

1. "A RELIGIOUS PEOPLE . . . A CHRISTIAN NATION"

Justice David J. Brewer, grandson of a New England Congregationalist minister and son of a Congregationalist missionary to Turkey, found a religious exemption to a generally applicable statute, the Alien Contract Labor Act of 1885, which did not provide any express exemption for religious employees. A unanimous Court supplied the exemption, finding it incredible that "a Congress of the United States intended to make it a misdemeanor for a church of this country to contract for the services of a christian minister residing in another nation." Brewer used the case as a vehicle for affirming what he declared to be the religion of America.

Holy Trinity Church v. United States
143 U.S. 457 (1892).

Plaintiff in error is a corporation, duly organized and incorporated as a religious society under the laws of the State of New York. E. Walpole Warren was, prior to September 1887, an alien residing in England. In that month the plaintiff in error made a contract with him, by which he was to remove to the city of New York and enter into its service as rector and pastor; and in pursuance of such contract, Warren did so remove and enter upon such service. It is claimed by the United States that this contract on the part of the plaintiff in error was forbidden by the act of February 26, 1885, 23 Stat. 332, c. 164, and an action was commenced to recover the penalty prescribed by that act. The Circuit Court held that the contract was within the prohibition of the statute, and rendered judgment accordingly, and the single question presented for our determination is whether it erred in that conclusion.

The first section describes the act forbidden, and is in these words: *"Be it enacted by the Senate and House of Representatives of the United States of America in Congress assembled,* That from and after the passage of this act it shall be unlawful for any person, company, partnership, or corporation, in any manner whatsoever, to prepay the transportation, or in any way assist or encourage the importation or migration of any alien or aliens, any foreigner or foreigners, into the United States, its Territories, or the District of Columbia, under contract or agreement, parol or special, express or implied, made previous to the importation or migration of such alien or aliens, foreigner or foreigners, to perform labor or service of any kind in the United States, its Territories, or the District of Columbia."

It must be conceded that the act of the corporation is within the letter of this section, for the relation of rector to his church is one of service, and implies labor on the one side with compensation on the other. Not only are the general words labor and service both used, but also, as it were to guard against any narrow interpretation and emphasize a breadth of meaning, to them is added "of any kind;" and, further, as noticed by the Circuit Judge in his opinion, the fifth section, which makes specific exceptions, among them professional actors, artists, lecturers, singers and domestic servants, strengthens the idea that every other kind of labor and service was intended to be reached by the first section. While there is great force to this reasoning, we cannot think Congress intended to denounce with penalties a transaction like that in the present case. It is a familiar rule, that a thing may be within the letter of the statute and yet not within the statute, because not within its spirit, nor within the intention of its makers. This has been often asserted, and the reports are full of cases illustrating its application. This is not the substitution of the will of the judge for that of the legislator, for frequently words of general meaning are used in a statute, words broad enough to include an act in question, and yet a consideration of the whole legislation, or of the circumstances surrounding its enactment, or of the absurd results which follow from giving such broad meaning to the words, makes it unreasonable to believe that the legislator intended to include the particular act....

We find, therefore, that the title of the act, the evil which was intended to be remedied, the circumstances surrounding the appeal to Congress, the reports of the committee of each house, all concur in affirming that the intent of Congress was simply to stay the influx of this cheap unskilled labor.

But beyond all these matters no purpose of action against religion can be imputed to any legislation, state or national, because this is a religious people. This is historically true. From the discovery of this continent to the present hour, there is a single voice making this affirmation. The commission to Christopher Columbus, prior to his sail westward, is from "Ferdinand and Isabella, by the grace of God, King and Queen of Castile," etc., and recites that "it is hoped that by God's assistance some of the continents and islands in the ocean will be discovered," etc. The first colonial grant, that made to Sir Walter Raleigh in 1584, was from "Elizabeth, by the grace of God, of England, Fraunce and Ireland, queene, defender of the faith," etc.; and the grant authorizing him to enact statutes for the government of the proposed colony provided that "they be not against the true Christian faith nowe professed in the Church of England." The first charter of Virginia, granted by King James I in 1606, after reciting the application of certain parties for a charter, commenced the grant in these words: "We, greatly commending, and graciously accepting of, their Desires for the Furtherance of so noble a Work, which may, by the Providence of Almighty God, hereafter tend to the Glory of his Divine Majesty, in propagating of Christian Religion to such People, as yet live in Darkness and miserable Ignorance of the true Knowledge and Worship of God, and may in time bring the Infidels and Savages, living in those parts, to human Civility, and to a settled and quiet Government; DO, by these our Letters–Patents, graciously accept of, and agree to, their humble and well-intended Desires."

Language of similar import may be found in the subsequent charters of that colony, from the same king, in 1609 and 1611; and the same is true of the various charters granted to the other colonies. In language more or less emphatic is the establishment of the Christian religion declared to be one of the purposes of the grant. The celebrated compact made by the Pilgrims in the Mayflower, 1620, recites: "Having undertaken for the Glory of God, and Advancement of the Christian Faith, and the Honour of our King and Country, a Voyage to plant the first Colony in the northern Parts of Virginia; Do by these Presents, solemnly and mutually, in the Presence of God and one another, covenant and combine ourselves together into a civil Body Politick, for our better Ordering and Preservation, and Furtherance of the Ends aforesaid."

The fundamental orders of Connecticut, under which a provisional government was instituted in 1638–1639, commence with this declaration: "Forasmuch as it hath pleased the All-mighty God by the wise disposition of his diuyne pruidence so to Order and dispose of things that we the Inhabitants and Residents of Windsor, Hartford and Wethersfield are now cohabiting and dwelling in and vppon the River of Conectecotte and the Lands thereunto adioyneing; And well knowing where a people are gathered togather the word of God requires that to mayntayne the peace and vnion of such a people there should be an orderly and decent Gouerment established according to God, to order and dispose of the affayres of the people at all seasons as occation shall require; doe therefore assotiate and conioyne our selues to be as one Publike State or Comonwelth; and doe, for our selues and our Successors and such as shall be adioyned to vs att any tyme hereafter, enter into Combination and Confederation togather, to mayntayne and presearue the liberty and purity of the gospell of our Lord Jesus wch we now p^{r}fesse, as also the disciplyne of the Churches, wch according to the truth of the said gospell is now practised amongst vs."

In the charter of privileges granted by William Penn to the province of Pennsylvania, in 1701, it is recited: "Because no People can be truly happy, though under the greatest Enjoyment of Civil Liberties, if abridged of the Freedom of their Consciences, as to their Religious Profession and Worship; And Almighty God being the only Lord of Conscience, Father of Lights and Spirits; and the Author as well as Object of all divine Knowledge, Faith and Worship, who only doth enlighten the Minds, and persuade and convince the Understandings of People, I do hereby grant and declare," etc.

Coming nearer to the present time, the Declaration of Independence recognizes the presence of the Divine in human affairs....

And in the famous case of *Vidal v. Girard's Executors* (1844), this court, while sustaining the will of Mr. Girard, with its provision for the creation of a college into which no minister should be permitted to enter, observed: "It is also said, and truly, that the Christian religion is a part of the common law of Pennsylvania."

If we pass beyond these matters to a view of American life as expressed by its laws, its business, its customs and its society, we find everywhere a clear recognition of the same truth. Among other matters note the following: The form of oath universally prevailing, concluding with an appeal to the Almighty; the custom of opening sessions of all deliberative bodies and most conventions with prayer; the prefatory words of all wills, "In the name of God, amen;" the laws respecting the observance of the Sabbath, with the general cessation of all secular business, and the closing of courts, legislatures, and other similar public assemblies on that day; the churches and church organizations which abound in every city, town and hamlet; the multitude of charitable organizations existing everywhere under Christian auspices; the gigantic missionary associations, with general support, and aiming to establish Christian missions in every quarter of the globe. These, and many other matters which might be noticed, add a volume of unofficial declarations to the mass of organic utterances that this is a Christian nation. In the face of all these, shall it be believed that a Congress of the United States intended to make it a misdemeanor for a church of this country to contract for the services of a Christian minister residing in another nation?

Suppose in the Congress that passed this act some member had offered a bill which in terms declared that, if any Roman Catholic church in this country should contract with Cardinal Manning to come to this country and enter into its service as pastor and priest or any Episcopal church should enter into a like contract with Canon Farrar; or any Baptist church should make similar arrangements with Rev. Mr. Spurgeon; or any Jewish synagogue with some eminent Rabbi, such contract should be adjudged unlawful and void, and the church making it be subject to prosecution and punishment, can it be believed that it would have received a minute of approving thought or a single vote? Yet it is contended that such was in effect the meaning of this statute. The construction invoked cannot be accepted as correct. It is a case where there was presented a definite evil, in view of which the legislature used general terms with the purpose of reaching all phases of that evil, and thereafter, unexpectedly, it is developed that the general language thus employed is broad enough to reach cases and acts which the whole history and life of the country affirm could not have been intentionally legislated against. It is the duty of the courts, under those circumstances, to say that, however broad the language of the statute may be, the act, although within the letter, is not within the intention of the legislature, and therefore cannot be within the statute. *The judgment will be reversed, and the case remanded for further proceedings in accordance with this opinion.*

NOTES AND QUESTIONS

For a careful description of the context of this case, see Steven K. Green, "Justice David Josiah Brewer and the 'Christian Nation' Maxim," 63 *Alb. L. Rev.* 427 (1999), and Carol Chomsky, "Unlocking the Mysteries of Holy Trinity:

Spirit, Letter, and History in Statutory Interpretation," 100 *Colum. L. Rev.* 901 (2000). Would the Court reach the same result today without express congressional authorization of an exemption for religion? See *Employment Division v. Smith* [Chapter Eleven, section 10]. Could Congress enact an exemption for clergy that does not offend against the nonestablishment principle as the Court now construes it? See *Texas Monthly, Inc. v. Bullock* [Chapter Eleven, section 1]; but see *Thomas v. Review Board* [Chapter Eleven, section 4].

What could the assertion that America is a religious people or, more particularly, a Christian nation mean? Perhaps the claim is a historical one. The texts cited above by Justice Brewer support the proposition that the Spanish and British empires had religious as well as political motives for planting colonies in this part of the world. There is also strong historical support for the claim that religion has also been a powerful influence on American culture and society not only during the founding period, but also on a continuing basis. See, e.g. Norman Cousins, *In God We Trust: The Religious Beliefs and Ideas of the American Founding Fathers* (1958); Jon Butler, *Awash in a Sea of Faith: Christianizing the American People* (1990) (illustrating the impact of religion upon culture in America precisely when secularism was prevailing as a cultural construct in Europe). On the influence of religion on the abolitionist movement, see Chapter Eight above. On the influence of religion on the Civil Rights movement, see Chapter Fifteen below. And see Robert T. Handy, *A Christian America: Protestant Hopes and Historical Realities* (1984); Mark A. Noll, Nathan A. Hatch, and George W. Marsden, *The Search for Christian America* (1989); but see Franklin H. Littell, *From State Church to Pluralism: A Protestant Interpretation of Religion in American History*, xxvi (1971) ("The whole image of early America as a 'Christian nation' . . . is a lie that must be struck down. . . . in her early years as a nation she was overwhelmingly unchurched and heathen, regardless of pretensions and public claims."); and James E. Beumler, "Social Teachings of the Presbyterian Church," *Church and Society* 83 (Nov./Dec. 1984) ("We have no right to claim that ours is and always has been a Christian nation.").

Or does the claim mean that "the citizenry of the United States is one of the most religious-perhaps even the most religious-of the citizenries of the world's advanced industrial democracies." Michael J. Perry, "Religious Arguments in Public Political Debate," 29 *Loyola L.A. L. Rev.* 1421 (1996). This is an empirical claim for which one must turn to sociologists of religion. See, e.g., Andrew Greeley, "The Persistence of Religion," *Cross Currents*, 24 (Spring 1995); George Gallup; *The Religious Life of Young Americans* (1992); George Gallup, *The Role of the Bible in American Society* (1990); Gallup, *Religion in America* (1990); Gallup, *100 Questions and Answers* (1989).

Would the Court today write as Justice Brewer did? In 1984 Justice Brennan, dissenting in *Lynch v. Donnelly* [Chapter Thirteen, section 6], condemned Justice Brewer's assertion as "arrogant." In 1992 Justice Scalia, dissenting in *Lee v. Weisman* [Chapter Fourteen, section 2], referred to *Holy Trinity Church* as an "aberration." In 1988 Justice O'Connor wrote about the case differently in a letter she came to regret. Annetta Conant, a political activist from Arizona, had written to the justice inquiring whether America is a Christian nation. Justice O'Connor replied in the affirmative, citing *Holy Trinity Church* and two other decisions. In January of 1989 Conant cited O'Connor's letter in support of a resolution adopted by the Arizona Republican

Party declaring the United States a Christian nation based on the laws of the Bible. Several scholars and commentators criticized the tone and content of the justice's letter. Prof. Laurence Tribe thought it "improper for Supreme Court justices to answer inquiries of a potentially politically charged kind in ways that could obviously be misused." Bruce Fein, a conservative court watcher, said the letter was "grossly improper" and "borders on the inexcusable." See Al Kamen, "2 Experts Fault O'Connor for Letter," *Wash. Post*, Mar. 15, 1989, at A3. See also Edwin M. Yoder, Jr., Justice O'Connor's Unfortunate Letter, Wash. Post, Mar. 19, 1989, at C7, and Alan Dershowitz, "A 'Christian Nation': O'Connor's Letter Aids Religious Bigots," *Seattle Times*, Apr. 17, 1989. O'Connor expressed regret that her letter "to an acquaintance ... was used in a political debate." "Arizona Furor Over Justice's Letter About Christianity," *San Francisco Chronicle*, Mar. 16, 1989. One commentator defended the letter. Cal Thomas, "The justice is on solid ground," *The San Diego Union–Tribune*, Mar. 23, 1989. Was the justice on solid ground, or did she do the right thing by apologizing? Five years before this episode O'Connor had proposed that claims of violation of the nonestablishment principle should be evaluated by an "endorsement" test which would inquire whether a "reasonable observer" would "fairly understand" government action to "sen[d] a message to nonadherents that they are outsiders, not full members of the political community." See *Lynch v. Donnelly* [Chapter Thirteen, section 6]. Assuming for a moment that the justice's letter is "government action," does it pass her endorsement test?

2.   Aid to a Church-Related Hospital

Federal aid to a hospital owned and operated by a Catholic religious order was litigated in the 1890s. The petitioner, Joseph Bradfield, appearing in his own behalf, won in the supreme court of the District of Columbia, but lost in the Court of Appeals. He appealed to the Supreme Court of the United States. The Republican administration of William McKinley vigorously defended the propriety of the grant. The opinion for a unanimous Court was delivered by Justice Rufus W. Peckham, an upstate New Yorker of long-established Protestant stock.

Bradfield v. Roberts

175 U.S. 291 (1899).

This was a suit in equity, brought by the appellant to enjoin the defendant from paying any moneys to the directors of Providence Hospital in the city of Washington, under an agreement entered into between the Commissioners of the District of Columbia and the directors of the hospital, by virtue of the authority of an act of Congress, because of the alleged invalidity of the agreement for the reasons stated in the bill of complaint. In that bill complainant represents that he is a citizen and taxpayer of the United States and a resident of the District of Columbia, that the defendant is the Treasurer of the United States, and the object of the suit is to enjoin him from paying to or on account of Providence Hospital, in the city of Washington, District of Columbia, any moneys belonging to the United

States, by virtue of a contract between the Surgeon General of the Army and the directors of that hospital, or by virtue of an agreement between the Commissioners of the District of Columbia and such directors, under the authority of an appropriation contained in the sundry civil appropriation bill for the District of Columbia, approved June 4, 1897.

Complainant further alleged in his bill: "That the said Providence Hospital is a private eleemosynary corporation, and that to the best of the complainant's knowledge and belief it is composed of members of a monastic order or sisterhood of the Roman Catholic Church, and is conducted under the auspices of said church; that the title to its property is vested in the 'Sisters of Charity of Emmitsburg, Maryland;' that it was incorporated by a special act of Congress approved April 8, 1864, whereby, in addition to the usual powers of bodies corporate and politic, it was invested specially with 'full power and all the rights of opening and keeping a hospital in the city of Washington for the care of such sick and invalid persons as may place themselves under the treatment and care of said corporation.'

"That in view of the sectarian character of said Providence Hospital and the specific and limited object of its creation, the said contract between the same and the Surgeon General of the Army and also the said agreement between the same and the Commissioners of the District of Columbia are unauthorized by law, and, moreover, involve a principle and a precedent for the appropriation of the funds of the United States for the use and support of religious societies, contrary to the article of the Constitution which declares that Congress shall make no law respecting a religious establishment, and also a precedent for giving to religious societies a legal agency in carrying into effect a public and civil duty which would, if once established, speedily obliterate the essential distinction between civil and religious functions.

"That the complainant and all other citizens and taxpayers of the United States are injured by reason of the said contract and the said agreement, in virtue whereof the public funds are being used and pledged for the advancement and support of a private and sectarian corporation, and that they will suffer irreparable damage if the same are allowed to be carried into full effect by means of payments made through or by the said defendant out of the Treasury of the United States, contrary to the Constitution and declared policy of the Government."

Mr. Joseph Bradfield, appellant, in person for appellant.

Mr. Assistant Attorney General Hoyt for appellee. *Mr. Attorney General* was on his brief.

Justice Peckham, after stating the facts, delivered the opinion of the court.

Passing the various objections made to the maintenance of this suit on account of an alleged defect of parties, and also in regard to the character in which the complainant sues, merely that of a citizen and taxpayer of the United States and a resident of the District of Columbia, we come to the main question as to the validity of the agreement between the Commissioners of the District and the directors of the hospital, founded upon the appropriation contained in the act of Congress, the contention being that the agreement if carried out would result in an appropriation by Congress of money to a religious society, thereby violating the constitutional provision which forbids Congress from passing any law respecting an establishment of religion. Art. I of the Amendments to the Constitution.

The appropriation is to be found in the general appropriation act for the government of the District of Columbia, approved March 3, 1897, c. 387, 29 Stat. 665, 679. It reads: "For two isolating buildings, to be constructed, in the discretion of the Commissioners of the District of Columbia, on the grounds of two hospitals, and to be operated as a part of such hospitals, thirty thousand dollars." Acting under the authority of this appropriation the Commissioners entered into the agreement in question.

As the bill alleges that Providence Hospital was incorporated by an act of Congress, approved April 8, 1864, c. 50, 13 Stat. 43, and assumes to give some of its provisions, the act thus referred to is substantially made a part of the bill, and it is therefore set forth in the margin.

The act shows that the individuals named therein and their successors in office were incorporated under the name of "The Directors of Providence Hospital," with power to receive, hold and convey personal and real property, as provided in its first section. By the second section the corporation was granted "full power and all the rights of opening and keeping a hospital in the city of Washington for the care of such sick and invalid persons as may place themselves under the treatment and care of the said corporation." The third section gave it full power to make such by-laws, rules and regulations that might be necessary for the general accomplishment of the objects of the hospital, not inconsistent with the laws in force in the District of Columbia. Nothing is said about religion or about the religious faith of the incorporators of this institution in the act of incorporation. It is simply the ordinary case of the incorporation of a hospital for the purposes for which such an institution is generally conducted. It is claimed that the allegation in the complainant's bill, that the said "Providence Hospital is a private eleemosynary corporation, and that to the best of complainant's knowledge and belief it is composed of members of a monastic order or sisterhood of the Roman Catholic Church, and is conducted under the auspices of said church; that the title to its property is vested in the Sisters of Charity of Emmitsburg, Maryland," renders the agreement void for the reason therein stated, which is that Congress has no power to make "a law respecting a religious establishment," a phrase which is not synonymous with that used in the Constitution, which prohibits the passage of a law "respecting an establishment of religion."

If we were to assume, for the purpose of this question only, that under this appropriation an agreement with a religious corporation of the tenor of this agreement would be invalid, as resulting indirectly in the passage of an act respecting an establishment of religion, we are unable to see that the complainant in his bill shows that the corporation is of the kind described, but on the contrary he has clearly shown that it is not.

The above-mentioned allegations in the complainant's bill do not change the legal character of the corporation or render it on that account a religious or sectarian body. Assuming that the hospital is a private eleemo-synary corporation, the fact that its members, according to the belief of the complainant, are members of a monastic order or sisterhood of the Roman Catholic Church, and the further fact that the hospital is conducted under the auspices of said church, are wholly immaterial, as is also the allegation regarding the title to its property. The statute provides as to its property and makes no provision for its being held by any one other than itself. The facts above stated do not in the least change the legal character of the hospital, or make a religious corporation out of a purely secular one as constituted by the law of its being. Whether the individuals who compose the corporation under its charter happen to be all Roman Catholics, or all Methodists, or Presbyterians, or Unitarians, or members of any other religious organization, or of no organization at all, is of not the slightest consequence with reference to the law of its incorporation, nor can the individual beliefs upon religious matters of the various incorporators be inquired into. Nor is it material that the hospital may be conducted under the auspices of the Roman Catholic Church. To be conducted under the auspices is to be conducted under the influence or patronage of that church. The meaning of the allegation is that the church exercises great and perhaps controlling influence over the management of the hospital. It must, however, be managed pursuant to the law of its being. That the influence of any particular church may be powerful over the members of a non-sectarian and secular corporation, incorporated for a certain defined purpose and with clearly stated powers, is surely not sufficient to convert such a corporation into a religious or sectarian body. That fact does not alter the legal character of the corporation, which is incorporated under an act of Congress, and its powers, duties and character are to be solely measured by the charter under which it alone has any legal existence. There is no allegation that its hospital work is confined to members of that church or that in its management the hospital has been conducted so as to violate its charter in the smallest degree. It is simply the case of a secular corporation being managed by people who hold to the doctrines of the Roman Catholic Church, but who nevertheless are managing the corporation according to the law under which it exists. The charter itself does not limit the exercise of its corporate powers to the members of any particular religious denomination, but on the contrary those powers are to be exercised in favor of any one seeking the ministrations of that kind of an institution. All that can be said of the corporation itself is that it has been incorporated by an act of Congress, and for its legal powers and duties that act must be exclusively referred to. As stated in the opinion of the Court of Appeals, this corporation "is not declared the trustee of any church or religious society. Its property is to be acquired in its own name and for its own purposes; that property and its business are to be managed in its own way, subject to no visitation, supervision or control by any ecclesiastical authority whatever, but only to that of the Government which created it. In respect then of its creation, organization, management and ownership of property it is an ordinary private corporation whose rights are determinable by the law of the land, and the religious opinions of whose members are not subjects of inquiry."

It is not contended that Congress has no power in the District to appropriate money for the purpose expressed in the appropriation, and it is not doubted that it has power to authorize the Commissioners of the District of Columbia to enter into a contract with the trustees of an incorporated hospital for the purposes mentioned in the agreement in this case, and the only objection set up is the alleged "sectarian character of the hospital and the specific and limited object of its creation."

The other allegations in complainant's bill are simply statements of his opinion in regard to the results necessarily flowing from the appropriation in question when connected with the agreement mentioned.

The act of Congress, however, shows there is nothing sectarian in the corporation, and "the specific and limited object of its creation" is the opening and keeping a hospital in the city of Washington for the care of such sick and invalid persons as may place themselves under the treatment and care of the corporation. To make the agreement was within the discretion of the Commissioners, and was a fair exercise thereof.

The right reserved in the third section of the charter to amend, alter or repeal the act leaves full power in Congress to remedy any abuse of the charter privileges.

Without adverting to any other objections to the maintenance of this suit, it is plain that complainant wholly fails to set forth a cause of action, and the bill was properly dismissed by the Court of Appeals, and its decree will, therefore, be *Affirmed.*

NOTES AND QUESTIONS

Many hospitals in America today are owned and operated by religious communities. Many federal and state programs provide financial assistance for health care. These programs include Hill–Burton funds for the construction or renovation of hospitals, Medicare funds for the treatment of persons eligible for medical benefits under the Social Security Act, as amended, Medicaid funds for the treatment of indigents, and funded research at university medical schools. Are these programs at religiously affiliated hospitals permissible under the rationale offered in *Bradfield*?

3. THE FIRST SCHOOL CASE

In the 1870s, during the Grant administration, the government set out to educate the Indians by "contract schools," federally funded schools largely operated under religious auspices. Catholic schools came to predominate. The Indian Rights Association, a philanthropic Protestant enterprise founded in 1882, proposed, as an alternative, compulsory federal education, where the Indians would be "Americanized" and the educational influence would be mainline Protestant American. The Indian Rights Association's leader, Herbert Welsh, painted an unfavorable contrast between "Roman control of our Indian schools" and "the American Public School idea," Francis P. Prucha, *The Churches and the Indian Schools, 1888–1912* 3–31 (1979).

The American Protective Association (APA) was founded in 1887 in reaction to Catholic immigration. *See* Gustavus Myers, *History of Bigotry in the United States* (rev. ed. 1960), John Higham, *Strangers in the Land: Patterns of American Nativism, 1860–1925* (1988), and Anson Phelps Stokes, *Church and State in the United States* 830–837 (1950). The APA made the Catholic influence on the Indian schools one of its major issues. In 1894, after the Catholic schools had received over $3 million of federal money, the APA attacks led to congressional attacks on the annual appropriation. The Cleveland administration met the outcry by a plan to phase out the contract schools in favor of federal schools. In 1896, Daniel M. Browning, Commissioner for Indian Affairs, instructed an Indian agent: "It is your duty first to build up and maintain the Government Day Schools ... the Indian parents have no right to designate which school their children shall attend." *Id.* 58. The ruling was seen as a near-fatal blow to the Catholic schools.

In a pattern familiar to students of American politics, the Cleveland administration—Democrats and so confident of the Catholic vote—cultivated the Protestants. The Roosevelt administration—Republican and anxious to woo Catholics—revoked the Browning ruling in 1902. *Id.* 62. In 1904 the Bureau of Catholic Indian Missions, the first national Catholic lobby, proposed to the administration that the United States use tribal funds to support the mission schools. Roosevelt agreed if the Indians would petition for this use. The Catholic Bureau drew up formal legal petitions. Many Indians affixed their mark. The Indian Rights Association and the American Baptist Home Missionary Society protested to the President. William Hare, the Episcopal bishop of South Dakota, suggested that the Sioux sue. His efforts resulted in a letter signed by a Sioux, Reuben Quick Bear, asking the Indian Rights Association for legal assistance. The association estimated the cost of a suit to be between $500 and $1,000 and hesitated. *Id.* 84–92.

Rebuffed in Congress and by the Roosevelt administration, the association's law committee in 1905 finally voted to bring suit against Francis Leupp, Roosevelt's Commissioner for Indian Affairs, and to pay for the litigation. Reuben Quick Bear was chosen and two other Sioux were recruited as plaintiffs. *Id.* 151–157. The Justice Department turned over defense of the case to special counsel chosen and compensated by the Catholic Bureau. *Id.* 153–154. A prototypical civil rights case, *Quick Bear v. Leupp*, set nominal plaintiffs against a nominal defendant while the interested ideological parties paid for the litigation and directed the strategy.

The history was set out in the answer filed by the United States:

1. The United States had approved the creation of Catholic Mission Schools in order "to encourage the education and civilization of the Indians through the work of religious organizations." The Act of 1819 appropriated $10,000 for such schools as the War Department approved [Chapter Seven, section 6A].

2. From 1819 to 1870 "the principal educational work" among the Indians was conducted by religious societies "aided more or less by the Government."

3. In 1870 Congress appropriated $100,000 which was used for contracts with various denominations to educate the Indians. In 1876 Congress began to make a general appropriation each year for the same purpose.

4. In 1894 objection was made to appropriating money for education "in sectarian institutions." The secretary of the interior agreed with the "intense feeling of opposition to sectarian education, which is showing itself all over the land," but concluded it would be impracticable to abandon the policy instantly; he recommended a decrease of 20 percent per year. General appropriation of public money for the sectarian schools stopped in 1899.

5. The money now being paid by the United States came from "Trust Funds" set up when the government bought land from the Indians and "Treaty Funds" set up by treaty. Appropriation of money for admittedly "sectarian schools" was classed under the heading "Fulfilling Treaty Stipulations with and Support of Indian Tribes." The money was regarded as the Indians' but was disbursed for their benefit by the secretary of the interior.

6. The treaty with the Sioux, made April 29, 1868, bound the United States to provide a schoolhouse and teacher for every thirty children.

7. On February 3, 1905, President Theodore Roosevelt wrote the Interior Department that the Indians "were entitled as a matter of moral right to have the moneys coming to them used for the education of their children at the schools of their choice." When petitions were signed by 212 Sioux Indians indicating that they wanted the Catholic schools to continue, the Department accordingly executed a contract with the Bureau of Catholic Indian Missions, using the 212 Sioux' proportionate share of the Trust Fund and Treaty Fund.

8. The amount in litigation was $27,000 due under such contract, executed July 1, 1905, for the education of 250 Indian pupils at St. Francis Mission School, Rosebud Reservation, South Dakota, at $108 per pupil per year.

On appeal to the Supreme Court, defendants argued:

1. "A religious establishment, however, is not synonymous with the establishment of religion." See *Bradfield v. Roberts* [section 2 above]. A school, like a hospital, is neither an establishment of religion nor a religious establishment, although along with secular education there might be, as there commonly is, instruction in morality and religion, just as in hospital there would be religious ministrations. *Id.* 74.

2. Not to let the Indians choose their own schools "perverts the supposed general spirit of the constitutional provisions into a means of prohibiting the free exercise of religion." *Id.* 77.

The opinion of a unanimous Court was delivered by Chief Justice Melville W. Fuller, a fairly high-church Episcopalian.

Quick Bear v. Leupp

210 U.S. 50 (1908).

We concur in the decree of the Court of Appeals of the District and the reasoning by which its conclusion is supported, as set forth in the opinion of Wright, J., speaking for the court.

The validity of the contract for $27,000 is attacked on the ground that all contracts for sectarian education among the Indians are forbidden by certain provisos contained in the Indian Appropriation Acts of 1895, 1896, 1897, 1898 and 1899. But if those provisos relate only to the appropriations made by the Government out of the public moneys of the United States raised by taxation from persons of all creeds and faiths, or none at all, and appropriated gratuitously for the purpose of education among the Indians, and not to "Tribal Funds," which belong to the Indians themselves, then the contract must be sustained. The difference between one class of appropriations and the other has long been recognized in the annual appropriation acts. The gratuitous appropriation of public moneys for the purpose of Indian education has always been made under the heading "Support of Schools," whilst the appropriation of the "Treaty Fund" has always been under the heading "Fulfilling Treaty Stipulations and Support of Indian Tribes," and that from the "Trust Fund" is not in the Indian Appropriation Acts at all. One class of appropriations relates to public moneys belonging to the Government; the other to moneys which belong to the Indians and which is administered for them by the Government....

As has been shown, in 1868 the United States made a treaty with the Sioux Indians, under which the Indians made large cessions of land and other rights. In consideration of this the United States agreed that for every thirty children a house should be provided and a teacher competent to teach the elementary branches of our English education should be furnished for twenty years. In 1877, in consideration of further land cessions, the United States agreed to furnish all necessary aid to assist the Indians in the work of civilization and furnish them schools and instruction in mechanical and agricultural arts, as provided by the Treaty of 1868. In 1889 Congress extended the obligation of the treaty for twenty years, subject to such modifications as Congress should deem most effective, to secure the Indians equivalent benefits of such education. Thereafter, in every annual Indian appropriation act, there was an appropriation to carry out the terms of this treaty, under the heading "Fulfilling Treaty Stipulations with and Support of Indian Tribes."

These appropriations rested on different grounds from the gratuitous appropriations of public moneys under the heading "Support of Schools." The two subjects were separately treated in each act, and, naturally, as they are essentially different in character. One is the gratuitous appropriation of public moneys for the purpose of Indian education, but the "Treaty Fund" is not public money in this sense. It is the Indians' money, or at least is dealt with by the Government as if it belonged to them, as morally it does. It differs from the "Trust Fund" in this: The "Trust Fund" has been set aside for the Indians and the income expended for their benefit, which expenditure required no annual appropriation. The whole amount due the Indians for certain land cessions was appropriated in one lump sum by the act of 1889, 25 Stat. 888, chap. 405. This "Trust Fund" is held for the Indians and not distributed *per capita*, being held as property in common. The money is distributed in accordance with the discretion of the Secretary of the Interior, but really belongs to the Indians. The President declared it to be the moral right of the Indians to have this "Trust Fund" applied to the education of the Indians in the schools of their choice, and the same view was entertained by the Supreme Court of the District of Columbia and the Court of Appeals of the District. But the "Treaty Fund" has exactly the same characteristics. They are moneys belonging really to the Indians. They are the price of land ceded by the Indians to the Government. The only difference is that in the "Treaty Fund" the debt to the Indians created and secured by the treaty is paid by annual appropriations. They are not gratuitous appropriations of public moneys, but the payment, as we repeat, of a treaty debt in installments. We perceive no justification for applying the proviso or declaration of policy to the payment of treaty obligations, the two things being distinct and different in nature and having no relation to each other, except that both are technically appropriations.

Some reference is made to the Constitution, in respect to this contract with the Bureau of Catholic Indian Missions. It is not contended that it is unconstitutional, and it could not be. *Bradfield v. Roberts* [section 2 above]. But it is contended that the spirit of the Constitution requires that the declaration of policy that the Government "shall make no appropriation whatever for education in any sectarian schools" should be treated as applicable, on the ground that the actions of the United States were to always be undenominational, and that, therefore, the Government can never act in a sectarian capacity, either in the use of its own funds or in that of the funds of others, in respect of which it is a trustee; hence that even the Sioux trust fund cannot be applied for education in Catholic schools, even though the owners of the fund so desire it. But we cannot concede the proposition that Indians cannot be allowed to use their own money to educate their children in the schools of their own choice because the Government is necessarily undenominational, as it cannot make any law respecting an establishment of religion or prohibiting the free exercise thereof. The Court of Appeals well said:

"The 'Treaty' and 'Trust' moneys are the only moneys that the Indians can lay claim to as matter of right; the only sums on which they are entitled to rely as theirs for education; and while these moneys are not delivered to them in hand, yet the money must not only be provided, but be expended, for their benefit and in part for their education; it seems inconceivable that Congress should have intended to prohibit them from receiving religious education at their own cost if they so desired it; such an intent would be one 'to prohibit the free exercise of religion' amongst the Indians, and such would be the effect of the construction for which the complainants contend."

The *cestuis que trust* cannot be deprived of their rights by the trustee in the exercise of power implied. *Decree affirmed.*

NOTES AND QUESTIONS

Relying on *Bradfield*, the Court rejected the contention in *Quick Bear* that the federal contract with the Bureau of Catholic Indian Missions violated the nonestablishment principle. Was the Court correct in intimating that to prohibit the Indians from "receiving religious education at their own cost if they so desired it" would "prohibit the free exercise of religion amongst the Indians." Is this case sui generis because of the Indian trust fund? Should the source fund from which a benefit is drawn within the federal treasury determine the constitutionality of subsidizing education, or should the focus be on what kind of education is being funded? Does *Quick Bear* teach that the religious character of a school does not by itself and without more render all forms of assistance in that school impermissible? See *Agostini v. Felton* and *Mitchell v. Helms* [Chapter Fourteen, section 1].

4. THE CHURCHES AND THE FEDERAL INCOME TAX

The first income tax after passage of the Sixteenth Amendment exempted from tax the income of any "corporation or association organized and operated exclusively for religious, charitable, scientific or educational purposes, no part of the net income of which inures to the benefit of any private stockholder or individual," 38 Stat. 172 (1913). In *Brushaber v. Union Pacific Railroad*, 240 U.S. 1 (1916), the case that upheld the power of Congress under the Sixteenth Amendment to set different rates of income tax for different classes, Chief Justice Edward Douglas White, a Catholic, swept away all objections to the lines drawn by Congress. No special mention was made of the charitable exemption or the benefits thereby accorded to religious groups.

5. THE CHURCHES AND THE DRAFT

Selective Draft Law Cases

245 U.S. 366 (1918).

■ CHIEF JUSTICE WHITE delivered the opinion of the court.

The act exempted from subjection to the draft designated United States and state officials as well as those already in the military or naval service of the United States, regular or duly ordained ministers of religion and theological students under the conditions provided for, and, while relieving from military service in the strict sense the members of religious sects as enumerated whose tenets excluded the moral right to engage in war, nevertheless subjected such persons to the performance of service of a non-combatant character to be defined by the President....

It remains only to consider contentions which, while not disputing power, challenge the act because of the repugnancy to the Constitution supposed to result from some of its provisions.... And we pass without anything but statement the proposition that an establishment of a religion or an interference with the free exercise thereof repugnant to the First Amendment resulted from the exemption clauses of the act to which we at the outset referred, because we think its unsoundness is too apparent to require us to do more....

NOTES AND QUESTIONS

The draft law challenged in the case above provided exemption from service to members of bonafide peace churches. Is this sort of exemption permissible? Is a challenge of such a statute as a violation of both the free exercise and nonestablishment principles so apparently unsound as to require nothing more from the Court than to characterize it in this fashion? Does this approach contain the core problem of an establishment, that one group (pacifists) are preferred over another group (adherents to the justifiable war tradition)? [See Chapter Two, NOTE. *Christians and Military Service in the Early Church: From Pacifism to the Augustinian Tradition on Justifiable War*]. Does it also contain problems of excessive entanglement with religion? [See Chapter Six, section 2A, NOTE. *Madison and Excessive Entanglement of Government with Religion*].

First Amendment claims were generally given short shrift during the period of World War I; see *Schenck v. United States*, 249 U.S. 47 (1919), *Frohwerk v. United States*, 249 U.S. 204 (1919), *Debs v. United States*, 249 U.S. 211 (1919), and *Abrams v. United States*, 250 U.S. 616 (1919) (sustaining convictions for speeches or pamphlets of American war policy). During the Vietnam War period the Court gave stronger protection to freedom of speech. See *Brandenburg v. Ohio*, 395 U.S. 444 (1969) (prohibiting criminalization of speech that is not likely to provoke imminent lawless action). But during the same period the Court was almost as dismissive of the two claims mentioned above as the Court was during World War I. See *Gillette v. United States* [Chapter Eleven, section 4]. Why such judicial animus to conscientious objection to military service?

6. PROHIBITION

During World War I the movement to eliminate the general consumption of alcohol culminated in Congress on December 22, 1917, with the submission of the Eighteenth Amendment to the states for ratification. By January 1919, ratification had been voted by forty-six states.

United States Constitution, Amendment XVIII

After one year from the ratification of this article the manufacture, sale or transportation of intoxicating liquors within ... the United States ... for beverage purposes is hereby prohibited.

———

The Eighteenth Amendment was the triumph of a movement with strong religious roots reaching back to the temperance reformers of the 1820s like Lyman Beecher and William Lloyd Garrison. After the Civil War, reformers who believed alcoholism to be a national menace called for delegates from churches and Sunday schools, and from state temperance groups, to form a Prohibition Party; its first national convention was in 1872, Norman H. Clark, *Deliver Us from Evil: An Interpretation of American Prohibition* 69-70 (1976). Thereafter the movement was largely sustained by Baptists, Presbyterians,

Scandinavian Lutherans, and, above all, by Methodists. *Id*. 89. A "Woman's Crusade" in the 1870s attacked saloons with demonstrations and prayers in the street. In 1874 the Women's Christian Temperance Union was formed and in 1879, under President Frances Willard, it began to change the consciousness of the nation in a war against saloons. From New York to Kansas, the Republican party was affected by Prohibitionist pressures, usually identified with the churches. *Id*. 74, 89. In 1887, H.H. Rutherford, a minister using "individual Protestant churches as his basic organizational unit," led the way in designing legislation letting local governments abolish the saloon. *Id*. 94. The Anti–Saloon League was self-identified as "the Protestant church in action." Andrew Sinclair, *Prohibition: The Era of Excess* 65 (1962). The leader of the league's educational work, Ernest Cherrington, wrote that "The church voters' lists ... constituted the real key." Ernest Cherrington, *History of the Anti–Saloon League* 59 (1913).

The evils at which the Anti–Saloon League aimed—essentially the deleterious effects of alcoholism—were palpable: broken homes and broken lives, the loss of employment and the loss of self esteem by those who became addicted. In addition, the anti-alcohol crusaders played on the association of alcohol with sexual sin, arguing that alcohol lowered inhibitions and facilitated lust, while the saloons themselves were often centers for prostitution. Sinclair 51. Just as in the crusade against slavery, the danger to chastity—a high value in Western Christianity—gave added impetus to the preachers against the evil.

As in the case of slavery, there was a biblical argument against the reformers. Wine had an honored place in Scripture; Jesus himself had turned water into wine at Cana (John 2:1–11). The biblical arguments were met as the scriptural arguments for slavery had been met, by saying that the wine accepted by the Jews was different from modern beverages. Sinclair 70. A more serious religious problem that divided the religious camp was that Catholics used wine to celebrate Mass, Episcopalians and various Protestant churches to celebrate Holy Communion, and Jews to observe the sabbath, the Seder meals at Passover, and other religious commemorations. Complete prohibition of all alcohol intruded sharply into basic liturgical practices. A lower court did enforce an Oklahoma statute literally to prevent shipment of sacramental wine to a Catholic priest, but the decision was reversed by the Oklahoma Supreme Court. Clark 126. Making an exception for liturgical use was politic. In some cases the Catholic vote was crucial in closing saloons locally—for example, in Los Angeles and San Jose in 1916. *Id*. 108. These local victories underscored how important the role of religious fervor was to the outcome. In general, none of the adherents of the more liturgical religions—Catholics, Episcopalians, Jews—showed the appetite for the suspension of alcohol that characterized the more pietistic churches.

The Eighteenth Amendment, on its face, exacerbated the religious problem. A ban on "intoxicating liquors ... for beverage purposes," read literally, included all wine. No one could pretend that wine was not drunk when it was used liturgically; and it was capable of intoxicating. The National Prohibition Act (the Volstead Act) made criminal the manufacture, sale, delivery, or possession of any beverage containing over .5 percent alcohol, but it wrote a discreet gloss, for the sake of religion, on the Amendment. The statute excepted "liquor for nonbeverage purposes and wine for sacramental purposes."

National Prohibition Act (Volstead Act), 41 Stat. 311 (1919)

Nothing in this title shall be held to apply to the manufacture, importation, possession or distribution of wine for sacramental purposes, or like religious rites.

———

The sale of such wine, however, was forbidden "to any person not a rabbi, minister of the gospel, priest, or an officer duly authorized for the purpose by an church or congregation." Like the Income Tax and the Selective Draft Acts, the Volstead Act gave a special privilege to the clergy. Prohibition did not divide the country as profoundly as slavery had divided it, because self-image and basic views of humanity were not at issue. A type of sumptuary law was at stake; but the seriousness with which the movement developed was owed above all to religion.

7. HOSTILITY TO RELIGIOUS SCHOOLS

Two cases decided by the Court in the 1920s dealt with overt hostility to religious schools. In *Meyer v. Nebraska* (1923) the Court invalidated a Nebraska statute forbidding instruction in the German language. The primary target was Lutheran schools, but Catholics came to the assistance of the defendant. In *Pierce v. Society of Sisters* (1925) the Court struck down an Oregon constitutional amendment compelling attendance at public schools; the primary target was Catholic schools, but Lutherans and other religious voices, including the American Jewish Committee, were raised in protest.

In 1919 nineteen states prohibited the teaching of the German language in educational institutions. In almost all instances the ban on foreign language instruction was a generally applicable criminal statute; even universities fell within the reach of the law. Of the states with such laws, only New Hampshire exempted religious and other nonpublic schools. Iowa, Nebraska, and Ohio—the three states that enforced this law by imposing criminal sanctions on teachers in religious schools who disobeyed the statute out of religious motivation–expressly included religious schools within the scope of their statutes. *See Meyer v. State*, 107 Neb. 657, 187 N.W. 100 (1922); *Bartels v. State*, 191 Iowa 1060, 181 N.W. 508 (1921); and *Bohning v. Ohio*, 262 U.S. 404 (1923).

The intensity behind these statutes can be understood only by placing these laws in the context of the xenophobic hysteria that erupted in World War I and that prevailed throughout many regions of the country, but especially in the Midwest, for several years after the armistice in November 1918. The "Great War"–characterized by President Woodrow Wilson as one to "keep the world safe for democracy" and one "to end all wars"—generated hostility to all things German that was excessive even by the standards of war-time propaganda. The Germans were identified "with cruelty, ignorance, irreligion, sexual perversion, mendacity, and every other arguable vice." William G. Ross, *Forging New Freedoms: Nativism, Education, and the Constitution, 1917–1927* 30–31 (1994). "Kaiserism" had to be destroyed not only abroad, but also at home. "The widespread use of the German language was the most visible aspect of German ethnicity and became the primary target of anti-German hysteria." *Id.*

39. "Frankfurters" became "hot dogs," and "hamburgers" became "liberty steaks." Even if only one of these linguistic shifts took hold in popular culture, they both illustrate the absolutist rigor of those who wished to extirpate all traces of Germanic culture from American life.

A campaign begotten in patriotic opposition to a foreign foe soon became a full-scale attack upon religious communities and their schools. The two religious communities with the largest number of nonpublic schools–Catholics and Lutherans–became the most vociferous opponents of the legislation to restrict foreign-language instruction. *Id.* 67. Both groups did so in part because they correctly intuited that the control of the language used for instruction in their schools was a surrogate for a broader attack on their very existence.

During the War, Lutherans were subjected to regular attacks in one of Nebraska's leading newspapers. For example, one editorial viewed the German Lutheran clergy as "the mediums through which pro-German literature is being peddled" and "the minds of their congregations are being poisoned by the tenor of their sermons." *Lincoln Daily Star*, July 12, 1917, p. 6, col. 1, cited in Ross, *id.* 76. To lay the axe at the root of such imagined trouble, the paper urged the elimination of the teaching of German, "a traitorous device . . . promoted for the secret and insidious Germanization of this country, as part of the great propaganda for the Germanization of the world." *Star*, Oct. 7, 1917, p. 4, col. 1, cited in Ross 80.

The attacks came not only from an overzealous press, but also from the State Council of Defense, a twelve-member board charged with the task of recommending policies to sustain the war effort. In a climate in which several agitated for the abolition of German parochial schools on the view that "instruction in the catechism was merely a ruse for indoctrination in kaiserism," Ross 81. The Council advocated "Americanization" of the future generation by removing foreign languages from the schools, and the Americanization of entire ethnic communities by eliminating foreign languages from the most visible and powerful agents of ethnic culture, the churches. *Id.* 84.

At the urging of the Council the Nebraska adopted a Sedition Act in 1918 that required alien teachers and preachers to obtain a license from the nearest district court. *Id.* The very issue that had inspired the career of James Madison as an advocate for religious freedom–the licensing of preachers by the Crown in colonial Virginia [Chapter Six, section 1A]–was not even seen as problematical by the Nebraska legislature. After all, preachers were free to preach in English. The statute permitted local councils of defense to investigate the applicants for a license to preach. In these "hearings" the burden was on the applicants to prove their loyalty rather than upon the government to demonstrate a specific instance of an applicant's disloyalty. Judges who might have behaved as independent magistrates conscious of their oath of office were supine puppets of popular will directed at "alien teachers and preachers."

Catholics were also vilified during this period. "One anti-Catholic publication alleged in 1923, for example, that the pope could nullify laws enacted by Congress and the state legislatures. Universal public education, the journal urged, would 'quickly Americanize the alien Roman Catholic hordes.' Meanwhile, a Methodist bishop in Detroit declared that 'the parochial school is the most un-American institution in America and must be closed.' " *Id.* 68. Opposition to religious schools "attracted support from a broad spectrum of persons and organizations, ranging from the Ku Klux Klan to the Order of Free

Masons. It is natural that the Klan should have supported compulsory public
education, since the Klan that flourished during the 1920s was virulently anti-
Catholic... Believing that the Roman Catholic church was conspiring to
destroy democracy, many Klansmen worried that Rome would strike first at the
public schools, the foundation of democracy.... Masons [also] warned that
Roman Catholic education endangered democracy. 'Once concede that an alien
church can interfere with the education of the citizen, ... and you must
concede that an alien political committee or dictator can do the same.'" *Id.* 69–
70. Subject to such attacks themselves, Catholics allied themselves with the
Lutherans when the time came to challenge the Nebraska statute. *Id.* 97.
Arthur F. Mullen, a prominent Omaha attorney and devout Catholic, persuaded
the leaders of his church of the need to challenge the laws prohibiting the
teaching of German, and he served as lead counsel for the opponents of these
laws when the time came to challenge them in court.

On May 25, 1920 Frank Edgerton, the county attorney for Hamilton
county, Nebraska, conducted an unannounced and warrantless site inspection
of the Zion Parochial School to determine whether the Lutheran school was in
compliance with the statute. Robert T. Meyer, a Lutheran layman, was teaching Raymond Parpart, a child of 10 years, to read in German from a book of
German-language Bible stories. As Meyer later told his attorney, "I knew that,
if I changed into English language, [Edgerton] would say nothing. If I went on
in German he would ... arrest me. I told myself that I should not flinch. And I
did not flinch. I went on in German." Meyer's courage at that moment is
reminiscent of the famous words of Luther at Wittenburg: "Hier stehe ich. Ich
kann kein anders." "Here I stand. I can do nothing else." Meyer was tried and
convicted for violating the Nebraska statute. Echoing the anti-German xeno-
phobia of the day and reviving the distinction between belief and action, the
Nebraska Supreme Court, per Justice Flansburg, affirmed.

Meyer v. State

107 Neb. 657, 187 N. W. 100 (1922).

The whole question resolves itself to this: Does the statute interfere
with the right of religious freedom, by prohibiting the teaching of a foreign
language, when that language is taught with the idea and purpose of later
using it, at some other time or place or in the school itself, in religious
worship?

The salutary purpose of the statute is clear. The Legislature had seen
the baneful effects of permitting foreigners, who had taken residence in
this country, to rear and educate their children in the language of their
native land. The result of that condition was found to be inimical to our
own safety. To allow the children of foreigners, who had emigrated here, to
be taught from early childhood the language of the country of their parents
was to rear them with that language as their mother tongue. It was to
educate them so that they must always think in that language, and, as a
consequence, naturally inculcate in them the ideas and sentiments foreign
to the best interests of this country. The statute, therefore, was intended
not only to require that the education of all children be conducted in the
English language, but that, until they had grown into that language and

until it had become a part of them, they should not in the schools be taught any other language. The obvious purpose of this statute was that the English language should be and become the mother tongue of all children reared in this state. The enactment of such a statute comes reasonably within the police power of the state....

A thorough knowledge of the German language as would be gained by young children by a course of study in the schools would no doubt, as pointed out in the testimony, make more convenient the matter of religious worship with their parents, whose knowledge of English was limited; but is such a reason sufficient to override the salutary effect and purpose of the statute? If a foreign language can be taught to children of tender years, for the purpose of allowing them to worship in that language, under the guise that such instruction is religious teaching, then the statute is a nullity. Writing, reading, geography, and a variety of other subjects, could as well be called religious subjects whenever the purpose was declared to be to use the knowledge, thus attained, as an aid in religious worship.

Though the statute prohibits the study of the German language and may, to an extent, limit the younger children from as freely engaging in religious services, conducted in the German language, as otherwise might be the case, we cannot say that such restriction is unwarranted. The law in no way attempts to restrict religious teachings, nor to mold beliefs, nor interfere with the entire freedom of religious worship....

Whenever the actions of individuals, even though in pursuance of religious beliefs—in this case the teaching in the schools of the German language to children of tender years—are considered as not in harmony with the public welfare, then it is proper that those acts be curbed.

As said by Chief Justice Campbell in *Re Frazee*, 63 Mich. 396, 405, 30 N. W. 72, 75 (6 Am. St. Rep. 310): "We cannot accede to the suggestion that religious liberty includes the right to introduce and carry out every scheme or purpose which persons see fit to claim as part of their religious system. There is no legal authority to constrain belief, but no one can lawfully stretch his own liberty of action so as to interfere with that of his neighbors, or violate peace and good order. The whole criminal law might be practically superseded if, under pretext of liberty of conscience, the commission of crime is made a religious dogma. It is a fundamental condition of all liberty, and necessary to civil society, that all men must exercise their rights in harmony and must yield to such restrictions as are necessary to produce that result."

Though every individual is at liberty to adopt and to follow, with entire freedom, whatsoever religious beliefs appeal to him, that does not mean that he will be protected in every act he does which is consistent with those beliefs, for when his acts become inimical to the public welfare of the state the law may prohibit them, though they are acts done in pursuance of and in conformity with the religious scruples of that individual.

Though the statute prohibits the teaching of a foreign language in a parochial school, even when that language is to be used later in religious worship, held, that such restriction does not unlawfully interfere with the right of religious freedom in the school, or the incidental right to freely give religious instruction as guaranteed by the Constitution.

When, in a parochial school, a foreign language is taught from a book containing a religious text, the fact that the study of the language is mingled with the study of a religious subject does not afford the teacher protection as against the penalty imposed by the statute for the teaching of such language.

NOTES AND QUESTIONS

Note the stark alternative set up in this opinion. If the court concedes that government has no business regulating the language of religious teaching and worship, does that really mean that "The whole criminal law might be practically superseded if, under pretext of liberty of conscience, the commission of crime is made a religious dogma"? In this respect, does the opinion of the majority anticipate the fear of Justice Scalia in *Employment Division v. Smith* [Chapter Eleven, section 10] that vigorous judicial protection of religious freedom invites anarchy? In a dissent that presaged the holding of the Supreme Court in this case, Justice Charles B. Letton wrote that the legislature could not "interfere with the fundamental right of every American parent to control, in a degree not harmful to the state, the education of his child."

Neither the state court nor the United States Supreme Court mentioned the Religion Clause of the First Amendment. In *Permoli v. New Orleans*, 44 U.S. 589 (1845) the Court had expressly held that this provision protects only against acts of Congress. After the enactment of the Fourteenth Amendment, it is historically and textually more plausible to argue that deprivations of liberty, including religious freedom, by a state are prohibited by the Privileges or Immunities Clause of the Fourteenth Amendment. *See* Akhil Reed Amar, *The Bill of Rights: Creation and Reconstruction* 183–185, 254–257 (1998). That is precisely what Arthur F. Mullen, counsel for Robert Meyer, did when he argued before the Supreme Court that "religious freedom, freedom of conscience and freedom of speech come within 'the privileges and immunities' referred to in the fourteenth amendment." Ross, *Forging New Freedoms* 118 (1994). The Court was not as focused as Mullen's reply in oral argument. But the Court did acknowledge religious freedom, or "the right . . . to worship God according to the dictates of his own conscience," among "those *privileges* long recognized at common law as essential to the orderly pursuit of happiness by free men."

Does this line of argumentation have a future? The largest obstacle to the success of the claim that religious freedom is one of the privileges or immunities protected in the Fourteenth Amendment is that the Court butchered that text of the Constitution in the *Slaughter-House Cases*, 83 U.S. 36 (1873). Perhaps that is why the search began for another means of securing fundamental liberties against invasion by the states. In the 1920s the Court gradually began the process of incorporating provisions of the Bill of Rights against the states through the Due Process Clause. *See, e.g., Gitlow v. New York*, 268 U.S. 652 (1925) (freedom of speech); *Near v. Minnesota*, 283 U.S. 697 (1931) (freedom of press); *DeJonge v. Oregon*, 299 U.S. 353 (1937) (freedom of assembly and petition). The Court intimated that a state authority could be held accountable for a violation of the Religion Clause in *Hamilton v. Bd. of Regents of the University of California*, 293 U.S. 245, 262 (1934) [section 11 below], and formally adopted this position in *Cantwell v. Connecticut*, 310 U.S. 296, 300 (1940) [Chapter Eleven, section 1]. In *Meyer* and *Pierce*, the tool used to invalidate the assaults on religious education was substantive due process. Since this line of argument had been used primarily by corporations to protect property interests against state regulation, the litigants in *Meyer* and *Pierce* stressed injury to their property caused by the Nebraska statute and the Oregon initiative. But they also included a claim of deprivation of liberty; and the liberty they were referring to was unmistakably religious freedom, the freedom to teach and to worship in the manner that the church, not the state, deems fit.

The author of the Court's opinion in *Meyer, Pierce,* and a third case dealing with a prohibition of Asian language instruction in the territory of Hawaii, *Farrington v. Tokushige*, 273 U.S. 284 (1927), was Justice James C. McReynolds, a Protestant. McReynolds still breathed in some of the air that inspired the statute. He wrote: "The desire of the Legislature to foster a homogeneous people with American ideals prepared readily to understand current discussions of civic matters is easy to appreciate. Unfortunate experiences during the late war and aversion toward every character of truculent adversaries were certainly enough to quicken that aspiration." But even McReynolds found the means chosen by Nebraska and eighteen other legislatures to offend against the Constitution. Justices Oliver Wendell Holmes, Jr. and George Sutherland–an odd couple–dissented without opinion.

Meyer v. Nebraska

262 U.S. 390 (1923).

■ Mr. Justice McReynolds delivered the opinion of the Court.

The Supreme Court of the state affirmed the judgment of conviction. It declared the offense charged and established was 'the direct and intentional teaching of the German language as a distinct subject to a child who had not passed the eighth grade,' in the parochial school maintained by Zion Evangelical Lutheran Congregation, a collection of Biblical stories being used therefor. And it held that the statute forbidding this did not conflict with the Fourteenth Amendment, but was a valid exercise of the police power.... The problem for our determination is whether the statute as construed and applied unreasonably infringes the liberty guaranteed to the plaintiff in error by the Fourteenth Amendment: "No state ... shall deprive any person of life, liberty or property without due process of law."

While this court has not attempted to define with exactness the liberty thus guaranteed, the term has received much consideration and some of the included things have been definitely stated. Without doubt, it denotes not merely freedom from bodily restraint but also the right of the individual to contract, to engage in any of the common occupations of life, to acquire useful knowledge, to marry, establish a home and bring up children, to worship God according to the dictates of his own conscience, and generally to enjoy those privileges long recognized at common law as essential to the orderly pursuit of happiness by free men. [Cases omitted]. The established doctrine is that this liberty may not be interfered with, under the guise of protecting the public interest, by legislative action which is arbitrary or without reasonable relation to some purpose within the competency of the state to effect. Determination by the Legislature of what constitutes proper exercise of police power is not final or conclusive but is subject to supervision by the courts [case omitted].

The American people have always regarded education and acquisition of knowledge as matters of supreme importance which should be diligently promoted. The Ordinance of 1787 declares: 'Religion, morality and knowledge being necessary to good government and the happiness of mankind, schools and the means of education shall forever be encouraged.' [Chapter Seven, section 6A]. Corresponding to the right of control, it is the natural duty of the parent to give his children education suitable to their station in life; and nearly all the states, including Nebraska, enforce this obligation by compulsory laws.

Practically, education of the young is only possible in schools conducted by especially qualified persons who devote themselves thereto. The calling always has been regarded as useful and honorable, essential, indeed, to the public welfare. Mere knowledge of the German language cannot reasonably be regarded as harmful. Heretofore it has been commonly looked upon as helpful and desirable. Plaintiff in error taught this language in school as part of his occupation. His right thus to teach and the right of parents to engage him so to instruct their children, we think, are within the liberty of the amendment....

That the state may do much, go very far, indeed, in order to improve the quality of its citizens, physically, mentally and morally, is clear; but the individual has certain fundamental rights which must be respected. The protection of the Constitution extends to all, to those who speak other languages as well as to those born with English on the tongue. Perhaps it would be highly advantageous if all had ready understanding of our ordinary speech, but this cannot be coerced by methods which conflict with the Constitution—a desirable and cannot be promoted by prohibited means....

The desire of the Legislature to foster a homogeneous people with American ideals prepared readily to understand current discussions of civic matters is easy to appreciate. Unfortunate experiences during the late war and aversion toward every character of truculent adversaries were certainly enough to quicken that aspiration. But the means adopted, we think, exceed the limitations upon the power of the state and conflict with rights assured to plaintiff in error. The interference is plain enough and no adequate reason therefor in time of peace and domestic tranquility has been shown.

The power of the state to compel attendance at some school and to make reasonable regulations for all schools, including a requirement that they shall give instructions in English, is not questioned. Nor has challenge been made of the state's power to prescribe a curriculum for institutions which it supports. Those matters are not within the present controversy. Our concern is with the prohibition approved by the Supreme Court.... No emergency has arisen which renders knowledge by a child of some language other than English so clearly harmful as to justify its inhibition with the consequent infringement of rights long freely enjoyed. We are constrained to conclude that the statute as applied is arbitrary and without reasonable relation to any end within the competency of the state.

As the statute undertakes to interfere only with teaching which involves a modern language, leaving complete freedom as to other matters, there seems no adequate foundation for the suggestion that the purpose was to protect the child's health by limiting his mental activities. It is well known that proficiency in a foreign language seldom comes to one not instructed at an early age, and experience shows that this is not injurious to the health, morals or understanding of the ordinary child.

The judgment of the court below must be reversed and the cause remanded for further proceedings not inconsistent with this opinion. Reversed.

■ JUSTICE HOLMES and SUTHERLAND dissented.

NOTES AND QUESTIONS

In 1920 the people of Michigan defeated by a vote of 610,699 to 353,818 a proposal that would require all elementary school children to be educated in public schools. Michigan again rejected this proposal in 1924 by a vote of 760,571 to 421,472. So did the voters of Washington in the same year by a vote of 221,500 to 158,922. For a discussion of these campaigns, see Ross, *Forging New Freedoms* 134–147. In 1922, by a vote of 115,506 to 103,685, the people of Oregon passed an initiative into law whose effect would have been to end religious and other private schools in the state. The principal supporters of the initiative, the Imperial Council, A.A.O. Nobles Mystic Shrine, offered the following argument to the voters: "Our nation supports the public school for the sole purpose of self-preservation. The assimilation and education of foreign-born citizens in the principles of our government, the hopes and inspiration of our people, are best secured by and through attendance of all children in our public schools. We must now halt those coming to our country from forming groups, establishing schools, and thereby bringing up their children in an environment often antagonistic to the principles of our government. Mix the children of the foreign-born with the native-born, and the rich with the poor. Mix those with prejudices in the public school melting pot for a few years while their minds are plastic, and finally bring out the finished product—a true American." *Oregon School Cases—Complete Record* 732 (1925). For a discussion of the role of nativist bias on the part of the American Protective Association, the Ku Klux Klan, the Masonic Grand Lodge of Oregon, and the Oregon Federation of Patriotic Societies in this controversy, see Ross, *Forging New Freedoms* 148–156, 160; *see also* Lawrence J. Saalfeld, *Forces of Prejudice in Oregon* (1984); David A. Horowitz, "Social Morality and Personal Revitalization: Oregon's Ku Klux Klan in the 1920s," 90 *Ore. Hist. Q.* 369 (1989); Malcolm Clark, Jr., "The Bigot Disclosed: Ninety Years of Nativism," 75 *Ore. Hist. Q.* 167 (1974).

As in Nebraska, the Catholic church took a lead role in organizing a challenge to the Oregon initiative. The strategy was to seek an injunction in federal court against Governor William Pierce prohibiting him from carrying out the terms of the initiative. The lead plaintiffs do not have personal names.

They are two corporate entities engaged in the lawful business of educating children: Society of the Sisters of the Holy Names of Jesus and Mary, and the Hill Military Academy (a private school whose litigation expenses were borne by the Knights of Columbus). A three-judge federal court held the law unconstitutional because it would unreasonably encroach on the lawful business of the schools. 296 F. 928 (D. Ore. 1924).

Like Arthur Mullen, the attorney for Robert Meyer, William D. Guthrie, the attorney for the Sisters, was a Catholic. Unlike Mullen, Guthrie was a Wall Street lawyer used to representing corporations. He had persuaded the Court to reject the first income tax (a modest 1%) in 1895. Perhaps his experience on Wall Street led him to select corporate entities as the clients in the test-case litigation. Mullen complained that the failure to join students or teachers as plaintiffs would invite a decision based wholly on the property rights of corporations. "The inherent and inalienable right belongs to the people the Lord made, not the people the state made," Mullen declared. Ross 162. Guthrie taught constitutional law at Columbia and served as President of the New York State Bar Association. His basic theory of the case was stated in a letter to J. P. Kavanaugh, his co-counsel in Oregon: "we must stand on the Fourteenth Amendment and its guaranty that no person shall be deprived of liberty without due process of law." In his brief Guthrie stressed the historic contribution of religious schools and colleges—all, in principle, he contended, threatened by the act. He went on to invoke the rights of parents—"those rights, which the statute seriously abridges and impairs, are of the very essence of personal liberty and freedom." *Oregon School Cases—Complete Record* 518 (1925). He said these rights were not held today in the slight esteem they were by Plato and by the Spartans, except in "Soviet Russia."

On appeal, counsel for Governor Pierce avoided any mention of the nativist attacks on the Catholic schools and on the loyalty and patriotism of Catholic citizens that were offered in the official state ballot cited above. Instead he urged a "rational basis" for an initiative clearly grounded in irrational hostility: "The voters of Oregon who adopted this law had the right to act on the belief that the fact that the great increase in juvenile crime in the United States followed so closely after the great increase in the number of children in the United States who were not attending public schools, was more than a coincidence. The voters in Oregon might also have based their action in adopting this law upon the alarm which they felt at the rising tide of religious suspicions in this country, and upon their belief that the basic cause of such religious feelings was the separation of children along religious lines during the most susceptible years of their lives, with the inevitable awakening of a consciousness of separation, and a distrust and suspicion of those from whom they were so carefully guarded. The voters of Oregon might have felt that the mingling together, during a portion of their education, of the children of all races and sects, might be the best safeguard against future internal dissentions and consequent weakening of the community against foreign dangers." *Pierce v. Society of Sisters*, 268 U.S. 510, 524–525 (1925). Citing the *Permoli* case from 1845, he also argued: "The statute does not interfere with religious identity. The American people as a whole have unalterably determined that there shall be an absolute and unequivocal separation of church and state, and that the public schools shall be maintained and conducted free from influences in favor of any religious organization, sect, creed or belief." *Id.* 512–513. He also urged that the Sisters and the military academy lacked standing to sue for violation of personal liberties since no parents or children or teachers were joined as parties to the litigation. And he argued that the predicate of *Meyer*–substantive due process–was misplaced since the Fourteenth Amendment was enacted primarily to protect the right of the recently emancipated African Americans.

A formidable array of religious organizations filed briefs amicus curiae in support of the schools. They included the American Jewish Committee, a board of the Protestant Episcopal Church, and a local conference of Seventh-day Adventists. In the most trenchant of these briefs, Louis Marshall wrote for the American Jewish Committee that the Oregon initiative would "confer upon the public schools a monopoly of education." He argued: "Recognizing in the main the great merit of our public schools system, it is nevertheless unthinkable that public schools alone shall, by legislative compulsion rather than by their own merits, be made the only medium of education in this country. Such a policy would speedily lead to their deterioration. The absence of the right of selection would at once lower the standards of education. If the children of the country are to be educated in accordance with an undeviating rule of uniformity and by a single method, then eventually our nation would consist of mechanical Robots and standardized Babbitts." *Oregon School Cases—A Complete Record* 614–15 (1925).

In *Pierce* the Court was unanimous. Justice McReynolds again delivered the opinion of the Court. It cited *Meyer*, and again focused on the liberty of parents. Like the court below and Guthrie's general line of argument, McReynolds avoided invoking the First Amendment.

Pierce v. Society of Sisters

268 U.S. 510 (1925).

The challenged Act, effective September 1, 1926, requires every parent, guardian or other person having control or charge or custody of a child between eight and sixteen years to send him "to a public school for the period of time a public school shall be held during the current year" in the district where the child resides; and failure so to do is declared a misdemeanor. There are exemptions—not specially important here—for children who are not normal, or who have completed the eighth grade, or who reside at considerable distances from any public school, or whose parents or guardians hold special permits from the County Superintendent. The manifest purpose is to compel general attendance at public schools by normal children, between eight and sixteen, who have not completed the eighth grade. And without doubt enforcement of the statute would seriously impair, perhaps destroy, the profitable features of appellees' business and greatly diminish the value of their property.

Appellee, the Society of Sisters, is an Oregon corporation, organized in 1880, with power to care for orphans, educate and instruct the youth, establish and maintain academies or schools, and acquire necessary real and personal property. It has long devoted its property and effort to the secular and religious education and care of children, and has acquired the valuable good will of many parents and guardians. It conducts interdependent primary and high schools and junior colleges, and maintains orphanages for the custody and control of children between eight and sixteen. In its primary schools many children between those ages are taught the subjects usually pursued in Oregon public schools during the first eight years. Systematic religious instruction and moral training according to the tenets of the Roman Catholic Church are also regularly provided. All courses of study, both temporal and religious, contemplate continuity of training under appellee's charge; the primary schools are essential to the system and the most profitable. It owns valuable buildings, especially constructed and equipped for school purposes. The business is remunerative—the annual income from primary schools exceeds thirty thousand dollars—and the successful conduct of this requires long time contracts with teachers and parents. The Compulsory Education Act of 1922 has already caused the withdrawal from its schools of children who would otherwise continue, and their income has steadily declined. The appellants, public officers, have proclaimed their purpose strictly to enforce the statute.

After setting out the above facts the Society's bill alleges that the enactment conflicts with the right of parents to choose schools where their children will receive appropriate mental and religious training, the right of the child to influence the parents' choice of a school, the right of schools and teachers therein to engage in a useful business or profession, and is accordingly repugnant to the Constitution and void. And, further, that unless enforcement of the measure is enjoined the corporation's business and property will suffer irreparable injury.

Appellee, Hill Military Academy, is a private corporation organized in 1908 under the laws of Oregon, engaged in owning, operating and conducting for profit an elementary, college preparatory and military training school for boys between the ages of five and twenty-one years. The average attendance is one hundred, and the annual fees received for each student amount to some eight hundred dollars. The elementary department is divided into eight grades, as in the public schools; the college preparatory department has four grades, similar to those of the public high schools; the courses of study conform to the requirements of the State Board of Education. Military instruction and training are also given, under the supervision of an Army officer. It owns considerable real and personal property, some useful only for school purposes. The business and incident good will are very valuable. In order to conduct its affairs long time contracts must be made for supplies, equipment, teachers and pupils. Appellants, law officers of the State and County, have publicly announced that the Act of November 7, 1922, is valid and have declared their intention to enforce it. By reason of the statute and threat of enforcement appellee's business is being destroyed and its property depreciated; parents and guardians are refusing to make contracts for the future instruction of their sons, and some are being withdrawn.

The Academy's bill states the foregoing facts and then alleges that the challenged Act contravenes the corporation's rights guaranteed by the Fourteenth Amendment and that unless appellants are restrained from proclaiming its validity and threatening to enforce it irreparable injury will result. The prayer is for an appropriate injunction.

No answer was interposed in either cause, and after proper notices they were heard by three judges on motions for preliminary injunctions upon the specifically alleged facts. The court ruled that the Fourteenth Amendment guaranteed appellees against the deprivation of their property without due process of law consequent upon the unlawful interference by appellants with the free choice of patrons, present and prospective. It declared the right to conduct schools was property and that parents and guardians, as a part of their liberty, might direct the education of children by selecting reputable teachers and places. Also, that these schools were not unfit or harmful to the public, and that enforcement of the challenged statute would unlawfully deprive them of patronage and thereby destroy their owners' business and property. Finally, that the threats to enforce the Act would continue to cause irreparable injury; and the suits were not premature.

No question is raised concerning the power of the State reasonably to regulate all schools, to inspect, supervise and examine them, their teachers and pupils; to require that all children of proper age attend some school, that teachers shall be of good moral character and patriotic disposition, that certain studies plainly essential to good citizenship must be taught, and that nothing be taught which is manifestly inimical to the public welfare.

The inevitable practical result of enforcing the Act under consideration would be destruction of appellees' primary schools, and perhaps all other private primary schools for normal children within the State of Oregon. These parties are engaged in a kind of undertaking not inherently harmful, but long regarded as useful and meritorious. Certainly there is nothing in the present records to indicate that they have failed to discharge their obligations to patrons, students or the State. And there are no peculiar circumstances or present emergencies which demand extraordinary measures relative to primary education.

Under the doctrine of *Meyer v. Nebraska*, we think it entirely plain that the Act of 1922 unreasonably interferes with the liberty of parents and guardians to direct the upbringing and education of children under their control. As often heretofore pointed out, rights guaranteed by the Constitution may not be abridged by legislation which has no reasonable relation to some purpose within the competency of the State. The fundamental theory of liberty upon which all governments in this Union repose excludes any general power of the State to standardize its children by forcing them to accept instruction from public teachers only. The child is not the mere creature of the State; those who nurture him and direct his destiny have the right, coupled with the high duty, to recognize and prepare him for additional obligations.... *Affirmed*.

NOTES AND QUESTIONS

Perhaps because of the way that Guthrie framed the case, McReynolds gave more attention in *Pierce* to the property rights of the school owners than to the liberty interests of parents and guardians. But the most memorable line of his opinion is its ringing conclusion: "The child is not the mere creature of the State." If those who nurture children have a right and a duty to "prepare them for the obligations of life," does the State have any affirmative duty to assist parents in this task at least by remaining neutral or nondiscriminatory when it distributes secular benefits? *See Cochran* [section 10 below] *Agostini v. Felton* and *Mitchell v. Helms* [Chapter Fourteen, section 1].

8. The First Division on Sexual Morals

Protestants and Catholics had in general agreed on what Christian sexual morality required. They had differed on divorce, but as far back as 1906 Justice Edward Douglass White, a Catholic, had written a majority opinion for the Supreme Court limiting a state's right to grant divorce to a nonresident of the state, but recognizing the "inherent power" of the state "over the marriage relation, its formation and dissolutions." *Haddock v. Haddock*, 201 U.S. 562, 569 (1906). White's view differed from the teaching of Pope Leo XIII in the encyclical *Arcanum*, February 10, 1880, *Acta Sanctae Sedis* 12:385, at 390–391; but White's position reflected an American consensus.

Statutes permitting sterilization became popular in the 1920s. Catholic moralists denounced the laws. In 1927 the Virginia statute authorizing compulsory sterilization of the feeble-minded came before the Supreme Court in the case of Carrie Buck. The majority opinion in *Buck v. Bell*, 274 U.S. 200 (1927) was written by Oliver Wendell Holmes, Jr. Holmes was one of the few members ever appointed to the Court who was openly agnostic about God and skeptical of revealed religion. As he wrote Harold Laski on January 11, 1929, "I regard [man] as I do the other species (except that my private interests are with his) having for his main business to live and propagate, and for his main interests food and sex." Mark De Wolfe Howe, ed., 2 *Holmes-Laski Letters* 1125 (1953). As Holmes worked on the case, he wrote Laski on April 25, 1927: "My lad tells me the religious are astir." *Id.* 938. However, when Holmes upheld the statute, there was but one dissenter: Justice Pierce Butler, the only Catholic on the Court, who dissented without opinion. Holmes confided to Laski, May 12, 1927: "[I] felt that I was getting near to the first principle of real reform. I say merely getting near. I don't mean that the surgeon's knife is the ultimate symbol." *Id.* 942.

9. Enforcement of Church Law

The proper interpretation of a trust to celebrate mass was litigated in the Supreme Court of the Philippines, from whose decision an appeal lay to the Supreme Court of the United States. The unanimous opinion of the Court was delivered by Justice Louis Brandeis. Brandeis was of Jewish antecedents and for that reason had been opposed by anti-Semites when named to the Court by President Wilson. He was a devoted Zionist, but he was not religiously Jewish, *see* Allon Gal, *Brandeis of Boston* 188–207 (1980). His opinion deferred to the canon law of the Catholic church, at the same time insisting that the secular courts had jurisdiction over the controversy and could override a church tribunal where there was "fraud, collusion, or arbitrariness."

Gonzalez v. Roman Catholic Archbishop of Manila

280 U.S. 1 (1929).

■ JUSTICE BRANDEIS delivered the opinion of the Court.

This case is here on certiorari to the Supreme Court of the Philippine Islands. The subject matter is a collative chaplaincy in the Roman Catholic Archdiocese of Manila, which has been vacant since December 1910. The main question for decision are whether the petitioner is legally entitled to be appointed the chaplain and whether he shall recover the surplus income accrued during the vacancy.

Raul Rogerio Gonzalez, by his guardian *ad litem*, brought the suit against the Archbishop in the Court of First Instance of Manila, on August 5, 1924. He prayed for judgment declaring the petitioner the lawful heir to the chaplaincy and its income; establishing the right of the petitioner and his successors to be appointed to and receive the income of the chaplaincy during their infancy whenever it may be vacant and, pending such appointment, to receive the income for their maintenance and support; declaring the trust character of the property and ordering it to be so recorded; directing the Archbishop to appoint the petitioner chaplain and to account to him for the income of the property from 1910 on; and directing the defendant to pay the petitioner 1,000 pesos a month pending the final determination of the case. The trial court directed the Archbishop to appoint the petitioner chaplain; and ordered payment to him of 173,725 pesos ($86,862.50), that sum being the aggregate net income of the chaplaincy during the vacancy, less the expense of having the prescribed masses celebrated in each year. It reserved the petitioner any legal right he may have to proceed in the proper court for cancellation of the certificate of registration of the property in the name of the Archbishop. The Supreme Court of the Philippine Islands reversed the judgment on February 4, 1928, and absolved the Archbishop from the complaint, "without prejudice to the right of proper persons in interest to proceed for independent relief," in respect to the income accrued during the vacancy, or in respect to the reformation of the certificate of registration so as to show the fiduciary character of the title. . . .

The chaplaincy was founded in 1820, under the will of Doña Petronila de Guzman. By it, she requested "the Father chaplain to celebrate sixty masses annually" in behalf of the souls of her parents, brothers, sisters and herself. The deed of foundation, which was executed by the testamentary executor of Doña Petronila, provided that "said property is segregated from temporal properties and transferred to the spiritual properties of this Archbishopric, without its being possible to alienate or convert the property as such into any other estate for any cause, even though it be of a more pious character, . . . so that by virtue of this Deed of Foundation canonical collation may be conferred on the said appointed chaplain." By appropriate proceedings an ecclesiastical decree approved "the foundation of the chaplaincy with all the circumstances and conditions provided for in said clause (of the will) and in the deed of foundation, as well as the imposition (charge) of seventeen hundred pesos against said building, converting said sum into spiritual property of a perpetual character subject to the ecclesiastical forum and jurisdiction." . . . .

Raul was presented to the Archbishop for appointment in 1922. The Archbishop refused to appoint him, on the ground that he did not then have "the qualifications required for chaplain of the said chaplaincy." He added: "The grounds of my conclusion are the very canons of the new Code of Canon Law. Among others, I can mention canon 1442 which says: 'Simple chaplaincies or benefices are conferred upon clergymen of the secular clergy,' in connection with canon 108, paragraph 1, 'Clergymen are those already initiated in the first tonsure' and canon 976, paragraph 1, 'No one can be promoted to first tonsure before he has begun the course in theology.' In view of the Canon as above mentioned, and other reasons which may be adduced, I believe that the boy, Raul Gonzalez, is not legally (ecclesiastically speaking) capacitated to the enjoyment of a chaplaincy."

Ever since the Council of Trent (1545–1563), it has been the law of the church that no one can be appointed to a collative chaplaincy before his fourteenth year. When Raul was presented for appointment, he was in his tenth year. He was less than twelve when this suit was begun. He was fourteen when the trial court entered its judgment. It is also urged on behalf of the Archbishop that at no time since that Council could one be lawfully appointed who lacked elementary knowledge of Christian Doctrine.

The new Codex Juris Canonici, which was adopted in Rome in 1917 and was promulgated by the Church to become effective in 1918, provides that no one shall be appointed to a collative chaplaincy who is not a cleric, Can. 1442. It requires students for the priesthood to attend a seminary; and prescribes their studies, Can. 1354, 1364. It provides that in order to be a cleric one must have had "prima tonsura," Can. 108, par. 1; that in order to have "prima tonsura" one must have begun the study of theology, Can. 976, par. 1; and that in order to study theology one must be a "bachiller," that is, must have obtained the first degree in the sciences and liberal arts, Can. 1365. It also provides that no one may validly receive ordination unless in the opinion of the ordinary he has the necessary qualifications, Can. 968, par. 1, 1464. Petitioner concedes that the chaplaincy here involved is a collative one; and that Raul lacked, at the time of his presentment and of the commencement of the suit, the age qualification required by the Canon Law in force when the chaplaincy was founded. It is also conceded that he lacked, then, and at the time of the entry of the judgment, other qualifications of a candidate for a collative chaplaincy essential, if the new Codex was applicable.

Raul's contention, in effect, is that the nearest male relative in descent from the foundress and the first chaplain, willing to be appointed chaplain, is entitled to enjoy the revenues of the foundation, subject only to the duty of saying himself the sixty masses in each year, if he is qualified so to do, or of causing them to be said by a qualified priest and paying the customary charge therefor out of the income. He claims that the provisions of the new Codex are not applicable and that his rights are to be determined by the Canon Law in force at the time the chaplaincy was founded and that the judgment of the trial court should be reinstated, because he possessed at the time of the entry of the judgment all the qualifications required by the Canon Law in force in 1820.... He contends that to deprive him of his alleged right to the chaplaincy because of a change made in 1918 in the Canon Law would violate the Constitution of the United States, the Treaty with Spain of 1898, and the Organic Act of the Philippine Islands.

The trial court rested its judgment for Raul largely on the ground that he possessed, at the time of its entry, the qualifications required by the Canon Law in force when the chaplaincy was founded; and that, hence, he was entitled both to be appointed chaplain and to recover the income accrued during the vacancy, even though he did not possess the qualifications prescribed by the new Codex then otherwise in force. The Supreme Court held that to give effect to the provisions of the new Codex would not impair the obligation of the contract made in 1820, as it was an implied term of the deed of foundation that the qualifications of a chaplain should be such as the church authorities might prescribe from time to time; and that, since Raul confessedly did not possess the qualifications prescribed by the new Codex which had been promulgated before he was presented, he could not be appointed.

First. The Archbishop interposes here, as he did below, an objection to the jurisdiction of the Philippine courts. He insists that, since the chaplaincy is confessedly a collative one, its property became spiritual property of a perpetual character subject to the jurisdiction of the ecclesiastical forum; and that thereby every controversy concerning either the right to appointment or the right to the income was removed from the jurisdiction of secular courts. The objection is not sound. The courts have jurisdiction of the parties. For the Archbishop is a juristic person amenable to the Philippine courts for the enforcement of any legal right; and the petitioner asserts such a right. There is jurisdiction of the subject matter. For the petitioner's claim is, in substance, that he is entitled to the relief sought as the beneficiary of a trust.

The fact that the property of the chaplaincy was transferred to the spiritual properties of the Archbishopric affects not the jurisdiction of the court, but the terms of the trust. *Watson v. Jones* [Chapter Eight, section 5]. The Archbishop's claim in this respect is that by an implied term of the gift, the property, which was to be held by the church, should be administered in such manner and by such persons as may be prescribed by the church from time to time. Among the church's laws which are thus claimed to be applicable are those creating tribunals for the determination of ecclesiastical controversies. Because the appointment is a canonical act, it is the function of the church authorities to determine what the essential qualifications of a chaplain are and whether the candidate possesses them. In the absence of fraud, collusion, or arbitrariness, the decisions of the proper church tribunals on matters purely ecclesiastical, although affecting civil rights, are accepted in litigation before the secular courts as conclusive, because the parties in interest made them so by contract or otherwise. Under like circumstances, effect is given in the courts to the determinations of the judicatory bodies established by clubs and civil associations.

Second. The Archbishop contended that Raul lacked even the minimum of training and knowledge of Christian Doctrine made indispensable by the Canon Law in force in 1820; that his confessed lack of the essential age at the time of the presentment and also at the time of the institution of the suit were unsurmountable obstacles to the granting of the prayer for appointment to the chaplaincy; and, moreover, that the failure to take an appeal to the Pope from the decision of the Archbishop, as provided by the Canon Law, precluded resort to legal proceedings. We have no occasion to consider the soundness of these contentions. For we are of opinion that the Canon Law in force at the time of the presentation governs, and the lack of the qualification prescribed by it is admitted. Neither the foundress, nor the church authorities, can have intended that the perpetual chaplaincy created in 1820 should, in respect to the qualifications of an incumbent, be forever administered according to the canons of the church which happened to be in force at that date. The parties to the foundation clearly contemplated that the Archbishop would, before ordination, exercise his judgment as to the fitness of the applicant; and they must have contemplated that, in the course of the centuries, the standard of fitness would be modified.

When the new Codex was promulgated in 1918 Raul was only six years old and had not yet been presented. If he had been presented, he obviously could not have been appointed. No right was then being enjoyed by him of which the promulgation of the new Codex deprived him. When he was presented later, he was ineligible under the then existing Canon Law. In concluding that Raul lacked the qualifications essential for a chaplain the Archbishop appears to have followed the controlling Canon Law. There is not even a suggestion that he exercised his authority arbitrarily.

Third. Raul urges that, even though he is not entitled to be appointed chaplain, he is entitled to recover the surplus net income earned during the vacancy. Indeed, it is the property rights involved that appear to be his main consideration. The value of the property in 1820 was about 1,700 pesos. The annual net income was then 180 pesos, a sum sufficient only to defray the annual expense of sixty masses. The annual net income has grown to about 12,000 pesos; and the annual expense of the sixty masses does not now exceed 300 pesos. In each year during the vacancy the masses have been duly celebrated. The surplus income accruing during the vacancy has been used by the Archbishop currently for pious purposes, namely, education. By canon 1481 of the new Codex the surplus income of a chaplaincy, after deducting expenses of the acting chaplain, must one-half be added to the endowment or capital and one-half to the repair of the church, unless there is a custom of using the whole for some common good to the diocese. The use made of the surplus of this chaplaincy was in accordance with what was claimed to be the long established custom of the Archdiocese. Both the custom and the specific application made of this surplus have been approved by the Holy See. The Supreme Court held that since Raul had sought the income only as an incident of the chaplaincy, he could not recover anything.

Raul's claim, which is made even in respect to income accrued prior to his birth, is rested upon some alleged right by inheritance, although his father is still living. The intention of the foundress, so far as expressed, was that the income should be applied to the celebration of masses and to the living of the chaplain, who should preferably be the nearest male relative in the line of descent from herself or the first chaplain. The claim that Raul individually is entitled as nearest relative to the surplus by inheritance is unsupported by anything in the deed of gift or the applicable law. Since Raul is not entitled to be appointed chaplain, he is not entitled to a living from the income of the chaplaincy. . . . *Affirmed.*

Who should decide whether a church official has acted "arbitrarily"? Although Justice Brandeis did a fairly good job of reading the canons of the church in this case, does a secular judge have any business doing so? Is the jurisdictional defense of the church insignificant? See *Watson v. Jones* [Chapter Eight, section 5] and *Serbian Eastern Orthodox Diocese for the United States of America and Canada v. Milivojevich,* 426 U.S. 696 (1976) [Chapter Twelve, section 3].

10.   THE FIRST SCHOOL BOOKS CASE

Louisiana in 1928 supplied free school books to all school children in the state. Taxpayers in Shreveport and Baton Rouge challenged the constitutionality of the action and appealed from a decision of the Louisiana Supreme Court to the United States Supreme Court. They argued: "if the furnishing of textbooks free to children attending private schools is not considered an aid to such private schools, but as incidental to the state educational system, then it logically follows that the tuition of the children attending such schools could be paid; their transportation to and from such schools could be provided; the salaries of the instructors could be paid in part or in whole; and finally, the buildings themselves could be erected,—with state funds; all of which, under the reasoning evinced in the statutes of Louisiana, might be justified on the ground that it is the interest of the State to see that its youth are educated." Justice Charles Evans Hughes, the son of a Baptist minister, delivered the opinion of a unanimous Supreme Court.

Cochran v. Board of Education

281 U.S. 370 (1930).

Act No. 100 of 1928 provided that the severance tax fund of the State, after allowing funds and appropriations as required by the state constitution, should be devoted "first, to supplying school books to the school children of the State." The Board of Education was directed to provide "school books for school children free of cost to such children." Act No. 143 of 1928 made appropriations in accordance with the above provisions.

The Supreme Court of the State, following its decision in *Borden v. Louisiana State Board of Education,* 168 La. 1005, held that these acts were not repugnant to either the state or the Federal Constitution.

No substantial Federal question is presented under section 4 of Article IV of the Federal Constitution guaranteeing to every State a republican form of government, as questions arising under this provision are political, not judicial, in character. *State of Ohio ex rel. Bryant v. Akron Metropolitan Park District,* and cases there cited.

The contention of the appellant under the Fourteenth Amendment is that taxation for the purchase of school books constituted a taking of private property for a private purpose. *Loan Association v. Topeka*, 20 Wall. 655. The purpose is said to be to aid private, religious, sectarian, and other schools not embraced in the public educational system of the State by furnishing text-books free to the children attending such private schools. The operation and effect of the legislation in question were described by the Supreme Court of the State as follows (168 La., p. 1020):

"One may scan the acts in vain to ascertain where any money is appropriated for the purchase of school books for the use of any church, private, sectarian or even public school. The appropriations were made for the specific purpose of purchasing school books for the use of the school children of the state, free of cost to them. It was for their benefit and the resulting benefit to the state that the appropriations were made. True, these children attend some school, public or private, the latter, sectarian or nonsectarian, and that the books are to be furnished them for their use, free of cost, whichever they attend. The schools, however, are not the beneficiaries of these appropriations. They obtain nothing from them, nor are they relieved of a single obligation, because of them. The school children and the state alone are the beneficiaries. It is also true that the sectarian schools, which some of the children attend, instruct their pupils in religion, and books are used for that purpose, but one may search diligently the acts, though without result, in an effort to find anything to the effect that it is the purpose of the state to furnish religious books for the use of such children.... What the statutes contemplate is that the same books that are furnished children attending public schools shall be furnished children attending private schools. This is the only practical way of interpreting and executing the statutes, and this is what the state board of education is doing. Among these books, naturally, none is to be expected, adapted to religious instruction."

The Court also stated, although the point is not of importance in relation to the Federal question, that it was "only the use of the books that is granted to the children, or, in other words, the books are lent to them."

Viewing the statute as having the effect thus attributed to it, we can not doubt that the taxing power of the State is exerted for a public purpose. The legislation does not segregate private schools, or their pupils, as its beneficiaries or attempt to interfere with any matters of exclusively private concern. Its interest is education, broadly; its method, comprehensive. Individual interests are aided only as the common interest is safeguarded. Judgment affirmed.

NOTES AND QUESTIONS

The "test" announced in this case appears to be that aid to education of children attending religious schools is permissible if it is cannot be "adapted to religious instruction" and "does not segregate private schools" as beneficiaries. Relying on *Cochran*, the New York legislature authorized a program of loaning secular textbooks to children attending religious schools. This program was sustained in *Board of Education v. Allen* [Chapter Fourteen, section 1] and in several cases citing it. Several cases have also focused on the breadth of the beneficiary class as an indication of whether the nonestablishment principle is violated. Contrast, e.g., *Committee for Public Education and Religious Liberty v. Nyquist* with *Mueller v. Allen* [Chapter Fourteen, section 1]. In *Agostini v. Felton*, Justice O'Connor wrote there is no impermissible financial incentive to advance religion when "aid is allocated on the basis of neutral, secular criteria that neither favor nor disfavor religion, and is made available to both religious and secular beneficiaries on a nondiscriminatory basis." [Chapter Fourteen, section 1]. Is this a principled way of approaching the issue of aid to religious schools?

11. CONSCIENTIOUS OBJECTORS

Rosika Schwimmer, a forty-nine-year-old Hungarian immigrant applying for naturalization, declared, "I am not willing to bear arms." She asserted, "My 'cosmic consciousness of belonging to the human family' is shared by all those who believe that all human beings are the children of God." Denial of her naturalization application was upheld by Pierce Butler, writing for a majority of six that the duty of citizens to defend their government by arms was a "fundamental principle of the Constitution."

United States v. Schwimmer

279 U.S. 644 (1929).

■ JUSTICE HOLMES, with whom JUSTICE BRANDEIS joined, dissented.

I would suggest that the Quakers have done their share to make the country what it is, that many citizens agree with the applicant's belief and that I had not supposed hitherto that we regretted our inability to expel them because they believe more than some of us do in the teachings of the Sermon on the Mount.

■ JUSTICE SANFORD also dissented.

In 1929 Douglas Clyde Macintosh, a Canadian, applied for naturalization. He was a Baptist minister who had served as chaplain at the front in World War I; he was now Dwight Professor of Theology at Yale. He declared he would not support the United States "right or wrong" or promise to take up arms in its defense. He "could not put allegiance to the government of any country before allegiance to the will of God."

The Second Circuit, per Judge Martin Manton, ordered him admitted to citizenship, 42 F.2d 845 (1930). The government took the case to the Supreme Court, arguing it was indistinguishable from *Schwimmer*. On Macintosh's behalf, John W. Davis argued that the free exercise of religion "embraces human conduct expressive of the relation between man and God." Davis asserted there was a constitutional immunity against bearing arms in a war if one has "conscientious religious scruples against doing so." Justice George

Sutherland characterized Davis's argument as astonishing: "Of course, there is no such principle in the Constitution, fixed or otherwise." Sutherland relied upon *Holy Trinity Church* [section 1 above] in his opinion for the Court.

United States v. Macintosh

283 U.S. 605 (1931).

When he speaks of putting his allegiance to the will of God above his allegiance to the government, it is evident, in the light of his entire statement, that he means to make his own *interpretation* of the will of God the decisive test which shall conclude the government and stay its hand. We are a Christian people (*Holy Trinity Church v. United States*, 143 U.S. 457, 470–471), according to one another the equal right of religious freedom, and acknowledging with reverence the duty of obedience to the will of God. But, also, we are a Nation with the duty to survive; a Nation whose Constitution contemplates war as well as peace; whose government must go forward upon the assumption, and safely can proceed upon no other, that unqualified allegiance to the Nation and submission and obedience to the laws of the land, as well those made for war as those made for peace, are not inconsistent with the will of God.

■ CHIEF JUSTICE HUGHES, with whom JUSTICES HOLMES, BRANDEIS, and STONE— a weighty minority–dissented.

The essence of religion is belief in a relation to God involving duties superior to those arising from any human relation. As was stated by Mr. Justice Field, in *Davis v. Beason* [Chapter Nine]: "The term 'religion' has reference to one's views of his relations to his Creator, and to the obligations they impose of reverence for his being and character, and of obedience to his will." One cannot speak of religious liberty, with proper appreciation of its essential and historic significance, without assuming the existence of a belief in supreme allegiance to the will of God. Professor Macintosh, when pressed by the inquiries put to him, stated what is axiomatic in religious doctrine. And, putting aside dogmas with their particular conceptions of deity, freedom of conscience itself implies respect for an innate conviction of paramount duty. The battle for religious liberty has been fought and won with respect to religious beliefs and practices, which are not in conflict with good order, upon the very ground of the supremacy of conscience within its proper field. What that field is, under our system of government, presents in part a question of constitutional law and also, in part, one of legislative policy in avoiding unnecessary clashes with the dictates of conscience. There is abundant room for enforcing the requisite authority of law as it is enacted and requires obedience, and for maintaining the conception of the supremacy of law as essential to orderly government, without demanding that either citizens or applicants for citizenship shall assume by oath an obligation to regard allegiance to God as subordinate to allegiance to civil power. The attempt to exact such a promise, and thus to bind one's conscience by the taking of oaths or the submission to tests, has been the cause of many deplorable conflicts. The Congress has sought to avoid such conflicts in this country by respecting our happy tradition. In no sphere of legislation has the intention to prevent such clashes been more conspicuous than in relation to the bearing of arms. It would require strong evidence that the Congress intended a reversal of its policy in prescribing the general terms of the naturalization oath. I find no such evidence.

Nor is there ground, in my opinion, for the exclusion of Professor Macintosh because his conscientious scruples have particular reference to wars believed to be unjust. There is nothing new in such an attitude. Among the most eminent statesmen here and abroad have been those who condemned the action of their country in entering into wars they thought to be unjustified. Agreements for the renunciation of war presuppose a preponderant public sentiment against wars of aggression. If, while recognizing the power of Congress, the mere holding of religious or conscientious scruples against all wars should not disqualify a citizen from holding office in this country, or an applicant otherwise qualified from being admitted to citizenship, there would seem to be no reason why a reservation of religious or conscientious objection to participation in wars believed to be unjust should constitute such a disqualification.

Apart from the terms of the oath, it is said that the respondent has failed to meet the requirement of "attachment to the principles of the Constitution." Here, again, is a general phrase which should be construed, not in opposition to, but in accord with, the theory and practice of our Government in relation to freedom of conscience. What I have said as to the provisions of the oath I think applies equally to this phase of the case.

QUESTIONS

Can any religious believer give "unqualified allegiance to the Nation"? See the flag salute cases, *Gobitis* and *Barnette* [Chapter Eleven, section 3]. Is the Court competent to assess whether such allegiance is "consistent with the will of God"? Did the Court give to Macintosh "the equal right of religious freedom, and acknowledg[e] with reverence [his] duty of obedience to the will of God"?

The Regents of the University of California required all male students to complete one course in military service and tactics. The Methodist Episcopal church in its General Conference of 1928 had declared, "We renounce war as an instrument of national policy." Two Methodist students, sons of ministers, asserting their religious belief "that war, training for war, and military training are immoral," were suspended from the university for failing to take the prescribed course. The supreme court of California sustained the Regents. The two Methodists appealed to the Supreme Court, contending that free exercise of religion was protected against the states by the First Amendment and that the principle of free exercise "must afford protection to outward manifestations of religious belief." The Court implicitly agreed with this contention, but would not formally embrace this position until *Cantwell v. Connecticut* (1940) [Chapter Eleven, section 1].

Pierce Butler, a Catholic, delivered the opinion of the Supreme Court in Hamilton v. Regents of the University of California, 293 U.S. 245 (1934). He cited the naturalization cases of *Schwimmer* and *Macintosh* to show that there was no unconstitutional infringement of religious belief for a government to require willingness to bear arms. If Butler were aware of the tradition within his church of honoring martyrs who declined to serve in the Roman army [Chapter One, section 10], would that have made a difference in how he approached this case?

Concurring in the opinion, Justice Benjamin Cardozo—a humanist of Jewish background—found nothing contrary to "the free exercise of religion as the phrase was understood by the founders of the nation, and by the generations that have followed.... One who is a martyr to a principle—which may turn out in the end to be a delusion or an error—does not prove by his martyrdom that he has kept within the law." Were the Macabees deluded or erroneous when they refused to "keep within the law" required of them by their Hellenistic overlords [Chapter One, section 5]? When Cardozo invoked the founders' understanding of free exercise of religion, did those founders include James Madison, author of the First Amendment [Chapter Six, section 1]? In light of the fact that–from the earliest period of the republic—conscientious objectors have had statutory protection for declining to bear arms, does the failure to secure that right in the text of the Bill of Rights mean that there is no basis for such legislation in the free exercise principle?

Shortly after World War II, *Schwimmer* and *Macintosh* were reversed in *Girouard v. United States*, 328 U.S. 61 (1946) [Chapter Eleven, section 4].

*

PART THREE

CONTEMPORARY CONTROVERSIES

Sacred Duties

1. Preaching From House to House and Distributing Religious Literature

Matthew 28:16-20

Now the eleven disciples went to Galilee, to the mountain to which Jesus had directed them. When they saw him, they worshiped him; but some doubted. And Jesus came and said to them, "All authority in heaven and on earth has been given to me. Go therefore and make disciples of all nations, baptizing them in the name of the Father and of the Son and of the Holy Spirit, and teaching them to obey everything that I have commanded you. And remember, I am with you always, to the end of the age."

NOTE

Many Christian communities rely on the text above, known as the "Great Commission," as the principal biblical basis for a variety of activities relating to sharing their religious faith with others. But the constitutional challenges of a single religious group, the Jehovah's Witnesses, to state regulation of religion were the catalyst that first brought the subject of this section, and indeed, the interpretation of free exercise of religion, to the United States Supreme Court. The challenges occurred at a time when the Court was reading other First Amendment freedoms into the meaning of "the due process of law" guarantee of the Fourteenth Amendment. Like the eighteenth-century Baptists, the Jehovah's Witnesses were an evangelical group outside the mainline Protestant churches. Like the nineteenth-century Mormons, the Witnesses were tightly knit. Like twentieth-century Catholics, they were ruled by a supreme authority. Like the Mennonites, the Witnesses were pioneers of civil liberty while being severe in maintaining orthodoxy within their own ranks. *See* M. James Penton, *Apocalypse Delayed* 62–68 (1985). Paradoxically they were to attack the hypocrisy of all "religionists" while claiming their own freedom from regulation that interfered with their own free exercise of "religion."

In 1880, in Pittsburgh, Charles Taze Russell began the publication of *Zion's Watch Tower and Herald of Christ's Presence*, teaching that the Second Coming of Christ was imminent. Book salesmen who were believers—"colporteurs," to use the term earlier applied to evangelical distributors of the Bible—sold Russell's works throughout the United States and Britain. By the eve of World War I, the *Watch Tower* had 45,000 subscribers. James A. Beckford, *The Trumpet of Prophecy: A Sociological Study of Jehovah's Witnesses* 1–18 (1975).

On Russell's death in 1916, Joseph Franklin Rutherford succeeded him as president of the Watch Tower Bible and Tract Society, the New York corporation that held title to all church property. Rutherford was a lawyer, once a special judge in Missouri, and customarily called Judge Rutherford. The next year Rutherford was indicted under the Espionage Act of 1917 for conspiracy to obstruct recruiting and to cause insubordination in the armed forces. Evidence supporting the charge was his publication of *The Finished Mystery*, a book that attacked "patriotism" as one of "the great untruths" of Satan, denounced war as murder, and declared that no issue was worth a single life. At the trial the government clinched its case by showing Rutherford's activity "advising men subject to the draft to claim their exemption and to refuse to perform any duty in camp if they were drafted." *Rutherford v. United States*, 258 F. 855, 865 (2d Cir. 1919). For his book and his advice, Rutherford and six other defendants were sentenced to twenty years in the federal penitentiary. On appeal, by a vote of 2–1, the convictions were set aside on the ground of a prejudicial act by the trial judge (sentencing an evasive witness for contempt). *Id.* 863. The First Amendment was not invoked. The government did not renew the prosecution. Other Jehovah's Witnesses received long prison sentences for distributing *The Finished Mystery, e.g., Stephens v. United States*, 261 F. 590 (9th Cir. 1919) (distributors had "a disloyal and wicked" purpose). But Judge Rutherford himself had had an unforgettable experience of the justice administered by the appellate courts of the United States.

Jehovah's Witnesses were prosecuted for selling their literature without a license as early as 1928. Prior to this time, the Witnesses had accepted the conventional view that Paul, in Romans 13:1, commanding obedience to the "powers," had meant the civil authorities [Chapter One, section 6]. Now in 1929 Judge Rutherford interpreted "the powers" to be obeyed as being God and Christ. Penton 139. In the 1930s the conflict between the Witnesses and local licensing authorities increased, and Rutherford in 1933 ordered that all adverse court decisions be appealed. In 1935 he set up a legal department under Olin R. Moyle, a Witness, to coordinate the defense of Witnesses. David R. Manwaring, *Render unto Caesar: The Flag–Salute Controversy* 26–27 (1962).

The Witnesses saturated communities—usually on Sundays, their day off from their ordinary occupation—with their tracts, ignoring local restrictions as infringements of their duty to carry out a divine command. In 1937 the Supreme Court, invoking the Mormon cases [Chapter Nine], unanimously dismissed for want of federal jurisdiction, leaving religiously motivated distributors of literature unprotected. *Coleman v. City of Griffin*, 302 U.S. 636 (1937). The next year, however, by a vote of 8–0, the Supreme Court invalidated the Griffin ordinance on the ground that it unconstitutionally abridged the Witnesses' freedom of speech and the freedom of the press. *Lovell v. City of Griffin*, 303 U.S. 444 (1938). These freedoms were characterized by Chief Justice Charles Evans Hughes as "among the fundamental personal rights" protected by the Fourteenth Amendment, while the Court still left a purely religious right without protection. The victory was largely the work of the American Civil Liberties Union (then called the American Liberties Union), which had come to the Witnesses' assistance. In 1939 the Court, 8–1, struck down four more municipal ordinances as abridgements of the freedom of speech and of the press. *Schneider v. Irvington*, 308 U.S. 147 (1939). Not, however, until 1940 did the Supreme Court address affirmatively the claim of free exercise of religion.

The Witnesses were now represented by Hayden C. Covington, a young Texan Witness, with whom Rutherford had replaced Moyle; he was to have a remarkable career in Supreme Court litigation, winning thirty-six cases in the next fifteen years. Penton 88. Without mentioning *Coleman*—unanimously decided only three years earlier—the Supreme Court in effect overruled it. More remarkably, the Court—composed of Hughes, McReynolds, Stone, and Roberts, whose appointments antedated the New Deal, and Roosevelt's appointees Black, Reed, Frankfurter, Douglas, and Murphy—was in complete agreement.

Cantwell v. Connecticut

310 U.S. 296 (1940).

Mr. Hayden C. Covington, with whom *Mr. Joseph F. Rutherford* was on the brief, for appellants and petitioner.

Messrs. Francis A. Pallotti, Attorney General, and *Edwin S. Pickett*, with whom *Messrs. William L. Hadden, Richard F. Corkey*, Assistant Attorney General, and *Luke H. Stapleton* were on the brief, for the State of Connecticut, appellee and respondent.

■ JUSTICE ROBERTS delivered the opinion of the Court.

Newton Cantwell and his two sons, Jesse and Russell, members of a group known as Jehovah's Witnesses, and claiming to be ordained ministers, were arrested in New Haven, Connecticut, and each was charged by information in five counts, with statutory and common law offenses. After trial in the Court of Common Pleas of New Haven County each of them was convicted on the third count, which charged a violation of § 6294 of the General Statutes of Connecticut, and on the fifth count, which charged commission of the common law offense of inciting a breach of the peace. On appeal to the Supreme Court the conviction of all three on the third count was affirmed. The conviction of Jesse Cantwell, on the fifth count, was also affirmed, but the conviction of Newton and Russell on that count was reversed and a new trial ordered as to them....

The facts adduced to sustain the convictions on the third count follow. On the day of their arrest the appellants were engaged in going singly from house to house on Cassius Street in New Haven. They were individually equipped with a bag containing books and pamphlets on religious subjects, a portable phonograph and a set of records, each of which, when played, introduced, and was a description of, one of the books. Each appellant asked the person who responded to his call for permission to play one of the records. If permission was granted he asked the person to buy the book described and, upon refusal, he solicited such contribution towards the publication of the pamphlets as the listener was willing to make. If a contribution was received a pamphlet was delivered upon condition that it would be read.

Cassius Street is in a thickly populated neighborhood, where about ninety per cent of the residents are Roman Catholics. A phonograph record, describing a book entitled "Enemies," included an attack on the Catholic religion. None of the persons interviewed were members of Jehovah's Witnesses.

The statute under which the appellants were charged provides:

"No person shall solicit money, services, subscriptions or any valuable thing for any alleged religious, charitable or philanthropic cause, from other than a member of the organization for whose benefit such person is soliciting or within the county in which such person or organization is located unless such cause shall have been approved by the secretary of the public welfare council. Upon application of any person in behalf of such cause, the secretary shall determine whether such cause is a religious one or is a bona fide object of charity or philanthropy and conforms to reasonable standards of efficiency and integrity, and, if he shall so find, shall approve the same and issue to the authority in charge a certificate to that effect. Such certificate may be revoked at any time. Any person violating any provision of this section shall be fined not more than one hundred dollars or imprisoned not more than thirty days or both...."

First. We hold that the statute, as construed and applied to the appellants, deprives them of their liberty without due process of law in contravention of the Fourteenth Amendment. The fundamental concept of liberty embodied in that Amendment embraces the liberties guaranteed by the First Amendment. The First Amendment declares that Congress shall make no law respecting an establishment of religion or prohibiting the free exercise thereof. The Fourteenth Amendment has rendered the legislatures of the states as incompetent as Congress to enact such laws. The constitutional inhibition of legislation on the subject of religion has a double aspect. On the one hand, it forestalls compulsion by law of the acceptance of any creed or the practice of any form of worship. Freedom of conscience and freedom to adhere to such religious organization or form of worship as the individual may choose cannot be restricted by law. On the other hand, it safeguards the free exercise of the chosen form of religion. Thus the Amendment embraces two concepts—freedom to believe and freedom to act. The first is absolute but, in the nature of things, the second cannot be. Conduct remains subject to regulation for the protection of society. The freedom to act must have appropriate definition to preserve the enforcement of that protection. In every case the power to regulate must be so exercised as not, in attaining a permissible end, unduly to infringe the protected freedom. No one would contest the proposition that a State may not, by statute, wholly deny the right to preach or to disseminate religious views. Plainly such a previous and absolute restraint would violate the terms of the guarantee. It is equally clear that a State may by general and non-discriminatory legislation regulate the times, the places, and the manner of soliciting upon its streets, and of holding meetings thereon; and may in other respects safeguard the peace, good order and comfort of the community, without unconstitutionally invading the liberties protected by the Fourteenth Amendment. The appellants are right in their insistence that the Act in question is not such a regulation. If a certificate is procured, solicitation is permitted without restraint but, in the absence of a certificate, solicitation is altogether prohibited.

The appellants urge that to require them to obtain a certificate as a condition of soliciting support for their views amounts to a prior restraint on the exercise of their religion within the meaning of the Constitution. The State insists that the Act, as construed by the Supreme Court of

Connecticut, imposes no previous restraint upon the dissemination of religious views or teaching but merely safeguards against the perpetration of frauds under the cloak of religion. Conceding that this is so, the question remains whether the method adopted by Connecticut to that end transgresses the liberty safeguarded by the Constitution.

The general regulation, in the public interest, of solicitation, which does not involve any religious test and does not unreasonably obstruct or delay the collection of funds, is not open to any constitutional objection, even though the collection be for a religious purpose. Such regulation would not constitute a prohibited previous restraint on the free exercise of religion or interpose an inadmissible obstacle to its exercise.

It will be noted, however, that the Act requires an application to the secretary of the public welfare council of the State; that he is empowered to determine whether the cause is a religious one, and that the issue of a certificate depends upon his affirmative action. If he finds that the cause is not that of religion, to solicit for it becomes a crime. He is not to issue a certificate as a matter of course. His decision to issue or refuse it involves appraisal of facts, the exercise of judgment, and the formation of an opinion. He is authorized to withhold his approval if he determines that the cause is not a religious one. Such a censorship of religion as the means of determining its right to survive is a denial of liberty protected by the First Amendment and included in the liberty which is within the protection of the Fourteenth.

The State asserts that if the licensing officer acts arbitrarily, capriciously, or corruptly, his action is subject to judicial correction. Counsel refer to the rule prevailing in Connecticut that the decision of a commission or an administrative official will be reviewed upon a claim that "it works material damage to individual or corporate rights, or invades or threatens such rights, or is so unreasonable as to justify judicial intervention, or is not consonant with justice, or that a legal duty has not been performed." It is suggested that the statute is to be read as requiring the officer to issue a certificate unless the cause in question is clearly not a religious one; and that if he violates his duty his action will be corrected by a court.

To this suggestion there are several sufficient answers. The line between a discretionary and a ministerial act is not always easy to mark and the statute has not been construed by the state court to impose a mere ministerial duty on the secretary of the welfare council. Upon his decision as to the nature of the cause, the right to solicit depends. Moreover, the availability of a judicial remedy for abuses in the system of licensing still leaves that system one of previous restraint which, in the field of free speech and press, we have held inadmissible. A statute authorizing previous restraint upon the exercise of the guaranteed freedom by judicial decision after trial is as obnoxious to the Constitution as one providing for like restraint by administrative action.

Nothing we have said is intended even remotely to imply that, under the cloak of religion, persons may, with impunity, commit frauds upon the public. Certainly penal laws are available to punish such conduct. Even the exercise of religion may be at some slight inconvenience in order that the

State may protect its citizens from injury. Without doubt a State may protect its citizens from fraudulent solicitation by requiring a stranger in the community, before permitting him publicly to solicit funds for any purpose, to establish his identity and his authority to act for the cause which he purports to represent. The State is likewise free to regulate the time and manner of solicitation generally, in the interest of public safety, peace, comfort or convenience. But to condition the solicitation of aid for the perpetuation of religious views or systems upon a license, the grant of which rests in the exercise of a determination by state authority as to what is a religious cause, is to lay a forbidden burden upon the exercise of liberty protected by the Constitution.

Second. We hold that, in the circumstances disclosed, the conviction of Jesse Cantwell on the fifth count must be set aside. Decision as to the lawfulness of the conviction demands the weighing of two conflicting interests. The fundamental law declares the interest of the United States that the free exercise of religion be not prohibited and that freedom to communicate information and opinion be not abridged. The State of Connecticut has an obvious interest in the preservation and protection of peace and good order within her borders. We must determine whether the alleged protection of the State's interest, means to which end would, in the absence of limitation by the Federal Constitution, lie wholly within the State's discretion, has been pressed, in this instance, to a point where it has come into fatal collision with the overriding interest protected by the federal compact.

Conviction on the fifth count was not pursuant to a statute evincing a legislative judgment that street discussion of religious affairs, because of its tendency to provoke disorder, should be regulated, or a judgment that the playing of a phonograph on the streets should in the interest of comfort or privacy be limited or prevented. Violation of an Act exhibiting such a legislative judgment and narrowly drawn to prevent the supposed evil, would pose a question differing from that we must here answer. Such a declaration of the State's policy would weigh heavily in any challenge of the law as infringing constitutional limitations. Here, however, the judgment is based on a common law concept of the most general and undefined nature. The court below has held that the petitioner's conduct constituted the commission of an offense under the state law, and we accept its decision as binding upon us to that extent.

The offense known as breach of the peace embraces a great variety of conduct destroying or menacing public order and tranquility. It includes not only violent acts but acts and words likely to produce violence in others. No one would have the hardihood to suggest that the principle of freedom of speech sanctions incitement to riot or that religious liberty connotes the privilege to exhort others to physical attack upon those belonging to another sect. When clear and present danger of riot, disorder, interference with traffic upon the public streets, or other immediate threat to public safety, peace, or order, appears, the power of the State to prevent or punish is obvious. Equally obvious is it that a State may not unduly suppress free communication of views, religious or other, under the guise of conserving desirable conditions. Here we have a situation analogous to a conviction under a statute sweeping in a great variety of conduct under a general and indefinite characterization, and leaving to the executive and judicial branches too wide a discretion in its application.

Having these considerations in mind, we note that Jesse Cantwell, on April 26, 1938, was upon a public street, where he had a right to be, and where he had a right peacefully to impart his views to others. There is no showing that his deportment was noisy, truculent, overbearing or offensive. He requested of two pedestrians permission to play to them a phonograph record. The permission was granted. It is not claimed that he intended to insult or affront the hearers by playing the record. It is plain that he wished only to interest them in his propaganda. The sound of the phonograph is not shown to have disturbed residents of the street, to have drawn a crowd, or to have impeded traffic. Thus far he had invaded no right or interest of the public or of the men accosted.

The record played by Cantwell embodies a general attack on all organized religious systems as instruments of Satan and injurious to man; it then singles out the Roman Catholic Church for strictures couched in terms which naturally would offend not only persons of that persuasion, but all others who respect the honestly held religious faith of their fellows. The hearers were in fact highly offended. One of them said he felt like hitting Cantwell and the other that he was tempted to throw Cantwell off the street. The one who testified he felt like hitting Cantwell said, in answer to the question "Did you do anything else or have any other reaction?" "No, sir, because he said he would take the victrola and he went." The other witness testified that he told Cantwell he had better get off the street before something happened to him and that was the end of the matter as Cantwell picked up his books and walked up the street.

Cantwell's conduct, in the view of the court below, considered apart from the effect of his communication upon his hearers, did not amount to a breach of the peace. One may, however, be guilty of the offense if he commit acts or make statements likely to provoke violence and disturbance of good order, even though no such eventuality be intended. Decisions to this effect are many, but examination discloses that, in practically all, the provocative language which was held to amount to a breach of the peace consisted of profane, indecent, or abusive remarks directed to the person of the hearer. Resort to epithets or personal abuse is not in any proper sense communication of information or opinion safeguarded by the Constitution, and its punishment as a criminal act would raise no question under that instrument.

We find in the instant case no assault or threatening of bodily harm, no truculent bearing, no intentional discourtesy, no personal abuse. On the contrary, we find only an effort to persuade a willing listener to buy a book or to contribute money in the interest of what Cantwell, however misguided others may think him, conceived to be true religion.

In the realm of religious faith, and in that of political belief, sharp differences arise. In both fields the tenets of one man may seem the rankest error to his neighbor. To persuade others to his own point of view, the pleader, as we know, at times, resorts to exaggeration, to vilification of men who have been, or are, prominent in church or state, and even to false statement. But the people of this nation have ordained in the light of history, that, in spite of the probability of excesses and abuses, these liberties are, in the long view, essential to enlightened opinion and right conduct on the part of the citizens of a democracy.

The essential characteristics of these liberties is, that under their shield many types of life, character, opinion and belief can develop unmolested and unobstructed. Nowhere is this shield more necessary than in our own country for a people composed of many races and of many creeds. There are limits to the exercise of these liberties. The danger in these times from the coercive activities of those who in the delusion of racial or religious conceit would incite violence and breaches of the peace in order to deprive others of their equal right to the exercise of their liberties, is emphasized by events familiar to all. These and other transgressions of those limits the States appropriately may punish.

Although the contents of the record not unnaturally aroused animosity, we think that, in the absence of a statute narrowly drawn to define and punish specific conduct as constituting a clear and present danger to a substantial interest of the State, the petitioner's communication, considered in the light of the constitutional guarantees, raised no such clear and present menace to public peace and order as to render him liable to conviction of the common law offense in question.

The judgment affirming the convictions on the third and fifth counts is reversed and the cause is remanded for further proceedings not inconsistent with this opinion. *Reversed.*

NOTE

The Religion of the Justices. Some authors have explored the religious views of the Justices. See, e.g., Michael E. Smith, "The Special Place of Religion in the Constitution," *1983 Sup. Ct. Rev.* 83, 105–118, and Sanford Levinson, *Constitutional Faith* (1988). By and large, though, the religion of the Justices is a taboo subject in legal analysis. Why? The religious makeup of the Court that took the momentous step of *Cantwell* was as follows. Five members had had Protestant upbringing but were no longer identified with the specific tenets of any church. Chief Justice Hughes's religious evolution is representative. He was the son of a Baptist minister in upstate New York and had himself taught Sunday School at the Fifth Avenue Baptist Church in New York City. But in his own words, "I had long since ceased to attach any importance to what many regard as the distinctive tenets of the denomination. Rather, I cherished the nobler tradition of the Baptists as protagonists in the struggle for religious liberty. I wished to throw what influence I had to the support of Christian institutions." The others were as follows: Black (former Baptist, sometimes attending services at a Unitarian Universalist church), Douglas (former Presbyterian and ex-born-again Christian), McReynolds (identified only as "Protestant"); and Stone (former Congregationalist). Two justices were members in a specific Protestant denomination: Reed was a Methodist, and Roberts was an Episcopalian. Murphy was a somewhat anticlerical Catholic. Frankfurter had a

Jewish background, but belonged to no Jewish congregation; he told the theologian Reinhold Niebuhr that he was a "believing unbeliever." Like Hughes, Douglas was a minister's son. The attitudes toward religion expressed by the Court correspond with fairly closely to the spiritual outlook of the majority of the Court, unchurched, unsympathetic to mainline orthodoxies, open to spiritual currents, basically theistic and vaguely in favor of "Christian" ideas.

Sources for the religions of the Justices: Hugo Black, Jr., *My Father: A Remembrance* 104, 176 (1975); Roger K. Newman, *Hugo Black: A Biography* 521 (1994); William O. Douglas, *Go East, Young Man* 4, 109–111 (1974); Liva Baker, *Felix Frankfurter* 18–19 (1969); Merlo Pusey, *Charles Evans Hughes* 1–2, 110 (1951); J. Woodford Howard, *Mr. Justice Murphy* 444–445, 455–456 (1968); John D. Fassett, *New Deal Justice: The Life of Stanley Reed of Kentucky* 28 (1994); Alpheus Thomas Mason, *Harlan Fiske Stone: Pillar of the Law* 29, 79, 807 (1956); *Biographical Dictionary of the Federal Judiciary* (1976) (McReynolds, 191, Roberts, 237); *see also* Michael S. Ariens and Robert A. Destro, *Religious Liberty in a Pluralistic Society* 276–77 (1996).

Murdock v. Pennsylvania

319 U.S. 105 (1943).

> *Mr. Hayden C. Covington* for petitioner.
>
> *Mr. Fred B. Tiescher* for respondent.

■ JUSTICE DOUGLAS delivered the opinion of the Court.

Petitioners spread their interpretations of the Bible and their religious beliefs largely through the hand distribution of literature by full or part time workers. They claim to follow the example of Paul, teaching "publickly, and from house to house." Acts 20:20. They take literally the mandate of the Scriptures, "Go ye into all the world, and preach the gospel to every creature." Mark 16:15. In doing so they believe that they are obeying a commandment of God.

The hand distribution of religious tracts is an age-old form of missionary evangelism—as old as the history of printing presses. It has been a potent force in various religious movements down through the years. This form of evangelism is utilized today on a large scale by various religious sects whose colporteurs carry the Gospel to thousands upon thousands of homes and seek through personal visitations to win adherents to their faith.[1] It is more than preaching; it is more than distribution of religious

---

1. The General Conference of Seventh-day Adventists, who filed a brief *amicus curiae* on the reargument of *Jones v. Opelika*, has given us the following data concerning their literature ministry: This denomination has 83 publishing houses throughout the world, issuing publications in over 200 languages. Some 9,256 separate publications were issued in 1941. By printed and spoken word, the Gospel is carried into 412 countries in 824 languages. 1942 Yearbook, p. 287. During December 1941, a total of 1,018 colporteurs operated in North America. They delivered during that month $97,997.19 worth of gospel literature, and for the whole year of 1941 a total of $790,610.36—an average per person of about $65 per month. Some of these were students and temporary workers. Colporteurs of this denomination receive half of their collections, from which they must pay their

literature. It is a combination of both. Its purpose is as evangelical as the revival meeting. This form of religious activity occupies the same high estate under the First Amendment as do worship in the churches and preaching from the pulpits. It has the same claim to protection as the more orthodox and conventional exercises of religion. It also has the same claim as the others to the guarantees of freedom of speech and freedom of the press.

The integrity of this conduct or behavior as a religious practice has not been challenged. Nor do we have presented any question as to the sincerity of petitioners in their religious beliefs and practices, however misguided they may be thought to be. Moreover, we do not intimate or suggest in respecting their sincerity that any conduct can be made a religious rite and by the zeal of the practitioners swept into the First Amendment. *Reynolds v. United States* and *Davis v. Beason* [Chapter Nine] denied any such claim to the practice of polygamy and bigamy. Other claims may well arise which deserve the same fate. We only hold that spreading one's religious beliefs or preaching the Gospel through distribution of religious literature and through personal visitations is an age-old type of evangelism with as high a claim to constitutional protection as the more orthodox types. The manner in which it is practiced at times gives rise to special problems with which the police power of the states is competent to deal. See for example *Cox v. New Hampshire* and *Chaplinsky v. New Hampshire* [citations omitted]. But that merely illustrates that the rights with which we are dealing are not absolutes. *Schneider v. State* [citation omitted]. We are concerned, however, in these cases merely with one narrow issue. There is presented for decision no question whatsoever concerning punishment for any alleged unlawful acts during the solicitation. Nor is there involved here any question as to the validity of a registration system for colporteurs and other solicitors. The cases present a single issue—the constitutionality of an ordinance which as construed and applied requires religious colporteurs to pay a license tax as a condition to the pursuit of their activities.

The alleged justification for the exaction of this license tax is the fact that the religious literature is distributed with a solicitation of funds. Thus it was stated, in *Jones v. Opelika*, that when a religious sect uses "ordinary commercial methods of sales of articles to raise propaganda funds," it is proper for the state to charge "reasonable fees for the privilege of canvassing." Situations will arise where it will be difficult to determine whether a particular activity is religious or purely commercial. The distinction at times is vital. As we stated only the other day, in *Jamison v. Texas* [citation omitted], "The states can prohibit the use of the streets for the distribution of purely commercial leaflets, even though such leaflets may have 'a civic appeal, or a moral platitude' appended. *Valentine v. Chrestensen* [citation omitted]. They may not prohibit the distribution of handbills in the pursuit

---

traveling and living expenses. Colporteurs are specially trained and their qualifications equal those of preachers. In the field, each worker is under the supervision of a field missionary secretary to whom a weekly report is made. After fifteen years of continuous service, each colporteur is entitled to the same pension as retired ministers. And see Howell, *The Great Advent Movement* (1935), 72–75.

of a clearly religious activity merely because the handbills invite the purchase of books for the improved understanding of the religion or because the handbills seek in a lawful fashion to promote the raising of funds for religious purposes." But the mere fact that the religious literature is "sold" by itinerant preachers rather than "donated" does not transform evangelism into a commercial enterprise. If it did, then the passing of the collection plate in church would make the church service a commercial project. The constitutional rights of those spreading their religious beliefs through the spoken and printed word are not to be gauged by standards governing retailers or wholesalers of books. The right to use the press for expressing one's views is not to be measured by the protection afforded commercial handbills. It should be remembered that the pamphlets of Thomas Paine were not distributed free of charge. It is plain that a religious organization needs funds to remain a going concern. But an itinerant evangelist, however misguided or intolerant he may be, does not become a mere book agent by selling the Bible or religious tracts to help defray his expenses or to sustain him. Freedom of speech, freedom of the press, freedom of religion are available to all, not merely to those who can pay their own way. As we have said, the problem of drawing the line between a purely commercial activity and a religious one will at times be difficult. On this record it plainly cannot be said that petitioners were engaged in a commercial rather than a religious venture. It is a distortion of the facts of record to describe their activities as the occupation of selling books and pamphlets. And the Pennsylvania court did not rest the judgments of conviction on that basis, though it did find that petitioners "sold" the literature. The Supreme Court of Iowa in *State v. Mead* described the selling activities of members of this same sect as "merely incidental and collateral" to their "main object which was to preach and publicize the doctrines of their order." That accurately summarizes the present record.

We do not mean to say that religious groups and the press are free from all financial burdens of government. See *Grosjean v. American Press Co.* [citation omitted]. We have here something quite different, for example, from a tax on the income of one who engages in religious activities or a tax on property used or employed in connection with those activities. It is one thing to impose a tax on the income or property of a preacher. It is quite another thing to exact a tax from him for the privilege of delivering a sermon. . . . Reversed.

■ JUSTICES REED, ROBERTS, FRANKFURTER and JACKSON dissented.

■ JUSTICE JACKSON, concurring in the result in *Douglas v. City of Jeannette* and dissenting in *Murdock v. Pennsylvania*:

From the record in *Douglas* we learn: In 1939, a "Watch Tower Campaign" was instituted by Jehovah's Witnesses in Jeannette, Pennsylvania, an industrial city of some 16,000 inhabitants. [In a footnote Justice Jackson cited census data indicating that about 50% of the residents of Westoreland County affiliated with a religious body at the time were Roman Catholics]. Each home was visited, a bell was rung or the door knocked upon, and the householder advised that the Witness had important information. If the householder would listen, a record was played on the phonograph. Its subject was "Snare and Racket." The following words are representative of its contents: "Religion is wrong and a snare because it deceives the people, but that does not mean that all who follow religion are willingly bad. Religion is a racket because it has long been used and is still used to extract money from the people upon the theory and promise that the paying over of money to a priest will serve to relieve the party paying from punishment after death and further insure his salvation." This line of attack is taken by the Witnesses generally upon all denominations, especially the Roman Catholic. The householder was asked to buy a variety of literature for a price or contribution. The price would be twenty-five cents for the books and smaller sums for the pamphlets. Oftentimes, if he was unwilling to purchase, the book or pamphlet was given to him anyway.

When this campaign began, many complaints from offended householders were received, and three or four of the Witnesses were arrested. Thereafter, the "zone servant" in charge of the campaign conferred with the Mayor. He told the Mayor it was their right to carry on the campaign and showed him a decision of the United States Supreme Court, said to have that effect, as proof of it. The Mayor told him that they were at liberty to distribute their literature in the streets of the city and that he would have no objection if they distributed the literature free of charge at the houses, but that the people objected to their attempt to force these sales, and particularly on Sunday. The Mayor asked whether it would not be possible to come on some other day and to distribute the literature without selling it. The zone servant replied that that was contrary to their method of "doing business" and refused. He also told the Mayor that he would bring enough Witnesses into the City of Jeannette to get the job done whether the Mayor liked it or not. The Mayor urged them to await the outcome of an appeal which was then pending in the other cases and let the matter take its course through the courts. This, too, was refused, and the threat to bring more people than the Mayor's police force could cope with was repeated.

On Palm Sunday of 1939, the threat was made good. Over 100 of the Witnesses appeared. They were strangers to the city and arrived in upwards of twenty-five automobiles. The automobiles were parked outside the city limits, and headquarters were set up in a gasoline station with telephone facilities through which the director of the campaign could be notified when trouble occurred. He furnished bonds for the Witnesses as they were arrested. As they began their work, around 9:00 o'clock in the morning, telephone calls began to come in to the Police Headquarters, and complaints in large volume were made all during the day. They exceeded the number that the police could handle, and the Fire Department was called out to assist. The Witnesses called at homes singly and in groups, and some of the homes complained that they were called upon several times. Twenty-one Witnesses were arrested. Only those were arrested where definite proof was obtainable that the literature had been offered for sale or a sale had been made for a price. Three were later discharged for inadequacies in this proof, and eighteen were convicted. The zone servant furnished appeal bonds.

The national structure of the Jehovah's Witness movement is also somewhat revealed in this testimony. At the head of the movement in this country is the Watch Tower Bible & Tract Society, a corporation organized under the laws of Pennsylvania, but having its principal place of business in Brooklyn, N.Y. It prints all pamphlets, manufactures all books, supplies all phonographs and records, and provides other materials for the Witnesses. It "ordains" these Witnesses by furnishing each, on a basis which does not clearly appear, a certificate that he is a minister of the Gospel. Its output is large and its revenues must be considerable. Little is revealed of its affairs. One of its "zone servants" testified that its correspondence is signed only with the name of the corporation and anonymity as to its personnel is its policy. The assumption that it is a "non-profit charitable" corporation may be true, but it is without support beyond mere assertion. In none of these cases has the assertion been supported by such usual evidence as a balance sheet or an income statement. What its manufacturing costs and revenues are, what salaries or bonuses it pays, what contracts it has for supplies or services we simply do not know. The effort of counsel for Jeannette to obtain information, books and records of the local "companies" of Witnesses engaged in the Jeannette campaign in the trial was met by contradictory statements as to the methods and meaning of such meager accounts as were produced.

The publishing output of the Watch Tower corporation is disposed of through converts, some of whom are full-time and some part-time ministers. These are organized into groups or companies under the direction of "zone servants." It is their purpose to carry on in a thorough manner so that every home in the communities in which they work may be regularly visited three or four times a year. The full-time Witnesses acquire their literature from the Watch Tower Bible & Tract Society at a figure which enables them to distribute it at the prices printed thereon with a substantial differential. Some of the books they acquire for 5¢ and dispose of for a contribution of 25¢. On others, the margin is less. Part-time ministers have a differential between the 20¢ which they remit to the Watch Tower Society and the 25¢ which is the contribution they ask for the books. We are told that many of the Witnesses give away a substantial quantity of the literature to people who make no contributions. Apart from the fact that this differential exists and that it enables the distributors to meet in whole or in part their living expenses, it has proven impossible in these cases to learn the exact results of the campaigns from a financial point of view. There is evidence that the group accumulated a substantial amount from the differentials, but the tracing of the money was not possible because of the failure to obtain records and the failure, apparently, to keep them.

The literature thus distributed is voluminous and repetitious. Characterization is risky, but a few quotations will indicate something of its temper.

Taking as representative the book "Enemies," of which J. F. Rutherford, the lawyer who long headed this group, is the author, we find the following: "The greatest racket ever invented and practiced is that of religion. The most cruel and seductive public enemy is that which employs religion to carry on the racket, and by which means the people are deceived and the name of Almighty God is reproached. There are numerous systems of religion, but the most subtle, fraudulent and injurious to humankind is that which is generally labeled the 'Christian religion,' because it has the appearance of a worshipful devotion to the Supreme Being, and thereby easily misleads many honest and sincere persons." It analyzes the income of the Roman Catholic hierarchy and announces that it is "the great racket, a racket that is greater than all other rackets combined." It also says under the chapter heading "Song of the Harlot Referring now to the foregoing Scriptural definition of *harlot:* What religious system exactly fits the prophecies recorded in God's Word? There is but one answer, and that is, The Roman Catholic Church organization.... Those close or nearby and dependent upon the main organization, being of the same stripe, picture the Jewish and Protestant clergy and other allies of the Hierarchy who tag along behind the Hierarchy at the present time to do the bidding of the old 'whore'.... Says the prophet of Jehovah: 'It shall come to pass in that day, that Tyre (modern Tyre, the Roman Catholic Hierarchy organization) shall be forgotten.' Forgotten by whom? By her former illicit paramours who have committed fornication with her." Throughout the literature, statements of this kind appear amidst scriptural comment and prophecy, denunciation of demonology, which is used to characterize the Roman Catholic religion, criticism of government and those in authority, advocacy of obedience to the law of God instead of the law of man, and an interpretation of the law of God as they see it.

The spirit and temper of this campaign is most fairly stated perhaps in the words, again of Rutherford, in his book "Religion": "God's faithful servants go from house to house to bring the message of the kingdom to those who reside there, omitting none, not even the houses of the Roman Catholic Hierarchy, and there they give witness to the kingdom because they are commanded by the Most High to do so. 'They shall enter in at the windows like a thief.' They do not loot nor break into the houses, but they set up their phonographs before the doors and windows and send the message of the kingdom right into the houses into the ears of those who might wish to hear and while those desiring to hear are hearing, some of the 'sourpusses' are compelled to hear. Locusts invade the homes of the people and even eat the varnish off the wood and eat the wood to some extent. Likewise God's faithful witnesses, likened unto locusts, get the kingdom message right into the house and they take the veneer off the religious things that are in that house, including candles and 'holy water', remove the superstition from the minds of the people, and show them that the doctrines that have been taught to them are wood, hay and stubble, destructible by fire, and they cannot withstand the heat. The people are enabled to learn that 'purgatory' is a bogeyman, set up by the agents of Satan to frighten the people into the religious organizations, where they may be fleeced of their hard-earned money. Thus the kingdom message plagues the religionists, and the clergy find that they are unable to prevent it. Therefore, as described by the prophet, the message comes to them like a thief that enters in at the windows, and this message is a warning to those who are on the inside that Jesus Christ has come, and they remember his warning words, to wit: 'Behold, I come as a thief.' (Revelation 16:15.) The day of Armageddon is very close, and that day comes upon the world in general like a thief in the night.''

The day of Armageddon, to which all of this is prelude, is to be a violent and bloody one, for then shall be slain all "demonologists," including most of those who reject the teachings of Jehovah's Witnesses.

In the *Murdock* case, on another Sunday morning of the following Lent, we again find the Witnesses in Jeannette, travelling by twos and threes and carrying cases for the books and phonographs. This time eight were arrested, as against the 21 arrested on the preceding Palm Sunday involved in the *Douglas* case.

In the *Struthers* case, we find the Witness knocking on the door of a total stranger at 4:00 on Sunday afternoon, July 7th. The householder's fourteen year old son answered, and, at the Witness's request, called his mother from the kitchen. His mother had previously become "very much disgusted about going to the door" to receive leaflets, particularly since another person had on a previous occasion called her to the door and told her, as she testified, "that I was doomed to go to hell because I would not let this literature in my home for my children to read." She testified that the Witness "shoved in the door" the circular being distributed, and that she "couldn't do much more than take" it, and she promptly tore it up in the presence of the Witness, for while she believed "in the worship of God," she did not "care to talk to everybody" and did not "believe that anyone needs to be sent from door to door to tell us how to worship." The record in the *Struthers* case is even more sparse than that in the *Murdock* case, but the householder did testify that at the time she was given the circular the Witness "told me that a number of them were in jail and would I call the Chief of Police and ask that their workers might be released."

Such is the activity which it is claimed no public authority can either regulate or tax. This claim is substantially, if not quite, sustained today. I dissent—a disagreement induced in no small part by the facts recited.

NOTE

Massachusetts law prohibited children from selling newspapers or magazines on the streets. Sarah Prince, an ordained Jehovah's Witness, permitted her ward Betty, a girl of nine, "to engage in the preaching work" receiving contributions for the *Watch Tower* on the streets of Brockton. Betty believed that failure to do the work would condemn her "to everlasting destruction at Armageddon." Convicted of aiding a minor to violate the statute, Sarah Prince contended that her own freedom to raise the child and Betty's free exercise of religion had been unconstitutionally compromised.

Citing *Reynolds* and *Davis* [Chapter Nine], Justice Wiley B. Rutledge wrote for the Court: "But the family itself is not beyond regulation in the public interest, as against a claim of religious liberty." He upheld the state's right to protect children from work on the streets, adding: "Parents may be free to become martyrs themselves. But it does not follow that they are free, in identical circumstances, to make martyrs of their children.... " Justices

Jackson, Roberts, and Frankfurter agreed with the result but not with the opinion making age the criterion for regulation of religion. Only Justice Murphy, a Catholic, dissented.

Prince v. Massachusetts

321 U.S. 158 (1944).

■ Murphy, J., dissenting.

No chapter in human history has been so largely written in terms of persecution and intolerance as the one dealing with religious freedom. From ancient times to the present day, the ingenuity of man has known no limits in its ability to forge weapons of oppression for use against those who dare to express or practice unorthodox religious beliefs. And the Jehovah's Witnesses are living proof of the fact that even in this nation, conceived as it was in the ideals of freedom, the right to practice religion in unconventional ways is still far from secure. Theirs is a militant and unpopular faith, pursued with a fanatical zeal. They have suffered brutal beatings; their property has been destroyed; they have been harassed at every turn by the resurrection and enforcement of little used ordinances and statutes. To them, along with other present-day religious minorities, befalls the burden of testing our devotion to the ideals and constitutional guarantees of religious freedom. We should therefore hesitate before approving the application of a statute that might be used as another instrument of oppression. Religious freedom is too sacred a right to be restricted or prohibited in any degree without convincing proof that a legitimate interest of the state is in grave danger.

NOTE

Retreat from Murdock? Texas provided an exemption from the imposition of sales tax on "[p]eriodicals that are published or distributed by a religious faith and that consist wholly of writings promulgating the teaching of the faith and books that consist wholly of writings sacred to a religious faith." Tex. Tax Code Ann. § 151.312 (1982). In *Texas Monthly, Inc. v. Bullock*, 489 U.S. 1 (1989) [Chapter Thirteen, section 3], the Court ruled that this provision violated the Establishment Clause. Justice Brennan, joined by Justices Marshall and Stevens, were of the view that the exemption lacked a secular objective because it was available only to religious publications and did not confer similar benefits for nonreligious publications or groups. Justice Blackmun, joined by Justice O'Connor, filed a separate concurring opinion, reserving the question of whether "the Free Exercise Clause requires a tax exemption for the sale of religious literature by a religious organization." Justice Scalia, joined by Chief Justice Rehnquist, and Justice Kennedy, dissented because he could "find no basis in the text of the Constitution, the decisions of this Court, or the traditions of our people for disapproving this longstanding and widespread practice." He described the opinions of Justices Brennan and Blackmun as a "judicial demolition project" that departed significantly from the Court's holding in *Walz v. Tax Comm'n of New York City*, 397 U.S. 664 (1970). [Chapter Thirteen, section 3] where the Court "considered and rejected an

Establishment Clause challenge that was in all relevant respects identical." In *Walz* numerous religious organizations filed briefs amicus curiae urging that tax exemption for "property used exclusively for purposes of religious worship" be sustained. In *Texas Monthly* no religious organization filed an amicus brief urging that the sales and use tax exemption on religious literature be sustained. The only amicus briefs filed—on behalf of the American Booksellers Association, the Magazine Publishers of America, and the American Civil Liberties Union—urged reversal of the lower court, or invalidation of the Texas provision.

Within months the question that Justices Blackmun and O'Connor had thought open in *Texas Monthly* was resolved in a case that squarely presented the objection that taxation of distribution of religious literature by an evangelist to members of his own faith violated the free exercise provision.

Jimmy Swaggart Ministries v. California State Board of Equalization

493 U.S. 378 (1990).

Michael W. McConnell, argued the cause for appellant. With him on the brief were *Charles R. Ajalat, Edward McGlynn Gaffney, Jr., William J. Treeby* and *Jesse H. Choper*.

Richard E. Nielsen, Deputy Attorney General of California, argued the cause for appellee. With him on the brief were *John K. Van de Kamp*, Attorney General, and *Neal J. Gobar*, Deputy Attorney General.

Briefs of amici curiae urging reversal were filed for the Association for Public Justice by *Bradley P. Jacob*; for the Evangelical Council for Financial Accountability et al. by *Samuel E. Ericsson, Michael J. Woodruff*, and *Forest D. Montgomery*; for the International Society for Krishna Consciousness of California, Inc., by *David M. Liberman, Robert C. Moest*, and *Barry A. Fisher*; for the National Council of Churches of Christ in the U.S.A. by *Douglas Laycock*; and for the National Taxpayers Union by *Gale A. Norton*.

Steven R. Shapiro filed a brief for the American Civil Liberties Union as amicus curiae urging affirmance. Briefs of amici curiae were filed for the National Conference of State Legislatures et al. by *Benna Ruth Solomon* and *Charles Rothfeld*; and for Watchtower Bible and Tract Society of New York, Inc., by *James M. McCabe* and *Donald T. Ridley*.

■ JUSTICE O'CONNOR delivered the opinion of the Court.

This case presents the question whether the Religion Clauses of the First Amendment prohibit a State from imposing a generally applicable sales and use tax on the distribution of religious materials by a religious organization.

California's Sales and Use Tax Law requires retailers to pay a sales tax "[f]or the privilege of selling tangible personal property at retail." A "sale" includes any transfer of title or possession of tangible personal property for consideration.

The use tax, as a complement to the sales tax, reaches out-of-state purchases by residents of the State. It is "imposed on the storage, use, or other consumption in this state of tangible personal property purchased from any retailer," at the same rate as the sales tax (6 percent). Although the use tax is imposed on the purchaser, it is generally collected by the retailer at the time the sale is made. Neither the State Constitution nor the State Sales and Use Tax Law exempts religious organizations from the sales and use tax, apart from a limited exemption for the serving of meals by religious organizations.

During the tax period in question (1974 to 1981), appellant Jimmy Swaggart Ministries was a religious organization incorporated as a Louisiana nonprofit corporation and recognized as such by the Internal Revenue Service pursuant to § 501(c)(3) of the Internal Revenue Code of 1954, as amended, and by the California State Controller pursuant to the Inheritance Tax and Gift Tax Laws of the State of California. Appellant's constitution and bylaws provide that it "is called for the purpose of establishing and maintaining an evangelistic outreach for the worship of Almighty God." This outreach is to be performed "by all available means, both at home and in foreign lands," and "shall specifically include evangelistic crusades; missionary endeavors; radio broadcasting (as owner, broadcaster, and placement agency); television broadcasting (both as owner and broadcaster); and audio production and reproduction of music; audio production and reproduction of preaching; audio production and reproduction of teaching; writing, printing and publishing; and, any and all other individual or mass media methods that presently exist or may be devised in the future to proclaim the good news of Jesus Christ."

From 1974 to 1981, appellant conducted numerous "evangelistic crusades" in auditoriums and arenas across the country in cooperation with local churches. During this period, appellant held 23 crusades in California—each lasting 1 to 3 days, with one crusade lasting 6 days—for a total of 52 days. At the crusades, appellant conducted religious services that included preaching and singing. Some of these services were recorded for later sale or broadcast. Appellant also sold religious books, tapes, records, and other religious and nonreligious merchandise at the crusades.

Appellant also published a monthly magazine, "The Evangelist," which was sold nationwide by subscription. The magazine contained articles of a religious nature as well as advertisements for appellant's religious books, tapes, and records. The magazine included an order form listing the various items for sale in the particular issue and their unit price, with spaces for purchasers to fill in the quantity desired and the total price. Appellant also offered its items for sale through radio, television, and cable television broadcasts, including broadcasts through local California stations.

In 1980, appellee Board of Equalization of the State of California (Board) informed appellant that religious materials were not exempt from the sales tax and requested appellant to register as a seller to facilitate reporting and payment of the tax. Appellant responded that it was exempt from such taxes under the First Amendment. In 1981, the Board audited appellant and advised appellant that it should register as a seller and report and pay sales tax on all sales made at its California crusades. The Board also opined that appellant had a sufficient nexus with the State of California to require appellant to collect and report use tax on its mail-order sales to California purchasers.

Based on the Board's review of appellant's records, the parties stipulated "that [appellant] sold for use in California tangible personal property for the period April 1, 1974, through December 31, 1981, measured by payment to [appellant] of $1,702,942.00 for mail order sales from Baton Rouge, Louisiana and $240,560.00 for crusade merchandise sales in California." These figures represented the sales and use in California of merchandise with specific religious content—Bibles, Bible study manuals, printed sermons and collections of sermons, audiocassette tapes of sermons, religious books and pamphlets, and religious music in the form of songbooks, tapes, and records. Based on the sales figures for appellant's religious materials, the Board notified appellant that it owed sales and use taxes of $118,294.54, plus interest of $36,021.11, and a penalty of $11,829.45, for a total amount due of $166,145.10. Appellant did not contest the Board's assessment of tax liability for the sale and use of certain nonreligious merchandise, including such items as "T-shirts with JSM logo, mugs, bowls, plates, replicas of crown of thorns, ark of the covenant, Roman coin, candlesticks, Bible stand, pen and pencil sets, prints of religious scenes, bud vase, and communion cups."

Appellant filed a petition for redetermination with the Board, reiterating its view that the tax on religious materials violated the First Amendment. Following a hearing and an appeal to the Board, the Board deleted the penalty but otherwise redetermined the matter without adjustment in the amount of $118,294.54 in taxes owing, plus $65,043.55 in interest. Pursuant to state procedural law, appellant paid the amount and filed a petition for redetermination and refund with the Board. The Board denied appellant's petition, and appellant brought suit in state court, seeking a refund of the tax paid.

The trial court entered judgment for the Board, ruling that appellant was not entitled to a refund of any tax. The California Court of Appeal affirmed, and the California Supreme Court denied discretionary review. We noted probable jurisdiction, and now affirm.

II

Appellant's central contention is that the State's imposition of sales and use tax liability on its sale of religious materials contravenes the First Amendment's command, made applicable to the States by the Fourteenth Amendment, to "make no law respecting an establishment of religion, or prohibiting the free exercise thereof." Appellant challenges the Sales and Use Tax Law under both the Free Exercise and Establishment Clauses.

A

The Free Exercise Clause, we have noted, "withdraws from legislative power, state and federal, the exertion of any restraint on the free exercise of religion. Its purpose is to secure religious liberty in the individual by prohibiting any invasions thereof by civil authority." *Schempp* [Chapter Fourteen, section 2]. Indeed, "[a] regulation neutral on its face may, in its application, nonetheless offend the constitutional requirement for governmental neutrality if it unduly burdens the free exercise of religion." *Yoder* [section 7 below]. Our cases have established that "[t]he free exercise inquiry asks whether government has placed a substantial burden on the observation of a central religious belief or practice and, if so, whether a compelling governmental interest justifies the burden." *Hernandez v. Commissioner* [discussed in Note. *Equal Tax Treatment of Religious Groups,* below].

Appellant relies almost exclusively on our decisions in *Murdock* and *Follett* for the proposition that a State may not impose a sales or use tax on the evangelical distribution of religious material by a religious organization. Appellant contends that the State's imposition of use and sales tax liability on it burdens its evangelical distribution of religious materials in a manner identical to the manner in which the evangelists in *Murdock* and *Follett* were burdened.

We reject appellant's expansive reading of *Murdock* and *Follett* as contrary to the decisions themselves. In *Murdock,* we considered the constitutionality of a city ordinance requiring all persons canvassing or soliciting within the city to procure a license by paying a flat fee. Reversing the convictions of Jehovah's Witnesses convicted under the ordinance of soliciting and distributing religious literature without a license, we explained: "The hand distribution of religious tracts is an age-old form of missionary evangelism ... [and] has been a potent force in various religious movements down through the years. This form of evangelism is utilized today on a large scale by various religious sects whose colporteurs carry the Gospel to thousands upon thousands of homes and seek through personal visitations to win adherents to their faith. It is more than preaching; it is more than distribution of religious literature. It is a combination of both. Its purpose is as evangelical as the revival meeting. This form of religious activity occupies the same high estate under the First Amendment as do worship in the churches and preaching in the pulpits." Accordingly, we held that "spreading one's religious beliefs or preaching the Gospel through distribution of religious literature and through personal visitations is an age-old type of evangelism with as high a claim to constitutional protection as the more orthodox types."

We extended *Murdock* the following Term by invalidating, as applied to "one who earns his livelihood as an evangelist or preacher in his home town," an ordinance (similar to that involved in *Murdock*) that required all booksellers to pay a flat fee to procure a license to sell books. *Follett.* Reaffirming our observation in *Murdock* that " 'the power to tax the exercise of a privilege is the power to control or suppress its enjoyment,' " we reasoned that "[t]he protection of the First Amendment is not restricted to orthodox religious practices any more than it is to the expression of orthodox economic views. He who makes a profession of evangelism is not in a less preferred position than the casual worker."

Our decisions in these cases, however, resulted from the particular nature of the challenged taxes—flat license taxes that operated as a prior restraint on the exercise of religious liberty. In *Murdock*, for instance, we emphasized that the tax at issue was "a license tax—a flat tax imposed on the exercise of a privilege granted by the Bill of Rights," and cautioned that "[w]e do not mean to say that religious groups and the press are free from all financial burdens of government.... We have here something quite different, for example, from a tax on the income of one who engages in religious activities or a tax on property used or employed in connection with those activities." In *Follett*, we reiterated that a preacher is not "free from all financial burdens of government, including taxes on income or property" and, "like other citizens, may be subject to general taxation."

Significantly, we noted in both cases that a primary vice of the ordinances at issue was that they operated as prior restraints of constitutionally protected conduct: "In all of these cases [in which license taxes have been invalidated] the issuance of the permit or license is dependent on the payment of a license tax. And the license tax is fixed in amount and unrelated to the scope of the activities of petitioners or to their realized revenues. It is not a nominal fee imposed as a regulatory measure to defray the expenses of policing the activities in question. It is in no way apportioned. It is a flat license tax levied and collected as a condition to the pursuit of activities whose enjoyment is guaranteed by the First Amendment. Accordingly, it restrains in advance those constitutional liberties of press and religion and inevitably tends to suppress their exercise. That is almost uniformly recognized as the inherent vice and evil of this flat license tax." *Murdock*. "The exaction of a tax as a condition to the exercise of the great liberties guaranteed by the First Amendment is as obnoxious as the imposition of a censorship or a previous restraint." *Follett*. Thus, although *Murdock* and *Follett* establish that appellant's form of religious exercise has "as high a claim to constitutional protection as the more orthodox types," *Murdock*, those cases are of no further help to appellant. Our concern in *Murdock* and *Follett*—that a flat license tax would act as a precondition to the free exercise of religious beliefs—is simply not present where a tax applies to all sales and uses of tangible personal property in the State....

We also note that just last Term a plurality of the Court rejected the precise argument appellant now makes. In *Texas Monthly* [this section above] Justice Brennan, writing for three Justices, held that a state sales tax exemption for religious publications violated the Establishment Clause. In so concluding, the plurality further held that the Free Exercise Clause did not prevent the State from withdrawing its exemption, noting that "[t]o the extent that our opinions in *Murdock* and *Follett* might be read ... to suggest that the States and the Federal Government may never tax the sale of religious or other publications, we reject those dicta." Justice White, concurring in the judgment, concluded that the exemption violated the Free Press Clause because the content of a publication determined its tax-exempt status. Justice Blackmun, joined by Justice O'Connor, concurred in the plurality's holding that the tax exemption at issue in that case contravened the Establishment Clause, but reserved the question whether "the Free Exercise Clause requires a tax exemption for the sale of religious literature by a religious organization; in other words, defining the ultimate scope of *Follett* and *Murdock* may be left for another day.'' In this case, of course, California has not chosen to create a tax exemption for religious materials, and we therefore have no need to revisit the Establishment Clause question presented in *Texas Monthly*.

We do, however, decide the free exercise question left open by Justice Blackmun's concurrence in *Texas Monthly* by limiting *Murdock* and *Follett* to apply only where a flat license tax operates as a prior restraint on the free exercise of religious beliefs. As such, *Murdock* and *Follett* plainly do not support appellant's free exercise claim. California's generally applicable sales and use tax is not a flat tax, represents only a small fraction of any retail sale, and applies neutrally to all retail sales of tangible personal property made in California. California imposes its sales and use tax even if the seller or the purchaser is charitable, religious, nonprofit, or state or local governmental in nature [cases omitted]. Thus, the sales and use tax is not a tax on the right to disseminate religious information, ideas, or beliefs per se; rather, it is a tax on the privilege of making retail sales of tangible personal property and on the storage, use, or other consumption of tangible personal property in California. For example, California treats the sale of a Bible by a religious organization just as it would treat the sale of a Bible by a bookstore; as long as both are in-state retail sales of tangible personal property, they are both subject to the tax regardless of the motivation for the sale or the purchase. There is no danger that appellant's religious activity is being singled out for special and burdensome treatment.

Moreover, our concern in *Murdock* and *Follett* that flat license taxes operate as a precondition to the exercise of evangelistic activity is not present in this case, because the registration requirement, and the tax itself do not act as prior restraints—no fee is charged for registering, the tax is due regardless of preregistration, and the tax is not imposed as a precondition of disseminating the message. Thus, unlike the license tax in *Murdock*, which was ''in no way apportioned'' to the ''realized revenues'' of the itinerant preachers forced to pay the tax, *see also Texas Monthly*, the tax at issue in this case is akin to a generally applicable income or property tax, which *Murdock* and *Follett* specifically state may constitutionally be imposed on religious activity.

In addition to appellant's misplaced reliance on *Murdock* and *Follett*, appellant's free exercise claim is also in significant tension with the Court's decision last Term in *Hernandez*, holding that the Government's disallowance of a tax deduction for religious ''auditing'' and ''training'' services did not violate the Free Exercise Clause. The Court reasoned that ''[a]ny burden imposed on auditing or training ... derives solely from the fact that, as a result of the deduction denial, adherents have less money to gain access to such sessions. This burden is no different from that imposed by any public tax or fee; indeed, the burden imposed by the denial of the 'contribution or gift' deduction would seem to pale by comparison to the overall federal income tax burden on an adherent.'' There is no evidence in this case that collection and payment of the tax violates appellant's sincere religious beliefs. California's nondiscriminatory Sales and Use Tax Law requires only that appellant collect the tax from its California purchasers and remit the tax money to the State. The only burden on appellant is the claimed reduction in income resulting from the presumably lower demand for appellant's wares (caused by the marginally higher price) and from the costs associated with administering the tax. As the Court made clear in *Hernandez*, however, to the extent that imposition of a generally applicable tax merely decreases the amount of money appellant has to spend on its religious activities, any such burden is not constitutionally significant. *Hernandez; Texas Monthly; Bob Jones University* [Chapter Fourteen, section 3].

Appellant contends that the availability of a deduction (at issue in *Hernandez*) and the imposition of a tax (at issue here) are distinguishable, but in both cases adherents base their claim for an exemption on the argument that an "incrementally larger tax burden interferes with their religious activities." It is precisely this argument—rather than one applicable only to deductions—that the Court rejected in *Hernandez*. At bottom, though we do not doubt the economic cost to appellant of complying with a generally applicable sales and use tax, such a tax is no different from other generally applicable laws and regulations—such as health and safety regulations—to which appellant must adhere.

Finally, because appellant's religious beliefs do not forbid payment of the sales and use tax, appellant's reliance on *Sherbert* [section 5 below], and its progeny is misplaced, because in no sense has the State " 'condition[ed] receipt of an important benefit upon conduct proscribed by a religious faith, or . . . denie[d] such a benefit because of conduct mandated by religious belief, thereby putting substantial pressure on an adherent to modify his behavior and to violate his beliefs.' " *Hobbie v. Unemployment Appeals Comm'n of Florida* [section 5 below] (quoting *Thomas v. Review Bd.* [section 4 below]). Appellant has never alleged that the mere act of paying the tax, by itself, violates its sincere religious beliefs.

We therefore conclude that the collection and payment of the generally applicable tax in this case imposes no constitutionally significant burden on appellant's religious practices or beliefs. The Free Exercise Clause accordingly does not require the State to grant appellant an exemption from its generally applicable sales and use tax. Although it is of course possible to imagine that a more onerous tax rate, even if generally applicable, might effectively choke off an adherent's religious practices, cf. *Murdock*, (the burden of a flat tax could render itinerant evangelism "crushed and closed out by the sheer weight of the toll or tribute which is exacted town by town"), we face no such situation in this case. Accordingly, we intimate no views as to whether such a generally applicable tax might violate the Free Exercise Clause. . . . *Affirmed.*

NOTES AND QUESTIONS

1. *The Chilling Effect of Imposing Use Tax on Itinerant Evangelists.* The headquarters of the Jimmy Swaggart Ministries is located in Baton Rouge, Louisiana. The ministry has never maintained an office or had any employees

in California other than during the evangelistic crusades referred to above. Nonetheless, the State also imposed use tax liability on the ministry for the estimated retail value of religious items such as Bibles and religious tapes from its headquarters in Louisiana to religious adherents in California. The ministry contended that this part of the State's imposition of taxation violated the Commerce and Due Process Clauses because, as an out-of-state distributor, it had an insufficient nexus to the State. See *National Geographic Society v. California Bd. of Equalization*, 430 U.S. 551, 554 (1977); *National Bellas Hess, Inc. v. Department of Revenue of Illinois*, 386 U.S. 753, 756–760 (1967). Although this portion of the tax liability ($1.7 million) was far greater than the liability the State claimed to have arisen from the sale of Bibles and other religious literature at the crusades within the State ($240,560), the Court declined to reach the merits of this claim. It took the view that the claim was procedurally barred, noting that the California courts had ruled that the ministry should have raised this objection in its initial papers before the tax authority. If mere entrance into a state to preach a religious crusade is all that it takes to subject all future distribution of religious literature to out-of-state religious adherents to state and local use tax, does this precedent chill the duty of evangelists to preach from house to house?

2. *Equal tax treatment of religious groups.* In *Swaggart Ministries* Justice O'Connor relied on *Hernandez v. Commissioner*, 490 U.S. 680 (1989) for the proposition that "generally applicable administrative and recordkeeping regulations may be imposed on religious organization without running afoul of the Establishment Clause." Justice O'Connor had dissented in *Hernandez*, in part because she doubted that the government was in fact applying its taxing power evenhandedly. But this concern did not trouble her a year later in *Swaggart Ministries*, where she repeatedly characterized the sales and use tax as "generally applicable," without any support for that conclusion in the record. On the assumption that the government may not impose a tax burden on any religious community that it does not also impose on all other religious communities, must the Witnesses collect sales tax every time they "sell" a copy of *Watchtower* or *Awake* in California or another state that taxes such transactions? Are the devotees of Krishna Consciousness supposed to do so when they distribute a copy of the *Bagavad-Gita* and receive a contribution for their ministry of Sankirtan [section 2 below]? Are Christian communities supposed to file quarterly tax returns on all "sales" of Bibles or of religious literature from pamphlet racks in the foyer of their churches? Are Jews supposed to account for the contribution to a synagogue for a seat at High Holy day services as though this were a "sale"? Would your answer to any of these questions implicate the government in "excessive entanglement with religion," a concern usually raised in cases involving the funding of religious schools [Chapter Fourteen, section 1]? After protracted negotiations with the religious community in the *Hernandez* case, the Internal Revenue Service reached an agreement in 1995 that allows members of the Church of Scientology a tax deduction for religious "auditing" and "training" services. Does this development change your answer to any of the other questions in this note? To your view of *Swaggart Ministries*? Is *Swaggart Ministries* consistent with *Cantwell*? With *Murdock* and *Follett*? If so, do *Cantwell, Murdock* and *Follett* have much vitality?

2.   PREACHING IN THE PUBLIC SQUARE

Acts of the Apostles 5: 17–23, 25–29, 32, 42

Then the high priest ... arrested the apostles and put them in the public prison. But during the night an angel of the Lord opened the prison doors, brought them out, and said, "Go, stand in the temple and tell the people the whole message about this life." When they heard this, they entered the temple at daybreak and went on with their teaching. When the high priest and those with him arrived, they called together the council and the whole body of the elders of Israel, and sent to the prison to have them brought. But when the temple police went there, they did not find them in the prison; so they returned and reported, "We found the prison securely locked and the guards standing at the doors, but when we opened them, we found no one inside." Then someone arrived and announced, "Look, the men whom you put in prison are standing in the temple and teaching the people!" Then the captain went with the temple police and brought them before the council. The high priest questioned them, saying, "We gave you strict orders not to teach in this name, yet here you have filled Jerusalem with your teaching." But Peter and the apostles answered, "We must obey God rather than any human authority. And we are witnesses to these things, and so is the Holy Spirit whom God has given to those who obey him." And every day in the temple and at home they did not cease to teach and proclaim Jesus as the Messiah.

———

In the passage cited above, the leaders of the new Christian movement were under an order not to preach their message publicly. Arrested for defiance of this order, they mysteriously escape from prison and resume the public preaching of their message. The text serves as a warning against efforts to "privatize" religion, or to confine it exclusively to the home.

The theologian David Tracy has written that religion is "the single subject about which many intellectuals can feel free to be ignorant. Often abetted by the churches, they need not study religion, for 'everybody' already knows what religion is: It is a private consumer product that some people seem to need. Its former social role was poisonous. Its present privatization is harmless enough to wish it well from a civilized distance. Religion seems to be the sort of thing one likes 'if that's the sort of thing one likes.'" David Tracy, *The Analogical Imagination* 13 (1981); *see also* Richard S. Myers, "The Supreme Court and the Privatization of Religion," 41 *Cath. U. L. Rev.* 19 (1991); and Gerard V. Bradley, "Dogmatomachy—A 'Privatization' Theory of the Religion Clause Cases," 30 *St. Louis U. L.J.* 275 (1986); *but see* Ruti Teitel, "A Critique of Religion as Politics in the Public Sphere," 77 *Cornell L.J.* 747 (1993); and Suzanne Sherry, "Religion and the Public Square: Making Democracy Safe for Religious Minorities," 47 *DePaul L.Rev.* 499 (1998).

Debates about the "privatization" thesis have also formed a major current in contemporary sociological studies of religion in American life. *See, e.g.,*

Robert N. Bellah, et. al., *Habits of the Heart: Individualism and Commitment in American Life* (1985); Peter Berger, *Modernization and Religion* (1981); Perry Dane, "The Public, the Private, and the Sacred: Variations on a Theme of Nomos and Narrative," 8 *Cardozo Stud. L. & Literature* 15 (1996); Mary Douglas and Steven Tipton, eds., *Religion and America: Spiritual Life in a Secular Age* (1983); Jeffrey Hadden and Theodore E. Long, eds., *Religion and Religiosity in America: Studies in Honor of Joseph H. Fichter* (1983); Stephen Hart, "Privatization in American Religion and Society," 47 *Sociological Analysis: A Journal in the Sociology of Religion* 319 (1987); and Stephen Holmes, "Jean Bodin: The Paradox of Sovereignty and the Privatization of Religion," in J. Roland Pennock & John W. Chapman, eds., *Religion, Morality, and the Law* (1988).

Richard John Neuhaus coined a catchy phrase, "the naked public square," to describe the rise of the ideology of secularism that "would exclude religion and religiously grounded values from the conduct of public business." Neuhaus, *The Naked Public Square: Religion and Democracy in America* xi (1984). Neuhaus extended this metaphor to criticize the vacuum with respect to political and spiritual truth that is created once the religious voice is excluded from political discourse. The relation between religion and politics in America is explored below in Chapter Fifteen. Here we lay the groundwork for the metaphor of the "public square" in the literal attempt of religious communities in America to spread their message by preaching and distributing religious literature in the public streets and parks. Note the persistent effort of governmental authorities to remove religious communities from open public fora.

In *Niemotko v. Maryland*, 340 U.S. 268 (1951) and *Poulos v. New Hampshire*, 345 U.S. 395 (1953), the Court clarified that religious groups were entitled to use city streets and parks for meetings and rallies. In *Marsh v. Alabama*, 326 U.S. 501 (1946), the Court had ruled that, even where a company owned a whole town, it could not assert its private property interests in such a way as to restrict the "fundamental libert[y]" of a Witness to use the sidewalks of a downtown block in this town to distribute religious literature. The State of Alabama was deemed to be an actor in the case because a deputy sheriff, who served as the town's policeman, had arrested Mrs. Marsh for trespass. Noting that freedom of the press and of religion occupy a "preferred position," the Court reversed her criminal conviction.

Like the Witnesses who go door to door to preach their message, the International Society for Krishna Consciousness, Inc., a religious society, teaches its members the practice of Sankirtan, a religious ritual in which its members greet members of the public by giving them flowers or small American flags, distribute or sell the society's religious literature, and seek donations to support the Krishna religion. The society and Joseph Beca, head of its temple in Minneapolis, sought an injunction against the application to the society and its members of a rule of the Minnesota Agricultural Society governing the state fair. Minnesota State Fair Rule 6.05 provides: "Sale or distribution of any merchandise, including printed or written material except under license issued [by] the Society and/or from a duly-licensed location shall be a misdemeanor." The rule required all persons or groups selling or distributing literature to do so in licensed booths. Represented by Barry Fisher, the Krishna devotees prevailed in the Supreme Court of Minnesota, which held the rule an unconstitutional restriction of Sankirtan in violation of the free exercise clause. 299 N.W. 2d 79 (1980). Professor Laurence Tribe represented the Krishna devotees in the United States Supreme Court, where he characterized the case as one involving free speech rights and equal access to a public forum. The equal access claim did not prevail.

Heffron v. International Society for Krishna Consciousness, Inc.

452 U.S. 640 (1981)

■ JUSTICE WHITE delivered the opinion of the Court.

The Fair is a major public event and attracts visitors from all over Minnesota as well as from other parts of the country. During the past five years, the average total attendance for the 12–day Fair has been 1,320,000 persons. The average daily attendance on weekdays has been 115,000 persons and on Saturdays and Sundays 160,000. . . .

[T]he First Amendment does not guarantee the right to communicate one's views at all times and places or in any manner that may be desired. . . . "We have often approved restrictions of that kind provided that they are justified without reference to the content of the regulated speech, that they serve a significant governmental interest, and that in doing so they leave open ample alternative channels for communication of the information." [citations omitted]. The issue here is whether Rule 6.05 is a permissible restriction on the place and manner of communicating the views of the Krishna religion, more specifically, whether the [Minnesota Agricultural] Society may require the members of ISKCON who desire to practice Sankirtan at the State Fair to confine their distribution, sales, and solicitation activities to a fixed location.

NOTES AND QUESTIONS

The Court held that the restrictions were a reasonable expression of the state's interest in the orderly movement of the visitors to the fair on the 125 acres fairground. The Minnesota Supreme Court had seen little danger of disorder resulting from an exception for the followers of Krishna. But the Supreme Court said that they had no claim to a special exemption as compared to the claims of other religions who also distribute literature and solicit funds. None of our cases suggest that the inclusion of peripatetic solicitation as part of a church ritual entitles church members to solicitation rights in a public forum superior to those of members of other religious groups that raise money but do not purport to ritualize the process. Nor for present purposes do religious organizations enjoy rights to communicate, distribute, and solicit on the fairgrounds superior to those of other organizations having social, political, or other ideological messages to proselytize. These nonreligious organizations seeking support for their activities are entitled to rights equal to those of religious groups to enter a public forum and spread their views, whether by soliciting funds or by distributing literature.

Justices Brennan, Blackmun, Marshall, and Stevens dissented. Justice Brennan contended that the Court's treatment of the Sankirtan issue was "seemingly inconsistent with prior case law.... Our cases are clear that governmental regulations which interfere with the exercise of specific religious beliefs or principles should be scrutinized with particular care," citing *Sherbert v. Verner* [section 5 below] and *Wisconsin v. Yoder* [section 7 below]. Is *Heffron* consistent with *Cantwell*? With *Murdock*?

The County of Los Angeles adopted a resolution that prohibited "First Amendment activity" at the Los Angeles International Airport. In *Commissioners of the City of Los Angeles v. Jews for Jesus, Inc.*, 482 U.S. 569 (1987) the Court focused on the rather obvious difficulty with a governmental proscription as overbroad as this one, postponing for another day the issue whether a publicly owned airport facility was a public forum.

In *International Society for Krishna Consciousness v. Lee*, 505 U.S. 672 (1992), the Court resolved the issue it had left open in *Jews for Jesus*. The case involved restrictions placed upon the freedom of the Krishna devotees to distribute religious literature in the three airports that serve the metropolitan New York area. The Court relied on a formalistic division of the public forum into fora that are truly public and those which are only quasi-public or limited in the access to the public to a particular purpose. One difficulty with the attempt to overlay this distinction among fora on the Krishna case is that the airport authority allows the use of the airports for all sorts of speech, including political speech and commercial speech. Candidates for political office often hold news conferences at the airports. Business deals are frequently negotiated in the airports. And vendors of secular newspapers and magazines are given stalls to sell their goods. Does this raise a problem of equal access, even to a limited public forum?

In *United States v. Kokinda*, 497 U.S. 720 (1990), a plurality of the Court ruled that the sidewalk in front of a post office is not a "traditional public forum" for purposes of expressive activity. In *United States v. Grace*, 461 U.S. 171 (1983), the Court reversed a conviction under 40 U.S.C. § 13k, prohibiting expressive activity "in the Supreme Court Buildings or grounds." The Court invalidated the application of the statute to a woman carrying a sign displaying the text of the first amendment on the sidewalks around the Court. Earlier in the same Term the Court noted that sidewalks "by long tradition or by government fiat have been devoted to assembly and debate." *Perry Education Assn. v. Perry Local Educators' Assn.*, 460 U.S. 37, 45 (1983). In *Grace*, however, the Court did not stress this traditional role of sidewalks as a space for expressive activity. Instead, it advanced the curious view that the sidewalks around the Court look like other sidewalks and have no barriers indicating that access to them is restricted in any way. Should these things matter? Should the content of a protester's message in front of the Court, whether religious or secular, matter?

In ancient Rome the central road leading to the forum, where both political and commercial business was routinely conducted, was called the Via Sacra or the Sacred Path, because religious temples were also found in the heart of the forum. Does the contemporary exclusion of some religious communities from publicly owned facilities such as airports reflect a bias in favor of a "naked public square"?

3.   WORSHIP OF A GRAVEN IMAGE

Exodus 20:3–5

You shall have no other gods before me. You shall not make yourself a graven image, or any likeness of anything ... you shall not bow down to them or serve them.

———

At the same time that the Jehovah's Witnesses were challenging restrictions on their evangelizing activity, they were challenging laws and regulations requiring their children to salute the flag. They succeeded where other religious groups had failed. As early as 1918 a Mennonite in Ohio was convicted of not keeping his nine-year-old daughter in school when she was sent home for refusing to salute. A school teacher in Nebraska who was a member of the Church of God was also fired for refusing. In 1925 the state of Washington committed a nine-year-old boy to a juvenile home when he obeyed his parents, members of the Elijah Voice Society, in not saluting at school. In 1928 in Delaware thirty-eight Mennonite children were expelled for not saluting, David R. Manwaring, *Render unto Caesar* 11–14 (1962).

Jehovah's Witnesses did not take a militant stand against saluting until 1935. In that year Judge Rutherford denounced the exaltation of Hitler in Germany (where the Witnesses were being persecuted) and eventually Rutherford singled out the salute "Heil Hitler" as idolatry. On October 6, 1935, in a national radio broadcast, Rutherford praised Carleton B. Nicholls, Jr., a third-grade student in Lynn, Massachusetts, who had refused to salute the flag, "declaring himself," Rutherford said, "for Jehovah God and his kingdom." Manwaring 30–31.

In at least thirty states the salute of the flag was required by statute or custom. After Rutherford's speech the children of Witnesses throughout the country refused to conform. By mid–1936, 120 such children had been expelled; by 1939, the number had passed 200. Manwaring 56. The state courts universally refused to recognize that the Witnesses had a protected constitutional right. Chief Justice Arthur Rugg's opinion upholding Carleton Nicholls's expulsion was typical. He wrote: "The pledge of allegiance to the flag ... has nothing to do with religion. There is nothing in the salute or the pledge of allegiance which constitutes an act of idolatry, or which approaches to any religious observance." *Nicholls v. Lynn*, 297 Mass. 65, 71, 7 N.E. 2d 577, 580 (1937). When twelve-year-old Dorothy Leoles was expelled in Georgia for failure to salute, the Supreme Court dismissed her appeal "for the want of a substantial federal question." *Leoles v. Landers*, 302 U.S. 656 (1937). The American Civil Liberties Union aided the Witnesses and actually handled most of their cases, and in New Jersey provided a model brief; but New Jersey, too, upheld an expulsion, and the Supreme Court dismissed the appeal. *Hering v. State Board of Education*, 303 U.S. 624 (1938).

The first full-dress treatment of the issue in the Supreme Court began with the action of the school board in Minersville, Pennsylvania, a depressed coal town (pop. 8,686). In October 1935 the board expelled Lillian Gobitis, twelve, and William Gobitis, ten, for failing to salute. The children then attended a

Kingdom School, run by the Witnesses, thirty miles distant. Their father, Walter, sought legal help to reinstate the children, and in May 1937, Olin R. Moyle and the ACLU initiated a federal suit to reinstate them. Outside groups such as the Patriotic Order of the Sons of America helped finance the school board in its opposition. Manwaring 81–93. District Judge Albert B. Maris, a Quaker, ruled on June 18, 1938, that the school board had violated the Fourteenth Amendment, 24 F. Supp. 271 (E.D. Pa. 1938). The Third Circuit affirmed, in an opinion by William Clark, a Presbyterian. 108 F. 2d 683 (3d Cir. 1939).

In the Supreme Court, Rutherford argued for the Gobitises that "the issue" was "the arbitrary totalitarian rule of the State versus full devotion and obedience to the THEOCRATIC GOVERNMENT or Kingdom of Jehovah God under Christ Jesus His anointed King." An ACLU *amicus* brief, written by George K. Gardner of Harvard Law School, argued that under *Reynolds v. United States* [Chapter 9] an innocuous religious belief could not be punished. The brief of the Bill of Rights Committee of the American Bar Association—another *amicus curiae*—was written by Grenville Clark and Louis Lusky; it invoked a famous footnote by Justice Harlan Stone in *United States v. Carolene Products Co.*, 304 U.S. 144, 152 n.4 (1938), calling for "more searching judicial inquiry" in cases of "prejudice against discrete and insular minorities." The distinction between judicial intervention to invalidate economic regulations—a type of intervention long criticized by liberals—and intervention on behalf of discrete and insular minorities was crucial if a Supreme Court already half made up of New Dealers was to respond. Lusky, who served as a judicial clerk for Justice Stone in that Term, drafted the famous "footnote 4." Stone was the sole dissenter in the first flag salute case.

Two weeks before *Gobitis* was decided, the Court held unanimously for the Witnesses in *Cantwell* [section 1 above]. But it was not an augury. Chief Justice Hughes dominated the Court's discussion of the case, and he denied that there was any infringement of religion, *see* Merlo Pusey, 2 *Charles Evan Hughes* 672–673 (1951). Hughes assigned the writing of the opinion to Felix Frankfurter. Frankfurter was to describe himself in the sequel to *Gobitis* as one "who belongs to the most vilified and persecuted minority in history," the Jews. He was also an immigrant from Austria–Hungary to the United States and a zealous upholder of judicial restraint in approaching the constitutionality of legislation. As he put it himself on December 5, 1942, "As one who has no ties with any formal religion, perhaps the feelings that underlie religious forms for me run into intensification of my feelings about American citizenship," *quoted in* Baker, *Felix Frankfurter* 290 (1969).

Note, in particular, that the Court's opinion states that the Fourteenth Amendment not only absorbed the free exercise provision of the First Amendment but also the prohibition on laws respecting an establishment of religion. This statement, uncontested by any member of the Court, was to survive long after *Gobitis* was gone.

Minersville School District v. Gobitis

310 U.S. 586 (1940).

Mr. Joseph W. Henderson, with whom *Messrs. John B. McGurl, Thomas F. Mount,* and *George M. Brodhead, Jr.* were on the brief, for petitioners.

Messrs. Joseph F. Rutherford and *George K. Gardner* argued the cause, and with the former *Mr. Hayden Covington* was on the brief, for respondents.

By leave of Court, briefs of *amici curiae* were filed on behalf of the Committee on the Bill of Rights, of the American Bar Association, consisting of *Messrs. Douglas Arant, Zechariah Chafee, Jr., Grenville Clark, Osmer C. Fitts, Lloyd K. Garrison, George I. Haight, Monte M. Leman, Ross L. Malone, Jr., Burton W. Musser, Joseph A. Padway,* and *Charles P. Taft*; and by *Messrs. George K. Gardner, Arthur Garfield Hays, Osmond K. Fraenkel, William G. Fennell, Jerome M. Britchey,* and *Alexander H. Frey,* on behalf of the American Civil Liberties Union, urging affirmance.

■ JUSTICE FRANKFURTER delivered the opinion of the Court.

Centuries of strife over the erection of particular dogmas as exclusive or all-comprehending faiths led to the inclusion of a guarantee for religious freedom in the Bill of Rights. The First Amendment, and the Fourteenth through its absorption of the First, sought to guard against repetition of those bitter religious struggles by prohibiting the establishment of a state religion and by securing to every sect the free exercise of its faith. So pervasive is the acceptance of this precious right that its scope is brought into question, as here, only when the conscience of individuals collides with the felt necessities of society.

Certainly the affirmative pursuit of one's convictions about the ultimate mystery of the universe and man's relation to it is placed beyond the reach of law. Government may not interfere with organized or individual expression of belief or disbelief. Propagation of belief—or even of disbelief—in the supernatural is protected, whether in church or chapel, mosque or synagogue, tabernacle or meeting-house. Likewise the Constitution assures generous immunity to the individual from imposition of penalties for offending, in the course of his own religious activities, the religious views of others, be they a minority or those who are dominant in government. *Cantwell* [section 1 above].

But the manifold character of man's relations may bring his conception of religious duty into conflict with the secular interests of his fellow-men. When does the constitutional guarantee compel exemption from doing what society thinks necessary for the promotion of some great common end, or from a penalty for conduct which appears dangerous to the general good? To state the problem is to recall the truth that no single principle can answer all of life's complexities. The right to freedom of religious belief, however dissident and however obnoxious to the cherished beliefs of others—even of a majority—is itself the denial of an absolute. But to affirm that the freedom to follow conscience has itself no limits in the life of a society would deny that very plurality of principles which, as a matter of history, underlies protection of religious toleration. Our present task, then, as so often the case with courts, is to reconcile two rights in order to prevent either from destroying the other. But, because in safeguarding conscience we are dealing with interests so subtle and so dear, every possible leeway should be given to the claims of religious faith.

In the judicial enforcement of religious freedom we are concerned with a historic concept. See Mr. Justice Cardozo in *Hamilton v. Regents* [Chapter Ten, section 11]. The religious liberty which the Constitution protects has never excluded legislation of general scope not directed against doctrinal loyalties of particular sects. Judicial nullification of legislation cannot be justified by attributing to the framers of the Bill of Rights views for which there is no historic warrant. Conscientious scruples have not, in the course of the long struggle for religious toleration, relieved the individual from obedience to a general law not aimed at the promotion or restriction of religious beliefs. The mere possession of religious convictions which contradict the relevant concerns of a political society does not relieve the citizen from the discharge of political responsibilities. The necessity for this adjustment has again and again been recognized. In a number of situations the exertion of political authority has been sustained, while basic considerations of religious freedom have been left inviolate. *Reynolds v. United States, Davis v. Beason* [Chapter Nine] *Selective Draft Law Cases, Hamilton v. Regents* [Chapter Ten, section 11]. In all these cases the general laws in question, upheld in their application to those who refused obedience from religious conviction, were manifestations of specific powers of government deemed by the legislature essential to secure and maintain that orderly, tranquil, and free society without which religious toleration itself is unattainable. Nor does the freedom of speech assured by Due Process move in a more absolute circle of immunity than that enjoyed by religious freedom. Even if it were assumed that freedom of speech goes beyond the historic concept of full opportunity to utter and to disseminate views, however heretical or offensive to dominant opinion, and includes freedom from conveying what may be deemed an implied but rejected affirmation, the question remains whether school children, like the Gobitis children, must be excused from conduct required of all the other children in the promotion of national cohesion. We are dealing with an interest inferior to none in the hierarchy of legal values. National unity is the basis of national security. To deny the legislature the right to select appropriate means for its attainment presents a totally different order of problem from that of the propriety of subordinating the possible ugliness of littered streets to the free expression of opinion through distribution of handbills.

Situations like the present are phases of the profoundest problem confronting a democracy—the problem which Lincoln cast in memorable dilemma: "Must a government of necessity be too *strong* for the liberties of its people, or too *weak* to maintain its own existence?" No mere textual reading or logical talisman can solve the dilemma. And when the issue demands judicial determination, it is not the personal notion of judges of what wise adjustment requires which must prevail.

Unlike the instances we have cited, the case before us is not concerned with an exertion of legislative power for the promotion of some specific need or interest of secular society—the protection of the family, the promotion of health, the common defense, the raising of public revenues to defray the cost of government. But all these specific activities of government presuppose the existence of an organized political society. The ultimate foundation of a free society is the binding tie of cohesive sentiment.

Such a sentiment is fostered by all those agencies of the mind and spirit which may serve to gather up the traditions of a people, transmit them from generation to generation, and thereby create that continuity of a treasured common life which constitutes a civilization. "We live by symbols." The flag is the symbol of our national unity, transcending all internal differences, however large, within the framework of the Constitution. This Court has had occasion to say that " ... the flag is the symbol of the Nation's power, the emblem of freedom in its truest, best sense.... it signifies government resting on the consent of the governed; liberty regulated by law; the protection of the weak against the strong; security against the exercise of arbitrary power; and absolute safety for free institutions against foreign aggression."

The case before us must be viewed as though the legislature of Pennsylvania had itself formally directed the flag-salute for the children of Minersville; had made no exemption for children whose parents were possessed of conscientious scruples like those of the Gobitis family; and had indicated its belief in the desirable ends to be secured by having its public school children share a common experience at those periods of development when their minds are supposedly receptive to its assimilation, by an exercise appropriate in time and place and setting, and one designed to evoke in them appreciation of the nation's hopes and dreams, its sufferings and sacrifices. The precise issue, then, for us to decide is whether the legislatures of the various states and the authorities in a thousand counties and school districts of this country are barred from determining the appropriateness of various means to evoke that unifying sentiment without which there can ultimately be no liberties, civil or religious. To stigmatize legislative judgment in providing for this universal gesture of respect for the symbol of our national life in the setting of the common school as a lawless inroad on that freedom of conscience which the Constitution protects, would amount to no less than the pronouncement of pedagogical and psychological dogma in a field where courts possess no marked and certainly no controlling competence. The influences which help toward a common feeling for the common country are manifold. Some may seem harsh and others no doubt are foolish. Surely, however, the end is legitimate. And the effective means for its attainment are still so uncertain and so unauthenticated by science as to preclude us from putting the widely prevalent belief in flag-saluting beyond the pale of legislative power. It mocks reason and denies our whole history to find in the allowance of a requirement to salute our flag on fitting occasions the seeds of sanction for obeisance to a leader.

The wisdom of training children in patriotic impulses by those compulsions which necessarily pervade so much of the educational process is not for our independent judgment. Even were we convinced of the folly of such a measure, such belief would be no proof of its unconstitutionality. For ourselves, we might be tempted to say that the deepest patriotism is best engendered by giving unfettered scope to the most crochety beliefs. Perhaps it is best, even from the standpoint of those interests which ordinances like the one under review seek to promote, to give to the least popular sect leave from conformities like those here in issue. But the courtroom is not the arena for debating issues of educational policy. It is not our province to choose among competing considerations in the subtle process of securing effective loyalty to the traditional ideals of democracy, while respecting at the same time individual idiosyncracies among a people so diversified in racial origins and religious allegiances. So to hold would in effect make us the *school board for the country*. That authority has not been given to this Court, nor should we assume it.

We are dealing here with the formative period in the development of citizenship. Great diversity of psychological and ethical opinion exists among us concerning the best way to train children for their place in society. Because of these differences and because of reluctance to permit a single, iron-cast system of education to be imposed upon a nation compounded of so many strains, we have held that, even though public education is one of our most cherished democratic institutions, the Bill of Rights bars a state from compelling all children to attend the public schools. *Pierce v. Society of Sisters* [Chapter Ten, section 7]. But it is a very different thing for this Court to exercise censorship over the conviction of legislatures that a particular program or exercise will best promote in the minds of children who attend the common schools an attachment to the institutions of their country.

What the school authorities are really asserting is the right to awaken in the child's mind considerations as to the significance of the flag contrary to those implanted by the parent. In such an attempt the state is normally at a disadvantage in competing with the parent's authority, so long—and this is the vital aspect of religious toleration—as parents are unmolested in their right to counteract by their own persuasiveness the wisdom and rightness of those loyalties which the state's educational system is seeking to promote. Except where the transgression of constitutional liberty is too plain for argument, personal freedom is best maintained—so long as the remedial channels of the democratic process remain open and unobstructed—when it is ingrained in a people's habits and not enforced against popular policy by the coercion of adjudicated law. That the flag-salute is an allowable portion of a school program for those who do not invoke conscientious scruples is surely not debatable. But for us to insist that, though the ceremony may be required, exceptional immunity must be given to dissidents, is to maintain that there is no basis for a legislative judgment that such an exemption might introduce elements of difficulty into the school discipline, might cast doubts in the minds of the other children which would themselves weaken the effect of the exercise.

The preciousness of the family relation, the authority and independence which give dignity to parenthood, indeed the enjoyment of all freedom, presuppose the kind of ordered society which is summarized by our flag. A society which is dedicated to the preservation of these ultimate values of civilization may in self-protection utilize the educational process for inculcating those almost unconscious feelings which bind men together in a comprehending loyalty, whatever may be their lesser differences and difficulties. That is to say, the process may be utilized so long as men's right to believe as they please, to win others to their way of belief, and their right to assemble in their chosen places of worship for the devotional ceremonies of their faith, are all fully respected.

Judicial review, itself a limitation on popular government, is a fundamental part of our constitutional scheme. But to the legislature no less than to courts is committed the guardianship of deeply-cherished liberties. Where all the effective means of inducing political changes are left free from interference, education in the abandonment of foolish legislation is itself a training in liberty. To fight out the wise use of legislative authority in the forum of public opinion and before legislative assemblies rather than to transfer such a contest to the judicial arena, serves to vindicate the self-confidence of a free people. *Reversed.*

■ JUSTICE MCREYNOLDS concurred in the result.

■ JUSTICE STONE dissented.

HISTORICAL NOTE

The Path to Barnette: Repudiation of Gobitis, Persecution of the Witnesses, and the Struggle against Totalitarianism during World War II. Although the Court was nearly unanimous in *Gobitis,* the opinion was repudiated roundly in many journals of opinion. The *New Republic*, which Frankfurter had helped found, said the Court had come "dangerously close" to being the victim of war hysteria. *Christian Century*, a liberal Protestant magazine, said, "Courts that will not protect even Jehovah's Witnesses will not long protect anybody." *America*, a Jesuit journal, said that the Court had permitted destruction of "one of the most precious rights under the Federal and our State Constitutions." The *Harvard Educational Review* said the decision subordinated the civil liberties of minorities to "the will of the majority." Thirty-nine law reviews discussed the decision, thirty-one of them critically. Few decisions of the Court in modern times have met with such across-the-board intellectual rejection. Manwaring 149–157.

The Jehovah's Witnesses were already unpopular. Before the decision came down on June 3, 1940, they had been victims of several incidents of mob violence in Texas. After the decision, individual Witnesses were attacked in Maine (beatings, burning of the Kingdom Hall in Kennebunk); West Virginia (forced drinking of castor oil); Wyoming (tarring and feathering); Nebraska (castration); Arkansas (shooting); Illinois, Indiana, Maryland, Mississippi, Oregon (mob attacks). Forty percent of the incidents occurred in two states, Oklahoma and Texas. Small towns, not tolerant of outsiders, were the usual sites. *Id.* 163–173.

Legal measures against the Witnesses added to their woes. Many communities adopted new flag salute requirements. In Indiana two women Witnesses were sentenced to 2-to-10 years in prison for "flag desecration" because they had distributed literature opposing the salute; their convictions were ultimately overturned. *McKee v. State*, 219 Ind. 247, 37 N.E. 2d 940 (1941). The Mississippi legislature, declaring that "the very life and existence of these United States and the state of Mississippi are threatened" by Germany, Italy, and Japan, made it a felony, punishable by imprisonment until the end of the war, to teach or distribute literature "which reasonably tends to create an attitude of stubborn refusal to salute, honor, or respect the flag." A Witness, R. E. Taylor, was sentenced under the statute. Affirming his conviction, 3–3, the Supreme Court of Mississippi rejected Taylor's claim of free exercise of religion, declaring that religion's "primary object is a haven of rest after 'life's fitful fever is over.' It is a fallacy of the rankest kind to assume that loyalty to one's country and its flag is attributing to them any aspect of divinity or omnipotent power," *Taylor v. State*, 194 Miss. 1, 34, 11 So. 2d 663, 673 (1943), *rev'd.*, *Taylor v. Mississippi*, 319 U.S. 583 (1943). In at least thirty-one states legal steps were taken to expel nonsaluting Witness children from the public schools. Manwaring 187. Planned by no central authority, unintended by the Supreme Court, overshadowed by World War II, the legal and illegal persecution of Witnesses from 1941 to 1943 was the greatest outbreak of religious intolerance in twentieth-century America.

Three state courts (Kansas, Minnesota, and Washington) refused to follow the reasoning of *Gobitis* and excused nonsaluters. The Civil Rights Section of the Justice Department on May 4, 1942, advised United States attorneys that they should take steps with local officials "to the end that official vigilantism violative of freedom of worship may be avoided." *Id.* 181. In the Supreme Court itself, dissenting in *Jones v. Opelika*, 316 U.S. 584 (1942), Justices Black, Douglas, and Murphy went out of their way to say: "Since we joined in the opinion in the *Gobitis* case, we think this is an appropriate occasion to state that we now believe that it was also wrongly decided . . . ." *Id.* 623–624.

Unflinching loyalty to the nation-state, such as that illustrated at the Nuremberg rallies with their massive displays of Nazi swastika flags, took on a different resonance in a country that had gone to war against totalitarian regimes. Richard Danzig, "Justice Frankfurter's Opinions in the Flag Salute Cases: Blending Logic and Psychologic in Constitutional Decisionmaking," 36 *Stan. L. Rev.* 675 (1984); and Peter Irons, *The Courage of Their Convictions* 15–24 (1988).

Hayden Covington saw the opportunity. Two months after this dissent, in August 1942, a class action was filed on behalf of Witnesses challenging the constitutionality of an order of the West Virginia Board of Education. The order had been adopted earlier in the year, quoted liberally from *Gobitis*, and required the salute from school children; a number of Witnesses had already been expelled. Walter Barnette, the father of two such children, was enlisted as the plaintiff. Manwaring 208–211. A three-judge federal court, in an opinion by John J. Parker, enjoined enforcement of the board's order, 47 F. Supp. 251 (S.D. W. Va. 1942). The state appealed, unenthusiastically.

Hayden Covington drew on the earlier briefs in *Gobitis*, invoked Daniel 3 and Esther 3 on the duty to obey God and not worship idols, and boldly attacked Frankfurter's opinion. In oral argument he compared *Gobitis* to *Dred Scott*. The Bill of Rights Committee of the American Bar Association and the ACLU filed strong supporting briefs. Manwaring 217–224. The decision was announced on June 13, 1943, Flag Day.

West Virginia State Bd. of Education v. Barnette

319 U.S. 624 (1943).

Mr. Hayden C. Covington for appellees.

Mr. W. Holt Wooddell, Assistant Attorney General of West Virginia, with whom *Mr. Ira J. Partlow* was on the brief, for appellants.

Briefs of *amici curiae* were filed on behalf of the Committee on the Bill of Rights, of the American Bar Association, consisting of *Messrs. Douglas Arant, Julius Birge, William D. Campbell, Zechariah Chafee, Jr., L. Stanley Ford, Abe Fortas, George I. Haight, H. Austin Hauxhurst, Monte M. Lemann, Alvin Richards, Earl F. Morris, Burton W. Musser,* and *Basil O'Connor*; and by *Messrs. Osmond K. Fraenkel, Arthur Garfield Hays,* and *Howard B. Lee,* on behalf of the American Civil Liberties Union, urging affirmance; and by *Mr. Ralph B. Gregg,* on behalf of the American Legion, urging reversal.

■ JUSTICE JACKSON delivered the opinion of the Court.

Following the decision by this Court on June 3, 1940, in *Minersville School District v. Gobitis,* the West Virginia legislature amended its statutes to require all schools therein to conduct courses of instruction in history, civics, and in the Constitutions of the United States and of the State "for the purpose of teaching, fostering and perpetuating the ideals, principles and spirit of Americanism, and increasing the knowledge of the organization and machinery of the government." Appellant Board of Education was directed, with advice of the State Superintendent of Schools, to "prescribe the courses of study covering these subjects" for public schools. The Act made it the duty of private, parochial and denominational schools to prescribe courses of study "similar to those required for the public schools."

The Board of Education on January 9, 1942, adopted a resolution containing recitals taken largely from the Court's *Gobitis* opinion and ordering that the salute to the flag become "a regular part of the program of activities in the public schools," that all teachers and pupils "shall be required to participate in the salute honoring the Nation represented by the Flag; provided, however, that refusal to salute the Flag be regarded as an act of insubordination, and shall be dealt with accordingly."

The resolution originally required the "commonly accepted salute to the Flag" which it defined. Objections to the salute as "being too much like Hitler's" were raised by the Parent and Teachers Association, the Boy and Girl Scouts, the Red Cross, and the Federation of Women's Clubs. Some modification appears to have been made in deference to these objections, but no concession was made to Jehovah's Witnesses. What is now required is the "stiff-arm" salute, the saluter to keep the right hand raised with palm turned up while the following is repeated: "I pledge allegiance to the Flag of the United States of America and to the Republic for which it stands; one Nation, indivisible, with liberty and justice for all."

Failure to conform is "insubordination" dealt with by expulsion. Readmission is denied by statute until compliance. Meanwhile the expelled child is "unlawfully absent" and may be proceeded against as a delinquent. His parents or guardians are liable to prosecution, and if convicted are subject to fine not exceeding $50 and jail term not exceeding thirty days.

Appellees, citizens of the United States and of West Virginia, brought suit in the United States District Court for themselves and others similarly situated asking its injunction to restrain enforcement of these laws and regulations against Jehovah's Witnesses. The Witnesses are an unincorporated body teaching that the obligation imposed by law of God is superior to that of laws enacted by temporal government. Their religious beliefs include a literal version of Exodus 20:4–5, which says: "Thou shalt not make unto thee any graven image, or any likeness of anything that is in heaven above, or that is in the earth beneath, or that is in the water under the earth; thou shalt not bow down thyself to them nor serve them." They consider that the flag is an "image" within this command. For this reason they refuse to salute it. . . .

The very purpose of a Bill of Rights was to withdraw certain subjects from the vicissitudes of political controversy, to place them beyond the reach of majorities and officials and to establish them as legal principles to be applied by the courts. One's right to life, liberty, and property, to free speech, a free press, freedom of worship and assembly, and other fundamental rights may not be submitted to vote; they depend on the outcome of no elections.

In weighing arguments of the parties it is important to distinguish between the due process clause of the Fourteenth Amendment as an instrument for transmitting the principles of the First Amendment and those cases in which it is applied for its own sake. The test of legislation which collides with the Fourteenth Amendment, because it also collides with the principles of the First, is much more definite than the test when only the Fourteenth is involved. Much of the vagueness of the due process clause disappears when the specific prohibitions of the First become its standard. The right of a State to regulate, for example, a public utility may well include, so far as the due process test is concerned, power to impose all of the restrictions which a legislature may have a "rational basis" for adopting. But freedoms of speech and of press, of assembly, and of worship may not be infringed on such slender grounds. They are susceptible of restriction only to prevent grave and immediate danger to interests which the State may lawfully protect. It is important to note that while it is the Fourteenth Amendment which bears directly upon the State it is the more specific limiting principles of the First Amendment that finally govern this case.

Nor does our duty to apply the Bill of Rights to assertions of official authority depend upon our possession of marked competence in the field where the invasion of rights occurs. True, the task of translating the majestic generalities of the Bill of Rights, conceived as part of the pattern of liberal government in the eighteenth century, into concrete restraints on officials dealing with the problems of the twentieth century, is one to disturb self-confidence. These principles grew in soil which also produced a philosophy that the individual was the center of society, that his liberty was attainable through mere absence of governmental restraints, and that government should be entrusted with few controls and only the mildest supervision over men's affairs. We must transplant these rights to a soil in which the *laissez-faire* concept or principle of non-interference has withered at least as to economic affairs, and social advancements are increasingly sought through closer integration of society and through expanded and strengthened governmental controls. These changed conditions often deprive precedents of reliability and cast us more than we would choose upon our own judgment. But we act in these matters not by authority of our competence but by force of our commissions. We cannot, because of modest estimates of our competence in such specialties as public education, withhold the judgment that history authenticates as the function of this Court when liberty is infringed.

Lastly, and this is the very heart of the *Gobitis* opinion, it reasons that "National unity is the basis of national security," that the authorities have "the right to select appropriate means for its attainment," and hence reaches the conclusion that such compulsory measures toward "national unity" are constitutional. *Id.* at 595. Upon the verity of this assumption depends our answer in this case.

National unity as an end which officials may foster by persuasion and example is not in question. The problem is whether under our Constitution compulsion as here employed is a permissible means for its achievement.

Struggles to coerce uniformity of sentiment in support of some end thought essential to their time and country have been waged by many good as well as by evil men. Nationalism is a relatively recent phenomenon but at other times and places the ends have been racial or territorial security, support of a dynasty or regime, and particular plans for saving souls. As first and moderate methods to attain unity have failed, those bent on its accomplishment must resort to an ever-increasing severity. As governmental pressure toward unity becomes greater, so strife becomes more bitter as to whose unity it shall be. Probably no deeper division of our people could proceed from any provocation than from finding it necessary to choose what doctrine and whose program public educational officials shall compel youth to unite in embracing. Ultimate futility of such attempts to compel coherence is the lesson of every such effort from the Roman drive to stamp out Christianity as a disturber of its pagan unity, the Inquisition, as a means to religious and dynastic unity, the Siberian exiles as a means to Russian unity, down to the fast failing efforts of our present totalitarian enemies. Those who begin coercive elimination of dissent soon find themselves exterminating dissenters. Compulsory unification of opinion achieves only the unanimity of the graveyard.

It seems trite but necessary to say that the First Amendment to our Constitution was designed to avoid these ends by avoiding these beginnings. There is no mysticism in the American concept of the State or of the nature or origin of its authority. We set up government by consent of the governed, and the Bill of Rights denies those in power any legal opportunity to coerce that consent. Authority here is to be controlled by public opinion, not public opinion by authority.

The case is made difficult not because the principles of its decision are obscure but because the flag involved is our own. Nevertheless, we apply the limitations of the Constitution with no fear that freedom to be intellectually and spiritually diverse or even contrary will disintegrate the social organization. To believe that patriotism will not flourish if patriotic ceremonies are voluntary and spontaneous instead of a compulsory routine is to make an unflattering estimate of the appeal of our institutions to free minds. We can have intellectual individualism and the rich cultural diversities that we owe to exceptional minds only at the price of occasional eccentricity and abnormal attitudes. When they are so harmless to others or to the State as those we deal with here, the price is not too great. But freedom to differ is not limited to things that do not matter much. That would be a mere shadow of freedom. The test of its substance is the right to differ as to things that touch the heart of the existing order.

If there is any fixed star in our constitutional constellation, it is that no official, high or petty, can prescribe what shall be orthodox in politics, nationalism, religion, or other matters of opinion or force citizens to confess by word or act their faith therein. If there are any circumstances which permit an exception, they do not now occur to us.

We think the action of the local authorities in compelling the flag salute and pledge transcends constitutional limitations on their power and invades the sphere of intellect and spirit which it is the purpose of the First Amendment to our Constitution to reserve from all official control.

The decision of this Court in *Minersville School District v. Gobitis* and the holdings of those few *per curiam* decisions which preceded and foreshadowed it are overruled, and the judgment enjoining enforcement of the West Virginia Regulation is *Affirmed*.

Justices Roberts and Reed adhere to the views expressed by the Court in *Minersville School District v. Gobitis*, 310 U.S. 586, and are of the opinion that the judgment below should be reversed.

■ JUSTICE FRANKFURTER dissented.

NOTES AND QUESTIONS

1. *Extending Barnette to Teachers.* In 1977 the Massachusetts legislature proposed a bill that would require "each teacher at the commencement of the first class of each day in all grades in all public schools" to lead the class in a group recitation of the Pledge of Allegiance to the Flag. The Massachusetts Constitution allows the Supreme Judicial Court to render advisory opinions on proposed legislation. In response to a request for such an opinion from the Governor, the court expressed the view that the legislation would violate the First Amendment, citing *Barnette* and *Wooley. Opinions of the Justices*, 372 Mass. 874, 363 N.E. 2d 251 (1977). Do you agree with this extension of *Barnette*? May government employees be required to say things that children would not be required to say? Justice Frankfurter wrote in *Gobitis*: "The flag is the symbol of our national unity, transcending all internal differences, however large, within the framework of the Constitution." Illustrating that the flag salute controversy continues to have powerful effects in the political life of "the republic for which [the flag] stands," in one of the debates during the presidential campaign of 1988, then Vice–President George Bush attacked his

opponent, Governor Michael Dukakis of Massachusetts, for agreeing to abide by the court's decision in the opinion referred to above.

2. *Coerced speech on a license plate.* In *Wooley v. Maynard*, 430 U.S. 705 (1977) a Jehovah's Witness objected to the motto of New Hampshire, "Live Free or Die," engraved on the license plates of that state. He was convicted for defacing his license plate by removing the offending words. The Court held that the State may not compel its citizens to "use their private property as . . . a 'mobile billboard' for the States's ideological message."

3. *Not Being Photographed.* In *Quaring v. Peterson*, 728 F. 2d 1121 (8th Cir. 1984), Frances J. Quaring, a Christian, held the belief that the commandment against "any graven image or likeness of anything" (Ex. 20:4; Deut. 5:8) prohibited her from having a likeness of anything in creation. She possessed no photographs, did not own a television set, and would permit no pictures of any kind, even on canned food, within her home. She refused to comply with Nebraska's requirement that her driver's license carry her photograph. In an action to obtain the license without complying, the Eighth Circuit, 2–1, held that the statute burdened Quaring's free exercise of religion (she needed the car in her work) and that Nebraska had not shown a compelling state interest in requiring the photograph. Quaring's claim was upheld by the Supreme Court, which affirmed by a vote of 4–4, *Jensen v. Quaring*, 472 U.S. 478 (1985). If you were the ninth justice in the case, how would you vote? Why?

4. *Not Receiving a Social Security Number as a Personal Identifier.* Stephen Roy applied for and received benefits under the Aid to Families with Dependent Children (AFDC) program and the Food Stamp program, but he refused to comply with the federal statutory requirement that he furnish the state welfare agency with the Social Security numbers of each member of his household as a condition of receiving benefits. He contended that obtaining a Social Security number for his 2–year-old daughter, Little Bird of the Snow, would violate his Native American religious beliefs because it would "rob the spirit" of his daughter and prevent her from attaining greater spiritual power. The agency then stopped the benefits payable to Roy on his daughter's behalf and sought to reduce his level of food stamps. Roy sued, arguing that the Free Exercise Clause entitled him to an exemption from the requirement that he identify his child by means of a social security number.

The district court denied Roy's claim for damages and benefits, but granted injunctive relief because it believed that the public interest in maintaining an efficient and fraud resistant system could be achieved without requiring Little Bird of the Snow to use a social security number. In *Bowen v. Roy,* 476 U.S. 693 (1986), Chief Justice Burger wrote for the Court: "Roy may no more prevail on his religious objection to the Government's use of a Social Security number for his daughter than he could on a sincere religious objection to the size or color of the Government's filing cabinets. The Free Exercise Clause affords an individual protection from certain forms of governmental compulsion; it does not afford an individual a right to dictate the conduct of the Government's internal procedures." Right result? Why? The decision on the particular facts in *Roy* was not as significant as the discussion that this case engendered about the appropriate standard for reviewing claims of violation of the free exercise clause. In *Sherbert v. Verner* [section 5 below], the Court held that in order to prevail over a claim that a government regulation burdened free exercise of religion, the government would have to demonstrate that the regulation in question was demanded by a "compelling governmental interest" and that the government had no "less restrictive alternative" to the regulation. In *Roy* Solicitor General Charles Fried argued in the government's brief for a significant departure from this test. Three justices agreed with Fried's argument. Joined by Justices Powell and Rehnquist, Chief Justice Burger wrote in his plurality opinion: "Absent proof of an intent to discriminate against particular religious beliefs or against religion in general, the Government meets its burden when it demonstrates that a challenged requirement for governmental benefits, neutral and uniform in its application, is a reasonable means of promoting a legitimate public interest." This position represented a shift for the Chief Justice, who had written in *Yoder* [section 7 below]: "Only those interests of the highest order and those not otherwise served can overbalance legitimate claims to the free exercise of religion." In *Roy* five justices (Brennan, White, Marshall, Blackmun, and O'Connor) expressly rejected this view of the appropriate standard. Justice O'Connor, joined by Justices Brennan and Marshall, wrote in a concurring and dissenting opinion that the standard proposed by the Chief Justice "has no basis in precedent and relegates a serious First Amendment value to the barest level of minimal scrutiny that the Equal Protection Clause already provides." The discussion in *Roy* proved to be a turning point in judicial enforcement of free exercise. In two subsequent cases, *O'Lone v. Estate of Shabazz* [section 9 below] and *Lyng v. Northwest Indian Cemetery Protective Ass'n* [section 11 below], the Court paid formal lip service to the *Sherbert* test, but rendered it fairly toothless. In *Employment Division v. Smith* [section 10 below], a majority of the Court explicitly rejected the compelling interest and least restrictive alternative tests in free exercise challenges to generally applicable laws.

4. NOT KILLING, NOT HELPING, NOT REGISTERING IN WAR

Deuteronomy 5:17

You shall not kill.

Joshua 11: 16–20, 23

So Joshua took all that land: the hill country and all the Negeb and all the land of Goshen and the lowland and the Arabah and the hill country of Israel and its lowland, from Mount Halak, which rises toward Seir, as far as Baal-gad in the valley of Lebanon below Mount Hermon. He took all their kings, struck them down, and put them to death. Joshua made war a long time with all those kings. There was not a town that made peace with the Israelites, except the Hivites, the inhabitants of Gibeon; all were taken in battle. For it was the LORD's doing to harden their hearts so that they would come against Israel in battle, in order that they might be utterly destroyed, and might receive no mercy, but be exterminated, just as the LORD had commanded Moses.... So Joshua took the whole land, according to all that the LORD had spoken to Moses; and Joshua gave it for an inheritance to Israel according to their tribal allotments. And the land had rest from war.

Psalm 34:14

Depart from evil, and do good;
seek peace, and pursue it.

Psalm 120:6–7

Too long have I had my dwelling
among those who hate peace.

I am for peace;
but when I speak,
they are for war.

Psalm 122: 6–9

Pray for the peace of Jerusalem:
"May they prosper who love you.

Peace be within your walls,
and security within your towers."

For the sake of my relatives and friends
I will say, "Peace be within you."

For the sake of the house of the LORD our God,
I will seek your good.

Isaiah 2: 3–4

For out of Zion shall go forth instruction,
and the word of the LORD from Jerusalem.
He shall judge between the nations,
and shall arbitrate for many peoples;
they shall beat their swords into plowshares,
and their spears into pruning hooks;
nation shall not lift up sword against nation,
neither shall they learn war any more.

The Gospel according to Matthew 5: 9

Blessed are the peacemakers, for they will be called children of God.

The Gospel according to Matthew 5: 21–26

"You have heard that it was said to those of ancient times, 'You shall not murder'; and 'whoever murders shall be liable to judgment.' But I say to you that if you are angry with a brother or sister, you will be liable to judgment; and if you insult a brother or sister, you will be liable to the council; and if you say, 'You fool,' you will be liable to the hell of fire. So when you are offering your gift at the altar, if you remember that your brother or sister has something against you, leave your gift there before the altar and go; first be reconciled to your brother or sister, and then come and offer your gift. Come to terms quickly with your accuser while you are on the way to court with him, or your accuser may hand you over to the judge, and the judge to the guard, and you will be thrown into prison. Truly I tell you, you will never get out until you have paid the last penny."

The Gospel according to Matthew 5: 38–42

"You have heard that it was said, 'An eye for an eye and a tooth for a tooth.' But I say to you, Do not resist an evildoer. But if anyone strikes you on the right cheek, turn the other also; and if anyone wants to sue you and take your coat, give your cloak as well; and if anyone forces you to go one mile, go also the second mile. Give to everyone who begs from you, and do not refuse anyone who wants to borrow from you."

Mahandas Ghandi, R.K. Prabhu and Rao, eds., *Mind of Mahatma Ghandi* (3d ed. 1968)

You can return blow for blow if you are not brave enough to follow the path of non-violence.

Mahandas Ghandi, D. G. Tendulkar, ed., 4 *Mahatma* 291 (2d ed. 1960)

It is the acid test of non-violence that in a non-violent conflict there is no rancour left behind, and in the end the enemies are converted into friends.

Mahandas Ghandi, *Young India*, Aug. 10 1925, 346.

Non-violence is "not a resignation from all real fighting against wickedness." On the contrary, the non-violence of my conception is a more active and real fight against wickedness than retaliation whose very nature is to increase wickedness. I contemplate a mental and, therefore, a moral opposition to immoralities. I seek entirely to blunt the edge of the tyrant's sword, not by putting up against it a sharper-edged weapon, but by disappointing his expectation that I would be offering physical resistance. The resistance of the soul that I should offer would elude him. It would at first dazzle him and at last compel recognition from him, which recognition would not humiliate him but would uplift him. It may be urged that this is an ideal state. And so it is.

NOTES AND QUESTIONS

There is no system of military conscription at present. A period in which the issue of conscientious objection is not an urgent need may, however, be just the right moment to contemplate what religious freedom might require if conscription were to return. *See, e.g.,* Kent Greenawalt, "Conscientious Objection," in James E. Wood, Jr., *Religion and the State: Essays in Honor of Leo Pfeffer* 247 (1985).

1. *Classical sources for conscientious objection.* May a government official– typically a member of a local draft board–inquire as to the reasons why an individual seeks an exemption from military service? Suppose the applicant for exemption cites "The Bible" as the basis for his views. May the government official probe the applicant's familiarity with texts like those mentioned above? For what purpose, to determine the sincerity of the applicant? Can this end be served by requiring alternative service? See Greenawalt, "Conscientious Objection" 262–64.

The classical Mosaic commandment above prohibits intentional homicide. It is better translated as "You shall not murder." *See* John Howard Yoder, "Exodus 20:13-'Thou Shalt Not Kill,'" 34 *Interpretation* 394–99 (1980); Dale Patrick, *Old Testament Law* 53–54 (1985). Does this text ground an exemption from military service?

The summary of the conquest of Canaan by the ancient Israelites found in the book of Joshua suggests a swift military campaign, a Blitzkrieg. In the ancient world—before the sacred and the secular were sharply differentiated—war was regarded as a religious affair, not only in Israel but in all of its surrounding cultures. *See, e.g.,* Roland deVaux, *Ancient Israel: Its Life and Institutions* 247–54 (1961). For example, the author of Joshua emphasizes the theme of the "holy war," according to which God himself helps the army of Israel by throwing the enemy into disordered panic (Josh. 10:10; cf. Exodus 15:3; 23:27f.). For a careful study of this theme, *see* Gerhard von Rad *Holy War in Ancient Israel* (1991). The book of the Bible immediately after Joshua–the book of Judges—also contains narratives of occasional conflicts between the Israelites and the resident Cannaanites, but it suggests that the occupation of Canaan was a more gradual process of infiltration. Neither book is meant to serve as an eyewitness account of military history. Do texts such as this "prove" that a biblical believer must be willing to be a warrior?

On the other hand, the Psalms cited above and the text from the prophet Isaiah indicate the yearning of ancient Israel for an era of peace in which the instruments of warfare would be transformed into agricultural tools and in which "nation shall not lift up sword against nation, neither shall they learn war any more." Do these texts provide counterweight to the text from Joshua? Do they mean that biblical believers must be pacifists?

In the Gospel according to Matthew, Jesus is presented as a new "prophet like Moses" offering a new interpretation of Torah on a new mountain top like Sinai. The passages from this sermon cited above highlight Jesus's blessing of peacemakers and his transformation of the Mosaic rules on anger and retaliation. May a Christian–or, for that matter, a non-Christian who accepts the validity of this portion of the New Testament–rely on texts such as these to ground his objection to military service?

Ghandi's teaching offers perhaps the most effective example of non-violent resistance in recent history. Its effect, bringing down the British Empire–the mightest imperial force in the world at the time—in India was astonishing. At its core, Ghandi's spirituality is Hindu, but he was familiar with the teachings of Jesus on non-violence, primarily through reading Leon Tolstoy. Ghandi described Jesus as "a prince among passive resisters." May a conscientious objector rely upon the teachings of Ghandi?

Is there a danger in letting government officials probe into the religious basis for an exemption? *See United States v. Ballard,* 322 U.S. 78 (1944) [Chapter Twelve, section 1].

2. *Pacifism and Justifiable War.* Must a conscientious objector be opposed to every imaginable use of force to resolve international conflict? Followers of Jesus in the early period of church history took seriously his teaching about non-violence and could not for that reason serve in the Roman army. Others refused to serve on the ground that soldiers were obliged to take an oath of loyalty to the emperor as lord, an oath inconsistent with the central command

of Deuteronomy 5:7 "You shall have no other god to set against me" and with the fundamental Christian belief that Jesus is Lord (Rom. 1:4; 1 Cor. 12:3). When Christianity became the official religion of the empire, Christians began to ponder not whether it was ever permissible to serve in the imperial army, but whether the State could ever wage war (*jus ad bellum*), and if so, whether there were any limits that the Christian religion placed on the conduct of warfare (*jus in bello*). The principal articulator of a theory of justifiable war was St. Augustine of Hippo. A modern commentator summarizes Augustine's theory as follows. "[T]hree kinds of war were morally defensible: a defensive war against aggression, a war to gain just reparations for a previous wrong, and a war to recover stolen property. But historical circumstances alone did not create the conditions for a 'just' war. A properly constituted authority must decide that the resort to war is necessary. Once that decision has been made, it is the soldier's duty to obey. Further, war must be waged with a 'right intention': not for revenge, or lust for glory and spoils, but with a sober commitment to conduct the war as an instrument of punishment necessary to protect the innocent and to prevent malefactors from doing worse. Right intentions would be expressed, not only in the decision to go to war, but also in the just conduct of a war. Here, 'the rules were taken from classical antiquity. Faith must be kept with the enemy. There should be no wanton violence, profanation of temples, looting, massacre, or conflagration. Vengeance, atrocities, and reprisals were excluded, though ambush was allowed.' Thus, Augustine, who counseled against self-defense in the case of individual threat, outlined the skeleton of a just-war theory rooted in a moral passion for peace as the tranquility of order." George Weigel, *Tranquilitas Ordinis: The Present Failure and Future Promise of American Catholic Thought on War and Peace* 29 (1987) (citations omitted). For a fuller discussion, see Chapter Two above, NOTE. *Christians and Military Service in the Early Church: From Pacifism to the Augustinian Tradition on Justifiable War.*

After centuries of reflection on the justification of war, there is now fairly strong consensus in international law that war may be justified only if: (1) declared and waged by legitimate authority, (2) resorted to after all efforts to resolve the conflict peacefully have failed, (3) waged for a just cause (e.g., restoration of peace and justice) and with reasonable hope of success (4) waged within the principle of proportionality, according to which the good sought to be achieved must outweigh the evil inherent in all war, and (5) waged within the limits of the law of war, providing, for example, immunity for noncombatants. Weigel 41. May a conscientious objector–whether or not he is religious–rely on these criteria in seeking an exemption from military service? Or must conscientious exemption be limited to pacifists? If so, does that conclusion create a governmental preference for one religious view over another? Assume that a draft board agrees that an applicant should be exempt under the theory of a justifiable war. Should the exemption go any further than the scope of the objection? For example, if a person asserts that he cannot in good conscience serve in a particular theater of war be excused from all forms of military service? See Greenawalt, "Conscientious Objection" 274, note 30.

Professor Greenawalt concludes: "The demand that people stand ready to kill others and to sacrifice their own lives is the most severe demand a society can place on its citizens. The first part of that demand, the readiness to kill others, is in tension with the Christian religious tradition that has largely underlain American culture. That is not to say that most Christians at any time in the country's history have believed killing is morally wrong, only that the perfectionist ethics of the gospels and the pacifist inclinations of the early church pose a serious question about whether such killing can be justified." Id. 257. Does this statement capture the development in church history and in international law relating to the theory of justifiable war?

Resolution on Conscientious Objection, First Continental Congress (1775)

As there are some people, who, from religious principles, cannot bear arms in any case, this Congress intend no violence to their consciences, but earnestly recommend it to them, to contribute liberally in this time of universal calamity, to the relief of their distressed brethren in the several colonies, and do all other services to their oppressed Country, which they can consistently with their religious principles. Worthington C. Ford, ed., 2 *Journals of the Continental Congress, 1774–1789* 189 (19__).

James Madison's Proposed Constitutional Amendment on Conscientious Objection (1789)

No person religiously scrupulous of bearing arms shall be compelled to render military service in person. Joseph Gales, ed., 1 *The Debates and Proceedings in the Congress of the United States* 451 (1856).

––––––––

Madison's proposal was responsive to the concern raised by three ratifying conventions that conscientious objectors might be compelled to render military service. The proposed language was not adopted, on the ground that it was sufficient to leave this matter to the states; several state constitutions already included provisions of this sort. There was no military conscription in the War of 1812 or in the Mexican–American War. Both the national Congress and the Confederacy resorted to conscription during the Civil War. The federal statute made provision for exemption of members of designated pacifist denominations. This approach was followed when the country entered World War I.

Selective Service Act of 1917, 40 Stat. 76, 78 (1917)

The Act provided exemption from combatant duty for members of "any well-recognized religious sect or organization at present organized and existing and whose existing creed or principles forbid its members to participate in war in any form."

––––––––

As noted above, the Court summarily dismissed a constitutional challenge to this statute based on the nonestablishment principle. *Selective Draft Law Cases*, 245 U.S. 366 (1918) [Chapter Ten, section 5]. Right result? Limiting the exemption for conscientious objection to members of a pacifist church has the advantage of making it easier for the government to determine those to whom the exemption applies, but is administrative convenience a standard of constitutionality? Is membership in a traditional pacifist church, such as the Society of

Friends, an assurance of the pacifist convictions of the member? Does a membership requirement exclude a non-member of pacifist groups from the exemption, even though the non-member has virtually identical convictions as those held by members of pacifist groups? Would the membership requirement have the effect of encouraging people to join a particular religious community? Does this violate the nonestablishment principle? As the nation braced for World War II, Congress abandoned the requirement of membership in a traditional peace church, and enacted the following language.

The Selective Draft Act of 1940, 54 Stat. 885 (1940)

Nothing contained in this Act shall be construed to require any person to be subject to combatant training and service in the land or naval forces of the United States who, by reason of religious training and belief, is conscientiously opposed to participation in war in any form. Any such person claiming such exemption from combatant training and service because of such conscientious objections whose claim is sustained by the local board shall, if he is inducted into the land or naval forces under this Act, be assigned to noncombatant service as defined by the President, or shall, if he is found to be conscientiously opposed to participation in such noncombatant service, in lieu of such induction, be assigned to work of national importance under civilian direction.

———

Between 25,000 and 50,000 men who objected to bearing arms in war were assigned in the armed services to noncombatant duty in food supply, communications, or the Medical Corps; the largest single religious group were some 12,000 Seventh-day Adventists. Mulford Q. Sibley and Philip E. Jacob, *Conscription of Conscience: The American State and the Conscientious Objector, 1940–1947* 86–90 (1952). Those who qualified under the statute but were unwilling to be in the military—about 12,000 in all—worked for the Civilian Public Service (CPS). CPS work was in forestry and conservation camps; in hospitals and mental institutions; on government survey teams and on private farms. The work was 40 to 96 hours a week and was without pay. *Id.* 112, 124. The better CPS camps were run by "the Historic Peace Churches"—the Friends, the Mennonites, and the Brethren—as agents of the government. *Id.* 111. The camp programs included religious indoctrination by the churches in charge of the camps. *Id.* 173. The constitutional problem involved in making men labor without pay was brushed aside by the courts, *e.g.*, *Roodenko v. United States*, 147 F.2d 752 (10th Cir. 1944), *cert. denied*, 324 U.S. 860 (1945). The constitutional problem of letting churches act as custodial agencies of the government does not seem to have been judicially addressed. The majority but by no means all of those in the CPS were themselves members of the Peace Churches. The Peace Churches as government agents were, in the eyes of two academic authorities, mice yoked to a cat. Sibley and Jacob 471.

The Selective Draft of 1940 was substantially broader than that of 1917. Instead of exempting only members of "any well-recognized religious sect," all that it required was "religious training and belief." The Circuit Courts divided on what constituted "religious training and belief." Judge Augustus N. Hand—

Learned Hand's brother—drew a distinction between religious beliefs and political conviction.

United States v. Kauten

133 F.2d 703, 708 (2d Cir. 1943).

■ HAND, CIRCUIT JUDGE.

Religious belief arises from a sense of the inadequacy of reason as a means of relating the individual to his fellow-men and to his universe—a sense common to men in the most primitive and in the most highly civilized societies. It accepts the aid of logic but refuses to be limited by it. It is a belief finding expression in a conscience which categorically requires the believer to disregard elementary self-interest and to accept martyrdom in preference to transgressing its tenets. . . .

There is a distinction between a course of reasoning resulting in a conviction that a particular war is inexpedient or disastrous and a conscientious objection to participation in any war under any circumstances. The latter, and not the former, may be the basis of exemption under the Act. The former is usually a political objection, while the latter, we think, may justly be regarded as a response of the individual to an inward mentor, call it conscience or God, that is for many persons at the present time the equivalent of what has always been thought a religious impulse.

NOTES AND QUESTIONS

The dictum was applied in *United States ex rel. Phillips v. Downer*, 135 F.2d 521 (2d Cir. 1943), in recognizing as a conscientious objector Randolph G. Phillips, who said he had been influenced to oppose "the killing of men" by the Lord's Prayer, the Ten Commandments, and the Sermon on the Mount, and by "historians and poets from Plato to Shaw." Arguably to the contrary, the Ninth Circuit en banc upheld denial of conscientious objector status to Herman Berman, whose objections to war had been learned from two Socialists, Norman Thomas and Eugene Debs, who were serious Christians. *Berman v. United States*, 156 F.2d 377 (9th Cir. 1946). Denying certiorari, 329 U.S. 795 (1946), the Supreme Court declined the opportunity to clarify the law.

The Supreme Court grappled with conscientious objection only indirectly. In *In re Summers*, 325 U.S. 561 (1945), 5–4, per Justice Stanley F. Reed, it upheld the right of Illinois to deny Clyde Wilson Summers admission to the bar because he refused to take an oath to support the constitution of Illinois. Summers had refused because of his conscientious objection to bearing arms as the Illinois constitution required in time of war; his refusal had led the bar's Committee on Character and Fitness to refuse to certify him. Invoking *Hamilton v. Regents* [Chapter Ten, section 11], Justice Reed said that any exemption from military service for conscientious objectors was "by grace of Congressional recognition of their beliefs." He found no violation of "the principles of religious freedom." Dissenting, Justice Black quoted the Sermon on the Mount, the Holmes dissent in *Schwimmer* [Chapter Ten, section 11], and the Hughes dissent in *Macintosh* [Chapter Ten, section 11].

Less than a year later, in *Girouard v. United States*, 328 U.S. 61 (1946), the *Schwimmer* and *Macintosh* dissents became the law as the Court, 5–3 per Justice Douglas, interpreted the Nationality Act of 1940 not to bar a conscientious objector from citizenship. James Louis Girouard, a Seventh-day Adventist, had served as a non-combatant in the armed services during the war, as had approximately 10,000 members of his church. Justice Douglas noted that service to the country could be manifest in a variety of ways: "The bearing of arms, important as it is, is not the only way in which our institutions may be supported and defended, even in times of great peril. Total war in its modern form dramatizes as never before the great cooperative effort necessary for victory." The Court also scrutinized the oath required of aliens and noted that it did not expressly require that they promise to bear arms. "Nor has Congress expressly made any such finding a prerequisite to citizenship. To hold that it is required is to read it into the Act by implication. But we could not assume that Congress intended to make such an abrupt and radical departure from our traditions." Douglas concluded, to the contrary, that the "respect by Congress over the years for the conscience of those having religious scruples against bearing arms is cogent evidence of the meaning of the oath. It is recognition by Congress that even in time of war one may truly support and defend our institutions though he stops short of using weapons of war." Chief Justice Stone, the sole dissenter in *Gobitis* [section 3 above], joined by Justice Frankfurter, the author of *Gobitis*, and Justice Reed, dissented. Does *Girouard* also reverse *Hamilton* [Chapter Ten, section 11] and *Summers* [above] by implication? If not, may a state university require all male students to complete one course in military service and tactics? And may a state prohibit an applicant for the Bar from becoming a lawyer if he is conscientiously opposed to bearing arms in defense of the nation?

During the war the law was clear that only those who could come within the terms of the draft law's exemption would be exempted. But the exemption was sometimes interpreted by local boards with prejudice against particular religious groups, *e.g.*, in Oklahoma, against the Mennonites and Brethren. Sibley and Jacob 65. In other cases boards acted capriciously, *see* Francis Heiser (a lawyer who represented many conscientious objectors), "The Law Versus the Conscientious Objector," 20 *U.Chi.L.Rev.* 441 (1953). Administrative appeal corrected some injustices but was limited. Judicial review of classifications by local boards was extremely narrow until 1946, when—at the behest of a Jehovah's Witness represented by Hayden Covington—the Supreme Court permitted challenge of a classification as a defense in a criminal prosecution. *Estep v. United States*, 327 U.S. 114 (1946).

Beyond prejudice and caprice, there was the inadequacy of the exemption. It did not extend to those who refused to register at all. Of these, 300 were criminally prosecuted, one-third of them Black Muslims. Sibley and Jacob 334. Roman Catholics who objected to the war as "unjust" but did not object to war "in any form" were occasionally prosecuted. Above all, the Jehovah's Witnesses did not fit the exemption. Witnesses did not object to the wars ordered by God in the Bible and so appeared not to object to war "in any form." They did object to fighting "Satan's war" for America. They regularly made the claim that each Witness was a minister of the Gospel. Herbert Hewitt Stroup, *The Jehovah's Witnesses* 165–166 (1945). They pitched their main constitutional case during the war on this point and lost. *Cox v. United States* [Chapter Twelve, section 2]. In Germany at the same time the Witnesses were being sent to lunatic asylums or to Dachau for refusal to serve. M. James Penton, *Apocalypse Delayed* 142 (1985). The United States was not as harsh, but over 5,000 Witnesses were imprisoned for their refusal to serve; no other church produced so many martyrs to conscience. Sibley and Jacob 84.

Well after World War II, the Court was prepared to back the draft law without greater sensitivity to religious beliefs. In *Gara v. United States,* 340 U.S. 857 (1950), a student at a Mennonite college had decided not to register for the draft. When the FBI came to arrest him, Gara, the dean of men, a practicing Quaker, told him, "Stand by your principles. Don't let them coerce you into registering." Gara was convicted of the felony of aiding and abetting a refusal to register. His free exercise claim was overridden by the government's interest in draft registration. 178 F.2d 38 (6th Cir. 1949). The Supreme Court, 4–4, affirmed without opinion. If you were the ninth justice, how would you vote? Why?

In 1955 the Witnesses made a notable breach in the draft law in *Sicurella v. United States,* 348 U.S. 385 (1955), where a Witness willing to engage in theocratic war commanded by God was held to be opposed to participation in war "in any form" within the meaning of the draft act. The Court's conclusion suggested how constitutional issues could be avoided by imaginative construction of the congressional exemption. Justice Tom C. Clark wrote the opinion; Justices Reed and Minton dissented. *Sicurella* was apt precedent when a new kind of conscientious objector appeared in litigation. The cases, significantly, arose in the 1950s when the United States was at peace. Equally significantly, they were decided when the Vietnam War was becoming unpopular.

United States v. Seeger

380 U.S. 163 (1965).

Solicitor General Archibald Cox argued the cause for the United States in all cases. *Assistant Attorney General Miller* was with him on the briefs in all cases. *Ralph S. Spritzer* was with him on the briefs in Nos. 50 and 51, and *Marshall Tamor Golding* was with him on the briefs in No. 50.

Duane B. Beeson argued the cause and filed a brief for petitioner in No. 29.

Kenneth W. Greenawalt argued the cause and filed a brief for respondent in No. 50.

Herman Alderstein argued the cause and filed a brief for respondent in No. 51.

Briefs of *amici curiae*, urging affirmance in Nos. 50 and 51 and reversal in No. 29, were filed by *Alfred Lawrence Toombs* and *Melvin L. Wulf* for the American Civil Liberties Union, and by *Leo Pfeffer, Shad Polier, Will Maslow,* and *Joseph B. Robison* for the American Jewish Congress. Briefs of *amici curiae*, urging affirmance in No. 50, were filed by *Herbert A. Wolff, Leo Rose, Nanette Dembitz* and *Nancy F. Wechsler* for the American Ethical Union, and by *Tolbert H. McCarroll, Lester Forest* and *Paul Blanshard* for the American Humanist Association.

■ JUSTICE CLARK delivered the opinion of the Court.

No. 50: Seeger was convicted in the District Court for the Southern District of New York of having refused to submit to induction in the armed forces. He was originally classified 1–A in 1953 by his local board, but this classification was changed in 1955 to 2–S (student) and he remained in this status until 1958 when he was reclassified 1–A. He first claimed exemption as a conscientious objector in 1957 after successive annual renewals of his student classification. Although he did not adopt verbatim the printed Selective Service System form, he declared that he was conscientiously opposed to participation in war in any form by reason of his "religious" belief; that he preferred to leave the question as to his belief in a Supreme Being open, "rather than answer 'yes' or 'no' "; that his "skepticism or disbelief in the existence of God" did "not necessarily mean lack of faith in anything whatsoever"; that his was a "belief in and devotion to goodness and virtue for their own sakes, and a religious faith in a purely ethical creed." He cited such personages as Plato, Aristotle and Spinoza for support of his ethical belief in intellectual and moral integrity "without belief in God, except in the remotest sense." His belief was found to be sincere, honest, and made in good faith; and his conscientious objection to be based upon individual training and belief, both of which included research in religious and cultural fields. Seeger's claim, however, was denied solely because it was not based upon a "belief in a relation to a Supreme Being" as required by § 6 (j) of the Act. At trial Seeger's counsel admitted that Seeger's belief was not in relation to a Supreme Being as commonly understood, but contended that he was entitled to the exemption because "under the present law Mr. Seeger's position would also include definitions of religion which have been stated more recently," and could be "accommodated" under the definition of religious training and belief in the Act. He was convicted and the Court of Appeals reversed, holding that the Supreme Being requirement of the section distinguished "between internally derived and externally compelled beliefs" and was, therefore, an "impermissible classification" under the Due Process Clause of the Fifth Amendment.

No. 51: Jakobson was also convicted in the Southern District of New York on a charge of refusing to submit to induction. On his appeal the Court of Appeals reversed on the ground that rejection of his claim may have rested on the factual finding, erroneously made, that he did not believe in a Supreme Being as required by § 6 (j).

Jakobson was originally classified 1–A in 1953 and intermittently enjoyed a student classification until 1956. It was not until April 1958 that he made claim to noncombatant classification (1–A–0) as a conscientious objector. He stated on the Selective Service System form that he believed in a "Supreme Being" who was "Creator of Man" in the sense of being "ultimately responsible for the existence of" man and who was "the Supreme Reality" of which "the existence of man is the *result*" (emphasis in original). He explained that his religious and social thinking had developed after much meditation and thought. He had concluded that man must be "partly spiritual" and, therefore, "partly akin to the Supreme Reality"; and that his "most important religious law" was that "no man ought ever to willfully sacrifice another man's life as a means to any other end. . . ." In

December 1958 he requested a 1–0 classification since he felt that participation in any form of military service would involve him in "too many situations and relationships that would be a strain on [his] conscience that [he felt he] must avoid." He submitted a long memorandum of "notes on religion" in which he defined religion as the *"sum and essence of one's basic attitudes to the fundamental problems of human existence,"* (emphasis in the original); he said that he believed in "Godness" which was "the Ultimate Cause for the fact of the Being of the Universe"; that to deny its existence would but deny the existence of the universe because "anything that Is, has an Ultimate Cause for its Being." There was a relationship to Godness, he stated, in two directions, *i.e.,* "vertically, towards Godness directly," and "horizontally, towards Godness through Mankind and the World." He accepted the latter one. The Board classified him 1–A–0 and Jakobson appealed. The hearing officer found that the claim was based upon a personal moral code and that he was not sincere in his claim. The Appeal Board classified him 1–A. It did not indicate upon what ground it based its decision, *i.e.,* insincerity or a conclusion that his belief was only a personal moral code. The Court of Appeals reversed, finding that his claim came within the requirements of § 6 (j). Because it could not determine whether the Appeal Board had found that Jakobson's beliefs failed to come within the statutory definition, or whether it had concluded that he lacked sincerity, it directed dismissal of the indictment.

No. 29: Forest Britt Peter was convicted in the Northern District of California on a charge of refusing to submit to induction. In his Selective Service System form he stated that he was not a member of a religious sect or organization; he failed to execute section VII of the questionnaire but attached to it a quotation expressing opposition to war, in which he stated that he concurred. In a later form he hedged the question as to his belief in a Supreme Being by saying that it depended on the definition and he appended a statement that he felt it a violation of his moral code to take human life and that he considered this belief superior to his obligation to the state. As to whether his conviction was religious, he quoted with approval Reverend John Haynes Holmes' definition of religion as "the consciousness of some power manifest in nature which helps man, in the ordering of his life in harmony with its demands ... [; it] is the supreme expression of human nature; it is man thinking his highest, feeling his deepest, and living his best." The source of his conviction he attributed to reading and meditation "in our democratic American culture, with its values derived from the western religious and philosophical tradition." *Ibid.* As to his belief in a Supreme Being, Peter stated that he supposed "you could call that a belief in the Supreme Being or God. These just do not happen to be the words I use." In 1959 he was classified 1–A, although there was no evidence in the record that he was not sincere in his beliefs. After his conviction for failure to report for induction the Court of Appeals, assuming *arguendo* that he was sincere, affirmed. . . .

Few would quarrel, we think, with the proposition that in no field of human endeavor has the tool of language proved so inadequate in the communication of ideas as it has in dealing with the fundamental questions of man's predicament in life, in death or in final judgment and retribution.

This fact makes the task of discerning the intent of Congress in using the phrase "Supreme Being" a complex one. Nor is it made the easier by the richness and variety of spiritual life in our country. Over 250 sects inhabit our land. Some believe in a purely personal God, some in a supernatural deity; others think of religion as a way of life envisioning as its ultimate goal the day when all men can live together in perfect understanding and peace. There are those who think of God as the depth of our being; others, such as the Buddhists, strive for a state of lasting rest through self-denial and inner purification; in Hindu philosophy, the Supreme Being is the transcendental reality which is truth, knowledge and bliss. Even those religious groups which have traditionally opposed war in every form have splintered into various denominations: from 1940 to 1947 there were four denominations using the name "Friends," Selective Service System Monograph No. 11, Conscientious Objection 13 (1950); the "Church of the Brethren" was the official name of the oldest and largest church body of four denominations composed of those commonly called Brethren, *id.*, at 11; and the "Mennonite Church" was the largest of 17 denominations, including the Amish and Hutterites, grouped as "Mennonite bodies" in the 1936 report on the Census of Religious Bodies, *id.*, at 9. This vast panoply of beliefs reveals the magnitude of the problem which faced the Congress when it set about providing an exemption from armed service. It also emphasizes the care that Congress realized was necessary in the fashioning of an exemption which would be in keeping with its long-established policy of not picking and choosing among religious beliefs.

In spite of the elusive nature of the inquiry, we are not without certain guidelines. In amending the 1940 Act, Congress adopted almost intact the language of Chief Justice Hughes in *United States v. Macintosh* [Chapter Ten, section 11]: "The essence of religion is belief in a relation to *God* involving duties superior to those arising from any human relation" (emphasis supplied). By comparing the statutory definition with those words, however, it becomes readily apparent that the Congress deliberately broadened them by substituting the phrase "Supreme Being" for the appellation "God." And in so doing it is also significant that Congress did not elaborate on the form or nature of this higher authority which it chose to designate as "Supreme Being." By so refraining it must have had in mind the admonitions of the Chief Justice when he said in the same opinion that even the word "God" had myriad meanings for men of faith: "[P]utting aside dogmas with their particular conceptions of deity, freedom of conscience itself implies respect for an innate conviction of paramount duty. The battle for religious liberty has been fought and won with respect to religious beliefs and practices, which are not in conflict with good order, upon the very ground of the supremacy of conscience within its proper field."

Moreover, the Senate Report on the bill specifically states that § 6(j) was intended to re-enact "substantially the same provisions as were found" in the 1940 Act. That statute, of course, refers to "religious training and belief" without more. Admittedly, all of the parties here purport to base their objection on religious belief. It appears, therefore, that we need only look to this clear statement of congressional intent as set out in the report.

Under the 1940 Act it was necessary only to have a conviction based upon religious training and belief; we believe that is all that is required here. Within that phrase would come all sincere religious beliefs which are based upon a power or being, or upon a faith, to which all else is subordinate or upon which all else is ultimately dependent. The test might be stated in these words: A sincere and meaningful belief which occupies in the life of its possessor a place parallel to that filled by the God of those admittedly qualifying for the exemption comes within the statutory definition. This construction avoids imputing to Congress an intent to classify different religious beliefs, exempting some and excluding others, and is in accord with the well-established congressional policy of equal treatment for those whose opposition to service is grounded in their religious tenets. . . .

In summary, Seeger professed "religious belief" and "religious faith." He did not disavow any belief "in a relation to a Supreme Being"; indeed he stated that "the cosmic order does, perhaps, suggest a creative intelligence." He decried the tremendous "spiritual" price man must pay for his willingness to destroy human life. In light of his beliefs and the unquestioned sincerity with which he held them, we think the Board, had it applied the test we propose today, would have granted him the exemption. We think it clear that the beliefs which prompted his objection occupy the same place in his life as the belief in a traditional deity holds in the lives of his friends, the Quakers. We are reminded once more of Dr. Tillich's thoughts: "And if that word [God] has not much meaning for you, translate it, and speak of the depths of your life, of the source of your being, of your ultimate concern, *of what you take seriously without any reservation.* Perhaps, in order to do so, you must forget everything traditional that you have learned about God." Tillich, *The Shaking of the Foundations* 57 (1948) (emphasis supplied). It may be that Seeger did not clearly demonstrate what his beliefs were with regard to the usual understanding of the term "Supreme Being." But as we have said Congress did not intend that to be the test. We therefore affirm the judgment in No. 50.

In *Jakobson*, No. 51, the Court of Appeals found that the registrant demonstrated that his belief as to opposition to war was related to a Supreme Being. We agree and affirm that judgment.

We reach a like conclusion in No. 29. It will be remembered that Peter acknowledged "some power manifest in nature . . . the supreme expression" that helps man in ordering his life. As to whether he would call that belief in a Supreme Being, he replied, "you could call that a belief in the Supreme Being or God. These just do not happen to be the words I use." We think that under the test we establish here the Board would grant the exemption to Peter and we therefore reverse the judgment in No. 29.

————

Is Congress entitled to give special protection to freedom of religious conscience, finding in its exercise a particular moral and social value, and citing as justification for its actions the recognition of this value in the free exercise clause of the First Amendment? Is it entitled to extend this protection even though it must frankly be recognized that to do so results in some advantage to religious belief and indirectly disadvantages those who do not profess the particular religious belief protected? John H. Mansfield, "Conscientious Objection—1964 Term," in Donald A. Gianella, ed., 1965 *Religion and Public Order* 74–75. In *Seeger*, Mansfield observed, the Supreme Court virtually merged the conscientious and the religious. An amendment to the Act in 1967, subsequent to the Court's decision in the *Seeger* case, deleted the reference to a "Supreme Being" but continued to provide that "religious training and belief" does not include "essentially political, sociological, or philosophical views, or a merely personal moral code." 81 Stat. 104, U.S.C. App § 456(j). The statute was interpreted as follows.

Selective Service Act of 1967, 81 Stat. 104, 50 U.S.C. App. § 456(j)

After the Court's decision in the *Seeger* case, Congress amended the Act in 1967, deleting the reference to a "Supreme Being," but continuing to provide that "religious training and belief" does not include "essentially political, sociological, or philosophical views, or a merely personal moral code." The statute was interpreted as follows.

Welsh v. United States

398 U.S. 333 (1970).

J.B. Tietz argued the cause and filed briefs for petitioner. *Solicitor General Erwin Griswold* argued the cause for the United States. With him on the brief were *Assistant Attorney General Wilson, Francis X. Beytagh, Jr.,* and *Beatrice Rosenberg*.

■ JUSTICE BLACK announced the judgment of the Court and delivered an opinion in which JUSTICE DOUGLAS, JUSTICE BRENNAN, and JUSTICE MARSHALL join.

The petitioner, Elliott Ashton Welsh II, was convicted by a United States District Judge of refusing to submit to induction into the Armed Forces in violation of 50 U.S.C. App. § 462 (a), and was on June 1, 1966, sentenced to imprisonment for three years. One of petitioner's defenses to the prosecution was that § 6 (j) of the Universal Military Training and Service Act exempted him from combat and noncombat service because he was "by reason of religious training and belief ... conscientiously opposed to participation in war in any form." After finding that there was no religious basis for petitioner's conscientious objector claim, the Court of Appeals, Judge Hamley dissenting, affirmed the conviction. We granted certiorari chiefly to review the contention that Welsh's conviction should be set aside on the basis of this Court's decision in *United States v. Seeger* [above]. For the reasons to be stated, and without passing upon the constitutional arguments that have been raised, we vote to reverse this conviction because of its fundamental inconsistency with *Seeger*....

The controlling facts in this case are strikingly similar to those in *Seeger*.... In the case before us the Government seeks to distinguish our holding in *Seeger* on basically two grounds, both of which were relied upon by the Court of Appeals in affirming Welsh's conviction. First, it is stressed that Welsh was far more insistent and explicit than Seeger in denying that his views were religious. For example, in filling out their conscientious objector applications, Seeger put quotation marks around the word "religious," but Welsh struck the word "religious" entirely and later characterized his beliefs as having been formed "by reading in the fields of history and sociology." The Court of Appeals found that Welsh had "denied that his objection to war was premised on religious belief" and concluded that "[t]he Appeal Board was entitled to take him at his word." We think this attempt to distinguish *Seeger* fails for the reason that it places undue emphasis on the registrant's interpretation of his own beliefs. The Court's statement in *Seeger* that a registrant's characterization of his own belief as "religious" should carry great weight does not imply that his declaration that his views are nonreligious should be treated similarly. When a registrant states that his objections to war are "religious," that information is highly relevant to the question of the function his beliefs have in his life. But very few registrants are fully aware of the broad scope of the word "religious" as used in § 6 (j), and accordingly a registrant's statement that his beliefs are nonreligious is a highly unreliable guide for those charged with administering the exemption. Welsh himself presents a case in point. Although he originally characterized his beliefs as nonreligious, he later upon reflection wrote a long and thoughtful letter to his Appeal Board in which he declared that his beliefs were "certainly religious in the ethical sense of the word." He explained: "I believe I mentioned taking of life as not being, for me, a religious wrong. Again, I assumed Mr. [Brady (the Department of Justice hearing officer)] was using the word 'religious' in the conventional sense, and, in order to be perfectly honest did not characterize my belief as 'religious.' "

The Government also seeks to distinguish *Seeger* on the ground that Welsh's views, unlike Seeger's, were "essentially political, sociological, or philosophical views or a merely personal moral code." As previously noted, the Government made the same argument about Seeger, and not without reason, for Seeger's views had a substantial political dimension.... In this case, Welsh's conscientious objection to war was undeniably based in part on his perception of world politics. In a letter to his local board, he wrote: "I can only act according to what I am and what I see. And I see that the military complex wastes both human and material resources, that it fosters disregard for (what I consider a paramount concern) human needs and ends; I see that the means we employ to 'defend' our 'way of life' profoundly change that way of life. I see that in our failure to recognize the political, social, and economic realities of the world, we, *as a nation,* fail our responsibility *as a nation."* We certainly do not think that § 6 (j)'s exclusion of those persons with "essentially political, sociological, or philosophical views or a merely personal moral code" should be read to exclude those who hold strong beliefs about our domestic and foreign affairs or even those whose conscientious objection to participation in all wars is founded to a substantial extent upon considerations of public policy. The two groups of registrants that obviously do fall within these exclusions from the exemption are those whose beliefs are not deeply held and those whose objection to war does not rest at all upon moral, ethical, or religious principle but instead rests solely upon considerations of policy, pragmatism, or expediency. In applying § 6 (j)'s exclusion of those whose views are "essentially political, sociological, or philosophical" or of those who have a "merely personal moral code," it should be remembered that these exclusions are definitional and do not therefore restrict the category of persons who are conscientious objectors by "religious training and belief." Once the Selective Service System has taken the first step and determined under the standards set out here and in *Seeger* that the registrant is a "religious" conscientious objector, it follows that his views cannot be "essentially political, sociological, or philosophical." Nor can they be a "merely personal moral code." *Seeger.*

Welsh stated that he "believe[d] the taking of life—anyone's life—to be morally wrong." In his original conscientious objector application he wrote the following: "I believe that human life is valuable in and of itself; in its living; therefore I will not injure or kill another human being. This belief (and the corresponding 'duty' to abstain from violence toward another person) is not 'superior to those arising from any human relation.' On the contrary: *it is essential to every human relation.* I cannot, therefore, conscientiously comply with the Government's insistence that I assume duties which I feel are immoral and totally repugnant." Welsh elaborated his beliefs in later communications with Selective Service officials. On the basis of these beliefs and the conclusion of the Court of Appeals that he held them "with the strength of more traditional religious convictions," we think Welsh was clearly entitled to a conscientious objector exemption. Section 6(j) requires no more. That section exempts from military service all those whose consciences, spurred by deeply held moral, ethical, or religious beliefs, would give them no rest or peace if they allowed themselves to become a part of an instrument of war. The judgment is *Reversed.*

■ Justice Harlan, concurring in the result.

The constitutional question that must be faced in this case is whether a statute that defers to the individual's conscience only when his views emanate from adherence to theistic religious beliefs is within the power of Congress. Congress, of course, could, entirely consistently with the requirements of the Constitution, eliminate all exemptions for conscientious objectors. Such a course would be wholly "neutral" and, in my view, would not offend the Free Exercise Clause, for reasons set forth in my dissenting opinion in *Sherbert v. Verner* [section 5 below]; See *Jacobson v. Massachusetts*, 197 U.S. 11, 29 (1905) (dictum); cf. *McGowan v. Maryland* [Chapter Thirteen, section 2]; *Davis v. Beason* [Chapter Nine]; *Hamilton v. Board of Regents* [Chapter Ten, section 11]; *Reynolds v. United States* [Chapter Nine]; Kurland, Of Church and State and the Supreme Court, 29 U. Chi. L. Rev. 1 (1961). However, having chosen to exempt, it cannot draw the line between theistic or nontheistic religious beliefs on the one hand and secular beliefs on the other. Any such distinctions are not, in my view, compatible with the Establishment Clause of the First Amendment.

■ Justice White, with whom Chief Justice Burger and Justice Stewart join, dissenting.

Whether or not *United States v. Seeger*, 380 U.S. 163 (1965), accurately reflected the intent of Congress in providing draft exemptions for religious conscientious objectors to war, I cannot join today's construction of § 6 (j) extending draft exemption to those who disclaim religious objections to war and whose views about war represent a purely personal code arising not from religious training and belief as the statute requires but from readings in philosophy, history, and sociology. Our obligation in statutory construction cases is to enforce the will of Congress, not our own; and as Mr. Justice Harlan has demonstrated, construing § 6 (j) to include Welsh exempts from the draft a class of persons to whom Congress has expressly denied an exemption.

NOTES AND QUESTIONS

1.   *Marxist Communism as a Religion.* Writers on communism have frequently characterized it as a religion, *e.g.*, Joseph Schumpeter, *Capitalism, Socialism, and Democracy* 5–8 (1950); Robert C. Tucker, *Philosophy and Myth in Karl Marx* 21–27 (1972). Like all serious systems, it claims to be true. It offers a comprehensive account of human relations and a Marxist morality. It propounds a way of life. It is propagated by the Communist party of the Soviet Union and by other communist parties. Analogies are easily drawn between the communist hierarchy, agents, and missionaries and Christian hierarchies, agents, and missionaries. Communism offers "social salvation," where a general elimination of injustice will occur, instead of an after-death salvation where justice will be done. Its founders are its prophets; the end predicted is apocalyptic. Its belief in the inevitability of class warfare and the victory of the proletariat is a form of predestination. Indeed, many of Marx's own images and ideas were drawn from the Bible. Reinhard Buchbinder, *Bibelzitate, Bibelanspielungen, Bibelparodien, theologische Vergleiche und Analogien bei Marx und Engels* 28–45 (1976). Marx, for example, says, "Materialism is the only-begotten son of Great Britain," *Id.* 118, parodying John 1:18. "All the important dogmas of the Church—the Trinity, Creation, Original Sin, Incarnation of the Son of God and Redemption of man, the Church or Mystical Body of Christ as a perfect society, the consummation of history through Christ—have been found 'transposed in Marxism to a register of atheistic humanism.' " Jean–Yves Calvez, *La Pensée de Karl Marx* 594 (1950).

Communism is not treated as a religion for purposes of the First Amendment. Once God is eliminated from a definition of religion, why does not communism qualify? The most obvious objection is that it does not claim to be one. But that is true of SCI/TM, *Malnak v. Yogi* [Chapter Fourteen, section 2]. Suppose, in a change of strategy, the Communist Party, U.S.A., should make the claim. Would its political character disqualify it? Is Islam less a religion because of its political importance to many Middle Eastern governments?

2.   *Selective Conscientious Objection.* As opposition to the Vietnam War reached a fevor pitch, a different claim of conscience arose. Many objectors to the Vietnam War were not traditional pacifists who maintain it is never permissible to use force in the resolution of international disputes. Instead, their position was that war is sometimes morally permissible or even necessary, but is not morally justifiable in other circumstances. This position is known as "selective conscientious objection," or SCO.

Gordon C. Zahn's *In Solitary Witness: The Life and Death of Franz Jägerstätter* (1964), telling the story of an Austrian Catholic executed for refusing to fight for Hitler, had shown that a simple, saintly man could choose death rather than participate in an unjust war. Vietnam not only led to conscientious objection by persons from traditional peace churches; it also led Catholics and other Christians who teach that war is sometimes morally justifiable to be more assertive of their conscientious scruples to a war that many Catholics, including the Catholic Bishops of the United States, found to be unjust under the teaching of the Second Vatican Council, discussed below.

Ralph Potter, a Protestant theologian at the Harvard Divinity School, wrote an important essay applying the just war tradition to the Vietnam War, *War and Moral Discourse* (1969). Potter also argued that the public interest would be served by legislation permitting SCO on the ground that the government should prize such independence as the expression "of the integrity which is the ground of other virtues," "Conscientious Objection to Particular Wars," in Donald Gianella, ed., *Religion and the Public Order* 87 (1968). Others were unconvinced; *see* John A. Rohr, *Prophets Without Honor: Public Policy and the Selective Conscientious Objector* (1971) (selective conscientious objectors are like the prophets: they must expect to be stoned for their prophecies).

John Courtney Murray, the leading Catholic writer on conscience and the state, would not condemn the Vietnam War himself but would defend the right to conscientiously object to it. A member of President Johnson's Advisory Commission on Selective Service, he thus took a minority position on the commission, Murray. "War and Conscience," in James Finn, ed., *A Conflict of Loyalties: The Case for Selective Conscientious Objection* 19–30 (1968). As Murray saw, Congress was hostile to the selective objector, and the selective objection was often wrongly read as a political, not a religious contention. *Id.* 25.

A year after *Welsh,* the Court took two cases relating to this issue. Guy Porter Gillette resembled Elliot Welsh in two respects: his opposition to the Vietnam war was "spurred by deeply held moral, ethical, or religious beliefs" that the Court had to construe broadly in order to come within its construction of the statute; and like Welsh, he refused to obey an order of induction into the armed services. Louis Negre had studied for the priesthood in a Catholic seminary. He was familiar with the condemnation of unjust wars announced in the Second Vatican Council: "Any act of war aimed indiscriminately at the destruction of entire cities or of extensive areas along with their population is a crime against God and man himself. It merits unequivocal and unhesitating condemnation." Pastoral Constitution on the Church in the Modern World, Par. 80, Walter Abbott, ed., *The Documents of Vatican II* 294 (1966). Applying this teaching to the facts of the Vietnam War, Negre concluded that this particular war could no longer be justified and that he could not conscientiously serve in it. Negre was thus unlike Welsh in two respects: he did not object to military service as such and was already in the Army when he refused the orders of his commanding officer, General Stanley Larsen, to report for duty in Vietnam; and Negre's refusal to obey the order to serve in Vietnam was not based on a vague, Tillichian sense of "the Ground of Being," but on the express teaching of his church on the morality of conflicts such as the Vietnam War. There is another significant difference between *Welsh* and *Gillette.* In *Welsh* the

Court gave an expansive, creative reading of the statute. In *Gillette* and *Negre* the Court took an unnuanced, literalistic approach to the words in the statute granting exempt status to those who "conscientiously opposed to participation in war in any form." Professor Greenawalt, who had represented the respondent in *United States v. Seeger*, served as Deputy Solicitor General while the *Gillette* and *Negre* cases were litigated. He describes the arguments for and against SCO in Greenawalt, "All or Nothing at All: The Defeat of Selective Conscientious Objection," 1971 *Supreme Court Review* 31, 46–47.

Gillette v. United States, Negre v. Larsen

401 U.S. 437 (1971).

Conrad J. Lynn argued the cause for petitioner in no. 85. With him on the brief were *Leon Friedman, Marvin M. Karpatkin*, and *Melvin L. Wulf. Richard Harrington* argued the cause for petitioner in No. 325. With him on the briefs were *Leigh Athearn, Stuart J. Land*, and *John T. Noonan, Jr.*

Solicitor General Erwin Griswold argued the cause for the United States and for the other respondents in both cases. With him on the briefs were *Assistant Attorney General Wilson* and *Beatrice Rosenberg.*

George T. Altman, pro se, filed a brief as *amicus curiae* in both cases. *Leo Rosen* filed a brief for the American Ethical Union as *amicus curiae* in No. 85. Briefs of *amici curiae* in No. 325 were filed by *Charles H. Tuttle* and *Thomas A. Shaw, Jr.*, for the National Council of the Churches of Christ in the U.S.A. et al.; by *Peter J. Donnici* for the Executive Board of the National Federation of Priests' Councils; by *Joseph B. Robison, Ephraim Margolin, Stanley J. Friedman, Seymour Farber*, and *Edwin J. Lukas* for the American Jewish Congress, by *Michael N. Pollet* and *Elsbeth Levy Bothe* for Louis P. Font; and by the American Friends Service Committee.

■ JUSTICE MARSHALL delivered the opinion of the Court.

These cases present the question whether conscientious objection to a particular war, rather than objection to war as such, relieves the objector from responsibilities of military training and service. Specifically, we are called upon to decide whether conscientious scruples relating to a particular conflict are within the purview of established provisions relieving conscientious objectors to war from military service. Both petitioners also invoke constitutional principles barring government interference with the exercise of religion and requiring governmental neutrality in matters of religion. . . .

For purposes of determining the statutory status of conscientious objection to a particular war, the focal language of § 6 (j) is the phrase, "conscientiously opposed to participation in war in any form." This language, on a straightforward reading, can bear but one meaning; that conscientious scruples relating to war and military service must amount to conscientious opposition to participating personally in any war and all war. See *Welsh v. United States* [above] (concurring in result). See also *United States v. Kauten* [above]. It matters little for present purposes whether the words, "in any form," are read to modify "war" or "participation." On the first reading, conscientious scruples must implicate "war in any form," and an objection involving a particular war rather than all war would plainly not be covered by § 6 (j). On the other reading, an objector must oppose "participation in war." It would strain good sense to read this phrase otherwise than to mean "participation in all war." For the word "war" would still be used in an unqualified, generic sense, meaning war as such. Thus, however the statutory clause be parsed, it remains that conscientious objection must run to war in any form. . . .

The critical weakness of petitioners' establishment claim arises from the fact that § 6 (j), on its face, simply does not discriminate on the basis of religious affiliation or religious belief, apart of course from beliefs concerning war. The section says that anyone who is conscientiously opposed to all war shall be relieved of military service. The specified objection must have a grounding in "religious training and belief," but no particular sectarian affiliation or theological position is required. The Draft Act of 1917, § 4, 40 Stat. 78, extended relief only to those conscientious objectors affiliated with some "well-recognized religious sect or organization" whose principles forbade members' participation in war, but the attempt to focus on particular sects apparently broke down in administrative practice, *Welsh v. United States* [above] (concurring in result), and the 1940 Selective Training and Service Act, § 5 (g), 54 Stat. 869, discarded all sectarian restriction. Thereafter Congress has framed the conscientious objector exemption in broad terms compatible with "its long-established policy of not picking and choosing among religious beliefs." *United States v. Seeger* [above].

Thus, there is no occasion to consider the claim that when Congress grants a benefit expressly to adherents of one *religion,* courts must either nullify the grant or somehow extend the benefit to cover all religions. For § 6 (j) does not single out any religious organization or religious creed for special treatment. Rather petitioners' contention is that since Congress has recognized one sort of conscientious objection concerning war, whatever its religious basis, the Establishment Clause commands that another, different objection be carved out and protected by the courts. . . .

Apart from the Government's need for manpower, perhaps the central interest involved in the administration of conscription laws is the interest in maintaining a fair system for determining "who serves when not all serve." When the Government exacts so much, the importance of fair, evenhanded, and uniform decisionmaking is obviously intensified. The Government argues that the interest in fairness would be jeopardized by expansion of § 6 (j) to include conscientious objection to a particular war. The contention is that the claim to relief on account of such objection is intrinsically a claim of uncertain dimensions, and that granting the claim in theory would involve a real danger of erratic or even discriminatory decisionmaking in administrative practice.

A virtually limitless variety of beliefs are subsumable under the rubric, "objection to a particular war. . . ."

To be sure, the Free Exercise Clause bars "governmental regulation of religious beliefs as such," *Sherbert v. Verner* [section 5 below], or interference with the dissemination of religious ideas. See *Fowler v. Rhode Island* [Chapter Thirteen, section 1]; *Follett v. McCormick* [section 1 above], *Murdock v. Pennsylvania* [section 1 above]. It prohibits misuse of secular governmental programs "to impede the observance of one or all religions or . . . to discriminate invidiously between religions, . . . even though the burden may be characterized as being only indirect." *Braunfield v. Brown*, [Chapter Thirteen, section 2] (opinion of Warren, C.J.). And even as to neutral prohibitory or regulatory laws having secular aims, the Free Exercise Clause may condemn certain applications clashing with imperatives of religion and conscience, when the burden on First Amendment values is not justifiable in terms of the Government's valid aims. See *id.;* *Sherbert v. Verner* [section 5 below]. See generally Clark, Guidelines for the Free Exercise Clause, 83 Harv. L. Rev. 327 (1969). However, the impact of conscription on objectors to particular wars is far from unjustified. The conscription laws, applied to such persons as to others, are not designed to interfere with any religious ritual or practice, and do not work a penalty against any theological position. The incidental burdens felt by persons in petitioners' position are strictly justified by substantial governmental interests that relate directly to the very impacts questioned. And more broadly, of course, there is the Government's interest in procuring the manpower necessary for military purposes, pursuant to the constitutional grant of power to Congress to raise and support armies. Art. 1, § 8. *Affirmed.*

■ JUSTICE DOUGLAS, dissenting.

The question, Can a conscientious objector, whether his objection be rooted in "religion" or in moral values, be required to kill? has never been answered by the Court. *Hamilton v. Regents* [Chapter Ten, section 11], did no more than hold that the Fourteenth Amendment did not require a State to make its university available to one who would not take military training. *United States v. Macintosh*, [Chapter Ten, section 11] denied naturalization to a person who "would not promise in advance to bear arms in defense of the United States unless he believed the war to be morally justified." The question of compelling a man to kill against his conscience was not squarely involved. Most of the talk in the majority opinion concerned "serving in the armed forces of the Nation in time of war." Such service can, of course, take place in noncombatant roles. The ruling was that such service is "dependent upon the will of Congress and not upon the scruples of the individual, except as Congress provides." The *dicta* of the Court in the *Macintosh* case squint towards the denial of Gillette's claim, though as I have said, the issue was not squarely presented.

Yet if dicta are to be our guide, my choice is the dicta of Chief Justice Hughes who, dissenting in *Macintosh*, spoke as well for Justices Holmes, Brandeis, and Stone [Chapter Ten, section 11]. . . .

I had assumed that the welfare of the single human soul was the ultimate test of the vitality of the First Amendment.

■ JUSTICE DOUGLAS was the only dissenting voice in both cases.

Negre v. Larsen

401 U.S. 437 (1971).

■ Douglas, J., dissenting.

I approach the facts of this case with some diffidence, as they involve doctrines of the Catholic Church in which I was not raised. But we have on one of petitioner's briefs an authoritative lay Catholic scholar, Dr. John T. Noonan, Jr., and from that brief I deduce the following: Under the doctrines of the Catholic Church a person has a moral duty to take part in wars declared by his government so long as they comply with the tests of his church for just wars.[1] Conversely, a Catholic has a moral duty not to participate in unjust wars.[2]

The Fifth Commandment, "Thou shall not kill," provides a basis for the distinction between just and unjust wars. In the 16th century Francisco Victoria, Dominican master of the University of Salamanca and pioneer in international law, elaborated on the distinction. "If a subject is convinced of the injustice of a war, he ought not to serve in it, even on the command of his prince. This is clear, for no one can authorize the killing of an innocent person." He realized not all men had the information of the prince and his counsellors on the causes of a war, but where "the proofs and tokens of the injustice of the war may be such that ignorance would be no excuse even to the subjects" who are not normally informed, that ignorance will not be an excuse if they participate. Today, well over 400 years later, the Baltimore Catechism makes an exception to the Fifth Commandment for a "soldier fighting a just war."

No one can tell a Catholic that this or that war is either just or unjust. This is a personal decision that an individual must make on the basis of his own conscience after studying the facts.[5]

---

1. The theological basis for this was explained by Pope John XXIII in Part II of *Pacem in Terris* ¶ 46 (Paulist Press, 1963): "Human society can be neither well-ordered nor prosperous unless it has some people invested with legitimate authority to preserve its institutions.... These however derive their authority from God, as St. Paul teaches in the words, *There exists no authority except from God*. These words of St. Paul are explained thus by St. John Chrysostom: ... *What I say is, that it is the divine wisdom and not mere chance, that has ordained that there should be government, that some should command and others obey*." ¶ 50 adds: "When, in fact, men obey their rulers, it is not at all as men that they obey them, but through their obedience it is God ... since He has decreed that men's dealings with one another should be regulated by an order which He Himself has established."

2. "Since the right to command is required by the moral order and has its source in God, it follows that, if civil authorities legislate for or allow anything that is contrary to that order and therefore contrary to the will of God, neither the laws made nor the authorizations granted can be binding on the consciences of the citizens, since *we must obey God rather than men*." *Id.*, at ¶ 51.

5. Pope Paul VI in § 16 of the Pastoral Constitution on the Church in the Modern World states: "Deep within his conscience man discovers a law which he has not laid upon himself but which he must obey. Its voice, ever calling him to love and to do what is good and avoid evil, tells him inwardly at the right moment to do this or to shun that. For man has in his heart a law inscribed by God. His dignity lies in observing this law, and by it he will be judged."

Like the distinction between just and unjust wars, the duty to obey conscience is not a new doctrine in the Catholic Church. When told to stop preaching by the Sanhedrin, to which they were subordinate by law, "Peter and the apostles answered and said, 'We must obey God rather than men.'" That duty has not changed. Pope Paul VI has expressed it as follows: "On his part, man perceives and acknowledges the imperatives of the divine law through the mediation of conscience. In all his activity a man is bound to follow his conscience, in order that he may come to God, the end and purpose of life."

NOTES AND QUESTIONS

1. *Hidden Judicial Preferences*? Both claimants for SCO status, Guy Gillette and Louis Negre, argued that a construction of section 6(j) limited to pacifists would offend against the nonestablishment principle by preferring an ethics of complete nonviolence over the religiously grounded belief that some, but not all, wars are justifiable. In *Seeger* the Court noted that Congress had framed the conscientious objector exemption in broad terms compatible with "its long-established policy of not picking and choosing among religious beliefs." In *Gillette* Justice Marshall wrote that "6(j) does not single out any religious organization or religious creed for special treatment" and that his construction of the statute did "not work a penalty against any theological position." Do you agree? Does Marshall's view of the draft law, in effect, prefer pacifism and impose a penalty upon selective conscientious objection based on the just war doctrine?

2. Toothless "Compelling Interest" Scrutiny? To prevail against a claimed violation of free exercise, the Court held in *Sherbert v. Verner* [section 5 below] that the government must pursue a compelling interest with the alternative least restrictive of religious freedom. The compelling interest test was imported into free exercise analysis from the field where Marshall was the most prominent and successful litigator of the twentieth century, racial classifications adjudicated under the Equal Protection Clause. In *Gillette* Marshall wrote that the burden on free exercise must be "strictly justified by substantial governmental interests." Did Marshall show that the burden on an SCO was justified in this way? Is "maintaining a fair system" a compelling interest? Is achieving "manpower goals" during an undeclared war? Marshall wrote that granting the claim of SCO entailed "the real danger of erratic or even discriminatory decisionmaking in administrative practice." Is this danger–whether real or imaginary–a compelling interest? Would the lawyer who led the team that produced the result in *Brown v. Bd. of Education* and in many other cases that marked the end of Jim Crow laws have accepted the contention of a school board attorney that desegregating the public schools should not be constitutionally required because it would entail a "real danger of erratic or even discriminatory decisionmaking in administrative practice"? Two commentators have warned of the danger that judges too readily "accept unsupported government assertions about the nature and strength of its interests, without reckoning the likely burdens in each case on free exercise." Mary Ann Glendon and Raul Yanes, "Structural Free Exercise," 90 *Mich. L. Rev.* 477, 532 (1991). Did Marshall avoid this danger?

3. *Mischaracterizing the Complexity of Religious Claims?* Justice Marshall described SCO as "intrinsically a claim of uncertain dimensions." Did this characterization of the SCO position reflect that it has deep roots in religious ethics since at least the early fifth century of the common era and that its its refined form has entered into over a hundred treaties and covenants in international law, as well as into the Field Manual for the armed forces? For a succinct statement of the content of the SCO position, as well as an explanation of the reasons for its development within Christianity, *see* Chapter Two above, Note. *Christians and Military Service in the Early Church: From Pacifism to the Augustinian Tradition on Justifiable War;* for a treatment of the limits placed by public international law on the use of force, *see* Thomas Ehrlich and Mary Ellen O'Connell, *International Law and the Use of Force* (1993). Did the Court confuse the issue of sincerity of a particular objector with the legitimacy of the moral and legal stance of the just war tradition? Compare *United States v. Berg*, 310 F. Supp. 1157 (D. Me. 1970). Eugene Alfred Berg, a former seminarian, was a practicing Catholic who believed in the just war doctrine taught by his church. He took the position that, given the present means of warfare, the conditions for a just war can no longer be met. Shortly before the *Negre* case, Judge Edward Gignoux found that a draft board's denial of Berg's claim for CO status had no basis in fact since—in the court's perception—Berg opposed war "in any form." Right result after *Negre*? Why or why not?

4. *Denial of Benefits for Conscientious Objectors.* William Robert Robison was a conscientious objector to all military service; in 1966 he was so classified by his local board and assigned to work at Peter Bent Brigham Hospital, Boston, for two years. When, on the completion of his service, he was denied educational support by the Veterans' Administration, he attacked as unconstitutional the statute that gave such benefits to veterans of military service but denied them to conscientious objectors. In *Johnson v. Robison,* 415 U.S. 361 (1974) the Court, per Justice Brennan, found the statute neither to deny equal protection of the laws nor to be an unconstitutional burden on Robison's free exercise of religion. Justice Brennan had written in *Sherbert v. Verner* [section 5 below] that a State may not force a sabbatarian "to choose between following the precepts of her religion and forfeiting [welfare] benefits, on the one hand, and abandoning one of the precepts of her religion in order to accept work, on the other hand. Governmental imposition of such a choice puts the same kind of burden upon the free exercise of religion as would a fine imposed against appellant for her Saturday worship." In *Robison,* he found only "an incidental burden," adding "if, indeed, any burden exists at all." In *Sherbert* Brennan wrote that "no showing merely of a rational relationship to some colorable state interest would suffice; in this highly sensitive constitutional area, '[o]nly the gravest abuses, endangering paramount interests, give occasion for permissible limitation.'" In *Robison,* Brennan wrote that the government's interest "in raising and supporting armies" was "clearly sufficient" to justify imposition of the burden. Justice Douglas dissented. He thought that the burden was undeniable; he saw no government interest except the financial one of not having to pay the educational benefits and declared, "That in my view is an invidious discrimination and a penalty on those who assert their religious scruples...."

5. *Pacifist convictions and the manufacture of weapons.* Eddie C. Thomas, a Jehovah's Witness, was transferred from work fabricating sheet steel for a variety of uses to a department making turrets for tanks. Thomas refused the

job on the ground that his religious convictions forbade his involvement in the manufacture of weapons. He was fired and sought unemployment compensation. The state attempted to undermine the importance or "centrality" of Thomas's claim to the faith of Jehovah's Witnesses by adducing evidence that other Witnesses were willing to work in an armaments plant. The Supreme Court of Indiana held that his unemployment was "voluntary" and not for "good cause." *Thomas v. Review Bd. of Indiana Employment Security Division*, 391 N.E. 2d 1127 (Ind. 1979). In *Thomas v. Review Board*, 450 U.S. 707 (1981), Chief Justice Burger wrote for the Court that *Sherbert* controlled and that the state was not entitled to burden Thomas's exercise of religious liberty in this way. Although Burger had introduced the concept of centrality in his opinion in *Wisconsin v. Yoder* [section seven below], he repudiated it in *Thomas*: "it is not within the judicial function and judicial competence to inquire whether the petitioner or his fellow worker more correctly perceived the commands of their common faith. Courts are not arbiters of scriptural interpretation. The narrow function of a reviewing court in this context is to determine whether there was an appropriate finding that [Thomas] terminated his work because of an honest conviction that such work was forbidden by his religion." As in *Bowen v. Roy* [section 3 above], the Court expressly rejected the extreme view of the lower court that any accommodation of a free exercise claim would constitute an impermissible establishment of religion. In a solo dissent Justice Rehnquist addressed the view that there is a "tension" between the two principles imbedded in the Religion Clause, nonestablishment and free exercise.

Thomas v. Review Board

450 U.S. 707 (1981).

■ REHNQUIST, J. dissenting.

The Court correctly acknowledges that there is a "tension" between the Free Exercise and Establishment Clauses of the First Amendment of the United States Constitution. Although the relationship of the two Clauses has been the subject of much commentary, the "tension" is of fairly recent vintage, unknown at the time of the framing and adoption of the First Amendment. The causes of the tension, it seems to me, are threefold. First, the growth of social welfare legislation during the latter part of the 20th century has greatly magnified the potential for conflict between the two Clauses, since such legislation touches the individual at so many points in his life. Second, the decision by this Court that the First Amendment was "incorporated" into the Fourteenth Amendment and thereby made applicable against the States, *Stromberg v. California*, 283 U.S. 359 (1931); *Cantwell v. Connecticut* [section 1 above] similarly multiplied the number of instances in which the "tension" might arise. The third, and perhaps most important, cause of the tension is our overly expansive interpretation of *both* Clauses. By broadly construing both Clauses, the Court has constantly narrowed the channel between the Scylla and Charybdis through which any state or federal action must pass in order to survive constitutional scrutiny.

None of these developments could have been foreseen by those who framed and adopted the First Amendment. The First Amendment was adopted well before the growth of much social welfare legislation and at a time when the Federal Government was in a real sense considered a government of limited delegated powers. Indeed, the principal argument against adopting the Constitution *without* a "Bill of Rights" was not that such an enactment would be *undesirable*, but that it was *unnecessary* because of the limited nature of the Federal Government. So long as the Government enacts little social welfare legislation, as was the case in 1791, there are few occasions in which the two Clauses may conflict. Moreover, as originally enacted, the First Amendment applied only to the Federal Government, not the government of the States. *Barron v. Baltimore*, 7 Pet. 243 (1833). The Framers could hardly anticipate *Barron* being superseded by the "selective incorporation" doctrine adopted by the Court, a decision which greatly expanded the number of statutes which would be subject to challenge under the First Amendment. Because those who drafted and adopted the First Amendment could not have foreseen either the growth of social welfare legislation or the incorporation of the First Amendment into the Fourteenth Amendment, we simply do not know how they would view the scope of the two Clauses.

NOTE

The Danger of Loose Metaphors. Scylla was a dangerous rock on the southern tip of Italy; Charybdis was a nearby whirlpool in the narrow Straits of Messina between Sicily and the Italian mainland. These navigational perils were represented as female monsters in ancient mythology. In *The Odyssey*, Homer describes Scylla as a "horrible monster" past whom "no crew can boast that they ever sailed without loss, since from every passing vessel she snatches a man with each of her [six] heads and so bears off her prey." Homer, *The Odyssey* 191 (E.V. Rieu trans. 1946). Charybdis is depicted as a "dread monster" who "sucks the dark waters down three times a day, and spews them up three times." Odysseus's divine guide, Circe, prays that heaven will keep him and his crew from this spot "when she is at her work, for not even the Earthshaker [Poseidon] could save you from disaster." *Id*. 191–92. The metaphor adopted by Rehnquist and later by Justice Scalia in his dissent in *Texas Monthly, Inc v. Bullock* [section 1 above] implies a negative connotation for both parts of the Religion Clause. These justices imagine nonestablishment and free exercise not as related manifestations of an identical principle of freedom, but as twin perils or dangers neither of which can be evaded without risking the other. Both Rehnquist and Scalia frequently invoke "those who framed and adopted the First Amendment," but none of the framers of the Religion Clause advanced the strange view that one portion of the Clause imperiled the other. *See* Michael J. Paulsen, "Religion, Equality, and the Constitution: An Equal Protection Approach to Establishment Clause Adjudication," 61 Notre Dame L. Rev. 311 (1986).

5. KEEPING HOLY THE SABBATH

Deuteronomy 5: 12–15

Keep the sabbath day holy as the Lord your God commanded you. You have six days to labor and do all your work. But the seventh day is a sabbath of the Lord your God; that day you shall not do any work, neither you, your son or your daughter, your slave or your slave-girl, your ox, your ass, or any of your cattle, nor the alien within your gates, so that your slaves and slave-girls may rest as you do. Remember that you were slaves in Egypt and the Lord your God brought you out with a strong hand and an outstretched arm, and for that reason the Lord your God commanded you to keep the sabbath day.

———

Sabbath observance is also considered below under the principle of double effect [Chapter Thirteen, section 2]. Here it is considered under the rubric of employment law. The two chief instances in which conflicts over Sabbath observance arise are unemployment compensation for a sabbatarian who is discharged for Sabbath observance, and the general duty under Title VII binding private employers to make reasonable accommodation for the religious practices and beliefs, including Sabbath observance, of their employees. Like *Gillette* and *Negre*, the case that follows can be seen as the conferral of a benefit on one religion, a benefit considerably less significant than exemption from military duty.

Sherbert v. Verner

374 U.S. 398 (1963).

William D. Donnelly argued the cause and filed briefs for appellant.

Daniel R. McLeod, Attorney General of South Carolina, argued the cause for appellees. With him on the brief was *Victor S. Evans*, Assistant Attorney General.

Briefs of *amici curiae*, urging reversal, were filed by *Morris B. Abram, Edwin J. Lukas, Arnold Forster, Melvin L. Wulf, Paul Hartman, Theodore Leskes* and *Sol Rabkin* for the American Jewish Committee et al., and by *Leo Pfeffer, Lewis H. Weinstein, Albert Wald, Shad Polier, Ephraim S. London, Samuel Lawrence Brennglass* and *Jacob Sheinkman* for the Synagogue Council of America et al.

■ JUSTICE BRENNAN delivered the opinion of the Court.

Appellant, a member of the Seventh-day Adventist Church, was discharged by her South Carolina employer because she would not work on Saturday, the Sabbath Day of her faith. When she was unable to obtain other employment because from conscientious scruples she would not take Saturday work, she filed a claim for unemployment compensation benefits under the South Carolina Unemployment Compensation Act. That law provides that, to be eligible for benefits, a claimant must be "able to work and ... available for work"; and, further, that a claimant is ineligible for benefits "[i]f ... he has failed, without good cause ... to accept available suitable work when offered him by the employment office or the employer.... " The appellee Employment Security Commission, in administrative proceedings under the statute, found that appellant's restriction upon her availability for Saturday work brought her within the provision disqualifying for benefits insured workers who fail, without good cause, to accept "suitable work when offered . . . by the employment office or the employer . . . . . " The Commission's finding was sustained by the Court of Common Pleas for Spartanburg County. That court's judgment was in turn affirmed by the South Carolina Supreme Court; which rejected appellant's contention that, as applied to her, the disqualifying provisions of the South Carolina statute abridged her right to the free exercise of her religion secured under the Free Exercise Clause of the First Amendment through the Fourteenth Amendment. The State Supreme Court held specifically that appellant's ineligibility infringed no constitutional liberties because such a construction of the statute "places no restriction upon the appellant's freedom of religion nor does it in any way prevent her in the exercise of her right and freedom to observe her religious beliefs in accordance with the dictates of her conscience" [citation omitted]. We noted probable jurisdiction of appellant's appeal. We reverse the judgment of the South Carolina Supreme Court and remand for further proceedings not inconsistent with this opinion. . . .

The door of the Free Exercise Clause stands tightly closed against any governmental regulation of religious beliefs as such, *Cantwell v. Connecticut* [section 1 above]. Government may neither compel affirmation of a repugnant belief, *Torcaso v. Watkins*, [Chapter Twelve, section 1]; nor penalize or discriminate against individuals or groups because they hold religious views abhorrent to the authorities, *Fowler v. Rhode Island* [Chapter Thirteen, section 1]. . . .

We turn first to the question whether the disqualification for benefits imposes any burden on the free exercise of appellant's religion. We think it is clear that it does. In a sense the consequences of such a disqualification to religious principles and practices may be only an indirect result of welfare legislation within the State's general competence to enact; it is true that no criminal sanctions directly compel appellant to work a six-day week. But this is only the beginning, not the end, of our inquiry. For "[i]f the purpose or effect of a law is to impede the observance of one or all religions or is to discriminate invidiously between religions, that law is constitutionally invalid even though the burden may be characterized as being only indirect." *Braunfeld v. Brown* [Chapter Thirteen, section 2]. Here not only is it apparent that appellant's declared ineligibility for benefits derives solely from the practice of her religion, but the pressure upon her to forego that practice is unmistakable. The ruling forces her to choose between following the precepts of her religion and forfeiting benefits, on the one hand, and abandoning one of the precepts of her religion in order to accept work, on the other hand. Governmental imposition of such a choice puts the same kind of burden upon the free exercise of religion as would a fine imposed against appellant for her Saturday worship.

Nor may the South Carolina court's construction of the statute be saved from constitutional infirmity on the ground that unemployment compensation benefits are not appellant's "right" but merely a "privilege." It is too late in the day to doubt that the liberties of religion and expression may be infringed by the denial of or placing of conditions upon a benefit or privilege [cases omitted].... In *Speiser v. Randall*, 357 U.S. 513 (1958), we emphasized that conditions upon public benefits cannot be sustained if they so operate, whatever their purpose, as to inhibit or deter the exercise of First Amendment freedoms.... "To deny an exemption to claimants who engage in certain forms of speech is in effect to penalize them for such speech." *Id.*, at 518. Likewise, to condition the availability of benefits upon this appellant's willingness to violate a cardinal principle of her religious faith effectively penalizes the free exercise of her constitutional liberties....

We must next consider whether some compelling state interest enforced in the eligibility provisions of the South Carolina statute justifies the substantial infringement of appellant's First Amendment right. It is basic that no showing merely of a rational relationship to some colorable state interest would suffice; in this highly sensitive constitutional area, "[o]nly the gravest abuses, endangering paramount interests, give occasion for permissible limitation," *Thomas v. Collins*, 323 U.S. 516, 530 (1945).... No such abuse or danger has been advanced in the present case. The appellees suggest no more than a possibility that the filing of fraudulent claims by unscrupulous claimants feigning religious objections to Saturday work might not only dilute the unemployment compensation fund but also hinder the scheduling by employers of necessary Saturday work. But that possibility is not apposite here because no such objection appears to have been made before the South Carolina Supreme Court, and we are unwilling to assess the importance of an asserted state interest without the views of the state court. Nor, if the contention had been made below, would the record appear to sustain it; there is no proof whatever to warrant such fears of malingering or deceit as those which the respondents now advance. Even if consideration of such evidence is not foreclosed by the prohibition against judicial inquiry into the truth or falsity of religious beliefs, *United States v. Ballard* [Chapter Twelve, section 1]—a question as to which we intimate no view since it is not before us—it is highly doubtful whether such evidence would be sufficient to warrant a substantial infringement of religious liberties. For even if the possibility of spurious claims did threaten to dilute the fund and disrupt the scheduling of work, it would plainly be incumbent upon the appellees to demonstrate that no alternative forms of regulation would combat such abuses without infringing First Amendment rights.

In these respects, then, the state interest asserted in the present case is wholly dissimilar to the interests which were found to justify the less direct burden upon religious practices in *Braunfeld v. Brown*, [Chapter Twelve, section 2]. The Court recognized that the Sunday closing law which that decision sustained undoubtedly served "to make the practice of [the Orthodox Jewish merchants'] ... religious beliefs more expensive." But the statute was nevertheless saved by a countervailing factor which finds no equivalent in the instant case—a strong state interest in providing one uniform day of rest for all workers. That secular objective could be achieved, the Court found, only by declaring Sunday to be that day of rest. Requiring exemptions for Sabbatarians, while theoretically possible, appeared to present an administrative problem of such magnitude, or to afford the exempted class so great a competitive advantage, that such a requirement would have rendered the entire statutory scheme unworkable. In the present case no such justifications underlie the determination of the state court that appellant's religion makes her ineligible to receive benefits.

In holding as we do, plainly we are not fostering the "establishment" of the Seventh-day Adventist religion in South Carolina, for the extension of unemployment benefits to Sabbatarians in common with Sunday worshippers reflects nothing more than the governmental obligation of neutrality in the face of religious differences, and does not represent that involvement of religious with secular institutions which it is the object of the Establishment Clause to forestall. . . .

In view of the result we have reached under the First and Fourteenth Amendments' guarantee of free exercise of religion, we have no occasion to consider appellant's claim that the denial of benefits also deprived her of the equal protection of the laws in violation of the Fourteenth Amendment.

The judgment of the South Carolina Supreme Court is reversed and the case is remanded for further proceedings not inconsistent with this opinion.

■ Justice Stewart, concurring in the result.

To require South Carolina to so administer its laws as to pay public money to the appellant under the circumstances of this case is thus clearly to require the State to violate the Establishment Clause as construed by this Court. This poses no problem for me, because I think the Court's mechanistic concept of the Establishment Clause is historically unsound and constitutionally wrong. I think the process of constitutional decision in the area of the relationships between government and religion demands considerably more than the invocation of broad-brushed rhetoric of the kind I have quoted. And I think that the guarantee of religious liberty embodied in the Free Exercise Clause affirmatively requires government to create an atmosphere of hospitality and accommodation to individual belief or disbelief. In short, I think our Constitution commands the positive protection by government of religious freedom—not only for a minority, however small—not only for the majority, however large—but for each of us.

South Carolina would deny unemployment benefits to a mother unavailable for work on Saturdays because she was unable to get a babysitter. Thus, we do not have before us a situation where a State provides unemployment compensation generally, and singles out for disqualification only those persons who are unavailable for work on religious grounds. This is not, in short, a scheme which operates so as to discriminate against religion as such. But the Court nevertheless holds that the State must prefer a religious over a secular ground for being unavailable for work— that state financial support of the appellant's religion is constitutionally required to carry out "the governmental obligation of neutrality in the face of religious differences. . . ."

Yet in cases decided under the Establishment Clause the Court has decreed otherwise. It has decreed that government must blind itself to the differing religious beliefs and traditions of the people. With all respect, I think it is the Court's duty to face up to the dilemma posed by the conflict between the Free Exercise Clause of the Constitution and the Establishment Clause as interpreted by the Court. It is a duty, I submit, which we owe to the people, the States, and the Nation, and a duty which we owe to ourselves. For so long as the resounding but fallacious fundamentalist rhetoric of some of our Establishment Clause opinions remains on our books, to be disregarded at will as in the present case, or to be undiscriminatingly invoked as in the *Schempp* case [Chapter Fourteen, section 2], so long will the possibility of consistent and perceptive decision in this most difficult and delicate area of constitutional law be impeded and impaired. And so long, I fear, will the guarantee of true religious freedom in our pluralistic society be uncertain and insecure. . . .

■ JUSTICE HARLAN, joined by Justice White, dissenting.

The South Carolina Supreme Court has uniformly applied this law in conformity with its clearly expressed purpose. It has consistently held that one is not "available for work" if his unemployment has resulted not from the inability of industry to provide a job but rather from personal circumstances, no matter how compelling. The reference to "involuntary unemployment" in the legislative statement of policy, whatever a sociologist, philosopher, or theologian might say, has been interpreted not to embrace such personal circumstances. . . .

In the present case all that the state court has done is to apply these accepted principles. Since virtually all of the mills in the Spartanburg area were operating on a six-day week, the appellant was "unavailable for work," and thus ineligible for benefits, when personal considerations prevented her from accepting employment on a full-time basis in the industry and locality in which she had worked. The fact that these personal considerations sprang from her religious convictions was wholly without relevance to the state court's application of the law. Thus in no proper sense can it be said that the State discriminated against the appellant on the basis of her religious beliefs or that she was denied benefits *because* she was a Seventh-day Adventist. She was denied benefits just as any other claimant would be denied benefits who was not "available for work" for personal reasons.

With this background, this Court's decision comes into clearer focus. What the Court is holding is that if the State chooses to condition unemployment compensation on the applicant's availability for work, it is constitutionally compelled to *carve out an exception*—and to provide benefits—for those whose unavailability is due to their religious convictions. Such a holding has particular significance in two respects.

First, despite the Court's protestations to the contrary, the decision necessarily overrules *Braunfeld v. Brown* [Chapter Thirteen, section 2], which held that it did not offend the "Free Exercise" Clause of the Constitution for a State to forbid a Sabbatarian to do business on Sunday. The secular purpose of the statute before us today is even clearer than that involved in *Braunfeld*. And just as in *Braunfeld*—where exceptions to the Sunday closing laws for Sabbatarians would have been inconsistent with the purpose to achieve a uniform day of rest and would have required case-by-case inquiry into religious beliefs—so here, an exception to the rules of eligibility based on religious convictions would necessitate judicial examination of those convictions and would be at odds with the limited purpose of the statute to smooth out the economy during periods of industrial instability. Finally, the indirect financial burden of the present law is far less than that involved in *Braunfeld*. Forcing a store owner to close his business on Sunday may well have the effect of depriving him of a satisfactory livelihood if his religious convictions require him to close on Saturday as well. Here we are dealing only with temporary benefits, amounting to a fraction of regular weekly wages and running for not more than 22 weeks. Clearly, any differences between this case and *Braunfeld* cut against the present appellant.

NOTES AND QUESTIONS

1. *Duty of Reasonable Accommodation of Employee's Religious Practices and Beliefs.* Title VII of the Civil Rights Act of 1964, as amended, makes it unlawful for an employer to discriminate against an employee on account of religion. Religion is defined to include "practice, as well as belief, unless an employer demonstrates that he is unable to reasonably accommodate ... without undue hardship to [his] business," 42 U.S.C. § 2000 e(j). Larry G. Hardison was a new member of the Worldwide Church of God, which teaches that the Sabbath must be observed without work from sunset on Friday to sunset on Saturday. Hardison worked at the central TWA supply depot, which operated twenty-four hours a day, seven days a week. He refused to work on Saturday, he did not have the seniority necessary to get off on Saturday, the union rejected TWA's request to waive the seniority rules, and he was fired. The District Court ruled for TWA. The Eighth Circuit found that Title VII had been violated. The United States, the American Civil Liberties Union, the Seventh-day Adventists, and Leo Pfeffer for the Central Conference of American Rabbis were among those urging affirmance. In *Trans World Airlines v. Hardison*, 432 U.S. 63 (1967), the Court, per Justice White, held that TWA could not have accommodated Hardison without undue hardship. White wrote that an employer's duty of reasonable accommodation does not include more than minimal costs, and that an employer need not assign substitute employees in violation of a seniority system worked out in a collective bargaining agreement. To give him Saturday off, the Court observed, would mean that "the privilege of having Saturday off would be allocated according to religious beliefs." Justices Brennan and Marshall dissented. *Sherbert* involved the termination of public welfare benefits; *Hardison* involved a statutory mandate on private employers to accommodate religion in the workplace. Putting this obvious difference aside, is *Hardison* consistent with *Sherbert*?

2. *Legislative Accommodation of Sabbath Observance.* When Connecticut changed its Sunday laws in 1976, it enacted a statute prohibiting an employer from requiring more than six days' employment in a calendar week. The statute added, "No person who states that a particular day of the week is observed as his Sabbath may be required by his employer to work on such day." Donald Thornton, a Presbyterian and a department store manager for Caldor, Inc., a chain of department stores, was ordered to work on Sundays. He did so

on thirty-one Sundays in two years before notifying Caldor that Sunday was his Sabbath and refusing to work on that day. He was demoted, resigned, and sued Caldor. The highest court of Connecticut held the statute to be an unconstitutional establishment of religion. *Caldor, Inc. v. Thorton*, 191 Conn. 336, 464 A.2d 785 (1983). *Lemon v. Kurtzman* [Chapter Fourteen, section 1] dealt with public funding of religious education, but the Court wrote more expansively, suggesting three general criteria for determining any violation of the nonestablishment principle: lack of secular purpose, a primary effect that advanced or inhibited religion, and excessive entanglement of the government in religion. The lower court rested its conclusion on the lack of secularity. The secular purpose of the Sunday laws upheld in *McGowan* [Chapter Thirteen, section 2], the court said, was to establish a *common* day of rest. Here the benefit of being able to choose one's day off was conferred only on religious persons, on those who had a "Sabbath" to observe. In *Estate of Thornton v. Caldor, Inc.*, 472 U.S. 703 (1985), the Court affirmed, 8–1. Chief Justice Burger, the author of *Lemon*, emphasized that the statute was weighted in favor of Sabbath observers and made no allowances for inconvenience or economic hardship of the employer. Its primary effect was to advance "a particular religious practice." Justice O'Connor, joined by Justice Marshall, concurred in the result on the view that the statute has "an impermissible effect because it conveys a message of endorsement of the Sabbath observance." But she expressly reserved the question of the constitutionality of § 701(j) of Title VII [section 6 below], expressing the view that this provision "calls for reasonable rather than absolute accommodation and extends that requirement to all religious beliefs and practices rather than protecting only the Sabbath observance." Justice Rehnquist dissented without opinion.

3. *Religious Conversion.* After two and one-half years of working for her employer, Paula Hobbie informed her employer that she was to be baptized into the Seventh-day Adventist Church and would no longer be able to work on her Sabbath for religious reasons. When she subsequently refused to work scheduled shifts on Friday evenings and Saturdays, her employer discharged her. Hobbie then filed a claim for unemployment compensation, which a claims examiner denied for "misconduct connected with [her] work." The only factual difference between Paula Hobbie and Adell H. Sherbert was that Hobbie had recently converted to the Seventh-day Adventist faith. The state court summarily affirmed the Unemployment Appeals Commission. In *Hobbie v. Unemployment Appeals Commission of Florida*, 480 U.S. 136 (1987), the Supreme Court reversed. Justice Brennan, the author of *Sherbert*, noted: "the Appeals Commission asks us to single out the religious convert for different, less favorable treatment than that given an individual whose adherence to his or her faith. We decline to do so.... [The timing of Hobbie's conversion is immaterial to our determination that her free exercise rights have been burdened; the salient inquiry under the Free Exercise Clause is the burden involved."

4. *Membership in a Religious Community.* William Frazee refused a temporary retail position offered him by Kelly Services because the job would have required him to work Sunday and Frazee told Kelly that as a Christian he could not work on "the Lord's day." Frazee's subsequent application for unemployment benefits was denied, as was his appeal. The Department of Employment Security's Board of Review stated that a refusal of work "based solely on an individual's personal belief is personal and noncompelling and does not render

the work unsuitable." Both the state trial court and the appellate court rejected Frazee's free exercise claim. In *Frazee v. Illinois Department of Unemployment Security*, 489 U.S. 829 (1989) the Court unanimously reversed. Justice White stated that none of the Court's decisions about unemployment compensation benefits turned on the fact that the claimant was a member of a particular religious sect or on any tenet of the sect involved that forbade the work the claimant refused to perform. Rather, the "judgments in those cases rested on the fact that each of the claimants had a sincere belief that religion required him or her to refrain from the work in question."

6. RELIGION IN THE WORKPLACE

NOTE

Religion in the Federal Workplace. On August 14, 1997, President Clinton issued a Presidential Directive containing Guidelines on Religious Exercise and Religious Expression in the Federal Workplace. 33 *Weekly Comp. Presidential Docs.* 1247 (Aug. 18, 1997). These guidelines are limited in scope, applying to "civilian executive branch agencies, officials, and employees in the Federal workplace," when these employees "are acting in their personal capacity within the Federal workplace and the public does not have regular exposure to the workplace." While attempting to avoid the appearance, to a reasonable observer, of an official endorsement or denigration of religion or of a particular religion, the guidelines clarify that federal "agencies may not regulate employees' personal religious expression on the basis of its content or viewpoint." Even where the government may have an interest in efficiency of public service that might outweigh an employee's private speech, the guidelines notes that agencies should exercise this authority to regulate private speech "evenhandedly and with restraint." Federal employees may engage in private religious expression in personal work areas; for example, "an employee may keep a Bible or Koran on her private desk and read it during breaks." And employees are permitted to express their religious convictions to other employees, subject to only to regulation based on "reasonable predictions of disruption, ... not merely hypothetical concerns, having little basis in fact, that the speech will have a deleterious effect on workplace efficiency." Consistent with the spirit of the No Religious Test provision, U.S. Const., Art. VI, and the prohibition of employment discrimination on the basis of religion found in Title VII of the Civil Rights Act of 1964, the Guidelines state: "No agency within the executive branch may promote, refuse to promote, hire, refuse to hire, or otherwise favor or disfavor, an employee or potential employee because of his or her religion, religious beliefs, or views concerning religion." The Guidelines prohibit a supervisor from exerting any form of coercion, explicitly or implicitly, of a Federal employee's participation or nonparticipation in religious activities. And they apply the law against hostile work environment and harassment to "protect Federal employees from being subjected to religiously discriminatory intimidation, or pervasive or sever religious ridicule or insult, whether by supervisors or fellow workers." The document notes that Title VII imposes a duty on all covered employers, including the government, to make reasonable accommodation of the religious practices and beliefs of employees. Thus "an agency must adjust work schedules to accommodate an employee's religious observance—for example, Sabbath or religious holiday observance—if an adequate substitute is available, or if the employee's absence would not otherwise impose an undue burden on the agency"; employees may wear religious garb (e.g., yarmulke, crucifix, or hijab) if it does not unduly interfere with the functioning of the workplace [section 8 below]; and employees may gather on their own time for prayer and Bible study in an empty conference room. One sentence tracks the provisions of the Religious Freedom Restoration Act of 1993 [section 10 below]: "In those cases where an agency's work rule imposes a substantial burden on a particular employee's exercise of religion, the agency must go further: an agency should grant the employee an exemption from that rule, unless the agency has a compelling interest in denying the exemption and there is no less restrictive means of furthering that interest." One of the examples offered under this guideline is that an "applicant for employment in a governmental agency who is a Jehovah's Witness should not be compelled, contrary to her religious beliefs, to take a loyalty oath whose form is religiously objectionable."

NOTE

Prohibition against Employment Discrimination on the Basis of Religion The Civil Rights Act of 1964 was enacted under the power of Congress to regulate commerce among the several states. Hence the prohibition against unfair employment practices in Title VII of this Act binds all private employers that affect interstate commerce and that employ "fifteen or more employees for each working day in each of twenty or more calendar weeks in the current or preceding calendar year." 42 U.S.C. § 2000e(b). Under the statute, it is an unfair employment practice "to fail or refuse to hire or to discharge any individual, or otherwise discriminating against any individual with respect to his compensation, terms, conditions, or privileges of employment, because of such individual's race, color, *religion*, sex, or national origin." 42 U.S.C. § 2000e–2(a). See also Michael Wolf, Bruce Friedman, and Daniel Sutherland, *Religion in the Workplace* (1998).

NOTE

Affirmative Duty of Private Employers to Accommodate Religious Beliefs and Practices of Employees. In addition to the negative prohibition against employment discrimination on the basis of religion, the definition section of Title VII places an affirmative duty of accommodation on employers by defining the term "religion" to include "all aspects of religious observance and practice, as well as belief, unless an employer demonstrates that he is unable to reasonably accommodate to an employee's or prospective employee's religious observance or practice without undue hardship on the conduct of the employer's business." 42 U.S.C. § 2000e(j). As noted above [section 5 above], an employer's statutory duty of reasonable accommodation of religion was narrowed considerably in *Trans World Airlines v. Hardison.* In the following case the employer was eager to bring religion into the workplace. Too eager, in the view of one of his employees, the EEOC, and the courts. Jake and Helen Townley are "born again believers in the Lord Jesus Christ" who "are unable to separate God from any portion of their daily lives, including their activities at the Townley company." In 1963, when the Townley's founded a company that manufactures mining equipment, they made a covenant with God that their business "would be a Christian, faith-operated business." The company reflects its founders' covenant with God in several ways: "[it] encloses a Gospel tract in every piece of outgoing mail; it prints Biblical verses on all company invoices, purchase orders, and other commercial documents; it gives financial support to various churches and missionaries; and it holds a devotional service once a week during work hours.... They typically last from thirty to forty-five minutes, and may include prayer, thanksgiving to God, singing, testimony, and scripture reading, as well as discussion of business related matters. Townley required all employees to attend the weekly services [compensating them for the time spent in this exercise]; failure to attend was regarded as equivalent to not attending work." One of the employees, Louis Pelvas, sought to be excused from the weekly devotionals on the ground that he was an atheist. The management replied that attendance was mandatory under a provision of the employee handbook that Pelvas had signed, but that he could sleep or read the newspaper during the services. Pelvas continued to attend the services, but filed a religious discrimination charge with the EEOC and left the company two months later.

EEOC v. Townley Engineering & Manufacturing Co.

859 F.2d 610 (9th Cir. 1988).

H. Edward Dean argued for the Defendant–Appellant.

Lorraine C. Davis, Assistant General Counsel, Equal Employment Opportunity Commission, argued for the Plaintiff–Appellee.

■ SNEED, CIRCUIT JUDGE:

Townley argues both that Title VII was not intended to apply to this employment policy [of holding devotional prayer services in the workplace], and that the proposed application of Title VII would violate the Free Exercise Clause of the First Amendment. It is clear that applying Title VII to the devotional services "would give rise to serious constitutional questions." See *NLRB v. Catholic Bishop of Chicago*, 440 U.S. 490, 501 (1979). Therefore, we may not find it applicable unless there is an "affirmative intention of Congress clearly expressed" that it should be so applied. *Id.*; see *EEOC v. Fremont Christian School*, 781 F.2d 1362, 1365 (9th Cir. 1986); *EEOC v. Pacific Press Publishing Ass'n*, 676 F.2d 1272, 1276 (9th Cir. 1982).

We hold that Congress did clearly intend for Title VII to cover Townley's mandatory devotional services. Sections 701(j) and 703(a) of Title VII make clear that requiring employees over their objections to attend devotional services cannot be reconciled with Title VII's prohibition against religious discrimination. Furthermore, we hold that Congress did not intend section 702's exemption for religious corporations to shield corporations such as Townley. We do hold, however, that Jake and Helen Townley have certain rights under the Free Exercise Clause that Title VII cannot infringe....

We have read sections 703(a) and 701(j) as creating a two-part frame-work in religious practice cases. First, the plaintiff must establish a prima facie case of religious discrimination.[5] [A]fter the plaintiff has made out a prima facie case, the burden shifts to the employer "to prove that [it] made good faith efforts to accommodate [the employee's] religious beliefs and, if those efforts were unsuccessful, to demonstrate that [it was] unable reason-ably to accommodate his beliefs without undue hardship." *Anderson v. General Dynamics Convair Aerospace Div.*, 589 F.2d 397, 401 (9th Cir. 1978)....

Pelvas proposed that Townley accommodate his religious objections to the devotional services by excusing him from attendance. The district court found that this accommodation would have caused Townley no undue hardship. It stated, "Excusing Pelvas from the mandatory devotional services would have cost Townley nothing in the operation of its business activities, and would not have disrupted other workers." 675 F. Supp. at 568. We agree.

Townley argues that the district court should have considered the spiritual hardship the accommodation would have caused. We acknowledge that spiritual costs can exist. Congress has so recognized by its enactment of sections 702 and 701 (e). Townley is, of course, right when it says, "Cost cannot always be measured in terms of dollars. Spiritual 'costs' must also be given consideration...." Appellant's Brief at 27. It is very doubtful, however, that such "costs" can impose on a corporate employer the required level of hardship....

Townley, the corporate entity, must connect the asserted spiritual hardship to an adverse impact on the conduct of the business. "A claim of undue hardship cannot be supported by merely conceivable or hypothetical hardships; instead, it must be supported by proof of 'actual imposition on coworkers or disruption of the work routine.' " *Tooley v. Martin–Marietta Corp.*, 648 F.2d 1239, 1243 (9th Cir.), cert. denied, 454 U.S. 1098 (1981).

The Court cited *Hardison* for the proposition that Title VII does not require rights of coworkers to be infringed in order to accommodate employee's religious practice. And it ruled that Section 702 of Title VII (excluding religious corporations, associations, educational institutions, and societies from Title

---

5. We have stated that plaintiffs must meet a three-part test to establish a prima facie case of religious discrimination under sections 703(a) and 701(j).... The employee must show that (1) a bona fide religious belief of the employee conflicted with an employ-ment policy; (2) the employee informed the employer of the conflict; and (3) the employee was penalized in some way because of the conflict. We note that although we have occa-sionally used language implying that the em-ployer must discharge the employee because of the conflict, we have never in fact required that the employee's penalty for observing his or her faith be so drastic. The threat of discharge (or of other adverse employment practices) is a sufficient penalty (cases omit-ted). An employee does not cease to be dis-criminated against because he temporarily gives up his religious practice and submits to the employment policy. See *American Postal Workers Union v. Postmaster General*, 781 F.2d 772, 774–75 (9th Cir. 1986).

VII's prohibition against religious discrimination, 42 U.S.C. § 2000e–1, was inapplicable to a secular company like Townley.

———

■ Noonan, Circuit Judge, dissenting.

The EEOC could not exempt the Townley Manufacturing Company to the disadvantage of Pelvas if the effect of exemption were to coerce Pelvas to practice the company's religion or to give up his own.

No such showing of coercion has been made. According to Pelvas he was explicitly told that if he attended the prescribed meetings he could wear ear plugs and read a book or sleep. Wearing ear plugs, he was not exposed to hearing a word of doctrine subversive of his atheism. Reading a book or sleeping, he was not participating in any form of worship.

One can readily imagine gatherings of worshippers where merely entering the church or crossing the temple door in their company would be a symbolic act committing one to worship. Compulsion to attend such gatherings would be deeply offensive to the conscience. One can readily imagine schoolchildren summoned to an auditorium and subjected to religious propaganda. Compulsion of the children would be equally obnoxious to religious freedom. But the gatherings to which Pelvas has objected took place on company property during company time; and he was no child but a mature man. Presence at the gathering was not a religious act nor, as far as the record shows, a symbolic association with worship nor subjection to a religious message. Indeed what Pelvas was permitted to do was the antithesis of worship, the opposite of indoctrination. He was allowed to disassociate himself in the most public way from the devotional services that were conducted. He was allowed to turn off and shut out the inspirational message. If he had been discharged or penalized or even ostracized for such behavior he and the EEOC would have cause for complaint. But in fact there has been no showing that such acts as he was permitted to perform, contemptuous as they were of the services, have been or would have been the subject of discipline or disadvantage to Pelvas. The Townley Manufacturing Company has already accommodated Pelvas' conscientious unwillingness to participate in its services.

NOTES AND QUESTIONS

1. *Observance of Religious Holidays.* The Ansonia Board of Education had employed Ronald Philbrook as a teacher for four years before Philbrook was baptized into the Worldwide Church of God. The tenets of the church require members to refrain from their employment during designated holy days, a practice that caused Philbrook to miss approximately six schooldays each year. Pursuant to a collective bargaining agreement between the Board and the teachers' union, Philbrook would first use up his three days of annual leave and then either take unauthorized paid leave, schedule required hospital visits on holy days, or work on those days. Philbrook repeatedly asked the Board to adopt the policy of allowing three days of personal business leave for religious

observance or, in the alternative, to allow him to pay the cost of a substitute and receive full pay for additional days off for religious observance. The Board consistently rejected both proposals and Philbrook ultimately sued in District Court under Title VII of the Civil Rights Act of 1964, particularly § 701(j) of the Act which requires employers to "reasonably accommodate to an employee's ... religious observance or practice without undue hardship on the conduct of the employer's business."

The District Court concluded that Philbrook had failed to make a case because the Board had not placed him in a position of violating his religion or losing his job. However, the Court of Appeals found that Philbrook had established a prima facie case of discrimination and reversed and remanded. In *Ansonia Bd. of Education v. Philbrook*, 479 U.S. 60 (1986), the Court, per Justice Rehnquist, stated that both lower courts had applied an erroneous view of the law. An employer has met its obligation under § 701(j) when it demonstrates that it has offered a reasonable accommodation to the employee. The employer does not need to show that each of the employee's alternative accommodations would result in undue hardship. Therefore, the Court directed the lower court to consider on remand whether the collective bargaining agreement is a reasonable accommodation of Philbrook's religious beliefs. Is *Philbrook* consistent with *Sherbert* [section five above]? With *Thomas v. Review Board* [section four above]?

2. *Accommodation of Religious Beliefs of a Federal Grantee.* The Hill–Burton Act, 42 U.S.C. § 291 *et seq.*, provides substantial federal funds through the states to hospitals, including those operated by religious orders. After a district court in 1972 enjoined St. Vincent's Hospital in Billings, Montana, from prohibiting a sterilization at the hospital, Congress amended the act in 1973 to provide that receipt of Hill–Burton money "does not authorize any court or any public official" to require the recipient to "make its facilities available for the performance of any sterilization procedure or abortion" contrary to the recipient's "religious beliefs or moral convictions." Health Programs Extension Act of 1973, Pub.L. 93–45, Title IV, § 401(b), 87 Stat. 91, 95 (1973), 42 U.S.C. § 300a, 7(a). Barbara Ann Chrisman sued the religious order operating Sacred Heart Hospital in Eugene, Oregon, alleging that refusal to perform a tubal ligation was the deprival of a civil right secured by 28 U.S.C. § 1343. Sacred Heart Hospital had received $691,913 in Hill–Burton funds as part of a total construction budget of $8,035,241. In *Chrisman v. Sisters of St. Joseph of Peace*, 506 F. 2d 308 (9th Cir. 1974), the court, per Judge Eugene Wright, held that the congressional proviso was not an unconstitutional establishment of religion. Citing *Sherbert*, Judge Wright concluded that "Congress quite properly sought to protect the freedom of religion of those with religious or moral scruples...."

3. (A) *The Church as Employer: Union Representation and Collective Bargaining.* In *National Labor Relations Board v. The Catholic Bishop of Chicago*, 440 U.S. 490 (1979), the NLRB asserted that the National Labor Relations Act gave it jurisdiction over parochial schools. Writing for the Court, Chief Justice Burger indicated that the Court wished to avoid the "serious constitutional questions" that would arise if the board had to adjudicate unfair labor charges against such schools and had to consider the defense of religious mission that would be raised by religious administrators. Quoting *Lemon* [Chapter Fourteen, section 1], the Court said, "Religious authority necessarily pervades the school

system." The "very process of inquiry," the Court said, might "impinge on rights guaranteed by the Religion Clauses." The Board would have to decide what were "terms and conditions of employment" and therefore mandatory subjects of collective bargaining. The Court raised the possibility of "the Board's inquiry" involving "sensitive issues that open the door to conflicts between clergy, administrators and the Board, or conflicts with negotiators for unions." The Court concluded that it was unwilling to include church-operated schools within the NLRB's jurisdiction, absent an "affirmative intention of Congress clearly expressed" to that effect. Finding congressional intent clear on the matter, Justice Brennan, joined by White, Marshall, and Blackmun, dissented. *Compare Holy Trinity Church* [Chapter Ten, section 1]. *Catholic Bishop of Chicago* left open the question of whether lay teachers at religious schools may organize a union under state labor laws, known as "little Wagner Acts." In *Catholic High School Ass'n of the Archdiocese of New York v. Culvert*, 753 F.2d 1161 (2d Cir. 1985), the court, per Judge Richard J. Cardamone, noted that the New York legislature had in 1968 amended the state statute to include teachers at religious schools within the jurisdiction of the State Labor Relations Board, and suggested that the Court's refusal in *Catholic Bishop of Chicago* to apply the NLRA to religious schools means that the NLRA does not preempt application of little Wagner Acts to religious schools. Does this follow from *Catholic Bishop of Chicago,* or reflect a departure from the constitutional concerns expressed by Burger? For a thoughtful analysis of the concept of "church autonomy" in the labor area, see Douglas Laycock, "Towards a General Theory of the Religion Clauses: The Case of Church Labor Relations and the Right to Church Autonomy," 81 *Colum.L.Rev.* 1373 (1981).

In *Buckley v. Archdiocese of Rockville Centre,* 992 F. Supp. 586 (E.D.N.Y. Feb. 5, 1998) the court held that there is no jurisdiction under Title IX of the Education Amendments of 1972 (prohibiting discrimination on the basis of sex in federally funded educational programs) over religious schools and religious orders, as they receive no federal funding. Different result if students attending a religious school receive a federal scholarship under a voucher scheme? *See* Note. *Educational Vouchers, Tuition Tax Credits, and Opportunity Scholarships.* [Chapter Fourteen, section 1]

(B) *The Church as Employer: Unemployment Insurance.* In *St. Martin Evangelical Lutheran Church v. South Dakota,* 451 U.S. 772 (1981), the Court unanimously held that an exception in the Federal Unemployment Tax for services performed in the employ of "a church or a convention or association of churches" should be read to include an elementary school that was not a legal entity separate from the parish church and a secondary school owned by the Wisconsin Evangelical Lutheran Synod. The majority opinion, by Justice Blackmun, laid stress on construing the statute "to avoid raising doubts of its constitutionality." Americans United for Separation of Church and State and the United States Catholic Conference—not typical allies in Religion Clause litigation—joined as *amici* urging this result.

(C) *The Church as Employer: Minimum Wage Laws.* The Tony & Susan Alamo Foundation is a nonprofit religious organization that derives its income largely from the operation of commercial businesses staffed by the Foundation's "associates," most of whom are drug addicts or criminals in a rehabilitation program operated by the Foundation. These workers received no cash salaries, but the Foundation provided them with food, clothing, shelter, and other benefits. The Secretary of Labor filed an action against the Foundation, alleging violations of the minimum wage, overtime, and recordkeeping provisions of the Fair Labor Standards Act [FLSA].In *Tony & Susan Alamo Foundation v. Secretary of Labor*, 471 U.S. 290 (1985), a unanimous Court, per Justice White, held the provisions of the FLSA applicable to the Foundation. Noting that the Foundation's businesses serve the general public in competition with ordinary commercial enterprises, the Court found the Foundation to be an "enterprise" within the meaning of 29 U.S.C. § 203(r), which defines that term as "the related activities performed . . . by any person or persons for a common business purpose." In *Catholic Bishop of Chicago* the Court thought that the "very process of inquiry" into the religious nature of the schools whose employees sought union representation might "impinge on rights guaranteed by the Religion Clauses." Seeking to avoid "serious constitutional questions," the Court required an "affirmative intention of Congress clearly expressed" before applying the NLRA to religious schools. Perceiving "no 'significant risk' of an infringement on First Amendment rights" in *Tony and Susan Alamo Foundation,* the Court did not "require any clearer expression of congressional intent to regulate these activities." It was sufficient that the FLSA contains no express or implied exception for commercial activities conducted by religious or other nonprofit organizations, and that the Labor Department had consistently interpreted the Act to reach such businesses. for the Court to conclude that the religious character of the Foundation did not place it beyond the Act's reach. Addressing the constitutional question, White wrote: "[T]he Free Exercise Clause does not require an exemption from a governmental program unless, at a minimum, inclusion in the program actually burdens the claimant's freedom to exercise religious rights." The Court cited the testimony of two associates in the program: "[N]o one ever expected any kind of compensation, and the thought is totally vexing to my soul. It would defeat my whole purpose." "I believe it would be offensive to me to even be considered to be forced to take a wage. . . . I believe it offends my right to worship God as I choose." The Court noted that the FLSA does not require cash payments to employees, and that— even if it did—"there is nothing in the Act to prevent the associates from returning the amounts to the Foundation, provided that they do so voluntarily." Hence the Court concluded that the application of the FLSA to the Foundation would not interfere with the associates' right to freely exercise their religious beliefs. At one level, this approach seems consistent with Justice White's emphasis on the individual claimant in *Frazee* [section 5 above]. *Alamo Foundation*, however, did not involve a claim by an individual for accommodation of his free exercise rights, but a suit against a church by the government. Two commentators have observed that "construing the free exercise provision as mainly protecting individual rights, largely ignoring its associational and institutional dimensions" contains a latent danger of subordinating free exercise to the nonestablishment principle. Glendon and Yanes, "Structural Free Exercise," 90 *Mich. L. Rev.* 477, 490 (1991). Even if you think that the results in *Frazee* and *Alamo Foundation* are correct, was the Court attentive to this danger? See *Kedroff v. Saint Nicholas Cathedral of the Russian Orthodox Church in North America*, 344 U.S. 94 (1952) [Chapter Twelve, section 3].

(D) *The Church as Employer*: *Employment Discrimination*: Title VII of the Civil Rights Act of 1964, as amended, 42 U.S.C. § 2000e et seq., contains three separate provisions exempting religious employers under various circumstances from general provisions of the Act. The narrowest provision is § 703(e)(1), which provides: "it shall not be an unlawful employment practice for an employer to hire and employ employees ... on the basis of his religion, sex, or national origin in those certain instances where religion, sex, or national origin is a bona fide occupational qualification reasonably necessary to the normal operation of that particular business or enterprise." 42 U.S.C. § 2000e–2(e)(1). EEOC guidelines on this provision state that the "bona fide occupational qualification," or BFOQ, as to sex, is to be construed narrowly. 29 CFR 1604.1(a); *see Pan American World Airways, Inc. v. Diaz* 442 F.2d 385 (5th Cir. 1971), cert. denied, 404 U.S. 950 (1971) (invalidating exclusion of males from positions as flight attendants). Presumably the same term would be construed narrowly as to religion; that is, a religious employer would need to demonstrate some clear connection between the religious convictions of the employee and the characteristics of the position that require it.

Susan Dolter was an English teacher at a Catholic high school affiliated with the archdiocese of Dubuque. Single, she became pregnant. She was dismissed for this reason. She sued under Title VII, alleging discrimination based on sex. In *Dolter v. Wahlert High School*, 483 F. Supp. 266 (N.D. Iowa, 1980), the court denied the defendant's motion to dismiss. It held that the school could dismiss any teacher who violated the Church's moral teaching by engaging in premarital sex, but the school could not discharge only women who did so. If the school was concerned only with the visible effect of pregnancy, it could give a woman teacher a paid leave of absence. The court said the trial would determine whether Susan Dolter's conduct was such that she did not possess the "bona fide occupational qualifications" for the job and so fell within an exception to the law on sex discrimination.

In contrast to *Dolter, see Maguire v. Marquette University*, 627 F. Supp. 1499 (E.D. Wis. 1986), aff'd, 814 F.2d 1213 (7th Cir. 1987). Marjorie Maguire was denied an appointment as associate professor of theology at a Jesuit University and claimed that the denial was unlawful sex discrimination. The university's defense was that Maguire's views were incompatible with the university's religious mission. The court found *McClure* [this section below] applicable, and ruled that the free exercise clause would be violated by ordering the university to hire Maguire.

Section 703(e)(2) allows "a school, college, university, or other educational institution or institution of learning to hire and employ employees of a particular religion if such school, college, university, or other educational institution or institution of learning is, in whole or in substantial part, owned, supported, controlled, or managed by a particular religion or by a particular religious corporation, association, or society, or if the curriculum of such school, college, university, or other educational institution or institution of learning is directed toward the propagation of a particular religion." 42 U.S.C. § 2000e–2(e)(2). The Kamehameha Schools were established under an educational trust established by the will of Bernice Pauahi Bishop, which specifies that all trustees shall be "persons of the Protestant religion" and which directs that Hawaiian children be educated free of cost in an atmosphere permeated by the Protestant faith. Students attending the schools operated by the Bishop Estate participate in daily prayer, are strongly encouraged to participate in religious organizations, and must attend and pass religious education courses to advance from grade to grade and to graduate from the schools. In an authoritative construction of the will, the Hawaii Supreme Court noted that Mrs. Bishop's entire will is "permeated with expressions of interest in the exposition of the Protestant religion." *Murray v. Kobayashi*, 431 P.2d 940, 942 (Haw. 1967). In *Kamehameha Schools v. EEOC*, 990 F.2d 458 (9th Cir.), *cert. denied*, 510 U.S. 963 (1993), the court did not cite *Amos* [below], but it created a strict test for determining whether a school is religious for purposes of the section 703(e)(2) exemption, and determined that the Kamehameha Schools do not qualify under this provision.

The most important exemption for religious employers is § 702, which provides: "This subchapter [Title VII] shall not apply ... to a religious corporation, association, educational institution, or society with respect to the employment of individuals of a particular religion to perform work connected with the carrying on by such corporation, association, educational institution, or society of its activities." 42 U.S.C. § 2000e–1. In the 1964 version of the Act, § 702 exempted only the *religious activities* of religious employers from the statutory proscription against religious discrimination in employment. In 1972 Congress amended this provision, extending the exemption to *all activities* of religious organizations. Senator Sam Ervin, one of the sponsors of the amendment, explained that the purpose of the amendment was to "take the political hands of Caesar off of the institutions of God, where they have no place to be." 118 Cong. Rec. 4503 (1972).

The question presented in the following case focused on the application of the exemption "to the secular nonprofit activities of religious organizations." In his opinion for the Court, Justice White referred to the fact that the case involved a "nonprofit activity." White did not cite *Alamo Foundation* [this section above], even though his opinion in that case expressly addressed the distinction between for-profit and not-for-profit activities. In separate concurring opinions, Justices Brennan and O'Connor emphasized that the exemption is limited to not-for-profit activities of a religious organization.

Corporation of Presiding Bishop of the Church of Jesus Christ of Latter-day Saints et al. v. Amos et al., (No. 86–179), and United States v. Amos et al., (No. 86–401)

483 U.S. 327 (1987).

Rex E. Lee argued the cause for appellants in No. 86–179. With him on the briefs were *Wilford W. Kirton, Jr., Dan S. Bushnell, M. Karlynn Hinman, Benjamin W. Heineman, Jr., Carter G. Phillips,* and *Ronald S. Flagg*. Assistant Attorney General *Reynolds* argued the cause for the United States in No. 86–401. With him on the briefs were Solicitor General *Fried*, Deputy Solicitor General *Ayer*, Deputy Assistant Attorney General *Carvin*, and *Andrew J. Pincus*.

David B. Watkiss argued the cause for appellees in both cases. With him on the brief were *Elizabeth T. Dunning, John A. Powell, Joan E. Bertin,* and *John E. Harvey*.

Briefs of amici curiae urging reversal were filed for the American Association of Presidents of Independent Colleges and Universities et al. by *Edward McGlynn Gaffney, Jr.*; for the American Jewish Congress by *Marc*

D. Stern and *Amy Adelson*; for the Baptist Joint Committee on Public Affairs by *Donald R. Brewer* and *Oliver S. Thomas*; for the Catholic League for Religious and Civil Rights by *Steven Frederick McDowell*; for the Christian Legal Society et al. by *Michael W. McConnell, Michael J. Woodruff, Samuel E. Ericsson, Kimberlee W. Colby, Philip E. Draheim*, and *Forest D. Montgomery*; for the General Conference of Seventh-day Adventists by *Warren L. Johns, Walter E. Carson*, and *Melvin B. Sabey*; for the National Jewish Commission on Law and Public Affairs by *Nathan Lewin* and *Dennis Rapps*; for the United States Catholic Conference by *John A. Liekweg* and *Mark E. Chopko*; and for the Council on Religious Freedom by *Lee Boothby, James M. Parker, Robert W. Nixon*, and *Rolland Truman*.

Briefs of amici curiae urging affirmance were filed for the American Federation of Labor and Congress of Industrial Organizations et al. by *Michael H. Gottesman, Robert M. Weinberg, David M. Silberman*, and *Lawrence Gold*; for the Anti–Defamation League of B'nai B'rith by *Harold P. Weinberger, Justin J. Finger, Jeffrey P. Sinensky, Jill L. Kahn, Ruti G. Tietel*, and *Meyer Eisenberg*; for the Employment Law Center of the Legal Aid Society of San Francisco by *Joan M. Graff, Robert Barnes*, and *Robert E. Borton*; and for the Women's Legal Defense Fund et al. by *Donna Lenhoff*.

Jordan W. Lorence filed a brief for Concerned Women of America as amicus curiae.

■ JUSTICE WHITE delivered the opinion of the Court.

Section 702 of the Civil Rights Act of 1964, 78 Stat. 255, as amended, 42 U.S.C. § 2000e–1, exempts religious organizations from Title VII's prohibition against discrimination in employment on the basis of religion. The question presented is whether applying the § 702 exemption to the secular nonprofit activities of religious organizations violates the Establishment Clause of the First Amendment. The District Court held that it does, and these cases are here on direct appeal pursuant to 28 U.S.C. § 1252. We reverse.

I

The Deseret Gymnasium (Gymnasium) in Salt Lake City, Utah, is a nonprofit facility, open to the public, run by the Corporation of the Presiding Bishop of The Church of Jesus Christ of Latter-day Saints (CPB), and the Corporation of the President of The Church of Jesus Christ of Latter-day Saints (COP). The CPB and the COP are religious entities associated with The Church of Jesus Christ of Latter-day Saints (Church), an unincorporated religious association sometimes called the Mormon or LDS Church.

Appellee Mayson worked at the Gymnasium for some 16 years as an assistant building engineer and then as building engineer. He was discharged in 1981 because he failed to qualify for a temple recommend, that is, a certificate that he is a member of the Church and eligible to attend its temples.[4]

---

4. Temple recommends are issued only to individuals who observe the Church's standards in such matters as regular church attendance, tithing, and abstinence from coffee, tea, alcohol, and tobacco.

Mayson and others purporting to represent a class of plaintiffs brought an action against the CPB and the COP alleging, among other things, discrimination on the basis of religion in violation of § 703 of the Civil Rights Act of 1964, 42 U.S.C. § 2000e–2. The defendants moved to dismiss this claim on the ground that § 702 shields them from liability. The plaintiffs contended that if construed to allow religious employers to discriminate on religious grounds in hiring for nonreligious jobs, § 702 violates the Establishment Clause.

The District Court first considered whether the facts of these cases require a decision on the plaintiffs' constitutional argument. Starting from the premise that the religious activities of religious employers can permissibly be exempted under § 702, the court developed a three-part test to determine whether an activity is religious.[6] Applying this test to Mayson's situation, the court found: first, that the Gymnasium is intimately connected to the Church financially and in matters of management; second, that there is no clear connection between the primary function which the Gymnasium performs and the religious beliefs and tenets of the Mormon Church or church administration; and third, that none of Mayson's duties at the Gymnasium are "even tangentially related to any conceivable religious belief or ritual of the Mormon Church or church administration." The court concluded that Mayson's case involves nonreligious activity.

The court next considered the plaintiffs' constitutional challenge to 702. Applying the three-part test set out in *Lemon v. Kurtzman* [Chapter Fourteen, section 1] the court first held that § 702 has the permissible secular purpose of "assuring that the government remains neutral and does not meddle in religious affairs by interfering with the decisionmaking process in religions...." The court concluded, however, that § 702 fails the second part of the *Lemon* test because the provision has the primary effect of advancing religion. Among the considerations mentioned by the court were: that § 702 singles out religious entities for a benefit, rather

---

6. The District Court described the test as follows: "First, the court must look at the tie between the religious organization and the activity at issue with regard to such areas as financial affairs, day-to-day operations and management. Second, whether or not there is a close and substantial tie between the two, the court next must examine the nexus between the primary function of the activity in question and the religious rituals or tenets of the religious organization or matters of church administration. If there is substantial connection between the activity in question and the religious organization's religious tenets or matters of church administration and the tie under the first part of the test is close, the court does not need to proceed any further and may declare the activity religious.... However, where the tie between the religious entity and activity in question is either close or remote under the first prong of the test and the nexus between the primary function of the activity in question and the religious tenets or rituals of the religious organization or matters of church administration is tenuous or non-existent, the court must engage in a third inquiry. It must consider the relationship between the nature of the job the employee is performing and the religious rituals or tenets of the religious organization or matters of church administration. If there is a substantial relationship between the employee's job and church administration or the religious organization's rituals or tenets, the court must find that the activity in question is religious. If the relationship is not substantial, the activity is not religious."

than benefiting a broad grouping of which religious organizations are only a part; that § 702 is not supported by long historical tradition; and that § 702 burdens the free exercise rights of employees of religious institutions who work in nonreligious jobs. Finding that § 702 impermissibly sponsors religious organizations by granting them "an exclusive authorization to engage in conduct which can directly and immediately advance religious tenets and practices," the court declared the statute unconstitutional as applied to secular activity. The court entered summary judgment in favor of Mayson ... and ordered him reinstated with backpay....

II

"This Court has long recognized that the government may (and sometimes must) accommodate religious practices and that it may do so without violating the Establishment Clause." *Hobbie v. Unemployment Appeals Comm'n of Fla.* [section 5 above]. It is well established, too, that "the limits of permissible state accommodation to religion are by no means co-extensive with the noninterference mandated by the Free Exercise Clause." *Walz v. Tax Comm'n* [Chapter Thirteen, section 3]. There is ample room under the Establishment Clause for "benevolent neutrality which will permit religious exercise to exist without sponsorship and without interference." *Id.* At some point, accommodation may devolve into "an unlawful fostering of religion," *Hobbie*, but these are not such cases, in our view....

Lemon requires first that the law at issue serve a "secular legislative purpose." This does not mean that the law's purpose must be unrelated to religion—that would amount to a requirement "that the government show a callous indifference to religious groups," *Zorach v. Clauson* [Chapter Fourteen, section 2] and the Establishment Clause has never been so interpreted. Rather, *Lemon*'s "purpose" requirement aims at preventing the relevant governmental decisionmaker—in this case, Congress—from abandoning neutrality and acting with the intent of promoting a particular point of view in religious matters.

Under the *Lemon* analysis, it is a permissible legislative purpose to alleviate significant governmental interference with the ability of religious organizations to define and carry out their religious missions. Appellees argue that there is no such purpose here because § 702 provided adequate protection for religious employers prior to the 1972 amendment, when it exempted only the religious activities of such employers from the statutory ban on religious discrimination. We may assume for the sake of argument that the pre–1972 exemption was adequate in the sense that the Free Exercise Clause required no more. Nonetheless, it is a significant burden on a religious organization to require it, on pain of substantial liability, to predict which of its activities a secular court will consider religious. The line is hardly a bright one, and an organization might understandably be concerned that a judge would not understand its religious tenets and sense of mission.[14] Fear of potential liability might affect the way an organization carried out what it understood to be its religious mission.

14. The present cases are illustrative of the difficulties: the distinction between Des- eret Industries, and the Gymnasium is rather fine. Both activities are run on a nonprofit

After a detailed examination of the legislative history of the 1972 amendment, the District Court concluded that Congress' purpose was to minimize governmental "interfer[ence] with the decision-making process in religions." We agree with the District Court that this purpose does not violate the Establishment Clause.

The second requirement under *Lemon* is that the law in question have "a principal or primary effect ... that neither advances nor inhibits religion." Undoubtedly, religious organizations are better able now to advance their purposes than they were prior to the 1972 amendment to § 702. But religious groups have been better able to advance their purposes on account of many laws that have passed constitutional muster: for example, the property tax exemption at issue in *Walz v. Tax Comm'n,* or the loans of schoolbooks to schoolchildren, including parochial school students, upheld in *Board of Education v. Allen* [Chapter Fourteen, section 1]. A law is not unconstitutional simply because it allows churches to advance religion, which is their very purpose. For a law to have forbidden "effects" under Lemon, it must be fair to say that the government itself has advanced religion through its own activities and influence. As the Court observed in *Walz,* "for the men who wrote the Religion Clauses of the First Amendment the 'establishment' of a religion connoted sponsorship, financial support, and active involvement of the sovereign in religious activity."

The District Court appeared to fear that sustaining the exemption would permit churches with financial resources impermissibly to extend their influence and propagate their faith by entering the commercial, profit-making world. The cases before us, however, involve a nonprofit activity instituted over 75 years ago in the hope that "all who assemble here, and who come for the benefit of their health, and for physical blessings, [may] feel that they are in a house dedicated to the Lord." Dedicatory Prayer for the Gymnasium [cited by the District Court]. These cases therefore do not implicate the apparent concerns of the District Court. Moreover, we find no persuasive evidence in the record before us that the Church's ability to propagate its religious doctrine through the Gymnasium is any greater now than it was prior to the passage of the Civil Rights Act in 1964. In such circumstances, we do not see how any advancement of religion achieved by the Gymnasium can be fairly attributed to the Government, as opposed to the Church.[15]

basis, and the CPB and the COP argue that the District Court failed to appreciate that the Gymnasium as well as Deseret Industries is expressive of the Church's religious values.

15. Undoubtedly, Mayson's freedom of choice in religious matters was impinged upon, but it was the Church ... and not the Government, who put him to the choice of changing his religious practices or losing his job. This is a very different case than *Estate of Thornton v. Caldor, Inc.* [section 5 above].

In *Caldor,* the Court struck down a Connecticut statute prohibiting an employer from requiring an employee to work on a day designated by the employee as his Sabbath. In effect, Connecticut had given the force of law to the employee's designation of a Sabbath day and required accommodation by the employer regardless of the burden which that constituted for the employer or other employees. See *Hobbie* [section 5 above]. In the present cases, appellee Mayson was not legal-

We find unpersuasive the District Court's reliance on the fact that § 702 singles out religious entities for a benefit. Although the Court has given weight to this consideration in its past decisions, it has never indicated that statutes that give special consideration to religious groups are per se invalid. That would run contrary to the teaching of our cases that there is ample room for accommodation of religion under the Establishment Clause. Where, as here, government acts with the proper purpose of lifting a regulation that burdens the exercise of religion, we see no reason to require that the exemption come packaged with benefits to secular entities. . . .

It cannot be seriously contended that § 702 impermissibly entangles church and state; the statute effectuates a more complete separation of the two and avoids the kind of intrusive inquiry into religious belief that the District Court engaged in this case. The statute easily passes muster under the third part of the *Lemon* test.

Appellees argue that § 702 creates danger of political divisiveness along political lines. As the Court stated in *Lynch v. Donnelly* [Chapter Thirteen, section 6]: "This Court has not held that political divisiveness alone can serve to invalidate otherwise permissible conduct. And we decline to so hold today. This case does not involve a direct subsidy to church-sponsored schools or colleges, or other religious institutions, and hence no inquiry into political divisiveness is even called for, *Mueller v. Allen*" [Chapter Fourteen, section 1]. The judgment of the District Court is reversed, and the cases are remanded for further proceedings consistent with this opinion. It is so ordered.

■ JUSTICE BRENNAN, with whom JUSTICE MARSHALL joins, concurring in the judgment.

I write separately to emphasize that my concurrence in the judgment rests on the fact that these cases involve a challenge to the application of § 702's categorical exemption to the activities of a nonprofit organization. I believe that the particular character of nonprofit activity makes inappropriate a case-by-case determination whether its nature is religious or secular. . . .

These cases present a confrontation between the rights of religious organizations and those of individuals. Any exemption from Title VII's proscription on religious discrimination necessarily has the effect of burdening the religious liberty of prospective and current employees. An exemption says that a person may be put to the choice of either conforming to certain religious tenets or losing a job opportunity, a promotion, or, as in these cases, employment itself. The potential for coercion created by such a provision is in serious tension with our commitment to individual freedom of conscience in matters of religious belief.

ly obligated to take the steps necessary to qualify for a temple recommend, and his discharge was not required by statute. We find no merit in appellees' contention that § 702 "impermissibly delegates governmental power to religious employees and conveys a message of governmental endorsement of religious discrimination."

At the same time, religious organizations have an interest in autonomy in ordering their internal affairs, so that they may be free to: "select their own leaders, define their own doctrines, resolve their own disputes, and run their own institutions. Religion includes important communal elements for most believers. They exercise their religion through religious organizations, and these organizations must be protected by the [Free Exercise] Clause." Laycock, *Towards a General Theory of the Religion Clauses: The Case of Church Labor Relations and the Right to Church Autonomy*, 81 Colum. L. Rev. 1373, 1389 (1981). See also *Serbian Eastern Orthodox Diocese v. Milivojevich* [Chapter Twelve, section 3] (church has interest in effecting binding resolution of internal governance disputes); *Kedroff v. Saint Nicholas Cathedral*, [Chapter Twelve, section 3] (state statute purporting to transfer administrative control from one church authority to another violates Free Exercise Clause). For many individuals, religious activity derives meaning in large measure from participation in a larger religious community. Such a community represents an ongoing tradition of shared beliefs, an organic entity not reducible to a mere aggregation of individuals. Determining that certain activities are in furtherance of an organization's religious mission, and that only those committed to that mission should conduct them, is thus a means by which a religious community defines itself. Solicitude for a church's ability to do so reflects the idea that furtherance of the autonomy of religious organizations often furthers individual religious freedom as well.

The authority to engage in this process of self-definition inevitably involves what we normally regard as infringement on free exercise rights, since a religious organization is able to condition employment in certain activities on subscription to particular religious tenets. We are willing to countenance the imposition of such a condition because we deem it vital that, if certain activities constitute part of a religious community's practice, then a religious organization should be able to require that only members of its community perform those activities.

This rationale suggests that, ideally, religious organizations should be able to discriminate on the basis of religion only with respect to religious activities, so that a determination should be made in each case whether an activity is religious or secular.... What makes the application of a religious-secular distinction difficult is that the character of an activity is not self-evident. As a result, determining whether an activity is religious or secular requires a searching case-by-case analysis. This results in considerable ongoing government entanglement in religious affairs. Furthermore, this prospect of government intrusion raises concern that a religious organization may be chilled in its free exercise activity. While a church may regard the conduct of certain functions as integral to its mission, a court may disagree. A religious organization therefore would have an incentive to characterize as religious only those activities about which there likely would be no dispute, even if it genuinely believed that religious commitment was important in performing other tasks as well. As a result, the community's process of self-definition would be shaped in part by the prospects of litigation. A case-by-case analysis for all activities therefore would both produce excessive government entanglement with religion and create the danger of chilling religious activity.

The risk of chilling religious organizations is most likely to arise with respect to nonprofit activities. The fact that an operation is not organized as a profit-making commercial enterprise makes colorable a claim that it is not purely secular in orientation. In contrast to a for-profit corporation, a nonprofit organization must utilize its earnings to finance the continued provision of the goods or services it furnishes, and may not distribute any surplus to the owners. See generally Hansmann, *The Role of Nonprofit Enterprise*, 89 Yale L. J. 835 (1980). This makes plausible a church's contention that an entity is not operated simply in order to generate revenues for the church, but that the activities themselves are infused with a religious purpose. Furthermore, unlike for-profit corporations, nonprofits historically have been organized specifically to provide certain community services, not simply to engage in commerce. Churches often regard the provision of such services as a means of fulfilling religious duty and of providing an example of the way of life a church seeks to foster.

Nonprofit activities therefore are most likely to present cases in which characterization of the activity as religious or secular will be a close question. If there is a danger that a religious organization will be deterred from classifying as religious those activities it actually regards as religious, it is likely to be in this domain. This substantial potential for chilling religious activity makes inappropriate a case-by-case determination of the character of a nonprofit organization, and justifies a categorical exemption for nonprofit activities. Such an exemption demarcates a sphere of deference with respect to those activities most likely to be religious. It permits infringement on employee free exercise rights in those instances in which discrimination is most likely to reflect a religious community's self-definition. . . .

■ JUSTICE O'CONNOR, concurring in the judgment.

In *Wallace v. Jaffree* [Chapter Fourteen, section 2], I noted a tension in the Court's use of the *Lemon* test to evaluate an Establishment Clause challenge to government efforts to accommodate the free exercise of religion: "On the one hand, a rigid application of the *Lemon* test would invalidate legislation exempting religious observers from generally applicable government obligations. By definition, such legislation has a religious purpose and effect in promoting the free exercise of religion. On the other hand, judicial deference to all legislation that purports to facilitate the free exercise of religion would completely vitiate the Establishment Clause. Any statute pertaining to religion can be viewed as an 'accommodation' of free exercise rights."

In my view, the opinion for the Court leans toward the second of the two unacceptable options described above. While acknowledging that "undoubtedly, religious organizations are better able now to advance their purposes than they were prior to the 1972 amendment to § 702," the Court seems to suggest that the "effects" prong of the Lemon test is not at all implicated as long as the government action can be characterized as "allowing" religious organizations to advance religion, in contrast to government action directly advancing religion. This distinction seems to me to obscure far more than to enlighten. Almost any government benefit to religion could be recharacterized as simply "allowing" a religion to better advance itself, unless perhaps it involved actual proselytization by government agents. In nearly every case of a government benefit to religion, the religious mission would not be advanced if the religion did not take advantage of the benefit; even a direct financial subsidy to a religious organization would not advance religion if for some reason the organization failed to make any use of the funds. It is for this same reason that there is little significance to the Court's observation that it was the Church rather than the Government that penalized Mayson's refusal to adhere to Church doctrine. The Church had the power to put Mayson to a choice of qualifying for a temple recommend or losing his job because the Government had lifted from religious organizations the general regulatory burden imposed by § 702. . . .

As I have suggested in earlier opinions, the inquiry framed by the *Lemon* test should be "whether government's purpose is to endorse religion and whether the statute actually conveys a message of endorsement." *Wallace* [Chapter Fourteen, section 2]. To ascertain whether the statute conveys a message of endorsement, the relevant issue is how it would be perceived by an objective observer, acquainted with the text, legislative history, and implementation of the statute. *Id*. Of course, in order to perceive the government action as a permissible accommodation of religion, there must in fact be an identifiable burden on the exercise of religion that can be said to be lifted by the government action. The determination whether the objective observer will perceive an endorsement of religion "is not a question of simple historical fact. Although evidentiary submissions may help answer it, the question is, like the question whether racial or sex-based classifications communicate an invidious message, in large part a legal question to be answered on the basis of judicial interpretation of social facts." *Lynch v. Donnelly* [Chapter Thirteen, section 6]. . . .

These cases involve a Government decision to lift from a nonprofit activity of a religious organization the burden of demonstrating that the particular nonprofit activity is religious as well as the burden of refraining from discriminating on the basis of religion. Because there is a probability that a nonprofit activity of a religious organization will itself be involved in the organization's religious mission, in my view the objective observer should perceive the Government action as an accommodation of the exercise of religion rather than as a Government endorsement of religion. . . .

NOTES AND QUESTIONS

1. *Employment of Clergy.* Mrs. Billie B. McClure, an officer (minister) in the Salvation Army, alleged sex discrimination when the Army terminated her as an officer. In *McClure v. Salvation Army*, 460 F.2d 553 (5th Cir. 1972), *cert. denied*, 409 U.S. 846 (1972), the Court of Appeals, per James P. Coleman, held that a serious constitutional doubt would arise if Title VII were interpreted to apply to the employment relation between a church and a minister. The court invoked the line of cases from *Watson v. Jones* [Chapter Eight, section 5] to

Kedroff and *Kreshik* [Chapter Twelve, section 3], noting *Kedroff's* recognition of "a spirit of freedom for religious organizations." As noted above, one court applied the *McClure* rationale to a lay teacher at a Jesuit university. *Maguire v. Marquette University*, 814 F.2d 1213 (7th Cir. 1987). On the ground that "secular authority may not take sides in internal ecclesiastical disputes," another court held that the "ministerial exception" applied to the decision to refuse tenure to a Catholic nun teaching canon law at a pontifical university that trains priests. *EEOC v. Catholic University of America*, 83 F. 3d 455 (D.C. Cir. 1996). The same court held that the EEOC's two-year investigation of the nun's sex discrimination claim against the university constituted an "excessive entanglement" of the government with religion, impermissible under *Lemon v. Kurtzman* [Chapter Fourteen, section 1]. *See also Rayburn v. General Conference of Seventh–Day Adventists*, 772 F.2d 1164 (4th Cir. 1985); *Hutchinson v. Thomas*, 789 F.2d 392 (6th Cir. 1986); and *Scharon v. St. Luke's Episcopal Presbyterian Hospitals*, 929 F.2d 360 (8th Cir. 1991).

Other lower courts have limited *McClure* to the specific context of ordained ministers, repeatedly stating the duty of religious organizations to comply with various labor regulations governing the employment of personnel other than clergy, narrowly defined. *See, e.g., EEOC v. Mississippi College*, 626 F.2d 477 (5th Cir. 1980) (religious college subject to sex discrimination claim filed under Title VII by professor of sociology); *Catholic High School Ass'n of the Archdiocese of New York v. Culvert*, 753 F.2d 1161 (2d Cir. 1985) (religious schools subject to jurisdiction of State Labor Relations Board); *DeMarco v. Holy Cross High School*, 4 F.3d 166 (2d Cir. 1993) (lay teacher may bring action against religious school under Age Discrimination in Employment Act); and *Geary v. Visitation of the Blessed Virgin Mary Parish School*, 7 F.3d 324 (3d Cir. 1993) (application of Age Discrimination in Employment Act to lay faculty member at religious school does not entail significant risk of entanglement in religion if court does not question validity of employer's religious beliefs and does not choose between competing religious visions of parties). Note that none of the statutory exemptions mentioned in the note above refer to discrimination on the basis of race or sex, but only allow a religious employer to take into account the religious convictions of an employee. Does *Amos* inform these decisions?

2. *Ordination of Women.* Could a woman seeking ordination in a religious community that limits the ministry or rabbinate to men prevail on a Title VII sex discrimination claim? Professor Becker has suggested that "government subsidies of mostly-patriarchal religion" are constitutionally suspect. Is this view strengthened by the holding *in Virginia v. United States*, 518 U.S. 515 (1996), that when a court reviews an official classification based on gender under equal protection analysis, it must determine whether proffered justification is "exceedingly persuasive"? If a church does meet the state action requirement under the Fourteenth Amendment, what would that do to the nonestablishment principle? Becker argues that banning "tax exemptions and postal subsidies and award of government contracts to religious organizations that close leadership positions to women" is a "moderate" change compared to "proscribing all religious subsidies or requiring state regulation of religion to eliminate sexism." *See* Mary Becker, "The Politics of Women's Wrongs and the Bill of 'Rights': A Bicentennial Perspective," 59 *U. Chi. L. Rev.* 453 (1992). According to Becker, this result is compelled by *Bob Jones University v. United States* [Chapter Fourteen, section 3], which stripped a university of its tax-exempt status because of a religiously grounded policy of student discipline

forbidding interracial dating or marriage. Before *Bob Jones University*, one commentator anticipated Becker's suggestion, but concluded that it is unrealistic to expect this development to occur; *see* Jane Vandeventer Goldman, "Taxing Sex Discrimination: Revoking Tax Benefits of Organizations Which Discriminate on the Basis of Sex," 1976 *Ariz. St. L. J.* 641. One of the rationales for the result in *Bob Jones University* is that an organization claiming exemption under IRC § 501(c)(3) is governed by the law of charitable trusts and must accordingly not maintain a purpose "contrary to public policy." The Court acknowledged that "determinations of public benefit and public policy are sensitive matters with serious implications for the institutions affected; a declaration that a given institution is not 'charitable' should be made only where there can be no doubt that the activity involved is contrary to a fundamental public policy. But there can no longer be any doubt that racial discrimination in education violates deeply and widely accepted views of elementary justice." The Court concluded that Bob Jones University did not meet the public policy requirement, since its "racial policies violated the clearly defined public policy, rooted in our Constitution, condemning racial discrimination and, more specifically, the government policy against subsidizing racial discrimination in education, public or private." Is there a similar federal interest in eliminating gender restrictions on ordination to ministry in a religious community? Can an affirmative answer to this question be reconciled with *Watson v. Jones* [Chapter Eight, section 5] or the church autonomy cases like *Kedroff* and *Kreshik* [Chapter Twelve, section 3]?

7.   EDUCATING ONE'S CHILDREN

NOTE

The Old Order Amish. Not the Jehovah's Witnesses but a smaller and older denomination of Christians was the protagonist in the establishment of the free exercise of religion in regard to education—the right that the Court had stopped short of asserting in *Meyer v. Nebraska* and *Pierce v. Society of Sisters* [Chapter Ten, section 6]. The Amish were a branch of the Mennonites who in 1693 under the leadership of Jacob Ammann of Erlanbach, Switzerland, had set up a stricter church community, characterized by the rigorous shunning of sinners. Immigrating to America between 1720 and 1775, they settled chiefly in Pennsylvania. John A. Hostetler, *Amish Society* 31–57 (1980). By the 1960s Amish settlements existed also in Maryland, Ohio, Indiana, Iowa, Kansas, and Wisconsin. The Old Order Amish, a division of the original movement, were the strictest of all, combining a devotion to the Bible with an agricultural way of life, the use of German as their language, a distinctive dress that went back to the eighteenth century, and a commitment to pacifism.

Grouped in nearly self-sufficient units forming small self-governed commonwealths, the Amish conceive of themselves as bodies of Christians "suspended in a tension-field between obedience to an all-knowing and all-powerful Creator on the one hand and the fear of disobedience on the other," *Id.* 21. For the Amish, knowledge unrelated to their agricultural life, leads to pride, and pride is destructive sin. Learning the world's ways and mingling with the proud endanger salvation. Love requires a close and closed community with like-minded brothers and sisters, the elect of God who are "a chosen generation" (1 Peter 2:9).

Public education as such was not objectionable to the Amish when such education first appeared in the form of rural neighborhood schoolhouses. Amish children generally attended grammar schools in the nineteenth century. In the twentieth century, however, compulsory secondary schools and consolidated high school districts were seen by the Amish as a threat. Secondary schools went beyond reading, writing, and arithmetic that Amish life found useful. The consolidated districts brought Amish and non-Amish together. In adolescence, when sexual temptations were perceived as acute, the Amish saw their children thrown together with the proud, immodestly dressed, disobedient children of the world. When, in the 1960s, decisions of the Supreme Court banished prayer and religious reading of the Bible from the schools, and the teaching of evolution became general, Amish distress with the public high school became acute. *See* Joseph Stoll (editor of *The Blackboard Bulletin*, an Amish parochial school journal), "Who Shall Educate Our Children?," in Albert N. Keim, ed., *Compulsory Education and the Amish: The Right Not to be Modern* 27–42 (1975).

As early as 1914, Amish were jailed and fined in Ohio for refusing to send their children to a new consolidated high school. Keim, "From Erlanbach to New Glarus," in Keim, 14–15. For the next fifty years similar sporadic persecutions were patiently endured. In the few cases that drew opinions from appellate courts, the Amish claim of religious freedom was almost universally rejected. In 1966 the Kansas Supreme Court upheld the conviction of LeRoy Garber for not sending his fifteen-year-old daughter Sharon to the public school; the Supreme Court of the United States denied review, *State v. Garber*, 197 Kan. 567, 419 P.2d 896 (1966), *cert. denied and appeal dismissed*, 389 U.S. 51 (1967).

The Amish bore these trials, disliking litigation and usually reluctant to let others litigate in their behalf. Hostetler in Keim 100. In Pennsylvania, a compromise with the state was worked out in 1955. Amish teenagers were permitted to attend an Amish vocational school three hours a week, doing their homework in agricultural or domestic projects under their parents' supervision. Hostetler, *Amish Society* 258. In Iowa local authorities in 1965 used force to take Amish pupils to the public high school. General public outrage led Iowa to compromise. Donald A. Erickson, "Showdown at an Amish Schoolhouse," in Keim, 43–83. The Iowa case led William C. Lindholm, a Lutheran pastor, to form the National Committee for Amish Religious Freedom.

On Christmas Eve, 1968, Pastor Lindholm asked William B. Ball, a Catholic lawyer, to defend Amish arrested in New Glarus, Wisconsin, for not sending their children to high school. Ball, a Pennsylvanian, proposed that Wisconsin compromise as Pennsylvania had; to his surprise the state refused. He went to trial in Green County, Wisconsin, in March 1969, relying chiefly on *Sherbert* [section 5]. He was able to introduce John Hostetler as an expert witness on how Amish religious belief required rejection of the high school, and Donald Erickson as a witness on the education accomplished by an Amish upbringing. Erickson also testified, "I have never seen a school that impressed me either as a culturally or religiously neutral school." Hostetler, "the most superb witness we could have had," was asked by the prosecution: "What's the point of education? Isn't it to get ahead in the world?" Hostetler replied: "It all depends on which world." Ball also put on the county sheriff to testify that he did not know of any teenage criminals who were Amish, and the county welfare supervisor to testify how little the Amish burdened the welfare system. Ball lost in the local court and the intermediate court, but won in the Wisconsin Supreme Court. Again, to his surprise, the state refused to yield, appealing to the Supreme Court of the United States and arguing that "the religion" whose free exercise was protected by the First Amendment was worship, not "a way of life." By the standard of *Reynolds v. United States* [Chapter Nine], the state was right. But Ball laid the groundwork for a different approach, and the Supreme Court, affirming, virtually tracked the testimony the trial had elicited. *See* William B. Ball, "Building a Landmark Case," in Keim 114–123. As you read this case, ask whether religious freedom played a significant role in the outcome. In *Employment Division v. Smith* [section 10 below], Justice Scalia suggested that religious freedom did not constitute the rationale for the outcome in *Yoder*, which he characterized as a "hybrid" case involving religious freedom and parental liberty. Would the Yoders have prevailed as secular parents without a free exercise claim? Does Scalia's reading of *Yoder* turn religious freedom into something like Hamburger Helper, a meal stretcher without any independent protein value? See James D. Gordon III, "Free Exercise on the Mountaintop," 79 *Calif. L. Rev.* 91 (1991) ("the *Smith* Court mistreated precedent, used shoddy reasoning, and, except in the unemployment compensation area, deprived the free exercise clause of any independent significance").

Wisconsin v. Yoder

406 U.S. 205 (1972).

John W. Calhoun, Assistant Attorney General of Wisconsin, argued the cause for Petitioner. With him on the briefs were *Robert W. Warren*, Attorney General, and *William H. Wilker*, Assistant Attorney General.

William B. Ball argued the cause for respondents. With him on the brief was *Joseph G. Skelly*.

Briefs of *amici curiae* urging affirmance were filed by *Donald E. Showalter* for the Mennonite Central Committee; by *Boardman Noland* and *Lee Boothby*, for the General Conference of Seventh–Day Adventists; by *William S. Ellis* for the National Council of the Churches of Christ; by *Nathan Lewin* for the National Jewish Commission on Law and Public Affairs; and by *Leo Pfeffer* for the Synagogue Council of America.

▮ CHIEF JUSTICE BURGER delivered the opinion of the Court.

On petition of the State of Wisconsin, we granted the writ of certiorari in this case to review a decision of the Wisconsin Supreme Court holding that respondents' convictions of violating the State's compulsory school-attendance law were invalid under the Free Exercise Clause of the First Amendment to the United States Constitution made applicable to the States by the Fourteenth Amendment. For the reasons hereafter stated we affirm the judgment of the Supreme Court of Wisconsin.

Respondents Jonas Yoder and Wallace Miller are members of the Old Order Amish religion, and respondent Adin Yutzy is a member of the

Conservative Amish Mennonite Church. They and their families are residents of Green County, Wisconsin. Wisconsin's compulsory school-attendance law required them to cause their children to attend public or private school until reaching age 16 but the respondents declined to send their children, ages 14 and 15, to public school after they completed the eighth grade. The children were not enrolled in any private school, or within any recognized exception to the compulsory-attendance law, and they are conceded to be subject to the Wisconsin statute.

On complaint of the school district administrator for the public schools, respondents were charged, tried, and convicted of violating the compulsory-attendance law in Green County Court and were fined the sum of $5 each. Respondents defended on the ground that the application of the compulsory-attendance law violated their rights under the First and Fourteenth Amendments. The trial testimony showed that respondents believed, in accordance with the tenets of Old Order Amish communities generally, that their children's attendance at high school, public or private, was contrary to the Amish religion and way of life. They believed that by sending their children to high school, they would not only expose themselves to the danger of the censure of the church community, but, as found by the county court, also endanger their own salvation and that of their children. The State stipulated that respondents' religious beliefs were sincere.

In support of their position, respondents presented as expert witnesses scholars on religion and education whose testimony is uncontradicted. They expressed their opinions on the relationship of the Amish belief concerning school attendance to the more general tenets of their religion, and described the impact that compulsory high school attendance could have on the continued survival of Amish communities as they exist in the United States today. The history of the Amish sect was given in some detail, beginning with the Swiss Anabaptists of the 16th century who rejected institutionalized churches and sought to return to the early, simple, Christian life de-emphasizing material success, rejecting the competitive spirit, and seeking to insulate themselves from the modern world. As a result of their common heritage, Old Order Amish communities today are characterized by a fundamental belief that salvation requires life in a church community separate and apart from the world and worldly influence. This concept of life aloof from the world and its values is central to their faith.

A related feature of Old Order Amish communities is their devotion to a life in harmony, with nature and the soil, as exemplified by the simple life of the early Christian era that continued in America during much of our early national life. Amish beliefs require members of the community to make their living by farming or closely related activities. Broadly speaking, the Old Order Amish religion pervades and determines the entire mode of life of its adherents. Their conduct is regulated in great detail by the *Ordnung*, or rules, of the church community. Adult baptism, which occurs in late adolescence, is the time at which Amish young people voluntarily undertake heavy obligations, not unlike the Bar Mitzvah of the Jews, to abide by the rules of the church community.

Amish objection to formal education beyond the eighth grade is firmly grounded in these central religious concepts. They object to the high school, and higher education generally, because the values they teach are in marked variance with Amish values and the Amish way of life; they view secondary school education as an impermissible exposure of their children to a "worldly" influence in conflict with their beliefs. The high school tends to emphasize intellectual and scientific accomplishments, self-distinction, competitiveness, worldly success, and social life with other students. Amish society emphasizes informal learning-through-doing; a life of "goodness," rather than a life of intellect; wisdom, rather than technical knowledge; community welfare, rather than competition; and separation from, rather than integration with, contemporary worldly society.

Formal high school education beyond the eighth grade is contrary to Amish beliefs, not only because it places Amish children in an environment hostile to Amish beliefs with increasing emphasis on competition in class work and sports and with pressure to conform to the styles, manners, and ways of the peer group, but also because it takes them away from their community, physically and emotionally, during the crucial and formative adolescent period of life. During this period, the children must acquire Amish attitudes favoring manual work and self-reliance and the specific skills needed to perform the adult role of an Amish farmer or housewife. They must learn to enjoy physical labor. Once a child has learned basic reading, writing, and elementary mathematics, these traits, skills, and attitudes admittedly fall within the category of those best learned through example and "doing" rather than in a classroom. And, at this time in life, the Amish child must also grow in his faith and his relationship to the Amish community if he is to be prepared to accept the heavy obligations imposed by adult baptism. In short, high school attendance with teachers who are not of the Amish faith—and may even be hostile to it—interposes a serious barrier to the integration of the Amish child into the Amish religious community. Dr. John Hostetler, one of the experts on Amish society, testified that the modern high school is not equipped, in curriculum or social environment, to impart the values promoted by Amish society.

The Amish do not object to elementary education through the first eight grades as a general proposition because they agree that their children must have basic skills in the "three R's" in order to read the Bible, to be good farmers and citizens, and to be able to deal with non-Amish people when necessary in the course of daily affairs. They view such a basic education as acceptable because it does not significantly expose their children to worldly values or interfere with their development in the Amish community during the crucial adolescent period. While Amish accept compulsory elementary education generally, wherever possible they have established their own elementary schools in many respects like the small local schools of the past. In the Amish belief higher learning tends to develop values they reject as influences that alienate man from God.

On the basis of such considerations, Dr. Hostetler testified that compulsory high school attendance could not only result in great psychological harm to Amish children, because of the conflicts it would produce, but would also, in his opinion, ultimately result in the destruction of the Old Order Amish church community as it exists in the United States today. The testimony of Dr. Donald A. Erickson, an expert witness on education, also showed that the Amish succeed in preparing their high school age children to be productive members of the Amish community. He described their system of learning through doing the skills directly relevant to their adult roles in the Amish community as "ideal" and perhaps superior to ordinary high school education. The evidence also showed that the Amish have an excellent record as law-abiding and generally self-sufficient members of society.

Although the trial court in its careful findings determined that the Wisconsin compulsory school-attendance law "does interfere with the freedom of the Defendants to act in accordance with their sincere religious belief" it also concluded that the requirement of high school attendance until age 16 was a "reasonable and constitutional" exercise of governmental power, and therefore denied the motion to dismiss the charges. The Wisconsin Circuit Court affirmed the convictions. The Wisconsin Supreme Court, however, sustained respondents' claim under the Free Exercise Clause of the First Amendment and reversed the convictions. A majority of the court was of the opinion that the State had failed to make an adequate showing that its interest in "establishing and maintaining an educational system overrides the defendants' right to the free exercise of their religion."

I

There is no doubt as to the power of a State, having a high responsibility for education of its citizens, to impose reasonable regulations for the control and duration of basic education. See, *e.g., Pierce v. Society of Sisters,* [Chapter Ten, section 7]. Providing public schools ranks at the very apex of the function of a State. Yet even this paramount responsibility was, in *Pierce,* made to yield to the right of parents to provide an equivalent education in a privately operated system. There the Court held that Oregon's statute compelling attendance in a public school from age eight to age 16 unreasonably interfered with the interest of parents in directing the rearing of their offspring, including their education in church-operated schools. As that case suggests, the values of parental direction of the religious upbringing and education of their children in their early and formative years have a high place in our society. See also *Ginsberg v. New York,* 390 U. S. 629, 639 (1968); *Meyer v. Nebraska* [Chapter Ten, section 7]; cf. *Rowan v. Post Office Dept.,* 397 U. S. 728 (1970). Thus, a State's interest in universal education, however highly we rank it, is not totally free from a balancing process when it impinges on fundamental rights and interests, such as those specifically protected by the Free Exercise Clause of the First Amendment, and the traditional interest of parents with respect to the religious upbringing of their children so long as they, in the words of *Pierce,* "prepare [them] for additional obligations."

II

We come then to the quality of the claims of the respondents concerning the alleged encroachment of Wisconsin's compulsory school-attendance statute on their rights and the rights of their children to the free exercise of the religious beliefs they and their forebears have adhered to for almost three centuries. In evaluating those claims we must be careful to determine whether the Amish religious faith and their mode of life are, as they claim, inseparable and interdependent. A way of life, however virtuous and admirable, may not be interposed as a barrier to reasonable state regulation of education if it is based on purely secular considerations to have the protection of the Religion Clauses, the claims must be rooted in religious belief. Although a determination of what is a "religious" belief or practice entitled to constitutional protection may present a most delicate question, the very concept of ordered liberty precludes allowing every person to make his own standards on matters of conduct in which society as a whole has important interests. Thus, if the Amish asserted their claims because of their subjective evaluation and rejection of the contemporary secular values accepted by the majority, much as Thoreau rejected the social values of his time and isolated himself at Walden Pond, their claims would not rest on a religious basis. Thoreau's choice was philosophical and personal rather than religious, and such belief does not rise to the demands of the Religion Clauses.

Giving no weight to such secular considerations, however, we see that the record in this case abundantly supports the claim that the traditional way of life of the Amish is not merely a matter of personal preference, but one of deep religious conviction, shared by an organized group, and intimately related to daily living. That the Old Order Amish daily life and religious practice stem from their faith is shown by the fact that it is in response to their literal interpretation of the Biblical injunction from the Epistle of Paul to the Romans, "be not conformed to this world...." This command is fundamental to the Amish faith. Moreover, for the Old Order Amish, religion is not simply a matter of theocratic belief. As the expert witnesses explained, the Old Order Amish religion pervades and determines virtually their entire way of life, regulating it with the detail of the Talmudic diet through the strictly enforced rules of the church community.

The record shows that the respondents' religious beliefs and attitude toward life, family, and home have remained constant—perhaps some would say static—in a period of unparalleled progress in human knowledge generally and great changes in education. The respondents freely concede, and indeed assert as an article of faith, that their religious beliefs and what we would today call "life style" have not altered in fundamentals for centuries. Their way of life in a church-oriented community, separated from the outside world and "worldly" influences, their attachment to nature and the soil, is a way inherently simple and uncomplicated, albeit difficult to preserve against the pressure to conform. Their rejection of telephones, automobiles, radios, and television, their mode of dress, of speech, their habits of manual work do indeed set them apart from much of contemporary society; these customs are both symbolic and practical.

As the society around the Amish has become more populous, urban, industrialized, and complex, particularly in this century, government regulation of human affairs has correspondingly become more detailed and pervasive. The Amish mode of life has thus come into conflict increasingly with requirements of contemporary society exerting a hydraulic insistence on conformity to majoritarian standards. So long as compulsory education laws were confined to eight grades of elementary basic education imparted in a nearby rural schoolhouse, with a large proportion of students of the Amish faith, the Old Order Amish had little basis to fear that school attendance would expose their children to the worldly influence they reject. But modern compulsory secondary education in rural areas is now largely carried on in a consolidated school, often remote from the student's home and alien to his daily home life. As the record so strongly shows, the values and programs of the modern secondary school are in sharp conflict with the fundamental mode of life mandated by the Amish religion; modern laws requiring compulsory secondary education have accordingly engendered great concern and conflict. . . .

IV

. . . The State's argument proceeds without reliance on any actual conflict between the wishes of parents and children. It appears to rest on the potential that exemption of Amish parents from the requirements of the compulsory-education law might allow some parents to act contrary to the best interests of their children by foreclosing their opportunity to make an intelligent choice between the Amish way of life and that of the outside world. The same argument could, of course, be made with respect to all church schools short of college. There is nothing in the record or in the ordinary course of human experience to suggest that non-Amish parents generally consult with children of ages 14–16 if they are placed in a church school of the parents' faith.

Indeed it seems clear that if the State is empowered, as *parens patriae*, to "save" a child from himself or his Amish parents by requiring an additional two years of compulsory formal high school education, the State will in large measure influence, if not determine, the religious future of the child. Even more markedly than in *Prince* [section 1 above], therefore, this case involves the fundamental interest of parents, as contrasted with that of the State, to guide the religious future and education of their children. The history and culture of Western civilization reflect a strong tradition of parental concern for the nurture and upbringing of their children. This primary role of the parents in the upbringing of their children is now established beyond debate as an enduring American tradition. . . . *Affirmed.*

■ Justices Powell and Rehnquist took no part in the case.

■ Justice Douglas, dissenting in part:

The views of the two children in question were not canvassed by the Wisconsin courts. The matter should be explicitly reserved so that new hearings can be held on remand of the case.

I think the emphasis of the Court on the "law and order" record of this Amish group of people is quite irrelevant. A religion is a religion irrespective of what the misdemeanor or felony records of its members might be. I am not at all sure how the Catholics, Episcopalians, the Baptists, Jehovah's

Witnesses, the Unitarians, and my own Presbyterians would make out if subjected to such a test. It is, of course, true that if a group or society was organized to perpetuate crime and if that is its motive, we would have rather startling problems akin to those that were raised when some years back a particular sect was challenged here as operating on a fraudulent basis. *United States v. Ballard* [Chapter Thirteen, section 1]. But no such factors are present here, and the Amish, whether with a high or low criminal record, certainly qualify by all historic standards as a religion within the meaning of the First Amendment.

The Court rightly rejects the notion that actions, even though religiously grounded, are always outside the protection of the Free Exercise Clause of the First Amendment. In so ruling, the Court departs from the teaching of *Reynolds v. United States* [Chapter Nine], where it was said concerning the reach of the Free Exercise Clause of the First Amendment, "Congress was deprived of all legislative power over mere opinion, but was left free to reach actions which were in violation of social duties or subversive of good order." In that case it was conceded that polygamy was a part of the religion of the Mormons. Yet the Court said, "It matters not that his belief [in polygamy] was a part of his professed religion: it was still belief, and belief only."

Action, which the Court deemed to be antisocial, could be punished even though it was grounded on deeply held and sincere religious convictions. What we do today, at least in this respect, opens the way to give organized religion a broader base than it has ever enjoyed; and it even promises that in time *Reynolds* will be overruled.

NOTES AND QUESTIONS

1. *Amish and Caring for the Elderly.* Part of the Amish religious ethic is to bear one another's burdens (Galatians 6:2) and, in particular, to relieve the wants of the old and the enfeebled (1 Timothy 5:8). Consequently they see no need for social security and have the view that as the government's intervention in these matters is wrong, it is sinful to receive social security benefits or pay the social security tax. In *United States v. Lee,* 455 U.S. 252 (1982), they challenged the tax as a burden on their religious freedom. The Supreme Court unanimously rejected the challenge. Chief Justice Burger wrote that not all governmentally imposed burdens on religion were unconstitutional. In his dissent in *Yoder* Justice Douglas suggested that the logic of that case required the overruling of *Reynolds* [Chapter Nine]. Far from overruling *Reynolds*, the Chief Justice cited it as support for the conclusion he reached in *Lee* that the government's interest in having a national, compulsory social security system outweighed the rights of religious conscience. Does this characterization of the case reflect a tendency to overgeneralize the interest of the government and to trivialize the interest of the religious claimant? Is *Lee* in tension with *Yoder*?

2. *Christian Schools.* Biblically based schools, often called Christian Schools and generally operated by Baptists, have fared differently in different states, to some degree because of different state statutes, to some degree because of the courts' greater or lesser sensitivity to the Baptists' free exercise claims. Their position has been that the Bible shows that God has given parents the

obligation and right of educating their children, *see, e.g.*, Deuteronomy 6:6–7, Proverbs 22:6, Ephesians 6:4; that in the exercise of this religious right they have instituted schools that are pervasively religious, not secular schools with religious instruction tacked on; that the state has no power to regulate the curriculum of the schools or the credentials of those who teach there; and that the school and the church are one, so that the state can no more prescribe for the one than for the other.

In *State v. Faith Baptist Church of Louisville, Nebraska*, 207 Neb. 802, 301 N.W. 2d 571 (1981), *appeal dismissed for want of a substantial federal question*, 454 U.S. 803 (1981), the church ran the Faith Christian School, an elementary and secondary educational enterprise that employed a curriculum supplied by Accelerated Christian Education (A.C.E.), consisting of a series of booklets with instructional information and self-test questions, all with a biblical orientation. For example, a social studies booklet was devoted to Chapter 1 of Genesis; a mathematics booklet interspersed biblical citations and sayings with problems in addition and subtraction. The school refused to supply the state with the names of the students at the school; to get approval of its curriculum; or to employ accredited teachers. The court granted the injunction sought by the state against the operation of the school.

The church and the school were one building. In defiance of a court order closing the building on weekdays to prevent its use as a school, a group of parishioners attended the building and conducted a prayer Union Representation and vigil. Police removed them by force. A federal court held that these parishioners had a cause of action against the officers because the officers had interfered with their right of worship. *McCurry v. Tesch*, 738 F.2d 271 (8th Cir. 1984), *cert. denied*, 469 U.S. 1211 (1985). For a short summary of the controversy, *see* Richard E. Shugrue, "An Approach to Mutual Respect: The Christian Schools Controversy," 18 *Creighton L. Rev.* 219 (1984–85); Comment, "*State v. Faith Baptist Church: State Regulation of Religious Education*," 15 *Creighton L. Rev.*183 (1981); *see also* "In Nebraska, the War Between Church and State Rages On," *Christianity Today* 32 (Feb. 17, 1984); "Fundamentalists Leave Jail, But Nebraska Church Schools Are Still in Trouble," *Christianity Today* 64 (Apr. 6, 1984); "Is the Nebraska School Trouble Finally Over?" *Christianity Today* 40 (July 13, 1984). For an account by one of the fundamentalist participants, *see* H. E. Rowe, *The Day They Padlocked the Church* (1983).

Iowa reached a conclusion like Nebraska's. In *Johnson v. Charles City Community Schools Board of Education*, 368 N.W. 2d 74 (Iowa 1985), *cert. denied, Pruessner v. Benton*, 474 U.S. 1033 (1985), the court explicitly agreed with *Faith Baptist* (above), and rejected "the Amish exception" to compulsory attendance that the legislature had provided. The court observed: "Sincerity of belief is the only factor wholly common to both the Amish and these plaintiffs. The beliefs of the plaintiffs are greatly less interwoven with their daily mode of life. The Amish culture is greatly more isolated from mainstream American life. Plaintiffs' children, for all the distinctive religious convictions they will be given, will live, compete for jobs, work, and move about in a diverse and complex society."

On the other hand, in *State v. Whisner*, 47 Ohio St. 2d 181, Ohio Ops. 3d 105, 351 N.E. 2d 750 (1976), the Reverend Levi Whisner, pastor of Tabernacle Christian Church in Bradford, Ohio, testified that the church and the Tabernacle Christian School were "the same." Parents convicted for failing to send their children to a school conforming to minimum state standards were acquitted on appeal. The court cited *Yoder* and found that the state had not ever attempted to justify its interest in applying its minimum standards to a religious school.

Similarly, in *Bangor Baptist Church v. State of Maine, Department of Educational and Cultural Services*, 576 F. Supp. 1299, 1335 (D. Me. 1983), the church and the administrators of the Bangor Christian School were granted an injunction against Maine officials prohibiting the officials from bringing actions against the plaintiffs "on the ground that they have induced habitual truancy through their statements to parents that the education of their children is a religious duty and that the state should have no role in regulating the education of Christian children." Not coincidentally, William B. Ball represented the successful churches in Ohio and Maine.

Compare State v. Heart Ministries, Inc., 227 Kan. 244, 607 P.2d 1102 (1980), *appeal dismissed for want of a substantial federal question*, 449 U.S. 802 (1980). The Reverend William Cowell and his wife Carol operated the Victory Village Home for Girls. According to his testimony Cowell believed that corporal punishment (including beating with belts and boards) is required by Scripture. He did not believe in preparing financial statements or an annual audit of accounts, but believed that God would provide. For these reasons he objected to state regulation of the enterprise and to payment of the state license fee of $5 per year. The Court held that "licensing is necessary and the fee reasonable" and found no need to go into the defendants' religious objections to the regulations that affected their discipline of the children and their financial practices.

Accord Roloff Evangelistic Enterprises, Inc. v. State, 556 S.W. 2d 856 (Tex. App. 1977) (Child Care Licensing Act held enforceable against children's home operated by the Reverend Lester Roloff, who contended, "We cannot comply with this standard since we are not responsible to the State in this matter of raising the children"), *appeal dismissed for want of substantial federal question*, 439 U.S. 803 (1978).

3. *Home Schooling.* In *Yoder* Chief Justice Burger stressed: "if the Amish asserted their claims because of their subjective evaluation and rejection of the contemporary secular values accepted by the majority, much as Thoreau rejected the social values of his time and isolated himself at Walden Pond, their claims would not rest on a religious basis. Thoreau's choice was philosophical and personal rather than religious, and such belief does not rise to the demands of the Religion Clauses." Must the motivation for the exemption from compulsory school attendance be religiously grounded, as it was in *Yoder*? Does the same logic that undergirds *Yoder* also support a broad constitutional mandate, grounded in concerns of parental liberty recognized in *Pierce* [Chapter Ten, section 7] or in free speech concerns, requiring all parents to be free from criminal prosecution for educating their own children in their own home? Under the logic of *Texas Monthly, Inc. v. Bullock* [section 1 above], must exemption from prosecution be provided for parents who are not motivated to educate their children at home for religious reasons? *See* Stephen Arons, "The Separation of School and State: *Pierce* Reconsidered," 40 *Harv. Ed. Rev.* 70 (1970). Arons's argument was difficult to reconcile with the clear emphasis on religion in *Yoder*. Has Justice Scalia strengthened Arons's argument by insisting in *Smith* [section 10 below] that the real reason for the result in *Yoder* was

parental liberty, not religious freedom? Many states permit—either by statute or by judicial decree—parents to educate their children at home. Some states even encourage the practice by providing textbooks and other assistance to parents willing to provide this form of intensive tutoring for their children. For an explanation and defense of home schooling, *see,* e.g., Stephen G. Gilles, "On Educating Children: A Parentalist Manifesto," 63 *U. Chi. L.Rev.* 937 (1996); Jon S. Lerner, "Protecting Home Schooling through the *Casey* Undue Burden Standard," 62 *U. Chi. L.Rev.* 363 (1995); Joseph P. Tocco, "Home Schooling in Michigan: Is There a Fundamental Right to Teach Your Children at Home?," 71 *U. Det. Mercy L.Rev.* 1053 (1994); Jack Macmullan, "The Constitutionality of State Home Schooling Statutes," 31 *Vill. L.Rev.* 1309 (1994).

4. *Free Exercise Where Parents Disagree or Disappear.* Do constitutional criteria apply where the custody of a child is at stake and the parents are of different religions? Six states say religion is to be considered among elements determining "the best interests" of the child, *see* Note, "The Establishment Clause and Religion in Child Custody Disputes: Factoring Religion into the Best Interest Equation," 82 *Mich. L.Rev.* 1702 (1984), a note critical of the statutes. Consider *Schreifels v. Schreifels*, 47 Wash. 2d 409, 287 P.2d 1001 (1955). John and Violet were husband and wife. Violet fell passionately in love with John's brother, Anthony, and left with him, taking with her the four children. In an action by John to recover custody of the children, the court said, "Adultery, whether promiscuous or not, violates the Ten Commandments and the statutes of this state." The court also took note that John was a devout practicing Catholic and observed that the children while with Violet were "not being given religious training in any denomination and that fact should be considered, together with the mother's misconduct, in awarding custody." *Contra Bonjour v. Bonjour*, 592 P.2d 1233 (Alaska 1979). Randall and Lindsey Bonjour were divorced. Both remarried. Randall and his second wife were devout Protestants; Lindsey was a non-churchgoing Christian and her new husband a non-Christian. The trial judge, applying the Alaska statute that stated that "the best interests" of the child include "religious" needs, gave weight to Randall's religious practice in awarding him custody of five-year-old Michael Joseph Bonjour. The trial judge made no special finding as to the boy's religious needs. The Supreme Court of Alaska, per Chief Justice Robert Boocheever, remanded, distinguishing between acceptable judicial recognition of the actual religious preference of a "mature child" and unconstitutional decision by a judge based on the judge's own view of what religious beliefs and practices were favorable to the child's welfare.

Is the case different where the issue is the placement of children in orphanages? In *Wilder v. Sugarman*, 385 F. Supp. 1013 (S.D.N.Y. 1974), six children by their guardians *ad litem*, represented by the New York Civil Liberties Union and the Legal Aid Society of Brooklyn, challenged the New York statute on placement, claiming that the statute discriminated against blacks and Protestants. The defendants—over thirty in number—included New York City and a number of individual institutions such as the Hebrew Children's Home, Lutheran Community Services, and the St. Cabrini Home.

The three-judge court (Walter R. Mansfield, Harold R. Ryler, Jr., and Kevin T. Duffy) in a long *per curiam* opinion, traced the care of orphans in New York back to the Dutch colony, where "poor relief [was] provided through ecclesiastical bodies." The pioneering New York statute of 1875, which removed children from almshouses, directed that they be placed with orphanages controlled by "persons of the same religious faith as the parents," as far as practicable; the settled policy of the state became one to care for such children by state payments to the institutions. In 1921 the principle of matching institution to parental religion was made part of the New York constitution, Art. 6, sec. 18; the principle was left in the constitution by popular vote in 1961. By statute in 1970 the religious preference of the parent was to be matched "so far as consistent with the best interest of the child and where practicable." The statutory language was interpreted by the Court of Appeals of New York to mean that religious matching was desirable but not mandatory. *Dickens v. Ernesto*, 30 N.Y. 2d 61, 65–66, 330 N.Y.S. 2d 346, 348, 281 N.E. 2d 153, 155 (1972), *appeal dismissed for want of a substantial federal question*, 407 U.S. 917 (1972). The present case was different from *Dickens* in that it challenged state funding of the religiously matched institution. The total amount was substantial: the state spent $194 million annually on these programs. The court asked if this expenditure, coupled with the attention given religious matching, did not amount to an impermissible establishment of religion.

At the same time the court recognized that the state was acting as a surrogate parent for the children it placed. As surrogate parent, the state had the duty "of fulfilling the child's Free Exercise rights." To deny the child spiritual training would be governmental interference with religion.

Finding the free exercise and establishment clauses "in conflict," the court said it would opt for the "benevolent neutrality" recommended by *Walz* [Chapter Thirteen, section 3], and so for practical accommodation. In practical terms, the court saw no alternative for the children apart from "the pervasively religious atmosphere" of the institutions that housed many of them: "Although plaintiffs suggest that non-sectarian homes, agencies or institutions be established, no clue is furnished as to where any such existing facilities might be found or how the capital funds for construction and staffing of new facilities might be provided." The court held that the New York statutes represent "a fair and reasonable accommodation between the Establishment and Free Exercise clauses of the Constitution." No appeal was taken.

In *Kendall v. Kendall*, 426 Mass. 238, 687 N.E. 2d 1228 (1997), the court sustained a trial court award of joint custody to the parents that included a judgment restricting exposure of the children, who had been raised in the Jewish faith, to the father's Fundamentalist Christian beliefs. The court ruled that this decree did not violate either free exercise or establishment concerns. Consistent with *Hobbie* [section 5 above]?

8. WEARING RELIGIOUS GARB

S. Simcha Goldman, an Orthodox Jew and ordained rabbi, was an Air Force captain serving as a psychologist at March Air Force Base. At all times he wore a yarmulke, a head-covering expressing submission to God. *See* S. R. Hirsch, *Hirsch Siddur* 14 (1969 ed.). The Air Force has comprehensive regulations concerning what headgear its personnel may wear and when they can wear it. When Goldman was ordered to stop wearing the yarmulke, he sought an injunction against enforcement of the regulations. The District Court granted the injunction. The court of appeals reversed, observing that the Air Force regulations were "necessarily arbitrary" and that the Air Force had "no concrete interest separate from the effect of strict enforcement itself," *Goldman v. Secretary of Defense*, 734 F. 2d 1531 (D.C. Cir. 1984). Circuit Judge Abner Mikva, himself a Jew, sat on the panel in the court of appeals, and noted for his colleagues on the bench that the practice of wearing a yarmulke is followed by some, but not all, Jews. Of what possible relevance was this piece of information to the determination of Goldman's case? *See* Isaac Klein, *A Guide to Jewish Religious Practice* 51–52 (1979). In a later case a panel of the same circuit invalidated on equal protection grounds the Department of Defense regulations prohibiting persons with homosexual orientation from serving in the Navy. *Steffan v. Aspin*, 8 F. 3d 57 (D.C. Cir. 1993), aff'd en banc sub nom. *Steffan v. Perry*, 41 F. 3d 677 (D.C. Cir. 1994). Without any sense of irony, Judge Mikva cited the circuit court opinion in *Goldman*, commenting on the case: "A strong and independent military is essential to the national security, and courts should not lightly overturn military judgments as to the best means of ensuring that security." Was Goldman's wearing of a yarmulke "essential to the national security"? The Supreme Court, 5–4, held against Goldman.

Goldman v. Weinberger

475 U.S. 503 (1986).

Nathan Lewin argued the cause for petitioner. With him on the brief were *David J. Butler* and *Dennis Rapps*.

Kathryn A. Oberly argued the cause for respondents. With her on the brief were *Solicitor General Fried, Assistant Attorney General Willard, Deputy Solicitor General Geller*, and *Anthony J. Steinmeyer*.

Briefs of *amici curiae* urging reversal were filed for the American Jewish Committee et al. by *Samuel Eric Hans Ericsson, Kimberlee Wood Colby, Samuel Rabinove*, and *Richard T. Foltin*; for the American Jewish Congress et al. by *Ronald A. Krauss* and *Marc D. Stern*; for the Anti-Defamation League of B'nai B'rith by *Daniel P. Levitt, Justin J. Finger*, and *Jeffrey P. Sinensky*; and for the Catholic League for Religious and Civil Rights by *Steven Frederick McDowell*.

W. Charles Bundren, Guy O. Farley, Jr., John W. Whitehead, Thomas O. Kotouc, Wendell R. Bird, and *William B. Hollberg* filed a brief for the Rutherford Institute et al. as *amici curiae*.

■ JUSTICE REHNQUIST delivered the opinion of the Court.

. . . The considered professional judgment of the Air Force is that the traditional outfitting of personnel in standardized uniforms encourages the subordination of personal preferences and identities in favor of the overall group mission. Uniforms encourage a sense of hierarchical unity by tending to eliminate outward individual distinctions except for those of rank. The Air Force considers them as vital during peacetime as during war because its personnel must be ready to provide an effective defense on a moment's notice; the necessary habits of discipline and unity must be developed in advance of trouble. We have acknowledged that "[t]he inescapable demands of military discipline and obedience to orders cannot be taught on battlefields; the habit of immediate compliance with military procedures and orders must be virtually reflex with no time for debate or reflection." *Chappell v. Wallace,* 462 U.S., at 300.

To this end, the Air Force promulgated AFR 35–10, a 190–page document, which states that "Air Force members will wear the Air Force uniform while performing their military duties, except when authorized to wear civilian clothes on duty." The rest of the document describes in minute detail all of the various items of apparel that must be worn as part of the Air Force uniform. It authorizes a few individualized options with respect to certain pieces of jewelry and hair style, but even these are subject to severe limitations. In general, authorized headgear may be worn only out of doors. Indoors, "[h]eadgear [may] not be worn except by armed security police in the performance of their duties." A narrow exception to this rule exists for headgear worn during indoor religious ceremonies. In addition, military commanders may in their discretion permit visible religious headgear and other such apparel in designated living quarters and nonvisible items generally. *See* Department of Defense Directive 1300.17 (June 18, 1985).

Petitioner Goldman contends that the Free Exercise Clause of the First Amendment requires the Air Force to make an exception to its uniform dress requirements for religious apparel unless the accoutrements create a "clear danger" of undermining discipline and esprit de corps. He asserts that in general, visible but "unobtrusive" apparel will not create such a danger and must therefore be accommodated. He argues that the Air Force failed to prove that a specific exception for his practice of wearing an unobtrusive yarmulke would threaten discipline. He contends that the Air Force's assertion to the contrary is mere *ipse dixit*, with no support from actual experience or a scientific study in the record and is contradicted by expert testimony that religious exceptions to AFR 35–10 are in fact desirable and will increase morale by making the Air Force a more humane place.

But whether or not expert witnesses may feel that religious exceptions to AFR 35–10 are desirable is quite beside the point. The desirability of dress regulations in the military is decided by the appropriate military officials, and they are under no constitutional mandate to abandon their considered professional judgment. Quite obviously, to the extent the regulations do not permit the wearing of religious apparel such as a yarmulke, a practice described by petitioner as silent devotion akin to prayer, military life may be more objectionable for petitioner and probably others. But the First Amendment does not require the military to accommodate such practices in the face of its view that they would detract from the uniformity sought by the dress regulations. The Air Force has drawn the line essentially between religious apparel which is visible and that which is not, and we hold that those portions of the regulations challenged here reasonably and evenhandedly regulate dress in the interest of the military's perceived need for uniformity. The First Amendment therefore does not prohibit them from being applied to petitioner even though their effect is to restrict the wearing of the headgear required by his religious beliefs.

The judgment of the Court of Appeals is *Affirmed*.

■ JUSTICE STEVENS, with whom JUSTICE WHITE and JUSTICE POWELL join, concurring.

Captain Goldman presents an especially attractive case for an exception from the uniform regulations that are applicable to all other Air Force personnel. His devotion to his faith is readily apparent. The yarmulke is a familiar and accepted sight. In addition to its religious significance for the wearer, the yarmulke may evoke the deepest respect and admiration—the symbol of a distinguished tradition and an eloquent rebuke to the ugliness of anti-Semitism. Captain Goldman's military duties are performed in a setting in which a modest departure from the uniform regulation creates almost no danger of impairment of the Air Force's military mission. Moreover, on the record before us, there is reason to believe that the policy of strict enforcement against Captain Goldman had a retaliatory motive— he had worn his yarmulke while testifying on behalf of a defendant in a court-martial proceeding. Nevertheless, as the case has been argued, I believe we must test the validity of the Air Force's rule not merely as it applies to Captain Goldman but also as it applies to all service personnel who have sincere religious beliefs that may conflict with one or more military commands.

Justice Brennan is unmoved by the Government's concern "that while a yarmulke might not seem obtrusive to a Jew, neither does a turban to a Sikh, a saffron robe to a Satchidananda Ashram–Integral Yogi, nor do dreadlocks to a Rastafarian." He correctly points out that "turbans, saffron robes, and dreadlocks are not before us in this case," and then suggests that other cases may be fairly decided by reference to a reasonable standard based on "functional utility, health and safety considerations, and the goal of a polished, professional appearance." As the Court has explained, this approach attaches no weight to the separate interest in uniformity itself. Because professionals in the military service attach great importance to that plausible interest, it is one that we must recognize as legitimate and rational even though personal experience or admiration for the performance of the "rag-tag band of soldiers" that won us our freedom in the revolutionary war might persuade us that the Government has exaggerated the importance of that interest.

The interest in uniformity, however, has a dimension that is of still greater importance for me. It is the interest in uniform treatment for the members of all religious faiths. The very strength of Captain Goldman's claim creates the danger that a similar claim on behalf of a Sikh or a Rastafarian might readily be dismissed as "so extreme, so unusual, or so faddish an image that public confidence in his ability to perform his duties will be destroyed." If exceptions from dress code regulations are to be granted on the basis of a multifactored test such as that proposed by Justice Brennan, inevitably the decisionmaker's evaluation of the character and the sincerity of the requestor's faith—as well as the probable reaction of the majority to the favored treatment of a member of that faith—will play a critical part in the decision. For the difference between a turban or a dreadlock on the one hand, and a yarmulke on the other, is not merely a difference in "appearance"—it is also the difference between a Sikh or a Rastafarian, on the one hand, and an Orthodox Jew on the other. The Air Force has no business drawing distinctions between such persons when it is enforcing commands of universal application.

As the Court demonstrates, the rule that is challenged in this case is based on a neutral, completely objective standard—visibility. It was not motivated by hostility against, or any special respect for, any religious faith. An exception for yarmulkes would represent a fundamental departure from the true principle of uniformity that supports that rule. For that reason, I join the Court's opinion and its judgment.

■ JUSTICE BRENNAN, with whom JUSTICE MARSHALL joins, dissenting.

Simcha Goldman invokes this Court's protection of his First Amendment right to fulfill one of the traditional religious obligations of a male Orthodox Jew—to cover his head before an omnipresent God. The Court's response to Goldman's request is to abdicate its role as principal expositor of the Constitution and protector of individual liberties in favor of credulous deference to unsupported assertions of military necessity. I dissent.

It is not the province of the federal courts to second-guess the professional judgments of the military services, but we are bound by the Constitution to assure ourselves that there exists a rational foundation for assertions of military necessity when they interfere with the free exercise of religion. "The concept of military necessity is seductively broad," *Glines*, 444 U.S., at 369 (Brennan, J., dissenting), and military decisionmakers themselves are as likely to succumb to its allure as are the courts and the general public. Definitions of necessity are influenced by decisionmakers' experiences and values. As a consequence, in pluralistic societies such as ours, institutions dominated by a majority are inevitably, if inadvertently, insensitive to the needs and values of minorities when these needs and values differ from those of the majority. The military, with its strong ethic of conformity and unquestioning obedience, may be particularly impervious to minority needs and values. A critical function of the Religion Clauses of the First Amendment is to protect the rights of members of minority religions against quiet erosion by majoritarian social institutions that dismiss minority beliefs and practices as unimportant, because unfamiliar. It is the constitutional role of this Court to ensure that this purpose of the First Amendment be realized.

The Court and the military services have presented patriotic Orthodox Jews with a painful dilemma—the choice between fulfilling a religious obligation and serving their country. Should the draft be reinstated, compulsion will replace choice. Although the pain the services inflict on Orthodox Jewish servicemen is clearly the result of insensitivity rather than design, it is unworthy of our military because it is unnecessary. The Court and the military have refused these servicemen their constitutional rights; we must hope that Congress will correct this wrong.

■ JUSTICE O'CONNOR, with whom JUSTICE MARSHALL joins, dissenting.

The first question that the Court should face here . . . is whether the interest that the Government asserts against the religiously based claim of the individual is of unusual importance. It is perfectly appropriate at this step of the analysis to take account of the special role of the military. The mission of our armed services is to protect our Nation from those who would destroy all our freedoms. I agree that, in order to fulfill that mission, the military is entitled to take some freedoms from its members. As the Court notes, the military " 'must insist upon a respect for duty and a discipline without counterpart in civilian life.' " (quoting *Schlesinger v. Councilman*, 420 U.S. 738 (1975)). The need for military discipline and esprit de corps is unquestionably an especially important governmental interest.

But the mere presence of such an interest cannot, as the majority implicitly believes, end the analysis of whether a refusal by the Government to honor the free exercise of an individual's religion is constitutionally acceptable. A citizen pursuing even the most noble cause must remain within the bounds of the law. So, too, the Government may, even in pursuing its most compelling interests, be subject to specific restraints in doing so. The second question in the analysis of a Free Exercise claim under this Court's precedents must also be reached here: will granting an exemption of the type requested by the individual do substantial harm to the especially important governmental interest?

In the rare instances where the military has not consistently or plausibly justified its asserted need for rigidity of enforcement, and where the individual seeking the exemption establishes that the assertion by the military of a threat to discipline or esprit de corps is in his or her case completely unfounded, I would hold that the Government's policy of uniformity must yield to the individual's assertion of the right of free exercise of religion. On the facts of this case, therefore, I would require the Government to accommodate the sincere religious belief of Captain Goldman. Napoleon may have been correct to assert that, in the military sphere, morale is to all other factors as three is to one, but contradicted assertions of necessity by the military do not on the scales of justice bear a similarly disproportionate weight to sincere religious beliefs of the individual.

I respectfully dissent.

■ JUSTICE BLACKMUN also dissented.

NOTES AND QUESTIONS

1. *Characterization of Constitutional Claims.* As Justice Stevens intimates in his concurring opinion, there was evidence in the record of the *Goldman* case that Captain Goldman's commanding officer [CO] had raised no objection whatever to Goldman's wearing a yarmulke under his military cap until Captain Goldman had a disagreement with his CO over an unrelated issue at a court-martial. If the CO's order had been addressed as retaliatory or as anti-Semitic hostility targeted at Jews, would the Court have reached the same result? On the general significance of characterization, *see* Kenneth F. Ripple, *Constitutional Litigation* 4–42 (1984).

2. *Congressional Response: Regulating the Military through the Spending Power.* Congress has the power "to lay and collect Taxes ... [and] to pay the

Debts and provide for the common Defence and general Welfare," U.S. Const, art. I, § 8, cl. 1, and the power "to make Rules for the Government and Regulation of the land and naval Forces." U.S. Const., art. I, § 8, cl. 14. In his dissent in *Goldman* Justice Brennan suggested that the Court's "credulous deference to unsupported assertions of military necessity" was subject to Congressional action that would "correct this wrong." After the ruling of the circuit court, several Jewish organizations sought relief from Congress, which promptly ordered the Secretary of Defense to establish a study group "to examine ways to minimize the potential conflict between the interests of members of the armed forces in abiding by their religious tenets and the military interest in maintaining discipline." The study group concluded that "dress and appearance ... within the military ... contribute significantly to building discipline, individual morale, unit cohesion, and service esprit de corps." But it also concluded that non-visible items of apparel should be permitted "when they do not constitute health or safety hazards." The Department of Defense promulgated a regulation in 1985 allowing the wearing of a yarmulke "unless military necessity dictated otherwise." Dept. of Defense Directive 1300.17, *Accommodation of Religious Practices Within the Military Services* (1985). A year later the Supreme Court ruled in *Goldman*. In 1988 Congress relied upon its spending power to provide that members of the armed forces may wear items of religious apparel whole in uniform, except where the Secretary of Defense determines that donning such apparel would interfere with the performance of military duties, or where the apparel is not neat or conservative. National Defense Authorization Act for Fiscal Year 1988 and 1989, 101 Stat. 1019, 1086–87, 10 U.S.C. § 774. Is this statute a permissible accommodation of a religious belief or—as Justice Stevens intimated in his concurring opinion in *Goldman*—an unconstitutional benefit to members of a particular religious group? *See* Dwight H. Sullivan, "The Congressional Response to *Goldman v. Weinberger*," 121 *Mil. L.Rev.* 125 (1988); Kenneth Lasson, "Religious Liberty in the Military: The First Amendment under 'Friendly Fire,'" 9 *J. L. & Relig.* 471, 484–88 (1992).

3. *Religious Garb in the Courtroom.* A trial court in New York ruled that Mayer Weinberger, "a devout adherent of the Jewish faith," had to remove his yarmulke or leave the courtroom. In *Close-It–Enterprises, Inc. v. Weinberger*, 64 A.D. 2d 686, 407 N.Y.S. 2d 587 (1978) the Appellate Division of the New York Supreme Court reversed, reasoning that a court may not put a person to a choice between access to the tribunal and the free exercise of religion. In a previous ruling the New York Court of Appeals upheld a trial judge's order barring a Roman Catholic priest-lawyer from wearing his collar while acting as a Legal Aid Society attorney in a criminal trial. *La Rocca v. Lane*, 37 N.Y. 2d 575, 376 N.Y.S. 2d 93, 338 N.E. 2d 606 (1975), *cert. denied*, 424 U.S. 968 (1976). Chief Judge Breitel wrote that a "lawyer is subject to the regulation of the Judge in matters of attire when that regulation is reasonably related to the preservation of order and decorum in the courtroom, the protection of parties and witnesses, and generally to the furtherance of the administration of justice." He suggested that "a juror might view differently statements made by a member of the clergy than those made by others, and might ascribe a greater measure of veracity and personal commitment to the rightness of the client's cause." And he concluded that "the risk that a fair trial could not be had" outweighed the "incidental limitation" of the defense counsel's right to free exercise of religion by compelling him "to remove the symbol of his religious

calling, a requirement of his calling which is not unconditional or beyond dispensation." Catholics observe the practice of fasting and abstaining from eating meat on the Fridays of Lent, but dispensation may be had from this practice. Does that mean that the state may require a Catholic to eat meat on a Friday in Lent? The *Weinberger* court distinguished *LaRocca* on the ground that no objection had been made by the opposing party to the wearing of a yarmulke, while the district attorney had objected to Father LaRocca's wearing of his Roman collar. Is this distinction crucial? Three years later Father LaRocca was again barred from wearing his Roman collar while representing a defendant before the grand jury. When Father LaRocca renewed his motion at trial, the district attorney again objected, but this time the court ruled in favor of the priest, invoking *McDaniel v. Paty* [Chapter Fifteen, section 2] as authorizing it to take a new look at the issue. *People v. Rodriquez*, 424 N.Y.S. 2d 600, 101 Misc. 2d 536 (1979). La Rocca cited the canon law mandating the wearing of the collar in a public forum and the recent pronouncement of Pope John Paul II that a priest should manifest his uniqueness by his dress. Responding to the district attorney's claim of prejudice, the court pointed out that the same prosecutor's office had "strenuously opposed a defendant's motion seeking to prevent a Catholic priest from wearing his clerical collar while testifying as a prosecution witness" in *People v. Ramirez*, September 11, 1979. The priest filed a civil rights action in federal court, seeking declaratory and injunctive relief from the orders barring the wearing of his Roman collar in court. Inter alia, LaRocca argued that the inconsistency between his case and *Weinberger* violated equal protection. The federal courts rejected the priest's claims. *LaRocca v. Gold*, 662 F. 2d 144 (2d Cir. 1981)

4. *Religious Garb and Prison Ministry*. Sister Helen Prejean has given a vivid account of her ministry to prisoners on death row in Louisiana. Prejean, *Dead Man Walking: An Eyewitness Account of the Death Penalty in the United States* (1993). This ministry sometimes involves her appearance in courts and before the State Parole Board as a witness for the prisoners. May the state require her to refrain from wearing any distinctive religious garb when she or other women like her engage in such ministry?

5. *Religious Garb and the Classroom*. Janet Cooper, a convert to the Sikh faith and a special education teacher in the Eugene public schools, donned white clothes and a white turban and wore them while teaching her sixth and eighth grade classes. In a letter to the staff of the school where she taught, she wrote that she would wear the turban and often wear white clothing as part of her religious practice, and that she had explained this and other changes in her life to her students. The superintendent of schools warned Cooper that her conduct was in violation of an Oregon statute that reads as follows: "No teacher in any public school shall wear any religious dress while engaged in the performance of duties as a teacher." ORS 342.650. In *Cooper v. Eugene School District No. 4J*, 301 Or. 358, 723 P. 2d 298 (1986), Justice Hans Linde acknowledged that the 1923 predecessor to ORS 342.650 dates from the period of anti-Catholic intolerance that behind us the initiative measure against private schools struck down in *Pierce v. Society of Sisters* [Chapter Ten, section 7]. Linde noted that the compatibility of religious dress with the role of public school teachers is an old issue under state laws and constitutions, generally involving teaching by nuns while wearing the habits of their orders. Linde concluded that the Oregon statute against religious dress in the classroom is

permissible to avoid the appearance of sectarian influence, favoritism, or official approval in the public school. Right result? Why?

6. *Religious Garb on the Basketball Court.* The Illinois High School Association adopted a facially neutral, generally-applicable rule that prohibits players from wearing hats or other headgear in basketball competition. The rule is grounded in a safety concern in preventing the wearing of headgear that might fall off in the heat of play and cause a player to fall. The Association was unwilling to allow for an exception for Orthodox Jews pinning a yarmulke to their heads with bobby pins. In *Menora v. Illinois High School Association*, 683 F. 2d 1030 (7th Cir. 1982), the court upheld the general rule, but remanded the case to the district court with directions to allow the Jewish students an opportunity to propose a form of secured headcovering that complied with Jewish law but also met the safety concern of the Association. The author of the opinion, Judge Richard Posner, well known for his ability to discern an economic dimension in cases where others might not, wrote that "free exercise of religion does not mean costless exercise of religion"; but he added that the state "may not make the exercise of religion unreasonably costly."

9.   RELIGIOUS OBSERVANCES IN PRISON

Introduction: *First Amendment Rights of Prisoners.* In *Cooper v. Pate*, 378 U.S. 546 (1964), *Cruz v. Beto*, 405 U.S. 319 (1972) (per curiam), and *Pell v. Procunier*, 417 U.S. 817, 822 (1974), the Court clarified that "inmates clearly retain protections afforded by the First Amendment, including its directive that no law shall prohibit the free exercise of religion." These holdings are supported by empirical research showing that participation in religious activities is a persistent and noncontingent inhibiter of adult crime. T. David Evans et al., "Religion and Crime Reexamined: The Impact of Religion, Secular Controls, and Social Ecology on Adult Criminology," 33 *Criminology* 195 (1995). However qualified by countervailing governmental interests, free exercise of religion is important to the rehabilitation of inmates and to the reduction of recidivism rates. Walter H. Moberly, *The Ethics of Punishment* (1968); R.A. Duff, "Expression, Penance and Reform," in J.G. Murphy, ed., *Punishment and Reformation* (3d ed. 1995).

Imprisonment is a powerful metaphor for the exile from the homeland experienced by Jews over the centuries. The prototype of such exiles was the Babylonian captivity, which began in 586 BCE, when the conqueror Nebuchadrezzar destroyed the Jerusalem Temple and dispersed or deported much of the population of Judah to Babylon. In 538 BCE, Cyrus the Persian conquered the Babylonians and issued an edict permitting the Jews to return to Jerusalem. Writing shortly after this return of the released captives to Israel, a prophet suggests that the purpose of fasting is not to achieve mere external compliance with the rules governing fasting on Yom Kippur, the day of atonement (Lev. 23:26–32), or on special days to commemorate national misfortunes (Zechariah 7:1–5; 8:18–19). Rather, this prophet states, the fasting that pleases the Lord opens people to social justice, mercy, and sharing. Note that the duties of social justice include liberation of the captives.

Isaiah 58:6–7

Is not this the fast that I choose:
    to loose the bonds of injustice,
    to undo the thongs of the yoke,
to let the oppressed go free,
    and to break every yoke?

Is it not to share your bread with the hungry,
    and bring the homeless poor into your house;
when you see the naked, to cover them,
    and not to hide yourself from your own kin?

————

In the following passage the prophet describes his mission as one of declaring the forgiveness and restoration of the people and the rebuilding of Jerusalem as "release to the prisoners."

Isaiah 61:1–2

The spirit of the Lord GOD is upon me,
because the LORD has anointed me;
he has sent me to bring good news to the oppressed,
to bind up the brokenhearted,
to proclaim liberty to the captives,
and release to the prisoners. . . .

They shall build up the ancient ruins,
they shall raise up the former devastations;
they shall repair the ruined cities,
the devastations of many generations.

————

The Gospel according to Luke 4:16–22 records that Jesus read this passage from Isaiah at a sabbath service at the synagogue in his home town of Nazareth. In this story Jesus accepted as his own the Isaian description of the prophetic mission as proclamation of liberty to the captives. In the following passage the coming reign of God is described as a judgment (in Greek, a crisis). Evildoers are not mentioned. The separation that occurs in this judgment is between pious people who failed to recognize God's presence in categories of human need and those who acted compassionately to relieve the needs of their fellow humans. The needy include those in prison.

Matthew 25:34–40

When the Son of Man comes in his glory, and all the angels with him, then he will sit on the throne of his glory. All the nations will be gathered before him, and he will separate people one from another as a shepherd separates the sheep from the goats, and he will put the sheep at his right hand and the goats at the left. Then the king will say to those at his right hand, "Come, you that are blessed by my Father, inherit the kingdom prepared for you from the foundation of the world; for I was hungry and you gave me food, I was thirsty and you gave me something to drink, I was a stranger and you welcomed me, I was naked and you gave me clothing, I was sick and you took care of me, I was in prison and you visited me." Then the righteous will answer him, "Lord, when was it that we saw you hungry and gave you food, or thirsty and gave you something to drink? And when was it that we saw you a stranger and welcomed you, or naked and gave you clothing? And when was it that we saw you sick or in prison and visited you?" And the king will answer them, "Truly I tell you, just as you did it to one of the least of these who are members of my family, you did it to me."

———

The Letter to the Hebrews is anonymous. It is the only epistle in the New Testament that does not begin with a greeting with the name of its author. In fact, it reads more like a sermon than a letter. The Letter refers in 10:32–34 to an unidentified persecution, perhaps that of Nero in 64 CE [Chapter One, section 6], so the letter must follow that event. It is usually dated around 85 CE. The following exhortation illustrates that by the end of first century Christians felt bound to their fellow Christians imprisoned for their faith.

Hebrews 13:3

Remember those who are in prison, as though you were in prison with them; those who are being tortured, as though you yourselves were being tortured.

NOTES AND QUESTIONS

1. *Prison Ministry and Religiously Motivated Prison Reform.* Guided by the teachings of religious texts such as those cited above, believers have long explored the social implications of their faith. This has led them not only to engage in ministry to those in prison, but also to promote prison reform. *See* Kenneth Scott Latourette, *A History of Christianity* 980–82, 1032, 1336 (1953). For a discussion of the relationship between biblical teaching and prison reform, *see* Lee Griffith, *The Fall of the Prison: Biblical Perspectives on Prison Abolition* (1993).

As noted above in Chapter One, many biblical characters and writers received punishment at the hands of the ruling authorities. Several biblical authors composed their writings while under arrest or behind prison walls and bars, experiencing first hand the deprivation of liberty at the heart of incarceration, and the other forms of punishment routinely meted out in jails. *See, e.g.,* Ephesians; Philippians; Colossians; 2 Timothy; Philemon. Over the centuries other believers have also experienced the harsh conditions of incarceration, and these experiences contributed to the shape of their ministries, sometimes spawning reform movements that resulted in significant changes in prison conditions. *See* Henry James Nicoll, *Great Movements, and Those Who Achieved Them* 1–47 (1882). On other occasions a believer's incarceration has produced highly influential literature. For example, during an incarceration in 1963, the Reverend Martin Luther King, Jr. wrote his famous *Letter from Birmingham*

Jail. Its stirring rhetoric calling for the liberation of those held captive by racial discrimination was all the more credible because written by a pastor behind bars for his nonviolent protest against racial injustice [Chapter Fifteen, section 3]. Another famous jailhouse experience was that of Charles Colson, a White House lawyer convicted of felonies associated with the abuse of power in the Watergate scandal. Colson's religious conversion while in prison led him to launch a ministry known as Prison Fellowship, which serves prisoners and their families and which seeks to address the conditions of incarceration in America.

Religious groups and revival movements frequently provided the impetus in America for prison reform. William Penn and other Quakers were advocates of prison reform early in American history. At a time when capital punishment was common even for relatively minor offenses, Penn abolished all capital offenses except murder; and he ordered labor as a punishment for crime. In 1787, a group of Quakers established the first prison reform group, the Philadelphia Society for Alleviating the Miseries of Public Prisons. This organization existed to create a humanitarian penitentiary that operated under the "obligations of benevolence." *See* Larry E. Sullivan, *The Prison Reform Movement: Forlorn Hope* 4–9 (1990); Norval Morris and David J. Rothman, eds., *The Oxford History of the Prison: The Practice of Punishment in Western Society* 95–97 (1995). Out of the eighteenth century revivals in England, John Howard emerged as a leader in prison reform. A close friend of the Methodist preacher John Wesley, Howard labored to change the appalling conditions in European prisons, and he inspired several acts of the English Parliament to improve these conditions. *See* Howard, *The State of the Prisons* (1777); *Account of the Principal Lazarettos in Europe* (1789). Out of the Second Awakening—a revivalist movement from the last decade of the eighteenth century through the first decades of the nineteenth century—the Reverend Louis Dwight and others became leaders of humanitarian causes aimed at improving conditions of prisoners. *See* Sydney E. Ahlstrom, 2 *A Religious History of the American People* 87 (1975). Later in the century Dorothea Dix had a profound impact on penology with her *Remarks on Prisons* (1845).

Beyond its role in prison reform, religion has also played an important role in meeting the needs of prisoners. For example, many prisons have staff chaplains who minister to the religious needs of prisoners. Prisoners have relatively easy access to clergy and others involved in various types of prison ministry. For a discussion of the role of the clergy in the rehabilitation of criminal offenders, *see* Morris & Rothman 85–86, 95–97, 116–119.

2. *Dietary Laws of Jews and Muslims*. In *Kahane v. Carlson*, 527 F.2d 492 (2d Cir. 1975), the court required prison officials to demonstrate that their refusal to provide kosher food for Orthodox Jewish prisoners was the least restrictive means of achieving a compelling penological interest. The court impliedly rejected the approach of a district court in the same circuit that upheld the view that the cost of providing kosher meals was a compelling governmental interest. *United States v. Huss*, 394 F. Supp. 752 (S.D.N.Y. 1975). After *Employment Division v. Smith* [section 10 below] shifted the standards for determining a free exercise violation, one appellate court intimated that a Muslim prisoner's request for a pork-free diet might be rejected since the government's interest need not be "compelling." *Hunafa v. Murphy*, 907 F.2d 46 (7th Cir. 1990). This case was cited in the hearings before Congress on the

Religious Freedom Restoration Act of 1993 [section 10 below] as an example of the need for the legislation.

3. *Islam and the Practice of Jumu'ah*. Islam, a major world religion was promulgated by the prophet Muhammad in Arabia in the seventh century C.E. The basic belief of Islam is expressed in the *shahadah*: "There is no God but Allah, and Muhammad is his prophet." The word *islam* literally means surrender, and indicates acceptance of the will of Allah by the believer, called a Muslim (from the active participle of *islam*). Islam, a major world religion was revealed to Prophet Muhammad in Arabia in the seventh century CE. The basic belief of Islam is expressed in the shahadah: "There is no god but God ("Allah" in Arabic), and Muhammad is his Prophet." The word "Islam" literally means surrender, and indicates acceptance of the will of God by the believer, called a Muslim (from the active participle of *islam*). This has been often misunderstood as an injunction to be passive. In fact, the surrender simply indicates a recognition that all human action is subject to divine will.

Islamic doctrine, law, and thinking is based primarily upon the *Qur'an* (literally, "that which is read or recited"), regarded as the Word of God delivered by the archangel Gabriel to Prophet Muhammad. Divine revelation began in Mecca, where the Prophet lived, and continued in Madina after he fled to it (the "*hijirah*") to escape persecution by his own powerful tribe in Mecca. The Islamic calendar begins with this event; thus the year 622 CE = 1 AH, or Anno Hegirae (year of the *hijirah*).

Secondary sources of Islamic law and thought include: (1) the *sunnah* (the example and words of the Prophet); (2) *ijma'* (consensus of the community); and (3) *ijtihad* (literally, to exert oneself), or individual endeavor to find the legal or doctrinal solution to a new problem by means of deductive reasoning by analogy to other matters.

The five pillars of Islam, or duties to be observed by Muslims are: (1) the profession of faith in the *shahadah,* (2) five daily prayers, (3) *zakat* (similar to tithing), (4) fasting during the month of Ramadan, and (5) a pilgrimage to Mecca. Some of these pillars, such as fasting, pilgrimage and zakat, are subject to the ability of the individual to perform them. For example, ill health exempts a person from fasting, if a poor person is fed instead. The pilgrimage is a duty of those who are healthy enough to perform it and can financially afford it. The five prayers referred to above include a noon prayer known as *salat az-zuhr*. On Friday, it is encouraged that this noon prayer (*salat*) is performed with other Muslims in the mosque. It is called the *Jum'ah* prayer. When Muslims enter a mosque, they are encouraged to salute it by praying two *raka'hs* to God (a unit of prayer involving bowing and kneeling).

They are also encouraged to follow the Prophet's *sunna* by performing two additional *rak'ahs* to God. The *juma'h* service begins, as usual, with a call to prayer (*adhan*), followed by a *khutbah* (sermon) usually given by the leader of the prayer (imam), and divided into two parts, the first of which is long. Sometimes, another person delivers one of the two parts. The *khutbah* is followed by two *rak'ahs*.

Islamic beliefs and practices are critical to the understanding of the following case. In the statement of facts the Court referred to the text from the *Qur'an* cited below and to an amicus brief for Imam Jamil Abdullah Al-Amin et al., which explained these beliefs and practices. Did the Court take these positions seriously in its legal analysis? Why did 31 State Attorneys General urge the Court to rule in favor of the warden? Why did many of these state officials oppose the Religious Freedom Restoration Act of 1993 without an amendment barring prisoners from invoking its protections [section 10 below], and why did so many of these state officials oppose the Religious Land Use and Institutionalized Persons Act of 2000 [section 11 below], which includes state prisoners within the scope of its protection?

The Qur'an, 62:9–10

O you who believe! When the call is made for prayer on Friday, then hasten to the remembrance of God and leave off worldly commerce; that is better for you, if you but knew. And when the prayer is ended, then disperse freely through the land and seek of God's bounty, and remember God frequently, that you may prosper.

O'Lone v. Estate of Shabazz

482 U.S. 342 (1987).

Laurie M. Hodian, Deputy Attorney General of New Jersey, argued the cause for petitioners. With her on the briefs were *W. Cary Edwards*, Attorney General, and *James J. Ciancia*, Assistant Attorney General.

Roger Clegg argued the cause for the United States as *amicus curiae* urging reversal. With him on the brief were *Solicitor General Fried*, *Assistant Attorney General Weld*, and *Deputy Solicitor General Bryson*.

James Katz argued the cause and filed a brief for respondents.

A brief of *amici curiae* urging reversal was filed for the Commonwealth of Pennsylvania et al. by *LeRoy S. Zimmerman*, Attorney General of Pennsylvania, *Amy Zapp*, Deputy Attorney General, *John G. Knorr III*, Senior Deputy Attorney General, and *Andrew S. Gordon*, Chief Deputy Attorney General, *Charles A. Graddick*, Attorney General of Alabama, *Ronald W. Lorensen*, Acting Attorney General of Alaska, *Robert K. Corbin*, Attorney General of Arizona, *Steven Clark*, Attorney General of Arkansas, *John K. Van de Kamp*, Attorney General of California, *Duane Woodard*, Attorney General of Colorado, *Charles M. Oberly III*, Attorney General of Delaware, *Jim Smith*, Attorney General of Florida, *Corinne K. A. Watanabe*, Attorney General of Hawaii, *James T. Jones*, Attorney General of Idaho, *Linley E. Pearson*, Attorney General of Indiana, *Robert P. Stephan*, Attorney General of Kansas, *William J. Guste, Jr.*, Attorney General of Louisiana, *Stephen H. Sachs*, Attorney General of Maryland, *Francis X. Bellotti*, Attorney General of Massachusetts, *Frank J. Kelley*, Attorney General of Michigan, *Hubert H. Humphrey III*, Attorney General of Minnesota, *Edwin Lloyd Pittman*, Attorney General of Mississippi, *William L. Webster*, Attorney General of Missouri, *Robert M. Spire*, Attorney General of Nebraska, *Brian McKay*, Attorney General of Nevada, *Lacy H. Thornburg*, Attorney General of North Carolina, *Nicholas J. Spaeth*, Attorney General of North Dakota, *Anthony J. Celebrezze, Jr.*, Attorney General of Ohio, *Dave Frohnmayer*, Attorney General of Oregon, *T. Travis Medlock*, Attorney General of South Carolina, *Mark V. Meierhenry*, Attorney General of South Dakota, *W. J. Michael Cody*, Attorney General of Tennessee, *Mary Sue Terry*, Attorney General of Virginia, *Kenneth O. Eikenberry*, Attorney General of Washington, *A. G. McClintock*, Attorney General of Wyoming, and *James R. Murphy*, Acting Corporate Counsel of the District of Columbia.

Briefs of *amici curiae* urging affirmance were filed for the American Civil Liberties Union et al. by *Eric Neisser, Alvin J. Bronstein, David B. Goldstein, Edward I. Koren*, and *Elizabeth Alexander*; for the American Jewish Congress et al. by *Marc D. Stern* and *Amy Adelson*; for the Catholic League for Religious and Civil Rights et al. by *Steven Frederick McDowell*; for the Christian Legal Society et al. by *Michael J. Woodruff* and *Samuel E. Ericsson*; for the Prisoners' Rights Project of the Legal Aid Society of the city of New York et al. by *Philip L. Weinstein, David A. Lewis*, and *Stephen M. Latimer*; for Imam Jamil Abdullah Al–Amin et al. by *Ellen J. Winner, James G. Abourezk*, and *Albert P. Mokhiber*; and for Len Marek et al. by *Steven C. Moore* and *Walter R. Echo–Hawk*.

■ CHIEF JUSTICE REHNQUIST delivered the opinion of the Court in which JUSTICES WHITE, POWELL, O'CONNOR, and SCALIA joined.

This case requires us to consider once again the standard of review for prison regulations claimed to inhibit the exercise of constitutional rights. Respondents, members of the Islamic faith, were prisoners in New Jersey's Leesburg State Prison.[1] They challenged policies adopted by prison officials which resulted in their inability to attend Jumu'ah, a weekly Muslim congregational service regularly held in the main prison building and in a separate facility known as "the Farm." Jumu'ah is commanded by the Koran and must be held every Friday after the sun reaches its zenith and before the Asr, or afternoon prayer. There is no question that respondents' sincerely held religious beliefs compelled attendance at Jumu'ah. We hold that the prison regulations here challenged did not violate respondents' rights under the Free Exercise Clause of the First Amendment to the United States Constitution.

Inmates at Leesburg are placed in one of three custody classifications. Maximum security and "gang minimum" security inmates are housed in the main prison building, and those with the lowest classification—full minimum—live in "the Farm." Both respondents were classified as gang minimum security prisoners when this suit was filed, and respondent Mateen was later classified as full minimum. [The Court described changes in prison policy relating to classification of prisoners that prompted this litigation]. . . .

Significant problems arose with those inmates assigned to outside work details. Some avoided reporting for their assignments, while others found reasons for returning to the main building during the course of the workday (including their desire to attend religious services). Evidence showed that the return of prisoners during the day resulted in security risks and administrative burdens that prison officials found unacceptable. Because details of inmates were supervised by only one guard, the whole

---

1. Respondent Shabazz died on January 15, 1986.

detail was forced to return to the main gate when one prisoner desired to return to the facility. The gate was the site of all incoming foot and vehicle traffic during the day, and prison officials viewed it as a high security risk area. When an inmate returned, vehicle traffic was delayed while the inmate was logged in and searched.

In response to these burdens, Leesburg officials took steps to ensure that those assigned to outside details remained there for the whole day. Thus, arrangements were made to have lunch and required medications brought out to the prisoners, and appointments with doctors and social workers were scheduled for the late afternoon. These changes proved insufficient, however, and prison officials began to study alternatives. After consulting with the director of social services, the director of professional services, and the prison's imam and chaplain, prison officials in March 1984 issued a policy memorandum which prohibited inmates assigned to outside work details from returning to the prison during the day except in the case of emergency.

The prohibition of returns prevented Muslims assigned to outside work details from attending Jumu'ah. Respondents filed suit under 42 U.S.C. § 1983, alleging that the prison policies unconstitutionally denied them their Free Exercise rights under the First Amendment, as applied to the States through the Fourteenth Amendment. The District Court, applying the standards announced in an earlier decision of the Court of Appeals for the Third Circuit, concluded that no constitutional violation had occurred. The District Court decided that Standard 853 and the March 1984 prohibition on returns "plausibly advance" the goals of security, order, and rehabilitation. It rejected alternative arrangements suggested by respondents, finding that "no less restrictive alternative could be adopted without potentially compromising a legitimate institutional objective."

The Court of Appeals, *sua sponte* hearing the case en banc, decided that its earlier decision relied upon by the District Court was not sufficiently protective of prisoners' free exercise rights, and went on to state that prison policies could be sustained only if: "the state . . . show[s] that the challenged regulations were intended to serve, and do serve, the important penological goal of security, and that no reasonable method exists by which [prisoners'] religious rights can be accommodated without creating bona fide security problems. The expert testimony of prison officials should be given due weight, but such testimony is not dispositive of the issue whether no reasonable adjustment is possible. . . . Where it is found that reasonable methods of accommodation can be adopted without sacrificing either the state's interest in security or the prisoners' interest in freely exercising their religious rights, the state's refusal to allow the observance of a central religious practice cannot be justified and violates the prisoner's first amendment rights." *Shabazz v. O'Lone*, 782 F.2d 416, 420 (CA3 1986) (footnotes omitted).

In considering whether a potential method of accommodation is reasonable, the court added, relevant factors include cost, the effects of overcrowding, understaffing, and inmates' demonstrated proclivity to unruly conduct. The case was remanded to the District Court for reconsideration under the standards enumerated in the opinion. We granted certiorari to consider the important federal constitutional issues presented by the Court of Appeals' decision, and to resolve apparent confusion among the Courts of Appeals on the proper standards to be applied in considering prisoners' free exercise claims.

Several general principles guide our consideration of the issues presented here. First, "convicted prisoners do not forfeit all constitutional protections by reason of their conviction and confinement in prison" (cases omitted). Inmates clearly retain protections afforded by the First Amendment, *Pell v. Procunier*, 417 U.S. 817, 822 (1974), including its directive that no law shall prohibit the free exercise of religion. See *Cruz v. Beto*, 405 U.S. 319 (1972) (*per curiam*). Second, "lawful incarceration brings about the necessary withdrawal or limitation of many privileges and rights, a retraction justified by the considerations underlying our penal system." *Price v. Johnston*, 334 U.S. 266, 285 (1948). The limitations on the exercise of constitutional rights arise both from the fact of incarceration and from valid penological objectives—including deterrence of crime, rehabilitation of prisoners, and institutional security [cases omitted].

In considering the appropriate balance of these factors, we have often said that evaluation of penological objectives is committed to the considered judgment of prison administrators, "who are actually charged with and trained in the running of the particular institution under examination" [cases omitted]. To ensure that courts afford appropriate deference to prison officials, we have determined that prison regulations alleged to infringe constitutional rights are judged under a "reasonableness" test less restrictive than that ordinarily applied to alleged infringements of fundamental constitutional rights. We recently restated the proper standard: "When a prison regulation impinges on inmates' constitutional rights, the regulation is valid if it is reasonably related to legitimate penological interests." *Turner v. Safley*, 482 U.S. 84 (1987). This approach ensures the ability of corrections officials "to anticipate security problems and to adopt innovative solutions to the intractable problems of prison administration," *ibid.*, and avoids unnecessary intrusion of the judiciary into problems particularly ill suited to "resolution by decree." [cases omitted].

We think the Court of Appeals decision in this case was wrong when it established a separate burden on prison officials to prove "that no reasonable method exists by which [prisoners'] religious rights can be accommodated without creating bona fide security problems." (Prison officials should be required "to produce convincing evidence that they are unable to satisfy their institutional goals in any way that does not infringe inmates' free exercise rights"). Though the availability of accommodations is relevant to the reasonableness inquiry, we have rejected the notion that "prison officials . . . have to set up and then shoot down every conceivable alternative method of accommodating the claimant's constitutional complaint." *Turner v. Safley*. By placing the burden on prison officials to disprove the availability of alternatives, the approach articulated by the Court of Appeals fails to reflect the respect and deference that the United States Constitution allows for the judgment of prison administrators.

Turning to consideration of the policies challenged in this case, we think the findings of the District Court establish clearly that prison officials have acted in a reasonable manner. *Turner v. Safley* drew upon our previous decisions to identify several factors relevant to this reasonableness determination. First, a regulation must have a logical connection to legitimate governmental interests invoked to justify it. The policies at issue here clearly meet that standard. The requirement that full minimum and gang minimum prisoners work outside the main facility was justified by concerns of institutional order and security, for the District Court found that it was "at least in part a response to a critical overcrowding in the state's prisons, and ... at least in part designed to ease tension and drain on the facilities during that part of the day when the inmates were outside the confines of the main buildings." We think it beyond doubt that the standard is related to this legitimate concern.

The subsequent policy prohibiting returns to the institution during the day also passes muster under this standard. Prison officials testified that the returns from outside work details generated congestion and delays at the main gate, a high risk area in any event. Return requests also placed pressure on guards supervising outside details, who previously were required to "evaluate each reason possibly justifying a return to the facilities and either accept or reject that reason." Rehabilitative concerns further supported the policy; corrections officials sought a simulation of working conditions and responsibilities in society. Chief Deputy Ucci testified: "One of the things that society demands or expects is that when you have a job, you show up on time, you put in your eight hours, or whatever hours you are supposed to put in, and you don't get off.... If we can show inmates that they're supposed to show up for work and work a full day, then when they get out at least we've done something." These legitimate goals were advanced by the prohibition on returns; it cannot seriously be maintained that "the logical connection between the regulation and the asserted goal is so remote as to render the policy arbitrary or irrational." *Turner v. Safley.*

Our decision in *Turner* also found it relevant that "alternative means of exercising the right ... remain open to prison inmates." There are, of course, no alternative means of attending Jumu'ah; respondents' religious beliefs insist that it occur at a particular time. But the very stringent requirements as to the time at which Jumu'ah may be held may make it extraordinarily difficult for prison officials to assure that every Muslim prisoner is able to attend that service. While we in no way minimize the central importance of Jumu'ah to respondents, we are unwilling to hold that prison officials are required by the Constitution to sacrifice legitimate penological objectives to that end.... [W]e think it appropriate to see whether under these regulations respondents retain the ability to participate in other Muslim religious ceremonies. The record establishes that respondents are not deprived of all forms of religious exercise, but instead freely observe a number of their religious obligations. The right to congregate for prayer or discussion is "virtually unlimited except during working hours," and the state-provided imam has free access to the prison. Muslim prisoners are given different meals whenever pork is served in the prison cafeteria. Special arrangements are also made during the month-long observance of Ramadan, a period of fasting and prayer. During Ramadan, Muslim prisoners are awakened at 4 a.m. for an early breakfast, and receive dinner at 8:30 each evening. We think this ability on the part of respondents to participate in other religious observances of their faith supports the conclusion that the restrictions at issue here were reasonable....

We take this opportunity to reaffirm our refusal, even where claims are made under the First Amendment, to "substitute our judgment on ... difficult and sensitive matters of institutional administration," *Block v. Rutherford*, 468 U.S. 576, 588 (1984), for the determinations of those charged with the formidable task of running a prison. Here the District Court decided that the regulations alleged to infringe constitutional rights were reasonably related to legitimate penological objectives. We agree with the District Court, and it necessarily follows that the regulations in question do not offend the Free Exercise Clause of the First Amendment to the United States Constitution. The judgment of the Court of Appeals is therefore *Reversed*.

■ Justice Brennan filed a dissenting opinion, in which Justices Marshall, Blackmun, and Stevens joined.

The religious ceremony that these respondents seek to attend is not presumptively dangerous, and the prison has completely foreclosed respondents' participation in it. I therefore would require prison officials to demonstrate that the restrictions they have imposed are necessary to further an important government interest, and that these restrictions are no greater than necessary to achieve prison objectives.... Even were I to accept the Court's standard of review, however, I would remand the case to the District Court, since that court has not had the opportunity to review respondents' claim under the new standard established by this Court in *Turner*. As the record now stands, the reasonableness of foreclosing respondents' participation in Jumu'ah has not been established.

I

... In reviewing a prisoner's claim of the infringement of a constitutional right, we must therefore begin from the premise that, as members of this society, prisoners retain constitutional rights that limit the exercise of official authority against them. See *Bell v. Wolfish*, 441 U.S. 520, 545 (1979). At the same time, we must acknowledge that incarceration by its nature changes an individual's status in society. Prison officials have the difficult and often thankless job of preserving security in a potentially explosive setting, as well as of attempting to provide rehabilitation that prepares some inmates for re-entry into the social mainstream. Both these demands require the curtailment and elimination of certain rights.

The challenge for this Court is to determine how best to protect those prisoners' rights that remain. Our objective in selecting a standard of review is therefore *not*, as the Court declares, "to ensure that courts afford appropriate deference to prison officials." The Constitution was not adopted as a means of enhancing the efficiency with which government officials conduct their affairs, nor as a blueprint for ensuring sufficient reliance on administrative expertise. Rather, it was meant to provide a bulwark against infringements that might otherwise be justified as necessary expedients of governing. The practice of Europe, wrote James Madison, was "charters of liberty ... granted by power"; of America, "charters of power granted by liberty." 6 *Writings of James Madison* 83 (G. Hunt ed. 1906). While we must give due consideration to the needs of those in power, this Court's role is to ensure that fundamental *restraints* on that power are enforced.

In my view, adoption of "reasonableness" as a standard of review for *all* constitutional challenges by inmates is inadequate to this task. Such a standard is categorically deferential, and does not discriminate among degrees of deprivation.... Various "factors" may be weighed differently in each situation, but the message to prison officials is clear: merely act "reasonably" and your actions will be upheld. If a directive that officials act "reasonably" were deemed sufficient to check all exercises of power, the Constitution would hardly be necessary. Yet the Court deems this single standard adequate to restrain *any* type of conduct in which prison officials might engage....

[I]f the activity in which inmates seek to engage is presumptively dangerous, or if a regulation merely restricts the time, place, or manner in which prisoners may exercise a right, a prison regulation will be invalidated only if there is no reasonable justification for official action. Where exercise of the asserted right is not presumptively dangerous, however, and where the prison has completely deprived an inmate of that right, then prison officials must show that "a particular restriction is necessary to further an important governmental interest, and that the limitations on freedoms occasioned by the restrictions are no greater than necessary to effectuate the governmental objective involved".....

To the extent that prison is meant to inculcate a respect for social and legal norms, a requirement that prison officials persuasively demonstrate the need for the absolute deprivation of inmate rights is consistent with that end. Furthermore, prison officials are in control of the evidence that is essential to establish the superiority of such deprivation over other alternatives. It is thus only fair for these officials to be held to a stringent standard of review in such extreme cases.

The prison in this case has completely prevented respondent inmates from attending the central religious service of their Muslim faith.... The State has neither demonstrated that the restriction is necessary to further an important objective nor proved that less extreme measures may not serve its purpose. Even if I accepted the Court's standard of review, however, I could not conclude on this record that prison officials have proved that it is reasonable to preclude respondents from attending Jumu'ah.

In *Turner*, the Court set forth a framework for reviewing allegations that a constitutional right has been infringed by prison officials. The Court found relevant to that review "whether there are alternative means of exercising the right that remain open to prison inmates." The Court in this case acknowledges that "respondents' sincerely held religious beliefs compe[l] attendance at Jumu'ah," and concedes that there are "no alternative means of attending Jumu'ah." Nonetheless, the Court finds that prison policy does not work a complete deprivation of respondents' asserted religious right, because respondents have the opportunity to participate in other religious activities. This analysis ignores the fact that, as the District Court found, Jumu'ah is the central religious ceremony of Muslims, "comparable to the Saturday service of the Jewish faith and the Sunday service of the various Christian sects." As with other faiths, this ceremony provides a special time in which Muslims "assert their identity as a community covenanted to God." Brief for Imam Jamil Abdullah Al–Amin et al. as *Amici Curiae* 32. As a result: "unlike other Muslim prayers which are performed individually and can be made up if missed, the Jumu'ah is obligatory, cannot be made up, and must be performed in congregation. The Jumu'ah is therefore regarded as the central service of the Muslim religion, and the obligation to attend is commanded by the Qur'an, the central book of the Muslim religion."

In *Turner*, the Court found that the practices of the Federal Bureau of Prisons were relevant to the availability of reasonable alternatives to the policy under challenge.... [I]t is therefore worth noting that Federal Bureau of Prisons regulations require the adjustment of work assignments to permit inmate participation in religious ceremonies, absent a threat to "security, safety, and good order." The Bureau's Directive implementing the regulations on Religious Beliefs and Practices of Committed Offenders (1986), states that, with respect to scheduling religious observances, "the more central the religious activity is to the tenets of the inmate's religious faith, the greater the presumption is for relieving the inmate from the institution program or assignment." Furthermore, the Chaplain Director of the Bureau has spoken directly to the issue of participation of Muslim inmates in Jumu'ah:

"Provision is made, by policy, in all Bureau facilities for the observance of Jumu'ah by all inmates in general population who wish to keep this faith practice. The service is held each Friday afternoon in the general time frame that corresponds to the requirements of Islamic jurisprudence....

"Subject only to restraints of security and good order in the institution all routine and normal work assignments are suspended for the Islamic inmates to ensure freedom to attend such services....

"In those institutions where the outside work details contain Islamic inmates, they are permitted access to the inside of the institution to attend the Jumu'ah."

That Muslim inmates are able to participate in Jumu'ah throughout the entire federal prison system suggests that the practice is, under normal circumstances, compatible with the demands of prison administration. Indeed, the Leesburg State Prison permitted participation in this ceremony for five years, and experienced no threats to security or safety as a result. In light of both standard federal prison practice and Leesburg's own past practice, a reasonableness test in this case demands at least minimal substantiation by prison officials that alternatives that would permit participation in Jumu'ah are infeasible....

[The respondents offered four specific proposals as less restrictive alternatives within the teaching of *Sherbert* [section 5 above]: (1) that gang minimum prisoners be assigned to an alternative inside work detail on Friday, (2) that gang minimum inmates be assigned to work details inside the main building on a regular basis, (3) that gang minimum inmates be assigned to Saturday or Sunday work details, which would allow them to make up any time lost by attending Jumu'ah on Friday, and (4) that minimum security inmates living at the Farm be assigned to jobs either in the Farm building or in its immediate vicinity. On the third proposal Justice Brennan noted:]

The record provides no indication ... of the number of Muslims that would seek such a work detail, the current number of weekend details, or why it would be infeasible simply to reassign current Saturday or Sunday workers to Friday, rather than create additional details. The prison is able to arrange work schedules so that Jewish inmates may attend services on Saturday and Christian inmates may attend services on Sunday. Despite the fact that virtually all inmates are housed in the main building over the weekend, so that the demand on the facility is greater than at any other time, the prison is able to provide sufficient staff coverage to permit Jewish and Christian inmates to participate in their central religious ceremonies. Given the prison's duty to provide Muslims a "reasonable opportunity of pursuing [their] faith comparable to the opportunity afforded fellow prisoners who adhere to conventional religious precepts," *Cruz v. Beto*, 405 U.S. 319, 322 (1972), prison officials should be required to provide more than mere assertions of the infeasibility of weekend details for Muslim inmates.

[On the fourth proposal Brennan noted:]

[P]rison officials stated that such an arrangement might create an "affinity group" of Muslims representing a threat to prison authority. Officials pointed to no such problem in the five years in which Muslim inmates were permitted to assemble for Jumu'ah, and in which the alternative Friday work detail was in existence. Nor could they identify any threat resulting from the fact that during the month of Ramadan all Muslim prisoners participate in both breakfast and dinner at special times. Furthermore, there was no testimony that the concentration of Jewish or Christian inmates on work details or in religious services posed any type of "affinity group" threat. As the record now stands, prison officials have declared that a security risk is created by a grouping of Muslim inmates in the least dangerous security classification, but not by a grouping of maximum security inmates who are concentrated in a work detail inside the main building, and who are the only Muslims assured of participating in Jumu'ah. Surely, prison officials should be required to provide at least some substantiation for this facially implausible contention.... [P]rison officials should be required at a minimum to identify the basis for their assertions....

Incarceration by its nature denies a prisoner participation in the larger human community. To deny the opportunity to affirm membership in a spiritual community, however, may extinguish an inmate's last source of hope for dignity and redemption. Such a denial requires more justification than mere assertion that any other course of action is infeasible. While I would prefer that this case be analyzed under the approach set out in Part I, *supra*, I would at a minimum remand to the District Court for an analysis of respondents' claims in accordance with the standard enunciated by the Court in *Turner* and in this case. I therefore dissent.

NOTES AND QUESTIONS

1. *The Progressive Eclipse of Strict Scrutiny in Free Exercise Cases.* As noted above, the Court began to move away from vigorous protection of religious freedom in *Bowen v. Roy* [section 3 above]. Solicitor General Fried persuaded three members of the Court–Chief Justice Burger and Justices Powell and Rehnquist—to abandon the strict scrutiny standard announced in *Sherbert*. Chief Justice Burger had written in *Yoder* [section 7 above]: "Only *those interests of the highest order* and those not otherwise served can overbalance legitimate claims to the free exercise of religion." In *Bowen v. Roy* he wrote: "the Government meets its burden [in free exercise cases] when it demonstrates that a challenged requirement for governmental benefits, neutral and uniform in its application, is a *reasonable means of promoting a legitimate public interest*" [emphasis added]. A majority of the Court [Justices Brennan, White, Marshall, Blackmun, and O'Connor] expressly rejected this view of the appropriate standard. In *O'Lone* Justices White and O'Connor joined Chief Justice Rehnquist in adopting a reasonableness standard, at least for free exercise claims presented by prisoners. Justice Brennan, the author of *Sherbert*, argued that the prison officials had not met the least restrictive alternative standard with respect to the four alternatives proposed by the Muslim prisoners. The Rehnquist opinion for a majority of the Court ignored this issue. In *Employment Division v. Smith* [section 10 below] Justice Scalia cited the Court's silence in *O'Lone* as evidence that the Court had abandoned strict scrutiny in free exercise cases.

2. *Equal Treatment of Religious Observances by Prisoners.* In *Larson v. Valente* [Chapter Fifteen, section 1] Justice Brennan wrote: "The clearest command of the Establishment Clause is that one religious denomination cannot be officially preferred over another." In his dissent in *O'Lone* he wrote: "Jumu'ah therefore cannot be regarded as one of several essentially fungible religious practices. The ability to engage in other religious activities cannot obscure the fact that the denial at issue in this case is absolute: respondents are completely foreclosed from participating in the core ceremony that reflects their membership in a particular religious community. If a Catholic prisoner were prevented from attending Mass on Sunday, few would regard that deprivation as anything but absolute, even if the prisoner were afforded other opportunities to pray, to discuss the Catholic faith with others, and even to avoid eating meat on Friday if that were a preference." Should accommodation of the religious observances of prisoners depend on the religious community of which they are a member? Does a rule favoring members of one group over another entail difficulties of breeding resentment among prisoners? Are such rules are likely to create difficulties of prison discipline? Should judges defer to wardens once they invoke a talisman like "prison discipline" or "prison security"?

3. *Congressional Response: Religious Freedom Restoration Act of 1993.* As noted above, several state Attorneys General urged the Court to adopt a

deferential standard with respect to prison officials in the *O'Lone* case. At the time of the consideration of the Religious Freedom Restoration Act [section 10 below], these Attorneys General urged the Senate to adopt an amendment to the legislation that would have expressly excluded prisoners from the terms of its coverage. Attorney General Janet Reno and several State Attorneys General opposed the amendment on the view that it is possible to accommodate the fundamental religious rights of prisoners without impairing legitimate governmental interests. Senators Coats, Danforth, Dole, Hatch, Hatfield, Kennedy, and Lieberman spoke of the importance of religious free exercise to prisoners, citing the scriptural texts noted above. 139 *Cong. Rec.* S14461–01 (Oct. 27, 1993). The Senate rejected the proposed amendment by a vote of 58–41. Four years later the Court invalidated the application of RFRA to the States. *City of Boerne v. Flores* 521 U.S. 507 (1997) [section 11 below]. In response to this decision Congress enacted a new law imposing the compelling interest standard on conflicts involving "people under the control of others," such as prisoners and nursing home patients. Religious Land Use and Institutionalized Persons Act of 2000, Pub. L. 106–274, 114 Stat. 803 [section 11 below].

10. Consuming Peyote

Introduction. *Exemptions in Drug Laws for Ceremonial Use of Peyote by Native Americans.* The Federal Government and several States provide exemptions for the religious use of peyote. Thus 21 CFR § 1307.31 (1989) states: "The listing of peyote as a controlled substance in Schedule I does not apply to the nondrug use of peyote in bona fide religious ceremonies of the Native American Church, and members of the Native American Church so using peyote are exempt from registration. Any person who manufactures peyote for or distributes peyote to the Native American Church, however, is required to obtain registration annually and to comply with all other requirements of law." Justice Blackmun's dissent in *Employment Division v. Smith*, 494 U.S. 872, 912, n. 5 (1990) noted that "23 States, including many that have significant Native American populations, have statutory or judicially crafted exemptions in their drug laws for religious use of peyote." *See, e.g.*, Ariz. Rev. Stat. Ann. §§ 13–3402(B)(1)-(3); Colo. Rev. Stat. § 12–22–317(3); N.M. Stat. Ann. § 30–31–6(D). For an example of an exemption for Native Americans in a judicial decision, see the opinion of Justice Matthew O. Tobriner in *People v. Woody*, 61 Cal. 2d 716, 40 Cal. Rptr. 69, 394 P. 2d 813 (1964) (acquitting Navajos for use of peyote in sacred ceremonies "as a sacramental symbol similar to bread and wine in certain Christian churches," noting that the state had failed to show any compelling interest to override the religious claim). For a description of modern use of peyote among Native Americans, *see* Omer C. Stewart, *Peyote Religion: A History* 327–336 (1987); for a description of peyote ceremonies, *see* Edward F. Anderson, *Peyote: The Divine Cactus* 41–65 (1980); Tony Hillerman, *People of Darkness* 153 (1980); and Dennis Tedlock & B. Tedlock eds., *Teachings from the American Earth: Indian Religion and Philosophy* 96–104 (1975); for the view that religious peyote use has been helpful in overcoming alcoholism, *see* Pascarosa & Futterman, "Ethnopsychedelic Therapy for Alcoholics: Observations in the Peyote Ritual of the Native American Church," 8 *J. of Psychedelic Drugs*, No. 3, 215 (1976), and Albaugh & Anderson, "Peyote in the

Treatment of Alcoholism among American Indians," 131 *Am. J. Psychiatry* 1247 (1974).

In the following case, Alfred Smith and Galen Black, members of the Native American Church, were fired from their jobs with a private drug rehabilitation organization because they ingested peyote for sacramental purposes at a ceremony of their church. When Smith and Black applied for unemployment compensation, the Employment Division of the Department of Human Resources determined that they were ineligible for benefits because they had been discharged for work-related "misconduct." At the time of the litigation Oregon did not provide a statutory exemption similar to that discussed above. In the first phase of the litigation [*Smith I*], the Oregon courts declined to reach the issue of whether such an exemption is constitutionally required. The Oregon Supreme Court ruled that the purpose of the "misconduct" provision under which Smith and Black had been disqualified was not to enforce the State's criminal laws but to preserve the financial integrity of the compensation fund. Citing *Sherbert* [section 5 above] and *Thomas* [section four above], the court concluded that Smith and Black were entitled to payment of unemployment benefits, on the ground that the purpose of the "misconduct" provision was inadequate to justify the burden that disqualification imposed on their religious practice. *Smith v. Employment Div., Dept. of Human Resources*, 301 Ore. 209, 217–219, 721 P. 2d 445, 449–450 (1986). The Supreme Court granted certiorari, 480 U.S. 916 (1987). Noting that the Oregon Supreme Court had not decided whether sacramental use of peyote was in fact proscribed by Oregon's controlled substance law, and that this issue was a matter of dispute between the parties, the Court vacated the judgment of the lower court and remanded for further proceedings. *Employment Division v. Smith*, 485 U.S. 660 (1988) (*Smith I*). On remand, the Oregon Supreme Court held that religiously inspired use of peyote fell within the prohibition of the Oregon statute, which "makes no exception for the sacramental use" of the drug. 307 Ore. 68, 72–73, 763 P. 2d 146, 148 (1988). It then considered whether that prohibition was valid under the Free Exercise Clause, and concluded that it was not. The court reaffirmed its previous ruling that the State could not deny unemployment benefits to respondents for having engaged in that practice. The Supreme Court again granted certiorari. 489 U.S. 1077 (1989). Unlike *Bowen v. Roy* [section 3 above], where the Solicitor General argued for a change of the standard governing free exercise claims, *Smith II* took the parties by surprise in the sense that neither the Attorney General of Oregon nor any of the parties anticipated that the Court would use this case as a vehicle for radically altering the standard governing the evaluation of a claimed violation of free exercise. This important doctrinal shift was neither briefed nor argued.

Employment Division v. Smith

494 U.S. 872 (1990).

Dave Frohnmayer, Attorney General of Oregon, argued the cause for petitioners. With him on the briefs were *James E. Mountain, Jr.*, Deputy Attorney General, *Virginia L. Linder*, Solicitor General, and *Michael D. Reynolds*, Assistant Solicitor General.

Craig J. Dorsay argued the cause and filed briefs for respondents.

Briefs of amici curiae urging affirmance were filed for the American Civil Liberties Union et al. by *Steven R. Shapiro* and *John A. Powell*; for the American Jewish Congress by *Amy Adelson, Lois C. Waldman, and Marc D. Stern*; for the Association on American Indian Affairs et al. by *Steven C. Moore* and *Jack Trope*; and for the Council on Religious Freedom by *Lee Boothby* and *Robert W. Nixon*.

■ Justice Scalia delivered the opinion of the Court.

This case requires us to decide whether the Free Exercise Clause of the First Amendment permits the State of Oregon to include religiously in-spired peyote use within the reach of its general criminal prohibition on use of that drug, and thus permits the State to deny unemployment benefits to persons dismissed from their jobs because of such religiously inspired use. . . .

II

Respondents' claim for relief rests on our decisions in *Sherbert v. Verner* [section 5] *Thomas v. Review Bd.* [section 4] and *Hobbie v. Unem-ployment Appeals Comm'n* [section 5], in which we held that a State could not condition the availability of unemployment insurance on an individual's willingness to forgo conduct required by his religion. As we observed in *Smith I*, however, the conduct at issue in those cases was not prohibited by law. We held that distinction to be critical, for "if Oregon does prohibit the religious use of peyote, and if that prohibition is consistent with the Federal Constitution, there is no federal right to engage in that conduct in Oregon," and "the State is free to withhold unemployment compensation from respondents for engaging in work-related misconduct, despite its religious motivation." Now that the Oregon Supreme Court has confirmed that Oregon does prohibit the religious use of peyote, we proceed to consider whether that prohibition is permissible under the Free Exercise Clause.

A

The free exercise of religion means, first and foremost, the right to believe and profess whatever religious doctrine one desires. Thus, the First Amendment obviously excludes all "governmental regulation of religious beliefs as such." *Sherbert* [section 5 above]. The government may not compel affirmation of religious belief, *Torcaso* [Chapter Twelve, section 1], punish the expression of religious doctrines it believes to be false, *Ballard* [Chapter Twelve, section 1], impose special disabilities on the basis of religious views or religious status, *McDaniel v. Paty*, [Chapter Fifteen, section 2], *Fowler v. Rhode Island* [Chapter Thirteen, section 1], *Larson v. Valente* [Chapter Fifteen, section 1], or lend its power to one or the other side in controversies over religious authority or dogma, *Presbyterian Church in U. S., Kedroff*, and *Serbian Eastern Orthodox Diocese* [Chapter Twelve, section 3].

But the "exercise of religion" often involves not only belief and profession but the performance of (or abstention from) physical acts: assembling with others for a worship service, participating in sacramental use of bread and wine, proselytizing, abstaining from certain foods or certain modes of transportation. It would be true, we think (though no case of ours has involved the point), that a State would be "prohibiting the free exercise [of religion]" if it sought to ban such acts or abstentions only when they are engaged in for religious reasons, or only because of the religious belief that they display. It would doubtless be unconstitutional, for example, to ban the casting of "statues that are to be used for worship purposes," or to prohibit bowing down before a golden calf.

Respondents in the present case, however, seek to carry the meaning of "prohibiting the free exercise [of religion]" one large step further. They contend that their religious motivation for using peyote places them beyond the reach of a criminal law that is not specifically directed at their religious practice, and that is concededly constitutional as applied to those who use the drug for other reasons. They assert, in other words, that "prohibiting the free exercise [of religion]" includes requiring any individual to observe a generally applicable law that requires (or forbids) the performance of an act that his religious belief forbids (or requires). As a textual matter, we do not think the words must be given that meaning. It is no more necessary to regard the collection of a general tax, for example, as "prohibiting the free exercise [of religion]" by those citizens who believe support of organized government to be sinful, than it is to regard the same tax as "abridging the freedom . . . of the press" of those publishing companies that must pay the tax as a condition of staying in business. It is a permissible reading of the text, in the one case as in the other, to say that if prohibiting the exercise of religion (or burdening the activity of printing) is not the object of the tax but merely the incidental effect of a generally applicable and otherwise valid provision, the First Amendment has not been offended [omitting cases].

Our decisions reveal that the latter reading is the correct one. We have never held that an individual's religious beliefs excuse him from compliance with an otherwise valid law prohibiting conduct that the State is free to regulate. On the contrary, the record of more than a century of our free exercise jurisprudence contradicts that proposition. As described succinctly by Justice Frankfurter in *Gobitis* [section 3 above]: "Conscientious scruples have not, in the course of the long struggle for religious toleration, relieved the individual from obedience to a general law not aimed at the promotion or restriction of religious beliefs. The mere possession of religious convictions which contradict the relevant concerns of a political society does not relieve the citizen from the discharge of political responsibilities." We first had occasion to assert that principle in *Reynolds* [Chapter Nine] where we rejected the claim that criminal laws against polygamy could not be constitutionally applied to those whose religion commanded the practice. "Laws," we said, "are made for the government of actions, and while they cannot interfere with mere religious belief and opinions, they may with practices. . . . Can a man excuse his practices to the contrary because of his religious belief? To permit this would be to make the professed doctrines of religious belief superior to the law of the land, and in effect to permit every citizen to become a law unto himself."

Subsequent decisions have consistently held that the right of free exercise does not relieve an individual of the obligation to comply with a "valid and neutral law of general applicability on the ground that the law proscribes (or prescribes) conduct that his religion prescribes (or proscribes)." *United States v. Lee* [section 7 above]; see *Gobitis* (collecting cases). In *Prince* [section 1 above] we held that a mother could be prosecuted under the child labor laws for using her children to dispense literature in the streets, her religious motivation notwithstanding. We found no constitutional infirmity in "excluding [these children] from doing there what no other children may do." In *Braunfeld* [Chapter Thirteen, section 2] we upheld Sunday-closing laws against the claim that they burdened the religious practices of persons whose religions compelled them to refrain from work on other days. In *Gillette* [section 4 above] we sustained the military Selective Service System against the claim that it violated free exercise by conscripting persons who opposed a particular war on religious grounds.

Our most recent decision involving a neutral, generally applicable regulatory law that compelled activity forbidden by an individual's religion was *United States v. Lee* [section 7 above]. There, an Amish employer, on behalf of himself and his employees, sought exemption from collection and payment of Social Security taxes on the ground that the Amish faith prohibited participation in governmental support programs. We rejected the claim that an exemption was constitutionally required. There would be no way, we observed, to distinguish the Amish believer's objection to Social Security taxes from the religious objections that others might have to the collection or use of other taxes. "If, for example, a religious adherent believes war is a sin, and if a certain percentage of the federal budget can be identified as devoted to war-related activities, such individuals would have a similarly valid claim to be exempt from paying that percentage of the income tax. The tax system could not function if denominations were allowed to challenge the tax system because tax payments were spent in a manner that violates their religious belief. . . ."

The only decisions in which we have held that the First Amendment bars application of a neutral, generally applicable law to religiously motivated action have involved not the Free Exercise Clause alone, but the Free Exercise Clause in conjunction with other constitutional protections, such as freedom of speech and of the press (citing *Cantwell, Murdock, Follett* [section 1 above]) or the right of parents (citing *Pierce* [Chapter Ten, section 7] and *Yoder* [section 7 above]). Some of our cases prohibiting compelled expression, decided exclusively upon free speech grounds, have also involved freedom of religion (citing *Wooley* and *Barnette* [section 3 above]). And it is easy to envision a case in which a challenge on freedom of association grounds would likewise be reinforced by Free Exercise Clause concerns. Cf. *Roberts v. United States Jaycees*, 468 U.S. 609, 622 (1984) ("An individual's freedom to speak, to worship, and to petition the government for the redress of grievances could not be vigorously protected from interference by the State [if] a correlative freedom to engage in group effort toward those ends were not also guaranteed").

The present case does not present such a hybrid situation, but a free exercise claim unconnected with any communicative activity or parental right. Respondents urge us to hold, quite simply, that when otherwise prohibitable conduct is accompanied by religious convictions, not only the convictions but the conduct itself must be free from governmental regulation. We have never held that, and decline to do so now. There being no contention that Oregon's drug law represents an attempt to regulate religious beliefs, the communication of religious beliefs, or the raising of one's children in those beliefs, the rule to which we have adhered ever since *Reynolds* [Chapter Nine] plainly controls. . . .

B

Respondents argue that even though exemption from generally applicable criminal laws need not automatically be extended to religiously motivated actors, at least the claim for a religious exemption must be evaluated under the balancing test set forth in *Sherbert* [section 5 above]. Under the *Sherbert* test, governmental actions that substantially burden a religious practice must be justified by a compelling governmental interest. Applying that test we have, on three occasions, invalidated state unemployment compensation rules that conditioned the availability of benefits upon an applicant's willingness to work under conditions forbidden by his religion (citing *Sherbert, Thomas*, and *Hobbie* [section 5 above]). We have never invalidated any governmental action on the basis of the *Sherbert* test except the denial of unemployment compensation. Although we have sometimes purported to apply the *Sherbert* test in contexts other than that, we have always found the test satisfied (citing *United States v. Lee* and *Gillette*). In recent years we have abstained from applying the *Sherbert* test (outside the unemployment compensation field) at all. In *Bowen v. Roy* [section 3 above] we declined to apply *Sherbert* analysis to a federal statutory scheme that required benefit applicants and recipients to provide their Social Security numbers. The plaintiffs in that case asserted that it would violate their religious beliefs to obtain and provide a Social Security number for their daughter. We held the statute's application to the plaintiffs valid regardless of whether it was necessary to effectuate a compelling interest. In *Lyng* [section 11 below] we declined to apply *Sherbert* analysis to the Government's logging and road construction activities on lands used for religious purposes by several Native American Tribes, even though it was undisputed that the activities "could have devastating effects on traditional Indian religious practices." In *Goldman* [section 8 above] we rejected application of the *Sherbert* test to military dress regulations that forbade the wearing of yarmulkes. In *O'Lone* [section 9 above] we sustained, without mentioning the *Sherbert* test, a prison's refusal to excuse inmates from work requirements to attend worship services.

Even if we were inclined to breathe into *Sherbert* some life beyond the unemployment compensation field, we would not apply it to require exemptions from a generally applicable criminal law. The *Sherbert* test, it must be recalled, was developed in a context that lent itself to individualized governmental assessment of the reasons for the relevant conduct. As a plurality of the Court noted in *Roy*, a distinctive feature of unemployment compensation programs is that their eligibility criteria invite consideration of the particular circumstances behind an applicant's unemployment: "The statutory conditions [in *Sherbert* and *Thomas*] provided that a person was not eligible for unemployment compensation benefits if, 'without good cause,' he had quit work or refused available work. The 'good cause' standard created a mechanism for individualized exemptions.... " As the plurality pointed out in *Roy*, our decisions in the unemployment cases stand for the proposition that where the State has in place a system of individual exemptions, it may not refuse to extend that system to cases of "religious hardship" without compelling reason.

Whether or not the decisions are that limited, they at least have nothing to do with an across-the-board criminal prohibition on a particular form of conduct.... We conclude today that the sounder approach, and the approach in accord with the vast majority of our precedents, is to hold the test inapplicable to such challenges. The government's ability to enforce generally applicable prohibitions of socially harmful conduct, like its ability to carry out other aspects of public policy, "cannot depend on measuring the effects of a governmental action on a religious objector's spiritual development." *Lyng*. To make an individual's obligation to obey such a law contingent upon the law's coincidence with his religious beliefs, except where the State's interest is "compelling"—permitting him, by virtue of his beliefs, "to become a law unto himself," *Reynolds*—contradicts both constitutional tradition and common sense.

The "compelling government interest" requirement seems benign, because it is familiar from other fields. But using it as the standard that must be met before the government may accord different treatment on the basis of race, or before the government may regulate the content of speech, is not remotely comparable to using it for the purpose asserted here (omitting cases). What it produces in those other fields—equality of treatment and an unrestricted flow of contending speech—are constitutional norms; what it would produce here—a private right to ignore generally applicable laws—is a constitutional anomaly.

Nor is it possible to limit the impact of respondents' proposal by requiring a "compelling state interest" only when the conduct prohibited is "central" to the individual's religion. It is no more appropriate for judges to determine the "centrality" of religious beliefs before applying a "compelling interest" test in the free exercise field, than it would be for them to determine the "importance" of ideas before applying the "compelling interest" test in the free speech field. What principle of law or logic can be brought to bear to contradict a believer's assertion that a particular act is "central" to his personal faith? Judging the centrality of different religious practices is akin to the unacceptable "business of evaluating the relative merits of differing religious claims." *Lee* (Stevens, J., concurring). As we reaffirmed only last Term, "[i]t is not within the judicial ken to question the centrality of particular beliefs or practices to a faith, or the validity of particular litigants' interpretations of those creeds." *Hernandez* [section 1 above]. Repeatedly and in many different contexts, we have warned that courts must not presume to determine the place of a particular belief in a religion or the plausibility of a religious claim (citing *Thomas, Presbyterian Church, Jones v. Wolf*, and *Ballard*).[4]

If the "compelling interest" test is to be applied at all, then, it must be applied across the board, to all actions thought to be religiously commanded. Moreover, if "compelling interest" really means what it says (and watering it down here would subvert its rigor in the other fields where it is applied), many laws will not meet the test. Any society adopting such a system would be courting anarchy, but that danger increases in direct proportion to the society's diversity of religious beliefs, and its determination to coerce or suppress none of them. Precisely because "we are a cosmopolitan nation made up of people of almost every conceivable religious preference," *Braunfeld* [Chapter Thirteen, section 2], and precisely because we value and protect that religious divergence, we cannot afford the luxury of deeming presumptively invalid, as applied to the religious objector, every regulation of conduct that does not protect an interest of the highest order. The rule respondents favor would open the prospect of constitutionally required religious exemptions from civic obligations of almost every conceivable kind—ranging from compulsory military service, to the payment of taxes, to health and safety regulation such as manslaughter and child neglect laws, compulsory vaccination laws, drug laws, and traffic laws; to social welfare legislation such as minimum wage laws, child labor laws, animal cruelty laws, environmental protection laws, and laws providing for equality of opportunity for the races (citing cases). The First Amendment's protection of religious liberty does not require this.[5]

---

4. While arguing that we should apply the compelling interest test in this case, Justice O'Connor nonetheless agrees that "our determination of the constitutionality of Oregon's general criminal prohibition cannot, and should not, turn on the centrality of the particular religious practice at issue." This means, presumably, that compelling-interest scrutiny must be applied to generally applicable laws that regulate or prohibit any religiously motivated activity, no matter how unimportant to the claimant's religion. Earlier in her opinion, however, Justice O'Connor appears to contradict this, saying that the proper approach is "to determine whether the burden on the specific plaintiffs before us is constitutionally significant and whether the particular criminal interest asserted by the State before us is compelling." "Constitutionally significant burden" would seem to be "centrality" under another name. In any case, dispensing with a "centrality" inquiry is utterly unworkable. It would require, for example, the same degree of "compelling state interest" to impede the practice of throwing rice at church weddings as to impede the practice of getting married in church. There is no way out of the difficulty that, if general laws are to be subjected to a "religious practice" exception, both the importance of the law at issue and the centrality of the practice at issue must reasonably be considered.

Nor is this difficulty avoided by Justice Blackmun's assertion that "although ... courts should refrain from delving into questions whether, as a matter of religious doctrine, a particular practice is 'central' to the religion, ... I do not think this means that the courts must turn a blind eye to the severe impact of a State's restrictions on the adherents of a minority religion." As Justice Blackmun's opinion proceeds to make clear, inquiry into "severe impact" is no different from inquiry into centrality. He has merely substituted for the question "How important is X to the religious adherent?" the question "How great will be the harm to the religious adherent if X is taken away?" There is no material difference.

5. Justice O'Connor contends that the "parade of horribles" in the text only "demonstrates ... that courts have been quite capable of ... strik[ing] sensible balances between religious liberty and competing state interests." But the cases we cite have struck "sensible balances" only because they have

Values that are protected against government interference through enshrinement in the Bill of Rights are not thereby banished from the political process. Just as a society that believes in the negative protection accorded to the press by the First Amendment is likely to enact laws that affirmatively foster the dissemination of the printed word, so also a society that believes in the negative protection accorded to religious belief can be expected to be solicitous of that value in its legislation as well. It is therefore not surprising that a number of States have made an exception to their drug laws for sacramental peyote use.... But to say that a nondiscriminatory religious-practice exemption is permitted, or even that it is desirable, is not to say that it is constitutionally required, and that the appropriate occasions for its creation can be discerned by the courts. It may fairly be said that leaving accommodation to the political process will place at a relative disadvantage those religious practices that are not widely engaged in; but that unavoidable consequence of democratic government must be preferred to a system in which each conscience is a law unto itself or in which judges weigh the social importance of all laws against the centrality of all religious beliefs.

Because respondents' ingestion of peyote was prohibited under Oregon law, and because that prohibition is constitutional, Oregon may, consistent with the Free Exercise Clause, deny respondents unemployment compensation when their dismissal results from use of the drug. The decision of the Oregon Supreme Court is accordingly reversed. It is so ordered.

■ JUSTICE O'CONNOR, with whom JUSTICE BRENNAN, JUSTICE MARSHALL, and JUSTICE BLACKMUN join as to Parts I and II, concurring in the judgment.*

Although I agree with the result the Court reaches in this case, I cannot join its opinion. In my view, today's holding dramatically departs from well-settled First Amendment jurisprudence, appears unnecessary to resolve the question presented, and is incompatible with our Nation's fundamental commitment to individual religious liberty.

II

The Court today extracts from our long history of free exercise precedents the single categorical rule that "if prohibiting the exercise of religion ... is ... merely the incidental effect of a generally applicable and otherwise valid provision, the First Amendment has not been offended." Indeed, the Court holds that where the law is a generally applicable criminal prohibition, our usual free exercise jurisprudence does not even

all applied the general laws, despite the claims for religious exemption. In any event, Justice O'Connor mistakes the purpose of our parade: it is not to suggest that courts would necessarily permit harmful exemptions from these laws (though they might), but to suggest that courts would constantly be in the business of determining whether the "severe impact" of various laws on religious practice (to use Justice Blackmun's terminology) or the "constitutiona[l] significan[ce]" of the "burden on the specific plaintiffs" (to use Justice O'Connor's terminology) suffices to permit us to confer an exemption. It is a parade of horribles because it is horrible to contemplate that federal judges will regularly balance against the importance of general laws the significance of religious practice.

* Although Justice Brennan, Justice Marshall, and Justice Blackmun join Parts I and II of this opinion, they do not concur in the judgment.

apply. To reach this sweeping result, however, the Court must not only give a strained reading of the First Amendment but must also disregard our consistent application of free exercise doctrine to cases involving generally applicable regulations that burden religious conduct.

A

The Free Exercise Clause of the First Amendment commands that "Congress shall make no law . . . prohibiting the free exercise [of religion]." In *Cantwell* [section 1 above] we held that this prohibition applies to the States by incorporation into the Fourteenth Amendment and that it categorically forbids government regulation of religious beliefs. As the Court recognizes, however, the "free exercise" of religion often, if not invariably, requires the performance of (or abstention from) certain acts; cf. 3 *A New English Dictionary on Historical Principles* 401–402 (J. Murray ed. 1897) (defining "exercise" to include "[t]he practice and performance of rites and ceremonies, worship, etc.; the right or permission to celebrate the observances (of a religion)" and religious observances such as acts of public and private worship, preaching, and prophesying). "[B]elief and action cannot be neatly confined in logic-tight compartments." *Yoder* [section 7 above]. Because the First Amendment does not distinguish between religious belief and conduct, conduct motivated by sincere religious belief, like the belief itself, must be at least presumptively protected by the Free Exercise Clause.

The Court today, however, interprets the Clause to permit the government to prohibit, without justification, conduct mandated by an individual's religious beliefs, so long as that prohibition is generally applicable. But a law that prohibits certain conduct—conduct that happens to be an act of worship for someone—manifestly does prohibit that person's free exercise of his religion. A person who is barred from engaging in religiously motivated conduct is barred from freely exercising his religion. Moreover, that person is barred from freely exercising his religion regardless of whether the law prohibits the conduct only when engaged in for religious reasons, only by members of that religion, or by all persons. It is difficult to deny that a law that prohibits religiously motivated conduct, even if the law is generally applicable, does not at least implicate First Amendment concerns.

The Court responds that generally applicable laws are "one large step" removed from laws aimed at specific religious practices. The First Amendment, however, does not distinguish between laws that are generally applicable and laws that target particular religious practices. Indeed, few States would be so naive as to enact a law directly prohibiting or burdening a religious practice as such. Our free exercise cases have all concerned generally applicable laws that had the effect of significantly burdening a religious practice. If the First Amendment is to have any vitality, it ought not be construed to cover only the extreme and hypothetical situation in which a State directly targets a religious practice. As we have noted in a slightly different context, " '[s]uch a test has no basis in precedent and relegates a serious First Amendment value to the barest level of minimum scrutiny that the Equal Protection Clause already provides.' " *Hobbie* [section 5 above], quoting *Bowen v. Roy* [section 3 above] (opinion concurring in part and dissenting in part).

To say that a person's right to free exercise has been burdened, of course, does not mean that he has an absolute right to engage in the conduct. Under our established First Amendment jurisprudence, we have recognized that the freedom to act, unlike the freedom to believe, cannot be absolute. See, e.g., *Cantwell* [section 1 above]; *Reynolds* [Chapter Nine]. Instead, we have respected both the First Amendment's express textual mandate and the governmental interest in regulation of conduct by requiring the government to justify any substantial burden on religiously motivated conduct by a compelling state interest and by means narrowly tailored to achieve that interest. See *Hernandez* [section 1 above]; *Hobbie* [section 5 above]; *United States v. Lee* [section 7 above]; *Thomas* [section 4 above]; *McDaniel v. Paty* [Chapter Fifteen, section 2]; *Yoder* [section 7 above]; *Gillette,* [section 4 above]; *Sherbert* [section 5 above]; *Roy* [section 3 above]; *Barnette* [section 3 above]. The compelling interest test effectuates the First Amendment's command that religious liberty is an independent liberty, that it occupies a preferred position, and that the Court will not permit encroachments upon this liberty, whether direct or indirect, unless required by clear and compelling governmental interests "of the highest order," *Yoder.* "Only an especially important governmental interest pursued by narrowly tailored means can justify exacting a sacrifice of First Amendment freedoms as the price for an equal share of the rights, benefits, and privileges enjoyed by other citizens." *Roy.*

The Court attempts to support its narrow reading of the Clause by claiming that "[w]e have never held that an individual's religious beliefs excuse him from compliance with an otherwise valid law prohibiting conduct that the State is free to regulate." But as the Court later notes, as it must, in cases such as *Cantwell* and *Yoder* we have in fact interpreted the Free Exercise Clause to forbid application of a generally applicable prohibition to religiously motivated conduct. See *Cantwell, Yoder.* Indeed, in *Yoder* we expressly rejected the interpretation the Court now adopts (citation omitted).

The Court endeavors to escape from our decisions in *Cantwell* and *Yoder* by labeling them "hybrid" decisions, but there is no denying that both cases expressly relied on the Free Exercise Clause (citation omitted), and that we have consistently regarded those cases as part of the mainstream of our free exercise jurisprudence. Moreover, in each of the other cases cited by the Court to support its categorical rule, we rejected the particular constitutional claims before us only after carefully weighing the competing interests. *Prince* [section 1 above] (state interest in regulating children's activities justifies denial of religious exemption from child labor laws); *Braunfeld* [Chapter Thirteen, section 2] (state interest in uniform day of rest justifies denial of religious exemption from Sunday closing law); *Gillette* [section 4 above] (state interest in military affairs justifies denial of religious exemption from conscription laws); *Lee* (state interest in comprehensive Social Security system justifies denial of religious exemption from mandatory participation requirement). That we rejected the free exercise claims in those cases hardly calls into question the applicability of First Amendment doctrine in the first place. Indeed, it is surely unusual to judge the vitality of a constitutional doctrine by looking to the win-loss record of the plaintiffs who happen to come before us.

B

... The Court today gives no convincing reason to depart from settled First Amendment jurisprudence. There is nothing talismanic about neutral laws of general applicability or general criminal prohibitions, for laws neutral toward religion can coerce a person to violate his religious conscience or intrude upon his religious duties just as effectively as laws aimed at religion. Although the Court suggests that the compelling interest test, as applied to generally applicable laws, would result in a "constitutional anomaly," the First Amendment unequivocally makes freedom of religion, like freedom from race discrimination and freedom of speech, a "constitutional nor[m]," not an "anomaly." Nor would application of our established free exercise doctrine to this case necessarily be incompatible with our equal protection cases.... We have in any event recognized that the Free Exercise Clause protects values distinct from those protected by the Equal Protection Clause. See *Hobbie*. As the language of the Clause itself makes clear, an individual's free exercise of religion is a preferred constitutional activity. *See, e.g.*, McConnell, Accommodation of Religion, 1985 *S. Ct. Rev.* 1, 9 ("[T]he text of the First Amendment itself 'singles out' religion for special protections"). A law that makes criminal such an activity therefore triggers constitutional concern—and heightened judicial scrutiny—even if it does not target the particular religious conduct at issue.... The Court's parade of horribles not only fails as a reason for discarding the compelling interest test, it instead demonstrates just the opposite: that courts have been quite capable of applying our free exercise jurisprudence to strike sensible balances between religious liberty and competing state interests.

Finally, the Court today suggests that the disfavoring of minority religions is an "unavoidable consequence" under our system of government and that accommodation of such religions must be left to the political process. In my view, however, the First Amendment was enacted precisely to protect the rights of those whose religious practices are not shared by the majority and may be viewed with hostility. The history of our free exercise doctrine amply demonstrates the harsh impact majoritarian rule has had on unpopular or emerging religious groups such as the Jehovah's Witnesses and the Amish. Indeed, the words of Justice Jackson in *Barnette* (overruling *Gobitis*) are apt: "The very purpose of a Bill of Rights was to withdraw certain subjects from the vicissitudes of political controversy, to place them beyond the reach of majorities and officials and to establish them as legal principles to be applied by the courts. One's right to life, liberty, and property, to free speech, a free press, *freedom of worship* and assembly, and other fundamental rights may not be submitted to vote; they depend on the outcome of no elections." See also *Ballard* [Chapter Twelve, section 1] ("The Fathers of the Constitution were not unaware of the varied and extreme views of religious sects, of the violence of disagreement among them, and of the lack of any one religious creed on which all men would agree. They fashioned a charter of government which envisaged the widest possible toleration of conflicting views"). The compelling interest test reflects the First Amendment's mandate of preserving religious liberty to the fullest extent possible in a pluralistic society. For the Court to deem this command a "luxury" is to denigrate "[t]he very purpose of a Bill of Rights."

III

The Court's holding today not only misreads settled First Amendment precedent; it appears to be unnecessary to this case. I would reach the same result applying our established free exercise jurisprudence.

A

There is no dispute that Oregon's criminal prohibition of peyote places a severe burden on the ability of respondents to freely exercise their religion. Peyote is a sacrament of the Native American Church and is regarded as vital to respondents' ability to practice their religion. As we noted in *Smith I*, the Oregon Supreme Court concluded that "the Native American Church is a recognized religion, that peyote is a sacrament of that church, and that respondent's beliefs were sincerely held." Under Oregon law, as construed by that State's highest court, members of the Native American Church must choose between carrying out the ritual embodying their religious beliefs and avoidance of criminal prosecution. That choice is, in my view, more than sufficient to trigger First Amendment scrutiny.

There is also no dispute that Oregon has a significant interest in enforcing laws that control the possession and use of controlled substances by its citizens. See, e. g., *Sherbert; Yoder* (citations omitted). As we recently noted, drug abuse is "one of the greatest problems affecting the health and welfare of our population" and thus "one of the most serious problems confronting our society today." *Treasury Employees v. Von Raab*, 489 U.S. 656, 668, 674 (1989). Indeed, under federal law (incorporated by Oregon law in relevant part, see Ore. Rev. Stat. § 475.005(6) (1987)), peyote is specifically regulated as a Schedule I controlled substance, which means that Congress has found that it has a high potential for abuse, that there is no currently accepted medical use, and that there is a lack of accepted safety for use of the drug under medical supervision. See 21 U.S.C. § 812(b)(1).... In light of our recent decisions holding that the governmental interests in the collection of income tax, *Hernandez*, a comprehensive Social Security system, *Lee,* and military conscription, *Gillette,* are compelling, respondents do not seriously dispute that Oregon has a compelling interest in prohibiting the possession of peyote by its citizens.

B

Thus, the critical question in this case is whether exempting respondents from the State's general criminal prohibition "will unduly interfere with fulfillment of the governmental interest" (citations omitted). Although the question is close, I would conclude that uniform application of Oregon's criminal prohibition is "essential to accomplish," *Lee*, its overriding interest in preventing the physical harm caused by the use of a Schedule I controlled substance. Oregon's criminal prohibition represents that State's judgment that the possession and use of controlled substances, even by only one person, is inherently harmful and dangerous. Because the health effects caused by the use of controlled substances exist regardless of the motivation of the user, the use of such substances, even for religious purposes, violates the very purpose of the laws that prohibit them. Moreover, in view of the societal interest in preventing trafficking in controlled substances, uniform application of the criminal prohibition at issue is essential to the effectiveness of Oregon's stated interest in preventing any possession of peyote.... For these reasons, I believe that granting a selective exemption in this case would seriously impair Oregon's compelling interest in prohibiting possession of peyote by its citizens. Under such circumstances, the Free Exercise Clause does not require the State to accommodate respondents' religiously motivated conduct....

I would therefore adhere to our established free exercise jurisprudence and hold that the State in this case has a compelling interest in regulating peyote use by its citizens and that accommodating respondents' religiously motivated conduct "will unduly interfere with fulfillment of the governmental interest." *Lee*. Accordingly, I concur in the judgment of the Court.

■ JUSTICE BLACKMUN, with whom JUSTICE BRENNAN and JUSTICE MARSHALL join, dissenting.

This Court over the years painstakingly has developed a consistent and exacting standard to test the constitutionality of a state statute that burdens the free exercise of religion. Such a statute may stand only if the law in general, and the State's refusal to allow a religious exemption in particular, are justified by a compelling interest that cannot be served by less restrictive means.

Until today, I thought this was a settled and inviolate principle of this Court's First Amendment jurisprudence. The majority, however, perfunctorily dismisses it as a "constitutional anomaly." As carefully detailed in Justice O'Connor's concurring opinion, the majority is able to arrive at this view only by mischaracterizing this Court's precedents. The Court discards leading free exercise cases such as *Cantwell* and *Yoder* as "hybrid." The Court views traditional free exercise analysis as somehow inapplicable to criminal prohibitions (as opposed to conditions on the receipt of benefits), and to state laws of general applicability (as opposed, presumably, to laws that expressly single out religious practices). The Court cites cases in which, due to various exceptional circumstances, we found strict scrutiny inapposite, to hint that the Court has repudiated that standard altogether. In short, it effectuates a wholesale overturning of settled law concerning the Religion Clauses of our Constitution. One hopes that the Court is aware of the consequences, and that its result is not a product of overreaction to the serious problems the country's drug crisis has generated.

This distorted view of our precedents leads the majority to conclude that strict scrutiny of a state law burdening the free exercise of religion is a "luxury" that a well-ordered society cannot afford, and that the repression of minority religions is an "unavoidable consequence of democratic government." I do not believe the Founders thought their dearly bought freedom from religious persecution a "luxury," but an essential element of liberty—and they could not have thought religious intolerance "unavoidable," for they drafted the Religion Clauses precisely in order to avoid that intolerance.

For these reasons, I agree with Justice O'Connor's analysis of the applicable free exercise doctrine, and I join parts I and II of her opinion. As she points out, "the critical question in this case is whether exempting respondents from the State's general criminal prohibition 'will unduly interfere with fulfillment of the governmental interest.'" *Lee.* I do disagree, however, with her specific answer to that question.

I

In weighing the clear interest of respondents Smith and Black in the free exercise of their religion against Oregon's asserted interest in enforcing its drug laws, it is important to articulate in precise terms the state interest involved. It is not the State's broad interest in fighting the critical "war on drugs" that must be weighed against respondents' claim, but the State's narrow interest in refusing to make an exception for the religious, ceremonial use of peyote. See *Thomas* ("focus of the inquiry" concerning State's asserted interest must be "properly narrowed"); *Yoder*, ("Where fundamental claims of religious freedom are at stake," the Court will not accept a State's "sweeping claim" that its interest in compulsory education is compelling; despite the validity of this interest "in the generality of cases, we must searchingly examine the interests that the State seeks to promote ... and the impediment to those objectives that would flow from recognizing the claimed Amish exemption"). Failure to reduce the competing interests to the same plane of generality tends to distort the weighing process in the State's favor. See Clark, Guidelines for the Free Exercise Clause, 83 *Harv. L.Rev.* 327, 330–331 (1969) ("The purpose of almost any law can be traced back to one or another of the fundamental concerns of government: public health and safety, public peace and order, defense, revenue. To measure an individual interest directly against one of these rarified values inevitably makes the individual interest appear the less significant"); Pound, A Survey of Social Interests, 57 *Harv. L. Rev.* 1, 2 (1943) ("When it comes to weighing or valuing claims or demands with respect to other claims or demands, we must be careful to compare them on the same plane ... [or else] we may decide the question in advance in our very way of putting it").

The State's interest in enforcing its prohibition, in order to be sufficiently compelling to outweigh a free exercise claim, cannot be merely abstract or symbolic. The State cannot plausibly assert that unbending application of a criminal prohibition is essential to fulfill any compelling interest, if it does not, in fact, attempt to enforce that prohibition. In this case, the State actually has not evinced any concrete interest in enforcing its drug laws against religious users of peyote. Oregon has never sought to prosecute respondents, and does not claim that it has made significant enforcement efforts against other religious users of peyote. The State's asserted interest thus amounts only to the symbolic preservation of an unenforced prohibition. . . .

The carefully circumscribed ritual context in which respondents used peyote is far removed from the irresponsible and unrestricted recreational use of unlawful drugs.[6] The Native American Church's internal restrictions on, and supervision of, its members' use of peyote substantially obviate the State's health and safety concerns. . . .

Moreover, just as in *Yoder*, the values and interests of those seeking a religious exemption in this case are congruent, to a great degree, with those the State seeks to promote through its drug laws. Not only does the church's doctrine forbid nonreligious use of peyote; it also generally advocates self-reliance, familial responsibility, and abstinence from alcohol. See Brief for Association on American Indian Affairs et al. as Amici Curiae 33–34 (the church's "ethical code" has four parts: brotherly love, care of family, self-reliance, and avoidance of alcohol (quoting from the church membership card)). There is considerable evidence that the spiritual and social support provided by the church has been effective in combating the tragic effects of alcoholism on the Native American population (citations omitted). Far from promoting the lawless and irresponsible use of drugs, Native American Church members' spiritual code exemplifies values that Oregon's drug laws are presumably intended to foster.

The State also seeks to support its refusal to make an exception for religious use of peyote by invoking its interest in abolishing drug trafficking. There is, however, practically no illegal traffic in peyote. See *Olsen v. Drug Enforcement Administration*, 878 F. 2d 1458, 1463, 1467 (D.C. Cir. 1989) (quoting DEA Final Order to the effect that total amount of peyote seized and analyzed by federal authorities between 1980 and 1987 was 19.4 pounds; in contrast, total amount of marijuana seized during that period was over 15 million pounds). Also, the availability of peyote for religious use, even if Oregon were to allow an exemption from its criminal laws, would still be strictly controlled by federal regulations, see 21 U.S.C. §§ 821–823 (registration requirements for distribution of controlled substances); 21 CFR § 1307.31 (1989) (distribution of peyote to Native American Church subject to registration requirements), and by the State of Texas, the only State in which peyote grows in significant quantities. Peyote simply is not a popular drug; its distribution for use in religious rituals has nothing to do with the vast and violent traffic in illegal narcotics that plagues this country.

---

6. In this respect, respondents' use of peyote seems closely analogous to the sacramental use of wine by the Roman Catholic Church. During Prohibition, the Federal Government exempted such use of wine from its general ban on possession and use of alcohol. See National Prohibition Act, Title II, § 3, 41 Stat. 308. However compelling the Government's then general interest in prohibiting the use of alcohol may have been, it could not plausibly have asserted an interest sufficiently compelling to outweigh Catholics' right to take communion.

Respondents believe, and their sincerity has never been at issue, that the peyote plant embodies their deity, and eating it is an act of worship and communion. Without peyote, they could not enact the essential ritual of their religion. See Brief for Association on American Indian Affairs et al. as Amici Curiae 5–6 ("To the members, peyote is consecrated with powers to heal body, mind and spirit. It is a teacher; it teaches the way to spiritual life through living in harmony and balance with the forces of the Creation. The rituals are an integral part of the life process. They embody a form of worship in which the sacrament Peyote is the means for communicating with the Great Spirit").

If Oregon can constitutionally prosecute them for this act of worship, they, like the Amish, may be "forced to migrate to some other and more tolerant region." *Yoder*. This potentially devastating impact must be viewed in light of the federal policy—reached in reaction to many years of religious persecution and intolerance—of protecting the religious freedom of Native Americans. See American Indian Religious Freedom Act, 92 Stat. 469, 42 U.S.C. § 1996 (1982 ed.) ("[I]t shall be the policy of the United States to protect and preserve for American Indians their inherent right of freedom to believe, express, and exercise the traditional religions ... , including but not limited to access to sites, use and possession of sacred objects, and the freedom to worship through ceremonials and traditional rites"). Congress recognized that certain substances, such as peyote, "have religious significance because they are sacred, they have power, they heal, they are necessary to the exercise of the rites of the religion, they are necessary to the cultural integrity of the tribe, and, therefore, religious survival." H.R. Rep. No. 95–1308, p. 2 (1978).

The American Indian Religious Freedom Act, in itself, may not create rights enforceable against government action restricting religious freedom, but this Court must scrupulously apply its free exercise analysis to the religious claims of Native Americans, however unorthodox they may be. Otherwise, both the First Amendment and the stated policy of Congress will offer to Native Americans merely an unfulfilled and hollow promise.

III

For these reasons, I conclude that Oregon's interest in enforcing its drug laws against religious use of peyote is not sufficiently compelling to outweigh respondents' right to the free exercise of their religion. Since the State could not constitutionally enforce its criminal prohibition against respondents, the interests underlying the State's drug laws cannot justify its denial of unemployment benefits. Absent such justification, the State's regulatory interest in denying benefits for religiously motivated "misconduct," is indistinguishable from the state interests this Court has rejected in *Frazee, Hobbie, Thomas*, and *Sherbert*. The State of Oregon cannot, consistently with the Free Exercise Clause, deny respondents unemployment benefits.

I dissent.

NOTES AND QUESTIONS

1. *State Legislative Response to Smith: Exempting Ceremonial Use of Peyote from Oregon's Criminal Law.* In his brief in *Smith*, the Attorney General of Oregon, Dave Frohnmayer, argued that "the public interest in controlling the use and availability of dangerous drugs is compelling" and that "government cannot accommodate religious use exemptions from criminal laws regulating dangerous drugs." Pet. Brief at 11, 16. As noted above, Justice O'Connor concluded: "Although the question is close, . . . uniform application of Oregon's criminal prohibition is 'essential to accomplish' its overriding interest in preventing the physical harm caused by the use of a Schedule I controlled substance." After winning in the Supreme Court on a theory he did not advocate (the elimination of the compelling interest standard in free exercise cases), Attorney General Frohnmayer testified before a committee of the Oregon Legislature against the theory he did advocate in the Court, urging the legislature to exempt the sacramental use of peyote by members of the Native American Church. The legislature granted the exemption. Or. Rev. Stat. § 475.992(5) (1993). What does this shift say about the claim that Oregon had a compelling interest in enforcing its drug laws against Native American consuming peyote in a ceremony of their church? If the state really thought that the use of peyote by Natives under these circumstances was so "dangerous" that it could not be accommodated when the brief was being written, why did this "compelling interest" disappear so swiftly after *Smith*?

2. *Scholarly Response to Smith.* Immediately after *Smith*, several scholars vigorously attacked the decision. *See,e.g.,* James D. Gordon III, "Free Exercise at the Mountaintop," 79 *Cal. L.Rev.* 91 (1991); Douglas Laycock, "The Remnants of Free Exercise," 1990 *Sup. Ct. Rev.* 1; Michael McConnell, "Free Exercise Revisionism and the Smith Decision," 57 *U. Chi. L.Rev.* 1109 (1990); but *see* William P. Marshall, "In Defense of *Smith* and Free Exercise Revisionism," 58 *U. Chi. L Rev.* 308 (1991).

3. *Congressional Response to Smith.* Virtually all significant religious communities united with prominent civil liberties organizations to form a Coalition for the Free Exercise of Religion, for the purpose of persuading Congress to enact legislation providing a statutory right to more secure protection of free exercise of religion that the *Smith* court deemed necessary under the First Amendment. Congress held hearings, documented several instances of post-*Smith* violations of religious freedom stemming from laws of general applicability, and then enacted—with broad bipartisan support (unanimous in the House, 97–3 in the Senate)—the Religious Freedom Restoration Act [RFRA], which President Clinton signed on November 16, 1993. The essential features of the Act follow.

The Religious Freedom Restoration Act,
42 U.S.C. §§ 2000bb–2000bb–4 (1993)

§ 2000bb. *Congressional findings and declaration of purposes*

(a) *Findings.* The Congress finds that (1) the framers of the Constitution, recognizing free exercise of religion as an unalienable right, secured its protection in the First Amendment to the Constitution; (2) laws "neutral" toward religion may burden religious exercise as surely as laws intended to interfere with religious exercise; (3) governments should not substantially burden religious exercise without compelling justification; (4)

in *Employment Division v. Smith*, 494 U.S. 872 (1990) the Supreme Court virtually eliminated the requirement that the government justify burdens on religious exercise imposed by laws neutral toward religion; and (5) the compelling interest test as set forth in prior Federal court rulings is a workable test for striking sensible balances between religious liberty and competing prior governmental interests.

(b) *Purposes*. The purposes of this chapter are—(1) to restore the compelling interest test as set forth in *Sherbert v. Verner*, 374 U.S. 398 (1963) and *Wisconsin v. Yoder*, 406 U.S. 205 (1972) and to guarantee its application in all cases where free exercise of religion is substantially burdened; and

(2) to provide a claim or defense to persons whose religious exercise is substantially burdened by government.

§ 2000bb–1. *Free exercise of religion protected*

(a) In general. Government shall not substantially burden a person's exercise of religion even if the burden results from a rule of general applicability, except as provided in subsection (b) of this section.

(b) Exception. Government may substantially burden a person's exercise of religion only if it demonstrates that application of the burden to the person—(1) is in furtherance of a compelling governmental interest; and (2) is the least restrictive means of furthering that compelling governmental interest.

(c) Judicial relief. A person whose religious exercise has been burdened in violation of this section may assert that violation as a claim or defense in a judicial proceeding and obtain appropriate relief against a government. Standing to assert a claim or defense under this section shall be governed by the general rules of standing under article III of the Constitution.

§ 2000bb–2. *Definitions*

As used in this chapter—(1) the term "government" includes a branch, department, agency, instrumentality, and official (or other person acting under color of law) of the United States, a State, or a subdivision of a State; (2) the term "State" includes the District of Columbia, the Commonwealth of Puerto Rico, and each territory and possession of the United States; (3) the term "demonstrates" means meets the burdens of going forward with the evidence and of persuasion; and (4) the term "exercise of religion" means the exercise of religion under the First Amendment to the Constitution.

§ 2000bb–3. *Applicability*

(a) In general. This chapter applies to all Federal and State law, and the implementation of that law, whether statutory or otherwise, and whether adopted before or after November 16, 1993.

(b) Rule of construction. Federal statutory law adopted after November 16, 1993 is subject to this chapter unless such law explicitly excludes such application by reference to this chapter.

(c) Religious belief unaffected. Nothing in this chapter shall be construed to authorize any government to burden any religious belief.

§ 2000bb–4. *Establishment clause unaffected.*

Nothing in this chapter shall be construed to affect, interpret, or in any way address that portion of the First Amendment prohibiting laws respecting the establishment of religion (referred to in this section as the "Establishment Clause"). Granting government funding, benefits, or exemptions, to the extent permissible under the Establishment Clause, shall not constitute a violation of this chapter. As used in this section, the term "granting," used with respect to government funding, benefits, or exemptions, does not include the denial of government funding, benefits, or exemptions.

For interpretive guides to RFRA, *see* Douglas Laycock & Oliver S. Thomas, "Interpreting the Religious Freedom Restoration Act," 73 *Tex. L.Rev.* 209 (1994), and Thomas C. Berg, "What Hath Congress Wrought? An Interpretive Guide to the Religious Freedom Restoration Act," 39 *Vill. L.Rev.* 1 (1994).

A year after enacting RFRA, Congress addressed the sacramental use of peyote by American Indians.

The American Indian Religious Freedom Act, 42 U.S.C. 1996a (1994)

Traditional Indian religious use of peyote.

(a) *Congressional findings and declarations*

The Congress finds and declares that—(1) for many Indian people, the traditional ceremonial use of the peyote cactus as a religious sacrament has for centuries been integral to a way of life, and significant in perpetuating Indian tribes and cultures; (2) since 1965, this ceremonial use of peyote by Indians has been protected by Federal regulation; (3) while at least 28 States have enacted laws which are similar to, or are in conformance with, the Federal regulation which protects the ceremonial use of peyote by Indian religious practitioners, 22 States have not done so, and this lack of uniformity has created hardship for Indian people who participate in such religious ceremonies; (4) the Supreme Court of the United States, in the case of *Employment Division v. Smith*, 494 U.S. 872 (1990), held that the First Amendment does not protect Indian practitioners who use peyote in Indian religious ceremonies, and also raised uncertainty whether this religious practice would be protected under the compelling State interest standard; and (5) the lack of adequate and clear legal protection for the religious use of peyote by Indians may serve to stigmatize and marginalize Indian tribes and cultures, and increase the risk that they will be exposed to discriminatory treatment.

(b) *Use, possession, or transportation of peyote*

(1) Notwithstanding any other provision of law, the use, possession, or transportation of peyote by an Indian for bona fide traditional ceremonial purposes in connection with the practice of a traditional Indian religion is

lawful, and shall not be prohibited by the United States or any State. No Indian shall be penalized or discriminated against on the basis of such use, possession or transportation, including, but not limited to, denial of otherwise applicable benefits under public assistance programs.

(2) This section does not prohibit such reasonable regulation and registration by the Drug Enforcement Administration of those persons who cultivate, harvest, or distribute peyote as may be consistent with the purposes of this section and section 1996 of this title....

(4) Nothing in this section shall prohibit any Federal department or agency, in carrying out its statutory responsibilities and functions, from promulgating regulations establishing reasonable limitations on the use or ingestion of peyote prior to or during the performance of duties by sworn law enforcement officers or personnel directly involved in public transportation or any other safety-sensitive positions where the performance of such duties may be adversely affected by such use or ingestion. Such regulations shall be adopted only after consultation with representatives of traditional Indian religions for which the sacramental use of peyote is integral to their practice. Any regulation promulgated pursuant to this section shall be subject to the balancing test set forth in section 3 of the Religious Freedom Restoration Act (Public Law 103–141; 42 U.S.C. 2000bb–1).

(5) This section shall not be construed as requiring prison authorities to permit, nor shall it be construed to prohibit prison authorities from permitting, access to peyote by Indians while incarcerated within Federal or State prison facilities.

(6) Subject to the provisions of the Religious Freedom Restoration Act (Public Law 103–141; 42 U.S.C. 2000bb–1), this section shall not be construed to prohibit States from enacting or enforcing reasonable traffic safety laws or regulations.

(7) Subject to the provisions of the Religious Freedom Restoration Act (Public Law 103–141; 42 U.S.C. 2000bb–1), this section does not prohibit the Secretary of Defense from promulgating regulations establishing reasonable limitations on the use, possession, transportation, or distribution of peyote to promote military readiness, safety, or compliance with international law or laws of other countries. Such regulations shall be adopted only after consultation with representatives of traditional Indian religions for which the sacramental use of peyote is integral to their practice.

(c) *Definitions*

For purposes of this section—

(1) the term "Indian" means a member of an Indian tribe;

(2) the term "Indian tribe" means any tribe, band, nation, pueblo, or other organized group or community of Indians, including any Alaska Native village (as defined in, or established pursuant to, the Alaska Native Claims Settlement Act (43 U.S.C. 1601 et seq.)), which is recognized as eligible for the special programs and services provided by the United States to Indians because of their status as Indians;

(3) the term "Indian religion" means any religion—(A) which is practiced by Indians, and (B) the origin and interpretation of which is from within a traditional Indian culture or community; and

(4) the term "State" means any State of the United States, and any political subdivision thereof.

(d) *Protection of rights of Indians and Indian tribes*

Nothing in this section shall be construed as abrogating, diminishing, or otherwise affecting—

(1) the inherent rights of any Indian tribe;

(2) the rights, express or implicit, of any Indian tribe which exist under treaties, Executive orders, and laws of the United States;

(3) the inherent right of Indians to practice their religions; and

(4) the right of Indians to practice their religions under any Federal or State law.

---

11.   PRESERVING SACRED LAND AND SACRED SPACE

INTRODUCTION. *The Sacredness of Land.* In the Hebrew Bible, Canaan is deemed "holy land" because it is part of the divine promise to the ancient patriarch Abraham and all his descendants: "I will give to you, and to your offspring after you, the land where you are now an alien, all the land of Canaan, for a perpetual holding; and I will be their God." Gen. 17:8; *see also* Gen. 12:7; 15:7; 23; 28:4. This religious belief continues to create contentious difficulties in Israel, Jordan, and Palestine to this day, since the descendants of Abraham include rival communities stemming from Abraham but divided for centuries for both religious and political reasons.

The seventeenth-century Puritans appropriated these texts about the promise of land to the descendants of Abraham to refer to America as a new promised land, or new Canaan, for God's elect [Chapter Five, section 2]. After the annexation of Texas by the Act of March 1, 1845, 5 Stat. 797, the Puritan view of the land was enlarged. The European settlers in the new world were now thought to have a "Manifest Destiny" to rule the continent from coast to coast. Within five years the dream became a reality. California entered the Union in 1850. The claim of white control of the continent had "devastating consequences"–to borrow a phrase from Justice O'Connor in the case below–for the culture and the very survival of the American Indians.

The claim embodied three conflicts with the beliefs of the Natives about the land. First, the white settlers assumed that English royal charters or "purchases" from other European rulers (such as Napoleon Bonaparte, who ceded to President Thomas Jefferson the lands drained by the Mississippi River in the Louisiana Purchase) were all they needed to lay hold of the new world. A notable exception to this general rule was Roger Williams, who accused the magistrates of the Massachusetts Bay colony of lacking any authority in the new land because no one had purchased it from the Natives. Williams was tried for heresy on this charge and for denouncing the connection between the colony's government and the church. Found guilty, he was exiled from the colony. When he went to Rhode Island, he was befriended by Narraganset Indians, whom he insisted on paying for the land he occupied. *See* Edwin Scott Gaustad, *A Religious History of America* 64–65 (1966). Second, as the "heresy" of Roger Williams illustrates, the specific English attitudes toward property ownership (e.g., deeds entitling one not simply to use, but also to possession of the land) contrasted sharply with the attitudes of the Natives. Third, the white settlers knew little and cared less about the religious views of the Native Americans about the sacred character of the land. This disjunction has remained problematical, despite scores of treaties pledging respect for the Indians' way of life. The cultural divide led eventually to violence. From the massacre of the Pequot tribe in Connecticut in 1637 by a military band led by Governor John Endicott of the Massachusetts Bay Colony to the nineteenth-century wars of removal of the Native Americans from the land, the white settlers relentlessly pursued a goal of complete domination of the continent. A culture clash resulted in massive loss of life that Simon Wiesenthal describes as genocide. See Ward Churchill, "Genocide of Native Population in the United States," in *Israel W. Charney, Ed., 2 Encyclopedia of Genocide* 435 (1999).

■ JUSTICE BRENNAN noted in his dissent in the case below: "Where dogma lies at the heart of western religions, Native American faith is inextricably bound to the use of land. The site-specific nature of Indian religious practice derives from the Native American perception that land is itself a sacred, living being. *See* Suagee, 'American Indian Religious Freedom and Cultural Resources Management: Protecting Mother Earth's Caretakers,' 10 *Am. Ind. L.Rev.* 1, 10 (1982). Rituals are performed in prescribed locations not merely as a matter of traditional orthodoxy, but because land, like all other living things, is unique, and specific sites possess different spiritual properties and significance. Within this belief system, therefore, land is not fungible; indeed, at the time of the Spanish colonization of the American southwest, 'all ... Indians held in some form a belief in a sacred and indissoluble bond between themselves and the land in which their settlements were located.' E. Spicer, *Cycle of Conquest: The Impact of Spain, Mexico, and the United States on the Indians of the United States* 576 (1962).

"For the Indians [in *Lyng*], the most sacred of lands is the high country where, they believe, pre-human spirits moved with the coming of humans to the earth. Because these spirits are seen as the source of religious power, or 'medicine,' many of the tribes' rituals and practices require frequent journeys to the area. Thus, for example, religious leaders preparing for the complex of ceremonies that underlie the tribes' World Renewal efforts must travel to specific sites in the high country in order to attain the medicine necessary for successful renewal. Similarly, individual tribe members may seek curative powers for the healing of the sick, or personal medicine for particular purposes such as good luck in singing, hunting, or love. A period of preparation generally precedes such visits, and individuals must select trails in the sacred area according to the medicine they seek and their abilities, gradually moving to increasingly more powerful sites, which are typically located at higher altitudes. Among the most powerful of sites are Chimney Rock, Doctor Rock, and Peak 8, all of which are elevated rock outcroppings. Ceremonies are communal efforts undertaken for specific purposes in accordance with instructions handed down from generation to generation. Commentaries on or interpretations of the rituals themselves are deemed absolute violations of the ceremonies, whose value lies not in their ability to explain the natural world or to enlighten individual believers but in their efficacy as protectors and enhancers of tribal existence."

In sharp contrast to this spiritual view of the land in dispute in the case below, Justice O'Connor approached the issue principally as the right of the government "to use what is, after all, *its* land." The United States Forest Service had upgraded 49 miles of previously unpaved roads in the Six Rivers National Forest in northern California. It proposed to create a paved 75–mile road linking two small California towns, Gasquet and Orleans (hence known as the G–O road). The conflict in this case centered on a six-mile paved segment through the Chimney Rock section of land that Justice O'Connor acknowledged "has historically been used for religious purposes by Yurok, Karok, and Tolowa Indians." O'Connor also noted that the proposed project would have "devastating effects on traditional Indian religious practices," and she assumed that "the threat to the efficacy of at least some religious practices [of the Indians] is extremely grave."

Lyng v. Northwest Indian Cemetery Protective Association

485 U.S. 439 (1988).

Andrew J. Pincus argued the cause for petitioners. With him on the briefs were *Solicitor General Fried, Acting Assistant Attorney General Marzulla, Deputy Solicitor General Ayer, Robert L. Klarquist,* and *Jacques B. Gelin.*

Marilyn B. Miles argued the cause for respondents. With her on the brief for the Indian respondents was *Stephen V. Quesenberry. John K. Van de Kamp,* Attorney General, *R.H. Connett,* Assistant Attorney General, and *Edna Walz,* Deputy Attorney General filed a brief for respondent State of California.

Briefs of amici curiae urging reversal were filed for the State of Hawaii et al. by *Kenneth O. Eikenberry,* Attorney General of Washington, *Timothy R. Malone, Nixon Handy,* and *Mark S. Green,* Assistant Attorneys General, *Warren Price III,* Attorney General of Hawaii, *Roger A. Tellinghuisen,* Attorney General of South Dakota, and *David Wilkinson,* Attorney General of Utah; for the Colorado Mining Association et al. by *Lawrence E. Stevens* and *Patrick J. Garver;* for the Howonquet Community Association et al. by *Ronald A. Zumbrun* and *Robin L. Rivett;* and for the city of Williams, Arizona, by *Gary Verburg.*

Briefs of amici curiae urging affirmance were filed for the American Civil Liberties Union Foundation et al. by *John A. Powell, Steven R. Shapiro, Paul L. Hoffman, Mark D. Rosenbaum, Alan L. Schlosser, Edward M. Chen, Matthew A. Coles,* and *Stephen L. Pevar;* for the American Jewish Congress et al. by *Marc D. Stern, Lois C. Waldman,* and *Amy Adelson;* and for the Christian Legal Society et al. by *Michael J. Woodruff, Samuel Rabinove, Richard T. Foltin,* and *Jordan Lorence.*

Steven C. Moore filed a brief for the National Congress of American Indians et al. as amici curiae.

■ Justice O'Connor delivered the opinion of the Court, in which Chief Justice Rehnquist, and Justices White, Stevens, and Scalia joined.

This case requires us to consider whether the First Amendment's Free Exercise Clause forbids the Government from permitting timber harvesting in, or constructing a road through, a portion of a National Forest that has traditionally been used for religious purposes by members of three American Indian tribes in northwestern California. We conclude that it does not.

I

... In 1977, the Forest Service issued a draft environmental impact statement that discussed proposals for upgrading an existing unpaved road that runs through the Chimney Rock area. In response to comments on the draft statement, the Forest Service commissioned a study of American Indian cultural and religious sites in the area.... The commissioned study, which was completed in 1979, found that the entire area "is significant as an integral and indispensible [sic] part of Indian religious conceptualization and practice." Specific sites are used for certain rituals, and "successful use of the [area] is dependent upon and facilitated by certain qualities of the physical environment, the most important of which are privacy, silence, and an undisturbed natural setting." The study concluded that constructing a road along any of the available routes "would cause serious and irreparable damage to the sacred areas which are an integral and necessary part of the belief systems and lifeway of Northwest California Indian peoples." Accordingly, the report recommended that the G–O road not be completed.

In 1982, the Forest Service decided not to adopt this recommendation, and it prepared a final environmental impact statement for construction of the road. The Regional Forester selected a route that avoided archeological sites and was removed as far as possible from the sites used by contemporary Indians for specific spiritual activities. Alternative routes that would have avoided the Chimney Rock area altogether were rejected because they would have required the acquisition of private land, had serious soil stability problems, and would in any event have traversed areas having ritualistic value to American Indians. At about the same time, the Forest Service adopted a management plan allowing for the harvesting of significant amounts of timber in this area of the forest. The management plan provided for one-half mile protective zones around all the religious sites identified in the report that had been commissioned in connection with the G–O road.

After exhausting their administrative remedies, respondents—an Indian organization, individual Indians, nature organizations and individual members of those organizations, and the State of California—challenged both the road-building and timber-harvesting decisions in the United States District Court for the Northern District of California. Respondents claimed that the Forest Service's decisions violated the Free Exercise Clause, several federal statutes, and governmental trust responsibilities to Indians living on the Hoopa Valley Reservation.

After a trial, the District Court issued a permanent injunction forbidding the Government from constructing the Chimney Rock section of the G–O road or putting the timber-harvesting management plan into effect. The court ... concluded that both projects would breach the Government's trust responsibilities to protect water and fishing rights reserved to the Hoopa Valley Indians.

While an appeal was pending before the United States Court of Appeals for the Ninth Circuit, Congress enacted the California Wilderness Act of 1984, Pub. L. 98–425, 98 Stat. 1619. Under that statute, much of the property covered by the Forest Service's management plan is now designated a wilderness area, which means that commercial activities such as timber harvesting are forbidden. The statute exempts a narrow strip of land, coinciding with the Forest Service's proposed route for the remaining segment of the G–O road, from the wilderness designation. The legislative history indicates that this exemption was adopted "to enable the completion of the Gasquet–Orleans Road project if the responsible authorities so decide." S. Rep. No. 98–582, p. 29 (1984).

A panel of the Ninth Circuit affirmed in part. The panel unanimously rejected the District Court's conclusion that the Government's proposed actions would breach its trust responsibilities to Indians on the Hoopa Valley Reservation. The panel also vacated the injunction to the extent that it had been rendered moot by the California Wilderness Act, which now prevents timber harvesting in certain areas covered by the District Court's order. The District Court's decision, to the extent that it rested on statutory grounds, was otherwise unanimously affirmed.

By a divided decision, the District Court's constitutional ruling was also affirmed. Relying primarily on the Forest Service's own commissioned study, the majority found that construction of the Chimney Rock section of the G–O road would have significant, though largely indirect, adverse effects on Indian religious practices. The majority concluded that the Government had failed to demonstrate a compelling interest in the completion of the road, and that it could have abandoned the road without thereby creating "a religious preserve for a single group in violation of the establishment clause." The majority apparently applied the same analysis to logging operations that might be carried out in portions of the Chimney Rock area not covered by the California Wilderness Act. ("Because most of the high country has now been designated by Congress as a wilderness area, the issue of logging becomes less significant, although it does not disappear").

III

A

It is undisputed that the Indian respondents' beliefs are sincere and that the Government's proposed actions will have severe adverse effects on the practice of their religion. Respondents contend that the burden on their religious practices is heavy enough to violate the Free Exercise Clause unless the Government can demonstrate a compelling need to complete the G–O road or to engage in timber harvesting in the Chimney Rock area. We disagree. In *Bowen v. Roy* [section 3 above] we considered a challenge to a federal statute that required the States to use Social Security numbers in administering certain welfare programs. . . .

The building of a road or the harvesting of timber on publicly owned land cannot meaningfully be distinguished from the use of a Social Security number in *Roy*. In both cases, the challenged government action would interfere significantly with private persons' ability to pursue spiritual fulfillment according to their own religious beliefs. In neither case, however, would the affected individuals be coerced by the Government's action into violating their religious beliefs; nor would either governmental action penalize religious activity by denying any person an equal share of the rights, benefits, and privileges enjoyed by other citizens.

We are asked to distinguish this case from *Roy* on the ground that the infringement on religious liberty here is "significantly greater," or on the ground that the government practice in *Roy* was "purely mechanical" whereas this case involves "a case-by-case substantive determination as to how a particular unit of land will be managed." Brief for Indian Respondents 33–34. Similarly, we are told that this case can be distinguished from *Roy* because "the government action is not at some physically removed location where it places no restriction on what a practitioner may do." Brief for Respondent State of California 18. . . .

These efforts to distinguish *Roy* are unavailing. This Court cannot determine the truth of the underlying beliefs that led to the religious objections here or in *Roy*, see *Hobbie* [section 5 above], and accordingly cannot weigh the adverse effects on the [Roys] and compare them with the adverse effects on respondents. Without the ability to make such comparisons, we cannot say that the one form of incidental interference with an individual's spiritual activities should be subjected to a different constitutional analysis than the other.

Respondents insist, nonetheless, that the courts below properly relied on a factual inquiry into the degree to which the Indians' spiritual practices would become ineffectual if the G–O road were built. They rely on several cases in which this Court has sustained free exercise challenges to government programs that interfered with individuals' ability to practice their religion (citing *Yoder* [section 7 above], *Sherbert* [section 5 above] *Thomas* [section 4 above], and *Hobbie* [section 4 above]).

Even apart from the inconsistency between *Roy* and respondents' reading of these cases, their interpretation will not withstand analysis. It is true that this Court has repeatedly held that indirect coercion or penalties on the free exercise of religion, not just outright prohibitions, are subject to scrutiny under the First Amendment. Thus, for example, ineligibility for unemployment benefits, based solely on a refusal to violate the Sabbath, has been analogized to a fine imposed on Sabbath worship. *Sherbert*. This does not and cannot imply that incidental effects of government programs, which may make it more difficult to practice certain religions but which have no tendency to coerce individuals into acting contrary to their religious beliefs, require government to bring forward a compelling justification for its otherwise lawful actions. The crucial word in the constitutional text is "prohibit": "For the Free Exercise Clause is written in terms of what the government cannot do to the individual, not in terms of what the individual can exact from the government." *Sherbert* (Douglas, J., concurring).

Whatever may be the exact line between unconstitutional prohibitions on the free exercise of religion and the legitimate conduct by government of its own affairs, the location of the line cannot depend on measuring the effects of a governmental action on a religious objector's spiritual development. The Government does not dispute, and we have no reason to doubt, that the logging and road-building projects at issue in this case could have devastating effects on traditional Indian religious practices. Those practices are intimately and inextricably bound up with the unique features of the Chimney Rock area, which is known to the Indians as the "high country." Individual practitioners use this area for personal spiritual development; some of their activities are believed to be critically important in advancing the welfare of the tribe, and indeed, of mankind itself. The Indians use this area, as they have used it for a very long time, to conduct a wide variety of specific rituals that aim to accomplish their religious goals. According to their beliefs, the rituals would not be efficacious if conducted at other sites than the ones traditionally used, and too much disturbance of the area's natural state would clearly render any meaningful continuation of traditional practices impossible. To be sure, the Indians themselves were far from unanimous in opposing the G–O road, and it seems less than certain that construction of the road will be so disruptive that it will doom their religion. Nevertheless, we can assume that the threat to the efficacy of at least some religious practices is extremely grave. . . .

However much we might wish that it were otherwise, government simply could not operate if it were required to satisfy every citizen's religious needs and desires. A broad range of government activities—from social welfare programs to foreign aid to conservation projects—will always be considered essential to the spiritual well-being of some citizens, often on the basis of sincerely held religious beliefs. Others will find the very same activities deeply offensive, and perhaps incompatible with their own search for spiritual fulfillment and with the tenets of their religion. The First Amendment must apply to all citizens alike, and it can give to none of them a veto over public programs that do not prohibit the free exercise of religion. The Constitution does not, and courts cannot, offer to reconcile the various competing demands on government, many of them rooted in sincere religious belief, that inevitably arise in so diverse a society as ours. That task, to the extent that it is feasible, is for the legislatures and other institutions. Cf. The Federalist No. 10 (suggesting that the effects of religious factionalism are best restrained through competition among a multiplicity of religious sects).

One need not look far beyond the present case to see why the analysis in *Roy*, but not respondents' proposed extension of *Sherbert* and its progeny, offers a sound reading of the Constitution. Respondents attempt to stress the limits of the religious servitude that they are now seeking to impose on the Chimney Rock area of the Six Rivers National Forest. While defending an injunction against logging operations and the construction of a road, they apparently do not at present object to the area's being used by recreational visitors, other Indians, or forest rangers. Nothing in the principle for which they contend, however, would distinguish this case from another lawsuit in which they (or similarly situated religious objectors) might seek to exclude all human activity but their own from sacred areas of the public lands. The Indian respondents insist that "privacy during the power quests is required for the practitioners to maintain the purity needed for a successful journey." Brief for Indian Respondents 8. Similarly: "The practices conducted in the high country entail intense meditation and require the practitioner to achieve a profound awareness of the natural environment. Prayer seats are oriented so there is an unobstructed view, and the practitioner must be surrounded by undisturbed naturalness." No disrespect for these practices is implied when one notes that such beliefs could easily require de facto beneficial ownership of some rather spacious tracts of public property. Even without anticipating future cases, the diminution of the Government's property rights, and the concomitant subsidy of the Indian religion, would in this case be far from trivial: the District Court's order permanently forbade commercial timber harvesting, or the construction of a two-lane road, anywhere within an area covering a full 27 sections (i.e. more than 17,000 acres) of public land.

The Constitution does not permit government to discriminate against religions that treat particular physical sites as sacred, and a law forbidding the Indian respondents from visiting the Chimney Rock area would raise a different set of constitutional questions. Whatever rights the Indians may have to the use of the area, however, those rights do not divest the Government of its right to use what is, after all, its land. Cf. *Roy*, (O'Connor, J., concurring in part and dissenting in part) (distinguishing between the Government's use of information in its possession and the Government's requiring an individual to provide such information).

B

Nothing in our opinion should be read to encourage governmental insensitivity to the religious needs of any citizen. The Government's rights to the use its own land, for example, need not and should not discourage it from accommodating religious practices like those engaged in by the Indian respondents. Cf. *Sherbert* (Harlan, J., dissenting). [O'Connor cited as evidence of such accommodation the commissioning of the study of the effect of the project on the cultural and religious value of the Chimney Rock area, noting that the "423–page report was so sympathetic to the Indians' interests that it has constituted the principal piece of evidence relied on by respondents' throughout this litigation" and that "the Forest Service did not in the end adopt the report's recommendation that the project be abandoned."]

Except for abandoning its project entirely, and thereby leaving the two existing segments of road to deadend in the middle of a National Forest, it is difficult to see how the Government could have been more solicitous. Such solicitude accords with "the policy of the United States to protect and preserve for American Indians their inherent right of freedom to believe, express, and exercise the traditional religions of the American Indian ... including but not limited to access to sites, use and possession of sacred objects, and the freedom to worship through ceremonials and traditional rites." American Indian Religious Freedom Act (AIRFA), Pub. L. 95–341, 92 Stat. 469, 42 U.S.C. § 1996.

[Noting that the sponsor of this legislation, Representative Udall of Arizona, had emphasized during the discussion in the House of Representatives that the bill would not "confer special religious rights on Indians," would "not change any existing State or Federal law," and in fact "has no teeth in it," O'Connor concluded: "Nowhere in the law is there so much as a hint of any intent to create a cause of action or any judicially enforceable individual rights."]

C

The dissent proposes an approach to the First Amendment that is fundamentally inconsistent with the principles on which our decision rests. Notwithstanding the sympathy that we all must feel for the plight of the Indian respondents, it is plain that the approach taken by the dissent cannot withstand analysis. On the contrary, the path towards which it points us is incompatible with the text of the Constitution, with the precedents of this Court, and with a responsible sense of our own institutional role.

The dissent begins by asserting that the "constitutional guarantee we interpret today ... is directed against *any* form of government action that frustrates or inhibits religious practice." (emphasis added). The Constitution, however, says no such thing. Rather, it states: "Congress shall make no law ... *prohibiting* the free exercise [of religion]" (emphasis added).

... The dissent now offers to distinguish *Roy* by saying that the Government was acting there "in a purely internal manner," whereas land-use decisions "are likely to have substantial external effects." Whatever the source or meaning of the dissent's distinction, it has no basis in *Roy*. Robbing the spirit of a child, and preventing her from attaining greater spiritual power, is both a "substantial external effect" and one that is remarkably similar to the injury claimed by respondents in the case before us today. The dissent's reading of *Roy* would effectively overrule that decision, without providing any compelling justification for doing so.

The dissent also misreads *Yoder*. The statute at issue in that case prohibited the Amish parents, on pain of criminal prosecution, from providing their children with the kind of education required by the Amish religion. The statute directly compelled the Amish to send their children to public high schools "contrary to the Amish religion and way of life." The Court acknowledged that the statute might be constitutional, despite its coercive nature, if the state could show with sufficient "particularity how its admittedly strong interest in compulsory education would be adversely affected by granting an exemption to the Amish".... [T]here is nothing whatsoever in the *Yoder* opinion to support the proposition that the "impact" on the Amish religion would have been constitutionally problematic if the statute at issue had not been coercive in nature.

Perceiving a "stress point in the longstanding conflict between two disparate cultures," the dissent attacks us for declining to "balance these competing and potentially irreconcilable interests, choosing instead to turn this difficult task over to the federal legislature." Seeing the Court as the arbiter, the dissent proposes a legal test under which it would decide which public lands are "central" or "indispensable" to which religions, and by implication which are "dispensable" or "peripheral," and would then decide which government programs are "compelling" enough to justify "infringement of those practices." We would accordingly be required to weigh the value of every religious belief and practice that is said to be threatened by any government program. Unless a "showing of 'centrality,' " is nothing but an assertion of centrality, the dissent thus offers us the prospect of this Court holding that some sincerely held religious beliefs and practices are not "central" to certain religions, despite protestations to the contrary from the religious objectors who brought the lawsuit. In other words, the dissent's approach would require us to rule that some religious adherents misunderstand their own religious beliefs. We think such an approach cannot be squared with the Constitution or with our precedents, and that it would cast the judiciary in a role that we were never intended to play.

IV

The decision of the court below, according to which the First Amendment precludes the Government from completing the G–O road or from permitting timber harvesting in the Chimney Rock area, is reversed. In order that the District Court's injunction may be reconsidered in light of this holding, and in the light of any other relevant events that may have intervened since the injunction issued, the case is remanded for further proceedings consistent with this opinion. It is so ordered.

■ Justice Kennedy took no part in the consideration or decision of this case.

■ Justice Brennan, with whom Justices Marshall and Blackmun join, dissenting.

" 'The Free Exercise Clause,' " the Court explains today, " 'is written in terms of what the government cannot do to the individual, not in terms of what the individual can exact from the government.' "(quoting *Sherbert* (Douglas, J., concurring)). Pledging fidelity to this unremarkable constitutional principle, the Court nevertheless concludes that even where the Government uses federal land in a manner that threatens the very existence of a Native American religion, the Government is simply not "doing" anything to the practitioners of that faith. Instead, the Court believes that Native Americans who request that the Government refrain from destroying their religion effectively seek to exact from the Government de facto beneficial ownership of federal property. These two astonishing conclusions follow naturally from the Court's determination that federal land-use decisions that render the practice of a given religion impossible do not burden that religion in a manner cognizable under the Free Exercise

Clause, because such decisions neither coerce conduct inconsistent with religious belief nor penalize religious activity. The constitutional guarantee we interpret today, however, draws no such fine distinctions between types of restraints on religious exercise, but rather is directed against any form of governmental action that frustrates or inhibits religious practice. Because the Court today refuses even to acknowledge the constitutional injury respondents will suffer, and because this refusal essentially leaves Native Americans with absolutely no constitutional protection against perhaps the gravest threat to their religious practices, I dissent.

I

For at least 200 years and probably much longer, the Yurok, Karok, and Tolowa Indians have held sacred an approximately 25 square-mile area of land situated in what is today the Blue Creek Unit of Six Rivers National Forest in northwestern California. As the Government readily concedes, regular visits to this area, known to respondent Indians as the "high country," have played and continue to play a "critical" role in the religious practices and rituals of these tribes. Brief for Petitioner 3. Those beliefs, only briefly described in the Court's opinion, are crucial to a proper understanding of respondents' claims.

As the Forest Service's commissioned study, the Theodoratus Report, explains, for Native Americans religion is not a discrete sphere of activity separate from all others, and any attempt to isolate the religious aspects of Indian life "is in reality an exercise which forces Indian concepts into non-Indian categories." Thus, for most Native Americans, "the area of worship cannot be delineated from social, political, cultural and other areas of Indian lifestyle." American Indian Religious Freedom, Hearings on S. J. Res. 102 before the Select Committee on Indian Affairs, 95th Cong., 2d Sess., 86 (statement of Barney Old Coyote, Crow Tribe). A pervasive feature of this lifestyle is the individual's relationship with the natural world; this relationship, which can accurately though somewhat incompletely be characterized as one of stewardship, forms the core of what might be called, for want of a better nomenclature, the Indian religious experience. While traditional western religions view creation as the work of a deity "who institutes natural laws which then govern the operation of physical nature," tribal religions regard creation as an ongoing process in which they are morally and religiously obligated to participate. Native Americans fulfill this duty through ceremonies and rituals designed to preserve and stabilize the earth and to protect humankind from disease and other catastrophes. Failure to conduct these ceremonies in the manner and place specified, adherents believe, will result in great harm to the earth and to the people whose welfare depends upon it. . . .

II

The Court does not for a moment suggest that the interests served by the G–O road are in any way compelling, or that they outweigh the destructive effect construction of the road will have on respondents' religious practices. Instead, the Court embraces the Government's contention that its prerogative as landowner should always take precedence over a claim that a particular use of federal property infringes religious practices. Attempting to justify this rule, the Court argues that the First Amendment bars only outright prohibitions, indirect coercion, and penalties on the free exercise of religion. All other "incidental effects of government programs," it concludes, even those "which may make it more difficult to practice certain religions but which have no tendency to coerce individuals into acting contrary to their religious beliefs," simply do not give rise to constitutional concerns. Since our recognition nearly half a century ago that restraints on religious conduct implicate the concerns of the Free Exercise Clause, see *Prince* [section 1 above], we have never suggested that the protections of the guarantee are limited to so narrow a range of governmental burdens. The land-use decision challenged here will restrain respondents from practicing their religion as surely and as completely as any of the governmental actions we have struck down in the past, and the Court's efforts simply to define away respondents' injury as nonconstitutional is both unjustified and ultimately unpersuasive.

A

The Court ostensibly finds support for its narrow formulation of religious burdens in our decisions in *Hobbie, Thomas,* and *Sherbert.* In those cases, the laws at issue forced individuals to choose between adhering to specific religious tenets and forfeiting unemployment benefits on the one hand, and accepting work repugnant to their religious beliefs on the other. The religions involved, therefore, lent themselves to the coercion analysis the Court espouses today, for they proscribed certain conduct such as munitions work (*Thomas*) or working on Saturdays (*Sherbert, Hobbie*) that the unemployment benefits laws effectively compelled. In sustaining the challenges to these laws, however, we nowhere suggested that such coercive compulsion exhausted the range of religious burdens recognized under the Free Exercise Clause.

Indeed, in *Yoder,* we struck down a state compulsory school attendance law on free exercise grounds not so much because of the affirmative coercion the law exerted on individual religious practitioners, but because of "the *impact* that compulsory high school attendance could have on the continued survival of Amish communities" (emphasis added). Like respondents here, the Amish view life as pervasively religious and their faith accordingly dictates their entire lifestyle. Detailed as their religious rules are, however, the parents in *Yoder* did not argue that their religion expressly proscribed public education beyond the eighth grade; rather, they objected to the law because "the values . . . of the modern secondary school are in sharp conflict with the fundamental mode of life mandated by the Amish religion." (emphasis added). By exposing Amish children "to a 'worldly' influence in conflict with their beliefs," and by removing those children "from their community, physically and emotionally, during the crucial and formative adolescent period of life" when Amish beliefs are inculcated, the compulsory school law posed "a very real threat of undermining the Amish community and religious practice." Admittedly, this threat arose from the compulsory nature of the law at issue, but it was the "impact" on religious practice itself, not the source of that impact, that led us to invalidate the law. . . .

The harm to the practitioners is the same regardless of the manner in which the Government restrains their religious expression, and the Court's fear that an "effects" test will permit religious adherents to challenge governmental actions they merely find "offensive" in no way justifies its refusal to recognize the constitutional injury citizens suffer when governmental action not only offends but actually restrains their religious practices. Here, respondents have demonstrated that the Government's proposed activities will completely prevent them from practicing their religion, and such a showing, no less than those made out in *Hobbie, Thomas, Sherbert*, and *Yoder*, entitles them to the protections of the Free Exercise Clause.

B

Nor can I agree with the Court's assertion that respondents' constitutional claim is foreclosed by our decision in *Roy*. There, applicants for certain welfare benefits objected to the use of a Social Security number in connection with the administration of their two year old daughter's application for benefits, contending that such use would "rob the [child's] spirit" and thus interfere with her spiritual development. In rejecting that challenge, we stated that "the Free Exercise Clause simply cannot be understood to require the Government to conduct its own internal affairs in ways that comport with the religious beliefs of particular citizens." Accordingly, we explained that *Roy* could "no more prevail on his religious objection to the Government's use of a Social Security number for his daughter than he could on a sincere religious objection to the size or color of the Government's filing cabinets. The Free Exercise Clause affords an individual protection from certain forms of governmental compulsion; it does not afford an individual a right to dictate the conduct of the Government's *internal procedures*." (emphasis added).

Today the Court professes an inability to differentiate *Roy* from the present case, suggesting that "the building of a road or the harvesting of timber on publicly owned land cannot be meaningfully distinguished from the use of a Social Security number." I find this inability altogether remarkable. In *Roy*, we repeatedly stressed the "internal" nature of the Government practice at issue: noting that Roy objected to "the widespread use of the social security number by the federal or state governments *in their computer systems*," (emphasis added), we likened the use of such recordkeeping numbers to decisions concerning the purchase of office equipment. When the Government processes information, of course, it acts in a purely internal manner, and any free exercise challenge to such internal recordkeeping in effect seeks to dictate how the Government conducts its own affairs.

Federal land-use decisions, by contrast, are likely to have substantial external effects that government decisions concerning office furniture and information storage obviously will not, and they are correspondingly subject to public scrutiny and public challenge in a host of ways that office equipment purchases are not. Indeed, in the American Indian Religious Freedom Act (AIRFA), 42 U.S.C. § 1996, Congress expressly recognized the adverse impact land-use decisions and other governmental actions frequently have on the site-specific religious practices of Native Americans, and the Act accordingly directs agencies to consult with Native American religious leaders before taking actions that might impair those practices. . . .

[I]n AIRFA Congress explicitly acknowledged that federal "policies and regulations" could and often did "intrude upon [and] interfere with" site-specific Native American religious ceremonies, and in *Roy* we recognized that this Act—"with its emphasis on protecting the freedom to believe, express, and exercise a religion—accurately identifies the mission of the Free Exercise Clause itself." Ultimately, in *Roy* we concluded that, however much the Government's recordkeeping system may have offended Roy's sincere religious sensibilities, he could not challenge that system under the Free Exercise Clause because the Government's practice did not "in any degree impair his freedom to believe, express, and exercise "his religion" (quoting AIRFA). That determination distinguishes the injury at issue here, which the Court finds so "remarkably similar" to Roy's, for respondents have made an uncontroverted showing that the proposed construction and logging activities will impair their freedom to exercise their religion in the greatest degree imaginable, and Congress has "accurately identified" such injuries as falling within the scope of the Free Exercise Clause. The Court's reading of *Roy*, therefore, simply cannot be squared with our endorsement—in that very same case—of this congressional determination. More important, it lends no support to the Court's efforts to narrow both the reach and promise of the Free Exercise Clause itself.

C

In the final analysis, the Court's refusal to recognize the constitutional dimension of respondents' injuries stems from its concern that acceptance of respondents' claim could potentially strip the Government of its ability to manage and use vast tracts of federal property. In addition, the nature of respondents' site-specific religious practices raises the specter of future suits in which Native Americans seek to exclude all human activity from such areas. These concededly legitimate concerns lie at the very heart of this case, which represents yet another stress point in the longstanding conflict between two disparate cultures—the dominant western culture, which views land in terms of ownership and use, and that of Native Americans, in which concepts of private property are not only alien, but contrary to a belief system that holds land sacred. Rather than address this conflict in any meaningful fashion, however, the Court disclaims all responsibility for balancing these competing and potentially irreconcilable interests, choosing instead to turn this difficult task over to the federal legislature. Such an abdication is more than merely indefensible as an institutional matter: by defining respondents' injury as "non-constitutional," the Court has effectively bestowed on one party to this conflict the unilateral authority to resolve all future disputes in its favor, subject only to the Court's toothless exhortation to be "sensitive" to affected religions.

In my view, however, Native Americans deserve—and the Constitution demands—more than this....

I believe it appropriate, therefore, to require some showing of "centrality" before the Government can be required either to come forward with a compelling justification for its proposed use of federal land or to forego that use altogether. "Centrality," however, should not be equated with the survival or extinction of the religion itself. In *Yoder*, for example, we treated the objection to the compulsory school attendance of adolescents as "central" to the Amish faith even though such attendance did not prevent or otherwise render the practice of that religion impossible, and instead simply threatened to "undermine" that faith. Because of their perceptions of and relationship with the natural world, Native Americans consider all land sacred. Nevertheless, the Theodoratus Report reveals that respondents here deemed certain lands more powerful and more directly related to their religious practices than others. Thus, in my view, while Native Americans need not demonstrate, as respondents did here, that the Government's land-use decision will assuredly eradicate their faith, I do not think it is enough to allege simply that the land in question is held sacred. Rather, adherents challenging a proposed use of federal land should be required to show that the decision poses a substantial and realistic threat of frustrating their religious practices. Once such a showing is made, the burden should shift to the Government to come forward with a compelling state interest sufficient to justify the infringement of those practices.

The Court today suggests that such an approach would place courts in the untenable position of deciding which practices and beliefs are "central" to a given faith and which are not, and invites the prospect of judges advising some religious adherents that they "misunderstand their own religious beliefs." In fact, however, courts need not undertake any such inquiries: like all other religious adherents, Native Americans would be the arbiters of which practices are central to their faith, subject only to the normal requirement that their claims be genuine and sincere. The question for the courts, then, is not whether the Native American claimants understand their own religion, but rather, whether they have discharged their burden of demonstrating, as the Amish did with respect to the compulsory school law in *Yoder*, that the land-use decision poses a substantial and realistic threat of undermining or frustrating their religious practices. Ironically, the Court's apparent solicitude for the integrity of religious belief and its desire to forestall the possibility that courts might second-guess the claims of religious adherents leads to far greater inequities than those the Court postulates: today's ruling sacrifices a religion at least as old as the Nation itself, along with the spiritual well-being of its approximately 5,000 adherents, so that the Forest Service can build a six-mile segment of road that two lower courts found had only the most marginal and speculative utility, both to the Government itself and to the private lumber interests that might conceivably use it....

III

Today, the Court holds that a federal land-use decision that promises to destroy an entire religion does not burden the practice of that faith in a manner recognized by the Free Exercise Clause. Having thus stripped respondents and all other Native Americans of any constitutional protection against perhaps the most serious threat to their age-old religious practices, and indeed to their entire way of life, the Court assures us that nothing in its decision "should be read to encourage governmental insensitivity to the religious needs of any citizen." I find it difficult, however, to imagine conduct more insensitive to religious needs than the Government's determination to build a marginally useful road in the face of uncontradicted evidence that the road will render the practice of respondents' religion impossible. Nor do I believe that respondents will derive any solace from the knowledge that although the practice of their religion will become "more difficult" as a result of the Government's actions, they remain free to maintain their religious beliefs. Given today's ruling, that freedom amounts to nothing more than the right to believe that their religion will be destroyed. The safeguarding of such a hollow freedom not only makes a mockery of the " 'policy of the United States to protect and preserve for American Indians their inherent right of freedom to believe, express, and exercise their traditional religions,' " (quoting AIRFA), it fails utterly to accord with the dictates of the First Amendment. I dissent.

NOTES AND QUESTIONS

1. *Congressional Protection of the Religious Freedom of American Indians.* In *Plessy v. Ferguson*, 163 U.S. 537 (1896), Justice Brown suggested that "the enforced separation of the two races stamps the colored race with a badge of inferiority ... not by reason of anything found in the act, but solely because the colored race chooses to put that construction upon it." *Id.* 551. As if it were the recently emanicipated slaves, disenfranchised at the end of Reconstruction in 1877 who begged southern legislatures to impose laws requiring the enforced separation of the races! And as if white supremacy and black inferiority were not the very purpose of Jim Crow laws, but were simply the feelings that "the colored race" chose to put on things! In modern parlance, the discourse of the *Plessy* Court reflected an astonishing degree of insensitivity. Taking up this theme, Justice O'Connor wrote in *Lyng*: "Nothing in our opinion should be read to encourage governmental insensitivity to the religious needs of any citizen." Was her opinion—which bluntly acknowledged that "the logging and road-building projects at issue in this case could have devastating effects on traditional Indian religious practices"—a model of governmental sensitivity? In any normal relationship who decides whether behavior is sensitive, the one engaged in the conduct at issue or the one impacted by the behavior? If in the view of a religious community the judiciary appears insensitive to its religious needs, may it turn to the political branches for protection? Within months after *Lyng*, Congress—acting under its spending power, U.S. Const., Art. I, § 8, cl. 1—withheld authorization from the Secretary of the Interior to build the proposed G–O road. Amendments to Department of the Interior and Related Agencies Appropriations Act, Pub. L. 100–446, 102 Stat. 1826 (Sept. 27, 1988); *see* H.R. Rep. No. 713, 100th Cong., 2d Sess. 72 (1988) ("prohibit[ing] the use of funds for construction of the Gasquet–Orleans (G–O) road in California, pending further review of the issue of Indian religious rights that would be significantly affected by the road construction"). The motivation for this

legislative response could have been as much to curb public subsidy of the private interests of the logging industry as it was to protect the religious freedom of Native Americans, but the effect at least was more "sensitive" to the religious needs of the American Indians.

Of what practical use is the American Indian Religious Freedom Act, 42 U.S.C. § 1996? After decisions such as *Lyng* and *Smith* revealed that this statute provided no judicially enforceable rights or remedies, Congress amended the act in 1994 to provide stronger and more specific statutory protection for the religious practices of Native Americans. 42 U.S.C. § 1996a [section 10 above]. *See* Anastasia P. Winslow, "Sacred Standards: Honoring the Establishment Clause in Protecting Native American Sites," 38 *Ariz. L.Rev.* 1291 (1996).

2. *The Sacredness of Space and the Historical Landmarking of Church Buildings.* A church building can be a deep expression of religious beliefs. *See, e.g.,* Angela C. Carmella, "Houses of Worship and Religious Liberty: Constitutional Limits to Landmark Preservation and Architectural Review," 36 *Vill. L.Rev.* 401 (1991); *see also* Thomas Pak, "Free Exercise, Free Expression, and Landmark Preservation," 91 *Colum. L. Rev.* 1813 (1991); and Robert L. Crewdson, "Ministry and Mortar: Historic Preservation and the First Amendment after *Barwick*," 33 *J. Urb. & Contemp. L.* 137 (1988). This theological view of church art, including church architecture, is reflected in the Second Vatican Council's Declaration on the Sacred Liturgy, ¶ 124: "When churches are to be built, let great care be taken that they be suitable for the celebration of liturgical services and for the active participation of the faithful." Walter Abbott, ed., *The Documents of Vatican II* 175 (1966). It is also reflected in the biblical readings and prayers that attend the consecration of a church building.

When the government directly interferes with the manner in which a religious community gathers to worship and pray, has the government entangled itself excessively in the life of a religious community? Article 2 of the Massachusetts Declaration of Rights, unchanged since 1780, provides: "It is the right as well as the duty of all men in society, publicly and at stated seasons to worship the SUPREME BEING, the great Creator and Preserver of the Universe. And no subject shall be hurt, molested, or restrained, in his person, liberty, or estate for worshipping GOD in the manner and season most agreeable to the dictates of his own conscience, or for his religious profession or sentiments; provided he doth not disturb the public peace or obstruct them in their religious worship." Relying on this provision of the State Constitution in *Society of Jesus of New England v. Boston Landmark Commission*, 409 Mass. 38, 564 N.E. 2d 571 (1990), the Massachusetts Supreme Judicial Court invalidated an order of a city commission that sought to prohibit the Jesuits from changing the interior space of a church in conformity with the teachings of Vatican II.

Should the fact that theological self-understandings of religious communities are at stake in the architecture of sacred buildings impede the movement to include religious buildings within the power of the government to preserve buildings, even of rather recent vintage, for their "historic value"? In *First Covenant Church of Seattle v. City of Seattle*, 120 Wash. 2d 203, 840 P.2d 174 (1992) the court, on remand after *Smith*, again held that application of landmark preservation ordinance to exterior of church building violates free exercise guarantees of First Amendment and of the state constitution. The court noted that "First Covenant claims, and no one disputes, that its church building itself 'is an expression of Christian belief and message' and that conveying religious beliefs is part of the building's function." Should a church's willingness to allow a building to be landmarked make a difference? *See Rector, Wardens & Members of Vestry of St. Bartholomew's Church v. New York*, 914 F. 2d 348 (2d Cir. 1990), cert. denied, 499 U.S. 905 (1991) (denying exemption from landmarks preservation ordinance in light of *Smith II*).

Professor Carmella was not only a leading commentator urging restraint in the application of landmarking laws to church buildings, but also a leading architect in the deconstruction or demolition of RFRA. *See* Eugene Gressman and Angela C. Carmella, "The RFRA Revision of the Free Exercise Clause," 57 *Ohio St. L.J.* 65 (1996 ("The RFRA is a congressional arrow aimed directly at the heart of the independent judicial function of constitutional interpretation."). *See also* William W. VanAlstyne, "The Failure of the Religious Freedom Restoration Act Under Section 5 of the Fourteenth Amendment," 46 *Duke L.J.* 291 (1996); Christopher L. Eisgruber and Lawrence G. Sager, "Why the Religious Freedom Restoration Act Is Unconstitutional," 69 *N.Y.U.L. Rev.* 437 (1994); and Marci Hamilton, "The Religious Freedom Restoration Act: Letting the Fox into the Henhouse Under Cover of Section 5 of the Fourteenth Amendment," 16 *Cardozo L.Rev.* 357 (1994). In particular, the critics of RFRA argued two difficulties with the statute. First, the doctrine of separation of powers prohibits congressional legislation that appeared to "reverse" legislatively a judgment of the Court. Second, they argued, Congress exceeded its enforcement power in section five of the Fourteenth Amendment by enacting so broad a statute affecting virtually all state and local laws.

Both of these claims were pressed in the following case. On the record before it, the Court could only address the second claim, the application of RFRA to the states, but it provided expansive dicta on the first point. In *South Carolina v. Katzenbach*, 383 U.S. 301 (1966) and *Katzenbach v. Morgan*, 384 U.S. 641 (1966), the Court sustained the Voting Rights Act of 1965 in opinions that held that Congress may enact rules enforcing the Civil War Amendments broader than those which the judiciary thinks are required on its interpretation of the Constitution. Sensing a retreat from the *Katzenbach* cases, Professor Hamilton cited the dissents from these cases frequently in her brief. The Court took the hint, and limited *Katzenbach* to its precise facts. It focused its concern on the limits on congressional power to enforce the provisions of the Fourteenth Amendment against the states, and ignored the underlying substantive claim of Archbishop Flores that a religious community may determine for itself how to design a place of worship without the interference of the government. After the statement of the facts, the only allusion that Justice Kennedy made to this issue was to acknowledge that various witnesses (including Professor Nadine Strossen, President of the ACLU, and Professors Gaffney and Laycock) during the congressional hearings on RFRA had testified that "historic preservation laws (like the one at issue here), as an incident of their normal operation, have adverse effects on churches and synagogues."

City of Boerne v. Flores

521 U.S. 507 (1997).

Marci A. Hamilton argued the cause for the Petitioner. *Jeffrey S. Sutton*, State Solicitor of Ohio, argued for Ohio, Arizona, Colorado, Delaware, Florida, Hawaii, Idaho, Mississippi, Nevada, New Hampshire, North Carolina, Oklahoma, the Commonwealth of Pennsylvania, and the Territories of American Samoa, Guam and The Virgin Islands, as amici curiae by special leave of the Court.

Douglas Laycock argued the cause for Respondent Flores. *Walter Dellinger* argued the cause for Intervenor–Respondent United States.

Briefs amicus curiae were filed in support of the Petitioner by *Robert J. Bruno* on behalf of Children's Healthcare Is a Legal Duty, Inc., and American Professional Society on the Abuse of Children; by *John H. Beisner, Barton S. Aronson, Paul W. Edmondson, Valerie Granfield, Elizabeth S. Merritt,* & *Laura S. Nelson Roush,* on behalf of National Trust for Historic Preservation in the United States & National Trust for Historic Preservation; by *Jay S. Bybee, Ronald D. Maines,* & *R. Shawn Gunnarson,* on behalf of the Clarendon Foundation.

Briefs amicus curiae were filed in Support of Respondents by *N. Lee Cooper, Stuart H. Newberger, Joseph N. Onek,* & *Matthew F. Pawa* on behalf of the American Bar Association; *Jay Alan Sekulow, Keith A. Fournier, James M. Henderson, Francis J. Manion, Thomas P. Monaghan, John G. Stepanovich,* & *Walter M. Weber* for the American Center for Law & Justice; by *Kevin J. Hasson, Eric W. Treene,* & *Roman P. Storzer* on behalf of the Becket Fund for Religious Liberty; by *Marc D. Stern,* American Jewish Congress, *Oliver S. Thomas,* National Council of Churches, *J. Brent Walker* & *Melissa Rogers,* Baptist Joint Committee on Public Affairs, *Steven T. McFarland,* Christian Legal Society, *Aron U. Raskas* & *Nathan J. Diament,* Union of Orthodox Jewish Congregations of America, *Michael Farris,* Home School Defense Association, *Samuel Rabinove* & *Richard Foltin,* American Jewish Committee; *Elliot Mincberg,* People for the American Way, *David Zwiebel,* Agudath Israel, *Steven R. Shapiro,* American Civil Liberties Union, *Steven K. Green,* Americans United for Separation of Church and State, & *Jack F. Trope,* Association of American Indian Affairs, on behalf of the Coalition for the Free Exercise of Religion ; by *Nathan Lewin, Mathew S. Nosanchuk,* & Dennis Rapps, on behalf of the National Jewish Commission on Law and Public Affairs; by *Nancie G. Marsulla* & *Barry C. Hodge,* on behalf of Defenders of Property Rights; *Norman J. Chachkin, Elaine R. Jones, David T. Goldberg,* & *Theodore M. Shaw,* on behalf of NAACP Legal Defense and Educational Fund, Inc.; by *William Bentley Ball* & *Richard E. Connell* on behalf of National Committee for Amish Religious Freedom; by *Michael Joseph Woodruff, Stephen M. Clarke, Isaac M. Jaroslawicz, J. Matthew Szymanski,* & *Scott J. Ward,* on behalf of Prison Fellowship Ministries and the Aleph Institute; by *Mark E. Chopko, Jeffrey Hunter Moon,* & *Michael W. McConnell* on behalf of the United States Catholic Conference, the Evangelical Lutheran Church in America, the Orthodox Church in America, and the Evangelical Covenant Church.

Thurston Greene filed a brief amicus curiae in support of neither party.

■ JUSTICE KENNEDY delivered the opinion of the Court, in which CHIEF JUSTICE REHNQUIST and JUSTICES STEVENS, THOMAS, and GINSBURG, JJ., joined, and in all but Part III–A–1 of which JUSTICE SCALIA joined.

A decision by local zoning authorities to deny a church a building permit was challenged under the Religious Freedom Restoration Act of 1993 (RFRA), 107 Stat. 1488, 42 U.S.C. § 2000bb et seq. The case calls into question the authority of Congress to enact RFRA. We conclude the statute exceeds Congress' power.

I

Situated on a hill in the city of Boerne, Texas, some 28 miles northwest of San Antonio, is St. Peter Catholic Church. Built in 1923, the church's structure replicates the mission style of the region's earlier history. The church seats about 230 worshippers, a number too small for its growing parish. Some 40 to 60 parishioners cannot be accommodated at some Sunday masses. In order to meet the needs of the congregation the Archbishop of San Antonio gave permission to the parish to plan alterations to enlarge the building.

A few months later, the Boerne City Council passed an ordinance authorizing the city's Historic Landmark Commission to prepare a preservation plan with proposed historic landmarks and districts. Under the ordinance, the Commission must preapprove construction affecting historic landmarks or buildings in a historic district.

Soon afterwards, the Archbishop applied for a building permit so construction to enlarge the church could proceed. City authorities, relying on the ordinance and the designation of a historic district (which, they argued, included the church), denied the application. The Archbishop brought this suit challenging the permit denial in the United States District Court for the Western District of Texas.

The complaint contained various claims, but to this point the litigation has centered on RFRA and the question of its constitutionality. The Archbishop relied upon RFRA as one basis for relief from the refusal to issue the permit. The District Court concluded that by enacting RFRA Congress exceeded the scope of its enforcement power under § 5 of the Fourteenth Amendment. The court certified its order for interlocutory appeal and the Fifth Circuit reversed, finding RFRA to be constitutional. We granted certiorari and now reverse.

II

Congress enacted RFRA in direct response to the Court's decision in *Employment Div. v. Smith*, [section 10 above]. There we considered a Free Exercise Clause claim brought by members of the Native American Church who were denied unemployment benefits when they lost their jobs because they had used peyote. Their practice was to ingest peyote for sacramental purposes, and they challenged an Oregon statute of general applicability which made use of the drug criminal. In evaluating the claim, we declined to apply the balancing test set forth in *Sherbert* [section 5 above] under which we would have asked whether Oregon's prohibition substantially burdened a religious practice and, if it did, whether the burden was justified by a compelling government interest. We stated: "Government's ability to enforce generally applicable prohibitions of socially harmful conduct ... cannot depend on measuring the effects of a governmental action on a religious objector's spiritual development. To make an individual's obligation to obey such a law contingent upon the law's coincidence with his religious beliefs, except where the State's interest is 'compelling' ... contradicts both constitutional tradition and common sense.'' (internal quotation marks and citation omitted).

The application of the *Sherbert* test, the *Smith* decision explained, would have produced an anomaly in the law, a constitutional right to ignore neutral laws of general applicability. The anomaly would have been accentuated, the Court reasoned, by the difficulty of determining whether a particular practice was central to an individual's religion. We explained, moreover, that it "is not within the judicial ken to question the centrality of particular beliefs or practices to a faith, or the validity of particular litigants' interpretations of those creeds.'' (internal quotation marks and citation omitted).

The only instances where a neutral, generally applicable law had failed to pass constitutional muster, the *Smith* Court noted, were cases in which other constitutional protections were at stake. *Yoder* [section 7 above].... The *Smith* decision acknowledged the Court had employed the *Sherbert* test in considering free exercise challenges to state unemployment compensation rules .. in *Sherbert, Thomas* [section 4 above], and *Hobbie* [section 5 above]. Those cases, the Court explained, stand for "the proposition that where the State has in place a system of individual exemptions, it may not refuse to extend that system to cases of religious hardship without compelling reason.'' (internal quotation marks omitted)....

These points of constitutional interpretation were debated by Members of Congress in hearings and floor debates. Many criticized the Court's reasoning, and this disagreement resulted in the passage of RFRA [for the essential provisions of the Act, see section 10 above]. In accordance with RFRA's usage of the term, we shall use "state law" to include local and municipal ordinances.

III

A

Under our Constitution, the Federal Government is one of enumerated powers. *McCulloch v. Maryland*, 17 U.S. 316, 405 (1819); *see also* The Federalist No. 45 (J. Madison). The judicial authority to determine the constitutionality of laws, in cases and controversies, is based on the premise that the "powers of the legislature are defined and limited; and that those limits may not be mistaken, or forgotten, the constitution is written.'' *Marbury v. Madison*, 5 U.S. 137, 176 (1803).

Congress relied on its Fourteenth Amendment enforcement power in enacting the most far reaching and substantial of RFRA's provisions, those which impose its requirements on the States. *See* Religious Freedom Restoration Act of 1993, S. Rep. No. 103–111, pp. 13–14 (1993) (Senate Report); H.R. Rep. No. 103–88, p. 9 (1993) (House Report). The Fourteenth Amendment provides, in relevant part: "Section 1.... No State shall make or enforce any law which shall abridge the privileges or immunities of citizens of the United States; nor shall any State deprive any person of life, liberty, or property, without due process of law; nor deny to any person within its jurisdiction the equal protection of the laws . . . . . Section 5. The Congress shall have power to enforce, by appropriate legislation, the provisions of this article." The parties disagree over whether RFRA is a proper exercise of Congress' § 5 power "to enforce" by "appropriate legislation" the constitutional guarantee that no State shall deprive any person of "life, liberty, or property, without due process of law" nor deny any person "equal protection of the laws."

In defense of the Act respondent contends, with support from the United States as amicus, that RFRA is permissible enforcement legislation. Congress, it is said, is only protecting by legislation one of the liberties guaranteed by the Fourteenth Amendment's Due Process Clause, the free exercise of religion, beyond what is necessary under *Smith*. It is said the congressional decision to dispense with proof of deliberate or overt discrimination and instead concentrate on a law's effects accords with the settled understanding that § 5 includes the power to enact legislation designed to prevent as well as remedy constitutional violations. It is further contended that Congress' § 5 power is not limited to remedial or preventive legislation.

All must acknowledge that § 5 is "a positive grant of legislative power" to Congress, *Katzenbach v. Morgan*, 384 U.S. 641, 651(1966). In *Ex parte Virginia*, 100 U.S. 339, 345–346 (1880), we explained the scope of Congress' § 5 power in the following broad terms: "Whatever legislation is appropriate, that is, adapted to carry out the objects the amendments have in view, whatever tends to enforce submission to the prohibitions they contain, and to secure to all persons the enjoyment of perfect equality of civil rights and the equal protection of the laws against State denial or invasion, if not prohibited, is brought within the domain of congressional power." Legislation which deters or remedies constitutional violations can fall within the sweep of Congress' enforcement power even if in the process it prohibits conduct which is not itself unconstitutional and intrudes into "legislative spheres of autonomy previously reserved to the States." *Fitzpatrick v. Bitzer*, 427 U.S. 445, 455 (1976). For example, the Court upheld a suspension of literacy tests and similar voting requirements under Congress' parallel power to enforce the provisions of the Fifteenth Amendment, see U.S. Const., Amdt. 15, § 2, as a measure to combat racial discrimination in voting, *South Carolina v. Katzenbach*, 383 U.S. 301, 308 (1966), despite the facial constitutionality of the tests under *Lassiter v. Northampton County Bd. of Elections*, 360 U.S. 45 (1959). We have also concluded that other measures protecting voting rights are within Congress' power to enforce the Fourteenth and Fifteenth Amendments, despite the burdens those measures placed on the States. *South Carolina v. Katzenbach* (upholding several provisions of the Voting Rights Act of 1965); *Katzenbach v. Morgan* (upholding ban on literacy tests that prohibited certain people schooled in Puerto Rico from voting) (other cases omitted).

It is also true, however, that "as broad as the congressional enforcement power is, it is not unlimited." *Oregon v. Mitchell* (opinion of Black, J.).

In assessing the breadth of § 5's enforcement power, we begin with its text. Congress has been given the power "to enforce" the "provisions of this article." We agree with respondent, of course, that Congress can enact legislation under § 5 enforcing the constitutional right to the free exercise of religion. The "provisions of this article," to which § 5 refers, include the Due Process Clause of the Fourteenth Amendment. Congress' power to enforce the Free Exercise Clause follows from our holding in *Cantwell* [section 1 above] that the "fundamental concept of liberty embodied in [the Fourteenth Amendment's Due Process Clause] embraces the liberties guaranteed by the First Amendment."

Congress' power under § 5, however, extends only to "enforcing" the provisions of the Fourteenth Amendment. The Court has described this power as "remedial," *South Carolina v. Katzenbach*. The design of the Amendment and the text of § 5 are inconsistent with the suggestion that Congress has the power to decree the substance of the Fourteenth Amendment's restrictions on the States. Legislation which alters the meaning of the Free Exercise Clause cannot be said to be enforcing the Clause. Congress does not enforce a constitutional right by changing what the right is. It has been given the power "to enforce," not the power to determine what constitutes a constitutional violation. Were it not so, what Congress would be enforcing would no longer be, in any meaningful sense, the "provisions of [the Fourteenth Amendment]."

While the line between measures that remedy or prevent unconstitutional actions and measures that make a substantive change in the governing law is not easy to discern, and Congress must have wide latitude in determining where it lies, the distinction exists and must be observed. There must be a congruence and proportionality between the injury to be prevented or remedied and the means adopted to that end. Lacking such a connection, legislation may become substantive in operation and effect. History and our case law support drawing the distinction, one apparent from the text of the Amendment.

1

[Justice Kennedy offered an interpretation of the legislative history surrounding the adoption of the Fourteenth Amendment that he said "confirms the remedial, rather than substantive, nature of the Enforcement Clause."]

————

As enacted, the Fourteenth Amendment confers substantive rights against the States which, like the provisions of the Bill of Rights, are self-executing. Cf. *South Carolina v. Katzenbach*. The power to interpret the Constitution in a case or controversy remains in the Judiciary.

2

[Justice Kennedy discussed the Court's earliest cases on the Fourteenth Amendment, which he said confirmed "the remedial and preventive nature of Congress' enforcement power, and the limitation inherent in the power." He acknowledged that "the specific holdings of these early cases might have been superseded or modified" (citing *Heart of Atlanta Motel, Inc. v. United States* and *United States v. Guest*) but concluded that the "treatment of Congress' § 5 power [in these early cases] as corrective or preventive, not definitional, has not been questioned" even in recent cases such as *South Carolina v. Katzenbach* and *Oregon v. Mitchell*.]

————

There is language in our opinion in *Katzenbach v. Morgan* which could be interpreted as acknowledging a power in Congress to enact legislation that expands the rights contained in § 1 of the Fourteenth Amendment. This is not a necessary interpretation, however, or even the best one. [Unlike RFRA, *Morgan*] rested on unconstitutional discrimination by New York and Congress' reasonable attempt to combat it. If Congress could define its own powers by altering the Fourteenth Amendment's meaning, no longer would the Constitution be "superior paramount law, unchangeable by ordinary means." It would be "on a level with ordinary legislative acts, and, like other acts, ... alterable when the legislature shall please to alter it." *Marbury v. Madison*. Under this approach, it is difficult to conceive of a principle that would limit congressional power. Shifting legislative majorities could change the Constitution and effectively circumvent the difficult and detailed amendment process contained in Article V.

We now turn to consider whether RFRA can be considered enforcement legislation under § 5 of the Fourteenth Amendment.

B

Respondent contends that RFRA is a proper exercise of Congress' remedial or preventive power. The Act, it is said, is a reasonable means of protecting the free exercise of religion as defined by *Smith*. It prevents and remedies laws which are enacted with the unconstitutional object of targeting religious beliefs and practices. See *Church of the Lukumi Babalu Aye* [section 12 below] ("[A] law targeting religious beliefs as such is never permissible"). To avoid the difficulty of proving such violations, it is said, Congress can simply invalidate any law which imposes a substantial burden on a religious practice unless it is justified by a compelling interest and is the least restrictive means of accomplishing that interest. If Congress can prohibit laws with discriminatory effects in order to prevent racial discrimination in violation of the Equal Protection Clause (citations omitted), then it can do the same, respondent argues, to promote religious liberty.

While preventive rules are sometimes appropriate remedial measures, there must be a congruence between the means used and the ends to be achieved. The appropriateness of remedial measures must be considered in light of the evil presented. Strong measures appropriate to address one harm may be an unwarranted response to another, lesser one.

A comparison between RFRA and the Voting Rights Act is instructive. In contrast to the record which confronted Congress and the judiciary in the voting rights cases, RFRA's legislative record lacks examples of modern instances of generally applicable laws passed because of religious bigotry. The history of persecution in this country detailed in the hearings mentions no episodes occurring in the past 40 years (citations to congressional hearing on RFRA omitted). It is difficult to maintain that they are examples of legislation enacted or enforced due to animus or hostility to the burdened religious practices or that they indicate some widespread pattern of religious discrimination in this country. Congress' concern was with the incidental burdens imposed, not the object or purpose of the legislation (citations to legislative history omitted). This lack of support in the legislative record, however, is not RFRA's most serious shortcoming. Judicial deference, in most cases, is based not on the state of the legislative record Congress compiles but "on due regard for the decision of the body constitutionally appointed to decide." *Oregon v. Mitchell* (opinion of Harlan, J.). As a general matter, it is for Congress to determine the method by which it will reach a decision.

Regardless of the state of the legislative record, RFRA cannot be considered remedial, preventive legislation, if those terms are to have any meaning. RFRA is so out of proportion to a supposed remedial or preventive object that it cannot be understood as responsive to, or designed to prevent, unconstitutional behavior. It appears, instead, to attempt a substantive change in constitutional protections. Preventive measures prohibiting certain types of laws may be appropriate when there is reason to believe that many of the laws affected by the congressional enactment have a significant likelihood of being unconstitutional. . . .

RFRA is not so confined. Sweeping coverage ensures its intrusion at every level of government, displacing laws and prohibiting official actions of almost every description and regardless of subject matter. RFRA's restrictions apply to every agency and official of the Federal, State, and local Governments. RFRA applies to all federal and state law, statutory or otherwise, whether adopted before or after its enactment. RFRA has no termination date or termination mechanism. Any law is subject to challenge at any time by any individual who alleges a substantial burden on his or her free exercise of religion. . . .

The stringent test RFRA demands of state laws reflects a lack of proportionality or congruence between the means adopted and the legitimate end to be achieved. If an objector can show a substantial burden on his free exercise, the State must demonstrate a compelling governmental interest and show that the law is the least restrictive means of furthering its interest. Claims that a law substantially burdens someone's exercise of religion will often be difficult to contest (citations omitted). Requiring a State to demonstrate a compelling interest and show that it has adopted the least restrictive means of achieving that interest is the most demanding test known to constitutional law. If " 'compelling interest' really means what it says . . . many laws will not meet the test. . . . [The test] would open the prospect of constitutionally required religious exemptions from civic obligations of almost every conceivable kind." *Smith*. Laws valid under *Smith* would fall under RFRA without regard to whether they had the object of stifling or punishing free exercise. We make these observations not to reargue the position of the majority in *Smith* but to illustrate the substantive alteration of its holding attempted by RFRA. Even assuming RFRA would be interpreted in effect to mandate some lesser test, say one equivalent to intermediate scrutiny, the statute nevertheless would require searching judicial scrutiny of state law with the attendant likelihood of invalidation. This is a considerable congressional intrusion into the States' traditional prerogatives and general authority to regulate for the health and welfare of their citizens.

The substantial costs RFRA exacts, both in practical terms of imposing a heavy litigation burden on the States and in terms of curtailing their traditional general regulatory power, far exceed any pattern or practice of unconstitutional conduct under the Free Exercise Clause as interpreted in *Smith*. Simply put, RFRA is not designed to identify and counteract state laws likely to be unconstitutional because of their treatment of religion. In most cases, the state laws to which RFRA applies are not ones which will have been motivated by religious bigotry. . . . It is a reality of the modern regulatory state that numerous state laws, such as the zoning regulations at issue here, impose a substantial burden on a large class of individuals. When the exercise of religion has been burdened in an incidental way by a law of general application, it does not follow that the persons affected have been burdened any more than other citizens, let alone burdened because of their religious beliefs. In addition, the Act imposes in every case a least restrictive means requirement—a requirement that was not used in the pre-*Smith* jurisprudence RFRA purported to codify—which also indicates that the legislation is broader than is appropriate if the goal is to prevent and remedy constitutional violations.

When Congress acts within its sphere of power and responsibilities, it has not just the right but the duty to make its own informed judgment on the meaning and force of the Constitution. This has been clear from the early days of the Republic. In 1789, when a Member of the House of Representatives objected to a debate on the constitutionality of legislation based on the theory that "it would be officious" to consider the constitutionality of a measure that did not affect the House, James Madison explained that "it is incontrovertibly of as much importance to this branch of the Government as to any other, that the constitution should be preserved entire. It is our duty." 1 Annals of Congress 500 (1789). Were it otherwise, we would not afford Congress the presumption of validity its enactments now enjoy.

Our national experience teaches that the Constitution is preserved best when each part of the government respects both the Constitution and the proper actions and determinations of the other branches. When the Court has interpreted the Constitution, it has acted within the province of the Judicial Branch, which embraces the duty to say what the law is. *Marbury v. Madison*. When the political branches of the Government act against the background of a judicial interpretation of the Constitution already issued, it must be understood that in later cases and controversies the Court will treat its precedents with the respect due them under settled principles, including stare decisis, and contrary expectations must be disappointed.

RFRA was designed to control cases and controversies, such as the one before us; but as the provisions of the federal statute here invoked are beyond congressional authority, it is this Court's precedent [in *Smith*], not RFRA, which must control.

It is for Congress in the first instance to "determine whether and what legislation is needed to secure the guarantees of the Fourteenth Amendment," and its conclusions are entitled to much deference. *Morgan.* Congress' discretion is not unlimited, however, and the courts retain the power, as they have since *Marbury v. Madison*, to determine if Congress has exceeded its authority under the Constitution. Broad as the power of Congress is under the Enforcement Clause of the Fourteenth Amendment, RFRA contradicts vital principles necessary to maintain separation of powers and the federal balance. The judgment of the Court of Appeals sustaining the Act's constitutionality is *reversed*. It is so ordered.

■ JUSTICE STEVENS, concurring.

In my opinion, the Religious Freedom Restoration Act of 1993 (RFRA) is a "law respecting an establishment of religion" that violates the First Amendment to the Constitution.

If the historic landmark on the hill in Boerne happened to be a museum or an art gallery owned by an atheist, it would not be eligible for an exemption from the city ordinances that forbid an enlargement of the structure. Because the landmark is owned by the Catholic Church, it is claimed that RFRA gives its owner a federal statutory entitlement to an exemption from a generally applicable, neutral civil law. Whether the Church would actually prevail under the statute or not, the statute has provided the Church with a legal weapon that no atheist or agnostic can obtain. This governmental preference for religion, as opposed to irreligion, is forbidden by the First Amendment. *Wallace v. Jaffree* [Chapter Fourteen, section 2].

■ JUSTICE SCALIA, with whom JUSTICE STEVENS joins, concurring in part.

■ [JUSTICE SCALIA offered specific replies to the claim of JUSTICE O'CONNOR that historical materials support a result contrary to the one reached in *Smith*. He concluded:]

It seems to me that the most telling point made by the dissent is to be found, not in what it says, but in what it fails to say. Had the understanding in the period surrounding the ratification of the Bill of Rights been that the various forms of accommodation discussed by the dissent were constitutionally required (either by State Constitutions or by the Federal Constitution), it would be surprising not to find a single state or federal case refusing to enforce a generally applicable statute because of its failure to make accommodation. Yet the dissent cites none—and to my knowledge, and to the knowledge of the academic defenders of the dissent's position, none exists.

■ JUSTICE O'CONNOR, with whom JUSTICE BREYER joins except as to a portion of Part I, dissenting.

I dissent from the Court's disposition of this case. I agree with the Court that the issue before us is whether the Religious Freedom Restoration Act (RFRA) is a proper exercise of Congress' power to enforce § 5 of the Fourteenth Amendment. But as a yardstick for measuring the constitutionality of RFRA, the Court uses its holding in *Smith*, the decision that prompted Congress to enact RFRA as a means of more rigorously enforcing the Free Exercise Clause. I remain of the view that *Smith* was wrongly decided, and I would use this case to reexamine the Court's holding there. Therefore, I would direct the parties to brief the question whether *Smith* represents the correct understanding of the Free Exercise Clause and set the case for reargument. If the Court were to correct the misinterpretation of the Free Exercise Clause set forth in *Smith*, it would simultaneously put our First Amendment jurisprudence back on course and allay the legitimate concerns of a majority in Congress who believed that *Smith* improperly restricted religious liberty. We would then be in a position to review RFRA in light of a proper interpretation of the Free Exercise Clause.

I

[Justice O'Connor stated agreement with much of the Court's opinion, including the proposition that Congress lacks the "power to decree the substance of the Fourteenth Amendment's restrictions on the States" and the "ability independently to define or expand the scope of constitutional rights by statute."]

————

This recognition does not, of course, in any way diminish Congress' obligation to draw its own conclusions regarding the Constitution's meaning. Congress, no less than this Court, is called upon to consider the requirements of the Constitution and to act in accordance with its dictates. But when it enacts legislation in furtherance of its delegated powers, Congress must make its judgments consistent with this Court's exposition of the Constitution and with the limits placed on its legislative authority by provisions such as the Fourteenth Amendment.

The Court's analysis of whether RFRA is a constitutional exercise of Congress' § 5 power is premised on the assumption that *Smith* correctly interprets the Free Exercise Clause. This is an assumption that I do not accept. I continue to believe that *Smith* adopted an improper standard for deciding free exercise claims. In *Smith*, five Members of this Court—without briefing or argument on the issue—interpreted the Free Exercise Clause to permit the government to prohibit, without justification, conduct mandated by an individual's religious beliefs, so long as the prohibition is generally applicable. Contrary to the Court's holding in that case, however, the Free Exercise Clause is not simply an antidiscrimination principle that protects only against those laws that single out religious practice for unfavorable treatment. *See Smith* (O'Connor, J., concurring in judgment). Rather, the Clause is best understood as an affirmative guarantee of the right to participate in religious practices and conduct without impermissible governmental interference, even when such conduct conflicts with a neutral, generally applicable law. Before *Smith*, our free exercise cases were generally in keeping with this idea: where a law substantially burdened religiously motivated conduct—regardless whether it was specifically targeted at religion or applied generally—we required government to justify that law with a compelling state interest and to use means narrowly tailored to achieve that interest (citations omitted).

The Court's rejection of this principle in *Smith* is supported neither by precedent nor by history. The decision has harmed religious liberty (citations omitted).

Stare decisis concerns should not prevent us from revisiting our holding in *Smith*.... Accordingly, I believe that we should reexamine our holding in *Smith*, and do so in this very case. In its place, I would return to a rule that requires government to justify any substantial burden on religiously motivated conduct by a compelling state interest and to impose that burden only by means narrowly tailored to achieve that interest.

II

... The historical evidence casts doubt on the Court's current interpretation of the Free Exercise Clause. The record instead reveals that its drafters and ratifiers more likely viewed the Free Exercise Clause as a guarantee that government may not unnecessarily hinder believers from freely practicing their religion, a position consistent with our pre-*Smith* jurisprudence....

A

[Justice O'Connor acknowledged that "it is not exactly clear what the Framers [of the free exercise provision] thought the phrase signified." But, she argued:] "a variety of sources supplement the legislative history and shed light on the original understanding of the Free Exercise Clause. These materials suggest that—contrary to *Smith*—the Framers did not intend simply to prevent the Government from adopting laws that discriminated against religion. Although the Framers may not have asked precisely the questions about religious liberty that we do today, the historical record indicates that they believed that the Constitution affirmatively protects religious free exercise and that it limits the government's ability to intrude on religious practice."

B

[Justice O'Connor explored the origins of the free exercise principle in American colonial history. She concluded:]

[E]arly in our country's history, several colonies acknowledged that freedom to pursue one's chosen religious beliefs was an essential liberty. Moreover, these colonies appeared to recognize that government should interfere in religious matters only when necessary to protect the civil peace or to prevent "licentiousness." In other words, when religious beliefs conflicted with civil law, religion prevailed unless important state interests militated otherwise. Such notions parallel the ideas expressed in our pre-*Smith* cases—that government may not hinder believers from freely exercising their religion, unless necessary to further a significant state interest.

C

[Justice O'Connor explored the re-emergence of the principles expounded in these early charters over a century later in state constitutions that were adopted in the flurry of constitution-drafting that followed the American Revolution, noting that by 1789, "every State but Connecticut had incorporated some version of a free exercise clause into its constitution." After citing several of the provisions relating to free exercise in the state constitutions, she concluded:]

————

The language used in these state constitutional provisions and the Northwest Ordinance strongly suggests that, around the time of the drafting of the Bill of Rights, it was generally accepted that the right to "free exercise" required, where possible, accommodation of religious practice. If not—and if the Court was correct in *Smith* that generally applicable laws are enforceable regardless of religious conscience—there would have been no need for these documents to specify, as the New York Constitution did, that rights of conscience should not be "construed as to excuse acts of licentiousness, or justify practices inconsistent with the peace or safety of [the] State." Such a proviso would have been superfluous. Instead, these documents make sense only if the right to free exercise was viewed as generally superior to ordinary legislation, to be overridden only when necessary to secure important government purposes.

D

[Justice O'Connor argued that the practice of the colonies and early States "bears out the conclusion that, at the time the Bill of Rights was ratified, it was accepted that government should, when possible, accommodate religious practice."]

E

[Noting that "the writings of the early leaders who helped to shape our Nation provide a final source of insight into the original understanding of the Free Exercise Clause," Justice O'Connor discussed the thoughts of James Madison, Thomas Jefferson, George Washington, Oliver Ellsworth, and Isaac Backus. She distilled three general principles from their writings.]

————

First, these early leaders accorded religious exercise a special constitutional status. The right to free exercise was a substantive guarantee of individual liberty, no less important than the right to free speech or the right to just compensation for the taking of property.... Second, all agreed that government interference in religious practice was not to be lightly countenanced. Finally, all shared the conviction that 'true religion and good morals are the only solid foundation of public liberty and happiness.' (quoting Continental Congress).... To give meaning to these ideas—particularly in a society characterized by religious pluralism and pervasive regulation—there will be times when the Constitution requires government to accommodate the needs of those citizens whose religious practices conflict with generally applicable law.

III

The Religion Clauses of the Constitution represent a profound commitment to religious liberty. Our Nation's Founders conceived of a Republic receptive to voluntary religious expression, not of a secular society in which religious expression is tolerated only when it does not conflict with a generally applicable law. As the historical sources discussed above show, the Free Exercise Clause is properly understood as an affirmative guarantee of the right to participate in religious activities without impermissible governmental interference, even where a believer's conduct is in tension with a law of general application. Certainly, it is in no way anomalous to accord heightened protection to a right identified in the text of the First Amendment. For example, it has long been the Court's position that freedom of speech—a right enumerated only a few words after the right to free exercise—has special constitutional status. Given the centrality of freedom of speech and religion to the American concept of personal liberty, it is altogether reasonable to conclude that both should be treated with the highest degree of respect.

Although it may provide a bright line, the rule the Court declared in *Smith* does not faithfully serve the purpose of the Constitution. Accordingly, I believe that it is essential for the Court to reconsider its holding in *Smith*—and to do so in this very case. I would therefore direct the parties to brief this issue and set the case for reargument.

I respectfully dissent from the Court's disposition of this case.

■ JUSTICES SOUTER and BREYER each filed short dissents.

NOTES AND QUESTIONS

1. *Judicial Respect for Constitutional Decision Making by the Coordinate Branches of Government.* In *Employment Division v. Smith* [section 10 above], Justice Scalia wrote: "Values that are protected against government interference through enshrinement in the Bill of Rights are not thereby banished from the political process. Just as a society that believes in the negative protection accorded to the press by the First Amendment is likely to enact laws that affirmatively foster the dissemination of the printed word, so also a society that believes in the negative protection accorded to religious belief can be expected to be solicitous of that value in its legislation as well." Was the Court respectful of the solicitude of a nearly unanimous Congress when it invalidated RFRA in *Boerne?* Shortly after the enactment of RFRA, Professor Paulsen wrote: "In a system of coordinate interpretive power, each branch should be guided in the exercise of its independent interpretation by a principle of deference to the considered views of the other branches, and by a responsibility of reasonable

accommodation of its independent views to those of the others." Michael Stokes Paulsen, "The Most Dangerous Branch: Executive Power to Say What the Law Is," 83 *Geo. L.J.* 217, 332 (1994). After *Boerne* Judge Noonan wrote: "It is because of the Court's view of the limited meaning of Free Exercise that the Court can treat RFRA—which offers no definition of Free Exercise, which on its face appears to be a procedural measure establishing a standard of proof and allocating the duty of meeting it—can treat RFRA as a definition made by Congress of a constitutional right. The Court went on to accord the congressional effort no deference, indeed to treat the act of Congress as a kind of usurpation of the judicial power to say what the Constitution means. Does Congress have no power in the area of religion? Free Exercise exists in the First Amendment as a negative on Congress. The power of Congress to act towards the states in matters of religion arises from the Fourteenth Amendment as interpreted by the Supreme Court, which in 1940 effected the basic shift in federal-state relations that the Court now views with suspicion." Noonan, "Free Exercise at the Stake," 84 *Va. L.Rev.* 459, 472–473 (1998). In a similar vein Professor McConnell wrote after *Boerne*: "[W]hen Congress has addressed and resolved a constitutional question, the Court should not overturn that interpretation without a powerful justification." Michael W. McConnell, "Institutions and Interpretation: A Critique of City of Boerne v. Flores," 111 *Harv. L.Rev.* 153, 187 (1997). On the other hand, Professor Currie was emphatically of the view that on grounds of separation of powers and federalism, "Section 5 of the Fourteenth Amendment empowers Congress to enforce its provisions, not to revise them.... Congress cannot tell the Court what the Constitution means." David P. Currie, "RFRA," 39 *Wm & Mary L.Rev.* 637 (1998).

Is the Court's reliance upon *Marbury v. Madison* well placed? If "it is emphatically the province and duty of the judiciary to say what the law is," *Marbury,* do the other branches have any significant role to play in determining the constitutionality of legislation? If this role is stronger after the adoption of the Fourteenth Amendment, which does not empower the judiciary, but Congress to enforce the amendment by appropriate *legislation?* Who should normally determine the appropriateness of legislation, judges or elected officials? The author of *Marbury,* Chief Justice Marshall, noted in *McCulloch v. Maryland* that once it is established that Congress has legislative authority, the scope of that power is broad. Congress, thought it "necessary and proper" to create a national bank. *McCulloch* upheld this decision, even though there is no text expressly conferring power on Congress to establish a bank. Should the Court defer to the Congressional determination of what is "necessary and proper" for the protection of free exercise rights that are *expressly* protected in the First Amendment and made a part of the Fourteenth Amendment either as part of the liberty protected by the Due Process Clause, *Cantwell* [section 1 above] or as Professor Amar argues, as a privilege or immunity of national citizenship? See Akhil Reed Amar, *The Bill of Rights* [Chapter Eight, section 6]? On the other hand, Profesor Currie was of the view that "[i]n demanding 'a congruence and proportionality between the injury to be prevented or remedied and the means adopted to that end,' [*Flores*] the Court in *Flores* set forth an attractive new test to serve notice that it would no longer blindly accept untenable congressional pretenses that a particular measure was 'appropriate' to enforce the Civil War amendments-or 'necessary and proper' to protect interstate or foreign commerce. Nothing less would be consistent with *Marbury v. Madison.*" David P. Currie, "RFRA," 39 *Wm & Mary L.Rev.* 637, 640 (1998).

2. *The Nonpersecution Principle.* Occasionally a justice will describe the avoidance of religious persecution as the purpose of the free exercise principle. For example, dissenting in *Prince v. Massachusetts* [section 1 above], Justice Murphy wrote: "No chapter in human history has been so largely written in terms of persecution and intolerance as the one dealing with religious freedom." Dissenting in *Employment Division v. Smith* [section 10 above], Justice Blackmun wrote: "I do not believe the Founders thought their dearly bought freedom from religious persecution a 'luxury,' but an essential element of liberty." In *Church of the Lukumi Babalu Aye* [section 12 below], Justice Kennedy identified a "fundamental nonpersecution principle of the First Amendment ... that government may not enact laws that suppress religious belief or practice." So well understood is this principle, he wrote, that "few violations are recorded in our opinions." He offered two examples, the refusal of Tennessee to allow clergy members to serve in public office, *McDaniel v. Paty* [Chapter Fifteen, section 2]; and the selective refusal by the City of Pawtucket to allow the Jehovah's Witnesses to use its public parks for public addresses at a religious meeting, *Fowler v. Rhode Island* [Chapter Thirteen, section 1]. The ordinance was not void on its face, but in its discriminatory application to an unpopular religious group. Is viewpoint discrimination the same as religious persecution? If so, then why did Justice Kennedy omit the refusal by the University of Missouri to allow a religious group to use its facilities on the same basis that it allowed other groups, *Widmar v. Vincent* [Chapter Fourteen, section 3B]? Or why did he not mention the refusal of public school district to allow student-initiated, student-led, prayer groups to meet at the school on the same basis as nonreligious extra-curricular groups, *Board of Education of the Westside Community Schools v. Mergens* [Chapter Fourteen, section 2]? Or why did he not mention the refusal of a school district to allow a religious film to be shown to the public at its facilities on the same basis as nonreligious films, *Lamb's Chapel v. Center Moriches Union Free School District* [Chapter Fourteen, section 2]? Or why did he not mention the refusal of the University of Virginia to allow the funding of a student newspaper with a religious viewpoint on the same basis as other nonreligious student papers, *Rosenberger v. Rector and Visitors of the University of Virginia* [Chapter Fourteen, section 3B]?

Justice Kennedy did add to his list of cases involving "persecution" the municipal ordinances enacted by the City of Hialeah that were at issue in the Santeria case. If those municipal ordinances were seen as "persecution," why did he not see a violation of the "fundamental principle" of nonpersecution in *City of Boerne v. Flores*? Kennedy acknowledged these critical facts in *Boerne*: "The church seats about 230 worshippers, a number too small for its growing parish. Some 40 to 60 parishioners cannot be accommodated at some Sunday masses." Archbishop Flores then approved a project to construct a larger sanctuary. The city replied with an ordinance that had the effect of by denying permission to build a larger structure to accommodate those who had to be turned away because of the small size of the church. Kennedy's definition of "persecution" includes "suppress[ing] religious belief or practice." Since the Boerne ordinance had the admitted effect of "suppressing religious belief or practice" for those denied the opportunity to participate in the Mass, why was this not another example of "persecution"? Is the nonpersecution principle like hard core pornography, capable of being known when seen but escaping clear definition, *Jacobellis v. State of Ohio*, 378 U.S. 184, 197 (1964), and thus incapable of serving as a principled way of measuring when free exercise is violated?

Why did Justice Kennedy scour the extensive hearings in search of "the history of persecution in this country"? Does it matter that "the hearings mention[ed] no episodes [of persecution] occurring in the past 40 years"? Is that number invoked to avoid the egregious examples of persecution aimed at the Jehovah's Witnesses a little more than 40 years ago? At the time of the flag salute controversy, these atrocities included beatings, tarring and feathering, castration, and shootings [section 1 above]; during World War II persecution of the Witnesses included mass imprisonment for conscientious objection to military service [section 4 above]. "[I]f one uses Madisonian criteria, Free Exercise has recently been violated when school children in Iowa, Maine, Nebraska, and Ohio were denied by local authorities the right to attend Christian schools, not to mention the burden placed upon the Amish in the 1970s that was alleviated only by *Wisconsin v. Yoder*. The Court would be suffering from amnesia not recollecting these crushing weights laid on conscience in the contemporary United States." John T. Noonan, Jr., "Free Exercise at the Stake," 472.

Justice Kennedy noted that Professor Laycock, who argued the *Boerne* case on behalf of Archbishop Flores, acknowledged in his testimony on RFRA before the Subcommittee on Civil and Constitutional Rights of the House Committee on the Judiciary that "deliberate persecution is not the usual problem in this country." 102d Cong., 2d Sess., 331–334 (1993); *see also* House Report 2 ("[L]aws directly targeting religious practices have become increasingly rare"). Kennedy correctly discerned that "the emphasis of the hearings was on laws of general applicability which place incidental burdens on religion." In light of the fact that *Employment Division v. Smith*—the decision of the Court that the hearings were addressing—was not an instance of "persecution" (or was it?), that should cause no great surprise. The whole point of the hearings was to create a remedy for persons whose free exercise of religion had been burdened not by intentional discrimination of the sort at issue in the *Babalu Aye* case below, but by laws of general applicability. Will not the impact of government regulation on sacred duties more typically arise from such generally applicable statutes than from statutes in which legislators include in the statement of purpose an intent to inflict injury upon a religious community? Will not such generally applicable statutes be typically enacted enacted without any attention to their differential impact upon believers, or much reflection by legislators about the possible negative consequences of these statutes for vital concerns of diverse religious communities?

Finally, Justice Kennedy acknowledged in *Boerne* that "Madison did not say that duties to the Creator are precedent only to those laws specifically directed at religion, nor did he strive simply to prevent deliberate acts of persecution or discrimination." Is this an important historical clue that nonpersecution is not really a good standard for determining a violation of the positive good that Madison insisted upon, both in Virginia [Chapter Six, section 1A] and in the First Congress, "free exercise of religion"?

3. *Scholarly Response to Boerne*. Scholars who had written against the constitutionality of RFRA were unsurprisingly supportive of the outcome in *Boerne*. *See, e.g.*, Christopher L. Eisgruber & Lawrence G. Sager, "Congressional Power and Religious Liberty after City of Boerne V. Flores," 1997 *Sup. Ct. Rev.* 79; Marci A. Hamilton, "The Religious Freedom Restoration Act Is Unconstitution-

al, Period," 1 *U. Pa. J. Const. L.* 1 (1998); Ira C. Lupu, "Why the Congress Was Wrong and the Court Was Right–Reflections on City of Boerne v. Flores," 39 *Wm. & Mary L.Rev.* 793 (1998) For scholarly commentary critical of the case, *see* David Cole, "The Value of Seeing Things Differently: Boerne v. Flores and Congressional Enforcement of the Bill of Rights," 1997 *Sup. Ct. Rev.* 31; Robert F. Drinan, "Reflections on the Demise of the Religious Freedom Restoration Act," 86 Geo. L. J. 101 (1997); Douglas Laycock, "Conceptual Gulfs in City of Boerne v. Flores," 39 Wm. & Mary L. J. 743 (1998); Michael W. McConnell, "Institutions and Interpretation: A Critique of City of Boerne v. Flores," 111 *Harv. L.Rev.* 153 (1997); and John T. Noonan, Jr., "Religious Liberty At the Stake," 84 *Va. L.Rev.* 459 (1998).

4. *Congressional Response to Boerne.* Shortly after *Boerne* was decided, the Coalition for Free Exercise of Religion met again with Congressional leaders, who promised hearings to develop a fuller record of the violation of religious freedom by state and local government. May Congress assert a standard for judicial review predicated upon some other explicit grant of power than the Enforcement Clause of the Fourteenth Amendment? Shortly after *Boerne*, the same coalition of religious communities that had supported RFRA initiated efforts to explore new legislation designed to overcome the hurdles to constitutionality the Court found in *Boerne*. The 105th Congress held hearings in the House and Senate Judiciary Committees, but did not report out any legislation.

In the next Congress, consensus was reached on legislation designed to provide a remedy for religious communities experiencing conflicts with zoning boards, and to individuals in prisons and nursing homes. President Clinton signed it on September 22, 2000. Its principal provisions follow.

Religious Land Use and Institutionalized Persons Act of 2000, Pub. L. 106–274, 114 Stat 803.

SEC. 2.   PROTECTION OF LAND USE AS RELIGIOUS EXERCISE.

(a) SUBSTANTIAL BURDENS.—

(1) GENERAL RULE.—No government shall impose or implement a land use regulation in a manner that imposes a substantial burden on the religious exercise of a person, including a religious assembly or institution, unless the government demonstrates that imposition of the burden on that person, assembly, or institution—(A) is in furtherance of a compelling governmental interest; and (B) is the least restrictive means of furthering that compelling governmental interest. . . .

(b) DISCRIMINATION AND EXCLUSION.—

(1) EQUAL TERMS.—No government shall impose or implement a land use regulation in a manner that treats a religious assembly or institution on less than equal terms with a nonreligious assembly or institution.

(2) NONDISCRIMINATION.—No government shall impose or implement a land use regulation that discriminates against any assembly or institution on the basis of religion or religious denomination.

(3) EXCLUSIONS AND LIMITS.—No government shall impose or implement a land use regulation that—(A) totally excludes religious

assemblies from a jurisdiction; or (B) unreasonably limits religious assemblies, institutions, or structures within a jurisdiction. . . .

SEC. 3. PROTECTION OF RELIGIOUS EXERCISE OF INSTITUTION-ALIZED PERSONS.

(a) GENERAL RULE.—No government shall impose a substantial burden on the religious exercise of a person residing in or confined to an institution, as defined in section 2 of the Civil Rights of Institutionalized Persons Act (42 U.S.C. 1997), even if the burden results from a rule of general applicability, unless the government demonstrates that imposition of the burden on that person—(1) is in furtherance of a compelling governmental interest; and (2) is the least restrictive means of furthering that compelling governmental interest. . . .

―――――

In an attempt to avoid the finding of unconstitutionality that attached to RFRA in *City of Boerne v. Flores* [above], Congress grounded its power to legislate in this way not upon the enforcement power of the Fourteenth Amendment, but upon the spending power and the power to regulate commerce among the several states. Thus the Act is triggered when a substantial burden is imposed upon religious exercise in a program or activity that receives Federal financial assistance, or when the burden would affect commerce "even if the burden results from a rule of general applicability." The Act also attempts to fall within the rationale of *Employment Division v. Smith* by stating that its provisions are triggered when a "substantial burden is imposed in the implementation of a land use regulation or system of land use regulations, under which a government makes, or has in place formal or informal procedures or practices that permit the government to make, individualized assessments of the proposed uses for the property involved." It also tries to avoid another problem for protection of religious liberty identified in *Smith:* "The term 'religious exercise' includes any exercise of religion, whether or not compelled by, or central to, a system of religious belief." Is this legislation constitutional? Why or why not?

5. *State Constitutions and State Religious Freedom Statutes.* The jurisdiction of the United States Supreme Court is limited to federal questions. Rule 10, Rules of the Supreme Court. Thus it may not reverse a decision based exclusively on State constitutional grounds. *See, e.g., Pruneyard Shopping Center v. Robins*, 447 U.S. 74 (1980); *Michigan v. Long*, 463 U.S. 1032 (1983). For a discussion of the role of state constitutional interpretation in dialogue with federal constitutional interpretation, Stuart G. Parsell, Note, Revitalization of the Free Exercise of Religion Under State Constitutions: A Response to Employment Division v. Smith, 68 *Notre Dame L.Rev.* 747 (1993); Tracey Levy, Comment, Rediscovering Rights: State Courts Reconsider the Free Exercise Clauses of Their Own Constitutions in the Wake of Employment Division v. Smith, 67 *Temp. L.Rev.* 1017 (1994). *See generally* G. Alan Tarr & Mary C.A. Porter, *State Supreme Courts in State and Nation* (1988); Jennifer Friesen, *State Constitutional Law: Litigating Individual Rights, Claims and Defenses* (2d ed. 1995); William J. Brennan, Jr., "State Constitutions and the Protection of Individual Rights," 90 *Harv. L.Rev.* 489 (1977); William J. Brennan, Jr., "The Bill of Rights and the States: The Revival of State Constitutions as

Guardians of Individual Rights," 61 *N.Y.U.L.Rev.* 535 (1986); Hans A. Linde, "First Things First: Rediscovering the States' Bill of Rights," 9 *U.Balt.L.Rev.* 379 (1980); and Hans A. Linde, "E Pluribus," 18 *Ga.L.Rev.* 165 (1984).

Every State has a Bill of Rights offering protection to free exercise of religion. Indeed, state charters with such guarantees existed before the adoption of the Bill of Rights in the federal constitution. For example, in *Society of Jesus of New England v. Boston Landmark Commission*, 409 Mass. 38, 564 N.E. 2d 571 (1990) [this section above], the Massachusetts Supreme Judicial Court relied not on the First Amendment to the federal constitution, but on Article 2 of the 1780 Massachusetts Declaration of Rights, for a result different from that reached in *Boerne*. For other examples of state supreme courts rejecting the *Smith* approach and interpreting their state constitutions to require the equivalent of strict scrutiny whenever a law significantly burdens the free exercise of religion, *see, e.g., Swanner v. Anchorage Equal Rights Comm'n*, 874 P.2d 274, 280–81 (Alaska 1994); and *State v. Hershberger*, 444 N.W.2d 282 (Minn. 1989), vacated, 495 U.S. 901 (1990); on remand, 462 N.W.2d 393 (Minn. 1990). Does Justice O'Connor's discussion of State Constitutions in *Boerne* contain a generous clue about how to proceed after *Smith* and *Boerne*? Now that the U.S. Supreme Court has invalidated RFRA as applied to the States, why should lawyers concerned with adequate safeguards for free exercise bring such cases under the First Amendment to that court? Would a more effective litigation strategy be to press these claims under State constitutional provisions relating to religious freedom? For a rich source of State constitutional materials relating to free exercise, *see* Chester J. Antieau et al., *Religion Under the State Constitutions* (1965). For a more recent discussion of this theme, *see* Angela C. Carmella, "State Constitutional Protection of Religious Exercise: An Emerging Post–Smith Jurisprudence," 1993 *B.Y.U. L.Rev.* 275 (collecting and discussing state constitutional provisions relating to religious freedom). *And see* Mary Ann Glendon & Raul F. Yanes, "Structural Free Exercise," 90 *Mich.L.Rev.* 477, 536–37 (1991) (noting that "a richer interplay of provisions and narratives" comes into play when state constitutions are added to the interpretive mix).

In the oral argument in *Boerne*, Jeffrey Sutton, State Solicitor of Ohio, suggested that RFRA was unnecessary because the several States were already attentive to the protection of religious freedom. If a particular State fails to live up to this promise, should that fact warrant strong State legislation safeguarding free exercise?

12. ANIMAL SACRIFICE

INTRODUCTION. *Santeria*. The Santeria religion originated in the nineteenth century when hundreds of thousands of members of the Yoruba people were brought as slaves from eastern Africa to Cuba. Their traditional African religion absorbed significant elements of Roman Catholicism. The resulting fusion is Santeria, "the way of the saints." The Cuban Yoruba express their devotion to spirits, called *orishas*, through the iconography of Catholic saints, Catholic symbols are often present at Santeria rites, and Santeria devotees attend the Catholic sacraments. *See* 13 *The Encyclopaedia of Religion* 66 (M.

Eliade ed. 1987); 1 *Encyclopaedia of the American Religious Experience* 183 (C. Lippy & P. Williams eds. 1988).

The Santeria faith teaches that every individual has a destiny from God, a destiny fulfilled with the aid and energy of the *orishas*. The basis of the Santeria religion is the nurture of a personal relation with the *orishas*, and one of the principal forms of devotion is an animal sacrifice. The sacrifice of animals as part of religious rituals has ancient roots. *See* generally 12 *The Encyclopaedia of Religion* 554–556. Animal sacrifice is mentioned throughout the Old Testament, *see* 14 *Encyclopaedia Judaica* 600, 600–605 (1971), and it played an important role in the practice of Judaism before destruction of the second Temple in Jerusalem, *see id.*, at 605–612. In modern Islam, there is an annual sacrifice commemorating Abraham's sacrifice of a ram in the place of his son. *See* C. Glasse, *The Concise Encyclopaedia of Islam* 178 (1989); 7 *The Encyclopaedia of Religion* 456.

According to Santeria teaching, the *orishas* are powerful but not immortal. They depend for survival on the sacrifice. Sacrifices are performed at birth, marriage, and death rites, for the cure of the sick, for the initiation of new members and priests, and during an annual celebration. Animals sacrificed in Santeria rituals include chickens, pigeons, doves, ducks, guinea pigs, goats, sheep, and turtles. The animals are killed by the cutting of the carotid arteries in the neck. The sacrificed animal is cooked and eaten, except after healing and death rituals. *See* 13 *The Encyclopaedia of Religion* 66; M. Gonzalez–Wippler, *The Santeria Experience* 105 (1982).

Santeria adherents faced widespread persecution in Cuba, so the religion and its rituals were practiced in secret. The open practice of Santeria and its rites remains infrequent. *See* 13 *The Encyclopaedia of Religion* 67; M. Gonzalez–Wippler, *Santeria: The Religion* 3–4 (1989). The religion was brought to America most often by exiles from the Cuban revolution. The district court in the next case estimated that there are at least 50,000 practitioners in South Florida today. 723 F. Supp. 1467, 1470 (S.D. Fla. 1989).

Church of Lukumi Babalu Aye, Inc. v. City of Hialeah, Florida

508 U.S. 520 (1993).

Douglas Laycock argued the cause for the petitioners.

Richard G. Garrett argued the cause for the respondent.

Edward McGlynn Gaffney, Jr., filed a brief amicus curiae for the Baptist Joint Committee on Public Affairs, et al.

■ JUSTICE KENNEDY delivered the opinion of the Court with respect to Parts I, III, and IV, in which Chief Justice Rehnquist and Justices White, Stevens, Scalia, Souter, and Thomas joined, the opinion of the Court with respect to Part II–B, in which Chief Justice Rehnquist and Justices White, Stevens, Scalia, and Thomas joined, the opinion of the Court with respect to Parts II–A–1 and II–A–3, in which Chief Justice Rehnquist and Justices Stevens, Scalia, and Thomas joined, and an opinion with respect to Part II–A–2, in which Justice Stevens joined.

The principle that government may not enact laws that suppress religious belief or practice is so well understood that few violations are recorded in our opinions. *McDaniel v. Paty* [Chapter Fifteen, section 2]; *Fowler v. Rhode Island* [Chapter Thirteen, section 1]. Concerned that this fundamental nonpersecution principle of the First Amendment was implicated here, however, we granted certiorari. 503 U.S. (1992). Our review confirms that the laws in question were enacted by officials who did not understand, failed to perceive, or chose to ignore the fact that their official actions violated the Nation's essential commitment to religious freedom. The challenged laws had an impermissible object; and in all events the principle of general applicability was violated because the secular ends asserted in defense of the laws were pursued only with respect to conduct motivated by religious beliefs. We invalidate the challenged enactments and reverse the judgment of the Court of Appeals.

I

B

Petitioner Church of the Lukumi Babalu Aye, Inc. (Church), is a not-for-profit corporation organized under Florida law in 1973. The Church and its congregants practice the Santeria religion. The president of the Church is petitioner Ernesto Pichardo, who is also the Church's priest and holds the religious title of *Italero*, the second highest in the Santeria faith. In April 1987, the Church leased land in the city of Hialeah, Florida, and announced plans to establish a house of worship as well as a school, cultural center, and museum. Pichardo indicated that the Church's goal was to bring the practice of the Santeria faith, including its ritual of animal sacrifice, into the open. The Church began the process of obtaining utility service and receiving the necessary licensing, inspection, and zoning approvals. Although the Church's efforts at obtaining the necessary licenses and permits were far from smooth, it appears that it received all needed approvals by early August 1987.

The prospect of a Santeria church in their midst was distressing to many members of the Hialeah community, and the announcement of the plans to open a Santeria church in Hialeah prompted the city council to hold an emergency public session on June 9, 1987. . . .

[B]eginning with the enactments passed at the June 9 meeting. First, the city council adopted Resolution 87–66, which noted the "concern" expressed by residents of the city "that certain religions may propose to engage in practices which are inconsistent with public morals, peace or safety," and declared that "the City reiterates its commitment to a prohibition against any and all acts of any and all religious groups which are inconsistent with public morals, peace or safety." Next, the council approved an emergency ordinance, Ordinance 87–40, that incorporated in full, except as to penalty, Florida's animal cruelty laws. Fla. Stat. ch. 828 (1987). Among other things, the incorporated state law subjected to criminal punishment "whoever . . . unnecessarily or cruelly . . . kills any animal." § 828.12.

The city council desired to undertake further legislative action, but Florida law prohibited a municipality from enacting legislation relating to animal cruelty that conflicted with state law. § 828.27(4). To obtain clarification, Hialeah's city attorney requested an opinion from the attorney general of Florida as to whether § 828.12 prohibited "a religious group from sacrificing an animal in a religious ritual or practice" and whether the city could enact ordinances "making religious animal sacrifice unlawful." The attorney general responded in mid-July. He concluded that the "ritual sacrifice of animals for purposes other than food consumption" was not a "necessary" killing and so was prohibited by § 828.12. Fla. Op. Atty. Gen. 87–56, Annual Report of the Atty. Gen. 146, 147, 149 (1988)....

The city council responded at first with a hortatory enactment, Resolution 87–90, that noted its residents' "great concern regarding the possibility of public ritualistic animal sacrifices" and the state law prohibition. The resolution declared the city policy "to oppose the ritual sacrifices of animals" within Hialeah and announced that any person or organization practicing animal sacrifice "will be prosecuted."

In September 1987, the city council adopted three substantive ordinances addressing the issue of religious animal sacrifice. Ordinance 87–52 defined "sacrifice" as "to unnecessarily kill, torment, torture, or mutilate an animal in a public or private ritual or ceremony not for the primary purpose of food consumption," and prohibited owning or possessing an animal "intending to use such animal for food purposes." It restricted application of this prohibition, however, to any individual or group that "kills, slaughters or sacrifices animals for any type of ritual, regardless of whether or not the flesh or blood of the animal is to be consumed." The ordinance contained an exemption for slaughtering by "licensed establishments" of animals "specifically raised for food purposes." Declaring, moreover, that the city council "has determined that the sacrificing of animals within the city limits is contrary to the public health, safety, welfare and morals of the community," the city council adopted Ordinance 87–71. That ordinance defined sacrifice as had Ordinance 87–52, and then provided that "it shall be unlawful for any person, persons, corporations or associations to sacrifice any animal within the corporate limits of the City of Hialeah, Florida." The final Ordinance, 87–72, defined "slaughter" as "the killing of animals for food" and prohibited slaughter outside of areas zoned for slaughterhouse use. The ordinance provided an exemption, however, for the slaughter or processing for sale of "small numbers of hogs and/or cattle per week in accordance with an exemption provided by state law." All ordinances and resolutions passed the city council by unanimous vote. Violations of each of the four ordinances were punishable by fines not exceeding $500 or imprisonment not exceeding 60 days, or both.

Following enactment of these ordinances, the Church and Pichardo filed this action pursuant to 42 U.S.C. § 1983 in the United States District Court for the Southern District of Florida. Named as defendants were the city of Hialeah and its mayor and members of its city council in their individual capacities. Alleging violations of petitioners' rights under, *inter alia*, the Free Exercise Clause, the complaint sought a declaratory judgment and injunctive and monetary relief. . . .

After a 9–day bench trial, the District Court ruled for the city, finding no violation of petitioners' rights under the Free Exercise Clause. . . . Although acknowledging that "the ordinances are not religiously neutral," and that the city's concern about animal sacrifice was "prompted" by the establishment of the Church in the city, the District Court concluded that the purpose of the ordinances was not to exclude the Church from the city but to end the practice of animal sacrifice, for whatever reason practiced. The court also found that the ordinances did not target religious conduct "on their face," though it noted that in any event "specifically regulating [religious] conduct" does not violate the First Amendment "when [the conduct] is deemed inconsistent with public health and welfare." Thus, the court concluded that, at most, the ordinances' effect on petitioners' religious conduct was "incidental to [their] secular purpose and effect."

The district court found that animal sacrifices present (1) a substantial health risk both to participants and the general public, (2) an emotional injury to children who witness the sacrifice of animals,(3) cruel and unnecessary killing of animals, and (4) slaughter of animals outside of areas zoned for slaughterhouse use. Characterizing these interests as "compelling," the court "balanced the competing governmental and religious interests," and concluded that the governmental interests "fully justify the absolute prohibition on ritual sacrifice" accomplished by the ordinances. The court also concluded that no less restrictive alternative— e.g., regulation of disposal of the caracasses from the Santeria sacrifices— would be enforceable as a result of "the secret nature of the Santeria religion."

The Court of Appeals for the Eleventh Circuit affirmed in a one-paragraph *per curiam* opinion. The appellate court did not rely on the district court finding of a compelling interest in promoting the welfare of children, but stated simply that the ordinances were "consistent with the Constitution." It declined to address the effect of *Employment Div. v. Smith* [section 10 above] on the case, because the District Court "employed an arguably stricter standard" than that applied in *Smith*.

II

The city does not argue that Santeria is not a "religion" within the meaning of the First Amendment. Nor could it. Although the practice of animal sacrifice may seem abhorrent to some, "religious beliefs need not be acceptable, logical, consistent, or comprehensible to others in order to merit First Amendment protection." *Thomas v. Review Bd.* [section 4 above]. Given the historical association between animal sacrifice and religious worship, petitioners' assertion that animal sacrifice is an integral part of their religion "cannot be deemed bizarre or incredible." *Frazee* [section 5 above].

In addressing the constitutional protection for free exercise of religion, our cases establish the general proposition that a law that is neutral and of general applicability need not be justified by a compelling governmental interest even if the law has the incidental effect of burdening a particular religious practice. *Smith*. Neutrality and general applicability are interrelated, and, as becomes apparent in this case, failure to satisfy one requirement is a likely indication that the other has not been satisfied. A law failing to satisfy these requirements must be justified by a compelling governmental interest and must be narrowly tailored to advance that interest. These ordinances fail to satisfy the *Smith* requirements. We begin by discussing neutrality.

A

In our Establishment Clause cases we have often stated the principle that the First Amendment forbids an official purpose to disapprove of a particular religion or of religion in general. See, e.g., *Mergens* [Chapter Fourteen, section 2]. . . .

At a minimum, the protections of the Free Exercise Clause pertain if the law at issue discriminates against some or all religious beliefs or regulates or prohibits conduct because it is undertaken for religious reasons. See, *e.g.*, *Braunfeld v. Brown* [Chapter Thirteen, section 2]; *Fowler v. Rhode Island* [Chapter Thirteen, section 1]. Indeed, it was "historical instances of religious persecution and intolerance that gave concern to those who drafted the Free Exercise Clause." *Bowen v. Roy* [section 3 above] (citations omitted). In *McDaniel v. Paty* [Chapter Fifteen, section 2], for example, we invalidated a State law that disqualified members of the clergy from holding certain public offices, because it "imposed special disabilities on the basis of . . . religious status." On the same principle, in *Fowler v. Rhode Island*, we found that a municipal ordinance was applied in an unconstitutional manner when interpreted to prohibit preaching in a public park by a Jehovah's Witness but to permit preaching during the course of a Catholic mass or Protestant church service. See also *Niemotko v. Maryland* [section 2 above]. Cf. *Larson v. Valente* [Chapter Fifteen, section 1] (state statute that treated some religious denominations more favorably than others violated the Establishment Clause).

1

Although a law targeting religious beliefs as such is never permissible, *McDaniel v. Paty* [Chapter Fifteen, section 2], *Cantwell* [Chapter Eleven, section 1], if the object of a law is to infringe upon or restrict practices because of their religious motivation, the law is not neutral, see *Smith*; and it is invalid unless it is justified by a compelling interest and is narrowly tailored to advance that interest. There are, of course, many ways of demonstrating that the object or purpose of a law is the suppression of religion or religious conduct. To determine the object of a law, we must begin with its text, for the minimum requirement of neutrality is that a law not discriminate on its face. A law lacks facial neutrality if it refers to a religious practice without a secular meaning discernable from the language or context. . . .

Facial neutrality is not determinative. The Free Exercise Clause, like the Establishment Clause, extends beyond facial discrimination. The Clause "forbids subtle departures from neutrality," *Gillette* [Chapter Thirteen, section 4] and "covert suppression of particular religious beliefs," *Bowen v. Roy*. Official action that targets religious conduct for distinctive treatment cannot be shielded by mere compliance with the requirement of facial neutrality. The Free Exercise Clause protects against governmental hostility which is masked, as well as overt. "The Court must survey meticulously the circumstances of governmental categories to eliminate, as it were, religious gerrymanders." *Walz v. Tax Comm'n of New York City*, [Chapter Thirteen, section 3] (Harlan, J., concurring).

The record in this case compels the conclusion that suppression of the central element of the Santeria worship service was the object of the ordinances.... No one suggests, and on this record it cannot be maintained, that city officials had in mind a religion other than Santeria.

It becomes evident that these ordinances target Santeria sacrifice when the ordinances' operation is considered. Apart from the text, the effect of a law in its real operation is strong evidence of its object.... The subject at hand does implicate, of course, multiple concerns unrelated to religious animosity, for example, the suffering or mistreatment visited upon the sacrificed animals, and health hazards from improper disposal. But the ordinances when considered together disclose an object remote from these legitimate concerns. The design of these laws accomplishes instead a "religious gerrymander," *Walz* (Harlan, J., concurring), an impermissible attempt to target petitioners and their religious practices.

It is a necessary conclusion that almost the only conduct subject to Ordinances 87–40, 87–52, and 87–71 is the religious exercise of Santeria church members. The texts show that they were drafted in tandem to achieve this result.... The net result of the gerrymander is that few if any killings of animals are prohibited other than Santeria sacrifice, which is proscribed because it occurs during a ritual or ceremony and its primary purpose is to make an offering to the *orishas*, not food consumption. Indeed, careful drafting ensured that, although Santeria sacrifice is prohibited, killings that are no more necessary or humane in almost all other circumstances are unpunished.

Operating in similar fashion is Ordinance 87–52, which prohibits the "possession, sacrifice, or slaughter" of an animal with the "intent to use such animal for food purposes." This prohibition, extending to the keeping of an animal as well as the killing itself, applies if the animal is killed in "any type of ritual" and there is an intent to use the animal for food, whether or not it is in fact consumed for food. The ordinance exempts, however, "any licensed [food] establishment" with regard to "any animals which are specifically raised for food purposes," if the activity is permitted by zoning and other laws. This exception, too, seems intended to cover Kosher slaughter. Again, the burden of the ordinance, in practical terms, falls on Santeria adherents but almost no others: If the killing is—unlike most Santeria sacrifices—unaccompanied by the intent to use the animal for food, then it is not prohibited by Ordinance 87–52; if the killing is specifically for food but does not occur during the course of "any type of ritual," it again falls outside the prohibition; and if the killing is for food and occurs during the course of a ritual, it is still exempted if it occurs in a properly zoned and licensed establishment and involves animals "specifically raised for food purposes." A pattern of exemptions parallels the pattern of narrow prohibitions. Each contributes to the gerrymander.

Ordinance 87–40 incorporates the Florida animal cruelty statute, Fla. Stat. § 828.12 (1987). Its prohibition is broad on its face, punishing "whoever ... unnecessarily ... kills any animal." The city claims that this ordinance is the epitome of a neutral prohibition. Brief for Respondent 13–14. The problem, however, is the interpretation given to the ordinance by respondent and the Florida attorney general. Killings for religious reasons are deemed unnecessary, whereas most other killings fall outside the prohibition.... Further, because it requires an evaluation of the particular justification for the killing, this ordinance represents a system of "individualized governmental assessment of the reasons for the relevant conduct," *Smith*. As we noted in *Smith*, in circumstances in which individualized exemptions from a general requirement are available, the government "may not refuse to extend that system to cases of 'religious hardship' without compelling reason"....

We also find significant evidence of the ordinances' improper targeting of Santeria sacrifice in the fact that they proscribe more religious conduct than is necessary to achieve their stated ends....

3

In sum, the neutrality inquiry leads to one conclusion: The ordinances had as their object the suppression of religion. The pattern we have recited discloses animosity to Santeria adherents and their religious practices; the ordinances by their own terms target this religious exercise; the texts of the ordinances were gerrymandered with care to proscribe religious killings of animals but to exclude almost all secular killings; and the ordinances suppress much more religious conduct than is necessary in order to achieve the legitimate ends asserted in their defense. These ordinances are not neutral, and the court below committed clear error in failing to reach this conclusion.

B

We turn next to a second requirement of the Free Exercise Clause, the rule that laws burdening religious practice must be of general applicability. *Smith*. All laws are selective to some extent, but categories of selection are of paramount concern when a law has the incidental effect of burdening religious practice. The Free Exercise Clause "protects religious observers against unequal treatment," *Hobbie* (Stevens, J., concurring in judgment), and inequality results when a legislature decides that the governmental interests it seeks to advance are worthy of being pursued only against conduct with a religious motivation.

The principle that government, in pursuit of legitimate interests, cannot in a selective manner impose burdens only on conduct motivated by religious belief is essential to the protection of the rights guaranteed by the Free Exercise Clause....

Respondent claims that Ordinances 87–40, 87–52, and 87–71 advance two interests: protecting the public health and preventing cruelty to animals. The ordinances are underinclusive for those ends. They fail to prohibit non-religious conduct that endangers these interests in a similar or greater degree than Santeria sacrifice does. The underinclusion is substantial, not inconsequential. Despite the city's proffered interest in preventing cruelty to animals, the ordinances are drafted with care to forbid few killings but those occasioned by religious sacrifice. Many types of animal deaths or kills for nonreligious reasons are either not prohibited or approved by express provision. . . .

The city concedes that "neither the State of Florida nor the City has enacted a generally applicable ban on the killing of animals." Brief for Respondent 21. It asserts, however, that animal sacrifice is "different" from the animal killings that are permitted by law. According to the city, it is "self-evident" that killing animals for food is "important"; the eradication of insects and pests is "obviously justified"; and the euthanasia of excess animals "makes sense." These *ipse dixits* do not explain why religion alone must bear the burden of the ordinances, when many of these secular killings fall within the city's interest in preventing the cruel treatment of animals.

The ordinances are also underinclusive with regard to the city's interest in public health, which is threatened by the disposal of animal carcasses in open public places and the consumption of uninspected meat, see Brief for Respondent 32. Neither interest is pursued by respondent with regard to conduct that is not motivated by religious conviction. The health risks posed by the improper disposal of animal carcasses are the same whether Santeria sacrifice or some nonreligious killing preceded it. The city does not, however, prohibit hunters from bringing their kill to their houses, nor does it regulate disposal after their activity. . . . Improper disposal is a general problem that causes substantial health risks, but which respondent addresses only when it results from religious exercise.

The ordinances are underinclusive as well with regard to the health risk posed by consumption of uninspected meat. Under the city's ordinances, hunters may eat their kill and fisherman may eat their catch without undergoing governmental inspection. Likewise, state law requires inspection of meat that is sold but exempts meat from animals raised for the use of the owner and "members of his household and nonpaying guests and employees." Fla. Stat. § 585.88(1)(a) (1991). The asserted interest in inspected meat is not pursued in contexts similar to that of religious animal sacrifice.

Ordinance 87–72, which prohibits the slaughter of animals outside of areas zoned for slaughterhouses, is underinclusive on its face. The ordinance includes an exemption for "any person, group, or organization" that "slaughters or processes for sale, small numbers of hogs and/or cattle per week in accordance with an exemption provided by state law." See Fla. Stat. § 828.24(3) (1991). Respondent has not explained why commercial operations that slaughter "small numbers" of hogs and cattle do not implicate its professed desire to prevent cruelty to animals and preserve the public health. Although the city has classified Santeria sacrifice as slaughter, subjecting it to this ordinance, it does not regulate other killings for food in like manner.

We conclude, in sum, that each of Hialeah's ordinances pursues the city's governmental interests only against conduct motivated by religious belief. The ordinances "have every appearance of a prohibition that society is prepared to impose upon [Santeria worshippers] but not upon itself." *The Florida Star v. B. J. F.*, 491 U.S. 524, 542 (1989) (Scalia, J., concurring in part and concurring in judgment). This precise evil is what the requirement of general applicability is designed to prevent.

III

A law burdening religious practice that is not neutral or not of general application must undergo the most rigorous of scrutiny. To satisfy the commands of the First Amendment, a law restrictive of religious practice must advance " 'interests of the highest order' " and must be narrowly tailored in pursuit of those interests. *McDaniel v. Paty*, quoting *Yoder*. The compelling interest standard that we apply once a law fails to meet the *Smith* requirements is not "watered ... down" but "really means what it says." *Smith*. A law that targets religious conduct for distinctive treatment or advances legitimate governmental interests only against conduct with a religious motivation will survive strict scrutiny only in rare cases. It follows from what we have already said that these ordinances cannot withstand this scrutiny....

IV

The Free Exercise Clause commits government itself to religious tolerance, and upon even slight suspicion that proposals for state intervention stem from animosity to religion or distrust of its practices, all officials must pause to remember their own high duty to the Constitution and to the rights it secures. Those in office must be resolute in resisting importunate demands and must ensure that the sole reasons for imposing the burdens of law and regulation are secular. Legislators may not devise mechanisms, overt or disguised, designed to persecute or oppress a religion or its practices. The laws here in question were enacted contrary to these constitutional principles, and they are void. *Reversed.*

———

■ JUSTICE SCALIA, joined by CHIEF JUSTICE REHNQUIST, filed an opinion concurring in part and concurring in the judgment. He did not join section 2 of Part II–A "because it departs from the opinion's general focus on the object of the *laws* at issue to consider the subjective motivation of the *lawmakers*, *i.e.*, whether the Hialeah City Council actually *intended* to disfavor the religion of Santeria."

■ JUSTICE SOUTER also filed an opinion concurring in part and concurring in the judgment. He took the occasion to express his views on *Smith*, declining to join Part II of Justice Kennedy's opinion because of "doubts about whether the *Smith* rule merits adherence." For Souter, the *Smith* rule was not germane to the disposition of the Hialeah case. He also urged the Court to "re-examine the rule *Smith* declared," noting: "we have applied the same rigorous scrutiny to burdens on religious exercise resulting from the enforcement of formally neutral, generally applicable laws as we have applied to burdens caused by laws that single out religious exercise" (citing *McDaniel v. Paty, Yoder, Hernandez, Frazee, Hobbie, Bob Jones University, Lee, Thomas, Sherbert,* and *Cantwell*).

———

■ Justice Blackmun, joined by Justice O'Connor, concurring in the judgment.

[T]he First Amendment's protection of religion extends beyond those rare occasions on which the government explicitly targets religion (or a particular religion) for disfavored treatment, as is done in this case. In my view, a statute that burdens the free exercise of religion 'may stand only if the law in general, and the State's refusal to allow a religious exemption in particular, are justified by a compelling interest that cannot be served by less restrictive means.' *Smith* (dissenting opinion). The Court, however, applies a different test. It applies the test announced in *Smith*, under which 'a law that is neutral and of general applicability need not be justified by a compelling governmental interest even if the law has the incidental effect of burdening a particular religious practice.' I continue to believe that *Smith* was wrongly decided, because it ignored the value of religious freedom as an affirmative individual liberty and treated the Free Exercise Clause as no more than an antidiscrimination principle.

NOTES AND QUESTIONS

1. *The Nondiscrimination Principle.* Is the nondiscrimination principle open to a more generous interpretation than that placed on it in *Employment Division v. Smith* [section 10 above]? Need the nondiscrimination principle "ignore the value of religious freedom"? Could a rearticulated nondiscrimination principle be a means of reconciling the purposes of the nonestablishment and the free exercise provisions of the Religion Clause? For example, the Court has held that religious discrimination is expressly forbidden under the nonestablishment provision; *see, e.g., Larson v. Valente,* 456 U.S. 228 (1982) [Chapter Fifteen, section 1], and *Agostini v. Felton,* 521 U.S. 203 (1997) [Chapter Fourteen, section 1].

After *City of Hialeah,* could a city "protect public health and to forbid cruelty to animals, so long as its regulations are necessary to achieve those compelling purposes, and are not aimed exclusively at religious practices"? *See* Kenneth L. Karst, "Religious Freedom and Equal Citizenship: Reflections on Lukumi," 69 *Tul. L.Rev.* 335 (1994).

2. *Exercises of Religion Untreated by the Supreme Court.* The variety of ways in which religion may be exercised are as infinite as the imagination. Only a small number of these exercises have been pronounced on by the Supreme Court and, in relation to a given statute, been given the status of a protected right or been subordinated to the state. Is it fair to suppose that the Court has taken the cases that appeared to it to represent all issues of greatest social significance? It is apparent that to some degree the organizational abilities,

attitude toward litigation, and persistence of some religious groups have been factors in what cases get before the Court. Other exercises of religion may have struck lawyers and judges as so unusual, so eccentric, so bizarre as not to warrant much judicial attention. The prevailing perspective is captured in the title of an article by I. Beverly Lake, "Freedom to Worship Curiously," 1 *U. Fla. L.Rev.* 203 (1948), and in the title of an article by Stephen L. Carter, "Evolution, Creationism, and Treating Religion as a Hobby," 1987 *Duke L. J.* 977 (1987), expanded and reprinted in *The Culture of Disbelief* 23–43 (1993). But from the point of view of the believer a practice that is "curious" to the outsider may be a matter of divine commandment, evangelical precept, holy faith. The Court discussed the importance of allowing religious practices to be defined from an insider's perspective in *Amos* [section 6 above]. In *Thomas v. Review Bd.* [section 4 above] Chief Justice Burger wrote that "religious beliefs need not be acceptable, logical, consistent, or comprehensible to others in order to merit First Amendment protection." The following sections look at a few examples of practices that may seem curious to outsiders, and that have been adjudicated only by courts below the Supreme Court.

13. PRESERVING THE PURITY OF THE MEMBERSHIP

The Book of Deuteronomy speaks often of "purging evil" (e.g., intentional homicide, Deut. 19:13; false testimony, Deut. 19:19) from the midst of the people (*see also* Deut. 13:5; 17:7, 12; 21:9, 21; 22:21, 22, 24; 24:7). This concept came to influence the discipline of the Christian church. The earliest report of removing offenders from the church involved an incestuous marriage between two Christians at Corinth, a seaport town in Greece that the Apostle Paul had evangelized in the early 50s of the common era. In his first letter to the Corinthians, Paul wrote that Christians should not have recourse to the pagan courts of the Roman empire, but should settle their differences with one another in the spirit of familial love [Chapter One, section 5]. In the same letter Paul also wrote that the church must impose the discipline of separating the offending couple from the community. Both Roman law and biblical law (Deut. 22:20; 27:20; Lev. 18:7–8) forbade marriage between a man and his stepmother. But Paul is as much shocked by the complacency ("arrogance" in the translation below) of the congregation in tolerating this incestuous relationship as by the impropriety of the relationship itself. Paul goes on to list several categories of inappropriate behavior that, in his view, also merited the sanction of excommunication.

1 Corinthians 5:1–3, 11

It is actually reported that there is sexual immorality among you, and of a kind that is not found even among pagans; for a man is living with his father's wife. And you are arrogant! Should you not rather have mourned, so that he who has done this would have been removed from among you? . . . . But now I am writing to you not to associate with anyone who bears the name of brother or sister who is sexually immoral or greedy, or is an idolator, reviler, drunkard, or robber. Do not even eat with such a one.

Few religious communities today make a practice of excommunicating all offenders against all of these behaviors. But if a church decides to do so, should it not be free to exercise church discipline without the fear of being second-guessed by the government?

The Gospel according to Matthew addressed the issue of how to implement church discipline. The procedure for removing an offender from the community involves three steps. First, the offender is to be approached alone, since solitary reproof may have the desired effect of restoring the offender to the community without the need of public rebuke (*see* James 5: 19-20: "My brothers and sisters, if anyone among you wanders from the truth and is brought back by another, you should know that whoever brings back a sinner from wandering will save the sinner's soul from death and will cover a multitude of sins." If this effort is unsuccessful, then—on the warrant of Deut. 19:15—at least two witnesses must accompany the accuser. Only then is the dispute to be reported to the full community, which has power to bind and loose, a Hebraic idiom for excommunication.

Matthew 18:18–20

If another member of the church sins against you, go and point out the fault when the two of you are alone. If the member listens to you, you have regained that one. But if you are not listened to, take one or two others along with you, so that every word may be confirmed by the evidence of two or three witnesses. If the member refuses to listen to them, tell it to the church; and if the offender refuses to listen even to the church, let such a one be to you as a Gentile and a tax collector. Truly I tell you, whatever you bind on earth will be bound in heaven, and whatever you loose on earth will be loosed in heaven. Again, truly I tell you, if two of you agree on earth about anything you ask, it will be done for you by my Father in heaven. For where two or three are gathered in my name, I am there among them.

NOTES AND QUESTIONS

1. *Defamation Relating to Church Discipline*. Many churches assert a religious duty to purge their flock of members who offend in doctrine or practice. As the passages above suggest, there is ample biblical warrant for this practice. The refusal of communion and denial of admission to the church building has been held nonactionable, *Carter v. Papineau*, 222 Mass. 464, 111 N.E. 358 (1916) (no defamation, no tort of any kind when an Episcopal priest exercised his authority under the canons to refuse Holy Communion to one whom he deemed among "open, notorious, evil livers, or to have done any wrong to his neighbors by word or deed").

On the other hand, the Pennsylvania Supreme Court ordered a trial when Robert L. Bear sought equitable relief in Cumberland County when the Reformed Mennonite Church excommunicated him, and all members of the church shunned him. Bear alleged that his family was being destroyed because his wife and children could have no social or physical contact with him and that his business was in collapse because he could not hire workers, get a loan, or market his produce. The court refused to hold that the free exercise clause was a complete defense for the church, *Bear v. Reformed Mennonite Church*, 462 Pa. 330, 341 A.2d 105 (1975).

The American Law Institute's *Restatement (Second) of Torts* (1977) recognizes a conditional privilege to communicate an otherwise defamatory statement to others sharing a common interest in a subject. Section 596, comment *e*, recognizes that members of a religious association have a sufficient common interest "to support a privilege for communications among themselves concerning the qualifications of the officers and members and their participation in the activities of the society." The privilege is lost if the one publishing the defamatory matter acts in reckless disregard of its truth or falsity; or acts solely from spite or ill will; or makes excessive publication of the statement. In *Moyle v. Franz*, 293 N.Y. 842, 59 N.E. 2d 437, *affirming per curiam*, 267 App. Div. 423, 46 N.Y.S. 2d 667 (1944), a libel judgment of $15,000 against the publisher of *The Watchtower* and leaders of the Jehovah's Witnesses was sustained. The plaintiff was Olin R. Moyle, the lawyer who was the architect of the Witnesses' early constitutional litigation; the defendants were represented by Hayden Covington. In 1939 Moyle had written a long letter to Judge Rutherford criticizing him. The defendants published a notice in *The Watchtower* stating that Moyle was no longer in the society due to "his unfaithfulness to the kingdom interests, and to those who serve the kingdom"; and that Moyle now maligned those who trusted him "just as Judas had proved his unfaithfulness to Christ Jesus." The court laid stress on the fact that *The Watchtower* was available not only to Witnesses but to anyone willing to buy it. This "excessive" publication destroyed the "qualified privilege" to defame that the Witnesses as a religious society possessed. The court also held that the jury could find malice because several of the individual defamants had acquiesced in the statements about Moyle with little knowledge of the incidents to which the statements referred.

2. *Discipline Imposed on the Clergy*. Like the laity, members of the clergy are not immune from falling from grace, a fact explored in American literature at least since Nathaniel Hawthorne's classic novel about seventh-century Puritan Massachusetts, *The Scarlet Letter* (1850). Hawthorne's narrative focuses on the effect of sin on three persons: Rev. Arthur Dimmesdale and Hester Prynne, who have an adulterous affair, and Dr. Roger Chillingworth, Hester's revengeful husband, who swears to devote the rest of his life to discovering and exposing the identity of the man who injured him. Hester bears the full brunt of public responsibility for her wrongdoing; she is condemned to wear the scarlet letter "A" (for adultery) prominently on her clothing and to stand in the public stocks with her beautiful, but "illegitimate" child, Pearl, in her arms. Dimmesdale's sin goes undisclosed for seven years, when after delivering a powerful sermon the preacher identifies himself as Hester's lover and dies shortly thereafter. Hawthorne suggests that the undisclosed sin has a corrosive effect on the entire community, portrayed as harsh and unforgiving. Like old Chillingworth, the people are blind to the excess of their rage.

Similar issues of responsibility for misconduct and of the need for communal healing recur today. In recent years the trust that the faithful normally repose in their clergy has been eroded by a series of stories of serious abuse of that relationship. For example, there are instances of sexual misconduct by clergy members who have offered martial counselling to parishioners and had affairs with one of the partners in a distressed marriage. *See, e.g., Moses v.*

Episcopal Diocese of Colorado, 863 P. 2d 310 (Colo. 1993). When a minister or priest's sexual misconduct claims a child as its victim, the damage is all the greater. *See, e.g., Doe v. Redeemer Lutheran Church*, 531 N.W. 2d 897 (Minn. App. 1995) (failure to report information about pastor's sexual abuse of child); *Mrozka v. Archdiocese of St.Paul & Minneapolis*, 482 N.W. 2d 806 (Minn. App. 1992) (same, upholding award of punitive damages), rev. denied (Minn. 1992). *And see* generally William W. Bassett, *Religious Organizations and the Law*, Chapter 8 (discussing liability of religious organizations for torts such as fraud, deception in recruiting practices, libel and slander, sexual abuse of children, and sexual harassment of adults) (1997).

There is no doubt that churches may impose discipline on offending members of the clergy, whether on doctrinal or ethical grounds. In the wake of these scandals, however, some members of the clergy upon whom discipline has been imposed have sued their churches for defamation. Some courts have dismissed these actions, conferring virtual immunity from such litigation on the view that to do otherwise would interfere with a religious community's right to govern itself. *See, e.g., Farley v. Wisconsin Evangelical Lutheran Synod*, 821 F. Supp. 1286 (D. Minn. 1993); *Yaggie v. Indiana–Kentucky Synod*, 860 F. Supp. 1194 (W.D. Ky. 1994); and *Tran v. Fiorenza*, 934 S.W.2d 740 (Tex. Ct. App. 1996). Others have not. *See, e.g., Drevlow v. Lutheran Church Missouri Synod*, 991 F.2d 468 (8th Cir. 1993); and *Marshall v. Munro*, 845 P.2d 424 (Alaska 1994).

Assigning liability for the injuries suffered as a result of these cases of clergy misconduct has also raised difficult legal questions. For example, under standard principles of agency, a corporation is liable for the torts of the employees it controls or from whose conduct it derives financial benefit. But when a member of the clergy is engaged in misconduct that flagrantly violates his ordination promises, the religious community is hardly in control of the offensive behavior, and the community certainly does not benefit from the egregious misconduct of the clergy. *See* Edward McGlynn Gaffney, Jr., and Philip C. Sorensen, *Ascending Liability in Religious and Other Nonprofit Organization* (1984). No court has ever extended the tort of malpractice to the clergy. *See, e.g.*, Mark Chopko, "Ascending Liability of Religious Entities for the Actions of Others," 17 *Am. J. of Trial Adv.* 189, 335–36 (1993). But courts have imposed liability on a religious community for negligent supervision of a member of the clergy known to have problems that are likely to recur. *See, e.g., Moses v. Episcopal Diocese of Colorado* [this section above] (rejecting claim of clergy malpractice, but affirming claims of breach of fiduciary duty and negligent hiring and supervision), and *Doe v. Redeemer Lutheran Church* [this section above].

3. *Limits on Freedom of a Church to Impose Discipline on a Former Member.* In the Church of Christ a disciplinary procedure known as "withdrawal of fellowship" is carried out by the entire membership of a local congregation. When one member has violated the church's code of ethics and refuses to repent, the elders read aloud to the congregation the scriptures that were violated. The congregation then withdraws its fellowship from the wayward member by refusing to acknowledge that person's presence. According to the testimony of the church elders in *Guinn v. Church of Christ of Collinsville*, 775 P. 2d 766 (Okla. 1989), this process serves a dual purpose: it causes the transgressor to feel lonely and thus to desire repentance and a return to

fellowship with the other members; and secondly, it ensures that the church and its remaining members continue to be pure and free from sin.

A jury awarded $205,000 in actual damages and $185,000 in punitive damages against the church because three of its elders imposed discipline on the plaintiff, a single parent, for alleged sexual relations in violation of the church's prohibition against fornication. The plaintiff was publicly branded a fornicator when the scriptures she had violated were recited to the local congregation. As part of the disciplinary process the same information about her transgressions was sent to four other Church of Christ congregations in the area to be read aloud during services. On appeal, the Oklahoma Supreme Court affirmed the award of damages to the plaintiff. According to the Court, the "dispositive first-impression question presented is whether a state forensic inquiry into an alleged tortious act by a religious body against its former member is an unconstitutional usurpation of the church's prerogatives by a secular court and hence prohibited by the First Amendment." The Court answered this question in the negative.

The Court acknowledged that the religion clauses "prohibit both state and federal governments from inhibiting or supporting citizens' religious interests [and] were written in an effort to create an environment in which 'many types of life, character, opinion and belief ... could develop unmolested and unob-structed.'" *Cantwell v. Connecticut* [section 1 above]. Accordingly, the Court ruled that disciplinary actions taken by the elders against the plaintiff *before* she withdrew her membership from the Church of Christ did not constitute a threat to public safety, peace or order and hence did not justify state interference.

The Court noted that "a Church of Christ member can voluntarily join the church's flock but cannot then disassociate oneself from it." But the Court held that the right to withdraw one's implied consent to submit to the disciplinary decisions of a church is constitutionally unqualified; "its relinquishment requires a knowing and intelligent waiver." And it held that when the plaintiff "withdrew her membership from the church and thereby withdrew her consent to participate in a spiritual relationship in which she had implicitly agreed to submit to ecclesiastical supervision, those disciplinary actions thereafter taken by the elders against the plaintiff, which actively involved her in the church's will and command, were outside the purview of the first amendment protection and were the proper subject of state regulation."

4. *Religious Communities as "Voluntary Associations."* The term "voluntary association" is often applied loosely to religious communities. Although this term helps to clarify that the government may not coerce religious beliefs, does the term "voluntary association" capture all the nuances of a believer submitting to God's will made known in a religious community? For religious believers, is faith in God and willingness to do His will an optional thing in the same sense with which we might describe the decision either to purchase or refrain from purchasing a particular item at the store? Did the Court in *Guinn* give any weight to the teaching of the Church of Christ that "a member can voluntarily join the church's flock but cannot then disassociate oneself from it"? Should it? Although the *Guinn* court did not cite *Hobbie v. Unemployment Appeals Commission of Florida* [section 5] in its opinion, is *Guinn* consistent with the right of religious conversion protected in *Hobbie*?

14. AIDING THE ALIEN AND THE OPPRESSED

Exodus 22:21

You shall not wrong or oppress a resident alien, for you were aliens in the land of Egypt.

NOTES AND QUESTIONS

In addition to the passage above, biblical law (Ex. 23:9; Lev. 19:34; Dt. 10:19, 23:8) expressly enjoins special concern for the sojourner or stranger in the land (*ger* in Hebrew). Deuteronomy (5:15, 15:15, 16:12, 24:18,22) also invokes the memory of Israel's enslavement in Egypt as the basis for special concern for slaves (*'ebed* in Hebrew). *See* Harry P. Nasuti, "Identity, Identification, and Imitation: The Narrative Hermeneutics of Biblical Law," 4 *J. Law & Relig.* 9, 12–16 (1986).

Relying on scriptural passages such as these, and upon the Convention Relating to the Status of Refugees, 189 U.N.T.S. 137 (July 28, 1951; entered into force, Apr. 22, 1954) and the Protocol Relating to the Status of Refugees, 606 U.N.T.S. 267, 6 I.L.M. 78 (1967), several religious communities undertook efforts to provide hospitality and shelter for refugees from Guatemala and Salvador during a period of intense political upheaval in these countries. *See* Ignatius Bau, *This Ground Is Holy: Church Sanctuary and Central American Refugees* (1985); Ann Crittenden, *Sanctuary: A Story of American Conscience and the Law in Collision* (1988). The fundamental position of the American government was that the refugees were not fleeing political oppression, but were "economic refugees" seeking simply to better their lot in this country.

In *United States v. Elder*, 601 F. Supp. 1574 (S.D. Tex. 1985), John Elder was charged with unlawfully transporting three undocumented Salvadoran aliens. Elder was a practicing Catholic, the director of Casa Oscar Romero, which gave shelter to Salvadorans who had fled their country. The land for Casa Romero had been donated by the Catholic diocese of Brownsville. Parishes and congregations of various religious denominations contributed to the shelter's support. Elder believed he was performing his Christian duty in aiding those who fled brutality in El Salvador. John Fitzpatrick, Catholic bishop of Brownsville, and ministers of local Baptist, Lutheran, Methodist, and Presbyterian churches testified that such assistance was an expression of the Christian Gospel.

District Judge Hayden W. Head, Jr., ruled that Elder had shown in court that he was fulfilling his Christian duties as he saw them. Judge Head then ruled that the government's interest in a uniform immigration policy overrode Elder's free exercise claim and refused to dismiss the criminal charge against him. Elder was acquitted by the jury.

In another sanctuary case, the defendants were convicted. *United States v. Aguilar, et al.*, 871 F.2d 1436 (9th Cir. 1986).

In cases such as these presenting a conflict with free exercise of religion, *Sherbert* [section 5] requires that the government demonstrate that its interest is truly compelling or of a paramount order. Government attorneys often advocate for this conclusion by asserting the governmental interest at a very high and abstract level of generality. Here the Justice Department lawyers asserted that the governmental interest was either a "uniform immigration policy" or "national security." In these cases does it beg the question about the status of political refugees to invoke a "uniform immigration policy"? Is the security of the nation truly threatened by church groups attempting to provide hospitality and support for refugees from war-torn countries? Does it matter that religious communities claim that their awareness of the situation in Central America derives from first-hand accounts of members of their communities engaged in missionary or charitable endeavors in that region? Or may the government trump all contrary views by invoking the cloak of national security? Does it matter that Congress had, for a period in the 1980s relevant to these refugee cases, authorized public appropriations to support war in that region?

15. CARRYING SNAKES AND DRINKING POISON

Mark 16:15–18

And He [Jesus] said to them: "Go into the whole world and preach the Gospel to every creature. Whoever believes and is baptized will be saved; but whoever does not believe will be condemned. These signs will attend those who believe: in my name they shall cast out devils, they shall speak in new tongues; if they carry snakes or if they drink a lethal drink, it shall not harm them; they shall lay hands upon the sick and they shall be well."

NOTES AND QUESTIONS

The Dolly Pond Church of God with Signs Following was founded by George Went Hensley in 1909 at Sale Creek in Grasshopper Valley, Tennessee. A Pentecostal offshoot of Methodism, it spread as "The Holiness Church" in the rural South and Southeast. Hensley's conversion had begun with his handling of a rattlesnake without harm. He and his followers took literally the above verses of Mark. They handled rattlesnakes and drank poison as "signs that God said would follow the believers—signs to confirm the Word of God," *State ex rel. Swann v. Pack*, 527 S.W. 2d 99 (Tenn. 1975), *cert. denied*, 424 U.S. 954 (1976). The district attorney at Newport, Tennessee, sought an injunction prohibiting Pastor Liston Pack and certain elders of the Church from handling poisonous snakes or drinking strychnine. The trial court granted the injunction as to the snakes but not as to drinking the poison. The Supreme Court of Tennessee enjoined both practices.

The court said, "We recognize that to forbid snake handling is to remove the theological heart of the Holiness Church." But the court held that "the handling of snakes in a crowded church sanctuary, with virtually no safeguards" was a serious danger to the public health. The court continued, "Our state and nation have an interest in having a strong, healthy, robust, taxpaying citizenry capable of self-support and of bearing arms and adding to the resources and reserves of manpower." This interest in preserving the life of its citizens was too sufficient to support an injunction against drinking poison. The court said it considered and rejected restricting the church's practice to consenting adults only because it was "too fraught with danger to permit its pursuit in the frenzied atmosphere of an emotional church service." *Accord Harden v. State*, 188 Tenn. 17, 216 S.W.2d 708 (1948), enforcing against members of the Holiness Church a statute specifically criminalizing the displaying of a poisonous snake so as to endanger anyone. *Accord Hill v. State*, 38 Ala. App. 404, 88 So. 2d 880 (1956) *cert. denied*, 264 Ala. 697, 88 So. 2d 887 (1956) where the complaining witness was a minister of the same church as the defendant but did not believe in such acts of faith. *Accord Lawson v. Commonwealth*, 291 Ky. 437, 164 S.W.2d 972 (1942), where the statute forbade handling of even nonpoisonous snakes and directed its prohibition specifically at handling "in connection with any religious service or gathering."

Apart from most people's repugnance to snakes, do these cases fairly balance the religious claims of the believers against the danger the state is preventing? In the absence of a statute against suicide, how persuasive is the court's reason for enjoining the consumption of poison?

16. NOT EATING BLOOD

Genesis 9:4

Flesh, with the life thereof, which is the blood thereof, you shall not eat.

————

See also Leviticus 17:10; Deuteronomy 12:23.

The early Christian community struggled with the extent to which Gentile converts to the faith would be required to observe the Mosaic law. A meeting of the church leadership in Jerusalem in the middle of the first century CE, sometimes referred to as the "Council of Jerusalem," included the prohibition against eating blood among the "necessary things" for Christians to observe.

Acts 15:28–29

For it has seemed good to the Holy Spirit and to us to lay upon you no greater burden than these necessary things: That you abstain from meat offered to idols, and from blood, and from things strangled, and from sexual impurity.

NOTES AND QUESTIONS

As a consequence of these biblical injunctions, Jehovah's Witnesses concluded that they could not eat blood sausages or blood puddings. On July 1, 1945, *The Watchtower* interpreted the texts also to forbid blood transfusions as a kind of blood-eating, offensive to God. Penton, *Apocalypse Delayed* 153.

In *Application of the President and Directors of Georgetown College*, 331 F.2d 1000 (D.C. Cir. 1964), *cert. denied*, 377 U.S. 978 (1964), Judge Skelly Wright granted an emergency writ authorizing Georgetown Hospital to give a blood transfusion to Mrs. Jesse Jones, a twenty-five-year-old woman and the mother of a seven-month-old child. The opinion of the attending doctors was that she would die without a transfusion. Both she and her husband were

Jehovah's Witnesses. Mrs. Jones refused consent. Judge Wright visited Mrs. Jones in the hospital and asked her to consent. Her only audible reply was, "Against my will." Judge Wright balanced against her religious rights the interest of the state in preserving the parent of a child; the possible criminality of suicide; and the hospital and doctors' unwillingness to let her die. He also observed, "It was obvious that the woman was not in a mental condition to make a decision"; and he added that "[i]f the law undertook the responsibility of authorizing the transfusion without her consent, no problem would be raised with respect to her religious practices."

In *Raleigh Fitkin–Paul Morgan Memorial Hospital v. Anderson*, 42 N.J. 421, 201 A.2d 537 (1964), *cert. denied*, 377 U.S. 985 (1964), Willimina Anderson, a Jehovah's Witness, thirty-two weeks pregnant, refused a blood transfusion. The hospital applied for a court order, showing that it was probable that at some point in the pregnancy she would hemorrhage and that both she and the unborn child would die. Declaring that "[w]e are satisfied that the unborn child is entitled to the law's protection," the court ordered the appointment of a guardian who would consent on behalf of "the infant." *Accord Jefferson v. Griffin Spalding County Hospital Authority*, 274 S.E.2d 457 (Ga. 1981) (guardian appointed for thirty-nine week-old fetus whose mother, a member of the Shiloh Sanctified Holiness Baptist Church, refused on religious grounds to undergo a caesarean section; the evidence showed that the child stood a 99 percent chance of dying and the mother a 50 percent chance in the absence of a caesarean operation).

If the child is viewed as having a right to protection, the case accords with *Prince v. Massachusetts*, [section 1 above]. Is its rationale undermined by *Roe v. Wade*, 410 U.S. 113 (1973), recognizing a mother's right to abort her child? In *Aste v. Brooks*, 32 Ill. 2d 361, 205 N.E.2d 435 (1965), the court disapproved as a violation of the First Amendment a court-ordered transfusion to an objecting adult Witness, who had no minor children.

---

17. Healing by Prayer and Faith

Mark 16:17–18

And these signs will accompany those who believe: ... they will lay their hands on the sick, and they will recover.

James 5:14–16

Are any among you sick? They should call for the elders of the church and have them pray over them, anointing them with oil in the name of the Lord. The prayer of faith will save the sick, and the Lord will raise them up; and anyone who has committed sins will be forgiven. Therefore confess your sins to one another, and pray for one another, so that you may be healed. The prayer of the righteous is powerful and effective.

———

In *People v. Cole*, 219 N.Y. 98, 113 N.E. 790 (1916), Willis Vernon Cole was prosecuted for practicing medicine. The evidence was that he had been called on by a prospective client (actually an investigator for the New York Medical Society). She understood him to promise to "cure her eyes"; she had been wearing glasses for ten years. He told her to take off the glasses and prayed silently; he said that he himself had worn glasses for many years but had been healed by prayer. His testimony was that he had not said he could cure her, but that God could, that He was the only healer. He told her she could cure herself by cleansing fear, disharmony, and false thoughts from her consciousness, that "disease was like a shadow which flees before the light."

The applicable statute defined practicing medicine to include holding oneself out as able "to diagnose, treat, operate or prescribe for any human disease." The statute also said, "This article should not be construed to affect . . . the practice of the religious tenets of any church." Cole was a member of the Christian Science Church and a practitioner as defined by its rules. The court held that his good faith practice of Christian Science was a defense to the charge of unlawfully practicing medicine. Judge Benjamin Cardozo joined the court's opinion. Chief Justice Bartlett went beyond the court, declaring in his concurrence: "I deny the power of the Legislature to make it a crime to treat disease by prayer."

The rule has been otherwise as to the treatment of sick children by prayer. In *People v. Pierson*, 176 N.Y. 201, 68 N.E. 243 (1903), Luther Pierson was a member of the Christian Catholic Church of Chicago. He did not believe in physicians; he did believe that prayer would cure disease. His sixteen-month-old daughter contracted whooping cough, then pneumonia, and died. Even when her symptoms became "dangerous," Cole did not call a doctor, believing that divine healing would be accomplished by his prayer. He was convicted of the misdemeanor of willfully failing to provide medical attendance for his child. He invoked the free exercise of religion clause of the New York constitution. The court said, "But the law of nature, as well as the common law, devolves upon the parents the duty of caring for their young. . . ." The court applied the statute.

Under California criminal law it is a misdemeanor for a parent willfully not to furnish "necessary clothing, food, shelter or medical attendance or other remedial care for his or her child."

California Penal Code § 270, as amended (1976)

If a parent provides a minor with treatment by spiritual means through prayer alone in accordance with the tenets and practices of a recognized church or religious denomination, by a duly accredited practitioner thereof, such treatment shall constitute "other remedial care," as used in this section.

————

The statute was amended after the thirteen-year-old daughter of Florence Arnold, a member of the Church of the First Born, had died after intestinal blockage treated only by prayer. Mrs. Arnold had pleaded no contest to a charge of manslaughter. *Los Angeles Daily Journal*, Sept. 2, 1985, 22.

In 1984, in three separate cases in California, parents were charged with second-degree murder or with involuntary manslaughter when their children died from serious illnesses after prayer treatment by Christian Science practitioners and no medical treatment. *See State v. Walker, State v. Glaser, State v. Rippberger. Los Angeles Daily Journal,* Sept. 2, 1985, 1. The position of the prosecutors was that the definition of remedial care under section 270 did not prevent prosecution under the murder or manslaughter provision of the Penal Code. "Religious freedom is vital, but a balancing act is needed," one prosecutor said. In *Walker,* dismissal of the indictment was denied. *Walker v. Superior Court,* 222 Cal. Rptr. 87, 176 Cal. App. 3d 526 (1986), *aff'd,* 47 Cal. 3d 112, 253 Cal. Rptr. 1, 763 P.2d 852 (1988).

Massachusetts has a spiritual treatment statute that provides: "A child shall not be deemed to be neglected or lack physical care for the sole reason that he is being provided remedial treatment by spiritual means alone in accordance with the tenets and practice of a recognized church or religious denomination by a duly accredited practitioner thereof." As practicing Christian Scientists, David and Ginger Twitchell believe in healing by spiritual treatment. When their son Robyn was two and a half years old, he suffered a severe illness that prompted them to retain a Christian Science practitioner and a Christian Science nurse. Robyn died within five days of his illness, which was diagnosed as a perforation of his bowel which had been obstructed. The Commonwealth prosecuted the parents for involuntary manslaughter, and a jury convicted them on this charge. On appeal, the parents relied on the statute cited above, urging that it is a complete bar to any criminal charge. In *Commonwealth v. Twitchell,* 416 Mass. 114, 617 N.E. 2d 609 (1993), the court clarified that the common law of Massachusetts includes a parental duty to provide medical treatment for a minor known to be gravely ill. The court also held that the statute does not apply to involuntary manslaughter. The Court also noted that the Attorney General had issued an opinion in 1975 that answered in the negative the question "whether parents who fail to provide medical services to children ion the basis of religious beliefs will be subject to prosecution for such failure." The court reversed the parents' convictions on the ground that they were entitled to present evidence of their reliance on an official interpretation of the law as an affirmative defense to the crime. *See* also *State v. McKown,* 475 N.W. 2d 63 (Minn. 1991), cert. denied, 502 U.S. 1036 (1992) (spiritual healing exemption in child neglect statute is not a complete defense to manslaughter, but indictment of Christian Science parents dismissed on the ground that they have a due process right to adequate notice that their inaction might subject them to criminal liability). For a sympathetic account of the history and practice of the Christian Science faith, *see* Catharine Cookson, *Regulating Religion: The Courts and the Free Exercise Clause* 149–85 (2001).

CHAPTER TWELVE

BELIEF AND ORGANIZATION OF BELIEF

1. INVESTIGATION OF BELIEF

The cases involving the attempted regulation of religious activity often approach the question of the truth of a religious belief or the sincerity with which it is held. Analytically, many of them—*e.g.*, the cases on blood transfusions, peyote-chewing, faith-healing—could be classified under "investigation of belief." However, there is a small group of cases where the constitutionality of such investigations has been considered directly.

The I AM movement falls within the general classification of Theosophical religion. Guy Ballard, its founder, born in 1878, said that he had been visited on Mount Shasta, California, by a young man who offered him a cup of "Omnipotent Life" itself. The young man was a seventeenth-century occultist, St. Germain des Pres, an ascended master, that is, a mortal who had become a spirit and communicated with human beings on earth. St. Germain told Ballard about reincarnation, led him on an astral flight into his past lives, and taught him how to escape the wheel of reincarnation by contact with God. Jesus, distinguished from Christ, was perceived as another ascended master, of great help to mortals. Ballard and his wife Edna conveyed this teaching by *Unveiled Mysteries* (1934) and by classes which developed a membership in the movement, *see* J. Gordon Melton, ed., 2 *Encyclopedia of American Religion* 155–59 (1978). Ballard died in 1939. The movement faltered. Edna Ballard and the Ballards' son Donald were indicted for mail fraud. Represented by Horace Donnelly, a leading lawyer in the defense of mail fraud with many years service in the legal department of the Post Office, the Ballards demurred. Even if all the facts were exactly as the government charged, the Ballards asserted that the First Amendment gave them immunity from prosecution. The district court, per Judge Leon Yankovich, denied the demurrer and ordered the case to trial. The judge who presided at the trial, Judge J.F.T. O'Connor, ruled that the truth of the Ballards' beliefs would not be an issue, only their sincerity; in that way, he informed the defendants, their religion would not be on trial. The trial began in December of 1941 shortly before the bombing of Pearl Harbor and continued into January of 1942. Ralph Lazarus, Assistant U.S. Attorney, told the jury in closing argument that they were doing "a patriotic service" in assuring a better America to which her servicemen would return. He called "this Ballard racket" "a flim-flam scheme that has been unparalleled in history." Edna was "a glib prevaricator." Portions of the jury charge are contained in the opinion below. For a fuller description of the evidence adduced at trial, see John T. Noonan, Jr., *The Lustre of Our Country* 151–55 (1998). The jury convicted Edna Ballard of seven uses of the mail in the furtherance of a scheme to defraud, Donald of three. It is not possible to tell from the verdict about representations the jury found false under the mail fraud statute.

Noting that mail fraud consists in untrue, not insincere statements, the Ninth Circuit per Judge Clifton Matthews, reversed and remanded for a new trial. Edna Ballard was sentenced to a year in prison and a fine of $8,000; Donald to thirty days and a fine of $40. Both sentences were suspended, *Los Angeles Times*, June 22, 1943. The Ballards appealed.

United States v. Ballard

322 U.S. 78 (1944).

Solicitor General Fahy, with whom *Assistant Attorney General Tom C. Clark, Mr. Robert S. Erdahl*, and *Miss Beatrice Rosenberg* were on the brief, for the United States. *Messrs. Roland Rich Woolley* and *Joseph F. Rank,* with whom *Mr. Ralph C. Curren* was on the brief, for respondents.

■ JUSTICE DOUGLAS delivered the opinion of the Court.

Respondents were indicted and convicted for using, and conspiring to use, the mails to defraud. The indictment was in twelve counts. It charged a scheme to defraud by organizing and promoting the I Am movement through the use of the mails. The charge was that certain designated corporations were formed, literature distributed and sold, funds solicited, and memberships in the I Am movement sought "by means of false and fraudulent representations, pretenses and promises." The false representations charged were eighteen in number. It is sufficient at this point to say that they covered respondents' alleged religious doctrines or beliefs. They were all set forth in the first count. The following are representative:

> that Guy W. Ballard, now deceased, alias Saint Germain, Jesus, George Washington, and Godfre Ray King, had been selected and thereby designated by the alleged "ascertained masters," Saint Germain, as a divine messenger; and that the words of "ascended masters" and the words of the alleged divine entity, Saint Germain, would be transmitted to mankind through the medium of the said Guy W. Ballard; that Guy W. Ballard, during his lifetime, and Edna W. Ballard, and Donald Ballard, by reason of their alleged high spiritual attainments and righteous conduct, had been selected as divine messengers through which the words of the alleged "ascended masters," including the alleged Saint Germain, would be communicated to mankind under the teachings commonly known as the "I Am" movement;

> that Guy W. Ballard, during his lifetime, and Edna W. Ballard and Donald Ballard had, by reason of supernatural attainments, the power to heal persons of ailments and diseases and to make well persons afflicted with any diseases, injuries, or ailments, and did falsely represent to persons intended to be defrauded that the three designated persons had the ability and power to cure persons of those diseases normally classified as curable and also of diseases which are ordinarily classified by the medical profession as being incurable diseases; and did further represent that the three designated persons had in fact cured

either by the activity of one, either, or all of said persons, hundreds of persons afflicted with diseases and ailments;

Each of the representations enumerated in the indictment was followed by the charge that respondents "well knew" it was false. After enumerating the eighteen misrepresentations the indictment also alleged: "At the time of making all of the afore-alleged representations by the defendants, and each of them, the defendants, and each of them, well knew that all of said aforementioned representations were false and untrue and were made with the intention on the part of the defendants, and each of them, to cheat, wrong, and defraud persons intended to be defrauded, and to obtain from persons intended to be defrauded by the defendants, money, property, and other things of value and to convert the same to the use and the benefit of the defendants, and each of them."

The indictment contained twelve counts, one of which charged a conspiracy to defraud. The first count set forth all of the eighteen representations, as we have said. Each of the other counts incorporated and realleged all of them and added no additional ones. There was a demurrer and a motion to quash, each of which asserted, among other things, that the indictment attacked the religious beliefs of respondents and sought to restrict the free exercise of their religion in violation of the Constitution of the United States. These motions were denied by the District Court. Early in the trial, however, objections were raised to the admission of certain evidence concerning respondent's religious beliefs. The court conferred with counsel in absence of the jury and with the acquiescence of counsel for the United States and for respondents confined the issues on this phase of the case to the question of the good faith of respondents. At the request of counsel for both sides the court advised the jury of that action in the following language:

Now, gentlemen, here is the issue in this case:

First, the defendants in this case made certain representations of belief in a divinity and in a supernatural power. Some of the teachings of the defendants, representations, might seem extremely improbable to a great many people. For instance, the appearance of Jesus to dictate some of the works that we have had introduced in evidence, as testified to here at the opening transcription, or shaking hands with Jesus, to some people that might seem highly improbable. I point that out as one of the many statements.

Whether that is true or not is not the concern of this Court and is not the concern of the jury—and they are going to be told so in their instructions. As far as this Court sees the issue, it is immaterial what these defendants preached or wrote or taught in their classes. They are not going to be permitted to speculate on the actuality of the happening of those incidents. Now, I think I have made that as clear as I can. Therefore, the religious beliefs of these defendants cannot be an issue in this court.

The issue is: Did these defendants honestly and in good faith believe those things? If they did, they should be acquitted. I cannot make it any clearer than that.

If these defendants did not believe those things, they did not believe that Jesus came down and dictated, or that Saint Germain came down and dictated, did not believe the things that they wrote, the things that they preached, but used the mail for the purpose of getting money, the jury should find them guilty. Therefore, gentlemen, religion cannot come into this case.

The District Court reiterated that admonition in the charge to the jury and made it abundantly clear. The following portion of the charge is typical:

The question of the defendants' good faith is the cardinal question in this case. You are not to be concerned with the religious belief of the defendants, or any of them. The jury will be called upon to pass on the question of whether or not the defendants honestly and in good faith believed the representations which are set forth in the indictment, and honestly and in good faith believed that the benefits which they represented would flow from their belief to those who embraced and followed their teachings, or whether these representations were mere pretenses without honest belief on the part of the defendants or any of them, and, were the representations made for the purpose of procuring money, and were the mails used for this purpose.

As we have said, counsel for the defense acquiesced in this treatment of the matter, made no objection to it during the trial, and indeed treated it without protest as the law of the case throughout the proceedings prior to the verdict. Respondents did not change their position before the District Court after verdict and contend that the truth or verity of their religious doctrines or beliefs should have been submitted to the jury. In their motion for new trial they did contend, however, that the withdrawal of these issues from the jury was error because it was in effect an amendment of the indictment. That was also one of their specifications of errors on appeal. And other errors urged on appeal included the overruling of the demurrer to the indictment and the motion to quash, and the disallowance of proof of the truth of respondents' religious doctrines or beliefs.

The Circuit Court of Appeals reversed the judgment of conviction and granted a new trial, one judge dissenting. In its view the restriction of the issue in question to that of good faith was error. Its reason was that the scheme to defraud alleged in the indictment was that respondents made the eighteen alleged false representations and that to prove that defendants devised the scheme described in the indictment "it was necessary to prove that they schemed to make some, at least, of the (eighteen) representations ... and that some, at least, of the representations which they schemed to make were false." One judge thought that the ruling of the District Court was also error because it was "as prejudicial to the issue of honest belief as to the issue of purposeful misrepresentation."

The case is here on a petition for a writ of certiorari which we granted because of the importance of the question presented....

As we have noted, the Circuit Court of Appeals held that the question of the truth of the representations concerning respondents' religious doctrines or beliefs should have been submitted to the jury. And it remanded the case for a new trial. It may be that the Circuit Court of Appeals took that action because it did not think that the indictment could be properly construed as charging a scheme to defraud by means other than misrepresentations of respondents' religious doctrines or beliefs. Or that court may have concluded that the withdrawal of the issue of the truth of those religious doctrines or beliefs was unwarranted because it resulted in a substantial change in the character of the crime charged. But on whichever basis that court rested its action, we do not agree that the truth or verity of respondents' religious doctrines or beliefs should have been submitted to the jury. Whatever this particular indictment might require, the First Amendment precludes such a course, as the United States seems to concede. "The law knows no heresy, and is committed to the support of no dogma, the establishment of no sect." *Watson v. Jones,* [Chapter Eight, section 4]. The First Amendment has a dual aspect. It not only "forestalls compulsion by law of the acceptance of any creed or the practice of any form of worship" but also "safeguards the free exercise of the chosen form of religion." *Cantwell v. Connecticut* [Chapter Eleven, section 1]. "Thus the Amendment embraces two concepts,—freedom to believe and freedom to act. The first is absolute but, in the nature of things, the second cannot be." Freedom of thought, which includes freedom of religious belief, is basic in a society of free men. *Board of Education v. Barnette* [Chapter Eleven, section 3]. It embraces the right to maintain theories of life and of death and of the hereafter which are rank heresy to followers of the orthodox faiths. Heresy trials are foreign to our Constitution. Men may believe what they cannot prove. They may not be put to the proof of their religious doctrines or beliefs. Religious experiences which are as real as life to some may be incomprehensible to others. Yet the fact that they may be beyond the ken of mortals does not mean that they can be made suspect before the law. Many take their gospel from the New Testament. But it would hardly be supposed that they could be tried before a jury charged with the duty of determining whether those teachings contained false representations. The miracles of the New Testament, the Divinity of Christ, life after death, the power of prayer are deep in the religious convictions of many. If one could be sent to jail because a jury in a hostile environment found those teachings false, little indeed would be left of religious freedom. The Fathers of the Constitution were not unaware of the varied and extreme views of religious sects, of the violence of disagreement among them, and of the lack of any one religious creed on which all men would agree. They fashioned a charter of government which envisaged the widest possible toleration of conflicting views. Man's relation to his God was made no concern of the state. He was granted the right to worship as he pleased and to answer to no man for the verity of his religious views. The religious views espoused by respondents might seem incredible, if not preposterous, to most people. But if those doctrines are subject to trial before a jury charged with finding their truth or falsity, then the same can be done with the religious beliefs of any sect. When the triers of fact undertake that task, they enter a forbidden domain. The First Amendment does not select any one group or any one type of religion for preferred treatment. It puts them all in that position. *Murdock v. Pennsylvania* [Chapter Eleven, section 1]. As stated in *Davis v. Beason* [Chapter Nine], "With man's relations to his Maker and the obligations he may think they impose, and the manner in which an expression shall be made by him of his belief on those subjects, no interference can be permitted, provided always the laws of society, designed to secure its peace and prosperity, and the morals of its people, are not interfered with." See *Prince v. Massachusetts* [Chapter Eleven, section 1]. So we conclude that the District Court ruled properly when it withheld from the jury all questions concerning the truth or falsity of the religious beliefs or doctrines of respondents. . . .

The case was reversed and remanded to the Court of Appeals for consideration of other issues not before the Supreme Court.

■ Chief Justice Stone, dissenting.

I am not prepared to say that the constitutional guaranty of freedom of religion affords immunity from criminal prosecution for the fraudulent procurement of money by false statements as to one's religious experiences, more than it renders polygamy or libel immune from criminal prosecution. *Davis v. Beason* [Chapter Nine]; see *Chaplinsky v. New Hampshire* 315 U.S. 568, 572; cf *Patterson v. Colorado,* 205 U.S. 454, 462; *Near v. Minnesota,* 283 U.S. 697, 715. I cannot say that freedom of thought and worship includes freedom to procure money by making knowingly false statements about one's religious experiences. To go no further, if it were shown that a defendant in this case had asserted as a part of the alleged fraudulent scheme, that he had physically shaken hands with St. Germain in San Francisco on a day named, or that, as the indictment here alleges, by the exertion of his spiritual power he "had in fact cured . . . hundreds of persons afflicted with diseases and ailments," I should not doubt that it would be open to the Government to submit to the jury proof that he had never been in San Francisco and that no such cures had ever been effected. In any event I see no occasion for making any pronouncement on this subject in the present case.

■ Justice Roberts and Justice Frankfurter join in this opinion.

■ Justice Jackson, dissenting.

I should say the defendants have done just that for which they are indicted. If I might agree to their conviction without creating a precedent, I cheerfully would do so. I can see in their teachings nothing but humbug, untainted by any trace of truth. But that does not dispose of the constitutional question whether misrepresentation of religious experience or belief is prosecutable; it rather emphasizes the danger of such prosecutions.

The Ballard family claimed miraculous communication with the spirit world and supernatural power to heal the sick. They were brought to trial for mail fraud on an indictment which charged that their representations were false and that they "well knew" they were false. The trial judge, obviously troubled, ruled that the court could not try whether the statements were untrue, but could inquire whether the defendants knew them to be untrue; and, if so, they could be convicted.

I find it difficult to reconcile this conclusion with our traditional religious freedoms.

In the first place, as a matter of either practice or philosophy I do not see how we can separate an issue as to what is believed from considerations as to what is believable. The most convincing proof that one believes his statements is to show that they have been true in his experience. Likewise, that one knowingly falsified is best proved by showing that what he said happened never did happen. How can the Government prove these persons knew something to be false which it cannot prove to be false? If we try religious sincerity severed from religious verity, we isolate the dispute from the very considerations which in common experience provide its most reliable answer.

In the second place, any inquiry into intellectual honesty in religion raises profound psychological problems. William James, who wrote on these matters as a scientist, reminds us that it is not theology and ceremonies which keep religion going. Its vitality is in the religious experiences of many people. "If you ask what these experiences are, they are conversations with the unseen, voices and visions, responses to prayer, changes of heart, deliverances from fear, inflowings of help, assurances of support, whenever certain persons set their own internal attitude in certain appropriate ways."[1] If religious liberty includes, as it must, the right to communicate such experiences to others, it seems to me an impossible task for juries to separate fancied ones from real ones, dreams from happenings, and hallucinations from true clairvoyance. Such experiences, like some tones and colors, have existence for one, but none at all for another. They cannot be verified to the minds of those whose field of consciousness does not include religious insight. When one comes to trial which turns on any aspect of religious belief or representation, unbelievers among his judges are likely not to understand and are almost certain not to believe him.

And then I do not know what degree of skepticism or disbelief in a religious representation amounts to actionable fraud. James points out that "Faith means belief in something concerning which doubt is still theoretically possible." Belief in what one may demonstrate to the senses is not faith. All schools of religious thought make enormous assumptions, generally on the basis of revelations authenticated by some sign or miracle. The appeal in such matters is to a very different plane of credulity than is invoked by representations of secular fact in commerce. Some who profess belief in the Bible read literally what others read as allegory or metaphor, as they read Aesop's fables. Religious symbolism is even used by some with the same mental reservations one has in teaching of Santa Claus or Uncle Sam or Easter bunnies or dispassionate judges. It is hard in matters so mystical to say how literally one is bound to believe the doctrine he teaches

---

1. William James, Collected Essays and Reviews, pp. 427–8; see generally his *Variet-* *ies of Religious Experience* and *The Will to Believe.* See also Burton, *Heyday of a Wizard.*

and even more difficult to say how far it is reliance upon a teacher's literal belief which induces followers to give him money.

There appear to be persons—let us hope not many—who find refreshment and courage in the teachings of the "I Am" cult. If the members of the sect get comfort from the celestial guidance of their "Saint Germain," however doubtful it seems to me, it is hard to say that they do not get what they pay for. Scores of sects flourish in this country by teaching what to me are queer notions. It is plain that there is wide variety in American religious taste. The Ballards are not alone in catering to it with a pretty dubious product.

The chief wrong which false prophets do to their following is not financial. The collections aggregate a tempting total, but individual payments are not ruinous. I doubt if the vigilance of the law is equal to making money stick by over-credulous people. But the real harm is on the mental and spiritual plane. There are those who hunger and thirst after higher values which they feel wanting in their humdrum lives. They live in mental confusion or moral anarchy and seek vaguely for truth and beauty and moral support. When they are deluded and then disillusioned, cynicism and confusion follow. The wrong of these things, as I see it, is not in the money the victims part with half so much as in the mental and spiritual poison they get. But that is precisely the thing the Constitution put beyond the reach of the prosecutor, for the price of freedom of religion or of speech or of the press is that we must put up with, and even pay for, a good deal of rubbish.

Prosecutions of this character easily could degenerate into religious persecution. I do not doubt that religious leaders may be convicted of fraud for making false representations on matters other than faith or experience, as for example if one represents that funds are being used to construct a church when in fact they are being used for personal Purposes. But that is not this case, which reaches into wholly dangerous ground. When does less than full belief in a professed credo become actionable fraud if one is soliciting gifts or legacies? Such inquiries may discomfort orthodox as well as unconventional religious leachers, for even the most regular of them are sometimes accused of taking their orthodoxy with a grain of salt.

I would dismiss the indictment and have done with this business of judicially examining other People's faiths.

NOTES AND QUESTIONS

1. *The Surprise Ending: Judicial Witness for the Prosecution.* Agatha Christie's murder mystery, *Witness for the Prosecution*, has a surprise ending. So does the *Ballard* case. When the Court of Appeals issued its first ruling, Judge O'Connor took the highly unusual step of writing to the Solicitor General, Charles Fahy, a fellow Catholic. Noting that the attorneys for both sides had agreed repeatedly to accept his ruling that sincerity not truth was the issue to be tried, O'Connor expressed outrage at letting the defendants attack the ground rules they had accepted. When the government petitioned for reconsideration, the panel did not change its decision, but Chief Judge William Denman

now added a concurring opinion, in which he wrote: "The district court did not give its reason for its ruling and instruction. If the reason be because such facts could occur in no possible chain of natural causation, it is a denial to the religious of the right to prove one of the bases of their belief in the intervention of the supernatural in the daily lives of human beings—an obvious denial of the freedom of the First Amendment of the Constitution." The next day O'Connor wrote to Wendell Berge, the head of the Criminal Division in the Justice Department. He reported to Berge that the defense had accepted his ruling. Then in a moment of candor he acknowledged the implications of Judge Denman's opinion for his own religious community: "One great organization believes in the miracles of Lourdes—under this opinion it would be necessary for that particular organization, preaching this article of faith, to prove it in a court before a jury, or be subject to conviction, imprisonment or fine, or both." In his view, not the prosecution of the I Am religion as a fraud, but the decision of the Ninth Circuit was "probably the greatest blow delivered to religious freedom" in America. He sent a copy to Justice William O. Douglas at his home in Silver Spring, MD. Is judicial advocacy for the prosecution authorized by the law or supported in judicial ethics?

2. *The Subtext: Jamesian Definition of Religious Experience.* Justice Jackson explicitly relied upon William James's *The Varieties of Religious Experience,* but the Jamesian influence permeated *Ballard.* The "basic proposition" put forward by James is that "the mother sea and fountain head of all religion lie in the mystical experiences of the individual."

Judge Noonan writes: "Relentless in this focus, James does not get into the nature of 'the divine'—that would be overt theology—and he treats theology— and he treats individuals 'in their solitude,' that is, as they exist in their interior, in their private imaginations and hearts.

"James acknowledges that he is intentionally omitting the institutional branch of religion. He does so not merely to limit his subject but from hostility. He defines institutional religion 'as an external art, the art of winning the favor of the gods.' He stops just short of saying, 'Organized religion is the technique of bribing the gods.' From Prosecutor Lazarus describing the I AM movement as 'a racket' to Justice Jackson calling it 'humbug, untainted by any trace of truth,' the same Jamesian perspective ran through *Ballard.*

"Looking for religion in the feelings of individuals in their solitude, James employed a criterion. For feelings about the divine to be religious, they had to be 'serious,' that is, ideational commitments that were neither casual nor cynical. With this criterion James asked of religion what Wordsworth had earlier required of true poetry and Matthew Arnold had made the poetic touchstone: 'the high seriousness which comes from absolute sincerity.'

"The majority of judges in *Ballard* made the same move. The test of belief being religious was the sincerity with which the belief was held. No matter that insincerity was not a federal crime. The judges honored the First Amendment by not putting religious truth on trial. Silently they incorporated in their decisions the cultural, American, Jamesian preference for judging not the content of the belief but the manner in which the belief was held by an individual." Noonan, *Lustre* 168–69. Does this judicial definition of religion violate the nonestablishment principle? The free exercise principle? Both principles?

The next case involves the Church of Scientology, founded by an American named L. Ron Hubbard. In a series of pamphlets Hubbard sketched the central beliefs and practices of this movement under the rubric, "Dianetics." The government attacked many of the therapeutic techniques used by Scientologists as false healing. This litigation ensued. Judge Skelly Wright thought the relevance of *Ballard* to this case was "obvious."

Founding Church of Scientology v. United States

409 F.2d 1146 (D.C. Cir. 1969), *cert. denied*, 396 U.S. 963 (1969).

■ WRIGHT, CIRCUIT J.

The basic theory of Dianetics is that man possesses both a reactive mind and an analytic mind. The analytic mind is a superior computer, incapable of error, to which can be attributed none of the human misjudgments which create social problems and much individual suffering. These are traceable rather to the reactive mind, which is made up of "engrams," or patterns imprinted on the nervous system in moments of pain, stress or unconsciousness. These imprinted patterns may be triggered by stimuli associated with the original imprinting, and may then produce unconscious or conditioned behavior which is harmful or irrational.

Dianetics is not presented as a simple description of the mind, but as a practical science which can cure many of the ills of man. It terms the ordinary person, encumbered by the "engrams" of his reactive mind, as a "preclear," by analogy to a computer from which previously programmed instructions have not been erased. The goal of Dianetics is to make persons "clear," thus freeing the rational and infallible analytical mind. The benefits this will bring are set out in considerable and alluring detail. All mental disorders are said to be caused by "engrams," as are all psychosomatic disorders, and that concept is broadly defined.

A process of working toward "clear" is described as "auditing." This process was explicitly characterized as "therapy" in Hubbard's best-selling book *Dianetics: The Modern Science of Mental Health* (1950). The process involves conversation with an "auditor" who would lead the subject or "preclear" along his "time track," discovering and exposing "engrams" along the way. Though auditing is represented primarily as a method of improving the spiritual condition of man, rather explicit benefits to bodily health are promised as well. Hubbard has asserted that arthritis, dermatitis, asthma, some coronary difficulties, eye trouble, bursitis, ulcers and sinusitis are psychosomatic and can be cured, and further that tuberculosis is "perpetuated by engrams."

A few years after the appearance of Dianetics, Hubbard began to set forth the broader theories of Scientology. Dianetics was explicitly endorsed as part of Scientology, "that branch * * * that covers Mental Anatomy." Testimony by Scientology adherents at the trial made clear that they continue to uphold the theories of Dianetics, though they feel that there may have been some errors in early formulations.

With Scientology came much of the overlay which lends color to the characterization of the movement as a religious one. Hubbard has claimed kinship between his theories and those espoused by Eastern religions, especially Hinduism and Buddhism. He argues that man is essentially a free and immortal spirit (a "thetan" in Scientological terminology) which merely inhabits the "mest body" ("mest" is an acronym of the words matter, energy, space, time). Man is said to be characterized by the qualities of "beingness," "havingness," and "doingness." The philosophical theory was developed that the world is constructed on the relationships of "Affinity," "Reality" and "Communication," which taken together are denominated "the ARC Triangle."

On the more mundane level, early in the career of Scientology Hubbard's followers—at least those in the United States—began to constitute themselves into formal religious bodies. The Founding Church of Scientology of Washington, D.C., one of the appellants, was incorporated in the District of Columbia in 1955. A formal creed was promulgated and was made part of the Articles of Incorporation. From the literature of the movement in evidence at trial, it appears that the move toward formal religious organization disturbed some adherents of Scientology, who seem to have regarded it is an attempt to provide a legal cloak for the movement's activities. But Hubbard defended the church movement, disavowing mysticism or supernaturalism, but pointing out the kinship of his ideas with those of the Vedas and other Eastern religious doctrines.

From the evidence developed at trial, it appears that a major activity of the Founding Church and its affiliated organizations in the District of Columbia is providing "auditing" at substantial fees (at the time of trial $500 for a 25–hour course), to persons interested in Scientology. The affiliated Academy of Scientology is engaged in training auditors. Auditors are paid directly by the Church. There is no membership in the Church as such; persons are accepted for auditing on the basis of their interest in Scientology (and presumably their ability to pay for its benefits).

The Hubbard Electrometer, or E-meter, plays an essential, or at least important, part in the process of auditing. The E-meter is a skin galvanometer, similar to those used in giving lie detector tests. The subject or "preclear" holds in his hands two tin soup cans, which are linked to the electrical apparatus. A needle on the apparatus registers changes in the electrical resistance of the subject's skin. The auditor asks questions of the subject, and the movement of the needle is apparently used as a check of the emotional reaction to the questions. According to complex rules and procedures set out in Scientology publications, the auditor can interpret the movements of the needle after certain prescribed questions are asked, and use them in diagnosing the mental and spiritual condition of the subject. The E-meters are sold for about $125, and are advertised in Scientology publications available at the Distribution Center adjoining the Church.

The Scientology movement in the District of Columbia also offers the entire range of Scientology publications for sale. Over the years this literature has grown into a formidable *corpus*. Hubbard's two early books on Dianetics are sold, along with later treatises developing Scientology. A large number of pamphlets and tracts supplements the hardcover books. The movement has a monthly magazine, *Ability*, which at the time of trial had published over 100 numbers. In addition, "L. Ron Hubbard's Professional Auditors' Bulletins," numbering at least 80 at the time of trial, are collected and published in pamphlets. Much of this literature is before the court as exhibits in evidence, and a large proportion of it stands condemned by the District Court's decree as "false or misleading labeling" of the E-meter. . . .

The *Ballard* case does not hold merely that religious belief is protected. The Ballards engaged in action; they solicited money from their faithful. Rather the holding of the case seems to be that regulation of religious action which involves testing in court the truth or falsity of religious belief is barred by the First Amendment.

The relevance of *Ballard* to the case before us is obvious. Here the E-meter has been condemned, not because it is itself harmful, but because the representations made concerning it are "false or misleading." And the largest part of those representations is contained in the literature of Scientology describing the process of auditing which appellants have claimed, without contest from the Government, is part of the doctrine of their religion and central to its exercise. Thus if their claims to religious status are accepted, a finding that the seized literature misrepresents the benefits from auditing is a finding that their religious doctrines are false.

———————

[Judge Wright concluded that the Church of Scientology had made a prima facie case that it was a religion and that a jury finding of false labeling under the Food, Drug, and Cosmetics Act would not be upheld when the finding was based on the church's "doctrinal religious literature."]

In a civil suit by a former member of the church, La Venda Van Schaick alleged she was induced to become a Scientologist by false representation by the church as to "the nature of the Scientology movement" and "the context of Scientology doctrine." The church, invoking *Ballard*, moved to dismiss. Judge W. Arthur Garrity, Jr., ruled, "To treat Scientology as a religion . . . would be to ignore the allegations of the complaint." He ordered a hearing as to whether the church was a religion, *Van Schaick v. Church of Scientology*, 535 F. Supp. 1125 (D. Mass. 1982). This issue has now been resolved in favor of the Scientologists in this country, *see, e.g., Hernandez v. Commissioner of Internal Revenue*, 490 U.S. 680 (1989). And the IRS settled a long-standing dispute with the Church of Scientology, restoring its tax-exempt status in 1993. See Stephen Labaton, "Scientology Granted Tax Exemptions," *N.Y. Times*, Oct. 14, 1993, A2.

As of the late 1990s, however, the Church of Scientology was still experiencing difficulty getting itself recognized as a church rather than as a commercial enterprise in other countries, notably Germany. *See, e.g.*, David Briscoe, "Scientology Scrutiny Defended: Sect Not a Religion, German Panel Says," *Arizona Republican*, Feb. 28, 1998; "Police in Germany Raid Scientology Offices," *St. Petersburg Times*, Feb. 11, 1998; "Scientology Case Shifts in Germany," *Boston Globe*, Nov. 7, 1997; "Court Told to Decide Scientology's

Legal Status by Its Profits," *Chicago Tribune*, Nov. 11, 1997; "Bonn Aide to Discuss Scientology in US," *Washington Post*, Nov. 3, 1997; Editorial, "The Secrets of the Universe," *Wall St. J.*, Feb. 24, 1998, A22.

Not only believers but nonbelievers were found to be protected by the First Amendment, or as the famous Footnote 11 in the following case suggested, there was a religion called Secular Humanism.

Torcaso v. Watkins

367 U.S. 488 (1961).

Leo Pfeffer and *Lawrence Speiser* argued the cause for appellant. With them on the briefs were *Joseph A. Sickles, Carlton R. Sickles, Bruce N. Goldberg, Rowland Watts and George Kaufmann.*

Thomas B. Finan, Attorney General of Maryland, and *Joseph S. Kaufman*, Deputy Attorney General, argued the cause and filed a brief for appellee. *C. Ferdinand Sybert*, former Attorney General of Maryland, and *Stedman Prescott, Jr.*, former Deputy Attorney General, appeared with *Mr. Kaufman* on the motion to dismiss or affirm.

Briefs of *amici curiae*, urging reversal, were filed by *Herbert A. Wolff and Leo Rosen* for the American Ethical Union, and by *Herbert B. Ehrmann, Lawrence Peirez, Isaac G. McNatt, Abraham Blumberg, Arnold Forster, Paul Hartman, Theodore Leskes, Edwin J. Lukas and Sol Rabkin* for the American Jewish Committee et al.

■ JUSTICE BLACK delivered the opinion of the Court.

Article 37 of the Declaration of Rights of the Maryland Constitution provides: "[N]o religious test ought ever to be required as a qualification for any office of profit or trust in this State, other than a declaration of belief in the existence of God...." The appellant Torcaso was appointed to the office of Notary Public by the Governor of Maryland but was refused a commission to serve because he would not declare his belief in God. He then brought this action in a Maryland Circuit Court to compel issuance of his commission, charging that the State's requirement that he declare this belief violated "the First and Fourteenth Amendments to the Constitution of the United States...."[1] The Circuit Court rejected these federal constitutional contentions, and the highest court of the State, the Court of Appeals, affirmed, holding that the state constitutional provision is self-executing and requires declaration of belief in God as a qualification for office without need for implementing legislation. The case is therefore properly here on appeal under 28 U.S.C. § 1257(2).

There is, and can be, no dispute about the purpose or effect of the Maryland Declaration of Rights requirement before us—it sets up a religious test which was designed to and, if valid, does bar every person who

---

1. Appellant also claimed that the State's test oath requirement violates the provision of Art. VI of the Federal Constitution that "no religious Test shall ever be required as a Qualification to any Office or public Trust under the United States." Because we are reversing the judgment on other grounds, we find it unnecessary to consider appellant's contention that this provision applies to state as well as federal offices.

refuses to declare a belief in God from holding a public "office of profit or trust" in Maryland. The power and authority of the State of Maryland thus is put on the side of one particular sort of believers—those who are willing to say they believe in "the existence of God.". . . .

We repeat and again reaffirm that neither a State nor the Federal Government can constitutionally force a person "to profess a belief or disbelief in any religion." Neither can constitutionally pass laws or impose requirements which aid all religions as against non-believers,[10] and neither can aid those religions based on a belief in the existence of God as against those religions founded on different beliefs.[11]

In upholding the State's religious test for public office the highest court of Maryland said:

"The petitioner is not compelled to believe or disbelieve, under threat of punishment or other compulsion. True, unless he makes the declaration of belief he cannot hold public office in Maryland, but he is not compelled to hold office." The fact, however, that a person is not compelled to hold public office cannot possibly be an excuse for barring him from office by state-imposed criteria forbidden by the Constitution. This was settled by our holding in *Wieman v. Updegraff*, 344 U.S. 183. We there pointed out that whether or not "an abstract right to public employment exists," Congress could not pass a law providing " ' . . . that no federal employee shall attend Mass or take any active part in missionary work'."

This Maryland religious test for public office unconstitutionally invades the appellant's freedom of belief and religion and therefore cannot be enforced against him.

The judgment of the Court of Appeals of Maryland is accordingly reversed and the cause is remanded for further proceedings not inconsistent with this opinion. *Reversed and remanded.*

■ JUSTICE FRANKFURTER and JUSTICE HARLAN concur in the result.

10. In discussing Article VI in the debate of the North Carolina Convention on the adoption of the Federal Constitution, James Iredell, later a Justice of this Court, said: " . . . [I]t is objected that the people of America may, perhaps, choose representatives who have no religion at all, and that pagans and Mahometans may be admitted into offices. But how is it possible to exclude any set of men, without taking away that principle of religious freedom which we ourselves so warmly contend for?" And another delegate pointed out that Article VI "leaves religion on the solid foundation of its own inherent validity, without any connection with temporal authority; and no kind of oppression can take place." 4 Elliot, *Debates in the State Ratifying Conventions* 194, 200.

11. Among religions in this country that do not teach what would generally be considered a belief in the existence of God are Buddhism, Taoism, Ethical Culture, Secular Humanism, and others. See *Washington Ethical Society v. District of Columbia*, 101 U.S. App. D.C. 371, 249 F.2d 127; *Fellowship of Humanity v. County of Alameda*, 153 Cal. App. 2d 673, 315 P.2d 394; II Encyclopaedia of the Social Sciences 293; 4 Encyclopaedia Britannica (1957 ed.) 325–327; 21 *id.,* at 797; Archer, *Faiths Men Live By* (2d ed. revised by Purinton), 120–138, 254–313; 1961 World Almanac 695, 712; *Year Book of American Churches for 1961*, at 29, 47.

2.   Determination of Ecclesiastical Status

If religious belief may not be tested, may religions status be tested by the government employing criteria other than those employed by the religion in question? To determine whether a registrant was entitled to the statutory deferment from the draft given to students "preparing for the ministry in theological or divinity schools recognized as such," the New York director of Selective Service set up theological "panels" to advise the local draft boards. Irwin S. Levy, fifteen years old, was admitted to study at Mesifta Talmudic Seminary in Brooklyn. He was in his third of nine years of study when he became eighteen and eligible for the draft. The advisory panel, composed of "the most prominent men of the Jewish faith in the great City of New York" (according to a draft board member) recommended denial of exemption as a theological student. Irwin Levy contended that the panel favored Reformed and Conservative Judaism over Orthodox Judaism and that out of fifty bona fide seminarians at Mesifta it had recognized only one as deserving exemption. In *United States ex rel. Levy v. Cain*, 149 F.2d 338 (2d Cir. 1945), the Second Circuit, per Judge Learned Hand, ruled that the Board had improperly delegated its responsibility to the panel and ordered Levy released from the army. This decision was followed in *United States v. Samuels*, 151 F.2d 801 (3d Cir. 1945), a case involving two other Mesifta students, Jacob S. Samuels and Henry Horowitz. The Supreme Court unanimously reversed.

Eagles v. United States ex rel. Samuels

329 U.S. 304 (1946).

Irving S. Shapiro argued the cause for petitioner. *Meyer Kreeger* argued the cause for respondent.

■ Douglas, J., delivered the opinion of the Court.

It appears that the city director, in aid of these functions, established theological panels. It was thought desirable to give the selective service personnel the benefit of the advice of those familiar with the educational practices of various religious groups so that Selective Service might exercise a more informed judgment in evaluating claims to classifications in IV–D. Accordingly, theological panels were constituted, one of which consisted of prominent laymen and rabbis of the Jewish faith who gave advisory opinions on those who sought a IV–D classification on the grounds that they were either rabbis or students preparing for the ministry in the Jewish religion. The members of the panel were volunteers, as permitted by the regulations. And pursuant to the regulations each took the oath of office.

Samuels registered under the Act in February, 1942. In May and July, 1942, he filed with his local board questionnaires stating that he had had two years of high school education; that he was a student at the Mesifta Theological Seminary preparing for the rabbinate; that since 1940 his regular occupation was that of a clerk; that for the past two years he had been employed by a textile company; and that the job for which he was best fitted was that of a spiritual leader and a teacher of Hebrew or rabbinical duties. The local board was advised by the seminary that Samuels had attended there since he was six years old, that he had finished the eight-year elementary course and the four-year pre-rabbinical course, that he had been admitted to the rabbinical division in 1937, that he left the school in 1939 to seek employment, that he returned to the evening school in September, 1941, and that he was transferred to the day session in July, 1942, which, as later appeared, was a few days before the school closed for the summer.

In August, 1942, the local board classified him IV–D. In May, 1944, he was given a physical examination and found acceptable for military service. Thereafter the city director requested that he appear before the theological panel in respect to his claim to a IV–D classification. He appeared before the panel in June, 1944, stating, *inter alia,* that he expected to graduate from the seminary in 1945, that ill health caused him to leave the school in 1939, that between 1940 and 1942 he worked as a clerk, and that he returned to the seminary as a full-time student at about the time he filed his selective service questionnaire.

The panel reported that the seminary which Samuels attended was not preparing men exclusively for the rabbinate, that orthodox tradition encouraged advanced study of the subjects in which students for the ministry were trained, and that students ultimately intending to enter business or a profession of some non-rabbinic activity in the field of religion may be enrolled in the same classes as those preparing for the rabbinate. The panel stated that it therefore seemed essential to determine in each case what the registrant had in mind in pursuing his course of study; that to make that determination the character of the seminary, the sincerity of the registrant's declared purpose, his demeanor, and the impression as to his candor and honesty should be considered. It concluded that Samuels was not "preparing in good faith for a career of service in the practicing rabbinate."

[The Court said that the draft board had not abandoned its functions to the panel. The Court also said that there was evidence supporting the board's doubt that Samuels was "preparing in good faith for the rabbinate. A registrant might seek a theological school as a refuge for the duration of the war. Congress did not create the exemption in sec. 5(d) for him."]

Cox v. United States

332 U.S. 442 (1947).

Hayden C. Covington argued the cause and filed a brief for petitioners.

Irving S. Shapiro argued the cause for the United States. With him on the brief were *Solicitor General Perlman and Robert S. Erdahl.*

■ JUSTICE REED delivered the opinion of the Court.

Petitioner Cox registered under the Selective Training and Service Act on October 16, 1940, and in his questionnaire stated that he was 22 years old and had been employed as a truck driver since 1936. The local board classified him IV–F, as not physically fit for service, on January 31, 1941, and on March 10, 1942, changed the classification to I–A. Ten days later Cox filed a request for reclassification as IV–E (conscientious objector), stating that he had become a Jehovah's Witness in January 1942. The board at first rejected the claim, but on June 12 of the same year granted him the requested classification. Ten days later petitioner first made his claim for total exemption from service, claiming to be a minister of religion; the local board refused the exemption and its action was sustained by the board of appeal. On May 18, 1944, the board ordered Cox to report to camp, and on May 26 he complied and then immediately left camp and did not return.

Upon trial Cox's selective service file was received in evidence. It contained an ordination certificate from the Watch Tower Bible and Tract Society stating that Cox was "a duly ordained minister of the Gospel" and that his "entire time" was devoted to missionary work. The file also contained an affidavit of a company servant, Cox's church superior, dated October 29, 1942, stating that Cox "regularly and customarily serves as a minister by going from house to house and conducting Bible Studies and Bible Talks." There was also an affidavit by Cox, dated October 28, 1942, stating that he was enrolled in the "Pioneer service" on October 16 and that he was "able to average 150 hours per month to my ministerial duties without secular work." He added that "my entire time will be devoted to preaching the Gospel as a pioneer." Cox testified at the trial in October 1944 as to his duties as a minister that he preached from house to house, conducted funerals, and "instructed the Bible" in homes. No evidence was introduced showing the total amount of time Cox had spent in religious activities since October 16, 1942. Nor was there evidence of the secular activities of Cox nor the time employed in them. Although the selective service file was introduced in evidence, and the trial court denied the motion for a directed verdict, it does not appear that the trial judge examined the file to determine whether the action of the local board was arbitrary and capricious or without basis in fact. At that time the lower federal courts interpreted *Falbo v. United States,* 320 U.S. 549, as meaning that no judicial review of any sort could be had of a selective service order. In *Estep v. United States*, 327 U.S. 114, we held that a limited review could be obtained if the registrant had exhausted his administrative remedies, and the Circuit Court of Appeals in accordance with that decision reviewed the file of Cox and found that the evidence was "substantially in support" of the classification found by the board.

Petitioner Thompson also registered on October 16, 1940, claiming exemption as a minister. He stated in his questionnaire that he was 30 years old and that for the past 13 years he had operated a grocery store and had been a minister since August 1, 1940. At first the local board gave him a deferred classification because of dependency, but then changed his classification to IV–E. Thompson appealed to the board of appeal on November 5, 1943, explaining his duties as a minister and presenting a full statement of his argument that as a colporteur he was within the exemption for ministers as interpreted by selective service regulations. . . .

Section 5(d) of the Selective Training and Service Act provides that "regular or duly ordained ministers of religion" shall be exempt from training and service under the Act, and § 622.44 of Selective Service Regulations defines the terms "regular minister of religion" and "duly ordained minister of religion." In order to aid the local boards in applying the regulation, the Director of Selective Service issued Opinion No. 14 (amended) on November 2, 1942, which described the tests to be applied in determining whether Jehovah's Witnesses were entitled to exemption as ministers, regular or ordained. The opinion stated that Witnesses who were members of the Bethel Family (producers of religious supplies) or pioneers, devoting all or substantially all of their time to the work of teaching the tenets of their religion, generally were exempt, and appended a list of certain members of the Bethel Family and pioneers who were entitled to this exemption. None of these Witnesses were on the list. The opinion stated that members of the Bethel Family and pioneers whose names did not appear on the list, as well as all other Witnesses holding official titles in the organization, must be classified by the boards according to the facts in each case. The determining criteria were stated to be "whether or not they devote their lives in the furtherance of the beliefs of Jehovah's Witnesses, whether or not they perform functions which are normally performed by regular or duly ordained ministers of other religions, and, finally, whether or not they are regarded by other Jehovah's Witnesses in the same manner in which regular or duly ordained ministers of other religions are ordinarily regarded." The opinion further stated that the local board should place in the registrant's file "a record of all facts entering into its determination for the reason that it is legally necessary that the record show the basis of the local board's decision."

It will be observed that § 622.44 of the regulation makes "ordination" the only practical difference between a "regular" and a "duly ordained minister." This seems consistent with § 5 of the Act. We are of the view that the regulation conforms to the Act and that it is valid under the rule-making power conferred by § 10 (a). We agree, also, that Opinion 14 furnishes a proper guide to the interpretation of the Act and Regulations. *Affirmed.*

■ Mr. Justice Frankfurter concurs in the result.

■ Mr. Justice Douglas, with whom Mr. Justice Black concurs, dissenting:

It is not disputed that Jehovah's Witnesses constitute a religious sect or organization. We have, moreover, recognized that its door-to-door evangelism is as much religious activity as "worship in the churches and preaching from the pulpits." *Murdock v. Pennsylvania* [Chapter Eleven, section 1]. The Selective Service files of these petitioners establish, I think, their status as ministers of that sect. Their claims to that status are supported by affidavits of their immediate superiors in the local group and by their national headquarters. And each of them was spending substantial time in the religious activity of preaching their faith. If a person is in fact engaging in the ministry, his motives for doing so are quite immaterial.

To deny these claimants their statutory exemption is to disregard these facts or to adopt a definition of minister which contracts the classification provided by Congress.

The classification as a minister may not be denied because the registrant devotes but a part of his time to religious activity.

NOTES AND QUESTIONS

Is the relevant distinction between *Cox* and *Samuels*, on the one hand, and *Ballard,* on the other, that in the draft cases a "privilege" or "exemption" was being granted, while in *Ballard* the ordinary criminal law was being applied? How does the Court's view of the nonbinding effect of ecclesiastical determinations relate to the cases that follow, especially *Kedroff v. St. Nicholas Cathedral* [section 3 below], an opinion also written by Justice Reed?

The critical procedural issue in the next case was over the right to trial by jury. The text of the Sixth Amendment secures that right for "the accused." Knowing of hostility in New York to his fledgling religious movement, Reverend Sun Myung Moon, the founder and head of the Unification Church, waived his right to a jury trial and sought a bench trial. The government insisted on a jury trial. Does the government have a right to trial by jury? Was the Bill of Rights designed for the protection of the government against the people, or–as Yogi Berra would put it–vice versa the other way round?

The critical substantive issue was the tax liability of Rev. Moon for the interest income on large sums of money—$1.7 million over three years–that he deposited in the Chase Manhattan Bank in his own name. Many religious leaders hold property in their name for the use of the religious community. For example, Charles Wesley, the founder of Methodism, held the assets of his community in this way. Many states, including California, and Illinois, and New York, have enacted corporate sole statutes, which authorize the property of a hierarchical church such as a Catholic diocese to be held in the name of the local bishop. For example, the California statute provides: "A corporation sole may be formed under this part by the bishop, chief priest, presiding elder, or other presiding officer of any religious denomination, society, or church, for the purpose of administering and managing the affairs, property, and temporalities thereof." Calif. Bus. & Professions Code, § 10002; the powers of a corporation sole are set forth in § 10007.

The district court refused to give the following instruction requested by Moon: "There is evidence in the case tending to prove that the International Unification Church movement existed as an unincorporated association which was personified by Reverend Moon, founder and spiritual leader of the worldwide Unification Church movement, and which supported and directed the activities of the various national church entities in the United States and elsewhere."

The district judge instructed the jury as follows: "If you find that the funds in the Chase accounts were the property of International Unification Church Movement or were held in trust by Moon for the International Unification Church Movement and used for church purposes and that the interest on those funds also belonged to the International Unification Church Movement and were used by it, then that interest would not be taxable income to Moon."

Moon objected to the instruction: "If he used money for his own purposes that use would indicate lack of a trust relationship."

Did Moon receive the money as donations to the church? Was it intended to be held in his name in trust for the church? He was convicted of filing false federal income tax returns and was sentenced to eighteen months in prison. Represented by Professor Laurence Tribe, Moon argued that the First Amendment was violated because the trial court failed to charge the jury that it must accept as conclusive the Unification Church's definition of what the church considered a religious purpose. The Second Circuit, per Judge Richard J. Cardamone, rejected these arguments. It further held that "the doctrine of *Jones v. Wolf* [section 3 below] has no application to the facts of this case."

Judge Oakes dissented from the portion of Judge Cardamone's opinion relating to the trial judge's charge on the law of trusts. He noted first that the critical issue was whether the Chase Manhattan Fund and the Tong Il stock held in Moon's own name were church property or Moon's personal property. Oakes also noted that Moon's claim that he was holding the assets in trust was well preserved on the record in this case, both through a pretrial motion to dismiss and through a midtrial motion for a judgment of acquittal, and that in any event reversal is required for any defects in respect to the charge on the issue of beneficial ownership because that issue was "central to the determination of guilt or innocence" in the case. He then wrote as follows.

United States v. Moon

718 F.2d 1210 (2d Cir. 1983), *cert. denied,* 466 U.S. 971 (1984).

■ Oakes, J., dissenting in part.

The Reverend Moon submitted detailed instructions with supporting memoranda of law both on the general issue of beneficial ownership (No. 16) and on the specific issue whether an unincorporated religious association can be the beneficiary of a charitable trust (No. 15). Similarly, counsel pressed and elaborated upon his requests at the charging conference and made plain his disagreement with the proposed instruction submitted by the Government. . . .

[T]his case did not involve a claim that an ordinary, lay taxpayer held certain assets in a private trust for the benefit of another. On the contrary, the taxpayer here was the founder and leader of a worldwide movement which, regardless of what the observer may think of its views or even its motives, is nevertheless on its face a religious one, the members of which regard the taxpayer as the embodiment of their faith. Because Moon was the spiritual leader of the church, the issue whether he or the church beneficially owned funds in his name was not as crystal-clear as might seem at first glance to be the case. . . .

It appears that the assets in question came to Moon largely from members of his faith, and there was some evidence that the donors intended their contributions to be used by him for religious purposes. The religious context involved gives the case a special color. . . . [F]unds donated for the use of an individual involved in religious work may be considered gifts to the religious organization with which the individual is affiliated. . . .

The Reverend Moon's claim that he held the Chase Funds and the Tong Il stock as trustee for the Unification Church movement likewise raised the question whether the donors intended this property to be used for religious purposes. In this context, then, I think it was incumbent upon the court to make certain that the trust charge not only properly state the factual elements that were involved, but that it also clearly emphasize that the Government had the burden of proof beyond a reasonable doubt on this difficult issue.... While I by no means agree with the appellants' contention that New York law establishes a presumption that any assets given to a religious leader are held by him in a charitable trust, it at least permits of a finding to this effect.

This conclusion stems from the following facts. First, the law favors charitable trusts and will draw reasonable inferences and resolve ambiguities to find and uphold them [cases omitted]. Second, when a gift appears to have been made for charitable or religious purposes, the gift may be found to have been made in trust even if no trust language has been used and even if the gift was in form absolute. Third, there are numerous cases holding that a minister or other church official who held title to property in his own name did so as trustee for the church. Finally, where the source of the assets is a church source, added to the fact that the donee is a religious official, a trust may be imposed. Thus the key issue was whether the funds were given to Moon for his own use or for that of his international church movement, and whether, even though some of the funds were utilized for his own living purposes, the donors intended to permit such use.

[I]n referring to the fact that the jury should consider all the evidence on the issue whether the Unification Church movement existed and whether the movement or the Reverend Moon owned the funds in the Chase accounts and Tong Il stock, the court listed eight factors.... Listed among these, but not emphasized, was "the intent of the parties who caused the stock and funds to be transferred to Reverend Moon's name." Rather than simply including intent as one of the things for the jury to consider, the court in my view should have advised the jury to accord the greatest weight to this factor. The church source of the funds and Moon's role as church leader were likely to cast light on the issue of the donors' intent, and accordingly the charge should have specifically directed the jury's attention to them. The instruction as given allowed the jury to find against Moon on the issue of beneficial ownership without even considering the crucial issue of donors' intent.

[T]he court's instructions regarding the use or misuse of trust funds were at the very least confusing.... [W]hile it may be correct as a matter of law that a trustee who diverts trust property to his own use is taxable to the extent of the diversion, diversion was not charged in the indictment. Thus, evidence of diversion was irrelevant to the case. The diversion instruction, given over defense objection, was at variance with the theory on which the Reverend Moon was indicted and on which the entire case was tried.

[A] trust may exist even though the trustee is endowed with the freedom to use for his own personal benefit a portion of the funds he holds in trust and such use will not nullify the existence of the trust [cases omitted]. This is particularly true in the case of monies held in trust by religious leaders, since often use of such funds to pay a leader's living expenses are within the scope of the church's religious purposes. Moreover, the instruction failed to explain that, even if the Reverend Moon had improperly diverted some of the Chase funds to a nontrust use, such partial diversion could not make the entire corpus, and thus the interest thereon, taxable to him. The inclusion of the phrase "to the extent so diverted" in the diversion portion of the charge could not have conveyed this concept at all.

Finally, in my view the instructions shifted to the defendant the burden of proof on the issue of beneficial ownership. The jury was charged that "if" it found the Chase funds were the property of the International Unification Church movement or were held in trust by Moon for the movement, "then" the interest "would not be taxable income to Moon." The implication of this instruction was that Moon had to convince the jury that the property belonged to the movement [case omitted]. By saying that the donor's intent must be "clear and unambiguous," not only was the law of charitable trusts being misstated, but the burden of proof improperly placed upon the defendant was made heavy indeed....

Thus in a case where the crucial issue, and indeed the only real factual question, was whether property unquestionably held in Moon's own name was beneficially owned by him personally or was held by him on behalf of his international church movement, the charge fell short in several respects.

NOTE

When Moon applied for certiorari, his petition was supported by some forty organizations and individuals, among them the National Council of the Churches of Christ in the U.S.A., the Presbyterian Church (U.S.A.), the American Baptist Churches in the U.S.A., the African Methodist Episcopal Church, the National Association of Evangelicals, the Southern Christian Leadership Conference, the Catholic League for Religious and Civil Rights, and the Church of Jesus Christ of Latter-Day Saints. Having served as the first dean of the law school at Brigham Young University, and subsequently as the university's president, Rex Lee, the Solicitor General at the time of the *Moon* case, was a leading member of the Church of Jesus Christ of Latter-Day Saints who was obviously familiar with the history of the persecution of his religious community in the late nineteenth century [Chapter Nine]. Michael McConnell, a leading authority on religious freedom also served on the staff of the Solicitor General at the time. Lee asked McConnell to review the record for potential incursions upon religious freedom. Although both of these scholars and public servants were sensitive to the preservation of religious freedom, neither could see any difficulty with the lower court's handling of the case. They signed the brief in opposition to the granting of certiorari, and the Court denied the petition. 446 U.S. 971 (1984). Rev. Moon served a prison term of a year and a half. Would he have been prosecuted for failure to report the interest as income, and would a jury in Manhattan have convicted Rev. Moon if he were the Catholic Archbishop of New York?

---

3.   TITLE TO CHURCH PROPERTY

NOTES AND QUESTIONS

1.   *The Neutrality of Courts and State Action.* The Fourteenth Amendment rules action by the state. In *Shelley v. Kraemer*, 334 U.S. 1 (1948), the Supreme Court (6–0) held that when a state enforced a racially restrictive covenant, the judicial decree was state action and, as it enforced a discrimination against blacks, it was state action barred by the Fourteenth Amendment.

The Fourteenth Amendment has now been interpreted by the Court to bar state action establishing a religion. When a state court acts to decide an interchurch property dispute—whether or not the court uses the church rule or "neutral principles"—does the court's decree constitute state action? Is it state action establishing a religion? Is such establishment barred by the Fourteenth Amendment? If not, why not?

Shelley v. Kraemer produced much commentary pondering its implications and attempting to limit its logic, *see* Gerald Gunther, *Constitutional Law: Cases and Materials* 933–938 (1975). Justice Holmes once wrote that "a page of history is worth a volume of logic." *New York Trust Co. v. Eisner*, 256 U.S. 345, 349 (1921). History, not logic, has suggested that in the area of religion *Shelley's* clear holding cannot be applied literally.

Compare Gordon v. Gordon, 332 Mass. 197, 124 N.E. 2d 228 (1955), *cert. denied*, 349 U.S. 947 (1955). Joseph Gordon of Attleboro, an Orthodox Jew, provided by will that if any of his children should "marry a person not born in the Hebrew faith," the testamentary gift to that child was revoked. His son Harold married Veronica Albaugh, a woman raised as a Catholic who was undergoing instruction from rabbis at the time of her wedding and who a little later formally became a convert to Judaism. The court found the phrase "Hebrew faith" not to be too vague (disagreeing with modern English trust cases on this point), it found Veronica to be one not born in that faith, and it rejected Harold Gordon's contention that *Shelley v. Kraemer* prevented enforcement of his father's will. The Probate Court's decree excluded him from the beneficiaries under the will. *Accord, United States National Bank v. Snodgrass*, 202 Or. 530, 275 P.2d 860 (1954) (will enforced denying gift to daughter if she became a Catholic or married a Catholic).

2.   *Communist-Controlled Churches.* The Eastern Christian Churches have traditionally had a much closer identification with the state than any church is permitted to have with the American government. In 1721 the Orthodox Church in Russia was put under government control by the Ecclesiastical Regulation of Peter the Great. Its former mode of government by a patriarch and sobors (councils) was replaced by a bureaucratic institution called the Holy Governing Synod, which took an oath to the czar as "Supreme Judge" and which was supervised by a lay administrator, the chief procurator. *See* Robert K. Massie, *Peter the Great* 782 (1980); Dimitry Pospielovsky, *The Russian Church under the Soviet Regime 1917–1982* 1, 19, 25 (1984). With the abdica-

tion of Nicholas II, the church lost its temporal head. In November 1917 a sobor elected Tikhon Belavin as patriarch, giving him unrestricted administrative powers in case the new Soviet government made it impossible to convoke another sobor. Pospielovsky 1, 31, 36. In 1923 a schismatic group, the Renovationists, favored by the Soviet government, deposed Tikhon, now in prison, and set up a new administration. *Id.* 1, 56–58.

Tikhon had appointed Platon Rozhdestvensky archbishop of North America, with St. Nicholas Cathedral in New York as his seat. The Renovationists named John Kedrovsky to the same position (although he was married and so canonically ineligible to be a bishop), and on November 7, 1923, he entered the cathedral, announcing that as appointee of "the Soviet All–Living Church" he had come "to take control of all Russian Church property," *New York Times,* November 8, 1923, p. 21, col. 3. Platon was dismissed for counterrevolutionary acts "directed against the Soviet," *see St. Nicholas Cathedral v. Kreshik* [this section below]. Platon responded by calling a sobor of the North American clergy and faithful in Detroit in 1924. This sobor concluded that the patriarchate in Russia was under the coercion of the communists. The sobor relied on a decree issued by Tikhon in 1920 authorizing archdioceses to organize on a local basis if the activity of the patriarchate should stop and, "until the restitution of the Supreme Church government, decide definitely all affairs." The Detroit sobor recognized Platon as archbishop. However, the courts of New York recognized the Renovationists as the church and gave Kedrovsky possession of St. Nicholas Cathedral. *Kedrovsky, v. Rojdesvensky,* 214 App. Div. 483, 212 N.Y.S. 273 (1925), *affirmed* 242 N.Y. 547, 162 N.E. 421 (1926). Most Orthodox churches in America were transferred to boards of trustees headed by Platon and escaped Kedrovsky. Pospielovsky 2, 283, 283 n. 48.

Litigation resumed in 1945. By this time, Kedrovsky was dead, his son John Kedroff had taken over the cathedral, and the Renovationist Church had lost the support of the Soviet government and disappeared. Meanwhile, New York had amended its Religious Corporation Law confirming title in the Russian Orthodox Church in North America (*i.e.*, the Church governed by Platon and his successors since the Detroit sobor) as the lawful owner of all property held by the Orthodox Church before the Russian Revolution. The American group sued for possession of the cathedral.

Kedroff himself, having no defense, sought out a new claimant. This was Venyamin Fedchenkov, whose claim was through Sergii Stragorodsky. Sergii, since his release from prison in 1927 and his comprehensive declaration of loyalty to the Soviet government, had without canonical authority acted as the de facto ecclesiastical head of the Orthodox Church in Russia while his critics saw him as a puppet of the secret police. Pospielovsky 1, 71–72; 2, 485. Sergii removed Platon and appointed Fedchenkov archbishop of North America in 1933. *Id.* 2, 289. Soviet support shifted from the Renovationists to the Church headed by Sergii. In 1945, at the end of World War II a sobor was held for three days in Moscow, which recognized Aleksii Simansky, Sergii's successor, as patriarch and enacted a new administrative statute to govern the church; its effect was to make the patriarch supreme, *ibid.* at 2, 209–211. Aleksii supported Fedchenkov, and Fedchenkov supported Kedroff. In 1952 the case reached the Supreme Court.

Kedroff v. Saint Nicholas Cathedral of the Russian Orthodox Church in North America

344 U.S. 94 (1952).

Philip Adler argued the cause and filed the briefs for appellants.

Ralph Montgomery Arkush argued the cause and filed the brief for appellee.

■ JUSTICE REED delivered the opinion of the Court.

The right to the use and occupancy of a church in the city of New York is in dispute.

The right to such use is claimed by appellee, a corporation created in 1925 by an act of the Legislature of New York, Laws of New York 1925, c. 403, for the purpose of acquiring a cathedral for the Russian Orthodox Church in North America as a central place of worship and residence of the ruling archbishop "in accordance with the doctrine, discipline and worship of the Holy Apostolic Catholic Church of Eastern Confession as taught by the holy scriptures, holy tradition, seven oecumenical councils and holy fathers of that church."

The corporate right is sought to be enforced so that the head of the American churches, religiously affiliated with the Russian Orthodox Church, may occupy the Cathedral. At the present time that head is the Metropolitan of All America and Canada, the Archbishop of New York, Leonty, who like his predecessors was elected to his ecclesiastical office by a sobor of the American churches.

That claimed right of the corporation to use and occupancy for the archbishop chosen by the American churches is opposed by appellants who are in possession. Benjamin Fedchenkoff bases his right on an appointment in 1934 by the Supreme Church Authority of the Russian Orthodox Church, to wit, the Patriarch *locum tenens* of Moscow and all Russia and its Holy Synod, as Archbishop of the Archdiocese of North America and the Aleutian Islands. The other defendant-appellant is a priest of the Russian Orthodox Church, also acknowledging the spiritual and administrative control of the Moscow hierarchy. . . .

The Russian upheaval caused repercussions in the North American Diocese. That Diocese at the time of the Soviet Revolution recognized the spiritual and administrative control of Moscow. White Russians, both lay and clerical, found asylum in America from the revolutionary conflicts, strengthening the feeling of abhorrence of the secular attitude of the new Russian Government. The church members already here, immigrants and native-born, while habituated to look to Moscow for religious direction, were accustomed to our theory of separation between church and state. The Russian turmoil, the restraints on religious activities and the evolution of a new ecclesiastical hierarchy in the form of the "Living Church," deemed noncanonical or schismatic by most churchmen, made very difficult Russian administration of the American diocese. Furthermore, Patriarch Tikhon, on November 20, 1920, issued Decision No. 362 relating to church administration for troublesome times. This granted a large measure of autonomy, when the Russian ruling authority was unable to function, subject to "confirmation later to the Central Church Authority when it is re-established." Naturally the growing number of American-born members of the Russian Church did not cling to a hierarchy identified with their country of remote origin with the same national feeling that moved their immigrant ancestors. These facts and forces generated in America a separatist movement.

That movement brought about the arrangements at the Detroit Sobor of 1924 for a temporary American administration of the church on account of the disturbances in Russia.[8] This was followed by the declarations of autonomy of the successive sobors since that date, a spate of litigation concerning control of the various churches and occupancy of ecclesiastical positions, the New York legislation (known as Article 5–C, notes 2 and 3), and this controversy.

Delegates from the North American Diocese intended to be represented at an admittedly canonical Sobor of the Russian Orthodox Church held in 1945 at Moscow. They did not arrive in time on account of delays, responsibility for which has not been fixed. The following stipulation appears as to their later actions while at Moscow: "It is stipulated that Bishop Alexi and Father Dzvonchik, representing the local group of American Churches under Bishop Theophilus, appeared before the Patriarch and the members of his Synod in Moscow, presented a written report on the condition of the American Church, with a request for autonomy and a few days later received from the Patriarch the Ukase. . . ."

There came to the Russian Church in America this Ukase of the Moscow Patriarchy of February 14 or 16, 1945, covering Moscow's requirements for reunion of the American Orthodox Church with the Russian. It required for reunion that the Russian Church in America hold promptly an "all American Orthodox Church Sobor"; that it express the decision of the dioceses to reunite with the Russian Mother Church, declare the agreement of the American Orthodox Church to abstain "from political activities against the U.S.S.R." and so direct its parishes, and elect a Metropolitan subject to confirmation by the Moscow Patriarchy. The decree said, "In view of the distance of the American Metropolitan District from the

---

8. The attitude of the Russian Church in America will be made sufficiently plain by these extracts from their records of action taken at the Detroit Sobor, 1924:

"Point 1. Temporarily, until the convocation of the All Russian Sobor further indicated in Point 5, to declare the Russian Orthodox Diocese in America a self-governed Church so that it be governed by its own elected Archbishop by means of a Sobor of Bishops, a Council composed of those elected from the clergy and laity, and periodic Sobors of the entire American Church.

"Point 5. To leave the final regulation of questions arising form the relationship of the Russian and the American Churches to a future Sobor of the Russian Orthodox Church which will be legally convoked, legally elected, will sit with the participation of representatives of the American church under conditions of political freedom, guaranteeing the fullness and authority of its decisions for the entire Church, and will be recognized by the entire Oecumenical Orthodox Church as a true Sobor of the Russian Orthodox Church."

Russian Mother Church ... the Metropolitan–Exarch ... may be given some extended powers by the Moscow Patriarchy...."

The American congregations speaking through their Cleveland Sobor of 1946 refused the proffered arrangement and resolved in part: "That any administrative recognition of the Synod of the Russian Orthodox Church Abroad is hereby terminated, retaining, however, our spiritual and brotherly relations with all parts of the Russian Orthodox Church abroad...." This ended the efforts to compose the differences between the Mother Church and its American offspring, and this litigation followed. We understand the above factual summary corresponds substantially with the factual basis for determination formulated by the Court of Appeals of New York. From those circumstances it seems clear that the Russian Orthodox Church was, until the Russian Revolution, an hierarchical church with unquestioned paramount jurisdiction in the governing body in Russia over the American Metropolitanate. Nothing indicates that either the Sacred Synod or the succeeding Patriarchs relinquished that authority or recognized the autonomy of the American church. The Court of Appeals decision proceeds, we understand, upon the same assumption. That court did consider "whether there exists in Moscow at the present time a true central organization of the Russian Orthodox Church capable of functioning as the head of a free international religious body." It concluded that this aspect of the controversy had not been sufficiently developed to justify a judgment upon that ground.

The Religions Corporations Law. The New York Court of Appeals depended for its judgment, refusing recognition to Archbishop Benjamin, the appointee of the Moscow Hierarchy of the Russian Orthodox Church, upon Article 5–C of the Religious Corporations Law.[10] Certainly a legisla-

---

10. The Court said: "The Legislature has made a determination that the 'Russian Church in America' was the one which, to use our words in 249 New York at pages 77–78, was the trustee which 'may be relied upon to carry out more effectively and faithfully the purposes of this religious trust (*Carrier v. Carrier*, 226 N.Y. 114)' by reason of the changed situation of the patriarchate in Russia.... The courts have always recognized that it is the province of the Legislature to make the underlying findings of fact which give meaning and substance to its ultimate directives. The courts have traditionally refused to consider the wisdom or technical validity of such findings of fact, if there be some reasonable basis upon which they may rest."

The Legislature of the State of New York, like the Congress, must be deemed to have investigated the whole problem carefully before it acted. The Legislature knew that the central authorities of the Russian Orthodox Church in Russia had been suppressed after the 1917 revolution, and that the patri-

archate was later resurrected by the Russian Government. The Legislature, like Congress, knew the character and method of operation of international communism and the Soviet attitude toward things religious. The Legislature was aware of the contemporary views of qualified observers who have visited Russia and who have had an opportunity to observe the present status of the patriarchate in the Soviet system. The Legislature realized that the North American church, in order to be free of Soviet interference in its affairs, had declared its temporary administrative autonomy in 1924, pursuant to the ukase of 1920, while retaining full *spiritual* communion with the patriarchate, and that there was a real danger that those properties and temporalities long enjoyed and used by the Russian Orthodox Church worshippers in this State would be taken from them by the representatives of the patriarchate. On the basis of these facts, and the facts stated [above] and no doubt other facts we know not of, our Legislature concluded that the Moscow Patriarchate was no longer capable of functioning ture is free to act upon such information as it may have as to the necessity for legislation. But an enactment by a legislature cannot validate action which the Constitution prohibits, and we think that the statute here in question passes the constitutional limits. We conclude that Article 5–C undertook by its terms to transfer the control of the New York churches of the Russian Orthodox religion from the central governing hierarchy of the Russian Orthodox Church, the Patriarch of Moscow and the Holy Synod, to the governing authorities of the Russian Church in America, a church organization limited to the diocese of North America and the Aleutian Islands. This transfer takes place by virtue of the statute. Such a law violates the Fourteenth Amendment. It prohibits in this country the free exercise of religion. Legislation that regulates church administration, the operation of the churches, the appointment of clergy, by requiring conformity to church statutes "adopted at a general convention (sobor) held in the City of New York on or about or between October fifth to eighth, nineteen hundred thirty-seven, and any amendments thereto," prohibits the free exercise of religion. Although this statute requires the New York churches to "in all other respects conform to, maintain and follow the faith, doctrine, ritual, communion, discipline, canon law, traditions and usages of the Eastern Confession (Eastern Orthodox or Greek Catholic Church)," their conformity is by legislative fiat and subject to legislative will. Should the state assert power to change the statute requiring conformity to ancient faith and doctrine to one establishing a different doctrine, the invalidity would be unmistakable. . . .

[The Court then analyzed *Watson v. Jones* [Chapter Eight, section 5] and concluded:]

The opinion, however, radiates a spirit of freedom for religious organizations, an independence from secular control or manipulation—in short, power to decide for themselves, free from state interference, matters of church government as well as those of faith and doctrine. Freedom to select the clergy, where no improper methods of choice are proven, we think, must now be said to have federal constitutional protection as a part of the free exercise of religion against state interference. . . .

Legislative Power. The Court of Appeals of New York recognized, generally, the soundness of the philosophy of ecclesiastical control of church administration and polity but concluded that the exercise of that control was not free from legislative interference. That Court presented forcefully the argument supporting legislative power to act on its own knowledge of "the Soviet attitude toward things religious." It was said: "The Legislature realized that the North American church, in order to be free of Soviet interference in its affairs, had declared its temporary administrative autonomy in 1924, pursuant to the ukase of 1920, while retaining full *spiritual* communion with the patriarchate, and that there was a real danger that those properties and temporalities long enjoyed and used by

as a true religious body, but had become a tool of the Soviet Government primarily designed to implement its foreign policy. Whether we, as judges, would have reached the same conclusion is immaterial. It is sufficient that the Legislature reached it, after full consideration of all the facts."

the Russian Orthodox Church worshippers in this State would be taken from them by the representatives of the patriarchate.''

It was thought that *American Communications Assn. v. Douds*, 339 U.S. 382, supported the thesis that where there is some specific evil, found as a fact, ''some infringement upon traditional liberties was justifiable'' to effect a cure. On that reasoning it was thought permissible, in view ''of the changed situation of the patriarchate in Russia,'' to replace it with the Russian Church in America as the ruling authority over the administration of the church. The legal basis for this legislative substitution was found in the theory that the Russian Church in America ''was the trustee which 'may be relied upon to carry out more effectively and faithfully the purposes of this religious trust (*Carrier v. Carrier*, 226 N.Y. 114).' '' Mindful of the authority of the Court of Appeals in its interpretation of the powers of its own legislature and with respect for its standing and ability, we do not agree with its statement as to legislative power over religious organizations....

In upholding the validity of Article 5–C, the New York Court of Appeals apparently assumes Article 5–C does nothing more than permit the trustees of the Cathedral to use it for services consistent with the desires of the members of the Russian Church in America. Its reach goes far beyond that point. By fiat it displaces one church administrator with another. It passes the control of matters strictly ecclesiastical from one church authority to another. It thus intrudes for the benefit of one segment of a church the power of the state into the forbidden area of religious freedom contrary to the principles of the First Amendment. Such prohibition differs from the restriction of a right to deal with Government allowed in *Douds*, in that the Union in the *Douds* case had no such constitutionally protected right. New York's Article 5–C directly prohibits the free exercise of an ecclesiastical right, the Church's choice of its hierarchy.

We do not think that New York's legislative application of a *cy-pres* doctrine to this trust avoids the constitutional rule against prohibition of the free exercise of religion. *Late Corporation of Latter–Day Saints v. United States* [Chapter Nine], relied upon by the appellee, does not support its argument. There the Church of Jesus Christ of Latter–Day Saints had been incorporated as a religious corporation by the State of Deseret, with subsequent confirmation by the Territory of Utah. Its property was held for religious and charitable purposes. That charter was revoked by Congress and some of the property of the church was escheated to the United States for the use of the common schools of Utah. This Court upheld the revocation of the charter, relying on the reserved power of the Congress over the acts of territories. The seizure of the property was bottomed on the general rule that where a charitable corporation is dissolved for unlawful practices, the sovereign takes and distributes the property according to the *cy-pres* doctrine to objects of charity and usefulness, *e.g.*, schools. A failure of the charitable purpose could have the same effect. None of these elements exist to support the validity of the New York statute putting the Russian Orthodox churches of New York under the administration of the Russian Church in America.

The record before us shows no schism over faith or doctrine between the Russian Church in America and the Russian Orthodox Church. It shows administrative control of the North American Diocese by the Supreme Church Authority of the Russian Orthodox Church, including the appointment of the ruling hierarch in North America from the foundation of the diocese until the Russian Revolution. We find nothing that indicates a relinquishment of this power by the Russian Orthodox Church.

Ours is a government which by the "law of its being" allows no statute, state or national, that prohibits the free exercise of religion. There are occasions when civil courts must draw lines between the responsibilities of church and state for the disposition or use of property. Even in those cases when the property right follows as an incident from decisions of the church custom or law on ecclesiastical issues, the church rule controls. This under our Constitution necessarily follows in order that there may be free exercise of religion.

The decree of the Court of Appeals of New York must be reversed, and the case remanded to that court for such further action as it deems proper and not in contravention of this opinion. It is so ordered. Reversed and remanded.

■ JUSTICES FRANKFURTER and BLACK concurred in the result.

■ JUSTICE JACKSON, dissenting:

I shall not undertake to wallow through the complex, obscure and fragmentary details of secular and ecclesiastical history, theology, and canon law in which this case is smothered. To me, whatever the canon law is found to be and whoever is the rightful head of the Moscow patriarchate, I do not think New York law must yield to the authority of a foreign and unfriendly state masquerading as a spiritual institution. (See "The Soviet Propaganda Program," Staff Study No. 3, Senate Subcommittee on Overseas Information Programs of the United States, 82d Cong., 2d Sess.)

I have supposed that a State of this Union was entirely free to make its own law, independently of any foreign-made law, except as the Full Faith and Credit Clause of the Constitution might require deference to the law of a sister state or the Supremacy Clause require submission to federal law. I do not see how one can spell out of the principles of separation of church and state a doctrine that a state submit property rights to settlement by canon law. If there is any relevant inference to be drawn, I should think it would be to the contrary, though I see no obstacle to the state allowing ecclesiastical law to govern in such a situation if it sees fit.

NOTES AND QUESTIONS

1. Academic response to *Kedroff*. *Kedroff* had both academic and judicial consequences. Mark DeWolfe Howe celebrated Justice Reed's recognition that the freedom of religious exercise could reside in a church as well as in an individual. Howe saw this "liberty of self-government" of a church as linked to the institutional pluralism recommended by John Neville Figgis. Figgis, *Churches in the Modern State* (1913); *see also* Maurice G. Tucker, *John Neville*

Figgis (1950*); see* Howe, "Foreword: Political Theory and the Nature of Liberty, The Supreme Court, 1952 Term," 67 *Harvard L. Rev.* 91–95 (1953). Howe made nothing of the anomaly that the church whose liberty was affirmed was the kind of church to which the New York courts now turned their attention.

2. *Judicial Response to Kedroff.* The highest court of New York read *Kedroff* to leave open the question whether "the Patriarchate, though nominally re-established" could function "except as an arm or agent of an antireligious civil government," *St. Nicholas Cathedral v. Kedroff,* 306 N.Y. 38, 53, 114 N.E.2d 197, 206 (1953). The case was remanded for trial. On appeal from a decision in favor of the Moscow Patriarchate, the Court of Appeals reviewed the evidence and held, 4–3, by Chief Judge Albert Conway, that the Moscow Patriarchate had ceased to exist by 1924 when the Detroit sobor took place; that, pursuant to Tikhon's grant of authority in 1920, the North American archdiocese had acted properly to protect the property held in trust for the Orthodox Church; that the present Moscow Patriarchate was a tool of the Soviet government; and that to permit the Moscow Patriarchate to exercise jurisdiction over St. Nicholas Cathedral would be a "perversion of the implied trust to which it was dedicated." The court further noted that the Moscow Patriarchate in biblical language had attacked the United States as "the fornicatrix of the resurrected Babylon," "the Washington Cain," and "the beast of the Apocalypse." The court saw its duty as protecting seizure of church property "by agents of a foreign atheistic State acting in the name and guise of a church administration they have infiltrated and subverted. What worse violation of the religious liberties of our people can be envisioned than to require that they subject themselves to the ecclesiastical rule of persons acting for a godless foreign regime as the price of continued use of their churches?" *St. Nicoholas Cathedral v. Kreshik,* 7 N.Y. 2d 191, 196 N.Y.S. 2d 655, 164 N.E. 2d 687 (1959).

The Supreme Court, summarily and indeed almost contemptuously, reversed *per curiam.* The decision, the Court declared, "rests on the same premises which were found to have underlain the enactment of the statute struck down in *Kedroff.*" The Court cited *Shelley v. Kraemer* [this section], to indicate that it made no difference that the state action was by a court rather than the legislature. The ruling in *Kedroff* was "controlling," *Kreshik v. St. Nicholas Cathedral,* 363 U.S. 190 (1960).

Compare Romanian Orthodox Missionary Episcopate of America v. Trutza, 205 F.2d 107 (6th Cir. 1953), *cert. denied,* 346 U.S. 915 (1953). In 1936 a council of the Romanian Orthodox Church enacted a statute providing that "the Holy Synod" in Bucharest was "the supreme authority" in the church. In 1947, after the communists had taken over Romania, the Romanian Orthodox Missionary Episcopate of America voted to suspend the 1936 statute as it affected the Church in America. In 1951 it declared the Church in Romania to be "completely enslaved by the political rulers" and itself to be administratively and spiritually autonomous. The court, per Judge Florence Allen, refused to give a bishop named by the church in Romania the property claimed by the now-autonomous American church. Judge Allen wrote: "We also think that this conclusion is in accord with the spirit, if not with the letter, of the *Kedroff* case, which declares that 'Freedom to select the clergy, where no improper methods of choice are proven ... must now be said to have federal constitutional protection as a part of the free exercise of religion against state interference.'

Since this is true as to protection against the interference of an individual American state, we think it should be equally true as to protection against the domination and interference of a foreign state."

Query. Can this case be reconciled with *Kreshik*? If the Nazis had taken over the Vatican, killed the pope, and arranged the election of a new pope, would the *Kreshik* court have turned over Catholic churches in the United States to his nominees?

Despite the warning in the Russian Orthodox cases about the dangers of judicial interpretation of religious doctrine, several state courts continued to invoke the "departure from doctrine" rule in the resolution of church property disputes. In effect these courts awarded contested church property to the faction that seemed in its eyes closest to the original teachings of a religious body. As in the abolitionist period, when the slavery issue divided the churches north and south, so also political issues began to trouble religious communities in the twentieth century. For example, one Presbyterian group split from the General Assembly as much because of that body's affiliation with the National Council of Churches of Christ in the U.S.A., an ecumenical body that had opposed the Vietnam war, as for its position in favor of the ordination of women. A jury decided that the General Assembly had substantially departed from the doctrine of the Presbyterian Church and could not therefore deprive the local congregation of the property. The Supreme Court of Georgia affirmed this verdict.

Presbyterian Church in the United States v. Mary Elizabeth Blue Hull Memorial Presbyterian Church

393 U.S. 440 (1969).

Charles L. Gowen argued the cause for petitioners. With him on the brief were *Robert B. Troutman and Frank S. Cheatham, Jr.*

Owen H. Page argued the cause for respondents and filed a brief for respondents Eastern Heights Presbyterian Church et al. *Richard T. Cowan, Frank B. Zeigler,* and *James Edward McAleer* filed a brief for respondent Mary Elizabeth Blue Hull Memorial Presbyterian Church.

Briefs of *amici curiae,* urging reversal, were filed by *George Wilson McKeag* for William Thompson, Stated Clerk of the General Assembly of the United Presbyterian Church in the United States et al., and by *Jackson A. Dykman* and *Harry G. Hill, Jr.,* for the Right Rev. John E. Hines, Presiding Bishop of the Protestant Episcopal Church in the United States.

Briefs of *amici curiae,* urging affirmance, were filed by *William J. McLeod, Jr.,* and *W.J. Williamson, pro se,* for Williamson, Secretary of Concerned Presbyterians, Inc., and by *Alfred J. Schweppe* for Laurelhurst United Presbyterian Church, Inc., et al.

■ Justice Brennan delivered the opinion of the Court.

This is a church property dispute which arose when two local churches withdrew from a hierarchical general church organization. Under Georgia law the right to the property previously used by the local churches was made to turn on a civil court jury decision as to whether the general church abandoned or departed from the tenets of faith and practice it held at the time the local churches affiliated with it. The question presented is whether the restraints of the First Amendment, as applied to the States through the Fourteenth Amendment, permit a civil court to award church property on the basis of the interpretation and significance the civil court assigns to aspects of church doctrine.

Petitioner, Presbyterian Church in the United States, is an association of local Presbyterian churches governed by a hierarchical structure of tribunals which consists of, in ascending order, (1) the Church Session, composed of the elders of the local church; (2) the Presbytery, composed of several churches in a geographical area; (3) the Synod, generally composed of all Presbyteries within a State; and (4) the General Assembly, the highest governing body.

A dispute arose between petitioner, the general church, and two local churches in Savannah, Georgia—the respondents, Hull Memorial Presbyterian Church and Eastern Heights Presbyterian Church—over control of the properties used until then by the local churches. In 1966, the membership of the local churches, in the belief that certain actions and pronouncements of the general church were violations of that organization's constitution and departures from the doctrine and practice in force at the time of affiliation,[1] voted to withdraw from the general church and to reconstitute the local churches as an autonomous Presbyterian organization. The ministers of the two churches renounced the general church's jurisdiction and authority over them, as did all but two of the ruling elders. In response, the general church, through the Presbytery of Savannah, established an Administrative Commission to seek a conciliation. The dissident local churchmen remained steadfast; consequently, the Commission acknowledged the withdrawal of the local leadership and proceeded to take over the local churches' property on behalf of the general church until new local leadership could be appointed.

The local churchmen made no effort to appeal the Commission's action to higher church tribunals—the Synod of Georgia or the General Assembly. Instead, the churches filed separate suits in the Superior Court of Chatham County to enjoin the general church from trespassing on the disputed property, title to which was in the local churches. The cases were consolidated for trial. The general church moved to dismiss the actions and cross-

---

1. The opinion of the Supreme Court of Georgia summarizes the claimed violations and departures from petitioner's original tenets of faith and practice as including the following: "ordaining of women as ministers and ruling elders, making pronouncements and recommendations concerning civil, economic, social and political matters, giving support to the removal of Bible reading and prayers by children in the public schools, adopting certain Sunday School literature and teaching neo-orthodoxy alien to the Confession of Faith and Catechisms, as originally adopted by the general church, and causing all members to remain in the National Council of Churches of Christ and willingly accepting its leadership which advocated named practices, such as the subverting of parental authority, civil disobedience and intermeddling in civil affairs"; also "that the general church has ... made pronouncements in matters involving international issues such as the Vietnam conflict and has disseminated publications denying the Holy Trinity and violating the moral and ethical standards of the faith."

claimed for injunctive relief in its own behalf on the ground that civil courts were without power to determine whether the general church had departed from its tenets of faith and practice. The motion to dismiss was denied, and the case was submitted to the jury on the theory that Georgia law implies a trust of local church property for the benefit of the general church on the sole condition that the general church adhere to its tenets of faith and practice existing at the time of affiliation by the local churches.[2] Thus, the jury was instructed to determine whether the actions of the general church "amount to a fundamental or substantial abandonment of the original tenets and doctrines of the [general church], so that the new tenets and doctrines are utterly variant from the purposes for which the [general church] was founded." The jury returned a verdict for the local churches, and the trial judge thereupon declared that the implied trust had terminated and enjoined the general church from interfering with the use of the property in question. The Supreme Court of Georgia affirmed. We granted certiorari to consider the First Amendment questions raised. We reverse. . . .

[T]he First Amendment severely circumscribes the role that civil courts may play in resolving church property disputes. It is obvious, however, that not every civil court decision as to property claimed by a religious organization jeopardizes values protected by the First Amendment. Civil courts do not inhibit free exercise of religion merely by opening their doors to disputes involving church property. And there are neutral principles of law, developed for use in all property disputes, which can be applied without "establishing" churches to which property is awarded. But First Amendment values are plainly jeopardized when church property litigation is made to turn on the resolution by civil courts of controversies over religious doctrine and practice. If civil courts undertake to resolve such controversies in order to adjudicate the property dispute, the hazards are ever present of inhibiting the free development of religious doctrine and of implicating secular interests in matters of purely ecclesiastical concern. Because of these hazards, the First Amendment enjoins the employment of organs of government for essentially religious purposes, *Abington School District v. Schempp* [Chapter Fourteen, section 2]: the Amendment therefore commands civil courts to decide church property disputes without resolving underlying controversies over religious doctrine. Hence, States, religious organizations, and individuals must structure relationships involving church property so as not to require the civil courts to resolve ecclesiastical questions.

The Georgia courts have violated the command of the First Amendment. The departure-from-doctrine element of the implied trust theory which they applied requires the civil judiciary to determine whether actions of the general church constitute such a "substantial departure" from the

---

2. This theory derives from principles fashioned by English courts. See *e.g., Craigdallie v. Aikman,* 1 Dow 1, 3 Eng. Rep. 601 (II. L. 1813) (Scot.); *Attorney General ex rel. Mander v. Pearson,* 3 Mer. 353, 36 Eng. Rep. 135 (Ch. 1817). For the subsequent development of the implied trust theory in English courts, see Note, Judicial Intervention in Disputes Over the Use of Church Property, 75 Harv. L. Rev. 1142, 1148–1149 (1962).

tenets of faith and practice existing at the time of the local churches' affiliation that the trust in favor of the general church must be declared to have terminated. This determination has two parts. The civil court must first decide whether the challenged actions of the general church depart substantially from prior doctrine. In reaching such a decision, the court must of necessity make its own interpretation of the meaning of church doctrines. If the court should decide that a substantial departure has occurred, it must then go on to determine whether the issue on which the general church has departed holds a place of such importance in the traditional theology as to require that the trust be terminated. A civil court can make this determination only after assessing the relative significance to the religion of the tenets from which departure was found. Thus, the departure-from-doctrine element of the Georgia implied trust theory requires the civil court to determine matters at the very core of a religion— the interpretation of particular church doctrines and the importance of those doctrines to the religion. Plainly, the First Amendment forbids civil courts from playing such a role.

Since the Georgia courts on remand may undertake to determine whether petitioner is entitled to relief on its cross-claims, we find it appropriate to remark that the departure-from-doctrine element of Georgia's implied trust theory can play *no* role in any future judicial proceedings. The departure-from-doctrine approach is not susceptible of the marginal judicial involvement contemplated in *Gonzalez.* Gonzalez' rights under a will turned on a church decision, the Archbishop's, as to church law, the qualifications for the chaplaincy. It was the archbishopric, not the civil courts, which had the task of analyzing and interpreting church law in order to determine the validity of Gonzalez' claim to a chaplaincy. Thus, the civil courts could adjudicate the rights under the will without interpreting or weighing church doctrine but simply by engaging in the narrowest kind of review of a specific church decision—*i.e.*, whether that decision resulted from fraud, collusion, or arbitrariness. Such review does not inject the civil courts into substantive ecclesiastical matters. In contrast, under Georgia's departure-from-doctrine approach, it is not possible for the civil courts to play so limited a role. Under this approach, property rights do not turn on a church decision as to church doctrine. The standard of departure-from-doctrine, though it calls for resolution of ecclesiastical questions, is a creation of state, not church, law. Nothing in the record suggests that this state standard has been interpreted and applied in a decision of the general church. Any decisions which have been made by the general church about the local churches' withdrawal have at most a tangential relationship to the state-fashioned departure-from-doctrine standard. A determination whether such decisions are fraudulent, collusive, or arbitrary would therefore not answer the questions posed by the state standard. To reach those questions would require the civil courts to engage in the forbidden process of interpreting and weighing church doctrine. Even if the general church had attempted to apply the state standard, the civil courts could not review and enforce the church decision without violating the Constitution. The First Amendment prohibits a State from employing religious organizations as an arm of the civil judiciary to perform the function of interpreting and applying state standards. See *Abington School District v. Schempp*. Thus, a civil court may no more review a church decision applying a state departure-from-doctrine standard than it may apply that standard itself.

The judgment of the Supreme Court of Georgia is reversed, and the case is remanded for further proceedings not inconsistent with this opinion. *It is so ordered.*

■ JUSTICE HARLAN, concurring.

I am in entire agreement with the Court's rejection of the "departure-from-doctrine" approach taken by the Georgia courts, as that approach necessarily requires the civilian courts to weigh the significance and the meaning of disputed religious doctrine. I do not, however, read the Court's opinion to go further to hold that the Fourteenth Amendment forbids civilian courts from enforcing a deed or will which expressly and clearly lays down conditions limiting a religious organization's use of the property which is granted. If, for example, the donor expressly gives his church some money on the condition that the church never ordain a woman as a minister or elder, or never amend certain specified articles of the Confession of Faith, he is entitled to his money back if the condition is not fulfilled. In such a case, the church should not be permitted to keep the property simply because church authorities have determined that the doctrinal innovation is justified by the faith's basic principles. Cf. *Watson v. Jones* [Chapter Eight, section 5].

On this understanding, I join the Court's opinion.

Maryland and Virginia Eldership of the Churches of God v. Church of God at Sharpsburg, Inc.

396 U.S. 367 (1970).

Alfred L. Scanlan, James H. Booser, and *Charles O.Fisher* for appellants.

Arthur G.Lambert for appellees.

■ PER CURIAM.

In resolving a church property dispute between appellants, representing the General Eldership, and appellees, two secessionist congregations, the Maryland Court of Appeals relied upon provisions of state statutory law governing the holding of property by religious corporations, upon language in the deeds conveying the properties in question to the local church corporations, upon the terms of the charters of the corporations, and upon provisions in the constitution of the General Eldership pertinent to the ownership and control of church property. Appellants argue primarily that the statute, as applied, deprived the General Eldership of property in violation of the First Amendment. Since, however, the Maryland court's resolution of the dispute involved no inquiry into religious doctrine, appellees' motion to dismiss is granted, and the appeal is dismissed for want of a substantial federal question. *It is so ordered.*

■ JUSTICE BRENNAN, with whom JUSTICE DOUGLAS and JUSTICE MARSHALL join, concurring.

I join the *per curiam* but add these comments. We held in *Presbyterian Church in the United States v. Mary Elizabeth Blue Hull Memorial Presbyterian Church* [this section above] that "First Amendment values are plainly jeopardized when church property litigation is made to turn on the resolution by civil courts of controversies over religious doctrine and practice. If civil courts undertake to resolve such controversies in order to adjudicate the property dispute, the hazards are ever present of inhibiting the free development of religious doctrine and of implicating secular interests in matters of purely ecclesiastical concern.... [T]he [First] Amendment therefore commands civil courts to decide church property disputes without resolving underlying controversies over religious doctrine." It follows that a State may adopt *any* one of various approaches for settling church property disputes so long as it involves no consideration of doctrinal matters, whether the ritual and liturgy of worship or the tenets of faith.

Thus the States may adopt the approach of *Watson v. Jones*, [Chapter Eight, section 5], and enforce the property decisions made within a church of congregational polity "by a majority of its members or by such other local organism as it may have instituted for the purpose of ecclesiastical government," and within a church of hierarchical polity by the highest authority that has ruled on the dispute at issue,[1] unless "express terms" in the "instrument by which the property is held" condition the property's use or control in a specified manner.[2] Under *Watson* civil courts do not inquire whether the relevant church governing body has power under religious law to control the property in question. Such a determination, unlike the identification of the governing body, frequently necessitates the interpretation of ambiguous religious law and usage. To permit civil courts to probe deeply enough into the allocation of power within a church so as to decide where religious law places control over the use of church property would violate the First Amendment in much the same manner as civil determination of religious doctrine.[3] Similarly, where the identity of the

---

1. Under the *Watson* definition, congregational polity exists when "a religious congregation ... , by the nature of its organization, is strictly independent of other ecclesiastical associations, and so far as church government is concerned, owes no fealty or obligation to any higher authority." Hierarchical polity, on the other hand, exists when "the religious congregation ... is but a subordinate member of some general church organization in which there are superior ecclesiastical tribunals with a general and ultimate power of control more or less complete, in some supreme judicatory

over the whole membership of that general organization."

2. Except that "express terms" cannot be enforced if enforcement is constitutionally impermissible under *Presbyterian Church*. Any language in *Watson* that may be read to the contrary must be disapproved. Only express conditions that may be effected without consideration of doctrine are civilly enforceable.

3. Except that civil tribunals may examine church rulings alleged to be the product of "fraud, collusion, or arbitrariness."

governing body or bodies that exercise general authority within a church is a matter of substantial controversy, civil courts are not to make the inquiry into religious law and usage that would be essential to the resolution of the controversy. In other words, the use of the *Watson* approach is consonant with the prohibitions of the First Amendment only if the appropriate church governing body can be determined without the resolution of doctrinal questions and without extensive inquiry into religious polity.

"[N]eutral principles of law, developed for use in all property disputes," *Presbyterian Church* [this section] provide another means for resolving litigation over religious property. Under the "formal title" doctrine, civil courts can determine ownership by studying deeds, reverter clauses, and general state corporation laws. Again, however, general principles of property law may not be relied upon if their application requires civil courts to resolve doctrinal issues. For example, provisions in deeds or in a denomination's constitution for the reversion of local church property to the general church, if conditioned upon a finding of departure from doctrine, could not be civilly enforced.[4]

A third possible approach is the passage of special statutes governing church property arrangements in a manner that precludes state interference in doctrine. Such statutes must be carefully drawn to leave control of ecclesiastical polity, as well as doctrine, to church governing bodies. *Kedroff v. St. Nicholas Cathedral* [this section above].

NOTE

Serbian Schism. Serbian Orthodox in the United States were originally a mission within the Russian Orthodox Church. Pospielovsky 2, 281. After the Russian Revolution, the Serbs set up a Serbian Orthodox Church with a patriarch in Belgrade, ruling all the Orthodox in the new state of Yugoslavia. In 1921 the governing body of this new church, the Holy Council of Bishops, set up a diocese in North America. The Constitution of the Church provided that the diocese stand "under the jurisdiction of the Serbian Orthodox Church in spiritual and hierarchical respects." The constitution of the diocese stated that it enjoyed full administrative freedom while belonging "canonically" to the Serbian Orthodox Church. See Djuro J. Vrga and Frank J. Fahey, *Changes and Socio–Religious Conflict in an Ethnic Minority Group: The Serbian Orthodox Church in America* 29 (1975).

In 1963, Dionysius, the bishop of the diocese in North America, was suspended by the authorities of the church in Yugoslavia. He declared, "I do not recognize this communist decision from Belgrade." An assembly of the American and Canadian diocese then called for "the cancellation of canonical hierarchical unity with the Mother Church in the Fatherland and the mainte-

---

Gonzales v. Roman Catholic Archbishop [Chapter Ten, section 9].

4. Thus a State that normally resolves disputes over religious property by applying general principles of property law would have to use a different method in cases involving such provisions, perhaps that defined in *Watson*. By the same token, States following the *Watson* approach would have to find another ground for decision, perhaps the applications of general property law, when identification of the relevant church governing body is impossible without immersion in doctrinal issues or extensive inquiry into church polity.

nance of only a spiritual unity of prayer,'' *Id*. 30–31. The members of the diocese divided. Over two-thirds of the old immigrants favored canonical unity with the Mother Church and over two-thirds of the post-World War II immigrants, deeply distrustful of the modern Yugoslav state, wanted the break. *Id*. 36. Litigation in Illinois finally led to the Supreme Court.

Serbian Eastern Orthodox Diocese for the United States of America and Canada v. Milivojevich

426 U.S. 696 (1976).

Albert E. Jenner, Jr., argued the cause for petitioners. With him on the briefs were *Keith F. Bode, Robert L. Graham, Thomas J. Karacic,* and *Henry D. Fisher.*

Leo J. Sullivan III argued the cause for respondents. With him on the brief were *Richard J. Smith* and *Jerome H. Torshen.*

■ JUSTICE BRENNAN delivered the opinion of the Court.

In 1963, the Holy Assembly of Bishops and the Holy Synod of the Serbian Orthodox Church (Mother Church) suspended and ultimately removed respondent Dionisije Milivojevich (Dionisije) as Bishop of the American–Canadian Diocese of that Church, and appointed petitioner Bishop Firmilian Ocokoljich (Firmilian) as Administrator of the Diocese, which the Mother Church then reorganized into three Dioceses. In 1964 the Holy Assembly and Holy Synod defrocked Dionisije as a Bishop and cleric of the Mother Church. In this civil action brought by Dionisije and the other respondents in Illinois Circuit Court, the Supreme Court of Illinois held that the proceedings of the Mother Church respecting Dionisije were procedurally and substantively defective under the internal regulations of the Mother Church and were therefore arbitrary and invalid. The State Supreme Court also invalidated the Diocesan reorganization into three Dioceses. We granted certiorari to determine whether the actions of the Illinois Supreme Court constituted improper judicial interference with decisions of the highest authorities of a hierarchical church in violation of the First and Fourteenth Amendments. We hold that the inquiries made by the Illinois Supreme Court into matters of ecclesiastical cognizance and polity and the court's actions pursuant thereto contravened the First and Fourteenth Amendments. We therefore reverse. . . .

The conclusion of the Illinois Supreme Court that the decisions of the Mother Church were ''arbitrary'' was grounded upon an inquiry that persuaded the Illinois Supreme Court that the Mother Church had not followed its own laws and procedures in arriving at those decisions. We have concluded that whether or not there is room for ''marginal civil court review'' under the narrow rubrics of ''fraud'' or ''collusion'' when church tribunals act in bad faith for secular purposes, no ''arbitrariness'' exception—in the sense of an inquiry whether the decisions of the highest ecclesiastical tribunal of a hierarchical church complied with church laws and regulations—is consistent with the constitutional mandate that civil courts are bound to accept the decisions of the highest judicatories of a religious organization of hierarchical polity on matters of discipline, faith, internal organization, or ecclesiastical rule, custom, or law. For civil courts to analyze whether the ecclesiastical actions of a church judicatory are in that sense "arbitrary" must inherently entail inquiry into the procedures that canon or ecclesiastical law supposedly requires the church judicatory to follow, or else into the substantive criteria by which they are supposedly to decide the ecclesiastical question. But this is exactly the inquiry that the First Amendment prohibits; recognition of such an exception would undermine the general rule that religious controversies are not the proper subject of civil court inquiry, and that a civil court must accept the ecclesiastical decisions of church tribunals as it finds them. *Watson* itself [Chapter Eight, section 5] requires our conclusion in its rejection of the analogous argument that ecclesiastical decisions of the highest church judicatories need only be accepted if the subject matter of the dispute is within their "jurisdiction." . . .

Indeed, it is the essence of religious faith that ecclesiastical decisions are reached and are to be accepted as matters of faith whether or not rational or measurable by objective criteria. Constitutional concepts of due process, involving secular notions of "fundamental fairness" or impermissible objectives, are therefore hardly relevant to such matters of ecclesiastical cognizance.

The constitutional evils that attend upon any "arbitrariness" exception in the sense applied by the Illinois Supreme Court to justify civil court review of ecclesiastical decisions of final church tribunals are manifest in the instant case. The Supreme Court of Illinois recognized that all parties agree that the Serbian Orthodox Church is a hierarchical church, and that the sole power to appoint and remove Bishops of the Church resides in its highest ranking organs, the Holy Assembly and the Holy Synod.[9] Indeed,

9. Plaintiffs argue and defendant Bishop Dionisije does not dispute that the Serbian Orthodox Church is a hierarchical and episcopal church. Moreover, the parties agree that in cases involving hierarchical churches the decisions of the proper church tribunals on questions of discipline, faith or ecclesiastical rule, though affecting civil rights, are accepted as conclusive in disputes before civil courts. . . . All parties maintain that the sole limitation on this rule, when civil courts entertain the 'narrowest kind of review,' occurs when the decision of the church tribunal is claimed to have resulted from fraud, collusion or arbitrariness. 60 Ill. 2d 477, 501, 328 N.E. 2d 268, 280 (1975).

Respondents conceded as much at oral argument. Tr. of Oral Arg. 24–25, 39–40. The hierarchical nature of the relationship between the American–Canadian Diocese and the Mother Church is confirmed by the fact that respondent corporations were organized under the provisions of the Illinois Religious

Corporations Act governing the incorporation of religious societies that are subordinate parts of larger church organizations. Similarly, the Diocese's subordinate nature was manifested in resolutions of the Diocese which Dionisije supported, and by Dionisije's submission of corporate bylaws, proposed constitutional changes, and final judgments of the Diocesan Ecclesiastical Court to the Holy Synod or Holy Assembly for approval. Moreover, when Dionisije was originally elevated to Bishop, he signed an Episcopal–Hierarchical Oath by which he swore that he would "always be obedient to the Most Holy Assembly," and: "Should I transgress against whatever I promised here, or should I be disobedient to the Divine Ordinances and Order of the Eastern Orthodox Church, or to the Most Holy Assembly (of Bishops) I, personally, will become a schismatic and should I make the Diocese entrusted to me in any manner to become disobedient to the Most Holy Assembly (of Bishops), may I, in that final authority with respect to the promulgation and interpretation of all matters of church discipline and internal organization rests with the Holy Assembly, and even the written constitution of the Mother Church expressly provides:

"The Holy Assembly of Bishops, as the highest hierarchical body, is legislative authority in the matters of faith, officiation, church order (discipline) and internal organization of the Church, as well as the highest church juridical authority within its jurisdiction (Article 69 sec. 28)." Art. 57.

"All the decisions of the Holy Assembly of Bishops and of the Holy Synod of Bishops of canonical and church nature, in regard to faith, officiation, church order and internal organization of the church, are valid and final." Art. 64.

"The Holy Assembly of Bishops, whose purpose is noted in Article 57 of this Constitution:

"9) interprets canonical-ecclesiastical rules, those which are general and obligatory, and particular ones, and publishes their collections;

"12) prescribes the ecclesiastical-judicial procedure for all Ecclesiastical Courts;

"26) settles disputes of jurisdiction between hierarchical and church-self governing organs;

"27) ADJUDGES:

"A) In first and in final instances:

"a) disagreements between bishops and the Holy Synod, and between the bishops and the Patriarch;

"b) canonical offenses of the Patriarch;

"B) In the second and final instance:

"All matters which the Holy Synod of Bishops judged in the first instance." Art. 69.

Nor is there any dispute that questions of church discipline and the composition of the church hierarchy are at the core of ecclesiastical concern; the bishop of a church is clearly one of the central figures in such a hierarchy and the embodiment of the church within his Diocese, and the Mother Church constitution states that "[h]e is, according to the church canonical regulations, chief representative and guiding leader of all church spiritual life and church order in the diocese." Art. 13. . . .

Similar considerations inform our resolution of the second question we must address—the constitutionality of the Supreme Court of Illinois' holding that the Mother Church's reorganization of the American–Canadian

case, be defrocked of my rank and divested of the (episcopal) authority without any excuse or gainsay, and (may I) become an alien to the heavenly gift which is being given unto me by the Holy Spirit through the Consecration of the Laying of Hands." App. 1088.

Finally, the hierarchical relationship was confirmed by provisions in the constitutions of both the Diocese and the Mother Church.

Diocese into three Dioceses was invalid because it was " 'in clear and palpable excess of its own jurisdiction.' " Essentially, the court premised this determination on its view that the early history of the Diocese "manifested a clear intention to retain independence and autonomy in its administrative affairs while at the same time becoming ecclesiastically and judicially an organic part of the Serbian Orthodox Church," and its interpretation of the constitution of the American–Canadian Diocese as confirming this intention. It also interpreted the constitution of the Serbian Orthodox Church, which was adopted after the Diocesan constitution, in a manner consistent with this conclusion.

This conclusion was not, however, explicitly based on the "fraud, collusion, or arbitrariness" exception. Rather, the Illinois Supreme Court relied on purported "neutral principles" for resolving property disputes which would "not in any way entangle this court in the determination of theological or doctrinal matters." Nevertheless the Supreme Court of Illinois substituted its interpretation of the Diocesan and Mother Church constitutions for that of the highest ecclesiastical tribunals in which church law vests authority to make that interpretation. This the First and Fourteenth Amendments forbid. *Reversed.*

■ CHIEF JUSTICE BURGER and JUSTICE WHITE concurred in the judgment.

■ JUSTICE REHNQUIST, with whom JUSTICE STEVENS joins, dissenting.

The Court's opinion, while long on the ecclesiastical history of the Serbian Orthodox Church, is somewhat short on the procedural history of this case. A casual reader of some of the passages in the Court's opinion could easily gain the impression that the State of Illinois had commenced a proceeding designed to brand Bishop Dionisije as a heretic, with appropriate pains and penalties. But the state trial judge in the Circuit Court of Lake County was not the Bishop of Beauvais, trying Joan of Arc for heresy [Chapter Four, section 2]; the jurisdiction of his court was invoked by petitioners themselves, who sought an injunction establishing their control over property of the American–Canadian Diocese of the church located in Lake County.

The jurisdiction of that court having been invoked for such a purpose by both Petitioners and respondents, contesting claimants to Diocesan authority, it was entitled to ask if the real Bishop of the American–Canadian Diocese would please stand up. The protracted proceedings in the Illinois courts were devoted to the ascertainment of who that individual was, a question which the Illinois courts sought to answer by application of the canon law of the church, just as they would have attempted to decide a similar dispute among the members of any other voluntary association. The Illinois courts did not in the remotest sense inject their doctrinal preference into the dispute. They were forced to decide between two competing sets of claimants to church office in order that they might resolve a dispute over real property located within the State. Each of the claimants had requested them to decide the issue. Unless the First Amendment requires control of disputed church property to be awarded solely on the basis of ecclesiastical paper title, I can find no constitutional infirmity in the judgment of the Supreme Court of Illinois.

Unless civil courts are to be wholly divested of authority to resolve conflicting claims to real property owned by a hierarchical church, and such claims are to be resolved by brute force, civil courts must of necessity make some factual inquiry even under the rules the Court purports to apply in this case. We are told that "a civil court must accept the ecclesiastical decisions of church tribunals as it finds them." But even this rule requires that proof be made as to what these decisions are, and if proofs on that issue conflict the civil court will inevitably have to choose one over the other. In so choosing, if the choice is to be a rational one, reasons must be adduced as to why one proffered decision is to prevail over another. Such reasons will obviously be based on the canon law by which the disputants have agreed to bind themselves, but they must also represent a preference for one view of that law over another.

If civil courts, consistently with the First Amendment, may do that much, the question arises why they may not do what the Illinois courts did here regarding the defrockment of Bishop Dionisije, and conclude, on the basis of testimony from experts on the canon law at issue, that the decision of the religious tribunal involved was rendered in violation of its own stated rules of procedure. Suppose the Holy Assembly in this case had a membership of 100; its rules provided that a bishop could be defrocked by a majority vote of any session at which a quorum was present, and also provided that a quorum was not to be less than 40. Would a decision of the Holy Assembly attended by 30 members, 16 of whom voted to defrock Bishop Dionisije, be binding on civil courts in a dispute such as this? The hypothetical example is a clearer case than the one involved here, but the principle is the same. If the civil courts are to be bound by any sheet of parchment bearing the ecclesiastical seal and purporting to be a decree of a church court, they can easily be converted into handmaidens of arbitrary lawlessness.

NOTES AND QUESTIONS

If the Orthodox in America could not break from the Russian Orthodox Church and be recognized by an American legislature (*Kedroff*) or court (*Kedrick*), how can an American court recognize the Serbian Orthodox Church which has no higher pedigree? Are both *Kedroff* and *Milivojevich* putting "paper title" above religious realities? The answer provides a clue to the approach in the following case.

Jones v. Wolf

443 U.S. 595 (1979).

E. Barrett Prettyman, Jr., argued the cause for petitioners. With him on the briefs were *Allen R. Snyder, Walter A. Smith, Jr., John B. Harris, Jr., T. Reese Watkins*, and *H.T. O'Neal, Jr.*

Frank C. Jones argued the cause for respondents. With him on the brief were *Wallace Miller, Jr., W. Warren Plowden, Jr.*, and *Edward S. Sell, Jr.*

Briefs of *amici curiae* urging reversal were filed by *Samuel W. Witwer, Sr.,* and *Samuel W. Witwer, Jr.,* for the General Council on Finance and Administration of the United Methodist Church; by *J. D. Todd, Jr., and David A. Quattlebaum III* for the Presbyterian Church in the United States; and by *George Wilson McKeag* and *Gregory M. Harvey* for William P. Thompson et al.

George E. Reed and *Patrick F. Geary* filed a brief for the United States Catholic Conference as *amicus curiae.*

■ JUSTICE BLACKMUN delivered the opinion of the Court.

This case involves a dispute over the ownership of church property following a schism in a local church affiliated with a hierarchical church organization. The question for decision is whether civil courts, consistent with the First and Fourteenth Amendments to the Constitution, may resolve the dispute on the basis of "neutral principles of law," or whether they must defer to the resolution of an authoritative tribunal of the hierarchical church.

The Vineville Presbyterian Church of Macon, Ga., was organized in 1904, and first incorporated in 1915. Its corporate charter lapsed in 1935, but was revived and renewed in 1939, and continues in effect at the present time.

The property at issue and on which the church is located was acquired in three transactions, and is evidenced by conveyances to the "Trustees of [or 'for'] Vineville Presbyterian Church and their successors in office," or simply to the "Vineville Presbyterian Church." The funds used to acquire the property were contributed entirely by local church members. Pursuant to resolutions adopted by the congregation, the church repeatedly has borrowed money on the property. This indebtedness is evidenced by security deeds variously issued in the name of the "Trustees of the Vineville Presbyterian Church," or, again, simply the "Vineville Presbyterian Church."

In the same year it was organized, the Vineville church was established as a member church of the Augusta–Macon Presbytery of the Presbyterian Church in the United States (PCUS). The PCUS has a generally hierarchical or connectional form of government, as contrasted with a congregational form. Under the polity of the PCUS, the government of the local church is committed to its Session in the first instance, but the actions of this assembly or "court" are subject to the review and control of the higher church courts, the Presbytery, Synod, and General Assembly, respectively. The powers and duties of each level of the hierarchy are set forth in the constitution of the PCUS, the Book of Church Order, which is part of the record in the present case.

On May 27, 1973, at a congregational meeting of the Vineville church attended by a quorum of its duly enrolled members, 164 of them, including the pastor, voted to separate from the PCUS. Ninety-four members opposed the resolution. The majority immediately informed the PCUS of the action, and then united with another denomination, the Presbyterian Church in America. Although the minority remained on the church rolls for three years, they ceased to participate in the affairs of the Vineville church and conducted their religious activities elsewhere.

In response to the schism within the Vineville congregation, the Augusta–Macon Presbytery appointed a commission to investigate the dispute and, if possible, to resolve it. The commission eventually issued a written ruling declaring that the minority faction constituted "the true congregation of Vineville Presbyterian Church," and withdrawing from the majority faction "all authority to exercise office derived from the [PCUS]." The majority took no part in the commission's inquiry, and did not appeal its ruling to a higher PCUS tribunal.

Representatives of the minority faction sought relief in federal court, but their complaint was dismissed for want of jurisdiction. They then brought this class action in state court, seeking declaratory and injunctive orders establishing their right to exclusive possession and use of the Vineville church property as a member congregation of the PCUS. The trial court, purporting to apply Georgia's "neutral principles of law" approach to church property disputes, granted judgment for the majority. The Supreme Court of Georgia, holding that the trial court had correctly stated and applied Georgia law, and rejecting the minority's challenge based on the First and Fourteenth Amendments, affirmed. We granted certiorari.

... The primary advantages of the neutral-principles approach are that it is completely secular in operation, and yet flexible enough to accommodate all forms of religious organization and polity. The method relies exclusively on objective, well-established concepts of trust and property law familiar to lawyers and judges. It thereby promises to free civil courts completely from entanglement in questions of religious doctrine, polity, and practice. Furthermore, the neutral-principles analysis shares the peculiar genius of private-law systems in general—flexibility in ordering private rights and obligations to reflect the intentions of the parties. Through appropriate reversionary clauses and trust provisions, religious societies can specify what is to happen to church property in the event of a particular contingency, or what religious body will determine the ownership in the event of a schism or doctrinal controversy. In this manner, a religious organization can ensure that a dispute over the ownership of church property will be resolved in accord with the desires of the members.

This is not to say that the application of the neutral-principles approach is wholly free of difficulty. The neutral-principles method, at least as it has evolved in Georgia, requires a civil court to examine certain religious documents, such as a church constitution, for language of trust in favor of the general church. In undertaking such an examination, a civil court must take special care to scrutinize the document in purely secular terms, and not to rely on religious precepts in determining whether the document indicates that the parties have intended to create a trust. In addition, there may be cases where the deed, the corporate charter, or the constitution of the general church incorporates religious concepts in the provisions relating to the ownership of property. If in such a case the interpretation of the instruments of ownership would require the civil court to resolve a religious controversy, then the court must defer to the resolution of the doctrinal issue by the authoritative ecclesiastical body. *Serbian Orthodox Diocese* [this section above].

On balance, however, the promise of nonentanglement and neutrality inherent in the neutral-principles approach more than compensates for what will be occasional problems in applications. These problems, in addition, should be gradually eliminated as recognition is given to the obligation of "States, religious organizations, and individuals [to] structure relationships involving church property so as not to require the civil courts to resolve ecclesiastical questions." *Presbyterian Church* [this section above]. We therefore hold that a State is constitutionally entitled to adopt neutral principles of law as a means of adjudicating a church property dispute.

The dissent would require the States to abandon the neutral-principles method, and instead would insist as a matter of constitutional law that whenever a dispute arises over the ownership of church property, civil courts must defer to the "authoritative resolution of the dispute within the church itself." It would require, first, that civil courts review ecclesiastical doctrine and polity to determine where the church has "placed ultimate authority over the use of the church property." After answering this question, the courts would be required to "determine whether the dispute has been resolved within that structure of government and, if so, what decision has been made." They would then be required to enforce that decision. We cannot agree, however, that the First Amendment requires the States to adopt a rule of compulsory deference to religious authority in resolving church property disputes, even where no issue of doctrinal controversy is involved.

The dissent suggests that a rule of compulsory deference would somehow involve less entanglement of civil courts in matters of religious doctrine, practice, and administration. Under its approach, however, civil courts would always be required to examine the polity and administration of a church to determine which unit of government has ultimate control over church property. In some cases, this task would not prove to be difficult. But in others, the locus of control would be ambiguous, and "[a] careful examination of the constitutions of the general and local church, as well as other relevant documents, [would] be necessary to ascertain the form of governance adopted by the members of the religious association." In such cases, the suggested rule would appear to require "a searching and therefore impermissible inquiry into church polity." *Serbian Orthodox Diocese.* The neutral-principles approach, in contrast, obviates entirely the need for an analysis or examination of ecclesiastical polity or doctrine in settling church property disputes.

The dissent also argues that a rule of compulsory deference is necessary in order to protect the free exercise rights "of those who have formed the association and submitted themselves to its authority." This argument assumes that the neutral principles method would somehow frustrate the free-exercise rights of the members of a religious association. Nothing could be further from the truth. The neutral-principles approach cannot be said to "inhibit" the free exercise of religion, any more than do other neutral provisions of state law governing the manner in which churches own property, hire employees, or purchase goods. Under the neutral-principles approach, the outcome of a church property dispute is not foreordained. At any time before the dispute erupts, the parties can ensure, if they so desire, that the faction loyal to the hierarchical church will retain the church property. They can modify the deeds or the corporate charter to include a right of reversion or trust in favor of the general church. Alternatively, the constitution of the general church can be made to recite an express trust in favor of the denominational church. The burden involved in taking such steps will be minimal. And the civil courts will be bound to give effect to the result indicated by, the parties, provided it is embodied in some legally cognizable form....

Neither the trial court nor the Supreme Court of Georgia ... explicitly stated that it was adopting a presumptive rule of majority representation. Moreover, there are at least some indications that under Georgia law the process of identifying the faction that represents the Vineville church involves considerations of religious doctrine and polity. Georgia law requires that "church property be held according to the terms of the church government," and provides that a local church affiliated with a hierarchical religious association "is part of the whole body of the general church and is subject to the higher authority of the organization and its laws and regulations." *Carnes v. Smith*, 236 Ga., at 33, 38, 222 S.E.2d at 325, 328; see Ga. Code §§ 22–5507, 22–5508 (1978). All this may suggest that the identity of the "Vineville Presbyterian Church" named in the deeds must be determined according to terms of the Book of Church Order, which sets out the laws and regulations of churches affiliated with the PCUS. Such a determination, however, would appear to require a civil court to pass on questions of religious doctrine,[7] and to usurp the function of the commission appointed by the Presbytery, which already has determined that petitioners represent the "true congregation" of the Vineville church. Therefore, if Georgia law provides that the identity of the Vineville church is to be determined according to the "laws and regulations" of the PCUS, then the First Amendment requires that the Georgia courts give deference to the presbyterial commission's determination of that church's identity.[8]

---

7. Issues of church doctrine and polity pervade the provisions of the Book of Church Order of the Presbyterian Church (1972) dealing with the identity of the local congregation. The local church corporation consists of "all the communing members on the active roll" of the church. *Id.*, § 6–2; The "active roll," in turn, is composed "of those admitted to the Lord's Table who are active in the church's life and work." § 8–7. The Session is given the power "to suspend or exclude from the Lord's Supper those found delinquent, according to the Rules of Discipline." § 15–6 (2). See § 111–2. The Session is sub- ject to "the review and control" of the Presbytery, § 14–5, as a part of the Presbytery's general authority to "order whatever pertains to the spiritual welfare of the churches under its care." § 16–7 (19).

8. There is no suggestion in this case that the decision of the commission was the product of "fraud" or "collusion." See *Serbian Orthodox Diocese v. Milivojevich,* [above]. In the absence of such circumstances, "the First and Fourteenth Amendments mandate that civil courts shall not disturb the decisions of the highest ecclesiastical tribunal

This Court, of course, does not declare what the law of Georgia is. Since the grounds for the decision that respondents represent the Vineville church remain unarticulated, the judgment of the Supreme Court of Georgia is vacated, and the case is remanded for further proceedings not inconsistent with this opinion. *It is so ordered.*

■ JUSTICE POWELL, with whom the CHIEF JUSTICE, JUSTICE STEWART, and JUSTICE WHITE join, dissenting.

This case presents again a dispute among church members over the control of a local church's property. Although the Court appears to accept established principles that I have thought would resolve this case, it superimposes on these principles a new structure of rules that will make the decision of these cases by civil courts more difficult. The new analysis also is more likely to invite intrusion into church polity forbidden by the First Amendment.

I

The Court begins by stating that "[t]his case involves a dispute over the ownership of church property," suggesting that the concern is with legal or equitable ownership in the real property sense. But the ownership of the property of the Vineville church is not at issue. The deeds place title in the Vineville Presbyterian Church, or in trustees of that church, and none of the parties has questioned the validity of those deeds. The question actually presented is which of the factions within the local congregation has the right to control the actions of the titleholder, and thereby to control the use of the property, as the Court later acknowledges.

Since 1872, disputes over control of church property usually have been resolved under principles established by *Watson v. Jones*, [Chapter Eight, section 5]. Under the new and complex, two-stage analysis approved today, a court instead first must apply newly defined "neutral principles of law" to determine whether property titled to the local church is held in trust for the general church organization with which the local church is affiliated. If it is, then the court will grant control of the property to the councils of the general church. If not, then control by the local congregation will be recognized. In the latter situation, if there is a schism in the local congregation, as in this case, the second stage of the new analysis becomes applicable. Again, the Court fragments the analysis into two substeps for the purpose of determining which of the factions should control the property.

As this new approach inevitably will increase the involvement of civil courts in church controversies, and as it departs from long-established precedents, I dissent.

A

The first stage in the "neutral principles of law" approach operates as a restrictive rule of evidence. A court is required to examine the deeds to the church property, the charter of the local church (if there is one), the

within a church of hierarchical polity, but must accept such decisions as binding on them, in their application to the religious issues of doctrine or polity before them."

book of order or discipline of the general church organization, and the state statutes governing the holding of church property. The object of the inquiry, where the title to the property is in the local church, is "to determine whether there [is] any basis for a trust in favor of the general church." The court's investigation is to be "completely secular rel[ying] exclusively on objective, well-established concepts of trust and property law familiar to lawyers and judges." Thus, where religious documents such as church constitutions or books of order must be examined "for language of trust in favor of the general church," "a civil court must take special care to scrutinize the document in purely secular terms, and not to rely on religious precepts in determining whether the document indicates that the parties have intended to create a trust." It follows that the civil courts using this analysis may consider the form of religious government adopted by the church members for the resolution of intrachurch disputes *only* if that polity has been stated, in express relation to church property, in the language of trust and property law.[1]

One effect of the Court's evidentiary rule is to deny to the courts relevant evidence as to the religious polity—that is, the form of governance—adopted by the church members. The constitutional documents of churches tend to be drawn in terms of religious precepts. Attempting to read them "in purely secular terms" is more likely to promote confusion than understanding. Moreover, whenever religious polity has not been expressed in specific statements referring to the property of a church, there will be no evidence of that polity cognizable under the neutral-principles rule. Lacking such evidence, presumably a court will impose some rule of church government derived from state law. In the present case, for example, the general and unqualified authority of the Presbytery over the actions of the Vineville church had not been expressed in secular terms of control of its property. As a consequence, the Georgia courts could find no acceptable evidence of this authoritative relationship, and they imposed instead a congregational form of government determined from state law.

This limiting of the evidence relative to religious government cannot be justified on the ground that it "free[s] civil courts completely from entanglement in questions of religious doctrine, polity, and practice." For unless the body identified as authoritative under state law resolves the underlying dispute in accord with the decision of the church's own authority, the state court effectively will have reversed the decisions of doctrine and practice made in accordance with church law. The schism in the Vineville church,

---

1. Despite the Court's assertion to the contrary, this "neutral principles" approach was not approved by the Court in dismissing the appeal in *Maryland & Va. Eldership v. Sharpsburg Church*, [this section above]. The state court there examined the constitution of the general church, the charters of the local churches, the deeds to the property at issue, and the relevant state statutes. But it did not restrict its inquiry to a search for statements expressed in the language of trust and property law. Rather the state court canvassed all of these sources, and others, see *Maryland & Va. Eldership v. Sharpsburg Church*, for information about the basic polity of the Church of God. Having concluded that the local congregations retained final authority over their property, it awarded judgment accordingly. Contrary to the statement of the Court in the present case that such an inquiry into church polity requires analysis of "ecclesiastical ... doctrine, the Maryland court's resolution of the dispute involved no inquiry into religious doctrine."

for example, resulted from disagreements among the church members over questions of doctrine and practice. Under the Book of Church Order, these questions were resolved authoritatively by the higher church courts, which then gave control of the local church to the faction loyal to that resolution. The Georgia courts, as a matter of state law, granted control to the schismatic faction, and thereby effectively reversed the doctrinal decision of the church courts. This indirect interference by the civil courts with the resolution of religious disputes within the church is no less proscribed by the First Amendment than is the direct decision of questions of doctrine and practice.[2]

When civil courts step in to resolve intrachurch disputes over control of church property, they will either support or overturn the authoritative resolution of the dispute within the church itself. The new analysis, under the attractive banner of "neutral principles," actually invites the civil courts to do the latter. The proper rule of decision, that I thought had been settled until today, requires a court to give effect in all cases to the decisions of the church government agreed upon by the members before the dispute arose.

B

The Court's basic neutral-principles approach, as a means of isolating decisions concerning church property from other decisions made within the church, relies on the concept of a trust of local church property in favor of the general church. Because of this central premise, the neutral-principles rule suffices to settle only disputes between the central councils of a church organization and a unanimous local congregation. Where, as here, the neutral-principles inquiry reveals no trust in favor of the general church, and the local congregation is split into factions, the basic question remains unresolved: which faction should have control of the local church.

The Court acknowledges that the church law of the Presbyterian Church in the United States (PCUS), of which the Vineville church is a part, provides for the authoritative resolution of this question by the Presbytery. Indeed, the Court indicates that Georgia, consistently with the

---

2. The neutral-principles approach appears to assume that the requirements of the Constitution will be satisfied if civil courts are forbidden to consider certain types of evidence. The First Amendment's Religion Clauses, however, are meant to protect churches and their members from civil law interference, not to protect the courts from having to decide difficult evidentiary questions. Thus, the evidentiary rules to be applied in cases involving intrachurch disputes over church property should be fashioned to avoid interference with the resolution of the dispute within the accepted church government. The neutral-principles approach consists instead of a rule of evidence that ensures that in some cases the courts will impose a form of church government and a doctrinal resolution at odds with that reached by the church's own authority.

The neutral-principles approach creates other difficulties. It imposes on the organization of churches additional legal requirements which in some cases might inhibit their formation by forcing the organizers to confront issues that otherwise might never arise. It also could precipitate church property disputes, for existing churches may deem it necessary, in light of today's decision, to revise their constitutional documents, charters, and deeds to include a specific statement of church polity in the language of property and trust law.

First Amendment, may adopt the *Watson v. Jones* rule of adherence to the resolution of the dispute according to church law—a rule that would necessitate reversal of the judgment for the respondents. But instead of requiring the state courts to take this approach, the Court approves as well an alternative rule of state law: the Georgia courts are said to be free to "adop[t] a presumptive rule of majority representation, defeasible upon a showing that the identity of the local church is to be determined by some other means." This showing may be made by proving that the church has "provid[ed], in the corporate charter or the constitution of the general church, that the identity of the local church is to be established in some other way."

On its face, this rebuttable presumption also requires reversal of the state court's judgment in favor of the schismatic faction. The polity of the PCUS commits to the Presbytery the resolution of the dispute within the local church. Having shown this structure of church government for the determination of the identity of the local congregation, the petitioners have rebutted any presumption that this question has been left to a majority vote of the local congregation.

The Court nevertheless declines to order reversal. Rather than decide the case here in accordance with established First Amendment principles, the Court leaves open the possibility that the state courts might adopt some restrictive evidentiary rule that would render the petitioners' evidence inadequate to overcome the presumption of majority control. But, aside from a passing reference to the use of the neutral-principles approach developed earlier in its opinion, the Court affords no guidance as to the constitutional limitations on such an evidentiary rule; the state courts, it says, are free to adopt any rule that is constitutional. "Indeed, the state may adopt any method of overcoming the majoritarian presumption, so long as the use of that method does not impair free-exercise rights or entangle the civil courts in matters of religious controversy." In essence, the Court's instructions on remand therefore allow the state courts the choice of following the long-settled rule of *Watson v. Jones* or of adopting some other rule—unspecified by the Court—that the state courts view as consistent with the First Amendment. Not only questions of state law but also important issues of federal constitutional law thus are left to the state courts for their decision, and, if they depart from *Watson v. Jones*, they will travel a course left totally uncharted by this Court.

NOTES AND QUESTIONS

1. *After* Wolf. *Wolf* predictably led to results that would not have been reached before. The First Presbyterian Church of Schenectady, incorporated in 1803, withdrew from the national church because of the latter's alleged support of radical political groups. The local church had title to the property. Following neutral-principles, the Court of Appeals awarded the local church the property. The national church argued that the book of Order said that "whenever a local church is dissolved," the property was to go to the hierarchical organization; but the court said that the local church had not been dissolved. The court said that to find an implied trust for the national church would require a forbidden

inquiry into church doctrine, *First Presbyterian Church of Schenectady v. United Presbyterian Church in the United States of America*, 62 N.Y. 2d 110, 476 N.Y.S. 2d 86, 464 N.E. 2d 454 (1984), *cert. denied*, 105 S.Ct. 514 (1984).

Compare this contemporaneous California case: Four Episcopal churches in Los Angeles—St. Matthias, St. Mary's, Our Saviour, and Holy Apostles—left the Protestant Episcopal Church after the Church's general convention accepted the ordination of women. The Protestant Episcopal Diocese and the Protestant Episcopal Church in the United States sued to recover the property. The court found that the most recently incorporated church, Holy Apostles, had articles of incorporation explicitly declaring that on its "dissolution" its property would inure to the benefit of the diocese. The court found that a "constructive dissolution" had occurred and that the diocese now took the property under this "express trust."

The other three churches were incorporated without any such provision but with a provision in their articles that the constitution, canons, and discipline of the diocese would always form part of their articles. The court said, "We think such declarations no more restrictive of future amendments to the articles of incorporation than would be similar statements in an automobile dealer's articles that it would always distribute General Motors products and always be bound by General Motors rules and policies . . . " The court also said, "If a Kentucky Fried Chicken franchisee secedes from its national affiliation to join a Tennessee Fried Chicken operation, neutral principles of law do not recognize any claim by the ex-franchisor.... " Finding no express trust in favor of the diocese or the national church, the court permitted St. Matthias, St. Mary's, and Our Saviour to leave with the property, *Protestant Episcopal Church v. Barker*, 115 Cal. App.3d 599, 171 Cal. Rptr. 541 (1981), *cert. denied*, 454 U.S. 864 (1981).

In the light of *Wolf*, the Supreme Court of Minnesota applied "neutral principles" to a dispute within the Serbian Eastern Orthodox Church. The majority of parishioners of St. Sava in South St. Paul, Minnesota, had remained loyal to the American diocese headed by Bishop Dionisije Milivojevich. The Minnesota court ruled in their favor, finding that the United States Supreme Court in *Milivojevich* [above] had explicitly said, "Whether corporate bylaws or other documents governing the individual property-holding corporations may affect any desired disposition of the Diocesan property is a question not before us." The Minnesota court found that title to the property was in the name of the church of St. Sava and that the charter and bylaws of that church gave control to a majority of the congregation. The generally hierarchical constitution of the Serbian Eastern Orthodox Church did not override these local provisions, *Piletich v. Deretich*, 328 N.W. 2d 696 (Minn. 1982). Would *Kedroff v. St. Nicholas Cathedral* [this section above] have been decided differently under *Wolf*? The corporation backed by the American diocese held the title.

In a single footnote the Supreme Court of Colorado summed up the confused state of the law *after Jones v. Wolf*.

Bishop of Colorado v. Mote
716 P.2d 85, 96 n. 10 (Colo. 1986).

Most courts faced with a post-*Jones* church property dispute did not have to choose between the polity approach and the neutral principles approach without precedential guidance. They simply noted that prior case law or statutes in their state required or suggested that one or the other approach be utilized. *E.g., Harris v. Apostolic Overcoming Holy Church of God, Inc.*, 457 So.2d 385, 387 (Ala. 1984) (neutral principles); *Protestant Episcopal Church in the Diocese of Los Angeles v. Barker*, 115 Cal. App.3d 599, 171 Cal. Rptr. 541, 548–49, *cert. denied*, 454 U.S. 864 (1981) (neutral principles); *New York Annual Conference of the United Methodist Church v. Fisher*, 182 Conn. 272, 438 A.2d 62, 68 (1980) (polity approach); *Grutka v. Clifford*, 445 N.E.2d 1015, 1019 (Ind. App. 1983), *cert. denied*, 465 U.S. 1006 (1984) (neutral principles); *Fluker Community Church v. Hitchens*, 419 So.2d 445, 447–48 (La.1982) (neutral principles); *Graffam v. Wray*, 437 A.2d 627, 634 (Me.1981) (neutral principles); *Babcock Memorial Presbyterian Church v. Presbytery of Baltimore*, 296 Md. 573, 464 A.2d 1008, 1016 (1983), *cert. denied*, 465 U.S. 1027, 104 S.Ct. 1287, 79 L. Ed.2d 689 (1984) (neutral principles); *Antioch Temple, Inc. v. Parekh*, 383 Mass. 854, 422 N.E.2d 1337, 1340–42 (1981) (polity); *Bennison v. Sharp*, 121 Mich. App. 705, 329 N.W. 2d 466, 474 (1982) (polity); *Piletich v. Deretich*, 328 N.W. 2d 696, 701–02 (Minn.1982) (neutral principles); *Protestant Episcopal Church v. Graves*, 83 N.J. 572, 417 A.2d 19, 23–24 (1980), *cert. denied sub nom. Moore v. Protestant Episcopal Church*, 449 U.S. 1131 (1981) (polity); *Southside Tabernacle v. Pentecostal Church of God*, 32 Wash. App. 814, 650 P.2d 231, 235 (1982) (polity); *Church of God of Madison v. Noel*, 318 S.E. 2d 920, 923–24 (W. Va. 1984) (polity). A few courts chose a neutral principles approach after deciding not to follow more or less explicit polity precedents. *E.g.,York v. First Presbyterian Church of Anna*, 130 Ill. App. 3d 611, 85 Ill. Dec. 756, 474 N.E. 2d 716 (1984), *cert. denied*, 474 U.S. 864 (1985); *Presbytery of Elijah Parish Lovejoy v. Jaeggi*, 682 S.W. 2d 465 (Mo.1984), *cert. denied*, 471 U.S. 1117 (1985); *Presbytery of Beaver–Butler v. Middlesex Presbyterian Church*, 507 Pa. 255, 489 A.2d 1317, *cert. denied*, 474 U.S. 887 (1985); *Foss v. Dykstra*, 319 N.W. 2d 499 (S.D. 1982). And in *Fonken v. Community Church of Kamrar*, 339 N.W. 2d 810 (Iowa 1983), the Iowa Supreme Court had no precedent requiring the selection of one approach over the other, but the court avoided the issue by applying both polity and neutral principles (reaching the same result) without expressing a preference for either one.

————

Applying this doctrine in this case, the Colorado Court of Appeals opted for majority rule as the neutral principle and held for the majority in a local church seceding from the Protestant Episcopal Church in the United States. The Colorado Supreme Court, invoking another neutral principle it found apposite, reversed: the local church articles of incorporation and by-laws, "along with relevant provisions in the canons of the general church," demonstrated a trust in favor of the general church. Note that the Colorado court saw no difficulty in interpreting church canons as part of its application of neutral property law.

In *Primate and Bishops' Synod of the Russian Orthodox Church Outside of Russia v. Russian Orthodox Church of the Holy Resurrection, Inc.*, 418 Mass. 1001, 636 N.E. 2d 211 (1994), the state courts found that a local dissident congregation could, on the basis of a democratic election that violated the canons of the church, decide to terminate its relationship with one of the oldest hierarchical churches in the world, and still retain ownership of the church property after leaving the church. In its petition for certiorari, the Bishops who form the legal and spiritual leadership of the church urged the Court to reconsider *Jones v. Wolf*, noting multiple conflicts among the circuits on how to characterize the governance of a church after *Jones*. This is true even of churches whose polity is manifestly hierarchical, such as the Presbyterians and the Episcopalians. For example, after spending enormous sums of money in legal fees to insure that all congregations of its church would have legal documents complying with the "neutral-principles" approach suggested in *Jones v. Wolf*, the Presbyterian Church (U.S.A.) was nonetheless viewed variously as hierarchical in Maryland and as congregational in Pennsylvania. Compare *Babcock Memorial Presbyterian Church v. Presbytery of Baltimore*, 296 Md. 573, 464 A.2d 1008, 1016 (1983), *cert. denied*, 465 U.S. 1027 (1984) with *Presbytery of Beaver–Butler v. Middlesex Presbyterian Church*, 507 Pa. 255, 489 A.2d 1317, *cert. denied*, 474 U.S. 887 (1985). And the Protestant Episcopal Church in the United States is viewed as episcopal in Michigan and as congregational in Kentucky. Compare *Bennison v. Sharp*, 121 Mich. App. 705, 329 N.W. 2d 466 (1982) with *Bjorkman and St. John's Protestant Episcopal Church of Bellevue v. The Protestant Episcopal Church in the United States of America of the Diocese of Lexington*, 759 S.W. 2d 583 (1988). Fortunately for the Presbyterians, the Kentucky Supreme Court seemed to recall [perhaps from *Watson*?] that the Presbyerians are a hierarchical church; *see Cumberland Presbytery of the Synod of the Mid–West of the Cumberland Presbyterian Church v. Branstetter et al.*, 824 S.W. 2d 417 (Ky. 1992). Several churches, including the Presbyterian Church (U.S.A.), filed a brief amicus curiae in the Russian Orthodox case, urging the Court to grant review. The Court denied certiorari. 513 U.S. 1121 (1995).

When a judicial decree has the effect of transforming centuries-old beliefs of religious communities about how they should be governed, is that "neutral"? One danger of the "neutral principles" approach is its inherent subjectivity. A judge may select a "neutral" ground for determining the result in a case when another ground is equally available that would not have the intrusive effect of telling a church that its polity does not matter. Note, moreover, that it is virtually impossible for a congregational community to be transformed by "neutral principles" into a hierarchical one. Transformations of church order and governance generally run in the opposite direction. Shall churches that have thought of themselves since the apostolic era as governed by elders or bishops be told by secular judges that they are really governed by the majority rule of the local congregation? Does this constitute an implicit establishment of congregation policy and inhibit the free exercise of hierarchial polity? Are such results "neutral" because they promote general societal values such as fairness or democracy?

2. *Rights of Churches to "New Property."* Is the name of a church protected by the law against unfair competition? Yes, according to *Purcell v. Summer*, 145 F.2d 979, 985 (4th Cir. 1944). The Methodist Episcopal South Church merged with two other churches to form the United Methodist Church. Dissident members who formed their own church using the old name were held to infringe the rights of the now merged church. Is *Purcell* good law in the light of *Wolf*?

Can religious materials constitute a protectable trade secret? No, according to *Religious Technology Center v. Wollersheim, et. al.,* 796 F.2d. 1076 (9th Cir. 1986). (Church of Scientology denied injunction against ex-members who established the Church of the New Civilization using materials taken from the church of Scientology. The court held that the value of the confidential materials was "spiritual," not commercial.)

Who own the copyright in sacred texts? Congress has the power to enact laws "to promote the progress of . . . useful Arts by securing for limited times to Authors . . . the exclusive Right to their respective Writings," U.S. Const., Art. I, sec. 8, cl. 8. Can a law enacted under this power be problematic under the Religion clause? *Costello Publishing Co., Inc. v. Rotelle,* 670 F.2d 1035 (D.C. Cir. 1981), involved a dispute over the control of distribution of *Morning and Evening Prayer,* an English translation of the official prayer-book of the Catholic church. Maintaining that a version of this prayer-book was "unauthorized," an official in the United States Catholic Conference wrote to several retailers urging them not to buy that version. When orders dried up, the publisher brought an antitrust action against the conference. Various foreign Episcopal Conferences intervened and counterclaimed, alleging that the publisher had infringed their copyright and had engaged in unfair trade practices. The district court, June L. Green, dismissed the counterclaims, but ruled for defendants on the antitrust issues. The Court of Appeals, per Judge Patricia Wald, reversed to allow a full airing of the intervenors' counterclaim on copyright infringement by the publisher. Holding, moreover, that there is no blanket religious exemption from antitrust laws, the court ruled that in an antitrust case against a religious organization, the courts must carefully assess the nature and extent of the antitrust violations, including their market impact, against the religious goals sought to be implemented before deciding that the activities are exempt. The court also ruled that–in order to avoid avoiding excessive entanglement in religious affairs–constitutional questions were to be deferred until the copyright and, if necessary, antitrust questions were resolved. Does this judicial resolution avoid excessive entanglement of the judiciary in religious matters? Would a better solution have been reached if all of the parties gathered to reflect prayerfully on a text recorded in all four Gospels: Jesus driving the money changers from the Temple (Matthew 21:12–13; Mark 11:15–19; Luke 19:45–48; John 2:13–17)?

Who owns the copyright in sacred music? In *F.E.L. Publications v. National Conference of Catholic Bishops,* 466 F.Supp. 1034 (N.D. Ill. 1978), a publisher of religious music filed a complaint against the national organization of bishops alleging that "pirated" hymnals had been published, distributed or sold without permission of plaintiff and without acknowledgment of the source of hymnals or hymns contained in it. Would you dismiss this complaint or let it proceed to trial? Why?

Were the parties in these cases faithful to the teaching of the Apostle Paul in 1 Corinthians 6:1–8 [Chapter One, section 6] that believers with a grievance against other believers should resolve the dispute within the religious community, rather than seek a judgment from a secular tribunal?

CHAPTER THIRTEEN

"AFFIRMATIVELY TO HELP GUARANTEE": DOUBLE EFFECT

The principle of double effect has a long history in moral argumentation. Essentially it is this. If a single act has both good and evil effects, the act is good if one intends the good effect and if the good effect is proportionately greater than the evil effect. A classic example is a person defending himself from an attempt on his life. With a single blow he strikes the aggressor, intending to defend himself. The effects of the blow are the death of the aggressor and the safety of his victim. The good effect of securing the victim's safety outweighs the evil effect of killing the aggressor.

This simple principle applies in a large number of situations where moral judgments must be made, see Peter Knauer, "The Hermeneutic Function of the Principle of Double Effect," 12 *Natural Law Forum* 132 (1967). The following cases suggest that an analogous analysis could be adopted in many cases where a state practice has the constitutionally protected effect of permitting the free exercise of religion and the constitutionally prohibited effect of establishing religion.

1. DOUBLE DUTY PARKS

Fowler v. Rhode Island

345 U.S. 67 (1953).

Hayden C. Covington argued the cause and filed a brief for appellant.

Raymond J. Pettine, Assistant Attorney General of Rhode Island, argued the cause for appellee. With him on the brief was *William E. Powers*, Attorney General.

■ JUSTICE DOUGLAS delivered the opinion of the Court.

The City of Pawtucket, Rhode Island, has an ordinance which reads as follows: "No person shall address any political or religious meeting in any public park; but this section shall not be construed to prohibit any political or religious club or society from visiting any public park in a body, provided that no public address shall be made under the auspices of such club or society in such park."

Jehovah's Witnesses, a religious sect, assembled in Slater Park of Pawtucket for a meeting which at the trial was conceded to be religious in character. About 400 people attended, 150 being Jehovah's Witnesses.

613

Appellant is a minister of this sect, residing in Arlington, Massachusetts. He was invited to Pawtucket as a visiting minister to give a talk before the Pawtucket congregation of Jehovah's Witnesses. Appellant accepted the invitation, attended the meeting in the park, and addressed it over two loudspeakers. It was a quiet, orderly meeting with no disturbances or breaches of the peace whatsoever.

Appellant's address was entitled 'The Pathway to Peace.' He discussed the futility of efforts being made to establish peace in the world. And then, according to his uncontradicted testimony he 'launched forth into the scriptural evidence to show where we were on the string of time; that we hard reached the end of this wicked system of things.' Appellant had been talking only a few minutes when he was arrested by the police and charged with violating the ordinance set forth above. He was tried and found guilty over objections that the ordinance as so construed and applied violated the First and the Fourteenth Amendments of the Constitution. He was fined $5. His conviction was affirmed by the Rhode Island Supreme Court....

Appellant's sect has conventions that are different from the practices of other religious groups. Its religious service is less ritualistic, more unorthodox, less formal than some. But apart from narrow exceptions not relevant here (*Reynolds v. United States* [Chapter Nine]; *Davis v. Beason* [Chapter Nine]) it is no business of courts to say that what is a religious practice or activity for one group is not religion under the protection of the First Amendment. Nor is it in the competence of courts under our constitutional scheme to approve, disapprove, classify, regulate, or in any manner control sermons delivered at religious meetings. Sermons are as much a part of a religious service as prayers. They cover a wide range and have as great a diversity as the Bible or other Holy Book from which they commonly take their texts. To call the words which one minister speaks to his congregation a sermon, immune from regulation, and the words of another minister an address, subject to regulation, is merely an indirect way of preferring one religion over another. That would be precisely the effect here if we affirmed this conviction in the face of the concession made during oral argument. Baptist, Methodist, Presbyterian, or Episcopal ministers, Catholic priests, Moslem mullahs, Buddhist monks could all preach to their congregations in Pawtucket's parks with impunity. But the hand of the law would be laid on the shoulder of a minister of this unpopular group for performing the same function.

The judgment is reversed and the cause is remanded to the Supreme Court of Rhode Island for proceedings not inconsistent with this opinion. *Reversed.*

■ Justice Frankfurter concurs in the opinion of the Court, except insofar as it may derive support from the First Amendment. For him it is the Equal–Protection–of–the–Laws Clause of the Fourteenth Amendment that condemns the Pawtucket ordinance as applied in this case.

■ Justice Jackson concurs in the result.

NOTES AND QUESTIONS

1. *Do You Know Religious Persecution When You See It?*. In *Church of the Lukumi Babalu Aye, Inc. City of Hialeah* [Chapter Eleven, section 12], Justice Kennedy identified *Fowler v. Rhode Island* as an example of religious "persecution." The treatment of the Witnesses in this case surely seems unfair, but it was mild in comparison to the treatment of the Witnesses at the time of the flag salute controversy [Chapter Eleven, section 3], yet Justice Kennedy joined the opinion in *Employment Division v. Smith* that relied twice on *Gobitis* [Chapter Eleven, section 3] without acknowledging its reversal by *Barnette* [Chapter Eleven, section 3]. And as atrocious as the treatment of the Witnesses in the 1940s was, it is pale by comparison to the violence perpetrated against the Mormons from the mid to the late nineteenth century [Chapter Nine], yet Justice Kennedy joined the opinion the Court in *Smith* that relied on the principal Mormon case, *Reynolds v. United States*. Does the Pawtucket ordinance in *Fowler* target a particular religious community or is it what Justice Scalia described in *Employment Division v. Smith* [Chapter Eleven, section 10] as a "law of general applicability"?

2. *Use of Public Parks for Papal Mass. O'Hair v. Andrus*, 613 F. 2d 931 (D.C. Cir. 1979). Madalyn Murray O'Hair, an avowed atheist, sought to enjoin the celebration of Mass by Pope John Paul II on the National Mall in Washington, D.C., on October 7, 1979. The cost of the Park Police service for the occasion was estimated to be between $100,000 and $150,000, plus $28,000 for related services; the Catholic Archdiocese of Washington was to pay over $400,000 to construct the platform for the Mass and to provide fencing, electrical equipment, and the like. The Park Service issued about 100 permits annually for religious services on national park land within the District of Columbia. The court, per Judge Harold Leventhal, found the National Mall to be a public park that has regularly been made available to all major demonstrations presenting First Amendment values." It refused to issue the injunction.

Compare Gilfillan v. City of Philadelphia, 637 F. 2d 924 (3rd Cir. 1980), *cert. denied*, 451 U.S. 987 (1981). A taxpayer and the Philadelphia branch of the American Civil Liberties Union sought to enjoin Philadelphia from building a platform where the pope would say Mass. The construction went ahead, the archdiocese of Philadelphia agreeing that it would pay if the city lost. The plaintiffs did not challenge city expenditures of about $1,000,000 to build a platform to welcome the pope at the airport and provide police on the pope's parade route; nor did they challenge his use of Logan Circle, a public place. They did challenge the $200,000 spent to build the platform and a cross and to surround the platform with shrubbery and flowers.

The city asserted that it had the secular purposes of protecting the pope and of reaping "a public relations bonanza" from his presence. The Third Circuit, 2–1, per Judge Max Rosenn, held that the challenged expenditures were an unconstitutional establishment of religion. Applying the tests of *Lemon* [Chapter Fourteen, section 1], the court held that the purpose and effect of putting up the platform was to advance religion, and that the joint planning of the city with the archdiocese of Philadelphia was "entanglement." Judge Ruggero J. Aldisert dissented, maintaining that the pope was not only a religious leader but the head of a civil, if "theocratic," state.

2. DOUBLE DUTY DAYS

McGowan v. Maryland

366 U.S. 420 (1961).

Harry Silbert argued the cause for appellants. With him on the brief were *A. Jerome Diener* and *Sidney Schlachman. John Martin Jones, Jr.,* Special Assistant Attorney General of Maryland, argued the cause for appellee. With him on the brief was *C. Ferdinand Sybert*, Attorney General.

■ CHIEF JUSTICE WARREN delivered the opinion of the Court.

The issues in this case concern the constitutional validity of Maryland criminal statutes, commonly known as Sunday Closing Laws or Sunday Blue Laws. These statutes, with exceptions to be noted hereafter, generally proscribe all labor, business and other commercial activities on Sunday. The questions presented are whether the classifications within the statutes bring about a denial of equal protection of the law, whether the laws are so vague as to fail to give reasonable notice of the forbidden conduct and therefore violate due process, and whether the statutes are laws respecting an establishment of religion or prohibiting the free exercise thereof.

Appellants are seven employees of a large discount department store located on a highway in Anne Arundel County, Maryland. They were indicted for the Sunday sale of a three-ring loose-leaf binder, a can of floor wax, a stapler and staples, and a toy submarine in violation of [the statute]. Generally, this section prohibited, throughout the State, the Sunday sale of all merchandise except the retail sale of tobacco products, confectioneries, milk, bread, fruits, gasoline, oils, greases, drugs and medicines, and newspapers and periodicals. Recently amended, this section also now excepts from the general prohibition the retail sale in Anne Arundel County of all foodstuffs, automobile and boating accessories, flowers, toilet goods, hospital supplies and souvenirs. It now further provides that any retail establishment in Anne Arundel County which does not employ more than one person other than the owner may operate on Sunday. . . .

[T]he "Establishment" Clause does not ban federal or state regulation of conduct whose reason or effect merely happens to coincide or harmonize with the tenets of some or all religions. In many instances, the Congress or state legislatures conclude that the general welfare of society, wholly apart from any religious considerations, demands such regulation. Thus, for temporal purposes, murder is illegal. And the fact that this agrees with the dictates of the Judaeo–Christian religions while it may disagree with others does not invalidate the regulation. So too with the questions of adultery and polygamy. *Davis v. Beason, Reynolds v. United States* [Chapter Nine]. The same could be said of theft, fraud, etc., because those offenses were also proscribed in the Decalogue.

Thus, these broad principles have been set forth by this Court. Those cases dealing with the specific problems arising under the "Establishment" Clause which have reached this Court are few in number. The most extensive discussion of the "Establishment" Clause's latitude is to be found in *Everson v. Board of Education* [Chapter Fourteen, section 1]....

Sunday Closing Laws, like those before us, have become part and parcel of this great governmental concern wholly apart from their original purposes or connotations. The present purpose and effect of most of them is to provide a uniform day of rest for all citizens; the fact that this day is Sunday, a day of particular significance for the dominant Christian sects, does not bar the State from achieving its secular goals. To say that the States cannot prescribe Sunday as a day of rest for these purposes solely because centuries ago such laws had their genesis in religion would give a constitutional interpretation of hostility to the public welfare rather than one of mere separation of church and State.... *Affirmed.*

■ JUSTICE FRANKFURTER delivered a concurring opinion.

■ JUSTICE DOUGLAS dissented.

NOTES AND QUESTIONS

1. *Blue Laws and Free Exercise.* Sunday closing laws were also challenged as impairing the free exercise of religion. The plaintiffs, Orthodox Jews, sought to enjoin enforcement of the Pennsylvania Sunday law on the grounds that it penalized their observance of their Sabbath. In *Braunfeld v. Brown*, 366 U.S. 599 (1961) the plaintiffs–Orthodox Jews–were put to a Hobson's choice: either giving up their Sabbath observance by keeping their businesses open Saturdays or closing Saturdays and Sundays and being at a serious economic disadvantage. Citing *Reynolds* [Chapter Nine] and *Prince,* [Chapter Eleven, section 1], the Court, per Chief Justice Earl Warren, sustained the statute as imposing "only an indirect burden on the exercise of religion" in the course of accomplishing a lawful state purpose that could not be accomplished without imposing the burden. Justice Brennan concurred in part and dissented in part and Justice Stewart dissented, asserting that the state could secure a day of rest while allowing an exception for Sabbatarians. Justice Douglas also dissented. Right result? Consistent with *Sherbert v. Verner* [Chapter Eleven, section 5]?

2. *Religious Holidays.* As noted above [Chapter Eleven, section 6], employers have an affirmative duty of to accommodate religious practices and beliefs of their employees under § 701(j) of Title VII of the Civil Rights Act of 1964 [Chapter Eleven, section 7]. This includes observance of religious holidays. For example, it is within the spirit of this provision when employers try to accommodate observant Jews on Yom Kippur or devout Christians on Good Friday. Must this duty of reasonable accommodation be decided on a case by case basis, or may a city or State with a large population of members of a particular religious community simply decide on an economic basis to give all public employees the day off on a prominent religious holiday? In *Metzl v. Leininger*, 57 F.3d 618 (7th Cir. 1995), the court invalidated an Illinois statute that made Good Friday a public holiday. Is this result consistent with § 701(j)? Is the observance of Thanksgiving or Christmas as a national holiday impermis-

sible? Is it possible to avoid a religious gerrymander of time? See *Lynch v. Donnelly* [section 6 below].

3. *State Stimulus to a Religious Divorce.* Under Jewish law a woman is validly divorced only if she receives a bill of divorce or *get* from her husband. If she marries again without it, she commits adultery and any child she bears is a illegitimate under Jewish law. No similar stigmas attach to the undivorced husband. Husbands consequently are in a position to extract concessions from their civilly divorced wives who need the *get* to remarry without religious opprobrium. Tyrannical husbands can even deny the *get* out of malice, keeping their ex-wives forever in a position where they cannot conscientiously marry. To remedy this situation, New York, at the request of Orthodox and Conservative Jewish groups, enacted in 1983 a statute that provides that a spouse, married by a clergyman or rabbi and seeking an annulment or divorce, must allege that "he or she has taken or . . . will take, prior to the entry of final judgment, all steps solely within his or her power to remove any barrier to the defendant's remarriage following the annulment or divorce," *New York Domestic Relations Law*, sec. 253. The statute further specifies that such steps do not include applying to a church tribunal (thus letting out Catholics) and that barriers include "any religious or conscientious restraint or inhibition imposed on a party to a marriage . . . by reason of the other party's withholding of any voluntary act." The New York Court of Appeals sustained the statute against a constitutional challenge. *Avitzur v. Avitzur*, 58 N.Y. 2d 108, 446 N.E. 2d 136, 459 N.Y.S. 2d 572 (1983), cert. denied 464 U.S. 817 (1983)

Does the statute have a double effect? Does the secular effect outweigh the religious?

3. DOUBLE DUTY PROPERTY

Walz v. Tax Commission of the City of New York

397 U.S. 664 (1970).

Edward J. Ennis argued the cause for appellant. *J. Lee Rankin* argued the cause for appellee. With him on the brief were *Stanley Buchsbaum* and *Edith I. Spivack.*

Briefs of *amici curiae* urging reversal were filed by *Osmond K. Fraenkel, Marvin M. Karpatkin, Norman Dorsen, Mr. Ennis,* and *Melvin L. Wulf* for the American Civil Liberties Union, and by *Lola Boswell* for Madalyn Murray O'Hair and *James H. Anderson, Jr.,* for the Society of Separationists, Inc.

Briefs of *amici curiae* urging affirmance were filed by *Louis J. Lefkowitz,* Attorney General, *Samuel A. Hirshowitz,* First Assistant Attorney General, and *Julius Greenfield,* Assistant Attorney General, for the State of New York, joined by the Attorneys General for their respective States as follows: *MacDonald Gallion* of Alabama, *Gary K. Nelson* of Arizona, *Joe Purcell* of Arkansas, *Duke W. Dunbar* of Colorado, *Robert K. Killian* of Connecticut, *David P. Buckson* of Delaware, *Earl Faircloth* of Florida, *Bertram T. Kanbara* of Hawaii, *William J. Scott* of Illinois, *Theodore L.*

Sendak of Indiana, *Richard C. Turner* of Iowa, *Kent Frizzel* of Kansas, *John B. Breckinridge* of Kentucky, *Jack P. F. Gremillion* of Louisiana, *James S. Erwin* of Maine, *Francis B. Burch* of Maryland, *Frank J. Kelley* of Michigan, *A. F. Summer* of Mississippi, *John C. Danforth* of Missouri, *Robert L. Woodahl* of Montana, *Clarence A. H. Meyer* of Nebraska, *Arthur J. Sills* of New Jersey, *James A. Maloney* of New Mexico, *Robert B. Morgan* of North Carolina, *Helgi Johanneson* of North Dakota, *Paul W. Brown* of Ohio, *William C. Sennett* of Pennsylvania, *Herbert F. De Simone* of Rhode Island, *Gordon Mydland* of South Dakota, *George F. McCanless* of Tennessee, *Crawford C. Martin* of Texas, *James M. Jeffords* of Vermont, *Robert Y. Button* of Virginia, *Slade Gorton* of Washington, *Robert W. Warren* of Wisconsin, and *James E. Barrett* of Wyoming, and by *Santiago C. Soler–Favale*, Attorney General of Puerto Rico; by *Franklin C. Salisbury* for Protestants and Other Americans United for Separation of Church and State; by *Noel Thompson* for the Parish Hall School, Inc.; by *Charles H. Tuttle* and *Thomas A. Shaw, Jr.*, for the National Council of the Churches of Christ in the United States; by *Anthony L. Fletcher, Stephen B. Clarkson, John Miles Evans, George F. Mackey, William G. Rhines, William Sherman*, and *H. Richard Schumacher* for the Episcopal Diocese of New York et al.; by *William R. Consedine, George E. Reed, Alfred L. Scanlan, Arthur E. Sutherland,* and *Charles M. Whelan* for the United States Catholic Conference; by *Marvin Braiterman* for the Synagogue Council of America et al.; by *Nathan Lewin* and *Julius Berman* for the National Jewish Commission on Law and Public Affairs; by *Joseph B. Friedman* for the Baptist Joint Committee on Public Affairs; and by *Roy L. Cole* for the Baptist General Convention of Texas.

■ Chief Justice Burger delivered the opinion of the Court.

Appellant, owner of real estate in Richmond County, New York, sought an injunction in the New York courts to prevent the New York City Tax Commission from granting property tax exemptions to religious organizations for religious properties used solely for religious worship. The exemption from state taxes is authorized by Art. 16, § 1, of the New York Constitution, which provides in relevant part: "Exemptions from taxation may be granted only by general laws. Exemptions may be altered or repealed except those exempting real or personal property used exclusively for religious, educational or charitable purposes as defined by law and owned by any corporation or association organized or conducted exclusively for one or more of such purposes and not operating for profit."

The essence of appellant's contention was that the New York City Tax Commission's grant of an exemption to church property indirectly requires the appellant to make a contribution to religious bodies and thereby violates provisions prohibiting establishment of religion under the First Amendment which under the Fourteenth Amendment is binding on the States.

Appellee's motion for summary judgment was granted and the Appellate Division of the New York Supreme Court, and the New York Court of Appeals affirmed. We noted probable jurisdiction, and affirm.

The Court has struggled to find a neutral course between the two Religion Clauses, both of which are cast in absolute terms, and either of which, if expanded to a logical extreme, would tend to clash with the other. For example, in *Zorach v. Clauson* [Chapter Fourteen, section 2], Mr. Justice Douglas, writing for the Court, noted: "The First Amendment, however, does not say that in every and all respects there shall be a separation of Church and State.... We sponsor an attitude on the part of government that shows no partiality to any one group and that lets each flourish according to the zeal of its adherents and the appeal of its dogma."

Mr. Justice Harlan expressed something of this in his dissent in *Sherbert v. Verner* [Chapter Eleven, section 42], saying that the constitutional neutrality imposed on us "is not so narrow a channel that the slightest deviation from an absolutely straight course leads to condemnation."

The course of constitutional neutrality in this area cannot be an absolutely straight line; rigidity could well defeat the basic purpose of these provisions, which is to insure that no religion be sponsored or favored, none commanded, and none inhibited. The general principle deducible from the First Amendment and all that has been said by the Court is this: that we will not tolerate either governmentally established religion or governmental interference with religion. Short of those expressly proscribed governmental acts there is room for play in the joints productive of a benevolent neutrality which will permit religious exercise to exist without sponsorship and without interference.

Each value judgment under the Religion Clauses must therefore turn on whether particular acts in question are intended to establish or interfere with religious beliefs and practices or have the effect of doing so. Adherence to the policy of neutrality that derives from an accommodation of the Establishment and Free Exercise Clauses has prevented the kind of involvement that would tip the balance toward government control of churches or governmental restraint on religious practice.

Adherents of particular faiths and individual churches frequently take strong positions on public issues including, as this case reveals in the several briefs *amici*, vigorous advocacy of legal or constitutional positions. Of course, churches as much as secular bodies and private citizens have that right. No perfect or absolute separation is really possible; the very existence of the Religion Clauses is an involvement of sorts—one that seeks to mark boundaries to avoid excessive entanglement.

The hazards of placing too much weight on a few words or phrases of the Court is abundantly illustrated within the pages of the Court's opinion in *Everson* [Chapter Fourteen, section 1]. Mr. Justice Black, writing for the Court's majority, said the First Amendment "means at least this: Neither a state nor the Federal Government can ... pass laws which aid one religion, aid all religions, or prefer one religion over another." Yet he had no difficulty in holding that: "Measured by these standards, we cannot say that the First Amendment prohibits New Jersey from spending tax-raised funds to pay the bus fares of parochial school pupils as a part of a general program under which it pays the fares of pupils attending public and other schools. *It is undoubtedly true that children are helped to get to church schools. There is even a possibility that some of the children might not be sent to the church schools if the parents were compelled to pay their children's bus fares out of their own pockets....*" (Emphasis added).

The Court did not regard such "aid" to schools teaching a particular religious faith as any more a violation of the Establishment Clause than providing "state-paid policemen, detailed to protect children ... [at the schools] from the very real hazards of traffic...."

Mr. Justice Jackson, in perplexed dissent in *Everson*, noted that "the undertones of the opinion, advocating complete and uncompromising separation ... seem utterly discordant with its conclusion...." Perhaps so. One can sympathize with Mr. Justice Jackson's logical analysis but agree with the Court's eminently sensible and realistic application of the language of the Establishment Clause. In *Everson* the Court declined to construe the Religion Clauses with a literalness that would undermine the ultimate constitutional objective as illuminated by history. Surely, bus transportation and police protection to pupils who receive religious instruction "aid" that particular religion to maintain schools that plainly tend to assure future adherents to a particular faith by having control of their total education at an early age. No religious body that maintains schools would deny this as an affirmative if not dominant policy of church schools. But if as in *Everson* buses can be provided to carry and policemen to protect church school pupils, we fail to see how a broader range of police and fire protection given equally to all churches, along with nonprofit hospitals, art galleries, and libraries receiving the same tax exemption, is different for purposes of the Religion Clauses.

Similarly, making textbooks available to pupils in parochial schools in common with public schools was surely an "aid" to the sponsoring churches because it relieved those churches of an enormous aggregate cost for those books. Supplying of costly teaching materials was not seen either as manifesting a legislative purpose to aid or as having a primary effect of aid contravening the First Amendment. *Board of Education v. Allen* [Chapter Fourteen, section 1]. In so holding the Court was heeding both its own prior decisions and our religious tradition. Mr. Justice Douglas, in *Zorach v. Clauson*, after recalling that we "are a religious people whose institutions presuppose a Supreme Being," went on to say: "We make room for as wide a variety of beliefs and creeds as the spiritual needs of man deem necessary.... *When the state encourages religious instruction ... it follows the best of our traditions.* For it then respects the religious nature of our people and accommodates the public service to their spiritual needs." (Emphasis added.)

With all the risks inherent in programs that bring about administrative relationships between public education bodies and church-sponsored schools, we have been able to chart a course that preserved the autonomy and freedom of religious bodies while avoiding any semblance of established religion. This is a "tight rope" and one we have successfully traversed.

II

The legislative purpose of the property tax exemption is neither the advancement nor the inhibition of religion; it is neither sponsorship nor hostility. New York, in common with the other States, has determined that certain entities that exist in a harmonious relationship to the community at large, and that foster its "moral or mental improvement," should not be inhibited in their activities by property taxation or the hazard of loss of those properties for nonpayment of taxes. It has not singled out one particular church or religious group or even churches as such; rather, it has granted exemption to all houses of religious worship within a broad class of property owned by nonprofit, quasi-public corporations which include hospitals, libraries, playgrounds, scientific, professional, historical, and patriotic groups. The State has an affirmative policy that considers these groups as beneficial and stabilizing influences in community life and finds this classification useful, desirable, and in the public interest. Qualification for tax exemption is not perpetual or immutable; some tax-exempt groups lose that status when their activities take them outside the classification and new entities can come into being and qualify for exemption.

Governments have not always been tolerant of religious activity, and hostility toward religion has taken many shapes and forms—economic, political, and sometimes harshly oppressive. Grants of exemption historically reflect the concern of authors of constitutions and statutes as to the latent dangers inherent in the imposition of property taxes; exemption constitutes a reasonable and balanced attempt to guard against those dangers. The limits of permissible state accommodation to religion are by no means co-extensive with the noninterference mandated by the Free Exercise Clause. To equate the two would be to deny a national heritage with roots in the Revolution itself. See *Sherbert* [Chapter Eleven, section 5] (Harlan, J., dissenting); *Braunfeld v. Brown* [Chapter Thirteen, section 2]. See generally Kauper, "The Constitutionality of Tax Exemptions for Religious Activities" in Dallin Oaks ed., *The Wall Between Church and State* 95 (1963). We cannot read New York's statute as attempting to establish religion; it is simply sparing the exercise of religion from the burden of property taxation levied on private profit institutions.

We find it unnecessary to justify the tax exemption on the social welfare services or "good works" that some churches perform for parishioners and others—family counselling, aid to the elderly and the infirm, and to children. Churches vary substantially in the scope of such services; programs expand or contract according to resources and need. As public-sponsored programs enlarge, private aid from the church sector may diminish. The extent of social services may vary, depending on whether the church serves an urban or rural, a rich or poor constituency. To give emphasis to so variable an aspect of the work of religious bodies would introduce an element of governmental evaluation and standards as to the worth of particular social welfare programs, thus producing a kind of continuing day-to-day relationship which the policy of neutrality seeks to minimize. Hence, the use of a social welfare yardstick as a significant element to qualify for tax exemption could conceivably give rise to confrontations that could escalate to constitutional dimensions.

Determining that the legislative purpose of tax exemption is not aimed at establishing, sponsoring, or supporting religion does not end the inquiry, however. We must also be sure that the end result—the effect—is not an excessive government entanglement with religion. The test is inescapably one of degree. Either course, taxation of churches or exemption, occasions some degree of involvement with religion. Elimination of exemption would tend to expand the involvement of government by giving rise to tax valuation of church property, tax liens, tax foreclosures, and the direct confrontations and conflicts that follow in the train of those legal processes.

Granting tax exemptions to churches necessarily operates to afford an indirect economic benefit and also gives rise to some, but yet a lesser, involvement than taxing them. In analyzing either alternative the questions are whether the involvement is excessive, and whether it is a continuing one calling for official and continuing surveillance leading to an impermissible degree of entanglement. Obviously a direct money subsidy would be a relationship pregnant with involvement and, as with most governmental grant programs, could encompass sustained and detailed administrative relationships for enforcement of statutory or administrative standards, but that is not this case. The hazards of churches supporting government are hardly less in their potential than the hazards of government supporting churches; each relationship carries some involvement rather than the desired insulation and separation. We cannot ignore the instances in history when church support of government led to the kind of involvement we seek to avoid.

The grant of a tax exemption is not sponsorship since the government does not transfer part of its revenue to churches but simply abstains from demanding that the church support the state. No one has ever suggested that tax exemption has converted libraries, art galleries, or hospitals into arms of the state or put employees "on the public payroll." There is no genuine nexus between tax exemption and establishment of religion. As Mr. Justice Holmes commented in a related context "a page of history is worth a volume of logic." *New York Trust Co. v. Eisner*, 256 U.S. 345, 349 (1921). The exemption creates only a minimal and remote involvement between church and state and far less than taxation of churches. It restricts the fiscal relationship between church and state, and tends to complement and reinforce the desired separation insulating each from the other.

Separation in this context cannot mean absence of all contact; the complexities of modern life inevitably produce some contact and the fire and police protection received by houses of religious worship are no more than incidental benefits accorded all persons or institutions within a State's boundaries, along with many other exempt organizations. The appellant has not established even an arguable quantitative correlation between the payment of an ad valorem property tax and the receipt of these municipal benefits.

All of the 50 States provide for tax exemption of places of worship, most of them doing so by constitutional guarantees. For so long as federal income taxes have had any potential impact on churches—over 75 years—religious organizations have been expressly exempt from the tax. Such treatment is an "aid" to churches no more and no less in principle than the real estate tax exemption granted by States. Few concepts are more deeply embedded in the fabric of our national life, beginning with pre-Revolutionary colonial times, than for the government to exercise at the very least this kind of benevolent neutrality toward churches and religious exercise generally so long as none was favored over others and none suffered interference.

It is significant that Congress, from its earliest days, has viewed the Religion Clauses of the Constitution as authorizing statutory real estate tax exemption to religious bodies. In 1802 the 7th Congress enacted a taxing statute for the County of Alexandria, adopting the 1800 Virginia statutory pattern which provided tax exemptions for churches. 2 Stat. 194.[5] As early as 1813 the 12th Congress refunded import duties paid by religious societies on the importation of religious articles.[6] During this period the City Council of Washington, D.C., acting under congressional authority, Act of Incorporation, § 7, 2 Stat. 197 (May 3, 1802), enacted a series of real and personal property assessments that uniformly exempted church property.[7] In 1870 the Congress specifically exempted all churches in the District of Columbia and appurtenant grounds and property "from any and all taxes or assessments, national, municipal, or county." Act of June 17, 1870, 16 Stat. 153.[8]

It is obviously correct that no one acquires a vested or protected right in violation of the Constitution by long use, even when that span of time covers our entire national existence and indeed predates it. Yet an unbroken practice of according the exemption to churches, openly and by affirmative state action, not covertly or by state inaction, is not something to be lightly cast aside. Nearly 50 years ago Mr. Justice Holmes stated: "If a thing has been practised for two hundred years by common consent, it will

---

5. In 1798 Congress passed an Act to provide for the valuation of lands and dwelling houses. All existing state exemptions were expressly excluded from the aforesaid valuation and enumeration. Act of July 9, 1798, § 8, 1 Stat. 585. Subsequent levies of direct taxes expressly or impliedly incorporated existing state exemptions. Act of July 14, 1798, § 2, 1 Stat. 598 (express incorporation of state exemption). See Act of Aug. 2, 1813, § 4, 3 Stat. 71; Act of Jan. 9, 1815, § 5, 3 Stat. 166 (express incorporation of state exemptions).

6. See 6 Stat. 116 (1813), relating to plates for printing Bibles. See also 6 Stat. 346 (1826) relating to church vestments, furniture, and paintings; 6 Stat. 162 (1816), Bible plates; 6 Stat. 600 (1834), and 6 Stat. 675 (1836), church bells.

7. See, *e.g.*, Acts of the Corporation of the City of Washington, First Council, c. V. approved Oct. 6, 1802, p. 13; Acts of the Corporation of the City of Washington, Second Council, § 1, approved Sept.12, 1803, p. 13; Acts of the Corporation of the City of Washington, Third Council, § 1, approved Sept. 5, 1804, p. 13. Succeeding Acts of the Corporation of the City of Washington. Thirteenth Council, c. 19 § 2, approved July 27, 1815, p. 24

8. Subsequent Acts of Congress carried over the substance of the exemption. Act of July 12, 1876, § 8, 19 Stat. 85; Act of March 3, 1877, § 8, 19 Stat. 399; Act of August 15, 1916, 39 Stat. 514; D.C. Code Ann. § 47–801a (1967).

need a strong case for the Fourteenth Amendment to affect it...." *Jackman v. Rosenbaum Co.*, 260 U.S. 22, 31 (1922).

Nothing in this national attitude toward religious tolerance and two centuries of uninterrupted freedom from taxation has given the remotest sign of leading to an established church or religion and on the contrary it has operated affirmatively to help guarantee the free exercise of all forms of religious belief. Thus, it is hardly useful to suggest that tax exemption is but the "foot in the door" or the "nose of the camel in the tent" leading to an established church. If tax exemption can be seen as this first step toward "establishment" of religion, as Mr. Justice Douglas fears, the second step has been long in coming. Any move that realistically "establishes" a church or tends to do so can be dealt with "while this Court sits."

Mr. Justice Cardozo commented in *The Nature of the Judicial Process* 51 (1921) on the "tendency of a principle to expand itself to the limit of its logic"; such expansion must always be contained by the historical frame of reference of the principle's purpose and there is no lack of vigilance on this score by those who fear religious entanglement in government.

The argument that making "fine distinctions" between what is and what is not absolute under the Constitution is to render us a government of men, not laws, gives too little weight to the fact that it is an essential part of adjudication to draw distinctions, including fine ones, in the process of interpreting the Constitution. We must frequently decide, for example, what are "reasonable" searches and seizures under the Fourth Amendment. Determining what acts of government tend to establish or interfere with religion falls well within what courts have long been called upon to do in sensitive areas.

It is interesting to note that while the precise question we now decide has not been directly before the Court previously, the broad question was discussed by the Court in relation to real estate taxes assessed nearly a century ago on land owned by and adjacent to a church in Washington, D.C.[9] At that time Congress granted real estate tax exemptions to buildings devoted to art, to institutions of public charity, libraries, cemeteries, and "church buildings, and grounds actually occupied by such buildings." In denying tax exemption as to land owned by but not used for the church, but rather to produce income, the Court concluded: "In the exercise of this [taxing] power, Congress, like any State legislature unrestricted by constitutional provisions, may at its discretion wholly exempt certain classes of property from taxation, or may tax them at a lower rate than other property." *Gibbons v. District of Columbia*, 116 U.S. 404, 408 (1886).

It appears that at least up to 1885 this Court, reflecting more than a century of our history and uninterrupted practice, accepted without discussion the proposition that federal or state grants of tax exemption to churches were not a violation of the Religion Clauses of the First Amendment. As to the New York statute, we now confirm that view. *Affirmed.*

■ Justice Brennan, concurring:

---

9. *Gibbons v. District of Columbia*, 116 U.S. 404 (1886). Cf. *Washington Ethical Society v. District of Columbia*, 101 U.S. App. D.C. 371, 249 F.2d 127 (1957).

The existence from the beginning of the Nation's life of a practice, such as tax exemptions for religious organizations, is not conclusive of its constitutionality. But such practice is a fact of considerable import in the interpretation of abstract constitutional language. On its face, the Establishment Clause is reasonably susceptible of different interpretations regarding the exemptions. This Court's interpretation of the clause, accordingly, is appropriately influenced by the reading it has received in the practices of the Nation. As Mr. Justice Holmes observed in an analogous context, in resolving such questions of interpretation "a page of history is worth a volume of logic." *New York Trust Co. v. Eisner*, 256 U.S. 345, 349 (1921). The more longstanding and widely accepted a practice, the greater its impact upon constitutional interpretation. History is particularly compelling in the present case because of the undeviating acceptance given religious tax exemptions from our earliest days as a Nation. Rarely if ever has this Court considered the constitutionality of a practice for which the historical support is so overwhelming. . . .

Government has two basic secular purposes for granting real property tax exemptions to religious organizations. First, these organizations are exempted because they, among a range of other private, nonprofit organizations contribute to the well-being of the community in a variety of nonreligious ways, and thereby bear burdens that would otherwise either have to be met by general taxation, or be left undone, to the detriment of the community. . . .

Second, government grants exemptions to religious organizations because they uniquely contribute to the pluralism of American society by their religious activities. Government may properly include religious institutions among the variety of private, nonprofit groups that receive tax exemptions, for each group contributes to the diversity of association, viewpoint, and enterprise essential to a vigorous, pluralistic society. See *Washington Ethical Society v. District of Columbia*, 101 U.S. App. D.C. 371, 373, 249 F.2d 127, 129 (1957). To this end, New York extends its exemptions not only to religious and social service organizations but also to scientific, literary, bar, library, patriotic, and historical groups, and generally to institutions "organized exclusively for the moral or mental improvement of men and women." The very breadth of this scheme of exemptions negates any suggestion that the State intends to single out religious organizations for special preference. The scheme is not designed to inject any religious activity into a nonreligious context, as was the case with school prayers. No particular activity of a religious organization—for example, the propagation of its beliefs—is specially promoted by the exemptions. They merely facilitate the existence of a broad range of private, non-profit organizations, among them religious groups, by leaving each free to come into existence, then to flourish or wither, without being burdened by real property taxes. . . .

Finally, I do not think that the exemptions "use essentially religious means to serve governmental ends, where secular means would suffice." The means churches use to carry on their public service activities are not "essentially religious" in nature. They are the same means used by any purely secular organization—money, human time and skills, physical facilities. It is true that each church contributes to the pluralism of our society through its purely religious activities, but the state encourages these activities not because it champions religion *per se* but because it values religion among a variety of private, nonprofit enterprises that contribute to the diversity of the Nation. Viewed in this light, there is no nonreligious substitute for religion as an element in our societal mosaic, just as there is no nonliterary substitute for literary groups.

■ Justice Harlan, concurring:

This legislation neither encourages nor discourages participation in religious life and thus satisfies the voluntarism requirement of the First Amendment. Unlike the instances of school prayers, *Abington School Dist. v. Schempp* [Chapter Fourteen, section 2], and *Engel v. Vitale*, or "released time" programs, *Zorach v. Clauson* [Chapter Fourteen, section 2] and *McCollum v. Board of Education* [Chapter Fourteen, section 2], the State is not "utilizing the prestige, power, and influence" of a public institution to bring religion into the lives of citizens (Goldberg, J., concurring).

The statute also satisfies the requirement of neutrality. Neutrality in its application requires an equal protection mode of analysis. The Court must survey meticulously the circumstances of governmental categories to eliminate, as it were, religious gerrymanders. In any particular case the critical question is whether the circumference of legislation encircles a class so broad that it can be fairly concluded that religious institutions could be thought to fall within the natural perimeter.

The statute that implements New York's constitutional provision for tax exemptions to religious organizations has defined a class of nontaxable entities whose common denominator is their nonprofit pursuit of activities devoted to cultural and moral improvement and the doing of "good works" by performing certain social services in the community that might otherwise have to be assumed by government. Included are such broad and divergent groups as historical and literary societies and more generally associations "for the moral or mental improvement of men." The statute by its terms grants this exemption in furtherance of moral and intellectual diversity and would appear not to omit any organization that could be reasonably thought to contribute to that goal.

To the extent that religious institutions sponsor the secular activities that this legislation is designed to promote, it is consistent with neutrality to grant them an exemption just as other organizations devoting resources to these projects receive exemptions. I think, moreover, in the context of a statute so broad as the one before us, churches may properly receive an exemption even though they do not themselves sponsor the secular-type activities mentioned in the statute but exist merely for the convenience of their interested members. As long as the breadth of exemption includes groups that pursue cultural, moral, or spiritual improvement in multifarious secular ways, including, I would suppose, groups whose avowed tenets may be antitheological, atheistic, or agnostic, I can see no lack of neutrality in extending the benefit of the exemption to organized religious groups.[1]

■ JUSTICE DOUGLAS, dissenting:

Engel v. Vitale [Chapter Fourteen, section 2] was as disruptive of traditional state practices as was *Stromberg*. Prior to *Stromberg*, a State could arrest an unpopular person who made a rousing speech on the charge of disorderly conduct. Since *Stromberg*, that has been unconstitutional. And so the revolution occasioned by the Fourteenth Amendment has progressed as Article after Article in the Bill of Rights has been incorporated in it and made applicable to the States.

Hence the question in the present case makes irrelevant the "two centuries of uninterrupted freedom from taxation," referred to by the Court. If history be our guide, then tax exemption of church property in this country is indeed highly suspect, as it arose in the early days when the church was an agency of the state. See W. Torpey, *Judicial Doctrines of Religious Rights in America* 171 (1948). The question here, though, concerns the meaning of the Establishment Clause and the Free Exercise Clause made applicable to the States for only a few decades at best.

With all due respect the governing principle is not controlled by *Everson v. Board of Education* [Chapter Fourteen, section 1]. *Everson* involved the use of public funds to bus children to parochial as well as to public schools. Parochial schools teach religion yet they are also educational institutions offering courses competitive with public schools. They prepare students for the professions and for activities in all walks of life. Education in the secular sense was combined with religious indoctrination at the parochial schools involved in *Everson*. Even so, the *Everson* decision was five to four and, though one of the five, I have since had grave doubts about it, because I have become convinced that grants to institutions teaching a sectarian creed violate the Establishment Clause. See *Engel* (Douglas, J., concurring).

This case, however, is quite different. Education is not involved. The financial support rendered here is to the church, the place of worship. A tax exemption is a subsidy. Is my Brother Brennan correct in saying that we would hold that state or federal grants to churches, say, to construct the edifice itself would be unconstitutional? What is the difference between that kind of subsidy and the present subsidy?....

The religiously used real estate of the churches today constitutes a vast domain. See M. Larson & C. Lowell, *The Churches: Their Riches, Revenues,*

---

1. While I would suppose most churches devote part of their resources to secular community projects and conventional charitable activities, it is a question of fact, a fact that would only be relevant if we had before us a statute framed more narrowly to include only "charities" or a limited class of organizations, and churches. In such a case, depending on the administration of the exemption, it might be that the granting of an exemption to religion would turn out to be improper. This would depend, I believe, on what activities the church in fact sponsored. It would also depend, I think, on whether or to what extent the exemption were accorded to secular social organizations, conceived to benefit their own membership but also engaged in incidental general philanthropic or cultural undertakings.

and Immunities (1969). Their assets total over $141 billion and their annual income at least $22 billion. *Id.*, at 232. And the extent to which they are feeding from the public trough in a variety of forms is alarming. *Id.*, c. 10.

We are advised that since 1968 at least five States have undertaken to give subsidies to parochial and other private schools—Pennsylvania, Ohio, New York, Connecticut, and Rhode Island. And it is reported that under two federal Acts, the Elementary and Secondary Education Act of 1965, 79 Stat. 27, and the Higher Education Act of 1965, 79 Stat. 1219, *billions of dollars* have been granted to parochial and other private schools.

The federal grants to elementary and secondary schools under 79 Stat. 27 were made to the States which in turn made advances to elementary and secondary schools. Those figures are not available.

But the federal grants to private institutions of higher education are revealed in Department of Health, Education, and Welfare (HEW), Digest of Educational Statistics 10 (1969). These show in billions of dollars the following:[15]

1965–66	$1.4
1966–67	$1.6
1967–68	$1.7
1968–69	$1.9
1969–70	$2.1

It is an old, old problem. Madison adverted to it: "Are there not already examples in the U.S. of ecclesiastical wealth equally beyond its object and the foresight of those who laid the foundation of it? In the U.S. there is a double motive for fixing limits in this case, because wealth may increase not only from additional gifts, but from exorbitant advances in the value of the primitive one. In grants of vacant lands, and of lands in the vicinity of growing towns & Cities the increase of value is often such as if foreseen, would essentially controul the liberality confirming them. The people of the U.S. owe their Independence & their liberty, to the wisdom of descrying in the minute tax of 3 pence on tea, the magnitude of evil comprized in the precedent. Let them exert the same wisdom, in watching agst every evil lurking under plausible disguises, and growing up from small beginnings."[17]

---

15. These totals include all types of federal aid—physical plants, dormitory construction, laboratories, libraries, lunch programs, fellowships and scholarships, etc. Of the total federal outlays for education only two-fifths are for programs administered by the Office of Education, other parts of the Department of HEW account for one-fifth. The rest of the outlays are distributed among 24 federal departments and agencies, of which the largest shares are accounted for by the Department of defense, the Veterans Administration, the National Science Foundation, and the Office of Economic Opportunity. U.S. Bureau of the Budget, Special Analysis, Federal Education Program, 1971 Budget, Special Analysis I, pt. 2, p. 115 (Feb. 1970).

17. In 1875 President Grant in his State of the Union Message referred to the vast amounts of untaxed church property: "In 1850, I believe, the church property of the United States which paid no tax, municipal or State, amounted to about $83,000,000. In 1860 the amount had doubled; in 1875 it is

If believers are entitled to public financial support, so are nonbelievers. A believer and nonbeliever under the present law are treated differently because of the articles of their faith. Believers are doubtless comforted that the cause of religion is being fostered by this legislation. Yet one of the mandates of the First Amendment is to promote a viable, pluralistic society and to keep government neutral, not only between sects, but also between believers and nonbelievers. The present involvement of government in religion may seem *de minimis*. But it is, I fear, a long step down the Establishment path. Perhaps I have been misinformed. But as I have read the Constitution and its philosophy, I gathered that independence was the price of liberty.

I conclude that this tax exemption is unconstitutional.

NOTES AND QUESTIONS

1. Several local communities–from Erie, Pennsylvania to Berkeley, California—have recently reconsidered some form of taxation on religious communities. In Colorado an initiative was placed on the ballot to remove the tax-exempt status of religious organizations. Thus far these efforts to tax religious property have been defeated on policy grounds. Are there any sound constitutional considerations that should inform these debates?

2. *Is a tax exemption a "subsidy"?* The majority opinion by Chief Justice Burger stated that "direct money subsidy would be a relationship pregnant with involvement and, as with most governmental grant programs, could encompass sustained and detailed administrative relationships for enforcement of statutory or administrative standards, but that is not this case." Only Justice Douglas, dissenting, was of the view that a tax exemption is a subsidy.

IRC § 501(c)(3) places limits on substantial lobbying by exempt organizations. In *Regan v. Taxation with Representation*, 461 U.S. 540 (1983), the Court, per Justice Rehnquist, sustained these limits. Taxation with Representation [TWR] wanted to use deductible contributions to support its lobbying activities. Justice Rehnquist wrote: "To evaluate TWR's claims, it is necessary to understand the effect of the tax exemption system enacted by Congress. Both tax exemptions and tax-deductibility are a form of *subsidy* that is administered through the tax system. A tax exemption has much the same effect as a *cash grant* to the organization of the amount of tax it would have to pay on its income. Deductible contributions are similar to cash grants of the amount of a portion of the individual's contributions. The system Congress has enacted provides this kind of *subsidy* to non profit civic welfare organizations generally, and an additional *subsidy* to those charitable organizations that do not engage in substantial lobbying. In short, Congress chose not to *subsidize* lobbying as extensively as it chose to *subsidize* other activities that non profit organizations undertake to promote the public welfare." (emphasis added).

In the years between *Walz* and *Taxation with Representation* tax attorneys became accustomed to thinking of an accounting category in federal and state

about $1,000,000,000. By 1900, without check, it is safe to say this property will reach a sum exceeding $3,000,000,000. So vast a sum, receiving all the protection and benefits of Government without bearing its proportion of the burdens and expenses of the same, will not be looked upon acquiescently by those who have to pay the taxes."

budgets that described all forms of wealth not taxed by the government (e.g., personal exemptions, deductions, and credits) as a form of "tax expenditure." *See* Stanley Surrey, *Pathways to Tax Reform: The Concept of Tax Expenditures* (1973). This category may be very useful in attempting to evaluate public policy on housing. One could, for example, calculate the amount of revenue lost to the Treasury as a result of the deduction for interest on mortgages, and compare that total to the cost of all direct expenditures on housing in federal programs administered by the Department of Housing and Urban Development. But how is this device relevant to the exemption of religious organizations from the payment of federal income tax, 26 U.S.C. § 501(c)(3)? Is the government not generally prohibited by the nonestablishment provision from making any direct cash expenditures to churches for religious purposes?

An exemption from the payment of taxation might be better described simply as a privilege or immunity—in this case, an ancient one—whereby the government restrains its taxing power to acknowledge that it should not take *from* the churches any portion of its voluntary contributions precisely because the government cannot contribute direct cash grants *to* the churches for religious purposes. The personal income of church members is, of course, subject to taxation; only the portion of their income that they give away to religious organizations does not qualify under the definition of "income" for tax purposes. *See* Boris I. Bittker, "Churches, Taxes, and the Constitution," 78 Yale L. J.1285 (1969); Boris I. Bittker and George K. Radhert, "The Exemption of Nonprofit Organizations from Federal Income Taxation," 81 Yale L. J. 299 (1976); Dean M. Kelley, "Tax Exemption and the Free Exercise of Religion," in James E. Wood, Jr., *Religion and the State: Essays in Honor of Leo Pfeffer* 323–358 (1985).

In the following cases note the drift toward thinking of every tax benefit as a "subsidy." In *Texas Monthly, Inc. v. Bullock*, 489 U.S. 1 (1989), Justice Brennan described the result in *Mueller v. Allen* [Chapter Fourteen, section 1] as follows: "we upheld a state income tax deduction for the cost of tuition, transportation, and nonreligious textbooks paid by a taxpayer for the benefit of a dependent. To be sure, the deduction aided parochial schools and parents whose children attended them, as well as nonsectarian private schools and their pupils' parents. We did not conclude, however, that this *subsidy* deprived the law of an overriding secular purpose or effect." He described the result in *Walz* [this section above] as according "sizable tax savings [to] religious groups." He analyzed the exemption from sales tax on the distribution of religious literature at issue in *Texas Monthly* as follows: "Every tax exemption constitutes a *subsidy* that affects nonqualifying taxpayers, forcing them to become 'indirect and vicarious donors.' *Bob Jones University v. United States* [Chapter Fourteen, section 3], *Regan v. Taxation with Representation of Wash.* Insofar as that *subsidy* is conferred upon a wide array of nonsectarian groups as well as religious organizations in pursuit of some legitimate secular end, the fact that religious groups benefit incidentally does not deprive the *subsidy* of the secular purpose and primary effect mandated by the Establishment Clause. However, when government directs a *subsidy* exclusively to religious organizations that is not required by the Free Exercise Clause and that either burdens nonbeneficiaries markedly or cannot reasonably be seen as removing a significant state-imposed deterrent to the free exercise of religion, as Texas has done, it 'provide[s] unjustifiable awards of assistance to religious organizations' and cannot but 'conve[y] a message of endorsement' to slighted members of the community. This is particularly true where, as here, the *subsidy* is targeted at writings that promulgate the teachings of religious faiths" (emphasis added).

In *Rosenberger v. Rector and Visitors of the University of Virginia*, 515 U.S. 819 (1995) [Chapter Fourteen, section 3], Justice Thomas wrote in his concurring opinion: "A tax exemption in many cases is economically and functionally indistinguishable from a direct monetary subsidy. In one instance, the government relieves religious entities (along with others) of a generally applicable tax; in the other, it relieves religious entities (along with others) of some or all of the burden of that tax by returning it in the form of a cash subsidy. Whether the benefit is provided at the front or back end of the taxation process, the financial aid to religious groups is undeniable. The analysis under the Establishment Clause must also be the same: 'Few concepts are more deeply embedded in the fabric of our national life, beginning with pre-Revolutionary colonial times, than for the government to exercise at the very least this kind of benevolent neutrality toward churches and religious exercise. . . .' *Walz*." In a footnote Thomas invoked Professor Surrey's concept of "tax expenditure," a concept "based upon recognition of the fact that a government can appropriate money to a particular person or group by using a special, narrowly directed tax deduction or exclusion, instead of by using its ordinary direct spending mechanisms. For example, a government with a general income tax, wanting to add $7,000 to the spendable income of a preacher whose top tax rate is 30%, has two ways of subsidizing him. The government can send the preacher a check for $10,000 and tax him on all of his income, or it can authorize him to reduce his taxable income by $23,333.33 [resulting in a tax saving of $7,000]. If the direct payment were itself taxable and did not alter his tax bracket, the preacher would receive the same benefit from the tax deduction as he would from the direct payment," citing Wolfman, Tax Expenditures: From Idea to Ideology, 99 *Harv. L. Rev.* 491, 491–492 (1985). Thomas acknowledged his tax professor at Yale Law School, Professor Bittker, as "certainly a leading scholar in the tax field," but argued that the dissent's reliance on Bittker is "misplaced in this context. Early criticism of the tax expenditure concept focused on the difficulty of drawing a dividing line between what is or is not a special provision. Professor Boris Bittker, for example, argued that since no tax is all inclusive, exemptions from any tax could not be described as the equivalent of subsidies. Boris I. Bittker, 'Churches, Taxes and the Constitution,' 78 *Yale L. J.* 1285 (1969). This wholesale rejection of tax expenditure analysis was short-lived and attracted few supporters. Rather, the large body of literature about tax expenditures accepts the basic concept that special exemptions from tax function as subsidies. The current debate focuses on whether particular items are correctly identified as tax expenditures and whether incentive provisions are more efficient when structured as tax expenditures rather than direct spending programs."

In the same opinion Justice Thomas refuted Justice Souter's reliance on James Madison's opposition to Patrick Henry's proposal of a tax for the support of a teacher of Christian religion [Chapter Six, section 1A]. Thomas appears to be denying any analytical difference between refraining from collecting a tax and an affirmative exercise of the spending power. Justice Brennan, concurring in *Walz*, drew a distinction between the willingness of both Madison and Jefferson to support *tax exemption* in Virginia on the one hand, and their strong opposition to Henry's proposal to *spend tax dollars* for teachers of religion. Would Thomas be on firmer ground both historically and as a matter of tax theory if reassessed his opinion of Professor Bittker's contribution on this theme?

4.   Double Duty Books

In *Jimmy Swaggart Ministries* [Chapter Eleven, section 1], the Court ruled that it does not violate the free exercise provision to impose sales and use taxes on the distribution of religious literature by an evangelist. The Court also ruled that the extensive regulation of the taxpayer inherent in the most complicated form of all taxes does not constitute a violation of the nonestablishment provision.

Jimmy Swaggart Ministries v. California State Board of Equalization

493 U.S. 378 (1990).

Justice O'Connor delivered the Opinion of the Court [see Chapter Eleven, section 1]

Appellant also contends that application of the sales and use tax to its sale of religious materials violates the Establishment Clause because it fosters " 'an excessive government entanglement with religion,' " *Lemon v. Kurtzman* [Chapter Fourteen, section 1]. Appellant alleges, for example, that the present controversy has featured on-site inspections of appellant's evangelistic crusades, lengthy on-site audits, examinations of appellant's books and records, threats of criminal prosecution, and layers of administrative and judicial proceedings.

The Establishment Clause prohibits "sponsorship, financial support, and active involvement of the sovereign in religious activity." *Walz* [section 3 above]. The "excessive entanglement" prong of the tripartite purpose-effect-entanglement *Lemon* test requires examination of "the character and purposes of the institutions that are benefited, the nature of the aid that the State provides, and the resulting relationship between the government and the religious authority"; see also *Walz* (separate opinion of Harlan, J.) (warning of "programs, whose very nature is apt to entangle the state in details of administration"). Indeed, in *Walz* we held that a tax exemption for "religious organizations for religious properties used solely for religious worship," as part of a general exemption for nonprofit institutions, did not violate the Establishment Clause. In upholding the tax exemption, we specifically noted that taxation of religious properties would cause at least as much administrative entanglement between government and religious authorities as did the exemption: "Either course, taxation of churches or exemption, occasions some degree of involvement with religion. Elimination of exemption would tend to expand the involvement of government by giving rise to tax valuation of church property, tax liens, tax foreclosures, and the direct confrontations and conflicts that follow in the train of these legal processes. Granting tax exemptions to churches necessarily operates to afford an indirect economic benefit and also gives rise to some, but yet a lesser, involvement than taxing them. In analyzing either alternative the questions are whether the involvement is excessive, and whether it is a continuing one calling for official and continuing surveillance leading to an impermissible degree of entanglement." The issue presented, therefore, is whether the imposition of sales and use tax liability in this case on appellant results in "excessive" involvement between appellant and the State and "continuing surveillance leading to an impermissible degree of entanglement."

At the outset, it is undeniable that a generally applicable tax has a secular purpose and neither advances nor inhibits religion, for the very essence of such a tax is that it is neutral and nondiscriminatory on questions of religious belief. Thus, whatever the precise contours of the Establishment Clause, see *County of Allegheny v. American Civil Liberties Union of Pittsburgh*, [section 6 below]; *Bowen v. Kendrick*, [section 7 below], its undisputed core values are not even remotely called into question by the generally applicable tax in this case.

Even applying the "excessive entanglement" prong of the *Lemon* test, however, we hold that California's imposition of sales and use tax liability on appellant threatens no excessive entanglement between church and state. First, we note that the evidence of administrative entanglement in this case is thin. Appellant alleges that collection and payment of the sales and use tax impose severe accounting burdens on it. The Court of Appeal, however, expressly found that the record did not support appellant's factual assertions, noting that appellant "had a sophisticated accounting staff and had recently computerized its accounting and that [appellant] in its own books and for purposes of obtaining a federal income tax exemption segregated 'retail sales' and 'donations.' "

Second, even assuming that the tax imposes substantial administrative burdens on appellant, such administrative and recordkeeping burdens do not rise to a constitutionally significant level. Collection and payment of the tax will of course require some contact between appellant and the State, but we have held that generally applicable administrative and recordkeeping regulations may be imposed on religious organization without running afoul of the Establishment Clause. *See Hernandez* ("[Routine regulatory interaction [such as application of neutral tax laws] which involves no inquiries into religious doctrine, . . . no delegation of state power to a religious body, . . . and no 'detailed monitoring and close administrative contact' between secular and religious bodies, . . . does not of itself violate the nonentanglement command"); *Tony and Susan Alamo Foundation* [Chapter Eleven, section 6] ("The Establishment Clause does not exempt religious organizations from such secular governmental activity as fire inspections and building and zoning regulations, *Lemon,* and the recordkeeping requirements of the Fair Labor Standards Act, while perhaps more burdensome in terms of paperwork, are not significantly more intrusive into religious affairs"). To be sure, we noted in *Tony and Susan Alamo Foundation* that the recordkeeping requirements at issue in that case "applied only to commercial activities undertaken with a 'business purpose,' and would therefore have no impact on petitioners' own evangelical activities," but that recognition did not bear on whether the generally applicable regulation was nevertheless "the kind of government surveillance the Court has previously held to pose an intolerable risk of government entanglement with religion."

The fact that appellant must bear the cost of collecting and remitting a generally applicable sales and use tax—even if the financial burden of such costs may vary from religion to religion—does not enmesh government in religious affairs. Contrary to appellant's contentions, the statutory scheme requires neither the involvement of state employees in, nor on-site continuing inspection of, appellant's day-to-day operations. There is no "official and continuing surveillance," *Walz*, by government auditors. The sorts of government entanglement that we have found to violate the Establishment Clause have been far more invasive than the level of contact created by the administration of neutral tax laws. Cf. *Aguilar v. Felton* [Chapter Fourteen, section 1]; *Larkin v. Grendel's Den* [Chapter Fifteen, section 2]. Most significantly, the imposition of the sales and use tax without an exemption for appellant does not require the State to inquire into the religious content of the items sold or the religious motivation for selling or purchasing the items, because the materials are subject to the tax regardless of content or motive. From the State's point of view, the critical question is not whether the materials are religious, but whether there is a sale or a use, a question which involves only a secular determination. Thus, this case stands on firmer ground than *Hernandez*, because appellant offers the items at a stated price, thereby relieving the State of the need to place a monetary value on appellant's religious items. Compare [the Court's opinion in] *Hernandez* (where no comparable good or service is sold in the marketplace, Internal Revenue Service looks to cost of providing the good or service) with [Justice O'Connor's dissent in *Hernandez*] ("It becomes impossible ... to compute the 'contribution' portion of a payment to charity where what is received in return is not merely an intangible, but an intangible (or, for that matter a tangible) that is not bought and sold except in donative contexts"). Although appellant asserts that donations often accompany payments made for the religious items and that items are sometimes given away without payment (or only nominal payment), it is plain that, in the first case, appellant's use of "order forms" and "price lists" renders illusory any difficulty in separating the two portions and that, in the second case, the question is only whether any particular transfer constitutes a "sale." Ironically, appellant's theory, under which government may not tax "religious core" activities but may tax "nonreligious" activities, would require government to do precisely what appellant asserts the Religion Clauses prohibit: "determine which expenditures are religious and which are secular." *Lemon.*

Accordingly, because we find no excessive entanglement between government and religion in this case, we hold that the imposition of sales and use tax liability on appellant does not violate the Establishment Clause.... *Affirmed.*

NOTES AND QUESTIONS

1. *Governmental Entanglement with Religion.* Is *Jimmy Swaggart Ministries* consistent with *Walz*? The answer to this question turns, in part, on your

assessment of when governmental entanglement in religious matters becomes "excessive." One of the concerns underlying James Madison's Memorial and Remonstrance against Patrick Henry's proposal to fund a teacher of Christian religion was the involvement that government would have with religion [Chapter Six, section 1C]. In *Walz* [this section above] the Court referred to this concern as a way of discerning whether a program has the effect of advancing religion; it sustained tax exemption in part because that would engender less contact between government and religion than a program of tax assessment and foreclosures and the like. A year later in a school funding case, *Lemon v. Kurtzman*, [Chapter Fourteen, section 1], the Court made excessive entanglement a separate criterion for measuring violations of the nonestablishment provision and relied on this standard to invalidate of state financial assistance to religious education. In several cases relying on this test the Court did not require a record of actual entanglement of the government in religious education. For example, in *Aguilar v. Felton* [Chapter Fourteen, section 1] the Court invalidated a federal program in which public school teachers offered remedial reading and mathematics instruction in parochial schools to children of low-income parents. In over twenty years of the operation of this program in New York City, there was no evidence that any government employee had ever succumbed to the religious influence of the school or had altered in any way the instruction of children in reading and mathematics. In a companion case, *Grand Rapids School District v. Ball* [Chapter Fourteen, section 1] no provision was made for detailed monitoring of the sort that led to the finding of excessive entanglement in *Aguilar*. But that did not keep the Court from indulging repeatedly in unsupported speculation about what *may* have been the case: "the challenged public school programs operating in the religious schools *may* impermissibly advance religion . . . [or they] *may* provide a crucial symbolic link between government and religion, thereby enlisting—at least in the eyes of impressionable youngsters—the powers of government to the support of the religious denomination operating the school." Without any evidence that the public school teachers participating in the programs were engaged in religious instruction in any way, the Court added that these teachers "*may* become involved in intentionally or inadvertently inculcating particular religious tenets or beliefs." "Teachers in such an atmosphere *may* well subtly (or overtly) conform their instruction to the environment in which they teach, . . . [and] the pressures of the environment *might* alter his behavior." Thus mere *fear* that an improbable result *might occur* sufficed to invalidate programs under the Establishment Clause. Justice O'Connor became one of the sharpest critics of the test; see, e.g., her dissent in *Grand Rapids*. By contrast, when a claim of excessive entanglement was raised in the context of a free exercise violation in *Swaggart Ministries*, the Court rejected the argument that extensive monitoring of the church constituted "excessive entanglement." Justice O'Connor made light of the entanglement concern by making compliance with state sales and use tax regulations look easy. One of her characteristics as a judge is careful scrutiny of details in records. In this instance, she did not discuss facts in the record critical to a determination of governmental entanglement. For example, there are over 8,000 taxing jurisdictions in the country, with rates that vary depending on the zip code within which the purchaser lives, and even on the amount of the sale. The Court gave the mistaken impression that there is only one rate of sales and use tax in California, when the record disclosed that there were several rates. And the Court even turned the ministry's effort to calculate its tax liability—through weekly lease of a complicated software program at enormous expense—into support for its conclusion that "the evidence of administrative entanglement in this case is thin." If this evidence is thin, why is it that no evidence at all is required by those who want to rely on the entanglement test when the government is not imposing a burden on religion, but is conferring a benefit on society by educating children in a religious school?

The entanglement test remains one of the standards for adjudicating claims but in two recent decisions, *Agostini v. Felton* and *Mitchell v. Helms* [Chapter Fourteen, section 1], the Court recast the entanglement inquiry as simply one criterion relevant to determining a statute's effect. Commentators have criticized the subjective, ad hoc character of this test, which by its very terms is transgressed only if a majority of the court regards a governmental contact with religion to be "excessive." *See* Kenneth Ripple, "The Entanglement Test of the Establishment Clause: A Ten Year Assessment," 27 *U.C.L.A. L. Rev.* 1195 (1980). Judge Ripple concluded that the entanglement test had become "a criterion without an internal discipline" and an "undisciplined judicial methodology." Do you agree?

5. DOUBLE DUTY CHAPLAINS

Marsh v. Chambers

463 U.S. 783 (1983).

Shanler D. Cronk, Assistant Attorney General of Nebraska, argued the cause for petitioners. With him on the briefs was *Paul L. Douglas,* Attorney General.

Herbert J. Friedman argued the cause for respondent. With him on the brief were *Stephen L. Pevar, Burt Neuborne, and Charles S. Sims.*

■ CHIEF JUSTICE BURGER delivered the opinion of the Court.

The question presented is whether the Nebraska Legislature's practice of opening each legislative day with a prayer by a chaplain paid by the State violates the Establishment Clause of the First Amendment.

I

The Nebraska Legislature begins each of its sessions with a prayer offered by a chaplain who is chosen biennially by the Executive Board of the Legislative Council and paid out of public funds.[1] Robert E. Palmer, a Presbyterian minister, has served as chaplain since 1965 at a salary of $319.75 per month for each month the legislature is in session.

---

1. Rules of the Nebraska Unicameral, Rules 1, 2, and 21. These prayers are recorded in the Legislative Journal and, upon the vote of the legislature, collected from time to time into prayerbooks, which are published at public expense. In 1975, 200 copies were printed; prayerbooks were also published in 1978 (200 copies), and in 1979 (100 copies). In total, publication costs amounted to $458.56.

Ernest Chambers is a member of the Nebraska Legislature and a taxpayer of Nebraska. Claiming that the Nebraska Legislature's chaplaincy practice violates the Establishment Clause of the First Amendment, he brought this action under 42 U.S.C. § 1983, seeking to enjoin enforcement of the practice.[2] After denying a motion to dismiss on the ground of legislative immunity, the District Court held that the Establishment Clause was not breached by the prayers, but was violated by paying the chaplain from public funds. It therefore enjoined the legislature from using public funds to pay the chaplain; it declined to enjoin the policy of beginning sessions with prayers. Cross-appeals were taken.[3]

The Court of Appeals for the Eighth Circuit rejected arguments that the case should be dismissed on Tenth Amendment, legislative immunity, standing, or federalism grounds. On the merits of the chaplaincy issue, the court refused to treat respondent's challenges as separable issues as the District Court had done. Instead, the Court of Appeals assessed the practice as a whole because "[p]arsing out [the] elements" would lead to "an incongruous result."

Applying the three-part test of *Lemon* [Chapter Fourteen, section 1], the court held that the chaplaincy practice violated all three elements of the test: the purpose and primary effect of selecting the same minister for 16 years and publishing his prayers was to promote a particular religious expression; use of state money for compensation and publication led to entanglement. Accordingly, the Court of Appeals modified the District Court's injunction and prohibited the State from engaging in any aspect of its established chaplaincy practice.

We granted certiorari limited to the challenge to the practice of opening sessions with prayers by a state-employed clergyman, and we reverse.

II

The opening of sessions of legislative and other deliberative public bodies with prayer is deeply embedded in the history and tradition of this country. From colonial times through the founding of the Republic and ever since, the practice of legislative prayer has coexisted with the principles of disestablishment and religious freedom. In the very courtrooms in which the United States District Judge and later three Circuit Judges heard and decided this case, the proceedings opened with an announcement that concluded, "God save the United States and this Honorable Court." The same invocation occurs at all sessions of this Court.

2. Respondent named as defendants State Treasurer Frank Marsh, Chaplain Palmer, and the members of the Executive Board of the Legislative Council in their official capacity. All appear as petitioners before us.

3. The District Court also enjoined the State from using public funds to publish the prayers holding that this practice violated the Establishment Clause. Petitioners have represented to us that they did not challenge this facet of the District Court's decision, Tr. of Oral Arg. 19–20. Accordingly, no issue as to publishing these prayers is before us.

The tradition in many of the Colonies was, of course, linked to an established church,[5] but the Continental Congress, beginning in 1774, adopted the traditional procedure of opening its sessions with a prayer offered by a paid chaplain. Although prayers were not offered during the Constitutional Convention,[6] the First Congress, as one of its early items of business, adopted the policy of selecting a chaplain to open each session with prayer. Thus, on April 7, 1789, the Senate appointed a committee "to take under consideration the manner of electing Chaplains." S. Jour., 1st Cong., 1st Sess., 10 (1820 ed.). On April 9, 1789, a similar committee was appointed by the House of Representatives. On April 25, 1789, the Senate elected its first chaplain, *id.,* at 16; the House followed suit on May 1, 1789, H. R. Jour., 1st Cong., 1st Sess., 26 (1826 ed.). A statute providing for the payment of these chaplains was enacted into law on September 22, 1789.[7] 2 Annals of Cong. 2180 § 4, 1 Stat. 71.[8]

On September 25, 1789, three days after Congress authorized the appointment of paid chaplains, final agreement was reached on the language of the Bill of Rights, S.Jour. at 88; H. R. Jour. at 121.[9] Clearly the men who wrote the First Amendment Religion Clause did not view paid legislative chaplains and opening prayers as a violation of that Amendment,

5. The practice in Colonies with established churches is, of course, not dispositive of the legislative prayer question. The history of Virginia is instructive, however, because that Colony took the lead in defining religious rights. In 1776, the Virginia Convention adopted a Declaration of Rights that included, as Article 16, a guarantee of religious liberty that is considered the precursor of both the Free Exercise and Establishment Clauses. 1 B. Schwartz, *The Bill of Rights: A Documentary History* 231–236 (1971); S. Cobb, *The Rise of Religious Liberty in America* 491–492 (1970). Virginia was also among the first to disestablish its church. Both before and after disestablishment, however, Virginia followed the practice of opening legislative sessions with prayer. See, *e.g.,* J. House of Burgesses 34 (Nov. 20, 1712); Debates of the Convention of Virginia 470 (June 2, 1788) (ratification convention); J. House of Delegates of Va. 3 (June 24, 1788) (state legislature). Rhode Island's experience mirrored that of Virginia. That Colony was founded by Roger Williams, who was among the first of his era to espouse the principle of religious freedom. Cobb, *supra,* at 426. As early as 1641, its legislature provided for liberty of conscience. *Id.,* at 430. Yet the sessions of its ratification convention, like Virginia's, began with prayers, see W. Staples, *Rhode Island in the Continental Congress, 1765–1790,* p. 668 (1870) (reprinting May 26, 1790, minutes of the convention).

6. History suggests that this may simply have been an oversight. At one point, Benjamin Franklin suggested that "henceforth prayers imploring the assistance of Heaven, and its blessings on our deliberations, be held in this Assembly every morning before we proceed to business." His proposal was rejected not because the Convention was opposed to prayer, but because it was thought that a midstream adoption of the policy would highlight prior omissions and because "[t]he Convention had no funds."

7. The statute provided: "[T]here shall be allowed to each chaplain of Congress ... five hundred dollars per annum during the session of Congress." This salary compares favorably with the Congressmen's own salaries of $6 for each day of attendance, 1 Stat. 70–71.

8. It bears note that James Madison, one of the principal advocates of religious freedom in the Colonies and a drafter of the Establishment Clause, was one of those appointed to undertake this task by the House of Representatives, H.R.Jour., at 11–12; and voted for the bill authorizing payment of the chaplains, 1 Annals of Cong. 891 (1789).

9. Interestingly, September 25, 1789, was also the day that the House resolved to request the President to set aside a Thanksgiving Day to acknowledge "the many signal favors of Almighty God," H.R.Jour., at 123. See also S.Jour., at 88.

for the practice of opening sessions with prayer has continued without interruption ever since that early session of Congress.[10] It has also been followed consistently in most of the states,[11] including Nebraska, where the institution of opening legislative sessions with prayer was adopted even before the State attained statehood. Neb. Jour. of Council, General Assembly, 1st Sess., 16 (Jan. 22, 1855).

Standing alone, historical patterns cannot justify contemporary violations of constitutional guarantees, but there is far more here than simply historical patterns. In this context, historical evidence sheds light not only on what the draftsmen intended the Establishment Clause to mean, but also on how they thought that Clause applied to the practice authorized by the First Congress-their actions reveal their intent. An Act "passed by the first Congress assembled under the Constitution, many of whose members had taken part in framing that instrument, ... is contemporaneous and weighty evidence of its true meaning." *Wisconsin v. Pelican Ins. Co.,* 127 U.S. 265, 297 (1888)....

In light of the unambiguous and unbroken history of more than 200 years, there can be no doubt that the practice of opening legislative sessions with prayer has become part of the fabric of our society. To invoke Divine guidance on a public body entrusted with making the laws is not, in these

10. The chaplaincy was challenged in the 1850's by "sundry petitions praying Congress to abolish the office of chaplain," S.Rep. No. 376, 32d Cong., 2d Sess., 1 (1853). After consideration by the Senate Committee on the Judiciary, the Senate decided that the practice did not violate the Establishment Clause, reasoning that a rule permitting Congress to elect chaplains is not a law establishing a national church and that the chaplaincy was no different from Sunday Closing Laws, which the Senate thought clearly constitutional. In addition, the Senate reasoned that since prayer was said by the very Congress that adopted the Bill of Rights, the Founding Fathers could not have intended the First Amendment to forbid legislative prayer or viewed prayer as a step toward an established church. *Id.,* at 2–4. In any event, the 35th Congress abandoned the practice of electing chaplains in favor of inviting local clergy to officiate, see Cong. Globe, 35th Cong., 1st Sess., 14, 27–28 (1857). Elected chaplains were reinstituted by the 36th Congress, Cong. Globe, 36th Cong., 1st Sess., 162 (1859) *id.,* at 1016 (1860).

11. See Brief for National Conference of State Legislatures as *Amicus Curiae.* Although most state legislatures begin their sessions with prayer, most do not have a formal rule requiring this procedure. But see, *e.g.* Alaska Legislature Uniform Rules 11 and

17 (1981) (providing for opening invocation); Ark. Rule of Senate 18 (1983); Colo. Legislator's Handbook, H.R. Rule 44 (1982); Idaho Rules of H.R. and Joint Rules 2 and 4 (1982); Ind. H.R. Rule 10 (1983); Kan. Rule of Senate 4 (1983); Kan. Rule of H.R. 103 (1983); Ky. General Assembly H. Res. 2 (1982); La. Rules of Order, Senate Rule 10.1. (1983); La. Rules of Order, H.R. Rule 8.1 (1982); Me. Senate and House Register, Rule of H.R. 4 (1983); Md. Senate and House of Delegates Rules 1 (1982 and 1983); Mo. Rules of Legislature, Joint Rule 1–1 (1983); N.H. Manual for the General Court of N.H., Rule of H.R. 52(a) (1981); N.D. Senate and H.R. Rules 101 and 301 (1983); Ore. Rule of Senate 4.01 (1983); Ore. Rule of H.R. 4.01 (1983) (opening session only); 104 Pa. Code § 11.11 (1983), 107 Pa. Code § 21.17 (1983); S.D. Official Directory and Rules of Senate and H.R., Joint Rule of the Senate and House 4–1 (1983); Tenn. Permanent Rules of Order of the Senate 1 and 6 (1981–1982) (provides for admission into Senate chamber of the "Chaplain of the Day"); Tex. Rule of H.R. 2, § 6 (1983); Utah Rules of Senate and H.R. 4.04 (1983); Va. Manual of Senate and House of Delegates, Rule of Senate 21(a) (1982) (session opens with "period of devotions"); Wash. Permanent Rule of H.R. 15 (1983); Wyo. Rule of Senate 4–1 (1983); Wyo. Rule of H.R. 2–1 (1983). See also P. Mason, Manual of Legislative Procedure § 586(2) (1979).

circumstances, an "establishment" of religion or a step toward establishment; it is simply a tolerable acknowledgment of beliefs widely held among the people of this country. As Justice Douglas observed, "[we are a religious people whose institutions presuppose a Supreme Being." *Zorach v. Clauson* [Chapter Fourteen, section 2]. . . .

Nor is the compensation of the chaplain from public funds a reason to invalidate the Nebraska Legislature's chaplaincy; remuneration is grounded in historic practice initiated ... by the same Congress that drafted the Establishment Clause of the First Amendment. The Continental Congress paid its chaplain, see, *e.g.*, 6 J. Continental Cong. 887 (1776), as did some of the states, see, *e.g.*, Debates of the Convention of Virginia 470 (June 26, 1788). Currently, many state legislatures and the United States Congress provide compensation for their chaplains, Brief for National Conference of State Legislatures as *Amicus Curiae* 3; 2 U.S.C. §§ 61d and 84–2; H. R. Res. 7, 96th Cong., 1st Sess. (1979).[18] Nebraska has paid its chaplain for well over a century, see 1867 Neb. Laws 85, § § 2–4 (June 21, 1867), reprinted in Neb. Gen. Stat. 459 (1873). The content of the prayer is not of concern to judges where, as here, there is no indication that the prayer opportunity has been exploited to proselytize or advance any one, or to disparage any other, faith or belief. That being so, it is not for us to embark on a sensitive evaluation or to parse the content of a particular prayer. *Reversed.*

■ Justice Brennan, with whom Justice Marshall joins, dissenting.

That the "purpose" of legislative prayer is preeminently religious rather than secular seems to me to be self-evident. "To invoke Divine guidance on a public body entrusted with making the laws," is nothing but a religious act. Moreover, whatever secular functions legislative prayer might play-formally opening the legislative session, getting the members of the body to quiet down, and imbuing them with a sense of seriousness and high purpose-could so plainly be performed in a purely nonreligious fashion that to claim a secular purpose for the prayer is an insult to the perfectly honorable individuals who instituted and continue the practice. . . .

More fundamentally, however, any practice of legislative prayer, even if it might look "nonsectarian" to nine Justices of the Supreme Court, will inevitably and continuously involve the State in one or another religious debate.[39] Prayer is serious business—serious theological business—and it is

18. The states' practices differ widely. Like Nebraska, several states choose a chaplain who serves for the entire legislative session. In other states, the prayer is offered by a different clergyman each day. Under either system, some states pay their chaplains and others do not. For States providing for compensation statutorily or by resolution, see, *e.g.*, Cal. Gov't Code Ann. §§ 9170, 9171, 9320 (West 1980), and S. Res. No. 6, 1983–1984 Sess.; Colo. H.R. J., 54th Gen. Assembly, 1st Sess., 17–19 (Jan. 5, 1983); Conn. Gen. Stat. Ann. § 2–9 (1983–1984); Ga. H.R.

Res. No. 3, § 1(c) (1983); Iowa Code § 2.11 (1983); Mo. Rev. Stat. § 21.150 (1978); Nev. Rev. Stat. § 218.200 (1981); N.J. Stat. Ann. § 52:11–2 (West 1970); N.M. Const., Art. IV, § 9; Okla. Stat. Ann., Tit. 74, §§ 291.12 and 292.1 (West Supp. 1982–1983); Vt. Stat. Ann., Tit. 2, § 19 (Supp. 1982); Wis. Stat. Ann. § 13.125 (West Supp. 1982).

39. See generally Cahn, "On Government and Prayer," 37 N. Y. U. L. Rev. 981 (1962); Hearings, ["Prayer in Public Schools and Buildings–Federal Court Jurisdiction, not a mere "acknowledgment of beliefs widely held among the people of this country" for the State to immerse itself in that business.[40] Some religious individuals or groups find it theologically problematic to engage in joint religious exercises predominantly influenced by faiths not their own.[41] Some might object even to the attempt to fashion a "nonsectarian" prayer.[42] Some would find it impossible to participate in any "prayer opportunity," marked by Trinitarian references.[43] Some would find a prayer *not* invoking the name of Christ to represent a flawed view of the relationship between human beings and God.[44] Some might find any petitionary prayer to be improper.[45] Some might find any prayer that lacked a petitionary element to be deficient.[46] Some might be troubled by what they consider shallow public prayer,[47] or nonspontaneous prayer,[48] or

Hearings before the Subcommittee on Courts, Civil Liberties, and the Administration of Justice of the House Committee on the Judiciary," 96th Cong., 2d Sess., 46–47 (1980) (testimony of M. William Howard, President of the National Council of the Churches of Christ in the U.S.A.) (hereinafter Hearings)] ("there is simply no such thing as 'nonsectarian' prayer ... "). Cf. N.Y. Times, Sept. 4, 1982, p. 8, col. 2 ("Mr. [Jerry] Falwell [founder of the organization 'Moral Majority']) is quoted as telling a meeting of the Religious Newswriters Association in New Orleans that because members of the Moral Majority represented a variety of denominations, 'if we ever opened a Moral Majority meeting with prayer, silent or otherwise, we would disintegrate' ").

40. I put to one side, not because of its irrelevance, but because of its obviousness, the fact that any official prayer will pose difficulties both for nonreligious persons and for religious persons whose faith does not include the institution of prayer, see, *e.g.*, H. Smith, *The Religions of Man* 138 (Perennial Library ed. 1965) (discussing Theravada Buddhism).

41. See, *e.g.*, Hearings 46–47 (testimony of M. Howard) ("We are told that [school] prayers could be 'nonsectarian,' or that they could be offered from various religious traditions in rotation. I believe such a solution is least acceptable to those most fervently devoted to their own religion"); S. Freehof, *Modern Reform Responsa* 71 (1971) (ecumenical services not objectionable in principle, but they should not take place too frequently); J. Bancroft, *Communication in Religious Worship with Non–Catholics* (1943).

42. See, *e.g.*, Hearings, at 47 (testimony of M. Howard) (nonsectarian prayer, even if

were possible, would likely be "offensive to devout members of all religions").

43. See, *e.g.*, S. Freehof, *Reform Responsa* 115 (1960).

44. See *e.g.*, D. Bloesch, *The Struggle of Prayer* 36–37 (1980) (hereinafter Bloesch) ("Because our Savior plays such a crucial role in the life of prayer, we should always pray having in mind his salvation and intercession. We should pray not only in the spirit of Christ but also in the name of Christ.... To pray in his name means that we recognize that our prayers cannot penetrate the tribunal of God unless they are presented to the Father by the Son, our one Savior and Redeemer"); cf. Fischer, "The Role of Christ in Christian Prayer," 41 *Encounter* 153, 155–156 (1980). As the Court points out, Reverend Palmer eliminated the Christological references in his prayers after receiving complaints from some of the State Senators. Suppose, however, that Reverend Palmer had said that he could not in good conscience omit some references. Should he have been dismissed? And, if so, what would have been the implications of *that* action under both the Establishment and the Free Exercise Clauses?

45. See, *e.g.*, *Meister Eckhart* 88–89 (R. Blakney Trans. 1941); Thomas Merton, *Contemplative Prayer* (1971); J. Williams, *What Americans Believe and How they Worship* 412–413 (3d ed. 1969) (hereinafter Williams) (discussing Christian Science belief that only proper prayer is prayer of communion).

46. See, *e.g.*, Bloesch 72–73; Stump, "Petitionary Prayer," 16 Am. Philosophical Q. 81 (1979); Wells, "Prayer: Rebelling Against the Status Quo," *Christianity Today*, Nov. 2, 1979, pp. 32–34.

47. See, *e.g.*, Matthew 6:6 ("But thou, when thou prayest, enter into thy closet, and prayer without adequate spiritual preparation or concentration.[49] Some might, of course, have *theological* objections to any prayer sponsored by an organ of government.[50] Some might object on theological grounds to the level of political neutrality generally expected of government-sponsored invocational prayer.[51] And some might object on theological grounds to the Court's requirement that prayer, even though religious, not be proselytizing.[52] If these problems arose in the context of a religious objection to some otherwise decidedly secular activity, then whatever remedy there is would have to be found in the Free Exercise Clause. But, in this case, we are faced with potential religious objections to an activity at the very center of religious life, and it is simply beyond the competence of government, and inconsistent with our conceptions of liberty, for the State to take upon itself the role of ecclesiastical arbiter.

IV

The argument is made occasionally that a strict separation of religion and state robs the Nation of its spiritual identity. I believe quite the contrary. It may be true that individuals cannot be "neutral" on the question of religion.[53] But the judgment of the Establishment Clause is that neutrality by the organs of *government* on questions of religion is both possible and imperative. Alexis de Tocqueville wrote the following concerning his travels through this land in the early 1830's:

"The religious atmosphere of the country was the first thing that struck me on arrival in the United States....

In France I had seen the spirits of religion and of freedom almost always marching in opposite directions. In America I found them intimately linked together in joint reign over the same land.

My longing to understand the reason for this phenomenon increased daily.

To find this out, I questioned the faithful of all communions; I particularly sought the society of clergymen, who are the depositaries of the various creeds and have a personal interest in their survival.... I expressed my astonishment and revealed my doubts to each of them; I found that they all agreed with each other except about details; all thought that the main reason for the quiet sway of religion over their country was the complete separation of church and state. I have no hesitation in stating

when thou hast shut thy door, pray to thy Father which is in secret; and thy Father which seeth in secret shall reward thee openly").

48. See *e.g.*, Williams 274–275 (discussing traditional Quaker practice).

49. See *e.g.*, Heschel, *Man's Quest for God* (1954) at 53; Heiler, *supra* n. 24, at 283–285.

50. See, *e.g.*, Williams 256; 3 Stokes 133–134; Hearings, at 65–66 (statement of Baptist Joint Committee on Public Affairs).

51. See, *e.g.*, Reinhold Niebuhr, *Faith and Politics* 100 (R. Stone ed. 1968) ("A genuinely prophetic religion speaks a word of judgment against every ruler and every nation, even against good rulers and good nations").

52. See, *e.g.*, Bloesch 159 ("World evangelization is to be numbered among the primary goals in prayer, since the proclaiming of the gospel is what gives glory to God").

53. See William James, *The Will to Believe* 1–31 (1st ed. 1897).

that throughout my stay in America I met nobody, lay or cleric, who did not agree about that." *Democracy in America* 295 (G. Lawrence trans., J. Mayer ed., 1969) [Chapter Seven, section 7].

More recent history has only confirmed de Tocqueville's observations. If the Court had struck down legislative prayer today, it would likely have stimulated a furious reaction. But it would also, I am convinced, have invigorated both the "spirit of religion" and the "spirit of freedom."

I respectfully dissent.

■ JUSTICE STEVENS also dissented.

NOTES AND QUESTIONS

1. *Military Chaplains.* West Point, Annapolis, and Colorado Springs all had regulations requiring cadets and midshipmen at the respective service academies to attend weekly Protestant, Catholic, or Jewish chapel services. Conscientious objectors were excused. In a class action on behalf of all the students, the regulations were held to violate the establishment clause. The government's claim was that "the sole purpose of chapel attendance is to develop in the cadets, through observation of the impact of religion on the lives of others during actual worship services, that sensitivity to religious emotion which is required of a military leader." The Court of Appeals doubted that the purpose was "wholly secular," finding in the regulations "an outright encouragement of religious worship," *Anderson v. Laird,* 466 F. 2d 283 (D.C. Cir. 1972) (2–1 decision), *cert. denied,* 409 U.S. 1076 (1972).

The premises of *Anderson* were taken further in a suit brought by two students at the Harvard Law School who sought declaratory and injunctive relief against continuation of the Army's chaplaincy program as violative of the nonestablishment provision. District Judge Joseph M. McLaughlin, granted summary judgment for the government and dismissed their complaint. 582 F.Supp. 463 (E.D.N.Y. 1984). The Court of Appeals relied on a mix of historical and pragmatic arguments.

Katcoff v. Marsh

755 F. 2d. 223 (2nd Cir. 1985).

■ MANSFIELD, CIRCUIT JUDGE.

We affirm except to the extent that the order applies to a few specific aspects of the program, which we reverse and remand for further proceedings.

Congress, in the exercise of its powers under Art. I § 8, of the Constitution to provide for the conduct of our national defense, has established an Army for the purpose of "preserving the peace and security, and providing for the defense, of the United States," 10 U.S.C. § 3062(a), and has directed that the "organized peace establishment of the Army" consist of all organizations and persons "necessary to form the basis for a complete and immediate mobilization for the national defense in the event of a national emergency," 10 U.S.C. § 3062(d). It has specifically authorized that as part of this establishment there be "Chaplains in the Army," who shall include the Chief of Chaplains, and commissioned and other officers of the Army appointed as chaplains. 10 U.S.C. § 3073. Under 10 U.S.C § 3547 each chaplain is required, when practicable, to hold religious services for the command to which he is assigned and to perform burial services for soldiers who die while in that command. The statute also obligates the commanding officer to furnish facilities, including transportation, to assist a chaplain in performing his duties.

In providing our armed forces with a military chaplaincy Congress has perpetuated a facility that began during Revolutionary days before the adoption of our Constitution, and that has continued ever since then, with the size of the chaplaincy growing larger in proportion to the increase in the size of our Army. When the Continental Army was formed those chaplains attached to the militia of the 13 colonies became part of our country's first national army. P. Thompson, 1 *The United States Army Chaplaincy*, xix (1978). On July 29, 1775, the Continental Congress authorized that a Continental Army chaplain be paid, II Cont.Cong.Jour. 220 (1775), and within a year General George Washington directed that regimental Continental Army chaplains be procured. V *The Writings of George Washington From The Original Manuscript Sources* 244–45 (J. Fitzgerald ed. 1932).

Upon the adoption of the Constitution and before the December 1791 ratification of the First Amendment Congress authorized the appointment of a commissioned Army chaplain. Act of March 3, 1791, Ch. XXVIII, § 5,1 Stat. 222. Since then, as the Army has increased in size the military chaplaincy has been extended and Congress has increased the number of Army chaplains. *See, e.g.,* Act of April 12, 1808, 2 Stat. 481; Act of January 11, 1812, 2 Stat. 671; Act of July 5, 1838, Ch. CLXII, § 18, 5 Stat. 259; Act of February 11, 1847, Ch. VIII, § 7,9 Stat. 124; Act of February 11, 1847, 9 Stat. 123; Act of July 22, 1861, Ch. IX, § 9, 12 Stat. 270.

In 1981 the Army had approximately 1,427 active-duty commissioned chaplains, 10 auxiliary chaplains, 1,383 chaplain's assistants, and 48 Directors of Religious Education. These chaplains are appointed as commissioned officers with rank and uniform but without command. 10 U.S.C. §§ 3293, 3581. Before an applicant may be appointed to the position of chaplain he must receive endorsement from an ecclesiastical endorsing agency recognized by the Armed Forces Chaplains Board, of which there are 47 in the United States, representing 120 denominations. In addition to meeting the theological standards of the endorsing agency the applicant must also meet minimum educational requirements established by the Department of Defense, which are more stringent than those of some religious denominations having endorsing agencies and are designed to insure the applicant's ability to communicate with soldiers of all ranks and to administer religious programs. In deciding upon the denominations of chaplains to be appointed the Office of the Chief of Chaplains establishes quotas based on the denominational distribution of the population of the United States as a whole. The entire civilian church population rather than the current military religious population is used in order to assure that in the event of war or total mobilization the denominational breakdown will accurately reflect that of the larger-sized Army.

Upon his appointment the chaplain, except for a number of civilian clerics provided voluntarily or by contract, is subject to the same discipline and training as that given to other officers and soldiers. He is trained in such subjects as Army organization, command relationships, supply, planning, teaching, map-reading, types of warfare, security, battlefield survival, and military administration. When ordered with troops into area, including a combat zone under fire, he must obey. He must be prepared to meet problems inherent in Army life, including how to handle trauma, death or serious injury of soldiers on the field of battle, marital and family stresses of military personnel, tending the wounded or dying, and psychological treatment of soldiers' drug or alcohol abuse as well as the alleviation of tensions between soldiers and their commanders. On the other hand, the chaplain is not required to bear arms or receive training in weapons. Under Articles 33 and 35 of the Geneva Conventions Relative to Treatment of Prisoners of War "chaplains" are accorded a non-combatant status, which means that they are not to be considered prisoners of war and they may exercise their ministry among prisoners of war. Promotion of a chaplain within the military ranks is based solely on his military performance and not on his effectiveness as a cleric.

The primary function of the military chaplain is to engage in activities designed to meet the religious needs of a pluralistic military community, including military personnel and their dependents. In view of the Army's huge size (some 788,000 soldiers and 1,300,000 dependents in 1981) and its far-flung distribution (291,000 soldiers stationed abroad and many in remote areas of the United States) the task is an important and formidable one. The Army consists of a wide spectrum of persons of different ethnic, racial and religious backgrounds who go into military service from varied social, economic and educational environments. The great majority of the soldiers in the Army express religious preferences. About 80% are under 30 years of age and a large number are married. As a result it has become necessary to provide religious facilities for soldiers of some 86 different denominations (footnote showing distribution of Army chaplains by denominations omitted). A sample survey of military personnel made by the Army in 1979 revealed the following religious preferences among enlisted personnel:

Protestant	38.5%
Catholic	22.5%
Mormon	2.5%
Eastern Orthodox	0.5%
Moslem	1.0%
Jewish	0.7%
Buddhist	0.7%
Other religions not listed	19.3%
No religious preference	14.3%

Aside from the problems arising out of the sheer size and pluralistic nature of the Army, its members experience increased needs for religion as the result of being uprooted from their home environments, transported often thousands of miles to territories entirely strange to them, and confronted there with new stresses that would not otherwise have been encountered if they had remained at home. In 1981 approximately 37% of the Army's active duty soldiers, amounting to 293,000 persons, were stationed overseas in locations such as Turkey, Sinai, Greece, or Korea. In most of these areas the Judeo–Christian faiths of most American soldiers are hardly represented at all by local clergy and the average soldier is separated from the local populace by a linguistic and cultural wall. Within the United States the same problem exists in a somewhat different way in that, although the linguistic or cultural barrier may be absent, local civilian clergy in the rural areas where most military camps are centered are inadequate to satisfy the soldiers' religious needs because they are too few in number for the task and are usually of different religious denominations from those of most of the nearby troops.

The problem of meeting the religious needs of Army personnel is compounded by the mobile, deployable nature of our armed forces, who must be ready on extremely short notice to be transported from bases (whether or not in the United States) to distant parts of the world for combat duty in fulfillment of our nation's international defense commitments. Unless there were chaplains ready to move simultaneously with the troops and to tend to their spiritual needs as they face possible death, the soldiers would be left in the lurch, religiously speaking. In the opinion of top generals of the Army and those presently in the chaplaincy, unless chaplains were made available in such circumstances the motivation, morale and willingness of soldiers to face combat would suffer immeasurable harm and our national defense would be weakened accordingly.

Many soldiers in the Army also suffer serious stresses from other causes attributable largely to their military service, which can be alleviated by counseling and spiritual assistance from a leader of their respective faiths. Among these are tensions created by separation from their homes, loneliness when on duty in strange surroundings involving people whose language or customs they do not share, fear of facing combat or new assignments, financial hardships, personality conflicts, and drug, alcohol or family problems. The soldier faced with any of these problems at home would usually be able to consult his spiritual adviser. The Army seeks to furnish the same services through military chaplains. In doing so the Army has proceeded on the premise that having uprooted the soldiers from their natural habitats it owes them a duty to satisfy their Free Exercise rights, especially since the failure to do so would diminish morale, thereby weakening our national defense.

To meet the religious needs of our armed forces Army chaplains and their assistants engage in a wide variety of services to military personnel and their families who wish to use them. No chaplain is authorized to proselytize soldiers or their families. The chaplain's principal duties are to conduct religious services (including periodic worship, baptisms, marriages, funerals and the like), to furnish religious education to soldiers and their families, and to counsel soldiers with respect to a wide variety of personal problems. In addition the chaplain, because of his close relationship with the soldiers in his unit, often serves as a liaison between the soldiers and their commanders, advising the latter of racial unrest, drug or alcohol abuse, and other problems affecting the morale and efficiency of the unit, and helps to find solutions. In some areas the Army also makes available religious retreats, in which soldiers voluntarily withdraw for a short period from the routine activities of daily living to another location for spiritual reflection and renewal.

For this comprehensive religious program involving hundreds of thousands of soldiers and their families, the Army has a large and fairly elaborate administrative organization, including not only the chaplains but also supporting personnel, facilities, publications, and other supplies. The Chief of Chaplains, a major general of the Army, is in general supervision and management of the Army's chaplaincy. His office contains three divisions: (1) Administration and Management, which, among other things, maintains liaison with religious and secular organizations, (2) Plans, Programs and Policies, and (3) Personnel and Ecclesiastical Relations. These divisions work closely with the Department of Defense Armed Forces Chaplains Board. Over the years the Army has built or acquired more than 500 chapels which are used for the conduct of religious services of many different denominations. In addition it has built more than 100 Religious Educational Facilities, which are used for religious services and classes in religious education for soldiers and members of their families of all ages (including children). The Army has purchased and made available for voluntary use by various denominations numerous chaplain's kits, vocational kits, communion sets and vestments, and religious publications (including Holy Scriptures and Prayer Books for Jewish Personnel, the New Testament of our Lord and Savior Jesus Christ, and a Book of Worship), and has developed a Cooperative Curriculum for Religious Education of the Armed Forces. Professional education and training has also been furnished to Army chaplains.

In view of the huge task faced in providing religion to our armed forces the Army has, in addition to chaplains, employed civilians to assist them in carrying out the program. These include Directors of Religious Education, assistants to chaplains, organists, voluntary religious teachers who participate in its voluntary religious education program, a small number of "auxiliary chaplains" and civilian or "contract clergy" who are employed to perform denominational services for the military community when military and operational requirements permit and chaplains for such denominations or religions are unavailable on the military installation.

The great majority of the chaplaincy's services, facilities, and supplies are procured by the Army through funds appropriated by Congress, which amounted to over $85 million for the fiscal year 1981, of which more than $62 million was used to pay the salaries and other compensation of chaplains, chaplain's assistants and auxiliary chaplains. Much smaller amounts were paid for the services of contract chaplains ($332,000), directors of religious education ($221,000), and organists and choir directors ($412,000). Some $7.7 million of non-appropriated funds, representing voluntary contributions or designated offerings from soldiers and their dependents, were also used in the fiscal year 1981 to provide for the needs of the Army's chaplaincy program. Generally speaking, non-appropriated funds are used for denominational activities such as the purchase of sacred items and literature and the salaries of organists and the choir directors.

[The plaintiffs conceded that "some chaplaincy" was essential and proposed a civilian system that the court found so inherently impractical as to border on the frivolous. The court concluded:]

Lastly, even if plaintiffs' proposal were feasible it would, assuming the *Lemon* standard advanced by the plaintiffs were held applicable, violate the Establishment Clause. The Army, financed by Congress, would to at least some extent still be commanding the civilian chaplains and supporting them with taxpayer-provided "logistical support, coordination and training in military affairs" (Appellants' Reply Br. 18), including transport, food and facilities.

We find that the more appropriate standard of relevancy to our national defense and reasonable necessity is met by the great majority of the Army's existing chaplaincy activities. The purpose and effect of the program is to make religion, religious education, counseling and religious facilities available to military personnel and their families under circumstances where the practice of religion would otherwise be denied as a practical matter to all or a substantial number. As a result, the morale of our soldiers, their willingness to serve, and the efficiency of the Army as an instrument for our national defense rests in substantial part on the military chaplaincy, which is vital to our Army's functioning.

In a few areas, however, the reasonable necessity for certain activities of the military chaplaincy is not readily apparent. For instance, it appears that in some large urban centers, such as at the Pentagon in Washington, D.C., in New York City and San Francisco, government funds may be used to provide military chaplains, facilities and retreats to "armchair" military personnel who, like other government civil servants, commute daily to their homes and spend their free hours (including weekends) in locations where civilian clergy and facilities are just as available to them as to other non-military citizens. Plaintiffs also assert that government-financed Army chaplains and facilities are provided to retired military personnel and their families. If the ability of such personnel to worship in their own communities is not inhibited by their military service and funds for these chaplains and facilities would not otherwise be expended, the justification for a governmental program of religious support for them is questionable and, notwithstanding our deference to Congress in military matters, requires a showing that they are relevant to and reasonably necessary for the conduct of our national defense by the Army. A remand therefore becomes necessary to determine whether, according to the standard we have outlined, government financing of a military chaplaincy in these limited areas for the purposes indicated is constitutionally permissible.

NOTES AND QUESTIONS

1. *Military Chaplains as Religious Educators*. Judge Mansfield included religious education as one of the functions of military chaplains. Does this raise a

concern in light of James Madison's struggle against Patrick Henry's proposal to fund a teacher of Christian religion [Chapter Six, section 1C]? From *Everson v. Bd. of Education* to *Mitchell v. Helms* [Chapter Fourteen, section 1] a central concern of the Court has been to nullify public expenditures for governmental indoctrination in religion. Are these cases distinguishable from the military chaplaincy case? For the view that religious organizations should sponsor chaplains to those who serve in the military, but that the government should not have priests, ministers, rabbis, and other members of the clergy on its payroll, see John Swomley, "Government Chaplaincies and the Separation of Church and State," in James E. Wood, Jr., *Religion and the State: Essays in Honor of Leo Pfeffer* 235–45 (1985); and see Harvey Cox, ed., *Military Chaplains, From a Religious Military to a Military Religion* (1971).

6. DOUBLE DUTY DISPLAYS

Lynch v. Donnelly

465 U.S. 668 (1984).

William F. McMahon argued the cause for petitioners. With him on the briefs were *Richard P. McMahon* and *Spencer W. Viner*.

Solicitor General Lee argued the cause for the United States as *amicus curiae* urging reversal. With him on the brief were *Assistant Attorney General McGrath, Deputy Solicitor General Bator, Deputy Assistant Attorney General Kuhl*, and *Kathryn A. Oberly*.

Amato A. DeLuca argued the cause for respondents. With him on the brief were *Sandra A. Blanding, Burt Neuborne, E. Richard Larson*, and *Norman Dorsen*.

■ CHIEF JUSTICE BURGER delivered the opinion of the Court.

We granted certiorari to decide whether the Establishment Clause of the First Amendment prohibits a municipality from including a crèche, or Nativity scene, in its annual Christmas display.

I

Each year, in cooperation with the downtown retail merchants' association, the city of Pawtucket, R.I., erects a Christmas display as part of its observance of the Christmas holiday season. The display is situated in a park owned by a nonprofit organization and located in the heart of the shopping district. The display is essentially like those to be found in hundreds of towns or cities across the Nation—often on public grounds—during the Christmas season. The Pawtucket display comprises many of the figures and decorations traditionally associated with Christmas, including, among other things, a Santa Claus house, reindeer pulling Santa's sleigh, candy-striped poles, a Christmas tree, carolers, cutout figures representing such characters as a clown, an elephant, and a teddy bear, hundreds of colored lights, a large banner that reads "SEASONS GREETINGS," and the crèche at issue here. All components of this display are owned by the city.

The crèche, which has been included in the display for 40 or more years, consists of the traditional figures, including the Infant Jesus, Mary and Joseph, angels, shepherds, kings, and animals, all ranging in height from 5" to 5'. In 1973, when the present crèche was acquired, it cost the city $1,365; it now is valued at $200. The erection and dismantling of the crèche costs the city about $20 per year; nominal expenses are incurred in lighting the crèche. No money has been expended on its maintenance for the past 10 years.

Respondents, Pawtucket residents and individual members of the Rhode Island affiliate of the American Civil Liberties Union, and the affiliate itself, brought this action in the United States District Court for Rhode Island, challenging the city's inclusion of the crèche in the annual display. The District Court held that the city's inclusion of the crèche in the display violates the Establishment Clause, which is binding on the states through the Fourteenth Amendment. The District Court found that, by including the crèche in the Christmas display, the city has "tried to endorse and promulgate religious beliefs," and that "erection of the crèche has the real and substantial effect of affiliating the City with the Christian beliefs that the crèche represents." This "appearance of official sponsorship," it believed, "confers more than a remote and incidental benefit on Christianity." Last, although the court acknowledged the absence of administrative entanglement, it found that excessive entanglement has been fostered as a result of the political divisiveness of including the crèche in the celebration. The city was permanently enjoined from including the crèche in the display.

A divided panel of the Court of Appeals for the First Circuit affirmed. We granted certiorari, and we reverse. . . .

The concept of a "wall" of separation is a useful figure of speech probably deriving from views of Thomas Jefferson. [Chapter Seven, section 1]. The metaphor has served as a reminder that the Establishment Clause forbids an established church or anything approaching it. But the metaphor itself is not a wholly accurate description of the practical aspects of the relationship that in fact exists between church and state.

No significant segment of our society and no institution within it can exist in vacuum or in total or absolute isolation. . . .

Our history is replete with official references to the value and invocation of Divine guidance in deliberations and pronouncements of the Founding Fathers and contemporary leaders. Beginning in the early colonial period long before Independence, a day of Thanksgiving was celebrated as a religious holiday to give thanks for the bounties of Nature as gifts from God. President Washington and his successors proclaimed Thanksgiving, with all its religious overtones, a day of national celebration and Congress made it a National Holiday more than a century ago [Chapter Seven, section 1]. That holiday has not lost its theme of expressing thanks for Divine aid any more than has Christmas lost its religious significance.

Executive Orders and other official announcements of Presidents and of the Congress have Proclaimed both Christmas and Thanksgiving National Holidays in religious terms. And, by Acts of Congress, it has long been the practice that federal employees are released from duties on these National Holidays, while being paid from the same public revenues that provide the compensation of the Chaplains of the Senate and the House and the military services. *See* J. Res. 5, 23 Stat. 516. Thus, it is clear that Government has long recognized—indeed it has subsidized—holidays with religious significance.

Other examples of reference to our religious heritage are found in the statutorily prescribed national motto "In God We Trust," 36 U.S.C. § 186, which Congress and the President mandated for our currency, see 31 U.S.C. § 5112(d)(1) (1982 ed.), and in the language "One nation under God," as part of the Pledge of Allegiance to the American flag. That pledge is recited by many thousands of public school children—and adults—every year.

Art galleries supported by public revenues display religious paintings of the 15th and 16th centuries, predominantly inspired by one religious faith. The National Gallery in Washington, maintained with Government support, for example, has long exhibited masterpieces with religious messages, notably the Last Supper, and paintings depicting the Birth of Christ, the Crucifixion, and the Resurrection, among many others with explicit Christian themes and messages.[4] The very chamber in which oral arguments on this case were heard is decorated with a notable and permanent—not seasonal—symbol of religion: Moses with the Ten Commandments. Congress has long provided chapels in the Capitol for religious worship and meditation.

There are countless other illustrations of the Government's acknowledgment of our religious heritage and governmental sponsorship of graphic manifestations of that heritage. Congress has directed the President to proclaim a National Day of Prayer each year "on which [day] the people of the United States may turn to God in prayer and meditation at churches, in groups, and as individuals." 36 U.S.C. § 169h. Our Presidents have repeatedly issued such Proclamations.[5] Presidential Proclamations and messages have also issued to commemorate Jewish Heritage Week, Presidential Proclamation No. 4844, 3 CFR 30 (1982), and the Jewish High Holy Days, 17 Weekly Comp. Of Pres. Doc. 1058 (1981). One cannot look at even this brief résumé without finding that our history is pervaded by expressions of religious beliefs such as are found in *Zorach* [Chapter Fourteen, section 2]. Equally pervasive is the evidence of accommodation of all faiths and all forms of religious expression, and hostility toward none. Through

---

4. The National Gallery regularly exhibits more than 200 similar religious paintings.

5. See, *e.g.*, Presidential Proclamation No. 5017, 48 Fed. Reg. 4261 (1983); Presidential Proclamation No. 4795, 3 CFR 109 (1981); Presidential Proclamation No. 4379, 3 CFR 486 (1971–1975 Comp.); Presidential Proclamation No. 4087, 3 CFR 81 (1971–1975 Comp.); Presidential Proclamation No. 3812, 3 CFR 155 (1966–1970 Comp.); Presidential Proclamation No. 3501, 3 CFR 228 (1959–1963 Comp.).

this accommodation, as Justice Douglas observed, governmental action has "follow[ed] the best of our traditions" and "respect[ed] the religious nature of our people."

III

This history may help explain why the Court consistently has declined to take a rigid, absolutist view of the Establishment Clause. We have refused "to construe the Religion Clauses with a literalness that would undermine the ultimate constitutional objective *as illuminated by history.*" *Walz* [Chapter Thirteen, section 3] (emphasis added). In our modern, complex society, whose traditions and constitutional underpinnings rest on and encourage diversity and pluralism in all areas, an absolutist approach in applying the Establishment Clause is simplistic and has been uniformly rejected by the Court.

Rather than mechanically invalidating all governmental conduct or statutes that confer benefits or give special recognition to religion in general or to one faith—as an absolutist approach would dictate—the Court has scrutinized challenged legislation or official conduct to determine whether, in reality, it establishes a religion or religious faith, or tends to do so. See *Walz*. Joseph Story wrote a century and a half ago: "The real object of the [First] Amendment was ... to prevent any national ecclesiastical establishment, which should give to an hierarchy the exclusive patronage of the national government." 3 J. Story, Commentaries on the Constitution of the United States 728 (1833).

In each case, the inquiry calls for line-drawing; no fixed, *per se* rule can be framed. The Establishment Clause like the Due Process Clauses is not a precise, detailed provision in a legal code capable of ready application. The purpose of the Establishment Clause "was to state an objective, not to write a statute." *Walz,* at 668. The line between permissible relationships and those barred by the Clause can no more be straight and unwavering than due process can be defined in a single stroke or phrase or test. The Clause erects a "blurred, indistinct, and variable barrier depending on all the circumstances of a particular relationship." *Lemon* [Chapter Fourteen, section1].

In the line-drawing process we have often found it useful to inquire whether the challenged law or conduct has a secular purpose, whether its principal or primary effect is to advance or inhibit religion, and whether it creates an excessive entanglement of government with religion. *Lemon.* But, we have repeatedly emphasized our unwillingness to be confined to any single test or criterion in this sensitive area.... The narrow question is whether there is a secular purpose for Pawtucket's display of the crèche. The display is sponsored by the city to celebrate the Holiday and to depict the origins of that Holiday. These are legitimate secular purposes. The District Court's inference, drawn from the religious nature of the crèche, that the city has no secular purpose was, on this record, clearly erroneous.

The District Court found that the primary effect of including the crèche is to confer a substantial and impermissible benefit on religion in general and on the Christian faith in particular. Comparisons of the relative benefits to religion of different forms of governmental support are elusive and difficult to make. But to conclude that the primary effect of including the crèche is to advance religion in violation of the Establishment Clause would require that we view it as more beneficial to and more an endorsement of religion, for example, than expenditure of large sums of public money for textbooks supplied throughout the country to students attending church-sponsored schools, *Board of Education v. Allen* [Chapter Fourteen, section 1]; expenditure of public funds for transportation of students to church-sponsored schools, *Everson v. Board of Education* [Chapter Fourteen, section 1]; federal grants for college buildings of church-sponsored institutions of higher education combining secular and religious education, *Tilton v. Richardson* [Chapter Fourteen, section 3]; noncategorical grants to church-sponsored colleges and universities, *Roemer v. Board of Public Works* [Chapter Fourteen, section 3]; and the tax exemptions for church properties sanctioned in *Walz v. Tax Comm'n*, [section 3 above]. It would also require that we view it as more of an endorsement of religion than the Sunday Closing Laws upheld in *McGowan v. Maryland*, [section 2 above]; the release time program for religious training in *Zorach v. Clauson* [Chapter Fourteen, section 2]; and the legislative prayers upheld in *Marsh v. Chambers* [section 5 above]....

Of course the crèche is identified with one religious faith but no more so than the examples we have set out from prior cases in which we found no conflict with the Establishment Clause. See, *e.g., McGowan v. Maryland*; *Marsh v. Chambers*. It would be ironic, however, if the inclusion of a single symbol of a particular historic religious event, as part of a celebration acknowledged in the Western world for 20 centuries, and in this country by the people, by the Executive Branch, by the Congress, and the courts for 2 centuries, would so "taint" the city's exhibit as to render it violative of the Establishment Clause. To forbid the use of this one passive symbol—the crèche—at the very time people are taking note of the season with Christmas hymns and carols in public schools and other public places, and while the Congress and legislatures open sessions with prayers by paid chaplains would be a stilted overreaction contrary to our history and to our holdings. If the presence of the crèche in this display violates the Establishment Clause, a host of other forms of taking official note of Christmas, and of our religious heritage, are equally offensive to the Constitution....

We hold that, notwithstanding the religious significance of the crèche, the city of Pawtucket has not violated the Establishment Clause of the First Amendment. Accordingly, the judgment of the Court of Appeals is reversed. *It is so ordered.*

■ JUSTICE O'CONNOR, concurring. What is crucial is that a government practice not have the effect of communicating a message of government endorsement or disapproval of religion. It is only practices having that effect, whether intentionally or unintentionally, that make religion relevant, in reality or public perception, to status in the political community. [O'Connor characterized the issue in *Lynch* as "whether Pawtucket has endorsed Christianity by its display of the crèche." Noting that practices such as legislative prayer [section 5 above], Thanksgiving as a public holiday, the motto "in God we trust" on currency, and the prayer opening court sessions ("God save the United States and this honorable court") do not convey "government approval of particular religious beliefs," O'Connor concluded that Pawtucket did not intend to communicate any official endorsement of Christianity in displaying the crèche, and that the effect or "objective" meaning of any statement made by the crèche in the community did not actually convey official endorsement of Christianity by the city.]

■ JUSTICE BRENNAN, with whom JUSTICES MARSHALL, BLACKMUN, and STEVENS join, dissenting:

... The inclusion of a crèche in Pawtucket's otherwise secular celebration of Christmas clearly violates these principles. Unlike such secular figures as Santa Claus, reindeer, and carolers, a nativity scene represents far more than a mere "traditional" symbol of Christmas. The essence of the crèche's symbolic purpose and effect is to prompt the observer to experience a sense of simple awe and wonder appropriate to the contemplation of one of the central elements of Christian dogma—that God sent His Son into the world to be a Messiah. Contrary to the Court's suggestion, the crèche is far from a mere representation of a "particular historic religious event." It is, instead, best understood as a mystical re-creation of an event that lies at the heart of Christian faith. To suggest, as the Court does, that such a symbol is merely "traditional" and therefore no different from Santa's house or reindeer is not only offensive to those for whom the crèche has profound significance,[19] but insulting to those who insist for religious or personal reasons that the story of Christ is in no sense a part of "history" nor an unavoidable element of our national "heritage."[20]

For these reasons, the crèche in this context simply cannot be viewed as playing the same role that an ordinary museum display does. The Court seems to assume that prohibiting Pawtucket from displaying a crèche would be tantamount to prohibiting a state college from including the Bible or Milton's Paradise Lost in a course on English literature. But in those cases the religiously inspired materials are being considered solely as literature. The purpose is plainly not to single out the particular religious beliefs that may have inspired the authors, but to see in these writings the outlines of a larger imaginative universe shared with other forms of literary expression.[21] The same may be said of a course devoted to the study of art; when the course turns to Gothic architecture, the emphasis is not on the religious beliefs which the cathedrals exalt, but rather upon the "aesthetic consequences of [such religious] thought."[22]

19. Many Christian commentators have voiced strong objections to what they consider to be the debasement and trivialization of Christmas through too close a connection with commercial and public celebrations. See, e.g., Kelley, "Beyond Separation of Church and State," 5 *J. Church & State* 181 (1963). See generally Barnett [*The American Christmas*] 55–57.

20. *See* A. Stokes & L. Pfeffer, *Church and State in the United States* 383 (rev. ed.

1964); R. Morgan, *The Supreme Court and Religion* 126 (1972); Barnett 68 (discussing opposition by Jews and other non-Christian religious groups to public celebrations of Christmas). *See also* Talmage, [*Disputation and Dialogue* (1985)].

21. See N. Frye, *The Secular Scripture* 14–15 (1976).

22. O. von Simson, *The Gothic Cathedral* 27 (1956). See also E. Panofsky, *Meaning in the Visual Arts* (1974). Compare Jus-

In this case, by contrast, the crèche plays no comparable secular role. Unlike the poetry of Paradise Lost which students in a literature course will seek to appreciate primarily for esthetic or historical reasons, the angels, shepherds, Magi, and infant of Pawtucket's nativity scene can only be viewed as symbols of a particular set of religious beliefs. It would be another matter if the crèche were displayed in a museum setting, in the company of other religiously inspired artifacts, as an example, among many, of the symbolic representation of religious myths. In that setting, we would have objective guarantees that the crèche could not suggest that a particular faith had been singled out for public favor and recognition. The effect of Pawtucket's crèche, however, is not confined by any of these limiting attributes. In the absence of any other religious symbols or of any neutral disclaimer, the inescapable effect of the crèche will be to remind the average observer of the religious roots of the celebration he is witnessing and to call to mind the scriptural message that the nativity symbolizes. The fact that Pawtucket has gone to the trouble of making such an elaborate public celebration and of including a crèche in that otherwise secular setting inevitably serves to reinforce the sense that the city means to express solidarity with the Christian message of the crèche and to dismiss other faiths as unworthy of similar attention and support. . . .

By insisting that such a distinctly sectarian message is merely an unobjectionable part of our "religious heritage," the Court takes a long step backwards to the days when Justice Brewer could arrogantly declare for the Court that "this is a Christian nation." *Church of Holy Trinity v. United States* [Chapter Ten, section 1]. Those days, I had thought, were forever put behind us by the Court's decision in *Engel v. Vitale* [Chapter Fourteen, section 2], in which we rejected a similar argument advanced by the State of New York that its Regent's Prayer was simply an acceptable part of our "spiritual heritage."

NOTES AND QUESTIONS

1. *Holiday Sequels.* The Scarsdale Crèche Committee, an association of seven Catholic and Protestant churches, annually displayed during the Christmas season a set of figures, 1/2 foot to 3 1/2 feet in height, depicting Christ in the manger, sculptured in wood at a cost of $1,600. The display was at Boniface Circle, a public park in the center of the business area. Boniface Circle was also used by Christmas carol singers. Other public buildings of Scarsdale were also used for religious purposes; for example, Wayside Cottage, a publicly owned building, was used for Bahai, Catholic, Jewish, and Unitarian services.

After litigation was begun to ban the placing of the crèche on Boniface Circle as unconstitutional, the Scarsdale authorities became uneasy about it and eventually decided themselves not to allow it; their feeling was "that because the symbol was religious it should not be on *any* public land." The

---

tice Jackson's explanation of his view that the study of religiously inspired material can, in the correct setting, be made a part of a secular educational program: "[m]usic without sacred music, architecture minus the ca-

thedral, or painting without the scriptural themes would be eccentric and incomplete, even from a secular point of view." *Illinois ex rel. McCollum v. Board of Education,* [Chapter Fourteen, section 2].

Crèche Committee and twelve others, mainly residents of Scarsdale, sued to override the denial.

In *McCreary v. Stone*, 739 F.2d 716 (2d Cir. 1984), judgment aff'd by equally divided court sub nom. *Bd. of Trustees of Village of Scarsdale v. McCreary*, 471 U.S. 83 (1985), the Second Circuit, per Lawrence W. Pierce, ruled that an injunction should issue prohibiting Scarsdale from "relying on the establishment clause as a reason for prohibiting the erection of a crèche at Boniface Circle, a traditional public forum." The court said that the absence of Santa Claus and other secular figures did not distinguish the Scarsdale case from *Lynch*; in each case the context was that of the celebration of Christmas; the advancement of religion was incidental; the erection of a visible sign disclaiming sponsorship by Scarsdale was sufficient disassociation from the government. The court added that any special impact on children as persons unable to understand that the town was being neutral had not been established.

The problem of religious displays on public property continued to trouble the lower courts. A Christmas tree, standing alone, was deemed permissible as "typifying the secular celebration of Christmas." *American Civil Liberties Union of Illinois v. St. Charles*, 794 F. 2d 265, 271 (7th Cir.), cert. denied, 479 U.S. 961 (1986). On the other hand, the presence of a nativity scene in the lobby of Chicago's City Hall "inevitably creates a clear and strong impression that the local government tacitly endorses Christianity." Despite a disclaimer to the contrary, the court reached this conclusion "[b]ecause City Hall is so plainly under government ownership and control, every display and activity in the building is implicitly marked with the stamp of government approval." *American Jewish Congress v. Chicago*, 827 F. 2d 120 (7th Cir. 1987).

The City of Pittsburgh and the County of Allegheny allowed two displays to be erected by private parties during the month of December. The first was a crèche depicting the Christian Nativity scene; its manger had at its crest an angel bearing a banner proclaiming "Gloria in Excelsis Deo," meaning "Glory to God in the Highest." The crèche was donated by the Holy Name Society, a Roman Catholic group, and bore a sign to that effect. It was placed on the grand staircase of the county courthouse. The second display was an 18-foot Chanukah menorah or candelabrum, which was placed just outside the City–County Building next to the city's 45-foot decorated Christmas tree. At the foot of the tree was a sign bearing the mayor's name and containing text declaring the city's "salute to liberty." The menorah is owned by Chabad, also known as Lubavitch, an organization of Orthodox Hasidic Jews who follow the teachings of the Lubavitch Rebbe. The City of Pittsburgh stored, erected, and removed the display each year. The ACLU sought an injunction against both displays on public property. Relying on *Lynch v. Donnelly*, the district court denied relief. The Court of Appeals reversed, holding that the crèche and the menorah in the present case must be understood as an impermissible governmental endorsement of Christianity and Judaism under *Lemon*.

A majority of the Supreme Court formally adopted the endorsement test proposed by Justice O'Connor in *Lynch*. Justice Blackmun cited post-*Lynch* decisions that had employed language of endorsement: *Wallace v. Jaffree* [Chapter Fourteen, section 2], *Edwards v. Aguillard* [Chapter Fourteen, section 2], and *School Dist. of Grand Rapids v. Ball* [Chapter Fourteen, section 1]. Noting that " 'endorsement' is not self-defining," Justice Blackmun wrote that the central meaning of the endorsement test is that "the government may not convey a message that religion or a particular religious belief is favored or preferred." Using this working definition, the Court ruled that the crèche, but not the menorah, has the impermissible effect of endorsing religion. The scholars are divided on the endorsement test. In favor of the test, see Beschle, "The Conservative as Liberal: The Religion Clauses, Liberal Neutrality, and the Approach of Justice O'Connor," 62 *Notre Dame L. Rev.* 151 (1987). Against the test, see Steven Smith, Symbols, "Perceptions, and Doctrinal Illusions: Establishment Neutrality and the 'No Endorsement' " Test, 86 *Mich. L. Rev.* 266 (1987).

The opinions generated in this case fill over a hundred pages in the United States Reports. The inability of the Court to coalesce around a sensible solution to this recurring difficulty is suggested by the summary of the case by the Reporter of Opinions: "Blackmun, J., announced the judgment of the Court and delivered the opinion of the Court with respect to Parts III–A, IV, and V, in which Brennan, Marshall, Stevens, and O'Connor, JJ., joined, an opinion with respect to Parts I and II, in which Stevens and O'Connor, JJ., joined, an opinion with respect to Part III–B, in which Stevens, J., joined, an opinion with respect to Part VII, in which O'Connor, J., joined, and an opinion with respect to Part VI, O'Connor, J., filed an opinion concurring in part and concurring in the judgment, in Part II of which Brennan and Stevens, JJ., joined. Brennan, J., filed an opinion concurring in part and dissenting in part, in which Marshall and Stevens, JJ., joined. Stevens, J., filed an opinion concurring in part and dissenting in part, in which Brennan and Marshall, JJ., joined. Kennedy, J., filed an opinion concurring in the judgment in part and dissenting in part, in which Rehnquist, C. J., and White and Scalia, JJ., joined." When the math and the Roman numerals are combined, five justices thought that the crèche inside the courthouse violated the Constitution, and six justices thought that the display of the menorah and the Christmas tree outside the courthouse was permissible.

In the opinion below, Justice Blackmun stressed the location of the crèche on the grand staircase, the "main," "most beautiful," and "most public" part of the courthouse. Should that matter? He also noted that the display was surrounded by flowers, and distinguished *Lynch* on this ground and because the crèche in Pawtucket had been surrounded with other figures: "a Santa Claus house, reindeer pulling Santa's sleigh, candy-striped poles, a Christmas tree, carolers, cutout figures representing such characters as a clown, an elephant, and a teddy bear, hundreds of colored lights, [and] a large banner that rea[d] 'SEASONS GREETINGS.' " Blackmun had dissented in *Lynch*, but needed to distinguish *Lynch* presumably because Justice O'Connor would not vote to reverse *Lynch*. Does the Court's focus on details such as these help resolve a recurrent problem, or trivialize constitutional adjudication and add fuel to future litigation?

Jews expressed outrage at the result in *Lynch* on the ground that the Nativity scene on government property sent them a message of second-class citizenship. See, e.g., Norman Redlich, "Separation of Church and State: The Burger Court's Tortuous Journey," 60 *Notre Dame L. Rev.* 1094, 1122–1126 (1985); Stephen M. Feldman, *Please Don't Wish Me a Merry Christmas: A Critical History of the Separation of Church and State* (1997). Jews were not the only ones offended by *Lynch*. As Justice Brennan's dissent suggested, believing Christians had cause for offense in the reduction of a major religious holiday (Christ's Mass) to the lowest secular common denominator in order to pass constitutional muster.

In *Allegheny County* Jews were divided, as was the Court, reflecting the diversity of opinion that has been a hallmark of Judaism over the centuries. Chabad, supported by the National Jewish Commission on Law and Public Affairs, wanted to be free to express Jewish faith by the public presence of a menorah. "Mainline" Jewish organizations, such as the American Jewish Committee and the American Jewish Congress, opposed the public display of the menorah. All observant Jews, not simply the Orthodox, had cause for puzzlement as the Court legitimated the menorah display as a secular phenomenon. Justice Blackmun described Chanukah as the commemoration of a "political rebellion." What is left out of this characterization is that this festival celebrates the courageous struggle of Judas Maccabeus and his followers to resist the Hellenization program of Antiochus Epiphanes [Chapter One, section 5]. Chanukah can be interpreted as a great moment to rejoice in religious freedom, but hardly as a time for intense secularization. The whole point of the rebellion was the rejection of secularization urged by the Hellenizers and their assimilated Jewish friends.

County of Allegheny v. ACLU, Greater Pittsburgh Chapter;
Chabad v. ACLU, Greater Pittsburgh Chapter;
City of Pittsburgh v. ACLU, Greater Pittsburgh Chapter

492 U.S. 573 (1989).

Peter Buscemi argued the cause for petitioners in Nos. 87–2050 and 88–96. With him on the briefs were *George M. Janocsko, Robert L. McTiernan, D.R. Pellegrini*, and *George R. Specter. Nathan Lewin* argued the cause for petitioner in No. 88–90 [*Chabad*]. With him on the briefs was *Charles H. Saul.*

Roslyn M. Litman argued the cause for respondents. With her on the brief for respondents American Civil Liberties Union et al. were *Jon Pushinsky, James B. Lieber, John A. Powell*, and *Steven R. Shapiro. Ruti Teitel, Jeffrey P. Sinensky, Steven M. Freeman, Richard E. Shevitz*, and *Jill L. Kahn* filed a brief for respondent Tunador.

Briefs of amici curiae urging reversal were filed for the United States by *Solicitor General Fried, Deputy Solicitor General Ayer*, and *Michael K. Kellogg*; for the city of Warren, Michigan, by *Robert E. Williams*; for Concerned Women for America by *Jordan W. Lorence, Cimron Campbell*, and *Wendell R. Bird*; for the National Jewish Commission on Law and Public Affairs by *Dennis Rapps* and *A. David Stern*; and for the National Legal Foundation by *Douglas W. Davis, Robert K. Skolrood*, and *William C. Wood, Jr.*

Briefs of amici curiae urging affirmance were filed for the American Jewish Committee et al. by *Samuel Rabinove, Richard T. Foltin, James G.*

Greilsheimer, Alan M. Klinger, David A. Stein, Lauren G. Klein, and *Lee Boothby*; and for the American Jewish Congress et al. by *Arlene Fickler, Marc D. Stern, Lois C. Waldman*, and *Amy Adelson*.

■ JUSTICE BLACKMUN announced the judgment of the Court....

This litigation began on December 10, 1986, when respondents, the Greater Pittsburgh Chapter of the American Civil Liberties Union and seven local residents, filed suit against the county and the city, seeking permanently to enjoin the county from displaying the crèche in the county courthouse and the city from displaying the menorah in front of the City–County Building. Respondents claim that the displays of the crèche and the menorah each violate the Establishment Clause of the First Amendment, made applicable to state governments by the Fourteenth Amendment. Chabad was permitted to intervene to defend the display of its menorah....

For a number of years, the city has had a large Christmas tree under the middle arch outside the Grant Street entrance. Following this practice, city employees on November 17, 1986, erected a 45–foot tree under the middle arch and decorated it with lights and ornaments. A few days later, the city placed at the foot of the tree a sign bearing the mayor's name and entitled "Salute to Liberty." Beneath the title, the sign stated: "During this holiday season, the city of Pittsburgh salutes liberty. Let these festive lights remind us that we are the keepers of the flame of liberty and our legacy of freedom."

At least since 1982, the city has expanded its Grant Street holiday display to include a symbolic representation of Chanukah, an 8–day Jewish holiday that begins on the 25th day of the Jewish lunar month of Kislev. The 25th of Kislev usually occurs in December, and thus Chanukah is the annual Jewish holiday that falls closest to Christmas Day each year. In 1986, Chanukah began at sundown on December 26.

According to Jewish tradition, on the 25th of Kislev in 164 B.C.E. (before the common era (165 B.C.)), the Maccabees rededicated the Temple of Jerusalem after recapturing it from the Greeks, or, more accurately, from the Greek-influenced Seleucid Empire, in the course of a political rebellion. Chanukah is the holiday which celebrates that event.

The Talmud explains the lamplighting ritual as a commemoration of an event that occurred during the rededication of the Temple. The Temple housed a seven-branch menorah, which was to be kept burning continuously. When the Maccabees rededicated the Temple, they had only enough oil to last for one day. But, according to the Talmud, the oil miraculously lasted for eight days (the length of time it took to obtain additional oil). To celebrate and publicly proclaim this miracle, the Talmud prescribes that it is a mitzvah (i.e., a religious deed or commandment), for Jews to place a lamp with eight lights just outside the entrance to their homes or in a front window during the eight days of Chanukah. Where practicality or safety from persecution so requires, the lamp may be placed in a window or inside the home. The Talmud also ordains certain blessings to be recited each night of Chanukah before lighting the lamp. One such benediction has been translated into English as "We are blessing God who has sanctified us and commanded us with mitzvot and has told us to light the candles of Hanukkah."....

[A]t the bottom line, the five Justices in concurrence and dissent in *Lynch* agreed upon the relevant constitutional principles: the government's use of religious symbolism is unconstitutional if it has the effect of endorsing religious beliefs, and the effect of the government's use of religious symbolism depends upon its context. These general principles are sound, and have been adopted by the Court in subsequent cases. Since *Lynch*, the Court has made clear that, when evaluating the effect of government conduct under the Establishment Clause, we must ascertain whether "the challenged governmental action is sufficiently likely to be perceived by adherents of the controlling denominations as an endorsement, and by the nonadherents as a disapproval, of their individual religious choices." *Grand Rapids* [Chapter Fourteen, section 1]. Accordingly, our present task is to determine whether the display of the crèche and the menorah, in their respective "particular physical settings," has the effect of endorsing or disapproving religious beliefs....

The fact that the crèche bears a sign disclosing its ownership by a Roman Catholic organization does not alter this conclusion. On the contrary, the sign simply demonstrates that the government is endorsing the religious message of that organization, rather than communicating a message of its own. But the Establishment Clause does not limit only the religious content of the government's own communications. It also prohibits the government's support and promotion of religious communications by religious organizations. Indeed, the very concept of "endorsement" conveys the sense of promoting someone else's message. Thus, by prohibiting government endorsement of religion, the Establishment Clause prohibits precisely what occurred here: the government's lending its support to the communication of a religious organization's religious message....

The government may acknowledge Christmas as a cultural phenomenon, but under the First Amendment it may not observe it as a Christian holy day by suggesting that people praise God for the birth of Jesus.[51] [Justice Blackmun concluded for the Court that the crèche display in this context endorses the Christian faith and must be permanently enjoined.]

The mere fact that Pittsburgh displays symbols of both Christmas and Chanukah does not end the constitutional inquiry. If the city celebrates both Christmas and Chanukah as religious holidays, then it violates the Establishment Clause. The simultaneous endorsement of Judaism and

---

51. Nor can the display of the crèche be justified as an "accommodation" of religion. See *Amos* [Chapter Eleven, section 6]. Government efforts to accommodate religion are permissible when they remove burdens on the free exercise of religion (O'Connor, J., concurring in judgment). The display of a crèche in a courthouse does not remove any burden on the free exercise of Christianity. Christians remain free to display crèches in their homes and churches. To be sure, prohibiting the display of a crèche in the courthouse deprives Christians of the satisfaction of seeing the government adopt their religious message as their own, but this kind of government affiliation with particular religious messages is precisely what the Establishment Clause precludes.

Christianity is no less constitutionally infirm than the endorsement of Christianity alone.

Conversely, if the city celebrates both Christmas and Chanukah as secular holidays, then its conduct is beyond the reach of the Establishment Clause. Because government may celebrate Christmas as a secular holiday, it follows that government may also acknowledge Chanukah as a secular holiday. Simply put, it would be a form of discrimination against Jews to allow Pittsburgh to celebrate Christmas as a cultural tradition while simultaneously disallowing the city's acknowledgment of Chanukah as a contemporaneous cultural tradition.[63] . . . .

[Justice Blackmun, joined by Justice O'Connor, concurring partly in the judgment, concluded that the display of an 18–foot menorah, in the setting of a 45–foot Christmas tree, did not endorse the Jewish faith and thus would not be enjoined. The four dissenters agreed that the menorah display was permissible, but for other reasons. Blackmun added:]

In the shadow of the tree, the menorah is readily understood as simply a recognition that Christmas is not the only traditional way of observing the winter-holiday season. In these circumstances, then, the combination of the tree and the menorah communicates, not a simultaneous endorsement of both the Christian and Jewish faiths, but instead, a secular celebration of Christmas coupled with an acknowledgment of Chanukah as a contemporaneous alternative tradition . . . .

Lynch v. Donnelly confirms, and in no way repudiates, the longstanding constitutional principle that government may not engage in a practice that has the effect of promoting or endorsing religious beliefs. The display of the crèche in the county courthouse has this unconstitutional effect. The display of the menorah in front of the City–County Building, however, does not have this effect, given its "particular physical setting."

The judgment of the Court of Appeals is affirmed in part and reversed in part, and the cases are remanded for further proceedings. It is so ordered.

■ JUSTICE O'CONNOR concurring in part and concurring in the judgment.

As a theoretical matter, the endorsement test captures the essential command of the Establishment Clause, namely, that government must not make a person's religious beliefs relevant to his or her standing in the political community by conveying a message "that religion or a particular religious belief is favored or preferred."

■ JUSTICE BRENNAN, with whom JUSTICE MARSHALL and JUSTICE STEVENS join, concurring in part and dissenting in part.

The uncritical acceptance of a message of religious pluralism also ignores the extent to which even that message may offend. Many religious faiths are hostile to each other, and indeed, refuse even to participate in

---

63. Thus, to take the most obvious of examples, if it were permissible for the city to display in front of the City–County Building a banner exclaiming "Merry Christmas," then it would also be permissible for the city to display in the same location a banner proclaiming "Happy Chanukah."

ecumenical services designed to demonstrate the very pluralism Justices Blackmun and O'Connor extol. To lump the ritual objects and holidays of religions together without regard to their attitudes toward such inclusiveness, or to decide which religions should be excluded because of the possibility of offense, is not a benign or beneficent celebration of pluralism: it is instead an interference in religious matters precluded by the Establishment Clause. The government-sponsored display of the menorah alongside a Christmas tree also works a distortion of the Jewish religious calendar. As Justice Blackmun acknowledges, "the proximity of Christmas [may] accoun[t] for the social prominence of Chanukah in this country." It is the proximity of Christmas that undoubtedly accounts for the city's decision to participate in the celebration of Chanukah, rather than the far more significant Jewish holidays of Rosh Hashanah and Yom Kippur. Contrary to the impression the city and Justices Blackmun and O'Connor seem to create, with their emphasis on "the winter-holiday season," December is not the holiday season for Judaism. Thus, the city's erection alongside the Christmas tree of the symbol of a relatively minor Jewish religious holiday, far from conveying "the city's secular recognition of different traditions for celebrating the winter-holiday season," (Blackmun, J.), or "a message of pluralism and freedom of belief," (O'Connor, J.), has the effect of promoting a Christianized version of Judaism. The holiday calendar they appear willing to accept revolves exclusively around a Christian holiday. And those religions that have no holiday at all during the period between Thanksgiving and New Year's Day will not benefit, even in a second-class manner, from the city's once-a-year tribute to "liberty" and "freedom of belief." This is not "pluralism" as I understand it.

■ Justice Stevens, with whom Justice Brennan and Justice Marshall join, concurring in part and dissenting in part.

Application of a strong presumption against the public use of religious symbols scarcely will "require a relentless extirpation of all contact between government and religion," (Kennedy, J., concurring in judgment in part and dissenting in part), for it will prohibit a display only when its message, evaluated in the context in which it is presented, is nonsecular. For example, a carving of Moses holding the Ten Commandments, if that is the only adornment on a courtroom wall, conveys an equivocal message, perhaps of respect for Judaism, for religion in general, or for law. The addition of carvings depicting Confucius and Mohammed may honor religion, or particular religions, to an extent that the First Amendment does not tolerate any more than it does "the permanent erection of a large Latin cross on the roof of city hall." (Kennedy, J., concurring in judgment in part and dissenting in part). Cf. *Stone v. Graham* [Chapter Fourteen, section 2]. Placement of secular figures such as Caesar Augustus, William Blackstone, Napoleon Bonaparte, and John Marshall alongside these three religious leaders, however, signals respect not for great proselytizers but for great lawgivers. It would be absurd to exclude such a fitting message from a courtroom, as it would to exclude religious paintings by Italian Renaissance masters from a public museum. Cf. *Lynch*, (Brennan, J., dissenting). Far from "border[ing] on latent hostility toward religion," (Kennedy, J., concurring in judgment in part and dissenting in part), this careful consideration of context gives due regard to religious and nonreligious members of our society. . . .

I cannot agree with the Court's conclusion that the display at Pittsburgh's City–County Building was constitutional. Standing alone in front of a governmental headquarters, a lighted, 45–foot evergreen tree might convey holiday greetings linked too tenuously to Christianity to have constitutional moment. Juxtaposition of this tree with an 18–foot menorah does not make the latter secular, as Justice Blackmun contends. Rather, the presence of the Chanukah menorah, unquestionably a religious symbol, gives religious significance to the Christmas tree. The overall display thus manifests governmental approval of the Jewish and Christian religions. Although it conceivably might be interpreted as sending "a message of pluralism and freedom to choose one's own beliefs," (O'Connor, J., concurring in part and concurring in judgment); accord (opinion of Blackmun, J.), the message is not sufficiently clear to overcome the strong presumption that the display, respecting two religions to the exclusion of all others, is the very kind of double establishment that the First Amendment was designed to outlaw. I would, therefore, affirm the judgment of the Court of Appeals in its entirety.

■ Justice Kennedy, with whom the Chief Justice, Justice White, and Justice Scalia join, concurring in the judgment in part and dissenting in part.

The majority holds that the County of Allegheny violated the Establishment Clause by displaying a crèche in the county courthouse, because the "principal or primary effect" of the display is to advance religion within the meaning of *Lemon* This view of the Establishment Clause reflects an unjustified hostility toward religion, a hostility inconsistent with our history and our precedents, and I dissent from this holding. The crèche display is constitutional, and, for the same reasons, the display of a menorah by the city of Pittsburgh is permissible as well. . . .

III

The majority invalidates display of the crèche, not because it disagrees with the interpretation of *Lynch* applied above, but because it chooses to discard the reasoning of the *Lynch* majority opinion in favor of Justice O'Connor's concurring opinion in that case. . . .

Even if *Lynch* did not control, I would not commit this Court to the test applied by the majority today. The notion that cases arising under the Establishment Clause should be decided by an inquiry into whether a " 'reasonable observer' " may " 'fairly understand' " government action to " 'sen[d] a message to nonadherents that they are outsiders, not full members of the political community,' " is a recent, and in my view most unwelcome, addition to our tangled Establishment Clause jurisprudence. . . . For the reasons expressed below, I submit that the endorsement test is flawed in its fundamentals and unworkable in practice. The uncritical adoption of this standard is every bit as troubling as the bizarre result it produces in the cases before us.

A

I take it as settled law that, whatever standard the Court applies to Establishment Clause claims, it must at least suggest results consistent with our precedents and the historical practices that, by tradition, have informed our First Amendment jurisprudence....

If the endorsement test, applied without artificial exceptions for historical practice, reached results consistent with history, my objections to it would have less force. But, as I understand that test, the touchstone of an Establishment Clause violation is whether nonadherents would be made to feel like "outsiders" by government recognition or accommodation of religion. Few of our traditional practices recognizing the part religion plays in our society can withstand scrutiny under a faithful application of this formula.

Some examples suffice to make plain my concerns. Since the Founding of our Republic, American Presidents have issued Thanksgiving Proclamations establishing a national day of celebration and prayer. The first such proclamation was issued by President Washington at the request of the First Congress, and "recommend[ed] and assign[ed]" a day "to be devoted by the people of these States to the service of that great and glorious Being who is the beneficent author of all the good that was, that is, or that will be," so that "we may then unite in most humbly offering our prayers and supplications to the great Lord and Ruler of Nations, and beseech Him to ... promote the knowledge and practice of true religion and virtue...." 1 J. Richardson, *A Compilation of Messages and Papers of the Presidents, 1789–1897*, p. 64 (1899). Most of President Washington's successors have followed suit, and the forthrightly religious nature of these proclamations has not waned with the years. President Franklin D. Roosevelt went so far as to "suggest a nationwide reading of the Holy Scriptures during the period from Thanksgiving Day to Christmas" so that "we may bear more earnest witness to our gratitude to Almighty God." Presidential Proclamation No. 2629, 58 Stat. 1160. It requires little imagination to conclude that these proclamations would cause nonadherents to feel excluded, yet they have been a part of our national heritage from the beginning.

Either the endorsement test must invalidate scores of traditional practices recognizing the place religion holds in our culture, or it must be twisted and stretched to avoid inconsistency with practices we know to have been permitted in the past, while condemning similar practices with no greater endorsement effect simply by reason of their lack of historical antecedent. Neither result is acceptable....

The result the Court reaches in these cases is perhaps the clearest illustration of the unwisdom of the endorsement test. Although Justice O'Connor disavows Justice Blackmun's suggestion that the minority or majority status of a religion is relevant to the question whether government recognition constitutes a forbidden endorsement, the very nature of the endorsement test, with its emphasis on the feelings of the objective observer, easily lends itself to this type of inquiry. If there be such a person as the "reasonable observer," I am quite certain that he or she will take away a salient message from our holding in these cases: the Supreme Court of the United States has concluded that the First Amendment creates classes of religions based on the relative numbers of their adherents. Those religions enjoying the largest following must be consigned to the status of least favored faiths so as to avoid any possible risk of offending members of minority religions. I would be the first to admit that many questions arising under the Establishment Clause do not admit of easy answers, but whatever the Clause requires, it is not the result reached by the Court today.

IV

The approach adopted by the majority contradicts important values embodied in the Clause. Obsessive, implacable resistance to all but the most carefully scripted and secularized forms of accommodation requires this Court to act as a censor, issuing national decrees as to what is orthodox and what is not. What is orthodox, in this context, means what is secular; the only Christmas the State can acknowledge is one in which references to religion have been held to a minimum. The Court thus lends its assistance to an Orwellian rewriting of history as many understand it. I can conceive of no judicial function more antithetical to the First Amendment.

A further contradiction arises from the majority's approach, for the Court also assumes the difficult and inappropriate task of saying what every religious symbol means. Before studying these cases, I had not known the full history of the menorah, and I suspect the same was true of my colleagues. More important, this history was, and is, likely unknown to the vast majority of people of all faiths who saw the symbol displayed in Pittsburgh. Even if the majority is quite right about the history of the menorah, it hardly follows that this same history informed the observers' view of the symbol and the reason for its presence. This Court is ill equipped to sit as a national theology board, and I question both the wisdom and the constitutionality of its doing so. Indeed, were I required to choose between the approach taken by the majority and a strict separationist view, I would have to respect the consistency of the latter. The suit before us is admittedly a troubling one. It must be conceded that, however neutral the purpose of the city and county, the eager proselytizer may seek to use these symbols for his own ends. The urge to use them to teach or to taunt is always present. It is also true that some devout adherents of Judaism or Christianity may be as offended by the holiday display as are nonbelievers, if not more so. To place these religious symbols in a common hallway or sidewalk, where they may be ignored or even insulted, must be distasteful to many who cherish their meaning.

For these reasons, I might have voted against installation of these particular displays were I a local legislative official. But we have no jurisdiction over matters of taste within the realm of constitutionally permissible discretion. Our role is enforcement of a written Constitution. In my view, the principles of the Establishment Clause and our Nation's historic traditions of diversity and pluralism allow communities to make reasonable judgments respecting the accommodation or acknowledgment of holidays with both cultural and religious aspects. No constitutional violation occurs when they do so by displaying a symbol of the holiday's religious origins.

NOTES AND QUESTIONS

1. *Christianized Judaism.* Noting that Rosh Hashanah and Yom Kippur are "far more significant Jewish holidays" than Chanukah, Justice Brennan read the opinions of Justices Blackmun and O'Connor as promoting a "Christianized version of Judaism" by their "emphasis on the winter holiday." If this reading is correct, do the Blackmun and O'Connor opinions fail to pass the endorsement test they espouse?

2. *Tangled entanglement.* Do you agree with Justice Kennedy that the endorsement test is a "most unwelcome addition to our tangled Establishment Clause jurisprudence ... flawed in its fundamentals and unworkable in practice"? Does it add anything to your understanding of the nonestablishment principle? Why did Justice Kennedy change his mind in *Lee v. Weisman* [Chapter Fourteen, section 2], where he employed the endorsement test in a 5–4 decision? To accommodate the view of Justice O'Connor, the author of the test in *Lynch?* Is Kennedy right in questioning "both the wisdom and the constitutionality of the Court functioning as a national theology board"? Does your answer shed any light on the ability of judges to sort out intrachurch property disputes under "neutral principles" [Chapter Twelve, section 3]?

3. *Public Display of the Cross.* On Christmas Eve, Christmas night, Easter in the Western calendar, and Easter in the Orthodox calendar, Los Angeles arranged the lights and blinds of the tower of City Hall so that each side formed a large cross, visible across the freeways. The practice, the city said, was "not in religious tribute, but more in a spirit of peace and good fellowship toward all mankind." The city similarly arranged a display of light on the tower showing the Heart and Easter Seal symbols when these funds had their charitable drives. No evidence was offered that the city had ever refused any similar request. The practice had gone on for thirty years as to the Christmas lighting; no evidence was presented that it had had any religious impact. In *Fox v. City of Los Angeles*, 22 Cal.3d 792, 150 Cal. Rptr. 867, 587 P.2d 663 (1978), the supreme court of California, 5–2, per Justice Frank Newman, held in a taxpayer's suit that the display violated the California Constitution, art. 1, sec. 4: "The Legislature shall make no law respecting an establishment of religion."

A local YMCA director who was an active Episcopalian proposed the erection of a Latin cross in a city-owned park in San Francisco. The city agreed, and placed a 103–foot by 36–foot concrete cross in Mount Davidson Park. In a dedication ceremony held in 1934, President Franklin D. Roosevelt pressed a golden telegraph key sending a signal from Washington, D.C. through a special direct circuit to illuminate the Cross. Fifty thousand people attended the event in the park, which took place on the eve of Palm Sunday in order to illuminate the Cross for Easter Week. In *Carpenter v. City & County of San Francisco*, 93 F.3d 627 (9th Cir. 1996), the court, per Judge Diarmuid O'Scannlain, ruled that the maintenance of the cross by the city violates the No Preference Clause of the California Constitution, art. I, § 4, which guarantees the "[f]ree exercise and enjoyment of religion without discrimination or preference."

A large cross on the crest of Skinner's Butte, a municipal park overlooking the city of Eugene, Oregon, was erected by two businesses and lighted at Christmas and Easter; it was ordered removed as a violation of both state and federal constitutions. The cross was then given to the city. In public ceremonies sponsored by the American Legion it was dedicated as a "Veteran's War Memorial." It was now lighted on national holidays and according to testimony continued to be seen by many people in Eugene as a religious symbol and was regarded by some as offensive for that reason. In *Eugene Sand and Gravel, Inc. v. City of Eugene*, 276 Or. 1007, 558 P.2d 338 (1976), the Oregon Supreme Court, 4–3, set aside its earlier decree, holding that the purpose of the display was secular, *cert. denied*, 434 U.S. 876 (1977).

A sixteen-foot tall cross, bearing a terra cotta figure of Jesus, was erected in 1927 in Wicker Memorial Park, located in North Township, Indiana, with a commemorative plaque bearing the following inscription: "As the inhabitants of the North Township repair to this park in years to come, as they are reinvigorated in body and mind by its use, as they are moved by the memory of the heroic deeds of those to whom it is dedicated, may they become partakers and promoters of the more noble, more exalted, more inspired American life. Calvin Coolidge." In 1955 the Knights of Columbus, a Catholic fraternal organization, added a memorial plaque to honor the deeds of those who gave their life in battle: "Dedicated to the memory of men and women whose love for this nation enabled them to make the supreme sacrifice of life itself in its defense." In *Gonzales v. North Township of Lake County, Indiana*, 4 F.3d 1412 (7th Cir. 1993), the court, per Judge William Bauer, rejected the township's claim that the crucifix was intended to act as a war memorial, and ruled that the original goal of the Knights of Columbus was to spread the Christian message. Finding no valid secular purpose for the display of the cross, the court held that it violated the nonestablishment provision, and ordered it removed from the public park. See also *American Civil Liberties Union v. Rabun*, 698 F.2d 1098 (11th Cir. 1983) (county-owned 35–foot by 26–foot cross dedicated at an Easter sunrise service was erected out of "religious stirrings and for a religious purpose," not for secular purpose of promoting tourism).

Lynch and *Allegheny County* were obviously resolved under the federal constitution and therefore do not control either *Fox* or *Carpenter*, both of which were decided under the California constitution. Are *Rabun* and *Gonzales* consistent with *Lynch* and *Allegheny County*?

4. *Another Cross: The Klan's Access to a Public Forum.* Ohio law makes Capitol Square, the Statehouse plaza in Columbus, a forum for discussion of public questions and for public activities, and gives the Capitol Square Review and Advisory Board responsibility for regulating access to the square. To use the square, a group must simply fill out an official application form and meet several speech-neutral criteria. Sensing that the cross has been used by the Ku Klux Klan not as a symbol of universal love, but of racial superiority and hatred, the Board denied, on Establishment Clause grounds, the application of the Klan to place an "unattended" cross on the square during the 1993 Christmas season. After the lower courts enjoined this denial of the Klan's application, the Board permitted the Klan to erect its cross. In *Capitol Square Review and Advisory Board v. Pinette*, 515 U.S. 753 (1995), the Court, per Justice Scalia, held that the Klan's display was private religious speech fully protected under the Free Speech Clause as secular private expression. See, e.g.,

Lamb's Chapel v. Center Moriches Union Free School Dist. 508 U.S. 384 (1993) [Chapter Fourteen, section 2H]. Because Capitol Square is a traditional public forum, the Board may regulate the content of the Klan's expression there only if such a restriction is necessary, and narrowly drawn, to serve a compelling state interest. Compliance with the Establishment Clause may be a state interest sufficiently compelling to justify content-based restrictions on speech. But the Court found that the factors considered determinative in striking down state restrictions on religious content in *Lamb's Chapel*, and *Widmar v. Vincent* [Chapter Fourteen, section 3] were present in this case as well. As *Lamb's Chapel*, and *Widmar*, the State did not sponsor the expression, the expression was made on government property that had been opened to the public for speech, and permission was requested through the same application process and on the same terms required of other private groups.

Justice Thomas wrote separately, agreeing with the Court's conclusion the Board's exclusion of the Klan's cross cannot be justified on Establishment Clause grounds. But he added: "[T]he fact that the legal issue before us involves the Establishment Clause should not lead anyone to think that a cross erected by the Ku Klux Klan is a purely religious symbol. The erection of such a cross is a political act, not a Christian one. There is little doubt that the Klan's main objective is to establish a racist white government in the United States. In Klan ceremony, the cross is a symbol of white supremacy and a tool for the intimidation and harassment of racial minorities, Catholics, Jews, Communists, and any other groups hated by the Klan. The cross is associated with the Klan not because of religious worship, but because of the Klan's practice of cross-burning."

7. Double Duty Social Service Programs

Bowen v. Kendrick

487 U.S. 589 (1988).

Solicitor General *Fried* argued the cause for appellant in Nos. 87–253 and 87–431, and for the federal appellee in No. 87–462. With him on the briefs were Assistant Attorney General Willard, Acting Assistant Attorney General *Spears*, Deputy Solicitor General *Ayer*, Deputy Assistant Attorney General *Cynkar*, *Lawrence S. Robbins, Michael Jay Singer, Jay S. Bybee, and Theodore C. Hirt. Michael W. McConnell* argued the cause for appellant in No. 87–775. With him on the briefs were *Edward R. Grant, Clarke D. Forsythe, Paul Arneson, and Michael J. Woodruff.*

Janet Benshoof argued the cause for appellees in Nos. 87–253, 87–431, and 87–775 and appellants in No. 87–462. With her on the briefs were *Lynn M. Paltrow, Nan D. Hunter, Rachael N. Pine, and Bruce J. Ennis, Jr.*

Briefs of amici curiae urging reversal were filed for the Attorney General of Arizona et al. by *Gary B. Born and James S. Campbell*; for the Catholic League for Religious and Civil Rights et al. by *Steven Frederick McDowell*; for the Institute for Youth Advocacy by *Gregory A. Loken*; for the National Jewish Commission on Law and Public Affairs by *Nathan*

Lewin and Dennis Rapps; for the National Right to Life Committee, Inc., by *James Bopp, Jr.*; for the Rutherford Institute et al. by *John W. Whitehead, David E. Morris, Alfred J. Lindh, Ira W. Still III, William B. Hollberg, Randall A. Pentiuk, Thomas W. Strahan, William Bonner, John F. Southworth, Jr., and W. Charles Bundren*; and for the United States Catholic Conference by *Mark E. Chopko and Philip H. Harris.*

Briefs of amici curiae urging affirmance were filed for the American Public Health Association et al. by *John H. Hall, Nadine Taub, and Judith Levin*; for the Baptist Joint Committee on Public Affairs et al. by *Oliver S. Thomas*; for the Committee for Public Education and Religious Liberty by *Leo Pfeffer*; for the Council on Religious Freedom by *Lee Boothby, Robert W. Nixon, and Rolland Truman*; for the National Coalition for Public Education and Religious Liberty et al. by *David B. Isbell, David H. Remes, and Herman Schwartz*; and for the NOW Legal Defense and Education Fund et al. by *Sarah E. Burns and Marsha Levick.* Briefs of amici curiae were filed for the Anti–Defamation League of B'nai B'rith et al. by *Ruti G. Teitel, Justin J. Finger, Jeffrey P. Sinensky, Meyer Eisenberg, and Steven M. Freeman*; for Catholic Charities, U.S.A., et al. by *Patrick Francis Geary*; and for the Unitarian Universalist Association et al. by *Patricia Hennessey.*

■ Rehnquist, C. J., delivered the opinion of the Court, in which White, O'Connor, Scalia, and Kennedy, JJ., joined.

This litigation involves a challenge to a federal grant program that provides funding for services relating to adolescent sexuality and pregnancy. Considering the federal statute both "on its face" and "as applied," the District Court ruled that the statute violated the Establishment Clause of the First Amendment insofar as it provided for the involvement of religious organizations in the federally funded programs. We conclude, however, that the statute is not unconstitutional on its face, and that a determination of whether any of the grants made pursuant to the statute violate the Establishment Clause requires further proceedings in the District Court.

The Adolescent Family Life Act (AFLA or Act), Pub. L. 97–35, 95 Stat. 578, 42 U.S.C. § 300z et seq., was passed by Congress in 1981 in response to the "severe adverse health, social, and economic consequences" that often follow pregnancy and childbirth among unmarried adolescents. Like its predecessor, the Adolescent Health Services and Pregnancy Prevention and Care Act of 1978, Pub. L. 95–626, Tit. VI, 92 Stat. 3595–3601 (Title VI), the AFLA is essentially a scheme for providing grants to public or nonprofit private organizations or agencies "for services and research in the area of premarital adolescent sexual relations and pregnancy." S.Rep. No. 97–161, p. 1 (1981) (hereinafter Senate Report). These grants are intended to serve several purposes, including the promotion of "self discipline and other prudent approaches to the problem of adolescent premarital sexual relations," the promotion of adoption as an alternative for adolescent parents, the establishment of new approaches to the delivery of care services for pregnant adolescents, and the support of research and demonstration projects "concerning the societal causes and consequences of adolescent premarital sexual relations, contraceptive use, pregnancy, and child rearing" [texts cited are from the AFLA, section citations omitted].

[Grant recipients are to provide two types of services: "care services" and "prevention services."] "Necessary services" include pregnancy testing and maternity counseling, adoption counseling and referral services, pre-natal and postnatal health care, nutritional information, counseling, child care, mental health services, and perhaps most importantly for present purposes, "educational services relating to family life and problems associated with adolescent premarital sexual relations."

In drawing up the AFLA and determining what services to provide under the Act, Congress was well aware that "the problems of adolescent premarital sexual relations, pregnancy, and parenthood are multiple and complex." Indeed, Congress expressly recognized that legislative or governmental action alone would be insufficient: "[S]uch problems are best approached through a variety of integrated and essential services provided to adolescents and their families by other family members, religious and charitable organizations, voluntary associations, and other groups in the private sector as well as services provided by publicly sponsored initiatives."

Accordingly, the AFLA expressly states that federally provided services in this area should promote the involvement of parents, and should "emphasize the provision of support by other family members, religious and charitable organizations, voluntary associations, and other groups." The AFLA implements this goal by providing that demonstration projects funded by the government "shall use such methods as will strengthen the capacity of families to deal with the sexual behavior, pregnancy, or parenthood of adolescents and to make use of support systems such as other family members, friends, religious and charitable organizations, and voluntary associations." . . .

In line with its purposes, the AFLA also imposes limitations on the use of funds by grantees. First, the AFLA expressly states that no funds provided for demonstration projects under the statute may be used for family planning services (other than counseling and referral services) unless appropriate family planning services are not otherwise available in the community. Second, the AFLA restricts the awarding of grants to "programs or projects which do not provide abortions or abortion counseling or referral," except that the program may provide referral for abortion counseling if the adolescent and her parents request such referral. Finally, the AFLA states that "grants may be made only to projects or programs which do not advocate, promote, or encourage abortion."

Since 1981, when the AFLA was adopted, the Secretary has received 1,088 grant applications and awarded 141 grants. Funding has gone to a wide variety of recipients, including state and local health agencies, private hospitals, community health associations, privately operated health care centers, and community and charitable organizations. It is undisputed that a number of grantees or subgrantees were organizations with institutional ties to religious denominations. . . .

The District Court in this lawsuit held the AFLA unconstitutional both on its face and as applied. Few of our cases in the Establishment Clause area have explicitly distinguished between facial challenges to a statute and attacks on the statute as applied. Several cases have clearly involved challenges to a statute "on its face." (citing *Edwards v. Aguillard* [Chapter Fourteen, section 2], *Wolman v. Walter* [Chapter Fourteen, section 1]; and *Committee for Public Education & Religious Liberty v. Nyquist* [Chapter Fourteen, section 1]).

In other cases we have, in the course of determining the constitutionality of a statute, referred not only to the language of the statute but also to the manner in which it had been administered in practice (citations omitted). . . .

As we see it, it is clear from the face of the statute that the AFLA was motivated primarily, if not entirely, by a legitimate secular purpose—the elimination or reduction of social and economic problems caused by teenage sexuality, pregnancy, and parenthood. Appellees cannot, and do not, dispute that, on the whole, religious concerns were not the sole motivation behind the Act, nor can it be said that the AFLA lacks a legitimate secular purpose. . . .

In adopting the AFLA, Congress expressly intended to expand the services already authorized by Title VI, to insure the increased participation of parents in education and support services, to increase the flexibility of the programs, and to spark the development of new, innovative services. These are all legitimate secular goals that are furthered by the AFLA's additions to Title VI, including the challenged provisions that refer to religious organizations. There simply is no evidence that Congress' "actual purpose" in passing the AFLA was one of "endorsing religion." *Edwards v. Aguillard*. Nor are we in a position to doubt that Congress' expressed purposes are "sincere and not a sham." *Id*.[12]

As usual in Establishment Clause cases, the more difficult question is whether the primary effect of the challenged statute is impermissible. Before we address this question, however, it is useful to review again just what the AFLA sets out to do. Simply stated, it authorizes grants to institutions that are capable of providing certain care and prevention services to adolescents. Because of the complexity of the problems that Congress sought to remedy, potential grantees are required to describe how they will involve other organizations, including religious organizations, in the programs funded by the federal grants. There is no requirement in the Act that grantees be affiliated with any religious denomination, although the Act clearly does not rule out grants to religious organizations.[13] The

---

12. We also see no reason to conclude that the AFLA serves an impermissible religious purpose simply because some of the goals of the statute coincide with the beliefs of certain religious organizations. See *Harris v. McRae* [Chapter Fifteen, section 4]; *McGowan v. Maryland* [section 2 above].

13. Indeed, the legislative history shows that Congress was aware that religious organizations had been grantees under Title VI and that it did not disapprove of that practice. The Senate Report states: "It

should be noted that under current law [Title VI], the Office of Adolescent Pregnancy Programs has made grants to two religious-affiliated organizations, two Christian organizations and several other groups that are indirectly affiliated with religious bodies. Religious affiliation is not a criterion for selection as a grantee under the adolescent family life program, but any such grants made by the Secretary would be a simple recognition that nonprofit religious organizations have a services to be provided under the AFLA are not religious in character, nor has there been any suggestion that religious institutions or organizations with religious ties are uniquely well qualified to carry out those services.[14] Certainly it is true that a substantial part of the services listed as necessary services under the Act involve some sort of education or counseling, but there is nothing inherently religious about these activities and appellees do not contend that, by themselves, the AFLA's "necessary services" somehow have the primary effect of advancing religion. Finally, it is clear that the AFLA takes a particular approach toward dealing with adolescent sexuality and pregnancy—for example, two of its stated purposes are to "promote self discipline and other prudent approaches to the problem of adolescent premarital sexual relations," and to "promote adoption as an alternative,"—but again, that approach is not inherently religious, although it may coincide with the approach taken by certain religions. . . .

Nothing in our previous cases prevents Congress from . . . recognizing the important part that religion or religious organizations may play in resolving certain secular problems. Particularly when, as Congress found, "prevention of adolescent sexual activity and adolescent pregnancy depends primarily upon developing strong family values and close family ties," it seems quite sensible for Congress to recognize that religious organizations can influence values and can have some influence on family life, including parents' relations with their adolescent children. . . .

[Appellees offer another] ground for objecting to the AFLA: the fact that it allows religious institutions to participate as recipients of federal funds. The AFLA defines an "eligible grant recipient" as a "public or nonprofit private organization or agency" which demonstrates the capability of providing the requisite services. As this provision would indicate, a fairly wide spectrum of organizations is eligible to apply for and receive funding under the Act, and nothing on the face of the Act suggests it is anything but neutral with respect to the grantee's status as a sectarian or purely secular institution. See Senate Report, at 16 ("Religious affiliation is not a criterion for selection as a grantee . . ."). In this regard, then, the AFLA is similar to other statutes that this Court has upheld against Establishment Clause challenges in the past (citations omitted). . . .

We note in addition that this Court has never held that religious institutions are disabled by the First Amendment from participating in publicly sponsored social welfare programs. To the contrary, in *Bradfield v. Roberts* [Chapter Ten, section 2], the Court upheld an agreement between the Commissioners of the District of Columbia and a religiously affiliated hospital whereby the Federal Government would pay for the construction of a new building on the grounds of the hospital. In effect, the Court

role to play in the provision of services to adolescents."

14. One witness before the Senate Committee testified that "projects which target hispanic and other minority populations are more accepted by the population if they include sectarian, as well as non-sectarian,

organizations in the delivery of those services." S.Rep., p. 10. This indicates not that sectarian grantees are particularly well qualified to perform AFLA services, but that the inclusion of both secular and sectarian grantees can improve the effectiveness of the Act's programs.

refused to hold that the mere fact that the hospital was "conducted under the auspices of the Roman Catholic Church" was sufficient to alter the purely secular legal character of the corporation, particularly in the absence of any allegation that the hospital discriminated on the basis of religion or operated in any way inconsistent with its secular charter. In the Court's view, the giving of federal aid to the hospital was entirely consistent with the Establishment Clause, and the fact that the hospital was religiously affiliated was "wholly immaterial." The propriety of this holding, and the long history of cooperation and interdependency between governments and charitable or religious organizations is reflected in the legislative history of the AFLA. See S. Rep. No. 98–496, p. 10 (1984) ("Charitable organizations with religious affiliations historically have provided social services with the support of their communities and without controversy"). . . .

Nor do we agree with the District Court that the AFLA necessarily has the effect of advancing religion because the religiously affiliated AFLA grantees will be providing educational and counseling services to adolescents. Of course, we have said that the Establishment Clause does "prohibit government-financed or government-sponsored indoctrination into the beliefs of a particular religious faith," *Grand Rapids* [Chapter Fourteen, section 1; note: *Grand Rapids* was reversed in *Agostini v. Felton*, Chapter Fourteen, section 1], and we have accordingly struck down programs that entail an unacceptable risk that government funding would be used to "advance the religious mission" of the religious institution receiving aid. *Meek v. Pittenger* [Chapter Fourteen, section 1; note: *Meek* was reversed *in Mitchell v. Helms*, Chapter Fourteen, section 1]. But nothing in our prior cases warrants the presumption adopted by the District Court that religiously affiliated AFLA grantees are not capable of carrying out their functions under the AFLA in a lawful, secular manner. . . .

We also disagree with the District Court's conclusion that the AFLA is invalid because it authorizes "teaching" by religious grant recipients on "matters [that] are fundamental elements of religious doctrine," such as the harm of premarital sex and the reasons for choosing adoption over abortion. On an issue as sensitive and important as teenage sexuality, it is not surprising that the Government's secular concerns would either coincide or conflict with those of religious institutions. But the possibility or even the likelihood that some of the religious institutions who receive AFLA funding will agree with the message that Congress intended to deliver to adolescents through the AFLA is insufficient to warrant a finding that the statute on its face has the primary effect of advancing religion. See *Lynch* [section 6 above]; *Harris v. McRae* [Chapter Fifteen, section 4]. Nor does the alignment of the statute and the religious views of the grantees run afoul of our proscription against "fund[ing] a specifically religious activity in an otherwise substantially secular setting." *Hunt v. McNair* [Chapter Fourteen, section 3]. The facially neutral projects authorized by the AFLA—including pregnancy testing, adoption counseling and referral services, prenatal and postnatal care, educational services, residential care, child care, consumer education, etc.—are not themselves "specifically religious activities," and they are not converted into such activities by the fact that they are carried out by organizations with religious affiliations.

[The Court also rejected three other argument against the validity of AFLA on its face: that the involvement of religious organizations in the Act has the impermissible effect of creating a "crucial symbolic link" between government and religion, that the AFLA lacks an express provision preventing the use of federal funds for religious purposes, and that the AFLA leads to an excessive government entanglement with religion.]

For the foregoing reasons we conclude that the AFLA does not violate the Establishment Clause "on its face."

We turn now to consider whether the District Court correctly ruled that the AFLA was unconstitutional as applied. . . .

On the merits of the "as applied" challenge, it seems to us that the District Court did not follow the proper approach in assessing appellees' claim that the Secretary is making grants under the Act that violate the Establishment Clause of the First Amendment. Although the District Court stated several times that AFLA aid had been given to religious organizations that were "pervasively sectarian," it did not identify which grantees it was referring to, nor did it discuss with any particularity the aspects of those organizations which in its view warranted classification as "pervasively sectarian."[15] The District Court did identify certain instances in which it felt AFLA funds were used for constitutionally improper purposes, but in our view the court did not adequately design its remedy to address the specific problems it found in the Secretary's administration of the statute. Accordingly, although there is no dispute that the record contains evidence of specific incidents of impermissible behavior by AFLA grantees, we feel that this lawsuit should be remanded to the District Court for consideration of the evidence presented by appellees insofar as it sheds light on the manner in which the statute is presently being administered. It is the latter inquiry to which the court must direct itself on remand.

We conclude, first, that the District Court erred in holding that the AFLA is invalid on its face, and second, that the court should consider on remand whether particular AFLA grants have had the primary effect of advancing religion. Should the court conclude that the Secretary's current practice does allow such grants, it should devise a remedy to insure that grants awarded by the Secretary comply with the Constitution and the statute. The judgment of the District Court is accordingly *Reversed.*

■ Justice O'Connor filed a concurring opinion.

■ Justice Kennedy, joined by Justice Scalia, filed a concurring opinion.

■ Justice Blackmun, joined by Justice Brennan, Justice Marshall and Justice Stevens, dissenting.

---

15. The closest the court came was to identify "at least ten AFLA grantees or subgrantees [that] were themselves 'religious organizations,' in the sense that they have explicit corporate ties to a particular religious faith and by-laws or policies that prohibit any deviation from religious doctrine." While these factors are relevant to the determination of whether an institution is "pervasively sectarian," they are not conclusive, and we do not find the court's conclusion that these institutions are "religious organizations" to be equivalent to a finding that their secular purposes and religious mission are "inextricably intertwined."

[Note the dissent's emphasis on details in the record that illustrated the transmission of a strong religious message in some of the federally funded programs.]

In 1981, Congress enacted the AFLA, thereby "involv[ing] families[,] ... religious and charitable organizations, voluntary associations, and other groups," in a broad-scale effort to alleviate some of the problems associated with teenage pregnancy. It is unclear whether Congress ever envisioned that public funds would pay for a program during a session of which parents and teenagers would be instructed: "You want to know the church teachings on sexuality.... You are the church. You people sitting here are the body of Christ. The teachings of you and the things you value are, in fact, the values of the Catholic Church." App. 226.

Or of curricula that taught: "The Church has always taught that the marriage act, or intercourse, seals the union of husband and wife, (and is a representation of their union on all levels). Christ commits Himself to us when we come to ask for the sacrament of marriage. We ask Him to be active in our life. God is love. We ask Him to share His love in ours, and God procreates with us, He enters into our physical union with Him, and we begin new life." *Id.*, at 372.

Or the teaching of a method of family planning described on the grant application as "not only a method of birth regulation but also a philosophy of procreation," and promoted as helping "spouses who are striving ... to transform their married life into testimony[,] ... to cultivate their matrimonial spirituality[, and] to make themselves better instruments in God's plan," and as "facilitat[ing] the evangelization of homes." *Id.* 385.

Whatever Congress had in mind [in enacting the AFLA], it enacted a statute that facilitated and, indeed, encouraged the use of public funds for [explicitly religious] instruction, by giving religious groups a central pedagogical and counseling role without imposing any restraints on the sectarian quality of the participation. As the record developed thus far in this litigation makes all too clear, federal tax dollars appropriated for AFLA purposes have been used, with Government approval, to support religious teaching. Today the majority upholds the facial validity of this statute and remands the action to the District Court for further proceedings concerning appellees' challenge to the manner in which the statute has been applied. Because I am firmly convinced that our cases require invalidating this statutory scheme, I dissent.

NOTES AND QUESTION

Charitable Choice. Section 104(j) of the Personal Responsibility and Work Opportunity Reconciliation Act of 1996, 42 U.S.C. S 604a, is known by the popular name of "Charitable Choice." This provision permits states to involve faith-based providers in the delivery of welfare services funded by the federal government through block grants to the states. Where the form of the assistance is indirect, such as by means of certificates or vouchers, the faith-based providers are not restricted as to their religious activities. Constitutional after *Bowen v. Kendrick*? Does the direct-indirect distinction matter after *Mitchell v.*

Helms [Chapter Fourteen, section 1]? For analysis of this legislation, see Carl H. Esbeck, "A Constitutional Case for Governmental Cooperation with Faith–Based Social Service Providers," 46 *Emory L. J.* 1 (1997); Esbeck, "The Neutral Treatment of Religion and Faith–Based Social Service Providers: Charitable Choice and Its Critics," in Derek Davis and Barry Hankins, eds., *Welfare Reform & Faith–Based Organizations* 173 (1999); Esbeck, "Myths, Miscues, and Misconceptions: No–Aid Separationism and the Establishment Clause," 13 *Notre Dame J. of Law, Ethics & Pub. Policy* 285 (1999); Alan E. Brownstein, "Interpreting The Religion Clauses In Terms Of Liberty, Equality, And Free Speech Values—A Critical Analysis Of 'Neutrality Theory' And 'Charitable Choice,'" 13 *Notre Dame J. L., Ethics & Pub. Policy* 243 (1999); Michelle P. Ryan, Comment, "Paved with Good Intentions: The Legal Consequences of the Charitable Choice Provision," 102 *Dickinson L. Rev.* 383 (1998); and Derek H. Davis, "Editorial: The Church–State Implications of the New Welfare Reform Act," 38 *J. Church & St.* 719 (1996).

CHAPTER FOURTEEN

EDUCATION

1. RELIGIOUS ELEMENTARY AND SECONDARY SCHOOLS

NOTE

What's in a Name?: The Problem with the "Pervasively Sectarian" Label. The Court and commentators routinely describe elementary and secondary schools of religious communities as "pervasively sectarian," see, e.g., cases in this section: *Lemon v. Kurtzman, Meek v. Pittenger, Aguilar v. Felton,* and *Grand Rapids School District v. Ball.* For a critique of this terminology, see Richard Baer, "The Supreme Court's Discriminatory Use of the Term 'Sectarian,'" 6 *J. L. & Politics* 449 (1990). In this section we refer to these schools simply as "religious schools."

This term avoids the negative connotation now imbedded in the term "sectarian." In the discourse of the sociology of religion, the term "sectarian" is sharply differentiated from the term "church." Ernst Troeltsch gave a problematic, but now classic, description of a church as "that type of organization which is overwhelmingly conservative, which to a certain extent accepts the secular order, and dominates the masses; in principle, therefore, it is universal, i.e. it desires to cover the whole life of humanity." Ernst Troeltsch, 1 *The Social Teachings of the Christian Church* 331 (1931). By contrast, Troeltsch describes sects as "comparably small groups; they aspire after personal inward perfection, and they aim at a direct personal fellowship between the members of each group.... Their attitude towards the world, the State, and Society may be indifferent, tolerant, or hostile, since they have no desire to control and incorporate these forms of social life; on the contrary, they tend to avoid them; their aim is usually rather to tolerate their presence alongside of their own body, or even to replace these social institutions by their own society." *Id.* (describing the sect type within medieval Catholicism). Sometimes the term "sectarian" can refer more narrowly to the radical wing of the Reformation, principally the Anabaptist movement led by Menno Simons [Chapter Five, section 1] and distinguished for its rejection both of infant baptism and of killing others at the command of the sovereign. Other Christians—both Catholic and Protestants—subjected Mennonites to persecution, including death, because of these beliefs; for a description of the sect type within Protestantism, see Troeltsch, 2 *The Social Teachings of the Christian Church* 691–807 (1931). In current legal and political discourse, however, the term "sectarian" is more fluid and much more pejorative, akin to the negative connotation of the term "cult." Once a perfectly harmless term describing the act of worship, "cult" has now come to be a term of contempt used to describe a religious community that one hates. "Sect" and "sectarian" may not be quite that strong, but they are often loaded terms when used by judges and journalists.

The term "religious school" avoids the circularity of the term "pervasively sectarian," which is frequently a substitute for serious empirical analysis of the actual effects that occur within an educational institution. The label "pervasively sectarian" school has come to mean an institution that may not receive public financial assistance even for transparently secular activities, because the Court thinks that these secular activities cannot be separated from religious ones at a "pervasively sectarian" school. Justice White challenged the loose use of the adverb "pervasively" in his dissent in *Lemon*: "Our prior cases have recognized the dual role of parochial schools in American society: they perform both religious and secular functions." It is simplistic to imagine that all religious schools fit a single profile of a "pervasively sectarian" institution, such as that articulated in *Committee for Public Education and Religious Liberty v. Nyquist* [this section below]. Religious schools reflect many different ways of integrating religion into the curriculum. This diversity is similar to the many different ways in which public schools integrate public morality into the curriculum, or fail to do so.

In *Mitchell v. Helms* [this section below] Justice Thomas wrote for a plurality of four justices that the time had come to dispense with the consideration of whether a recipient of aid is "pervasively sectarian." He acknowledged that there was a period in which that factor mattered, but concluded: "that period is one that the Court should regret, and it is thankfully long past." He offered three reasons for this conclusion. First, the term had become irrelevant. The Court had "not struck down an aid program in reliance on this factor since 1985, in *Aguilar* and *Ball* [this section below]," reversed or partially reversed in *Agostini* [this section below]. Second, "the religious nature of a recipient should not matter to the constitutional analysis, so long as the recipient adequately furthers the government's secular purpose." Third, "the inquiry into the recipient's religious views required by a focus on whether a school is pervasively sectarian is not only unnecessary but also offensive. It is well established, in numerous other contexts, that courts should refrain from trolling through a person's or institution's religious beliefs." Noting the origin of the label in the anti-Catholic atmosphere in which the Blaine Amendment was considered [Chapter Eight, section 7], see Green, "The Blaine Amendment Reconsidered," 36 *Am. J. Legal Hist.* 38 (1992), Justice Thomas concluded: "nothing in the Establishment Clause requires the exclusion of pervasively sectarian schools from otherwise permissible aid programs, and other doctrines of this Court bar it. This doctrine, born of bigotry, should be buried now."

The term "religious school" is more inclusive of the wide variety of religious communities that operate religious schools, including many who do not call their schools "parochial." That term is familiar to Roman Catholics and Lutherans, who operate religious schools on a large scale in conjunction with a local community known as a parish, the adjectival form of which is "parochial." But the term is not generally used among other Christian communities, such as Baptists, Calvinists, and Seventh-day Adventists, who also operate religious schools, or among Jews who operate yeshivoth or Hebrew day-schools.

Everson v. Board of Education of the Township of Ewing

330 U.S. 1 (1947).

Edward R. Burke and *E. Hilton Jackson* argued the cause for appellant. With *Mr. Burke* on the brief were *Challen B. Ellis, W.D. Jamieson* and *Kahl K. Spriggs.*

William H. Speer argued the cause for appellees. With him on the brief were *Porter R. Chandler* and *Roger R. Clisham.*

Briefs of *amici curiae* in support of appellant were filed by *E. Hilton Jackson* for the General Conference of Seventh-day Adventists et al.; by *Harry V. Osborne, Kenneth W. Greenawalt* and *Whitney N. Seymour* for the American Civil Liberties Union; and by *Milton T. Lasher* for the State Council of the Junior Order of United American Mechanics of New Jersey.

Briefs of *amici curiae* in support of appellees were filed by *George F. Barrett,* Attorney General of Illinois, *William C. Wines,* Assistant Attorney General of Illinois, and *James A. Emmert,* Attorney General of Indiana, for the States of Illinois and Indiana; by *Fred S. LeBlanc,* Attorney General, for the State of Louisiana; by *Clarence A. Barnes,* Attorney General, for the Commonwealth of Massachusetts; by *Edmund E. Shepherd,* Solicitor General, and *Daniel J. O'Hara,* Assistant Attorney General, for the State of Michigan; by *Nathaniel L. Goldstein,* Attorney General, and *Wendell P. Brown,* Solicitor General, for the State of New York; and by *James N. Vaughn* and *George E. Flood* for the National Council of Catholic Men et al.

■ JUSTICE BLACK delivered the opinion of the Court.

A New Jersey statute authorizes its local school districts to make rules and contracts for the transportation of children to and from schools. The appellee, a township board of education, acting pursuant to this statute, authorized reimbursement to parents of money expended by them for the bus transportation of their children on regular buses operated by the public transportation system. Part of this money was for the payment of transportation of some children in the community to Catholic parochial schools. These church schools give their students, in addition to secular education, regular religious instruction conforming to the religious tenets and modes of worship of the Catholic Faith. The superintendent of these schools is a Catholic priest.

The appellant, in his capacity as a district taxpayer, filed suit in a state court challenging the right of the Board to reimburse parents of parochial school students. He contended that the statute and the resolution passed pursuant to it violated both the State and the Federal Constitutions. That court held that the legislature was without power to authorize such payment under the state constitution. The New Jersey Court of Errors and Appeals reversed, holding that neither the statute nor the resolution passed pursuant to it was in conflict with the State constitution or the provisions of the Federal Constitution in issue.

The only contention here is that the state statute and the resolution, insofar as they authorized reimbursement to parents of children attending parochial schools, violate the Federal Constitution in these two respects, which to some extent overlap. *First.* They authorize the State to take by taxation the private property of some and bestow it upon others, to be used for their own private purposes. This, it is alleged, violates the due process clause of the Fourteenth Amendment. *Second.* The statute and the resolution forced inhabitants to pay taxes to help support and maintain schools which are dedicated to, and which regularly teach, the Catholic Faith. This is alleged to be a use of state power to support church schools contrary to the prohibition of the First Amendment which the Fourteenth Amendment made applicable to the states.

First.... It is much too late to argue that legislation intended to facilitate the opportunity of children to get a secular education serves no public purpose. *Cochran v. Louisiana State Board of Education,* [Chapter Ten, section 10]. The same thing is no less true of legislation to reimburse needy parents, or all parents, for payment of the fares of their children so that they can ride in public busses to and from schools rather than run the risk of traffic and other hazards incident to walking or "hitchhiking." Nor does it follow that a law has a private rather than a public purpose because it provides that tax-raised funds will be paid to reimburse individuals on account of money spent by them in a way which furthers a public program. Subsidies and loans to individuals such as farmers and home-owners, and to privately owned transportation systems, as well as many other kinds of businesses, have been commonplace practices in our state and national history....

Second. The New Jersey statute is challenged as a "law respecting an establishment of religion." The First Amendment, as made applicable to the states by the Fourteenth, *Murdock v. Pennsylvania,* [Chapter Eleven, section 1], commands that a state "shall make no law respecting an establishment of religion, or prohibiting the free exercise thereof...." These words of the First Amendment reflected in the minds of early Americans a vivid mental picture of conditions and practices which they fervently wished to stamp out in order to preserve liberty for themselves and for their posterity. Doubtless their goal has not been entirely reached; but so far has the Nation moved toward it that the expression "law respecting an establishment of religion," probably does not so vividly remind present-day Americans of the evils, fears, and political problems that caused that expression to be written into our Bill of Rights. Whether this New Jersey law is one respecting an "establishment of religion" requires an understanding of the meaning of that language, particularly with respect to the imposition of taxes....

This Court has previously recognized that the provisions of the First Amendment, in the drafting and adoption of which Madison and Jefferson played such leading roles, had the same objective and were intended to provide the same protection against governmental intrusion on religious liberty as the Virginia statute. *Reynolds v. United States* [Chapter Nine]; *Watson v. Jones* [Chapter Eight, section 5]; *Davis v. Beason* [Chapter Nine]. Prior to the adoption of the Fourteenth Amendment, the First Amendment did not apply as a restraint against the states. Most of them did soon provide similar constitutional protections for religious liberty. But some states persisted for about half a century in imposing restraints upon the free exercise of religion and in discriminating against particular religious groups. In recent years, so far as the provision against the establishment of a religion is concerned, the question has most frequently arisen in connection with proposed state aid to church schools and efforts to carry on religious teachings in the public schools in accordance with the tenets of a particular sect. Some churches have either sought or accepted state financial support for their schools. Here again the efforts to obtain state aid or acceptance of it have not been limited to any one particular faith. The state courts, in the main, have remained faithful to the language of their own constitutional provisions designed to protect religious freedom and to separate religions and governments. Their decisions, however, show the difficulty in drawing the line between tax legislation which provides funds for the welfare of the general public and that which is designed to support institutions which teach religion....

The "establishment of religion" clause of the First Amendment means at least this: Neither a state nor the Federal Government can set up a church. Neither can pass laws which aid one religion, aid all religions, or prefer one religion over another. Neither can force nor influence a person to go to or to remain away from church against his will or force him to profess a belief or disbelief in any religion. No person can be punished for entertaining or professing religious beliefs or disbeliefs, for church attendance or non-attendance. No tax in any amount, large or small, can be levied to support any religious activities or institutions, whatever they may be called, or whatever form they may adopt to teach or practice religion. Neither a state nor the Federal Government can, openly or secretly, participate in the affairs of any religious organizations or groups and *vice versa*. In the words of Jefferson, the clause against establishment of religion by law was intended to erect "a wall of separation between church and State." *Reynolds v. United States* [Chapter Nine].

We must consider the New Jersey statute in accordance with the foregoing limitations imposed by the First Amendment. But we must not strike that state statute down if it is within the State's constitutional power even though it approaches the verge of that power. New Jersey cannot consistently with the "establishment of religion" clause of the First Amendment contribute tax-raised funds to the support of an institution which teaches the tenets and faith of any church. On the other hand, other language of the amendment commands that New Jersey cannot hamper its citizens in the free exercise of their own religion. Consequently, it cannot exclude individual Catholics, Lutherans, Mohammedans, Baptists, Jews, Methodists, Non-believers, Presbyterians, or the members of any other faith, *because of their faith, or lack of it,* from receiving the benefits of public welfare legislation. While we do not mean to intimate that a state could not provide transportation only to children attending public schools, we must be careful, in protecting the citizens of New Jersey against state-established churches, to be sure that we do not inadvertently prohibit New Jersey from extending its general state law benefits to all its citizens without regard to their religious belief.

Measured by these standards, we cannot say that the First Amendment prohibits New Jersey from spending tax-raised funds to pay the bus fares of parochial school pupils as a part of a general program under which it pays the fares of pupils attending public and other schools. It is undoubtedly true that children are helped to get to church schools. There is even a possibility that some of the children might not be sent to the church schools if the parents were compelled to pay their children's bus fares out of their own pockets when transportation to a public school would have been paid for by the State. The same possibility exists where the state requires a local transit company to provide reduced fares to school children including those attending parochial schools, or where a municipally owned transportation system undertakes to carry all school children free of charge. Moreover, state-paid policemen, detailed to protect children going to and from church schools from the very real hazards of traffic, would serve much the same purpose and accomplish much the same result as state provisions intended to guarantee free transportation of a kind which the state deems to be best for the school children's welfare. And parents might refuse to risk their children to the serious danger of traffic accidents going to and from parochial schools, the approaches to which were not protected by policemen. Similarly, parents might be reluctant to permit their children to attend schools which the state had cut off from such general government services as ordinary police and fire protection, connections for sewage disposal, public highways and sidewalks. Of course, cutting off church schools from these services, so separate and so indisputably marked off from the religious function, would make it far more difficult for the schools to operate. But such is obviously, not the purpose of the First Amendment. That Amendment requires the state to be a neutral in its relations with groups of religious believers and non-believers; it does not require the state to be their adversary. State power is no more to be used so as to handicap religions than it is to favor them. . . .

The First Amendment has erected a wall between church and state. That wall must be kept high and impregnable. We could not approve the slightest breach. New Jersey has not breached it here. *Affirmed.*

NOTES AND QUESTIONS

1. *Secular Purpose as Public Purpose. Everson* was the first case to apply the nonestablishment provision to a state program. Justice Black did not use the term "secular purpose" that the Court would later enshrine *in Bd. of Education v. Allen* [section 1 below] and *Lemon v. Kurtzman* [section 1 below]. He did, however, write that "legislation to facilitate the opportunity of children to get a secular education serves ... [a] public purpose." In *Everson,* Black thought, the public was not being asked to support the transmission of religious meaning and value. Against exactions of that sort, the First Amendment had erected a "wall of separation of church and state." But in Black's view the nonestablishment provision was not offended by "legislation to reimburse needy parents, or all parents, for payment of the fares of their children to and from schools rather than run the risk of traffic and other hazards incident to walking or hitchhiking." Four members of the Court—Frankfurter, Rutledge,

Jackson, and Burton—would have gone further and held the bus transportation unconstitutional.

In one respect the secularity requirement is curious. The Court has never relied on this standard to invalidate any program, state or federal, providing financial assistance to religious education. In all of the cases in this section the Court has been quick to find a secular purpose for the challenged aid. Although the secularity might seem toothless, it embodies an important consideration about nonestablishment, the commitment that taxpayers should not be forced to pay for instruction in a religion in which they do not believe. See, e.g., William G. McLoughlin, 2 *New England Dissent: The Baptists and the Separation of Church and State, 1630–1833* 1004–1005 (1971); see also NOTE. *The Quest for a Test.*

2. *The Religion of the Justices.* Rutledge, the son of a fundamentalist Baptist minister in Kentucky, had in later life become a modern Unitarian, Fred Israel, "Wiley Rutledge," Leon Friedman and Fred L. Israel, eds., 4 *The Justices of the United States Supreme Court 1789–1969,* 2593–2594 (1995). He wrote an especially passionate dissent, declaring that "transportation, where it is needed, is as essential to education as any other element.... The only line that can be so drawn is one between more dollars and less. Certainly in this realm such a line can be no valid constitutional measure. Now, as in Madison's time, not the amount but the principle of assessment is wrong." As an appendix to his dissent, Rutledge had reprinted the Remonstrance drafted by Madison in 1785 [Chapter Six, section 3].

3. *Plaintiffs and Amici in the School Cases.* Justice Black had in 1925 been a member of the Ku Klux Klan and in 1926 he was the Klan's candidate for the Senate, see Gerald T. Dunne, *Hugo Black and the Judicial Revolution* 114–121 (1977). Commenting on this membership, Black's son has written: "The Ku Klux Klan and Daddy, so far as I could tell, only had one thing in common. He suspected the Catholic Church. He used to read all of Paul Blanshard's books exposing power abuse in the Catholic Church. He thought the popes and bishops had too much power and property" Hugo Black, Jr., *My Father: A Remembrance* 104 (1975). Shortly after *Everson* Paul Blanshard published a series of polemical articles in *The Nation* attacking the Catholic Church for "segregat[ing] Catholic school children from the rest of the children in a separate school system." Blanshard, *American Freedom and Catholic Power* 4 (1949). His book sold 165,000 copies within two years. It was "unquestionably the most widely read anti-Catholic polemic of the post-World War II years." Frank J. Sorauf, *The Wall of Separation: The Constitutional Politics of Church and State* 34 (1976). According to Blanshard, the Catholic Church was an alien and authoritarian institution, dominated by its hierarchy, whose power posed a threat to American democracy. Blanshard emphasized the intolerance of the church and its insistence that in an ideal society the state would repress heresy. *Id.* 294–296. The "outcome of the struggle between American democracy and the Catholic hierarchy," he wrote, "depends upon the survival and expansion of the public school.... [T]he Catholic hierarchy could never make the United States into a clerical state unless it captured the public-school system or regimented a majority of American children into its own parochial-school system." *Id.* 286. He added: It seems clear to me that there is no alternative for champions of traditional American democracy except to build a resistance movement designed to prevent the hierarchy from imposing its social policies

upon our schools, hospitals, government and family organization.... In the field of culture and information, the platform should stand for the American public school, from kindergarten through college, as the foundation of American democracy. *Id*. 303–304.

Part of "the resistance movement" was an organization called Protestants and Other Americans United for Separation of Church and State, in which Blanshard served as a staff member. Blanshard was one of the founders of POAU in the year of *Everson*, 1947. Prominent in this effort to "unite Americans" were the Scottish Rite Masons (Southern Jurisdiction). Sorauf, *The Wall of Separation* 54. POAU was a major participant in litigation designed to invalidate school legislation or practices favorable to Catholics. Its broader constituency was fundamentalist Protestant with a long tradition of antipopery. Its success reflected "a fear of the loss of Protestant hegemony in American society." *Id*. 33, 53.

A second major player in schools' litigation was the American Civil Liberties Union (ACLU). Three currents of thought were identifiable in the ACLU—"the separationism of Madison and Jefferson," ironically now most often found in New England Congregationalists and Unitarians; militant atheism rejecting all religion; and the secular humanism of groups like the Ethical Culture Society. The third current was probably the ACLU mainstream. It was antipathetic to "dogmatic and authoritative religions." *Id*. 32–33. The feeling of many ACLU members was captured by a leading American philosopher, John Dewey, when he urged no federal aid for Catholic schools lest encouragement be given "a powerful reactionary world organization in the most vital realm of democratic life. John Dewey, "S. 2499, Its Antidemocratic Implications," *The Nation's Schools* 39 (March 1947):20, 21. Funding of religious schools, Dewey wrote, "would create divisions among our people and would lead to permanent conflict among self-perpetuating blocs." Dewey did not hesitate to say that the encouragement of the schools of the Catholic Church brought with it "the resulting promulgation of principles inimical to democracy."

The third major participant in school litigation was the American Jewish Congress (AJC). Founded to work for Zionist objectives at the end of World War I, the AJC at the end of World War II reflected the concern of many Jews that they might be vulnerable in an America dominated by a Christian majority. Its membership was drawn from Conservative Judaism and Reform Judaism. Acting on its own behalf or for other organizations such as the Synagogue Council of America, the National Community Relations Advisory Committee, and the Committee for Public Education and Religious Liberty (PEARL), the AJC was the most active amicus of the three organizations. Leo Pfeffer, "Amici in Church–State Litigation," 44 *Law & Contemp. Probs.* 83, 86 (1981). The Orthodox did not belong, and in 1965 formed The Jewish Committee on Law and Political Action (COLPA), which opposed the AJC on support to religious schools. *Id*. 94.

4. *Can Catholics Be Trusted?* Ever since the Reformation in England a recurrent theme in English and American history has been the suspicion that Catholics could not be trusted to be loyal, either to the Crown in the English context or to democracy in the American context. Whether or not this mistrust was well founded in the past, there is less cause for suspicion of this sort ever since the major doctrinal shifts in the Second Vatican Council. The most pertinent documents are the *Declaration on Religious Liberty* and the *Declara-*

tion on the Relations of the Church to Non–Christian Religions. An American Jesuit, John Courtney Murray, drew on the American experience of religious liberty to challenge the Catholic theologians who had opposed religious freedom, *see* Murray, "Governmental Repression of Heresy." *Proceedings of the Catholic Theological Society of America* 161 (1948); and Murray, *We Hold These Truths: Catholic Reflections on the American Proposition* (1960). Although the Catholic Church had accepted the idea of religious liberty in practice, Murray's arguments met resistance from theologians who believed that the church could not formally repudiate the doctrine of the past [Chapter Two, section 4; Chapter Four, section 1]. *See* Donald E. Pelotte, *John Courtney Murray: Theologian In Conflict* 34–58 (1975). In the end, Murray's arguments prevailed. On December 7, 1965, the Second Vatican Council adopted, and Pope Paul VI approved, the *Declaration on Religious Liberty*, known from its opening words as *Dignitatis Humanae Personae* (Of the Dignity of the Person). The vote of the bishops was 2,308 to 70. The central teaching in this declaration reads as follows.

Vatican II, *Declaration on Religious Liberty* (1965)

This Vatican Synod has decreed that the human person has the right to religious freedom. This freedom means that all men are to be immune from coercion on the part of individuals or of social groups and of any human power, in such wise that no one is to be forced to act in a manner contrary to his own beliefs; nor is anyone to be restrained from acting in accordance with his own beliefs, whether privately or publicly, whether alone or in association with others, within due limits. The Council also declares that the right to religious freedom has its foundation in the very dignity of the human person, as this dignity is known through the revealed Word of God and by reason itself. This right of the human person to religious freedom is to be recognized in the constitutional law whereby society is governed and thus is to become a civil right. Walter Abbott, ed., *The Documents of the Second Vatican Council* 678–79 (1965).

The declaration made a fundamental commitment to religious freedom for every person. For commentary on this document, *see, e.g.,* John Courtney Murray, *The Problem of Religious Freedom* (1965); Pietro Pavan, "The Right to Religious Freedom in the Conciliar Declaration," in Neophytos Edelby & Tedoro Jiminez–Urresti, eds., *Religious Freedom* 37–52 (1966); Pietro Pavan, "Declaration on Religious Freedom," in Herbert Vorgrimler, ed., 4 *Commentary on the Documents of Vatican II* 49–86 (1969). American bishops, including Cardinals Richard Cushing of Boston, Albert Meyer of Chicago, Joseph Ritter of St. Louis, Lawrence Sheehan of Baltimore, and Francis Spellman of New York, Archbishop John Dearden of Detroit, and Bishops Francis Reh of Saginaw and John Wright of Pittsburgh, played an important supportive role at critical moments in the development of the document. *See,* e.g., Xavier Rynne, *The Third Session* 24–31, 254–63 (1964); Rynne, *The Fourth Session* 31–50 (1965); John T. Noonan, Jr., *The Lustre of Our Country: The American Experience of Religious Freedom* 329–53 (1998). Judge Noonan concludes this chapter: "the Declaration on Religious Freedom would not have come into existence without the American contribution and the experiment that began with Madison." *Id.* 353.

In a companion document, the *Declaration on the Relations of the Church to Non–Christian Religions*, *Nostra aetate* (In Our Time), on October 28, 1965, the Council recognized the common religious questions and aspirations of humankind, spoke with particular respect of Buddhism and Hinduism; acknowledged Islam as a religion that not only worshipped God but venerated Jesus and Mary; and gave special homage to the "great spiritual patrimony common to Jews and Christians" and condemned and deplored the persecutions in the past of the Jews. Ironically it was not the contemporary Catholic Church, but images derived from words and deeds of Catholics in earlier ages, that animated many of those still suspicious of its religious schools.

5. *Loan of Secular Textbooks to Children Attending Religious Schools. Everson* provided the basis for challenging state aid to religious schools. But only in the 1960s did a sustained challenge to such aid develop. The great majority of cases where POAU, ACLU, and AJC intervened were education cases. Pfeffer, "Amici in Church–State Litigation," 44 *Law & Contemp. Probs.* 83, 94 (1981).

The first major case was a setback to the challengers: *Board of Education v. Allen*, 392 U.S. 236 (1968). In 1965 New York required local public school boards to lend textbooks, designed for use in the public schools, to all school children in the district. A school board challenged the statute as a violation of the First Amendment. With the AJC, represented by Leo Pfeffer, and POAU as *amici*, on one side, and the United States and eight states, on the other, the case came before the Supreme Court, which, 6–3, upheld the statute. The case was decided on the pleadings and stipulated facts without a trial. The record, as the Court commented, was bare of information about the subsidized schools. Moreover, the validity of textbook loans had been established in *Cochran*, [Chapter Ten, section 10] in the days before the First Amendment was applied to the states. It was not an ideal case for the challengers. Justice White wrote for the Court that "this Court has long recognized that religious schools pursue two goals, religious instruction and secular education." Support of secular education was a legitimate state function.

The author of *Everson*, Justice Black, joined by Justices Douglas and Fortas, dissented: "the wall" must be left "high and impregnable." Evidently unaware of the teaching of Vatican II on religious liberty mentioned above, or even of Blanshard's begrudging acknowledgement of the significance of this document, *Paul Blanshard on Vatican II* 74–96 (1966), Black displayed his animosity to Catholicism: "It is true, of course, that the New York law does not as yet formally adopt or establish a state religion. But it takes a great stride in that direction and coming events cast their shadows before them. The same powerful sectarian religious propagandists who have succeeded in securing passage of the present law to help religious schools carry on their sectarian religious purposes can and doubtless will continue their propaganda, looking toward complete domination and supremacy of their particular brand of religion."

Black declared further that the First Amendment was based on the assumption that state aid to religious schools "generates discord, disharmony, hatred, and strife among our people." The idea was slightly reformulated in a note questioning *Allen* by Paul A. Freund of Harvard, who wrote: "While political debate and discussion is normally a wholesome process for reaching viable accommodations, political division on religious lines is one of the principal evils that the first amendment sought to forestall." Freund, "Public Aid to Parochial Schools," 82 *Harvard L. Rev.* 1680, 1692 (1969). Freund cited no authority for this proposition. It was to have a career in the Supreme Court [see NOTE. *Political Division along Religious Lines*, this section]. Freund also commented on "the elaborate minuet of the individual student's request for specific books and its approval by the public school board," and noted that new Pennsylvania legislation had replaced the minuet with direct aid to the schools: "all is now modern ballet, bold and muscular." He asked, "Will the Court re-score its composition to accommodate the new movement?" Pennsylvania was not alone in its new legislation. In the late 1960s, Connecticut, Louisiana, Michigan, New Jersey, Pennsylvania, and Rhode Island passed statutes designed to finance the secular parts of the curriculum of the non-public schools, *see* Donald A. Giannella, *"Lemon* and *Tilton:* The Bitter and the Sweet of Church–State Entanglement," 1971 *Supreme Court Review* 149. All of these states had substantial Catholic populations; Rhode Island had a Catholic majority. The statutes passed were tailored to anticipate constitutional objections. The objections were made in *Lemon* and the companion cases. Three years before reaching the merits of this claim, the Court had opened the door to litigation by taxpayers.

6.   *Standing to Challenge Violations of the Nonestablishment Provision (I).* In *Frothingham v. Mellon*, 262 U.S. 447 (1923), the court held that a taxpayer had no standing to object to an act of Congress she asserted to be unconstitutional; the effect of the government carrying out the act had a "remote, fluctuating and uncertain" impact on her tax burden; she had shown no cognizable injury. In *Doremus v. Board of Education*, 342 U.S. 429 (1952), *Frothingham* was followed and standing denied to a taxpayer objecting to a New Jersey statute authorizing Bible-reading in the public schools. In *Flast v. Cohen*, 392 U.S. 83 (1968), however, the Court permitted a taxpayer to sue to enjoin the inclusion of children attending religious schools in remedial reading and math programs funded under the federal Elementary and Secondary Education Act of 1965, the program at issue in *Aguilar v. Felton, Agostini v. Felton,* and *Mitchell v. Helms* [this section below]. The taxpayer claimed that the funds were being used to support religious schools in violation of the nonestablishment provision.

The court recognized a right in a taxpayer to litigate the unconstitutionality "only of exercises of congressional power under the taxing and spending clause of Article I, sec. 8, of the Constitution," and to do so only if the taxpayer could allege a specific constitutional restraint such as the nonestablishment provision. Justice Douglas, concurring, observed: "The mounting federal aid to sectarian schools is notorious and the subterfuges numerous." He advocated liberality in allowing standing to objecting taxpayers. Justices Stewart and Fortas also saw peculiar virtue in permitting claims by taxpayers raising objections under the nonestablishment provision. Justice Harlan, dissenting, saw no basis for seeing the nonestablishment provision as a more "specific" limitation than other constitutional commands. Only in "some Pickwickian sense" did Harlan find that the constitutional provisions speak to spending. For later developments, see NOTE. *Standing II* [Chapter Fifteen, section 4].

Lemon v. Kurtzman (No. 89)
Earley v. DiCenso (No. 569)
and Robinson v. DiCenso (No. 570)
403 U.S. 602 (1971).

Henry W. Sawyer III argued the cause and filed briefs for appellants in No. 89. *Edward Bennett Williams* argued the cause for appellants in No.

569. With him on the brief were *Jeremiah C. Collins and Richard P. McMahon. Charles F. Cottam* argued the cause for appellants in No. 570. With him on the brief were *Herbert F. DeSimone*, Attorney General of Rhode Island, and *W. Slater Allen, Jr.*, Assistant Attorney General.

J. Shane Creamer argued the cause for appellees Kurtzman et al. in No. 89. On the brief were *Fred Speaker*, Attorney General of Pennsylvania, *David W. Rutstein*, Deputy Attorney General, and *Edward Friedman. William B. Ball* argued the cause for appellee schools in No. 89. With him on the brief were *Joseph G. Skelly, James E. Gallagher, Jr., C. Clark Hodgson, Jr., Samuel Rappaport, Donald A. Semisch*, and *William D. Valente. Henry T. Reath* filed a brief for appellee Pennsylvania Association of Independent Schools in No. 89. *Leo Pfeffer* and *Milton Stanzler* argued the cause for appellees in Nos. 569 and 570. With them on the brief were *Harold E. Adams, Jr.*, and *Allan M. Shine.*

Briefs of *amici curiae* urging reversal in No. 89 were filed by *Mr. Pfeffer* for the American Association of School Administrators et al.; by *Henry C. Clausen* for United Americans for Public Schools; by *Samuel Rabinove, Arnold Forster, George Soll, Joseph B. Robison, Paul Hartman*, and *Sol Rabkin* for the American Jewish Committee et al.; by *Franklin C. Salisbury* for Protestants and Other Americans United for Separation of Church and State; by *J. Harold Flannery*, for the Center for Law and Education, Harvard University, et al.; and by *Peter L. Costas* and *Paul W. Orth* for the Connecticut State Conference of Branches of the NAACP et al.

Briefs of *amici curiae* urging affirmance in No. 89 were filed by *Acting Solicitor General Friedman, Assistant Attorney General Ruckelshaus, Robert V. Zener*, and *Donald L. Horowitz* for the United States; by *Paul W. Brown*, Attorney General of Ohio, *pro se*, and *Charles S. Lopeman*, First Assistant Attorney General, for the Attorney General of Ohio et al.; by *Levi Anderson* for the City of Philadelphia; by *Robert M. Landis* for the School District of Philadelphia; by the City of Pittsburgh; by *Bruce W. Kauffman, John M. Elliott*, and *Edward F. Mannino* for the City of Erie; by *James A. Kelly* for the School District of the City of Scranton; by *Charles M. Whelan, William R. Consedine, Alfred L. Scanlan, Arthur E. Sutherland*, and *Harmon Burns, Jr.*, for the National Catholic Educational Association et al.; by *Ethan A. Hitchcock* and *I.N.P. Stokes* for the National Association of Independent Schools, Inc.; by *Jerome H. Gerber* for the Pennsylvania State AFL–CIO, by *Thomas J. Ford, Edward J. Walsh, Jr.*, and *Theodore D. Hoffmann* for the Long Island Conference of Religious Elementary and Secondary School Administrators; by *Nathan Lewin* for the National Jewish Commission on Law and Public Affairs (COLPA); by *Stuart Hubbell* for Citizens for Educational Freedom; and by *Edward M. Koza, Walter L. Hill, Jr., Thomas R. Balaban*, and *William J. Pinkowski* for the Polish American Congress, Inc., et al.

The National Association of Laymen filed a brief as *amicus curiae* in No. 89. Briefs of *amici curiae* urging reversal in Nos. 569 and 570 were filed by *Acting Solicitor General Friedman, Assistant Attorney General Gray*, and *Messrs. Zener* and *Horowitz* for the United States, and by *Jesse*

H. Choper and Messrs. *Consedine, Whelan,* and *Burns* for the National Catholic Educational Association et al.

Briefs of *amici curiae* urging affirmance in Nos. 569 and 570 were filed by *Messrs. Rabinove, Robison, Forster,* and *Rabkin* for the American Jewish Committee et al.; by *Mr. Salisbury* for Protestants and Other Americans United for Separation of Church and State; by *Mr. Flannery* for the Center for Law and Education, Harvard University, et al.; and by *Messrs. Costas* and *Orth* for the Connecticut State Conference of Branches of the NAACP et al.

■ CHIEF JUSTICE BURGER delivered the opinion of the Court.

These two appeals raise questions as to Pennsylvania and Rhode Island statutes providing state aid to church-related elementary and secondary schools. Both statutes are challenged as violative of the Establishment and Free Exercise Clauses of the First Amendment and the Due Process Clause of the Fourteenth Amendment.

Pennsylvania has adopted a statutory program that provides financial support to nonpublic elementary and secondary schools by way of reimbursement for the cost of teachers' salaries, textbooks, and instructional materials in specified secular subjects. Rhode Island has adopted a statute under which the State pays directly to teachers in nonpublic elementary schools a supplement of 15% of their annual salary. Under each statute state aid has been given to church-related educational institutions. We hold that both statutes are unconstitutional.

I

The Rhode Island Statute

The Rhode Island Salary Supplement Act was enacted in 1969. It rests on the legislative finding that the quality of education available in nonpublic elementary schools has been jeopardized by the rapidly rising salaries needed to attract competent and dedicated teachers. The Act authorizes state officials to supplement the salaries of teachers of secular subjects in nonpublic elementary schools by paying directly to a teacher an amount not in excess of 15% of his current annual salary. As supplemented, however, a nonpublic school teacher's salary cannot exceed the maximum paid to teachers in the State's public schools, and the recipient must be certified by the state board of education in substantially the same manner as public school teachers.

In order to be eligible for the Rhode Island salary supplement, the recipient must teach in a nonpublic school at which the average per-pupil expenditure on secular education is less than the average in the State's public schools during a specified period. Appellant State Commissioner of Education also requires eligible schools to submit financial data. If this information indicates a per-pupil expenditure in excess of the statutory limitation, the records of the school in question must be examined in order to assess how much of the expenditure is attributable to secular education and how much to religious activity.[1]

The Act also requires that teachers eligible for salary supplements must teach only those subjects that are offered in the State's public schools. They must use "only teaching materials which are used in the public schools." Finally, any teacher applying for a salary supplement must first agree in writing "not to teach a course in religion for so long as or during such time as he or she receives any salary supplements" under the Act.

Appellees are citizens and taxpayers of Rhode Island. They brought this suit to have the Rhode Island Salary Supplement Act declared unconstitutional and its operation enjoined on the ground that it violates the Establishment and Free Exercise Clauses of the First Amendment. Appellants are state officials charged with administration of the Act, teachers eligible for salary supplements under the Act, and parents of children in church-related elementary schools whose teachers would receive state salary assistance.

A three-judge federal court was convened. It found that Rhode Island's nonpublic elementary schools accommodated approximately 25% of the State's pupils. About 95% of these pupils attended schools affiliated with the Roman Catholic church. To date some 250 teachers have applied for benefits under the Act. All of them are employed by Roman Catholic schools.

The court held a hearing at which extensive evidence was introduced concerning the nature of the secular instruction offered in the Roman Catholic schools whose teachers would be eligible for salary assistance under the Act. Although the court found that concern for religious values does not necessarily affect the content of secular subjects, it also found that the parochial school system was "an integral part of the religious mission of the Catholic Church."

The District Court concluded that the Act violated the Establishment Clause, holding that it fostered "excessive entanglement" between government and religion. In addition two judges thought that the Act had the impermissible effect of giving "significant aid to a religious enterprise." We affirm.

The Pennsylvania Statute

Pennsylvania has adopted a program that has some but not all of the features of the Rhode Island program. The Pennsylvania Nonpublic Elementary and Secondary Education Act was passed in 1968 in response to a crisis that the Pennsylvania Legislature found existed in the State's nonpublic schools due to rapidly rising costs. The statute affirmatively reflects the legislative conclusion that the State's educational goals could appropri-

---

1. The district Court found only one instance in which this breakdown between religious and secular expenses was necessary. The school in question was not affiliated with the Catholic church. The court found it un- likely that such determinations would be necessary with respect to Catholic schools because their heavy reliance on nuns kept their wage costs substantially below those of the public schools.

ately be fulfilled by government support of "those purely secular education-al objectives achieved through nonpublic education . . . ."

The statute authorizes appellee state Superintendent of Public Instruction to "purchase" specified "secular educational services" from nonpublic schools. Under the "contracts" authorized by the statute, the State directly reimburses nonpublic schools solely for their actual expenditures for teachers' salaries, textbooks, and instructional materials. A school seeking reimbursement must maintain prescribed accounting procedures that identify the "separate" cost of the "secular educational service." These accounts are subject to state audit. The funds for this program were originally derived from a new tax on horse and harness racing, but the Act is now financed by a portion of the state tax on cigarettes.

There are several significant statutory restrictions on state aid. Reimbursement is limited to courses "presented in the curricula of the public schools." It is further limited "solely" to courses in the following "secular" subjects: mathematics, modern foreign languages, physical science, and physical education. Textbooks and instructional materials included in the program must be approved by the state Superintendent of Public Instruction. Finally, the statute prohibits reimbursement for any course that contains "any subject matter expressing religious teaching, or the morals or forms of worship of any sect."

The Act went into effect on July 1, 1968, and the first reimbursement payments to schools were made on September 2, 1969. It appears that some $5 million has been expended annually under the Act. The State has now entered into contracts with some 1,181 nonpublic elementary and second-ary schools with a student population of some 535,215 pupils-more than 20% of the total number of students in the State. More than 96% of these pupils attend church-related schools, and most of these schools are affiliat-ed with the Roman Catholic church.

Appellants brought this action in the District Court to challenge the constitutionality of the Pennsylvania statute. The organizational plaintiffs-appellants are associations of persons resident in Pennsylvania declaring belief in the separation of church and state; individual plaintiffs-appellants are citizens and taxpayers of Pennsylvania. Appellant Lemon, in addition to being a citizen and a taxpayer, is a parent of a child attending public school in Pennsylvania. Lemon also alleges that he purchased a ticket at a race track and thus had paid the specific tax that supports the expenditures under the Act. Appellees are state officials who have the responsibility for administering the Act. In addition seven church-related schools are defen-dants-appellees.

A three-judge federal court was convened. The District Court held that the individual plaintiffs-appellants had standing to challenge the Act. The organizational plaintiffs-appellants were denied standing under *Flast v. Cohen* [Note. *Standing I*, this section above].

The court granted appellees' motion to dismiss the complaint for failure to state a claim for relief. It held that the Act violated neither the Establishment nor the Free Exercise Clause. We reverse . . . .

The language of the Religion Clauses of the First Amendment is at best opaque, particularly when compared with other portions of the Amendment. Its authors did not simply prohibit the establishment of a state church or a state religion, an area history shows they regarded as very important and fraught with great dangers. Instead they commanded that there should be "no law *respecting* an establishment of religion." A law may be one "respecting" the forbidden objective while falling short of its total realization. A law "respecting" the proscribed result, that is, the establishment of religion, is not always easily identifiable as one violative of the Clause. A given law might not *establish* a state religion but nevertheless be one "respecting" that end in the sense of being a step that could lead to such establishment and hence offend the First Amendment.

In the absence of precisely stated constitutional prohibitions, we must draw lines with reference to the three main evils against which the Establishment Clause was intended to afford protection: "sponsorship, financial support, and active involvement of the sovereign in religious activity." *Walz v. Tax Commission* [Chapter Thirteen, section 3].

Every analysis in this area must begin with consideration of the cumulative criteria developed by the Court over many years. Three such tests may be gleaned from our cases. **First, the statute must have a secular legislative purpose; second, its principal or primary effect must be one that neither advances nor inhibits religion; finally, the statute must not foster "an excessive government entanglement with religion."**

In *Walz*, the Court upheld state tax exemptions for real properly owned by religious organizations and used for religious worship. That holding, however, tended to confine rather than enlarge the area of permissible state involvement with religious institutions by calling for close scrutiny of the degree of entanglement involved in the relationship. The objective is to prevent, as far as possible, the intrusion of either into the precincts of the other.

Our prior holdings do not call for total separation between church and state; total separation is not possible in an absolute sense. Some relationship between government and religious organizations is inevitable. *Zorach v. Clauson* [section 2 below]; *Sherbert v. Verner* [Chapter Eleven, section 5] (Harlan, J., dissenting). Fire inspections, building and zoning regulations, and state requirements under compulsory school-attendance laws are examples of necessary and permissible contacts. Indeed, under the statutory exemption before us in *Walz*, the State had a continuing burden to ascertain that the exempt property was in fact being used for religious worship. Judicial caveats against entanglement must recognize that the line of separation, far from being a "wall," is a blurred, indistinct, and variable barrier depending on all the circumstances of a particular relationship.

This is not to suggest, however, that we are to engage in a legalistic minuet in which precise rules and forms must govern. A true minuet is a matter of pure form and style, the observance of which is itself the substantive end. Here we examine the form of the relationship for the light that it casts on the substance. In order to determine whether the government entanglement with religion is excessive, we must examine the character and purposes of the institutions that are benefitted, the nature of the aid that the State provides, and the resulting relationship between the government and the religious authority. Mr. Justice Harlan, in a separate opinion in *Walz,* echoed the classic warning as to "programs, whose very nature is apt to entangle the state in details of administration...." Here we find that both statutes foster an impermissible degree of entanglement.

(a) Rhode Island program

The District Court made extensive findings on the grave potential for excessive entanglement that inheres in the religious character and purpose of the Roman Catholic elementary schools of Rhode Island, to date the sole beneficiaries of the Rhode Island Salary Supplement Act.

The church schools involved in the program are located close to parish churches. This understandably permits convenient access for religious exercises since instruction in faith and morals is part of the total educational process. The school buildings contain identifying religious symbols such as crosses on the exterior and crucifixes, and religious paintings and statues either in the classrooms or hallways. Although only approximately 30 minutes a day are devoted to direct religious instruction, there are religiously oriented extracurricular activities. Approximately two-thirds of the teachers in these schools are nuns of various religious orders. Their dedicated efforts provide an atmosphere in which religious instruction and religious vocations are natural and proper parts of life in such schools. Indeed, as the District Court found, the role of teaching nuns in enhancing the religious atmosphere has led the parochial school authorities to attempt to maintain a one-to-one ratio between nuns and lay teachers in all schools rather than to permit some to be staffed almost entirely by lay teachers.

On the basis of these findings the District Court concluded that the parochial schools constituted "an integral part of the religious mission of the Catholic Church." The various characteristics of the schools make them "a powerful vehicle for transmitting the Catholic faith to the next generation." This process of inculcating religious doctrine is, of course, enhanced by the impressionable age of the pupils, in primary schools particularly. In short, parochial schools involve substantial religious activity and purpose.

The substantial religious character of these church-related schools gives rise to entangling church-state relationships of the kind the Religion Clauses sought to avoid. Although the District Court found that concern for religious values did not inevitably or necessarily intrude into the content of secular subjects, the considerable religious activities of these schools led the legislature to provide for careful governmental controls and surveillance by state authorities in order to ensure that state aid supports only secular education.

The dangers and corresponding entanglements are enhanced by the particular form of aid that the Rhode Island Act provides. Our decisions from *Everson* to *Allen* have permitted the States to provide church-related schools with secular, neutral, or non-ideological services, facilities, or materials. Bus transportation, school lunches, public health services, and secular textbooks supplied in common to all students were not thought to offend the Establishment Clause. We note that the dissenters in *Allen* seemed chiefly concerned with the pragmatic difficulties involved in ensuring the truly secular content of the textbooks provided at state expense.

In *Allen* the Court refused to make assumptions, on a meager record, about the religious content of the textbooks that the State would be asked to provide. We cannot, however, refuse here to recognize that teachers have a substantially different ideological character from books. In terms of potential for involving some aspect of faith or morals in secular subjects, a textbook's content is ascertainable, but a teacher's handling of a subject is not. We cannot ignore the danger that a teacher under religious control and discipline poses to the separation of the religious from the purely secular aspects of precollege education. The conflict of functions inheres in the situation. In our view the record shows these dangers are present to a substantial degree. The Rhode Island Roman Catholic elementary schools are under the general supervision of the Bishop of Providence and his appointed representative, the Diocesan Superintendent of Schools. In most cases, each individual parish, however, assumes the ultimate financial responsibility for the school, with the parish priest authorizing the allocation of parish funds. With only two exceptions, school principals are nuns appointed either by the Superintendent or the Mother Provincial of the order whose members staff the school. By 1969 lay teachers constituted more than a third of all teachers in the parochial elementary schools, and their number is growing. They are first interviewed by the superintendent's office and then by the school principal. The contracts are signed by the parish priest, and he retains some discretion in negotiating salary levels. Religious authority necessarily pervades the school system.

The schools are governed by the standards set forth in a "Handbook of School Regulations," which has the force of synodal law in the diocese. It emphasizes the role and importance of the teacher in parochial schools: "The prime factor for the success or the failure of the school is the spirit and personality, as well as the professional competency, of the teacher...." The Handbook also states that: "Religious formation is not confined to formal courses; nor is it restricted to a single subject area." Finally, the Handbook advises teachers to stimulate interest in religious vocations and missionary work. Given the mission of the church school, these instructions are consistent and logical.

Several teachers testified, however, that they did not inject religion into their secular classes. And the District Court found that religious values did not necessarily affect the content of the secular instruction. But what has been recounted suggests the potential if not actual hazards of this form of state aid. The teacher is employed by a religious organization, subject to the direction and discipline of religious authorities, and works in a system dedicated to rearing children in a particular faith. These controls are not lessened by the fact that most of the lay teachers are of the Catholic faith. Inevitably some of a teacher's responsibilities hover on the border between secular and religious orientation.

We need not and do not assume that teachers in parochial schools will be guilty of bad faith or any conscious design to evade the limitations imposed by the statute and the First Amendment. We simply recognize that a dedicated religious person, teaching in a school affiliated with his or her faith and operated to inculcate its tenets, will inevitably experience great difficulty in remaining religiously neutral. Doctrines and faith are not inculcated or advanced by neutrals. With the best of intentions such a teacher would find it hard to make a total separation between secular teaching and religious doctrine. What would appear to some to be essential to good citizenship might well for others border on or constitute instruction in religion. Further difficulties are inherent in the combination of religious discipline and the possibility of disagreement between teacher and religious authorities over the meaning of the statutory restrictions.

We do not assume, however, that parochial school teachers will be unsuccessful in their attempts to segregate their religious beliefs from their secular educational responsibilities. But the potential for impermissible fostering of religion is present. The Rhode Island Legislature has not, and could not, provide state aid on the basis of a mere assumption that secular teachers under religious discipline can avoid conflicts. The State must be certain, given the Religion Clauses, that subsidized teachers do not inculcate religion-indeed the State here has undertaken to do so. To ensure that no trespass occurs, the State has therefore carefully conditioned its aid with pervasive restrictions. An eligible recipient must teach only those courses that are offered in the public schools and use only those texts and materials that are found in the public schools. In addition the teacher must not engage in teaching any course in religion.

A comprehensive, discriminating, and continuing state surveillance will inevitably be required to ensure that these restrictions are obeyed and the First Amendment otherwise respected. Unlike a book, a teacher cannot be inspected once so as to determine the extent and intent of his or her personal beliefs and subjective acceptance of the limitations imposed by the First Amendment. These prophylactic contacts will involve excessive and enduring entanglement between state and church.

There is another area of entanglement in the Rhode Island program that gives concern. The statute excludes teachers employed by nonpublic schools whose average per-pupil expenditures on secular education equal or exceed the comparable figures for public schools. In the event that the total expenditures of an otherwise eligible school exceed this norm, the program requires the government to examine the school's records in order to determine how much of the total expenditures is attributable to secular education and how much to religious activity. This kind of state inspection and evaluation of the religious content of a religious organization is fraught with the sort of entanglement that the Constitution forbids. It is a relationship pregnant with dangers of excessive government direction of church schools and hence of churches. The Court noted "the hazards of government supporting churches" in *Walz,* and we cannot ignore here the danger that pervasive modern governmental power will ultimately intrude on religion and thus conflict with the Religion Clauses.

(b) Pennsylvania program

The Pennsylvania statute also provides state aid to church-related schools for teachers' salaries. The complaint describes an educational system that is very similar to the one existing in Rhode Island. According to the allegations, the church-related elementary and secondary schools are controlled by religious organizations, have the purpose of propagating and promoting a particular religious faith, and conduct their operations to fulfill that purpose. Since this complaint was dismissed for failure to state a claim for relief, we must accept these allegations as true for purposes of our review.

As we noted earlier, the very restrictions and surveillance necessary to ensure that teachers play a strictly nonideological role give rise to entanglements between church and state. The Pennsylvania statute, like that of Rhode Island, fosters this kind of relationship. Reimbursement is not only limited to courses offered in the public schools and materials approved by state officials, but the statute excludes "any subject matter expressing religious teaching, or the morals or forms of worship of any sect." In addition, schools seeking reimbursement must maintain accounting procedures that require the State to establish the cost of the secular as distinguished from the religious instruction.

The Pennsylvania statute, moreover, has the further defect of providing state financial aid directly to the church-related school. This factor distinguishes both *Everson* and *Allen,* for in both those cases the Court was careful to point out that state aid was provided to the student and his parents—not to the church-related school. *Allen; Everson.* In *Walz,* the Court warned of the dangers of direct payments to religious organizations: "Obviously a direct money subsidy would be a relationship pregnant with involvement and, as with most governmental grant programs, could encompass sustained and detailed administrative relationships for enforcement of statutory or administrative standards. . . ."

The history of government grants of a continuing cash subsidy indicates that such programs have almost always been accompanied by varying measures of control and surveillance. The government cash grants before us now provide no basis for predicting that comprehensive measures of surveillance and controls will not follow. In particular the government's post-audit power to inspect and evaluate a church-related school's financial records and to determine which expenditures are religious and which are secular creates an intimate and continuing relationship between church and state.

IV

A broader base of entanglement of yet a different character is presented by the divisive political potential of these state programs. In a community where such a large number of pupils are served by church-related schools, it can be assumed that state assistance will entail considerable political activity. Partisans of parochial schools, understandably concerned with rising costs and sincerely dedicated to both the religious and secular educational missions of their schools, will inevitably champion this cause and promote political action to achieve their goals. Those who oppose state aid, whether for constitutional, religious, or fiscal reasons, will inevitably respond and employ all the usual political campaign techniques to prevail. Candidates will be forced to declare and voters to choose. It would be unrealistic to ignore the fact that many people confronted with issues of this kind will find their votes aligned with their faith.

Ordinarily political debate and division, however vigorous or even partisan, are normal and healthy manifestations of our democratic system of government, but political division along religious lines was one of the principal evils against which the First Amendment was intended to protect. Freund, Comment, Public Aid to Parochial Schools, 82 Harv. L. Rev. 1680, 1692 (1969). The potential divisiveness of such conflict is a threat to the normal political process. *Walz* (separate opinion of Harlan, J.). See also *Allen* (Harlan, J., concurring); *Abington School District v. Schempp* [Chapter Fourteen, section 2] (Goldberg, J., concurring). To have States or communities divide on the issues presented by state aid to parochial schools would tend to confuse and obscure other issues of great urgency. We have an expanding array of vexing issues, local and national, domestic and international, to debate and divide on. It conflicts with our whole history and tradition to permit questions of the Religion Clauses to assume such importance in our legislatures and in our elections that they could divert attention from the myriad issues and problems that confront every level of government. The highways of church and state relationships are not likely to be one-way streets, and the Constitution's authors sought to protect religious worship from the pervasive power of government. The history of many countries attests to the hazards of religion's intruding into the political arena or of political power intruding into the legitimate and free exercise of religious belief.

Of course, as the Court noted in *Walz*, "[a]dherents of particular faiths and individual churches frequently take strong positions on public issues." *Walz*. We could not expect otherwise, for religious values pervade the fabric of our national life. But in *Walz* we dealt with a status under state tax laws for the benefit of all religious groups. Here we are confronted with successive and very likely permanent annual appropriations that benefit relatively few religious groups. Political fragmentation and divisiveness on religious lines are thus likely to be intensified.

The potential for political divisiveness related to religious belief and practice is aggravated in these two statutory programs by the need for continuing annual appropriations and the likelihood of larger and larger demands as costs and populations grow.

———

[The judgment of the Rhode Island District Court in the *De Censo* cases was affirmed; the judgment of the Pennsylvania District Court was reversed.]

■ JUSTICE DOUGLAS concurred in an opinion joined by JUSTICE BLACK. JUSTICES BRENNAN and WHITE also wrote separate concurrences. JUSTICE WHITE dissented in *Earley*. Justice Marshall took no part in *Lemon*, but concurred with Justice Douglas in *Earley*.

NOTES AND QUESTIONS

1. *Political Division along Religious Lines*. Chief Justice Burger endorsed Freund's idea that a principal evil envisaged by the First Amendment was political division on religious lines. Commentators noted that Freund himself offered no evidence in support of his assertion, and disagreed sharply with Freund's view and the Court's acceptance of it. *See, e.g.*, Edward McGlynn Gaffney, "Political Divisiveness Along Religious Lines: The Entanglement of the Court in Sloppy History and Bad Public Policy," 24 *St. Louis U. L.J.* 205 (1980). For example, far from thinking that the First Amendment enabled Congress to repress religious speech it deemed divisive, James Madison came to the First Congress because of partisan support by Baptists in Virginia [Chapter Six, section 3D]. Far from entertaining a bias against religious rights, Madison wrote: "In a free government, the security for civil rights must be the same as for religious rights." James Madison, Federalist No. 51, see also Federalist No. 10 in Jacob E. Cooke, ed., *The Federalist* 351 (1961). In Madison's view, the pluralism of contending religious voices is not a threat to the republic, but a safeguard against the tyranny of a religious majority "by comprehending in the society so many separate descriptions of citizens, as will render an unjust combination of a majority of the whole, very improbable, if not impracticable." *Id.* [See also Chapter Fifteen].

2. *Religious Schools since Lemon*. *Lemon* was a watershed, a substantial departure in analysis and mood from *Allen*. The Chief Justice's opinion picked up Freund's metaphor of a minuet and boldly proclaimed that the Court was committed not to form but to substance. Above all, the Court promulgated the three-pronged test that was to dominate the education cases and affect other First Amendment litigation about religion. The line followed in subsequent cases was as "blurred, indistinct, and variable" as *Lemon* had indicated.

From all sides of the spectrum of views on the nonestablishment provision, commentators have roundly criticized the jurisprudence of the Court on this provision as incoherent and even chaotic. For example, Professor Choper wrote: "Without cataloguing the school aid cases in detail, I think it is fair to say that application of the Court's three-prong test has generated ad hoc judgments which are incapable of being reconciled on any principled basis. For example, a provision for therapeutic and diagnostic health services to parochial school pupils by public employees is invalid if provided *in* the parochial school, but not if offered at a neutral site, even if in a mobile unit adjacent to the parochial school. Reimbursement to parochial schools for the expense of administering teacher-prepared tests required by state law is invalid, but the state may reimburse parochial schools for the expense of administering state-prepared tests. The state may lend school textbooks to parochial school pupils because, the court has explained, the books can be checked in advance for religious content and are 'self-policing'; but the state may not lend other seemingly self-policing instructional items such as tape recorders and maps. The state may pay the cost of bus transportation to parochial schools, which the Court has ruled are 'permeated' with religion; but the state is forbidden to pay for field trip transportation visits 'to governmental, industrial, cultural, and scientific centers designed to enrich the secular studies of students.' I hope that these illustrations are sufficiently striking to demonstrate the unpredictability of the Court's approach.'' Jesse H. Choper, ''The Religion Clauses of the First Amendment: Reconciling the Conflict,'' 41 *U. Pitt. L.Rev.* 673, 680–81 (1980). For other recitals of the confusing results in nonestablishment provision cases, see Antonin Scalia, ''On Getting It Wrong By Making It Look Easy,'' in Edward McGlynn Gaffney, ed., *Private Schools and the Public Good: Policy Alternatives for the Eighties* 174 (1981); Michael J. Paulsen, ''Religion, Equality, and the Constitution: An Equal Protection Approach to Establishment Clause Adjudication,'' 61 *Notre Dame L. Rev.* 311, 315–17 (1986); John Garvey, ''Another Way of Looking at School Aid,'' 1985 *Supreme Court Rev.* 61, 67; Phillip E. Johnson, ''Concepts and Compromises in First Amendment Religious Doctrine,'' 72 Calif. L. Rev. 817, 825–31 (1984); Note, ''The Supreme Court, Effect Inquiry, and Aid to Parochial Education,'' 37 *Stanford L. Rev.* 219, 234 (1984); and Leonard W. Levy, *The Establishment Clause: Religion and the First Amendment* 128–29 (1986). Can you find a principled way of reconciling the cases below?

In *Lemon v. Kurtzman*, 411 U.S. 192 (1973) (*Lemon II*), the District Court permitted Pennsylvania to reimburse the nonpublic schools for services rendered in the school year 1970–1971, although the payment would be made after June 28, 1971, when the Supreme Court had held the Pennsylvania statute unconstitutional. The successful parties in *Lemon* I challenged the reimbursement. The Supreme Court, 5–3, per CHIEF JUSTICE BURGER, upheld the District Court's exercise of discretion. The schools had relied on the statute. The decision in *Lemon* I was ''not clearly foreshadowed.'' The burden on the schools not getting reimbursement would be heavy. The ''constitutional interests at stake in *Lemon* I'' would not be compromised by a single payment and a single and final postaudit of the school's expenditures. JUSTICES DOUGLAS, BRENNAN, and STEWART dissented, insisting that the nonestablishment provision was violated if any money was paid: ''the subsidy today given to sectarian schools out of taxpayers' monies exceeds by far the 'three pence' which Madison condemned in his Remonstrance.''

On June 25, 1973, the Supreme Court decided *Committee for Public Education and Religious Liberty v. Nyquist*, 413 U.S. 756. Leo Pfeffer represented PEARL; amici supporting the New York law included the United States, represented by Solicitor General Erwin Griswold. The New York statute, enacted in 1972, provided:

1.   Money grants of $30 to $40 per pupil to nonpublic schools serving low-income families to maintain and repair school facilities ''to ensure the health'' of the students. The grants would not exceed 50 percent of per pupil cost in a public school.

2.   Reimbursement of $50 to $100 per nonpublic school pupil to parents with income of less than $5000. The reimbursement could not exceed 50 percent of the parents' outlay. The announced legislative purpose was to give educational options to low-income families and to prevent ''a massive increase in public school enrollment and costs'' by nonpublic school pupils transferring to public schools.

3.   A tax credit per nonpublic school pupil for parents with income of $25,000 or less; the credit, declining as income increased, amounted at the most to $50 per child. The legislature noted that the nonpublic schools already had

tax-exempt status and that voluntary contributions to them were already tax-deductible.

In New York State, there were 2,038 nonpublic schools. Of these, 1,415 were Catholic, 164 Jewish, 59 Lutheran, 49 Episcopal, 37 Seventh–Day Adventist, 18 other religions.

In an opinion by Justice Powell, the Court held each part of the New York law invalid:

1. The maintenance and repair provisions "violate the Establishment Clause because their effect, inevitably, is to subsidize and advance the religious mission of sectarian schools."

2. The effect of the reimbursement of the low-income parents was "to provide desired financial support for nonpublic, sectarian institutions." That the grants were to the parents, not to the schools; that they were reimbursements, and not prospective; that they paid only 50 percent of the parents' outlay; that they were designed to let low-income parents exercise their religion because "without state assistance their right to have their children educated in a religious environment is diminished or even denied"—all these considerations were taken up by the Court and found insufficient to justify "a step which can only be regarded as one 'advancing' religion."

3. The tax deduction was found to be equally "a charge made upon the state for the purpose of religious education." The Court rejected the analogy with property tax exemptions for churches. That exemption, it said, was based on history; this one was an innovation. The purpose of the property tax exemption, the Court asserted, was to minimize entanglement with the state; the benefit to the churches was "incidental." The exemption went to all charities; here the benefit was channelled "primarily" to sectarian schools.

Chief Justice Burger and Justice Rehnquist agreed with striking down the "maintenance and repair" provisions. JUSTICE WHITE dissented on all issues, and the Chief Justice and Justice Rehnquist joined him in finding that the decision on reimbursement and tax deduction ran counter to *Everson*, *Allen*, *Walz*, and *Quick Bear* [Chapter Ten, section 1]. The Chief Justice declared: "The essence of all these decisions, I suggest, is that government aid to individuals generally stands on an entirely different footing from direct aid to religious institutions." On the same day, in *Sloan v. Lemon*, 413 U.S. 825 (1973), the Court, 6–3, per Justice Powell, invalidated a similar statute passed by Pennsylvania after *Lemon I*.

A New York statute gave a cash grant of $27 to $45 per pupil to nonpublic schools to pay them for the cost of administering both examinations prepared by the state and internal examinations prepared by their own teachers. In *Levitt v. Committee for Public Education and Religious Liberty*, 413 U.S. 472 (1973), the Court, 8–1 (JUSTICE WHITE dissenting), upheld a challenge by PEARL, again represented by Leo Pfeffer. Chief Justice Burger suggested that the internal tests might "be drafted with an eye, unconsciously or otherwise, to inculcate students in the religious precepts of the sponsoring church." The Court also noted that there was no audit to determine whether the school's costs were less than the sums received. Accord, *New York v. Cathedral Academy*, 434 U.S. 125 (1977).

Pennsylvania had enacted a law in 1972 providing to all nonpublic school children textbooks and auxiliary services such as counselling, testing, remedial help, speech and hearing therapy, and to the schools instructional material such as maps, films, and laboratory equipment. In *Meek v. Pittenger*, 421 U.S. 349 (1975), the Court, 5–4, per Justice Stewart, upheld the textbook program, citing *Allen*. By a vote of 6–3, the Court held the auxiliary services and instructional aids program to be an unconstitutional establishment of religion. The Court emphasized that 75 percent of the nonpublic schools aided were church-related (they were in fact largely Catholic schools). The Court noted that in one year $12 million of aid had been disbursed to these schools through the loan of instructional materials.

The Court asserted that the professionals providing the auxiliary services on the premises of the nonpublic schools would have to be kept under surveillance to prevent impermissible fostering of religion. The Court also found "a serious potential for divisive conflict over the issue of aid to religion." Justice Brennan, joined by Justices Marshall and Douglas, dissented as to the validity of the textbook program, noting that an annual appropriation of $4.6 million had been made for it. They expressed a willingness to reverse *Allen* solely on the ground that it had been decided before the adoption of the political divisiveness test in *Lemon*. The author of *Lemon*, Chief Justice Burger, joined by Justices White and Rehnquist, dissented as to the invalidity of the other two programs. Justice Rehnquist wrote: "The Court apparently believes that the Establishment Clause of the First Amendment not only mandates religious neutrality on the part of government but also requires that this Court go further and throw its weight on the side of those who believe that our society as a whole should be a purely secular one." Leo Pfeffer represented the successful taxpayer; William Ball represented one of the losing defendants.

After *Meek v. Pittenger*, Ohio enacted a statute attempting to conform to the "criteria" announced in *Meek*. It appropriated $88 million for the first two years to provide nonpublic schools with a variety of aid. More than 96 percent of the schools were religious and more than 92 percent, Catholic. In *Wolman v. Walter*, 433 U.S. 229 (1977), the Court, per Justice Blackmun, upheld as constitutional the provision of textbooks; tests provided by examiners outside the schools; speech, hearing, and psychological diagnostic services; and therapeutic and remedial services provided off the premises, including as possible sites mobile units parked near the schools. The Court invalidated the provision of instructional materials and equipment, and paying for field trips to secular centers of interest. That the statute made the students, not the schools, the recipients of the instructional material was held to be irrelevant: it supported "the religious role of the schools."

Chief Justice Burger, joined by Justices White and Rehnquist, dissented as to the items disallowed. Justice Brennan dissented as to all the items allowed. Justice Marshall dissented as to most of the items allowed, including the secular textbooks, reiterating that *Allen* had not considered "the significance of the potential for political divisiveness inherent in programs of aid to sectarian schools." Justice Stevens dissented as to the textbooks and tests. Justice Powell, who had served for years as the attorney for the Board of Education in Richmond, Virginia, observed: "Our decisions in this troubling area ... often must seem arbitrary," but he thought "analytical tidiness" was not to be achieved by "blind absolutism." He would have allowed the field trip funding as indistinguishable from the bus services allowed by *Everson*. He would have permitted instructional materials that went directly to individual students.

Lines began to harden. Justices Brennan, Marshall, Blackmun, and Stevens formed a bloc opposed to any aid of any sort to children attending religious schools. Justice Powell became the critical fifth vote in *Regan*, *Mueller*, and *Aguilar* [this section below]. As Powell voted, so went the Court. Note the frequency with which Justice Rehnquist cited Justice Powell, the author of *Nyquist v. Allen*, in *Mueller v. Allen*.

Wolman was followed by *Committee for Public Education and Religious Liberty v. Regan*, 444 U.S. 646 (1980). After *Levitt*, New York had amended its statute to reimburse the nonpublic schools only for giving and grading state-prepared examinations and for making state-required reports. PEARL, represented by Leo Pfeffer, challenged this statute, too. The Court, 5–4, per Justice White, upheld the statute, declaring that *"Wolman v. Walter* controls this case,"* but acknowledging that the Court's "course sacrifices clarity and predictability for flexibility," and that this would continue to be true until "a single, more encompassing construction of the Establishment Clause" was reached. The author of *Wolman*, Justice Blackmun, joined by Justices Brennan, Marshall, and Stevens, dissented, seeing a "defection" from *Wolman* which he could attribute "only to a concern about the continuing and emotional controversy." In a separate dissent, Justice Stevens characterized the Court's present course as a "sisyphean task," and exhorted it to return to "the high and impregnable wall."

A Minnesota tax statute permitted all parents to deduct up to between $500 and $700 per child for the actual expenses incurred for tuition, textbooks, and transportation. Operating for over two decades without controversy, the statute was challenged as a violation of the nonestablishment provision.

Mueller v. Allen

463 U.S. 388 (1983).

William I. Kampf argued the cause for the petitioners. With him on the brief were *James A. Lee, Jr. Charles S. Sims,* and *Burt Neuborne. Douglas C. Blomgren,* Special Assistant Attorney General of Minnesota, argued the cause for respondents. With him on the brief were *Hubert H. Humphrey III,* Attorney General, *Catharine F. Haukedahl,* Special Assistant Attorney General, and *William P. Marshall. John R. Kenefick* filed a brief for respondents Becker et al. *Timothy P. Quinn* and *Andrew J. Eisenzimmer* filed a brief for respondents Berthiaume.

Briefs of amici curiae urging reversal were filed by *Lee Boothby* and *Robert W. Nixon* for Americans United for Separation of Church and State; by *John W. Baker* for Baptist Joint Committee on Public Affairs; by *Russell C. Brown* for the Minnesota Association of School Administrators; by *Henry C. Clausen* for United Americans for Public Schools; by *Robert Chanin, Laurence Gold, Nathan Z. Dershowitz,* and *Marc D. Stern* for the National Committee for Public Education & Religious Liberty et al.; and by *Gwendolyn H. Gregory, August Steinhilber,* and *Thomas A. Shannon* for the National School Boards Association.

Briefs of amici curiae urging affirmance were filed by Solicitor General *Lee* for the United States; by *Edward McGlynn Gaffney, Jr.,* for the Council of American Private Education et al.; by *Nathan Lewin, Daniel J. Chazin,* and *Dennis Rapps* for the National Jewish Commission on Law and Public Affairs (COLPA); by *David J. Young,* for Citizens for Educational Freedom; and by *Wilfred R. Caron, Edward Bennett Williams,* and *John A. Liekweg* for the United States Catholic Conference; by *Charles E. Rice* for the Catholic League for Religious & Civil Rights; by *John J. Donnelly* for Parents Rights, Inc.; and by *William H. Mellor III* and *Maxwell A. Miller* for Mountain States Foundation et al.

■ JUSTICE REHNQUIST delivered the opinion of the Court.

The general nature of our inquiry in this area has been guided, since the decision in *Lemon v. Kurtzman* by the "three-part" test laid down in that case [citing purpose-effect-entanglement test]. While this principle is well settled, our cases have also emphasized that it provides "no more than [a] helpful signpos[t]" in dealing with Establishment Clause challenges. *Hunt v. McNair* [section 3 below]. With this caveat in mind, we turn to the specific challenges raised against [the statute] under the *Lemon* framework.

Little time need be spent on the question of whether the Minnesota tax deduction has a secular purpose. Under our prior decisions, governmental assistance programs have consistently survived this inquiry even when they have run afoul of other aspects of the *Lemon* framework. See, *e.g., Lemon v. Kurtzman, Meek v. Pittenger, Wolman v. Walter.* This reflects, at least in part, our reluctance to attribute unconstitutional motives to the States, particularly when a plausible secular purpose for the State's program may be discerned from the face of the statute.

A State's decision to defray the cost of educational expenses incurred by parents regardless of the type of schools their children attend-evidences a purpose that is both secular and understandable. An educated populace is essential to the political and economic health of any community, and a State's efforts to assist parents in meeting the rising cost of educational expenses plainly serves this secular purpose of ensuring that the State's citizenry is well educated. Similarly, Minnesota, like other States, could conclude that there is a strong public interest in assuring the continued financial health of private schools, both sectarian and nonsectarian. By educating a substantial number of students such schools relieve public schools of a correspondingly great burden—to the benefit of all taxpayers. In addition, private schools may serve as a benchmark for public schools, in a manner analogous to the "TVA yardstick" for private power companies. As Justice Powell has remarked: "Parochial schools, quite apart from their sectarian purpose, have provided an educational alternative for millions of young Americans; they often afford wholesome competition with our public schools; and in some States they relieve substantially the tax burden incident to the operation of public schools. The State has, moreover, a legitimate interest in facilitating education of the highest quality for all children within its boundaries, whatever school their parents have chosen for them." *Wolman* (Powell, J., concurring in part, concurring in judgment in part, and dissenting in part). All these justifications are readily available to support [the statute], and each is sufficient to satisfy the secular purpose inquiry of *Lemon.*

We turn therefore to the more difficult but related question whether the Minnesota statute has "the primary effect of advancing the sectarian aims of the nonpublic schools." *Committee for Public Education v. Regan*; *Lemon v. Kurtzman*. In concluding that it does not, we find several features of the Minnesota tax deduction particularly significant. First, an essential feature of Minnesota's arrangement is the fact that [the statute] is only one among many deductions—such as those for medical expenses and charitable contributions—available under the Minnesota tax laws.[5] Our decisions consistently have recognized that traditionally "[l]egislatures have especially broad latitude in creating classifications and distinctions in tax statutes," *Regan v. Taxation With Representation of Wash.*, 461 U.S. 540, 547 (1983), in part because the "familiarity with local conditions" enjoyed by legislators especially enables them to "achieve an equitable distribution of the tax burden." *Madden v. Kentucky,* 309 U.S. 83, 88 (1940). Under our prior decisions, the Minnesota Legislature's judgment that a deduction for educational expenses fairly equalizes the tax burden of its citizens and encourages desirable expenditures for educational purposes is entitled to substantial deference.[6]

Other characteristics of [the statute] argue equally strongly for the provision's constitutionality. Most importantly, the deduction is available for educational expenses incurred by all parents, including those whose children attend public schools and those whose children attend nonsectarian private schools or sectarian private schools. Just as in *Widmar v. Vincent* [section 3 below], where we concluded that the State's provision of a forum neutrally "available to a broad class of nonreligious as well as religious speakers" does not "confer any imprimatur of state approval," so

---

5. Deductions for charitable contributions, allowed by Minnesota law include contributions to religious institutions, and exemptions from property tax for property used for charitable purposes under Minnesota law include property used for wholly religious purposes. In each case, it may be that religious institutions benefit very substantially from the allowance of such deductions. The Court's holding in *Walz* indicates, however, that this does not require the conclusion that such provisions of a State's tax law violate the Establishment Clause.

6. Our decision in *Committee for Public Education v. Nyquist* [this section above] is not to the contrary on this point. We expressed considerable doubt there that the "tax benefits" provided by New York law properly could be regarded as parts of a genuine system of tax laws. Plainly, the outright grants to low-income parents did not take the form of ordinary tax benefits. As to the benefits provided to middle-income parents, the Court said: "The amount of the deduction is unrelated to the amount of money actually

expended by any parent on tuition, but is calculated on the basis of a formula contained in the statute. The formula is apparently the product of a legislative attempt to assure that each family would receive a carefully estimated new benefit, and that the tax benefit would be comparable to, and compatible with, the tuition grant for lower income families." Indeed, the question whether a program having the elements of a "genuine tax deduction" would be constitutionally acceptable was expressly reserved in *Nyquist*, n. 49. While the economic consequences of the program in *Nyquist* and that in this case may be difficult to distinguish, we have recognized on other occasions that "the form of the [State's assistance to parochial schools must be examined] for the light that it casts on the substance." *Lemon v. Kurtzman*. The fact that the Minnesota plan embodies a "genuine tax deduction" is thus of some relevance, especially given the traditional rule of deference accorded legislative classifications in tax statutes.

here: "[t]he provision of benefits to so broad a spectrum of groups is an important index of secular effect."[7]

In this respect, as well as others, this case is vitally different from the scheme struck down in *Nyquist.* There, public assistance amounting to tuition grants, was provided only to parents of children in *nonpublic* schools. This fact had considerable bearing on our decision striking down the New York statute at issue; we explicitly distinguished both *Allen and Everson* on the grounds that "[i]n both cases the class of beneficiaries included *all* schoolchildren, those in public as well as those in private schools." (emphasis in original). Moreover, we intimated that "public assistance (e.g., scholarships) made available generally without regard to the sectarian-nonsectarian, or public-nonpublic nature of the institution benefitted," might not offend the Establishment Clause. We think the tax deduction adopted by Minnesota is more similar to this latter type of program than it is to the arrangement struck down in *Nyquist.* Unlike the assistance at issue in *Nyquist,* [the statute] permits *all* parents—whether their children attend public school or private—to deduct their children's educational expenses. As *Widmar* and our other decisions indicate, a program, like [the statute], that neutrally provides state assistance to a broad spectrum of citizens is not readily subject to challenge under the Establishment Clause.

We also agree with the Court of Appeals that, by channeling whatever assistance it may provide to parochial schools through individual parents, Minnesota has reduced the Establishment Clause objections to which its action is subject. It is true, of course, that financial assistance provided to parents ultimately has an economic effect comparable to that of aid given directly to the schools attended by their children. It is also true, however, that under Minnesota's arrangement public funds become available only as a result of numerous, private choices of individual parents of school-age children. For these reasons, we recognized in *Nyquist* that the means by which state assistance flows to private schools is of some importance: we said that "the fact that aid is disbursed to parents rather than to ... schools" is a material consideration in Establishment Clause analysis, albeit "only one among many factors to be considered." It is noteworthy that all but one of our recent cases invalidating state aid to parochial schools have involved the direct transmission of assistance from the State to the schools themselves. The exception, of course, was *Nyquist,* which, as discussed previously, is distinguishable from this case on other grounds. Where, as here, aid to parochial schools is available only as a result of decisions of individual parents no "imprimatur of state approval," *Widmar* [section 3 below] can be deemed to have been conferred on any particular religion, or on religion generally.

---

7. Likewise, in *Sloan v. Lemon* [this section above], where we held that a Pennsylvania statute violated the First Amendment, we emphasized that "the State [had] singled out a class of its citizens for a special econom-ic benefit." We also observed in *Widmar* [section 3 below] that "empirical evidence that religious groups will dominate [the school's] open forum" might be relevant to analysis under the Establishment Clause.

We find it useful, in the light of the foregoing characteristics of [the statute] to compare the attenuated financial benefits flowing to parochial schools from the section to the evils against which the Establishment Clause was designed to protect. These dangers are well described by our statement that " '[w]hat is at stake as a matter of policy [in Establishment Clause cases] is preventing that kind and degree of government involvement in religious life that, as history teaches us, is apt to lead to strife and frequently strain a political system to the breaking point.' " *Nyquist*, quoting *Walz* (opinion of Harlan, J.). It is important, however, to "keep these issues in perspective":

"At this point in the 20th century we are quite far removed from the dangers that prompted the Framers to include the Establishment Clause in the Bill of Rights. See *Walz*. The risk of significant religious or denominational control over our democratic processes—or even of deep political division along religious lines—is remote, and when viewed against the positive contributions of sectarian schools, any such risk seems entirely tolerable in light of the continuing oversight of this Court." *Wolman* [this section above] (Powell, J., concurring in part, concurring in judgment in part, and dissenting in part). The Establishment Clause of course extends beyond prohibition of a state church or payment of state funds to one or more churches. We do not think, however, that its prohibition extends to the type of tax deduction established by Minnesota. The historic purposes of the Clause simply do not encompass the sort of attenuated financial benefit, ultimately controlled by the private choices of individual parents, that eventually flows to parochial schools from the neutrally available tax benefit at issue in this.

Petitioners argue that, notwithstanding the facial neutrality of [the statute], in application the statute primarily benefits religious institutions. Petitioners rely, as they did below, on a statistical analysis of the type of persons claiming the tax deduction. They contend that most parents of public school children incur no tuition expenses, and that other expenses deductible under [the statute], are negligible in value; moreover, they claim that 96% of the children in private schools in 1978–1979 attended religiously affiliated institutions. Because of all this, they reason, the bulk of deductions taken under [the statute] will be claimed by parents of children in sectarian schools. Respondents reply that petitioners have failed to consider the impact of deductions for items such as transportation, summer school tuition, tuition paid by parents whose children attended schools outside the school districts in which they resided, rental or purchase costs for a variety of equipment, and tuition for certain types of instruction not ordinarily provided in public schools.

We need not consider these contentions in detail. We would be loath to adopt a rule grounding the constitutionality of a facially neutral law on annual reports reciting the extent to which various classes of private citizens claimed benefits under the law. Such an approach would scarcely provide the certainty that this field stands in need of, nor can we perceive principled standards by which such statistical evidence might be evaluated. Moreover, the fact that private persons fail in a particular year to claim the tax relief to which they are entitled—under a facially neutral statute—should be of little importance in determining the constitutionality of the statute permitting such relief.

Finally, private educational institutions, and parents paying for their children to attend these schools, make special contributions to the areas in which they operate. "Parochial schools, quite apart from their sectarian purpose, have provided an educational alternative for millions of young Americans; they often afford wholesome competition with our public schools: and in some States they relieve substantially the tax burden incident to the operation of public schools." *Wolman* (Powell, J., concurring in part, concurring in judgment in part, and dissenting in part). If parents of children in private schools choose to take especial advantage of the relief provided by [the statute], it is no doubt due to the fact that they bear a particularly great financial burden in educating their children. More fundamentally, whatever unequal effect may be attributed to the statutory classification can fairly be regarded as a rough return for the benefits, discussed above, provided to the State and all taxpayers by parents sending their children to Parochial schools. In the light of all this, we believe it wiser to decline to engage in the type of empirical inquiry into those persons benefitted by state law which petitioners urge.

Thus, we hold that the Minnesota tax deduction for educational expenses satisfies the primary effect inquiry of our Establishment Clause cases. *Affirmed.*

■ JUSTICES BRENNAN, MARSHALL, BLACKMUN, and STEVENS dissented.

The School District of Grand Rapids offered two programs to pupils in nonpublic schools. The Shared Time Program offered "remedial": and "enrichment" art, mathematics, music, reading, and physical education in the elementary schools. The teachers were full-time employees of the public schools hired in the usual way. About ten percent of a nonpublic school student's time would be spent in these courses. The Community Education Programs were taught in the nonpublic schools at the end of the regular school day and included arts and crafts, drama, and Spanish. The teachers were hired part-time by the School District and were usually full-time teachers at a religious school. The director of both programs was a public employee who worked out the schedule with the religious schools. Almost all of the schools benefitted were Catholic or Protestant.

Grand Rapids School District v. Ball

473 U.S. 373 (1985).

Kenneth F. Ripple, Special Assistant Attorney General of Michigan, argued the cause for petitioners. With him on the briefs were *William S. Farr, John R. Oostema, Stuart D. Hubbell, Frank J. Kelley*, Attorney General, *Louis J. Caruso*, Solicitor General, and *Gerald F. Young*, Assistant Attorney General.

Michael W. McConnell, argued the cause for the United States as amicus curiae urging reversal. With him on the brief were Solicitor General *Lee*, Acting Assistant Attorney General *Willard*, Deputy Solicitor General *Bator*, Deputy Assistant Attorney General *Kuhl, Anthony J. Steinmeyer*, and *Michael Jay Singer*.

A.E. Dick Howard argued the cause for respondents. On the brief was *Albert R. Dilley*.

Briefs of amici curiae urging reversal were filed for the National Jewish Commission on Law and Public Affairs (COLPA) by *Nathan Lewin, Dennis Rapps*, and *Daniel D. Chazin*; and for the United States Catholic Conference by *Wilfred R. Caron* and *John A. Liekweg*.

Briefs of amici curiae urging affirmance were filed for the American Jewish Congress et al. by *Marc D. Stern, Ronald A. Krauss, Jack D. Novik, Burt Neuborne, Charles S. Sims, Justin Finger,* and *Jeffrey Sinensky*; for Americans United for Separation of Church and State by *Lee Boothby*; and for the Baptist Joint Committee on Public Affairs et al. by *John W. Baker*.

■ Justice Brennan delivered the opinion of the Court.

Given that 40 of the 41 schools in this case are thus "pervasively sectarian," the challenged public-school programs operating in the religious schools may impermissibly advance religion in three different ways. First, the teachers participating in the programs may become involved in intentionally or inadvertently inculcating particular religious tenets or beliefs. Second, the programs may provide a crucial symbolic link between government and religion, thereby enlisting—at least in the eyes of impressionable youngsters—the powers of government to the support of the religious denomination operating the school. Third, the programs may have the effect of directly promoting religion by impermissibly providing a subsidy to the primary religious mission of the institutions affected....

Our cases have recognized that the Establishment Clause guards against more than direct, state-funded efforts to indoctrinate youngsters in specific religious beliefs. Government promotes religion as effectively when it fosters a close identification of its powers and responsibilities with those of any—or all—religious denominations as when it attempts to inculcate specific religious doctrines. If this identification conveys a message of government endorsement or disapproval of religion, a core purpose of the Establishment Clause is violated. See *Lynch v. Donnelly* (O'Connor, J., concurring) [Chapter Thirteen, section 3]; cf. *Abington School District v. Schempp,* [section 2 below] (history teaches that "powerful sects or groups might bring about a fusion of governmental and religious functions or a concert or dependency of one upon the other to the end that official support of the State or Federal Government would be placed behind the tenets of one or of all orthodoxies"). As we stated in *Larkin v. Grendel's Den, Inc.* [Chapter Fifteen, section 2]: "[T]he mere appearance of a joint exercise of legislative authority by Church and State provides a significant symbolic benefit to religion in the minds of some by reason of the power conferred." See also *Widmar v. Vincent* [section 3 below] (finding effect "incidental" and not "primary" because it "does not confer any imprimatur of state approval on religious sects or practices").

It follows that an important concern of the effects test is whether the symbolic union of church and state effected by the challenged governmental action is sufficiently likely to be perceived by adherents of the controlling denominations as an endorsement, and by the nonadherents as a disapproval, of their individual religious choices. The inquiry into this kind of effect must be conducted with particular care when many of the citizens perceiving the governmental message are children in their formative years. Cf. *Tilton v. Richardson* [section 3 below]. The symbolism of a union between church and state is most likely to influence children of tender years, whose experience is limited and whose beliefs consequently are the function of environment as much as of free and voluntary choice....

Petitioners claim that the aid here, like the textbooks in *Allen* flows primarily to the students, not to the religious schools. Of course, all aid to religious schools ultimately "flows to" the students, and petitioners' argument if accepted would validate all forms of nonideological aid to religious schools, including those explicitly rejected in our prior cases. Yet in *Meek*, we held unconstitutional the loan of instructional materials to religious schools and in *Wolman*, we rejected the fiction that a similar program could be saved by masking it as aid to individual students. *Wolman*. It follows *a fortiori* that the aid here, which includes not only instructional materials but also the provision of instructional services by teachers in the parochial school building, "inescapably, [has] the primary effect of providing a direct and substantial advancement of the sectarian enterprise." Where, as here, no meaningful distinction can be made between aid to the student and aid to the school, "the concept of a loan to individuals is a transparent fiction"....

Petitioners also argue that this "subsidy" effect is not significant in this case, because the Community Education and Shared Time programs supplemented the curriculum with courses not previously offered in the religious schools and not required by school rule or state regulation. Of course, this fails to distinguish the programs here from those found unconstitutional in *Meek*. As in *Meek*, we do not find that this feature of the program is controlling. First, there is no way of knowing whether the religious schools would have offered some or all of these courses if the public school system had not offered them first. The distinction between courses that "supplement" and those that "supplant" the regular curriculum is therefore not nearly as clear as petitioners allege. Second, although the precise courses offered in these programs may have been new to the participating religious schools, their general subject matter—reading, math, etc.—was surely a part of the curriculum in the past, and the concerns of the Establishment Clause may thus be triggered despite the "supplemental" nature of the courses. *Meek v. Pittenger*. Third, and most important, petitioners' argument would permit the public schools gradually to take over the entire secular curriculum of the religious school, for the latter could surely discontinue existing courses so that they might be replaced a year or two later by a Community Education or Shared Time course with the same content. The average religious school student, for instance, now spends 10 percent of the school day in Shared Time classes. But there is no principled basis on which this Court can impose a limit on the percentage of the religious-school day that can be subsidized by the public school. To let the genie out of the bottle in this case would be to permit ever larger segments of the religious school curriculum to be turned over to the public school system, thus violating the cardinal principle that the State may not in effect become the prime supporter of the religious school system. See *Lemon v. Kurtzman*.

III

We conclude that the challenged programs have the effect of promoting religion in three ways. The state-paid instructors, influenced by the pervasively sectarian nature of the religious schools in which they work, may subtly or overtly indoctrinate the students in particular religious tenets at public expense. The symbolic union of church and state inherent in the provision of secular, state-provided instruction in the religious school buildings threatens to convey a message of state support for religion to students and to the general public. Finally, the programs in effect subsidize the religious functions of the parochial schools by taking over a substantial portion of their responsibility for teaching secular subjects. For these reasons, the conclusion is inescapable that the Community Education and Shared Time programs have the "primary or principal" effect of advancing religion, and therefore violate the dictates of the Establishment Clause of the First Amendment.

Nonpublic schools have played an important role in the development of American education, and we have long recognized that parents and their children have the right to choose between public schools and available sectarian alternatives. As The Chief Justice noted in *Lemon v. Kurtzman,* "nothing we have said can be construed to disparage the role of church-related elementary and secondary schools in our national life. Their contribution has been and is enormous." But the Establishment Clause "rest[s] on the belief that a union of government and religion tends to destroy government and degrade religion." *Engel v. Vitale* [section 2 below]. Therefore,"[t]he Constitution decrees that religion must be a private matter for the individual, the family, and the institutions of private choice, and that while some involvement and entanglement are inevitable, lines must be drawn." *Lemon v. Kurtzman*. It is so ordered.

■ Chief Justice Burger concurred as to the Community Education Program but dissented as to the Shared Time Program, as did Justice O'Connor. Justice Rehnquist and Justice White dissented as to both programs.

———

The federal program challenged in *Flast v. Cohen* [Note: *Standing*, this action above] was decided on the merits in the following case, and in *Agostini v. Felton* (reversing *Aguilar*) and in *Mitchell v. Helms* (reversing *Meek v. Pittinger* and *Wolman v. Walter*). The last case dealt with computers and other instructional materials. The first two cases involved the provision of remedial education in reading and mathematics and more particularly whether each service could be provided by public school teachers on the premises of religious schools.

Aguilar v. Felton

473 U.S. 402 (1985).

Solicitor General *Lee* argued the cause for appellants in all cases. With him on the briefs for appellant in No. 84–238 were Acting Assistant Attorney General *Willard*, Deputy Solicitor General *Bator*, Deputy Assistant Attorney General *Kuhl, Anthony J. Steinmeyer,* and *Michael Jay Singer. Charles H. Wilson* filed a brief for appellant in No. 84–237. *Frederick A.O. Schwarz, Jr., Leonard Koerner*, and *Stephen J. McGrath* filed briefs for appellant in No. 84–239.

Stanley Geller argued the cause for appellees in all cases.

Briefs of amici curiae urging reversal were filed for the Council for American Private Education et al. by *Edward McGlynn Gaffney, Jr.*; for the Catholic League for Religious and Civil Rights by *Steven Frederick McDowell*; for Citizens for Educational Freedom by *Charles E. Rice*; for the National Jewish Commission on Law and Public Affairs (COLPA) by *Nathan Lewin, Dennis Rapps*, and *Daniel D. Chazin*; for Parents Rights, Inc., by John J. Donnelly; and for the United States Catholic Conference by *Wilfred R. Caron* and *Mark E. Chopko.*

Briefs of amici curiae urging affirmance were filed for the American Civil Liberties Union et al. by *Burt Neuborne, Charles Sims,* and *Marc D. Stern;* for Americans United for Separation of Church and State by *Lee Boothby;* and for the Anti–Defamation League of B'nai B'rith by *Justin J. Finger, Meyer Eisenberg,* and *Jeffrey P. Sinensky.*

■ JUSTICE BRENNAN delivered the opinion of the Court.

Title I of the Elementary and Secondary Education Act of 1965 authorizes the Secretary of Education to distribute financial assistance to local educational institutions to meet the needs of educationally deprived children from low income families. . . .

Since 1966 the City of New York has provided instructional services funded by Title I to parochial school students on the premises of parochial schools. . . . The programs conducted at these schools include remedial reading, reading skills, remedial mathematics, English as a second language and guidance services. These programs are carried out by regular employees of the public schools (teachers, guidance counselors, psychologists, psychiatrists, and social workers) who have volunteered to teach in the parochial schools. . . .

The critical elements of the entanglement proscribed in *Lemon* and *Meek* are thus present in this case. First, as noted above, the aid is provided in a pervasively sectarian environment. Second, because assistance is provided in the form of teachers, ongoing inspection is required to ensure the absence of a religious message. . . .

The administrative cooperation that is required to maintain the educational program at issue here entangles Church and State still another way that infringes interests at the heart of the Establishment Clause. Administrative personnel of the public and parochial school system must work together....

Affirmed.

■ Justice Powell, concurring.

[In his concurring opinion in *Wolman*, Justice Powell wrote: "The risk of significant religious or denominational control over our democratic processes—or even of deep political division along religious lines—is remote...." In *Aguilar*, after agreeing that there was an "excessive entanglement," Powell wrote differently.]

This risk of entanglement is compounded by the additional risk of political divisiveness stemming from the aid to religion at issue here.... There remains a considerable risk of continuing political strife over the propriety of direct aid to religious schools and the proper allocation of limited governmental resources. In states such as New York that have large and varied sectarian populations, one can be assured that politics will enter into any state decision to aid parochial schools....

The Title I program at issue in this case will also be invalid under the "effects" prong of the test adopted in *Lemon*.

■ Chief Justice Burger, dissenting.

Under the guise of protecting Americans from the evils of an Established Church such as those of the eighteenth century and earlier times, today's decision will deny countless school children desperately needed remedial teaching services funded under Title 1. What is disconcerting about the result reached today is that, in the face of the human cost entailed by this decision, the Court does not even attempt to identify any threat to religious liberty posed by the operation of Title I.... [Quoting the opinion of Judge Henry Friendly in the court of appeals, the Chief Justice noted that the Title I program in New York had "done so much good and little, if any, detectable harm."]

■ Justice Rehnquist, dissenting.

I dissent for the reason stated in my dissenting opinion in *Wallace v. Jaffree* [section 2 below].

■ Justice O'Connor, dissenting.

The abstract theories explaining why on-premises instruction might publicly advance religion dissolve in the face of experience in New York.... Indeed, in nineteen years there has never been a single incident in which a Title I instructor "subtly or overtly" attempted to "indoctrinate the students in particular religious tenets at public expense." [Justice O'Connor sharply criticized the entanglement test as the basis for much of the confusion in the Court's Establishment Clause cases].

■ Justice White also dissented.

NOTES AND QUESTIONS

1. *A Departure from Aguilar—On–Premises Assistance to Student with a Disability.* The Title I program invalidated in *Aguilar* was one of the chief components of the war on poverty begun in 1965. In enacting this legislation, Congress strove to help all children who fit into two categories of human need, economic disadvantage and educational disadvantage. Congress expressly stated that the programs should be available to all children, whether attending a public school or a religious school. 20 U.S.C. § 6321. In prohibiting the delivery of Title I remedial services on the premises of the schools attended by the intended beneficiaries, the court stopped the most effective manner of delivering these needed services to thousands of children from low-income families in New York City. Professor McConnell called *Aguilar* "a disaster" not only for the needy children and their families who were excluded from participation in the Title I program, but also for the legislation's social objectives. Michael W. McConnell, "Why 'Separation' Is Not the Key to Church–State Relations," *The Christian Century* (Jan. 18, 1989), 44. When *Aguilar* was handed down, it was estimated that some 20,000 economically disadvantaged children in the city of New York, and some 183,000 children nationwide would experience a decline in Title I services. See Leonard Levy, *The Establishment Clause* 176 (1986), and S. Rep. No. 100–222, p. 14 (1987), U.S. Code Cong. & Admin. News 1988, pp. 101, 114 (estimating that *Aguilar* costs have "resulted in a decline of about 35 percent in the number of private school children who are served").

The first departure from *Aguilar* came in the following Term, when the Court ruled unanimously in *Witters v. Washington Department of Services for the Blind* [section 3 below] that government assistance may even directly aid the nonsecular educational function of a religious school, something no one had sought in *Aguilar*. Since the aid in question was to a blind person seeking job rehabilitation by training for the ministry at the level of postsecondary education, commentators relied on this fact to conclude that the case had no impact on the funding of religious elementary and secondary education. That assumption crumbled in the next case.

Deaf since birth, James Zobrest attended grades one through five in a school for the deaf. While he attended grades six through eight in the local public school in Tucson, Arizona, the district furnished him with a sign-language interpreter. For religious reasons, his parents enrolled him for the ninth grade in Salpointe Catholic High School, and requested that the district supply him with an interpreter at Salpointe, pursuant to the Individuals with Disabilities Education Act (IDEA), 20 U.S.C. § 1400 et seq. The district referred the matter to the County Attorney, who concluded that providing an interpreter on the premises of a religious school would violate the United States Constitution. The Arizona Attorney General concurred in the County Attorney's opinion. On the strength of these opinions, the district declined to provide the requested interpreter. Represented by William Ball, who argued on behalf of the Pennsylvania program in *Lemon,* the parents sued for injunctive and declaratory relief and damages, alleging that the IDEA and the free exercise provision required the district to provide the interpreter, and that the nonestablishment provision did not bar this relief. The district court granted summary judgment to the district on the ground that the interpreter would act as a conduit for the child's religious inculcation, thereby promoting his religious development at government expense in violation of the nonestablishment provision. The Court of Appeals affirmed.

In *Zobrest v. Catalina Foothills School District*, 509 U.S. 1 (1993), the Court, per Chief Justice Rehnquist, held that the nonestablishment provision does not prevent a district from furnishing a disabled child enrolled in a religious school with a sign-language interpreter in order to facilitate his education. Government programs that neutrally provide benefits to a broad class of citizens defined without reference to religion are not readily subject to an nonestablishment provision challenge just because sectarian institutions may also receive an attenuated financial benefit [citing *Mueller* and *Witters*]. By according parents freedom to select a school of their choice, the statute ensures that a government-paid interpreter will be present in a sectarian school only as a result of individual parents' private decisions. Since "the IDEA creates no financial incentive for parents to choose a sectarian school, an interpreter's presence there cannot be attributed to state decisionmaking."

The Court held that the fact that a public employee will be physically present in a religious school does not by itself invalidate the assistance. The Chief Justice distinguished *Meek v. Pittenger* and *Grand Rapids v. Ball* on the ground that the programs challenged in those cases gave direct grants of government aid—instructional equipment and material, teachers, and guidance counselors—which relieved religious schools of costs they otherwise would have borne in educating their students. Here, said the Chief Justice, the child is the primary beneficiary, and the school receives only an incidental benefit. In addition, an interpreter, unlike a teacher or guidance counselor, neither adds to nor subtracts from the sectarian school's environment but merely interprets whatever material is presented to the class as a whole. There is no absolute bar to the placing of a public employee in a religious school. Is *Zobrest* consistent with *Aguilar*?

■ Justice Blackmun, joined by Justices Stevens, Souter, and O'Connor dissented on the view that the Court did not need to reach the constitutional question if the IDEA does not require the relief sought by the Zobrest's. Since the Court disagreed with the dissenters on this point and reached the merits of the constitutional question, Justice Blackmun, joined by Justice Souter, also expressed an opinion on the merits. "Until now," he wrote, "the Court never has authorized a public employee to participate directly in religious indoctrination. Yet that is the consequence of today's decision."

Blackmun read the leading precedents as follows. Under *Grand Rapids*, the nonestablishment provision "absolutely prohibit[s] government-financed or government-sponsored indoctrination into the beliefs of a particular religious faith." Under Justice O'Connor's concurring opinion in *Bowen v. Kendrick*, "[a]ny use of public funds to promote religious doctrines violates the Establishment Clause." Under *Meek*, citing *Lemon*, " 'The State must be certain, given the Religion Clauses, that subsidized teachers do not inculcate religion.' " Under *Levitt v. Committee for Public Education and Religious Liberty*, "[t]he State is constitutionally compelled to assure that the state-supported activity is not being used for religious indoctrination." He concluded: "In keeping with this restriction, our cases consistently have rejected the provision by government of any resource capable of advancing a school's religious mission. Although the Court generally has permitted the provision of 'secular and nonideological services unrelated to the primary, religion-oriented educational function of the sectarian school,' *Meek*, it has always proscribed the provision of benefits that afford even 'the opportunity for the transmission of sectarian views,' " *Wolman*.

Acknowledging that the distinctions drawn in the Court's cases "perhaps are somewhat fine," Blackmun insisted that "lines must be drawn." "And our cases make clear that government crosses the boundary when it furnishes the medium for communication of a religious message. If petitioners receive the relief they seek, it is beyond question that a state-employed sign-language interpreter would serve as the conduit for petitioner's religious education, thereby assisting Salpointe in its mission of religious indoctrination. But the Establishment Clause is violated when a sectarian school enlists 'the machinery of the State to enforce a religious orthodoxy.' *Lee v. Weisman* [section 2 below]."

2. *The Handwriting on the Aguilar Wall.* Shortly after *Zobrest*, the Court decided another case involving the delivery of services to children with disabilities. The case proved a significant turning point in the road from *Aguilar* to *Agostini*. Orthodox Hasidic Jews known as the Satmar community came to America as survivors of the Holocaust. In *Kiryas Joel Village School District v. Grumet*, 512 U.S. 687 (1994), the Court describes them as a "vigorously religious people who make few concessions to the modern world and go to great lengths to avoid assimilation into it." For further description of the Satmar Hasidim, see Jerome R. Mintz, *Hasidic People: A Place in the New World* 27–42, 206–15, 309–27 (1992); and Israel Rubin, *Satmar: An Island in the City* (1972). In this respect, the Satmar Hasidim are similar to the separatist tendencies of the Old Order Amish, whom the Court thought worthy of accommodation in *Yoder* [Chapter Eleven, section 7]. Prior to *Aguilar*, the local school district had agreed that disabled children within the Satmar religious community, like any disabled children, are eligible for special education classes. In the experience of this community, their children "were traumatized and mocked when they had to enter the unfamiliar world of the local public schools to receive such classes." Thomas C. Berg, "Slouching Towards Secularism: A Comment on Kiryas Joel School District v. Grumet," 44 *Emory L. J.* 433 (1995). Responding to this concern, the school district agreed to provide the special education classes on the premises of the schools operated by the Satmar community. When *Aguilar* threw this arrangement into doubt, the New York legislature agreed to create a unique, new school district with lines redrawn to include only the Hasidim. In *Kiryas Joel* the Court, 6–3, invalidated the creation of this special school district as a "religious gerrymander." See *Larkin v. Grendel's Den, Inc.* [Chapter Fifteen, section 2].

Five of the justices, however, acknowledged a measure of responsibility for the legislative redistricting, which would not have occurred except for the rule announced in *Aguilar* that a public school employee may not deliver services of a secular nature on the premises of a religious school. These justices stated in separate opinions that the time had come to review *Aguilar*. Justice O'Connor concurred separately, repeating the view expressed in her dissent in *Aguilar* that "if the government provides [special] education on-site at public schools and at nonsectarian private schools, it is only fair that it provide it on-site at sectarian schools as well. I thought this to be true in *Aguilar* … and I still believe it today." Noting that the pre-*Aguilar* delivery regime was "entirely permissible," she wrote that the Court "should, in a proper case, be prepared to reconsider *Aguilar*, in order to bring our Establishment Clause jurisprudence back to what I think is the proper track—government impartiality, not animosity, towards religion." In another concurring opinion, Justice Kennedy wrote that the single-religion school district issue presented in *Kiryas Joel* was "attributable in no small measure to what I believe were unfortunate rulings by this Court" in *Aguilar* and in *Grand Rapids*. Kennedy added that "the decisions in *Grand Rapids* and *Aguilar* may have been erroneous," and that "it may be necessary for us to reconsider them at a later date." Justice Scalia, joined by Chief Justice Rehnquist and Justice Thomas, wrote a dissent characterizing *Aguilar* as a case that is "hostile to our national tradition of accommodation" and that "should be overruled at the earliest opportunity." The only question now was how long *Aguilar* would last as a precedent. The answer came in *Agostini*: not long. The same parties who had been enjoined on remand in *Aguilar* from providing Title I services on the premises of a religious school sought relief from this injunction on the ground that *Aguilar* was no longer good law. *Agostini* also simplified the analysis. The focus, wrote Justice Sandra Day O'Connor, should be on whether an aid program has the impermissible "effect of advancing religion by creating a financial incentive to undertake religious indoctrination." Relying on *Witters* [this section above] and *Zobrest* [this section above], Justice O'Connor wrote that no incentive of this sort is present "where the aid is allocated on the basis of neutral, secular criteria that neither favor nor disfavor religion, and is made available to both religious and secular beneficiaries on a nondiscriminatory basis." Is this is principled way of deciding these cases?

Rachel Agostini, et al. v. Betty–Louise Felton, et al. Chancellor, Board of Education of the City of New York, et al. v. Betty–Louise Felton, et al.

521 U.S. 203 (1997).

Acting Solicitor General *Walter Dellinger* argued the cause for petitioners in all cases. With him on the briefs for the Secretary of Education were Acting Assistant Attorney General *Frank W. Hunger*, Deputy Solicitor General *Seth P. Waxman*, Deputy Assistant Attorney General *Stephen W. Preston, Paul R.Q. Wolfson, Michael Jay Singer* and *Howard S. Scher*. *Kevin T. Baine* and Emmet T. Flood filed briefs for petitioners Rachel Agostini et al. *Paul A. Crotty*, Corporation Counsel of the City of New York, *Leonard Koerner, Marilyn Richter*, and *Stephen J. McGrath* filed briefs for the Chancellor and Board of Education of the City of New York.

Stanley Geller argued the cause for respondents in all cases.

Briefs of amici curiae urging reversal were filed for the Becket Fund for Religious Liberty by *Kevin J. Hasson, Eric W. Treene*, and *Roman P. Storzer;* for the Christian Legal Society et al. by *Thomas C. Berg, Steven T. McFarland, Kimberlee Wood Colby, Samuel B. Casey,* and *Michael W. McConnell;* for the Knights of Columbus by *James W. Shannon, Jr., Pat A. Cipollone*, and *Carl A. Anderson;* for the National Jewish Commission on Law and Public Affairs (COLPA) by *Nathan Lewin* and *Dennis Rapps;* for the Pacific Legal Foundation by *Sharon L. Browne* and *Mark T. Gallagher;* for Sarah Peter et al. by *Michael Joseph Woodruff, Michael J. Paulsen,* and

Daniel L. Bowles; for the United States Catholic Conference by *John A. Liekweg* and *Jeffrey Hunter Moon*; and for United States Senator Robert F. Bennet by *Ronald D. Maines* and *Frederick Mark Gedicks.*

Briefs of amici curiae urging affirmance were filed for the American Jewish Congress et al. by *Marc D. Stern, Norman Redlich, Marvin E. Frankel,* and *David J. Strom;* for Americans United for Separation of Church and State and the American Civil Liberties Union by *Steven R. Shapiro, Arthur N. Eisenberg,* and *Steven K. Green;* and for the Council on Religious Freedom et al. by *Lee Boothby, Walter E. Carson, Harold J. Lance,* and *Robert W. Nixon.*

Briefs of amici curiae were filed for the Institute for Justice et al. by *William H. Mellor III, Clint Bolick, Richard D. Komer* and *Mark Synderman*; and for the New York County Lawyers Association Committee on Supreme Court by *H. Elliott Wales.*

■ JUSTICE O'CONNOR delivered the opinion of the Court, in which CHIEF JUSTICE REHNQUIST, and JUSTICES SCALIA, KENNEDY, and THOMAS joined.

In *Aguilar v. Felton* [this section above], this Court held that the Establishment Clause of the First Amendment barred the city of New York from sending public school teachers into parochial schools to provide remedial education to disadvantaged children pursuant to a congressionally mandated program. On remand, the District Court for the Eastern District of New York entered a permanent injunction reflecting our ruling. Twelve years later, petitioners—the parties bound by that injunction—seek relief from its operation. Petitioners maintain that *Aguilar* cannot be squared with our intervening Establishment Clause jurisprudence and ask that we explicitly recognize what our more recent cases already dictate: *Aguilar* is no longer good law. We agree with petitioners that *Aguilar* is not consistent with our subsequent Establishment Clause decisions and further conclude that, on the facts presented here, petitioners are entitled under Federal Rule of Civil Procedure 60(b)(5) to relief from the operation of the District Court's prospective injunction.

I

[Justice O'Connor discussed the purpose of Title I of the Elementary and Secondary Education Act of 1965: to "provid[e] full educational opportunity to every child regardless of economic background," citing the Senate Report. She noted the explicit legislative mandate that "the services provided to children attending private schools must be 'equitable in comparison to services and other benefits for public school children,' " that the Title I services themselves must be "secular, neutral, and nonideological," and [the federal regulation the aid to] "supplement, and in no case supplant, the level of services" already provided by the private school. O'Connor noted that the plan evaluated and rejected in *Aguilar* called for the provision of Title I services on private school premises during school hours, only public employees could serve as Title I instructors and counselors, and before any public employee could provide Title I instruction at a private school, she would be given a detailed set of written and oral instructions emphasizing the secular purpose of Title I and setting out the rules to be followed to ensure that this purpose was not compromised. "Specifically, employees would be told that (i) they were employees of the Board and accountable only to their public school supervisors; (ii) they had exclusive responsibility for selecting students for the Title I program and could teach only those children who met the eligibility criteria for Title I; (iii) their materials and equipment would be used only in the Title I program; (iv) they could not engage in team-teaching or other cooperative instructional activities with private school teachers; and (v) they could not introduce any religious matter into their teaching or become involved in any way with the religious activities of the private schools.... To ensure compliance with these rules, a publicly employed field supervisor was to attempt to make at least one unannounced visit to each teacher's classroom every month."

In a 5–4 decision, this Court [ruled in *Aguilar*] that the Board's Title I program necessitated an "excessive entanglement of church and state in the administration of [Title I] benefits." On remand, the District Court permanently enjoined the Board "from using public funds for any plan or program under [Title I] to the extent that it requires, authorizes or permits public school teachers and guidance counselors to provide teaching and counselling services on the premises of sectarian schools within New York City...."

In October and December of 1995, petitioners—the Board and a new group of parents of parochial school students entitled to Title I services—filed motions in the District Court seeking relief under Federal Rule of Civil Procedure 60(b) from the permanent injunction entered by the District Court on remand from our decision in Aguilar. Petitioners argued that relief was proper under Rule 60(b)(5) and our decision in *Rufo v. Inmates of Suffolk County Jail*, 502 U.S. 367 (1992), because the "decisional law [had] changed to make legal what the [injunction] was designed to prevent." Specifically, petitioners pointed to the statements of five Justices in *Board of Ed. of Kiryas Joel Village School Dist. v. Grumet*, 512 U.S. 687 (1994), calling for the overruling of *Aguilar*. The District Court denied the motion. The District Court recognized that petitioners, "at bottom," sought "a procedurally sound vehicle to get the [propriety of the injunction] back before the Supreme Court," and concluded that the "the Board ha[d] properly proceeded under Rule 60(b) to seek relief from the injunction." Despite its observations that "the landscape of Establishment Clause decisions has changed," and that "[t]here may be good reason to conclude that *Aguilar*'s demise is imminent," the District Court denied the Rule 60(b) motion on the merits because *Aguilar*'s demise had "not yet occurred." The Court of Appeals for the Second Circuit "affirmed substantially for the reasons stated in" the District Court's opinion. We granted certiorari, and now reverse....

III

A

The Court [in *Grand Rapids v. Ball*] acknowledged that the Shared Time program served a purely secular purpose, thereby satisfying the first part of the so-called *Lemon* test. Nevertheless, it ultimately concluded that the program had the impermissible effect of advancing religion. The Court found that the program violated the Establishment Clause's prohibition against "government-financed or government-sponsored indoctrination into the beliefs of a particular religious faith" in at least three ways. First, drawing upon the analysis in *Meek v. Pittenger*, the Court observed that "the teachers participating in the programs may become involved in intentionally or inadvertently inculcating particular religious tenets or beliefs." ... Accordingly, a majority found a " 'substantial risk' " that teachers—even those who were not employed by the private schools—might "subtly (or overtly) conform their instruction to the [pervasively sectarian] environment in which they [taught]." The danger of "state-sponsored indoctrination" was only exacerbated by the school district's failure to monitor the courses for religious content....

The presence of public teachers on parochial school grounds had a second, related impermissible effect: It created a "graphic symbol of the 'concert or union or dependency' of church and state," quoting *Zorach v. Clauson* [section 2 below], especially when perceived by "children in their formative years." The Court feared that this perception of a symbolic union between church and state would "conve[y] a message of government endorsement ... of religion" and thereby violate a "core purpose" of the Establishment Clause.

Third, the Court found that the Shared Time program impermissibly financed religious indoctrination by subsidizing "the primary religious mission of the institutions affected." The Court separated its prior decisions evaluating programs that aided the secular activities of religious institutions into two categories: those in which it concluded that the aid resulted in an effect that was "indirect, remote, or incidental" (and upheld the aid); and those in which it concluded that the aid resulted in "a direct and substantial advancement of the sectarian enterprise" (and invalidated the aid).... The *Ball* Court likewise placed no weight on the fact that the program was provided to the student rather than to the school. Nor was the impermissible effect mitigated by the fact that the program only supplemented the courses offered by the parochial schools.

The New York City Title I program challenged in *Aguilar* closely resembled the Shared Time program struck down in *Ball*, but the Court found fault with an aspect of the Title I program not present in *Ball*: The Board had "adopted a system for monitoring the religious content of publicly funded Title I classes in the religious schools." Even though this monitoring system might prevent the Title I program from being used to inculcate religion, the Court concluded, as it had in *Lemon* and *Meek*, that the level of monitoring necessary to be "certain" that the program had an exclusively secular effect would "inevitably resul[t] in the excessive entanglement of church and state," thereby running afoul of *Lemon*'s third prong.... In the majority's view, New York City's Title I program suffered from the "same critical elements of entanglement" present in *Lemon* and *Meek*: the aid was provided "in a pervasively sectarian environment ... in the form of teachers," requiring "ongoing inspection ... to ensure the absence of a religious message." Such "pervasive monitoring by public authorities in the sectarian schools infringes precisely those Establishment Clause values at the root of the prohibition of excessive entanglement." The Court noted two further forms of entanglement inherent in New York City's Title I program: the "administrative cooperation" required to implement Title I services and the "dangers of political divisiveness" that might grow out of the day-to-day decisions public officials would have to make in order to provide Title I services.

Distilled to essentials, the Court's conclusion that the Shared Time program in *Ball* had the impermissible effect of advancing religion rested on three assumptions: (i) any public employee who works on the premises of a religious school is presumed to inculcate religion in her work; (ii) the presence of public employees on private school premises creates a symbolic union between church and state; and (iii) any and all public aid that directly aids the educational function of religious schools impermissibly finances religious indoctrination, even if the aid reaches such schools as a consequence of private decisionmaking. Additionally, in *Aguilar* there was a fourth assumption: that New York City's Title I program necessitated an excessive government entanglement with religion because public employees who teach on the premises of religious schools must be closely monitored to ensure that they do not inculcate religion.

Our more recent cases have undermined the assumptions upon which *Ball* and *Aguilar* relied. To be sure, the general principles we use to evaluate whether government aid violates the Establishment Clause have not changed since *Aguilar* was decided. For example, we continue to ask whether the government acted with the purpose of advancing or inhibiting religion, and the nature of that inquiry has remained largely unchanged (citations omitted). Likewise, we continue to explore whether the aid has the "effect" of advancing or inhibiting religion. What has changed since we decided *Ball* and *Aguilar* is our understanding of the criteria used to assess whether aid to religion has an impermissible effect.

1

As we have repeatedly recognized, government inculcation of religious beliefs has the impermissible effect of advancing religion. Our cases subsequent to *Aguilar* have, however, modified in two significant respects the approach we use to assess indoctrination. First, we have abandoned the presumption erected in *Meek* and *Ball* that the placement of public employees on parochial school grounds inevitably results in the impermissible effect of state-sponsored indoctrination or constitutes a symbolic union between government and religion. In *Zobrest*, we examined whether the IDEA, 20 U.S.C. § 1400 et seq., was constitutional as applied to a deaf student who sought to bring his state-employed sign-language interpreter with him to his Roman Catholic high school. We held that this was permissible, expressly disavowing the notion that "the Establishment Clause [laid] down [an] absolute bar to the placing of a public employee in a sectarian school." "Such a flat rule, smacking of antiquated notions of 'taint,' would indeed exalt form over substance." We refused to presume that a publicly employed interpreter would be pressured by the pervasively sectarian surroundings to inculcate religion by "add[ing] to [or] sub-tract[ing] from" the lectures translated. In the absence of evidence to the contrary, we assumed instead that the interpreter would dutifully discharge her responsibilities as a full-time public employee and comply with the ethical guidelines of her profession by accurately translating what was said. Because the only government aid in *Zobrest* was the interpreter, who was herself not inculcating any religious messages, no government indoctrina-tion took place and we were able to conclude that "the provision of such assistance [was] not barred by the Establishment Clause." *Zobrest* there-fore expressly rejected the notion—relied on in *Ball* and *Aguilar*—that, solely because of her presence on private school property, a public employee will be presumed to inculcate religion in the students. *Zobrest* also implicit-ly repudiated another assumption on which *Ball* and *Aguilar* turned: that the presence of a public employee on private school property creates an impermissible "symbolic link" between government and religion. . . .

Second, we have departed from the rule relied on in *Ball* that all government aid that directly aids the educational function of religious schools is invalid. In *Witters v. Washington Dept. for Servs. for Blind* [section 3 below], we held that the Establishment Clause did not bar a State from issuing a vocational tuition grant to a blind person who wished to use the grant to attend a Christian college and become a pastor, missionary, or youth director. Even though the grant recipient clearly would use the money to obtain religious education, we observed that the tuition grants were " 'made available generally without regard to the sectarian-nonsectarian, or public-nonpublic nature of the institution bene-fitted.' " (citing *Nyquist*). The grants were disbursed directly to students, who then used the money to pay for tuition at the educational institution of their choice. In our view, this transaction was no different from a State's issuing a paycheck to one of its employees, knowing that the employee would donate part or all of the check to a religious institution. In both situations, any money that ultimately went to religious institutions did so "only as a result of the genuinely independent and private choices of" individuals. The same logic applied in *Zobrest*, where we allowed the State to provide an interpreter, even though she would be a mouthpiece for religious instruction, because the IDEA's neutral eligibility criteria ensured that the interpreter's presence in a sectarian school was a "result of the private decision of individual parents" and "[could] not be attributed to state decisionmaking". . . .

Zobrest and *Witters* make clear that, under current law, the Shared Time program in *Ball* and New York City's Title I program in *Aguilar* will not, as a matter of law, be deemed to have the effect of advancing religion through indoctrination. Indeed, each of the premises upon which we relied in *Ball* to reach a contrary conclusion is no longer valid. First, there is no reason to presume that, simply because she enters a parochial school classroom, a full-time public employee such as a Title I teacher will depart from her assigned duties and instructions and embark on religious indoctri-nation, any more than there was a reason in *Zobrest* to think an interpreter would inculcate religion by altering her translation of classroom lectures.

Certainly, no evidence has ever shown that any New York City Title I instructor teaching on parochial school premises attempted to inculcate religion in students. Thus, both our precedent and our experience require us to reject respondents' remarkable argument that we must presume Title I instructors to be "uncontrollable and sometimes very unprofessional." As discussed above, *Zobrest* also repudiates *Ball*'s assumption that the presence of Title I teachers in parochial school classrooms will, without more, create the impression of a "symbolic union" between church and state.... Justice Souter does not disavow the notion, uniformly adopted by lower courts, that Title I services may be provided to sectarian school students in off-campus locations, even though that notion necessarily presupposes that the danger of "symbolic union" evaporates once the services are provided off-campus. Taking this view, the only difference between a constitutional program and an unconstitutional one is the location of the classroom, since the degree of cooperation between Title I instructors and parochial school faculty is the same no matter where the services are provided. We do not see any perceptible (let alone dispositive) difference in the degree of symbolic union between a student receiving remedial instruction in a classroom on his sectarian school's campus and one receiving instruction in a van parked just at the school's curbside. To draw this line based solely on the location of the public employee is neither "sensible" nor "sound," and the Court in *Zobrest* rejected it. Nor under current law can we conclude that a program placing full-time public employees on parochial campuses to provide Title I instruction would impermissibly finance religious indoctrination. In all relevant respects, the provision of instructional services under Title I is indistinguishable from the provision of sign-language interpreters under the IDEA. Both programs make aid available only to eligible recipients. That aid is provided to students at whatever school they choose to attend....

We are also not persuaded that Title I services supplant the remedial instruction and guidance counselling already provided in New York City's sectarian schools. Although Justice Souter maintains that the sectarian schools provide such services and that those schools reduce those services once their students begin to receive Title I instruction, his claims rest on speculation about the impossibility of drawing any line between supplemental and general education, and not on any evidence in the record that the Board is in fact violating Title I regulations by providing services that supplant those offered in the sectarian schools. We are unwilling to speculate that all sectarian schools provide remedial instruction and guidance counselling to their students, and are unwilling to presume that the Board would violate Title I regulations by continuing to provide Title I services to students who attend a sectarian school that has curtailed its remedial instruction program in response to Title I. Nor are we willing to conclude that the constitutionality of an aid program depends on the number of sectarian school students who happen to receive the otherwise neutral aid. *Zobrest* did not turn on the fact that James Zobrest had, at the time of litigation, been the only child using a publicly funded sign-language interpreter to attend a parochial school. Accord, *Mueller v. Allen*.

What is most fatal to the argument that New York City's Title I program directly subsidizes religion is that it applies with equal force when those services are provided off-campus, and Aguilar implied that providing the services off-campus is entirely consistent with the Establishment Clause. . . . Because the incentive is the same either way, we find no logical basis upon which to conclude that Title I services are an impermissible subsidy of religion when offered on-campus, but not when offered off-campus. Accordingly, contrary to our conclusion in *Aguilar*, placing full-time employees on parochial school campuses does not as a matter of law have the impermissible effect of advancing religion through indoctrination. . . .

A number of our Establishment Clause cases have found that the criteria used for identifying beneficiaries . . . **might themselves have the effect of advancing religion by creating a financial incentive to undertake religious indoctrination.** *Witters* (upholding neutrally available program because it did not "create a financial incentive for students to undertake sectarian education"); *Zobrest* (upholding neutrally available IDEA aid because it "creates no financial incentive for parents to choose a sectarian school"). **This incentive is not present, however, where the aid is allocated on the basis of neutral, secular criteria that neither favor nor disfavor religion, and is made available to both religious and secular beneficiaries on a nondiscriminatory basis. Under such circumstances, the aid is less likely to have the effect of advancing religion.** See *Widmar v. Vincent* [section 3 below] ("The provision of benefits to so broad a spectrum of groups is an important index of secular effect").

In *Ball* and *Aguilar*, the Court gave this consideration no weight. Before and since those decisions, we have sustained programs that provided aid to all eligible children regardless of where they attended school. *Everson, Allen, Mueller, Witters, Zobrest*.

Applying this reasoning to New York City's Title I program, it is clear that Title I services are allocated on the basis of criteria that neither favor nor disfavor religion. The services are available to all children who meet the Act's eligibility requirements, no matter what their religious beliefs or where they go to school, 20 U.S.C. § 6312(c)(1)(F). The Board's program does not, therefore, give aid recipients any incentive to modify their religious beliefs or practices in order to obtain those services.

We turn now to *Aguilar*'s conclusion that New York City's Title I program resulted in an excessive entanglement between church and state. Whether a government aid program results in such an entanglement has consistently been an aspect of our Establishment Clause analysis. We have considered entanglement both in the course of assessing whether an aid program has an impermissible effect of advancing religion, *Walz*, and as a factor separate and apart from "effect," *Lemon*. Regardless of how we have characterized the issue, however, the factors we use to assess whether an entanglement is "excessive" are similar to the factors we use to examine "effect." That is, to assess entanglement, we have looked to "the character and purposes of the institutions that are benefitted, the nature of the aid that the State provides, and the resulting relationship between the government and religious authority." Similarly, we have assessed a law's "effect" by examining the character of the institutions benefitted (e.g., whether the religious institutions were "predominantly religious"), *Meek*, *Hunt v. McNair*, and the nature of the aid that the State provided (e.g., whether it was neutral and nonideological), see *Everson*, *Wolman*. Indeed, in *Lemon* itself, the entanglement that the Court found "independently" to necessitate the program's invalidation also was found to have the effect of inhibiting religion. ("[W]e cannot ignore here the danger that pervasive modern governmental power will ultimately intrude on religion ... "). Thus, it is simplest to recognize why entanglement is significant and treat it—as we did in *Walz*—as an aspect of the inquiry into a statute's effect.

Not all entanglements, of course, have the effect of advancing or inhibiting religion. Interaction between church and state is inevitable, *Walz*, and we have always tolerated some level of involvement between the two. Entanglement must be "excessive" before it runs afoul of the Establishment Clause.... See, e.g., *Bowen v. Kendrick* [Chapter Thirteen, section 7] (no excessive entanglement where government reviews the adolescent counselling program set up by the religious institutions that are grantees, reviews the materials used by such grantees, and monitors the program by periodic visits); *Roemer v. Board of Public Works of Md.*, (no excessive entanglement where state conducts annual audits to ensure that categorical state grants to religious colleges are not used to teach religion).... [T]he Court's finding of "excessive" entanglement in *Aguilar* rested on three grounds: (i) the program would require "pervasive monitoring by public authorities" to ensure that Title I employees did not inculcate religion; (ii) the program required "administrative cooperation" between the Board and parochial schools; and (iii) the program might increase the dangers of "political divisiveness."

Under our current understanding of the Establishment Clause, the last two considerations are insufficient by themselves to create an "excessive" entanglement. They are present no matter where Title I services are offered, and no court has held that Title I services cannot be offered off-campus (citations omitted). Further, the assumption underlying the first consideration has been undermined. In *Aguilar*, the Court presumed that full-time public employees on parochial school grounds would be tempted to inculcate religion, despite the ethical standards they were required to uphold. Because of this risk pervasive monitoring would be required.

But after *Zobrest* we no longer presume that public employees will inculcate religion simply because they happen to be in a sectarian environment. Since we have abandoned the assumption that properly instructed public employees will fail to discharge their duties faithfully, we must also discard the assumption that pervasive monitoring of Title I teachers is required. There is no suggestion in the record before us that unannounced monthly visits of public supervisors are insufficient to prevent or to detect inculcation of religion by public employees. Moreover, we have not found excessive entanglement in cases in which States imposed far more onerous burdens on religious institutions than the monitoring system at issue here. *Bowen.*

To summarize, New York City's Title I program does not run afoul of any of **three primary criteria we currently use to evaluate whether government aid has the effect of advancing religion: it does not result in governmental indoctrination; define its recipients by reference to religion; or create an excessive entanglement**. We therefore hold that a federally funded program providing supplemental, remedial instruction to disadvantaged children on a neutral basis is not invalid under the Establishment Clause when such instruction is given on the premises of sectarian schools by government employees pursuant to a program containing safeguards such as those present here. The same considerations that justify this holding require us to conclude that this carefully constrained program also cannot reasonably be viewed as an endorsement of religion. *Witters, Bowen.* Accordingly, we must acknowledge that *Aguilar*, as well as the portion of *Ball* addressing Grand Rapids' Shared Time program, are no longer good law. . . .

IV

To evaluate the Rule 60(b)(5) motion properly before us today in no way undermines "integrity in the interpretation of procedural rules" or signals any departure from "the responsive, non-agenda-setting character of this Court." (Ginsburg, J., dissenting). Indeed, under these circumstances, it would be particularly inequitable for us to bide our time waiting for another case to arise while the city of New York labors under a continuing injunction forcing it to spend millions of dollars on mobile instructional units and leased sites when it could instead be spending that money to give economically disadvantaged children a better chance at success in life by means of a program that is perfectly consistent with the Establishment Clause.

For these reasons, we reverse the judgment of the Court of Appeals and remand to the District Court with instructions to vacate its September 26, 1985, order.

It is so ordered.

■ JUSTICE SOUTER filed a dissenting opinion, in which JUSTICES STEVENS and GINSBURG joined, and in which JUSTICE BREYER joined as to Part II.

In this novel proceeding, petitioners seek relief from an injunction the District Court entered 12 years ago to implement our decision in *Aguilar v. Felton*. . . . The Court . . . [misreads] our more recent Establishment Clause cases, which the Court describes as having rejected the underpinnings of *Aguilar* and portions of *Aguilar*'s companion case, *School Dist. of Grand Rapids v. Ball*. The result is to repudiate the very reasonable line drawn in *Aguilar* and *Ball*, and to authorize direct state aid to religious institutions on an unparalleled scale, in violation of the Establishment Clause's central prohibition against religious subsidies by the government.

I respectfully dissent. . . .

I

I believe *Aguilar* was a correct and sensible decision, and my only reservation about its opinion is that the emphasis on the excessive entanglement produced by monitoring religious instructional content obscured those facts that independently called for the application of two central tenets of Establishment Clause jurisprudence. The State is forbidden to subsidize religion directly and is just as surely forbidden to act in any way that could reasonably be viewed as religious endorsement. *Ball* ("Although Establishment Clause jurisprudence is characterized by few absolutes, the Clause does absolutely prohibit government-financed or government-sponsored indoctrination into the beliefs of a particular religious faith"); ("Government promotes religion as effectively when it fosters a close identification of its powers and responsibilities with those of any—or all—religious denominations as when it attempts to inculcate specific religious doctrines."), citing *Lynch v. Donnelly* (O'Connor, J., concurring).

As is explained elsewhere, the flat ban on subsidization antedates the Bill of Rights and has been an unwavering rule in Establishment Clause cases, qualified only by the conclusion two Terms ago that state exactions from college students are not the sort of public revenues subject to the ban. See *Rosenberger v. Rector and Visitors of Univ. of Va.* [section 3 below]. The rule expresses the hard lesson learned over and over again in the American past and in the experiences of the countries from which we have come, that religions supported by governments are compromised just as surely as the religious freedom of dissenters is burdened when the government supports religion. "When the government favors a particular religion or sect, the disadvantage to all others is obvious, but even the favored religion may fear being 'taint[ed] ... with corrosive secularism.' The favored religion may be compromised as political figures reshape the religion's beliefs for their own purposes; it may be reformed as government largesse brings government regulation." *Lee v. Weisman* [section 2 below] (Blackmun, J., concurring)....

These principles were violated by the programs at issue in *Aguilar* and *Ball*, as a consequence of several significant features common to both Title I, as implemented in New York City before *Aguilar*, and the Grand Rapids Shared Time program: each provided classes on the premises of the religious schools, covering a wide range of subjects including some at the core of primary and secondary education, like reading and mathematics; while their services were termed "supplemental," the programs and their instructors necessarily assumed responsibility for teaching subjects that the religious schools would otherwise have been obligated to provide (citations omitted); while the programs offered aid to nonpublic school students generally (and Title I went to public school students as well), participation by religious school students in each program was extensive; and, finally, aid under Title I and Shared Time flowed directly to the schools in the form of classes and programs, as distinct from indirect aid that reaches schools only as a result of independent private choice (citations omitted).

What, therefore, was significant in *Aguilar* and *Ball* about the placement of state-paid teachers into the physical and social settings of the religious schools was not only the consequent temptation of some of those teachers to reflect the schools' religious missions in the rhetoric of their instruction, with a resulting need for monitoring and the certainty of entanglement. What was so remarkable was that the schemes in issue assumed a teaching responsibility indistinguishable from the responsibility of the schools themselves. The obligation of primary and secondary schools to teach reading necessarily extends to teaching those who are having a hard time at it, and the same is true of math. Calling some classes remedial does not distinguish their subjects from the schools' basic subjects, however inadequately the schools may have been addressing them.

What was true of the Title I scheme as struck down in *Aguilar* will be just as true when New York reverts to the old practices with the Court's approval after today. There is simply no line that can be drawn between the instruction paid for at taxpayers' expense and the instruction in any subject that is not identified as formally religious. While it would be an obvious sham, say, to channel cash to religious schools to be credited only against the expense of "secular" instruction, the line between "supplemental" and general education is likewise impossible to draw. If a State may constitutionally enter the schools to teach in the manner in question, it must in constitutional principle be free to assume, or assume payment for, the entire cost of instruction provided in any ostensibly secular subject in any religious school.... Judge Friendly's opinion for the Second Circuit [in *Aguilar*] made it expressly clear that there was no stopping place in principle once the public teacher entered the religious schools to teach their secular subjects. It may be objected that there is some subsidy in remedial education even when it takes place off the religious premises, some subsidy, that is, even in the way New York City has administered the Title I program after *Aguilar*. In these circumstances, too, what the State does, the religious school need not do; the schools save money and the program makes it easier for them to survive and concentrate their resources on their religious objectives. This argument may, of course, prove too much, but if it is not thought strong enough to bar even off-premises aid in teaching the basics to religious school pupils (an issue not before the Court in *Aguilar* or today), it does nothing to undermine the sense of drawing a line between remedial teaching on and off-premises. The off-premises teaching is arguably less likely to open the door to relieving religious schools of their responsibilities for secular subjects simply because these schools are less likely (and presumably legally unable) to dispense with those subjects from their curriculums or to make patently significant cut-backs in basic teaching within the schools to offset the outside instruction; if the aid is delivered outside of the schools, it is less likely to supplant some of what would otherwise go on inside them and to subsidize what remains. On top of that, the difference in the degree of reasonably perceptible endorsement is substantial. Sharing the teaching responsibilities within a school having religious objectives is far more likely to telegraph approval of the school's mission than keeping the State's distance would do. This is clear at every level. As the Court observed in *Ball*, "[t]he symbolism of a union between church and state [effected by placing the public school teachers into the religious schools] is most likely to influence children of tender years, whose experience is limited and whose beliefs consequently are the function of environment as much as of free and voluntary choice." *Ball*. When, moreover, the aid goes overwhelmingly to one religious denomination, minimal contact between state and church is the less likely to feed the resentment of other religions that would like access to public money for their own worthy projects.

In sum, if a line is to be drawn short of barring all state aid to religious schools for teaching standard subjects, the *Aguilar-Ball* line was a sensible one capable of principled adherence. It is no less sound, and no less necessary, today. . . .

II

The Court notes that aid programs providing benefits solely to religious groups may be constitutionally suspect, while aid allocated under neutral, secular criteria is less likely to have the effect of advancing religion. The opinion then says that *Ball* and *Aguilar* "gave this consideration no weight," and accordingly conflict with a number of decisions. But what exactly the Court thinks *Ball* and *Aguilar* inadequately considered is not clear, given that evenhandedness is a necessary but not a sufficient condition for an aid program to satisfy constitutional scrutiny. Title I services are available to all eligible children regardless whether they go to religious or public schools, but, as I have explained elsewhere and am not alone in recognizing, see, e.g., *Rosenberger* (O'Connor, J., concurring) and (Souter, J., dissenting), that fact does not define the reach of the Establishment Clause. If a scheme of government aid results in support for religion in some substantial degree, or in endorsement of its value, the formal neutrality of the scheme does not render the Establishment Clause helpless or the holdings in *Aguilar* and *Ball* inapposite. . . .

III

[T]he object of Title I is worthy without doubt, and the cost of compliance is high. In the short run there is much that is genuinely unfortunate about the administration of the scheme under *Aguilar*'s rule. But constitutional lines have to be drawn, and on one side of every one of them is an otherwise sympathetic case that provokes impatience with the Constitution and with the line. But constitutional lines are the price of constitutional government.

———

The Court had an opportunity to re-draw the constitutional lines in the following case. The plaintiffs challenged the "equitable participation" of religious schools in a federal program that provided funds to state educational agencies for distribution of computer hardware and software, library books, maps, charts, and other equipment to schools. Six Justices–in a plurality opinion by Justice Thomas and a concurring opinion by Justice O'Connor— agreed that the program is constitutional and that *Meek* and *Wolman* had to be reversed. Citing *Agostini*, Justice Thomas noted that the three "primary criteria" the Court currently uses to evaluate whether government aid has the

effect of advancing religion are whether it results in governmental indoctrination, defines its recipients by reference to religion, or creates an excessive
entanglement. As in *Agostini*, Justice Souter filed a vigorous dissent. He
gathered up details from prior cases that seemed like constitutional criteria and
announced an eleven-part test for determining whether a program of assistance
to religious schools violates the nonestablishment principle.

Guy Mitchell v. Mary L. Helms

120 S.Ct. 2530 (2000).

Michael W. McConnell argued the case for the petitioners. With him on
the briefs were *Steffen N. Johnson, Patricia A. Dean, Andrew T. Karron*,
and *John C. Massaro.*

Barbara D. Underwood argued on behalf of the United States in
support of petitioners.

Lee L. Boothby argued the case for the respondents. With him on the
brief was *Nicholas P. Miller.*

Michael D. Hess, Corporation Counsel of the City of New York, and
Stephen J. McGrath filed briefs for the City of New York and the Chancellor and Board of Education of the City of New York Board of Education of
the City of New York.

Briefs of amici curiae urging reversal were filed for the Arizona
Council for Academic Private Education, et al. by *Edward McGlynn Gaff-
ney, Jr.*, and *David Hessler;* for the Avi Chai Foundation by *Nathan Lewin*
and *Dennis Rapps*; for the Becket Fund for Religious Liberty by *Kevin J.
Hasson, Eric W. Treene*, and *Roman P. Storzer;* for the Catholic League for
Civil and Religious Rights by *Robert P. George*; for the Christian Legal
Society et al. by *Steven T. McFarland, Kimberlee Wood Colby,* and *Samuel
B. Casey*; for the Institute for Justice by *Clint Bolick*; for the Knights of
Columbus by *Pat A. Cipollone*, and Edmund T. Flood; for the National
Jewish Commission on Law and Public Affairs by *Dennis Rapps*; for Ohio,
Colorado, Florida, Illinois, Iowa, Kansas, Louisiana, Michigan, Mississippi,
Nebraska, New Jersey, South Carolina, and Virginia; by *Betty D. Montgom-
ery*, Attorney General of Ohio, and *Edward B. Foley*; for Pacific Legal
Foundation by *Sharon L. Browne*; for the United States Catholic Confer-
ence by *Mark E. Chopko John A. Liekweg* and *Jeffrey Hunter Moon*; for the
Washington Legal Foundation by *Daniel J. Popeo.*

Briefs of amici curiae urging affirmance were filed for the ACLU, et al.
by Drew S. Days, III; for the Baptist Joint Committee on Public Affairs by
Melissa Rogers; for the Interfaith Religious Liberty Foundation, et al. by
Derek Davis; for the National Education Association by *Robert H. Chanin*;
for the National Committee for Public Education and Religious Liberty
[PEARL] by *Marshall Beil*; and for the National School Boards Association
by *Julie Underwood.*

JUSTICE THOMAS announced the judgment of the Court and delivered an opinion, in which THE CHIEF JUSTICE, JUSTICE SCALIA, and JUSTICE KENNEDY join.

As part of a longstanding school aid program known as Chapter 2, the Federal Government distributes funds to state and local governmental agencies, which in turn lend educational materials and equipment to public and private schools, with the enrollment of each participating school determining the amount of aid that it receives. The question is whether Chapter 2, as applied in Jefferson Parish, Louisiana, is a law respecting an establishment of religion, because many of the private schools receiving Chapter 2 aid in that parish are religiously affiliated. We hold that Chapter 2 is not such a law.

I

A

Chapter 2 of the Education Consolidation and Improvement Act of 1981, as amended, has its origins in the Elementary and Secondary Education Act of 1965 (ESEA), and is a close cousin of the provision of the ESEA that we recently considered in *Agostini v. Felton* [above]. Like the provision at issue in *Agostini*, Chapter 2 channels federal funds to local educational agencies (LEA's), which are usually public school districts, via state educational agencies (SEA's), to implement programs to assist children in elementary and secondary schools. Among other things, Chapter 2 provides aid "for the acquisition and use of instructional and educational materials, including library services and materials (including media materials), assessments, reference materials, computer software and hardware for instructional use, and other curricular materials."

LEA's and SEA's must offer assistance to both public and private schools (although any private school must be nonprofit). Participating private schools receive Chapter 2 aid based on the number of children enrolled in each school, and allocations of Chapter 2 funds for those schools must generally be "equal (consistent with the number of children to be served) to expenditures for programs . . . for children enrolled in the public schools of the [LEA]." LEA's must in all cases "assure equitable participation" of the children of private schools "in the purposes and benefits" of Chapter 2. Further, Chapter 2 funds may only "supplement and, to the extent practical, increase the level of funds that would be made available from non-Federal sources." LEA's and SEA's may not operate their programs "so as to supplant funds from non-Federal sources."

Several restrictions apply to aid to private schools. Most significantly, the "services, materials, and equipment" provided to private schools must be "secular, neutral, and nonideological." In addition, private schools may not acquire control of Chapter 2 funds or title to Chapter 2 materials, equipment, or property. A private school receives the materials and equipment listed in [the statute] by submitting to the LEA an application detailing which items the school seeks and how it will use them; the LEA, if it approves the application, purchases those items from the school's allocation of funds, and then lends them to that school.

In Jefferson Parish (the Louisiana governmental unit at issue in this case), as in Louisiana as a whole, private schools have primarily used their allocations for nonrecurring expenses, usually materials and equipment. In the 1986—1987 fiscal year, for example, 44% of the money budgeted for private schools in Jefferson Parish was spent by LEA's for acquiring library and media materials, and 48% for instructional equipment. Among the materials and equipment provided have been library books, computers, and computer software, and also slide and movie projectors, overhead projectors, television sets, tape recorders, VCR's, projection screens, laboratory equipment, maps, globes, filmstrips, slides, and cassette recordings.

It appears that, in an average year, about 30% of Chapter 2 funds spent in Jefferson Parish are allocated for private schools. For the 1985—1986 fiscal year, 41 private schools participated in Chapter 2. For the following year, 46 participated, and the participation level has remained relatively constant since then. Of these 46, 34 were Roman Catholic; 7 were otherwise religiously affiliated; and 5 were not religiously affiliated.

B

Respondents filed suit in December 1985, alleging, among other things, that Chapter 2, as applied in Jefferson Parish, violated the Establishment Clause of the First Amendment of the Federal Constitution. The case's tortuous history over the next 15 years indicates well the degree to which our Establishment Clause jurisprudence has shifted in recent times, while nevertheless retaining anomalies with which the lower courts have had to struggle....

[Justice Thomas noted that in granting summary judgment for the plaintiffs in 1990, the district court had relied relied primarily on *Meek v. Pittenger*, and *Wolman v. Walter*, in which "the Court held unconstitutional programs that provided many of the same sorts of materials and equipment as does Chapter 2." In 1997 a different district judge granted summary judgment for the defendants on the ground that in a similar Chapter 2 case the Ninth Circuit had distinguished *Meek* and *Wolman* based on the percentage of schools receiving aid that were parochial but had also noted that *Meek* upheld "the massive provision of textbooks to parochial schools." *Walker v. San Francisco Unified School Dist.*, 46 F.3d 1449, 1468, n. 16 (9th Cir. 1995). Thomas noted: "although the Ninth Circuit did not explicitly hold that *Meek* and *Wolman* were no longer good law, its reasoning seemed to require that conclusion.... The Fifth Circuit acknowledged that *Agostini*, by recognizing our rejection of the rule that 'all government aid that directly assists the educational function of religious schools is invalid,' had rejected a premise of *Meek*, but [the Fifth Circuit] nevertheless concluded that *Agostini* had neither directly overruled *Meek* and *Wolman* nor rejected their distinction between textbooks and other in-kind aid. The Fifth Circuit therefore concluded that *Meek* and *Wolman* controlled, and thus it held Chapter 2 unconstitutional." The stage was thus set for a reconsideration of *Meek* and *Wolman,* which several amici urged the Court to undertake.]

II

The Establishment Clause of the First Amendment dictates that "Congress shall make no law respecting an establishment of religion." In the over 50 years since *Everson*, we have consistently struggled to apply these simple words in the context of governmental aid to religious schools. As we admitted in *Tilton*, "candor compels the acknowledgment that we can only dimly perceive the boundaries of permissible government activity in this sensitive area."

In *Agostini*, however, we brought some clarity to our case law, by overruling two anomalous precedents (one in whole, the other in part) and by consolidating some of our previously disparate considerations under a revised test. Whereas in *Lemon* we had considered whether a statute (1) has a secular purpose, (2) has a primary effect of advancing or inhibiting religion, or (3) creates an excessive entanglement between government and religion, in *Agostini* we modified *Lemon* for purposes of evaluating aid to schools and examined only the first and second factors. We acknowledged that our cases discussing excessive entanglement had applied many of the same considerations as had our cases discussing primary effect, and we therefore recast *Lemon*'s entanglement inquiry as simply one criterion relevant to determining a statute's effect. *Agostini*. We also acknowledged that our cases had pared somewhat the factors that could justify a finding of excessive entanglement. We then set out revised criteria for determining the effect of a statute: "To summarize, New York City's Title I program does not run afoul of any of three primary criteria we currently use to evaluate whether government aid has the effect of advancing religion: It does not result in governmental indoctrination; define its recipients by reference to religion; or create an excessive entanglement." *Id.*

In this case, our inquiry under *Agostini*'s purpose and effect test is a narrow one. Because respondents do not challenge the District Court's holding that Chapter 2 has a secular purpose, and because the Fifth Circuit also did not question that holding, we will consider only Chapter 2's effect. Further, in determining that effect, we will consider only the first two *Agostini* criteria, since neither respondents nor the Fifth Circuit has questioned the District Court's holding that Chapter 2 does not create an excessive entanglement. Considering Chapter 2 in light of our more recent case law, we conclude that it neither results in religious indoctrination by the government nor defines its recipients by reference to religion. We therefore hold that Chapter 2 is not a "law respecting an establishment of religion." In so holding, we acknowledge what both the Ninth and Fifth Circuits saw was inescapable—*Meek* and *Wolman* are anomalies in our case law. We therefore conclude that they are no longer good law.

A

As we indicated in *Agostini*, and have indicated elsewhere [citing *Zobrest, Rosenberger, Witters, Mueller,* and *Corporation of Presiding Bishop v. Amos*], the question whether governmental aid to religious schools results in governmental indoctrination is ultimately a question whether any religious indoctrination that occurs in those schools could reasonably be attributed to governmental action. We have also indicated that the answer to the question of indoctrination will resolve the question whether a program of educational aid "subsidizes" religion, as our religion cases use that term.

In distinguishing between indoctrination that is attributable to the State and indoctrination that is not, we have consistently turned to the principle of neutrality, upholding aid that is offered to a broad range of groups or persons without regard to their religion. If the religious, irreligious, and areligious are all alike eligible for governmental aid, no one would conclude that any indoctrination that any particular recipient conducts has been done at the behest of the government. For attribution of indoctrination is a relative question. If the government is offering assistance to recipients who provide, so to speak, a broad range of indoctrination, the government itself is not thought responsible for any particular indoctrination. To put the point differently, if the government, seeking to further some legitimate secular purpose, offers aid on the same terms, without regard to religion, to all who adequately further that purpose, *see Allen*, (discussing dual secular and religious purposes of religious schools), then it is fair to say that any aid going to a religious recipient only has the effect of furthering that secular purpose. The government, in crafting such an aid program, has had to conclude that a given level of aid is necessary to further that purpose among secular recipients and has provided no more than that same level to religious recipients.

As a way of assuring neutrality, we have repeatedly considered whether any governmental aid that goes to a religious institution does so "only as a result of the genuinely independent and private choices of individuals." *Agostini*. We have viewed as significant whether the "private choices of individual parents," as opposed to the "unmediated" will of government, *Ball,* determine what schools ultimately benefit from the governmental aid, and how much. For if numerous private choices, rather than the single choice of a government, determine the distribution of aid pursuant to neutral eligibility criteria, then a government cannot, or at least cannot easily, grant special favors that might lead to a religious establishment. Private choice also helps guarantee neutrality by mitigating the preference for pre-existing recipients that is arguably inherent in any governmental aid program, *see, e.g.*, Gilder, The Revitalization of Everything: The Law of the Microcosm, Harv. Bus. Rev. 49 (Mar./Apr. 1988), and that could lead to a program inadvertently favoring one religion or favoring religious private schools in general over nonreligious ones.

The principles of neutrality and private choice, and their relationship to each other, were prominent not only in *Agostini*, but also in *Zobrest, Witters*, and *Mueller.*... [In *Zobrest*] private choices helped to ensure neutrality, and neutrality and private choices together eliminated any possible attribution to the government even when the interpreter translated classes on Catholic doctrine.... In *Witters*, we held that the Establishment Clause did not bar a State from including within a neutral program providing tuition payments for vocational rehabilitation a blind person studying at a Christian college to become a pastor, missionary, or youth director....

The tax deduction for educational expenses that we upheld in *Mueller* was, in these respects, the same as the tuition grant in *Witters*. We upheld it chiefly because it "neutrally provides state assistance to a broad spectrum of citizens," and because "numerous, private choices of individual parents of school-age children" determined which schools would benefit from the deductions. We explained that "[w]here, as here, aid to parochial schools is available only as a result of decisions of individual parents no 'imprimatur of state approval' can be deemed to have been conferred on any particular religion, or on religion generally."

Agostini's second primary criterion for determining the effect of governmental aid is closely related to the first. The second criterion requires a court to consider whether an aid program "define[s] its recipients by reference to religion." As we briefly explained in *Agostini*, this second criterion looks to the same set of facts as does our focus, under the first criterion, on neutrality, but the second criterion uses those facts to answer a somewhat different question–whether the criteria for allocating the aid "creat[e] a financial incentive to undertake religious indoctrination." In *Agostini* we set out the following rule for answering this question: "This incentive is not present, however, where the aid is allocated on the basis of neutral, secular criteria that neither favor nor disfavor religion, and is made available to both religious and secular beneficiaries on a nondiscriminatory basis. Under such circumstances, the aid is less likely to have the effect of advancing religion."

We hasten to add, what should be obvious from the rule itself, that simply because an aid program offers private schools, and thus religious schools, a benefit that they did not previously receive does not mean that the program, by reducing the cost of securing a religious education, creates, under *Agostini's* second criterion, an "incentive" for parents to choose such an education for their children. For any aid will have some such effect. *See Allen, Everson, Mueller.*

B

Respondents inexplicably make no effort to address Chapter 2 under the *Agostini* test. Instead, dismissing *Agostini* as factually distinguishable, they offer two rules that they contend should govern our determination of whether Chapter 2 has the effect of advancing religion. They argue first, and chiefly, that "direct, nonincidental" aid to the primary educational mission of religious schools is always impermissible. Second, they argue that provision to religious schools of aid that is divertible to religious use is similarly impermissible. Respondents' arguments are inconsistent with our more recent case law, in particular *Agostini* and *Zobrest*, and we therefore reject them.

1

Although some of our earlier cases, particularly *Ball*, did emphasize the distinction between direct and indirect aid, the purpose of this distinction was merely to prevent "subsidization" of religion. As even the dissent all but admits, our more recent cases address this purpose not through the direct/indirect distinction but rather through the principle of private choice, as incorporated in the first *Agostini* criterion (i.e., whether any indoctrination could be attributed to the government). If aid to schools, even "direct aid," is neutrally available and, before reaching or benefiting any religious school, first passes through the hands (literally or figuratively) of numerous private citizens who are free to direct the aid elsewhere, the government has not provided any "support of religion." Although the presence of private choice is easier to see when aid literally passes through the hands of individuals–which is why we have mentioned directness in the same breath with private choice, *see, e.g., Agostini, Witters, Mueller*—there is no reason why the Establishment Clause requires such a form.

Indeed, *Agostini* expressly rejected the absolute line that respondents would have us draw. We there explained that "we have departed from the rule relied on in *Ball* that all government aid that directly assists the educational function of religious schools is invalid." *Agostini* relied primarily on *Witters* for this conclusion and made clear that private choice and neutrality would resolve the concerns formerly addressed by the rule in *Ball*. It was undeniable in *Witters* that the aid (tuition) would ultimately go to the Inland Empire School of the Bible and would support religious education. We viewed this arrangement, however, as no different from a government issuing a paycheck to one of its employees knowing that the employee would direct the funds to a religious institution. Both arrangements would be valid, for the same reason: "[A]ny money that ultimately went to religious institutions did so 'only as a result of the genuinely independent and private choices of' individuals." *Agostini* . . . .

2

Respondents also contend that the Establishment Clause requires that aid to religious schools not be impermissibly religious in nature or be divertible to religious use. We agree with the first part of this argument but not the second. Respondents' "no divertibility" rule is inconsistent with our more recent case law and is unworkable. So long as the governmental aid is not itself "unsuitable for use in the public schools because of religious content," *Allen*, and eligibility for aid is determined in a constitutionally permissible manner, any use of that aid to indoctrinate cannot be attributed to the government and is thus not of constitutional concern. And, of course, the use to which the aid is put does not affect the criteria governing the aid's allocation and thus does not create any impermissible incentive under *Agostini*'s second criterion. . . .

It is perhaps conceivable that courts could take upon themselves the task of distinguishing among the myriad kinds of possible aid based on the ease of diverting each kind. But it escapes us how a court might coherently draw any such line. It not only is far more workable, but also is actually related to real concerns about preventing advancement of religion by government, simply to require, as did *Zobrest, Agostini*, and *Allen*, that a program of aid to schools not provide improper content and that it determine eligibility and allocate the aid on a permissible basis.

C

[Justice Thomas addressed several factors that the dissent urged "depending on the facts of each case 'in all its particularity,' could be relevant to the constitutionality of a school-aid program." Thomas dismissed the concern for political divisiveness as one that "once occupied the Court but that post-*Aguilar* cases have rightly disregarded." Justice Thomas offered four reasons for rejecting consideration of whether a school that receives aid (or whose students receive aid) is "pervasively sectarian."]

First, its relevance in our precedents is in sharp decline. Although our case law has consistently mentioned it even in recent years, we have not struck down an aid program in reliance on this factor since 1985, in *Aguilar* and Ball. *Agostini* of course overruled *Aguilar* in full and *Ball* in part....

Second, the religious nature of a recipient should not matter to the constitutional analysis, so long as the recipient adequately furthers the government's secular purpose. If a program offers permissible aid to the religious (including the pervasively sectarian), the areligious, and the irreligious, it is a mystery which view of religion the government has established, and thus a mystery what the constitutional violation would be. The pervasively sectarian recipient has not received any special favor, and it is most bizarre that the Court would, as the dissent seemingly does, reserve special hostility for those who take their religion seriously, who think that their religion should affect the whole of their lives, or who make the mistake of being effective in transmitting their views to children.

Third, the inquiry into the recipient's religious views required by a focus on whether a school is pervasively sectarian is not only unnecessary but also offensive. It is well established, in numerous other contexts, that courts should refrain from trolling through a person's or institution's religious beliefs. *See Employment Div. v. Smith.* Yet that is just what this factor requires.... In addition, and related, the application of the "pervasively sectarian" factor collides with our decisions that have prohibited governments from discriminating in the distribution of public benefits based upon religious status or sincerity. *See Rosenberger, Lamb's Chapel, Widmar.*

Finally, hostility to aid to pervasively sectarian schools has a shameful pedigree that we do not hesitate to disavow. Although the dissent professes concern for "the implied exclusion of the less favored," the exclusion of pervasively sectarian schools from government-aid programs is just that, particularly given the history of such exclusion. Opposition to aid to "sectarian" schools acquired prominence in the 1870's with Congress's consideration (and near passage) of the Blaine Amendment, which would have amended the Constitution to bar any aid to sectarian institutions. Consideration of the amendment arose at a time of pervasive hostility to the Catholic Church and to Catholics in general, and it was an open secret that "sectarian" was code for "Catholic." See generally Green, The Blaine

Amendment Reconsidered, 36 Am. J. Legal Hist. 38 (1992).... In short, nothing in the Establishment Clause requires the exclusion of pervasively sectarian schools from otherwise permissible aid programs, and other doctrines of this Court bar it. This doctrine, born of bigotry, should be buried now....

III

Applying the two relevant *Agostini* criteria, we see no basis for concluding that Jefferson Parish's Chapter 2 program "has the effect of advancing religion." *Agostini*. Chapter 2 does not result in governmental indoctrination, because it determines eligibility for aid neutrally, allocates that aid based on the private choices of the parents of schoolchildren, and does not provide aid that has an impermissible content. Nor does Chapter 2 define its recipients by reference to religion.

Taking the second criterion first, it is clear that Chapter 2 aid "is allocated on the basis of neutral, secular criteria that neither favor nor disfavor religion, and is made available to both religious and secular beneficiaries on a nondiscriminatory basis." *Agostini*. Aid is allocated based on enrollment ... and allocations to private schools must "be equal (consistent with the number of children to be served) to expenditures for programs under this subchapter for children enrolled in the public schools of the [LEA]," 20 U.S.C. § 7372(b).

Chapter 2 satisfies the first *Agostini* criterion because it does not provide to religious schools aid that has an impermissible content. The statute explicitly bars anything of the sort, providing that all Chapter 2 aid for the benefit of children in private schools shall be "secular, neutral, and nonideological," and the record indicates that the Louisiana SEA and the Jefferson Parish LEA have faithfully enforced this requirement insofar as relevant to this case. The chief aid at issue is computers, computer software, and library books. The computers presumably have no pre-existing content, or at least none that would be impermissible for use in public schools. Respondents do not contend otherwise. Respondents also offer no evidence that religious schools have received software from the government that has an impermissible content.

IV

In short, Chapter 2 satisfies both the first and second primary criteria of *Agostini*. It therefore does not have the effect of advancing religion. For the same reason, Chapter 2 also "cannot reasonably be viewed as an endorsement of religion," *Agostini*. Accordingly, we hold that Chapter 2 is not a law respecting an establishment of religion. Jefferson Parish need not exclude religious schools from its Chapter 2 program. To the extent that *Meek* and *Wolman* conflict with this holding, we overrule them.

Our conclusion regarding *Meek* and *Wolman* should come as no surprise. The Court as early as *Wolman* itself left no doubt that *Meek* and *Allen* were irreconcilable, and we have repeatedly reaffirmed *Allen* since then, *see, e.g., Agostini*. In fact, *Meek*, in discussing the materials-and-equipment program, did not even cite *Allen*. Less than three years after

Wolman, we explained that *Meek* did not, despite appearances, hold that "all loans of secular instructional material and equipment inescapably have the effect of direct advancement of religion." *Regan*. Then, in *Mueller*, we conceded that the aid at issue in *Meek* and *Wolman* did "resembl[e], in many respects," the aid that we had upheld in *Everson* and *Allen*. Most recently, *Agostini*, in rejecting *Ball*'s assumption that "all government aid that directly assists the educational function of religious schools is invalid," *Agostini*, necessarily rejected a large portion (perhaps all) of the reasoning of *Meek* and *Wolman* in invalidating the lending of materials and equipment, for *Ball* borrowed that assumption from those cases. Today we simply acknowledge what has long been evident. . . .

The judgment of the Fifth Circuit is reversed. It is so ordered.

■ JUSTICE O'CONNOR, with whom JUSTICE BREYER joined, concurred in the judgment on the ground that *Agostini* "controls the constitutional inquiry respecting Title II presented here." The concurring justices also agreed with the plurality that "to the extent our decisions in *Meek* and *Wolman* are inconsistent with the Court's judgment today, . . . those decisions should be overruled."

Justice O'Connor, however, did not join the plurality opinion, offering two principal reasons for writing separately: "First, the plurality's treatment of neutrality comes close to assigning that factor singular importance in the future adjudication of Establishment Clause challenges to government school-aid programs. Second, the plurality's approval of actual diversion of government aid to religious indoctrination is in tension with our precedents and, in any event, unnecessary to decide the instant case."

On the first point, O'Connor argued that several other elements in *Agostini* were of constitutional significance: a lack of evidence of inculcation of religion by Title I instructors, the legal requirement that Title I services be supplemental to regular curricula, the finding that no Title I funds reached the coffers of religious schools' coffers, and that the aid had secular content and was distributed on the basis of wholly neutral criteria. She also noted that two of these criteria were present in *Zobrest, above*, where no government funds reached the religious school's coffers and where the aid did not relieve school of expense it otherwise would have assumed.

On the second point, O'Connor again cited her opinion in *Agostini* as evidence that the Court had not adopted the principle that aid to education in religious schools may advance the religious missions of those schools: "no evidence has ever shown that any New York City Title I instructor teaching on parochial school premises attempted to inculcate religion in students." She also cited Justice White in *Bd. of Education v. Allen*: "Nothing in this record supports the proposition that all textbooks, whether they deal with mathematics, physics, foreign languages, history, or literature, are used by the parochial schools to teach religion." And she noted that the purpose of the remand in *Bowen v. Kendrick, above*, was to "determine, after further factual development, whether aid recipients had used the government aid to support their religious objectives."

O'Connor objected that the logic of the plurality opinion "foreshadows the approval of direct monetary subsidies to religious organizations, even when they use the money to advance their religious objectives." In her view the "school-aid cases often pose difficult questions at the intersection of the neutrality and no-aid principles and therefore defy simple categorization under either rule." Citing her concurring opinion in *Rosenberger*, O'Connor concluded: "Resolution instead depends on the hard task of judging—sifting through the details and determining whether the challenged program offends the Establishment Clause. Such judgment requires courts to draw lines, sometimes quite fine, based on the particular facts of each case."

■ JUSTICE SOUTER, joined by JUSTICES STEVENS and GINSBURG, dissented. He criticized the plurality for taking a stance that "appears to take evenhandedness neutrality and in practical terms promote it to a single and sufficient test for the establishment constitutionality of school aid." Souter wrote that "evenhandedness of distribution is relevant in judging whether a benefit scheme so characterized should be seen as aiding a sectarian school's religious mission, but this neutrality is not alone sufficient to qualify the aid as constitutional." Since Justice O'Connor expressly agreed with the dissent on this matter, five justices remain of the view that something more than nondiscrimination or evenhandedness or neutrality must be taken into consideration in deciding cases involving aid to education in religious schools.

NOTES AND QUESTIONS

The Search for Coherence. As noted above, commentators on the cases applying the nonestablishment provision to religious education have not found them coherent. For example, Professor Choper has written: "There is broad consensus that a central threat to the religious freedom of individuals and groups—indeed, in the judgment of many the most serious infringement upon religious liberty—is posed by forcing them to pay taxes in support of as a religious establishment or religious activities." Jesse H. Choper, *Securing Religious Liberty* 16 (1995). The application of this general principle to the particular details of state and federal programs of assistance to various aspects of religious education, however, has left Choper and others utterly bewildered. Choper calls the post-*Lemon* case law "ad hoc judgments which are incapable of being reconciled on any principled basis." Is Choper right? Can you harmonize the cases? Consider this summary of what the Court has found permissible and impermissible in the half century since *Everson*.

Permissible:

Bus transportation to and from school: *Everson*, 1947

Secular textbooks: *Cochran*, 1930; *Allen*, 1968; *Lemon*, 1971 *Meek*, 1975; *Wolman*, 1975

Exemption from property tax: *Walz*, 1970

Lunches: *Lemon*, 1971 (dictum)

Diagnostic services: *Wolman*, 1977

Therapy off school grounds: *Wolman,* 1977

Counselling off school grounds: *Wolman,* 1977

Remedial instruction off school grounds: *Wolman,* 1977

Payments for use and grading of examinations prepared by state: *Regan,* 1980

Tax deduction for tuition and educational expenses available to all taxpayers: *Mueller,* 1983

Sign-language interpreter for deaf student on premises of religious high school: *Zobrest,* 1993

Remedial services on premises: *Agostini,* 1997 (reversing *Aguilar* and *Grand Rapids,* 1985)

Computer hardware and software, *Mitchell,* 2000

Instructional material such as maps, films, and laboratory equipment, provided to religious schools, *Mitchell,* 2000, reversing *Meek,* 1975

Instructional material, such as maps, magazines, tape recorders provided to children attending religious schools, *Mitchell,* 2000 reversing *Wolman,* 1977

Therapeutic services (counselling, testing, remedial help, speech and hearing therapy) on premises of religious schools, *Mitchell,* 2000 reversing *Meek,* 1975

Bus transportation for children attending religious schools to participate in educational field trips, such as visiting a museum or the State Legislature, *Mitchell,* 2000 reversing *Wolman,* 1977

Impermissible:

Reimbursement of religious schools for salaries of teachers of mathematics, modern foreign languages, physical science, and physical education, *Lemon,* 1971.

Instructional materials approved by state official and given to religious schools, *Lemon,* 1971

Salary supplements to teachers at religious schools who teach only subjects offered in public schools and who use only teaching materials used in the public schools, *Earley,* 1971

Grants to nonpublic schools serving low-income families to maintain and repair school facilities, *Nyquist,* 1973; *Sloan v. Lemon,* 1973

Tuition reimbursements ($50 cap) only for low-income parents of children attending religious schools, *Nyquist,* 1973

Tax credits ($50 cap) only for low-income parents of children attending religious schools, *Nyquist,* 1973

Payment for state-mandated examinations prepared by teachers at religious schools, *Levitt,* 1973; *New York v. Cathedral Academy,* 1977

Instructional material such as maps, films, and laboratory equipment, provided to religious schools, *Meek,* 1975, see *Mitchell,* 2000

Therapeutic services (counselling, testing, remedial help, speech and hearing therapy) on premises of religious schools, *Meek*, 1975, see *Mitchell*, 2000

Bus transportation for children attending religious schools to participate in educational field trips, such as visiting a museum or the State Legislature, *Wolman*, 1977, see *Mitchell*, 2000

Instructional material, such as maps, magazines, tape recorders provided to children attending religious schools, *Wolman*, 1977, see *Mitchell*, 2000

Exemption of religious literature from sales tax, without similar exemption for nonreligious literature, *Texas Monthly*, 1989

2. *Predictability*. If predictability is a desirable attribute of the law, is it easier to predict that educational vouchers providing support for all parents with schoolchildren, including those attending religious schools, would be permissible after *Mueller v. Allen* [this section above] or after *Mitchell v. Helms*? In *PEARL v. Regan*, Justice White acknowledged for a sharply divided Court that its "course sacrifices clarity and predictability for flexibility," and that this would continue to be true until "a single, more encompassing construction of the Establishment Clause" was reached. In *Agostini* a bare majority agreed with the proposition that there is no impermissible financial incentive to advance religion when "aid is allocated on the basis of neutral, secular criteria that neither favor nor disfavor religion, and is made available to both religious and secular beneficiaries on a nondiscriminatory basis." Did Justice O'Connor's formulation of the nondiscrimination principle fulfill Justice White's hope for "a single, more encompassing construction of the Establishment Clause" that may yield greater coherence in the case law? The plurality opinion of Justice Thomas in *Mitchell* cited O'Connor's opinion in *Agostini* frequently, but O'Connor filed a separate concurring opinion. Why? Because she thought the plurality opinion did not stress that public funds may not be channelled to religious groups for religious indoctrination? She emphasized this point in her concurring opinion, but she also underscored that it is permissible under *Witters, Zobrest*, and *Agostini* to foster "truly independent private choice." How should the Court rule on a voucher plan that on its face prohibits public funds from being channelled to religious groups for religious indoctrination, and that fosters "truly independent private choice"?

3. *Educational Vouchers or Scholarships*. Can the parental liberty interest advanced in *Meyer* and *Pierce* [Chapter Ten, section 7] and *Yoder* [Chapter Eleven, section 7] serve as the basis for financing greater freedom of educational choice? Around 1970 federal and state officials recognized that educational choice might be desirable and achievable. At that time the literature on the subject consisted of only a few brief sketches of contrasting "voucher" plans. A leading market economist at the University of Chicago advocated a laissez-faire approach to education that would give each parent the equivalent of the per pupil expenditure of the local public school district to be spent on education in any way the parent sees fit. Milton Friedman, *Capitalism and Freedom* 85 (1962); and see Henry Levin, "The Failure of the Public Schools and the Free Market Remedy," 2 *The Urban Rev.* 32 (June 1968). Sociologist Christopher Jencks also wrote a provocative essay, "Is the Public School Obsolete?," 2 *Public Interest* 18 (Winter 1966). Two educators, Theodore Sizer and Phillip Whitten, offered "A Proposal for a Poor Children's Bill of Rights" 5 *Psychology Today* 58 (1968). Two legal scholars, Professors Coons and Sugarman of the

University of California at Berkeley, advanced arguments for educational reform based on equality or fairness, with special concern for the poor, who have been least well served by our current educational system. See, e.g., John E. Coons and Stephen D. Sugarman, *Family Choice in Education: A Model State System for Vouchers* (1971); Coons and Sugarman, *Education by Choice: The Case for Family Control* (1978). In their latest writing on the subject, Coons and Sugarman note: "The extension of school choice to all families may proceed either in one giant step or bit-by-bit. One state may decide to give scholarships first to drop-outs; later it may extend these same rights to at-risk students, to minority students seeking integration, or to disabled students." Coons and Sugarman, *Scholarships for Children* 4 (1992). They proposed an initiative measure in California that would extend scholarships first to low-income families, as in *Nyquist*, and within a relatively brief time to all children.

Since the 1970s the literature both for and against vouchers has mushroomed. For arguments in favor of voucher proposals, see, e.g., John E. Chubb and Terry M. Moe, *Politics, Markets, and America's Schools* (1990); Abigail Thernstrom, *School Choice in Massachusetts* (1991); Sheldon Richman, *Separating School and State: How to Liberate America's Families* (1994); Peter W. Cookston, Jr. *School Choice: The Struggle for the Soul of American Education* (1994); and Michael A. Vaccari, Public Purpose and the Public Funding of Sectarian Educational Institutions: A More Rational Approach After Rosenberger and Agostini, 82 *Marq. L. Rev.* 1 (1998). For arguments against voucher proposals, see, e.g., Julie K. Underwood, "Choice Is Not a Panacea," 71 *Ed. L. Rep.* 599 (1992); Steven K. Green, "The Legal Argument Against Private School Choice," 62 *U. Cin. L. Rev.* 37 (1993); Carol L. Ziegler & Nancy M. Lederman, "School Vouchers: Are Urban Students Surrendering Rights for Choice?," 19 *Fordham Urb. L. J.* 813 (1993); Marilyn V. Yarbrough, "Still Separate and Still Unequal," 36 *Wm & Mary L. Rev.* 685 (1995); and Laura S. Underkuffler, "Vouchers And Beyond: The Individual As Causative Agent In Establishment Clause Jurisprudence," 75 *Ind. L.J.* 167 (2000).

If a voucher system available to a broad class of beneficiaries, as in *Mueller*, were adopted, would it pass constitutional muster under cases like *Mueller, Witters*, [section 3 below], *Zobrest, Rosenberger* [section 3 below] and *Agostini*? In his dissent in *Agostini*, Justice Souter wrote: "There is simply no line that can be drawn between the instruction paid for at taxpayers' expense and the instruction in any subject that is not identified as formally religious. While it would be an obvious sham, say, to channel cash to religious schools to be credited only against the expense of 'secular' instruction, the line between 'supplemental' and general education is likewise impossible to draw. If a State may constitutionally enter the schools to teach in the manner in question, it must in constitutional principle be free to assume, or assume payment for, the entire cost of instruction provided in any ostensibly secular subject in any religious school." Is this an argument for or against vouchers? Would vouchers be rejected under the rationale announced in *Nyquist*? In *Mueller*?

A voucher plan in Milwaukee originally skirted the constitutional issue by excluding religious schools. In 1995 the program was amended to include religious schools, on condition that these schools permit students to opt out of religious activities and classes. The Wisconsin Supreme Court sustained the amended school choice program under both the First Amendment and under various provisions of the state constitution. *Jackson v. Benson*, 218 Wis. 2d 835,

578 N.W. 2d 602, cert. denied, 119 S.Ct. 466 (1998). Applying the three *Lemon* tests, the court ruled that even though the amended statute allowed for payment of state funds to sectarian schools, the program has a valid secular purpose of providing low-income parents with an opportunity to have their children educated outside of the embattled public school system of Milwaukee; that the program did not have the primary effect of advancing religion since "beneficiaries were selected on a random basis from all pupils who applied and met religious-neutral criteria, participating private schools were selected on a religious-neutral basis, whether sectarian or nonsectarian, schools were prohibited from requiring participating students to participate in any religious activity, and public aid flowed to sectarian private schools only as a result of numerous private choices of individual parents;" and that the program's "requirement subjecting participating private schools to performance, reporting, and auditing standards would not result in an excessive governmental entanglement with religion, even though enforcement of standards required the Superintendent of Public Instruction to monitor quality of secular education at participating sectarian schools, where the Superintendent already monitored the quality of education at all sectarian private schools, and the program did not involve state in any way with schools' governance, curriculum, or day-to-day affairs." Right result? The court did not discuss whether the opt-out condition placed upon their participation in the program is constitutional. Is it? *See generally*, Michael W. McConnell, "The Selective Funding Problem: Abortions and Religious Schools," 104 *Harv. L. Rev.* 989 (1991).

The Milwaukee case generated intense interest as a vehicle for getting the issue of vouchers before the Supreme Court. In the Milwaukee case the Institute for Justice, of Washington, DC, and the Landmark Legal Foundation, Kansas City, MO filed briefs and argued on behalf of intervenor parents. Briefs amicus curiae urging the invalidity of the school choice program were filed by the American Civil Liberties Union; the American Jewish Congress; Americans United for Separation of Church & State; the Milwaukee Jewish Council for Community Relations and the Wisconsin Jewish Conference; the NAACP; People for the American Way; and the Wisconsin Education Association. Briefs in support of the constitutionality of the voucher program were filed by the Center for Education Reform, American Legislative Exchange, CEO America, Putting Children First, James Madison Institute for Public Policy Studies, Jewish Policy Center, "I Have a Dream" Foundation (Washington, D.C. Chapter), Institute for Public Affairs, Liberty Counsel, Maine School Choice Coalition, Pennsylvania Manufacturers Association, Reach Alliance, Arkansas Policy Foundation, North Carolina Education Reform Foundation, Texas Justice Foundation, Minnesota Business Partnership, Minnesotans for School Choice, Toussaint Institute, South Carolina Policy Counsel, and United New Yorkers for Choice in Education; by the Christian Legal Society, the Ethics and Religious Liberty Commission of the Southern Baptist Convention, the Lutheran Church–Missouri Synod, and the National Association of Evangelicals; by the Family Research Institute, Christian Defense Fund, Center for Public Justice, Family Research Council, Toward Tradition, Liberty Counsel and Focus on the Family.

Shortly after the Wisconsin case, the Arizona supreme court sustained A.R.S. § 43–1089, which allows a state tax credit of up to $500 for those who donate to school tuition organizations (STOs). *Kotterman v. Killian*, 193 Ariz. 273, 972 P. 2d 606 (1999), cert. denied, 120 S.Ct. 283 (1999). A similar array of interested parties participated in this litigation. Supporting the taxpayers who challenged the statute were the ACLU, the Arizona Education Association, Arizona School Boards Association, People for the American Way, and Americans United for Separation of Church and State. As in the Milwaukee case, the Institute for Justice represented parents as intervenors whose interests would be directly affected by the outcome of the case. The Arizona School Choice Trust also participated as an intervenor.

The Arizona court relied primarily upon *Mueller v. Allen*, in which Justice Rehnquist emphasized the fact that the benefits of Minnesota's tax deduction extended to a broad class of recipients, not just to the parents of private school children as in *Nyquist*. In *Kotterman* Chief Justice Zlaket wrote: "the Arizona tuition credit is available to all taxpayers who are willing to contribute to an STO. Any individual, not just a parent, may donate to the scholarship program. Thus, Arizona's class of beneficiaries is even broader than that found acceptable in *Mueller*, and clearly achieves a greater level of neutrality." Citing *Jackson v. Benson*, the Arizona court ruled that the tax scheme was permissible because religious schools were simply "one of many" institutions benefited. The taxpayers challenging the scheme attempted to distinguish *Mueller v. Allen* on the ground that the Minnesota statute upheld in *Mueller* involved a tax deduction, while the Arizona statute involved a tax credit. A deduction is subtracted from gross income, reducing the net amount on which a tax is assessed according to the taxpayer's marginal rate; a credit is taken directly from the tax as tentatively calculated. Noting that in *Nyquist*, Justice Powell wrote that the constitutionality of a tax benefit "does not turn ... on the label we accord it," Chief Justice Zlaket wrote in *Kotterman* that the distinction between a deduction and a credit is not "constitutionally significant." The *Kotterman* court also relied on *Witters* to sustain aid flowing to religious institutions "only as a result of the genuinely independent and private choices of aid recipients" and on *Zobrest* to uphold public support for a child's education in a religious school that was the result of the "private decision of individual parents". As in *Jackson*, the *Kotterman* court also rejected challenges to the statute based on the state constitution.

About half of Maine's school districts do not operate their own schools. Instead they provide tuition to resident families for use in other schools through the State's education tuition program. For decades these "other schools" included religious schools. In 1980 the Attorney General of Maine issued an opinion to the effect that inclusion of religious schools in this program violates the nonestablishment provision. Op. Me. Att'y Gen. 80–2. Pursuant to this opinion, the legislature amended the governing legislation in 1981, making religious schools ineligible for the program. 20–A M.R.S.A. 2951(2).

Five families from the town of Raymond, including Robert and Cynthia Bagley, enrolled their sons at Cheverus High School, a Catholic college preparatory school located in Portland and operated by the Jesuits. The parents requested that Raymond pay their sons' tuition at Cheverus. Citing the 1981 amendment to the statute, the school district denied their requests. The parents filed suit against Raymond, the Department of Education, and the Commissioner of Education, alleging that the defendants had violated their constitutional rights to nonestablishment of religion, free exercise of religion, and equal protection of the laws. As in *Jackson* and *Kotterman*, the *Bagley* case attracted many of the same interests groups, which filed amicus briefs for and against the relief sought by these families. The trial court granted summary judgment for the defendants, and the Supreme Judicial Court of Maine affirmed. *Bagley v. Raymond School District*, 728 A.2d 127 (Me. 1999), cert. denied, 120 S.Ct. 364 (1999). Right result after *Agostini* and *Mitchell*? See also *Chittenden Town School District v. Department of Education*, 169 Vt. 310, 738 A.2d 539 (1999), cert. denied sub nom. *Andrews v. Vermont Department of Education*, 120 S.Ct. 626 (1999).

Two cases are still unresolved at this point. The first, from Ohio, has been in litigation since 1995, when the Cleveland City School District experienced a fiscal crisis so severe that the United States District Court for the Northern District of Ohio ordered the State of Ohio to take over the administration of the district. In response to this crisis, a pilot program authorized James Goff, the State Superintendent of Public Instruction, to create a scholarship program to enable students to attend "alternative" schools, as well as a tutorial program for students attending the district's schools. Scholarship recipients, chosen by lot, receive a percentage of the tuition charged by the alternative school of their choice, up to a maximum of $2,500. Recipients whose family income is not more than two hundred percent of the federally established poverty level receive ninety percent of their school tuition, while recipients whose family income is above this "low income" threshold receive seventy-five percent of their school tuition. Receipt of scholarship money is accomplished in one of two ways. Where a scholarship recipient has chosen to attend a registered private school, the state delivers a check, made payable to the recipient's parents, to the chosen school. The parents must then endorse the check over to the school. Where the recipient has chosen an adjacent public school, the state issues a check made payable directly to the school. A team of lawyers from the ACLU, Americans United for Separation of Church and State, the Ohio Education Association, and People for the American Way assisted in representing Doris Simmons–Harris and other Ohio taxpayers in challenging the scholarship program in state court as violative of the federal and state constitutions. The Institute for Justice represented a group of intervenor parents known as Hope For Cleveland's Children. David Young and David Hessler, veterans from the *Wolman* litigation, represented intervenor schools. Finding the program constitutional, the trial court refused to enjoin its operation. Approximately 2,000 scholarships were awarded. Of the 53 alternative schools participating in the program, approximately 80% were religious schools.

As in the Milwaukee case, keen interest in the Cleveland case is reflected in amicus briefs. Supporting the plaintiffs challenging the scholarship program in Cleveland were the American Jewish Congress, the Anti–Defamation League of B'nai B'rith, and the National Committee for Public Education and Religious Liberty (PEARL). Amicus briefs supporting Superintendent Goff were filed by the Center for Educational Reform, the Becket Fund for Religious Liberty, Agudath Israel of America, Citizens for Educational Freedom, Parents Rights Organization, the Education Freedom Foundation, and the National Jewish Commission on Law and Public Affairs (COLPA).

In *Simmons–Harris v. Goff*, 1997 WL 217583, the Court of Appeals, per Judge Young, reversed. The court rejected the State's contention that the scholarship program should be considered in conjunction with the tutorial program: "The case law suggests that the appropriate question is whether a distinct governmental benefit is fully available for use in both sectarian and secular institutions." Relying on *Grand Rapids*, it found that "the secular and sectarian functions of the religious schools at issue in this case cannot be separated." It distinguished *Mueller* on the grounds that *Mueller* authorized a tax deduction, not a cash payment; and that the deduction in *Mueller* was available to all parents, while the Cleveland scholarship program is available only to parents choosing to send a child to a private school (none of the surrounding public school districts participated in the program). It distinguished *Witters* on the grounds that the scholarship program results in a "significant portion of the aid expended ... under the program as a whole" to religious schools; and that choosing between sending a child to a religious school or having the child remain in the troubled public school district is not a "genuinely independent and private choice of aid recipients" within the meaning of that phrase in *Witters*. It distinguished *Zobrest* on the ground that "the provision of a sign-language interpreter for a blind [sic] student" attending a religious school only "incidentally benefited" those schools. Plausible distinctions? Right result after *Agostini* and *Mitchell*?

The court also ruled that the program violated the state constitution, section 7, Art. I of which provides: "No person shall be compelled to attend, erect, or support any place of worship, or maintain any form of worship, against his consent; and no preference shall be given, by law, to any religious society; nor shall any interference with the rights of conscience be permitted." The court also found that the voucher program violated section 2, Article VI, which provides: "The general assembly shall make such provisions, by taxation, or otherwise, as, with the income arising from the school trust fund, will secure a thorough and efficient system of common schools throughout the State; but no religious or other sect, or sects, shall ever have any exclusive right to, or control of, any part of the school funds of this state."

The Supreme Court of Ohio affirmed in part and reversed in part. 86 Ohio St.3d 1, 711 N.E.2d 203 (1999). Relying primarily on *Agostini,* the court ruled that the school voucher program did not violate the federal nonestablishment provision, except for selection criteria which gave priority to students whose parents belonged to a religious group that supported a sectarian school, and it held that these selection criteria were severable from the rest of the statute. The state supreme court also held that the voucher program did not violate the school fund clause of the state constitution, or the provision of the state constitution establishing a thorough and efficient system of common schools, or the state constitution's uniformity clause. It did, however, affirm the finding of the court of appeals that the program violated the state constitution's one-subject rule, Oh. Const., Section 15(D), Art. II.

The Ohio legislature promptly enacted new legislation limited to the single subject of the Cleveland school situation. Knowing the view of the state court on the merits of the Cleveland voucher program, its opponents filed a challenge in the federal district court, which enjoined the program. *Simmons-Harris v. Zelman,* 72 F.Supp. 2d 834 (N.D.Ohio 1999) aff'd, 234 F.3d 945 (6th Cir.2000), reh. denied, cert. pending. The Sixth Circuit affirmed, 234 F.3d 945 (6th Cir.2000). This opinion is in apparent conflict with the ruling of the Ohio Supreme Court on the same federal question with the identical parties, and on the same federal question presented in the Milwaukee voucher case, *Jackson v. Benson,* 218 Wis.2d 835, 578 N.W.2d 602 (1998). If the Supreme Court grants review, what result? Why?

Several states, including California and Michigan, have considered various voucher proposals, but have not adopted them. In 1999 Florida became the first state to have a state-wide voucher program in operation. The purpose of the

Opportunity Scholarship Program is "to provide enhanced opportunity for students in this state to gain the knowledge and skills necessary for postsecondary education, a technical education, or the world of work. Fl. Stat. 229.0537(1). Does this state a valid secular, that is, public purpose?

Finding that "a student should not be compelled, against the wishes of the student's parent or guardian, to remain in a school found by the state to be failing for 2 years in a 4–year period," the Legislature has made available "opportunity scholarships in order to give parents and guardians the opportunity for their children to attend a public school that is performing satisfactorily or to attend an eligible private school when the parent or guardian chooses to apply the equivalent of the public education funds generated by his or her child to the cost of tuition in the eligible private school." The statute defines eligibility of a participating school as follows: "To be eligible to participate in the opportunity scholarship program, a private school must be a Florida private school, may be sectarian or nonsectarian, and must: (a) Demonstrate fiscal soundness by being in operation for one school year or provide the Department of Education with a statement by a certified public accountant confirming that the private school desiring to participate is insured and the owner or owners have sufficient capital or credit to operate the school for the upcoming year serving the number of students anticipated with expected revenues from tuition and other sources that may be reasonably expected. In lieu of such a statement, a surety bond or letter of credit for the amount equal to the opportunity scholarship funds for any quarter may be filed with the department. (b) Except for the first year of implementation, notify the Department of Education and the school district in whose service area the school is located of its intent to participate in the program under this section by May 1 of the school year preceding the school year in which it intends to participate. The notice shall specify the grade levels and services that the private school has available for the opportunity scholarship program. (c) Comply with the antidiscrimination provisions of 42 U.S.C. § 2000d. (d) Meet state and local health and safety laws and codes. (e) Accept scholarship students on an entirely random and religious-neutral basis without regard to the student's past academic history; however, the private school may give preference in accepting applications to siblings of students who have already been accepted on a random and religious-neutral basis. (f) Be subject to the instruction, curriculum, and attendance criteria adopted by an appropriate nonpublic school accrediting body and be academically accountable to the parent or guardian for meeting the educational needs of the student. The private school must furnish a school profile which includes student performance. (g) Employ or contract with teachers who hold a baccalaureate or higher degree, or have at least 3 years of teaching experience in public or private schools, or have special skills, knowledge, or expertise that qualifies them to provide instruction in subjects taught. (h) Comply with all state statutes relating to private schools. (i) Accept as full tuition and fees the amount provided by the state for each student. (j) Agree not to compel any student attending the private school on an opportunity scholarship to profess a specific ideological belief, to pray, or to worship. (k) Adhere to the tenets of its published disciplinary procedures prior to the expulsion of any opportunity scholarship student." Do these conditions upon an eligible institution suffice for purposes of predicting the likelihood that the program will be found constitutionally permissible? See *Holmes v. Bush*, 2000 WL 526364 (Fl. Cir. Ct. 2000).

2. Public Schools

A. Released Time for Religious Instruction

The protagonist of the first famous case on religion and the public schools has told her own story of how she came to bring the case. She notes that she was the granddaughter of a Presbyterian elder and was baptized a Lutheran. Her father, a Christian while she was growing up, became an active spokesman for rationalism. As an adult she regarded herself as a humanist. She had inherited the spirit of her mother, who named her for "the first exponent of woman's rights," Vashti, the wife of King Ahasuerus, who lost her position because she refused to obey the king's command to attend a royal drinking party (Esther 1:1–12), see Vashti Cromwell McCollum, *One Woman's Fight* 9–14 (1951).

In 1940, Champaign, Illinois, adopted a plan permitting Roman Catholic, Jewish, and mainline Protestant religious teaching in its schools. The McCollums' son, James Terry, a student in the fourth grade, wanted to attend the Protestant instruction. Vashti McCollum consented but found it to be "indoctrination." She withheld her consent when Jim was in the fifth grade, but the regular teacher told Jim she wanted the class "to be 100%" When he abstained, he was sent, during the religious instruction period, to a small music room and was conspicuous in his isolation, *id*. 17–20.

Vashti McCollum took her complaint to the superintendent of schools, a Methodist, who turned a deaf ear. She then consulted a young Unitarian minister who had criticized the religious education plan. He put her in touch with the Chicago Action Council, an offshoot of the Civil Liberties Union. With its help, she brought the case, braving the social difficulties of her stance in a college town in the Midwest Bible Belt and spending $5,000 of her own money on the case. Her husband, an instructor in the Horticultural Department of the University of Illinois, supported her without joining the suit. She received over 6,000 letters praising her or vilifying her, and she became for some "a godless atheist," for others a champion of freedom. *Id*. 16, 45, 190.

McCollum v. Board of Education

333 U.S. 203 (1948).

Walter F. Dodd and *Edward R. Burke* argued the cause for appellant. *Mr. Dodd* also filed a brief.

John L. Franklin and *Owen Rall* argued the cause and filed a brief for appellees.

Briefs of *amici curiae* urging reversal were filed by *Henry Epstein, Leo Pfeffer* and *Samuel Rothstein* for the Synagogue Council of America et al.; *Herbert A. Wolff* for the American Ethical Union; *E. Hilton Jackson, Challen B. Ellis, W. D. Jamieson* and *Kahl K. Spriggs* for the Joint Conference Committee on Public Relations of several Baptist conventions; *Edward C. Park* for the American Unitarian Association; *Kenneth W.*

Greenawalt, Leon Despres, Russell Whitman, John D. Miller, William L. Marbury, Thomas H. Eliot, Winthrop Wadleigh, Whitney N. Seymour, and *Gurney Edwards* for the American Civil Liberties Union; and *Homer Cummings* and *William D. Donnelly* for the General Conference of Seventh-day Adventists.

George F. Barrett, Attorney General of Illinois, and *William C. Wines,* Assistant Attorney General, filed a brief as *amici curiae,* urging affirmance.

Charles H. Tuttle filed a brief for the Protestant Council of New York City, as *amicus curiae.*

■ JUSTICE BLACK delivered the opinion of the Court.

This case relates to the power of a state to utilize its tax-supported public school system in aid of religious instruction insofar as that power may be restricted by the First and Fourteenth Amendments to the Federal Constitution.

The appellant, Vashti McCollum, began this action for mandamus against the Champaign Board of Education in the Circuit Court of Champaign County, Illinois. Her asserted interest was that of a resident and taxpayer of Champaign and of a parent whose child was then enrolled in the Champaign public schools. Illinois has a compulsory education law which, with exceptions, requires parents to send their children, aged seven to sixteen, to its tax-supported public schools where the children are to remain in attendance during the hours when the schools are regularly in session. Parents who violate this law commit a misdemeanor punishable by fine unless the children attend private or parochial schools which meet educational standards fixed by the State. District boards of education are given general supervisory powers over the use of the public school buildings within the school districts. Ill. Rev. Stat. ch. 122, §§ 123, 301 (1943).

Appellant's petition for mandamus alleged that religious teachers, employed by private religious groups, were permitted to come weekly into the school buildings during the regular hours set apart for secular teaching, and then and there for a period of thirty minutes substitute their religious teaching for the secular education provided under the compulsory education law. The petitioner charged that this joint public-school religious group program violated the First and Fourteenth Amendments to the United States Constitution. The prayer of her petition was that the Board of Education be ordered to "adopt and enforce rules and regulations prohibiting all instruction in and teaching of religious education in all public schools in Champaign School District Number 71, ... and in all public school houses and buildings in said district when occupied by public schools". . . .

Although there are disputes between the parties as to various inferences that may or may not properly be drawn from the evidence concerning the religious program, the following facts are shown by the record without dispute. In 1940 interested members of the Jewish, Roman Catholic, and a few of the Protestant faiths formed a voluntary association called the Champaign Council on Religious Education. They obtained permission from the Board of Education to offer classes in religious instruction to public school pupils in grades four to nine inclusive. Classes were made up of pupils whose parents signed printed cards requesting that their children be permitted to attend; they were held weekly, thirty minutes for the lower grades, forty-five minutes for the higher. The council employed the religious teachers at no expense to the school authorities, but the instructors were subject to the approval and supervision of the superintendent of schools. The classes were taught in three separate religious groups by Protestant teachers,[4] Catholic priests, and a Jewish rabbi, although for the past several years there have apparently been no classes instructed in the Jewish religion. Classes were conducted in the regular classrooms of the school building. Students who did not choose to take the religious instruction were not released from public school duties; they were required to leave their classrooms and go to some other place in the school building for pursuit of their secular studies. On the other hand, students who were released from secular study for the religious instructions were required to be present at the religious classes. Reports of their presence or absence were to be made to their secular teachers.[5]

The foregoing facts, without reference to others that appear in the record, show the use of tax-supported property for religious instruction and the close cooperation between the school authorities and the religious council in promoting religious education. The operation of the State's compulsory education system thus assists and is integrated with the program of religious instruction carried on by separate religious sects. Pupils compelled by law to go to school for secular education are released in part from their legal duty upon the condition that they attend the religious classes. This is beyond all question a utilization of the tax-established and tax-supported public school system to aid religious groups to spread their faith. And it falls squarely under the ban of the First Amendment (made applicable to the States by the Fourteenth) as we interpreted it in *Everson v. Board of Education* [section 1 above]. There we said: "Neither a state nor the Federal Government can set up a church. Neither can pass laws which aid one religion, aid all religions, or prefer one religion over another.[6] Neither can force or influence a person to go to or to remain away from

4. There were two teachers of the Protestant faith. One was a Presbyterian and had been a foreign missionary for that church. The second testified as follows: "I am affiliated with the Christian church. I also work in the Methodist Church and I taught at the Presbyterian. I am married to a Lutheran."

5. The director of the Champaign Council on Religious Education testified: "If any pupil is absent we turn in a slip just like any teacher would to the superintendent's office. The slip is a piece of paper with a number of hours in the school day and a square, and the teacher of the particular room for the particular hour records the absentees. It has their names and the grade and the section to which they belong. It is the same sheet that the geography and history teachers and all the other teachers use, and is furnished by the school."

6. The dissent, agreed to by four judges, said: "The problem then cannot be cast in terms of legal discrimination or its absence. This would be true, even though the state in giving aid should treat all religious instruction alike.... Again, it was the furnishing of 'contributions of money for the propagation of opinions which he disbelieves' that the fathers outlawed. That consequence and effect are not removed by multiplying to all-inclusiveness the sects for which support is exacted. The Constitution requires, not comprehensive identification of state with religion, but complete separation." *Everson v. Board of Education* [section 1 above].

church against his will or force him to profess a belief or disbelief in any religion. No person can be punished for entertaining or professing religious beliefs or disbeliefs, for church attendance or non-attendance. No tax in any amount, large or small, can be levied to support any religious activities or institutions, whatever they may be called, or whatever form they may adopt to teach or practice religion.[7] Neither a state nor the Federal Government can, openly or secretly, participate in the affairs of any religious organizations or groups and *vice versa*. In the words of Jefferson, the clause against establishment of religion by law was intended to erect 'a wall of separation between church and State.' " The majority in the *Everson* case, and the minority as shown by quotations from the dissenting views in our notes 6 and 7, agreed that the First Amendment's language, properly interpreted, had erected a wall of separation between Church and State. They disagreed as to the facts shown by the record and as to the proper application of the First Amendment's language to those facts.

Recognizing that the Illinois program is barred by the First and Fourteenth Amendments if we adhere to the views expressed both by the majority and the minority in the *Everson* case, counsel for the respondents challenge those views as dicta and urge that we reconsider and repudiate them. They argue that historically the First Amendment was intended to forbid only government preference of one religion over another, not an impartial governmental assistance of all religions. In addition they ask that we distinguish or overrule our holding in the *Everson* case that the Fourteenth Amendment made the "establishment of religion" clause of the First Amendment applicable as a prohibition against the States. After giving full consideration to the arguments presented we are unable to accept either of these contentions.

To hold that a state cannot consistently with the First and Fourteenth Amendments utilize its public school system to aid any or all religious faiths or sects in the dissemination of their doctrines and ideals does not, as counsel urge, manifest a governmental hostility to religion or religious teachings. A manifestation of such hostility would be at war with our national tradition as embodied in the First Amendment's guaranty of the free exercise of religion. For the First Amendment rests upon the premise that both religion and government can best work to achieve their lofty aims if each is left free from the other within its respective sphere. Or, as we said in the *Everson* case, the First Amendment has erected a wall between Church and State which must be kept high and impregnable.

Here not only are the State's tax-supported public school buildings used for the dissemination of religious doctrines. The State also affords sectarian groups an invaluable aid in that it helps to provide pupils for

---

7. The dissenting judges said: "In view of this history no further proof is needed that the Amendment forbids any appropriation, large or small, from public funds to aid or support any and all religious exercises. . . . Legislatures are free to make, and courts to sustain, appropriations only when it can be found that in fact they do not aid, promote, encourage or sustain religious teaching or observances, be the amount large or small." *Everson v. Board of Education* [section 1 above].

their religious classes through use of the State's compulsory public school machinery. This is not separation of Church and State.

The cause is reversed and remanded to the State Supreme Court for proceedings not inconsistent with this opinion. *Reversed and remanded.*

———

■ In language reminiscent of his opinion in the first flag salute case, *Gobitis* [Chapter Eleven, section 3], which had been overruled in *Barnette* [Chapter Eleven, section 3], JUSTICE FRANKFURTER wrote a separate opinion, joined by JUSTICES JACKSON, RUTLEDGE, and BURTON, the dissenters in *Everson*.

———

The public school is at once the symbol of our democracy and the most pervasive means for promoting our common destiny. In no activity of the State is it more vital to keep out divisive forces than in its schools, to avoid confusing, not to say fusing, what the Constitution sought to keep strictly apart. . . .

We renew our conviction that "we have staked the very existence of our country on the faith that complete separation between the state and religion is best for the state and best for religion." *Everson v. Board of Education* [section 1 above]. If nowhere else, in the relation between Church and State, "good fences make good neighbors."

———

■ JUSTICE JACKSON also wrote a separate opinion, concurring in JUSTICE FRANK-FURTER'S opinion and concurring in the result reached by the Court.

———

It is idle to pretend that this task is one for which we can find in the Constitution one word to help us as judges to decide where the secular ends and the sectarian begins in education. Nor can we find guidance in any other legal source. It is a matter on which we can find no law but our own prepossessions. If with no surer legal guidance we are to take up and decide every variation of this controversy, raised by persons not subject to penalty or tax but who are dissatisfied with the way schools are dealing with the problem, we are likely to have much business of the sort. And, more importantly, we are likely to make the legal "wall of separation between church and state" as winding as the famous serpentine wall designed by Mr. Jefferson for the University he founded.

———

■ JUSTICE REED dissented.

NOTE

Of Walls and Lines. In his opinion for the Court in *McCollum*, Justice Black again cited Jefferson's letter to the Danbury Baptists [Chapter Seven, section 1] with its metaphor about a "wall of separation between church and state." Why, especially after the tearing down of the Berlin Wall as a symbolic moment for freedom and the end of Cold War tensions, are Americans so enamored of the wall metaphor to describe the relationship between religious believers and the government? The Justices have not agreed about the composition of the wall. For Justice Black in *Everson* the wall was meant to be "high and impregnable." Justice Jackson lamented in *McCollum* that the wall was as "winding as the famous serpentine wall designed by Mr. Jefferson" at the University of Virginia. For Chief Justice Burger in *Lemon*, "the line of separation, far from being a 'wall,' is a blurred, indistinct, and variable barrier depending on all the circumstances of a particular relationship."

When Burger wrote that way in 1971, "strict separationists" were not content with their substantive victory, but took alarm at the shift in metaphor. James Madison suggested not a wall, but a line differentiating "the rights of religion and the Civil Authority." Letter of James Madison to the Reverend Jasper Adams, 1832, 9 *The Writings of James Madison* 484 (1910), reprinted in John F. Wilson and Donald L. Drakeman, eds., *Church and State in American History* 80–82 (2d ed. 1987). Historian Sidney E. Mead notes that Madison's metaphor of a line, unlike Jefferson's wall, "does not conjure up the image of a solid and unchanging structure built by the founders, but rather 'the path of a moving point, thought of as having length but not breadth.' " Mead, "Neither Church nor State: Reflections on James Madison's 'Line of Separation,' " 10 *J. Ch. & St.* 349, 350 (1968).

In his concurring opinion Justice Frankfurter was citing Robert Frost's famous poem, "Mending Wall." Did he read the poem carefully? It begins: "Something there is that doesn't love a wall." *The Complete Poems of Robert Frost* 39 (1995). In the poem two New England farmers annually rebuild a stone wall that nature and the work of hunters have eroded each winter. One farmer is quite content to engage in this spring-time ritual. The other farmer quietly wonders whether this annual wall-building is worth the bother. He, at least, stops to ask: "*Why* do they make good neighbors?". Before rebuilding or fortifying a wall, this farmer would "ask to know/ What I was walling in or walling out." Frost gives several generous hermeneutical clues about which farmer reflects his own views on wall-building. For example, unedited by Frankfurter, the full line of the poem cited by the justice reads: "*He only says*, 'Good fences make good neighbors.' " (emphasis added). At the conclusion of the poem, Frost notes that the unreflective farmer cited by Frankfurter "will not go behind his father's saying,/ And he likes having thought of it so well/ He says again, 'Good fences make good neighbors.' "

When the Court invalidated the released time program in *McCollum*, what was it "walling in or walling out"? For all its rhetoric about a "high and impregnable wall," the *Everson* Court sustained the bus transportation program challenged there. By contrast, the *McCollum* Court struck down the released time program challenged there, representing the first time that the Court had invalidated a state practice under the command against legislation respecting an establishment of religion recently "incorporated" against the state in *Everson*.

In a symposium on *McCollum* a prominent Jewish commentator supported the decision. Milton R. Konvitz, "Separation of Church and State: The First Freedom," 14 *Law & Contemp. Probs.* 44 (1949). Others attacked the Court's reasoning robustly. See Edward S. Corwin, "The Supreme Court as National School Board," 14 *Law & Contemp. Probs.* 1 (1949); John Courtney Murray, "Law or Presuppositions," 14 *Law & Contemp. Probs.* 23 (1949); and Russell N. Sullivan, "Religious Education in the Schools," 14 *Law & Contemp. Probs.* 92 (1949). Corwin, a leading political scientist at Princeton, suggested that Black's reliance on Jefferson's letter was flawed. Fr. Murray, whose views on religious freedom were later to prevail at the Second Vatican Council [section one above], picked up on Justice Jackson's candid acknowledgement that released time "is a matter on which we can find no law but our own prepossessions." And Murray roundly criticized Justice Black's use of history and his "sectarian idea of religion." Noting that released time programs had been working in "over 3,000 communities in forty-six states," Sullivan agreed with Justice Jackson that the Court was "likely to have much business" once it started down the path of behaving, in Corwin's term, as "a national school board." Sullivan thought the decision in *McCollum* was full of uncertainty that was bound to produce more litigation on the matter. His prediction proved correct. Soon another released time case was brought to the Court, this time with a different result, based on the location of the religious instruction, off the premises of the public school. As Justice Jackson feared, the wall was becoming not just "winding and serpentine," but "warped and twisted."

Zorach v. Clauson

343 U.S. 306 (1952).

Kenneth W. Greenawalt argued the cause for appellants. With him on the brief were *Leo Pfeffer* and *Edwin J. Lukas.*

Wendell P. Brown, Solicitor General, argued the cause for the Commissioner of Education of the State of New York, appellee. With him on the brief were *Nathaniel L. Goldstein*, Attorney General, and *Ruth Kessler Toch* and *John P. Powers*, Assistant Attorneys General.

Michael A. Castaldi argued the cause for the Board of Education of the City of New York, appellee. With him on the brief were *Dennis M. Hurley, Seymour B. Quel, Daniel T. Scannell* and *Arthur H. Kahn.*

Charles H. Tuttle argued the cause for the Greater New York Coordinating Committee on Released Time of Jews, Protestants and Roman Catholics, appellee. With him on the brief was *Porter R. Chandler.*

Briefs of *amici curiae* supporting appellees were filed on behalf of the States of California, by *Edmund G. Brown,* Attorney General, *William V. O'Connor,* Chief Deputy Attorney General, and *Howard S. Goldin,* Deputy Attorney General; Indiana, by *J. Emmett McManamon,* Attorney General; Kentucky, by *J.D. Buckman, Jr.,* Attorney General, and *M.B. Holifield,* Assistant Attorney General; Maine, by *Alexander A. LaFleur,* Attorney General; Massachusetts, by *Francis E. Kelley,* Attorney General, *Charles H. Walters,* Assistant Attorney General, and *William F. Marcella;* Oregon, by *George Neuner,* Attorney General, *Robert F. Maguire* and *William E.*

Dougherty; Pennsylvania, by *Robert E. Woodside,* Attorney General, and *Harry F. Stambaugh;* and West Virginia, by *William C. Marland,* Attorney General, and *Thomas J. Gillooly, T.D. Kauffelt* and *Eston B. Stephenson,* Assistant Attorneys General.

■ JUSTICE DOUGLAS delivered the opinion of the Court.

New York City has a program which permits its public schools to release students during the school day so that they may leave the school buildings and school grounds and go to religious centers for religious instruction or devotional exercises. A student is released on written request of his parents. Those not released stay in the classrooms. The churches make weekly reports to the schools, sending a list of children who have been released from public school but who have not reported for religious instruction. This "released time" program involves neither religious instruction in public school classrooms nor the expenditure of public funds. All costs, including the application blanks, are paid by the religious organizations. The case is therefore unlike *McCollum v. Board of Education,* which involved a "released time" program from Illinois. In that case the classrooms were turned over to religious instructors. We accordingly held that the program violated the First Amendment which (by reason of the Fourteenth Amendment) prohibits the states from establishing religion or prohibiting its free exercise.

Appellants, who are taxpayers and residents of New York City and whose children attend its public schools, challenge the present law, contending it is in essence not different from the one involved in the *McCollum* case. Their argument, stated elaborately in various ways, reduces itself to this: the weight and influence of the school is put behind a program for religious instruction; public school teachers police it, keeping tab on students who are released; the classroom activities come to a halt while the students who are released for religious instruction are on leave; the school is a crutch on which the churches are leaning for support in their religious training; without the cooperation of the schools this "released time" program, like the one in the *McCollum* case, would be futile and ineffective. The New York Court of Appeals sustained the law against this claim of unconstitutionality.

The briefs and arguments are replete with data bearing on the merits of this type of "released time" program. Views *pro* and *con* are expressed, based on practical experience with these programs and with their implications.[5] We do not stop to summarize these materials nor to burden the

---

5. See, *e.g.,* Beckes, Weekday Religious Education (National Conference of Christians and Jews, Human Relations Pamphlet No. 6); Butts, American Tradition in Religion and Education, pp. 188, 199; Moehlman, The Wall of Separation between Church and State, pp. 123, 155 ff.; Moehlman, The Church as Educator, pp. 103 ff.; Moral and Spiritual Values in the Public Schools (Educational Policies Commission, 1951); Newman, The Sectarian Invasion of Our Public Schools; Public School Time for Religious Education, 12 Jewish Education 130 (January, 1941); Religious Instruction On School Time, 7 Frontiers of Democracy 72 (1940); Released Time for Religious Education in New York City's Schools (Public Education Association, June 30, 1943); Released Time for Religious Education in New York City's Schools (Public Education Association, June 30, 1945); Released Time for Reliopinion with an analysis of them. For they involve considerations not germane to the narrow constitutional issue presented. They largely concern the wisdom of the system, its efficiency from an educational point of view, and the political considerations which have motivated its adoption or rejection in some communities. Those matters are of no concern here, since our problem reduces itself to whether New York by this system has either prohibited the "free exercise" of religion or has made a law "respecting an establishment of religion" within the meaning of the First Amendment.

It takes obtuse reasoning to inject any issue of the "free exercise" of religion into the present case. No one is forced to go to the religious classroom and no religious exercise or instruction is brought to the classrooms of the public schools. A student need not take religious instruction. He is left to his own desires as to the manner or time of his religious devotions, if any.

There is a suggestion that the system involves the use of coercion to get public school students into religious classrooms. There is no evidence in the record before us that supports that conclusion.[6] The present record indeed tells us that the school authorities are neutral in this regard and do no more than release students whose parents so request. If in fact coercion were used, if it were established that any one or more teachers were using their office to persuade or force students to take the religious instruction, a wholly different case would be presented.[7] Hence we put aside that claim of coercion both as respects the "free exercise" of religion and "an establishment of religion" within the meaning of the First Amendment.

Moreover, apart from that claim of coercion, we do not see how New York by this type of "released time" program has made a law respecting an establishment of religion within the meaning of the First Amendment. There is much talk of the separation of Church and State in the history of the Bill of Rights and in the decisions clustering around the First Amendment. See *Everson* [section 1 above]; *McCollum* [this section above]. There cannot be the slightest doubt that the First Amendment reflects the philosophy that Church and State should be separated. And so far as

gious Education in New York City Schools (Public Education Association, 1949); 2 Stokes, Church and State in the United States, pp. 523–548; The Status Of Religious Education In The Public Schools (National Education Association).

6. Nor is there any indication that the public schools enforce attendance at religious schools by punishing absentees from the released time programs for truancy.

7. Appellants contend that they should have been allowed to prove that the system is in fact administered in a coercive manner. The New York Court of Appeals declined to grant a trial on this issue, noting, *inter alia*, that appellants had not properly raised their claim in the manner required by state practice. This independent state ground for decision precludes appellants from raising the issue of maladministration in this proceeding (citations omitted).

The only allegation in the complaint that bears on the issue is that the operation of the program "has resulted and inevitably results in the exercise of pressure and coercion upon parents and children to secure attendance by the children for religious instruction." But this charge does not even implicate the school authorities. The New York Court of Appeals was therefore generous in labeling it a "conclusory" allegation. Since the allegation did not implicate the school authorities in the use of coercion, there is no basis for holding that the New York Court of Appeals under the guise of local practice defeated a federal right. . . .

interference with the "free exercise" of religion and an "establishment" of religion are concerned, the separation must be complete and unequivocal. The First Amendment within the scope of its coverage permits no exception; the prohibition is absolute. The First Amendment, however, does not say that in every and all respects there shall be a separation of Church and State. Rather, it studiously defines the manner, the specific ways, in which there shall be no concert or union or dependency one on the other. That is the common sense of the matter. Otherwise the state and religion would be aliens to each other—hostile, suspicious, and even unfriendly. Churches could not be required to pay even property taxes. Municipalities would not be permitted to render police or fire protection to religious groups. Policemen who helped parishioners into their places of worship would violate the Constitution. Prayers in our legislative halls; the appeals to the Almighty in the messages of the Chief Executive; the proclamations making Thanksgiving Day a holiday; "so help me God" in our courtroom oaths—these and all other references to the Almighty that run through our laws, our public rituals, our ceremonies would be flouting the First Amendment. A fastidious atheist or agnostic could even object to the supplication with which the Court opens each session: "God save the United States and this Honorable Court."

We would have to press the concept of separation of Church and State to these extremes to condemn the present law on constitutional grounds. The nullification of this law would have wide and profound effects. A Catholic student applies to his teacher for permission to leave the school during hours on a Holy Day of Obligation to attend a mass. A Jewish student asks his teacher for permission to be excused for Yom Kippur. A Protestant wants the afternoon off for a family baptismal ceremony. In each case the teacher requires parental consent in writing. In each case the teacher, in order to make sure the student is not a truant, goes further and requires a report from the priest, the rabbi, or the minister. The teacher in other words cooperates in a religious program to the extent of making it possible for her students to participate in it. Whether she does it occasionally for a few students, regularly for one, or pursuant to a systematized program designed to further the religious needs of all the students does not alter the character of the act.

We are a religious people whose institutions presuppose a Supreme Being. We guarantee the freedom to worship as one chooses. We make room for as wide a variety of beliefs and creeds as the spiritual needs of man deem necessary. We sponsor an attitude on the part of government that shows no partiality to any one group and that lets each flourish according to the zeal of its adherents and the appeal of its dogma. When the state encourages religious instruction or cooperates with religious authorities by adjusting the schedule of public events to sectarian needs, it follows the best of our traditions. For it then respects the religious nature of our people and accommodates the public service to their spiritual needs. To hold that it may not would be to find in the Constitution a requirement that the government show a callous indifference to religious groups. That would be preferring those who believe in no religion over those who do believe. Government may not finance religious groups nor undertake religious instruction nor blend secular and sectarian education nor use secular institutions to force one or some religion on any person. But we find no constitutional requirement which makes it necessary for government to be hostile to religion and to throw its weight against efforts to widen the effective scope of religious influence. The government must be neutral when it comes to competition between sects. It may not thrust any sect on any person. It may not make a religious observance compulsory. It may not coerce anyone to attend church, to observe a religious holiday, or to take religious instruction. But it can close its doors or suspend its operations as to those who want to repair to their religious sanctuary for worship or instruction. No more than that is undertaken here. . . . *Affirmed.*

■ Justice Black, dissenting.

I am aware that our *McCollum* decision on separation of Church and State has been subjected to a most searching examination throughout the country. Probably few opinions from this Court in recent years have attracted more attention or stirred wider debate. Our insistence on "a wall between Church and State which must be kept high and impregnable" has seemed to some a correct exposition of the philosophy and a true interpretation of the language of the First Amendment to which we should strictly adhere. With equal conviction and sincerity, others have thought the *McCollum* decision fundamentally wrong and have pledged continuous warfare against it. The opinions in the court below and the briefs here reflect these diverse viewpoints. In dissenting today, I mean to do more than give routine approval to our *McCollum* decision. I mean also to reaffirm my faith in the fundamental philosophy expressed in *McCollum* and *Everson* [section 1 above]. That reaffirmance can be brief because of the exhaustive opinions in those recent cases.

Difficulty of decision in the hypothetical situations mentioned by the Court, but not now before us, should not confuse the issues in this case. Here the sole question is whether New York can use its compulsory education laws to help religious sects get attendants presumably too unenthusiastic to go unless moved to do so by the pressure of this state machinery. That this is the plan, purpose, design and consequence of the New York program cannot be denied. The state thus makes religious sects beneficiaries of its power to compel children to attend secular schools. Any use of such coercive power by the state to help or hinder some religious sects or to prefer all religious sects over nonbelievers or vice versa is just what I think the First Amendment forbids. In considering whether a state has entered this forbidden field the question is not whether it has entered too far but whether it has entered at all. New York is manipulating its compulsory education laws to help religious sects get pupils. This is not separation but combination of Church and State.

The Court's validation of the New York system rests in part on its statement that Americans are "a religious people whose institutions presuppose a Supreme Being." This was at least as true when the First Amendment was adopted; and it was just as true when eight Justices of this Court invalidated the released time system in *McCollum* on the premise that a state can no more "aid all religions" than it can aid one.[4] It was precisely because Eighteenth Century Americans were a religious people divided into many fighting sects that we were given the constitutional mandate to keep Church and State completely separate. Colonial history had already shown that, here as elsewhere zealous sectarians entrusted with governmental power to further their causes would sometimes torture, maim and kill those they branded "heretics," "atheists" or "agnostics." The First Amendment was therefore to insure that no one powerful sect or combination of sects could use political or governmental power to punish dissenters whom they could not convert to their faith. Now as then, it is only by wholly isolating the state from the religious sphere and compelling it to be completely neutral, that the freedom of each and every denomination and of all nonbelievers can be maintained. It is this neutrality the Court abandons today when it treats New York's coercive system as a program which *merely* "encourages religious instruction or cooperates with religious authorities." The abandonment is all the more dangerous to liberty because of the Court's legal exaltation of the orthodox and its derogation of unbelievers.

Under our system of religious freedom, people have gone to their religious sanctuaries not because they feared the law but because they loved their God. The choice of all has been as free as the choice of those who answered the call to worship moved only by the music of the old Sunday morning church bells. The spiritual mind of man has thus been free to believe, disbelieve, or doubt, without repression, great or small, by the heavy hand of government. Statutes authorizing such repression have been stricken. Before today, our judicial opinions have refrained from drawing invidious distinctions between those who believe in no religion and those who do believe. The First Amendment has lost much if the religious follower and the atheist are no longer to be judicially regarded as entitled to equal justice under law.

State help to religion injects political and party prejudices into a holy field. It too often substitutes force for prayer, hate for love, and persecution for persuasion. Government should not be allowed, under cover of the soft euphemism of "co-operation," to steal into the sacred area of religious choice....

■ JUSTICE JACKSON, dissenting.

As one whose children, as a matter of free choice, have been sent to privately supported Church schools, I may challenge the Court's suggestion that opposition to this plan can only be antireligious, atheistic, or agnostic. My evangelistic brethren confuse an objection to compulsion with an

---

4. A state policy of aiding "all religions" necessarily requires a governmental decision as to what constitutes "a religion." Thus is created a governmental power to hinder certain religious beliefs by denying their character as such. See, *e.g.*, the Regulations of the New York Commissioner of Education providing that, "The courses in religious observance and education must be maintained and operated by or under the control of *duly constituted* religious bodies." (Emphasis added.) Art. 17, § 154, 1 N.Y. Official Code Comp. 683. This provides precisely the kind of censorship which we have said the Constitution forbids. *Cantwell v. Connecticut* [Chapter Eleven, section 1].

objection to religion. It is possible to hold a faith with enough confidence to believe that what should be rendered to God does not need to be decided and collected by Caesar.

The day that this country ceases to be free for irreligion it will cease to be free for religion—except for the sect that can win political power. The same epithetical jurisprudence used by the Court today to beat down those who oppose pressuring children into some religion can devise as good epithets tomorrow against those who object to pressuring them into a favored religion. And, after all, if we concede to the State power and wisdom to single out "duly constituted religious" bodies as exclusive alternatives for compulsory secular instruction, it would be logical to also uphold the power and wisdom to choose the true faith among those "duly constituted." We start down a rough road when we begin to mix compulsory public education with compulsory godliness.

A number of Justices just short of a majority of the majority that promulgates today's passionate dialectics joined in answering them in *Illinois ex rel. McCollum v. Board of Education* [above]. The distinction attempted between that case and this is trivial, almost to the point of cynicism, magnifying its nonessential details and disparaging compulsion which was the underlying reason for invalidity. A reading of the Court's opinion in that case along with its opinion in this case will show such difference of overtones and undertones as to make clear that the *McCollum* case has passed like a storm in a teacup. The wall which the Court was professing to erect between Church and State has become even more warped and twisted than I expected. Today's judgment will be more interesting to students of psychology and of the judicial processes than to students of constitutional law.

B. School Prayer and Devotional Reading of the Bible

In *McCollum* and *Zorach* [this section above], the Court dealt with the desires of religious parents and disallowed the presence of teachers with religion on the premises of public schools but allowed the children to leave the public schools for religious instruction elsewhere. The next case focused on whether the government could impose a "nondenominational prayer" for use in the public schools. Note that the prayer in question was controversial precisely because it tried to avoid displeasing anyone. Is the government the arbiter of what is acceptable in forms of worship? Can it do so without violating the nonestablishment provision? In 1962 and 1963 the Court answered these questions. The first decision dealt with a prayer composed by the government. The second dealt with the recitation of the Lord's prayer and with devotional reading of the Bible.

Engel v. Vitale

370 U.S. 421 (1962).

William J. Butler argued the cause for petitioners. With him on the briefs was *Stanley Geller*.

Bertram B. Daiker argued the cause for respondents. With him on the briefs was *Wilford E. Neier.*

Potter R. Chandler argued the cause for intervenors-respondents. With him on the briefs were *Thomas J. Ford* and *Richard E. Nolan.*

Charles A. Brind filed a brief for the Board of Regents of the University of the State of New York, as *amicus curiae*, in opposition to the petition for certiorari.

Briefs of *amici curiae*, urging reversal, were filed by *Herbert A. Wolff, Leo Rosen* and *Nancy Wechsler* for the American Ethical Union; *Louis Caplan, Edwin J. Lukas, Paul Hartman, Theodore Leskes* and *Sol Rabkin* for the American Jewish Committee et al.; and *Leo Pfeffer, Lewis H. Weinstein, Albert Waid, Shad Polier* and *Samuel Lawrence Brennglass* for the Synagogue Council of America et al.

A brief of *amici curiae*, urging affirmance, was filed by *Roger D. Foley*, Attorney General of Nevada, *Robert Pickrell*, Attorney General of Arizona, *Frank Holt*, Attorney General of Arkansas, *Albert L. Coles*, Attorney General of Connecticut, *Richard W. Ervin*, Attorney General of Florida, *Eugene Cook*, Attorney General of Georgia, *Frank Benson*, Attorney General of Idaho, *Edwin K. Steers*, Attorney General of Indiana, *William M. Ferguson*, Attorney General of Kansas, *Jack P. F. Gremillion*, Attorney General of Louisiana, *Thomas B. Finan*, Attorney General of Maryland, *Joe T. Patterson*, Attorney General of Mississippi, *William Maynard*, Attorney General of New Hampshire, *Arthur J. Sills*, Attorney General of New Jersey, *Earl E. Hartley*, Attorney General of New Mexico, *Leslie R. Burgum*, Attorney General of North Dakota, *David Stahl*, Attorney General of Pennsylvania, *J. Joseph Nugent*, Attorney General of Rhode Island, *Daniel R. McLeod*, Attorney General of South Carolina, *A. C. Miller*, Attorney General of South Dakota, *Will Wilson*, Attorney General of Texas, and *C. Donald Robertson*, Attorney General of West Virginia.

■ JUSTICE BLACK delivered the opinion of the Court.

The respondent Board of Education of Union Free School District No. 9, New Hyde Park, New York, acting in its official capacity under state law, directed the School District's principal to cause the following prayer to be said aloud by each class in the presence of a teacher at the beginning of each school day: "Almighty God, we acknowledge our dependence upon Thee, and we beg Thy blessings upon us, our parents, our teachers and our Country." This daily procedure was adopted on the recommendation of the State Board of Regents, a governmental agency created by the State Constitution to which the New York Legislature has granted broad supervisory, executive, and legislative powers over the State's public school system. These state officials composed the prayer which they recommended and published as a part of their "Statement on Moral and Spiritual Training in the Schools," saying: "We believe that this Statement will be subscribed to by, all men and women of good will, and we call upon all of them to aid in giving life to our program." . . . .

There can be no doubt that New York's state prayer program officially establishes the religious beliefs embodied in the Regents' prayer. The respondents' argument to the contrary which is largely based upon the contention that the Regents' prayer is "nondenominational" and the fact that the program, as modified and approved by state courts, does not require all pupils to recite the prayer but permits those who wish to do so to remain silent or be excused from the room, ignores the essential nature of the program's constitutional defects. Neither the fact that the prayer may be denominationally neutral nor the fact that its observance on the part of the students is voluntary can serve to free it from the limitations of the Establishment Clause, as it might from the Free Exercise Clause, of the First Amendment, both of which are operative against the States by virtue of the Fourteenth Amendment. Although these two clauses may in certain instances overlap, they forbid two quite different kinds of governmental encroachment upon religious freedom. The Establishment Clause, unlike the Free Exercise Clause, does not depend upon any showing of direct governmental compulsion and is violated by the enactment of laws which establish an official religion whether those laws operate directly to coerce nonobserving individuals or not. This is not to say, of course, that laws officially prescribing a particular form of religious worship do not involve coercion of such individuals. When the power, prestige and financial support of government is placed behind a particular religious belief, the indirect coercive pressure upon religious minorities to conform to the prevailing officially approved religion is plain. But the purposes underlying the Establishment Clause go much further than that. Its first and most immediate purpose rested on the belief that a union of government and religion tends to destroy government and to degrade religion. The history of governmentally established religion, both in England and in this country, showed that whenever government had allied itself with one particular form of religion, the inevitable result had been that it had incurred the hatred, disrespect and even contempt of those who held contrary beliefs. That same history showed that many people had lost their respect for any religion that had relied upon the support of government to spread its faith. The Establishment Clause thus stands as an expression of principle on the part of the Founders of our Constitution that religion is too personal, too sacred, too holy, to permit its "unhallowed perversion" by a civil magistrate. Another purpose of the Establishment Clause rested upon an awareness of the historical fact that governmentally established religions and religious persecutions go hand in hand. The Founders knew that only a few years after the Book of Common Prayer became the only accepted form of religious services in the established Church of England, an Act of Uniformity was passed to compel all Englishmen to attend those services and to make it a criminal offense to conduct or attend religious gatherings of any other kind[17]—a law which was consistently flouted by dissenting religious

---

17. 5 & 6 Edward VI, c. 1, entitled "An Act for the Uniformity of Service and Administration of Sacraments throughout the Realm." This Act was repealed during the reign of Mary but revived upon the accession of Elizabeth. See note 7, *supra*. The reasons which led to the enactment of this statute were set out in its preamble: "Where there hath been a very godly Order set forth by the Authority of Parliament, for Common Prayer and Administration of the Sacraments to be used in the Mother Tongue within the Church of *England*, agreeable to the Word of God and the Primitive Church, very comfort-groups in England and which contributed to widespread persecutions of people like John Bunyan who persisted in holding "unlawful [religious] meetings ... to the great disturbance and distraction of the good subjects of this kingdom...."[18] And they knew that similar persecutions had received the sanction of law in several of the colonies in this country soon after the establishment of official religions in those colonies.[19] It was in large part to get completely away from this sort of systematic religious persecution that the Founders brought into being our Nation, our Constitution, and our Bill of Rights with its prohibition against any governmental establishment of religion. The New York laws officially prescribing the Regents' prayer are inconsistent both with the purposes of the Establishment Clause and with the Establishment Clause itself.

It has been argued that to apply the Constitution in such a way as to prohibit state laws respecting an establishment of religious services in public schools is to indicate a hostility toward religion or toward prayer. Nothing, of course, could be more wrong. The history of man is inseparable from the history of religion. And perhaps it is not too much to say that since the beginning of that history many people have devoutly believed that "More things are wrought by prayer than this world dreams of." It was doubtless largely due to men who believed this that there grew up a sentiment that caused men to leave the cross-currents of officially established state religions and religious persecution in Europe and come to this country filled with the hope that they could find a place in which they could pray when they pleased to the God of their faith in the language they chose.[20] And there were men of this same faith in the power of prayer who

able to all good People desiring to live in Christian Conversation, and most profitable to the Estate of this Realm, upon the which the Mercy, Favour and Blessing of Almighty God is in no wise so readily and plenteously poured as by Common Prayers, due using of the Sacraments, and often preaching of the Gospel, with the Devotion of the Hearers: (1) And yet this notwithstanding, a great Number of People in divers Parts of this Realm, following their own Sensuality, and living either without Knowledge or due Fear of God, do willfully and damnably before Almighty God abstain and refuse to come to their Parish Churches and other Places where Common Prayer, Administration of the Sacraments, and Preaching of the Word of God, is used upon *Sundays* and other Days ordained to be Holydays."

18. Bunyan's own account of his trial is set forth in A Relation of the Imprisonment of Mr. John Bunyan, reprinted in *Grace Abounding and The Pilgrim's Progress* (Brown ed. 1907), at 103–132.

19. For a vivid account of some of these persecutions, see Wertenbaker, *The Puritan Oligarchy* (1947).

20. Perhaps the best example of the sort of men who came to this country for precisely that reason is Roger Williams, the founder of Rhode Island, who has been described as "the truest Christian amongst many who sincerely desired to be Christian." Parrington, *Main Currents in American Thought* (1930), Vol. 1, at p. 74. Williams, who was one of the earliest exponents of the doctrine of separation of church and state, believed that separation was necessary in order to protect the church from the danger of destruction which he thought inevitable flowed from control by even the best-intentioned civil authorities: "The unknowing zeale of *Constantine* and other Emperours, did more hurt to *Christ Jesus* his Crowne and Kingdome, then the raging fury of the most bloody *Neroes*. In the *persecutions* of the later, *Christians* were sweet and fragrant, like spice pounded and beaten in morters: But those *good* Emperours, persecuting some erroneous persons, *Arrius, & c.* and advancing the professours of some Truths of Christ (for there was no small number of *Truths* lost in those times) and maintaining their *Religion* by the materiall Sword, I say by this meanes led the fight for adoption of our Constitution and also for our Bill of Rights with the very guarantees of religious freedom that forbid the sort of governmental activity which New York has attempted here. These men knew that the First Amendment, which tried to put an end to governmental control of religion and of prayer, was not written to destroy either. They knew rather that it was written to quiet well-justified fears which nearly all of them felt arising out of an awareness that governments of the past had shackled men's tongues to make them speak only the religious thoughts that government wanted them to speak and to pray only to the God that government wanted them to pray to. It is neither sacrilegious nor antireligious to say that each separate government in this country should stay out of the business of writing or sanctioning official prayers and leave that purely religious function to the people themselves and to those the people choose to look to for religious guidance.[21] ... *Reversed and remanded.*

■ Justice Frankfurter took no part in the decision of this case.

■ Justice White took no part in the consideration or decision of this case.

■ Justice Douglas, concurring.

It is customary in deciding a constitutional question to treat it in its narrowest form. Yet at times the setting of the question gives it a form and content which no abstract treatment could give. The point for decision is whether the Government can constitutionally finance a religious exercise. Our system at the federal and state levels is presently honeycombed with such financing.[1] Nevertheless, I think it is an unconstitutional undertaking whatever form it takes....

Christianity was *ecclipsed,* and the Professors of it fell asleep...." Williams, *The Bloudy Tenent, of Persecution* [Chapter Five, section 2]. To Williams, it was no part of the business or competence of a civil magistrate to interfere in religious matters: "[W]hat imprudence and *indiscretion* is it in the most common affaires of Life, to conceive that *Emperours, Kings* and *Rulers* of the earth must not only be qualified with *politicall* and *state abilities* to *make* and *execute* such *Civill Lawes* which may concerne the common *rights, peace* and *safety* (which is worke and businesse, load and burthen enough for the ablest shoulders in the Commonweal) but also furnished with such *Spirituall* and heavenly *abilities* to governe the *Spirituall* and *Christian Commonweale....*" *Id.,* at 366. See also *id., at* 136–137.

21. There is of course nothing in the decision reached here that is inconsistent with the fact that school children and others are officially encouraged to express love for our country by reciting historical documents such as the Declaration of Independence which contain references to the Deity or by singing officially espoused anthems which in-

clude the composer's professions of faith in a Supreme Being, or with the fact that there are many manifestations in our public life of belief in God. Such patriotic or ceremonial occasions bear no true resemblance to the unquestioned religious exercise that the State of New York has sponsored in this instance.

1. "There are many 'aids' to religion in this country at all levels of government. To mention but a few at the federal level, one might begin by observing that the very First Congress which wrote the First Amendment provided for chaplains in both Houses and in the armed services. There is compulsory chapel at the service academies, and religious services are held in federal hospitals and prisons. The President issues religious proclamations. The Bible is used for the administration of oaths. N.Y.A. and W.P.A. funds were available to parochial schools during the depression. Veterans receiving money under the 'G.I.' Bill of 1944 could attend denominational schools, to which payments were made directly by the government. During World War II, federal money was contributed to denominational schools for the training of nurses. The benefits of the National School

■ JUSTICE STEWART, dissenting.

A local school board in New York has provided that those pupils who wish to do so may join in a brief prayer at the beginning of each school day, acknowledging their dependence upon God and asking His blessing upon them and upon their parents, their teachers, and their country. The Court today decides that in permitting this brief nondenominational prayer the school board has violated the Constitution of the United States. I think this decision is wrong.

The Court does not hold, nor could it, that New York has interfered with the free exercise of anybody's religion. For the state courts have made clear that those who object to reciting the prayer must be entirely free of any compulsion to do so, including any "embarrassments and pressures." Cf. *Barnette* [Chapter Eleven, section three]. But the Court says that in permitting school children to say this simple prayer, the New York authorities have established "an official religion."

With all respect, I think the Court has misapplied a great constitutional principle. I cannot see how an "official religion" is established by letting those who want to say a prayer say it. On the contrary, I think that to deny the wish of these school children to join in reciting this prayer is to deny them the opportunity of sharing in the spiritual heritage of our Nation.

NOTES AND QUESTIONS

1. *The End of Nonsectarianism? Engel* shattered "a common denominator" approach to Protestant Christianity that had reigned for decades as the de facto establishment in America. Robert E. Rodes, Jr., offered an alternative approach to a thin "national consensus." He argued that it could be found in commitment to "freedom" and to "dialogue." By commitment to freedom he meant "a recognition of a purpose in man that cannot be found through the means under the control of organized society," in Abraham Joshua Heschel's words an "openness to transcendence." By "dialogue" Rodes meant "conversation among persons of different beliefs, having for its purpose mutual understanding and respect, rather than agreement. To this end, it stresses personal affirmation, and eschews both apologetics and compromise.... [Dialogue's] development is largely the work of theologians, perhaps the most influential among them being Martin Buber." Rodes, "The Passing of Nonsectarianism: Some Reflections on the School Prayer Case," 38 *Notre Dame Law.* 115, 133–34

Lunch Act are available to students in private as well as public schools. The Hospital Survey and Construction Act of 1946 specifically made money available to non-public hospitals. The slogan 'In God We Trust' is used by the Treasury Department, and Congress recently added God to the pledge of allegiance. There is Bible-reading in the schools of the District of Columbia, and religious instruction is given in the District's National Training School for Boys. Religious organizations are exempt from the federal income tax and are granted postal privileges. Up to defined limits—15 per cent of the adjusted gross income of individuals and 5 per cent of the net income of corporations—contributions to religious organizations are deductible for federal income tax purposes. There are no limits to the deductibility of gifts and bequests to religious institutions made under the federal gift and estate tax laws. This list of federal 'aids' could easily be expanded, and of course there is a long list in each state." Fellman, The Limits of Freedom (1959), pp. 40–41.

(1963). Rodes recognized that both "freedom" and "dialogue" in his usage were religious, and he contended that the Constitution did not preclude their acceptance. He found their antecedents in what Tocqueville had written of the special place of religion and religious freedom in America [Chapter Seven, section 7].

Rodes concluded: "To sum up, the value of freedom and dialogue as the root principles in our national religious consensus lies in their conformity on the one hand to what is deepest and truest in our traditional aspirations as a people, and on the other hand to a recognition of those central mysteries of human existence to which the most important of religious affirmations are addressed. It would be comforting to be able to derive from this formulation of principles some consequences of practical application to the church-state problems currently facing our schools and our society. But I see these principles less as furnishing a logical basis for solving problems of this kind than as conducing to an atmosphere in which they may be solved. The profoundest consequence of a national religious consensus worked out in terms of freedom and dialogue is that it becomes the concern of every citizen that every other citizen live out his own deepest commitments to the fullest possible extent. It is in the context of heightened spiritual awareness afforded by such a living out that we await the manifestation of divine power whereby freedom may be consummated in salvation, dialogue in unity. And it is in this concern for such a living out that we may hope for a solution to our immediate problems of church and state." Does Rodes's approach make sense? Does it pass constitutional scrutiny?

The Williamsburg Charter was signed in Williamsburg,Virginia, on the bicentennial of the call by Virginia for a Bill of Rights in the national Constitution, with a provision guaranteeing religious liberty for all. National leaders of many different walks of life and reflecting many different perspectives endorsed the document "calling for a fresh consideration of religious liberty in our time." The Charter "sets forth a renewed national compact, in the sense of a solemn mutual agreement between parties, on how we view the place of religion in American life and how we should contend with each other's deepest differences in the public sphere. It is a call to a vision of public life that will allow conflict to lead to consensus, religious commitment to reinforce political civility. In this way, diversity is not a point of weakness but a source of strength." The Williamsburg Charter, 8 *J. L. & Relig.* 5, 7 (1990). This issue of the *Journal of Law and Religion* contains several essays about various aspects of the Charter; see also James Davison Hunter and Os Guinness eds., *Articles of Faith, Articles of Peace: The Religious Liberty Clauses and the American Public Philosophy* (1990).

2. *Religious Orders and Religious Garb in the Public Schools.* Chapter Eleven, section 8 explores the refusal of the government to allow a believer to wear religious garb as a violation of free exercise of religion. Here the focus is on whether the state may prohibit members of religious orders from wearing religious garb while teaching in a public school. In an early case on this theme the New York Court of Appeals said "that the effect of the costume worn by these Sisters of St. Joseph at all times in the presence of their pupils would be to inspire respect, if not sympathy, for the religious denomination to which they so manifestly belong," and so would violate New York's constitutional prohibition against the state aiding any school "wholly or in part" under the control of a religious denomination. *O'Connor v. Hendrick*, 184 N.Y. 421, 77

N.E. 612 (1906). But no prohibition existed against nuns being hired by a public school, and in the absence of state law or policy to the contrary, nuns in religious garb did teach in the public schools, see *Gerhardt v. Heid*, 66 N.D. 444, 267 N.W. 127 (1936) (Benedictine sisters in dark habits have religious liberty under the North Dakota Constitution to teach in the public schools). This decision was superseded by a popular referendum. Leo Pfeffer, *Church, State and Freedom* 413 (1953).

Post–*McCollum* scrutiny of areas that had relied on Catholic religious orders led to litigation in New Mexico, a state with a tradition of such reliance. In Mora County, Rio Arrida County, San Juan County, San Miguel County, Santa Fe County, and Taos County, New Mexico, a number of public schools had been staffed "for many years" by Sisters of the Most Precious Blood and other Catholic orders. The teachers, who wore religious habits, were employed as public school teachers. School was held in buildings rented from the Catholic archdiocese. The pupils were taught prayers and given religious instruction. Protestant parents complained and, eventually, in the period preceding the litigation, the protesters persuaded the State Board of Education to talk to the archbishop of Santa Fe. He directed that there should be no religious instruction during the school week. The objectors pressed their objections with a suit.

The trial court found that there was "no separation" between the state and the Catholic Church in New Mexico in the schools. The Supreme Court of New Mexico characterized the system as a "Catholic school system supported by public funds." It enjoined further operation of the system. *Zellers v. Huff*, 55 N.M. 501, 236 P.2d 949 (1951). A statute provided, "No teacher shall use any sectarian or denominational books in the schools, or teach sectarian doctrine in the schools; any teacher violating the provision of this section shall be immediately discharged, his certificate to teach school revoked, and be forever barred from receiving any school moneys and employment in the public schools in the state." The court applied the statute to the sisters found to have taught religion.

Janet Cooper, a public school teacher, wore white clothing and a white turban to show that she had become a Sikh. She explained to her pupils the religious significance of her dress. She refused to abandon the practice at the order of the superintendent of schools. Invoking an Oregon statute that prohibited the wearing of "religious dress" by a teacher on duty, ORS 324.650, the superintendent suspended the teacher and revoked her teaching certificate under the terms of ORS 324.655. In *Cooper v. Eugene School District No. 4J*, 301 Or. 358, 723 P. 2d 298 (1986), app. dismissed, 480 U.S. 942 (1987), the court, per Justice Linde, noted that the 1923 predecessor of the statute "dates from the period of anti-Catholic intolerance that also gave us the initiative measure against private schools struck down in *Pierce v. Society of Sisters* [Chapter Ten, section 7]." Justice Linde, a leader in the effort to reclaim state constitutional law, also noted that the "religion clauses of Oregon's Bill of Rights . . . are specifications of a larger vision of freedom for adversity of religious beliefs and modes of worship and freedom from state-supported official faiths or modes of worship." Nevertheless, the court sustained the statutory requirements, as applied not to occasional appearance in religious dress, but to "wearing religious dress as a regular or frequently repeated practice while teaching." The court found that the present law, adopted in 1965, "had [no] aim other than to maintain the religious neutrality in the public schools, to avoid giving children or their parents the impression that the school, through its teacher, approves and shares the religious commitment of one group and perhaps finds that of others less worthy." This purpose, the court held, does not contravene either Oregon's guarantees of religious freedom or the federal First Amendment.

Under *Hysong v. Gallitzin School Dist.*, 164 Pa. 629, 30 A. 482 (1894), the wearing of religious garb was held not to constitute "sectarian teaching." The legislature responded with a statute similar to that sustained by the Oregon Supreme Court in *Cooper*. The Pennsylvania Supreme Court sustained that statute in *Commonwealth v. Herr*, 229 Pa. 132, 78 A. 68 (1910) against the contention that it imposed a "religious test." In observance of the Qur'an, a devout Muslim covered her entire body except for her face and hands while working as a substitute public school teacher. In *United States v. Board of Educ. for the School Dist. of Philadelphia*, 911 F.2d 882 (3d Cir. 1990) the court relied upon *Cooper* to reject her claim that the application of the Pennsylvania religious garb statute to her violated the duty imposed by Title VII on employers to make reasonable accommodation of the religious practices and beliefs of employees [Chapter Eleven, section 6]. Right result? The Presidential directive on religion in the federal workplace [Chapter Eleven, section 8] clarifies that employees may wear religious garb (e.g., yarmulke, crucifix, or hijab) if it does not unduly interfere with the functioning of the workplace. Should this federal directive count for more in the construction of congressional legislation than an interpretation of state law? Should postal employees have greater rights of religious freedom in the workplace than public school teachers?

3. *The Bible in the Public Schools.* Horace Mann, the apostle of free public education, was an advocate of the use of the Bible in the public schools of Massachusetts. His final report as secretary of the State Board of Education declared: "[O]ur system earnestly inculcates all Christian morals; it founds its morals on the basis of religion; it welcomes the religion of the Bible: and in receiving the Bible, it allows it to do what it is allowed to do in no other system—*to speak for itself.*" Mann, *Twelfth Annual Report of the State Board of Education* (1848), in 4 *Life and Works of Horace Mann* 311–12 (1891) (emphasis in original). According to Mann, "I suppose there is not, at the present time, a single town in the Commonwealth in whose schools [the King James Bible] is not read," *Eleventh Annual Report* (1847). *Id.*177.

Church law forbade Catholics to read Scripture in a translation not approved by ecclesiastical authority. The King James Bible—the Bible normally used in public schools—was an unapproved translation. Besides minor and insubstantial disagreements, the King James version omitted several books of the Old Testament—part of Esther; Tobias; Maccabees—viewed as integral to it by Catholics. But as the Bible was never read in its entirety in the schools, the omitted parts would probably not have been read in any case. The real objection was the sense of believing Catholics that they should not have to use a Protestant text. In Boston in 1859 an eleven-year-old, Thomas Wall, refused to read the Ten Commandments from the King James Version and was beaten by his teacher. In an action of battery against the teacher, a Boston court held that the discipline was proper, *Commonwealth v. Cooke*, 7 *University of Pennsylvania Law Review (American Law Register)* 417 (Boston Police Ct. 1859). Outrage over the case led to changes in the membership of the Boston School

Committee, but in other Massachusetts communities compulsion was used on Catholics as late as 1865. Robert H. Lord, 2 *A History of the Archdiocese of Boston* 601–05 (1945).

The first appellate case came from Maine where a Catholic girl was expelled from the Ellsworth schools for refusing to read the King James version. Counsel vigorously argued that the legislature had no power to make "a religious test" for admission to school or to prefer Protestants over Catholics. The court declared that "reading the Bible is no more an interference with religious belief, than would reading the mythology of Greece or Rome be regarded as interfering with religious belief or an affirmance of the pagan creeds," *Donahoe v. Richards*, 38 Me. 379, 399 (1854). Responding directly to Bridget Donahoe's "conscientious religious scruples," which forbade her to read the text, the court noted that the Index of Prohibited Books forbade Catholics to read other books and declared, "The right of one sect to interdict or expurgate would place all schools in subordination to the sect interdicting or expurgating," Id 407. Counsel had argued why, "in the name of common sense and Christian charity," she should not have been allowed to read from the Catholic translation. Dismissing the action, the court recommended such charity to the school board: "Large masses of foreign population are among us, weak in the midst of our strength." Those entrusted with the duty of educating them should discharge their duty "with magnanimous liberality and Christian kindness." The Court cited the Golden Rule. *Id.* 413.

Jews came to complain about Bible reading as well. In a Louisiana case Jewish parents objected to the reading of any part of the New Testament in the public schools. Finding the practice of Bible reading to violate the state Constitution, the Louisiana Supreme Court declared the New Testament to be "the foundation and text-book of Christianity, based on the teachings contained therein that Christ is divine. And the lessons therefrom give a preference to Christians, and at the same time make a discrimination against the Jews." *Herold v. Parish Board,* 136 La. 1034, 1049, 68 So. 116, 121 (1915).

Fourteen state courts had upheld the legality of Bible reading, eight state courts had found it to violate state constitutions. Donald E. Boles, *The Bible, Religion and the Public Schools* 332 (1965). In all, thirty-seven states permitted Bible-reading, seventeen by statute. No momentum toward change in state practice was discernible. The earliest decision against this practice under state constitutional law had been in *Minor v. Board of Educ. of Cincinnati* (Superior Ct. Cincinnati, Feb. 1870), unreported but published separately under the title, *The Bible in the Common Schools* (1870). The most recent such case was in South Dakota in 1929. Boles, *id.* 355. A checkerboard pattern existed and had existed for a long time. Against this background the *Schempp* case was begun in 1959.

Unlike previous challenges, this case was brought in federal court and invoked the First Amendment. The plaintiffs, Edward and Sidney Schempp, were church-going Unitarians with three children, aged 18, 15, and 12 in the elementary schools of Abington, Pennsylvania. The theological doctrine of the Trinity, the divinity of Christ, and God as a vengeful Judge, the Schempps asserted to be in that part of Scripture that was contrary to their belief. The oldest, Ellory, had objected to the regular reading of ten verses of the Bible at the start of each school day, and he had first demonstrated his objections by reading the Qur'an to himself while the Bible was read aloud. The plaintiffs' expert witness, Solomon Grayzel, a rabbi and editor of the Jewish Publication Society, publisher of the *Holy Scriptures According to the Masoretic Text*, testified that "portions of the New Testament were offensive to Jewish tradition and that, from the standpoint of Jewish faith, the concept of Jesus Christ as the Son of God was 'practically blasphemous' "; also that portions of the New Testament "tended to bring the Jews into ridicule or scorn" and that such passages, unexplained, did psychological harm to Jewish children, *Schempp v. School District,* 177 F. Supp. 398, 401 (E.D. Pa. 1959). Luther A. Weigle, a Lutheran minister and dean emeritus of Yale Divinity School, testified for the defense that the Bible was nonsectarian "within the Christian faiths," and that the Bible was of great moral, literary, and historical value. A three-judge federal court, in an opinion by Chief Judge John Biggs, Jr., held the Bible-reading to be unconstitutional. While the case was awaiting decision by the Supreme Court, Pennsylvania amended its statute to make the reading optional for each student. The Supreme Court, on October 24, 1960—toward the close of a presidential campaign in which the religion of John F. Kennedy had been hotly contested—vacated the judgment and remanded the case to be decided in the light of the statutory change, 364 U.S. 298. Again the lower court enjoined the Bible-reading, 201 F. Supp. 815 (E.D. Pa. 1962). As it was appealed, *Engel* [this section above] was decided and foreshadowed what the Supreme Court would do here.

School District of Abington Township v. Schempp (No. 142)
Murray v. Curlett (No. 119)

374 U.S. 203 (1963).

John D. Killian III, Deputy Attorney General of Pennsylvania, and *Philip H. Ward III* argued the cause for appellants in No. 142. With them on the brief were David Stahl, Attorney General of Pennsylvania, *Percival R. Rieder* and *C. Brewster Rhoads.*

Henry W. Sawyer III argued the cause for appellees in No. 142. With him on the brief was *Wayland H. Elsbree.*

Leonard J. Kerpelman argued the cause and filed a brief for petitioners in No. 119.

Francis B. Burch and *George W. Baker, Jr.* argued the cause for respondents in No. 119. With them on the brief were *Nelson B. Seidman* and *Philip Z. Altfeld.*

Thomas B. Finan, Attorney General of Maryland, argued the cause for the State of Maryland, as amicus curiae, urging affirmance in No. 119. With him on the brief were *James P. Garland* and *Robert F. Sweeney,* Assistant Attorney Generals of Maryland. *Richmond M. Flowers,* Attorney General of Alabama, *Robert Pickrell*, Attorney General of Arizona, *Bruce Bennett*, Attorney General of Arkansas, *Richard W. Ervin*, Attorney General of Florida, *Eugene Cook*, Attorney General of Georgia, *Allan G. Shepard,* Attorney General of Idaho, *William M. Ferguson*, Attorney General of Kansas, *Jack P.F. Gremillion*, Attorney General of Louisiana, *Frank E. Hancock*, Attorney General of Maine, *Joe T. Patterson*, Attorney General of

Mississippi, *William Maynard*, Attorney General of New Hampshire, *Arthur J. Sills*, Attorney General of New Jersey, *Earl E. Hartley*, Attorney General of New Mexico, *Thomas Wade Burton*, Attorney General of North Carolina, *J. Joseph Nugent*, Attorney General of Rhode Island, *Daniel R. McLeod*, Attorney General of South Carolina, *Frank R. Farrar*, Attorney General of South Dakota, and *George F. McCanless*, Attorney General of Tennessee, joined in the brief of their respective States, as amici curiae.

Briefs of amici curiae, urging affirmance in No. 142 and reversal in No. 119, were filed by *Morris B. Abram, Edwin J. Lukas, Burnett Roth, Arnold Forster, Paul Hartman, Theodore Leskes* and *Sol Rabkin* for the American Jewish Committee et al.; by *Leo Pfeffer, Lewis H. Weinstein, Albert Wald, Shad Polier, Samuel Lawrence Brennglass* and *Theodore R. Mann* for the Synagogue Council of America et al.; and by *Herbert A. Wolff, Leo Rosen, Morris L. Ernst* and *Nancy F. Wechsler* for the American Ethical Union.

■ JUSTICE CLARK delivered the opinion of the court.

Applying the Establishment Clause principles to the cases at bar we find that the States are requiring the selection and reading at the opening of the school day of verses from the Holy Bible [*Schempp*] and the recitation of the Lord's Prayer by the students in unison [*Murray*]. These exercises are prescribed as part of the curricular activities of students who are required by law to attend school. They are held in the school buildings under the supervision and with the participation of teachers employed in those schools. None of these factors, other than compulsory school attendance, was present in the program upheld in *Zorach v. Clauson* [section 2A above]. The trial court in No. 142 had found that such an opening exercise is a religious ceremony and was intended by the State to be so. We agree with the trial court's finding as to the religious character of the exercises. Given that finding, the exercises and the law requiring them are in violation of the Establishment Clause.

There is no such specific finding as to the religious character of the exercises in No. 119, and the State contends (as does the State in No. 142) that the program is an effort to extend its benefits to all public school children without regard to their religious belief. Included within its secular purposes, it says, are the promotion of moral values, the contradiction to the materialistic trends of our times, the perpetuation of our institutions and the teaching of literature. The case came up on demurrer, of course, to a petition which alleged that the uniform practice under the rule had been to read from the King James version of the Bible and that the exercise was sectarian. The short answer, therefore, is that the religious character of the exercise was admitted by the State. But even if its purpose is not strictly religious, it is sought to be accomplished through readings, without comment, from the Bible. Surely the place of the Bible as an instrument of religion cannot be gainsaid, and the State's recognition of the pervading religious character of the ceremony is evident from the rule's specific permission of the alternative use of the Catholic Douay version as well as the recent amendment permitting nonattendance at the exercises. None of these factors is consistent with the contention that the Bible is here used either as an instrument for nonreligious moral inspiration or as a reference for the teaching of secular subjects.

The conclusion follows that in both cases the laws require religious exercises and such exercises are being conducted in direct violation of the rights of the appellees and petitioners.[9] Nor are these required exercises mitigated by the fact that individual students may absent themselves upon parental request, for that fact furnishes no defense to a claim of unconstitutionality under the Establishment Clause. See *Engel v. Vitale* [this section above]. Further, it is no defense to urge that the religious practices here may be relatively minor encroachments on the First Amendment. The breach of neutrality that is today a trickling stream may all too soon become a raging torrent and, in the words of Madison, "it is proper to take alarm at the first experiment on our liberties." Memorial and Remonstrance Against Religious Assessments [Chapter Six, section 3], quoted in *Everson*.

It is insisted that unless these religious exercises are permitted a "religion of secularism" is established in the schools. We agree of course that the State may not establish a "religion of secularism" in the sense of affirmatively opposing or showing hostility to religion, thus "preferring those who believe in no religion over those who do believe." *Zorach v. Clauson* [section 2A above]. We do not agree, however, that this decision in any sense has that effect. In addition, it might well be said that one's education is not complete without a study of comparative religion or the history of religion and its relationship to the advancement of civilization. It certainly may be said that the Bible is worthy of study for its literary and historic qualities. Nothing we have said here indicates that such study of the Bible or of religion, when presented objectively as part of a secular program of education, may not be effected consistently with the First Amendment. But the exercises here do not fall into those categories. They are religious exercises, required by the States in violation of the command of the First Amendment that the Government maintain strict neutrality, neither aiding nor opposing religion.

Finally, we cannot accept that the concept of neutrality, which does not permit a State to require a religious exercise even with the consent of the majority of those affected, collides with the majority's right to free exercise of religion.[10] While the Free Exercise Clause clearly prohibits the use of

---

9. It goes without saying that the laws and practices involved here can be challenged only by persons having standing to complain. But the requirements for standing to challenge state action under the Establishment Clause, unlike those relating to the Free Exercise Clause, do not include proof that particular religious freedoms are infringed. *McGowan v. Maryland* [Chapter Thirteen, section 2]. The parties here are school children and their parents, who are directly affected by the laws and practices against which their complaints are directed. These interests surely suffice to give the parties standing to complain. See *Engel, McCollum, Everson*. Compare *Doremus v. Board of Educ.*, 342 U.S. 429 (1952), which involved the same substantive issues presented here. The appeal was there dismissed upon the graduation of the school child involved and because of the appellants' failure to establish standing as taxpayers.

10. We are not of course presented with and therefore do not pass upon a situation such as military service, where the Government regulates the temporal and geographic state action to deny the rights of free exercise to *anyone*, it has never meant that a majority could use the machinery of the State to practice its beliefs. Such a contention was effectively answered by Mr. Justice Jackson for the Court in *Barnette* [Chapter Eleven, section 3]: "The very purpose of a Bill of Rights was to withdraw certain subjects from the vicissitudes of political controversy, to place them beyond the reach of majorities and officials and to establish them as legal principles to be applied by the courts. One's right to ... freedom of worship ... and other fundamental rights may not be submitted to vote; they depend on the outcome of no elections."

The place of religion in our society is an exalted one, achieved through a long tradition of reliance on the home, the church and the inviolable citadel of the individual heart and mind. We have come to recognize through bitter experience that it is not within the power of government to invade that citadel, whether its purpose or effect be to aid or oppose, to advance or retard. In the relationship between man and religion, the State is firmly committed to a position of neutrality....

The judgment in the Pennsylvania case was affirmed.

■ JUSTICES GOLDBERG and HARLAN concurred separately.

■ JUSTICE BRENNAN, concurring.

Attendance at the public schools has never been compulsory; parents remain morally and constitutionally free to choose the academic environment in which they wish their children to be educated. The relationship of the Establishment Clause of the First Amendment to the public school system is preeminently that of reserving such a choice to the individual parent, rather than vesting it in the majority of voters of each State or school district. The choice which is thus preserved is between a public secular education with its uniquely democratic values, and some form of private or sectarian education, which offers values of its own. In my judgment the First Amendment forbids the State to inhibit that freedom of choice by diminishing the attractiveness of either alternative—either by restricting the liberty of the private schools to inculcate whatever values they wish, or by jeopardizing the freedom of the public schools from private or sectarian pressures....

It has also been suggested that the "liberty" guaranteed by the Fourteenth Amendment logically cannot absorb the Establishment Clause because that clause is not one of the provisions of the Bill of Rights which in terms protects a "freedom" of the individual. See Corwin, *A Constitution of Powers in a Secular State* (1951), 113–116. The fallacy in this contention, I think, is that it underestimates the role of the Establishment Clause as a coguarantor, with the Free Exercise Clause, of religious liberty. The Framers did not entrust the liberty of religious beliefs to either clause alone. The Free Exercise Clause "was not to be the full extent of the Amendment's guarantee of freedom from governmental intrusion in matters of faith."

environment of individuals to a point that, unless it permits voluntary religious services to be conducted with the use of government facilities, military personnel would be unable to engage in the practice of their faiths.

McGowan v. Maryland [Chapter Thirteen, section 2] at 464 (opinion of Frankfurter, J.). . . .

The secular purposes which devotional exercises are said to serve fall into two categories—those which depend upon an immediately religious experience shared by the participating children; and those which appear sufficiently divorced from the religious content of the devotional material that they can be served equally by nonreligious materials. With respect to the first objective, much has been written about the moral and spiritual values of infusing some religious influence or instruction into the public school classroom.[56] To the extent that only *religious* materials will serve this purpose, it seems to me that the purpose as well as the means is so plainly religious that the exercise is necessarily forbidden by the Establishment Clause. The fact that purely secular benefits may eventually result does not seem to me to justify the exercises, for similar indirect nonreligious benefits could no doubt have been claimed for the released time program invalidated in *McCollum* [section 2A above].

The second justification assumes that religious exercises at the start of the school day may directly serve solely secular ends—for example, by fostering harmony and tolerance among the pupils, enhancing the authority of the teacher, and inspiring better discipline. To the extent that such benefits result not from the content of the readings and recitation, but simply from the holding of such a solemn exercise at the opening assembly or the first class of the day, it would seem that less sensitive materials might equally well serve the same purpose. I have previously suggested that *Torcaso* [Chapter Twelve, section 1] and the *Sunday Law Cases* [Chapter Thirteen, section 2] forbid the use of religious means to achieve secular ends where nonreligious means will suffice. That principle is readily applied to these cases. It has not been shown that readings from the speeches and messages of great Americans, for example, or from the documents of our heritage of liberty, daily recitation of the Pledge of Allegiance, or even the observance of a moment of reverent silence at the opening of class, may not adequately serve the solely secular purposes of the devotional activities without jeopardizing either the religious liberties of any members of the community or the proper degree of separation between the spheres of religion and government. Such substitutes would, I think, be unsatisfactory or inadequate only to the extent that the present activities do in fact serve religious goals. While I do not question the judgment of experienced educators that the challenged practices may well

56. See *e.g.*, Henry, *The Place of Religion in Public Schools* (1950); Martin, *Our Public Schools—Christian or Secular* (1952); Educational Policies Comm'n of the National Educational Assn., *Moral and Spiritual Values in the Public Schools* (1951), c. IV; Harner, *Religion's Place in General Education* (1949). Educators are by no means unanimous however, on this question. See Boles, *The Bible, Religion, and the Public Schools* (1961), 223–224. Compare George Washington's advice in his Farewell Address: "And let us with caution indulge the supposition, that morality can be maintained without religion. Whatever may be conceded to the influence of refined education on minds of peculiar structure, reason and experience both forbid us to expect that National morality can prevail in exclusion of religious principle." 35 *Writings of George Washington* (Fitzpatrick ed. 1940), 229. [Chapter Seven, section 2].

achieve valuable secular ends, it seems to me that the State acts unconstitutionally if it either sets about to attain even indirectly religious ends by religious means, or if it uses religious means to serve secular ends where secular means would suffice. . . .

It has been suggested that a tentative solution to these problems may lie in the fashioning of a "common core" of theology tolerable to all creeds but preferential to none.[64] But as one commentator has recently observed, "[h]istory is not encouraging to" those who hope to fashion a "common denominator of religion detached from its manifestation in any organized church." Sutherland, Establishment According to *Engel,* 76 Harv. L. Rev. 25, 51 (1962). Thus, the notion of a "common core" litany or supplication offends many deeply devout worshippers who do not find clearly sectarian practices objectionable. Father Gustav Weigel has recently expressed a widely shared view: "The moral code held by each separate religious community can reductively be unified, but the consistent particular believer wants no such reduction." And, as the American Council on Education warned several years ago, "The notion of a common core suggests a watering down of the several faiths to the point where common essentials appear. This might easily lead to a new sect—a public school sect—which would take its place alongside the existing faiths and compete with them." *Engel* is surely authority that nonsectarian religious practices, equally with sectarian exercises, violate the Establishment Clause. Moreover, even if the Establishment Clause were oblivious to nonsectarian religious practices, I think it quite likely that the "common core" approach would be sufficiently objectionable to many groups to be foreclosed by the prohibitions of the Free Exercise Clause. . . . [T]he line we must draw between the permissible and the impermissible is one which accords with history and faithfully reflects the understanding of the Founding Fathers. . . .

■ JUSTICE STEWART, dissenting.

Since the *Cantwell* [Chapter Eleven, section 1] pronouncement in 1940, this Court has only twice held invalid state laws on the ground that they were laws "respecting an establishment of religion" in violation of the Fourteenth Amendment. *McCollum v. Board of Education* [section 2A above]; *Engel v. Vitale* [section 2A above]. On the other hand, the Court has upheld against such a challenge laws establishing Sunday as a compulsory day of rest, *McGowan v. Maryland,* [Chapter Thirteen, section 2] and a law authorizing reimbursement from public funds for the transportation of parochial school pupils. *Everson v. Board of Education* [section 1 above].

---

64. See Abbott, "A Common Bible Reader for Public Schools," 56 Religious Education 20 (1961); Note, 22 Albany L. Rev. 156–157 (1958); 2 Stokes, *Church and State in the United States* (1950), 501–506 (describing the "common denominator" or "three faiths" plan and certain programs of instruction designed to implement the "common core" approach). The attempts to evolve a universal, nondenominational prayer are by no means novel. See, *e.g.,* Madison's letter to Edward Everett, March 19, 1823, commenting upon a "project of a prayer . . . intended to comprehend & conciliate College Students of every [Christian] denomination, by a Form composed wholly of texts & phrases of scripture." 9 *Writings of James Madison* (Hunt ed. 1910), 126. For a fuller description of this and other attempts to fashion a "common core" or nonsectarian exercise, *see Engel v. Vitale,* 18 Misc. 2d 659, 660–662, 191 N.Y.S. 2d 453, 459–460.

Unlike other First Amendment guarantees, there is an inherent limitation upon the applicability of the Establishment Clause's ban on state support to religion. That limitation was succinctly put in *Everson*: "State power is no more to be used so as to handicap religions than it is to favor them." And in a later case, this Court recognized that the limitation was one which was itself compelled by the free exercise guarantee. "To hold that a state cannot consistently with the First and Fourteenth Amendments utilize its public school system to aid any or all religious faiths or sects in the dissemination of their doctrines and ideals does not ... manifest a governmental hostility to religion or religious teachings. A manifestation of such hostility would be at war with our national tradition as embodied in the First Amendment's guaranty of the free exercise of religion." *McCollum*.

... Viewed in this light, it seems to me clear that the records in both of the cases before us are wholly inadequate to support an informed or responsible decision. Both cases involve provisions which explicitly permit any student who wishes, to be excused from participation in the exercises. There is no evidence in either case as to whether there would exist any coercion of any kind upon a student who did not want to participate. No evidence at all was adduced in the *Murray* case, because it was decided upon a demurrer. All that we have in that case, therefore, is the conclusory language of a pleading. While such conclusory allegations are acceptable for procedural purposes, I think that the nature of the constitutional problem involved here clearly demands that no decision be made except upon evidence. In the *Schempp* case the record shows no more than a subjective prophecy by a parent of what he thought would happen if a request were made to be excused from participation in the exercises under the amended statute. No such request was ever made, and there is no evidence whatever as to what might or would actually happen, nor of what administrative arrangements the school actually might or could make to free from pressure of any kind those who do not want to participate in the exercises. There were no District Court findings on this issue, since the case under the amended statute was decided exclusively on Establishment Clause grounds.

What our Constitution indispensably protects is the freedom of each of us, be he Jew or Agnostic, Christian or Atheist, Buddhist or Freethinker, to believe or disbelieve, to worship or not worship, to pray or keep silent, according to his own conscience, uncoerced and unrestrained by government. It is conceivable that these school boards, or even all school boards, might eventually find it impossible to administer a system of religious exercises during school hours in such a way as to meet this constitutional standard—in such a way as completely to free from any kind of official coercion those who do not affirmatively want to participate. But I think we must not assume that school boards so lack the qualities of inventiveness and good will as to make impossible the achievement of that goal.

I would remand both cases for further hearings.

NOTES AND QUESTIONS

1. *Original Intent and Impact Studies.* Some justices, notably Justice Scalia, lay great emphasis on discerning and remaining faithful to the "original intent" of the framers of the First Amendment. *See, e.g.,* Antonin Scalia, *A Matter of Interpretation: Federal Courts and the Law* (1997). At one point in his concurring opinion in *Schempp*, Justice Brennan appears to take this position: "[T]he line we must draw between the permissible and the impermissible is one which accords with history and faithfully reflects the understanding of the Founding Fathers." But later in his opinion Brennan wrote that an awareness of "the aims of the Founding Fathers [does] not always resolve concrete problems." Are both of Brennan's views correct? For a careful historical exploration of this theme, *see* Rodney K. Smith, *Public Prayer and the Constitution* (1987).

Another approach to the School Prayer decision is to analyze its actual impact on school boards throughout the country. According to two impact studies, no case during the Warren Court era (1953–1968) generated more intense reaction across the nation than *Schempp*, including the Court's controversial rulings on school desegregation, *Brown v. Board of Educ.*, 347 U.S. 483 (1954), the case requiring all states to adopt a rule of evidence excluding unlawfully seized evidence from admission at trial, *Mapp v. Ohio*, 367 U.S. 643 (1961), and the case requiring the police to warn a suspect being interrogated in custody of constitutional rights to remain silent and to have counsel, *Miranda v. Arizona*, 384 U.S. 436 (1966). See Kenneth Dolbeare and Phillip E. Hammond, *The School Prayer Decisions: From Court Policy to Local Practice* (1971), and William K. Muir, Jr., *Prayer in the Public Schools: Law and Attitude Change* (1967).

Congressional reaction to *Schempp* was swift and angry. Members of Congress denounced the decision. Senator Bricker proposed a constitutional amendment to overturn *Schempp*. Despite the support of leaders like Senator Everett Dirksen, this effort failed. Neither did it succeed when renewed twice again, in the 1970s and the 1980s. See NOTE. *Congressional Compromise: The Equal Access Act, but no Constitutional Amendment for "Voluntary Prayer"* [this section below]. But the Court had unleashed a firestorm of public criticism of its work on religion in public schools. The author of *Schempp*, Justice Tom Clark, went out on the stump to explain that the opinion did not say what several politicians and commentators said it meant.

C.   POSTING THE TEN COMMANDMENTS

A Kentucky statute required the posting of a copy of the Ten Commandments, purchased with private contributions, on the wall of each public classroom in the state. Effective June 17, 1978, this law provided: "It shall be the duty of the superintendent of public instruction, provided sufficient funds are available as provided in subsection (3) of this Section, to ensure that a durable, permanent copy of the Ten Commandments shall be displayed on a wall in each public elementary and secondary school classroom in the Commonwealth. The copy shall be sixteen (16) inches wide by twenty (20) inches high.

(2) In small print below the last commandment shall appear a notation concerning the purpose of the display, as follows: 'The secular application of the

Ten Commandments is clearly seen in its adoption as the fundamental legal code of Western Civilization and the Common Law of the United States.'

(3) The copies required by this Act shall be purchased with funds made available through voluntary contributions made to the state treasurer for the purposes of this Act." Ky. Rev. Stat. § 158.178 (1980). In an unsigned order the Court invalidated the statute for want of a secular purpose.

Stone v. Graham

449 U.S. 39 (1980).

■ PER CURIAM

Petitioners, claiming that this statute violates the Establishment and Free Exercise Clauses of the First Amendment, sought an injunction against its enforcement. The state trial court upheld the statute, finding that its "avowed purpose" was "secular and not religious," and that the statute would "neither advance nor inhibit any religion or religious group" nor involve the State excessively in religious matters. The Supreme Court of the Commonwealth of Kentucky affirmed by an equally divided court. 599 S.W. 2d 157 (1980). We reverse.

[The Court recited the familiar three-part test in *Lemon*]. If a statute violates any of these three principles, it must be struck down under the Establishment Clause. We conclude that Kentucky's statute requiring the posting of the Ten Commandments in public school rooms has no secular legislative purpose, and is therefore unconstitutional.

The Commonwealth insists that the statute in question serves a secular legislative purpose, observing that the legislature required the following notation in small print at the bottom of each display of the Ten Commandments: "The secular application of the Ten Commandments is clearly seen in its adoption as the fundamental legal code of Western Civilization and the Common Law of the United States."

The trial court found the "avowed" purpose of the statute to be secular, even as it labeled the statutory declaration "self-serving." Under this Court's rulings, however, such an "avowed" secular purpose is not sufficient to avoid conflict with the First Amendment. In *Schempp* [this section above], this Court held unconstitutional the daily reading of Bible verses and the Lord's Prayer in the public schools, despite the school district's assertion of such secular purposes as "the promotion of moral values, the contradiction to the materialistic trends of our times, the perpetuation of our institutions and the teaching of literature."

The preeminent purpose for posting the Ten Commandments on schoolroom walls is plainly religious in nature. The Ten Commandments are undeniably a sacred text in the Jewish and Christian faiths, and no legislative recitation of a supposed secular purpose can blind us to that fact. The Commandments do not confine themselves to arguably secular matters, such as honoring one's parents, killing or murder, adultery, stealing, false witness, and covetousness. See Exodus 20:12–17; Deuteronomy 5:16–21 [Chapter One, section 1]. Rather, the first part of the Commandments concerns the religious duties of believers: worshipping the Lord God alone, avoiding idolatry, not using the Lord's name in vain, and observing the Sabbath Day. See Exodus 20:1–11; Deuteronomy 5: 6–15 [Chapter One, section 2].

This is not a case in which the Ten Commandments are integrated into the school curriculum, where the Bible may constitutionally be used in an appropriate study of history, civilization, ethics, comparative religion, or the like. *Schempp* [section 2B above]. Posting of religious texts on the wall serves no such educational function. If the posted copies of the Ten Commandments are to have any effect at all, it will be to induce the schoolchildren to read, meditate upon, perhaps to venerate and obey, the Commandments. However desirable this might be as a matter of private devotion, it is not a permissible state objective under the Establishment Clause.

It does not matter that the posted copies of the Ten Commandments are financed by voluntary private contributions, for the mere posting of the copies under the auspices of the legislature provides the "official support of the State ... Government" that the Establishment Clause prohibits. *Schempp*; see *Engel v. Vitale* [section 2B above]. Nor is it significant that the Bible verses involved in this case are merely posted on the wall, rather than read aloud as in *Schempp and Engel,* for "it is no defense to urge that the religious practices here may be relatively minor encroachments on the First Amendment." *Schempp*. We conclude that [the Kentucky statute] violates the first part of the *Lemon* test, and thus the Establishment Clause of the Constitution.

The petition for a writ of certiorari is granted, and the judgment below is reversed. *It is so ordered.*

■ CHIEF JUSTICE BURGER and JUSTICE BLACKMUN dissent. They would grant certiorari and give this case plenary consideration.

■ JUSTICE STEWART dissents from this summary reversal of the courts of Kentucky, which, so far as appears, applied wholly correct constitutional criteria in reaching their decisions.

■ JUSTICE REHNQUIST, dissenting.

With no support beyond its own *ipse dixit,* the Court concludes that the Kentucky statute involved in this case "has *no* secular legislative purpose" (emphasis supplied), and that "[t]he preeminent purpose for posting the Ten Commandments on schoolroom walls is plainly religious in nature." This even though, as the trial court found, "[[t]he General Assembly thought the statute had a secular legislative purpose and specifically said so." The Court's summary rejection of a secular purpose articulated by the legislature and confirmed by the state court is without precedent in Establishment Clause jurisprudence.

NOTES AND QUESTIONS

1. *Transcendental Meditation as a Religion: Malnak v. Yogi,* 592 F.2d 197 (3d Cir. 1979). "The Science of Creative Intelligence—Transcendental Meditation"

(SCI/TM) was offered as an elective in five high schools using a textbook developed by Maharishi Mahesh Yogi and employing teachers trained by the World Plan Executive Council—United States, an organization promoting the teaching of SCI/TM. Essential to the practice of TM was a mantra personal to each participant. The mantra was obtained by each student in the course by compulsory attendance at a Puja, a ceremony sung in Sanskrit by a Hindu monk who made offerings to the deified Guru Dev. In an action brought by parents of school children and Americans United for Separation of Church and State, the court enjoined the course as an unconstitutional establishment of religion.

Concurring, Judge Arlin B. Adams pointed out the novelty of the case: the defendants argued that the Puja was a secular not a religious ceremony, common in Eastern cultures; they contended that TM was primarily a concentration or relaxation technique without "ultimate significance." Judge Adams observed that under a modern definition of religion, extractable from *Seeger, Welsh* [Chapter Eleven, section 4], and *Torcaso* [Chapter Twelve, section 1], there had been built an analogy with the traditional religions found in America. A religion laid claim to ultimate truth and to comprehensive truth and typically, though not necessarily, involved clergy, ceremonial observances, organization, and efforts at propagation. He found that SCI/TM "provides answers to questions concerning the nature both of world and man, the underlying sustaining force of the universe, and the way to unlimited happiness"—indeed what its adherents believed to be *"the way."* Consequently, it was sufficiently comprehensive and truth-asserting to be a religion. The trained teachers, organization for propagation, and Puja were sufficiently like the characteristics of older religious groups to confirm the finding that SCI/TM was a nontheistic religion.

D. MOMENTS OF SILENCE (OR PRAYER)

NOTES AND QUESTIONS

1. *Whispering in the Sounds of Silence.* In his concurring opinion in *Schempp*, Justice Brennan wrote: "the observance of a moment of reverent silence at the opening of class ... adequately serve[s] the secular purposes of the devotional activities without jeopardizing either the religious liberties of any members of the community or the proper degree of separation between the spheres of religion and government." What was presumptively unobjectionable in 1963 became controversial in the 1980s.

Several states authorize such moments of silence at the commencement of the public school day. When the Court turned to this issue in the next one, it had a statute before it that was more complicated. An Alabama Law enacted in 1978 authorized a one-minute period of silence in all public schools "for meditation." An amendment enacted in 1981 authorized a period of silence "for meditation *or voluntary prayer*." An amendment enacted in 1982 authorized teachers to lead "willing students" in a *prescribed prayer* to "Almighty God ... the Creator and Supreme Judge of the world." As to the later amendments, the Court could have issued a terse Per Curiam order, as it had done in *Stone v. Graham*, citing *Engel* and *Schempp* as controlling. Instead, it ordered full briefing and oral argument and issued a lengthy set of opinions. Perhaps this was because of the sharp display of disrespect for the Court by the district court, which held that the Court's decisions on the nonestablishment provision were "wrong" and that Alabama had the power to establish a state religion if it chose to do so. The Fifth Circuit reversed and the Supreme Court affirmed as to the 1982 statute with its prescribed prayer. The question left for decision was whether the 1981 statute authorizing "meditation or voluntary prayer" was an establishment of religion. The plaintiff was Ishmael Jaffree who filed the complaint on behalf of his children, two in the second grade, one in kindergarten. Jaffree stated that his children were exposed to ostracism for not participating in prayers led by the teachers and that the teachers refused to stop leading the prayers.

Wallace v. Jaffree

472 U.S. 38 (1985).

John S. Baker, Jr. argued the cause for the appellants and filed the brief for appellant Wallace in No. 83–812. *Thomas O. Kotouc* and *Thomas F. Parker IV* filed briefs for appellants in No. 83–929.

Deputy Solicitor General *Paul M. Bator* argued the cause for United States as amicus curiae urging reversal. With him on the brief were Solicitor General *Lee*, Assistant Attorney General *Reynolds, Michael W. McConnell*, and *Brian K. Landsburg*.

Ronnie L. Williams argued the cause and filed a brief for appellees.

Briefs of amici curiae urging reversal were filed for the State of Delaware et al. by *Charles M. Oberly III*, Attorney–General of Delaware, *Fred S. Silverman*, State Solicitor, and *Susan H. Kirk–Ryan* and *Barbara MacDonald*, Deputy Attorneys General, *Robert K. Corbin*, Attorney General of Arizona, *Linley E. Pearson*, Attorney General of Indiana, *William J. Guste, Jr.*, Attorney General of Louisiana, *Michael C. Turpen*, Attorney General of Oklahoma, and *Gerald L. Baliles*, Attorney General of Virginia; for the State of Connecticut by *Joseph I. Lieberman*, Attorney General, *Henry S. Cohn*, Assistant Attorney General, and *Clarine Nardi Riddle*; for the Center for Judicial Studies by *Charles E. Rice*; for the Christian Legal Society et al. by *Forest D. Montgomery* and *Samuel E. Ericsson*; for the Freedom Council by *James J. Knicely* and *John W. Whitehead*; for the Legal Foundation of America by *David Crump*; for the Moral Majority, Inc., by *William Bentley Ball* and *Philip J. Murren*; and for Winston C. Anderson et al., by *Alfred J. Mainini*.

Briefs of amici curiae urging affirmance were filed for the American Civil Liberties Union et al. by *Jack D. Novik, Burt Neuborne, John Sexton*, and *Nathan Z. Dershowitz*; for the American Jewish Congress et al., by *Marc D. Stern, Justin J. Finger*, and *Jeffrey P. Sinensky*; and for Lowell P. Weicker, Jr., by *Stanley A. Twardy, Jr.*

■ JUSTICE STEVENS delivered the opinion of the Court.

. . . In applying the purpose test, it is appropriate to ask "whether government's actual purpose is to endorse or disapprove of religion." In this case, the answer to that question is dispositive. For the record not only provides us with an unambiguous affirmative answer, but it also reveals that the enactment of [the 1981 statute authorizing meditation or voluntary prayer] was not motivated by any clearly secular purpose-indeed, the statute had no secular purpose....

The sponsor of the [1981 legislation], Senator Donald Holmes, inserted into the legislative record—apparently without dissent—a statement indicating that the legislation was an "effort to return voluntary prayer" to the public schools. Later Senator Holmes confirmed this purpose before the District Court. In response to the question whether he had any purpose for the legislation other than returning voluntary prayer to public schools, he stated, "No, I did not have no other purpose in mind." The State did not present evidence of *any* secular purpose.

The unrebutted evidence of legislative intent contained in the legislative record and in the testimony of the sponsor of [the 1981 statute] is confirmed by a consideration of the relationship between this statute and the two other measures that were considered in this case. The District Court found that the 1981 statute and its 1982 sequel had a common, nonsecular purpose. The wholly religious character of the later enactment is plainly evident from its text. When the differences between [the 1981 statute] and its 1978 predecessor, are examined, it is equally clear that the 1981 statute has the same wholly religious character.

There are only three textual differences between [these two statutes]: (1) the earlier statute applies only to grades one through six, whereas [the later statute] applies to all grades; (2) the earlier statute uses the word "shall" whereas [the later statute] uses the word "may"; (3) the earlier statute refers only to "meditation" whereas [the later statute] refers to "meditation or voluntary prayer." The first difference is of no relevance in this litigation because the minor appellees were in kindergarten or second grade during the 1981–1982 academic year. The second difference would also have no impact on this litigation because the mandatory language of [the 1981 statute] continued to apply to grades one through six. Thus, the only significant textual difference is the addition of the words "or voluntary prayer."

The legislative intent to return prayer to the public schools is, of course, quite different from merely protecting every student's right to engage in voluntary prayer during an appropriate moment of silence during the school day. The 1978 statute already protected that right, containing nothing that prevented any student from engaging in voluntary prayer during a silent minute of meditation. Appellants have not identified any secular purpose that was not fully served by [the 1978 statute] before the enactment of [the later statute]. Thus, only two conclusions are consistent with the text of [the 1981 statute]: (1) the statute was enacted to convey a message of State endorsement and promotion of prayer, or (2) the statute was enacted for no purpose. No one suggests that the statute was nothing but a meaningless or irrational act.

We must, therefore, conclude that the Alabama Legislature intended to change existing law and that it was motivated by the same purpose that the Governor's Answer to the Second Amended Complaint expressly admitted; that the statement inserted in the legislative history revealed; and that

Senator Holmes' testimony frankly described. The Legislature enacted [the 1981 statute] ... for the sole purpose of expressing the State's endorsement of prayer activities for one minute at the beginning of each school day. The addition of "or voluntary prayer" indicates that the State intended to characterize prayer as a favored practice. Such an endorsement is not consistent with the established principle that the Government must pursue a course of complete neutrality toward religion.

The importance of that principle does not permit us to treat this as an inconsequential case involving nothing more than a few words of symbolic speech on behalf of the political majority. For whenever the State itself speaks on a religious subject, one of the questions that we must ask is "whether the Government intends to convey a message of endorsement or disapproval of religion." ... Keeping in mind, as we must, "both the fundamental place held by the Establishment Clause in our constitutional scheme and the myriad, subtle ways in which Establishment Clause values can be eroded," we conclude that [the 1981 statute] violates the First Amendment.

The judgment of the Court of Appeals is affirmed. *It is so ordered.*

JUSTICE POWELL concurred, in order "to respond to criticism of the three-pronged *Lemon* test," which he described as "the only coherent test a majority of the Court has ever adopted."

JUSTICE O'CONNOR concurred, proposing "a refinement of the *Lemon* test," to the effect that the nonestablishment provision was violated "when the government makes adherence to religion relevant to a person's standing in the community." The government, she wrote, must not convey a message that religion or a particular religious belief is favored or preferred. See *Lynch v. Donnelly* (O'Connor, J., concurring) [Chapter Thirteen, section 6].After noting that twenty-five states permitted students to observe a moment of silence, she added that "moment of silence laws in many states should pass Establishment Clause scrutiny because they do not favor the child who chooses to pray during a moment of silence over the child who chooses to meditate or reflect."

■ CHIEF JUSTICE BURGER dissented.

Some who trouble to read the opinions in this case will find it ironic—perhaps even bizarre—that on the very day we heard arguments in this case, the Court's session opened with an invocation for Divine protection. Across the park a few hundred yards away, the House of Representatives and the Senate regularly open each session with a prayer. These legislative prayers are not just one minute in duration, but are extended, thoughtful invocations and prayers for Divine guidance. They are given, as they have been since 1789, by clergy appointed as official Chaplains and paid from the Treasury of the United States. Congress has also provided chapels in the Capitol, at public expense, where Members and others may pause for prayer, meditation—or a moment of silence.

Inevitably some wag is bound to say that the Court's holding today reflects a belief that the historic practice of the Congress and this Court is justified because members of the Judiciary and Congress are more in need of Divine guidance than are schoolchildren. Still others will say that all this controversy is "much ado about nothing," since no power on earth—

including this Court and Congress—can stop any teacher from opening the school day with a moment of silence for pupils to meditate, to plan their day—or to pray if they voluntarily elect to do so.

■ JUSTICE WHITE dissented, supporting "a basic reconsideration of our precedents."

■ JUSTICE REHNQUIST, dissenting.

Thirty-eight years ago this Court, in *Everson v. Board of Education* [section 1 above] summarized its exegesis of Establishment Clause doctrine thus: "In the words of Jefferson, the clause against establishment of religion by law was intended to erect 'a wall of separation between church and State.' *Reynolds v. United States* [Chapter Nine]. This language from *Reynolds,* a case involving the Free Exercise Clause of the First Amendment rather than the Establishment Clause, quoted from Thomas Jefferson's letter to the Danbury Baptist Association the phrase "I contemplate with sovereign reverence that act of the whole American people which declared that their legislature should 'make no law respecting an establishment of religion, or prohibiting the free exercise thereof,' thus building a wall of separation between church and State" [Chapter Seven, section 1].

It is impossible to build sound constitutional doctrine upon a mistaken understanding of constitutional history, but unfortunately the Establishment Clause has been expressly freighted with Jefferson's misleading metaphor for nearly forty years. Thomas Jefferson was of course in France at the time the constitutional amendments known as the Bill of Rights were passed by Congress and ratified by the states. His letter to the Danbury Baptist Association was a short note of courtesy, written fourteen years after the amendments were passed by Congress. He would seem to any detached observer as a less than ideal source of contemporary history as to the meaning of the Religion Clauses of the First Amendment.

Jefferson's fellow Virginian James Madison, with whom he was joined in the battle for the enactment of the Virginia Statute of Religious Liberty of 1786, did play as large a part as anyone in the drafting of the Bill of Rights. He had two advantages over Jefferson in this regard: he was present in the United States, and he was a leading member of the First Congress. But when we turn to the record of the proceedings in the First Congress leading up to the adoption of the Establishment Clause of the Constitution, including Madison's significant contributions thereto, we see a far different picture of its purpose than the highly simplified "wall of separation between church and State" [Chapter Seven, section 1]....

The repetition of this error in the Court's opinion in *McCollum* and, *inter alia, Engel* does not make it any sounder historically. Finally, in *Schempp,* the Court made the truly remarkable statement that "the views of Madison and Jefferson, preceded by Roger Williams came to be incorporated not only in the Federal Constitution but likewise in those of most of our States" (footnote omitted). On the basis of what evidence we have, this statement is demonstrably incorrect as a matter of history. And its repetition in varying forms in succeeding opinions of the Court can give it no more authority than it possesses as a matter of fact; *stare decisis* may bind courts as to matters of law, but it cannot bind them as to matters of history.

The true meaning of the Establishment Clause can only be seen in its history.... As drafters of our Bill of Rights, the Framers inscribed the principles that control today. Any deviation from their intentions frustrates the permanence of that Charter and will only lead to the type of unprincipled decisionmaking that has plagued our Establishment Clause cases since *Everson*.

The Framers intended the Establishment Clause to prohibit the designation of any church as a "national" one. The Clause was also designed to stop the Federal Government from asserting a preference for one religious denomination or sect over others. Given the "incorporation" of the Establishment Clause as against the States via the Fourteenth Amendment in *Everson*, States are prohibited as well from establishing a religion or discriminating between sects. As its history abundantly shows, however, nothing in the Establishment Clause requires government to be strictly neutral between religion and irreligion, nor does that Clause prohibit Congress or the States from pursuing legitimate secular ends through nondiscriminatory sectarian means.

The Court strikes down the Alabama statute ... because the State wished to "endorse prayer as a favored practice." It would come as much of a shock to those who drafted the Bill of Rights as it will to a large number of thoughtful Americans today to learn that the Constitution, as construed by the majority, prohibits the Alabama Legislature from "endorsing" prayer. George Washington himself, at the request of the very Congress which passed the Bill of Rights, proclaimed a day of "public thanksgiving and prayer, to be observed by acknowledging with grateful hearts the many and signal favors of Almighty God." [Chapter Seven, section 1]. History must judge whether it was the father of his country in 1789, or a majority of the Court today, which has strayed from the meaning of the Establishment Clause.

The State surely has a secular interest in regulating the manner in which public schools are conducted. Nothing in the Establishment Clause of the First Amendment, properly understood, prohibits any such generalized "endorsement" of prayer. I would therefore reverse the judgment of the Court of Appeals.

NOTES AND QUESTIONS

1. *The Irrelevance of Lemon.* Professor McConnell writes: "One striking fact about both the *Jaffree and Thornton* [Chapter Eleven, section 5] decisions is the irrelevance of the *Lemon* test." Michael W. McConnell, "Accommodation of Religion," 1985 *Supreme Court Review* 58. Do you agree? "The opinions in *Jaffree and Thornton,* despite their surface appearance, present no obstacles to the development of a principled doctrine of the accommodation of religion, under which the purposes of the Free Exercise and Establishment Clauses are harmonized." *Id.* 59. Do you agree?

2. *Pure Silence*. Two years after *Wallace*, the Court had an opportunity to clarify the permissibility of "pure" moment of silence statutes. A New Jersey statute challenged in *Karcher v. May*, 484 U.S. 72 (1987), did not have any of the complications of the Alabama statute invalidated in *Wallace v. Jaffree*, but the case had jurisdictional defects that led the Court to dismiss it on those grounds.

3. *The Court's Use of History*. From *Everson* [section 1 above] to *Lee v. Weisman* [section 2F below] and *Rosenberger v. Rector and Visitors of the University of Virginia* [section 3 below], the Court has been relying on various accounts of the history surrounding the adoption of the First Amendment in opinions interpreting the meaning of the nonestablishment provision. The Court's use of history has come under fire both by historians and by members of the Court. One of the principal difficulties voiced by historians is the selective character of the Court's reliance on history. See, e.g., Leonard W. Levy, *The Establishment Clause* (1986).

Even when the Court cites reliable accounts, such as Thomas Curry, *The First Freedoms* (1986), there is a tendency to refer the reader to pages in the cited volume that appear to bolster the Court's conclusion, and to ignore other materials in the same volume that cast doubt on the Court's reading of the past. Or it may cite a scholar who agrees with the Justice's perspective, but ignore other critical work that casts doubt on that perspective. For example, in his concurring opinion in *Lee v. Weisman* [section 2F below], Justice Souter frequently cited Professor Laycock, Douglas Laycock, " 'Nonpreferential' Aid to Religion: A False Claim About Original Intent," 27 *Wm. & Mary L. Rev.* 875 (1986), but ignored the contrary evidence offered by Professor Smith, Rodney K. Smith, "Nonpreferentialism in Establishment Clause Analysis: A Response to Professor Laycock," 65 *St. John's L. Rev.* 245 (1991), and Smith, "Getting Off on the Wrong Foot and Back on Again: A Reexamination of the History of the Framing of the Religion Clauses of the First Amendment and a Critique of the *Reynolds* and *Everson* Decisions," 20 *Wake Forest L. Rev.* 569, 590–591 (1984). Souter cited Levy's viewpoint on plural establishments, *The Establishment Clause* 1–62, 91–119 (1986), but ignored the powerful rebuttal of this view presented by one of Levy's finest Ph.D. candidates in history, Curry, *The First Freedoms* 208–22 (1986).

Concurring in *Rosenberger*, Justice Thomas challenged Justice Souter's use of the Assessment Controversy in Virginia for the conclusion that "the Framers intended to disable religious entities from participating on neutral terms in evenhanded government programs. The evidence that does exist points in the opposite direction."

In his dissent in *Jaffree*, Justice Rehnquist wrote that "history abundantly shows" that the nonestablishment provision does not require "government to be strictly neutral between religion and irreligion, nor does that Clause prohibit Congress or the States from pursuing legitimate secular ends through nondiscriminatory sectarian means." Rehnquist cited Robert L. Cord, *Separation of Church and State: Fact and Fiction* (1982), without mentioning any of Cord's critics, including Curry. In the same opinion in *Jaffree*, Rehnquist also wrote: "*stare decisis* may bind courts as to matters of law, but it cannot bind them as to matters of history." Which way does this statement cut, in favor of judicial excursions into history or to avoiding it? Cord has written: "the Supreme Court has used its American 'history'—and little else—to justify its present Establishment Clause requirements. That fact alone makes an historical analysis germane, if not crucial, to any re-examination of present Supreme Court policy." Robert Cord, "Church–State Separation: Restoring the 'No Preference' Doctrine of the First Amendment," *Harv. J. L. & Pub. Policy* (1986) 129, 131, n. 10. Do you agree?

In his dissenting opinion in *Lee v. Weisman*, Justice Scalia quoted Justice Brennan's concurring opinion in *Schempp*: "[T]he line we must draw between the permissible and the impermissible is one which accords with history and faithfully reflects the understanding of the Founding Fathers." But Scalia ignored another line from Brennan's opinion in *Schempp*: "But an awareness of history and an appreciation of the aims of the Founding Fathers do not always resolve concrete problems."

Sometimes a judicial slip borders on dishonest use of the past. For example, Justice Scalia obviously knows of the full impact of the second flag salute case, *Barnette*, [Chapter Eleven, section 3] which he relies upon in his dissent in *Lee v. Weisman*. Why did he rely twice in *Employment Division v. Smith* [Chapter Eleven, section 10] upon the first flag salute case, *Gobitis*, which *Barnette* had overruled?

For severe criticisms of the Court's constructions of history, see Gerard V. Bradley, *Church-State Relationships in America* (1987), and Mark DeWolfe Howe, *The Garden and the Wilderness* (1965). Professor Kurland criticized " 'law office history,' written the way brief writers write briefs, by picking and choosing statement and events favorable to the client's cause." Philip B. Kurland, "The Origins of the Religion Clauses of the Constitution," 27 *Wm. & Mary L. Rev.* 839, 842 (1986). Historians have voiced this objection at a more general level, noting that spurious accounts of the past, prepared by lawyers more for advocacy than for accuracy, have made their way unchecked into the Court's opinions. See, e.g., Charles Miller, *The Supreme Court and the Uses of History* (1969); William Wiecek, "Clio as Hostage: The United States Supreme Court and the Uses of History," 24 *Cal. W. L. Rev.* 227 (1988); Alfred Kelly, "Clio and the Court: An Illicit Love Affair," 1965 *Sup. Ct. Rev.* 119.

E.   STUDENT-INITIATED, STUDENT-LED PRAYER

NOTES AND QUESTIONS

1. *Congressional Compromise: The Equal Access Act, but no Constitutional Amendment for "Voluntary Prayer."* President Ronald Reagan recommended to Congress the enactment of a constitutional amendment permitting voluntary group prayer in the public schools, Message to Congress, 18 *Weekly Compilation of Presidential Documents* 664 (May 17, 1982). The measure did not get out of committee.

In the following year a bill entitled the Religious Speech Protection Act was introduced in the House. It was eventually replaced by the Equal Access Act, which provided protection not only for religious speech, but for all forms of speech by voluntary student groups. The legislation was thought necessary because lower federal courts were not willing to extend the logic of *Widmar v. Vincent* [section 3 below], requiring equal access for religious speech on the campus of a public university, to high school students. *Brandon v. Guilderland Bd. of Ed.*, 635 F.2d 971 (2d Cir. 1980), cert. denied, 454 U.S. 1123 (1981); *Lubbock Civil Liberties Union v. Lubbock Independent School Dist.*, 669 F.2d

1038 (5th Cir. 1982), cert. denied, 459 U.S. 1155 (1983), and *Bender v. Williamsport*, 741 F.2d 538 (3rd Cir., 1984), *vacated* on jurisdictional grounds, 475 U.S. 1132 (1986). The bill drew support from evangelicals, from some civil rights groups, and from organizations often suspicious of religion in the schools such as the Baptist Joint Committee on Public Affairs and the National Council of Churches. The bill was signed into law by President Reagan on August 11, 1984.

Equal Access Act, 98 Stat. 1302, 20 U.S.C. § 4071 et seq. (1984)

20 U.S.C. § 4071. Denial of equal access prohibited

(a) Restriction of limited open forum on basis of religious, political, philosophical, or other speech content prohibited.

It shall be unlawful for any public secondary school which receives Federal financial assistance and which has a limited open forum to deny equal access or a fair opportunity to, or discriminate against, any students who wish to conduct a meeting within that limited open forum on the basis of the religious, political, philosophical, or other content of the speech at such meetings.

(b) "Limited open forum" defined

A public secondary school has a limited open forum whenever such school grants an offering to or opportunity for one or more noncurriculum related student groups to meet on school premises during noninstructional time.

(c) Fair opportunity criteria

Schools shall be deemed to offer a fair opportunity to students who wish to conduct a meeting within its limited open forum if such school uniformly provides that—

(1) the meeting is voluntary and student-initiated;

(2) there is no sponsorship of the meeting by the school, the government, or its agents or employees;

(3) employees or agents of the school or government are present at religious meetings only in a nonparticipatory capacity;

(4) the meeting does not materially and substantially interfere with the orderly conduct of educational activities within the school; and

(5) nonschool persons may not direct, conduct, control, or regularly attend activities of student groups.

(d) Federal or State authority nonexistent with respect to certain rights

Nothing in this subchapter shall be construed to authorize the United States or any State or political subdivision thereof-

(1) to influence the form or content of any prayer or other religious activity;

(2) to require any person to participate in prayer or other religious activity;

(3) to expend public funds beyond the incidental cost of providing the space for student-initiated meetings;

(4) to compel any school agent or employee to attend a school meeting if the content of the speech at the meeting is contrary to the beliefs of the agent or employee;

(5) to sanction meetings that are otherwise unlawful;

(6) to limit the rights of groups of students which are not of a specified numerical size; or

(7) to abridge the constitutional rights of any person.

(e) Unaffected Federal financial assistance to schools

Notwithstanding the availability of any other remedy under the Constitution or the laws of the United States, nothing in this subchapter shall be construed to authorize the United States to deny or withhold Federal financial assistance to any school.

(f) Authority of schools with respect to order-and-discipline, well-being, and voluntary presence concerns

Nothing in this subchapter shall be construed to limit the authority of the school, its agents or employees, to maintain order and discipline on school premises, to protect the well-being of students and faculty, and to assure that attendance of students at meetings is voluntary.

§ 4072.   Definitions.

As used in this subchapter—

(1) The term "secondary school" means a public school which provides secondary education as determined by State law.

(2) The term "sponsorship" includes the act of promoting, leading, or participating in a meeting. The assignment of a teacher, administrator, or other school employee to a meeting for custodial purposes does not constitute sponsorship of the meeting.

(3) The term "meeting" includes those activities of student groups which are permitted under a school's limited open forum and are not directly related to the school curriculum.

(4) The term "noninstructional time" means time set aside by the school before actual classroom instruction begins or after actual classroom instruction ends.

NOTES AND QUESTIONS

1. *Protecting Claims of Conscience.* Note that the Equal Access Act protects not only religious speech, but also nonreligious speech. Dean Rodney K. Smith has suggested that the Court is moving toward using the term "conscience," as opposed to "religion," in nonestablishment provision analysis. Acknowledging that it is difficult "to predict with confidence the Court's direction," Smith sees in this move "a larger agenda for the Court—one that might well expand protection for religious and related liberty." Smith, "Conscience, Coercion and the Establishment of Religion: The Beginning of an End to the Wandering of a

Wayward Judiciary?" 43 *Case W. Res. L. Rev.* 917 (1993). He recognizes that the line of cases culminating in *Employment Division v. Smith* [Chapter Eleven, section 10] demonstates "the Court's reluctance to broaden the right of free exercise from religion to conscience." Hence he concludes that broader protection of conscience would have to be legislative, as was the case in the conscientious objector context [Chapter Eleven, section 4]. "By broadening the free exercise right to include matters of conscience, as well as religion, Congress could do much to help further human rights and would also be taking a significant step in the direction of creating a unified theory of the religion provision. Conscience-based theory also might eliminate the historic tension between the Free Exercise and Establishment Clauses." *See also* Michael J. Sandel, "Freedom of Conscience or Freedom of Choice?," in James D. Hunter & Os Guinness eds., *Articles of Peace: the Religious Liberty Clauses and the American Public Philosophy* 74 (1990).

The Anti–Defamation League of B'nai B'rith, which had litigated in all of the cases denying equal access to high school students and which opposed the legislation, now argued that the Equal Access Act was itself an unconstitutional establishment, enacted solely to promote prayer, entangling the public school in the supervision and arrangement of religious meetings, symbolically giving state support to religion, and in general violating the principle established by *McCollum* [this section above] that religion should be off the campus of a public school. See Anti–Defamation League, *Religion and the Public Schools* (1984) 9–15. Counsel for Bridget Mergens urged that she had a constitutional right to engage in student-initiated, student-led prayer on the premises of a public school. The Court thought it enough to uphold the constitutionality of the Equal Access Act.

Board of Education of the Westside Community Schools v. Mergens

496 U.S. 226 (1990).

Allen E. Daubman argued the cause for petitioners. With him on the briefs were *Verne Moore, Jr., Marc D. Stern*, and *Amy Adelson*.

Jay Alan Sekulow argued the cause for private respondents. With him on the brief were *Douglas W. Davis, Robert K. Skolrood, Douglas Veith*, and *Charles E. Rice*. Solicitor General *Kenneth Starr* argued the cause for the United States. With him on the brief were Acting Assistant Attorney General *Schiffer*, Deputy Solicitor General *Roberts*, and *Anthony J. Steinmeyer*.

Briefs of amici curiae urging reversal were filed for the American Jewish Committee et al. by *Samuel Rabinove, Richard T. Foltin*, and *Lee Boothby*; for People for the American Way by *William R. Weissman, David W. Danner*, and *Susan M. Liss*; for the Anti–Defamation League of B'nai B'rith et al. by *Richard E. Shevitz, Ruti G. Teitel, Meyer Eisenberg, Jeffrey P. Sinensky, Steven M. Freeman*, and *Jill L. Kahn*; and for the National School Boards Association by *Gwendolyn H. Gregory, August W. Steinhilber*, and *Thomas A. Shannon*.

Briefs of amici curiae urging affirmance were filed for the Baptist Joint Committee on Public Affairs et al. by *Douglas Laycock, Samuel E. Ericsson, Forest D. Montgomery, Oliver S. Thomas, J. Brent Walker*, and *Wilford W. Kirton, Jr.*; for the Catholic League for Religious and Civil Rights by *Nancy J. Gannon*; for Concerned Women for America by *Jordan W. Lorence, Cimron Campbell*, and *Wendell R. Bird*; for Christian Advocates Serving Evangelism by *Wendell R. Bird*; for the Knights of Columbus by *Kevin T. Baine* and *Kevin J. Hasson*; for the Rutherford Institute et al. by *John W. Whitehead*; for the Southern Center for Law & Ethics by *Albert L. Jordan*; for the United States Catholic Conference by *Mark E. Chopko* and *John A. Liekweg*; for Tara Lynn Burr et al. by *Michael W. McConnell, Robert Hale, Michael J. Woodruff, Kimberlee W. Colby, Edward McGlynn Gaffney, Jr., Thomas C. Hill, Robert J. Cynkar*, and *David L. White*; for *Richard Collin Mangrum*, pro se; and for Dr. David Moshman by *Andrew J. Ekonomou*. Briefs of amici curiae were filed for the Campus Crusade for Christ, Inc., by *Robert R. Thompson*; and for Specialty Research Associates, Inc., by *Thomas Patrick Monaghan*.

■ JUSTICE O'CONNOR delivered the opinion of the Court, except as to Part III.

This case requires us to decide whether the Equal Access Act, 98 Stat. 1302, 20 U.S.C. §§ 4071–4074, prohibits Westside High School from denying a student religious group permission to meet on school premises during noninstructional time, and if so, whether the Act, so construed, violates the Establishment Clause of the First Amendment.

I

Students at Westside High School are permitted to join various student groups and clubs, all of which meet after school hours on school premises. The students may choose from approximately 30 recognized groups on a voluntary basis.

School Board Policy 5610 concerning "Student Clubs and Organizations" recognizes these student clubs as a "vital part of the total education program as a means of developing citizenship, wholesome attitudes, good human relations, knowledge and skills." Board Policy 5610 also provides that each club shall have faculty sponsorship and that "clubs and organizations shall not be sponsored by any political or religious organization, or by any organization which denies membership on the basis of race, color, creed, sex or political belief." Board Policy 6180 on "Recognition of Religious Beliefs and Customs" requires that "[s]tudents adhering to a specific set of religious beliefs or holding to little or no belief shall be alike respected." In addition, Board Policy 5450 recognizes its students' "Freedom of Expression," consistent with the authority of the board....

In January 1985, respondent Bridget Mergens met with Westside's Principal, Dr. Findley, and requested permission to form a Christian club at the school. The proposed club would have the same privileges and meet on the same terms and conditions as other Westside student groups, except that the proposed club would not have a faculty sponsor. According to the students' testimony at trial, the club's purpose would have been, among other things, to permit the students to read and discuss the Bible, to have fellowship, and to pray together. Membership would have been voluntary and open to all students regardless of religious affiliation.

Findley denied the request, as did Associate Superintendent Tangdell.... The school officials explained that school policy required all student clubs to have a faculty sponsor, which the proposed religious club would not or could not have, and that a religious club at the school would violate the Establishment Clause. Respondents, by and through their parents as next friends, then brought this suit in the United States District Court for the District of Nebraska seeking declaratory and injunctive relief. They alleged that petitioners' refusal to permit the proposed club to meet at Westside violated the Equal Access Act, which prohibits public secondary schools that receive federal financial assistance and that maintain a "limited open forum" from denying "equal access" to students who wish to meet within the forum on the basis of the content of the speech at such meetings. Respondents further alleged that petitioners' actions denied them their First and Fourteenth Amendment rights to freedom of speech, association, and the free exercise of religion.

Petitioners responded that the Equal Access Act did not apply to Westside and that, if the Act did apply, it violated the Establishment Clause of the First Amendment and was therefore unconstitutional. The United States intervened in the action to defend the constitutionality of the Act.

The District Court entered judgment for petitioners. The court held that the Act did not apply in this case because Westside did not have a "limited open forum" as defined by the Act—all of Westside's student clubs, the court concluded, were curriculum-related and tied to the educational function of the school. The court rejected respondents' constitutional claims, reasoning that Westside did not have a limited public forum as set forth in *Widmar v. Vincent* [section 3 below] and that Westside's denial of respondents' request was reasonably related to legitimate pedagogical concerns, see *Hazelwood School Dist. v. Kuhlmeier*, 484 U.S. 260, 273 (1988).

The United States Court of Appeals for the Eighth Circuit reversed, [holding] that the District Court erred in concluding that all the existing student clubs at Westside were curriculum related. The Court of Appeals noted that the "broad interpretation" advanced by the Westside school officials "would make the [Equal Access Act] meaningless" and would allow any school to "arbitrarily deny access to school facilities to any unfavored student club on the basis of its speech content," which was "exactly the result that Congress sought to prohibit by enacting the [Act]." The Court of Appeals instead found that "[m]any of the student clubs at WHS, including the chess club, are noncurriculum-related." Accordingly, because it found that Westside maintained a limited open forum under the Act, the Court of Appeals concluded that the Act applied to "forbi[d] discrimination against [respondents'] proposed club on the basis of its religious content." The Court of Appeals then rejected petitioners' contention that the Act violated the Establishment Clause. Noting that the Act extended the decision in *Widmar* to public secondary schools, the Court of Appeals concluded that "[a]ny constitutional attack on the [Act] must therefore be predicated on the difference between secondary school students and university students." Because "Congress considered the difference in the maturity level of secondary students and university students before passing the [Act]," the Court of Appeals held, on the basis of Congress' factfinding, that the Act did not violate the Establishment Clause. We granted certiorari, and now affirm.

II

A

In *Widmar* we invalidated, on free speech grounds, a state university regulation that prohibited student use of school facilities " 'for purposes of religious worship or religious teaching.' " In doing so, we held that an "equal access" policy would not violate the Establishment Clause under our decision in *Lemon* . . . . We noted, however, that "[u]niversity students are, of course, young adults. They are less impressionable than younger students and should be able to appreciate that the University's policy is one of neutrality toward religion."

In 1984, Congress extended the reasoning of *Widmar* to public secondary schools.

B

The obligation to grant equal access to student groups is triggered if Westside maintains a "limited open forum"—i.e., if it permits one or more "noncurriculum related student groups" to meet on campus before or after classes. [Justice O'Connor focused on the term "noncurriculum related student group," not defined in the Act.] Because the purpose of granting equal access is to prohibit discrimination between religious or political clubs on the one hand and other noncurriculum-related student groups on the other, the Act is premised on the notion that a religious or political club is itself likely to be a noncurriculum-related student group. It follows, then, that a student group that is "curriculum related" must at least have a more direct relationship to the curriculum than a religious or political club would have . . . .

[T]he Act, which was passed by wide, bipartisan majorities in both the House and the Senate, reflects at least some consensus on a broad legislative purpose. The Committee Reports indicate that the Act was intended to address perceived widespread discrimination against religious speech in public schools, and, as the language of the Act indicates, its sponsors contemplated that the Act would do more than merely validate the status quo.

In light of this legislative purpose, we think that the term "noncurriculum related student group" is best interpreted broadly to mean any student group that does not directly relate to the body of courses offered by the school. In our view, a student group directly relates to a school's curriculum if the subject matter of the group is actually taught, or will soon be taught, in a regularly offered course; if the subject matter of the group concerns the body of courses as a whole; if participation in the group is required for a particular course; or if participation in the group results in academic credit.

For example, a French club would directly relate to the curriculum if a school taught French in a regularly offered course or planned to teach the subject in the near future.... The existence of such groups at a school would not trigger the Act's obligations.

On the other hand, unless a school could show that groups such as a chess club, a stamp collecting club, or a community service club fell within our description of groups that directly relate to the curriculum, such groups would be "noncurriculum related student groups" for purposes of the Act. The existence of such groups would create a "limited open forum" under the Act and would prohibit the school from denying equal access to any other student group on the basis of the content of that group's speech. Whether a specific student group is a "noncurriculum related student group" will therefore depend on a particular school's curriculum, but such determinations would be subject to factual findings well within the competence of trial courts to make....

C

[Applying this definition to the facts in *Mergens*, the Court found the Act triggered by the Westside's approximately 30 voluntary student clubs, such as Interact (a service club related to Rotary International); Chess Club, and Subsurfers (a club for students interested in scuba diving)].We therefore conclude that Westside permits "one or more noncurriculum related student groups to meet on school premises during noninstructional time." Because Westside maintains a "limited open forum" under the Act, it is prohibited from discriminating, based on the content of the students' speech, against students who wish to meet on school premises during noninstructional time....

The remaining statutory question is whether petitioners' denial of respondents' request to form a religious group constitutes a denial of "equal access" to the school's limited open forum. Although the school apparently permits respondents to meet informally after school, respondents seek equal access in the form of official recognition by the school. Official recognition allows student clubs to be part of the student activities program and carries with it access to the school newspaper, bulletin boards, the public address system, and the annual Club Fair. Given that the Act explicitly prohibits denial of "equal access ... to ... any students who wish to conduct a meeting within [the school's] limited open forum" on the basis of the religious content of the speech at such meetings, we hold that Westside's denial of respondents' request to form a Christian club denies them "equal access" under the Act.

Because we rest our conclusion on statutory grounds, we need not decide—and therefore express no opinion on—whether the First Amendment requires the same result.

III

Petitioners ... maintain that because the school's recognized student activities are an integral part of its educational mission, official recognition of respondents' proposed club would effectively incorporate religious activities into the school's official program, endorse participation in the religious club, and provide the club with an official platform to proselytize other students.

We disagree. In *Widmar*, we applied the three-part *Lemon* test to hold that an "equal access" policy, at the university level, does not violate the Establishment Clause.... First, we stated that a university's forum does not "confer any imprimatur of state approval on religious sects or practices." Indeed, the message is one of neutrality rather than endorsement; if a State refused to let religious groups use facilities open to others, then it would demonstrate not neutrality but hostility toward religion. "The Establishment Clause does not license government to treat religion and those who teach or practice it, simply by virtue of their status as such, as subversive of American ideals and therefore subject to unique disabilities." *McDaniel v. Paty* (Brennan, J., concurring in judgment) [Chapter Fifteen, section 2]. Second, we noted that "[t]he [University's] provision of benefits to [a] broad ... spectrum of groups"—both nonreligious and religious speakers—was "an important index of secular effect."

We think the logic of *Widmar* applies with equal force to the Equal Access Act. As an initial matter, the Act's prohibition of discrimination on the basis of "political, philosophical, or other" speech as well as religious speech is a sufficient basis for meeting the secular purpose prong of the *Lemon* test (citations omitted). Congress' avowed purpose—to prevent discrimination against religious and other types of speech—is undeniably secular (citations omitted)....

Petitioners' principal contention is that the Act has the primary effect of advancing religion. Specifically, petitioners urge that, because the student religious meetings are held under school aegis, and because the State's compulsory attendance laws bring the students together (and thereby provide a ready-made audience for student evangelists), an objective observer in the position of a secondary school student will perceive official school support for such religious meetings....

We disagree. First, ... there is a crucial difference between government speech endorsing religion, which the Establishment Clause forbids, and private speech endorsing religion, which the Free Speech and Free Exercise Clauses protect. We think that secondary school students are mature enough and are likely to understand that a school does not endorse or support student speech that it merely permits on a nondiscriminatory basis. Cf. *Tinker v. Des Moines Independent Community School Dist.*, 393 U.S. 503 (1969) (no danger that high school students' symbolic speech implied school endorsement); *Barnette*, [Chapter Eleven, section 3]. See generally Note, 92 Yale L. J. 499, 507–509 (1983) (summarizing research in adolescent psychology). The proposition that schools do not endorse everything they fail to censor is not complicated....

Indeed, we note that Congress specifically rejected the argument that high school students are likely to confuse an equal access policy with state sponsorship of religion. [citing Senate Report: "[S]tudents below the college level are capable of distinguishing between State-initiated, school sponsored, or teacher-led religious speech on the one hand and student-initiated, student-led religious speech on the other."] Given the deference due "the duly enacted and carefully considered decision of a coequal and representative branch of our Government," *Walters v. National Assn. of Radiation Survivors*, 473 U.S. 305, 319 (1985), we do not lightly second-guess such legislative judgments, particularly where the judgments are based in part on empirical determinations.

Second, we note that the Act expressly limits participation by school officials at meetings of student religious groups, and that any such meetings must be held during "noninstructional time." The Act therefore avoids the problems of "the students' emulation of teachers as role models" and "mandatory attendance requirements," *Edwards* [section 2G below]; *McCollum* [section 2A above]. To be sure, the possibility of student peer pressure remains, but there is little if any risk of official state endorsement or coercion where no formal classroom activities are involved and no school officials actively participate....

Third, the broad spectrum of officially recognized student clubs at Westside, and the fact that Westside students are free to initiate and organize additional student clubs, counteract any possible message of official endorsement of or preference for religion or a particular religious belief. Although a school may not itself lead or direct a religious club, a school that permits a student-initiated and student-led religious club to meet after school, just as it permits any other student group to do, does not convey a message of state approval or endorsement of the particular religion. Under the Act, a school with a limited open forum may not lawfully deny access to a Jewish students' club, a Young Democrats club, or a philosophy club devoted to the study of Nietzsche. To the extent that a religious club is merely one of many different student-initiated voluntary clubs, students should perceive no message of government endorsement of religion. Thus, we conclude that the Act does not, at least on its face and as applied to Westside, have the primary effect of advancing religion....

[The Court also rejected the claim that compliance with the Act would risk excessive entanglement between government and religion, noting that the Act forbids faculty monitors to direct or control the activities of student groups.]

Accordingly, we hold that the Equal Access Act does not on its face contravene the Establishment Clause. Because we hold that petitioners have violated the Act, we do not decide respondents' claims under the Free Speech and Free Exercise Clauses. For the foregoing reasons, the judgment of the Court of Appeals is affirmed. It is so ordered.

JUSTICE KENNEDY, joined by JUSTICE SCALIA filed an opinion concurring in the judgment. He agreed that the Act does not violate the nonestablishment provision. Rather than rest this conclusion on the three criteria in *Lemon*, he noted that since the accommodation of religion mandated by the Act is a neutral one, in the context of this case it suffices to inquire whether the Act violates either of two principles. First, the government cannot give direct benefits to religion in such a degree that it in fact establishes a state religion or religious faith, or tends to do so. *Allegheny* (Kennedy, J., concurring in judgment in part and dissenting in part). Any incidental benefits that accompany official recognition of a religious club under the Act's criteria do not lead to the establishment of religion under this standard. *Widmar*. Second, the government cannot coerce any student to participate in a religious activity. *Allegheny*. The Act also satisfies this standard, since nothing on its face or in the facts of this case demonstrates that its enforcement will pressure students to participate in such an activity.

JUSTICE MARSHALL, joined by JUSTICE BRENNAN, filed a separate statement concurring in the judgment. Although agreeing that the Act as applied to Westside could withstand nonestablishment provision scrutiny, Marshall concluded that "the inclusion of the Christian club in the type of forum presently established at the school, without more, will not assure government neutrality toward religion." The Marshall opinion introduced a tension between the free speech and nonestablishment provisions that did not surface in *Widmar*. Marshall suggested that the failure of a school to stand apart from religious speech can convey a message that the school endorses, rather than merely tolerates, that speech. He urged that the "particular vigilance" the Court had shown in monitoring compliance with the nonestablishment provision in elementary and secondary schools, *Edwards* should extend to monitoring the actual effects of an "equal access" policy. Why is such monitoring necessary in this context but fatal in the context of funding of religious elementary schools [section 1 above]? Marshall distinguished *Widmar* "in light of the substantially different character of the student forum at issue here." In *Widmar*, he said, the state university maintained a wide-open and independent forum, affording many ideological organizations access to school facilities; took concrete steps to assure that the university's name was not identified with the policies or programs of any student group; and emphasized the autonomy of its students. Marshall concluded that Westside must take steps to fully "disassociate itself from the Christian club's religious speech and avoid appearing to sponsor or endorse the club's goals." Marshall expressed the view that the high school "could, for example, entirely discontinue encouraging student participation in clubs and clarify that the clubs are not instrumentally related to the school's overall mission. Or, if Westside sought to continue its general endorsement of those clubs that did not engage in controversial speech, it could do so if it also affirmatively disclaimed endorsement of the Christian club."

JUSTICE STEVENS dissented on the ground that the avoidance of a "patently bizarre result" necessitated a negative answer to the question: "Can Congress really have intended to issue an order to every public high school in the Nation stating, in substance, that if you sponsor a chess club, a scuba diving club, or a French club—without having formal classes in those subjects—you must also open your doors to every religious, political, or social organization, no matter how controversial or distasteful its views may be?" He insisted that a "fair review of the legislative history" of the Act discloses that "Congress intended to recognize a much narrower forum than the Court has legislated into existence today."

Since Justice Stevens was of the view that the Act was not triggered on the facts of this case, it was unnecessary for him to reach the establishment provision question. Nevertheless, he thought it appropriate to point out that the question is much more difficult than deciding whether the Act might run afoul of the provision because of the danger that some students would mistakenly believe that the student-initiated religious clubs are sponsored by the school. According to Stevens, the Court's construction of the statute obliged it to answer a further question: "whether the Act violates the Establishment Clause by authorizing religious organizations to meet on high school grounds even when the high school's teachers and administrators deem it unwise to admit controversial or partisan organizations of any kind." Stevens concluded: "The Court's construction of this Act leads to a sweeping intrusion by the Federal Government into the operation of our public schools, and does so despite the absence of any indication that Congress intended to divest local school districts of their power to shape the educational environment. If a high school administration continues to believe that it is sound policy to exclude controversial groups, such as political clubs, the Ku Klux Klan, and perhaps gay rights advocacy groups, from its facilities, it now must also close its doors to traditional extracurricular activities that are noncontroversial but not directly related to any course being offered at the school. Congress made frequent reference to the primacy of local control in public education, and the legislative history of the Act is thus inconsistent with the Court's rigid definition of 'noncurriculum related groups.' Indeed, the very fact that Congress omitted any definition in the statute itself is persuasive evidence of an intent to allow local officials broad discretion in deciding whether or not to create limited public fora. I see no reason—and no evidence of congressional intent—to constrain that discretion any more narrowly than our holding in *Widmar* requires."

F. PRAYER AT GRADUATION CEREMONIES AND ATHLETIC CONTESTS

NOTES AND QUESTIONS

1. *Graduation Ceremonies*. James Grossberg and other graduating high school seniors and their parents sought an injunction against the saying of a short, audible prayer by representatives of the senior class at graduation ceremonies. Attendance at the ceremonies was voluntary; seniors could have their diplomas mailed to them. In *Grossberg v. Deusebio*, 380 F. Supp. 285 (E.D. Va. 1974), the court, per Judge Merhige, refused to grant the injunction, writing that the occasion was a ceremony geared primarily to the award of honors and diplomas. All other portions of the program are peripheral to this function.... I can hardly perceive that the few moments ... create any significant risk of significant aid to religion. Not every involvement of religion in public life is violative of the Establishment Clause." *Accord, Wood v. Mt. Lebanon Township School District*, 342 F. Supp. 1293 (W. D. Penn. 1972); *Wiest v. Mt. Lebanon School District* 457 Pa. 166, 320 A.2d 362 (1974), *cert. denied*, 419 U.S. 967 (1974).

For several years the principals of the Providence public schools have invited clergy to deliver invocations and benedictions at graduations. In the following case, Robert E. Lee, the principal of the Nathan Bishop Middle School, invited Rabbi David Gutterman to do so. Lee gave the rabbi a two-page pamphlet, prepared by the National Conference of Christians and Jews, giving general advice on inclusive prayer for civic occasions, and advised him that his prayers at graduation should be nonsectarian. Justice Kennedy viewed this as evidence that a state actor "directed and controlled the content of the prayers." Kennedy invoked *Engel* [this section above] for the proposition that "it is no part of the business of government to compose official prayers for any group of the American people to recite as a part of a religious program carried on by government." Rabbi Gutterman offered the following Invocation at the beginning of the ceremony: "God of the Free, Hope of the Brave: For the legacy of America where diversity is celebrated and the rights of minorities are protected, we thank You. May these young men and women grow up to enrich it. For the liberty of America, we thank You. May these new graduates grow up to guard it. For the political process of America in which all its citizens may participate, for its court system where all may seek justice we thank You. May those we honor this morning always turn to it in trust. For the destiny of America we thank You. May the graduates of Nathan Bishop Middle School so live that they might help to share it. May our aspirations for our country and for these young people, who are our hope for the future, be richly fulfilled. Amen." At the close of the ceremony he offered the following benediction: "O God, we are grateful to You for having endowed us with the capacity for learning which we have celebrated on this joyous commencement. Happy families give thanks for seeing their children achieve an important milestone. Send Your blessings upon the teachers and administrators who helped prepare them. The graduates now need strength and guidance for the future, help them to understand that we are not complete with academic knowledge alone. We must each strive to fulfill what You require of us all: To do justly, to love mercy, to walk humbly. We give thanks to You, Lord, for keeping us alive, sustaining us and allowing us to reach this special, happy occasion. Amen." Both the prayers and the pamphlet that Lee gave to Gutterman became focal points for a narrowly and—to gauge from the tone of Justice Scalia's dissent—sharply divided Court.

Counsel for the school principal and Solicitor General Kenneth Starr urged reconsideration of the *Lemon* test. The Court ruled that reassessment of *Lemon* was not required in order to decide this case, finding that the "pervasive" degree of government involvement with Rabbi Gutterman created "state-sponsored and state-directed religious exercise in public school" in violation of the Constitution. It acknowledged that "coercive pressures" on children, including peer pressure, in a secondary school setting might be "subtle and indirect," but nonetheless "as real as overt compulsion." But the Court did not jettison *Lemon* in favor of a coercion test. According to Kennedy, the principal's decision that an invocation and a benediction would be given was "as if a state statute decreed that the prayers must occur." And the principal's selection of Rabbi Gutterman to offer these two prayers was rife with "the potential for divisiveness over the choice of a particular member of the clergy to conduct the ceremony."

Lee v. Weisman

505 U.S. 577 (1992).

Charles J. Cooper argued the cause for petitioners. With him on the briefs were *Michael A. Carvin, Peter J. Ferrara, Robert J. Cynkar, Joseph A. Rotella* and *Jay Alan Sekulow*. Solicitor General *Starr* argued the cause for the United States as amicus curiae urging reversal. With him on the brief were Assistant Attorney General *Gerson*, Deputy Solicitor General *Roberts*, Deputy Assistant Attorney General *McGinnis*, and *Richard H. Seamon*. *Sandra A. Blanding* argued the cause for respondent. With her on the brief were *Steven R. Shapiro* and *John A. Powell*.

Briefs of amici curiae urging reversal were filed for the Board of Education of Alpine School District by *Brinton R. Burbridge* and *Merrill F. Nelson*; for the Christian Legal Society et al. by *Edward McGlynn Gaffney, Michael J. Woodruff, Samuel E. Ericsson,* and *Forest D. Montgomery*; for the Clarendon Foundation by *Kemp R. Harshman* and *Ronald D. Maines*; for Concerned Women for America et al. by *James Matthew Henderson, Sr., Jordan Lorence, Mark N. Troobnick,* and *Thomas Patrick Monaghan*; for Focus on the Family et al. by *Stephen H. Galebach* and *Laura D. Millman*; for the Liberty Counsel by *Mathew D. Staver*; for the National Jewish Commission on Law and Public Affairs by *Nathan Lewin* and *Dennis Rapps*; for the National Legal Foundation by *Robert K. Skolrood* and *Brian M. McCormick*; for the Rutherford Institute et al. by *John W. Whitehead, Alexis I. Crow, A. Eric Johnston, Stephen E. Hurst, Joseph Secola, Thomas S. Newberger, J. Brian Heller, Amy Dougherty, David Melton, Thomas W. Strahan, Robert R. Melnick, William Bonner, Larry Crain, W. Charles Bundren,* and *James Knicely*; for Specialty Research Associates, Inc., et al. by *Jordan Lorence*; for the Southern Baptist Convention Christian Life Commission by *Michael K. Whitehead* and *James M. Smart, Jr.*; and for the United States Catholic Conference by *Mark E. Chopko* and *Phillip H. Harris*.

Briefs of amici curiae urging affirmance were filed for Americans for Religious Liberty by *Ronald A. Lindsay*; and for the American Jewish Congress et al. by *Douglas Laycock*. Briefs of amici curiae were filed for the State of Delaware by *Charles M. Oberly III*, Attorney General of Delaware, *Michael F. Foster*, Solicitor General, *David S. Swayze*, and *David B. Ripsom*; for the Council on Religious Freedom et al. by *Lee Boothby, Robert W. Nixon, Walter E. Carson,* and *Rolland Truman*; for the Institute in Basic Life Principles by *Joe Reynolds*; for the National Coalition for Public Education and Religious Liberty et al. by *David B. Isbell* and *T. Jeremy Gunn*; and for the National School Boards Association by *Gwendolyn H. Gregory, August W. Steinhilber,* and *Thomas A. Shannon*.

■ Justice Kennedy delivered the opinion of the Court, in which Justices Blackmun, Stevens, O'Connor, and Souter joined.

School principals in the public school system of the city of Providence, Rhode Island, are permitted to invite members of the clergy to offer invocation and benediction prayers as part of the formal graduation ceremonies for middle schools and for high schools. The question before us is whether including clerical members who offer prayers as part of the official school graduation ceremony is consistent with the Religion Clauses of the First Amendment, provisions the Fourteenth Amendment makes applicable with full force to the States and their school districts.

I

A

In the Providence school system, most high school graduation ceremonies are conducted away from the school, while most middle school ceremonies are held on school premises.... The parties stipulate that attendance at graduation ceremonies is voluntary.... At Deborah's middle school ceremony ... the students stood for the Pledge of Allegiance and remained standing during the rabbi's prayers. Even on the assumption that there was a respectful moment of silence both before and after the prayers, the rabbi's two presentations must not have extended much beyond a minute each, if that.

The school board (and the United States, which supports it as amicus curiae) argued that these short prayers and others like them at graduation exercises are of profound meaning to many students and parents throughout this country who consider that due respect and acknowledgment for divine guidance and for the deepest spiritual aspirations of our people ought to be expressed at an event as important in life as a graduation. We assume this to be so in addressing the difficult case now before us, for the significance of the prayers lies also at the heart of Daniel and Deborah Weisman's case.

II

These dominant facts mark and control the confines of our decision: State officials direct the performance of a formal religious exercise at promotional and graduation ceremonies for secondary schools. Even for those students who object to the religious exercise, their attendance and participation in the state-sponsored religious activity are in a fair and real sense obligatory, though the school district does not require attendance as a condition for receipt of the diploma.

This case does not require us to revisit the difficult questions dividing us in recent cases, questions of the definition and full scope of the principles governing the extent of permitted accommodation by the State for the religious beliefs and practices of many of its citizens. See *Allegheny* [Chapter Thirteen, section 6]; *Wallace v. Jaffree* [section 2D above] *Lynch v. Donnelly* [Chapter Thirteen, section 6]. For without reference to those principles in other contexts, the controlling precedents as they relate to prayer and religious exercise in primary and secondary public schools compel the holding here that the policy of the city of Providence is an unconstitutional one. We can decide the case without reconsidering the general constitutional framework by which public schools' efforts to accommodate religion are measured. Thus we do not accept the invitation of petitioners and amicus the United States to reconsider our decision in *Lemon* [section 1 above]. The government involvement with religious activity in this case is pervasive, to the point of creating a state-sponsored and state-directed religious exercise in a public school. Conducting this formal religious observance conflicts with settled rules pertaining to prayer exercises for students, and that suffices to determine the question before us.

The principle that government may accommodate the free exercise of religion does not supersede the fundamental limitations imposed by the Establishment Clause. It is beyond dispute that, at a minimum, the Constitution guarantees that government may not coerce anyone to support or participate in religion or its exercise, or otherwise act in a way which "establishes a [state] religion or religious faith, or tends to do so." *Lynch* [Chapter Thirteen, section 6]; see also *Allegheny*, *Everson* [section 1 above]. The State's involvement in the school prayers challenged today violates these central principles.

That involvement is as troubling as it is undenied. A school official, the principal, decided that an invocation and a benediction should be given; this is a choice attributable to the State, and from a constitutional perspective it is as if a state statute decreed that the prayers must occur. The principal chose the religious participant, here a rabbi, and that choice is also attributable to the State. The reason for the choice of a rabbi is not disclosed by the record, but the potential for divisiveness over the choice of a particular member of the clergy to conduct the ceremony is apparent.

Divisiveness, of course, can attend any state decision respecting religions, and neither its existence nor its potential necessarily invalidates the State's attempts to accommodate religion in all cases. The potential for divisiveness is of particular relevance here though, because it centers around an overt religious exercise in a secondary school environment where subtle coercive pressures exist and where the student had no real alternative which would have allowed her to avoid the fact or appearance of participation.

The State's role did not end with the decision to include a prayer and with the choice of a clergyman. Principal Lee provided Rabbi Gutterman with a copy of the "Guidelines for Civic Occasions," and advised him that his prayers should be nonsectarian. Through these means the principal directed and controlled the content of the prayers. Even if the only sanction for ignoring the instructions were that the rabbi would not be invited back, we think no religious representative who valued his or her continued reputation and effectiveness in the community would incur the State's displeasure in this regard. It is a cornerstone principle of our Establishment Clause jurisprudence that "it is no part of the business of government to compose official prayers for any group of the American people to recite as a part of a religious program carried on by government," *Engel*, [section 2B above], and that is what the school officials attempted to do.

Petitioners argue, and we find nothing in the case to refute it, that the directions for the content of the prayers were a good-faith attempt by the school to ensure that the sectarianism which is so often the flashpoint for religious animosity be removed from the graduation ceremony. The concern is understandable, as a prayer which uses ideas or images identified with a particular religion may foster a different sort of sectarian rivalry than an invocation or benediction in terms more neutral. The school's explanation, however, does not resolve the dilemma caused by its participation. The question is not the good faith of the school in attempting to make the prayer acceptable to most persons, but the legitimacy of its undertaking that enterprise at all when the object is to produce a prayer to be used in a formal religious exercise which students, for all practical purposes, are obliged to attend. . . .

The First Amendment's Religion Clauses mean that religious beliefs and religious expression are too precious to be either proscribed or prescribed by the State. The design of the Constitution is that preservation and transmission of religious beliefs and worship is a responsibility and a choice committed to the private sphere, which itself is promised freedom to pursue that mission. . . .

These concerns have particular application in the case of school officials, whose effort to monitor prayer will be perceived by the students as inducing a participation they might otherwise reject. Though the efforts of the school officials in this case to find common ground appear to have been a good-faith attempt to recognize the common aspects of religions and not the divisive ones, our precedents do not permit school officials to assist in composing prayers as an incident to a formal exercise for their students. *Engel*. And these same precedents caution us to measure the idea of a civic religion against the central meaning of the Religion Clauses of the First Amendment, which is that all creeds must be tolerated and none favored. The suggestion that government may establish an official or civic religion as a means of avoiding the establishment of a religion with more specific creeds strikes us as a contradiction that cannot be accepted.

The degree of school involvement here made it clear that the graduation prayers bore the imprint of the State and thus put school-age children who objected in an untenable position. We turn our attention now to consider the position of the students, both those who desired the prayer and she who did not.

To endure the speech of false ideas or offensive content and then to counter it is part of learning how to live in a pluralistic society, a society which insists upon open discourse towards the end of a tolerant citizenry. And tolerance presupposes some mutuality of obligation. It is argued that our constitutional vision of a free society requires confidence in our own ability to accept or reject ideas of which we do not approve, and that prayer at a high school graduation does nothing more than offer a choice. By the time they are seniors, high school students no doubt have been required to attend classes and assemblies and to complete assignments exposing them to ideas they find distasteful or immoral or absurd or all of these. Against this background, students may consider it an odd measure of justice to be subjected during the course of their educations to ideas deemed offensive and irreligious, but to be denied a brief, formal prayer ceremony that the school offers in return. This argument cannot prevail, however. It overlooks a fundamental dynamic of the Constitution.

The First Amendment protects speech and religion by quite different mechanisms. Speech is protected by ensuring its full expression even when the government participates, for the very object of some of our most important speech is to persuade the government to adopt an idea as its own. The method for protecting freedom of worship and freedom of conscience in religious matters is quite the reverse. In religious debate or expression the government is not a prime participant, for the Framers deemed religious establishment antithetical to the freedom of all. The Free Exercise Clause embraces a freedom of conscience and worship that has close parallels in the speech provisions of the First Amendment, but the Establishment Clause is a specific prohibition on forms of state intervention in religious affairs with no precise counterpart in the speech provisions.... [I]n the hands of government what might begin as a tolerant expression of religious views may end in a policy to indoctrinate and coerce. A state-created orthodoxy puts at grave risk that freedom of belief and conscience which are the sole assurance that religious faith is real, not imposed....

As we have observed before, there are heightened concerns with protecting freedom of conscience from subtle coercive pressure in the elementary and secondary public schools. See, e.g., *Schempp* (Goldberg, J., concurring) [section 2B above]; *Edwards* [section 2G below]; *Mergens* (Kennedy, J., concurring) [section 2E above]. Our decisions in *Engel* and *Schempp* recognize, among other things, that prayer exercises in public schools carry a particular risk of indirect coercion.... What to most believers may seem nothing more than a reasonable request that the nonbeliever respect their religious practices, in a school context may appear to the nonbeliever or dissenter to be an attempt to employ the machinery of the State to enforce a religious orthodoxy.

We need not look beyond the circumstances of this case to see the phenomenon at work. The undeniable fact is that the school district's supervision and control of a high school graduation ceremony places public pressure, as well as peer pressure, on attending students to stand as a group or, at least, maintain respectful silence during the invocation and benediction. This pressure, though subtle and indirect, can be as real as any overt compulsion. Of course, in our culture standing or remaining silent can signify adherence to a view or simple respect for the views of others. And no doubt some persons who have no desire to join a prayer have little objection to standing as a sign of respect for those who do. But for the dissenter of high school age, who has a reasonable perception that she is being forced by the State to pray in a manner her conscience will not allow, the injury is no less real. There can be no doubt that for many, if not most, of the students at the graduation, the act of standing or remaining silent was an expression of participation in the rabbi's prayer. That was the very point of the religious exercise. It is of little comfort to a dissenter, then, to be told that for her the act of standing or remaining in silence signifies mere respect, rather than participation. What matters is that, given our social conventions, a reasonable dissenter in this milieu could believe that the group exercise signified her own participation or approval of it.

Finding no violation under these circumstances would place objectors in the dilemma of participating, with all that implies, or protesting. We do not address whether that choice is acceptable if the affected citizens are mature adults, but we think the State may not, consistent with the Establishment Clause, place primary and secondary school children in this position. Research in psychology supports the common assumption that adolescents are often susceptible to pressure from their peers towards conformity, and that the influence is strongest in matters of social convention (citations omitted). To recognize that the choice imposed by the State constitutes an unacceptable constraint only acknowledges that the government may no more use social pressure to enforce orthodoxy than it may use more direct means. . . .

Our society would be less than true to its heritage if it lacked abiding concern for the values of its young people, and we acknowledge the profound belief of adherents to many faiths that there must be a place in the student's life for precepts of a morality higher even than the law we today enforce. We express no hostility to those aspirations, nor would our oath permit us to do so. A relentless and all-pervasive attempt to exclude religion from every aspect of public life could itself become inconsistent with the Constitution. See *Schempp* (Goldberg, J., concurring). We recognize that, at graduation time and throughout the course of the educational process, there will be instances when religious values, religious practices, and religious persons will have some interaction with the public schools and their students. See *Mergens* [section 2E above]. But these matters, often questions of accommodation of religion, are not before us. The sole question presented is whether a religious exercise may be conducted at a graduation ceremony in circumstances where, as we have found, young graduates who object are induced to conform. No holding by this Court suggests that a school can persuade or compel a student to participate in a religious exercise. That is being done here, and it is forbidden by the Establishment Clause of the First Amendment.

For the reasons we have stated, the judgment of the Court of Appeals is *Affirmed*.

■ JUSTICE BLACKMUN, with whom JUSTICE STEVENS and JUSTICE O'CONNOR join, concurring.

[With respect to the proposed coercion test, Blackmun wrote:] The Court holds that the graduation prayer is unconstitutional because the State "in effect required participation in a religious exercise." Although our precedents make clear that proof of government coercion is not necessary to prove an Establishment Clause violation, it is sufficient. Government pressure to participate in a religious activity is an obvious indication that the government is endorsing or promoting religion. But it is not enough that the government restrain from compelling religious practices: It must not engage in them either. *Schempp* (Goldberg, J., concurring). The Court repeatedly has recognized that a violation of the Establishment Clause is not predicated on coercion. *Schempp, Wallace v. Jaffree*, (O'Connor, J., concurring in judgment), *Nyquist* [section 1 above] ("[P]roof of coercion . . . [is] not a necessary element of any claim under the Establishment

Clause"). The Establishment Clause proscribes public schools from "conveying or attempting to convey a message that religion or a particular religious belief is favored or preferred," *Allegheny*, even if the schools do not actually "impos[e] pressure upon a student to participate in a religious activity."[6] *Mergens* (Kennedy, J., concurring in part and concurring in judgment)....

There is no doubt that attempts to aid religion through government coercion jeopardize freedom of conscience. Even subtle pressure diminishes the right of each individual to choose voluntarily what to believe. Representative [Daniel] Carroll explained during congressional debate over the Establishment Clause: "[T]he rights of conscience are, in their nature, of peculiar delicacy, and will little bear the gentlest touch of governmental hand." 1 Annals of Cong. 757 (1789). Our decisions have gone beyond prohibiting coercion, however, because the Court has recognized that "the fullest possible scope of religious liberty," *Schempp*, (Goldberg, J., concurring), entails more than freedom from coercion....

■ [JUSTICE SOUTER, with whom JUSTICE STEVENS and JUSTICE O'CONNOR joined, concurring, joined the whole of the Court's opinion, and fully agreed "that prayers at public school graduation ceremonies indirectly coerce religious observance." He wrote separately to emphasize his views that "the Establishment Clause applies to governmental practices that do not favor one religion or denomination over others, and that state coercion of religious conformity, over and above state endorsement of religious exercise or belief, is not a necessary element of an Establishment Clause violation."]

I

B

Some have challenged [*Everson*] by reading the Establishment Clause to permit "nonpreferential" state promotion of religion. The challengers argue that, as originally understood by the Framers, "[t]he Establishment Clause did not require government neutrality between religion and irreligion nor did it prohibit the Federal Government from providing nondiscriminatory aid to religion." *Wallace* (Rehnquist, J., dissenting); see also R. Cord, *Separation of Church and State: Historical Fact and Current Fiction* (1988). While a case has been made for this position, it is not so convincing as to warrant reconsideration of our settled law; indeed, I find in the history of the Clause's textual development a more powerful argument supporting the Court's jurisprudence following *Everson*.

[Justice Souter reviewed the text of early drafts of the First Amendment.] Though it accepted much of the Senate's work on the Bill of Rights,

---

6. As a practical matter, of course, anytime the government endorses a religious belief there will almost always be some pressure to conform. "When the power, prestige and financial support of government is placed behind a particular religious belief, the indirect coercive pressure upon religious minorities to conform to the prevailing officially approved religion is plain." *Engel*.

the House rejected the Senate's version of the Establishment Clause and called for a joint conference committee, to which the Senate agreed. The House conferees ultimately won out, persuading the Senate to accept this as the final text of the Religion Clauses: "Congress shall make no law respecting an establishment of religion, or prohibiting the free exercise thereof." What is remarkable is that, unlike the earliest House drafts or the final Senate proposal, the prevailing language is not limited to laws respecting an establishment of "a religion," "a national religion," "one religious sect," or specific "articles of faith."[2] The Framers repeatedly considered and deliberately rejected such narrow language and instead extended their prohibition to state support for "religion" in general.

———

[Justice Souter espoused the view that Framers distinguished between preferential and nonpreferential establishments, citing Laycock, "Nonpreferential" Aid, 902–906; Leonard W. Levy, *The Establishment Clause* 1–62, 91–119 (1986). In particular Souter relied on the Virginia statute for religious freedom [Chapter Six, section 2], written by Jefferson and sponsored by Madison, as evidence that the Framers of the First Amendment condemned all establishments, however nonpreferentialist, by guaranteeing broadly that "no man shall be compelled to frequent or support any religious worship, place, or ministry whatsoever," including his own. The other piece of evidence cited by Souter is an 1822 letter from Madison to Edward Livingston stating that "religion & Govt. will both exist in greater purity, the less they are mixed together."]

What we thus know of the Framers' experience underscores the observation of one prominent commentator, that confining the Establishment Clause to a prohibition on preferential aid "requires a premise that the Framers were extraordinarily bad drafters—that they believed one thing but adopted language that said something substantially different, and that they did so after repeatedly attending to the choice of language" [citing Laycock, "Nonpreferential" Aid, 882–883]. We must presume, since there is no conclusive evidence to the contrary, that the Framers embraced the significance of their textual judgment.[3] Thus, on balance, history neither contradicts nor warrants reconsid-

2. Some commentators have suggested that by targeting laws respecting "an" establishment of religion, the Framers adopted the very nonpreferentialist position whose much clearer articulation they repeatedly rejected. See, e.g., R. Cord, *Separation of Church and State* 11–12 (1988). Yet the indefinite article before the word "establishment" is better seen as evidence that the Clause forbids any kind of establishment, including a nonpreferential one. If the Framers had wished, for some reason, to use the indefinite term to achieve a narrow meaning for the Clause, they could far more aptly have placed it before the word "religion." See Laycock, "Nonpreferential" Aid to Religion: A False Claim About Original Intent, 27 Wm. & Mary L. Rev. 875, 884–885 (1986).

3. In his dissent in *Wallace v. Jaffree*, the Chief Justice rested his nonpreferentialist interpretation partly on the post-ratification actions of the early National Government. Aside from the willingness of some (but not all) early Presidents to issue ceremonial religious proclamations, which were at worst trivial breaches of the Establishment Clause, he cited such seemingly preferential aid as a treaty provision, signed by Jefferson, authorizing federal subsidization of a Roman Catholic priest and church for the Kaskaskia Indians. But this proves too much, for if the Establishment Clause permits a special appropriation of tax money for the religious eration of the settled principle that the Establishment Clause forbids support for religion in general no less than support for one religion or some.

II

Petitioners rest most of their argument on a theory that, whether or not the Establishment Clause permits extensive nonsectarian support for religion, it does not forbid the state to sponsor affirmations of religious belief that coerce neither support for religion nor participation in religious observance. I appreciate the force of some of the arguments supporting a "coercion" analysis of the Clause. See *Allegheny* (opinion of Kennedy, J.); McConnell, "Coercion: The Lost Element of Establishment," 27 Wm. & Mary L.Rev. 933 (1986). But we could not adopt that reading without abandoning our settled law, a course that, in my view, the text of the Clause would not readily permit. Nor does the extratextual evidence of original meaning stand so unequivocally at odds with the textual premise inherent in existing precedent that we should fundamentally reconsider our course.

A

Over the years, this Court has declared the invalidity of many noncoercive state laws and practices conveying a message of religious endorsement. *Allegheny; Wallace v. Jaffree; Engel....*

Our precedents may not always have drawn perfectly straight lines. They simply cannot, however, support the position that a showing of coercion is necessary to a successful Establishment Clause claim....

B

One may fairly say, as one commentator has suggested, that the government brought prayer into the ceremony "precisely because some people want a symbolic affirmation that government approves and endorses their religion, and because many of the people who want this affirmation place little or no value on the costs to religious minorities." Laycock, "Summary and Synthesis: The Crisis in Religious Liberty," 60 Geo. Wash. L. Rev. 841, 844 (1992).

Petitioners would deflect this conclusion by arguing that graduation prayers are no different from Presidential religious proclamations and similar official "acknowledgments" of religion in public life. But religious invocations in Thanksgiving Day addresses and the like, rarely noticed, ignored without effort, conveyed over an impersonal medium, and directed at no one in particular, inhabit a pallid zone worlds apart from official prayers delivered to a captive audience of public school students and their families.... When public school officials, armed with the State's authority, convey an endorsement of religion to their students, they strike near the

---

activities of a particular sect, it forbids virtually nothing, [citing Laycock, " 'Nonpreferential' Aid" 915]. Although evidence of historical practice can indeed furnish valuable aid in the interpretation of contemporary language, acts like the one in question prove only that public officials, no matter when they serve, can turn a blind eye to constitutional principle.

core of the Establishment Clause. However "ceremonial" their messages may be, they are flatly unconstitutional.

■ JUSTICE SCALIA, with whom CHIEF JUSTICE REHNQUIST, JUSTICE WHITE, and JUSTICE THOMAS join, dissenting.

Three Terms ago, I joined an opinion recognizing that the Establishment Clause must be construed in light of the "[g]overnment policies of accommodation, acknowledgment, and support for religion [that] are an accepted part of our political and cultural heritage." That opinion affirmed that "the meaning of the Clause is to be determined by reference to historical practices and understandings." It said that "[a] test for implementing the protections of the Establishment Clause that, if applied with consistency, would invalidate longstanding traditions cannot be a proper reading of the Clause." *Allegheny* [Chapter Thirteen, section 6] (Kennedy, J., concurring in judgment in part and dissenting in part).

These views of course prevent me from joining today's opinion, which is conspicuously bereft of any reference to history. In holding that the Establishment Clause prohibits invocations and benedictions at public-school graduation ceremonies, the Court—with nary a mention that it is doing so—lays waste a tradition that is as old as public-school graduation ceremonies themselves, and that is a component of an even more long-standing American tradition of nonsectarian prayer to God at public celebrations generally. As its instrument of destruction, the bulldozer of its social engineering, the Court invents a boundless, and boundlessly manipulable, test of psychological coercion.... Today's opinion shows more forcefully than volumes of argumentation why our Nation's protection, that fortress which is our Constitution, cannot possibly rest upon the changeable philosophical predilections of the Justices of this Court, but must have deep foundations in the historic practices of our people.

I

The history and tradition of our Nation are replete with public ceremonies featuring prayers of thanksgiving and petition, *Lynch, Marsh,* [Chapter Thirteen, section 5] *Wallace v. Jaffree,* (Rehnquist, J., dissenting); *Engel* (Stewart, J., dissenting), but ... the Court is so oblivious to our history as to suggest that the Constitution restricts "preservation and transmission of religious beliefs ... to the private sphere."

From our Nation's origin, prayer has been a prominent part of governmental ceremonies and proclamations [Justice Scalia cited The Declaration of Independence [Chapter Six, section 3A], the inaugural addresses of George Washington, Thomas Jefferson, James Madison, and George Bush, and the proclamation of a national celebration of Thanksgiving by George Washington [Chapter Seven, section1]. Scalia also noted that "the other two branches of the Federal Government also have a long-established practice of prayer at public events," citing *Marsh,* and the practice of opening the Court's own sessions with the invocation "God save the United States and this Honorable Court" since the days of Chief Justice Marshall].

In addition to this general tradition of prayer at public ceremonies, there exists a more specific tradition of invocations and benedictions at public school graduation exercises....

II

The Court presumably would separate graduation invocations and benedictions from other instances of public "preservation and transmission of religious beliefs" on the ground that they involve "psychological coercion." I find it a sufficient embarrassment that our Establishment Clause jurisprudence regarding holiday displays, see *Allegheny*, has come to "requir[e] scrutiny more commonly associated with interior decorators than with the judiciary." *American Jewish Congress v. Chicago*, 827 F.2d 120, 129 (CA7 1987) (Easterbrook, J., dissenting). But interior decorating is a rock-hard science compared to psychology practiced by amateurs. A few citations of "[r]esearch in psychology" that have no particular bearing upon the precise issue here, cannot disguise the fact that the Court has gone beyond the realm where judges know what they are doing. The Court's argument that state officials have "coerced" students to take part in the invocation and benediction at graduation ceremonies is, not to put too fine a point on it, incoherent....

The opinion manifests that the Court itself has not given careful consideration to its test of psychological coercion. For if it had, how could it observe, with no hint of concern or disapproval, that students stood for the Pledge of Allegiance, which immediately preceded Rabbi Gutterman's invocation? The government can, of course, no more coerce political orthodoxy than religious orthodoxy. *Barnette* [Chapter Eleven, section 3]. Moreover, since the Pledge of Allegiance has been revised since *Barnette* to include the phrase "under God," recital of the Pledge would appear to raise the same Establishment Clause issue as the invocation and benediction. If students were psychologically coerced to remain standing during the invocation, they must also have been psychologically coerced, moments before, to stand for (and thereby, in the Court's view, take part in or appear to take part in) the Pledge. Must the Pledge therefore be barred from the public schools (both from graduation ceremonies and from the classroom) ? In *Barnette* we held that a public school student could not be compelled to recite the Pledge; we did not even hint that she could not be compelled to observe respectful silence—indeed, even to stand in respectful silence—when those who wished to recite it did so. Logically, that ought to be the next project for the Court's bulldozer....

III

The deeper flaw in the Court's opinion does not lie in its wrong answer to the question whether there was state-induced "peer-pressure" coercion; it lies, rather, in the Court's making violation of the Establishment Clause hinge on such a precious question. The coercion that was a hallmark of historical establishments of religion was coercion of religious orthodoxy and of financial support by force of law and threat of penalty. Typically, attendance at the state church was required; only clergy of the official church could lawfully perform sacraments; and dissenters, if tolerated, faced an array of civil disabilities. L. Levy, *The Establishment Clause* 4 (1986). Thus, for example, in the Colony of Virginia, where the Church of England had been established, ministers were required by law to conform to the doctrine and rites of the Church of England; and all persons were required to attend church and observe the Sabbath, were tithed for the public support of Anglican ministers, and were taxed for the costs of building and repairing churches. *Id.*

The Establishment Clause was adopted to prohibit such an establishment of religion at the federal level (and to protect state establishments of religion from federal interference).... But there is simply no support for the proposition that the officially sponsored nondenominational invocation and benediction read by Rabbi Gutterman—with no one legally coerced to recite them—violated the Constitution of the United States....

Thus, while I have no quarrel with the Court's general proposition that the Establishment Clause "guarantees that government may not coerce anyone to support or participate in religion or its exercise," I see no warrant for expanding the concept of coercion beyond acts backed by threat of penalty—a brand of coercion that, happily, is readily discernible to those of us who have made a career of reading the disciples of Blackstone rather than of Freud. The Framers were indeed opposed to coercion of religious worship by the National Government; but, as their own sponsorship of nonsectarian prayer in public events demonstrates, they understood that "[s]peech is not coercive; the listener may do as he likes." *American Jewish Congress v. Chicago*, 827 F.2d, at 132 (Easterbrook, J., dissenting)....

Beyond the fact, stipulated to by the parties, that attendance at graduation is voluntary, there is nothing in the record to indicate that failure of attending students to take part in the invocation or benediction was subject to any penalty or discipline. Contrast this with, for example, the facts of *Barnette*: Schoolchildren were required by law to recite the Pledge of Allegiance; failure to do so resulted in expulsion, threatened the expelled child with the prospect of being sent to a reformatory for criminally inclined juveniles, and subjected his parents to prosecution (and incarceration) for causing delinquency. To characterize the "subtle coercive pressures," allegedly present here as the "practical" equivalent of the legal sanctions in *Barnette* is ... well, let me just say it is not a "delicate and fact-sensitive" analysis....

IV

Our Religion Clause jurisprudence has become bedeviled (so to speak) by reliance on formulaic abstractions that are not derived from, but positively conflict with, our long-accepted constitutional traditions. Foremost among these has been the so-called *Lemon* test, which has received well-earned criticism from many Members of this Court (citations omitted). The Court today demonstrates the irrelevance of *Lemon* by essentially ignoring it, and the interment of that case may be the one happy byproduct of the Court's otherwise lamentable decision. Unfortunately, however, the

Court has replaced *Lemon* with its psycho-coercion test, which suffers the double disability of having no roots whatever in our people's historic practice, and being as infinitely expandable as the reasons for psychotherapy itself. . . .

Church and state would not be such a difficult subject if religion were, as the Court apparently thinks it to be, some purely personal avocation that can be indulged entirely in secret, like pornography, in the privacy of one's room. For most believers it is not that, and has never been. Religious men and women of almost all denominations have felt it necessary to acknowledge and beseech the blessing of God as a people, and not just as individuals, because they believe in the "protection of divine Providence," as the Declaration of Independence put it, not just for individuals but for societies [Chapter Six, Section 3A]; because they believe God to be, as Washington's first Thanksgiving Proclamation put it, the "Great Lord and Ruler of Nations." [Chapter Seven, section 1] One can believe in the effectiveness of such public worship, or one can deprecate and deride it. But the longstanding American tradition of prayer at official ceremonies displays with unmistakable clarity that the Establishment Clause does not forbid the government to accommodate it. . . .

The Founders of our Republic knew the fearsome potential of sectarian religious belief to generate civil dissension and civil strife. And they also knew that nothing, absolutely nothing, is so inclined to foster among religious believers of various faiths a toleration—no, an affection—for one another than voluntarily joining in prayer together, to the God whom they all worship and seek. Needless to say, no one should be compelled to do that, but it is a shame to deprive our public culture of the opportunity, and indeed the encouragement, for people to do it voluntarily. The Baptist or Catholic who heard and joined in the simple and inspiring prayers of Rabbi Gutterman on this official and patriotic occasion was inoculated from religious bigotry and prejudice in a manner that cannot be replicated. To deprive our society of that important unifying mechanism, in order to spare the nonbeliever what seems to me the minimal inconvenience of standing or even sitting in respectful nonparticipation, is as senseless in policy as it is unsupported in law.

For the foregoing reasons, I dissent.

NOTES AND QUESTIONS

1. *Student–Led Prayer at High School Graduation Ceremonies*. While *Lee* was pending, the Court held the petition for certiorari in another case dealing with prayer at graduation ceremonies. In *Jones v. Clear Creek Independent School Dist.*, 930 F.2d 416 (5th Cir.1991), the lower court had held that it is permissible for public high school seniors to choose student volunteers to deliver nonsectarian, nonproselytizing invocations at their graduation ceremonies. The Court vacated this judgment and remanded for further consideration in the light of *Lee*. 505 U.S. 1215 (1992). On remand, the court remained of the view that this practice was not prohibited by *Lee*. *Jones v. Clear Creek Indep. Sch. Dist*, 977 F.2d 963 (5th Cir. 1992), reh'g, denied, 983 F.2d 234 (5th Cir. 1992), cert. denied, 508 U.S. 967 (1993).

2. *Student-led Prayer at College Graduation Ceremonies.* Noting that the *Lee* Court expressly left open the question whether graduation prayer would be acceptable "if the affected citizens are mature adults," lower courts have ruled that college students are sufficiently mature to understand that prayer at the commencement ceremonies of a public university does not constitute official endorsement of religion, sustaining the practice of invocations and benedictions in that setting. See *Tanford v. Brand*, 104 F.3d 982 (7th Cir.), cert. denied, 522 U.S. 814 (1997); *Chaudhuri v. State of Tennessee*, 130 F.3d 232 (6th Cir. 1997) ("*Lee* attached particular importance to the youth of the audience and the risk of peer pressure and 'indirect coercion' in the primary and secondary school context"), cert. denied, 523 U.S. 1024 (1998).

3. *Student-led Prayer at Athletic Contests.* Allowing high school students to offer a prayer at their graduation ceremonies suggested to some that students might also select a representative who might lead the student body with some sort of inspirational, uplifting words before a major event in the social life of Texans, such as Friday night football contests. At one school district a student elected to the office of "student council chaplain" delivered a prayer over the public address system before each varsity football game for the entire season. Parents of children—one Catholic, the other Mormon—attending the school challenged this practice in the district court as a violation of the nonestablishment provision. While the suit was pending, the school district modified its policy, permitting but not requiring prayer initiated and led by a student at all home games. The district court sustained this amended policy, but entered an order modifying that policy to permit only "nonsectarian, nonproselytizing prayer." The Court of Appeals reversed, holding the football prayer policy invalid on its face.

Santa Fe Independent School District v. Jane Doe

120 S. Ct. 2266 (2000).

■ JUSTICE STEVENS delivered the opinion of the Court.

[Urging the "crucial difference between government speech endorsing religion, which the Establishment Clause forbids, and private speech endorsing religion, which the Free Speech and Free Exercise Clauses protect. *Mergens* [section 2E above]," the school district contended that the speech at issue was private, not public. Justice Stevens, who had dissented in *Mergens*, now "certainly agree[d] with that distinction," but wrote that "the pregame invocations should be regarded as 'private speech.'"]

These invocations are authorized by a government policy and take place on government property at government-sponsored school-related events. "[N]ot every message delivered under such circumstances is the government's own, [but] that the pregame ceremony was not the sort of government-created forum in which an individual's contribution is not government speech. The school officials did not "evince either 'by policy or by practice,' any intent to open the [pregame ceremony] to 'indiscriminate use,' ... by the student body generally." *Hazelwood School Dist. v. Kuhlmeier*, 484 U.S. 260, 270 (1988) (*quoting Perry Ed. Assn. v. Perry Local*

Educators' Assn., 460 U.S. 37, 47 (1983)). Rather, the school allows only one student, the same student for the entire season, to give the invocation.

. . .

[Justice Stevens ruled that the election of the "student council chaplain" by the student body did not cure the constitutional defect in this policy.]

. . .

[S]tudent election does nothing to protect minority views but rather places the students who hold such views at the mercy of the majority. Because "fundamental rights may not be submitted to vote; they depend on the outcome of no elections," *West Virginia Bd. of Ed. v. Barnette*, Chapter Eleven, section 3] the District's elections are insufficient safeguards of diverse student speech. . . . [W]hile Santa Fe's majoritarian election might ensure that most of the students are represented, it does nothing to protect the minority; indeed, it likely serves to intensify their offense. . . .

Moreover, the District has failed to divorce itself from the religious content in the invocations. It has not succeeded in doing so, either by claiming that its policy is "one of neutrality rather than endorsement" or by characterizing the individual student as the "circuit-breaker" in the process. Contrary to the District's repeated assertions that it has adopted a "hands-off" approach to the pregame invocation, the realities of the situation plainly reveal that its policy involves both perceived and actual endorsement of religion. In this case, as we found in *Lee* [this section above], the "degree of school involvement" makes it clear that the pregame prayers bear "the imprint of the State and thus put school-age children who objected in an untenable position". . . .

The decision whether to deliver a message is first made by majority vote of the entire student body, followed by a choice of the speaker in a separate, similar majority election. Even though the particular words used by the speaker are not determined by those votes, the policy mandates that the "statement or invocation" be "consistent with the goals and purposes of this policy," which are "to solemnize the event, to promote good sportsmanship and student safety, and to establish the appropriate environment for the competition."

In addition to involving the school in the selection of the speaker, the policy, by its terms, invites and encourages religious messages. The policy itself states that the purpose of the message is "to solemnize the event." A religious message is the most obvious method of solemnizing an event. Moreover, the requirements that the message "promote good citizenship" and "establish the appropriate environment for competition" further narrow the types of message deemed appropriate, suggesting that a solemn, yet nonreligious, message, such as commentary on United States foreign policy, would be prohibited. Indeed, the only type of message that is expressly endorsed in the text is an "invocation"–a term that primarily describes an appeal for divine assistance. In fact, as used in the past at Santa Fe High

School, an "invocation" has always entailed a focused religious message. Thus, the expressed purposes of the policy encourage the selection of a religious message, and that is precisely how the students understand the policy. The results of the elections described in the parties' stipulation make it clear that the students understood that the central question before them was whether prayer should be a part of the pregame ceremony. We recognize the important role that public worship plays in many communities, as well as the sincere desire to include public prayer as a part of various occasions so as to mark those occasions' significance. But such religious activity in public schools, as elsewhere, must comport with the First Amendment. . . .

■ CHIEF JUSTICE REHNQUIST, with whom JUSTICE SCALIA and JUSTICE THOMAS join, dissenting.

The Court distorts existing precedent to conclude that the school district's student-message program is invalid on its face under the Establishment Clause. But even more disturbing than its holding is the tone of the Court's opinion; it bristles with hostility to all things religious in public life. Neither the holding nor the tone of the opinion is faithful to the meaning of the Establishment Clause, when it is recalled that George Washington himself, at the request of the very Congress which passed the Bill of Rights, proclaimed a day of "public thanksgiving and prayer, to be observed by acknowledging with grateful hearts the many and signal favors of Almighty God" [Chapter Seven, section 1].

We do not learn until late in the Court's opinion that respondents in this case challenged the district's student-message program at football games before it had been put into practice. . . . [T]he question is not whether the district's policy may be applied in violation of the Establishment Clause, but whether it inevitably will be.

The Court, venturing into the realm of prophesy, decides that it "need not wait for the inevitable" and invalidates the district's policy on its face. To do so, it applies the most rigid version of the oft-criticized test of *Lemon* [section 1 above]. [Justice Rehnquist then described the "checkered career" of *Lemon*].

Even if it were appropriate to apply the *Lemon* test here, the district's student-message policy should not be invalidated on its face. . . .

First, the Court misconstrues the nature of the "majoritarian election" permitted by the policy as being an election on "prayer" and "religion." To the contrary, the election permitted by the policy is a two-fold process whereby students vote first on whether to have a student speaker before football games at all, and second, if the students vote to have such a speaker, on who that speaker will be. . . .

[A]ny speech that may occur as a result of the election process here would be private, not government, speech. The elected student, not the government, would choose what to say. Support for the Court's holding cannot be found in any of our cases. And it essentially invalidates all student elections. A newly elected student body president, or even a newly elected prom king or queen, could use opportunities for public speaking to say prayers. Under the Court's view, the mere grant of power to the students to vote for such offices, in light of the fear that those elected might publicly pray, violates the Establishment Clause.

Second, with respect to the policy's purpose, the Court holds that "the simple enactment of this policy, with the purpose and perception of school endorsement of student prayer, was a constitutional violation." But the policy itself has plausible secular purposes: "[T]o solemnize the event, to promote good sportsmanship and student safety, and to establish the appropriate environment for the competition." Where a governmental body "expresses a plausible secular purpose" for an enactment, "courts should generally defer to that stated intent." *Wallace* [section 2D above]; *see also Mueller v. Allen* [section 1 above]. The Court grants no deference to—and appears openly hostile toward—the policy's stated purposes, and wastes no time in concluding that they are a sham.

For example, the Court dismisses the secular purpose of solemnization by claiming that it "invites and encourages religious messages." *Cf. Lynch* [Chapter Thirteen, section 6], (discussing the "legitimate secular purposes of solemnizing public occasions"). The Court so concludes based on its rather strange view that a "religious message is the most obvious means of solemnizing an event." But it is easy to think of solemn messages that are not religious in nature, for example urging that a game be fought fairly. And sporting events often begin with a solemn rendition of our national anthem, with its concluding verse "And this be our motto: 'In God is our trust.'" Under the Court's logic, a public school that sponsors the singing of the national anthem before football games violates the Establishment Clause. Although the Court apparently believes that solemnizing football games is an illegitimate purpose, the voters in the school district seem to disagree. Nothing in the Establishment Clause prevents them from making this choice. . . .

The Court also relies on our decision in *Lee v. Weisman* [this section above], to support its conclusion. In *Lee*, we concluded that the content of the speech at issue, a graduation prayer given by a rabbi, was "directed and controlled" by a school official. In other words, at issue in *Lee* was government speech. Here, by contrast, the potential speech at issue, if the policy had been allowed to proceed, would be a message or invocation selected or created by a student. That is, if there were speech at issue here, it would be private speech. The "crucial difference between government speech endorsing religion, which the Establishment Clause forbids, and private speech endorsing religion, which the Free Speech and Free Exercise Clauses protect," applies with particular force to the question of endorsement. *Mergens*.

Had the policy been put into practice, the students may have chosen a speaker according to wholly secular criteria—like good public speaking skills or social popularity—and the student speaker may have chosen, on her own accord, to deliver a religious message. Such an application of the policy would likely pass constitutional muster. *See Lee*, (Souter, J., concurring) ("If the State had chosen its graduation day speakers according to wholly secular criteria, and if one of those speakers (not a state actor) had individually chosen to deliver a religious message, it would be harder to attribute an endorsement of religion to the State'')....

The policy at issue here may be applied in an unconstitutional manner, but it will be time enough to invalidate it if that is found to be the case. I would reverse the judgment of the Court of Appeals.

G.   SCIENCE AND RELIGION IN THE CURRICULUM

NOTES AND QUESTIONS

1. *The Quest for Tests*: *Secular Purpose, Nondiscrimination, Endorsement, and Neutrality*. As Justice Rehnquist noted, *Stone v. Graham* marked the first occasion that the Court had invalidated a practice on the ground that it lacked a valid secular purpose. As early as *McCollum*, Justice Black assumed that what was occurring in public schools is "secular teaching," which Black simply takes to mean "nonreligious." In *Zorach*, Justice Douglas took a similar approach: "Government may not finance religious groups nor undertake religious instruction nor blend secular and sectarian education nor use secular institutions to force one or some religion on any person." In *Schempp*, Justice Clark acknowledged that "the State may not establish a 'religion of secularism' in the sense of affirmatively opposing or showing hostility to religion, thus 'preferring those who believe in no religion over those who do believe,' " citing *Zorach*, but he denied that putting an end to devotional reading of the Bible in public schools would have that effect. Clark concluded his opinion in *Schempp* by announcing that "the purpose or effect [of a practice challenged under the Establishment Clause must not] be to aid or oppose, to advance or retard" religion. Thus was born the first of the three standards in the *Lemon* test.

The Court sometimes distinguishes carefully between "secular purpose" and the motivations guiding legislators to enact law. For example, Justice O'Connor who served for many years in the Arizona legislature, wrote in *Mergens* [section 2E above]: "Even if some legislators were motivated by a conviction that religious speech in particular was valuable and worthy of protection, that alone would not invalidate the Act, because what is relevant is the legislative purpose of the statute, not the possibly religious motives of the legislators who enacted the law." Justice Black, who served for many years in the United States Senate, was highly doubtful of the Court's ability to discern either a statute's purpose or the legislators' motives, and viewed both tasks as irrelevant to the judicial function.

The secular purpose test has never been relied upon to invalidate a program funding any aspect of religious schools. For example, in *Mueller v. Allen*, Justice Rehnquist wrote that the Court is "reluctan[t] to attribute unconstitutional motives to the States, particularly when a plausible secular purpose for the State's program may be discerned from the face of the statute." But the Court has relied exclusively on this criterion in four cases dealing with religion in the public schools: *Stone v. Graham* (posting of ten commandments); *Wallace v. Jaffree* (school prayer); *Epperson v. Arkansas* (ban on teaching of evolution); and *Edwards v. Aguillard* (equal treatment of "creation science"). In all four of these cases the Court held the challenged legislation unconstitutional on the sole ground that the act served no identified secular purpose and has as its primary purpose the promotion of a particular religious belief. As you consider these cases, ask what is meant by "secular." It is frequently (e.g., in

Wallace, Epperson and *Edwards*) taken to mean "nonreligious." It was used in this sense by the dissenters in *Bowers v. Hardwick* [Chapter Sixteen, section 3]: "The legitimacy of secular legislation depends ... on whether the State can advance some justification for its law beyond its conformity to religious doctrine."

The term "secular" is not self-defining. Although the Court and many commentators use "secular" loosely to mean "non-religious," this identification has been challenged as inaccurate and unjust. The Williamsburg Charter, a bicentennial document celebrating religious freedom, urges that " 'Secular purpose' should not mean 'non-religious purpose' but 'general public purpose.' Otherwise, the impression is gained that 'public is equivalent to secular; religion is equivalent to private.' Such equations are neither accurate nor just." The Williamsburg Charter, 8 *J. L. & Relig.* 5, 14 (1990).

The privatization of religion is not a neutral position, but a construct deriving from one of the many streams of what is loosely known as "Enlightenment philosophy." Professor Myers argues that "although secular rationalism is part of the American tradition, privileging that conception of rationality would do violence to the views of most Americans." Richard S. Myers, "The Supreme Court and the Privatization of Religion," 41 *Cath. U. L. Rev.* 19, 74 (1991); Phillip E. Johnson, "Concepts and Compromises in First Amendment Religious Doctrine," 72 *Calif. L. Rev.* 817 (1984); David Louisell, "Does the Constitution Require a Purely Secular Society?," 26 *Cath. U. L. Rev.* 20 (1976); and Frederick Mark Gedicks, "Some Political Implications of Religious Belief," 4 *Notre Dame J. L. Ethics & Pub. Policy* 419, 432–39 (1990) (discussing problem of alienating religious citizens).

One measure of whether legislation is "secular" in the sense of promoting a "general public purpose" is whether it is "discriminatory." This term, however, also needs refinement. Professor Kurland proposed a generation ago that legislation was impermissible if it either provided a benefit or imposed a burden on the basis of religion. Philip Kurland, "Of Church and State in the Supreme Court," 28 *U. Chi. L. Rev.* 1 (1961). No one adopted this formulation because it was too broad and undifferentiated. Accommodation of religion is sometimes mandatory under the free exercise clause; see, e.g., *Thomas v. Review Bd.* [Chapter Eleven, section 4]; *Sherbert v. Verner* [Chapter Eleven, section 5]; *Wisconsin v. Yoder* [Chapter Eleven, section 7]. And legislatures are free, within limits, to make accommodations of religion that are not constitutionally mandated; for example, Title VII imposes a duty on employers to make reasonable accommodation of the religious practices and beliefs of employees [Chapter Eleven, section 6]. Some commentators see accommodation in tension with the secularity requirement. Another way of viewing accommodation of religion is to see it as part of the "general public purpose" of the Religion Clause. In this perspective, the nonestablishment principle does not defeat or contradict free exercise. It faciliatates and enables it. See, e.g., Michael W. McConnell, "Accommodation of Religion," 1985 *Sup. Ct. Rev.* 1. In this perspective irrational discrimination against religion would be a violation of the secularity requirement. As Justice Brennan wrote in *Larson v. Valente* [Chapter Fifteen, section 1]: "*selective* legislative imposition of burdens and advantages upon particular denominations" is prohibited. "The clearest command of the Establishment Clause is that one religious denomination cannot be officially preferred over another.... Free exercise ... can be guaranteed only when legislators—and voters—are required to accord to their own religions the very same treatment given to small, new, or unpopular denominations."

Justice O'Connor has attempted to link the secular purpose requirement to her theory that governmental practices are invalid if they create a perception that government is endorsing or disapproving of religion. *Lynch v. Donnelly* [Chapter Thirteen, section 6]. For her, the "secularity" of a statute becomes questionable if the statute sends a symbolic message that nonadherents to any particular religion are "outsiders, not members of the political community." She wrote in *Wallace v. Jaffree*: "It is not a trivial matter, however, to require that the legislature manifest a secular purpose and omit all sectarian endorsements from its laws. That requirement is precisely tailored to the Establishment Clause's purpose of assuring that Government not intentionally endorse religion or a religious practice."

At first blush, O'Connor's proposal contains the promise of greater sensitivity for religious minorities. It is not, however, easy to apply the endorsement test meaningfully. See, for example, *Allegheny* [Chapter Thirteen, section 6], where the Court rescued the Menorah from the fate accorded a nativity creche by pronouncing that the Menorah is secular. For whom? For the observant Jews who erected the Menorah? Under the endorsement test, judges can get lost in the ambiguity of the cultural meaning of religious messages. Some commentators have criticized the endorsement test as an unmanageable judicial intrusion on the political process. For example, Professor Smith writes: "the very concept of 'alienation,' or symbolic exclusion, is difficult to grasp.... 'Alienation' might refer to nothing more than an awareness by an individual that she belongs to a religious minority, accompanied by a realization that at least on some issues she is unlikely to be able to prevail in the political process.... That awareness may be discomforting. But is it the sort of phenomenon for which constitutional law can provide an efficacious remedy? Constitutional doctrine that stifles the message will not likely alter the reality—or a minority's awareness of that reality." Steven D. Smith, *Foreordained Failure: The Quest for a Constitutional Principle of Religious Freedom* 164–65 , n. 66 (1995); see also Smith, "Symbols, Perceptions, and Doctrinal Illusions: Establishment Neutrality and the 'No Endorsement' Test," 86 *Mich. L. Rev.* 266 (1987); and Michael W. McConnell, "Religious Freedom at a Crossroads," 59 *U. Chi. L. Rev.* 115, 148–51 (1992).

In the same article Professor McConnell also argues that when "secular" is used loosely to mean "non-religious"—as it typically is by the Court and commentators—"It is no longer intellectually credible to maintain that secular liberalism is simply the 'neutral position.'" *Id.* 134. And see McConnell, "Accommodation of Religion: An Update and a Response to Critics," 60 *Geo. Wash. L. Rev.* 685, 740 (1992) (Religion Clause not an instrument for "collective relativism," but a guarantee that all sects and modes of beliefs, religious as well as secular, may compete for allegiance of the people, without official preference). Contra, Kathleen M. Sullivan, "Religion and Liberal Democracy," 59 *U. Chi. L. Rev.* 195, 197–99 (1992) (Constitution commands a "secular public order").

Dean Garvey argues that the Constitution protects and promotes free exercise of religion because religion is conceived of as valuable in its itself. Thus religious freedom is not a instrumental value deriving from or pointing to some larger principle, such as "neutrality." Instead, religious freedom is what ethicists call a "terminal value," something which is good in itself. It is not that neutrality requires a subprinciple of toleration of religious exercise at least under some conditions, but that the baseline of free exercise necessitates neutrality by the government toward religion. John Garvey, *What are Freedoms For?* (1997). Do you agree? Is toleration a robust virtue?

Neutrality is not self-defining either. In *Employment Division v. Smith* [Chapter Eleven, section 10], the Court adopted a formalistic approach to neutrality, requiring nothing more of the government than refraining from intentional, overt hostility to religion. In *City of Boerne v. Flores* [Chapter Eleven, section 11], this tendency became worse when the Court spoke of full-blown "religious persecution" as the standard for gauging a violation of religious liberty that Congress might rectify. The American idea of religious freedom does not tolerate, let alone support, official hostility to religion. See Edward McGlynn Gaffney, "Hostility to Religion, American–Style," 42 *DePaul L. Rev.* 263 (1992).

The concept of religious neutrality has meant more than the avoiding of intentional hostility. To have deeper meaning, governmental neutrality in religious matters must have substantive content. Professor Laycock defines "substantive neutrality" as follows: "the religion clauses require government to minimize the extent to which it either encourages or discourages religious belief or disbelief, practice or nonpractice, observance or nonobservance." Douglas Laycock, "Formal, Substantive, and Disaggregated Neutrality Toward Religion," 39 *DePaul L. Rev.* 993, 1001 (1990). The constitutional standard proposed by Professor Choper a generation ago promoted a similar understanding of neutrality. Jesse H. Choper, "Religion in the Public Schools: A Proposed Constitutional Standard," 47 *Minn. L. Rev.* 329 (1963) (governmental program unconstitutional if likely to result in compromising or influencing a student's religious or conscientious beliefs).

Some commentators doubt that neutrality is possible. For example, Professor Hitchcock has written: "The urge to ensure that non-belief does not suffer in comparison with belief has often led to practical and theoretical restrictions being placed on religion itself. The classical doctrine of strict separationism rests on an assumption that the state can and must be neutral. But in practice this is impossible. Values are necessary for the functioning of any society, and if they are not consciously adopted and publicly acknowledged they will be smuggled in surreptitiously and often unconsciously. Values are always in real or potential conflict, and the state inevitably favors some values over others." James Hitchcock, "Church, State and Moral Values: The Limits of American Pluralism," 44 *Law and Contemporary Problems* 3, 21 (1981). Do you agree? For strikingly different critiques of "neutrality," see Steven Smith, *Foreordained Failure*, 77–97, and Suzanna Sherry, "Lee v. Weisman: Paradox Redux," 1992 *Sup. Ct. Rev.* 123.

Berkeley sociologist Robert Bellah has called attention to "civil religion," exemplified in Lincoln's Second Inaugural [Chapter Eight, section 4]. Bellah defines "civil religion" as "that religious dimension, found I think in the life of every people, through which it interprets its historical experience in the light of transcendent reality." Bellah, *The Broken Covenant: American Civil Religion in Time of Trial* 3 (1967). Civil religion invokes the mythology of the nation, that is, not what is untrue but what transfigures reality "so that it provides moral and spiritual meaning." *Id. See also* Wilson Yates, "Separation of Church and State: Civil Religion and Crossings at the Border," 1 *Hamline L. Rev.* 67 (1978); Sanford Levinson, " 'The Constitution' in American Civil Religion," 1979 *Sup. Ct. Rev.* 123. Can the public schools teach civics, government, and history without presenting for acceptance "the civil religion of America"?

2.   *Science and Religion.* Almost as controversial as prayer in public schools is the science curriculum in public schools. The continuing debate over science and religion is reflected in the next two cases. The first case involved a claim by Susan Epperson that her freedom as a school teacher was diminished by a 1928 Arkansas "anti-evolution" statute prohibiting the teaching in its public schools and universities of the theory that man evolved from other species of life. Writing for a unanimous Court in *Epperson v. Arkansas*, Justice Abe Fortas linked this case to the famous trial of John Scopes in Dayton, Tennessee in the summer of 1925. Clarence Darrow represented Scopes, a football coach with no training in biology. The "Great Commoner," William Jennings Bryan, represented the State of Tennessee. He engaged in a "crusade" against the introduction of Darwinism into the curriculum because Darwin did not only depict humans as the progressive result of the evolutionary process, but believed that the Caucasian "race" was "finally, the highest type of all." Second, Bryan, a pacifist who had resigned as President Woodrow Wilson's Secretary of State in 1915 because of Wilson's rejection of the Kellogg–Briand pact on arbitration of international disputes, saw the ease with which Darwin's understanding of "survival of the fittest" was appropriated by advocates of Social Darwinism such as Charles Sumner to justify laissez-faire capitalism, imperialism, and militarism. Edward J. Larson, *Summer for the Gods: The Scopes Trial and America's Continuing Debate over Science and Religion* (1997). The jury convicted, which is what everyone wanted, so that an appeal could be framed. Bryan died shortly after the trial. On appeal, the Tennessee Supreme Court overturned the conviction, but left the statute standing. *Scopes v. State*, 154 Tenn. 105, 289 S.W. 363 (1927).

Abe Fortas was a young high school student in Memphis during the 1920s. He followed the Scopes trial closely, and was motivated by that experience to go to law school. Larson, *Summer for the Gods* 254. Larson notes that "[e]choes of the Scopes trial resounded through Epperson's appeal before the Supreme Court" and that "[a]llusions to the Scopes case ran through the oral arguments and media coverage as well." *Id.* 254–55. Memoranda in the Fortas Papers disclose that a majority of the justices voted in conference to overturn the Arkansas statute in *Epperson* on the ground that it was void for vagueness. Fortas was "almost alone" in arguing to reverse the lower court on establishment grounds. Id. 255. He asked to write the Court's opinion, which focused exclusively on the Establishment Clause. After acknowledging that the Arkansas statute "is presently more a curiosity than a vital fact of life," Fortas divined the "original purpose" of the Arkansas statute by importing into it language from "its antecedent, Tennessee's 'monkey law.' " For modern critiques of the Darwinian account of evolution (e.g., the failure to account for the emergence of new species through "slight, random variations"), see Philip E. Johnson, *Darwin on Trial* (1992); Johnson, *Defeating Darwinism* (1997), and Edward J. Larson, *Trial and Error: The American Controversy Over Creation and Evolution* (1989).

As in *Stone v. Graham* [section 2C above] and *Wallace v. Jaffree* [section 2D above] the statutes reviewed in *Epperson* and *Edwards v. Aguillard* [below] were invalidated on the ground that they lacked a secular purpose. Does either of the following considerations state a legitimate secular purpose for statutes such as those invalidated in *Epperson* and *Edwards*? Suppose a statute merely stated that "the purpose of this statute is to remove the controversial subject of human origins from the public schools." Drawing on his experience as a legislator at the time of the enactment of the statute invalidated in *Epperson*, Justice Black filed an opinion concurring in the judgment, restating his long-standing opposition to striking down statutes on account of their purpose, imagined or real. He wrote: "There is no reason I can imagine why a State is without power to withdraw from its curriculum any subject deemed too emotional and controversial for its public schools." Do you agree? Or suppose a statute recited that its purpose is "to keep young children from being taught something that the legislature has found to contain significant factual errors." Would that count as a secular purpose?

Epperson v. Arkansas

393 U.S. 97 (1968).

Eugene R. Warren argued the cause for appellants. With him on the brief was *Bruce T. Bullion*.

Don Langston, Assistant Attorney General of Arkansas, argued the cause for appellee. With him on the brief was *Joe Purcell*, Attorney General.

Briefs of *amici curiae*, urging reversal, were filed by *Leo Pfeffer, Melvin L. Wulf*, and *Joseph B. Robison* for the American Civil Liberties Union et al., and by *Philip J. Hirschkop* for the National Education Association of the United States et al.

■ JUSTICE FORTAS delivered the opinion of the Court.

I

This appeal challenges the constitutionality of the "anti-evolution" statute which the State of Arkansas adopted in 1928 to prohibit the teaching in its public schools and universities of the theory that man evolved from other species of life. The statute was a product of the upsurge of "fundamentalist" religious fervor of the twenties. The Arkansas statute was an adaptation of the famous Tennessee "monkey law" which that State adopted in 1925. The constitutionality of the Tennessee law was upheld by the Tennessee Supreme Court in the celebrated *Scopes* case in 1927.

The Arkansas law makes it unlawful for a teacher in any state-supported school or university "to teach the theory or doctrine that mankind ascended or descended from a lower order of animals," or "to adopt or use in any such institution a textbook that teaches" this theory.

Violation is a misdemeanor and subjects the violator to dismissal from his position.[2]

The present case concerns the teaching of biology in a high school in Little Rock. According to the testimony, until the events here in litigation, the official textbook furnished for the high school biology course did not have a section on the Darwinian Theory. Then, for the academic year 1965–1966, the school administration, on recommendation of the teachers of biology in the school system, adopted and prescribed a textbook which contained a chapter setting forth "the theory about the origin of man from a lower form of animal." . . .

The State's undoubted right to prescribe the curriculum for its public schools does not carry with it the right to prohibit, on pain of criminal penalty, the teaching of a scientific theory or doctrine where that prohibition is based upon reasons that violate the First Amendment. It is much too late to argue that the State may impose upon the teachers in its schools any conditions that it chooses, however restrictive they may be of constitutional guarantees. *Keyishian v. Board of Regents*, 385 U.S. 589, 605–606 (1967).

In the present case, there can be no doubt that Arkansas has sought to prevent its teachers from discussing the theory of evolution because it is contrary to the belief of some that the Book of Genesis must be the exclusive source of doctrine as to the origin of man. No suggestion has been made that Arkansas' law may be justified by considerations of state policy other than the religious views of some of its citizens.[15] It is clear that

2. Initiated Act No. 1, Ark. Acts 1929; Ark. Stat. Ann. §§ 80–1627, 80–1628 (1960 Repl. Vol.). The text of the law is as follows:

"§ 80–1627.—Doctrine of ascent or descent of man from lower order of animals prohibited.—It shall be unlawful for any teacher or other instructor in any University, College, Normal, Public School, or other institution of the State, which is supported in whole or in part from public funds derived by State and local taxation to teach the theory or doctrine that mankind ascended or descended from a lower order of animals and also it shall be unlawful for any teacher, textbook commission, or other authority exercising the power to select textbooks for above mentioned educational institutions to adopt or use in any such institution a textbook that teaches the doctrine or theory that mankind descended or ascended from a lower order of animals.

"§ 80–1628.—Teaching doctrine or adopting textbook mentioning doctrine—Penalties—Positions to be vacated.—Any teacher or other instructor or textbook commissioner who is found guilty of violation of this act by teaching the theory or doctrine mentioned in

section 1 hereof, or by using, or adopting any such textbooks in any such educational institution shall be guilty of a misdemeanor and upon conviction shall be fined not exceeding five hundred dollars; and upon conviction shall vacate the position thus held in any educational institutions of the character above mentioned or any commission of which he may be a member."

15. Former Dean Leflar of the University of Arkansas School of Law has stated that "the same ideological considerations underlie the anti-evolution enactment" as underlie the typical blasphemy statute. He says that the purpose of these statutes is an "ideological" one which "involves an effort to prevent (by censorship) or punish to presentation of intellectually significant matter which contradicts accepted social, moral or religious ideas." Leflar, Legal Liability for the Exercise of Free Speech, 10 Ark. L. Rev. 155, 158 (1956). See also R. Hofstadter & W. Metzger, The Development of Academic Freedom in the United States 320–366 (1955) (*passim*); H. Beale, A History of Freedom of Teaching in American Schools 202–207 (1941); Emerson & Haber, The *Scopes* Case in Modern fundamentalist sectarian conviction was and is the law's reason for existence.[16]

Its antecedent, Tennessee's "monkey law," candidly stated its purpose: to make it unlawful "to teach any theory that denies the story of the Divine Creation of man as taught in the Bible, and to teach instead that man has descended from a lower order of animals."[17] Perhaps the sensational publicity attendant upon the *Scopes* trial induced Arkansas to adopt less explicit language.[18] It eliminated Tennessee's reference to "the story of the Divine Creation of man" as taught in the Bible, but there is no doubt that the motivation for the law was the same: to suppress the teaching of a theory which, it was thought, "denied" the divine creation of man.

Arkansas' law cannot be defended as an act of religious neutrality. Arkansas did not seek to excise from the curricula of its schools and universities all discussion of the origin of man. The law's effort was confined to an attempt to blot out a particular theory because of its supposed conflict with the Biblical account, literally read. Plainly, the law is contrary to the mandate of the First, and in violation of the Fourteenth, Amendment to the Constitution.

The judgment of the Supreme Court of Arkansas is *Reversed.*

■ JUSTICE BLACK, concurring.

I am by no means sure that this case presents a genuinely justiciable case or controversy. Although Arkansas Initiated Act No. 1, the statute alleged to be unconstitutional, was passed by the voters of Arkansas in 1928, we are informed that there has never been even a single attempt by the State to enforce it. And the pallid, unenthusiastic, even apologetic

Dress, 27 U. Chi. L. Rev. 522 (1960); Waller, The Constitutionality of the Tennessee Anti-Evolution Act, 35 Yale L. J. 191 (1925) (*passim*); ACLU, The Gag on Teaching 7 (2d ed., 1937); J. Scopes & J. Presley, Center of the Storm 45–53 (1967).

16. The following advertisement is typical of the public appeal which was used in the campaign to secure adoption of the statute:

"THE BIBLE OR ATHEISM, WHICH?"

"All atheists favor evolution. If you agree with atheism vote against Act No. 1. If you agree with the Bible vote for Act No. 1. . . . Shall conscientious church members be forced to pay taxes to support teachers to teach evolution which will undermine the faith of their children? The Gazette said Russian Bolshevists laughed at Tennessee. True, and that sort will laugh at Arkansas. Who cares? Vote FOR ACT NO. 1." The Arkansas Gazette, Little Rock, Nov. 4, 1928, p. 12, cols. 4–5.

Letters from the public expressed the fear that teaching of evolution would be "subversive of Christianity," *id.,* Oct. 24,

1928, p. 7, col. 2; see also *id.,* Nov. 4, 1928, p. 19, col. 4; and that it would cause school children "to disrespect the Bible," *id.,* Oct. 27, 1928, p. 15, col. 5. One letter read: "The cosmogony taught by [evolution] runs contrary to that of Moses and Jesus, and as such is nothing, if anything at all, but atheism. . . . Now let the mothers and fathers of our state that are trying to raise their children in the Christian faith arise in their might and vote for this anti-evolution bill that will take it out of our tax supported schools. When they have saved the children, they have saved the state." *Id.,* at cols. 4–5.

17. Arkansas' law was adopted by popular initiative in 1928, three years after Tennessee's law was enacted and one year after the Tennessee supreme Court's decision in the *Scopes* case, *supra.*

18. In its brief, the State says that the Arkansas statute was passed with the holding of the *Scopes* case in mind. Brief for Appellee 1.

defense of the Act presented by the State in this Court indicates that the State would make no attempt to enforce the law should it remain on the books for the next century. Now, nearly 40 years after the law has slumbered on the books as though dead, a teacher alleging fear that the State might arouse from its lethargy and try to punish her has asked for a declaratory judgment holding the law unconstitutional. She was subsequently joined by a parent who alleged his interest in seeing that his two then school-age sons "be informed of all scientific theories and hypotheses...." But whether this Arkansas teacher is still a teacher, fearful of punishment under the Act, we do not know. It may be, as has been published in the daily press, that she has long since given up her job as a teacher and moved to a distant city, thereby escaping the dangers she had imagined might befall her under this lifeless Arkansas Act. And there is not one iota of concrete evidence to show that the parent-intervenor's sons have not been or will not be taught about evolution. The textbook adopted for use in biology classes in Little Rock includes an entire chapter dealing with evolution. There is no evidence that this chapter is not being freely taught in the schools that use the textbook and no evidence that the intervenor's sons, who were 15 and 17 years old when this suit was brought three years ago, are still in high school or yet to take biology. Unfortunately, however, the State's languid interest in the case has not prompted it to keep this Court informed concerning facts that might easily justify dismissal of this alleged lawsuit as moot or as lacking the qualities of a genuine case or controversy.

Notwithstanding my own doubts as to whether the case presents a justiciable controversy, the Court brushes aside these doubts and leaps headlong into the middle of the very broad problems involved in federal intrusion into state powers to decide what subjects and schoolbooks it may wish to use in teaching state pupils. While I hesitate to enter into the consideration and decision of such sensitive state-federal relationships, I reluctantly acquiesce. But, agreeing to consider this as a genuine case or controversy, I cannot agree to thrust the Federal Government's long arm the least bit further into state school curriculums than decision of this particular case requires.

NOTES AND QUESTIONS

1. *Was Epperson a Case or Controversy?* Justice Fortas wrote: "In the present case, there can be no doubt that Arkansas has sought to prevent its teachers from discussing the theory of evolution because it is contrary to the belief of some that the Book of Genesis must be the exclusive source of doctrine as to the origin of man." Although there is no basis for this assertion in the record in *Epperson*, Justice Brennan cited this line with approval in *Edwards*. Why did Justice Black concur separately in *Epperson*? Had the state of Arkansas ever attempted to enforce the law? Did biology textbooks in use at the time include materials on evolution? Was the case moot? Was Susan Epperson still a teacher at the time of the suit? Were the children still in school?

2. Justice Fortas clearly intended to free public schools from any restrictions against teaching evolution. Fortas failed to achieve this result because some

religious believers read his opinion simply as an invitation to be even-handed or "neutral" in the treatment of alternative views about the origins of the universe and of human life. They thought this goal could be achieved by offering instruction both in evolution and in creationist perspectives. They learned otherwise in *McLean v. Arkansas Bd. of Ed.*, 529 F. Supp. 1255 (E.D. Ark.1982), and in a subsequent case that considered the 1981 Louisiana "Balanced Treatment Act," requiring that teachers who taught "evolution science" must also teach "creation science." The Fifth Circuit, per Judge E. Grady Jolly, held the act unconstitutional. *Aguillard v. Edwards*, 765 F.2d 1251 (5th Cir. 1985). The statutory scheme, wrote Judge Jolly, "focusing on the religious *bête noire* of evolution, as it does, demonstrates the religious purpose of the statute. Indeed the Act continues the battle William Jennings Bryan carried to his grave." Law-office history again found its way into the United States Reports. The historical errors in *Epperson* were repeated in *Edwards*.

Edwards v. Aguillard

482 U.S. 578 (1987).

Wendell R. Bird, Special Assistant Attorney General of Georgia, argued the cause for appellants. With him on the briefs were *A. Morgan Brian, Jr.*, and *Thomas T. Anderson*, Special Assistant Attorneys General, *Kendall L. Vick*, and *Patricia Nalley Bowers*, Assistant Attorney General of Louisiana.

Jay Topkis argued the cause for appellees. With him on the brief was *John DiGiulio, Samuel I. Rosenberg, Allen Blumstein, Gerard E. Harper, Jack D. Novik, Burt Neuborne, Norman Dorsen, John Sexton*, and *Ron Wilson*.

Briefs of amici curiae urging reversal were filed for the Catholic League for Religious and Civil Rights by *Steven Frederick McDowell*; for the Christian Legal Society et al. by *Michael J. Woodruff, Kimberlee W. Colby, Samuel E. Ericsson, and Forest D. Montgomery*; and for Concerned Women for America by *Michael P. Farris* and *Jordan W. Lorence*.

Briefs of amici curiae urging affirmance were filed for the State of New York et al. by *Robert Abrams*, Attorney General of New York, *O.Peter Sherwood*, Solicitor General, *Paul M. Glickman, Jane Levine, Suzanne Lynn, and Marla Tepper*, Assistant Attorneys General, and *Neil F. Hartigan*, Attorney General of Illinois; for the American Association of University Professors et al. by *Ann H. Franke, Jacqueline W. Mintz, and Sheldon E. Steinbach*; for the American Federation of Teachers, AFL–CIO, by *Bruce A. Miller* and *Stuart M. Israel*; for the American Jewish Congress et al. by *Marvin E. Frankel, Marc D. Stern, and Ronald A. Krauss*; for Americans United for Separation of Church and State et al. by *Lee Boothby, Samuel Rabinove, Richard T. Foltin, and James M. Parker*; for the Anti–Defamation League of B'nai B'rith et al. *by Ruti G. Teitel, Justin J. Finger, Jeffrey P. Sinensky*, and *Steven M. Freeman*; for National Academy of Sciences by *Barry H. Garfinkel* and *Mark Herlihy*; for the New York Committee for Public Education and Religious Liberty by *Leo Pfeffer*; for People for the American Way et al. by *Timothy B. Dyk, A. Douglas Melamed*, and *Kerry*

W. Kircher; for the Spartacist League et al. by *Rachel H. Wolkenstein*; and for 72 Nobel Laureates et al. by *Walter B. Slocombe*.

Briefs of amici curiae were filed for the Rabbinical Alliance of America et al. by *John W. Whitehead* and *Larry L. Crain*; and for Reverend Bill McLean et al. by *Phillip E. Kaplan*.

■ JUSTICE BRENNAN delivered the opinion of the Court, in which JUSTICES MARSHALL, BLACKMUN, POWELL, and STEVENS joined, and in all but Part II of which JUSTICE O'CONNOR joined.

The question for decision is whether Louisiana's "Balanced Treatment for Creation—Science and Evolution—Science in Public School Instruction" Act (Creationism Act), La.Rev.Stat.Ann. §§ 17:286.1–17:286.y, is facially invalid as violative of the Establishment Clause of the First Amendment.

I

The Creationism Act forbids the teaching of the theory of evolution in public schools unless accompanied by instruction in "creation science." No school is required to teach evolution or creation science. If either is taught, however, the other must also be taught. The theories of evolution and creation science are statutorily defined as "the scientific evidences for [creation or evolution] and inferences from those scientific evidences."

Appellees, who include parents of children attending Louisiana public schools, Louisiana teachers, and religious leaders, challenged the constitutionality of the Act in District Court, seeking an injunction and declaratory relief. Appellants, Louisiana officials charged with implementing the Act, defended on the ground that the purpose of the Act is to protect a legitimate secular interest, namely, academic freedom.

II

[Justice Brennan recited the *Lemon* test, noting that "State action violates the Establishment Clause if it fails to satisfy any of these prongs" and that "the *Lemon* test has been applied in all cases since its adoption in 1971, except in *Marsh v. Chambers*." [Chapter Thirteen, section 5] He distinguished the Court's reliance upon historical acceptance of the practice sustained in *Marsh* from the task of determining the proper roles of church and state in public schools on the ground that "free public education was virtually nonexistent at the time the Constitution was adopted." Brennan observed that the Court has been "particularly vigilant in monitoring compliance with the Establishment Clause in elementary and secondary schools" because "[f]amilies entrust public schools with the education of their children, but condition their trust on the understanding that the classroom will not purposely be used to advance religious views that may conflict with the private beliefs of the student and his or her family" and because "[s]tudents in such institutions are impressionable and their attendance is involuntary." Brennan cited Justice Frankfurter's concurring opinion in *McCollum* [section 2A above]: "The public school is at once the symbol of our democracy and the most pervasive means for promoting our common destiny. In no activity of the State is it more vital to keep out divisive forces than in its schools...."]

III

Lemon's first prong focuses on the purpose that animated adoption of the Act. "The purpose prong of the *Lemon* test asks whether government's actual purpose is to endorse or disapprove of religion." *Lynch v. Donnelly* (O'Connor, J., concurring) [Chapter Thirteen, section 6]. A governmental intention to promote religion is clear when the State enacts a law to serve a religious purpose. This intention may be evidenced by promotion of religion in general, *Wallace v. Jaffree* [section 2D above], or by advancement of a particular religious belief, e.g., *Stone v. Graham* [section 2C above], *Epperson v. Arkansas*, [this section above] (holding that banning the teaching of evolution in public schools violates the First Amendment since "teaching and learning" must not "be tailored to the principles or prohibitions of any religious sect or dogma"). If the law was enacted for the purpose of endorsing religion, "no consideration of the second or third criteria [of *Lemon*] is necessary." *Wallace v. Jaffree* [section 2D above]. In this case, appellants have identified no clear secular purpose for the Louisiana Act.

True, the Act's stated purpose is to protect academic freedom. This phrase might, in common parlance, be understood as referring to enhancing the freedom of teachers to teach what they will. The Court of Appeals, however, correctly concluded that the Act was not designed to further that goal.[6] We find no merit in the State's argument that the "legislature may not [have] use[d] the terms 'academic freedom' in the correct legal sense. They might have [had] in mind, instead, a basic concept of fairness; teaching all of the evidence." Even if "academic freedom" is read to mean "teaching all of the evidence" with respect to the origin of human beings, the Act does not further this purpose. The goal of providing a more comprehensive science curriculum is not furthered either by outlawing the teaching of evolution or by requiring the teaching of creation science. The Act actually serves to diminish academic freedom by removing the flexibility to teach evolution without also teaching creation science, even if teachers determine that such curriculum results in less effective and comprehensive science instruction.

A

While the Court is normally deferential to a State's articulation of a secular purpose, it is required that the statement of such purpose be sincere and not a sham. *Wallace v. Jaffree*, (Powell, J., concurring) (O'Con-

---

6. The Court of Appeals stated that "[a]cademic freedom embodies the principle that individual instructors are at liberty to teach that which they deem to be appropriate in the exercise of their professional judgment." But, in the State of Louisiana, courses in public schools are prescribed by the State Board of Education and teachers are not free, absent permission, to teach courses different from what is required. "Academic freedom," at least as it is commonly understood, is not a relevant concept in this context. Moreover, as the Court of Appeals explained, the Act "requires, presumably upon risk of sanction or dismissal for failure to comply, the teaching of creation-science whenever evolution is taught. Although states may prescribe public school curriculum concerning science instruction under ordinary circumstances, the compulsion inherent in the Balanced Treatment Act is, on its face, inconsistent with the idea of academic freedom as it is universally understood."

nor, J., concurring in judgment); *Stone v. Graham* [section 2C above]. It is clear from the legislative history that the purpose of the legislative sponsor, Senator Bill Keith, was to narrow the science curriculum. During the legislative hearings, Senator Keith stated: "My preference would be that neither [creationism nor evolution] be taught." Such a ban on teaching does not promote—indeed, it undermines—the provision of a comprehensive scientific education.

It is equally clear that requiring schools to teach creation science with evolution does not advance academic freedom. The Act does not grant teachers a flexibility that they did not already possess to supplant the present science curriculum with the presentation of theories, besides evolution, about the origin of life. Indeed, the Court of Appeals found that no law prohibited Louisiana public school teachers from teaching any scientific theory. As the president of the Louisiana Science Teachers Association testified, "[a]ny scientific concept that's based on established fact can be included in our curriculum already, and no legislation allowing this is necessary." The Act provides Louisiana school teachers with no new authority. Thus the stated purpose is not furthered by it.

[Justice Brennan noted a similarity between the Alabama statute held unconstitutional in *Wallace* and the Creationism Act. Both, he suggested, had a stated purpose the Court rejected as insufficient, because an adopted law already provided for that purpose.] Thus, in this case, as in *Wallace*, "[a]ppellants have not identified any secular purpose that was not fully served by [existing state law] before the enactment of [the statute in question]."

Furthermore, the goal of basic "fairness" is hardly furthered by the Act's discriminatory preference for the teaching of creation science and against the teaching of evolution. While requiring that curriculum guides be developed for creation science, the Act says nothing of comparable guides for evolution. Similarly, resource services are supplied for creation science but not for evolution. Only "creation scientists" can serve on the panel that supplies the resource services. The Act forbids school boards to discriminate against anyone who "chooses to be a creation-scientist" or to teach "creationism," but fails to protect those who choose to teach evolution or any other non-creation science theory, or who refuse to teach creation science.

If the Louisiana Legislature's purpose was solely to maximize the comprehensiveness and effectiveness of science instruction, it would have encouraged the teaching of all scientific theories about the origins of humankind.[8] But under the Act's requirements, teachers who were once

---

8. The dissent concludes that the Act's purpose was to protect the academic freedom of students, and not that of teachers. Such a view is not at odds with our conclusion that if the Act's purpose was to provide comprehensive scientific education (a concern shared by students and teachers, as well as parents), that purpose was not advanced by the statute's provisions. Moreover, it is astonishing that the dissent, to prove its assertion, relies on a section of the legislation that was eventually deleted by the legislature. The dissent contends that this deleted section—which was explicitly rejected by the Louisiana Legislature—reveals the legislature's "obviously intended meaning of the statutory terms 'ac-free to teach any and all facets of this subject are now unable to do so. Moreover, the Act fails even to ensure that creation science will be taught, but instead requires the teaching of this theory only when the theory of evolution is taught. Thus we agree with the Court of Appeals' conclusion that the Act does not serve to protect academic freedom, but has the distinctly different purpose of discrediting "evolution by counterbalancing its teaching at every turn with the teaching of creationism...."

B

[Justice Brennan cited *Stone v. Graham*:] "The Ten Commandments are undeniably a sacred text in the Jewish and Christian faiths, and no legislative recitation of a supposed secular purpose can blind us to that fact." As a result, the contention that the law was designed to provide instruction on a "fundamental legal code" was "not sufficient to avoid conflict with the First Amendment." As in *Stone* and *Schempp,* we need not be blind in this case to the legislature's preeminent religious purpose in enacting this statute. There is a historic and contemporaneous link between the teachings of certain religious denominations and the teaching of evolution. It was this link that concerned the Court in *Epperson* which also involved a facial challenge to a statute regulating the teaching of evolution. In that case, the Court reviewed an Arkansas statute that made it unlawful for an instructor to teach evolution or to use a textbook that referred to this scientific theory. Although the Arkansas antievolution law did not explicitly state its predominant religious purpose, the Court could not ignore that "[t]he statute was a product of the upsurge of 'fundamentalist' religious fervor" that has long viewed this particular scientific theory as contradicting the literal interpretation of the Bible.[10] [After reviewing the history of antievolution statutes, Brennan determined that there can be no doubt that the motivation for the Arkansas law was the same as other anti-evolution statutes: "to suppress the teaching of a theory which, it was thought, 'denied' the divine creation of man." The Court found that there can be no legitimate state interest in protecting particular religions from scientific views "distasteful to them," and concluded "that the First Amendment does not permit the State to require that teaching and learning must be tailored to the principles or prohibitions of any religious sect or dogma."

These same historic and contemporaneous antagonisms between the teachings of certain religious denominations and the teaching of evolution

ademic freedom.'" Quite to the contrary, Boudreaux, the main expert relied on by the sponsor of the Act, cautioned the legislature that the words "academic freedom" meant "freedom to teach science." His testimony was given at the time the legislature was deciding whether to delete this section of the Act.

10. The Court evaluated the statute in light of a series of antievolution statutes adopted by state legislatures dating back to the Tennessee statute that was the focus of the celebrated Scopes trial in 1925. *Epperson.* The Court found the Arkansas statute comparable to this Tennessee "monkey law," since both gave preference to " 'religious establishments which have as one of their tenets or dogmas the instantaneous creation of man.' " (quoting *Scopes v. State*, 154 Tenn. 105, 126, 289 S.W. 363, 369 (1927) (Chambliss, J., concurring)).

are present in this case. The preeminent purpose of the Louisiana Legislature was clearly to advance the religious viewpoint that a supernatural being created humankind. The term "creation science" was defined as embracing this particular religious doctrine by those responsible for the passage of the Creationism Act. Senator Keith's leading expert on creation science, Edward Boudreaux, testified at the legislative hearings that the theory of creation science included belief in the existence of a supernatural creator (noting that "creation scientists" point to high probability that life was "created by an intelligent mind").[12] Senator Keith also cited testimony from other experts to support the creation-science view that "a creator [was] responsible for the universe and everything in it." The legislative history therefore reveals that the term "creation science," as contemplated by the legislature that adopted this Act, embodies the religious belief that a supernatural creator was responsible for the creation of humankind.

Furthermore, it is not happenstance that the legislature required the teaching of a theory that coincided with this religious view. The legislative history documents that the Act's primary purpose was to change the science curriculum of public schools in order to provide persuasive advantage to a particular religious doctrine that rejects the factual basis of evolution in its entirety. The sponsor of the Creationism Act, Senator Keith, explained during the legislative hearings that his disdain for the theory of evolution resulted from the support that evolution supplied to views contrary to his own religious beliefs. According to Senator Keith, the theory of evolution was consonant with the "cardinal principle[s] of religious humanism, secular humanism, theological liberalism, aetheistism [sic]." The state senator repeatedly stated that scientific evidence supporting his religious views should be included in the public school curriculum to redress the fact that the theory of evolution incidentally coincided with what he characterized as religious beliefs antithetical to his own. The legislation therefore sought to alter the science curriculum to reflect endorsement of a religious view that is antagonistic to the theory of evolution.

In this case, the purpose of the Creationism Act was to restructure the science curriculum to conform with a particular religious viewpoint. Out of many possible science subjects taught in the public schools, the legislature chose to affect the teaching of the one scientific theory that historically has been opposed by certain religious sects. As in *Epperson*, the legislature passed the Act to give preference to those religious groups which have as one of their tenets the creation of humankind by a divine creator. The "overriding fact" that confronted the Court in *Epperson* was "that Arkansas' law selects from the body of knowledge a particular segment which it proscribes for the sole reason that it is deemed to conflict with ... a particular interpretation of the Book of Genesis by a particular religious group." Similarly, the Creationism Act is designed either to promote the theory of creation science which embodies a particular religious tenet by

12. The lead witness at the hearings introducing the original bill, Luther Sunderland, described creation science as postulating "that everything was created by some intelligence or power external to the universe."

requiring that creation science be taught whenever evolution is taught or to prohibit the teaching of a scientific theory disfavored by certain religious sects by forbidding the teaching of evolution when creation science is not also taught. The Establishment Clause, however, "forbids *alike* the preference of a religious doctrine or the prohibition of theory which is deemed antagonistic to a particular dogma." Because the primary purpose of the Creationism Act is to advance a particular religious belief, the Act endorses religion in violation of the First Amendment.

We do not imply that a legislature could never require that scientific critiques of prevailing scientific theories be taught. Indeed, the Court acknowledged in *Stone* that its decision forbidding the posting of the Ten Commandments did not mean that no use could ever be made of the Ten Commandments, or that the Ten Commandments played an exclusively religious role in the history of Western Civilization. In a similar way, teaching a variety of scientific theories about the origins of humankind to schoolchildren might be validly done with the clear secular intent of enhancing the effectiveness of science instruction. But because the primary purpose of the Creationism Act is to endorse a particular religious doctrine, the Act furthers religion in violation of the Establishment Clause....

V

The Louisiana Creationism Act advances a religious doctrine by requiring either the banishment of the theory of evolution from public school classrooms or the presentation of a religious viewpoint that rejects evolution in its entirety. The Act violates the Establishment Clause of the First Amendment because it seeks to employ the symbolic and financial support of government to achieve a religious purpose. The judgment of the Court of Appeals therefore is *Affirmed*.

————

[JUSTICE POWELL served for years as Counsel to the Richmond Board of Education of Richmond, Virginia. He filed a concurring opinion, joined by JUSTICE O'CONNOR. He wrote separately "to emphasize that nothing in the Court's opinion diminishes the traditionally broad discretion accorded state and local school officials in the selection of the public school curriculum." Powell concluded:]

The fact that the Louisiana Legislature purported to add information to the school curriculum rather than detract from it as in *Epperson* does not affect my analysis. Both legislatures acted with the unconstitutional purpose of structuring the public school curriculum to make it compatible with a particular religious belief: the "divine creation of man."

That the statute is limited to the scientific evidences supporting the theory does not render its purpose secular. In reaching its conclusion that the Act is unconstitutional, the Court of Appeals "[did] not deny that the underpinnings of creationism may be supported by scientific evidence." And there is no need to do so. Whatever the academic merit of particular subjects or theories, the Establishment Clause limits the discretion of state officials to pick and choose among them for the purpose of promoting a particular religious belief. The language of the statute and its legislative history convince me that the Louisiana Legislature exercised its discretion for this purpose in this case.

II

Even though I find Louisiana's Balanced Treatment Act unconstitutional, I adhere to the view "that the States and locally elected school boards should have the responsibility for determining the educational policy of the public schools." *Board of Education, Island Trees Union Free School Dist. No. 26 v. Pico*, 457 U.S. 853, 893 (1982) (Powell, J., dissenting). A decision respecting the subject matter to be taught in public schools does not violate the Establishment Clause simply because the material to be taught " 'happens to coincide or harmonize with the tenets of some or all religions.' " *Harris v. McRae* [Chapter Fifteen, section 4]. In the context of a challenge under the Establishment Clause, interference with the decisions of these authorities is warranted only when the purpose for their decisions is clearly religious.

III

In sum, I find that the language and the legislative history of the Balanced Treatment Act unquestionably demonstrate that its purpose is to advance a particular religious belief. Although the discretion of state and local authorities over public school curricula is broad, "the First Amendment does not permit the State to require that teaching and learning must be tailored to the principles or prohibitions of any religious sect or dogma." *Epperson*.

■ JUSTICE WHITE, concurring in the judgment.

As it comes to us, this is not a difficult case. Based on the historical setting and plain language of the Act both courts construed the statutory words "creation science" to refer to a religious belief, which the Act required to be taught if evolution was taught. In other words, the teaching of evolution was conditioned on the teaching of a religious belief. Both courts concluded that the state legislature's primary purpose was to advance religion and that the statute was therefore unconstitutional under the Establishment Clause.

[I]f the meaning ascribed to a state statute by a court of appeals is a rational construction of the statute, we normally accept it.... Even if as an original matter I might have arrived at a different conclusion based on a reading of the statute and the record before us, I cannot say that the two courts below are so plainly wrong that they should be reversed.... If the Court of Appeals' construction is to be accepted, so is its conclusion that under our prior cases the Balanced Treatment Act is unconstitutional because its primary purpose is to further a religious belief by imposing certain requirements on the school curriculum. Unless, therefore, we are to reconsider the Court's decisions interpreting the Establishment Clause, I agree that the judgment of the Court of Appeals must be affirmed.

■ JUSTICE SCALIA, with whom CHIEF JUSTICE REHNQUIST joins, dissenting.

Even if I agreed with the questionable premise that legislation can be invalidated under the Establishment Clause on the basis of its motivation alone, without regard to its effects, I would still find no justification for today's decision. The Louisiana legislators who passed the Balanced Treatment Act, each of whom had sworn to support the Constitution, were well aware of the potential Establishment Clause problems and considered that aspect of the legislation with great care. After seven hearings and several months of study, resulting in substantial revision of the original proposal, they approved the Act overwhelmingly and specifically articulated the secular purpose they meant it to serve. Although the record contains abundant evidence of the sincerity of that purpose (the only issue pertinent to this case), the Court today holds, essentially on the basis of "its visceral knowledge regarding what must have motivated the legislators," (citing dissent in Court of Appeals) that the members of the Louisiana Legislature knowingly violated their oaths and then lied about it. I dissent.

I

This case arrives here in the following posture: The Louisiana Supreme Court has never been given an opportunity to interpret the Balanced Treatment Act, State officials have never attempted to implement it, and it has never been the subject of a full evidentiary hearing. We can only guess at its meaning. We know that it forbids instruction in either "creation-science" or "evolution-science" without instruction in the other, but the parties are sharply divided over what creation science consists of. Appellants insist that it is a collection of educationally valuable scientific data that has been censored from classrooms by an embarrassed scientific establishment. Appellees insist it is not science at all but thinly veiled religious doctrine. Both interpretations of the intended meaning of that phrase find considerable support in the legislative history....

I doubt whether that "purpose" requirement of *Lemon* is a proper interpretation of the Constitution; but even if it were, I could not agree with the Court's assessment that the requirement was not satisfied here. This Court has said little about the first component of the *Lemon* test. Almost invariably, we have effortlessly discovered a secular purpose for measures challenged under the Establishment Clause, typically devoting no more than a sentence or two to the matter. *Witters; Grand Rapids; Mueller; Larkin v. Grendel's Den, Inc.; Widmar; Committee for Public Education & Religious Liberty v. Regan; Wolman; Meek; Nyquist; Levitt; Tilton v. Richardson; Lemon.* In fact, only once before deciding *Lemon,* and twice since, have we invalidated a law for lack of a secular purpose. *Wallace; Stone v. Graham; Epperson.* Nevertheless, a few principles have emerged from our cases, principles which should, but to an unfortunately large extent do not, guide the Court's application of *Lemon* today. It is clear, first of all, that regardless of what "legislative purpose" may mean in other contexts, for the purpose of the *Lemon* test it means the "actual" motives of those responsible for the challenged action.... Thus, if those legislators who supported the Balanced Treatment Act in fact acted with a "sincere" secular purpose, the Act survives the first component of the *Lemon* test, regardless of whether that purpose is likely to be achieved by the provisions they enacted. . . .

The author of *Lemon* [Chief Justice Burger] writing for the Court, has said that invalidation under the purpose prong is appropriate when "there [is] no question that the statute or activity was motivated *wholly* by religious considerations." *Lynch v. Donnelly*. In all three cases in which we truck down laws under the Establishment Clause for lack of a secular purpose, we found that the legislature's sole motive was to promote religion. *Wallace; Stone v. Graham; Epperson*. Thus, the majority's invalidation of the Balanced Treatment Act is defensible only if the record indicates that the Louisiana Legislature had *no* secular purpose.

It is important to stress that the purpose forbidden by *Lemon* is the purpose to "advance religion" *Witters; Wallace; Nyquist; Levitt; Walz; Allen*. Our cases in no way imply that the Establishment Clause forbids legislators merely to act upon their religious convictions. We surely would not strike down a law providing money to feed the hungry or shelter the homeless if it could be demonstrated that, but for the religious beliefs of the legislators, the funds would not have been approved. Also, political activism by the religiously motivated is part of our heritage. Notwithstanding the majority's implication to the contrary, we do not presume that the sole purpose of a law is to advance religion merely because it was supported strongly by organized religions or by adherents of particular faiths. *Walz* [Chapter Thirteen, section 3]; *Harris v. McRae* [Chapter Fifteen, section 4].

Similarly, we will not presume that a law's purpose is to advance religion merely because it " 'happens to coincide or harmonize with the tenets of some or all religions,' " *Harris v. McRae* [Chapter Fifteen, section 4], or because it benefits religion, even substantially. We have, for example, turned back Establishment Clause challenges to restrictions on abortion funding, *Harris*, and to Sunday closing laws, *McGowan v. Maryland* [Chapter Thirteen, section 2], despite the fact that both "agre[e] with the dictates of [some] Judaeo–Christian religions." "In many instances, the Congress or state legislatures conclude that the general welfare of society, wholly apart from any religious considerations, demands such regulation." On many past occasions we have had no difficulty finding a secular purpose for governmental action far more likely to advance religion than the Balanced Treatment Act. *Mueller; Wolman; Meek; Nyquist; Lemon; Walz; Allen*. Thus, the fact that creation science coincides with the beliefs of certain religions, a fact upon which the majority relies heavily, does not itself justify invalidation of the Act.

Finally, our cases indicate that even certain kinds of governmental actions undertaken with the specific intention of improving the position of religion do not "advance religion" as that term is used in *Lemon*. Rather, we have said that in at least two circumstances government must act to advance religion, and that in a third it may do so.

First, since we have consistently described the Establishment Clause as forbidding not only state action motivated by the desire to advance religion, but also that intended to "disapprove," "inhibit," or evince "hostility" toward religion (citations omitted); and since we have said that governmental "neutrality" toward religion is the preeminent goal of the First Amendment, a State which discovers that its employees are inhibiting religion must take steps to prevent them from doing so, even though its purpose would clearly be to advance religion. *Walz.* Thus, if the Louisiana Legislature sincerely believed that the State's science teachers were being hostile to religion, our cases indicate that it could act to eliminate that hostility without running afoul of *Lemon* 's purpose test.

Second, we have held that intentional governmental advancement of religion is sometimes required by the Free Exercise Clause. For example, in *Hobbie, Thomas, Yoder*, and *Sherbert*, we held that in some circumstances States must accommodate the beliefs of religious citizens by exempting them from generally applicable regulations. We have not yet come close to reconciling *Lemon* and our Free Exercise cases, and typically we do not really try. See, e.g., *Hobbie, Thomas.* It is clear, however, that members of the Louisiana Legislature were not impermissibly motivated for purposes of the Lemon test if they believed that approval of the Balanced Treatment Act was *required* by the Free Exercise Clause.

We have also held that in some circumstances government may act to accommodate religion, even if that action is not required by the First Amendment. *Hobbie.* It is well established that "[t]he limits of permissible state accommodation to religion are by no means co-extensive with the noninterference mandated by the Free Exercise Clause." *Walz.* Thus, few would contend that Title VII of the Civil Rights Act of 1964, which both forbids religious discrimination by private-sector employers, and requires them reasonably to accommodate the religious practices of their employees, [Chapter Eleven, section 6] violates the Establishment Clause, even though its "purpose" is, of course, to advance religion, and even though it is almost certainly not required by the Free Exercise Clause. While we have warned that at some point, accommodation may devolve into "an unlawful fostering of religion," *Hobbie*, we have not suggested precisely (or even roughly) where that point might be. It is possible, then, that even if the sole motive of those voting for the Balanced Treatment Act was to advance religion, and its passage was not actually required, or even believed to be required, by either the Free Exercise or Establishment Clauses, the Act would nonetheless survive scrutiny under *Lemon*'s purpose test.

One final observation about the application of that test: Although the Court's opinion gives no hint of it, in the past we have repeatedly affirmed "our reluctance to attribute unconstitutional motives to the States." *Mueller*; see also *Lynch v. Donnelly* (Brennan, J., dissenting). Whenever we are called upon to judge the constitutionality of an act of a state legislature, "we must have 'due regard to the fact that this Court is not exercising a primary judgment but is sitting in judgment upon those who also have taken the oath to observe the Constitution and who have the responsibility for carrying on government.'" This is particularly true, we have said, where the legislature has specifically considered the question of a law's constitutionality.

With the foregoing in mind, I now turn to the purposes underlying adoption of the Balanced Treatment Act.

II

A

We have relatively little information upon which to judge the motives of those who supported the Act. About the only direct evidence is the statute itself and transcripts of the seven committee hearings at which it was considered. Unfortunately, several of those hearings were sparsely attended, and the legislators who were present revealed little about their motives. We have no committee reports, no floor debates, no remarks inserted into the legislative history, no statement from the Governor, and no postenactment statements or testimony from the bill's sponsor or any other legislators. Cf. *Wallace* [where the record contained such materials]. Nevertheless, there is ample evidence that the majority is wrong in holding that the Balanced Treatment Act is without secular purpose.

At the outset, it is important to note that the Balanced Treatment Act did not fly through the Louisiana Legislature on wings of fundamentalist religious fervor—which would be unlikely, in any event, since only a small minority of the State's citizens belong to fundamentalist religious denominations. See B. Quinn, H. Anderson, M. Bradley, P. Goetting, & P. Shriver, Churches and Church Membership in the United States 16 (1982)....

The vast majority of [the legislators] voted to approve a bill which explicitly stated a secular purpose; what is crucial is not their wisdom in believing that purpose would be achieved by the bill, but their sincerity in believing it would be.... [T]he Court today plainly errs in holding that the Louisiana Legislature passed the Balanced Treatment Act for exclusively religious purposes....

The Court seeks to evade the force of this expression of purpose by stubbornly misinterpreting it, and then finding that the provisions of the Act do not advance that misinterpreted purpose, thereby showing it to be a sham. The Court first surmises that "academic freedom" means "enhancing the freedom of teachers to teach what they will,"—even though "academic freedom" in that sense has little scope in the structured elementary and secondary curriculums with which the Act is concerned. Alternatively, the Court suggests that it might mean "maximiz[ing] the comprehensiveness and effectiveness of science instruction,"—though that is an exceedingly strange interpretation of the words, and one that is refuted on the very face of the statute. Had the Court devoted to this central question of the meaning of the legislatively expressed purpose a small fraction of the research into legislative history that produced its quotations of religiously motivated statements by individual legislators, it would have discerned quite readily what "academic freedom" meant: students' freedom from indoctrination. The legislature wanted to ensure that students would be free to decide for themselves how life began, based upon a fair and balanced presentation of the scientific evidence—that is, to protect "the right of each [student] voluntarily to determine what to believe (and what not to believe) free of any coercive pressures from the State." *Grand Rapids*....

In sum, even if one concedes, for the sake of argument, that a majority of the Louisiana Legislature voted for the Balanced Treatment Act partly in order to foster (rather than merely eliminate discrimination against) Christian fundamentalist beliefs, our cases establish that that alone would not suffice to invalidate the Act, so long as there was a genuine secular purpose as well. We have, moreover, no adequate basis for disbelieving the secular purpose set forth in the Act itself, or for concluding that it is a sham enacted to conceal the legislators' violation of their oaths of office. I am astonished by the Court's unprecedented readiness to reach such a conclusion, which I can only attribute to an intellectual predisposition created by the facts and the legend of *Scopes v. State*, 154 Tenn. 105, 289 S.W. 363 (1927)—an instinctive reaction that any governmentally imposed requirements bearing upon the teaching of evolution must be a manifestation of Christian fundamentalist repression. In this case, however, it seems to me the Court's position is the repressive one. The people of Louisiana, including those who are Christian fundamentalists, are quite entitled, as a secular matter, to have whatever scientific evidence there may be against evolution presented in their schools, just as Mr. Scopes was entitled to present whatever scientific evidence there was for it. Perhaps what the Louisiana Legislature has done is unconstitutional because there is no such evidence, and the scheme they have established will amount to no more than a presentation of the Book of Genesis. But we cannot say that on the evidence before us in this summary judgment context, which includes ample uncontradicted testimony that "creation science" is a body of scientific knowledge rather than revealed belief. Infinitely less can we say (or should we say) that the scientific evidence for evolution is so conclusive that no one could be gullible enough to believe that there is any real scientific evidence to the contrary, so that the legislation's stated purpose must be a lie. Yet that illiberal judgment, that *Scopes*-in-reverse, is ultimately the basis on which the Court's facile rejection of the Louisiana Legislature's purpose must rest.

Because I believe that the Balanced Treatment Act had a secular purpose, which is all the first component of the *Lemon* test requires, I would reverse the judgment of the Court of Appeals and remand for further consideration.

III

I have to this point assumed the validity of the *Lemon* "purpose" test. In fact, however, I think the pessimistic evaluation that The Chief Justice made of the totality of *Lemon* is particularly applicable to the "purpose" prong: it is "a constitutional theory [that] has no basis in the history of the amendment it seeks to interpret, is difficult to apply and yields unprincipled results...." *Wallace* (Rehnquist, J., dissenting).

Our cases interpreting and applying the purpose test have made such a maze of the Establishment Clause that even the most conscientious governmental officials can only guess what motives will be held unconstitutional. We have said essentially the following: Government may not act with the purpose of advancing religion, except when forced to do so by the Free Exercise Clause (which is now and then); or when eliminating existing governmental hostility to religion (which exists sometimes); or even when merely accommodating governmentally uninhibited religious practices, except that at some point (it is unclear where) intentional accommodation results in the fostering of religion, which is of course unconstitutional. But the difficulty of knowing what vitiating purpose one is looking for is as nothing compared with the difficulty of knowing how or where to find it. For while it is possible to discern the objective "purpose" of a statute (i.e., the public good at which its provisions appear to be directed), or even the formal motivation for a statute where that is explicitly set forth (as it was, to no avail, here), discerning the subjective motivation of those enacting the statute is, to be honest, almost always an impossible task. The number of possible motivations, to begin with, is not binary, or indeed even finite. In the present case, for example, a particular legislator need not have voted for the Act either because he wanted to foster religion or because he wanted to improve education. He may have thought the bill would provide jobs for his district, or may have wanted to make amends with a faction of his party he had alienated on another vote, or he may have been a close friend of the bill's sponsor, or he may have been repaying a favor he owed the majority leader, or he may have hoped the Governor would appreciate his vote and make a fundraising appearance for him, or he may have been pressured to vote for a bill he disliked by a wealthy contributor or by a flood of constituent mail, or he may have been seeking favorable publicity, or he may have been reluctant to hurt the feelings of a loyal staff member who worked on the bill, or he may have been settling an old score with a legislator who opposed the bill, or he may have been mad at his wife who opposed the bill, or he may have been intoxicated and utterly unmotivated when the vote was called, or he may have accidentally voted "yes" instead of "no," or, of course, he may have had (and very likely did have) a combination of some of the above and many other motivations. To look for the sole purpose of even a single legislator is probably to look for something that does not exist. . . .

[Justice Scalia posed a series of questions about where the Court might find evidence of an individual legislator's purpose, and how many legislators must have the invalidating intent.]

Because there are no good answers to these questions, this Court has recognized from Chief Justice Marshall, see *Fletcher v. Peck*, 6 Cranch 87, 130 (1810), to Chief Justice Warren, *United States v. O'Brien*, 391 U.S. 367, 383–384 (1968), that determining the subjective intent of legislators is a perilous enterprise. See also *Epperson* (Black, J., concurring). It is perilous, I might note, not just for the judges who will very likely reach the wrong result, but also for the legislators who find that they must assess the validity of proposed legislation—and risk the condemnation of having voted for an unconstitutional measure—not on the basis of what the legislation contains, nor even on the basis of what they themselves intend, but on the basis of what others have in mind. . . .

In the past we have attempted to justify our embarrassing Establishment Clause jurisprudence on the ground that it "sacrifices clarity and predictability for flexibility." *Regan.* One commentator has aptly characterized this as "a euphemism . . . for . . . the absence of any principled rationale." Choper, "The Religion Clauses of the First Amendment: Reconciling the Conflict," *41 U. Pitt. L. Rev.* 673, 681 (1980). I think it time that we sacrifice some "flexibility" for "clarity and predictability." Abandoning *Lemon* 's purpose test—a test which exacerbates the tension between the Free Exercise and Establishment Clauses, has no basis in the language or history of the Amendment, and, as today's decision shows, has wonderfully flexible consequences—would be a good place to start.

NOTES AND QUESTIONS

1. *Rewriting Schempp.* Even though *Schempp* had not relied on secular purpose doctrine to invalidate the reading of verses from the Holy Bible and the recitation of the Lord's Prayer by the students, Brennan cast doubt twenty years later on the proffer of such secular purposes as the "promotion of moral values, the contradiction to the materialistic trends of our times, the perpetuation of our institutions and the teaching of literature." Having recast *Schempp* in this light, he conjoined it with *Stone.*

2. *Is Critical Thinking Unconstitutional?* The controversy over evolution continues. Seven years after *Edwards*, a local school board in Louisiana adopted the following resolution: "Whenever, in classes of elementary or high school, the scientific theory of evolution is to be presented, whether from textbook, workbook, pamphlet, other written material, or oral presentation the following statement shall be quoted immediately before the unit of study begins as a disclaimer from endorsement of such theory.

"It is hereby recognized by the Tangipahoa Parish Board of Education, that the lesson to be presented, regarding the origin of life and matter, is known as the Scientific Theory of Evolution and should be presented to inform students of the scientific concept and not intended to influence or dissuade the Biblical version of Creation or any other concept.

"It is further recognized by the Board of Education that it is the basic right and privilege of each student to form his/her own opinion or maintain beliefs taught by parents on this very important matter of the origin of life and matter. Students are urged to exercise critical thinking and gather all information possible and closely examine each alternative toward forming an opinion."

Finding the purpose of encouraging critical thinking a "sham," *Edwards*, the district court ruled that the resolution lacked a plausible secular purpose, and the court enjoined the school board from enforcement of this policy. *Freiler v. Tangipahoa Parish Board of Education*, 975 F. Supp. 819 (E.D. La. 1997). Right result? Why? The Fifth Circuit affirmed, but on a different ground. It agreed with the district court that the assigned reason for the disclaimer—critical thinking—was a sham, but readily found other legitimate secular purposes such as disclaiming any orthodoxy of belief that could be inferred from the exclusive place of evolution in the curriculum, and reducing offense to any student or parent caused by the teaching of evolution. It found the disclaimer invalid because "the primary effect of the disclaimer is to protect and maintain a particular religious viewpoint, namely belief in the Biblical version of creation." 185 F.3d 337, 346 (5th Cir. 2000). The court concluded that the disclaimer failed the primary effect test, for three reasons: "(1) the juxtaposition of the disavowal of endorsement of evolution with an urging that students contemplate alternative theories of the origin of life; (2) the reminder that students have the right to maintain beliefs taught by their parents regarding the origin of life; and (3) the 'Biblical version of Creation' as the only alternative theory explicitly referenced in the disclaimer." *Id*. Right result? Why?

Only three justices were willing to hear the case. Joined by Chief Justice Rehnquist and Justice Thomas, Justice Scalia filed a dissent from the denial of certiorari. *Tangipahoa Parish Bd. of Education et al., v. Herb Freiler et al.*, 120 S.Ct. 2706 (2000). Noting that a majority of the Court had previously expressed disapproval of the *Lemon* test, Scalia would grant certiorari in this case "if only to take the opportunity to inter the *Lemon* test once for all." Scalia wrote that "the manner of [the Fifth Circuit's] application [of *Lemon*] so erroneous as independently to merit the granting of certiorari, if not summary reversal." For Scalia, far from advancing religion, the disclaimer merely "advance[s] freedom of thought." Scalia noted that this was not *Edwards* redivivus, but a case in which "the theory of evolution is the only theory actually taught." He thus concluded that "the disclaimer constitutes nothing more than 'simply a tolerable acknowledgment of beliefs widely held among the people of this country,' citing *Marsh v. Chambers* [Chapter Thirteen, section 5] and *Lynch v. Donnelly*, 465 U.S. 668, 673, (1984) ("Nor does the Constitution require complete separation of church and state; it affirmatively mandates accommodation, not merely tolerance, of all religions, and forbids hostility toward any"). Do you agree?

3. *Comprehensive Truth Claims*. Does not "modern science" lay claim to comprehensive truth about the earth? Are the tentative character of its claims and its abstention from statements as to "ultimate" causes what distinguish it from religion? Is the difference for those who find their truth only in science one of style more than substance? *See also Note: Marxist Communism as a Religion* [Chapter Eleven, section 4].

H.   USE OF PUBLIC SCHOOL PROPERTY BY RELIGIOUS SPEAKERS

A school district in New York allowed private groups to rent the facilities after hours. A religious group sought to use one of the facilities of the district to show a series of films and to conduct discussion about family values from a religious perspective. The district denied access to the public school facility because of the religious content of the message sought to be conveyed. In *Lamb's Chapel v. Center Moriches Union Free School District*, 508 U.S. 384 (1993), the Court, per Justice White, acknowledged that compliance with the nonestablishment provision may be a state interest sufficiently compelling to justify content-based restrictions on speech, but struck down state restrictions on religious content where the State did not sponsor the religious expression, the expression was made on government property that had been opened to the public for speech, and permission was requested through the same application process and on the same terms required of other private groups. According to the Court, the difference between forbidden government speech endorsing religion and protected private speech that does so is what distinguishes *Allegheny County* and *Lynch* from *Widmar*. Thus private religious speech is as fully protected under the Free Speech Clause as secular private expression, and that the use of a public school facility by a private religious group on neutral terms is not precluded by any of the three criteria announced in *Lemon*.

2. *The Vitality of Lemon.* Scholars have criticized the *Lemon* test and litigators have urged the Court to repudiate it. As of 2000, however, the Court has not done so. In *Lamb's Chapel,* Justice Scalia concurred in the judgment, but wrote sharply about the Court's continued reliance on *Lemon*: "Like some ghoul in a late-night horror movie that repeatedly sits up in its grave and shuffles abroad, after being repeatedly killed and buried, *Lemon* stalks our Establishment Clause jurisprudence once again, frightening the little children and school attorneys of the Center Moriches Union Free School District. Its most recent burial, only last Term, was, to be sure, not fully six-feet under: our decision in Lee v. Weisman [section 2F above], conspicuously avoided using the supposed 'test' but also declined the invitation to repudiate it. Over the years, however, no fewer than five of the currently sitting Justices have, in their own opinions personally driven pencils through the creature's heart (the author of today's opinion repeatedly), and a sixth has joined an opinion doing so. The secret of the *Lemon* test's survival, I think, is that it is so easy to kill. It is there to scare us (and our audience) when we wish it to do so, but we can command it to return to the tomb at will. When we wish to strike down a practice it forbids, we invoke it, see, e.g., *Aguilar* [section 1 above]; when we wish to uphold a practice it forbids, we ignore it entirely, see, e.g., *Marsh v. Chambers* [Chapter Thirteen, section 5]. Sometimes, we take a middle course, calling its three prongs 'no more than helpful signposts,' *Hunt v. McNair* [section 3A below]. Such a docile and useful monster is worth keeping around, at least in a somnolent state; one never knows when one might need him."

Scholars continue to be divided over the vitality of *Lemon.* For the view that *Lee v. Weisman,* in effect, replaced the *Lemon* test with a coercion test, *see* Michael J. Paulsen, "Lemon Is Dead," 43 *Case W. Res. L. Rev.* 795 (1993). In reply to Paulsen, Professor Conkle does not "defend all of the Court's applications of *Lemon*"; in particular, he acknowledges that "in the area of funding for parochial education, some of the Court's decisions have turned on exceedingly fine distinctions." But he argues that the essence of *Lemon* is multiple-variable, "context-specific case-by-case analysis of particular problems," and that in this sense *Lemon* is still pragmatically useful. Daniel O. Conkle, "*Lemon* Lives," 43 *Case W. Res. L. Rev.* 865 (1993). Noting that "lower courts continue to cite and rely upon [*Lemon*] regularly," Professor Lupu agrees with Conkle that *Lemon* is far from dead. Ira C. Lupu, "Which Old Witch?: A Comment on Professor Paulsen's Lemon is Dead," 43 *Case W. Res. L. Rev.* 883 (1993). Whether or not *Lemon* is dead or alive, after reviewing the cases in the first two sections of this Chapter, can you articulate a reasoned or principled approach to the funding of religious elementary and secondary schools or to the presence of religion in some form in the public schools?

3. HIGHER EDUCATION

A. INSTITUTIONAL ASSISTANCE AND STUDENT AID

Age has been a factor in free exercise cases, see, e.g., *Prince* [Chapter Eleven, section 1]. It has also played a role—indeed, a decisive one—in the area of education. Announced on the same day as the Court's decision in *Lemon* and by the same author, Chief Justice Burger, *Tilton* drew a bright line between elementary and secondary education on the one hand (where students were deemed highly impressionable and the schools "pervasively sectarian,") and postsecondary institutions (characterized by mature students and academic freedom). The line drawn in *Tilton* was to last. Until the *Columbia Union College* case, 159 F.3d 151 (4th Cir. 1998), now pending in the district court, no successful challenge had been mounted under the nonestablishment provision to various forms of financial assistance, federal or state, institutional or student-based, as long as the level of education was at a religious college or university. The statute sustained in *Tilton* was an Act of Congress providing federal aid for the construction of buildings at colleges and universities. It contained a proviso, lasting for twenty years after receipt of the grant, that the building could not be used for religious worship or "sectarian instruction." The Court nullified the proviso, on the view that the statute would violate the nonestablishment provision without it. The statute was silent about the presence of religious art in the buildings built with federal funds. The record contained evidence that none of the subsidized buildings at the four Catholic colleges in Connecticut sued in the case—Albertus Magnus, Annhurst, Fairfield, and Sacred Heart University—contained religious art. The Chief Justice turned this detail into a constitutional rule. The case was narrowly decided.

Tilton v. Richardson

403 U.S. 672 (1971).

Leo Pfeffer argued the cause for appellants. With him on the briefs were *Peter L. Costas*, *Paul W. Orth*, and *Jerry Wagner*.

Daniel M. Friedman argued the cause for appellees Richardson et al. On the brief were *Solicitor General Griswold, Assistant Attorney General Ruckelshaus, Robert V. Zener*, and *Donald L. Horowitz*. *F. Michael Ahern*, Assistant Attorney General of Connecticut, argued the cause for appellee Peterson. With him on the brief was *Robert K. Killian*, Attorney General. *Edward Bennett Williams* argued the cause for appellee colleges and universities. With him on the brief were *Jeremiah C. Collins, Howard T. Owens, Lawrence W. Iannotti*, and *Bruce Lewellyn*.

Briefs of *amici curiae* urging reversal were filed by *Franklin C. Salisbury* for Protestants and Other Americans United for Separation of Church and State, and by *Peter L. Costas* and *Paul W. Orth* for the Connecticut State Conference of Branches of the NAACP et al.

Briefs of *amici curiae* urging affirmance were filed by *Wilber G. Katz* and *John Holt Myers* for the American Council on Education et al., and by *Nathan Lewin* for the National Jewish Commission on Law and Public Affairs.

■ CHIEF JUSTICE BURGER announced the judgment of the Court and an opinion in which JUSTICE HARLAN, JUSTICE STEWART, and JUSTICE BLACKMUN join.

[Chief Justice Burger quoted the purpose of the Act of Congress "to assure colleges for American youth."] This expresses a legitimate secular objective entirely appropriate for governmental action.

The simplistic argument that every form of financial aid to church-sponsored activity violates the Religion Clauses was rejected long ago in *Bradfield v. Roberts* [Chapter Ten, section 2].... The Act itself was carefully drafted to ensure that the federal subsidized facilities would be devoted to the secular and not the religious functions of the recipient institutions.... Finally, this record fully supports the findings of the District Court that none of the four church-related institutions in this case has violated the statutory restrictions....

[Chief Justice Burger noted that two of the buildings involved were libraries where no classes were conducted; that one was a language laboratory; that one was a science building; and that one was a music, drama, and arts building]. There was no evidence that religion seeps into the use of any of these facilities.... Although appellants introduced several institutional documents that stated certain religious restrictions on what could be taught, other evidence showed that these restrictions were not in fact enforced and that the schools were characterized by an atmosphere of academic freedom rather than religious indoctrination.

[Burger rejected the appellant's use of a "hypothetical composite" profile of a "typical sectarian" institution. When considering whether there were "excessive entanglements," which had proved fatal in *Lemon*, Burger distinguished the colleges from elementary and secondary schools.]

There is substance to the contention that college students are less impressionable and less susceptible to religious indoctrination. Common observation would seem to support that view, and Congress may well have entertained it. The skepticism of the college student is not an inconsiderable barrier to any attempt or tendency to subvert the congressional objectives and limitations. Furthermore, by their very nature, college and postgraduate courses tend to limit the opportunities for sectarian influence by virtue of their own internal disciplines. Many church-related colleges and universities are characterized by a high degree of academic freedom and seek to evoke free and critical responses from their students.

The record here would not support a conclusion that any of these four institutions departed from this general pattern. All four schools are governed by Catholic religious organizations, and the faculties and student bodies at each are predominantly Catholic. Nevertheless, the evidence shows that non-Catholics were admitted as students and given faculty appointments. Not one of these four institutions requires its students to attend religious services. Although all four schools require their students to take theology courses, the parties stipulated that these courses are taught according to the academic requirements of the subject matter and the teacher's concept of professional standards....

The entanglement between church and state is also lessened here by the nonideological character of the aid that the Government provides. Our cases from *Everson* to *Allen* have permitted church-related schools to receive government aid in the form of secular, neutral, or nonideological services, facilities, or materials that are supplied to all students regardless of the affiliation of the school that they attend. In *Lemon* and *DiCenso* [section 1 above], however, the state programs subsidized teachers, either directly or indirectly. Since teachers are not necessarily religiously neutral, greater governmental surveillance would be required to guarantee that state salary aid would not in fact subsidize religious instruction. There we found the resulting entanglement excessive. Here, on the other hand, the Government provides facilities that are themselves religiously neutral. The risks of Government aid to religion and the corresponding need for surveillance are therefore reduced.

Finally, government entanglements with religion are reduced by the circumstance that, unlike the direct and continuing payments under the Pennsylvania program, and all the incidents of regulation and surveillance, the Government aid here is a one-time, single-purpose construction grant. There are no continuing financial relationships or dependencies, no annual audits, and no government analysis of an institution's expenditures on secular as distinguished from religious activities. Inspection as to use is a minimal contact.

No one of these three factors standing alone is necessarily controlling; cumulatively all of them shape a narrow and limited relationship with government which involves fewer and less significant contacts than the two state schemes before us in *Lemon* and *DiCenso*. The relationship therefore has less potential for realizing the substantive evils against which the Religion Clauses were intended to protect.

We think that cumulatively these three factors also substantially lessen the potential for divisive religious fragmentation in the political arena. This conclusion is admittedly difficult to document, but neither have appellants pointed to any continuing religious aggravation on this matter in the political processes. Possibly this can be explained by the character and diversity of the recipient colleges and universities and the absence of any intimate continuing relationship or dependency between government and religiously affiliated institutions. The potential for divisiveness inherent in the essentially local problems of primary and secondary schools is significantly less with respect to a college or university whose student constituency is not local but diverse and widely dispersed.

V

Finally, we must consider whether the implementation of the Act inhibits the free exercise of religion in violation of the First Amendment. Appellants claim that the Free Exercise Clause is violated because they are compelled to pay taxes, the proceeds of which in part finance grants under the Act. Appellants, however, are unable to identify any coercion directed at the practice or exercise of their religious beliefs. *Allen* [section 1 above]. Their share of the cost of the grants under the Act is not fundamentally distinguishable from the impact of the tax exemption sustained in *Walz* [Chapter Thirteen, section 3] or the provision of textbooks upheld in *Allen*.

We conclude that the Act does not violate the Religion Clauses of the First Amendment except that part of [the statute] providing a 20–year limitation on the religious use restrictions. We remand to the District Court with directions to enter a judgment consistent with this opinion. *Vacated and remanded.*

■ Justices Douglas, Black, and Marshall concurred in part and dissented in part.

NOTES AND QUESTIONS

1. *The Tilt of* Tilton. South Carolina authorized revenue bonds to assist institutions of higher learning to construct buildings except those to be used for worship or sectarian instruction. A taxpayer challenged the issue of the bonds for the benefit of the Baptist College at Charleston, a college whose trustees were elected by the South Carolina Baptist Convention. In *Hunt v. McNair*, 413 U.S. 734 (1973), the Supreme Court, 6–3, upheld the statute, finding it to pass the three-part *Lemon* test. The plaintiff had produced little evidence as to the Baptist College's actual curriculum; the usual opponents of state aid to religion did not enter the case. Justice Brennan, joined by Justices Douglas and Marshall, dissented, contending by borrowing funds from the Higher Education Authority, the college turned over to the state "a comprehensive and continuing surveillance" of its "educational, religious and fiscal affairs." On the same day as *Hunt,* Justice Powell also announced that all of the programs at issue in *Nyquist* were invalid under *Lemon*.

Maryland enacted an annual grant program for any private institution of higher learning in the state except ones awarding only theological degrees; none of the money received could be used "for sectarian purposes." The grants were supervised by the Maryland Council for Higher Education, which required the recipient colleges to segregate the grants and to certify that they had not been used for sectarian purposes. In the first year of the program, seventeen institutions, five of them church-related, received grants. Four taxpayers sued to prevent the grants being made to four Catholic colleges. In *Roemer v. Board of Public Works of Maryland*, 426 U.S. 736 (1976), the Court, 5–4, upheld the program. Applying *Lemon,* Justice Blackmun found that the program had a secular purpose, the support of private higher education; that the primary effect was not to advance religion because the encouragement of spiritual development at the four colleges was "only one secondary objective" of each college; that the review of the Maryland Council for High Education was not excessive entanglement; and that because other private institutions were also subsidized the danger of political divisiveness was not great. Justices White and Rehnquist concurred, agreeing that the purpose of the legislators was secular and labelling the entanglement test as superfluous.

Justices Brennan, Marshall, Stewart, and Stevens dissented. Justice Stevens referred "to the pernicious tendency of a state subsidy to tempt religious schools to compromise their religious mission without wholly abandoning it." There was no evidence in the record in *Roemer* to suggest that the religious colleges in Maryland had abandoned or even compromised their religious mission in order to receive state aid. On the contrary, the record disclosed that the colleges had required theology courses, that a number of teachers opened their classes with prayer, and that some members of the college faculties were members of religious orders. None of those facts deterred the Court from sustaining the aid. Should it have? The State of New York established a program of financial assistance for colleges in New York. Shortly after this program began, several religious colleges in New York shifted their corporate governance to a lay board of trustees. Should a strategic move of this sort count as evidence that these colleges had succumbed "to the pernicious tendency of a state subsidy to tempt religious schools to compromise their religious mission"? Is the fidelity of a religious community to its heritage a legitimate concern for a governmental official to take into account? Can it serve as a useful standard for judicial review [see "church autonomy cases," Chapter Twelve, section 3]? Protestants and Other Americans United and the ACLU were among the original plaintiffs, but were dismissed for lack of standing, 387 F. Supp. 1282, 1284 n.1 (D. Md. 1974); Leo Pfeffer filed an *amicus* brief for PEARL.

2. *State Student Aid Programs.* Nearly all states provide some form of financial aid to students in higher education, either in grants or in subsidized loans. POAU dropped the first three words from their title, "Protestants and Other," and became known simply as Americans United for Separation of Church and State. Dismissed as a party for lack of standing in *Tilton* and *Roemer,* the newly christened group was eager to litigate higher education cases, especially in Southern jurisdictions, where they hoped they would be able to create a record with instances of Bible-belt Christianity "seep[ing] into the use of any of these facilities," to use Chief Justice Burger's term in *Tilton.* When they solved the standing problem, they discovered that the trilogy of higher education cases—*Tilton, Hunt* and *Roemer*—now cut in favor of sustaining state loans and grants to students attending religious colleges and universities. The Court declined review. *Americans United for Separation of Church and State v. Blanton,* 433 F. Supp. 97 (M.D. Tenn.), *summarily aff'd,* 434 U.S. 803 (1977); *Smith v. Board of Governors of Univ. of North Carolina,* 429 F. Supp. 871 (W.D.N.C.), *summarily aff'd,* 434 U.S. 803 (1977)

Larry Witters applied for aid to the Washington Commission for the Blind, a state agency authorized to help the visually handicapped in obtaining education. Witters was a student at Inland Empire School of the Bible, a Christian college in Spokane. All the courses he wished to pursue were to enable him to serve as a youth minister. The commission denied him assistance on the ground that the Washington Constitution, Art. 1, sec. 11, provided that no public money should "be applied to any religious worship, exercise, or instruction." The Washington Supreme Court upheld the commission, but on federal constitutional grounds, citing and applying *Lemon* [section 1 above]. In *Witters v. Washington Department of Services for the Blind,* 474 U.S. 481 (1986), the Court reversed, finding no violation of the First Amendment. Justice Marshall wrote for a unanimous Court that the program comported with all three tests in *Lemon.* He noted: "Any aid provided under Washington's program that ultimately flows to religious institutions does so only as a result of the genuinely independent and private choices of aid recipients." One cannot say that the case is one of the blind leading the blind, but it would be difficult to believe that Witters's disability did not make even the staunchest defender of the "wall of separation" hesitate to hold help for him illegal. On remand, the Washington Supreme Court again upheld the ban on aid to Witters, this time on a nonreviewable state constitutional ground. 112 Wash. 2d 363, 771 P. 2d 1119 (1989).

Several states deny student aid to students attending "pervasively sectarian" colleges, Colo. Rev. Stat. § 23–3.5–101–106 (1998), or to students pursuing a theology degree, Wash. Rev. Code § 28B.10.814 (1994), or to "members of religious orders who are pursuing a course of study leading to a degree in theology, divinity or religious education," Wis. Stat. Ann. § 39.30(2)(d) (Supp.

1998–1999). The Court in *Roemer* sustained the Maryland capitation grant program, which provides financial aid, on a per student basis, to a wide range of private colleges. Although many of the colleges participating in this program are affiliated with religious institutions, the Maryland Higher Education Commission deemed Columbia Union College, a private liberal arts college affiliated with the Seventh-day Adventist Church, too "pervasively sectarian" to participate in the program. The college sued the members of the commission, seeking declaratory and injunctive relief that their exclusion of the college from this program violated the college's free speech, free exercise, and equal protection rights.

The District Court, 988 F.Supp. 897 (D.Md. 1998), and the Court of Appeals for the Fourth Circuit, 159 F.3d 151 (4th Cir. 1999), agreed that the commission's action infringed one or more of these rights. Relying on *Roemer,* both courts nonetheless concluded that exclusion of the college from this program could be justified by Maryland's compelling interest in enforcing the nonestablishment provision by ensuring that a "pervasively sectarian" institution did not benefit from public funds. The 4th Circuit ordered a trial to determine whether Columbia Union is "pervasively sectarian." The Supreme Court in *Lemon* invented the label "pervasively sectarian" to distinguish between schools that carefully segregate religious and secular activities and schools that consider their religious and educational missions indivisible and therefore require religion to permeate all activities. See Note. *What's in a Name?: The Problem with the "Pervasively Sectarian" Label* [section 1 above]. At trial, what sorts of empirical questions will the college need to answer in order to qualify for the assistance? Circuit Judge Diana Gribbon Motz suggested that the factfinder should probe whether "religious principles are important to the college" and whether "religious indoctrination is more than a secondary objective." Is that a legitimate inquiry for a secular court to undertake? Are matters such as these amenable to stipulation? How is a state agency to determine when indoctrination is a primary objective? If too many college students "believe," will the state deny funding? Does the nonestablishment provision allow state agencies to measure how seriously someone takes his or her religious convictions? The court hinted at ways in which the college could win the trial it ordered. For example, it suggested that because "only about 350 to 400 of Columbia Union's 1172 students" actually participate in its mandatory religious services, Columbia Union might not be pervasively sectarian. Is the college in danger of losing the financial aid if 500 students start attending services? Would it be in a better position to receive the aid if chapel attendance fell to 200? In a final plea to the commission, the college president asked a poignant question: "If we recant, would we qualify?" Should such a question be asked, let alone answered, in a land that cherishes free exercise of religion?

Chief Judge J. Harvie Wilkinson III dissented. "The majority's remand effectively dumps at the state's doorstep the volatile tasks of distinguishing between religious institutions and drawing controversial and delicate lines. Religious institutions will be without clear guidance as to when they might become too sectarian. The three Catholic colleges currently receiving funding— Mount Saint Mary's College & Seminary, the College of Notre Dame of Maryland, and Loyola College—must now worry about whether they will at some indefinable point offend the state by stepping over the sectarian edge. For example, Mount Saint Mary's appoints the Archbishop of Baltimore as an automatic trustee and requires that at least one-fourth of its trustees, including the Archbishop, be ordained priests. Notre Dame requires that just under one-third of its trustees be nuns. And Loyola's president must be a member of the Society of Jesus. May Mount Saint Mary's raise its requirement to one-half? May Notre Dame increase its to more than one-third? May Loyola include the same prerequisite in its search for a vice president? How are these colleges to know? It will be impossible for them to predict at what point sectarian influences of this type will tip the scales.... For religious institutions seeking Sellinger Program funds, the majority's remand simply raises more questions than it answers.

"The 'pervasively sectarian' test of *Hunt, Roemer,* and *Bowen* already places the judiciary in the uncomfortable role of determining just how religious an institution is, and requires that it draw somewhat arbitrary lines.... By requiring the district court to conduct a trial here, the majority has plunged government at all levels into the intimacies of religious faith."

The Supreme Court denied certiorari, perhaps because the case came before the Court in an interlocutory posture. 527 U.S. 1013 (1999). Dissenting from the denial of certiorari, Justice Thomas wrote that the Court should "scrap the 'pervasively sectarian' test and reaffirm that the Constitution requires, at a minimum, neutrality not hostility toward religion." Do you agree?

B.   EQUAL ACCESS

Both of the following cases involve the use of student activity fees at state universities. The first case turned on physical access to the campus. The second focused on access to a fund, established by student fees, that various student associations used for publishing student newspapers. Is the difference between physical access and access to money critical?

Shortly after *Tilton* was announced, the Board of Curators of the University of Missouri adopted a regulation that prohibits the use of University buildings or grounds "for purposes of religious worship or religious teaching." From 1973 until 1977 a registered religious group named Cornerstone regularly sought and received permission to conduct its meetings in University facilities. In 1977, however, the Dean of Students, Gary Widmar, informed the group that it could no longer meet in University buildings, citing the 1972 regulation. Eleven students sued Dean Widmar in federal court, alleging that the University's regulation discriminated against religious activity and discussion, in violation of their rights to free exercise of religion, equal protection, and freedom of speech under the First and Fourteenth Amendments to the Constitution of the United States.

The District Court upheld the regulation, finding it not only justified, but required, by the nonestablishment provision. Under *Tilton,* the court reasoned, the State could not provide facilities for religious use without giving prohibited support to an institution of religion. The court found religious speech entitled to less protection than other types of expression.

The Court of Appeals for the Eighth Circuit reversed. Rejecting the analysis of the district court, it viewed the regulation as a content-based discrimination against religious speech, for which it could find no compelling justification. The court held that the nonestablishment provision does not bar a policy of equal access, in which facilities are open to groups and speakers of all kinds. According to the Court of Appeals, the "primary effect" of such a policy would not be to advance religion, but rather to further the neutral purpose of developing students' " 'social and cultural awareness as well as [their] intellectual curiosity' " (quoting from the University bulletin's description of the student activities program).

Widmar v. Vincent

454 U.S. 263 (1981).

Ted D. Ayres argued the cause for petitioners. With him on the brief was *Jackson A. Wright.*

James M. Smart, Jr., argued the cause for respondents. With him on the brief was *Michael K. Whitehead.*

Briefs of amici curiae urging reversal were filed by *Joel H. Paget* for the Association for the Coordination of University Religious Affairs; by *Wilkes C. Robinson* and *Jane E. Nelson* for Bible Study; by *Edward McGlynn Gaffney, Jr.,* and *Kenneth F. Ripple* for the Center for Constitutional Studies et al.; by *Barry A. Fisher* for the Holy Spirit Association for the Unification of World Christianity; by *Nathan Lewin, Daniel D. Chazin*, and *Dennis Rapps* for the National Jewish Commission on Law and Public Affairs; and by *Wilfred R. Caron* for the United States Catholic Conference.

Briefs amici curiae were filed by *Earl W. Trent, Jr.*, for the Baptist Joint Committee on Public Affairs; by *J. Robert Brame, John W. Whitehead*, and *James J. Knicely* for the National Association of Evangelicals; and by *Donald L. Reidhaar* for the Regents of the University of California.

■ JUSTICE POWELL delivered the opinion of the court.

This case presents the question whether a state university, which makes its facilities generally available for the activities of registered student groups, may close its facilities to a registered student group desiring to use the facilities for religious worship and religious discussion.

I

It is the stated policy of the University of Missouri at Kansas City to encourage the activities of student organizations. The University officially recognizes over 100 student groups. It routinely provides University facilities for the meetings of registered organizations. Students pay an activity fee of $41 per semester (1978–1979) to help defray the costs to the University....

II

Through its policy of accommodating their meetings, the University has created a forum generally open for use by student groups. Having done so, the University has assumed an obligation to justify its discriminations and exclusions under applicable constitutional norms.[5] The Constitution

5. This Court has recognized that the campus of a public university, at least for its students, possesses many of the characteristics of a public forum. See generally, *Police*

forbids a State to enforce certain exclusions from a forum generally open to the public, even if it was not required to create the forum in the first place. See, *e.g., Madison Joint School District v. Wisconsin Employment Relations Comm'n* (although a State may conduct business in private session, "[w]here the State has opened a forum for direct citizen involvement," exclusions bear a heavy burden of justification); *Southeastern Promotions, Ltd v. Conrad* (because municipal theater was a public forum, city could not exclude a production without satisfying constitutional safeguards applicable to prior restraints).

The University's institutional mission, which it describes as providing a *"secular education"* to its students, does not exempt its actions from constitutional scrutiny. With respect to persons entitled to be there, our cases leave no doubt that the First Amendment rights of speech and association extend to the campuses of state universities. See, *e.g., Healy v. James*, 408 U.S. 169 (1972); *Tinker v. Des Moines Independent School District*, 393 U.S. 503 (1969); *Shelton v. Tucker*, 364 U.S. 479 (1960).

Here UMKC has discriminated against student groups and speakers based on their desire to use a generally open forum to engage in religious worship and discussion. These are forms of speech and association protected by the First Amendment. See, *e.g., Heffron v. International Society for Krishna Consciousness, Inc.* [Chapter Eleven, section 2]; *Niemotko v. Maryland* [Chapter Eleven, section 2]; *Saia v. New York*, 334 U.S. 558 (1948).[6]

Dept. of Chicago v. Mosley, 408 U.S. 92 (1972); *Cox v. Louisiana*, 379 U.S. 536 (1965). "The college classroom with its surrounding environs is peculiarly 'the marketplace of ideas.' " *Healy v. James*, 408 U.S. 169, 180 (1972). Moreover, the capacity of a group or individual "to participate in the intellectual give and take of campus debate . . . [would be] limited by denial of access to the customary media for communicating with the administration, faculty members, and other students." We therefore have held that students enjoy First Amendment rights of speech and association on the campus, and that the "denial [to particular groups] of use of campus facilities for meetings and other appropriate purposes" must be subjected to the level of scrutiny appropriate to any from of prior restraint.

At the same time, however, our cases have recognized that First Amendment rights must be analyzed "in light of the special characteristics of the school environment." *Tinker v. Des Moines Independent School District*, 393 U.S. 503, 506 (1969). We continue to adhere to that view. A university differs in significant respects from public forums such as streets or parks or even municipal theaters. A university's mission is education, and decisions of this Court have never denied

a university's authority to impose reasonable regulations compatible with that mission upon the use of its campus and facilities. We have not held, for example, that a campus must make all of its facilities equally available to students and non-students alike, or that a university must grant free access to all of its grounds or buildings.

6. The dissent argues that "religious worship" is not speech generally protected by the "free speech" guarantee of the First Amendment and the "equal protection" guarantee of the Fourteenth Amendment. If "religious worship" were protected "speech," the dissent reasons, "the Religion Clauses would be emptied of any independent meaning in circumstances in which religious practice took the form of speech." This is a novel argument. The dissent does not deny that speech *about* religion is speech entitled to the general protections of the First Amendment. It does not argue that descriptions of religious experiences fail to qualify as "speech." Nor does it repudiate last Term's decision in *Heffron v. International Society for Krishna Consciousness, Inc.*, which assumed that religious appeals to nonbelievers constituted protected "speech." Rather, the dissent seems to attempt a distinction between the kinds of religious speech explicitly protected by our

In order to justify discriminatory exclusion from a public forum based on the religious content of a group's intended speech, the University must therefore satisfy the standard of review appropriate to content-based exclusions. It must show that its regulation is necessary to serve a compelling state interest and that it is narrowly drawn to achieve that end. See *Carey v. Brown,* 447 U.S. 455, 461, 464–465 (1980).

III

In this case the University claims a compelling interest in maintaining strict separation of church and State. It derives this interest from the "Establishment Clauses" of both the Federal and Missouri Constitutions.

A

The University first argues that it cannot offer its facilities to religious groups and speakers on the terms available to other groups without violating the Establishment Clause of the Constitution of the United States. We agree that the interest of the University in complying with its constitutional obligations may be characterized as compelling. It does not follow, however, that an "equal access" policy would be incompatible with this Court's Establishment Clause cases. Those cases hold that a policy will not offend the Establishment Clause if it can pass a three-pronged test: "First, the [governmental policy] must have a secular legislative purpose; second, its principal or primary effect must be one that neither advances nor inhibits religion ...; finally, the [policy] must not foster 'an excessive government entanglement with religion.'" *Lemon v. Kurtzman* [section 1 above]. *See Committee for Public Education v. Regan* [section 1 above]; *Roemer v. Maryland Public Works Bd.* [section 3A above].

In this case two prongs of the test are clearly met. Both the District Court and the Court of Appeals held that an open-forum policy, including nondiscrimination against religious speech would have a secular purpose and would avoid entanglement with religion. But the District Court con-

---

cases and a new class of religious "speech act[s]," constituting "worship." There are at least three difficulties with this distinction.

First, the dissent fails to establish that the distinction has intelligible content. There is no indication when "singing hymns, reading scripture, and teaching biblical principles," cease to be "singing, teaching, and reading"—all apparently forms of "speech," despite their religious subject matter—and become unprotected "worship."

Second, even if the distinction drew an arguable principled line, it is highly doubtful that it would lie within the judicial competence to administer. Cf. *Fowler v. Rhode Island,* [Chapter Thirteen, section 1]. Merely to draw the distinction would require the university—and ultimately the courts—to inquire into the significance of words and prac-

tices to different religious faiths, and in varying circumstances by the same faith. Such inquiries would tend inevitably to entangle the State with religion in a manner forbidden by our cases. *Walz* [Chapter Thirteen, section 3].

Finally, the dissent fails to establish the *relevance* of the distinction on which it seeks to rely. The dissent apparently wishes to preserve the vitality of the Establishment Clause. But it gives no reason why the Establishment Clause, or any other provision of the Constitution, would require different treatment for religious speech designed to win religious converts, see *Heffron,* than for religious worship by persons already converted. It is far from clear that the State gives greater support in the latter case than in the former.

cluded, and the University argues here, that allowing religious groups to share the limited public forum would have the "primary effect" of advancing religion.

The University's argument misconceives the nature of this case. The question is not whether the creation of a religious forum would violate the Establishment Clause. The University has opened its facilities for use by student groups, and the question is whether it can now exclude groups because of the content of their speech. See *Healy v. James.* In this context we are unpersuaded that the primary effect of the public forum, open to all forms of discourse, would be to advance religion.

We are not oblivious to the range of an open forum's likely effects. It is possible—perhaps even foreseeable—that religious groups will benefit from access to University facilities. But this Court has explained that a religious organization's enjoyment of merely "incidental" benefits does not violate the prohibition against the "primary advancement" of religion. *Committee for Public Education v. Nyquist* [section 1 above]; see, *e.g., Roemer v. Maryland Public Works Bd.*; *Hunt v. McNair* [section 3A above]; *McGowan v. Maryland* [Chapter Thirteen, section 2].

We are satisfied that any religious benefits of an open forum at UMKC would be "incidental" within the meaning of our cases. Two factors are especially relevant.

First, an open forum in a public university does not confer any imprimatur of state approval on religious sects or practices. As the Court of Appeals quite aptly stated, such a policy "would no more commit the University . . . to religious goals" than it is "now committed to the goals of the Students for a Democratic Society, the Young Socialist Alliance," or any other group eligible to use its facilities.[14]

Second, the forum is available to a broad class of nonreligious as well as religious speakers; there are over 100 recognized student groups at UMKC. The provision of benefits to so broad a spectrum of groups is an important index of secular effect. See, *e.g., Wolman* [section 1 above]; *Nyquist* [section 1 above]. If the Establishment Clause barred the extension of general benefits to religious groups, "a church could not be protected by the police and fire departments, or have its public sidewalk kept in repair." *Roemer* [this section above] . . . . At least in the absence of empirical evidence that religious groups will dominate UMKC's open forum, we agree

---

14. University students are, of course, young adults. They are less impressionable than younger students and should be able to appreciate that the University's policy is one of neutrality toward religion. See *Tilton* [this section above]. The University argues that the Cornerstone students themselves admitted in affidavits that "[s]tudents know that if something is on campus, then it is a student organization, and they are more likely to feel comfortable attending a meeting." Affidavit of Florian Frederick Chess. In light of the large number of groups meeting on campus, however, we doubt students could draw any reasonable inference of University support from the mere fact of a campus meeting place. The University's student handbook already notes that the University's name will not "be identified in any way with the aims, policies, programs, products, or opinions of any organization or its members." 1980–1981 UMKC Student Handbook 25.

with the Court of Appeals that the advancement of religion would not be the forum's "primary effect."

B

Arguing that the State of Missouri has gone further than the Federal Constitution in proscribing indirect state support for religion, the University claims a compelling interest in complying with the applicable provisions of the Missouri constitution.

The Missouri courts have not ruled whether a general policy of accommodating student groups, applied equally to those wishing to gather to engage in religious and nonreligious speech, would offend the State Constitution. We need not, however, determine how the Missouri courts would decide this issue. It is also unnecessary for us to decide whether, under the Supremacy Clause, a state interest, derived from its own could ever outweigh free speech interests protected by the First Amendment. We limit our holding to the case before us.

On one hand, respondents' First Amendment rights are entitled to special constitutional solicitude. Our cases have required the most exacting scrutiny in cases in which a State undertakes to regulate speech on the basis of its content. See, *e.g., Carey v. Brown,* 447 U.S. 455 (1980); *Police Dept. of Chicago v. Mosley,* 408 U.S. 92 (1972). On the other hand, the state interest asserted here—in achieving greater separation of church and State than is already ensured under the Establishment Clause of the Federal constitution—is limited by the Free Exercise Clause and in this case by the Free Speech Clause as well. In this constitutional context, we are unable to recognize the State's interest as sufficiently "compelling" to justify content-based discrimination against respondents' religious speech.

IV

Our holding in this case in no way undermines the capacity of the University to establish reasonable time, place, and manner regulations. Nor do we question the right of the University to make academic judgments as to how best to allocate scarce resources or "to determine for itself on academic grounds who may teach, what may be taught, how it shall be taught, and who may be admitted to study." *Sweezy v. New Hampshire,* 354 U.S. 234, 263 (1957) (Frankfurter, J., concurring in result); see *University of California Regents v. Bakke,* 438 U.S. 265, 312–313 (1978) (opinion of Powell, J., announcing the judgment of the Court). Finally, we affirm the continuing validity of cases, *e.g., Healy v. James,* 408 U.S., at 188–189, that recognize a university's right to exclude even First Amendment activities that violate reasonable campus rules or substantially interfere with the opportunity of other students to obtain an education.

The basis for our decision is narrow. Having created a forum generally open to student groups, the University seeks to enforce a content-based exclusion of religious speech. Its exclusionary policy violates the fundamental principle that a state regulation of speech should be content-neutral, and the University is unable to justify this violation under applicable constitutional standards. For this reason, the decision of the Court of Appeals is *Affirmed*.

■ JUSTICE STEVENS concurred in the judgment.

■ JUSTICE WHITE, dissenting.

[After referring to *Stone v. Graham* [section 2C above], *Schempp* [section 2 above], *Engel* [section 2B above], and *Torcaso v. Watkins* [Chapter Twelve, section 1]. If the majority were right that no distinction may be drawn between verbal acts of worship and other verbal acts, all of these cases would have to be reconsidered. Although I agree that the line may be difficult to draw in many cases, surely the majority cannot seriously suggest that no line may ever be drawn. If that were the case, the majority would have to uphold the University's right to offer a class entitled "Sunday Mass." Under the majority's view such a class would be—as a matter of constitutional principle—indistinguishable from a class entitled "The History of the Catholic Church."

NOTES AND QUESTIONS

In *Mueller v. Allen* [section 1 above] Justice Rehnquist noted that the tax deduction for educational expenses was available to a broad beneficiary class on a neutral basis. He compared this financial benefit to the requirement in *Widmar* that a state university must afford both religious and nonreligious speakers equal access to a public forum. Several of the briefs in the following case urged a critical distinction between granting access to speaking forums on a content-neutral and viewpoint-neutral basis and providing economically valuable services to advance religious ideas. For this reason the case could as easily be analyzed under the category of subsidy as under the category of equal access.

Like *Agostini* [section 1 above], the next case provoked a sharp conflict on the Court between Justices emphasizing two principles articulated in *Everson* [section 1 above]: (1) the *nondiscrimination principle*, described by Justice Black as follows: "we must be careful, in protecting the citizens of New Jersey against state-established churches, to be sure that we do not inadvertently prohibit [the State] from extending its general state law benefits to all its citizens without regard to their religious belief" and (2), the *no-aid principle*, described by Black as follows: "No tax in any amount, large or small, can be levied to support any religious activities or institutions, whatever they may be called, or whatever form they may adopt to teach or practice religion."

In 1990 Ronald Rosenberger and other undergraduates at the University of Virginia formed a student organization known as Wide Awake Productions [WAP]. Shortly thereafter, WAP was approved as a "Contracting Independent Organization" [CIO], which meant that the organization, though independent of university control, could request payment of bills to third-party contractors for carrying out the purposes of the organization. The purposes of WAP are "to publish a magazine of philosophical and religious expression, to facilitate discussion which fosters an atmosphere of sensitivity to and tolerance of Christian viewpoints, and to provide a unifying focus for Christians of multicultural backgrounds." The organization publishes *Wide Awake: A Christian Perspective at the University of Virginia*. As the Court noted, "The paper's Christian viewpoint was evident from the first issue, in which its editors wrote that the journal offers a Christian perspective on both personal and community issues, especially those relevant to college students at the University of Virginia. The editors committed the paper to a two-fold mission: to challenge Christians to live, in word and deed, according to the faith they proclaim and to encourage students to consider what a personal relationship with Jesus Christ means. The first issue had articles about racism, crisis pregnancy, stress, prayer, C. S. Lewis' ideas about evil and free will, and reviews of religious music. In the next two issues, *Wide Awake* featured stories about homosexuality, Christian missionary work, and eating disorders, as well as music reviews and interviews with University professors. Each page of *Wide Awake*, and the end of each article or review, is marked by a cross. The advertisements carried in *Wide Awake* also reveal the Christian perspective of the journal. For the most part, the advertisers are churches, centers for Christian study, or Christian bookstores." WAP requested the Student Activities Fund to pay its printer $5,862 for the costs of printing its newspaper, which by 1992 had a circulation of 5,000 copies. The Appropriations Committee of the Student Council denied WAP's request on the ground that Wide Awake was a religious activity i.e., that the newspaper "promoted or manifested a particular belief in or about a deity or an ultimate reality." WAP appealed the denial to the full Student Council, contending that denial of support on the basis of the magazine's religious perspective violated the Constitution. The appeal was denied without further comment. In a letter signed by the Dean of Students, the Student Activities Committee sustained the denial of funding.

Having no further recourse within the University structure, WAP, Wide Awake, and three of its editors and members filed suit in federal court, alleging that refusal to authorize payment of the printing costs of the publication, solely on the basis of its religious editorial viewpoint, violated their rights to freedom of speech and press, to the free exercise of religion, and to equal protection of the law. The district court ruled for the University, holding that denial of support was not an impermissible content or viewpoint discrimination against the speech of the students. Disagreeing with the district court on this point, the Court of Appeals held that the University Guidelines refusing funding to religious activity did discriminate on the basis of content. It ruled that, while the State need not underwrite speech, there was a presumptive violation of the Speech Clause when viewpoint discrimination was invoked to deny third-party payment otherwise available to CIOs. The Court of Appeals, however, affirmed the judgment, concluding that the discrimination by the University was justified by the "compelling interest in maintaining strict separation of church and state." The question presented in the Supreme Court was "Whether the Establishment Clause compels a state university to exclude an otherwise eligible student publication from participation in the student activities fund, solely on the basis of its religious viewpoint, where such exclusion would violate the Speech and Press Clauses if the viewpoint of the publication were nonreligious." Pet. for Cert. i.

Rosenberger v. Rector and Visitors of the University of Virginia

515 U.S. 819 (1995).

Michael W. McConnell argued the cause for the petitioners; with him on the briefs was *Michael P. McDonald. John C. Jeffries, Jr.,* argued the cause for respondents; with him on the brief was *James J. Mingle.*

Briefs of amici curiae urging reversal were filed for the Commonwealth of Virginia by *James S. Gilmore III*, Attorney General, *David E. Anderson*, Chief Deputy Attorney General, *William Henry Hurd*, Deputy Attorney General, and *Alison Paige Landry*, Assistant Attorney General; for the American Center for Law and Justice by *Jay Alan Sekulow, James Matthew Henderson, Sr.,* and *Keith A. Fournier;* for the Catholic League for Political and Religious Rights by *Edward McGlynn Gaffney, Jr.;* for the Christian Legal Society et al. by *Douglas Laycock, Steven T. McFarland,* and *Samuel B. Casey;* and for the Intercollegiate Studies Institute *by Robert M. Rader* and *Donn C. Meindertsma.*

Briefs of amici curiae urging affirmance were filed for the American Civil Liberties Union et al. by *Marjorie Heins, Steven R. Shapiro,* and *Steven B. Pershing*; for Americans United for Separation of Church and State by *Steven K. Green, Samuel Rabinove, Jeffrey P. Sinensky,* and *Steven M. Freeman*; for the Baptist Joint Committee on Public Affairs et al. by *J. Brent Walker, Oliver S. Thomas, Elliott M. Mincberg, Melissa Rogers, David Saperstein,* and *Lois C. Waldma*; for the Council on Religious Freedom by *Lee Boothby, Walter E. Carson, Robert W. Nixon,* and *Rolland Truman*; for the National School Boards Association by *Gwendolyn H. Gregory, August W. Steinhilber,* and *Thomas A. Shanon*; for the Pacific Legal Foundation by *Anthony T. Caso* and *Deborah J. La Letra*; and for the Student Press Center by *S. Mark Goodman.*

■ JUSTICE KENNEDY delivered the opinion of the Court.

The University of Virginia, an instrumentality of the Commonwealth for which it is named and thus bound by the First and Fourteenth Amendments, authorizes the payment of outside contractors for the printing costs of a variety of student publications. It withheld any authorization for payments on behalf of petitioners for the sole reason that their student paper primarily promotes or manifests a particular belief in or about a deity or an ultimate reality. That the paper did promote or manifest views within the defined exclusion seems plain enough. The challenge is to the University's regulation and its denial of authorization, the case raising issues under the Speech and Establishment Clauses of the First Amendment. . . .

II

It is axiomatic that the government may not regulate speech based on its substantive content or the message it conveys. *Police Dept. of Chicago v. Mosley*, 408 U.S. 92, 96 (1972). . . . In the realm of private speech or expression, government regulation may not favor one speaker over another. *City Council of Los Angeles v. Taxpayers for Vincent*, 466 U.S. 789, 804 (1984). Discrimination against speech because of its message is presumed to be unconstitutional. *Turner Broadcasting System, Inc. v. FCC*, 512 U.S. 622 (1994). These rules informed our determination that the government offends the First Amendment when it imposes financial burdens on certain speakers based on the content of their expression. *Simon & Schuster, Inc. v. Members of N. Y. State Crime Victims Bd.*, 502 U.S. 105, 115 (1991). When the government targets not subject matter but particular views taken by speakers on a subject, the violation of the First Amendment is all the more blatant. *R.A.V. v. St. Paul*, 505 U.S. 377, 391 (1992). Viewpoint discrimination is thus an egregious form of content discrimination. The government must abstain from regulating speech when the specific motivating ideology or the opinion or perspective of the speaker is the rationale for the restriction. *Perry Ed. Assn. v. Perry Local Educators' Assn.*, 460 U.S. 37, 46 (1983).

These principles provide the framework forbidding the State from exercising viewpoint discrimination, even when the limited public forum is one of its own creation. In a case involving a school district's provision of school facilities for private uses, we declared that there is no question that the District, like the private owner of property, may legally preserve the property under its control for the use to which it is dedicate. *Lamb's Chapel v. Center Moriches Union Free School Dist.* [section 2H above]. Once it has opened a limited forum, the State must respect the lawful boundaries it has itself set. The State may not exclude speech where its distinction is not reasonable in light of the purpose served by the forum, nor may it discriminate against speech on the basis of its viewpoint. Thus, in determining whether the State is acting to preserve the limits of the forum it has created so that the exclusion of a class of speech is legitimate, we have observed a distinction between, on the one hand, content discrimination, which may be permissible if it preserves the purposes of that limited forum, and, on the other hand, viewpoint discrimination, which is presumed impermissible when directed against speech otherwise within the forum's limitations.

The SAF is a forum more in a metaphysical than in a spatial or geographic sense, but the same principles are applicable. *Lamb's Chapel....* Our conclusion was unanimous: It discriminates on the basis of viewpoint to permit school property to be used for the presentation of all views about family issues and child-rearing except those dealing with the subject matter from a religious standpoint.

The University does acknowledge (as it must in light of our precedents) that ideologically driven attempts to suppress a particular point of view are presumptively unconstitutional in funding, as in other contexts, but insists that this case does not present that issue because the Guidelines draw lines based on content, not viewpoint.... It is, in a sense, something of an understatement to speak of religious thought and discussion as just a viewpoint, as distinct from a comprehensive body of thought. The nature of our origins and destiny and their dependence upon the existence of a divine being have been subjects of philosophic inquiry throughout human history. We conclude, nonetheless, that here, as in *Lamb's Chapel*, viewpoint discrimination is the proper way to interpret the University's objections to *Wide Awake*. By the very terms of the SAF prohibition, the University does not exclude religion as a subject matter but selects for disfavored treatment those student journalistic efforts with religious editorial viewpoints. Religion may be a vast area of inquiry, but it also provides, as it did here, a specific premise, a perspective, a standpoint from which a variety of subjects may be discussed and considered. The prohibited perspective, not the general subject matter, resulted in the refusal to make third-party payments, for the subjects discussed were otherwise within the approved category of publications. . . .

The University's denial of WAP's request for third-party payments in the present case is based upon viewpoint discrimination not unlike the discrimination the school district relied upon in *Lamb's Chapel* and that we found invalid. The church group in *Lamb's Chapel* would have been qualified as a social or civic organization, save for its religious purposes. Furthermore, just as the school district in *Lamb's Chapel* pointed to nothing but the religious views of the group as the rationale for excluding its message, so in this case the University justifies its denial of SAF participation to WAP on the ground that the contents of *Wide Awake* reveal an avowed religious perspective. . . .

The University tries to escape the consequences of our holding in *Lamb's Chapel* by urging that this case involves the provision of funds rather than access to facilities. The University begins with the unremarkable proposition that the State must have substantial discretion in determining how to allocate scarce resources to accomplish its educational mission. Citing our decisions in *Rust v. Sullivan*, 500 U.S. 173 (1991), *Regan v. Taxation with Representation of Wash.*, 461 U.S. 540 (1983), and *Widmar*, the University argues that content-based funding decisions are both inevitable and lawful. Were the reasoning of *Lamb's Chapel* to apply to funding decisions as well as to those involving access to facilities, it is urged, its holding would become a judicial juggernaut, constitutionalizing the ubiquitous content-based decisions that schools, colleges, and other government entities routinely make in the allocation of public funds.

To this end the University relies on our assurance in *Widmar*. There, in the course of striking down a public university's exclusion of religious groups from use of school facilities made available to all other student groups, we stated: "Nor do we question the right of the University to make academic judgments as to how best to allocate scarce resources." The quoted language in *Widmar* was but a proper recognition of the principle that when the State is the speaker, it may make content-based choices. When the University determines the content of the education it provides, it is the University speaking, and we have permitted the government to regulate the content of what is or is not expressed when it is the speaker or when it enlists private entities to convey its own message. . . . We recognized that when the government appropriates public funds to promote a particular policy of its own it is entitled to say what it wishes. When the government disburses public funds to private entities to convey a governmental message, it may take legitimate and appropriate steps to ensure that its message is neither garbled nor distorted by the grantee.

It does not follow, however, and we did not suggest in *Widmar*, that viewpoint-based restrictions are proper when the University does not itself speak or subsidize transmittal of a message it favors but instead expends funds to encourage a diversity of views from private speakers. A holding that the University may not discriminate based on the viewpoint of private persons whose speech it facilitates does not restrict the University's own speech, which is controlled by different principles. *Mergens* [section 2E above]. . . .

The distinction between the University's own favored message and the private speech of students is evident in the case before us. . . . The University declares that the student groups eligible for SAF support are not the University's agents, are not subject to its control, and are not its responsibility. Having offered to pay the third-party contractors on behalf of private speakers who convey their own messages, the University may not silence the expression of selected viewpoints. . . . Vital First Amendment speech principles are at stake here. The first danger to liberty lies in granting the State the power to examine publications to determine whether or not they are based on some ultimate idea and if so for the State to classify them. The second, and corollary, danger is to speech from the chilling of individual thought and expression. That danger is especially real in the University setting, where the State acts against a background and tradition of thought and experiment that is at the center of our intellectual and philosophic tradition. In ancient Athens, and, as Europe entered into a new period of intellectual awakening, in places like Bologna, Oxford, and Paris, universities began as voluntary and spontaneous assemblages or concourses for students to speak and to write and to learn. The quality and creative power of student intellectual life to this day remains a vital measure of a school's influence and attainment. For the University, by regulation, to cast disapproval on particular viewpoints of its students risks the suppression of free speech and creative inquiry in one of the vital centers for the nation's intellectual life, its college and university campuses. . . .

Based on the principles we have discussed, we hold that the regulation invoked to deny SAF support, both in its terms and in its application to these petitioners, is a denial of their right of free speech guaranteed by the First Amendment. It remains to be considered whether the violation following from the University's action is excused by the necessity of complying with the Constitution's prohibition against state establishment of religion. We turn to that question

III

The Court of Appeals ruled that withholding SAF support from *Wide Awake* contravened the Speech Clause of the First Amendment, but proceeded to hold that the University's action was justified by the necessity of avoiding a violation of the Establishment Clause, an interest it found compelling. . . . It reasoned that because *Wide Awake* is a journal pervasively devoted to the discussion and advancement of an avowedly Christian theological and personal philosophy, the University's provision of SAF funds for its publication would send an unmistakably clear signal that the University of Virginia supports Christian values and wishes to promote the wide promulgation of such values.

If there is to be assurance that the Establishment Clause retains its force in guarding against those governmental actions it was intended to prohibit, we must in each case inquire first into the purpose and object of the governmental action in question and then into the practical details of the program's operation. Before turning to these matters, however, we can set forth certain general principles that must bear upon our determination.

A central lesson of our decisions is that a significant factor in upholding governmental programs in the face of Establishment Clause attack is their neutrality towards religion. We have decided a series of cases addressing the receipt of government benefits where religion or religious views are implicated in some degree. The first case in our modern Establishment Clause jurisprudence was *Everson* [section 1 above]. There we cautioned that in enforcing the prohibition against laws respecting establishment of religion, we must be sure that we do not inadvertently prohibit the government from extending its general state law benefits to all its citizens without regard to their religious belief. We have held that the guarantee of neutrality is respected, not offended, when the government, following neutral criteria and evenhanded policies, extends benefits to recipients whose ideologies and viewpoints, including religious ones, are broad and diverse (citations omitted). *Kiryas Joel* [section 1 above]; *Witters; Mueller; Widmar.* More than once have we rejected the position that the Establishment Clause even justifies, much less requires, a refusal to extend free speech rights to religious speakers who participate in broad-reaching government programs neutral in design. See *Lamb's Chapel; Mergens; Widmar.*

The governmental program here is neutral toward religion. There is no suggestion that the University created it to advance religion or adopted some ingenious device with the purpose of aiding a religious cause. The object of the SAF is to open a forum for speech and to support various student enterprises, including the publication of newspapers, in recognition of the diversity and creativity of student life. The University's SAF Guidelines have a separate classification for, and do not make third-party payments on behalf of, religious organizations, which are those whose purpose is to practice a devotion to an acknowledged ultimate reality or deity. The category of support here is for student news, information, opinion, entertainment, or academic communications media groups, of which Wide Awake was 1 of 15 in the 1990 school year. WAP did not seek a subsidy because of its Christian editorial viewpoint; it sought funding as a student journal, which it was.

The neutrality of the program distinguishes the student fees from a tax levied for the direct support of a church or group of churches. A tax of that sort, of course, would run contrary to Establishment Clause concerns dating from the earliest days of the Republic. The apprehensions of our predecessors involved the levying of taxes upon the public for the sole and exclusive purpose of establishing and supporting specific sects. The exaction here, by contrast, is a student activity fee designed to reflect the reality that student life in its many dimensions includes the necessity of wide-ranging speech and inquiry and that student expression is an integral part of the University's educational mission.... We must treat it, then, as an exaction upon the students. But the $14 paid each semester by the students is not a general tax designed to raise revenue for the University.

The SAF cannot be used for unlimited purposes, much less the illegitimate purpose of supporting one religion. Much like the arrangement in *Widmar*, the money goes to a special fund from which any group of students with CIO status can draw for purposes consistent with the University's educational mission; and to the extent the student is interested in speech, withdrawal is permitted to cover the whole spectrum of speech, whether it manifests a religious view, an antireligious view, or neither. Our decision, then, cannot be read as addressing an expenditure from a general tax fund. Here, the disbursements from the fund go to private contractors for the cost of printing that which is protected under the Speech Clause. This is a far cry from a general public assessment designed and effected to provide financial support for a church. . . .

The Court of Appeals (and the dissent) are correct to extract from our decisions the principle that we have recognized special Establishment Clause dangers where the government makes direct money payments to sectarian institutions. *Roemer; Hunt; Tilton* [section 3A above]; *Allen* [section 1 above]. The error is not in identifying the principle but in believing that it controls this case. Even assuming that WAP is no different from a church and that its speech is the same as the religious exercises conducted in *Widmar* (two points much in doubt), the Court of Appeals decided a case that was, in essence, not before it, and the dissent would have us do the same. We do not confront a case where, even under a neutral program that includes nonsectarian recipients, the government is making direct money payments to an institution or group that is engaged in religious activity. Neither the Court of Appeals nor the dissent, we believe, takes sufficient cognizance of the undisputed fact that no public funds flow directly to WAP's coffers.

It does not violate the Establishment Clause for a public university to grant access to its facilities on a religion-neutral basis to a wide spectrum of student groups, including groups which use meeting rooms for sectarian activities, accompanied by some devotional exercises. *Widmar; Mergens*. This is so even where the upkeep, maintenance, and repair of the facilities attributed to those uses is paid from a student activities fund to which students are required to contribute. *Widmar*. The government usually acts by spending money. Even the provision of a meeting room, as in *Mergens* and *Widmar*, involved governmental expenditure, if only in the form of electricity and heating or cooling costs. The error made by the Court of Appeals, as well as by the dissent, lies in focusing on the money that is undoubtedly expended by the government, rather than on the nature of the benefit received by the recipient. If the expenditure of governmental funds is prohibited whenever those funds pay for a service that is, pursuant to a religion-neutral program, used by a group for sectarian purposes, then *Widmar, Mergens*, and *Lamb's Chapel* would have to be overruled. Given our holdings in these cases, it follows that a public university may maintain its own computer facility and give student groups access to that facility, including the use of the printers, on a religion neutral, say first-come-first-served, basis. If a religious student organization obtained access on that religion-neutral basis and used a computer to compose or a printer or copy machine to print speech with a religious content or viewpoint, the State's action in providing the group with access would no more violate the Establishment Clause than would giving those groups access to an assembly hall. There is no difference in logic or principle, and no difference of constitutional significance, between a school using its funds to operate a facility to which students have access, and a school paying a third-party contractor to operate the facility on its behalf. The latter occurs here. The University provides printing services to a broad spectrum of student newspapers qualified as CIOs by reason of their officers and membership. Any benefit to religion is incidental to the government's provision of secular services for secular purposes on a religion-neutral basis. Printing is a routine, secular, and recurring attribute of student life.

By paying outside printers, the University in fact attains a further degree of separation from the student publication, for it avoids the duties of supervision, escapes the costs of upkeep, repair, and replacement attributable to student use, and has a clear record of costs. As a result, and as in *Widmar*, the University can charge the SAF, and not the taxpayers as a whole, for the discrete activity in question. It would be formalistic for us to say that the University must forfeit these advantages and provide the services itself in order to comply with the Establishment Clause. It is, of course, true that if the State pays a church's bills it is subsidizing it, and we must guard against this abuse. That is not a danger here, based on the considerations we have advanced and for the additional reason that the student publication is not a religious institution, at least in the usual sense of that term as used in our case law, and it is not a religious organization as used in the University's own regulations. It is instead a publication involved in a pure forum for the expression of ideas, ideas that would be both incomplete and chilled were the Constitution to be interpreted to require that state officials and courts scan the publication to ferret out views that principally manifest a belief in a divine being.

[Justice Kennedy noted that scrutinizing the content of student speech to determine whether it contains "too great a religious content" raises the specter of "governmental censorship, to ensure that all student writings and publications meet some baseline standard of secular orthodoxy."] As we recognized in *Widmar*, official censorship would be far more inconsistent with the Establishment Clause's dictates than would governmental provision of secular printing services on a religion-blind basis. . . .

To obey the Establishment Clause, it was not necessary for the University to deny eligibility to student publications because of their viewpoint. The neutrality commanded of the State by the separate Clauses of the First Amendment was compromised by the University's course of action. The viewpoint discrimination inherent in the University's regulation required public officials to scan and interpret student publications to discern their underlying philosophic assumptions respecting religious theory and belief. That course of action was a denial of the right of free speech and would risk fostering a pervasive bias or hostility to religion, which could undermine the very neutrality the Establishment Clause requires. There is no Establishment Clause violation in the University's honoring its duties under the Free Speech Clause. The judgment of the Court of Appeals must be, and is, *reversed*. It is so ordered.

■ JUSTICE O'CONNOR, concurring.

We have time and again held that the government generally may not treat people differently based on the God or gods they worship, or don't worship. *Kiryas Joel* (O'Connor, J., concurring). This insistence on government neutrality toward religion explains why we have held that schools may not discriminate against religious groups by denying them equal access to facilities that the schools make available to all. *Lamb's Chapel*; *Widmar*. Withholding access would leave an impermissible perception that religious activities are disfavored: the message is one of neutrality rather than endorsement; if a State refused to let religious groups use facilities open to others, then it would demonstrate not neutrality but hostility toward religion. *Mergens*. The Religion Clauses prohibit the government from favoring religion, but they provide no warrant for discriminating against religion. Neutrality, in both form and effect, is one hallmark of the Establishment Clause. As Justice Souter demonstrates, however, there exists another axiom in the history and precedent of the Establishment Clause. Public funds may not be used to endorse the religious message. *Bowen v. Kendrick* (Blackmun, J., dissenting) (O'Connor, J., concurring) [Chapter Thirteen, section 7]. Our cases have permitted some government funding of secular functions performed by sectarian organizations. *Kendrick*; *Roemer*; *Bradfield v. Roberts* [Chapter Ten, section 2]. These decisions, however, provide no precedent for the use of public funds to finance religious activities.

This case lies at the intersection of the principle of government neutrality and the prohibition on state funding of religious activities.... When two bedrock principles so conflict, understandably neither can provide the definitive answer. Reliance on categorical platitudes is unavailing. Resolution instead depends on the hard task of judging—sifting through the details and determining whether the challenged program offends the Establishment Clause. Such judgment requires courts to draw lines, sometimes quite fine, based on the particular facts of each case....

[In *Witters*] we thus resolved the conflict between the neutrality principle and the funding prohibition, not by permitting one to trump the other, but by relying on the elements of choice peculiar to the facts of that case. The aid to religion at issue here is the result of petitioner's private choice. No reasonable observer is likely to draw from the facts before us an inference that the State itself is endorsing a religious practice or belief.... [T]he decision [in *Everson*] reflected the need to rely on careful judgment—not simple categories—when two principles, of equal historical and jurisprudential pedigree, come into unavoidable conflict.

So it is in this case. The nature of the dispute does not admit of categorical answers, nor should any be inferred from the Court's decision today. Instead, certain considerations specific to the program at issue lead me to conclude that by providing the same assistance to Wide Awake that it does to other publications, the University would not be endorsing the magazine's religious perspective. [Justice O'Connor focused on three details in the record: (1) the independence of the student organizations from the university; (2) the distribution of financial assistance in a manner that ensures its use only for permissible purposes; and (3) the provision of assistance to many student groups with "widely divergent viewpoints." She noted that besides the general news publications, the university provided support to *The Yellow Journal,* a humor magazine that has targeted Christianity as a subject of satire, and *Al-Salam,* a publication to promote a better understanding of Islam to the university community. She concluded that this factual context "makes improbable any perception of government endorsement of the religious message.... Given this wide array of non-religious, anti-religious and competing religious viewpoints in the forum supported by the University, any perception that the University endorses one particular viewpoint would be illogical.]

The Court's decision today therefore neither trumpets the supremacy of the neutrality principle nor signals the demise of the funding prohibition in Establishment Clause jurisprudence.... When bedrock principles collide, they test the limits of categorical obstinacy and expose the flaws and dangers of a Grand Unified Theory that may turn out to be neither grand nor unified. The Court today does only what courts must do in many Establishment Clause cases—focus on specific features of a particular government action to ensure that it does not violate the Constitution. By withholding from Wide Awake assistance that the University provides generally to all other student publications, the University has discriminated on the basis of the magazine's religious viewpoint in violation of the Free Speech Clause. And particular features of the University's program—such as the explicit disclaimer, the disbursement of fund directly to third-party vendors, the vigorous nature of the forum at issue, and the possibility for objecting students to opt out—convince me that providing such assistance in this case would not carry the danger of impermissible use of public funds to endorse Wide Awake's religious message.

■ JUSTICE THOMAS, concurring.

I agree with the Court's opinion and join it in full, but I write separately to express my disagreement with the historical analysis put forward by the dissent. Although the dissent starts down the right path in consulting the original meaning of the Establishment Clause, its misleading application of history yields a principle that is inconsistent with our Nation's long tradition of allowing religious adherents to participate on equal terms in neutral government programs.

[Justice Thomas took specific exception to the dissent's reliance on the Virginia debate on the "Assessment Controversy" for the conclusion that "government must actively discriminate against religion." Thomas criticized the dissent for glossing over "the fundamental characteristic of the Virginia assessment bill that sparked the controversy: The assessment was to be imposed for the support of clergy in the performance of their function of teaching religion. Thus, the Bill Establishing a Provision for Teachers of the Christian Religion provided for the collection of a specific tax, the proceeds of which were to be appropriated 'by the Vestries, Elders, or Directors of each religious society ... to a provision for a Minister or

Teacher of the Gospel of their denomination, or the providing places of divine worship, and to none other use whatsoever.' " He concluded:]

Though our Establishment Clause jurisprudence is in hopeless disarray, this case provides an opportunity to reaffirm one basic principle that has enjoyed an uncharacteristic degree of consensus: The Clause does not compel the exclusion of religious groups from government benefits programs that are generally available to a broad class of participants. *Lamb's Chapel; Zobrest; Mergens; Texas Monthly; Witters; Mueller; Widmar.* Under the dissent's view, however, the University of Virginia may provide neutral access to the University's own printing press, but it may not provide the same service when the press is owned by a third party. Not surprisingly, the dissent offers no logical justification for this conclusion, and none is evident in the text or original meaning of the First Amendment.

If the Establishment Clause is offended when religious adherents benefit from neutral programs such as the University of Virginia's Student Activities Fund, it must also be offended when they receive the same benefits in the form of in-kind subsidies. The constitutional demands of the Establishment Clause may be judged against either a baseline of neutrality or a baseline of no aid to religion, but the appropriate baseline surely cannot depend on the fortuitous circumstances surrounding the form of aid. The contrary rule would lead to absurd results that would jettison centuries of practice respecting the right of religious adherents to participate on neutral terms in a wide variety of government-funded programs.

Our Nation's tradition of allowing religious adherents to participate in evenhanded government programs is hardly limited to the class of essential public benefits identified by the dissent. A broader tradition can be traced at least as far back as the First Congress, which ratified the Northwest Ordinance of 1787 [Chapter Seven, section 6]. Article III of that famous enactment of the Confederation Congress had provided: "Religion, morality, and knowledge ... being necessary to good government and the happiness of mankind, schools and the means of learning shall forever be encouraged." Congress subsequently set aside federal lands in the Northwest Territory and other territories for the use of schools. Many of the schools that enjoyed the benefits of these land grants undoubtedly were church-affiliated sectarian institutions as there was no requirement that the schools be public. See C. Antieau, A. Downey, & E. Roberts, *Freedom From Federal Establishment, Formation and Early History of the First Amendment Religion Clauses* 163 (1964). Nevertheless, early Congresses found no problem with the provision of such neutral benefits.

Numerous other government benefits traditionally have been available to religious adherents on neutral terms. Several examples may be found in the work of early Congresses, including copyright protection for the author and authors of any map, chart, book or books, Act of May 31, 1790, ch. 15, § 1, 1 Stat. 124, and a privilege allowing every printer of newspapers to send one paper to each and every other printer of newspapers within the United States, free of postage, Act of Feb. 20, 1792, ch. 7, § 21, 1 Stat. 232, 238. Neither of these laws made any exclusion for the numerous authors or printers who manifested a belief in or about a deity. Thus, history provides an answer for the constitutional question posed by this case, but it is not the one given by the dissent. The dissent identifies no evidence that the Framers intended to disable religious entities from participating on neutral terms in evenhanded government programs. The evidence that does exist points in the opposite direction and provides ample support for today's decision.

■ JUSTICE SOUTER, with whom JUSTICES STEVENS, GINSBURG, and BREYER join, dissenting.

The Court today, for the first time, approves direct funding of core religious activities by an arm of the State. It does so, however, only after erroneous treatment of some familiar principles of law implementing the First Amendment's Establishment and Speech Clauses, and by viewing the very funds in question as beyond the reach of the Establishment Clause's funding restrictions as such. Because there is no warrant for distinguishing among public funding sources for purposes of applying the First Amendment's prohibition of religious establishment, I would hold that the University's refusal to support petitioners' religious activities is compelled by the Establishment Clause. I would therefore affirm.

I

The central question in this case is whether a grant from the SAF to pay *Wide Awake's* printing expenses would violate the Establishment Clause. Although the Court does not dwell on the details of *Wide Awake's* message, it recognizes something sufficiently religious in the publication to demand Establishment Clause scrutiny. Although the Court places great stress on the eligibility of secular as well as religious activities for grants from the SAF, it recognizes that such evenhanded availability is not by itself enough to satisfy constitutional requirements for any aid scheme that results in a benefit to religion. Something more is necessary to justify any religious aid. Some members of the Court, at least, may think the funding permissible on a view that it is indirect, since the money goes to *Wide Awake's* printer, not through *Wide Awake's* own checking account. The Court's principal reliance, however, is on an argument that providing religion with economically valuable services is permissible on the theory that services are economically indistinguishable from religious access to governmental speech forums, which sometimes is permissible. But this reasoning would commit the Court to approving direct religious aid beyond anything justifiable for the sake of access to speaking forums. The Court implicitly recognizes this in its further attempt to circumvent the clear bar to direct governmental aid to religion. Different members of the Court seek to avoid this bar in different ways. The opinion of the Court makes the novel assumption that only direct aid financed with tax revenue is barred, and draws the erroneous conclusion that the involuntary Student Activities Fee is not a tax. . . . The resulting decision is in unmistakable tension with the accepted law that the Court continues to avow. . . .

[Justice Souter cited several examples of articles published in *Wide Awake.* He concluded:] This writing is no merely descriptive examination of religious doctrine or even of ideal Christian practice in confronting life's social and personal problems. Nor is it merely the expression of editorial opinion that incidentally coincides with Christian ethics and reflects a Christian view of human obligation. It is straightforward exhortation to enter into a relationship with God as revealed in Jesus Christ, and to satisfy a series of moral obligations derived from the teachings of Jesus Christ.... The subject is not the discourse of the scholar's study or the seminar room, but of the evangelist's mission station and the pulpit. It is nothing other than the preaching of the word, which (along with the sacraments) is what most branches of Christianity offer those called to the religious life.

Using public funds for the direct subsidization of preaching the word is categorically forbidden under the Establishment Clause, and if the Clause was meant to accomplish nothing else, it was meant to bar this use of public money. Evidence on the subject antedates even the Bill of Rights itself, as may be seen in the writings of Madison, whose authority on questions about the meaning of the Establishment Clause is well settled. *Nyquist; Everson.* Four years before the First Congress proposed the First Amendment, Madison gave his opinion on the legitimacy of using public funds for religious purposes, in the Memorial and Remonstrance Against Religious Assessments, which played the central role in ensuring the defeat of the Virginia tax assessment bill in 1786 and framed the debate upon which the Religion Clauses stand: "Who does not see that ... the same authority which can force a citizen to contribute three pence only of his property for the support of any one establishment, may force him to conform to any other establishment in all cases whatsoever?" James Madison, Memorial and Remonstrance [Chapter Six, section 3].

Madison wrote against a background in which nearly every Colony had exacted a tax for church support, the practice having become so commonplace as to shock the freedom-loving colonials into a feeling of abhorrence. *Everson.* Madison's Remonstrance captured the colonists' conviction that individual religious liberty could be achieved best under a government which was stripped of all power to tax, to support, or otherwise to assist any or all religions, or to interfere with the beliefs of any religious individual or group. Their sentiment as expressed by Madison in Virginia, led not only to the defeat of Virginia's tax assessment bill, but also directly to passage of the Virginia Bill for Establishing Religious Freedom, written by Thomas Jefferson. That bill's preamble declared that to compel a man to furnish contributions of money for the propagation of opinions which he disbelieves, is sinful and tyrannical, Jefferson, A Bill for Establishing Religious Freedom, reprinted in 5 The Founder's Constitution 84–85 (P. Kurland & R. Lerner eds. 1987), and its text provided that "no man shall be compelled to frequent or support any religious worship, place, or ministry whatsoever...." We have previously recognized that the provisions of the First Amendment, in the drafting and adoption of which Madison and Jefferson played such leading roles, had the same objective and were intended to provide the same protection against governmental intrusion on religious liberty as the Virginia statute. *Everson;* see also Laycock, Nonpreferential Aid to Religion: A False Claim About Original Intent, 27 Wm. & Mary L. Rev. 875, 921, 923 (1986) ("If the debates of the

1780's support any proposition, it is that the Framers opposed government financial support for religion.... They did not substitute small taxes for large taxes; three pence was as bad as any larger sum. The principle was what mattered. With respect to money, religion was to be wholly voluntary. Churches either would support themselves or they would not, but the government would neither help nor interfere"); T. Curry, *The First Freedoms* 217 (1986) ("At the time of the framing of the Bill of Rights, the belief that government assistance to religion, especially in the form of taxes, violated religious liberty had a long history"); J. Choper, *Securing Religious Liberty* 16 (1995) ("There is broad consensus that a central threat to the religious freedom of individuals and groups—indeed, in the judgment of many the most serious infringement upon religious liberty—is posed by forcing them to pay taxes in support of a religious establishment or religious activities")....

The principle against direct funding with public money is patently violated by the contested use of today's student activity fee. Like today's taxes generally, the fee is Madison's threepence. The University exercises the power of the State to compel as a student to pay it, see Jefferson's Preamble, and the use of any part of it for the direct support of religious activity thus strikes at what we have repeatedly held to be the heart of the prohibition on establishment....

In the doubtful cases (those not involving direct public funding), where there is initially room for argument about as a law's effect, evenhandedness serves to weed out those laws that impermissibly advance religion by channelling aid to it exclusively. Evenhandedness is therefore as a prerequisite to further enquiry into the constitutionality of as a doubtful law,[5] but evenhandedness goes no further. It does not guarantee success under Establishment Clause scrutiny.... Evenhandedness as one element of as a permissibly attenuated benefit is, of course, as a far cry from evenhandedness as a sufficient condition of constitutionality for direct financial support of religious proselytization, and our cases have unsurprisingly repudiated any such attempt to cut the Establishment Clause down to as a mere prohibition against unequal direct aid....

III

Since I cannot see the future I cannot tell whether today's decision portends much more than making as a shambles out of student activity fees in public colleges. Still, my apprehension is whetted by Chief Justice Burger's warning in *Lemon*: "in constitutional adjudication some steps, which when taken were thought to approach 'the verge,' have become the platform for yet further steps. as a certain momentum develops in constitutional theory and it can be as a 'downhill thrust' easily set in motion but difficult to retard or stop." I respectfully dissent.

5. In as a narrow band of cases at the polar extreme from direct funding cases, those involving essential public benefits commonly associated with living in an organized society (like police and fire protection, for example), evenhandedness may become important to ensuring that religious interests are not inhibited.

C. EXEMPTION

Section 501(c)(3) of the Internal Revenue Code exempts "corporations . . . organized and operated exclusively for religious, charitable . . . *or* educational purposes. . . ." from tax on their income. In the following case, the Court read the "or" to mean "*and*," thus requiring all exempt organizations to be "charitable," and importing the law of charitable trusts into the law of tax exemption. This interpretive move enabled the Court to require conformity of exempt organizations, including religious schools, to "public policy." Because the Court did not confine the definition of "public policy" very carefully, the case could serve as the basis for an expansive reading of authority to regulate religious schools because of their exempt status. One commentator has, for example, has proposed banning "tax exemptions and postal subsidies and award of government contracts to religious organizations that close leadership positions to women." *See* Mary Becker, "The Politics of Women's Wrongs and the Bill of 'Rights': as a Bicentennial Perspective," 59 *U. Chi. L. Rev.* 453 (1992).

Bob Jones, the President of Bob Jones University, is a fundamentalist pastor who read the stories about separation of the sons of Noah (Shem, Ham, and Japheth; Gen. 10:5,20,31) by language and land to require racial separation in today's world. Accordingly, Bob Jones University maintained until recently a policy of student discipline against racial intermarriage. Because no other religious university maintains a rule of student discipline remotely similar to this position, the rule announced in the case "may ultimately govern one set of facts and no other." Paul B. Stephan III, "Bob Jones University v. United States: Public Policy in Search of Tax Policy," 1983 *Sup. Ct. Rev.* 33.

Many years after the decision, Stephan's prediction that the rule in the case would be of very narrow application has proved more descriptive than Becker's desire to expand its scope beyond racial discrimination in education to issues such as the ordination of women [Chapter Eleven, section 6]. Which of these approaches make better sense to you? Why?

Bob Jones University v. United States (No. 81–3) Goldsboro Christian Schools, Inc. v. United States (No. 81–1)

461 U.S. 574 (1983).

William G. McNairy argued the cause for petitioner in No. 81–1. With him on the briefs were *Claude C. Pierce, Edward C. Winslow*, and *John H. Small. William Bentley Ball* argued the cause for petitioner in No. 81–3. With him on the briefs were *Philip J. Murren* and *Richard E. Connell.*

Assistant Attorney General *Reynolds* argued the cause for the United States in both cases. With him on the briefs were Acting Solicitor General *Wallace* and Deputy Assistant Attorney General *Cooper.*

William T. Coleman, Jr., pro se, by invitation of the Court, 456 U.S. 922, argued the cause as *amicus curiae* urging affirmance. With him on the brief were *Richard C. Warmer, Donald T. Bliss, John W. Stamper, Ira M. Feinberg*, and *Eric Schnapper.*

■ CHIEF JUSTICE BURGER delivered the opinion of the Court.

We granted certiorari to decide whether petitioners, nonprofit private schools that prescribe and enforce racially discriminatory admissions standards on the basis of religious doctrine, qualify as tax-exempt organizations under § 501(c)(3) of the Internal Revenue Code of 1954.

I

A

Until 1970, the Internal Revenue Service granted tax-exempt status to private schools, without regard to their racial admissions policies, under § 501(c)(3) of the Internal Revenue Code, and granted charitable deductions for contributions to such schools under § 170 of the Code.

On January 12, 1970, a three-judge District Court for the District of Columbia issued a preliminary injunction prohibiting the IRS from according tax-exempt status to private schools in Mississippi that discriminated as to admissions on the basis of race. *Green v. Kennedy,* 309 F. Supp. 1127, appeal dism'd *sub nom. Cannon v. Green,* 398 U.S. 956 (1970). Thereafter, in July 1970, the IRS concluded that it could "no longer legally justify allowing tax-exempt status [under § 501(c)(3)] to private schools which practice racial discrimination." IRS News Release, July 7, 1970. At the same time, the IRS announced that it could not "treat gifts to such schools as charitable deductions for income tax purposes [under § 170]." By letter dated November 30, 1970, the IRS formally notified private schools, including those involved in this litigation, of this change in policy, "applicable to all private schools in the United States at all levels of education."

On June 30, 1971, the three-judge District Court issued its opinion on the merits of the Mississippi challenge. *Green v. Connally,* 330 F. Supp. 1150, summarily aff'd *sub nom. Coit v. Green,* 404 U.S. 997 (1971). That court approved the IRS's amended construction of the Tax Code. The court also held that racially discriminatory private schools were not entitled to exemption under § 501(c)(3) and that donors were not entitled to deductions for contributions to such schools under § 170. The court permanently enjoined the Commissioner of Internal Revenue from approving tax-exempt status for any school in Mississippi that did not publicly maintain a policy of nondiscrimination.

The revised policy on discrimination was formalized in Revenue Ruling 71–447: "Both the courts and the Internal Revenue Service have long recognized that the statutory requirement of being 'organized and operated exclusively for religious, charitable, ... or educational purposes' was intended to express the basic common law concept [of 'charity'].... All charitable trusts, educational or otherwise, are subject to the requirement that the purpose of the trust may not be illegal or contrary to public policy." Based on the "national policy to discourage racial discrimination in education," the IRS ruled that "a [private] school not having a racially nondiscriminatory policy as to students is not 'charitable' within the common law concepts reflected in sections 170 and 501(c)(3) of the Code."

The application of the IRS construction of these provisions to petitioners, two private schools with racially discriminatory admissions policies, is now before us.

B

No. 81–3, Bob Jones University v. United States

Bob Jones University is a nonprofit corporation located in Greenville, S.C. Its purpose is "to conduct an institution of learning ... , giving special emphasis to the Christian religion and the ethics revealed in the Holy Scriptures." Certificate of Incorporation, Bob Jones University, Inc., of Greenville, S.C. The corporation operates a school with an enrollment of approximately 5,000 students, from kindergarten through college and graduate school. Bob Jones University is not affiliated with any religious denomination, but is dedicated to the teaching and propagation of its fundamentalist Christian religious beliefs. It is both a religious and educational institution. Its teachers are required to be devout Christians, and all courses at the University are taught according to the Bible. Entering students are screened as to their religious beliefs, and their public and private conduct is strictly regulated by standards promulgated by University authorities.

The sponsors of the University genuinely believe that the Bible forbids interracial dating and marriage. To effectuate these views, Negroes were completely excluded until 1971. From 1971 to May 1975, the University accepted no applications from unmarried Negroes but did accept applications from Negroes married within their race.

Following the decision of the United States Court of Appeals for the Fourth Circuit *in McCrary v. Runyon,* 515 F.2d 1082 (1975), aff'd, 427 U.S. 160 (1976), prohibiting racial exclusion from private schools, the University revised its policy. Since May 29, 1975, the University has permitted unmarried Negroes to enroll; but a disciplinary rule prohibits interracial dating and marriage. That rule reads:

"There is to be no interracial dating.

"1. Students who are partners in an interracial marriage will be expelled.

"2. Students who are members of or affiliated with any group or organization which holds as one of its goals or advocates interracial marriage will be expelled.

"3. Students who date outside of their own race will be expelled.

"4. Students who espouse, promote, or encourage others to violate the University's dating rules and regulations will be expelled."

The University continues to deny admission to applicants engaged in an interracial marriage or known to advocate interracial marriage or dating.

Until 1970, the IRS extended tax-exempt status to Bob Jones University under § 501(c)(3). By the letter of November 30, 1970, that followed the injunction issued in *Green v. Kennedy,* the IRS formally notified the

University of the change in IRS policy, and announced its intention to challenge the tax-exempt status of private schools practicing racial discrimination in their admissions policies.

After failing to obtain an assurance of tax exemption through administrative means, the University instituted an action in 1971 seeking to enjoin the IRS from revoking the school's tax-exempt status. That suit culminated in *Bob Jones University v. Simon*, 416 U.S. 725 (1974), in which this Court held that the Anti–Injunction Act of the Internal Revenue Code, 26 U.S.C. § 7421(a), prohibited the University from obtaining judicial review by way of injunctive action before the assessment or collection of any tax.

Thereafter, on April 16, 1975, the IRS notified the University of the proposed revocation of its tax-exempt status. On January 19, 1976, the IRS officially revoked the University's tax-exempt status, effective as of December 1, 1970, the day after the University was formally notified of the change in IRS policy. The University subsequently filed returns under the Federal Unemployment Tax Act for the period from December 1, 1970, to December 31, 1975, and paid a tax totalling $21 on one employee for the calendar year of 1975. After its request for a refund was denied, the University instituted the present action, seeking to recover the $21 it had paid to the IRS. The Government counterclaimed for unpaid federal unemployment taxes for the taxable years 1971 through 1975, in the amount of $489,675.59, plus interest.

The United States District Court for the District of South Carolina held that revocation of the University's tax-exempt status exceeded the delegated powers of the IRS, was improper under the IRS rulings and procedures, and violated the University's rights under the Religion Clauses of the First Amendment. The court accordingly ordered the IRS to pay the University the $21 refund it claimed and rejected the IRS's counterclaim.

The Court of Appeals for the Fourth Circuit, in a divided opinion, reversed. Citing *Green v. Connally* with approval, the Court of Appeals concluded that § 501(c)(3) must be read against the background of charitable trust law. To be eligible for an exemption under that section, an institution must be "charitable" in the common-law sense, and therefore must not be contrary to public policy. In the court's view, Bob Jones University did not meet this requirement, since its "racial policies violated the clearly defined public policy, rooted in our Constitution, condemning racial discrimination and, more specifically, the government policy against subsidizing racial discrimination in education, public or private." The court held that the IRS acted within its statutory authority in revoking the University's tax-exempt status. Finally, the Court of Appeals rejected petitioner's arguments that the revocation of the tax exemption violated the Free Exercise and Establishment Clauses of the First Amendment. The case was remanded to the District Court with instructions to dismiss the University's claim for a refund and to reinstate the IRS's counterclaim.

II

A

... When the Government grants exemptions or allows deductions all taxpayers are affected: the very fact of the exemption or deduction for the donor means that other taxpayers can be said to be indirect and vicarious "donors." Charitable exemptions are justified on the basis that the exempt entity confers a public benefit—a benefit which the society or the community may not itself choose or be able to provide, or which supplements and advances the work of public institutions already supported by tax revenues. History buttresses logic to make clear that, to warrant exemption under § 501(c)(3), an institution must fall within a category specified in that section and must demonstrably serve and be in harmony with the public interest. The institution's purpose must not be so at odds with the common community conscience as to undermine any public benefit that might otherwise be conferred.

B

We are bound to approach these questions with full awareness that determinations of public benefit and public policy are sensitive matters with serious implications for the institutions affected; a declaration that a given institution is not "charitable" should be made only where there can be no doubt that the activity involved is contrary to a fundamental public policy. But there can no longer be any doubt that racial discrimination in education violates deeply and widely accepted views of elementary justice. Prior to 1954, public education in many places still was conducted under the pall of *Plessy v. Ferguson,* 163 U.S. 537 (1896); racial segregation in primary and secondary education prevailed in many parts of the country. See, *e.g.,* Segregation and the Fourteenth Amendment in the States (B. Reams & P. Wilson eds. 1975). This Court's decision in *Brown v. Board of Education,* 347 U.S. 483 (1954), signalled an end to that era. Over the past quarter of a century, every pronouncement of this Court and myriad Acts of Congress and Executive Orders attest a firm national policy to prohibit racial segregation and discrimination in public education. . . .

The governmental interest at stake here is compelling. The Government has a fundamental, overriding interest in eradicating racial discrimination in education[29]—discrimination that prevailed, with official approval, for the first 165 years of this Nation's constitutional history. That governmental interest substantially outweighs whatever burden denial of tax benefits places on petitioners' exercise of their religious beliefs. The interests asserted by petitioners cannot be accommodated with that compelling governmental interest, see *United States v. Lee* [Chapter Eleven, section 6], and no "less restrictive means," see *Thomas v. Review Board* [Chapter Eleven, section 5], are available to achieve the governmental interest. . . . *Affirmed.*

■ JUSTICE POWELL, concurring in part and concurring in the judgment.

I write separately because I am troubled by the broader implications of the Court's opinion with respect to the authority of the IRS and its construction of §§ 170 and 501(c)(3) of the Internal Revenue Code. . . . I am unconvinced that the critical question in determining tax-exempt status

---

29. We deal here only with religious *schools*—not with churches or other purely religious institutions; here, the governmental interest is in denying public support to racial discrimination in education. . . .

is whether an individual organization provides a clear "public benefit" as defined by the Court.... Even more troubling to me is the element of conformity that appears to inform the Court's analysis. The Court asserts than an exempt organization must "demonstrably serve and be in harmony with the public interest," must have a purpose that comports with "the common community conscience," and must not act in a manner "affirmatively at odds with [the] declared position of the whole government." Taken together, these passages suggest that the primary function of a tax-exempt organization is to act on behalf of the Government in carrying out governmentally approved policies. In my opinion, such a view of § 501(c)(3) ignores the important role played by tax exemptions in encouraging diverse, indeed often sharply conflicting, activities and viewpoints. As Justice Brennan has observed, private, non-profit groups receive tax exemptions because "each group contributes to the diversity of association, viewpoint, and enterprise essential to a vigorous, pluralistic society." *Walz* (Brennan, J., concurring). Far from representing an effort to reinforce any perceived "common community conscience," the provision of tax exemptions to nonprofit groups is one indispensable means of limiting the influence of governmental orthodoxy on important areas of community life. Given the importance of our tradition of pluralism, "[t]he interest in preserving an area of untrammeled choice for private philanthropy is very great." *Jackson v. Statler Foundation*, 496 F. 2d 623, 639 (2d Cir. 1974) (Friendly, J., dissenting).

JUSTICE REHNQUIST, dissenting, was of the view that Congress "could deny tax-exempt status to educational institutions that promote racial discrimination," but, unlike the Court, was "convinced that Congress simply has failed to take this action and ... regardless of our view on the propriety of Congress' failure to legislate we are not constitutionally empowered to act for them."

NOTES AND QUESTIONS

1. *Mennonite Separationism.* The Court oftens exalts the concept of separationism, without acknowledging its roots in the religious community guided by Menno Simons [Chapter Five, section 1]. The amicus brief on behalf of the Mennonites put forward these considerations in the *Bob Jones University* case.

"There is in our consciousness a strong sense of an often torturous history, in which our predecessors passed through periods of extreme hardship and suffering, a history that includes the records of many martyrs who suffered for those tenets that still constitute our confession of faith. A notable feature of our church history is that of a church in a migratory status, migrating from one place, or nation, to another in search of religious consideration or toleration, a defenseless people looking for a place to be. This has left within us an extremely high regard for religious liberty. We consider the religious liberty that this nation concedes as possibly its greatest virtue.... The tremendous stress that we have faced and face when we find ourselves in conflict between the will of secular government and what we understand as the will of God constitutes one of the most difficult aspects of our religious experience."

"Our faith and understanding of scripture enjoin respect and obedience to the secular governments under which we live. We recognize them as institutions established by God for order in society. For that reason alone, without the added distress of punitive action for failure to do so, we always exercise ourselves to be completely law abiding. Our religious beliefs, however, are very deeply held. When these beliefs collide with the demands of society, our highest allegiance must be toward God, and we must say with men of God of the past, 'We must obey God rather than men,' and these are the crises from which we would be spared." Brief Amicus Curiae in Support of Petition for Writ of Certiorari on Behalf of Church of God in Christ, Mennonite 1–4. Does the Court adequately respond to the Mennonites' concerns?

2. *Change in Dating Policy at Bob Jones University.* In an interview on CNN's Larry King Live on March 3, 2000, the President of Bob Jones University announced an end to the university's half-century-old ban on interracial dating. Jim Davenport "Dating Decision Stuns Conservative Campus Break From Tradition Unexpected By Even Those Closest To President Of Bob Jones," *Augusta Chronicle*, March 5, 2000. Should the IRS reinstate the university's tax-exempt status? If so, what is left of the precedent above? Can the case cause mischief for exempt organizations that have no issue about compliance with nondiscrimination on the basis of race, but that do not conform to public policy, however that is to be defined?

3. *Accreditation of Religiously Affiliated Law Schools.* Like a number of states, Oklahoma prescribed as a condition for admission to the bar that the applicant have attended a school accredited by the American Bar Association. The ABA in 1981 refused to approve the accreditation of the law school of Oral Roberts University, which required applicants to the law school to sign a statement of Christian religious belief. The university sued, alleging that its free exercise of religion was being infringed. In *Oral Roberts University v. American Bar Association*, 8 Legal Aff. Manual 205 (N.D. Ill. 1981), the court found that the ABA was engaged in state action and that its action violated the First Amendment. Within the month the ABA revised its policy. Leonard J. Nelson III, "Religious Discrimination, Christian Mission, and Legal Education: The Implications of the Oral Roberts University Accreditation Controversy," 15 *Cumberland L. Rev.* 663, 679–680 (1985). *See also* April Cassou and Robert Curran, "Secular Orthodoxy and Sacred Freedoms: Accreditation of Church–Related Law Schools," 11 *J. of Coll. and Univ. L.* 293 (1984) (pointing to hostility in the Association of American Law Schools toward religious schools and speculating on the vulnerability of the AALS to antitrust suits); and Robert Destro, "ABA and AALS Accreditation: What's 'Religious Diversity' Got to Do With It?," 78 *Marq. L. Rev.* 427 (1995). And see Douglas Laycock and Susan E. Waelbroeck, "Academic Freedom and the Free Exercise of Religion," 66 *Texas L. Rev.* 1455 (1988); Michael W. McConnell, "Academic Freedom in Religious Colleges and Universities," 53 *L. & Contemp. Probs.* 303 (1990).

4. *The Importance of a Written Constitution.* Does the present state of affairs in America result primarily from the First Amendment and its interpretation by the Supreme Court or does it flow from other general social considerations? Consider the following from a book review by Noonan of St. John A. Robilliard, *Religion and the Law* (1984) in 33 *Am. J. of Comparative L.* 765 (1985).

Six areas exist in which religion is special and privileged by both British and American law: (1) taxation, both as to income tax and property tax, so that large financial benefits are governmentally bestowed on religious bodies; (2) charitable status, so that religion has the favored position of a public charity; (3) clerical status, so that, for example, clerics do not fall under the National Labor Relations Act in this country, and the Sex Discrimination Act in Britain has two exemptions relating to the ministry; (4) the celebration of Sunday, so that in both nations this Christian holy day is set aside as the usual day of rest even though a hodgepodge of exceptions make the day far from a Puritan sabbath in either country; (5) marriage, so that bigamy is a crime in Britain and in every state despite the number of Moslems in England and the general relaxation of laws on sex in both countries; (6) priestly services in state institutions, so that in both countries the armed forces and prisons have chaplains representing the major denominations. The different constitutional systems of the two countries have not resulted in substantially different results in these significant matters.

Three areas exist where there are some differences:

(1) The Church of England, still the established church of the land, has courts which can compel testimony and hold persons in contempt; decisions of these courts are part of the general law of England. The church's bishops are appointed by the Prime Minister although convention dictates that the government select from the church's nominees. Parliament is still able to control the church's liturgy and Prayer Book. In practice, the benefits the church receives are not large, and the government's normal deference to ecclesiastical preferences results in equally limited government interference. No comparable relationship exists in the United States.

(2) By the Education Act 1944, religious education is undertaken by English state schools according to "the agreed syllabus" for a given local area. The agreed syllabus is drawn up by such religious groups as the local education authorities choose to invite to write it; the invited groups must then agree unanimously, a provision that no doubt assures a certain blandness if not tepidity. Communism and humanism may form part of the content of the syllabus; Christianity is always a major part. A teacher may be dismissed for teaching contrary to the syllabus; in *Watson v. Hertfordshire County Council* (1977, unreported) a fundamentalist was discharged for teaching Genesis literally when the syllabus stipulated that it was symbolic.

In fact, an agreed syllabus is closely followed by only 17% of the schools; over half even ignore the statutory requirement that religious education be provided to all their pupils. Local option seems to have become *laissez-faire*. In the same way the Education Act 1944 requires that every day every school begin with "collective worship on the part of the pupils" in a way not distinctive of any particular religious denomination. In practice, as Robilliard reports, there is no uniformity as to what "collective worship" means, and worship varies from hymn singing to "happenings." The evidence also suggests no very general compliance with the requirement that the service occur daily.

At a formal level, the American scene is very different. The Supreme Court has meticulously purified the public schools of the Bible, the Ten Commandments, and prayer, Christian or nondenominational. One may, however, wonder if the practical results—since the Bible may still be studied in American schools as literature—are so different from a British "agreed syllabus"; and whether an American high school assembly, with the religious words of our national anthem still sung, is a different species of collective worship than a "happening" in a British state school. Statutory as well as constitutional law on public education is different in the two countries. Much more empirical information is needed before one can be certain of the true differences in practice.

(3) The Supreme Court has gone very far in interpreting the draft laws to recognize conscientious objection to war; in England the recognition of conscientious objection in 1916 and again in 1939 was left to special tribunals whose decisions could not be reviewed by the regular courts. On the face of it at least, the British C.O. has had to proceed on a much more ad hoc basis than his American counterpart. On the other hand, the American decisions are post-World War II, and British tribunals might behave similarly if a British draft law were now in force. Any difference is in the decisions of two different eras.

On other issues of conscience, there is some variation. Robilliard, basing himself on dicta in the Court of Appeal, believes that in Britain there is a right to suicide. But there is only a qualified right to refuse to perform an abortion, and conscientious objection to abortion is a bar to a doctor's advancement in gynecology. A Briton has a right to kill himself but no unqualified right to refrain from killing others. In America there is no generally recognized right to suicide, and there is a right, generally acknowledged by statutes, to refrain from committing an abortion. The difference appears to arise not from constitutional considerations but political realities: the right-to-life movement is far stronger in the United States than in Britain.

The chief difference produced by the different constitutional systems of the two countries appears to be the status of the Church of England, whose anomalous and not very significant privileges are owed to history. Robilliard speaks wistfully of "the absence of any clear landmark for the [British] courts, such as a Bill of Rights," but the Bill of Rights in America has led to blurrier and blurrier lines. Words in a constitution cannot create clarity. Nor is logic much help. It is over a century since Holmes observed that logic was not the life of the law, but the expectation that logic will rule dies hard. What the courts, the legislature, and the citizenry are doing in the field of religion is balancing values—values of faith, of tolerance, of tradition, of charity, etc. The balance is far more affected by economic structures, political movements, historical survivals, and the cultural level of the countries than by specific constitutional or statutory prescriptions.

CHAPTER FIFTEEN

Political Participation

1. The Rights of Churches

Kedroff v. St. Nicholas Cathedral [Chapter Thirteen, section 3] invalidated a statute because it prohibited "the free exercise of an ecclesiastical right, the Church's choice of its hierarchy." Mark De Wolfe Howe, then the leading academic authority on the law and churches, celebrated this sentence as recognizing "the liberty of the group as something different from the individual liberties of its members," Howe, "Foreword: Political Theory and the Nature of Liberty, The Supreme Court, 1952 Term," 67 *Harv.L.Rev.* 91, at 93 (1953). Howe saw the Court as acknowledging "a corporate liberty" for churches which political theorists such as John Neville Figgis had long ago claimed as their due. See Figgis, *Churches in the Modern State* (1913).

A large number of cases had, of course, recognized the religious rights of individuals because they were exercised on behalf of a group and as a group activity. For example, *Cantwell v. Connecticut* [Chapter Eleven, section 1], the first of these cases, identified Cantwell's sidewalk proselytizing as religious because he was a Jehovah's Witness. But it was his right to free exercise, not the Jehovah's Witnesses' as a body, that was vindicated. In this line of cases, *Wisconsin v. Yoder* [Chapter Eleven, section 5], is the most striking. The defendants prevailed because their way of life was part of a church's way of life. Again, however, it was the individual believers' rights that were asserted and upheld.

A Minnesota statute required all charitable organizations to register with the state and to report their receipts and costs of management and fundraising. The statute excepted "a religious society" that received more than half of its contributions from its members. The Holy Spirit Association for the Unification of World Christianity (Unification Church) and four followers of the church sought a declaration that the statute abridged their free exercise of religion. The state defended the statute on the ground that members of a religious organization would exercise sufficient control over a religious organization's activities when they contributed over half of the funds; the state did not have to exercise close supervision.

In *Larson v. Valente*, 456 U.S. 228 (1982), the Court, per Justice Brennan, found the state's rationale implausible. The Court took notice of the legislative discussion that indicated that the sponsors of the law did not want to reach a Catholic archdiocese and did want to reach the Unification Church. The Court held that the 50 percent rule "effects the *selective* legislative imposition of burdens and advantages upon particular denominations." According to Justice Brennan, "The clearest command of the Establishment Clause is that one religious denomination cannot be officially preferred over another.... Free exercise ... can be guaranteed only when legislators—and voters—are required to accord to their own religions the very same treatment given to small, new, or unpopular denominations." The Court held that by imposing heavier regulatory burdens on the Unification Church than on other religious communities, the Minnesota statute achieved an "official denominational preference" in violation of the nonestablishment provision. Justices Rehnquist, White, O'Connor, and Chief Justice Burger dissented on the ripeness of the case for constitutional adjudication; Justices Rehnquist and White dissented on the merits. Still left to be litigated was the basic question whether the Unification Church was a religious organization. Implicitly, however, the majority opinion recognized a corporate right in a church to protest denominational preferences by a state.

Coupled with *Kedroff, Larson* affords a basis for contending that churches as well as individuals are protected by the religion clause.

2. EXERCISE OF GOVERNMENTAL POWER BY CHURCHES AND MEMBERS OF THE CLERGY

In Larkin v. Grendel's Den, Inc., 459 U.S. 116 (1982), a Massachusetts law gave churches a discretionary power to veto liquor licenses within 500 feet of a church. Grendel's Den, a restaurant in Harvard Square, applied for a liquor license. The Holy Cross Armenian Catholic Church, ten feet away, objected; the license was denied. Grendel's Den sued the licensing boards. Represented by Professor Laurence Tribe of the Harvard Law School, the restaurant raised the issue that the statute was an establishment of religion. The Supreme Court, 8–1, per Chief Justice Burger, held that the statute had the primary and principal effect of advancing religion for two reasons: (1) the churches had the power to use their veto in a way that was not "religiously neutral"; (2) "the mere appearance of a joint exercise of legislative authority by Church and State provides a significant symbolic benefit to religion in the minds of some." Moreover, the Court said, the statute entangled the churches with the government: "The Framers did not set up a system of government in which important, discretionary governmental powers would be delegated to or shared with religious institutions." Justice Rehnquist dissented, noting that the state could absolutely ban liquor licenses within a given distance of a church and finding the Massachusetts statute "sensible."

See also State v. Celmer, 80 N.J. 405, 404 A.2d 1 (1979), *cert. denied,* 444 U.S. 951 (1979). The defendant was convicted of drunk driving in Ocean Grove municipal court. He challenged the state statutes that incorporated "The Ocean Grove Camp Meeting Association of the United Methodist Church" and gave this association power to construct and maintain public highways and to "preserve order" in Ocean Grove. The municipal court had been established by the Association, ten out of twenty-six of whose trustees had to be Methodist ministers. The court found it to be "first and foremost a religious organization" and concluded: "Such a fusion of secular and ecclesiastical power not only violates both the letter and the spirit of the First Amendment, it also runs afoul of the 'establishment clause' of our own State constitution, see N.J. Const. (1947) Art 1, ¶ 4."

Followers of the an Indian guru named Bhagwan lived in a spiritual community in Oregon. When they sought to incorporate as a city, the State of Oregon filed suit to block the move. The state alleged: "The primary purpose for establishing the City of Rajneeshpuram was to advance the religion of

Rajneeshism. The City was founded to fulfill a religious vision. The City was designed and functions as a spiritual mecca for followers of the Bhagwan worldwide. It serves as a monument to and the residence of the Bhagwan, and as a gathering place for followers at institutions of religious training and at three annual religious festivals." The state also contended that to pay public monies or provide public services to the City of Rajneeshpuram would violate the constitutions of Oregon and the United States. The defendants replied that the benefits to their religion were incidental, like police and fire services; and that to deny them the right to run the City of Rajneeshpuram would be to deny them the free exercise of their religion. District Judge Helen J. Frye granted the state's motion.

Oregon v. City of Rajneeshpuram

598 F. Supp. 1208 (D. Ore. 1984).

[T]he potential injury to the anti-establishment principle of the first amendment by the existence and operation of the City of Rajneeshpuram clearly outweighs the potential harm to the defendants' free exercise of religious rights. To deny defendants the right to operate a city is the only means of achieving a compelling state and federal interest—that of avoiding an establishment of religion.

NOTES AND QUESTIONS

1. *Disqualification of Clergy from Serving in Public Office.* In its first Constitution, in 1796, Tennessee disqualified ministers from serving as legislators. That disqualifying provision continued unchanged since its adoption. Tenn. Const. Art. 9, § 1. The state legislature applied this provision to candidates for delegate to the State's 1977 limited constitutional convention: "Any citizen of the state who can qualify for membership in the House of Representatives of the General Assembly may become a candidate for delegate to the convention...."

McDaniel, an ordained minister of a Baptist Church in Chattanooga, Tenn., filed as a candidate for delegate to the constitutional convention. An opposing candidate, Selma Cash Paty, sued in the Chancery Court for a declaratory judgment that McDaniel was disqualified from serving as a delegate and for a judgment striking his name from the ballot. Chancellor Franks of the Chancery Court held that the provision cited above violated the First and Fourteenth Amendments to the Federal Constitution and declared McDaniel eligible for the office of delegate. Accordingly, McDaniel's name remained on the ballot and in the ensuing election he was elected by a vote almost equal to that of three opposing candidates.

After the election, the Tennessee Supreme Court reversed the Chancery Court, holding that the disqualification of clergy imposed no burden upon "religious belief" and restricted "religious action ... [only] in the lawmaking process of government—where religious action is absolutely prohibited by the establishment clause...." The state interests in preventing the establishment of religion and in avoiding the divisiveness and tendency to channel political activity along religious lines, resulting from clergy participation in political affairs, were deemed by that court sufficiently weighty to justify the disqualification, notwithstanding the guarantee of the Free Exercise Clause.

McDaniel v. Paty

435 U.S. 618 (1978).

Frederic S. Le Clercq argued the cause and filed a brief for appellant.

Kenneth R. Herrell, Assistant Attorney General of Tennessee, argued the cause for appellees. With him on the brief for appellees Hassler et al. were *Brooks McLemore,* Attorney General, and *C. Hayes Cooney,* Chief Deputy Attorney General. *Philip C Lawrence* filed a brief for appellee Paty.

Leo Pfeffer, Abraham S. Goldstein, Joel Gora, George W. McKeag, John T. Redmond, James W. Respass, and *Thomas A. Shaw* filed a brief for the American Civil Liberties Union et al. as amici curiae urging reversal.

■ CHIEF JUSTICE BURGER announced the judgment of the Court and delivered an opinion in which Justice Powell, Justice Rehnquist, and Justice Stevens joined.

The question presented by this appeal is whether a Tennessee statute barring "Minister[s] of the Gospel, or priest[s] of any denomination whatever" from serving as delegates to the State's limited constitutional convention deprived appellant McDaniel, an ordained minister, of the right to the free exercise of religion guaranteed by the First Amendment and made applicable to the States by the Fourteenth Amendment. The First Amendment forbids all laws "prohibiting the free exercise" of religion.

II

A

The disqualification of ministers from legislative office was a practice carried from England by seven of the original States; later six new States similarly excluded clergymen from some political offices. 1 A. Stokes, Church and State in the United States 622 (1950) (hereafter Stokes). In England the practice of excluding clergy from the House of Commons was justified on a variety of grounds: to prevent dual officeholding, that is, membership by a minister in both Parliament and Convocation; to insure that the priest or deacon devoted himself to his "sacred calling" rather than to "such mundane activities as were appropriate to a member of the House of Commons"; and to prevent ministers, who after 1533 were subject to the Crown's powers over the benefices of the clergy, from using membership in Commons to diminish its independence by increasing the influence of the King and the nobility. *In re MacManaway,* [1951] A.C. 161, 164, 170–171.

The purpose of the several States in providing for disqualification was primarily to assure the success of a new political experiment, the separation of church and state. Stokes 622. Prior to 1776, most of the 13 Colonies had some form of an established, or government-sponsored, church. *Id.,* at 364–446. Even after ratification of the First Amendment, which prohibited the Federal Government from following such a course, some States continued pro-establishment provisions. See *id.,* at 408, 418–427, 444. Massachusetts, the last State to accept disestablishment, did so in 1833. *Id.,* at 426–427.

In light of this history and a widespread awareness during that period of undue and often dominant clerical influence in public and political affairs here, in England, and on the Continent, it is not surprising that strong views were held by some that one way to assure disestablishment was to keep clergymen out of public office. Indeed, some of the foremost political philosophers and statesmen of that period held such views regarding the clergy. Earlier, John Locke argued for confining the authority of the English clergy "within the bounds of the church, nor can it in any manner be extended to civil affairs; because the church itself is a thing absolutely separate and distinct from the commonwealth." 5 Works of John Locke 21 (C. Baldwin ed. 1824). Thomas Jefferson initially advocated such a position in his 1783 draft of a constitution for Virginia.[4] James Madison, however, disagreed and vigorously urged the position which in our view accurately reflects the spirit and purpose of the Religion Clauses of the First Amendment. Madison's response to Jefferson's position was: "Does not The exclusion of Ministers of the Gospel as such violate a fundamental principle of liberty by punishing a religious profession with the privation of a civil right? does it [not] violate another article of the plan itself which exempts religion from the cognizance of Civil power? does it not violate justice by at once taking away a right and prohibiting a compensation for it? does it not in fine violate impartiality by shutting the door [against] the Ministers of one Religion and leaving it open for those of every other." 5 Writings of James Madison 288 (G. Hunt ed. 1904).

Madison was not the only articulate opponent of clergy disqualification. When proposals were made earlier to prevent clergymen from holding public office, John Witherspoon, a Presbyterian minister, president of Princeton University, and the only clergyman to sign the Declaration of Independence, made a cogent protest and, with tongue in cheek, offered an amendment to a provision much like that challenged here: " 'No clergyman, of any denomination, shall be capable of being elected a member of the Senate or House of Representatives, because (here insert the grounds of offensive disqualification, which I have not been able to discover) Provided always, and it is the true intent and meaning of this part of the constitu-

---

4. 6 Papers of Thomas Jefferson 297 (J. Boyd ed. 1952). Jefferson later concluded that experience demonstrated there was no need to exclude clergy from elected office. In a letter to Jeremiah Moor in 1800, he stated: "[I]n the same scheme of a constitution [for Virginia which I prepared in 1783, I observe] an abridgment of the right of being elected, which after 17 years more of experience & reflection, I do not approve. It is the incapacitation of a clergyman from being elected. The clergy, by getting themselves established by law, & ingrafted into the machine of government, have been a very formidable engine against the civil and religious rights of man. They are still so in many countries & even in some of these United States. Even in 1783 we doubted the stability of our recent measures for reducing them to the footing of other useful callings. It now appears that our means were effectual. The clergy here seem to have relinquished all pretensions to privilege, and to stand on a footing with lawyers, physicians & c. They ought therefore to possess the same rights." 9 Works of Jefferson 143 (P. Ford ed. 1905).

tion, that if at any time he shall be completely deprived of the clerical character by those by whom he was invested with it, as by deposition for cursing and swearing, drunkenness or uncleanness, he shall then be fully restored to all the privileges of a free citizen; his offense [of being a clergyman] shall no more be remembered against him; but he may be chosen either to the Senate or House of Representatives, and shall be treated with all the respect due to his *brethren,* the other members of Assembly,' " Stokes 624–625.

As the value of the disestablishment experiment was perceived, 11 of the 13 States disqualifying the clergy from some types of public office gradually abandoned that limitation. New York, for example, took that step in 1846 after delegates to the State's constitutional convention argued that the exclusion of clergymen from the legislature was an "odious distinction." 2 C. Lincoln, The Constitutional History of New York 111–112 (1906). Only Maryland and Tennessee continued their clergy-disqualification provisions into this century and, in 1974, a District Court held Maryland's provision violative of the First and Fourteenth Amendments' guarantees of the free exercise of religion. *Kirkley v. Maryland,* 381 F. Supp. 327. Today Tennessee remains the only State excluding ministers from certain public offices.

The essence of this aspect of our national history is that in all but a few States the selection or rejection of clergymen for public office soon came to be viewed as something safely left to the good sense and desires of the people.

B

This brief review of the history of clergy-disqualification provisions also amply demonstrates, however, that, at least during the early segment of our national life, those provisions enjoyed the support of responsible American statesmen and were accepted as having a rational basis. Against this background we do not lightly invalidate a statute enacted pursuant to a provision of a state constitution which has been sustained by its highest court. The challenged provision came to the Tennessee Supreme Court clothed with the presumption of validity to which that court was bound to give deference.

However, the right to the free exercise of religion unquestionably encompasses the right to preach, proselyte, and perform other similar religious functions, or, in other words, to be a minister of the type McDaniel was found to be. *Murdock v. Pennsylvania,* [Chapter Eleven, section 1]; *Cantwell v. Connecticut* [Chapter Eleven, section 1]. Tennessee also acknowledges the right of its adult citizens generally to seek and hold office as legislators or delegates to the state constitutional convention. Tenn. Const. Art. 2, §§ 9, 25, 26; Tenn. Code Ann. §§ 8–1801, 8–1803 (Supp. 1977). Yet under the clergy-disqualification provision, McDaniel cannot exercise both rights simultaneously because the State has conditioned the exercise of one on the surrender of the other. Or, in James Madison's words, the State is "punishing a religious profession with the privation of a civil right." 5 Writings of James Madison, *supra,* at 288. In so doing, Tennessee has encroached upon McDaniel's right to the free exercise of religion. "[T]o condition the availability of benefits [including access to the ballot] upon this appellant's willingness to violate a cardinal principle of [his] religious faith [by surrendering his religiously impelled ministry] effectively penalizes the free exercise of [his] constitutional liberties." *Sherbert v. Verner* [Chapter Eleven, section 5].

If the Tennessee disqualification provision were viewed as depriving the clergy of a civil right solely because of their religious beliefs, our inquiry would be at an end. The Free Exercise Clause categorically prohibits government from regulating, prohibiting, or rewarding religious beliefs as such. *Sherbert, Cantwell.* In *Torcaso v. Watkins,* [Chapter Twelve, section 2], the Court reviewed the Maryland constitutional requirement that all holders of "any office of profit or trust in this State" declare their belief in the existence of God. In striking down the Maryland requirement, the Court did not evaluate the interests assertedly justifying it but rather held that it violated freedom of religious belief.

In our view, however, *Torcaso* does not govern. By its terms, the Tennessee disqualification operates against McDaniel because of his *status* as a "minister" or "priest." The meaning of those words is, of course, a question of state law.[5] And although the question has not been examined extensively in state-law sources, such authority as is available indicates that ministerial status is defined in terms of conduct and activity rather than in terms of belief.[6] Because the Tennessee disqualification is directed primarily at status, acts, and conduct it is unlike the requirement in *Torcaso,* which focused on *belief.* Hence, the Free Exercise Clause's absolute prohibition of infringements on the "freedom to believe" is inapposite here.

This does not mean, of course, that the disqualification escapes judicial scrutiny or that McDaniel's activity does not enjoy significant First Amendment protection. The Court recently declared in *Yoder* [Chapter Eleven, section 7]: "The essence of all that has been said and written on the subject is that only those interests of the highest order and those not otherwise served can overbalance legitimate claims to the free exercise of religion."

---

5. In this case, the Tennessee Supreme Court concluded that the disqualification of McDaniel did not interfere with his religious *belief.* But whether the ministerial status, as defined by state law, implicates the "freedom to act" or the absolute "freedom to believe," *Cantwell v. Connecticut* [Chapter Eleven, section 1], must be resolved under the Free Exercise Clause. Thus, although we consider the Tennessee court's resolution of that issue, we are not bound by it.

6. The Tennessee constitutional provision embodying the disqualification inferentially defines the ministerial profession in terms of its "duties," which include the "care

of souls." Tenn. Const., Art. 9, § 1. In this case, the Tennessee Supreme Court stated that the disqualification reaches those filling a "leadership role in religion," and those "dedicated to the full time *promotion* of the religious objectives of a particular religious sect." 547 S.W. 2d, at 903 (emphasis added). The Tennessee court, in defining "priest," also referred to the dictionary definition as "one who *performs* sacrificial, ritualistic, mediatorial, interpretative, or ministerial functions...." *Id.,* at 908 (quoting Webster's Third New International Dictionary 1799–1800 (1971)) (emphasis added).

Tennessee asserts that its interest in preventing the establishment of a state religion is consistent with the Establishment Clause and thus of the highest order. The constitutional history of the several States reveals that generally the interest in preventing establishment prompted the adoption of clergy disqualification provisions, see Stokes 622; Tennessee does not appear to be an exception to this pattern (Brennan, J., concurring in judgment). There is no occasion to inquire whether promoting such an interest is a permissible legislative goal, however, for Tennessee has failed to demonstrate that its views of the dangers of clergy participation in the political process have not lost whatever validity they may once have enjoyed. The essence of the rationale underlying the Tennessee restriction on ministers is that if elected to public office they will necessarily exercise their powers and influence to promote the interests of one sect or thwart the interests of another, thus pitting one against the others, contrary to the anti-establishment principle with its command of neutrality. See *Walz* [Chapter Thirteen, section 3]. However widely that view may have been held in the 18th century by many, including enlightened statesmen of that day, the American experience provides no persuasive support for the fear that clergymen in public office will be less careful of anti-establishment interests or less faithful to their oaths of civil office than their unordained counterparts.

We hold that § 4 of ch. 848 violates McDaniel's First Amendment right to the free exercise of his religion made applicable to the States by the Fourteenth Amendment. Accordingly, the judgment of the Tennessee Supreme Court is reversed, and the case is remanded to that court for further proceedings not inconsistent with this opinion. *Reversed and remanded.*

■ JUSTICE BLACKMUN took no part in the consideration of this case.

■ JUSTICE BRENNAN, joined by JUSTICE MARSHALL, concurring:

That public debate of religious ideas, like any other, may arouse emotion, may incite, may foment religious divisiveness and strife does not rob it of constitutional protection. *Cantwell v. Connecticut,* [Chapter Eleven, section 1]; *cf. Terminiello v. Chicago,* 337 U.S. 1, 4–5 (1949). The mere fact that a purpose of the Establishment Clause is to reduce or eliminate religious divisiveness or strife, does not place religious discussion, association, or political participation in a status less preferred than rights of discussion, association, and political participation generally. "Adherents of particular faiths and individual churches frequently take strong positions on public issues including ... vigorous advocacy of legal or constitutional positions. Of course, churches as much as secular bodies and private citizens have that right." *Walz* [Chapter Thirteen, section 3].

The State's goal of preventing sectarian bickering and strife may not be accomplished by regulating religious speech and political association. The Establishment Clause does not license government to treat religion and those who teach or practice it, simply by virtue of their status as such, as subversive of American ideals and therefore subject to unique disabilities. Cf. *Wieman v. Updegraff,* 344 U.S. 183 (1952). Government may not inquire into the religious beliefs and motivations of officeholders—it may not remove them from office merely for making public statements regarding religion, or question whether their legislative actions stem from religious conviction. Cf. *Bond v. Floyd*, 385 U.S. 116 (1966).

In short, government may not as a goal promote "safe thinking" with respect to religion and fence out from political participation those, such as ministers, whom it regards as overinvolved in religion. Religionists no less than members of any other group enjoy the full measure of protection afforded speech, association, and political activity generally. The Establishment Clause, properly understood, is a shield against any attempt by government to inhibit religion as it has done here; *Schempp* [Chapter Fourteen, section 2]. It may not be used as a sword to justify repression of religion or its adherents from any aspect of public life.

NOTES AND QUESTIONS

1. *Religion and Politics*. Justice Scalia wrote in his dissent in *Edwards v. Aguillard* [Chapter Fourteen, section 2]: "Our cases in no way imply that the Establishment Clause forbids legislators merely to act upon their religious convictions. We surely would not strike down a law providing money to feed the hungry or shelter the homeless if it could be demonstrated that, but for the religious beliefs of the legislators, the funds would not have been approved. Also, political activism by the religiously motivated is part of our heritage. Notwithstanding the majority's implication to the contrary, we do not presume that the sole purpose of a law is to advance religion merely because it was supported strongly by organized religions or by adherents of particular faiths. *Walz; Harris*. To do so would deprive religious men and women of their right to participate in the political process. Today's religious activism may give us the Balanced Treatment Act [at issue in *Edwards*], but yesterday's resulted in the abolition of slavery, and tomorrow's may bring relief for famine victims."

Scalia's comment addresses two distinct concerns, the rights of religiously minded citizens and groups to participate fully in the democratic process, and the extent to which religious concerns are legitimate in the legislative process. Despite the array of opinions in *McDaniel v. Paty*, there is fairly strong consensus on the first point. On the second point there are two difficulties, one practical and one theoretical. The practical problem is that under § 501(c)(3) of the Internal Revenue Code a religious organization is exempt from federal income tax only if it complies with two restraints in this provision. First, the tax code and accompanying regulations prohibit "substantial activities to influence legislation," as well as "substantial amounts of income" (imprecisely defined—the case law says that 5% is not substantial and 20% is substantial) on attempts to influence legislation. Second, the tax code and regulations impose an absolute prohibition against any form of participation in any political campaigns on behalf of candidates for public office. Political speech is generally regarded as at the core of what the First Amendment protects. See, e.g., *New York Times v. Sullivan*, 376 U.S. 254 (1964). Are such restraints unconstitutional conditions or are they necessary to effectuate a compelling governmental interest? What governmental interest? See generally Edward McGlynn Gaffney, Jr., "On Not Rendering to Caesar: The Unconstitutionality of Tax Regulation of Activities of Religious Organizations Relating to Politics," 40 *DePaul L. Rev.* 1 (1990); and Wilfred Caron and Deirdre Dessingue, "IRC § 501(c)(3): Practical and Constitutional Implications of 'Political' Activity Restraints," 2 *J. L. &*

Politics 169 (1985) (arguing that IRS regulations seriously impair the ability of religious organizations to participate in public debate on socio-moral issues of vital concern to the nation's welfare, and that they have an intimidating adverse effect on the pastoral mission of these organizations).

It might sound intuitively correct that religious bodies should avoid getting "too involved" in politics. For example, the political diversity of the membership of a church might counsel against rending the unity of the church by falsely assuming that all or even most of the members of the church are all of one political party or view. There can also be dangers in politicizing the religious message of a community. On the other hand, there are perils in avoiding any connection between a church's teaching and its practical implications in the real world. Thus John Baker, a representative of the Baptist Joint Committee on Public Affairs, testified before Congress as follows: "War and peace, human welfare, civil rights, abortion, and education are all public issues, but they have attributes which make them also religious issues. The list of these areas of governmental involvement with society which some of the churches assert also demand religious involvement is almost infinite." *Legislative Activity By Certain Types of Exempt Organizations*, Hearings Before the House Ways and Means Committee, 92d Cong., 2d Sess. 282 (1972).

With these religious views in mind, consider specific dimensions of the restraints on political activity imposed by § 501(c)(3) and the parallel regulations. 26 C.F.R. § 1.501(c)–1(c)(3)(iii). The prohibition is absolute. It extends to both direct and indirect participation or intervention in a political campaign, on behalf of or in opposition to any candidate. Such activity includes, but is not limited to, the publication or distribution of written or printed statements (such as a newsletter) or the making of oral statements on behalf of or in opposition to a candidate. Revenue rulings issued by the IRS strictly limit the role of religious organizations in voter education projects designed to inform the electorate of the views of candidates on issues of importance to members of the faith. See, e.g., Revenue Ruling 78–248, 1978–1 C.B. 154; Revenue Ruling 80–282, 1980–2 C.B. 178. The IRS has determined that it is permissible for an exempt organization to distribute questionnaires to candidates and to publish voter guides stating the position of candidates, but only if it is on a wide range of issues, Revenue Ruling 78–248, 1978–1 C.B. 154. According to the IRS, voter guides or questionnaires are impermissible if they "evidence a bias on certain issues," or concentrate on a "narrow range of issues," even if not expressly stating support or opposition for any candidate. Are these restraints permissible? Why or why not?

In the early 1970s—during the Vietnam War—some Members of Congress attempted to tighten the regulations relating to lobbying by exempt organizations. Several religious organizations testified that many problems facing the human community are not purely technical or tactical in nature, but contain important moral and religious dimensions worthy of consideration by policy makers. *Legislative Activity By Certain Types of Exempt Organizations*, Hearings Before the House Ways and Means Committee, 92d Cong., 2d Sess. (1972). The proposals to tighten restrictions on lobbying by religious bodies did not emerge from the committee.

The normative theoretical concern—the extent to which religious concerns are legitimate in the legislative process—has at least two sides to it. An example of a churchside view of this issue was voiced by the 200th General

Assembly of the Presbyterian Church (USA) in a 1989 policy statement that said: "Since the time of Calvin, Reformed Protestants have felt called to share their vision of God's intended order for the human community, and Presbyterians have recognized and acted on the responsibility to seek social justice and peace and to promote the biblical values of freedom and liberty as well as corporate responsibility within the political order.... In 'attempting to influence legislation' churches speak to the moral aspects of political issues. Such witness flows directly from fundamental faith and is integral to its free exercise. It is essential to the church's identity and mission, and to the moral authority of its pronouncement, that it speak as 'church' through its religious structures and leaders." *God Alone is Lord of the Conscience*, 10, 36, (1989), reprinted in 8 *J. L. & Relig.* 331, 335, 364–65 (1990). Dean Kelley, who served for decades as the executive for religious and civil liberty of the National Council of Churches of Christ in the U.S.A., wrote: "Churches are bound by their sense of mission, their consecrated obedience to God, to speak out on issues where the well-being of persons is at stake, to proclaim what they believe is the right and moral course for the whole society and what will benefit everyone, not just themselves or their members. Churches were doing this sort of thing before there were legislatures or lobbies, and they will continue to do so—despite whatever odds or obstacles—as long as there are churches." Dean M. Kelley, *Why Churches Should Not Pay Taxes* 86 (1977). See also statements of Jewish, Protestant, and Catholic leaders on religiously grounded witness on matters of social justice, including the civil right movement [section 3 below].

Professor Greenawalt expressed a different view of the theoretical concern: "A liberal society ... has no business dictating matters of religious belief and worship to its citizens. It cannot forbid or require forms of belief, it cannot preclude acts of worship that cause no secular harm, it cannot restrict expression about what constitutes religious truth. One needs only a modest extension of these uncontroversial principles to conclude that a liberal society should not rely on religious grounds to prohibit activities that either cause no secular harm or do not cause enough secular harm to warrant their prohibition." Kent Greenawalt, *Religious Convictions and Political Choice* 90–91 (1988). From *Everson* [Chapter Fourteen, section 1] to *Lee v. Weisman* [Chapter Fourteen, section 1], the Court has clarified that coercion of the sort described in the first two sentences of Professor Greenawalt certainly constitutes a violation of the nonestablishment provision. Does it follow that Greenawalt's third sentence is "only a modest extension"? Does his standard of non-reliance on religious grounds in the formation of public policy account for the numerous historical instances of vivid religious participation in American politics, from the dawn of the American revolution through the abolitionist movement [Chapter Eight] to the recent civil rights movement and the controversy over abortion [sections 3 & 4 below]? Note that he would not allow the government to prohibit activities that "do not cause enough secular harm to warrant their prohibition." Who should undertake this ad-hoc balancing to determine whether or not activities "cause enough secular harm to warrant prohibition," legislators or judges? Is that what the judges were doing in *Stone v. Graham* and *Wallace v. Jaffree* [Chapter Fourteen, section 2]? Greenawalt urges legislators not to present religious arguments in public political debate, lest such discourse will make some constituents "feel like second-class citizens ... imposed upon in the sense of being excluded." Id. 132, 157. Why should someone feel imposed upon if a disagreement over public policy is grounded, at least in part, on a difference in worldview involving religious as well as secular claims? As Professor Tushnet wrote: "Nonadherents who believe they are excluded from the political community are merely expressing the disappointment felt by everyone who has lost a fair fight in the arena of politics." Mark V. Tushnet, "The Constitution of Religion," 18 *Conn. L. Rev.* 701, 712 (1986). See discussion of the endorsement test in NOTE. *The Quest for Tests.* [Chapter Fourteen, section 2].

Professor Perry opposes the marginalization of religious discourse in political debate, writing: "Because of the role that religious arguments about the morality of human conduct inevitably play in the political process, it is important that such arguments, no less than secular moral arguments, be presented in—so that they can be tested in—public political debate. Moreover, it is impossible to construct 'an airtight barrier' between, on the one side, public culture generally—in which religiously based moral discourse is undeniably proper—and on the other, public debate specifically about controversial political issues." Michael J. Perry, *Religion in Politics: Constitutional and Moral Perspectives* 61 (1997). On the issue of religion in legislative judgments, however, Perry suggests that "in making a political choice about the morality of human conduct, especially a coercive political choice, legislators and others should not rely on a religious argument about the requirements of human well-being unless, in their view, a persuasive secular argument reaches the same conclusion about those requirements as the religious arguments." *Id.* 8. Under *McDaniel v. Paty,* Perry's first statement is a constitutional mandate. Is his second statement a counsel of prudence in a pluralistic society or a constitutional rule informing "secular purpose" doctrine? Writing in the early 1980s Professor Perry suggested that judicial review by the Supreme Court is "the institutionalization of prophecy." Michael J. Perry, *The Constitution, the Courts, and Human Rights* (1982). The prophetic voice to which Perry refers is not that of foretelling the future, but of telling forth a critical judgment in the here and now. Could one make this claim after cases like *United States v. Lee, Tony and Susan Alamo Foundation, Goldman, Shabazz, Lyng, Smith,* and *Boerne* [Chapter Eleven]?

---

3.   THE CIVIL RIGHTS MOVEMENT

The first meeting of what became the Southern Christian Leadership Conference (SCLC) was held at the call of four black ministers and one layman. They invited black churchmen and other black leaders to meet at the Ebenezer Baptist Church in Atlanta. The meeting, held in January 1957, developed working papers on busing, economic survival, and social protest against the discriminatory treatment of blacks. The papers stated: "We must recognize in this new period that *direct action is our most potent political weapon....* The campaign is based on the most stable social institution in Negro culture—the church," Aldon D. Morris, *The Origins of the Civil Rights Movement* (1984), 83–85 (emphasis in original).

The SCLC was the force that developed the infrastructure of the civil rights movement. It provided moral, material, and organizational support to local protesters, otherwise isolated and at a disadvantage with the white power structure. It produced among local communities "the mental attitudes conducive to protest." It led to large numbers of people wanting "freedom," *Id.* 77,

95–97. The "most magnificent accomplishment" of the SCLC was "the creation of a disciplined mass movement of Southern blacks," Bayard Ruskin, *Strategies for Freedom* (1976) 80.

No political movement in America succeeds alone. The SCLC was joined by the older National Association for the Advancement of Colored People and the newer Congress of Racial Equality, both organizations with Baptist Church support. Morris 120–138. The Student Nonviolent Coordinating Committee was founded in 1960 with help from SCLC. *Id.* 219–220. The American Friends Service Committee, the Fellowship for Reconciliation, and the Alabama Christian Movement for Human Rights all played supporting roles. The SCLC was central.

The SCLC had the following church connections:

1. Twenty-one of its original twenty-five officers were ordained ministers. *Id.* 80–87.

2. Its president, Martin Luther King, Jr., was a Baptist minister.

3. Its members (it had no individual members) were chiefly churches or church-related organizations. *Id.* 91.

4. Its characteristic form of meeting was a rally modeled on a church revival, featuring a charismatic minister, usually the Reverend King. *Id.* 91–92, 97.

5. Its imagery was religious—for example, Moses was put forward as an exemplar. The present state of subservience was seen as "Egypt," *Id.* 98.

6. Financing came largely from the churches, chiefly from "black church-oriented mass meetings outside the South." On September 4, 1959, Dr. King wrote to Rev. Wilber B. Miller: Most of my speaking is in the interest of raising funds for this conference. One of the methods that I have used in the past few months is that of selecting cities across the country and asking the ministerial groups to come together and sponsor a citywide meeting at which time I speak, and funds are raised through the churches and other organizations for the work of the Southern Christian Leadership Conference.

7. It transferred the emphasis of the preaching of black churches on acceptance of one's lot in this world to an emphasis on religion as having social significance. In doing so it used the traditional power of religious teachers to affect cultural consciousness. "The mass-based black church played the leading role in interpreting reality and providing moral standards for blacks." *Id.* 96.

For these reasons, the SCLC could be described by the Reverend Joseph Lowery, one of its founders, as "the black church coming alive." *Id.* 88.

The means adopted by this religious organization were political. Its strategy focused on franchising voters, with the aim of doubling the black vote in the South. To this end, the SCLC launched "The Crusade for Citizenship" in 1958, a movement to register blacks to vote. *Id.* 101–109. The kind of resistance that this movement could expect to meet is captured by the following letter to the Reverend George Lee, a leader in an earlier local voting registration drive in Humphreys County, Mississippi (shortly after receiving the letter, he was murdered): "Preacher, instead of preaching the Gospel, what you say you are called to do, you are preaching to Negroes here in Humphreys County to register and vote. You had better do what you claim that you were called to do, preach the Gospel." *Id.* 105.

A climactic moment in the drive for civil rights was the confrontation planned by the SCLC in Birmingham in 1963. The local head, the Reverend Fred Shuttlesworth, has described Birmingham as launching "a systematic, wholehearted battle against segregation which would set the pace for the nation." The confrontation succeeded because of the cohesion produced by "music, religious oratory, prayers, and shared symbols." *Id.* 251. By this date the SCLC had a budget of $1 million and a highly organized staff. The Birmingham demonstrators were carefully coordinated, with the 16th Street Baptist Church as headquarters; this church and three other Baptist churches provided the leadership with a starting constituency "of close to 5000." *Id.* 262. Martin Luther King, Jr., stayed out of jail by not participating in any street demonstration until Good Friday. He then chose this day to defy an injunction, and he was arrested. Addressing his "fellow clergymen" on April 16, 1963, he wrote from Birmingham City jail.

Martin Luther King, Jr., Letter from Birmingham Jail, April 16, 1963

Just as the apostle Paul left his village of Tarsus and carried the gospel of Jesus Christ to the far corners of the Greco–Roman world, so I am compelled to carry the gospel of freedom beyond my home town....

One may well ask how can you advocate breaking some laws and obeying others? I would agree with St. Augustine that "an unjust law is no law at all." ... To put it in the terms of St. Augustine, an unjust law is a human law that is not rooted in eternal law and natural law....

Was not Jesus Christ an extremist for love? ... Was not Amos an extremist for justice? ... Was not Paul an extremist for the Christian gospel? ... Was not Martin Luther an extremist? And John Bunyan? ... And Abraham Lincoln? ... And Thomas Jefferson?

There was a time when the church was very powerful. In those days the church was not merely a thermometer that recorded the ideas and principles of popular opinion; it was a thermostat that transformed the mores of society.... The Christians pressed on, in the conviction that they were a "colony of heaven," called to obey God rather than man.... By their effort and example they brought an end to such ancient evils as infanticide and gladiatorial contests.... I hope the church as a whole will meet the challenge of this decisive hour.

————

Nearly a million copies of this letter were distributed before King was bailed from jail. Morris 266. Following Birmingham, 758 demonstrations occurred in 186 cities across the South; 14,733 persons were arrested. A year later, the national government passed the Civil Rights Act of 1964. *Id.* 274. As effectively as the northern ministers of 1850, the black ministers of the Southern Christian Leadership Conference had intervened in American government.

The following statement about the connection between Judaism and social justice is by a rabbi who is director of the Religious Action Center of the Union of American Hebrew Congregations and a lawyer.

David Saperstein, "Jewish Perspectives on the Role of Religion in the Political Process," 1 *J. L. & Relig.* 220 (1983)

When the religious lobby is successful, and uniquely successful, it is only on those issues where there is an overwhelming consensus in the religious community on the substance and the priority of a particular issue. When this happens, the religious community can play an influential role in defining the public's moral perception of the particular issue in keeping with our traditional values and goals. Since millions of Americans look to religious leaders for such guidance, these leaders can often have a significant, occasionally determinative, impact on the political decision-making process. Key examples of this in American history include the outlawing of dueling, the antislavery movement, the temperance movement, the industrial reforms of the progressive era, the recognition of the labor movement, the generation of public and Congressional support for the United Nations, the civil rights movement, and the anti-Vietnam War movement. In recent years, the religious community has played a crucial role in the development of international food relief policy resulting from the 1974–1975 world hunger crisis and in originating and lobbying for the human rights provisos to the foreign aid bills in 1978.

When one analyzes the fundamental postulates and axioms which underlie the political vision of mainstream religious groups, it is clear that they are virtually indistinguishable from the postulates and axioms which underlie modern political liberalism. There is, however, one profound difference which I think is important to point out. Political liberalism presumes virtually complete freedom of the individual, or as John Stuart Mill's famous dictum asserts, you may do your own thing so long as you do not infringe on the freedom or rights of others. But the *Halakhah,* and most religious traditions today, categorically reject this idea. *Halakhah* has embodied the recognition that issues of law and morality involve not only the relationship of person-to-person but also the relationship of person-to-God.

––––––––

In a similar vein, a representative of the National Jewish Community Relations Advisory Council testified before Congress that each of its affiliates "regards its program as an expression of the tenets of the Jewish faith which it is organized to advance. Their activities are inspired by the Prophets' mandate to pursue justice. They believe that mandate governs [their lives] in all it aspects and requires those who adhere to the principles of Judaism to let their views be heard in support of justice for all." *Legislative Activity By Certain Types of Exempt Organizations*, Hearings Before the House Ways and Means Committee, 92d Cong., 2d Sess. 99 (1972).

In August of 2000 Sen. Joseph I. Lieberman became the first Jew in America to be nominated for the vice presidency. Lieberman is a religiously observant Orthodox Jew who is comfortable with the language of faith. Lieberman has used religious discourse both on the floor of the Senate and in stump speeches on the campaign trail. For example, at a Detroit church, he called for the creation of a role for religion in public life. "As a people, we need to reaffirm our faith and renew the dedication of our nation and ourselves to God and God's purpose," he said. And at the University of Notre Dame, he delivered a major address on religion and politics.

Senator Joseph I. Lieberman, Address at University of Notre Dame, October, 2000

We are still arguably the most religiously observant people on earth, and share a near universal belief in God. But you wouldn't know it from national public life today. The line between church and state is an important one and has always been hard for us to draw, but in recent years we have gone far beyond what the Framers ever imagined in separating the two. So much so that we have practically banished religious values and religious institutions from the public square and constructed a "discomfort zone" for even discussing our faith in public settings—ironically making religion one of the few remaining socially acceptable targets of intolerance.

————

Not all admire Lieberman's efforts to insert the sacred into the profane world of politics. The most prominent complaint came from a Jewish group, the Anti–Defamation League. See John Rivera, "Unease over faith in politics Campaign: The Anti–Defamation League says Joseph I. Lieberman, Al Gore and George W. Bush have stepped over the line in the way they have used religious references in the presidential race," *Baltimore Sun*, Sept. 7, 2000, 2A.

Compare the following statement by a Methodist pastor who served for many years as the executive director of the Christian Legal Society and who is now a law professor.

Lynn Buzzard, "The Evangelical Rediscovery of Law and Politics" 1 *J. L. & Relig.* 187, 199 (1983)

The practical consequence of this assertion that Christ is Lord of all is that the evangelical Christian community will resist the attempt to constrain its activities to what the secularist defines as "religion." Politics, art, science and philosophy are all part of the arena of activity by the believing community. The criticism of religious groups on the right based on their involvement in politics is particularly ill conceived. One may indeed debate their choice of issues or even the side they take on some, but no one emerging from the biblical tradition dare challenge their assertion that as believers they feel compelled to speak to the moral character and the political life of the nation.

————

The following is by the executive director of the Baptist Joint Committee on Public Affairs.

James M. Dunn, "The Christian as Political Activist," 81 *Liberty* 18 (July–August, 1986).

Where does one draw the line between mixing politics-religion and merging church-state? It is a popular question, often asked simply to shut off debate. The challenge works as a cutoff valve because there is no simple, easy, short answer.

The question implies a neat worldview in which everything is black or white, good or bad. This either-or mentality is not the exclusive disease of religious and political fundamentalists. In fact, a dualism infects American life. It insists upon every issue being divided from top to bottom by a vertical line with a right side and a wrong side.

Instead of this vertical line, a horizontal line with opposing views, differing ways of looking at things, or balancing consideration at either end is probably a more useful model. In many of the polarities, paradoxes, contradictions, or competing goods that complicate the church-state debate, one draws the line and then travels it, or draws the line and discovers that traveling the line is fraught with creative tension.

———

For other Protestant commentators, see Richard John Neuhaus, *The Naked Public Square* (1982); Richard John Neuhaus and Michael Cromartie, eds., *Piety and Politics: Evangelicals and Fundamentalists Confront the World* (1987); John Howard Yoder, *The Politics of Jesus* (1972); Dean Kelley, "The Intermeddling Manifesto, Or, The Role of Religious Bodies in Affecting Public Policy in the United States," 8 *J. L. & Relig.* 85 (1990); Michael W. McConnell, "Christ, Culture, and Courts: A Niebuhrian Examination of First Amendment Jurisprudence," 42 *DePaul L. Rev.* 191 (1992).

Compare the following by a leading Catholic writer.

Robert E. Rodes, Jr., "Pluralist Christendom and the Christian Civil Magistrate" 9 *Communio* 321, 329 (1982)

The aspiration to a fully human life requires a social agenda. Respect for people of other, or no, religious beliefs should not stop a Christian from formulating his social principles on the basis of a Christian understanding of human destiny and affairs. Indeed, such an understanding gives the firmest possible support to that very respect. That respect in turn gives a solid foundation not only to traditional educational and charitable endeavors, but also to continuing efforts to eliminate race discrimination, to provide the poor with decent homes and enough to eat, to secure to the worker both the psychological and the economic fruits of his labor, to promote a radical redistribution of income and resources, to resist unjust war, or to establish the right of the unborn to live. These are all matters on which Christians can make common cause with other people, but I believe that a Christian must base his own support for them on his own commitments.

———

For comments by other Catholic writers, see Michael J. Perry, *Religion in Politics: Constitutional and Moral Perspectives* (1997); Perry, *Love and Power: The Role of Religion and Morality in American Politics* (1991); Perry, *Morality, Politics, and Law: A Bicentennial Essay* (1988); Richard McBrien, *Caesar's Coin: Religion and Politics in America* (1987); John A. Coleman, *An American Strategic Theology* (1982); Joseph Bernardin, "The Role of the Religious Leader in the Development of Public Policy," 34 *DePaul L. Rev.* 1 (1984); David Hollenbach, "Contexts of the Political Role of Religion," 20 *San Diego L. Rev.* 877 (1993); Edward McGlynn Gaffney, Jr., "On Not Rendering to Caesar: The Unconstitutionality of Tax Regulation of Activities of Religious Organizations Relating to Politics," 40 *DePaul L. Rev.* 1, 9–16 (1990) (describing historic role of religion in American politics); Gaffney, "Politics Without Brackets on Religious Convictions: Michael Perry and Bruce Ackerman on Neutrality," 64 *Tulane L. Rev.* 1143 (1990) (describing role of religion in abolitionist movement, civil rights movement, and in immigration policy); Gaffney, "Biblical Religion and American Politics: Some Historical and Theological Reflections," 1 *J. Law & Relig.* 171 (1983).

4. Movements For and Against Abortion

Since the first century the Christian Church had regarded abortion as a serious sin. The Reformation produced no division on this point. At the beginning of the 1960s the churches, Protestant and Catholic, asserted the sanctity of life and rejected abortion for invading it, Noonan, *A Private Choice: Abortion in America in the Seventies* (1979) 59–61. When predominantly professional and secular organizations—the American Civil Liberties Union; the American Medical Association; Planned Parenthood of America—began to ask for changes in the abortion laws, a division occurred in the religious ranks. Some theological casuists found occasions on which abortion, although a grave act, could be justified by its preservation of other values. Some religious bodies objected to making abortion a matter of civil law.

The General Assembly of the Unitarian–Universalists in 1963 characterized existing statutes as "an affront to human life and dignity" and called for legalizing abortion for any "compelling reason, physical, psychological, mental, spiritual, or economic," Lawrence Lader, *Abortion* 100 (1967). In California nearly 1,300 Protestant ministers and Jewish rabbis called for change. *Id.* 147. Joseph Fletcher, an Episcopal priest and professor of Christian ethics at Episcopal Theological School, became a leader for reform and a director of the Association for the Study of Abortion, a spearhead of change. *Id.* 148. In 1971, the Eighth General Synod of the United Church of Christ called for legalization. In 1972, the General Conference of the United Methodist Church called for removal of "abortion from the criminal code." Noonan 61.

Ever since the "birth control" movement had taken shape in the United States under the leadership of Margaret Higgins Sanger, its most vocal and persistent opponent had been the Catholic Church. Despite the opposition of the Church, the movement had succeeded. Contraception had become widely accepted in the United States. American public policy supported contraception. The federal government paid for "family planning programs." Within the Catholic Church itself a strong strain of opinion argued for the moral acceptability of contraception. John T. Noonan, Jr., *Contraception: A History of its Treatment by the Catholic Theologians and Canonists* (1967).

When the abortion battle opened, it was entirely natural for the old birth controllers to see it as a replay of the battle over contraception. Their nemesis, the Catholic Church, appeared again to them as the principal foe. The scenario was clear. They would attack the Roman menace. Secular, Protestant, and Jewish opinion would rally to them. The Church's own ranks would divide. After a struggle, abortion would be triumphantly established as national policy.

In *Roe v. Wade,* 410 U.S. 113 (1973), the Court held the abortion laws to be an unconstitutional denial of liberty. The Court did not mention a First Amendment basis for its decision. But one commentator defended the decision on the ground that the existing abortion laws had been kept in place by the pressure of religious groups: "Whenever the views of organized religious groups have come to play a pervasive role in an entire subject's legislative consideration for reasons intrinsic to the subject matter as then understood," the legislature cannot act without favoring a particular religious doctrine and thereby 'establishing' a religion, "Laurence Tribe, "Foreword, The Supreme Court—1972 Term: Toward a Model of Roles in the Due Process of Life and Law," 87 *Harvard Law Review* 20, 23 (1973). Professor Tribe later changed his mind and repudiated this position. Tribe, American Constitutional Law 1349–50 (2d ed. 1987).

In the political sphere, the leaders of the movement to restrict abortion by law were often Protestants. The president of the largest anti-abortion group, the National Right to life Committee, Mildred Jefferson, was a Methodist. The president of Americans United for Life was George Huntston Williams, Hollis Professor of Divinity at Harvard Divinity School and an ordained Unitarian minister. The president of American Citizens Concerned for Life, Marjory Mecklenburg, was a Methodist. In the Congress, early sponsors of a Human Life Amendment included Senator Mark Hatfield, a Baptist, and Senator Harold Hughes, an ordained Methodist minister. Noonan *A Private Choice* 61. Near the end of the 1970s the most powerful and politically effective opposition to legalized abortion came from evangelical and fundamentalist Protestants; the Moral Majority put forward their position. The Church of Jesus Christ of Latter–Day Saints was an effective opponent in the states where the Mormons were numerous. Nevertheless, in the eyes of the proponents of the abortion liberty, the *bete noire* was still the Catholic Church.

In 1976 an amendment introduced to an appropriations act by Congressman Henry Hyde sharply restricted the federal funding of abortion. Immediately after the act's passage, Planned Parenthood of New York City sought a preliminary injunction prohibiting the Secretary of Health, Education, and Welfare from implementing the restrictions of the Hyde Amendment. Judge John Dooling, a federal district judge in Brooklyn, granted the injunction, making it applicable to the secretary's actions throughout the country. *McRae v. Mathews,* 421 F. Supp. 533 (E.D.N.Y. 1976). The case then went to trial.

Among the contentions of the plaintiff were (1) that the Hyde Amendment was an establishment of Catholic doctrine because it reflected Catholic religious teaching; and (2) that it was a denial of the free exercise of religion by those who believed that religious duty required them to secure an abortion. Judge Dooling, himself a Catholic, gave the plaintiffs wide latitude in introducing evidence to prove these points, including evidence on the religious habits of

Congressman Hyde. Over three years after the preliminary injunction had been granted, Judge Dooling gave his decision, making the injunction permanent. In *McRae v. Califano,* 491 F. Supp. 630 (E.D.N.Y. 1980) Judge Dooling. summarized the Catholic involvement in abortion politics as follows.

1. Testimony before the Subcommittee on Constitutional Amendments of the Senate Committee on the Judiciary in support of a constitutional amendment to protect the unborn child—Testimony on March 7, 1974, by the cardinal archbishops of Boston, Chicago, Los Angeles, and Philadelphia.

2. Promulgation on November 20, 1975, by the National Conference of Catholic Bishops of a "Pastoral Plan for Prolife Activities" recommending an educational effort; a pastoral effort, addressed to the specific needs of women with problems related to pregnancy and abortion; and a public policy effort to insure "effective legal protection for the right to life."

3. The Diocese of Fargo, North Dakota, had attempted to carry out this plan by instruction from the bishop to the clergy.

4. Many Catholic newspapers and magazines gave "a great deal of attention" to the Catholic position on abortion and solicited support for the enactment of constitutional and statutory provisions on abortion.

5. In the Archdiocese of Los Angeles the Feast of the Holy Innocents (December 28th) had been made the occasion in each year from 1971 to 1978 for a candlelit procession followed by the celebration of a Mass of Atonement.

6. In 1976–1977 the New York Right to life Committee had received $116,000 from "Respect Life" contributions solicited outside churches after mass.

7. The Minnesota Right to Life organizations were stated beneficiaries of the annual Catholic appeal collection of the Archdiocese of St. Paul.

8. Mary Peek, a candidate for the House of Representatives in Minnesota, "experienced an erosion of support" after criticism of her position on abortion and that she lost the election by 116 votes. Peek did not believe that there was any institutional coercion of Catholics but that the social disapprobation of abortion within the Catholic community, resulting from the hierarchically created atmosphere of disapproval, must to some extent carry through to the voting booth.

9. In 1972–1974 Minnesota Citizens Concerned for Life was particularly active in the Minnesota legislature and that it received support from Catholic parishioners, although it was nondenominational "and practically interdenominational."

10. A lobbyist for the National Committee for a Human Life Amendment, "the lobbying arm" of the National Conference of Catholic Bishops, kept in close touch with the Senate and House conferees on the abortion funding bill in 1977.

McRae v. Califano

491 F. Supp. 630 (E.D.N.Y. 1980)

■ DOOLING, J.

Religious motivation and allegiance to religiously perceived principle on the part of many legislators, on both sides of the issue, are easy and necessary inferences from the record and the legislative history. That does not signify that only religious motivation can explain the pro-life position nor does it signify that secular reasoning could not readily arrive at the pro-life principle. What finally influenced the votes of the decisive number of legislators cannot be said with any confidence to be religious motivation or religious conviction or will to make effective a religiously perceived principle of conduct or the influence of institutional religion and religious pleading or fear of reprisal from religiously oriented voters. What can be said is that an organized effort of institutional religion to influence the vote on the enactments in question on religious grounds was made, that it cannot be said that the effort did not influence a decisive number of votes through a combination of religious belief and principle on the part of some with a fear of political reprisal on the part of others, and that the narrow votes in both houses are open to the inference that in one or the other way the religious factor was decisive of the issue for enough legislators to affect the outcome of the voting. On the specific effect of Roman Catholic institutional intervention Representative Hyde said in his April 22, 1978, St. Louis speech:

> "It would be amusing (if it weren't so threatening) that the current crusade of the American Civil Liberties Union is to prove in Federal Court that the pro-life movement in America is a religious plot—specifically a Catholic plot—and hence a violation of the First Amendment. I should like to point out that while several Catholic voices—many Catholic voices—are heard in Congress on behalf of innocent prenatal life—the leading Senatorial pro-life spokesmen are mostly non-Catholic. I speak of Senator Jesse Helms of North Carolina, Senator Dick Schweiker of Pennsylvania.

> "The most prominent Catholics in the Senate—the senior senator from Massachusetts and the junior senator from New York—do not support our effort to stop the abortion tidal wave. The same sad truth applies to the celebrated Catholic governors of California and New York. In the House we have a Jesuit Priest Congressman who wears his Roman collar while casting votes to continue the use of taxpayers' money to pay for medicaid abortions. To my knowledge, he remains in good standing with his religious superiors. In a nearby state, one Catholic college invited a Senator who was a leader of the pro-abortion forces in Congress to address its graduating class last June. The point of all this I suggest, is that the outrage of abortion isn't all that disturbing to some influential Catholics. That is what Jacques Maritain calls 'kneeling to the world.'

"There is one nun based in Chicago who travels the country attacking me for opposing abortion. Occasionally, the newspapers give her coverage which I suggest ought to embarrass every Catholic."

When Representative Hyde voted in 1976 to override President Ford's veto of the 1976 enactment despite his agreement with the veto on the appropriations aspect of the bill (which exceeded the President's budget by $4 billion), he said:

"I am, nevertheless, voting to override the President's veto because within this legislation is a provision forbidding the use of Federal funds to pay for abortions. In starkest terms, the potential exists of saving some 300,000 lives which otherwise might be destroyed with the use of taxpayers' funds. The saving of these lives far outweighs the economic considerations involved in this legislation.". . .

Yet it would not be difficult to point to considerable pro-life argument that counted on the evident facts that the fetus begins in a union of living human cells and is from nearly the first moment a potential human being, and that its dependent existence, is, for all its dependence, separate life of human quality; and to pro-life argument that the "right to life"—the affirmation that only great reasons can justify frustrating the natural growth into being of rational human life—is separately significant, and that the reasons advanced for funding abortion are for the most part empty. Others argued that federal neutrality would be represented by not subsidizing abortion, that the right to choose abortion did not imply a right to have an abortion paid for from public funds. Others argued that if there was a public duty it was a duty to provide alternatives to abortion, and so to relieve poor women of the need to resort to the always tragic recourse of abortion.

The repeated use during the debates of "human life" terminology extended at times to referring to the immortal soul of the fetus, to invoking Herod's "slaughter of the innocent," and to emphasizing that the fetus is "defenseless," is "innocent." Much of this language is seen in the Roman Catholic literature already referred to, and it implies humanity in the fetus—for only rational beings can be "innocent" in moral terms. The language and references are specifically religious, but, again, much other argument was in the debates that was free of religious reference, whether or not the debaters were motivated by their religious convictions. Other parts of the debates are very insistent that the issue was a moral issue, and that the members had to, or ought to, vote their consciences. The pro-choice debaters, in their reference to the pro-life members' positions, frequently emphasized their respect for the pro-life members' views and, in so doing, manifested an evidently informed belief that the pro-life views were essentially religious. More broadly, the pro-life members at times portrayed abortion as one element of the moral decay that they saw about them in this country and against which they sought to rouse the Congress.

The charge that the pro-life members were seeking to impose their "morality" or their religious views on the Congress, and on poor women, and the counter-charge that the pro-choice members were preparing to require taxpayers to whom abortion was morally abhorrent to subsidize it with their taxes, resulted in frequent avowals by members of their religious affiliations; indeed, members did not hesitate to instance in aid of their arguments their own religious upbringing, their conduct of their own families, and their legal and medical professional experience with abortion. The positions of the various churches on abortion were referred to more than once. The pro-choice members argued that the abortion decision was a matter of individual conscience. And there was a recognition that in the minds of some members their religious beliefs did not really leave them a free vote.

The debates were often bitterly controversial, even inflamed; the members returned to the debate again and again with expressed reluctance but with unabated resolution. The members recognized that the debates were often emotion-charged, and much of the argument, even read in the black and white of the Congressional Record, is deeply felt, personal in tone, and consciously moralistic—because the speaker sees no escape from the moral issue or from its importance. The members were plainly aware, were made aware, of the pressures exerted upon them by their sense of their constituencies' views on the issue and of the religious setting in which the views were entertained and expressed.

The intense lobbying on both sides of the issue is reflected in the debates and made clear in the record. The members were fully aware of it, and the not infrequent references to the picketing, the March for Life, and the letters from the constituencies indicate general consciousness that the issue was one that had gained wide popular attention and recognition that their votes would be reported to their constituencies. While the overall impression is that the pro-life lobbying effort was better centralized and more strongly presented than the pro-choice lobbying, the pro-choice lobbying was effectively present and skillful. Remarkably, the issue cut across party lines, so that the lobbying effort had to be more personal than organizational in its address. To an extent the essentially non-partisan cast that the issue assumed seems to have cost the pro-choice advocates a substantial part of the Democratic support that might normally have been expected on a DHEW issue affecting medicaid. Representative Flood's 1976 change from opposition to support of the Hyde amendment is illustrative.

No measure of the effect of the lobbying is possible. The unanswered question is whether there would have been any abortion legislation if the pro-life group had not used the expedient of presenting the issue as a "rider" on the appropriation bill for 1976. The inference from the fact that the funding restriction has survived only as a rider for four successive years is that the expedient itself is responsible for the fund restrictions, and not any congressional consensus on abortion, or any fruition of effective lobbying effort. It is evident enough that the amendments are legislation on an appropriation bill, and that, although each side has charged the other with hostage taking, the reality has been that the pro-life forces have held the appropriation bills hostage until the amendments were passed. Yet that would not have been possible unless in one of the two bodies there was a consensus for abortion legislation. In a sense the amendments are enactments of the House of Representatives to which the Senate has acceded, with such amendments as it could negotiate, rather than risk the appropriation bills. . . .

As pointed out earlier, right to life language has found its way into a number of statutes, and, in the case of the pregnancy amendment to Title VII (Equal Employment Opportunities), 42 U.S.C. § 2000e(k), occasioned exchanges as bitter as many of those that occurred during the Hyde amendment debates. In addition to the other enactments referred to above, Public Law 95–444 of October 10, 1978, 92 Stat. 1067, added to the section enumerating the duties and functions of the Civil Rights Commission the provision:

"(f) Nothing in this or any other Act shall be construed as authorizing the Commission, its Advisory Committees, or any person under its supervision or control to appraise, or to study and collect information about, laws and policies of the Federal Government, or any other governmental authority in the United States, with respect to abortion."

The Commission had issued a report in 1975 on *The Constitutional Aspects of the Right to Limit Childbearing* which argued against legislation aimed at narrowing the effect of *Roe v. Wade*.

E

What ultimately emerges from the facts found in parts XII through XIV is that the major religions whose views were presented all regard abortion as presenting religiously framed questions of moral right, moral duty and conscience, that they are in disagreement on the appropriate rules of conduct but in agreement that abortion is a morally grave undertaking in any circumstances, and that their sharpest disagreement concerns the role of civil government.

———

Judge Dooling held that the Hyde Amendment did not violate the nonestablishment provision but that it did violate other parts of the Bill of Rights:

———

A woman's conscientious decision, in consultation with her physician, to terminate her pregnancy because that is medically necessary to her health, is an exercise of the most fundamental of rights, nearly allied to her right to be, surely part of the liberty protected by the Fifth Amendment, doubly protected when the liberty is exercised in conformity with religious belief and teaching protected by the First Amendment. To deny necessary medical assistance for the lawful and medically necessary procedure of abortion is to violate the pregnant woman's First and Fifth Amendment rights. The irreconcilable conflict of deeply and widely held views on this issue of individual conscience excludes any legislative intervention except that which protects each individual's freedom of conscientious decision and conscientious nonparticipation.

Judgment must be for plaintiffs.

—————

The Supreme Court reversed Judge Dooling's decision and vacated his nationwide injunction.

Harris v. McRae

448 U.S. 297 (1980).

Solicitor General McCree argued the cause for appellant. With him on the briefs were *Assistant Attorney General Daniel and Eloise E. Davies. Victor G. Rosenblum, Dennis J. Horan, John D. Gorby, Carl Anderson, Patrick A. Trueman, A. Lawrence Washburn, Jr., and Gerald E. Bodell* filed briefs for Buckley et al., appellees under this Court's Rule 10(4), in support of appellant.

Rhonda Copelon argued the cause for appellees McRae et al. With her on the briefs were *Nancy Stearns, Sylvia Law, Ellen K. Sawyer, Janet Benshoof, Judith Levin, Harriet Pilpel,* and *Eve Paul.*

Briefs of amici curiae urging reversal were filed by *John T Noonan, Jr.,* and *William B. Ball* for Representative Jim Wright et al.; and by *Wilfred R. Caron* and *Patrick F. Geary* for the United States Catholic Conference.

Briefs of *amici curiae* urging affirmance were filed by *Robert Abrams,* Attorney General, *Shirley Adelson Siegel,* Solicitor General, and *Peter Bienstock, Arnold D. Fleischer,* and *Barbara E. Levy,* Assistant Attorneys General, for the State of New York et al., joined by *Rufus L. Edmisten,* Attorney General of North Carolina, *William F. O'Connell,* Special Deputy Attorney General, and *Steven Mansfield Shaber,* Associate Attorney General, and *James A. Redden,* Attorney General of Oregon; by *Leo Pfeffer* for the American Ethical Union et al.; by *Barbara Ellen Handschu* for the Association of Legal Aid Attorneys of the City of New York—District 65—U.A.W. et al.; and by *Phyllis N. Segal* and *Judith L. Avner* for the National Organization for Women et al.

Briefs of *amici curiae* were filed by *Nadine Taub* for the Bergen-Passaic Health Systems Agency et al.; by *James G. Kolb* for the Coalition for Human Justice; by *Sanford Jay Rosen* for the National Council of Churches of Christ in the U.S.A.; and by *Sanford Jay Rosen* for the United Presbyterian Church in the U.S.A.

■ JUSTICE STEWART delivered the opinion of the Court.

The appellees argue that the Hyde Amendment contravenes rights secured by the Religion Clauses of the First Amendment. It is the appellees' view that the Hyde Amendment violates the Establishment Clause because it incorporates into law the doctrines of the Roman Catholic Church concerning the sinfulness of abortion and the time at which life commences. Moreover, insofar as a woman's decision to seek a medically necessary abortion may be a product of her religious beliefs under certain

Protestant and Jewish tenets, the appellees assert that the funding limitations of the Hyde Amendment impinge on the freedom of religion guaranteed by the Free Exercise Clause.

1

It is well settled that "a legislative enactment does not contravene the Establishment Clause if it has a secular legislative purpose, if its principal or primary effect neither advances nor inhibits religion, and if it does not foster an excessive governmental entanglement with religion." *Committee for Public Education v. Regan* [Chapter Fourteen, section 1]. Applying this standard, the District Court properly concluded that the Hyde Amendment does not run afoul of the Establishment Clause. Although neither a State nor the Federal Government can constitutionally "pass laws which aid one religion, aid all religions, or prefer one religion over another," *Everson v. Board of Education* [Chapter Fourteen, section 1], it does not follow that a statute violates the Establishment Clause because it "happens to coincide or harmonize with the tenets of some or all religions." *McGowan v. Maryland* [Chapter Thirteen, section 2]. That the Judaeo–Christian religions oppose stealing does not mean that a State or the Federal Government may not, consistent with the Establishment Clause, enact laws prohibiting larceny. *Ibid.* The Hyde Amendment, as the District Court noted, is as much a reflection of "traditionalist" values towards abortion, as it is an embodiment of the views of any particular religion. 491 F. Supp., at 741. See also *Roe v. Wade,* 410 U.S., at 138–141. In sum, we are convinced that the fact that the funding restrictions in the Hyde Amendment may coincide with the religious tenets of the Roman Catholic Church does not, without more, contravene the Establishment Clause.

We need not address the merits of the appellees' arguments concerning the Free Exercise Clause, because the appellees lack standing to raise a free exercise challenge to the Hyde Amendment. The named appellees fall into three categories: (1) the indigent pregnant women who sued on behalf of other women similarly situated, (2) the two officers of the Women's Division, and (3) the Women's Division itself. The named appellees in the first category lack standing to challenge the Hyde Amendment on free exercise grounds because none alleged, much less proved, that she sought an abortion under compulsion of religious belief. See *McGowan v. Maryland, supra,* at 429. Although the named appellees in the second category did provide a detailed description of their religious beliefs, they failed to allege either that they are or expect to be pregnant or that they are eligible to receive Medicaid. These named appellees, therefore, lack the personal stake in the controversy needed to confer standing to raise such a challenge to the Hyde Amendment. See *Warth v. Seldin,* 422 U.S. 490, 498–499.

Finally, although the Women's Division alleged that its membership includes "pregnant Medicaid eligible women who, as a matter of religious practice and in accordance with their conscientious beliefs, would choose but are precluded or discouraged from obtaining abortions reimbursed by Medicaid because of the Hyde Amendment," the Women's Division does not satisfy the standing requirements for an organization to assert the rights of its membership. One of those requirements is that "neither the claim asserted nor the relief requested requires the participation of individual members in the lawsuit." *Hunt v. Washington Apple Advertising Common*, 432 U.S. 333, 343. Since "it is necessary in a free exercise case for one to show the coercive effect of the enactment as it operates against him in the practice of his religion," *Schempp* [Chapter Fourteen, section 2], the claim asserted here is one that ordinarily requires individual participation. In the present case, the Women's Division concedes that "the permissibility, advisability and/or necessity of abortion according to circumstance is a matter about which there is diversity of view within ... our membership, and is a determination which must be ultimately and absolutely entrusted to the conscience of the individual before God." It is thus clear that the participation of individual members of the Women's Division is essential to a proper understanding and resolution of their free exercise claims. Accordingly, we conclude that the Women's Division, along with the other named appellees, lack standing to challenge the Hyde Amendment under the Free Exercise Clause.

■ JUSTICES BRENNAN, MARSHALL, BLACKMUN, and STEVENS dissented but did not focus on the religious issues.

———

Standing (II). The Department of Health, Education, and Welfare gave a surplus army hospital, appraised at $577,500, to Northeast Bible College. A "public benefit" allowance made by the department made the transfer gratuitous. The college—now known as Valley Forge Christian College—operated under the direction of the Assemblies of God. Its purpose was to train persons "for Christian service as either ministers or laymen." All its faculty had to have been "baptized in the Holy Spirit and be living consistent Christian lives; all members of the administration had to be affiliated with the Assemblies of God," *Id.* 468–469. Americans United (the former Protestants and Others United) sued to have the conveyance nullified on the ground that the gift had breached the nonestablishment provision. Americans United described itself as a nonprofit organization composed of 90,000 members who were taxpayers. The Third Circuit granted Americans United and four of its employees standing to sue not as taxpayers but as citizens, claiming "injury in fact" to "their shared individuated right to a government that 'shall make no law respecting the establishment of religion'," 619 F. 2d 252, 261 (1980). The Supreme Court, reversed. "The federal courts," JUSTICE REHNQUIST wrote, "were simply not constituted as ombudsmen of the general welfare." JUSTICE BRENNAN, joined by JUSTICES MARSHALL and BLACKMUN, dissented.

Valley Forge Christian College v. Americans United for Separation of Church and State

454 U.S. 464 (1982).

■ BRENNAN, J., dissenting.

[No] clear division can be drawn in this context between actions of the Legislative Branch and those of the Executive Branch. To be sure, the First

Amendment is phrased as a restriction on Congress' legislative authority; this is only natural since the Constitution assigns the authority to legislate and appropriate only to the Congress. But it is difficult to conceive of an expenditure for which the last governmental actor, either implementing directly the legislative will, or acting within the scope of legislatively delegated authority, is not an Executive Branch official. The First Amendment binds the Government as a whole, regardless of which branch is at work in a particular instance.

The Court's second purported distinction between this case and *Flast* [Chapter Fourteen, section 1] is equally unavailing. The majority finds it "decisive" that the Federal Property and Administrative Services Act of 1949 "was an evident exercise of Congress' power under the Property Clause, Art. IV, § 3, cl. 2," *ante,* at 480, while the Government action in *Flast* was taken under Art. 1, § 8. The Court relies on *United States v. Richardson,* 418 U.S. 166 (1974), and *Schlesinger v. Reservists Committee to Stop the War,* 418 U.S. 208 (1974), to support the distinction between the two Clauses, noting that those cases involved alleged deviations from the requirements of Art. 1, § 9, cl. 7, and Art. 1, § 6, cl. 2, respectively. The standing defect in each case was not, however, the failure to allege a violation of the Spending Clause; rather, the taxpayers in those cases had not complained of the distribution of Government largesse, and thus failed to meet the essential requirement of taxpayer standing recognized in *Doremus.*

It can make no constitutional difference in the case before us whether the donation to the petitioner here was in the form of a cash grant to build a facility....

■ JUSTICE STEVENS also dissented.

———

Valley Forge was followed in *Allen v. Wright,* 468 U.S. 737 (1984), a class action by black parents who maintained that the Internal Revenue Service unconstitutionally permitted racially discriminatory private schools to be tax-exempt. The Court found that the "denigration" suffered by the plaintiffs was not an actionable injury. Do *Valley Forge* and *Allen* bear on *Abortion Rights Mobilization v. Regan* [this section below]?

A group of twenty organizations headed by Americans United for Separation of Church and State sued to protest the establishment on January 10, 1984, of diplomatic relations between the United States and the Holy See. The case was dismissed on May 8, 1985, for lack of standing, *Americans United for Separation of Church and State v. Reagan,* 607 F. Supp. 747 (E.D. Pa. 1985), *aff'd,* 786 F.2d 194 (3rd Cir. 1986).

Abortion Rights Mobilization, Inc. v. Regan

544 F. Supp. 471 (S.D.N.Y. 1982).

■ JUDGE ROBERT L. CARTER:

Plaintiffs seek a declaration from the court that the political activities of the Roman Catholic Church and the inaction by the Secretary and the

Commissioner violate the Constitution and the Code. In addition, plaintiffs request an order requiring the government defendants to take all actions necessary to enforce the Constitution and the Code, including revocation of the church defendants' § 501(c)(3) status, collection of all taxes due, and notification to church contributors that they may not deduct such contributions.

Defendants challenge plaintiffs' standing to bring an action concerning the tax status of third parties. Plaintiffs respond by asserting three bases for their right to proceed: establishment clause standing, voter standing, and equal protection standing.

A. Article III Requirements

1. *Establishment Clause Standing.* The existence of Article III injury "often turns on the nature and source of the claim asserted." *Warth v. Seldin,* 422 U.S. at 500. The injury in fact requirement can be satisfied by a wide range of harms, including economic, aesthetic, environmental, or spiritual damage. *See, e.g., Gladstone, Realtors v. Village of Bellwood,* 441 U.S. 91, 111–12 (1979) (denial of right to interracial association); *Duke Power Co. v. Carolina Env. Study Group,* 438 U.S. at 73–74 (environmental and aesthetic consequences of pollution); *United States v. Students Challenging Regulatory Agency Procedures (SCRAP),* 412 U.S. 669, 686 (1973) (enjoyment of natural resources); *Schempp* [Chapter Fourteen, section 2] (spiritual values). There is no invariant meaning to the term "palpable injury"; the Constitution or a statute can create an interest that exists only in the legal regime, and damage to such an interest may fulfill the injury in fact requirement. *See Valley Forge* (Brennan, J., dissenting); *Joint Anti–Fascist Refugee Comm. v. McGrath,* 341 U.S. 123, 152 (1951) (Frankfurter, J., concurring).

Although the Supreme Court has recognized that violation of a person's "spiritual stake in the First Amendment values" of separation of church and state may inflict sufficient harm to satisfy the injury in fact test, *see Data Processing Service Organizations v. Camp,* 397 U.S. 150, 154, (1970), *citing Schempp,* it has cautioned that offense to one's sense of fidelity to separatist principles is an insufficient injury to bring suit for an alleged establishment clause violation. *See Valley Forge; Doremus v. Bd. of Education* [Chapter Fourteen, section 2]. Would-be plaintiffs must show that they are "directly affected by the laws and practices against which their complaints are directed." *Schempp* [Chapter Fourteen, section 2B].

The individual plaintiffs' concern about the establishment clause violations perpetrated by the defendants does not rise above the whistleblowing that the Supreme Court held, in *Valley Forge,* does not satisfy the injury requirement. Plaintiffs attempt to articulate injury in fact by linking the offending activity with their involvement in the abortion rights controversy. They describe the government action of which they complain as a subsidy to opponents of abortion that impacts on plaintiffs' particularized interest to preserve reproductive choice. Plaintiffs argue, in effect, that because they object to an establishment violation occurring in a particular arena of public controversy in which they are involved, they have suffered a discrete and palpable injury not experienced by the *Valley Forge* plaintiff. Plaintiffs' characterization of their injury shares the defect that caused the demise of the *Valley Forge* complaint. In both cases, plaintiffs described an interest that brought them to court, but they did not articulate an injury that they had suffered.

The clergy plaintiffs and the Women's Center for Reproductive Health ("Women's Center") have disclosed, in their affidavits, compelling and personalized injuries flowing from the tacit government endorsement of the Roman Catholic Church position on abortion that are sufficient to confer standing on them to complain of the alleged establishment clause violations. The clergy plaintiffs have devoted their lives to religious communities and beliefs that are denigrated by government favoritism to a different theology. They provide spiritual leadership to and care for the spiritual needs of their congregations. As part of these duties, they must counsel those in their care in accordance with religious laws that command consideration of abortion as the morally required response to pregnancy. The Women's Center provides guidance to women in decisionmaking on issues pertaining to family life, including childbearing. It was founded by Reverend Lutz along with others to put the principles of the Presbyterian Church into effect. As with the clergy plaintiffs, the Women's Center's religiously inspired mission is denigrated by government endorsement of a theology contrary to its guiding principles.

Tacit government endorsement of the Roman Catholic Church view of abortion hampers and frustrates these plaintiffs' ministries. The government need not silence these plaintiffs to cause discrete spiritual injury because official approval of an orthodoxy antithetical to their spiritual mission diminishes their position in the community, encumbers their calling in life, and obstructs their ability to communicate effectively their religious message. The spiritual values protected by the establishment clause can be injured without direct coercion against individuals, *see Engel v. Vitale* [Chapter Fourteen, section 2B] (indirect coercive pressure to conform to officially approved doctrine), even if plaintiffs have not alleged that particular religious freedoms have been infringed, *Schempp*. It is sufficient to establish injury in fact that plaintiffs can show, as the clergy plaintiffs have, that the challenged action adversely affects them in their daily lives.

These plaintiffs also clearly satisfy the second and third aspects of the Article III standing test—causation and redressability. Their injury flows directly from the federal defendants' allowing the church defendants the privilege of retaining § 501(c)(3) status while electioneering and denying this privilege to other religious organizations. The granting of a uniquely favored tax status to one religious entity is an unequivocal statement of preference that gilds the image of that religion and tarnishes all others. A decree ordering the termination of this illegal practice and restoring all sects to equal footing will redress this injury. Accordingly, the clergy plaintiffs and the Women's Center meet the Article III requirements for standing to raise claims under the establishment clause.

2.   *Voter standing.* In *Baker v. Carr*, 369 U.S. 186 (1962), the Supreme Court conferred "voter standing" on a group of Tennessee citizens challenging that state's apportionment scheme as "effecting a gross disproportion of representation to voting population." The plaintiffs asserted that the classification disfavored the voters in some counties by "placing them in a position of unjustifiable inequality *vis-a-vis*" voters in other counties. These allegations stated sufficient injury to satisfy the Article III standing requirements. . . .

Grounded in the equal protection safeguards of the fifth, rather than the fourteenth, amendment, plaintiffs' claims seem barely distinguishable from those involved in *Baker*. Both cases center on allegations that some arbitrary government action diluted the strength of voters in one group at the expense of those in another. Plaintiffs' injury is no less real because they claim discrimination based on issues rather than geography, nor is it relevant that the impact of allegedly harmful government conduct is felt during the battle over choosing representatives rather than in the number of representatives technically available to the aggrieved voters. The bottom line is that plaintiffs have alleged government action which has improperly biased the political process against the discrete group to which they belong.

———

The court dismissed the complaint as it related to the United States Catholic Conference (USCC) and the National Conference of Catholic Bishops (NCCB) on the ground that their enjoyment of the exemption did not violate the First Amendment; the government remained as a defendant. The plaintiffs subpoenaed all USCC and NCCB papers relating to the Pastoral Plan for Pro–Life Activities; all documents reflecting any contact with any candidate for any public office in the United States; and all documents reflecting financial support or involvement of the USCC, the NCCB, any archdiocese, diocese, parish church, or any church personnel with twelve pro-life organizations, Brief of the USCC and NCCB, amici curiae, *Abortion Rights Mobilization, Inc. v. Baker,* Second Circuit, 1985. Would a court order requiring production of such documents constitute "excessive entanglement" of the government with religion? In *NAACP v. Alabama,* 357 U.S. 449 (1958), the Court held that state-compelled disclosure of the membership list of the NAACP was an unconstitutional infringement of the right of association. For the view that nonprofit organizations should have an independent right of associational freedom that would function as a "rebuttable presumption" or a "constitutional oasis that the government can invade only for a very good reason," see Aviam Soifer, *Law and the Company We Keep* 100 (1995); see also Ronald R. Garet, "Communality and Existence: The Rights of Groups," 56 *S. Cal. L. Rev.* 1001 (1983); Charles Rice, *Freedom of Association* (1962).

Subsequently Judge Carter imposed a fine of $50,000 per day on the USCC and the NCCB for refusing to respond to subpoenas for documents sought by the plaintiffs in the case, *Abortion Rights Mobilization, Inc. v. Baker,* 110 F.R.D. 337 (S.D.N.Y. 1986). The Second Circuit stayed Judge Carter's order, but ruled that the Catholic Conference lacked standing to appeal the order since it was no longer a party, but only a subpoenaed witness, in the case. *In re United States Catholic Conference*, 824 F. 2d 156 (2d Cir. 1987). The Court granted the petitions for certiorari filed by the conference and by the government. A broad group of religious organizations, including the Synagogue Council of America and many Protestant communions that disagree with the teaching of the Catholic Church on abortion, joined an amicus brief written by Gaffney and Laycock. The brief argued that religious organizations must be free to announce their teachings on public issues with moral implications, without the threat of forfeiting their tax-exempt status.

Two questions were presented to the Supreme Court: whether the church had standing as a witness in the case to challenge Judge Carter's discovery order, and whether the plaintiffs had standing. The Supreme Court addressed only the first question, holding unanimously that the church had standing, and remanding the case to the Second Circuit to address the second question. *United States Catholic Conference v. Abortion Rights Mobilization, Inc.*, 487 U.S. 72 (1988). On remand, the Second Circuit ruled that the plaintiffs lacked standing to challenge the exempt status of the church, and hence that the district court lacked jurisdiction either to order extensive discovery from the conference or to compel the Secretary of the Treasury to revoke the conference's exempt status. 885 F.2d 1020 (2d Cir. 1989), cert. denied, 495 U.S. 918 (1990).

CHAPTER SIXTEEN

SEXUAL MORALS

---

1. POLYGAMY

NOTE. *Renewed Belief in Polygamy by "Fundamentalist" Mormons.* A group of Mormons, disassociated from the main church and sometimes referred to as "Fundamentalists," has practiced plural marriage in the twentieth century. One estimate places their current numbers at over 30,000 in the 1990s. *New York Times Sunday Magazine*, Dec. 14, 1997. Their publication *Truth* taught: "Plural marriage is one of the laws of heaven that has been restored." See *United States v. Barlow,* 56 F. Supp. 795 (D. Utah 1944), *app. dismissed,* 323 U.S. 805 (1944). They claimed to act on the basis of "the divinity of the Doctrine and the Covenants of the Church of Jesus Christ of Latter Day Saints (exclusive of the Manifests)." See *State v. Barlow,* 107 Utah 292, 153 P. 2d 647 (1944), *app. dismissed, Barlow v. Utah,* 324 U.S. 829 (1945). They were "strenuously opposed" by the Church of Jesus Christ of Latter–Day Saints. Note, "Interstate Immorality: the Mann Act and the Supreme Court," 56 *Yale L. J.* 718, 721 (1947).

Truth was indicted as obscene literature, but the indictment was quashed, *United States v. Barlow.* The State of Utah convicted several persons under a state statute of being guilty of "unlawful cohabitation with more than one person of the opposite sex," *State v. Barlow.* Among the defendants convicted in this case was Heber Kimball Cleveland, who became a defendant in the following federal case.

Cleveland v. United States

329 U.S. 14 (1946).

Claude T. Barnes argued the cause for petitioners. With him on the brief were *Ed. D. Hatch* and *O.A. Tangren.*

Assistant Solicitor General Judson argued the cause for the United States on the original argument, and *Robert M. Hitchcock* on the reargument. With *Mr. Judson* on the brief were *W. Marvin Smith, Robert S. Erdahl* and *Beatrice Rosenberg.*

■ JUSTICE DOUGLAS delivered the opinion of the Court.

Petitioners are members of a Mormon sect, known as Fundamentalists. They not only believe in polygamy; unlike other Mormons, they practice it. Each of petitioners, except Stubbs, has, in addition to his lawful wife, one or more plural wives. Each transported at least one plural wife across state lines, either for the purpose of cohabiting with her, or for the purpose of aiding another member of the cult in such a project. They were convicted of violating the Mann Act (36 Stat. 825, 18 U.S.C. § 398) on a trial to the court, a jury having been waived. The judgments of conviction were affirmed on appeal. The cases are here on petitions for certiorari which we granted in view of the asserted conflict between the decision below and *Mortensen v. United States*, 322 U.S. 369.

The Act makes an offense the transportation in interstate commerce of "any woman or girl for the purpose of prostitution or debauchery, or for any other immoral purpose."The decision turns on the meaning of the latter phrase, "for any other immoral purpose."

United States v. Bitty, 208 U.S. 393, involved a prosecution under a federal statute making it a crime to import an alien woman "for the purpose of prostitution or for any other immoral purpose." The act was construed to cover a case where a man imported an alien woman so that she should live with him as his concubine. Two years later the Mann Act was passed. Because of the similarity of the language used in the two acts, the *Bitty* case became a forceful precedent for the construction of the Mann Act. Thus one who transported a woman in interstate commerce so that she should become his mistress or concubine was held to have transported her for an "immoral purpose" within the meaning of the Mann Act. *Caminetti v. United States*, 242 U.S. 470.

It is argued that the *Caminetti* decision gave too wide a sweep to the Act; that the Act was designed to cover only the white slave business and related vices; that it was not designed to cover voluntary actions bereft of sex commercialism; and that in any event it should not be construed to embrace polygamy which is a form of marriage and, unlike prostitution or debauchery or the concubinage involved in the *Caminetti* case, has as its object parenthood and the creation and maintenance of family life. In support of that interpretation an exhaustive legislative history is submitted which, it is said, gives no indication that the Act was aimed at polygamous practices.

While *Mortensen v. United States* rightly indicated that the Act was aimed "primarily" at the use of interstate commerce for the conduct of the white slave business, we find no indication that a profit motive is a *sine qua non* to its application. Prostitution, to be sure, normally suggests sexual relations for hire. But debauchery has no such implied limitation. In common understanding the indulgence which that term suggests may be motivated solely by lust. And so we start with words which by their natural import embrace more than commercialized sex. What follows is "any other immoral purpose." Under the *ejusdem generis* rule of construction the general words are confined to the class and may not be used to enlarge it. But we could not give the words a faithful interpretation if we confined them more narrowly than the class of which they are a part.

That was the view taken by the Court in the *Bitty* and *Caminetti* cases. We do not stop to reexamine the *Caminetti* case to determine whether the Act was properly applied to the facts there presented. But we adhere to its holding, which has been in force for almost thirty years, that the Act, while primarily aimed at the use of interstate commerce for the purposes of commercialized sex, is not restricted to that end.

We conclude, moreover, that polygamous practices are not excluded from the Act. They have long been outlawed in our society. As stated in *Reynolds v. United States* [Chapter Nine]:"Polygamy has always been odious among the northern and western nations of Europe, and, until the establishment of the Mormon Church, was almost exclusively a feature of the life of Asiatic and of African people. At common law, the second marriage was always void (2 Kent, Com. 79), and from the earliest history of England polygamy has been treated as an offence against society."

As subsequently stated in *Mormon Church v. United States* [Chapter Nine], "The organization of a community for the spread and practice of polygamy is, in a measure, a return to barbarism. It is contrary to the spirit of Christianity and of the civilization which Christianity has produced in the Western world." And see *Davis v. Beason* [Chapter Nine]. Polygamy is a practice with far more pervasive influences in society than the casual, isolated transgressions involved in the *Caminetti* case. The establishment or maintenance of polygamous households is a notorious example of promiscuity. The permanent advertisement of their existence is an example of the sharp repercussions which they have in the community. We could conclude that Congress excluded these practices from the Act only if it were clear that the Act is confined to commercialized sexual vice. Since we cannot say it is, we see no way by which the present transgressions can be excluded. These polygamous practices have long been branded as immoral in the law. Though they have different ramifications, they are in the same genus as the other immoral practices covered by the Act....

It is also urged that the requisite criminal intent was lacking since petitioners were motivated by a religious belief. That defense claims too much. If upheld, it would place beyond the law any act done under claim of religious sanction. But it has long been held that the fact that polygamy is supported by a religious creed affords no defense in a prosecution for bigamy. *Reynolds*. Whether an act is immoral within the meaning of the statute is not to be determined by the accused's concepts of morality. Congress has provided the standard. The offense is complete if the accused intended to perform, and did in fact perform, the act which the statute condemns, viz., the transportation of a woman for the purpose of making her his plural wife or cohabiting with her as such.

We have considered the remaining objections raised and find them without merit. *Affirmed.*

JUSTICES BLACK and JACKSON think the cases should be reversed. They are of the opinion that affirmance requires extension of the rule announced in the *Caminetti* case and that the correctness of that rule is so dubious that it should at least be restricted to its particular facts. JUSTICE RUTLEDGE concurs in the result.

JUSTICE MURPHY, dissenting.

It is not my purpose to defend the practice of polygamy or to claim that it is morally the equivalent of monogamy. But it is essential to understand what it is, as well as what it is not. Only in that way can we intelligently decide whether it falls within the same genus as prostitution or debauchery.

There are four fundamental forms of marriage: (1) monogamy; (2) polygyny, or one man with several wives; (3) polyandry, or one woman with several husbands; and (4) group marriage. The term "polygamy" covers both polygyny and polyandry. Thus we are dealing here with polygyny, one of the basic forms of marriage. Historically, its use has far exceeded that of any other form. It was quite common among ancient civilizations and was referred to many times by the writers of the Old Testament; even today it is to be found frequently among certain pagan and non-Christian peoples of the world. We must recognize, then, that polygyny, like other forms of marriage, is basically a cultural institution rooted deeply in the religious beliefs and social mores of those societies in which it appears. It is equally true that the beliefs and mores of the dominant culture of the contemporary world condemn the practice as immoral and substitute monogamy in its place. To those beliefs and mores I subscribe, but that does not alter the fact that polygyny is a form of marriage built upon a set of social and moral principles. It must be recognized and treated as such.

The Court states that polygamy is "a notorious example of promiscuity." The important fact, however, is that, despite the differences that may exist between polygamy and monogamy, such differences do not place polygamy in the same category as prostitution or debauchery. When we use those terms we are speaking of acts of an entirely different nature, having no relation whatever to the various forms of marriage. It takes no elaboration here to point out that marriage, even when it occurs in a form of which we disapprove, is not to be compared with prostitution or debauchery or other immoralities of that character.

The Court's failure to recognize this vital distinction and its insistence that polygyny is "in the same genus" as prostitution and debauchery do violence to the anthropological factors involved. Even etymologically, the words "polygyny" and "polygamy" are quite distinct from "prostitution," "debauchery" and words of that ilk. There is thus no basis in fact for including polygyny within the phrase "any other immoral purpose" as used in this statute.

2. Marriage

In the mid 1950s an appeal was presented to the Court challenging the Jim Crow laws that prohibited racial intermarriage. The Court dismissed the appeal without briefing or argument "for want of a substantial federal question." *Naim v. Naim*, 350 U.S. 891 (1955), 350 U.S. 985 (1956). In light of the Court's momentous decision in *Brown v. Bd. of Education*, 347 U.S. 483 (1954), the Court was surely not giving its blessing upon laws that kept people from marrying across racial lines. Neither, however, was it cursing such laws, which were grounded, as the *Loving* case [below] illustrates, in the worst sort of racist bias.

One prominent commentator praised the Court for avoiding the issue at the time. Arguing that "the Negro community as a whole [could] hardly be said to be pressing hard" on this issue at the time, Professor Bickel offered the *Naim* case as an example of what he call the "passive virtues" that the Court needed to cultivate. Alexander M. Bickel, *The Least Dangerous Branch* 174 (1962). Professor Gunther, who barely escaped from Nazi Germany a year after the infamous Nuremberg Laws, took a different view. Gerald Gunther, "The Subtle Vices of the Passive Virtues," 64 *Colum. L. Rev.* 1, 16–17 (1964). The Court could only postpone the issue, which would not go away by ignoring it. Eventually it took a misecegenation case from Virginia and ruled unanimously to invalidate the law, as it had done in *Brown*.

Loving v. Virginia

388 U.S. 1 (1967).

Bernard S. Cohen and *Philip J. Hirschkop* argued the cause and filed a brief for appellants. *Mr. Hirschkop* argued *pro hac vice*, by special leave of Court.

R. D. McIlwaine III, Assistant Attorney General of Virginia, argued the cause for appellee. With him on the brief were *Robert Y. Button*, Attorney General, and *Kenneth C. Patty*, Assistant Attorney General.

William M. Marutani, by special leave of Court, argued the cause for the Japanese American Citizens League, as *amicus curiae,* urging reversal.

Briefs of *amici curiae*, urging reversal, were filed by *William M. Lewers and William B. Ball* for the National Catholic Conference for Interracial Justice et al.; by *Robert L. Carter* and *Andrew D. Weinberger* for the National Association for the Advancement of Colored People, and by *Jack Greenberg, James M. Nabrit III* and *Michael Meltsner* for the N.A.A.C.P. Legal Defense & Educational Fund, Inc.

T. W. Bruton, Attorney General, and *Ralph Moody*, Deputy Attorney General, filed a brief for the State of North Carolina, as *amicus curiae*, urging affirmance.

■ CHIEF JUSTICE WARREN delivered the opinion of the Court.

This case presents a constitutional question never addressed by this Court: whether a statutory scheme adopted by the State of Virginia to prevent marriages between persons solely on the basis of racial classifications violates the Equal Protection and Due Process Clauses of the Fourteenth Amendment. For reasons which seem to us to reflect the central meaning of those constitutional commands, we conclude that these statutes cannot stand consistently with the Fourteenth Amendment.

In June 1958, two residents of Virginia, Mildred Jeter, a Negro woman, and Richard Loving, a white man, were married in the District of Columbia pursuant to its laws. Shortly after their marriage, the Lovings returned to Virginia and established their marital abode in Caroline County. At the October Term, 1958, of the Circuit Court of Caroline County, a grand jury issued an indictment charging the Lovings with violating Virginia's ban on interracial marriages. On January 6, 1959, the Lovings pleaded guilty to the charge and were sentenced to one year in jail; however, the trial judge suspended the sentence for a period of 25 years on the condition that the Lovings leave the State and not return to Virginia together for 25 years. He stated in an opinion that: "Almighty God created the races white, black, yellow, malay and red, and he placed them on separate continents. And but for the interference with his arrangement there would be no cause for such marriages. The fact that he separated the races shows that he did not intend for the races to mix."

. . . There is patently no legitimate overriding purpose independent of invidious racial discrimination which justifies this classification. The fact that Virginia prohibits only interracial marriages involving white persons demonstrates that the racial classifications must stand on their own justification, as measures designed to maintain White Supremacy. We have consistently denied the constitutionality of measures which restrict the rights of citizens on account of race. There can be no doubt that restricting the freedom to marry solely because of racial classifications violates the central meaning of the Equal Protection Clause.

These statutes also deprive the Lovings of liberty without due process of law in violation of the Due Process Clause of the Fourteenth Amendment. The freedom to marry has long been recognized as one of the vital personal rights essential to the orderly pursuit of happiness by free men.

Marriage is one of the "basic civil rights of man," fundamental to our very existence and survival. *Skinner v. Oklahoma,* 316 U.S. 535, 541 (1942). See also *Maynard v. Hill,* 125 U.S. 190 (1888). To deny this fundamental freedom on so unsupportable a basis as the racial classifications embodied in these statutes, classifications so directly subversive of the principle of equality at the heart of the Fourteenth Amendment, is surely to deprive all the State's citizens of liberty without due process of law. The Fourteenth Amendment requires that the freedom of choice to marry not be restricted by invidious racial discriminations. Under our Constitution, the freedom to marry, or not marry, a person of another race resides with the individual and cannot be infringed by the State.

These convictions must be reversed. *It is so ordered.*

■ JUSTICE STEWART concurred in the judgment.

NOTES AND QUESTIONS

1. *Same–Sex Marriage.* Several persons of the same sex applied for a marriage license in Hawaii. The applications were denied solely on ground that they were of the same sex. They filed a complaint alleging that the denial of marriage licenses violated their rights to privacy and to equal protection guaranteed by the Hawaii Constitution. In *Baehr v. Lewin,* 74 Haw. 530, 852 P.2d 44 (1993) the Hawaii Supreme Court, per Justice Levinson, held that Article I, § 6 of the Hawaii Constitution, containing a right to privacy, does not protect a fundamental right to marriage for same-sex couples. The court reasoned that the "right to same-sex marriage is not so rooted in traditions and collective conscience of Hawaii's people that failure to recognize it would violate fundamental principles of liberty and justice; neither is the right to same-sex

marriage implicit in concept of ordered liberty, such that neither liberty nor justice would exist if it were sacrificed." Art. I, § 5 of the state constitution prohibits state-sanctioned discrimination against any person in exercise of his or her civil rights on basis of sex. The court ruled that the state statute restricting marital relation to male or female establishes a sex-based classification which is subject to "strict scrutiny" test in an equal protection challenge. The court remanded for further proceedings to determine whether the statute meets that rigorous standard.

While the *Baehr* case was pending, Congress enacted legislation that defined marriage as a relationship between a man and a woman. The purpose of this legislation is to limit the outcome of the Hawaii litigation to that state, so that no other state would bound to recognize a same-sex marriage allowed in Hawaii or any other State under the Full Faith and Credit Clause of the federal constitution. In 2000 the voters of Hawaii barred same-sex marriages. In the same year, the voters of California adopted Proposition 22, known as The Limit On Marriage Act. It reads: "Only marriage between a man and a woman is valid or recognized in California." A total of 33 states now forbid that practice.

For an account of the debate in Congress over the Defense of Marriage Act, see Joan Bisupic, "Once Unthinkable, Now Under Debate: Same–Sex Marriage Issue to Take Center Stage in Senate," *Wash. Post,* Sept. 3, 1996, A1. For a scholarly argument in favor of same-sex marriage, see e.g., William N. Eskridge, Jr., *The Case for Same–Sex Marriage: From Sexual Liberty to Civilized Commitment* (1996). For analysis that is critical of this development, see, e.g., David Coolidge, "Same–Sex Marriage? Baehr v. Miike and The Meaning of Marriage," 38 *So. Tex. L. Rev.* 1 (1997); and Raymond C. O'Brien, "Single–Gender Marriage: A Religious Perspective," 7 *Temple Pol. & Civ. Rts. L. Rev.* 429 (1998).

On December 20, 1999, the Supreme Court of Vermont ruled in *Baker v. State of Vermont,* 744 A. 2d 864 (Vt. 1999) that exclusion of same-sex couples from benefits and protections incident to marriage under state law violated the common benefits clause of the Vermont Constitution, Chap. 1, Art. 7. It ordered the Legislature to enact a law granting gay and lesbian couples the same rights and privileges as heterosexual married couples. Acting on the court's mandate, the committee unveiled a 22–page proposal that skirted the term "marriage" in favor of a far-reaching domestic partnership system that allows gay and lesbian couples to derive economic benefits from their relationship with a partner of the same sex. For an account of the controversy, see Elizabeth Mehren, "New Firestorm Erupts Over Vermont's Domestic Partner Plan Law: State appears poised to become first to enact same-sex benefits. Proposal is 'an assault on the institution of marriage,' Christian right official says. Vermont's Domestic Partner Plan Law, *Los Angeles Times,* Feb. 13, 2000, A14.

2. *The End of Marriage?* Holding a Massachusetts statute barring the distribution of contraceptives to single persons to be an unconstitutional invasion of privacy, Justice Brennan for the Court wrote that the rights of access "must be the same for the married and the unmarried alike," *Eisenstadt v. Baird,* 405 U.S. 438, 453 (1972). In a passage that seemed to go out of its way to challenge the religious metaphor of Genesis 2:24 that man and wife are one flesh, Justice Brennan added that "the marital couple is not an independent entity with a mind and heart of its own...."

Reviewing *Eisenstadt* and other decisions of the Supreme Court eroding on constitutional grounds the difference between marriage and nonmarriage, Noonan raised the question whether the legal status of marriage had rested on "covert religious assumptions," making for a consensus now shattered, Noonan, "The Family and the Supreme Court," 23 *Cath. U. L. Rev.* 255 (1973). This article concluded:

The Gingerbread Man, you may remember, was an exceptionally well-made work of human artifice. After outrunning many dangers he was taken on the tail of an old fox. The fox moved him from his tail to his back, from his back to his nose, and then threw him, topsy-turvy, in the air and on his descent began to eat him.

"I'm a quarter gone," cried the Gingerbread Man. Then, "I'm half gone," he cried. Then, "I'm three-quarters gone." And then there was silence.

If marriage had a tongue like the Gingerbread Man, what would it cry out now?

3. SODOMY

As early as 1964, a sentence of twenty to thirty years' imprisonment for a homosexual act of oral copulation was challenged as cruel and unusual punishment, unconstitutional under the Eighth Amendment. A federal court rejected the challenge although releasing the prisoner for lack of effective counsel at his trial. *Perkins v. State of North Carolina*, 234 F. Supp. 333 (W.D.N.C. 1964). After *Eisenstadt v. Baird*, 405 U.S. 438 (1972), it was argued, "If the right of privacy extends to the sexual conduct of unmarried heterosexuals, it's hard to see why it would not also apply to the private sexual conduct of homosexuals." Note, "The Constitutionality of Laws Forbidding Private Homosexual Conduct," 72 *Mich. L. Rev.* 1613, 1619 (1974). But a privacy right to homosexual conduct was rejected. *Doe v. Commonwealth's Attorney for Richmond*, 425 U.S. 901 (1976), *summarily affirming* 403 F. Supp. 1199 (E.D. Va. 1975); cf. *Dronenburg v. Zech*, 741 F. 2d 1388 (D.C. 1984) (per Bork, J.) (Navy's policy of mandatory discharge for homosexual conduct not unconstitutional).

Bowers v. Hardwick

478 U.S. 186 (1986).

Michael E. Hobbs, Georgia Senior Assistant Attorney General, for petitioner; with him on the brief were *Michael J. Bowers, Attorney General of Georgia; Marion 0. Gordon, First Asst. Attorney General of Georgia; and Daryl A. Robinson, Senior Asst. Attorney General of Georgia.*

Laurence H. Tribe for respondents; with him on the brief were *Kathleen M. Sullivan, Brian Koukoutchos, and Kathleen L. Wilde.*

■ JUSTICE WHITE delivered the opinion of the Court.

In August 1982, respondent was charged with violating the Georgia statute criminalizing sodomy by committing that act with another adult male in the bedroom of respondent's home. After a preliminary hearing, the District Attorney decided not to present the matter to the grand jury unless further evidence developed.

Respondent then brought suit in the Federal District Court, challenging the constitutionality of the statute insofar as it criminalized consensual sodomy. He asserted that he was a practicing homosexual, that the Georgia sodomy statute, as administered by the defendants, placed him in imminent danger of arrest, and that the statute for several reasons violates the Federal Constitution. . . .

This case does not require a judgment on whether laws against sodomy between consenting adults in general, or between homosexuals in particular, are wise or desirable. It raises no question about the right or propriety of state legislative decisions to repeal their laws that criminalize homosexual sodomy, or of state court decisions invalidating those laws on state constitutional grounds.* The issue presented is whether the Federal Constitution confers a fundamental right upon homosexuals to engage in sodomy and hence invalidates the laws of the many States that still make such conduct illegal and have done so for a very long time. The case also calls for some judgment about the limits of the Court's role in carrying out its constitutional mandate.

We first register our disagreement with the Court of Appeals and with respondent that the Court's prior cases have construed the Constitution to confer a right of privacy that extends to homosexual sodomy and for all intents and purposes have decided this case. The reach of this line of cases was sketched in *Carey v. Population Services International*, 431 U.S. 678, 685 (1977). *Pierce v. Society of Sisters* [Chapter Ten, section 7], and *Meyer v. Nebraska*, 262 U.S. 390 (1923), were described as dealing with child rearing and education; *Prince v. Massachusetts* [Chapter Eleven, section 1], with family relationships; *Skinner v. Oklahoma ex rel. Williamson*, 316 U.S. 535 (1942), with procreation; *Loving v. Virginia* [above], with marriage; *Griswold* [above], and *Eisenstadt* [above], with contraception; and *Roe v. Wade*, with abortion. The latter three cases were interpreted as construing the Due Process Clause of the Fourteenth Amendment to confer a fundamental individual right to decide whether or not to beget or bear a child. *Carey*.

Accepting the decisions in these cases and the above description of them, we think it evident that none of the rights announced in those cases bears any resemblance to the claimed constitutional right of homosexuals to engage in acts of sodomy that is asserted in this case. No connection between family, marriage, or procreation on the one hand and homosexual activity on the other has been demonstrated, either by the Court of Appeals or by respondent. Moreover, any claim that these cases nevertheless stand for the proposition that any kind of private sexual conduct between consenting adults is constitutionally insulated from state proscription is insupportable. Indeed, the Court's opinion in *Carey* twice asserted that the

* Editors' note: In *Powell v. State*, 510 S.E.2d 18 (1998), the Georgia Supreme Court reversed a conviction for sodomy on the ground that the sodomy statute violates the right of privacy guaranteed by the due process clause of the state constitution. Ga. Const., Art. 1, § 1, Par. 1.

privacy right, which the *Griswold* line of cases found to be one of the protections provided by the Due Process Clause, did not reach so far.

Precedent aside, however, respondent would have us announce, as the Court of Appeals did, a fundamental right to engage in homosexual sodomy. This we are quite unwilling to do. It is true that despite the language of the Due Process Clauses of the Fifth and Fourteenth Amendments, which appears to focus only on the processes by which life, liberty, or property is taken, the cases are legion in which those Clauses have been interpreted to have substantive content, subsuming rights that to a great extent are immune from federal or state regulation or proscription. Among such cases are those recognizing rights that have little or no textual support in the constitutional language. *Meyer, Prince*, and *Pierce* fall in this category, as do the privacy cases from *Griswold* to *Carey*.

Striving to assure itself and the public that announcing rights not readily identifiable in the Constitution's text involves much more than the imposition of the Justices' own choice of values on the States and the Federal Government, the Court has sought to identify the nature of the rights qualifying for heightened judicial protection. In *Palko v. Connecticut,* 302 U.S. 319, 325, 326 (1937), it was said that this category includes those fundamental liberties that are "implicit in the concept of ordered liberty," such that "neither liberty nor justice would exist if [they] were sacrificed." A different description of fundamental liberties appeared in *Moore v. East Cleveland,* 431 U.S. 494, 503 (1977) (opinion of Powell, J.), where they are characterized as those liberties that are "deeply rooted in this Nation's history and tradition." *Id.*, at 503 (Powell, J.). See also *Griswold.*

It is obvious to us that neither of these formulations would extend a fundamental right to homosexuals to engage in acts of consensual sodomy. Proscriptions against that conduct have ancient roots. See generally, Survey on the Constitutional Right to Privacy in the Context of Homosexual Activity, 40 Miami U. L. Rev. 521, 525 (1986). Sodomy was a criminal offense at common law and was forbidden by the laws of the original thirteen States when they ratified the Bill of Rights.[5] In 1868, when the

---

5. Criminal sodomy laws in effect in 1791:

Connecticut: Public Statute Laws of the State of Connecticut, 1808, Title LXVI, Ch. 1, § 2 (rev. 1672).

Delaware: 1 Laws of the State of Delaware, 1797, ch. 22, § 5 (passed 1719).

Georgia had no criminal sodomy statute until 1816, but sodomy was a crime at common law, and the General Assembly adopted the Common Law of England as the law of Georgia in 1784. The First Laws of the State of Georgia, pt. 1 (1981).

Maryland had no criminal sodomy statute in 1791. Maryland's Declaration of Rights, passed in 1776, however, stated that "the inhabitants of Maryland are entitled to the common law of England," and sodomy was a crime at common law. 4 Sources and Documents of United States Constitutions 372 (W. Swindler ed. 1975).

Massachusetts: Acts and Laws passed by the General Court of Massachusetts, ch. 14, Act of March 3, 1785.

New Hampshire passed its first sodomy statute in 1718. Acts and Laws of New Hampshire 1680–1726, p. 141 (1978).

Sodomy was a crime at common law in New Jersey at the time of the ratification of the Bill of Rights. The State enacted its first criminal sodomy law five years later. Acts of the Twentieth General Assembly, March 18, 1796, Ch. DC, § 7, p. 93.

Fourteenth Amendment was ratified, all but 5 of the 37 States in the Union had criminal sodomy laws.[6] In fact, until 1961, all 50 States outlawed sodomy, and today, 24 States and the District of Columbia continue to provide criminal penalties for sodomy performed in private and between consenting adults. Against this background, to claim that a right to engage in such conduct is "deeply rooted in this Nation's history and tradition" or "implicit in the concept of ordered liberty" is, at best, facetious.

New York: Laws of New York, ch. 21, p. 391 (passed 1787).

6. Criminal sodomy statutes in effect in 1868:

Alabama: Ala. Code, § 3604 (1867).

Arizona (Terr.): Howell Code, ch. 10, § 48 (1865).

Arkansas: Ark. Stat., ch. 51, Art. IV, § 5 (1858).

California: 1 Cal. Gen. Laws, ch. 99, § 48 (1865).

Colorado (Terr.): Colo. Rev. Stat., ch. 22, §§ 45, 46 (1868).

Connecticut: Conn. Gen. Stat., Tit. 122, ch. 7, § 124 (1866).

Delaware: Del. Code Ann., Tit. 20, ch. 131, § 7 (1852).

Florida: Acts and Resolutions, ch. 8, § 17 (1868).

Georgia: Ga. Code §§ 4286, 4287, 4290 (1867).

Kingdom of Hawaii: Hawaii Penal Code, ch. 13, § 11 (1868).

Illinois: Ill. Rev. Stat., div. 5, §§ 49, 50 (1845).

Kansas: Kan. (Terr.) Stat., ch. 53, § 7 (1855).

Kentucky: 1 Ky. Rev. Stat., ch. 28, Art. IV, § 11 (1860).

Louisiana: La. Rev. Stat., Crimes and Offenses, § 5 (1856).

Maine: Me. Rev. Stat., tit. XII, ch. 160, § 4 (1847).

Maryland: 1 Md. Code, Art. 30. § 201 (1860).

Massachusetts: Mass. Gen. Laws, ch. 165, § 18 (1860).

Michigan: Mich. Rev. Stat., Tit. 30, ch. 158. § 16 (1846).

Minnesota: Minn. Stat., ch. 96, § 13 (1859).

Mississippi: Miss. Rev. Code, ch. 64, Art. 238, § LII, art. 238 (1857).

Missouri: 1 Mo. Rev. Stat., ch. 50, Art. VIII, § 7 (1856).

Montana (Terr.): Mont. Laws, Criminal Practice Acts, ch. IV, § 44 (1864).

Nebraska (Terr.): Neb. Rev. Stat., Crim. Code, ch. 4, § 47 (1866).

Nevada (Terr.): Nev. Comp. Laws. ch. 28 § 45 (1862).

New Hampshire: N. H. Rev. Laws, Act. of June 19, 1812, § 5 (1815).

New Jersey: N. J. Rev. Stat., Tit. 8, ch. 1, § 9 (1847).

New York: 3 N. Y. Rev. Stat., pt. 4, ch. 1. tit. 5, art. 3, § 20 (1858).

North Carolina: N. C. Rev. Code. ch. 34, § 6 (1854).

Oregon: Laws of Ore., Crimes–Against Morality, etc., ch. 7, § 655 (1874).

Pennsylvania: Act of March 31, 1860, § 32, Pub. Law 392, in 1 Digest of Statute Law of Pa. 1700–1903 1011 (Purdon 1905).

Rhode Island: R. I. Gen. Stat., ch. 232, § 12 (1872).

South Carolina: Act of 1712, in 2 Stat. at Large of S. C. 1682–1716, p. 493 (1837). Tennessee: Tenn. Code, ch. 8, Art. 1, § 4843 (1858).

Texas: Tex. Rev. Stat., Penal Code, tit. 10, ch. 5, Art. 342 (1887) (passed 1860).

Vermont: Laws of the State of Vermont (1779).

Virginia: Va. Code, ch. 149, § 12 (1868).

West Virginia: W. Va. Code, ch. 149, § 12 (1860).

Wisconsin (Terr.): Wis. Stat., § 14 (1839).

* Editor's Note. As of 1993, 24 states retained sodomy statutes. See, e.g., Joyce Murdoch, "Laws Against Sodomy Survive in 24 States; As District Attempts Repeal, Maryland and Virginia Statutes Remain on the Books," *Wash. Post*, April 11, 1993, A20.

Nor are we inclined to take a more expansive view of our authority to discover new fundamental rights embedded in the Due Process Clause. The Court is most vulnerable and comes nearest to illegitimacy when it deals with judge-made constitutional law having little or no cognizable roots in the language or design of the Constitution. That this is so was painfully demonstrated by the face-off between the Executive and the Court in the 1930's, which resulted in the repudiation of much of the substantive gloss that the Court had placed on the Due Process Clause of the Fifth and Fourteenth Amendments. There should be, therefore, great resistance to expand the substantive reach of those Clauses, particularly if it requires redefining the category of rights deemed to be fundamental. Otherwise, the Judiciary necessarily takes to itself further authority to govern the country without express constitutional authority. The claimed right pressed on us today falls far short of overcoming this resistance.

Respondent, however, asserts that the result should be different where the homosexual conduct occurs in the privacy of the home. He relies on *Stanley v. Georgia,* 394 U.S. 557 (1969), where the Court held that the First Amendment prevents conviction for possessing and reading obscene material in the privacy of his home: "If the First Amendment means anything, it means that a State has no business telling a man, sitting alone in his house, what books he may read or what films he may watch."

Stanley did protect conduct that would not have been protected outside the home, and it partially prevented the enforcement of state obscenity laws; but the decision was firmly grounded in the First Amendment. The right pressed upon us here has no similar support in the text of the Constitution, and it does not qualify for recognition under the prevailing principles for construing the Fourteenth Amendment. Its limits are also difficult to discern. Plainly enough, otherwise illegal conduct is not always immunized whenever it occurs in the home. Victimless crimes, such as the possession and use of illegal drugs do not escape the law where they are committed at home. *Stanley* itself recognized that its holding offered no protection for the possession in the home of drugs, firearms, or stolen goods. And if respondent's submission is limited to the voluntary sexual conduct between consenting adults, it would be difficult, except by fiat, to limit the claimed right to homosexual conduct while leaving exposed to prosecution adultery, incest, and other sexual crimes even though they are committed in the home. We are unwilling to start down that road.

Even if the conduct at issue here is not a fundamental right, respondent asserts that there must be a rational basis for the law and that there is none in this case other than the presumed belief of a majority of the electorate in Georgia that homosexual sodomy is immoral and unacceptable. This is said to be an inadequate rationale to support the law. The law, however, is constantly based on notions of morality, and if all laws representing essentially moral choices are to be invalidated under the Due Process Clause, the courts will be very busy indeed. Even respondent makes no such claim, but insists that majority sentiments about the morality of homosexuality should be declared inadequate. We do not agree, and are unpersuaded that the sodomy laws of some 25 States should be invalidated on this basis.

Accordingly, the judgment of the Court of Appeals is *Reversed.*

■ CHIEF JUSTICE BURGER, concurring.

I join the Court's opinion, but I write separately to underscore my view that in constitutional terms there is no such thing as a fundamental right to commit homosexual sodomy.

As the Court notes, the proscriptions against sodomy have very "ancient roots." Decisions of individuals relating to homosexual conduct have been subject to state intervention throughout the history of Western Civilization. Condemnation of those practices is firmly rooted in Judeo–Christian moral and ethical standards. Homosexual sodomy was a capital crime under Roman law. See Code Theod. 9.7.6; Code Just. 9.9.31. See also D. Bailey, Homosexuality in the Western Christian Tradition 70–81 (1975). During the English Reformation when powers of the ecclesiastical courts were transferred to the King's Courts, the first English statute criminalizing sodomy was passed. 25 Hen. VIII, c. 6. Blackstone described "the infamous crime against nature" as an offense of "deeper malignity" than rape, an heinous act "the very mention of which is a disgrace to human nature," and "a crime not fit to be named." Blackstone's Commentaries 215. The common law of England, including its prohibition of sodomy, became the received law of Georgia and the other Colonies. In 1816 the Georgia Legislature passed the statute at issue here, and that statute has been continuously in force in one form or another since that time. To hold that the act of homosexual sodomy is somehow protected as a fundamental right would be to cast aside millennia of moral teaching.

This is essentially not a question of personal "preferences" but rather one of the legislative authority of the State. I find nothing in the Constitution depriving a State of the power to enact the statute challenged here.

■ JUSTICE POWELL concurred.*

■ JUSTICE BLACKMUN, with whom JUSTICE BRENNAN, JUSTICE MARSHALL, AND JUSTICE STEVENS join, dissenting.

We protect . . . rights [of privacy] not because they contribute, in some direct and material way, to the general public welfare, but because they form so central a part of an individual's life. "[T]he concept of privacy embodies the 'moral fact that a person belongs to himself and not others nor to society as a whole.'" *Thornburgh v. American Coll. of Obst. & Gyn.,* 476 U.S. 747, 777 (Stevens, J., concurring), quoting Fried, Correspondence, 6 Phil. & Pub. Affairs 288–289 (1977). And so we protect the decision

---

* Editor's Note: After retiring from the Court, Justice Powell addressed a group of law students at New York University. When asked whether there was any decision he made that he had doubts about in retrospect, Powell replied about *Hardwick*: "I think I probably made a mistake in that one." Professor Laurence Tribe, who argued the case on behalf of Hardwick, said: "The fact that a respected jurist who is indispensable to the majority conceded that on sober second thought he was probably wrong certainly will affect the way that future generations look at the decision," Ruth Marcus, "Powell Regrets Backing Sodomy Law," *Wash. Post,* Oct. 26, 1990, A3.

whether to marry precisely because marriage "is an association that promotes a way of life, not causes; a harmony in living, not political faiths; a bilateral loyalty, not commercial or social projects." *Griswold.* We protect the decision whether to have a child because parenthood alters so dramatically an individual's self-definition, not because of demographic considerations or the Bible's command to be fruitful and multiply. Cf. *Thornburgh v. American Coll. of Obst. & Gyn.* (Stevens, J., concurring). And we protect the family because it contributes so powerfully to the happiness of individuals, not because of a preference for stereotypical households. Cf. *Moore v. East Cleveland,* 431 U.S. 494, 500–506 (plurality opinion). The Court recognized in *Roberts,* 468 U.S., at 619, that the "ability independently to define one's identity that is central to any concept of liberty" cannot truly be exercised in a vacuum; we all depend on the "emotional enrichment of close ties with others."

Only the most willful blindness could obscure the fact that sexual intimacy is "a sensitive, key relationship of human existence, central to family life, community welfare, and the development of the human personality," *Paris Adult Theatre I v. Slayton,* 413 U.S. 49, 63 (1973); see also *Carey.* The fact that individuals define themselves in a significant way through their intimate sexual relationships with others suggests, in a Nation as diverse as ours, that there may be many "right" ways of conducting those relationships, and that much of the richness of a relationship will come from the freedom an individual has to *choose* the form and nature of these intensely personal bonds. See Karst, The Freedom of Intimate Association, 89 Yale L. J. 624, 637 (1980); cf *Eisenstadt; Roe v. Wade....*

The core of petitioner's defense of § 16–6–2, however, is that respondent and others who engage in the conduct prohibited by § 16–6–2 interfere with Georgia's exercise of the " 'right of the Nation and of the States to maintain a decent society,' " *Paris Adult Theater I.* Essentially, petitioner argues, and the Court agrees, that the fact that the acts described in § 16–6–2 "for hundreds of years, if not thousands, have been uniformly condemned as immoral" is a sufficient reason to permit a State to ban them today....

I cannot agree that either the length of time a majority has held its convictions or the passions with which it defends them can withdraw legislation from this Court's scrutiny. See, *e.g., Roe v. Wade; Loving v. Virginia; Brown v. Board of Education,* 347 U.S. 483 (1954).[7] As Justice

---

7. The parallel between *Loving* and this case is almost uncanny. There, too, the State relied on a religious justification for its law. Compare 388 U.S., at 3 (quoting trial court's statement that "Almighty God created the races white, black, yellow, malay and red, and he placed them on separate continents.... The fact that he separated the races shows that he did not intend for the races to mix"), with Brief for Petitioner 20–21 (relying on the Old and New Testaments and the writings of St. Thomas Aquinas to show that "traditional Judeo–Christian values proscribe such conduct"). There, too, defenders of the challenged statute relied heavily on the fact that when the Fourteenth Amendment was ratified, most of the States had similar prohibitions. Compare Brief for Appellee in *Loving v. Virginia,* O.T. 1966, No. 395, pp. 28–29, with *ante,* at 5–7 and n. 6. There, too, at the time the case came before the Court, many of the States still had criminal statutes concern-

Jackson wrote so eloquently for the Court in *Barnette* [Chapter Eleven, section 3], "we apply the limitations of the Constitution with no fear that freedom to be intellectually and spiritually diverse or even contrary will disintegrate the social organization.... [F]reedom to differ is not limited to things that do not matter much. That would be a mere shadow of freedom. The test of its substance is the right to differ as to things that touch the heart of the existing order." See also Karst, 89 Yale L. J., at 627. It is precisely because the issue raised by this case touches the heart of what makes individuals what they are that we should be especially sensitive to the rights of those whose choices upset the majority.

The assertion that "traditional Judeo–Christian values proscribe" the conduct involved, Brief for Petitioner 20, cannot provide an adequate justification for § 16–6–2. That certain, but by no means all, religious groups condemn the behavior at issue gives the State no license to impose their judgments on the entire citizenry. The legitimacy of secular legislation depends instead on whether the State can advance some justification for its law beyond its conformity to religious doctrine. See, *eg.*, *McGowan v. Maryland* [Chapter Thirteen, section 2]; *Stone v. Graham* [Chapter Fourteen, section 2]. Thus, far from buttressing his case, petitioner's invocation of Leviticus, Romans, St. Thomas Aquinas, and sodomy's heretical status during the Middle Ages undermines his suggestion that § 1 6–6–2 represents a legitimate use of secular coercive power.[8] A State can no more punish private behavior because of religious intolerance than it can punish such behavior because of racial animus. "The Constitution cannot control such prejudices, but neither can it tolerate them. Private biases may be outside the reach of the law, but the law cannot, directly or indirectly give them effect." *Palmore v. Sidoti,* 466 U.S. 429, 433 (1984). No matter how uncomfortable a certain group may make the majority of this Court, we have held that "[m]ere public intolerance or animosity cannot constitutionally justify the deprivation of a person's physical liberty." *O'Connor v. Donaldson,* 422 U.S. 563, 575 (1975). See also *City of Cleburne v. Cleburne*

---

ing the conduct at issue. Compare 388 U.S., at 6, n. 5 (noting that 16 States still outlawed interracial marriage), with *ante,* 6–7 (noting that 24 States and the District of Columbia have sodomy statutes). Yet the Court held, not only that the invidious racism of Virginia's law violated the Equal Protection Clause, see 388 U.S., at 7–12, but also that the law deprived the Lovings of due process by denying them the "freedom of choice to marry" that had "long been recognized as one of the vital personal rights essential to the orderly pursuit of happiness by free men." *Id.*, at 12.

8. The theological nature of the origin of Anglo–American antisodomy statutes is patent. It was not until 1533 that sodomy was made a secular offense in England. 25 Hen. VIII, cap. 6. Until that time, the offense was, in Sir James Stephen's words, "merely ecclesiastical." 2 J. Stephen, A History of the Criminal Law of England 430 (1883). Pollack and Maitland similarly observed that "[the crime against nature.... was so closely connected with heresy that the vulgar had but one name for both." 2 F. Pollack & F. Maitland, The History of English Law 554 (1895). The transfer of jurisdiction over prosecutions for sodomy to the secular courts seems primarily due to the alteration of ecclesiastical jurisdiction attendant on England's break with the Roman Catholic Church, rather than to any new understanding of the sovereign's interest in preventing or punishing the behavior involved. cf. E. Coke, The Third Part of the Institutes of the Laws of England. ch. 10 (1797).

Living Center, 473 U.S. 432 (1985); *U.S. Dept. of Agriculture v. Moreno,* 413 U.S. 528, 534 (1973).

NOTES AND QUESTIONS

1. *Romer v. Evans.* Various Colorado municipalities passed ordinances banning discrimination based on sexual orientation in housing, employment, education, public accommodations, health and welfare services, and other transactions and activities. Colorado voters then adopted by statewide referendum "Amendment 2" to the State Constitution, which precluded all legislative, executive, or judicial action at any level of state or local government designed to protect the status of persons based on their "homosexual, lesbian or bisexual orientation, conduct, practices or relationships." Colo. Const. Art. II, § 30b.

In *Romer v. Evans,* 517 U.S. 620 (1996), the Court, per Justice Kennedy, held that since the amendment had "the peculiar property of imposing a broad and undifferentiated disability on a single named group," it lacked a rational relationship to legitimate state interests. The Court noted that the amendment's immediate effect is to repeal all existing statutes, regulations, ordinances, and policies of state and local entities barring discrimination based on sexual orientation, and that its ultimate effect is to prohibit any governmental entity from adopting similar, or more protective, measures in the future absent state constitutional amendment. JUSTICE KENNEDY wrote: "A law declaring that in general it shall be more difficult for one group of citizens than for all others to seek aid from government is itself a denial of equal protection of the laws in the most literal sense.... If the constitutional conception of 'equal protection of the laws' means anything, it must at the very least mean that a bare desire to harm a politically unpopular group cannot constitute a legitimate governmental interest."

JUSTICE SCALIA, joined by CHIEF JUSTICE REHNQUIST and JUSTICE THOMAS, filed a dissent that concluded: "Today's opinion has no foundation in American constitutional law, and barely pretends to. The people of Colorado have adopted an entirely reasonable provision which does not even disfavor homosexuals in any substantive sense, but merely denies them preferential treatment. Amendment 2 is designed to prevent piecemeal deterioration of the sexual morality favored by a majority of Coloradans, and is not only an appropriate means to that legitimate end, but a means that Americans have employed before. Striking it down is an act, not of judicial judgment, but of political will." Is *Romer v. Evans* reconcilable with *Bowers v. Hardwick?*

*

BIBLIOGRAPHY

Abbreviations

CSEL Corpus scriptorum ecclesiasticorum latinorum (Vienna: C. Geroldi, 1866–).

PG J. P. Migne, *Patrologiae cursus completus. Series graeca* (Paris,: Migne, 1857–1866).

PL J. P. Migne, *Patrologiae cursus completus. Series latina* (Paris: Migne, 1844–1880).

RS Rolls Series or Rerum britanicarum medii aevi scriptores (London: Longmans, 1858–1896).

Abbott, Walter. "A Common Bible Reader for Public Schools," 56 Religious Education 20 (1961).

___, ed. *The Documents of the Second Vatican Council* (New York: Herder & Herder, 1965).

Abrams, Elliott. *Faith or Fear: How Jews Can Survive in a Christian America* (New York: Free Press, 1997).

American Civil Liberties Union. *The Gag on Teaching* (New York: ACLU, 2d ed. 1937).

Adams, John. *Diary and Autobiography of John Adams,* ed. L. H. Butterfield, Leonard C. Faber, etc. and Wendell D. Garrett (Cambridge: Belknap Press of Harvard University Press, 1961).

Ahlstrom, Sydney E. *A Religious History of the American People* (New Haven: Yale University Press, 1975).

Albaugh & Anderson. "Peyote in the Treatment of Alcoholism among American Indians," 131 *Am. J. Psychiatry* 1247 (1974).

Alberigo, Giuseppe, ed. *Conciliorum oecumenicorum decreta* (Basilae: Herder, 1962).

Alexander, Loveday C.A. "Rome, Early Christian Attitudes to," in David Noel Freedman, ed., *The Anchor Bible Dictionary* (Garden City, NY: Doubleday, 1992).

Alexander of Hales. "De conscientia." in Odon Lottin, *Psychologie et morale aux XIIe et XIIIe siecles* (Louvain: Abbaye du Mont César, 1945).

Alt, Albrecht. "The Origins of Israelite Law" in *Essays on Old Testament History and Religion* (Oxford: Blackwell, 1966).

Amar, Akhil Reed. *The Bill of Rights Creation and Reconstruction* (New Haven: Yale University Press, 1998).

American Law Institute. *Restatement of Torts, Second* (St. Paul, MN: American Law Institute Publishers, 1977).

Ames, Fisher. *Works,* ed. W. B. Allen (Indianapolis: Library Classics, 1983).

929

Anderson, Edward F. *Peyote: The Divine Cactus* (Tucson, AZ: University of Arizona Press, 1996).

Antieau, Chester J., Arthur T. Downey, and Edward C. Roberts. *Freedom from Federal Establishment* (Milwaukee: Bruce Publishing Co., 1964).

Antieau, Chester J., Phillip Mark Carroll, and Thomas Carroll Burke. *Religion Under the State Constitutions* (Brooklyn: Central Book Company, 1965).

Anti–Defamation League of B'nai B'rith. *ADL Law Report: Litigation Docket: 1986* (New York: ADL, 1986).

——. *Religion and the Public Schools* (New York: ADL, 1984).

Aquinas, Thomas. *Scriptum super quatuor libros in sententiarum Magister Petri Lombardi* (Parma, 1852–1873).

——. *Summa theologiae* (Rome: Petri Marietti, 1903).

——. *Summa theologiae in English Translation* (London: Eyre & Spottiswoode, 1964).

Ariens, Michael S. and Robert A. Destro. *Religious Liberty in a Pluralistic Society* (Durham, N.C.: Carolina Academic Press, 1996).

Aristotle. *Nichomachean Ethics,* tr. D. P. Chase (New York: E. P. Dutton, 1930).

Arons, Stephen. "The Separation of School and State: *Pierce* Reconsidered," 40 *Harvard Educational Review* 70 (1970).

Arrington, Leonard J. *Brigham Young: American Moses* (New York: Alfred A. Knopf, 1985).

——. *Great Basin Kingdom: An Economic History of the Latter-day Saints, 1830–1900* (Salt Lake City: University of Utah Press, 1993).

—— and Davis Bitton. *The Mormon Experience: A History of the Latter Day Saints* (New York: Alfred A. Knopf, 1979).

Asch, Ronald G. *The Thirty Years War: The Holy Roman Empire and Europe, 1618–1648* (New York: St. Martin's Press, 1997).

Augustine. *Letters, CSEL* 44.

——. *De Civitate Dei contra paganos (The City of God), CSEL* 40.

Backus, Isaac. *A History of New England with particular reference to the denomination of Christians called Baptists* (Newton, 1871; New York: Arno Press reprint, 1969).

Baer, Richard. "The Supreme Court's Discriminatory Use of the Term 'Sectarian,' " 6 *J. L. & Politics* 449 (1990).

Bainton, Roland H. *Christian Attitudes toward War and Peace: A Historical Survey and Critical Re-evaluation* (Nashville: Abingdon, 1960).

Baker, Liva. *Felix Frankfurter* (New York: Coward–McCann, 1969).

Ball, Milner. S. *Lying Down Together: Law, Metaphor and Theology* (Madison: University of Wisconsin Press, 1985).

Ball, William Bentley. "Building a Landmark Case," in Albert N. Keim, ed., *Compulsory Education and the Amish* (Boston: Beacon Press, 1975).

Baltzer, Klaus. *The Covenant Formulary* (Philadelphia: Fortress, 1971).

Barrett, C.K., ed. *New Testament Background: Selected Documents* (New York: Harper & Row, 1987).

Barclay, William. "Revelation 13, Great Themes of the New Testament," *Expository Times* 70 (1958/59).

Basler, Ray P., ed. *The Collected Works of Abraham Lincoln* (New Brunswick, NJ: Rutgers University Press, 1953–1990).

Bassett, William W. *Religious Organizations and the Law* (Deerfield, IL: Clark Boardman Callaghan, 1997)

Bathory, Dennis. *Political Theory as Public Confession: The Social and Political Thought of St. Augustine of Hippo* (New Brunswick, NJ: Transaction Books, 1981).

Bau, Ignatius. *This Ground Is Holy: Church Sanctuary and Central American Refugees* (New York: Paulist Press, 1985).

Baum, Gregory. *Is the New Testament Anti–Semitic? A Re-examination of the New Testament* (New York: Paulist Press, 1965).

Baus, Karl. *From the Apostolic Community to Constantine* (New York: Herder & Herder, 1965).

Beale, H. *A History of Freedom of Teaching in American Schools* (New York: C. Scribner's Sons, 1941).

Becker, Mary. "The Politics of Women's Wrongs and the Bill of 'Rights': A Bicentennial Perspective," 59 *U. Chi. L. Rev.* 453 (1992)

Beckford, James A. *The Trumpet of Prophecy: A Sociological Study of Jehovah's Witnesses* (Oxford: Basil Blackwell, 1975).

Beecher, Lyman. *Autobiography,* ed. Barbara M. Cross (Cambridge: Belknap Press of Harvard University Press, 1961).

Bellah, Robert N. *The Broken Covenant: American Civil Religion in Time of Trial* (New York: Seabury Press, 1967).

___ et. al. *Habits of the Heart: Individualism and Commitment in American Life* (New York: Harper & Row, 1986).

Bender, Harold S. "A Brief Biography of Menno Simons," *The Complete Writings of Menno Simons* (Scottdale, Pa.: Mennonite Publishing House, 1956).

Ben–Sasson, Haim Hillel. "Effects of Religious Animosity on the Jews," in Haim Hillel Ben–Sasson, ed., *A History of the Jewish People* (Cambridge: Harvard University Press, 1976).

Berg, Thomas C. "Slouching Towards Secularism: A Comment on Kiryas Joel School District v. Grumet," 44 *Emory L. J.* 433 (1995)

___. "What Hath Congress Wrought? An Interpretive Guide to the Religious Freedom Restoration Act," 39 *Vill. L. Rev.* 1 (1994).

Berger, Peter. *Modernisation and Religion* (Dublin, Ireland: Economic & Social Research Institute, 1981).

Bergh, Albert E., ed. *Writings of Thomas Jefferson* (1907).

Berman, Harold J. *Law and Revolution: The Formation of the Western Legal Tradition* (Cambridge: Harvard University Press, 1983).

Bernardin, Joseph. "The Role of the Religious Leader in the Development of Public Policy," 34 *DePaul L. Rev.* 1 (1984).

Beumler, James E. "Social Teachings of the Presbyterian Church," *Church and Society* 83 (Nov./Dec. 1984).

Black, Hugo, Jr. *My Father: A Remembrance* (New York: Random House, 1975).

Blackstone, William. *The Sovereignty of the Law: Selections from Blackstone's Commentaries on the Laws of England; edited with an introduction by Gareth Jones (Toronto: University of Toronto Press, 1973).*

Blakely, William Addison, ed. *American State Papers Bearing on Sunday Legislation* (1911, reprint: New York: Da Capo, 1970).

Blanshard, Paul. *American Freedom and Catholic Power* (Boston: Beacon Press, 1949).

Blenkinsopp, Joseph. "Deuteronomy," in Raymond E. Brown, Joseph A. Fitzmyer, and Roland E. Murphy, eds. *The New Jerome Biblical Commentary* (Englewood Cliffs, NJ: Prentice Hall, 1990).

___. *Ezra–Nehemiah* (Philadelphia: Westminster, 1988).

___. *The Pentateuch: An Introduction to the First Five Books of the Bible* (Garden City, NY: Doubleday, 1992).

___. *Wisdom and Law in the Old Testament* (Oxford: Oxford University Press, 1995).

Boles, Donald E. *The Bible, Religion, and the Public Schools* (Ames: Iowa State University Press, 1965).

Borden, Morton. *Jews, Turks, and Infidels* (Chapel Hill, NC: University of North Carolina Press, 1984).

Boyd, Julian P., ed. *Papers of Thomas Jefferson* (Princeton: Princeton University Press, 1950–___).

Bracton, Henri de. *Bracton's Notebook,* ed. F.W. Maitland (London: B. Quaritch, 1895).

___. *The Laws and Customs of England,* ed. Samuel Thorne (Cambridge: Belknap Press of Harvard University Press, 1968).

Bradley, Gerard V. *Church-State Relationships in America* (New York: Greenwood Press, 1987).

___. "Dogmatomachy—A "Privatization" Theory of the Religion Clause Cases," 30 *St. Louis U. L. J.* 275 (1986).

Bradley, Joseph. "Esoteric Thoughts on Religion and Religionism" (1876), in Charles Bradley, ed., *Miscellaneous Writings of Joseph Bradley* (Newark, NJ: L. J. Hardman, 1902).

Braude, William G., trans. *The Midrash on Psalms* (New Haven: Yale University Press, 1959).

Brennan, William J., Jr. "The Bill of Rights and the States: The Revival of State Constitutions as Guardians of Individual Rights," 61 *N.Y.U.L.Rev.* 535 (1986).

___. "State Constitutions and the Protection of Individual Rights," 90 *Harv.L.Rev.* 489 (1977).

Bridenbaugh, Carl. *Mitre and Sceptre: Transatlantic Faiths, Ideas, Personalities, and Politics* (New York: Oxford University Press, 1962).

Brock, Peter. *Pacifism in the United States, From the Colonial Era to the First World* (Princeton, NJ: Princeton University Press, 1968).

Brown, Peter. "Religious Coercion in the later Roman Empire: The Case of North Africa," *History* 48 (1963) 283–305.

___. "Saint Augustine's Attitude to Religious Coercion," *J. of Roman Studies* 54 (1964) 107–16.

Brown, Raymond E. "The Pater Noster as an Eschatological Prayer," *Theological Studies* 22 (1961) 175–208.

___. Joseph A. Fitzmyer, and Roland E. Murphy, eds. *The New Jerome Biblical Commentary* (Englewood Cliffs, NJ: Prentice–Hall, 2d ed. 1990).

Browne, William Hand, ed. "An Act Concerning Religion," *Archives of Maryland: Proceedings and Acts of the General Assembly of Maryland, January 1637–September 1664* (Annapolis, 1883).

Bruckner, Aleksander. "The Polish Reformation in the Sixteenth Century," in Mieczyslaw Giergielwic, ed., *Polish Civilization* (New York: New York University Press, 1979).

Buchbinder, Reinhard. *Bibelizitate, Bibelanspielungen, Bibelparodien, theologische Vergleiche und Analogien bei Marx und Engels* (Berlin: E. Schmidt, 1976).

Buckley, Thomas E. *Church and State in Revolutionary Virginia 1776–1787* (Charlottesville: University Press of Virginia, 1977).

Bullard, JohnVincent, ed. *Constitutions and Canons Ecclesiastical, 1604* (Milwaukee, Morehouse Publishing Co., 1934).

Bunyan, John. *A Relation of the Imprisonment of Mr. John Bunyan*, in Roger Sharrock, ed., *Grace Abounding to the Chief of sinners, and, The Pilgrim's Progress from this World to that which is to Come* (New York: Oxford University Press, 1966).

Burr, Nelson Rollin. *The Story of the Diocese of Connecticut* (Hartford, CT: Church Missions Publishing, 1962).

Bushman, Richard L. *Joseph Smith and the Beginnings of Mormonism* (Chicago: University of Illinois Press, 1984).

Butler, Jon. *Awash in a Sea of Faith: Christianizing the American People* (Cambridge: Harvard University Press, 1990).

Butterfield, L.H., Leonard C. Faber, Wendell D. Garrett, eds. *Diary and Autobiography of John Adams* (Cambridge: Belknap Press of Harvard University Press, 1961).

Buzzard, Lynn. "The Evangelical Rediscovery of Law and Politics." 1 *J. Law and Relig.* 187 (1983).

Cadbury, H.J. "Roman Law and the Trial of Paul," in *The Beginnings of Christianity* (London: Macmillan, 1933).

Cadoux, Cecil John. *The Early Christian Attitude to War* (New York: Seabury Press, 1982; orig. ed. 1919).

von Campenhausen, Hans. "Christians and Military Service in the Early Church," in *Tradition and Life in the Church: Essays and Lectures on Church History* (Philadelphia: Fortress, 1968).

———. "Augustine and the Fall of Rome" in *Tradition and Life in the Church.*

Carmella, Angela C. "Houses of Worship and Religious Liberty: Constitutional Limits to Landmark Preservation and Architectural Review," 36 *Vill. L. Rev.* 401 (1991).

———. "State Constitutional Protection of Religious Exercise: An Emerging Post–Smith Jurisprudence," 1993 *B.Y.U. L. Rev.* 275.

Carmichael, Calum. *Law & Narrative in the Bible: The Evidence of the Deuteronomic Laws and the Decalogue* (Ithaca: Cornell University Press, 1985).

Caron, Wilfred and Deirdre Dessingue. "IRC § 501(c)(3): Practical and Constitutional Implications of 'Political' Activity Restraints," 2 *J. L. & Politics* 169 (1985).

Carter, Stephen L. "Evolution, Creationism, and Treating Religion as a Hobby," 1987 *Duke L. J.* 977 (1987), expanded and reprinted in *The Culture of Disbelief* (1993).

———. *The Culture of Disbelief: How American Law and Politics Trivialize Religious Devotion* (New Haven: Yale University Press, 1993).

Cassidy, Richard. *Jesus, Politics and Society: A Study of Luke's Gospel* (Maryknoll, NY: Orbis, 1978).

———. *Society and Politics in the Acts of the Apostles* (Maryknoll, NY: Orbis, 1987).

Cassou, April Kestell and Robert Curran. "Secular Orthodoxy and Sacred Freedoms: Accreditation and Church–Related Schools." 11 *Journal of College and University Law* 293 (1984).

Chase, Harold, Samuel Krislov, Keith Boyum, and Jerry N. Clark. *Biographical Dictionary of the Federal Judiciary* (Detroit: Gale Research Co., 1976).

Chazan, Robert. *Daggers of Faith: Thirteenth–Century Christian Missionizing and Jewish Response* (Berkeley: University of California Press, 1989).

___. *In the Year 1096: The First Crusade and the Jews* (Philadelphia: Jewish Publication Society, 1996).

Cheney, Christopher R. *Pope Innocent III and England* (Stuttgart: A. Hierseman, 1976).

___ and F. W. Powicke. *Councils and Synods with Other Documents Relating to the English Church* (Oxford: Clarendon Press, 1964).

___ and W.H. Semple, eds. *Selected Letters of Pope Innocent III concerning England, 1198–1216* (London: T. Nelson, 1953).

Cherrington, Ernest. *History of the Anti–Saloon League* (Westerville, Ohio: American Issue Pub. Co., 1913).

Chester, Allan G. *Selected Sermons of Hugh Latimer* (Washington: University of Virginia Press, 1968).

Chomsky, Carol. "Unlocking the Mysteries of Holy Trinity: Spirit, Letter, and History in Statutory Interpretation," 100 *Colum. L. Rev.* 901 (2000).

Choper, Jesse H. "The Religion Clauses of the First Amendment: Reconciling the Conflict." 41 *University of Pittsburgh L. Rev.* 673 (1980).

___. "Religion in the Public Schools: A Proposed Constitutional Standard," 47 *Minn. L. Rev.* 329 (1963).

Chopko, Mark. "Ascending Liability of Religious Entities for the Actions of Others," 17 *Am. J. of Trial Adv.* 189 (1993).

Chubb, John E. and Terry M. Moe. *Politics, Markets, and America's Schools* (Washington, D.C.: Brookings Institution, 1990).

Clark, Norman H. *Deliver Us from Evil: An Interpretation of American Prohibition* (New York: W. W. Norton, 1976).

Clark, J. Morris. "Guidelines for the Free Exercise Clause," 83 *Harv. L. Rev.* 327 (1969).

Cohn, Norman. *Cosmos, Chaos, and the World to Come: The Ancient Roots of Apocalyptic Faith* (New Haven: Yale University Press, 1993).

Coke, Edward. *The Third Part of the Institutes of the Laws of England* (4th ed.) (London: John Streater, James Flesher, Henry Twyford, 1893).

Cole, David. "The Value of Seeing Things Differently: Boerne v. Flores and Congressional Enforcement of the Bill of Rights," 1997 *Sup. Ct. Rev.* 31.

Coleman, John A. *An American Strategic Theology* (New York: Paulist Press, 1982).

Collins, Adela Yarbro. "The Apocalypse (Revelation)," in Raymond E. Brown, Joseph A. Fitzmyer, and Roland E. Murphy, eds. *The New Jerome Biblical Commentary* (Englewood Cliffs, NJ: Prentice Hall, 1990).

Collins, John. *The Apocalyptic Imagination: An Introduction to the Jewish Matrix of Christianity* (New York: Crossroad, 1984).

Comment. "State v. Faith Baptist Church: State Regulation of Religious Education." 15 *Creighton L. Rev.* 183 (1981).

Conkle, Daniel O. "Lemon Lives," 43 *Case W. Res. L. Rev.* 865 (1993).

"Conscience Whigs." *How to Settle the Texas Question* (Boston: E. Wright, 1845).

Cookson, Catharine. *Regulating Religion: The Courts and the Free Exercise Clause* (New York: Oxford University Press, 2001).

Cookston, Peter W., Jr. *School Choice: The Struggle for the Soul of American Education* (New Haven: Yale University Press, 1994).

Coons, John E. and Stephen D. Sugarman. *Education by Choice: The Case for Family Control* (Berkeley, CA: University of California Press, 1978).

____. *Family Choice in Education: A Model State System for Vouchers* (Berkeley, CA: Institute of Governmental Studies, University of California, 1971).

____. *Scholarships for Children* (Berkeley, CA: Institute of Governmental Studies, University of California, 1992).

Cord, Robert. "Church–State Separation: Restoring the 'No Preference' Doctrine of the First Amendment." 9 *Harvard Journal of Law and Public Policy* 129 (1986).

____. *Separation of Church and State: Historical Fact and Current Fiction* (New York: Lambeth Press, 1982).

Corwin, Edward S. "The Supreme Court as National School Board," 14 *Law & Contemp. Probs.* 1 (1949).

Cousins, Norman. *In God We Trust: The Religious Beliefs and Ideas of the American Founding Fathers* (New York: Harper, 1958).

Cover, Robert M. *Justice Accused: Antislavery and the Judicial Process* (New Haven: Yale University Press, 1975).

____. "The Supreme Court 1982 Term–Foreword: Nomos and Narrative," 97 *Harv. L. Rev.* 1 (1983).

Crewdson, Robert L. "Ministry and Mortar: Historic Preservation and the First Amendment after Barwick," 33 *J. Urb. & Contemp. L.* 137 (1988).

Crittenden, Ann. *Sanctuary: A Story of American Conscience and the Law in Collision* (New York: Werdenfeld & Nicolson, 1988).

Cullmann, Oscar. *Jesus and the Revolutionaries* (New York: Harper & Row, 1970).

____. *New Testament Christology* (London: SCM, 1959).

____. "Paul and the State," in *The State in the New Testament* (New York: Scribner's, 1956).

Currie, David P. "RFRA," 39 *Wm & Mary L. Rev.* 637 (1998).

Curry, Thomas J. *The First Freedoms: Church and State in America to the Passage of the First Amendment* (New York: Oxford University Press, 1986).

Cushing, John D. "Notes on Disestablishment in Massachusetts, 1780–1833." 26 *William and Mary Quarterly* 169–90 (1969).

Cyprian. *De lapsis (The Lapsed), PL* 4.

Dalin, David G. and Jonathan D. Sarna, eds. *Religion and State in the American Jewish Experience: A Documentary History* (Notre Dame: University of Notre Dame Press, 1997).

Dane, Perry. "The Public, the Private, and the Sacred: Variations on a Theme of Nomos and Narrative," 8 *Cardozo Stud. L. & Literature* 15 (1996).

Danzig, Richard. "Justice Frankfurter's Opinions in the Flag Salute Cases: Blending Logic and Psychologic in Constitutional Decisionmaking," 36 *Stan. L. Rev.* 675 (1984).

Daube, David. "Responsibilities of Master and Disciples in the Gospels," *New Testament Studies* 19 (1972) 13.

Davidowitz, Lucy. *The War Against the Jews, 1933–1945* (New York: Holt, Rinehart, & Winston, 1975).

Deane, Herbert. *The Political and Social Ideas of St. Augustine* (New York: Columbia University Press, 1963).

Decter, Midge. "A Jew in Anti–Christian America," *First Things* 56 (Oct. 1995).

Dept. of Defense Directive 1300.17, *Accommodation of Religious Practices Within the Military Services* (1985).

Derrett, J. Duncan M. *Law in the New Testament* (London: Darton, Longman & Todd, 1970).

___. "Luke's Perspective on Tribute to Caesar," in Richard Cassidy and Philip Scharper eds. *Political Issues in Luke–Acts* (Maryknoll, NY: Orbis, 1983).

Dershowitz, Alan M. *The Vanishing American Jew* (Boston: Little Brown, 1997).

Destro, Robert. "ABA and AALS Accreditation: What's 'Religious Diversity' Got to Do With It?," 78 *Marq. L. Rev.* 427 (1995).

___, and Michael S. Ariens. *Religious Liberty in a Pluralistic Society* (Durham, N.C.: Carolina Academic Press, 1996).

deVaux, Roland. *Ancient Israel: Its Life and Institutions* (New York: McGraw–Hill, 1961).

Dewey, John. "S. 2499, Its Antidemocratic Implications." *The Nation's Schools* 39 (March 1947) 20–21.

Dix, Dorothea. *Remarks on Prisons* (Montclair, NJ: P. Smith, 1967).

Dolbeare, Kenneth and Phillip E. Hammond. *The School Prayer Decisions: From Court Policy to Local Practice* (Chicago: University of Chicago Press, 1971).

Doncoeur, P. and Y. Lanners. *La Rehabilitation de Jeanne La Purcelle. L'enquete ordonne par Charles VII en 1450 et le codicille de Guillaume Bouille* (Paris: Librairie d'Argences, 1956).

Dorff, Elliot N. and Arthur Rosett. *A Living Tree: The Roots and Growth of Jewish Law* (Albany: State University of New York Press, 1988).

Douglas, Mary and Steven Tipton, eds. *Religion and America: Spiritual Life in a Secular Age* (Boston: Beacon Press, 1983).

Douglas, William O. *Go East, Young Man* (New York: Random House, 1974).

Douglass, James W. *The Non–Violent Cross* (New York: Macmillan, 1968).

Dresser, Amos. "The Narrative of Amos Dresser," in John L. Thomas, ed. *Slavery Attacked: The Abolitionist Crusade* (Englewood Cliffs, NJ: Prentice–Hall, 1965).

Drinan, Robert F. "Reflections on the Demise of the Religious Freedom Restoration Act," 86 *Geo. L. J.* 101 (1997).

Driver, G.R. and J. C. Miles, eds. *The Babylonian Laws* (2 vols.) (Oxford, England: Clarendon Press, 1952–55).

Duff, R.A. "Expression, Penance and Reform," in J.G. Murphy, ed., *Punishment and Reformation* (Belmont, CA: Wadsworth Pub. Co., 3d ed. 1995).

Dunn, James M. "The Christian as Political Activist." *Liberty* 81 (July–August 1986) 18.

Dunne, Gerald T. *Hugo Black and the Judicial Revolution* (New York: Simon and Schuster, 1977).

Eckenrode, H. J. *Separation of Church and State in Virginia* (New York: Da Capo Press Reprint, 1971).

Edelby, Neophytos & Teodoro Jiminez–Urresti, eds. *Religious Freedom* (New York: Paulist Press, 1966).

Edwards, Mark U., Jr. *Luther's Last Battles: Politics and Polemics, 1531–46* (Ithaca: Cornell University Press, 1983).

Ehrlich, Thomas and Mary Ellen O'Connell. *International Law and the Use of Force* (Boston: Little, Brown, 1993).

Eidelberg, Shlomo, trans. *The Jews and the Crusaders: The Hebrew Chronicles of the First and Second Crusades* (Madison: University of Wisconsin Press, 1977).

Eisgruber, Christopher L. and Lawrence G. Sager. "Why the Religious Freedom Restoration Act Is Unconstitutional," 69 *N.Y.U.L. Rev.* 437 (1994).

Elliot, Jonathan. *The Debates in the Several State Conventions on the Adoption of the Federal Constitution* (Philadelphia: J. B. Lippincott, 1836).

Ellis, George D., ed. *Platforms of the Two Great Political Parties* (Washington, D.C.: Government Printing Office, 1928).

Elton, G. R. *Reform and Reformation: England, 1509–1558* (Cambridge: Harvard University Press, 1978).

Emerson, Thomas I. and David Haber. "The *Scopes* Case in Modern Dress," 27 *U. Chi. L. Rev.* 522 (1960).

Eppstein, John. *The Catholic Tradition of the Law of the Nations* (Washington, D.C.: Carnegie Endowment for International Peace by the Catholic Association for International Peace, 1935).

Eusebius. *Ecclesiastical History* (Cambridge: Cambridge University Press, 1898).

___. *The Life of Constantine, PL* 8.

Evans, T. David et al. "Religion and Crime Reexamined: The Impact of Religion, Secular Controls, and Social Ecology on Adult Criminology," 33 *Criminology* 195 (1995).

Fairman, Charles. "Does the Fourteenth Amendment Incorporate the Bill of Rights?," 2 *Stanford L. Rev.* 5 (1949).

Falk, Richard A. *Law, Morality, and War in the Contemporary World* (New York: Center of International Studies, Princeton University, 1963).

___. *Legal Order in a Violent World* (Princeton, NJ: Princeton University Press, 1968).

___. ed. & Samuel S. Kim. *The War System: An Interdisciplinary Approach,* (Boulder, CO: Westview Press, 1980).

___ & Saul H. Mendlovitz, eds. *The Strategy of World Order* (4 vols.) (New York: World Law Fund, 1966).

Farrand, Max, ed. *Record of the Federal Convention of 1787* (New Haven: Yale University Press, 1911).

Fassett, John D. *New Deal Justice: The Life of Stanley Reed of Kentucky* (New York: Vintage Press, 1994).

Fehrenbacher, Don E. *The Dred Scott Case: Its Significance in American Law and Politics* (New York: Oxford University Press, 1978).

Figgis, John Neville. *The Political Aspects of S. Augustine's City of God,* (London: Longmans, Green, 1921).

Fitzmyer, Joseph A. "The Letter to the Romans" and "A Life of Paul," in Raymond E. Brown, Joseph A. Fitzmyer, and Roland E. Murphy, eds. *The New Jerome Biblical Commentary,* (Englewood Cliffs, NJ: Prentice–Hall, 1990).

Flannery, Edward H. *The Anguish of the Jews* (New York: Macmillan, 1965).

Foliot, Gilbert. *Foliot to Thomas (1166), RS* 67.

Ford, Josephine Massyngberde. *Revelation* (Garden City, NY: Doubleday, 1975).

Ford, Worthington, ed. *Journals of the Continental Congress, 1774–1789* (Washington, D.C.: National Archives, 1958–59).

Foxe, John. *Acts and Monuments of these latter and perilous days* (London: George Seeley, 1870).

Frankena, R. "The Vassal–Treaties of Esarhaddon and the Dating of Deuteronomy," *Old Testament Studies* 14 (1965) 122–54.

Frend, W.H.C. *Martyrdom and Persecution in the Early Church* (Garden City, NY: Anchor Books, 1967).

Freund, Paul A. "Public Aid to Parochial Schools." 82 *Harv. L. Rev.* 1680 (1968).

Freyne, Seán. *The World of the New Testament* (Wilmington: Michael Glazier, 1989).

———. *Gallilee and Gospel* (Tübingen, Morh Siebeck, 2000).

Friedman, Milton. *Capitalism and Freedom* (Chicago: University of Chicago Press,1962).

Friedman, Wolfgang. "Hugo Grotius," in 3 *Encyclopedia of Philosophy* (New York: Macmillan, 1967).

Friesen, Jennifer. *State Constitutional Law: Litigating Individual Rights, Claims and Defenses* (Charlottesville: Michie, 2d ed. 1995).

Frost, Robert. *The Complete Poems of Robert Frost* (New York: Henry Holt, 1979).

Fuller, Reginald H. *The Foundations of New Testament Christology* (New York: Scribners, 1965).

"Fundamentalists Leave Jail, But Nebraska Church Schools Are Still in Trouble." *Christianity Today* (July 13, 1984).

Furniss, Norman F. *The Mormon Conflict, 1850–1859* (New Haven: Yale University Press, 1960).

Gaffney, Edward McGlynn, Jr. "Biblical Religion and American Politics: Some Historical and Theological Reflections," 1 *J. Law & Relig.* 171 (1983).

———. "Of Covenants Ancient and New: The Influence of Secular Law on Biblical Religion," 2 *J. Law & Relig.* 117 (1984).

———. "On Not Rendering to Caesar: The Unconstitutionality of Tax Regulation of Activities of Religious Organizations Relating to Politics," 40 *DePaul L. Rev.* 1 (1990)

———. "Political Divisiveness Along Religious Lines: The Entanglement of the Court in Sloppy History and Bad Public Policy," 24 *St. Louis U. L. J.* 205 (1980).

———. "Politics Without Brackets on Religious Convictions: Michael Perry and Bruce Ackerman on Neutrality," 64 *Tulane L. Rev.* 1143 (1990).

———, ed. *Private Schools and the Public Good: Policy Alternatives for the Eighties* (Notre Dame: University of Notre Dame Press, 1981).

___ and Philip C. Sorensen. *Ascending Liability in Religious and Other Nonprofit Organization* (Macon, GA: Mercer University Press, 1984).

Gager, John G. *The Origins of Anti–Semitism* (New York: Oxford University Press, 1983).

Gal, Allon. *Brandeis of Boston* (Cambridge: Harvard University Press, 1980).

Gales, Joseph, ed. *The Debates and Proceedings in the Congress of the United States* (Washington: Gales and Seaton, 1856).

Garnsey, Peter and Richard Saller. *The Roman Empire: Economy, Society and Culture* (London: Duckworth, 1987).

Garet, Ronald R. "Communality and Existence: The Rights of Groups," 56 *S. Cal. L. Rev.* 1001 (1983).

Garvey, John. "Another Way of Looking at School Aid," 1985 *Sup. Ct. Rev.* (1985).

___. *What are Freedoms For?* (Cambridge: Harvard University Press, 1996).

Gaustad, Edwin Scott. *A Religious History of America* (San Francisco: Harper & Row, 1990).

Gedicks, Frederick Mark. "Some Political Implications of Religious Belief," 4 *Notre Dame J.L. Ethics & Pub. Policy* 419 (1990).

Gero, Stephen. "*Miles Gloriosus*: The Christian and Military Service according to Tertullian," *Church History* 39 (1970) 285–98.

Gerstenberger, Erhard. *Wesen und Herkunft des Apodiktischen Reacts* (Neukirchen: Neukirchener Verlag, 1965).

Giannella, Donald A. "*Lemon* and *Tilton*: The Bitter and the Sweet of Church–State Entanglement." 1971 *Sup. Ct. Rev.* 147.

Gilles, Stephen G. "On Educating Children: A Parentalist Manifesto," 63 *U. Chi. L. Rev.* 937 (1996).

Given, James B. *Society and Homicide in Thirteenth Century England* (Stanford: Stanford University Press, 1977).

Glasse, Cyril. *The Concise Encyclopaedia of Islam* (San Francisco: Harper & Row, 1989).

Glendon, Mary Ann & Raul F. Yanes "Structural Free Exercise," 90 *Mich. L. Rev.* 477 (1991).

Goldin, Judah. *The Song at the Sea* (New Haven: Yale University Press, 1971).

Goldman, Jane Vandeventer. "Taxing Sex Discrimination: Revoking Tax Benefits of Organizations Which Discriminate on the Basis of Sex," 1976 *Ariz. St. L. J.* 641.

Gonzalez–Wippler, Migene. *The Santeria Experience* (St. Paul: Llewellyn Publications, 1992).

Goodel, William. "Slavery Tested by Its Own Code," 1 *Quarterly Anti–Slavery Magazine* 23 (1836).

Gordon, Cyrus H. "Gilgamesh Epic," in Bruce M. Metzger and Michael D. Coogan, eds., *The Oxford Companion to the Bible* 254 (New York: Oxford University Press, 1993)

Gordon, James D. III. "Free Exercise on the Mountaintop," 79 *Calif. L. Rev.* 91 (1991).

Gordon, Sarah Barringer. *The Mormon Question: Polygamy, Politics, and Constitutional Conflict in Nineteenth–Century America* (Chapel Hill, NC: University of North Carolina Press, 2001).

Gratian. *Concordia discordantium canonum (Harmony of Unharmonious Canons)* ed. Emil Friedberg (Leipzig: B. Tauchnitz, 1879).

Green, Beriah. "Letter to a Minister of the Gospel," 1 *Quarterly Anti–Slavery Magazine* 340 (1836).

Green, Steven K. "Justice David Josiah Brewer and the 'Christian Nation' Maxim," 63 *Alb. L. Rev.* 427 (1999).

___. "The Blaine Amendment Reconsidered," 36 *Am. J. Legal Hist.* 38 (1992).

___."The Legal Argument Against Private School Choice," 62 *U. Cin. L. Rev.* 37 (1993).

Greenawalt, Kent. "Conscientious Objection," in James E. Wood, Jr., ed., *Religion and the State: Essays in Honor of Leo Pfeffer* 247 (Waco, TX: Baylor University Press, 1985).

___. *Religious Convictions and Political Choice* (New York: Oxford University Press, 1988).

Gregory IX. *Decretales,* ed. Emil Friedberg (Leipzig: B. Tauchnitz, 1881).

Griffith, Lee. *The Fall of the Prison: Biblical Perspectives on Prison Abolition* (Eugene, OR: Wipf & Stock, 1999).

Grosseteste, Robert. *Letters, RS* 25.

Gunther, Gerald, and Kathleen Sullivan. *Constitutional Law: Cases and Materials* (New York: Foundation Press, 13th ed. 1997).

Hadden, Jeffrey and Theodore E. Long, eds. *Religion and Religiosity in America: Studies in Honor of Joseph H. Fichter* (New York: Crossroad, 1983).

Hahn, Ferdinand. *The Titles of Jesus in Christology* (Cleveland: World, 1969).

Hamilton, Marci A. "The Religious Freedom Restoration Act Is Unconstitutional, Period," 1 *U. Pa. J. Const. L.* 1 (1998).

___. "The Religious Freedom Restoration Act: Letting the Fox into the Henhouse Under Cover of Section 5 of the Fourteenth Amendment," 16 *Cardozo L. Rev.* 357 (1994).

Handy, Robert T. *A Christian America: Protestant Hopes and Historical Realities* (New York: Oxford University Press, 1984).

Hansen, Klaus J. *Quest for Empire: The Political Kingdom of God and the Council of Fifty in Mormon History* (East Lansing, MI: Michigan State University Press, 1970).

Hardy, B. Carmon. *Solemn Covenant: The Mormon Polygamous Passage* (Urbana, IL: University of Illinois Press, 1992).

Harnack, Adolph. *The Mission and Expansion of Christianity in the First Three Centuries* (New York: Harper, 1962).

___. *Militia Christi: The Christian Religion and the Military in the First Three Centuries* (Philadelphia: Fortress, 1981).

Harrelson, Walter. *The Ten Commandments and Human Rights* (Philadelphia: Fortress, 1980).

Hart, Stephen. "Privatization in American Religion and Society," *47 Sociological Analysis: A Journal in the Sociology of Religion* 319 (1987).

Hastings, Hugh. *Ecclesiastical Records of the State of New York* (Albany: James B. Lyon, 1901).

Hauerwas, Stanley. *Against the Nations: War and Survival in a Liberal Society* (New York: Harper & Row, 1985).

___. *The Peaceable Kingdom* (Notre Dame: University of Notre Dame Press, 1983).

Heinemann, Joseph. "The Background of Jesus' Prayer in the Jewish Liturgical Tradition," in Jakob J. Petruchowski and Michael Briocke, eds., *The Lord's Prayer and Jewish Liturgy* (New York: Seabury, 1978).

Heiser, Francis. "The Law Versus the Conscientious Objector," 20 *University of Chicago Law Review* 441 (1953).

Helgeland, John, Robert Daly, and J. Patout Burns. *Christians and the Military: The Early Experience* (Philadelphia: Fortress Press, 1985).

___. "Christians and the Roman Army: A.D. 173–337," *Church History* 43 (1974) 149–63.

Henry, Virgil. *The Place of Religion in Public Schools* (New York: Harper, 1950).

Herr, Moshe David. "Edom," in 6 *Encyclopaedia Judaica* 370–80 (New York: Macmillan, 1971).

Hill, John Edward Christopher. *Change and Continuity in Seventeenth Century England* (London: Weidenfeld & Nicolson, 1974).

Hillerman, Tony. *People of Darkness* (New York: Perennial Library, 1988).

Hillers, Delbert. *Covenant: The History of a Biblical Idea* (Baltimore: Johns Hopkins University Press, 1969).

___. "Revelation 13:18 and the Scroll from Murabba'at," *Bulletin of the American Schools of Oriental Research* 170 (1963) 65.

Hirsch, Samson Raphael. *Hirsch Siddur: The Order of Prayers for the Whole Year* (Eng. trans. Jerusalem: Feldheim, 1969).

Hitchcock, James. "Church, State and Moral Values: The Limits of American Pluralism," 44 *Law & Contemporary Problems* 3 (1981).

Hofstadter, Richard, and Walter Metzger. *The Development of Academic Freedom in the United States* (New York: Columbia University Press, 1955).

Hollenbach, David. "Contexts of the Political Role of Religion," 20 *San Diego L. Rev.* 877 (1993).

Holmes, Oliver Wendell, Jr. *Holmes-Laski Letters,* ed. Mark DeWolfe Howe (Cambridge: Harvard University Press, 1953).

Holmes, Stephen. "Jean Bodin: The Paradox of Sovereignty and the Privatization of Religion," in J. Roland Pennock & John W. Chapman, eds., *Religion, Morality, and the Law* (New York: New York University Press, 1988).

Holt, James C. *Magna Carta* (Cambridge: Cambridge University Press, 1965).

Hornus, Jean–Michel. *It is Not Lawful for Me to Fight* (Scottsdale, PA: Herald Press, 1980).

Hostetler, John A. *Amish Society* (Baltimore: Johns Hopkins University Press, 3d ed. 1980)

——. "The Cultural Context of the Wisconsin Case," in Albert N. Keim, ed., *Compulsory Education and the Amish: The Right Not to Be Modern* (Boston: Beacon Press, 1975).

House Ways and Means Committee, *Legislative Activity By Certain Types of Exempt Organizations*, Hearings, 92d Cong., 2d Sess. (1972).

Howard, J. Woodford. *Mr. Justice Murphy: A Political Biography* (Princeton: Princeton University Press, 1968).

Howard, John. *Account of the Principal Lazarettos in Europe* (Warrington: T. Cadell, 1789).

——. *The State of the Prisons* (New York: E.P. Dutton & Co., 1929).

Howe, Mark DeWolfe. "Foreword: Political Theory and the Nature of Liberty, The Supreme Court, 1952 Term." 67 *Harv. L. Rev.* 1 (1953).

——. *The Garden and the Wilderness: Religion and Government in American Constitutional History* (Chicago: University of Chicago Press, 1965).

Hunter, David. "A Decade of Research on Early Christians and Military Service," *Religious Studies Rev.* 18 (1991) 87–94.

Hunter, James Davison and Os Guinness eds. *Articles of Faith, Articles of Peace: The Religious Liberty Clauses and the American Public Philosophy* (Washington, D.C.: Brookings Institution, 1990).

Hutchinson, William T. and William M.E. Rachal, eds. *Papers of James Madison* (Chicago: University of Chicago Press, 1962).

Hutson, James H. *Supplement to Max Farrand's The Records of the Federal Convention of 1787* (New Haven, CT: Yale University Press, 1987).

"In Nebraska, the War Between Church and State Rages On," *Christianity Today* (February 17, 1984).

Innocent III. *Gesta Innocenti III, PL* 216.

___. *De miseria humanae conditionis (The Misery of the Human Condition)*, ed. Michele Maccarrone (Lucca: Thesaurus Mundi 1955).

___. *Selected Letters of Pope Innocent III Concerning England, 1198–1216*, ed. Christopher R. Cheney and W. H. Semple (New York: T. Nelson, 1953).

Irons, Peter. *The Courage of Their Convictions* (New York: Free Press, 1988).

"Is the Nebraska School Trouble Finally Over?," *Christianity Today* (July 13, 1984).

Isaac, Jules. *The Teaching of Contempt: Christian Roots of Anti–Semitism* (New York: Holt, Reinhart & Winston, 1964).

Isaac, Rhys. " 'The Rage of Malice of the Old Serpent Devil': The Dissenters and the Making and Remaking of the Virginia Statute for Religious Freedom," in Merrill Peterson and Robert Vaughn, eds., *The Virginia Statute for Religious Freedom: Its Evolution and Consequences in American History* (New York: Cambridge University Press, 1988).

Israel, Fred L. "Wiley Rutledge," in Leon Friedman and Fred L. Israel, eds., *The Justices of the United States Supreme Court 1789–1969* (New York: Chelsea House, 1969).

Jefferson, Thomas. *Autobiography, Writings*, ed. Albert E. Bergh (Washington, D.C.: Jefferson Memorial Association, 1907).

___. *Jefferson's Reports in Virginia Reports Annotated* (1903).

___. *Notes on Virginia. Works*, ed. Paul L. Ford (New York: C. P. Putnam's Sons, 1892).

___. *Papers*, ed. Julian P. Boyd (Princeton: Princeton University Press, 1950–___).

___. *The Works of Jefferson*, ed. Paul Leicester Ford (New York: G.P. Putnam's Sons, 1892–1905).

Jencks, Christopher. "Is the Public School Obsolete?," 2 *Public Interest* 18 (Winter 1966).

John of Salisbury. *The Letters of John of Salisbury*, ed. W. J. Millor and C. N. L. Brooke (Oxford: Clarendon Press, 1979).

___. *Policraticus*, ed. C. I. Webb (Oxford: Clarendon Press, 1909).

Johnson, James Turner. *Ideology, Reason and the Limitation of War: Secular and Religious Concepts, 1200–1740* (Princeton, NJ: Princeton University Press, 1975).

___. *The Quest for Peace: Three Moral Traditions in Western Cultural History* (Princeton, NJ: Princeton University Press, 1987).

Johnson, Luke. *The Acts of the Apostles* (Collegeville, Minn.: Liturgical Press, 1992).

Johnson, Philip E. "Concepts and Compromises in First Amendment Religious Doctrine," 72 *Calif. L. Rev.* 817 (1984).

＿. *Darwin on Trial* (Downers Grove, IL: InterVarsity Press, 1993).

＿. *Defeating Darwinism* (Downers Grove, IL: InterVarsity Press, 1997).

Johnson, Samuel. *Dictionary* (London: W. Strahan, 1755).

Josephus, Flavius. *The Antiquities of the Jews* in *The Works of Flavius Josephus*, trans. William Whiston (London: Winston, 1987).

＿. *The Jewish Wars* in *The Works of Flavius Josephus*, trans. William Whiston (London: Winston, 1987).

Journal of the First Session of the [U.S.] Senate, September 4, 1789 (Washington, 1820).

Journal of the Massachusetts Constitutional Convention of 1820 (Boston, 1853).

Karst, Kenneth L. "Religious Freedom and Equal Citizenship: Reflections on Lukumi," 69 *Tul. L. Rev.* 335 (1994).

Kauper, Paul G. and Steven C. Ellis. "Religious Corporations and the Law." 71 *Mich. L. Rev.* 1499 (1973).

Keim, Albert N. "From Erlanbach to New Glarus," in Albert N. Keim, ed., *Compulsory Education and the Amish: The Right Not to Be Modern* (Boston: Beacon Press, 1975).

Kelley, Dean M. "The Intermeddling Manifesto, Or, The Role of Religious Bodies in Affecting Public Policy in the United States," 8 *J. L. & Relig.* 85 (1990).

＿. *Why Churches Should Not Pay Taxes* (New York: Harper & Row, 1977).

Kelly, Alfred. "Clio and the Court: An Illicit Love Affair," 1965 *Sup. Ct. Rev.* 119.

Kelly, Henry Ansgar. *The Matrimonial Trials of Henry VIII* (Stanford: Stanford University Press, 1976).

Kent, James. *Commentaries on American Law* (New York: The Author, 1844).

King, Martin Luther. *Letter from Birmingham Jail* (Stamford, Conn.: Overbrook Press, 1968).

Klein, Isaac. *A Guide to Jewish Religious Practice* (New York: Jewish Theological Seminary of America, 1979).

Klibansky, Raymond. "Preface to John Locke." *Epistola de Tolerantia* (Oxford: Clarendon Press, 1968).

Knauer, Peter. "The Hermeneutic Function of the Principle of Double Effect." 12 *Natural Law Forum* 132 (1967).

Kneeland, Abner. *A View of the Trial, Conviction and Final Imprisonment in the Common Jail of the County of Suffolk, of Abner Kneeland, for the Alleged Crime of Blasphemy*, reproduced in Leonard W. Levy, *Blasphemy in Massachusetts* (New York: Da Capo, 1973).

Knibb, Michael A. *The First and Second Book of Esdras* (Cambridge: Cambridge University Press, 1979).

Knowles, David. *Thomas Becket* (Stanford: Stanford University Press, 1971).

Konvitz, Milton R. "Separation of Church and State: The First Freedom," 14 *Law & Contemp. Probs.* 44 (1949).

Kovacs, Maureen Gallery, trans. *The Epic of Gilgamesh* (Stanford, CA: Stanford University Press, 1989).

Kraeling, Carl. "The Episode of the Roman Standards at Jerusalem," *Harvard Theological Review* 35 (1942) 263.

Krey, August C., ed. *The First Crusade: The Accounts of Eyewitnesses and Participants* (Princeton, NJ: Princeton University Press, 1920).

Kurland, Philip. "Of Church and State in the Supreme Court," 28 *U. Chi. L. Rev.* 1 (1961).

——. "The Origins of the Religion Clauses of the Constitution," 27 *Wm. & Mary L. Rev.* 839 (1986).

Lactantius. *De mortibus persecutorum (The Deaths of the Persecutors), PL* 7.

Lader, Lawrence. *Abortion* (Boston: Beacon Press, 1967).

Lake, I. Beverly. "Freedom to Worship Curiously," 1 *U. Fla. L. Rev.* 203 (1948).

Langan, John. "The Elements of St. Augustine's Just War Theory," *Journal of Religious Ethics* 12 (1984) 19–38.

Laplatte, C. "Cauchon," *Dictionnaire d'histoire et de geographie ecclesiastiques* (Paris: Letouzey et An, 1953), vol. 12.

Larson, Edward J. *Summer for the Gods: The Scopes Trial and America's Continuing Debate over Science and Religion* (Cambridge: Harvard University Press, 1988).

——. *Trial and Error: The American Controversy Over Creation and Evolution* (New York: Oxford University Press, 1989).

Larson, Stan, ed. *Prisoner for Polygamy: The Memoirs and Letters of Rudger Clawson at the Utah Territorial Penitentiary, 1884–87* (Urbana, IL: University of Illinois Press, 1993).

Lash, Kurt T. "The Second Adoption of the Establishment Clause: The Rise of the Nonestablishment Principle," 27 *Ariz. St. L.J.* 1085 (1995).

——. "The Second Adoption of the Free Exercise Clause: Religious Exemptions under the Fourteenth Amendment," 88 *Northwestern L. Rev.* 1106 (1994).

Lasson, Kenneth. "Religious Liberty in the Military: The First Amendment under 'Friendly Fire,' " 9 *J. L. & Relig.* 471 (1992).

Latimer, Hugh. *Selected Sermons of Hugh Latimer,* ed. Allan G. Chester (Cranburynswick, NY: Folger Books, 1978).

Latourette, Kenneth Scott. *A History of Christianity* (New York: Harper & Brothers, 1953).

Laycock, Douglas. "Conceptual Gulfs in City of Boerne v. Flores," 39 *Wm. & Mary L. J.* 743 (1998).

——. "Continuity and Change in the Threat to Religious Liberty: The Reformation Era and the Late Twentieth Century," 80 *Minn. L. Rev.* 1052 (1996).

——. "Formal, Substantive, and Disaggregated Neutrality toward Religion," 39 *DePaul L. Rev.* 1 (1990).

——. "'Nonpreferential' Aid to Religion: A False Claim About Original Intent," 27 *Wm. & Mary L. Rev.* 875 (1986).

——. "The Remnants of Free Exercise," 1990 *Sup. Ct. Rev.* 1.

——. "Summary and Synthesis: The Crisis in Religious Liberty," 60 *Geo. Wash. L. Rev.* 841 (1992).

——. "Tax Exemptions for Racially Discriminatory Religious Schools," 60 *Texas L. Rev.* 259 (1982).

—— and Oliver S. Thomas. "Interpreting the Religious Freedom Restoration Act," 73 *Tex. L. Rev.* 209 (1994).

—— and Susan E. Waelbroeck. "Academic Freedom and the Free Exercise of Religion," 66 *Texas L. Rev.* 1455 (1988).

Lecler, Joseph. *Toleration and the Reformation,* trans. T. L. Weslow (New York: Association Press, 1960).

Leflar. "Legal Liability for the Exercise of Free Speech," 10 *Ark. L. Rev.* 155 (1956).

Lenihan, David A. "The Just War Theory in the Work of St. Augustine," *Augustininan Studies* 19 (1988) 37–70.

Leo XIII. *Arcanum, Acta Sanctae Sedis* 12:385–402 (February 10, 1880).

Lerner, Jon S. "Protecting Home Schooling through the *Casey* Undue Burden Standard," 62 *U. Chi. L. Rev.* 363 (1995).

Levin, Henry. "The Failure of the Public Schools and the Free Market Remedy," 2 *The Urban Rev.* 32 (June 1968).

Levinson, Sanford. "The Constitution in American Civil Religion." 1979 *Sup. Ct. Rev.* 123.

——. *Constitutional Faith* (Princeton, NJ: Princeton University Press, 1988).

Levy, Jacob. *Wörterbuch über die Talmudim und Midraschim: Neuhebräische und chaldaisches Wörterbuch* (Daarmstadt: Wissenschaftliche Buchgesellschaft, 1963).

Levy, Leonard W., ed. *Blasphemy* in *Massachusetts: Freedom of Conscience and the Abner Kneeland Case, A Documentary Record* (New York, Da Capo Press, 1973).

——. *Blasphemy: Verbal Offense against the Sacred, From Moses to Salman Rushdie* (New York: Knopf, 1993).

____. *The Establishment Clause: Religion and the First Amendment* (Chapel Hill: University of North Carolina Press, 1986).

____. *The Religion Clauses* (New York: Macmillan, 1986).

Levy, Tracey. "Rediscovering Rights: State Courts Reconsider the Free Exercise Clauses of Their Own Constitutions in the Wake of Employment Division v. Smith," 67 *Temp.L. Rev.* 1017 (1994).

Lieber, Francis. *Contributions to Political Science, Miscellaneous Writings* (Philadelphia: J. B. Lippincott, 1881).

____. *Manual of Political Ethics* (Boston: C. C. Brown and J. Little, 1839).

____. *On Civil Liberty and Self Government* (Philadelphia: J. B. Lippincott, 1859).

Lincoln, Abraham. *Collected Works,* ed. Roy P. Basler (New Brunswick, NJ: Rutgers University Press, 1953).

Linde, Hans A. "First Things First: Rediscovering the States' Bill of Rights," 9 *U.Balt.L.Rev.* 379 (1980).

____. "E Pluribus," 18 *Ga. L. Rev.* 165 (1984).

Linder, Amnon. *The Jews in Roman Imperial Legislation* (Detroit: Wayne State University Press, 1987).

Littell, Franklin H. *From State Church to Pluralism: A Protestant Interpretation of Religion in American History* (New York: Macmillan, 1971).

Loades, D. M. *The Oxford Martyrs* (London: Batsford, 1970).

Locke, John. *Epistola de Tolerantia (Letter on Toleration),* ed. Raymond Klibansky (Oxford: Clarendon Press, 1968).

____. *The Second Treatise of Government,* ed. J. W. Gough (Oxford: Basil Blackwell, 1966).

Lohfink, Norbert. "Deuteronomy," in *Interpreter's Dictionary of the Bible* (Nashville: Abingdon, 1976) 5:229–32.

Lord, Robert Howard. *A History of the Archdiocese of Boston* (New York: Sheed & Ward, 1945).

____. John E. Sexton, and Edward T. Harrington. *History of the Archdiocese of Boston* (Boston: Pilot Publishing Co., 1945).

Louisell, David. "Does the Constitution Require a Purely Secular Society?," 26 *Cath. U. L. Rev.* 20 (1976).

Lupu, Ira C. "Which Old Witch?: A Comment on Professor Paulsen's Lemon is Dead," 43 *Case W. Res. L. Rev.* 883 (1993).

____. "Why the Congress Was Wrong and the Court Was Right–Reflections on City of Boerne v. Flores," 39 *Wm. & Mary L. Rev.* 793 (1998).

MacGregor, G.H.C. *The New Testament Basis of Pacifism* (Nyack, NY: Fellowship, 1954).

MacMaster, Richard K., Samuel L. Horst, and Robert F. Ullie. *Conscience in Crisis: Mennonite and Other Peace Churches in America, 1739–1789* (Scottdale, Pa.: Herald Press, 1979).

Macmullan, Jack. "The Constitutionality of State Home Schooling Statutes," 31 *Vill. L. Rev.* 1309 (1994).

Madison, James. "Posthumously Published Essay," *Harper's* (March 1914).

____. *Papers of James Madison*, ed. William T. Hutchinson and William M. E. Rachal (Chicago: University of Chicago Press, 1962–____).

____. *Record of the Federal Convention of 1787*, ed. Max Farrand (New Haven: Yale University Press, 1911).

____. Alexander Hamilton, and John Jay. *The Federalist Papers* (Baltimore: Johns Hopkins University Press, 1960).

Magrath, C. Peter. "Chief Justice Waite and the 'Twin Relic': Reynolds v. United States," 18 *Vand. L. Rev.* 507 (1965).

Malone, Dumas. *Jefferson the President: First Term, 1801–1805* (Boston: Little Brown, 1970).

Mann, Horace. *Eleventh Annual Report of the State Board of Education* [in Massachusetts] (1847), in *Life and Works of Horace Mann* (Boston: Lee & Shepard, 1891).

____. *Twelfth Annual Report of the State Board of Education* [in Massachusetts] (1848), in *Life and Works of Horace Mann* (Boston: Lee & Shepard, 1891).

Mansfield, John H. "Conscientious Objection–1964 Term," in Donald A. Giannella, ed., *Religion and Public Order* (Chicago: University of Chicago Press, 1965).

Manwaring, David R. *Render unto Caesar: The Flag–Salute Controversy* (Chicago: University of Chicago Press, 1962).

Marcus, Jacob R. *The Colonial American Jew, 1492–1776* (Detroit: Wayne State University Press, 1970).

Markus, Robert A. "St. Augustine's Views of the 'Just War,'" in W.J. Shiels, ed., *The Church and War* (Oxford: Published for the Ecclesiastical History Society by B. Blackwell, 1983).

____. "*Coge intrare*: the Church and Political Power," in *Saeculum*.

____. *Saeculum: History and Society in the Theology of St Augustine* (Cambridge: Cambridge University Press, 1970).

Marshall, William P. "In Defense of *Smith* and Free Exercise Revisionism," 58 *U. Chi. L Rev.* 308 (1991).

Martin, R.P. *Carmen Christi: Philippians ii.5–11 in Recent Interpretation and in the Setting of Early Christian Worship* (Cambridge: Cambridge University Press, 1967).

Mason, Alpheus Thomas. *Harlan Fiske Stone: Pillar of the Law* (New York: Viking, 1956).

Massie, Robert K. *Peter the Great* (New York: Alfred A. Knopf, 1980).

McBrien, Richard. *Caesar's Coin: Religion and Politics in America* (New York: Macmillan,1987).

McCarthy, Dennis. *Covenant and Treaty* (Rome: Pontifical Biblical Institute, 1963).

____. *Old Testament Covenant: A Survey of Current Opinions* (Richmond: John Knox, 1972).

McCollum, Vashti Cromwell. *One Woman's Fight* (Garden City, NY: Doubleday, 1951).

McConnell, Michael W. "Academic Freedom in Religious Colleges and Universities," 53 *L. & Contemp. Probs.* 303 (1990).

____. "Accommodation of Religion." 1985 *Sup. Ct. Rev.* 1 (1985).

____. "Accommodation of Religion: An Update and a Response to Critics," 60 *Geo. Wash. L. Rev.* 685 (1992).

____. "Christ, Culture, and Courts: A Niebuhrian Examination of First Amendment Jurisprudence," 42 *DePaul L. Rev.* 191 (1992).

____. "Coercion: The Lost Element of Establishment," 27 *Wm. & Mary. L. Rev.* 933 (1986).

____. and Richard A. Posner, "An Economic Approach to Issues of Religious Freedom," 56 U. Chi. L. Rev. 1 (1989).

____. "Free Exercise Revisionism and the *Smith* Decision," 57 *U. Chi. L. Rev.* 1109 (1990).

____. "Institutions and Interpretation: A Critique of City of *Boerne v. Flores*," 111 *Harv. L. Rev.* 153, 187 (1997)

____. "Religious Freedom at a Crossroads," 59 *U. Chi. L. Rev.* 115 (1992).

____. "The Selective Funding Problem: Abortions and Religious Schools," 104 *Harv. L. Rev.* 989 (1991).

____. "Why 'Separation' Is Not the Key to Church–State Relations," *The Christian Century* (Jan. 18, 1989).

McKay, J.W. "Exodus XXIII 1–3, 6–8: A Decalogue for the Administration of Justice in the City Gate," *Vetus Testamentum* 21 (1971) 311–25.

McLaughlin, William G. *New England Dissent 1630–1833* (Cambridge: Harvard University Press, 1971).

Macmullen, Ramsey. *Constantine* (New York: Croom Helm, 1987).

Mead, Sidney E. "Neither Church nor State: Reflections on James Madison's 'Line of Separation,' " 10 *J. Ch. & St.* 349 (1968).

Melton, J. Gordon, ed. *Encyclopedia of American Religion* (Wilmington, N.C.: McGrath Publishing, 1978).

Mendenhall, George. "Covenant," in *Interpreter's Dictionary of the Bible* (Nashville: Abingdon, 1962) 1:714–23.

____. *Law and Covenant in the Ancient Near East* (Pittsburgh: Biblical Colloquium, 1955).

Meyer, Jacob C. *Church and State in Massachusetts from 1740 to 1833* (Cleveland, Ohio: Western Reserve University Press, 1930).

Milburn, R.L.P. "The Persecution of Domitian," *Church Q. Rev.* 139 (1945) 154–64.

Millard, Alan. "The Flood," in Bruce M. Metzger and Michael D. Coogan, eds., *The Oxford Companion to the Bible* 231 (New York: Oxford University Press, 1993).

Miller, Charles. *The Supreme Court and the Uses of History* (Cambridge: Belknap Press of Harvard University Press, 1969).

Miller, Perry. *Nature's Nation* (Cambridge: Harvard University Press, 1967).

___. *Roger Williams* (Indianapolis: Bobbs–Merrill, 1953).

Miller, William Lee. *The First Liberty: Religion and the American Republic* (New York: Alfred A. Knopf, 1986).

Millor, W.J., & Brooke, C.N.L. *The Letters of John of Salisbury* (London: T. Nelson, 1979).

Mintz, Jerome R. *Hasidic People: A Place in the New World* (Cambridge: Harvard University Press, 1992).

Mitchell, Joshua C. *The Fragility of Freedom: Tocqueville on Religion, Democracy, and the American Future* (Chicago: University of Chicago Press, 1995).

Moberly, Walter H. *The Ethics of Punishment* (Hamden, CT: Archon Books, 1968).

More, Thomas. *Correspondence of Sir Thomas More,* ed. Elizabeth Frances Rogers (Princeton: Princeton University Press, 1947).

___. *Utopia,* ed. Robert M. Adams (New York: W. W. Norton, 1976).

Morgan, Edmund S. *The Puritan Dilemma* (Boston: Little, Brown, 1958).

Morison, Samuel Eliot. "The Struggle over the Adoption of the Constitution of Massachusetts, 1780." Massachusetts Historical Society, *Proceedings* 50 (1916–1917).

___. "The Great Rebellion in Harvard College and the Resignation of President Kirkland." Colonial Society of America *Transactions* (1920).

Morris, Aldon D. *The Origins of the Civil Rights Movement* (New York: Free Press, 1984).

Morris, Norval and David J. Rothman, eds. *The Oxford History of the Prison: The Practice of Punishment in Western Society* (New York: Oxford University Press, 1995).

Mowinckel, Sigmund. *Le Décalogue* (Paris: Félix Alcan, 1927).

___. *The Psalms in Israel's Worship* (Nashville: Abingdon, 1962).

Muir, William K., Jr. *Prayer in the Public Schools: Law and Attitude Change* (Chicago: University of Chicago Press, 1967).

Mundhill, Robin R. *England's Jewish Solution: Experiment and Expulsion, 1262–1290* (New York: Cambridge University Press, 1998).

Murray, John Courtney. "Governmental Repression of Heresy." *Proceedings of the Catholic Theological Society of America* (1948) 161.

——. "Law or Presuppositions," 14 *Law & Contemp. Probs.* 23 (1949).

——. *The Problem of Religious Freedom* (Westminster, MD: Newman Press, 1965).

——. "War and Conscience," in James Finn, ed., A *Conflict of Loyalties: The Case for Selective Conscientious Objection* (New York: Pegasus, 1968).

——. *We Hold These Truths: Reflections on the American Experience* (New York: Sheed & Ward,1960).

Myers, Richard S. "The Supreme Court and the Privatization of Religion," 41 *Cath. U. L. Rev.* 19 (1991).

Nasuti, Harry P. "Identity, Identification, and Imitation: The Narrative Hermeneutics of Biblical Law," 4 *J. Law & Relig.* 9 (1986).

Neuhaus, Richard John, ed. *Jews in Unsecular America* (Grand Rapids: Eerdmans, 1987).

——. *The Naked Public Square: Religion and Democracy in America* (Grand Rapids: Eerdmans, 1986).

—— and Michael Cromartie, eds., *Piety and Politics: Evangelicals and Fundamentalists Confront the World* (Washington, D.C.: Ethics and Public Policy Center, 1987).

Neusner, Jacob. *The Death and Birth of Judaism* (New York: Basic Books, 1987).

——. *Judaism and Christianity in the Age of Constantine* (Chicago: University of Chicago Press, 1987).

——. *Judaism in the Matrix of Christianity* (Philadelphia: Fortress Press, 1986).

Newman, Roger K. *Hugo Black: A Biography* (New York: Pantheon Books, 1994).

Nicholson, E.W. "The Decalogue as the Direct Address of God." *Vetus Testamentum* 27 (1977) 422–33

Nicoll, Henry James. *Great Movements, and Those Who Achieved Them* (New York: Harper & Brothers, 1882).

Noll, Mark A., Nathan A. Hatch, and George W. Marsden, *The Search for Christian America* (Westchester, IL: Crossway Books, 1983).

Noonan, John T., Jr., "Book Review of Robilliard." 33 *Am. J. of Comparative L.* 765 (1985).

——. *Bribes* (New York: Macmillan, 1985).

——. *Contraception: A History of its Treatment by the Catholic Theologians and Canonists* (Cambridge: Harvard University Press, 1965).

——. "The Family and the Supreme Court." 23 *Catholic U. L. Rev.* 255 (1973).

____. *The Lustre of Our Country: The American Experience of Religious Freedom* (Berkeley: University of California Press, 1998).

____. *Persons and Masks of the Law: Jefferson, Wythe, Cardozo, and Holmes as Makers of the Masks* (New York: Farrar, Straus, and Giroux, 1976).

____. *A Private Choice: Abortion in America in the Seventies* (New York: Free Press, 1979).

____. "Quota of Imps," in Merrill Peterson and Robert Vaughn, eds., *The Virginia Statute for Religious Freedom: Its Evolution and Consequences in American History* (New York: Cambridge University Press, 1988).

____. "Religious Liberty At the Stake," 84 *Va. L. Rev.* 459 (1998).

Note. "The Establishment Clause and Religion in Child Custody Disputes: Factoring Religion into the Best Interest Equation." 82 *Mich. L. Rev.* 1702 (1984).

Note. "The Supreme Court, Effect Inquiry, and Aid to Parochial Education." 37 *Stanford L. Rev.* 219 (1984).

Novak, David. "American Jews and America: The Mission of Israel Revisited," in Richard John Neuhaus, ed., *Jews in Unsecular America* (Grand Rapids: Eerdmans, 1987).

Nuttall, Geoffrey. *Christian Pacifism in History* (Oxford: Blackwell, 1958).

O'Dea, Thomas. *The Mormons* (Chicago: University of Chicago Press, 1957).

O'Donovan, Oliver, *The Desire of Nations: Rediscovering the Roots of Political Theology* (New York: Cambridge University Press, 1996).

Oberman, Heiko A. *The Roots of Anti–Semitism in the Age of Renaissance and Reformation* (Philadelphia: Fortress Press, 1984).

Oesterreicher, John M. "Declaration on the Relationship of the Church to Non–Christian Religions," in Herbert Vorgrimler, ed., *Commentary on the Documents of Vatican II* (New York: Herder & Herder, 1969).

Pak, Thomas, "Free Exercise, Free Expression, and Landmark Preservation," 91 *Colum. L. Rev.* 1813 (1991).

Paludan, Phillip S. *A Covenant with Death* (Urbana: University of Illinois Press, 1975).

Parker, Geoffrey, ed. *The Thirty Years War* (New York: Routledge Press, 1997).

Parker, Theodore. "The Mexican War," in Parker, *The Slave Power* (Boston: American Unitarian Association, 1969).

____. *The Slave Power,* ed. James K. Hosner. (Boston: American Unitarian Association; reprint, New York: Arno Press, 1969).

____. *Works* (Boston: American Unitarian Association, 1907–1913).

Parkes, James. *Conflict of the Church and the Synagogue: A Study in the Origins of Anti-Semitism* (Cleveland: World, 1961).

Parsell, Stuart G. "Revitalization of the Free Exercise of Religion Under State Constitutions: A Response to Employment Division v. Smith," 68 *Notre Dame L. Rev.* 747 (1993).

Pascarosa and Futterman, "Ethnopsychedelic Therapy for Alcoholics: Observations in the Peyote Ritual of the Native American Church," 8 *J. of Psychedelic Drugs* 215 (1976).

Patrick, Dale. *Old Testament Law* (Richmond: John Knox, 1985).

Paulsen, Michael J. "Religion, Equality, and the Constitution: An Equal Protection Approach to Establishment Clause Adjudication," 61 *Notre Dame L. Rev.* 311 (1986).

——. "The Most Dangerous Branch: Executive Power to Say What the Law Is," 83 *Geo. L.J.* 217.

Pavan, Pietro. "Declaration on Religious Freedom," in Herbert Vorgrimler, ed., 4 *Commentary on the Documents of Vatican II* 49–86 (New York: Herder & Herder, 1969).

——. "The Right to Religious Freedom in Conciliar Declaration," in Neophytos Edelby & & Teodoro Jiminez–Urresti, eds. *Religious Freedom* 37–52 (New York: Paulist Press, 1966).

Pelikan, Jaroslav. *The Emergence of the Catholic Tradition (100–600)* (Chicago: University of Chicago Press, 1971).

Pelotte, Donald E. *John Courtney Murray: Theologian in Conflict* (New York: Paulist Press, 1976).

Penton, M. James. *Apocalypse Delayed* (Toronto: University of Toronto Press, 1985).

Pepys. Samuel. *Diary*, ed. Robert Latham and William Matthews (Berkeley: University of California Press, 1970).

Perkins, Pheme. "The Gospel According to John," in Raymond E. Brown, Joseph A. Fitzmyer, and Roland E. Murphy, eds. *The New Jerome Biblical Commentary*, ed. (Englewood Cliffs, NJ: Prentice–Hall, 2d ed. 1990).

——. *Reading the New Testament* (Paramus, NJ: Paulist Press, 1988).

Perry, Michael J. *The Constitution, the Courts, and Human Rights* (New Haven: Yale University Press, 1982).

——. *Love and Power: The Role of Religion and Morality in American Politics* (New York: Oxford University Press, 1991).

——. *Morality, Politics, and Law: A Bicentennial Essay* (New York: Oxford University Press, 1988).

——. *Religion in Politics: Constitutional and Moral Perspectives* (New York: Oxford University Press, 1997).

——. "Religious Arguments in Public Political Debate," 29 *Loyola L.A. L. Rev.* 1421 (1996).

Peterson, Merrill and Robert Vaughn, eds. *The Virginia Statute for Religious Freedom: Its Evolution and Consequences in American History* (New York: Cambridge University Press, 1988).

Pfeffer, Leo. "Amici in Church–State Litigation." 44 *Law & Contemporary Problems* 83 (1981).

___. *Church, State and Freedom* (Boston: Beacon Press, 1967).

Phelps, Amos A. *Lectures on Slavery and Its Remedy* (Boston: New England Anti–Slavery Society, 1834; republished St. Clair Shores, Mich.: Scholarly Press, 1970).

Phillips, Anthony. *Ancient Israel's Criminal Law: A New Approach to the Decalogue* (New York: Schocken, 1970).

Philo. *In Flaccum*, trans. C.D. Yonge (London: Hendrickson, 1993).

Pollack, F. & F. Maitland. *The History of English Law* (Cambridge: Cambridge University Press, 1903).

Pospielovsky, Dimitry. *The Russian Church under the Soviet Regime, 1917–1982* (Crestwood, NY: St. Vladimir's Seminary Press, 1984).

Potter, D.S. "Persecution in the Early Church," in David Noel Freedman, ed., *Anchor Bible Dictionary* (New York: Doubleday, 1997).

Potter, Ralph. "Conscientious Objection to Particular Wars," in Donald Giannella, ed., *Religion and the Public Order* (Ithaca: Cornell University Press, 1968).

___. *War and Moral Discourse* (Richmond: John Knox Press, 1969).

Powicke, F.W. and Christopher R. Cheney, eds. *Councils and Synods with Other Documents Relating to the English Church* (Oxford: Clarendon Press, 1964).

Presbyterian Church (USA). "God Alone is Lord of the Conscience," (1989), reprinted in 8 *J. L. & Relig.* 331 (1990).

Pritchard, James, ed. *Ancient Near Eastern Texts Relating to the Old Testament* (Princeton, NJ: Princeton University Press, 1969).

Prucha, Francis P. *The Churches and the Indian Schools 1888–1912* (Lincoln: University of Nebraska Press, 1979).

Pusey, Merlo. *Charles Evans Hughes* (New York: Macmillan, 1951).

Rabello, Alfredo Mordechai. "Theodosius I," 15 *Encyclopaedia Judaica* 1101 (New York: Macmillan, 1971).

___. "Theodosius II," 15 *Encyclopaedia Judaica* 1101–02 (New York: Macmillan, 1971).

Ramsay, Paul. *War and the Christian Conscience* (Durham, N.C.: Duke University Press, 1961).

Reiman, P.A. "Covenant, Mosaic," in *Interpreter's Dictionary of the Bible* (Nashville: Abingdon, 1976) 5:192–99.

Religion Case Reporter (1999–___; monthly synopses of leading cases organized topically; available from Paradigm Publications, Inc., 1358 East 24th Street, Brooklyn, NY 11210) www.paradigmpub.com

Religious Freedom Reporter: A Service of the Center for Law and Religious Freedom (1981–___; monthly synopses of leading cases organized topically; available from Campbell University, Church–State Resource Center, Norman Adrian Wiggins School of Law, 113 Main Street, Buies Creek, NC 27506).

Reorganized Church of Jesus Christ of Latter Day Saints. *Book of Doctrines and Covenants.* (Independence, Mo.: Herald Publishing House, 1970).

Reuther, Rosemary Radford. *Faith and Fratricide: The Theological Roots of Anti–Semitism* (New York: Seabury Press, 1974).

Rhodes, James Ford. *History of the United States* (New York: Macmillan, 1910).

Richardson, Herbert, ed. *Constitutional Issues in the Case of Rev. Moon* (New York: Edwin Mellen Press, 1984).

Rice, Charles. *Freedom of Association* (New York: New York University Press,1962).

Richardson, James D., ed. *Messages and Papers of the Presidents 1789–1897* (Washington, D.C.: Government Printing Office, 1896).

Richman, Sheldon. *Separating School and State: How to Liberate America's Families* (Fairfax, VA: Future of Freedom Foundation, 1994).

Riesenfeld, Harald. *The Gospel Traditions* (Philadelphia: Fortress, 1970).

Ripple, Kenneth F. *Constitutional Litigation* (Charlottesville: Michie, 1984).

Rodes, Robert E., Jr. *Lay Authority and Reformation in the English Church* (Notre Dame, Ind.: University of Notre Dame Press, 1982).

——. "Pluralist Christendom and the Christian Civil Magistrate," 8 *Capital U. L. Rev.* 413 (1979).

——. "The Passing of Nonsectarianism: Some Reflections on the School Prayer Case," 38 *Notre Dame Lawyer* 115 (1963).

Rohr, John A. *Prophets Without Honor, Public Policy and the Selective Conscientious Objector* (Nashville, Tenn.: Abingdon Press, 1971).

Rowe, H. Edward. *The Day They Padlocked the Church* (Shreveport, La.: Huntington House, 1983).

Rubin, Israel. *Satmar: An Island in the City* (Chicago: Quadrangle Books, 1972).

Runciman, Steven. *The History of the Crusades* (Cambridge: Cambridge University Press, 3 vols. 1951–54).

Ruskin, Bayard. *Strategies for Freedom* (New York: Columbia University Press, 1976).

Rynne, Xavier. *The Fourth Session* (New York: Farrar, Straus & Giroux, 1966).

——. *The Third Session* (New York: Farrar, Straus & Giroux, 1965).

Sandburg, Carl. *Abraham Lincoln* (New York: Harcourt, Brace, 1939).

Sande, Ken. *The Peacemaker: A Biblical Guide to Resolving Personal Conflict* (Grand Rapids: Baker, 1991).

Sandel, Michael J. "Freedom of Conscience or Freedom of Choice?," in James D. Hunter and Os Guinness eds., *Articles of Peace: The Religious Liberty Clauses and the American Public Philosophy* (Washington, DC: Brookings Institution, 1990).

Saperstein, David. "Jewish Perspectives on the Role of Religion in the Political Process." 1 *J. Law and Relig.* 220 (1983):220.

Sarna, Jonathan D. *"Christian America or Secular America?: The Church–State Dilemma of American Jews,"* in Richard John Neuhaus, ed., *Jews in Unsecular America* (Grand Rapids: Eerdmans, 1987).

Scalia, Antonin. *A Matter of Interpretation: Federal Courts and the Law* (Princeton, NJ: Princeton University Press, 1997).

Scarisbrick, J. J. *Henry VIII* (Berkeley: University of California Press, 1968).

Schneemelher, William, ed. *New Testament Apocrypha* (Louisville, KY: Westminster/John Knox Press, 1991).

Schreiber, Aaron M. *Jewish Law and Decision–Making: A Study Through Time* (Philadelphia: Temple University Press, 1979).

Schumpeter, Joseph. *Capitalism, Socialism, and Democracy* (New York: Harper & Row, 1950).

Scopes, J. & J. Presley. *Center of the Storm* (New York: Holt, Rinehart and Winston, 1967).

Second Vatican Council. *Acta Synodalia* (Rome: Vatican Polyglot Press, 1978).

____. *The Documents of the Second Vatican Council,* ed. Walter Abbott, trans., Joseph Gallagher (New York: Herder & Herder, 1966).

____. *Commentary on the Documents of Vatican II,* ed. Herbert Vorgrimler, (New York: Herder & Herder, 1969).

Sherman, Franklin, ed. *Luther's Works*, Vol. 47 ("The Christian in Society," IV) (Minneapolis: Fortress Press, 1971).

Sherry, Suzanna. "Lee v. Weisman: Paradox Redux," 1992 *Sup. Ct. Rev.* 123.

Sherwin–White, A.N. *Roman Society and Roman Law in the New Testament* (New York: Oxford University Press, 1973).

Shipps, Jan. *Mormonism: The Story of a New Religious Tradition* (Urbana, IL: University of Illinois Press, 1985).

Shirer,William L. *The Rise and Fall of the Third Reich: A History of Nazi Germany* (New York: Simon & Shuster, 1960).

Shugrue, Richard E. "An Approach to Mutual Respect: The Christian School Controversy." 18 *Creighton L. Rev.* 219 (1984).

Sibley, Mulford Q. and Philip E. Jacob. *Conscription of Conscience: The American State and the Conscientious Objector, 1940–1947* (Ithaca: Cornell University Press, 1952).

Simon, Karla W. "The Tax Exempt Status of Racially Discriminatory Religious Schools," 36 *Tax L. Rev.* 477 (1981).

Simons, Menno. "Een klare beantwoordinge over eene schrift Gelii Fabri," in John Christian Wenger, ed., *The Complete Writings of Menno Simons* (Scottdale, Pa.: Herald Press, 1966).

Sinclair, Andrew. *Prohibition: The Era of Excess* (Boston: Little, Brown, 1962).

Sizer, Theodore and Phillip Whitten. "A Proposal for a Poor Children's Bill of Rights," 5 *Psychology Today* 58 (1968).

Smith, Michael E. "The Special Place of Religion in the Constitution." 1983 *Sup. Ct. Rev.* 105.

Smith, Rodney K. "Conscience, Coercion and the Establishment of Religion: The Beginning of an End to the Wandering of a Wayward Judiciary?," 43 *Case W. Res. L. Rev.* 917 (1993).

——. "Getting Off on the Wrong Foot and Back on Again: A Reexamination of the History of the Framing of the Religious Clauses of the First Amendment and a Critique of the *Reynolds* and *Everson* Decisions," 20 *Wake Forest L. Rev.* 569 (1984).

——. "Nonpreferentialism in Establishment Clause Analysis: A Response to Professor Laycock," 65 *St. John's L. Rev.* 245 (1991).

——. *Public Prayer and the Constitution* (Wilmington, DE: Scholarly Resources, 1987).

Smith, Steven D. *Foreordained Failure: The Quest for a Constitutional Principle of Religious Freedom* (New York: Oxford University Press, 1995).

——. "Symbols, Perceptions, and Doctrinal Illusions: Establishment Neutrality and the 'No Endorsement' Test," 86 *Mich. L. Rev.* (1987).

Soifer, Aviam, *Law and the Company We Keep* (Cambridge: Harvard University Press, 1995).

Sorauf, Frank J. *The Wall of Separation* (Princeton: Princeton University Press, 1976).

Spicer, E. *Cycle of Conquest: The Impact of Spain, Mexico and the United States on the Indians of the United States* (Tucson: University of Arizona Press, 1962).

Spinoza, Baruch. *The Political Works,* ed. A.G. Wernham (Oxford: Clarendon Press, 1958).

Stamm, Johann and Maurice Andrew, *The Ten Commandments in Recent Research* (London: SCM, 1967).

Stephen, James Fitzjames. *A History of the Criminal Law of England* (London: Macmillan, 1883).

Stern, Menahem. "The Decrees Against the Jewish Religion and the Establishment of the Hasmonean State," in Haim Hillel Ben–Sasson, ed., *A History of the Jewish People* (Cambridge: Harvard University Press, 1976).

Stewart, Omer C. *Peyote Religion: A History* (Norman, OK: University of Oklahoma Press, 1987).

Stokes, Anson Phelps. *Church and State in the United States* (New York: Harper, 1950).

Stoll, Joseph. "Who Shall Educate Our Children?," in Albert N. Keim, ed., *Compulsory Education and the Amish: The Right Not to Be Modern* (Boston: Beacon Press, 1975).

Stroup, Herbert Hewitt. *The Jehovah's Witnesses* (New York: Columbia University Press, 1945).

Sturm, Douglas. "American Legal Realism and the Covenantal Myth: World Views in the Practice of Law," 31 *Mercer L. Rev.* 487 (1980).

Suagee, Dean B. "American Indian Religious Freedom and Cultural Resources Management: Protecting Mother Earth's Caretakers," 10 *Am. Ind. L. Rev.* 1 (1982).

Sullivan, Dwight H. "The Congressional Response to *Goldman v. Weinberger*," 121 *Mil. L. Rev.* 125 (1988).

Sullivan, Kathleen M. "Religion and Liberal Democracy," 59 *U. Chi. L. Rev.* 195 (1992).

Sullivan, Larry E. *The Prison Reform Movement: Forlorn Hope* (Boston: Twayne Publishers, 1990).

Sullivan, Russell N. "Religious Education in the Schools," 14 *Law & Contemp. Probs.* 92 (1949).

Swaney, Charles Baumer. *Episcopal Methodism and Slavery* (New York: Negro University Press, 1962; reprint of 1926 edition).

Swift, Louis J. *The Early Fathers on War and Military Service* (Wilmington, DE: M. Glazier, 1983).

———. "Augustine on War and Killing: Another View," *Harv. Theol. Rev.* 66 (1973) 369–83.

Synan, Edward A. *The Popes and the Jews in the Middle Ages* (New York: Macmillan, 1965).

Tarr, G. Alan & Mary C.A. Porter. *State Supreme Courts in State and Nation* (New Haven, CT: Yale University Press, 1988).

Taylor, Lily Ross. *The Divinity of the Roman Emperor* (Philadelphia: Porcupine Press, 1975).

Tedlock, Dennis & B. Tedlock, eds. *Teachings From the American Earth: Indian Religion and Philosophy* (New York: Liveright, 1975).

Teitel, Ruti. "A Critique of Religion as Politics in the Public Sphere," 77 *Cornell L. J.* 747 (1993).

Thayer, Eli. *A History of the Kansas Crusade: Its Friends and Its Foes* (New York: Harper & Brothers, 1889).

Theodosian Code, tr. Clyde Pharr (Princeton: Princeton University Press, 1952).

Thernstrom, Abigail. *School Choice in Massachusetts* (Boston: Pioneer Institute for Public Policy Research, 1991).

Thomas, John L., ed. "The Narrative of Amos Dresser," in *Slavery Attacked: The Abolitionist Crusade* (1965).

Thompson, Robert Ellis. *A History of the Presbyterian Churches in the United States* (New York: Christian Literature Co., 1895).

Thorne, Samuel E. Introduction, *The Laws and Customs of England* (Cambridge: The Belknap Press of Harvard University Press, 1968).

Thorpe, Francis Newton, ed. *Federal and State Constitutions* (Washington, D.C.: Government Printing Office, 1909).

Tillich, Paul. *The Shaking of the Foundations* (New York: C. Scribner's Sons, 1948).

Tocco, Joseph P. "Home Schooling in Michigan: Is There a Fundamental Right to Teach Your Children at Home?," 71 *U. Det. Mercy L. Rev.* 1053 (1994).

Tocqueville, Alexis de. *Democracy in America,* tr. Henry Reeves (Boston: J. Allyn, 1875).

___. *Oeuvres et correspondance ineditees* (Paris, 1861).

Tracy, David. *The Analogical Imagination* (New York: Crossroad, 1981).

Trevelyan, George Macaulay. *England under the Stuarts* (London: Methuen & Co., 1904; New York: Putnam, 6th ed.1914).

Tribe, Laurence H. "Foreword: Toward a Model of Roles in the Due Process of life and Law," 87 *Harv. L. Rev.* 1 (1973).

Trimble, Bruce R. *Chief Justice Waite* (Princeton: Princeton University Press, 1938).

Troeltsch, Ernst. *The Social Teachings of the Christian Church* (New York: The Macmillan Company, 1931).

Tucker, Robert C. *Philosophy and Myth in Karl Marx* (Cambridge: Harvard University Press, 1972).

Tushnet, Mark V. "The Constitution of Religion," 18 *Conn. L. Rev.* 701 (1986).

Underwood, Julie K. "Choice is Not a Panacea," 71 *Ed. L. Rep.* 599 (1992).

VanAlstyne, William W. "The Failure of the Religious Freedom Restoration Act Under Section 5 of the Fourteenth Amendment," 46 *Duke L. J.* 291 (1996).

Van Wagoner, Richard S. *Mormon Polygamy, A History* (Salt Lake City: Signature Books, 2d ed.1989).

Viteritti, Joseph P. "Choosing Equality: Religious Freedom and Educational Opportunity Under Constitutional Federalism," 15 *Yale L. & Policy Rev.* 113 (1996).

von Campenhausen, Hans. "Christians and Military Service in the Early Church," in *Tradition and Life in the Church: Essays and Lectures on Church History* (Philadelphia: Fortress Press, 1968).

von Rad, Gerhard. *Deuteronomy* (Philadelphia: Westminster, 1966).

____. *Holy War in Ancient Israel*, translated and edited by Marva J. Dawn; introduction by Ben C. Ollenburger (Grand Rapids: Eerdmans, 1991).

Vrga, Djuro J. and Frank J. Fahey. *Changes and Socio–Religious Conflict in an Ethnic Minority Group: The Serbian Orthodox Church in America* (San Francisco: R and E Research Associates, 1975).

Waller. "The Constitutionality of the Tennessee Anti–Evolution Act," 35 *Yale L.J.* 191 (1925).

Warren, W.L. *King John* (Berkeley: University of California Press, 1978).

Waszink, Jan Hendrik and J.C.M. Van Winden, eds. *Tertullian. De idololatria* (Leiden: E.J. Brill, 1987).

Weigel, George. *Tranquilitas Ordinis: The Present Failure and Future Promise of American Catholic Thought on War and Peace* (New York: Oxford University Press, 1987).

Weisbrod, Carol & Pamela Sheingorn. "Reynolds v. United States: Nineteenth–Century Forms of Marriage and the Status of Women," 10 *Conn. L. Rev.* 828 (1978).

Weld, Thomas Dwight. *The Bible Against Slavery* (New York: American Anti–Slavery Society, 1838).

Welles, Gideon. *Diary of Gideon Welles* (Boston: Houghton, Mifflin & Co., 1911).

Wiecek, William. "Clio as Hostage: The United States Supreme Court and the Uses of History," *24 Cal. W. L. Rev.* 227 (1988).

Wilken, Robert L. *John Chrysostom and the Jews: Rhetoric and Reality in the Late Fourth Century* (Berkeley: University of California Press, 1983).

____. *The Christians as the Romans Saw Them* (New Haven: Yale University Press, 1984).

Williams, George H. *Wilderness and Paradise in Christian Thought* (New York: Harper, 1962).

Williams, Roger. *The Bloudy Tenent, of Persecution, for cause of Conscience, discussed, in A Conference between Truth and Peace* (London, 1644).

____. *The Complete Writings of Roger Williams,* Perry Miller, ed. (New York: Russell & Russell, 1963).

____. *Letters of Roger Williams,* John Russell Bartlett, ed. (Providence: Printed for Narragansett Club, 1874).

Winthrop, John. *Papers* (Boston: Massachusetts Historical Society, 1931).

Wolfson, Harry. *The Philosophy of Spinoza* (New York: Schocken Books, 1969).

World Council of Churches. *The New Delhi Report* (Geneva: World Council of Churches, 1962).

Yarbrough, Marilyn V. "Still Separate and Still Unequal," 36 *Wm. & Mary L. Rev.* 685 (1995).

Yaseen, Leonard. *The Jesus Connection* (New York: Crossroad, 1986).

Yates, Wilson. "Separation of Church and State: Civil Religion and Crossings at the Border," 1 *Hamline L. Rev.* 67 (1978).

Yoder, John Howard. "Exodus 20:13–'Thou Shalt Not Kill,' " 34 *Interpretation* 394–399 (1980).

___. "The Constantinian Sources of Western Social Ethics," in *The Priestly Kingdom* (Notre Dame: University of Notre Dame Press, 1984).

___. *Nevertheless: The Varieties of Religious Pacifism* (Scottsdale, PA: Herald Press, 1992).

___. *The Politics of Jesus: Vicit Agnus Noster* (Grand Rapids: Eerdmans, 1972).

___. *When War is Unjust: Being Honest in Just–War Thinking.* (Maryknoll, NY: Orbis, 1996).

Zahn, Gordon C. *In Solitary Witness: The Life and Death of Franz Jägerstätter* (New York: Holt, Rinehart & Winston, 1964).

Ziegler, Carol L. and Nancy M. Lederman. "School Vouchers: Are Urban Students Surrendering Rights for Choice?," 19 *Fordham Urb. L. J.* 813 (1993).

*

INDEX

K

P

Satmar Hasidim, 716

Scalia, Antonin, Associate Justice (1986–___), opinions: 365, 417, 480–87, 526, 717, 810–13, 834–43, 888, 921

Scarisbrick, J. J., 105–06

Scarsdale, New York, 656–57

School prayer: cases, 799–818, proposed constitutional amendment proposed, 778

Schumpeter, Joseph, 408

Schwenckfeld, Caspar (1489–1561) and opposition to use of force in religious matters, 118

Schwenckfelders, 118, 196

Schwimmer, Rosika, 344

Science and religion in public school curriculum, 822–42

Scientology, 373, 567–70

Scottish Rite Masons, 685

Seabury, Samuel, Episcopal Bishop, 164

Second Awakening, and prison reform, 467

Secular humanism, 571 n. 11

Secular purpose requirement, 683–84, 693, 818–19, 828–41

Sekulow, Jay Alan, 517, 791, 801, 857

Selective conscientious objection, 408–15

Selective Draft Act of 1940, 397

Selective Service Act of 1917, 396

Selective Service Act of 1967, 405

Separation of church and state
    See Establishment of religion; Free Exercise; Wall of separation

Serbian Eastern Orthodox Church, 595–99

Sermon on the Mount, 344

Servetus, Michael

Seventh-day Adventists: 358 n. 1, 399, 415–16, 418, 701
    See Amicus Curiae briefs: General Conference of Seventh-day Adventist

Sexual morals: child custody, 455
    and religion: adultery or fornication, 5, 214, polygamy, Chapter 9 *passim*, 288–307, 912–15, marriage, 915–19, homosexuality, 919–27

Sexton, John, 782, 827

Shaftsbury, Lord, 138

Shared Time Program, 708

Shaw, Lemuel, Chief Justice of Massachusetts Supreme Judicial Court (1830–1860): blasphemy, 212
    Fugitive Slave Act of 1850, 261
    support of Unitarian ministers (1830), 243

Sherman, Roger (Connecticut), 196–97, 198, 200, 202

Sherry, Suzanne, 374

Shilo Sanctified Holiness Baptist Church, 555

Shunning, 444

Shuttlesworth, Fred, 893

Sibley, Mulford Q., 397

Sign language translator for deaf student in religious school, 714–16

Sikhs, 459

Silence, moment of, 782

Silvester, Rep. Peter, fear that Religion clause would abolish religion (1789), 198

Simons, Menno (1493–1559), and rejection of infant baptism and use of force, 118–22
    See Mennonites

Simpson, Matthew, Methodist Bishop, 272

Sin: cooperation in sin of slavery itself a sin according to abolitionists, 254–64
    coerced support of religion a sin according to President Jefferson, 169
    public acknowledgement of national transgressions necessary according to President Washington, 203

Sincerity of religious conviction, 558–66

"Single Issue" politics: abolition of slavery, 256–64
    civil rights movement, 891–94
    movements for and against abortion, 897–911

Sioux Indians, 318–19

Sisters of Charity, 313

Sisters of the Holy Names of Jesus and Mary, 334

Sisters of the Most Precious Blood, 768

Slavery: in Bible, 4, 16, 30
    religious liberty of slaves violated before adoption of Civil War Amendments, 283
    religious opposition to, 254–85
    religious policies: Methodists, 255, 270–72
    Presbyterians, 255, 272–73

Smart, James M., Jr., 851

Smith, Joseph, founding prophet of Church of Jesus Christ of Latter-Day Saints (1805–1844) 288

Smith, Rodney K., 787, 790

Smith, Stephen D., 821

Snake handling as religious practice, 553–54

Sobor, council of bishops in Orthodox Church, 580

Social legislation: impact on Religion Clause, 416, 418

Social Security number: and religious freedom, 390

Social Security tax: and religious exemption for Amish, 452

Socinians, 118

Sodomy, 106, 919–27

Solicitation of money, 358, 366, 376, 880

Sorauf, Frank J., 684

Souter, David H., Associate Justice, (1990–___), 726–30, 740, 807–10, 868–70

South Carolina, state constitution and federal bill of rights: 188, 191
    cases: 418, 517, 847, 871

South Dakota, case: 431

Southern Christian Leadership Conference, 891–93

Soviet All Living Church, 581

Soviet Union, and control of Russian Orthodox Church, 580–81
    See Russian Orthodox Church

Y

Z

*

BIBLICAL INDEX

997

†